TERMINAL LANCE

ULTIMATE OMNIBUS

Also by Maximilian Uriarte

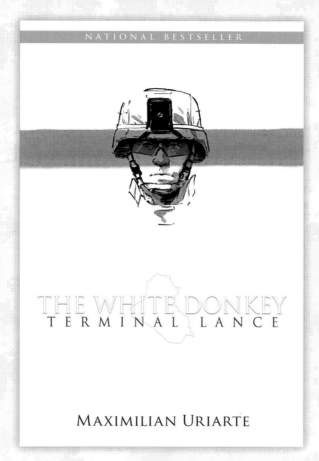

NATIONAL BESTSELLER

THE WHITE DONKEY
TERMINAL LANCE

MAXIMILIAN URIARTE

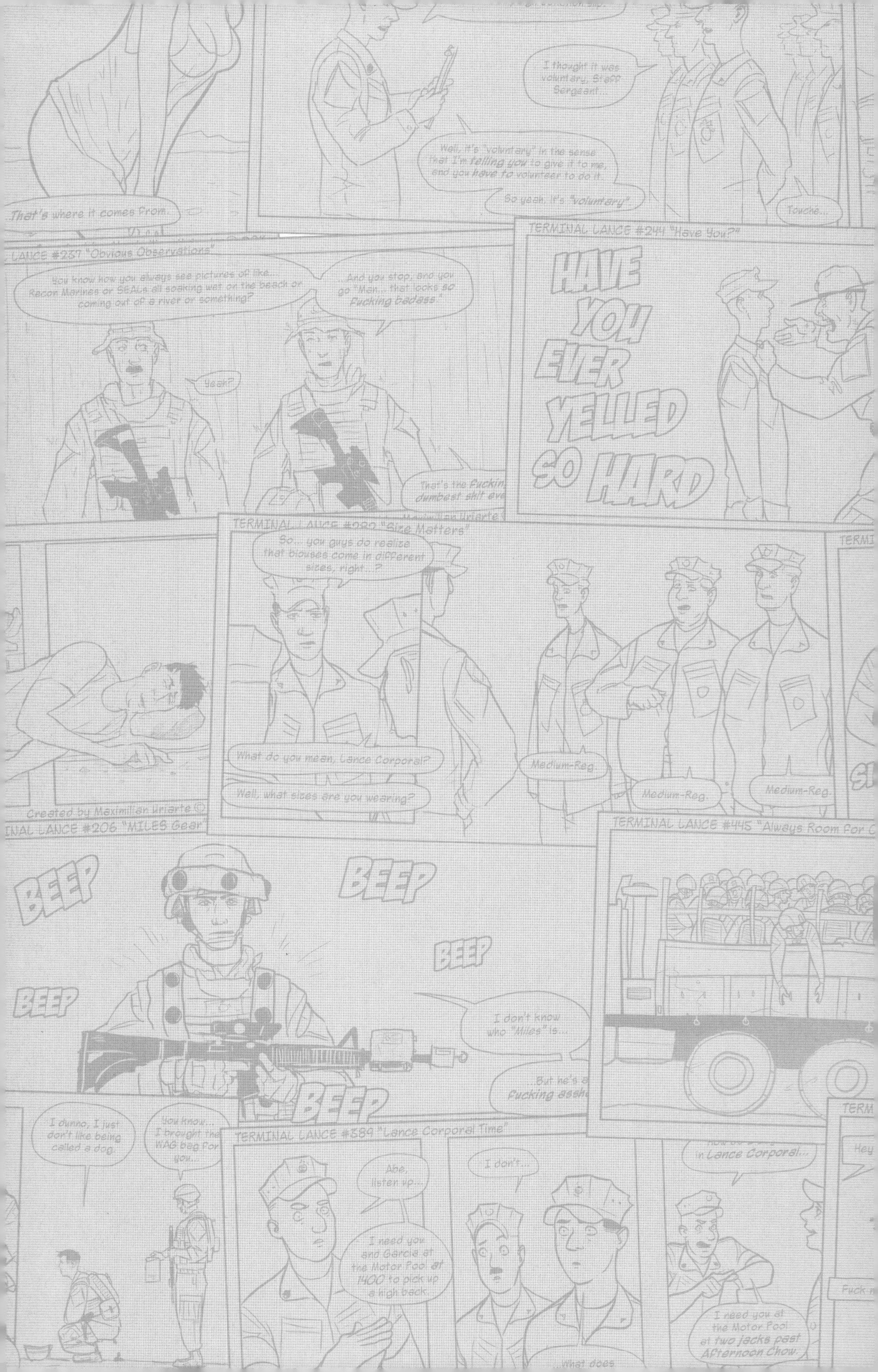

...That's where it comes from.
I thought it was voluntary, Staff Sergeant...
Well, it's "voluntary" in the sense that I'm telling you to give it to me, and you have to volunteer to do it.
So yeah, it's "voluntary".
Touché...
LANCE #237 "Obvious Observations"
You know how you always see pictures of like... Recon Marines or SEALs all soaking wet on the beach or coming out of a river or something?
Yeah?
...And you stop, and you go "Man... that looks so fucking badass."
That's the fuckin dumbest shit eve
TERMINAL LANCE #244 "Have You?"
HAVE YOU EVER YELLED SO HARD
TERMINAL LANCE #282 "Size Matters"
So... you guys do realize that blouses come in different sizes, right...?
What do you mean, Lance Corporal?
Well, what sizes are you wearing?
Medium-Reg.
Medium-Reg.
Medium-Reg.
Created by Maximilian Uriarte ©
INAL LANCE #206 "MILES Gear"
BEEP
BEEP
BEEP
BEEP
BEEP
I don't know who "Miles" is...
...But he's a fucking assh
TERMINAL LANCE #445 "Always Room For
I dunno, I just don't like being called a dog.
You know... I brought the WAG bag for you...
TERMINAL LANCE #389 "Lance Corporal Time"
Abe, listen up...
I need you and Garcia at the Motor Pool at 1400 to pick up a high back.
I don't...
...What does
in Lance Corporal...
I need you at the Motor Pool at two jacks past Afternoon Chow.
Hey
Fuck

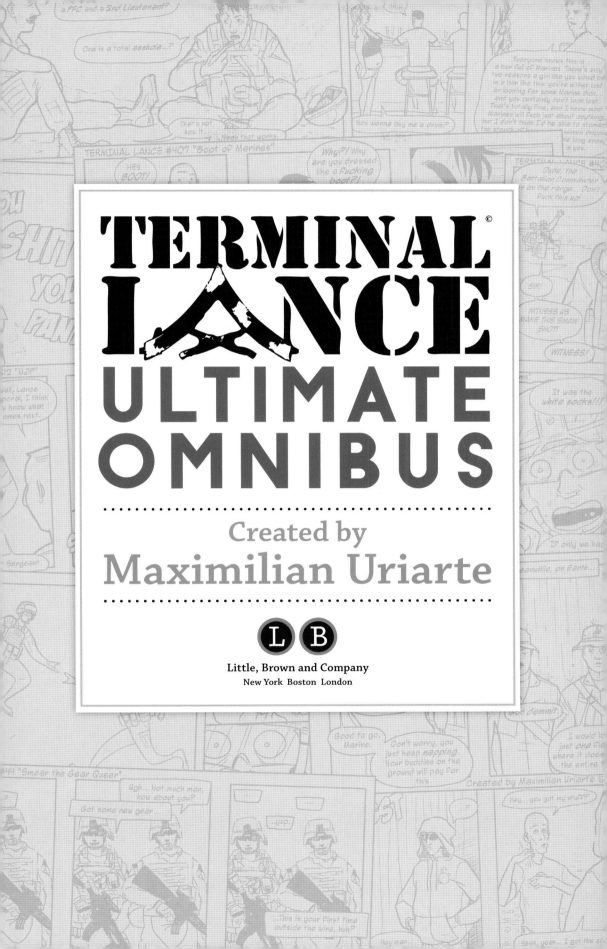

TERMINAL LANCE

ULTIMATE
OMNIBUS

Created by
Maximilian Uriarte

L B

Little, Brown and Company
New York Boston London

Copyright © 2018 by Maximilian Uriarte

Hachette Book Group supports the right to free expression and the value of copyright. The purpose of copyright is to encourage writers and artists to produce the creative works that enrich our culture.

The scanning, uploading, and distribution of this book without permission is a theft of the author's intellectual property. If you would like permission to use material from the book (other than for review purposes), please contact permissions@hbgusa.com. Thank you for your support of the author's rights.

Little, Brown and Company
Hachette Book Group
1290 Avenue of the Americas, New York, NY 10104
littlebrown.com

First Edition: April 2018

Little, Brown and Company is a division of Hachette Book Group, Inc. The Little, Brown name and logo are trademarks of Hachette Book Group, Inc.

The publisher is not responsible for websites (or their content) that are not owned by the publisher.

The Hachette Speakers Bureau provides a wide range of authors for speaking events. To find out more, go to hachettespeakersbureau.com or call (866) 376-6591.

All strips were previously published on terminallance.com or in the *Marine Corps Times*.

Interior book design by Jason Snyder

ISBN 978-0-316-41224-7
LCCN 2017958898

10 9 8 7 6 5 4 3 2 1

WOR

Printed in the United States of America

DEDICATED TO THE LANCE CORPORALS
OF THE MARINE CORPS

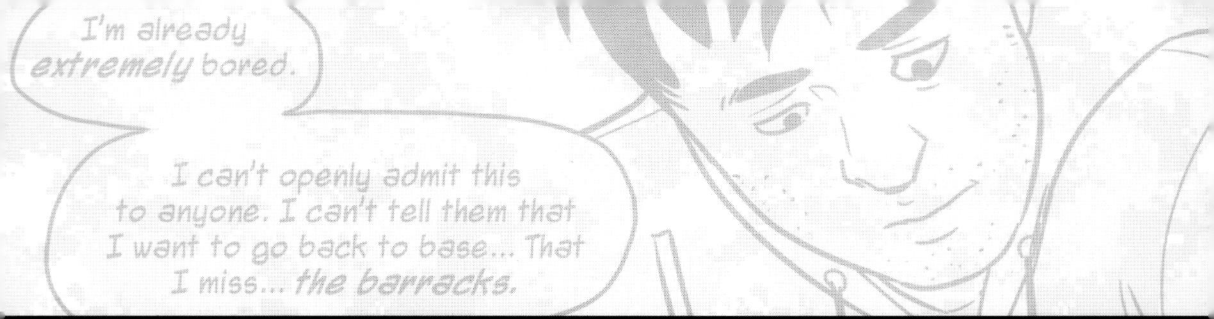
I'm already extremely bored.
I can't openly admit this to anyone. I can't tell them that I want to go back to base... That I miss... the barracks.

Foreword from Paul Szoldra

Duffel Blog creator

There must be something in the water in Hawaii.

Back in 2003, I walked off a plane onto the island of Oahu and headed to the Kaneohe Marine Corps base where I had been assigned with 3rd Battalion, 3rd Marines. I was stationed there for three years.

A short time after I left, a Marine I had never met did the same. His name was Maximilian Uriarte, and, like me, he was always questioning the things around him. "Why are we doing it this way?" he probably asked his fellow Marines.

This doesn't make any sense, he and I would think, while standing outside in formation for hours on end waiting for the commanding officer to show up.

But soon Max progressed from being a minor annoyance to his platoon sergeant to becoming the creator of the incredibly successful *Terminal Lance* comic strip. For Max, it wasn't enough to talk about the trials and tribulations of infantry life to just the fellow Marines in his platoon.

He had to do something. He had to build something new that would unite all Marines in their shared experiences, and give them a hearty laugh in the process.

And build it, he did.

As for me, well, I later created the military satire site known as Duffel Blog, for much the same reasons as Max. I had things I wanted to say and that was the platform that did it. And Max's creation is directly responsible for my own. His courage, dedication, and hilarious comics inspired me to go down a similar path, and for that, I'll forever be grateful.

I never had the pleasure of serving with Max, since we both just missed each other in our paths to Hawaii. But thankfully, we met after I moved to the San Francisco Bay Area in 2013. I recall our first meeting as being slightly awkward. We walked around Union Square, two internet friends, talking about what we were up to and chatting about our time in the Marines.

But that awkwardness was quickly dashed as I realized how alike we were. We had similar outlooks on life, agreed on a number of contentious issues, and most strikingly, did not have enough time in the world for all the ideas we had in our heads. That's the most amazing thing about Max.

He has more ideas for new projects than he can count. He'll never be satisfied with just *Terminal Lance,* which dwarfs all other military comics and counts top officers at Headquarters Marine Corps among its readership.

Put simply, Max's drive to create new and even more exciting things is what makes him Max.

And the crazy thing is that he instinctively knows what will work, and he hits home runs just about every time. Whether that's a new strip idea, or completely blowing past his goal on Kickstarter for his *New York Times*–bestselling book, *The White Donkey,* Max's drive should be an inspiration to all Marines, veterans, and civilians alike.

Max and I are now real-life friends. He sometimes texts me something he's working on, or asks for my advice regarding an upcoming project. He dutifully listens to my advice and then usually takes the opposite approach, so much so that I now laughingly tell him, "Well, that's what I think, but I know you're not going to do that."

And yet, that never offends me. Because I know Max. He has blazed his own trail for so long without my advice that he already knows the way.

With this book of the complete *Terminal Lance,* you'll see rather quickly why Max has been so successful. He speaks to the issues of Marines with authenticity and biting humor, because he has been there right alongside them.

He loves the Marine Lance Corporal, and he has never forgotten to focus singularly on that person with everything he creates. And I'm thankful that, even with the strip's Lance Corporal focus, a former sergeant like me can get the humor and enjoy it all the same.

But, I wonder as I write this, about seven years after *Terminal Lance* was born, what will come next and credit its inspiration to Max?

Hopefully nothing has changed with the water in Hawaii.

Author's Note

When I created Terminal Lance *back in 2010*, I never could have foreseen what it would become over the years. What began as a humble three-panel comic strip and a rambling blog soon became a staple of Marine Corps culture.

The strip, which was once considered taboo by the military establishment, has since been embraced by Marines stationed in every clime and place from every rank and rate. Now, it is hard to imagine a Corps before the age of social media and before the biting critique that this comic presented. Few people were willing to publicly go against the grain of Marine Corps culture, and the few outlets and comic strips that existed seemed like extensions of a self-indulgent Public Affairs office rather than something that truly challenged the Marines' own image.

It might not seem like it now, but at the time of its original publication, *Terminal Lance* was quite subversive. Marines are prideful people and are generally unwelcoming of anything that challenges that pride.

But I'm proud to say that the strip quickly grew in popularity. I suppose it's hard to be mad at something when you know it's true, and it's doubly difficult when that something makes you laugh.

With that said, *Terminal Lance* is a product of its time, and the last seven years have seen enormous social change, both in the military and in the country as a whole.

For example, in late 2010, President Obama repealed the long-standing "Don't Ask, Don't Tell" policy that expelled many service members based on their sexual orientation. For the first time in American history, openly gay men and women were allowed to serve in the United States Armed Forces without fear.

Terminal Lance has found itself in the unique position to speak directly to a large population of active-duty service members. For this reason, I have tried my best to provide a comforting voice in the face of rapid change. In the case of the DADT repeal, I did a comic strip (*Terminal Lance* #34 "It's Already Gay") pointing out how absurd it is to be upset at the new order when being in the Marine Corps is already extremely gay in itself.

It is because of strips like these that *Terminal Lance* has earned itself a reputation for being one of the few military voices that has been outspoken in its support of social progress.

With that said, *Terminal Lance* is still a product of its time, and I started this comic at the age of twenty-two. My own viewpoints on varying subjects have shifted over time, with the times. Some of the comics in this collection are perhaps outdated in their humor, language, artwork, or their political stance, but they are presented here as they were created. It is with this knowledge that I hope the comics are appreciated for what they are:

The examination and characterization of the often absurd experience of being a United States Marine infantryman.

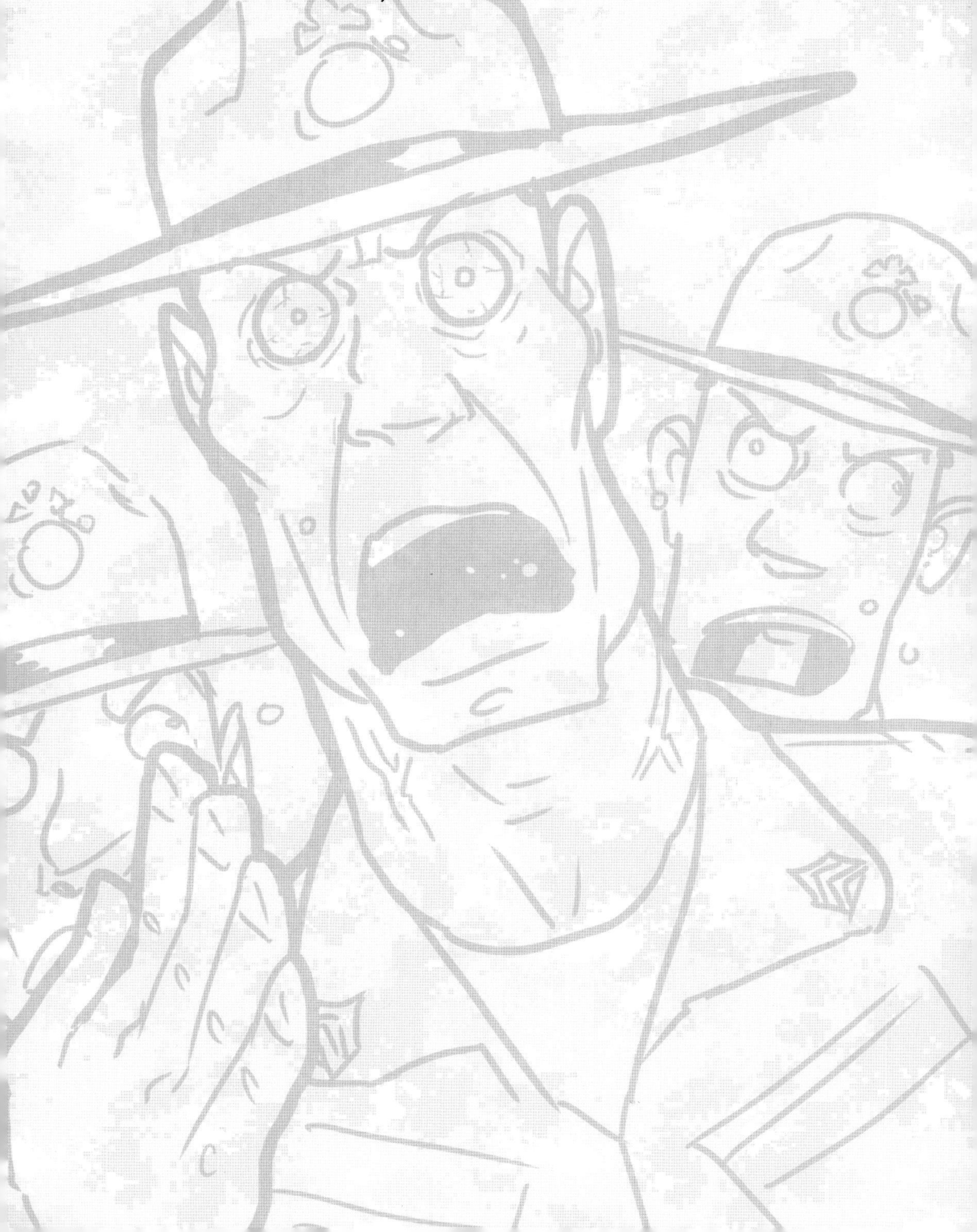

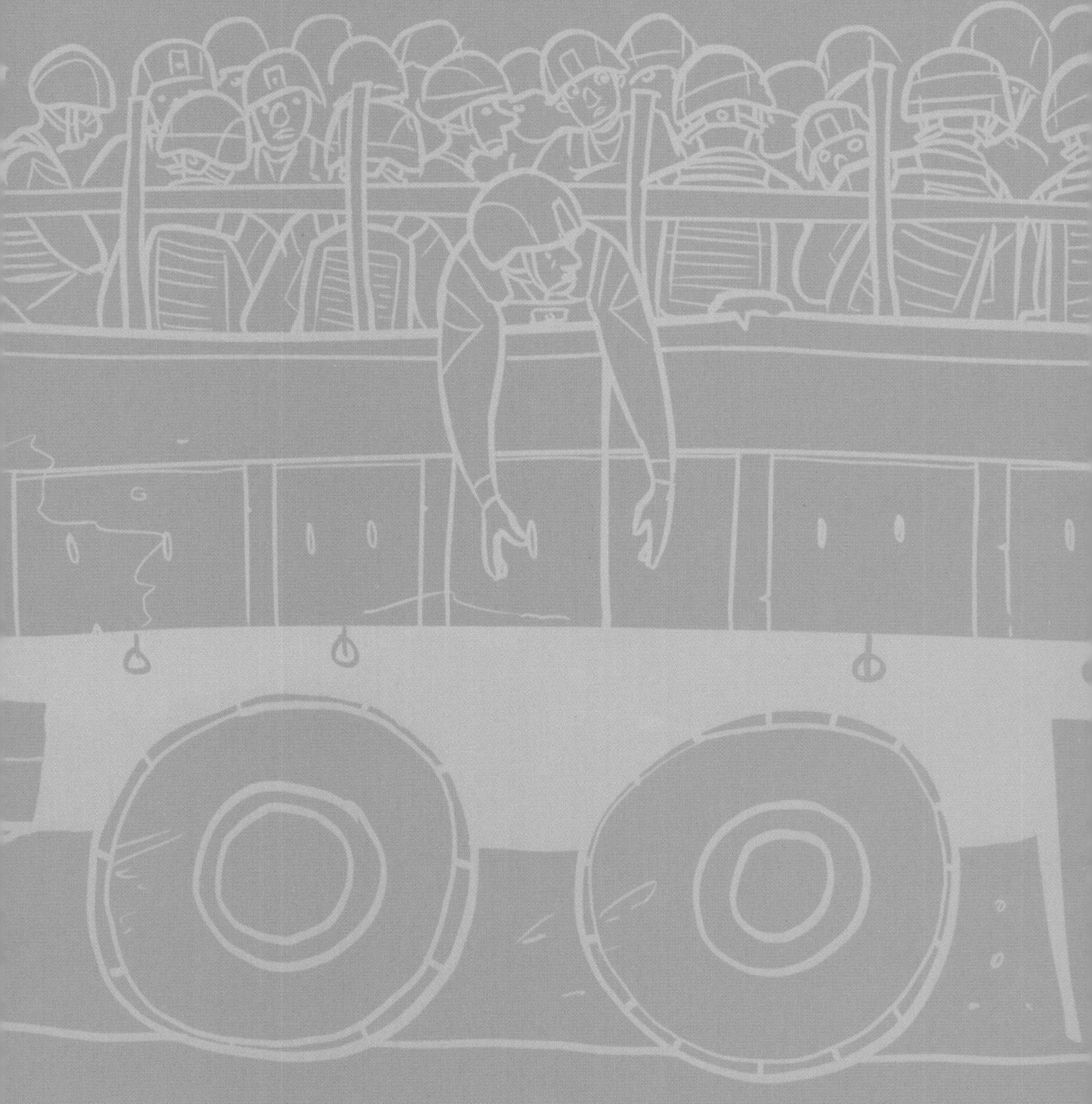

PART 1
REGULAR STRIPS

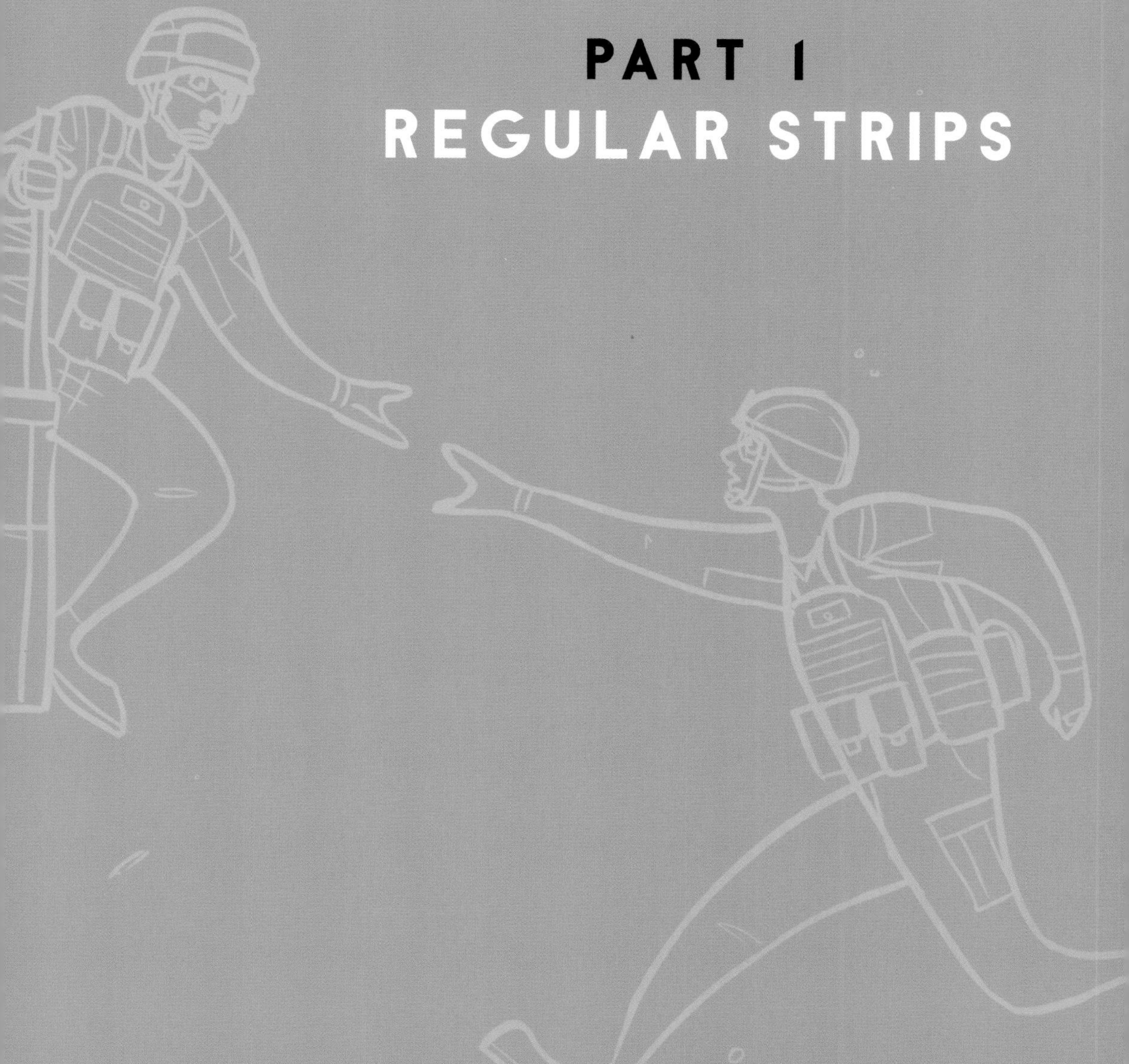

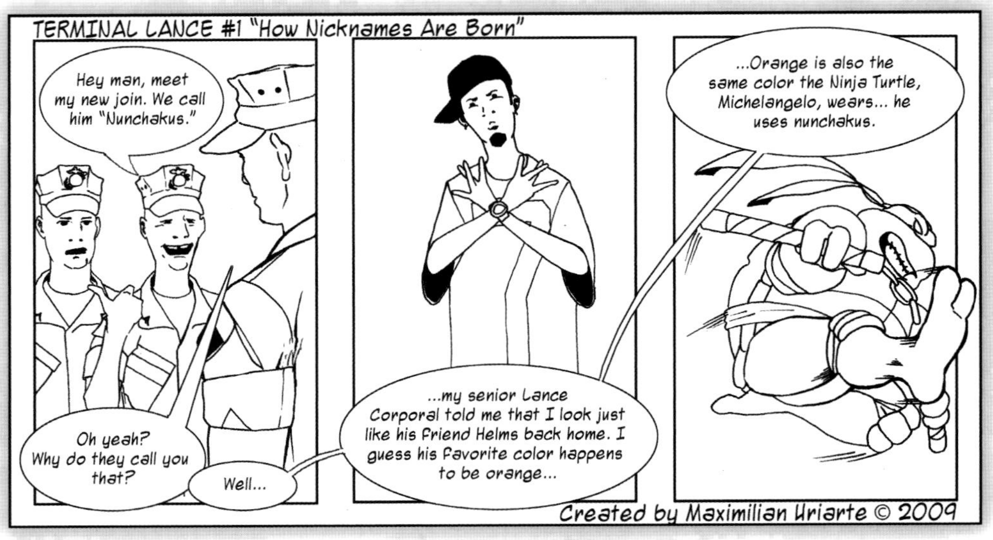
TERMINAL LANCE #1 "How Nicknames Are Born"
Hey man, meet my new join. We call him "Nunchakus."
Oh yeah? Why do they call you that?
Well...
...my senior Lance Corporal told me that I look just like his friend Helms back home. I guess his favorite color happens to be orange...
...Orange is also the same color the Ninja Turtle, Michelangelo, wears... he uses nunchakus.
Created by Maximilian Uriarte © 2009

1 "How Nicknames Are Born"

Good morning Marines and anyone else who decides to read this!

So this was the first post, the first comic, the launch of *Terminal Lance* officially. This comic was inspired by my experiences with the crazy nicknames that get invented around here. We've all seen it happen, standing around in a circle talking—one sentence leads to the next, one connection to another, and suddenly you have a nickname for someone that has nothing to do with what you were originally talking about.

One example I can think of specifically is my friend Bill. My section leader at the time decided that Bill looked like the character Bill from *King of the Hill*, so he declared him "Bill," even though his real name has absolutely no similarity.

I suppose I was always lucky, as my last name was too hard for my seniors to pronounce so they started calling me by my first name—Max. And thus, I became known as my actual name.

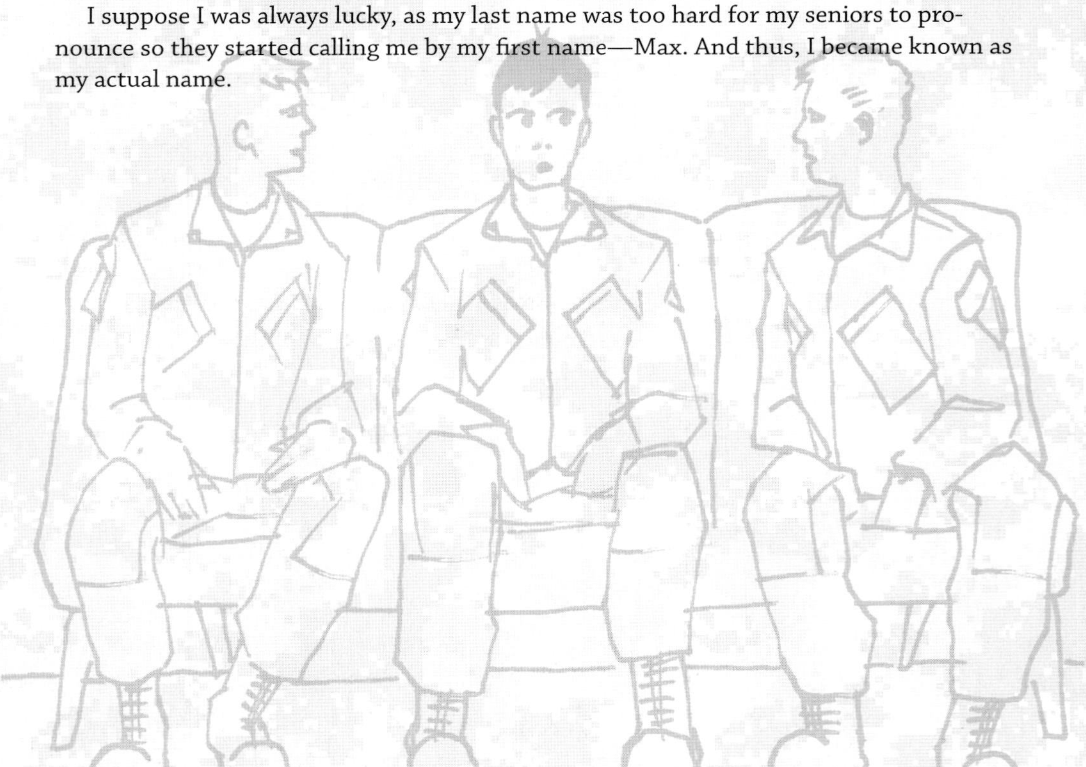

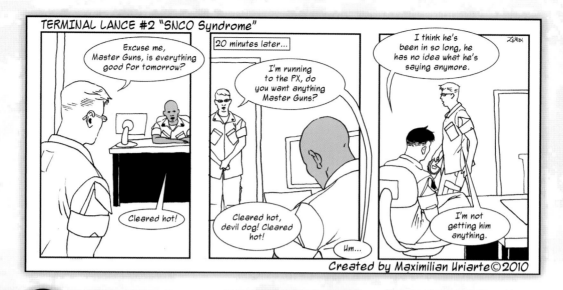

TERMINAL LANCE #2 "SNCO Syndrome"
Excuse me, Master Guns, is everything good for tomorrow?
Cleared hot!
20 minutes later...
I'm running to the PX, do you want anything Master Guns?
Cleared hot, devil dog! Cleared hot!
Um...
I think he's been in so long, he has no idea what he's saying anymore.
I'm not getting him anything.
Created by Maximilian Uriarte©2010

2 "SNCO Syndrome"

I find the many dialects of the Marine Corps to be interesting, or at least entertaining. It's strange how once someone goes into boot camp and gets shat out the other side, his entire vocabulary is often reduced to a bunch of nonsensical grunts and half-phrases. Some of these people continue to talk like this for years, and their vocabularies certainly suffer for it. I refer to this as "SNCO Syndrome." (Staff Non-Commissioned Officer.) Keep in mind that not all Staff NCO's suffer from this.

Some, however, retain this mode of thought and speech for the rest of their lives. This comic is actually inspired by a true story. I had a Master Guns (Master Gunnery Sergeant) who would literally say "Cleared Hot!" in place of most of his vocabulary. Sometimes it made sense, most of the time it didn't. I know how it affected the work environment, which is to say, not really at all. However, I can't imagine that, were the man to return home and continue yelling "Cleared Hot!" at the most inappropriate times, it would end well. These things carry on all over the Corps, though; my recruiter used to end every sentence and answer every question with "Good to Go." Other words permeate the barracks and chow halls of the Marine Corps, such as "Hello, Roger," and the almost always inappropriate "Kill," or its extended version: "Kill Bodies." I think what bothers me the most about "Kill" as a response is that it's never the people who've actually killed someone that use it.

Whatever the case, I think all Marines—SNCO's and motivated junior enlisted—could stand to expand their vocabularies. If you're the kind of person that answers a question with "Semper Fi," you probably need to be on medication. Still, whether you love it or hate it, Marine-speak is universally understood by Marines alike.

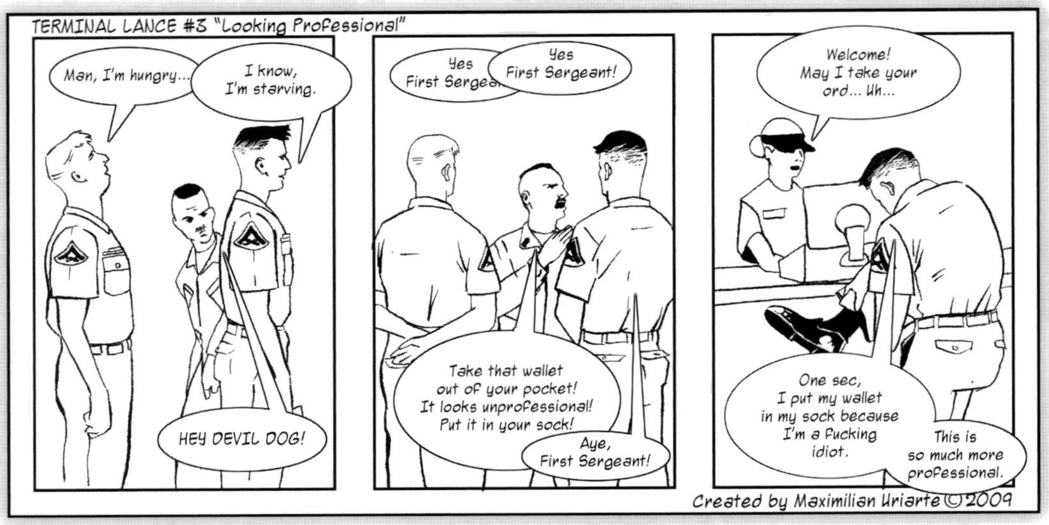
TERMINAL LANCE #3 "Looking Professional"
Man, I'm hungry...
I know, I'm starving.
HEY DEVIL DOG!
Yes First Sergeant!
Yes First Sergeant!
Take that wallet out of your pocket! It looks unprofessional! Put it in your sock!
Aye, First Sergeant!
Welcome! May I take your ord... Uh...
One sec, I put my wallet in my sock because I'm a fucking idiot.
This is so much more professional.
Created by Maximilian Uriarte ©2009

3 "Looking Professional"

I always found the rules surrounding what we are allowed to do while in uniform sort of silly. We can't have things in our pockets and we can't carry anything in our right hand. Technically, we can't even hold the hand of our loved ones while in uniform. For an organization that prides itself on practicality and adaptability in combat, the military practices none of that regarding the wearing of service uniforms.

Today's service uniforms are really nothing more than modernized versions of the ones that the Marines of old used to wear. Back then, however, I don't think anyone cared if you used your pockets to store items, as that is why pockets exist. Yes, I am stating this as a fact: Pockets exist to store items on your person. This concept is extremely hard for some of the more hardcore regulation-thumpers to grasp. The idea that you could honestly get in trouble for putting your wallet in your back pocket is completely absurd to anyone outside of the service.

This happens all the time: We get corrected for doing something that would seem practical enough in your uniform. Not just the Service Alphas, Bravos, and Chucks—but in cammies as well. Have you ever tried to put your hands in your pocket on a cold field op? Or tried to wear a backpack or some other carry-able storage device using the straps provided only to be yelled at by some random, butt-hurt Staff NCO? Of course, you have! But we're all used to it. Regulations are regulations, and some people truly pride themselves on their ability to angrily enforce them.

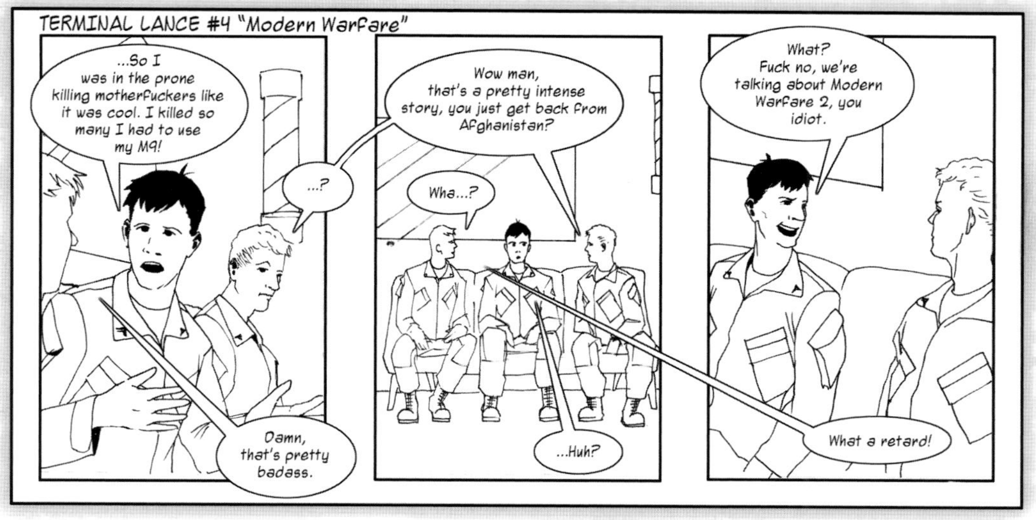
TERMINAL LANCE #4 "Modern Warfare"
...So I was in the prone killing motherfuckers like it was cool. I killed so many I had to use my M9!
...?
Damn, that's pretty badass.
Wow man, that's a pretty intense story, you just get back from Afghanistan?
Wha...?
...Huh?
What? Fuck no, we're talking about Modern Warfare 2, you idiot.
What a retard!

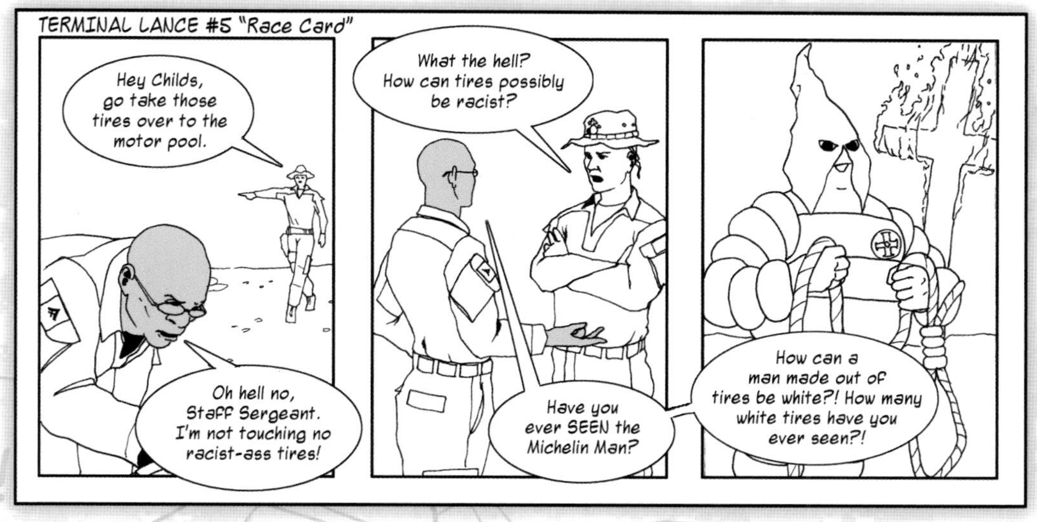
TERMINAL LANCE #5 "Race Card"
Hey Childs, go take those tires over to the motor pool.
Oh hell no, Staff Sergeant. I'm not touching no racist-ass tires!
What the hell? How can tires possibly be racist?
Have you ever SEEN the Michelin Man?
How can a man made out of tires be white?! How many white tires have you ever seen?!

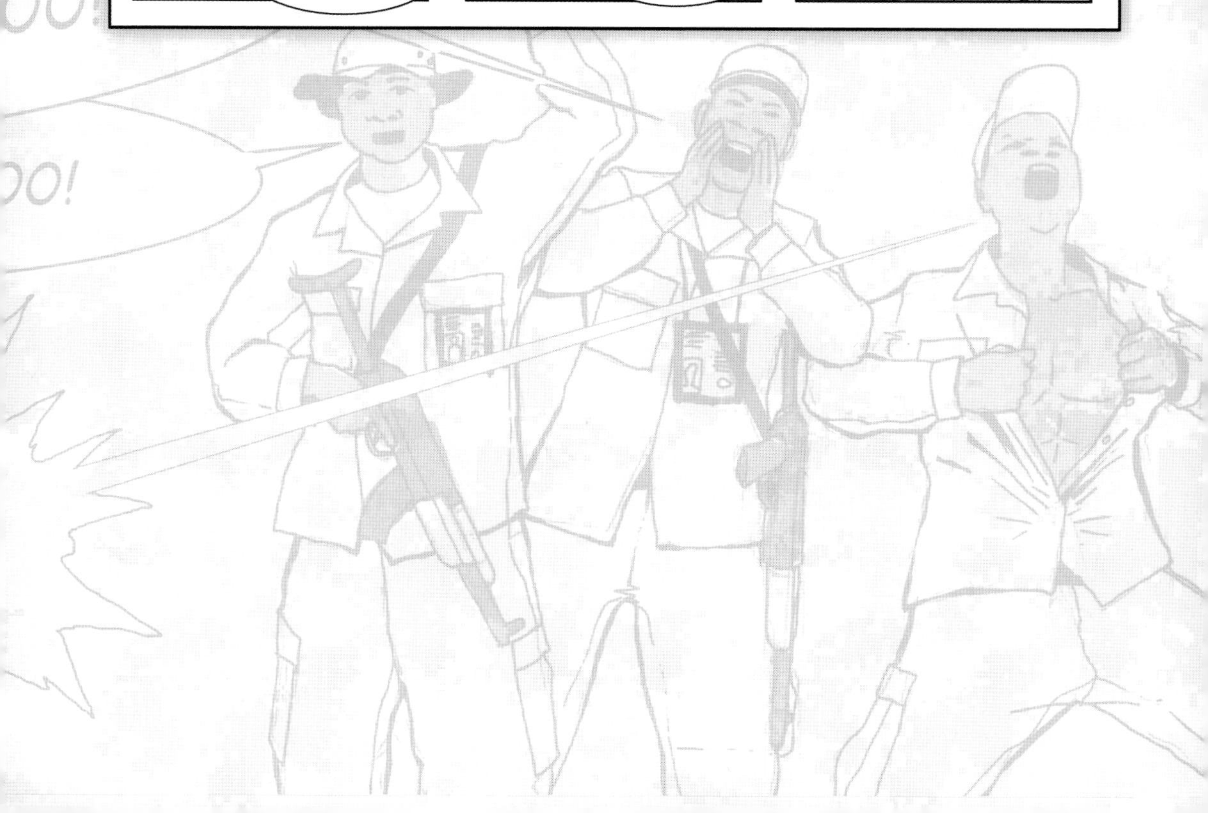

TERMINAL LANCE #6 "Jambo!" (If you went to Iraq, you'll get it.)

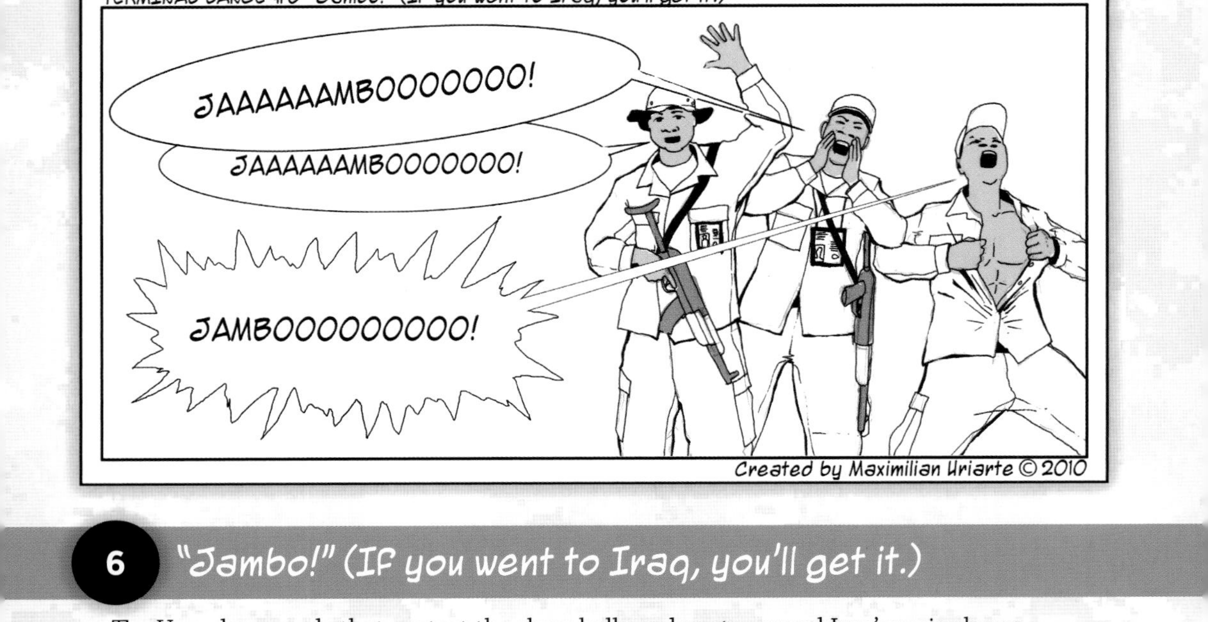
JAAAAAAMBOOOOOOO!
JAAAAAAMBOOOOOOO!
JAMBOOOOOOOOOO!

Created by Maximilian Uriarte © 2010

6 "Jambo!" (If you went to Iraq, you'll get it.)

The Ugandan guards that protect the chow halls and posts around Iraq's major bases always brought joy to me. I remember my days in the turret fondly, riding past the guard posts and yelling "Jambo!" from my hole atop the MRAP as we cruised around Camp Fallujah. I was always reciprocated with an even more enthusiastic reply of "JAAAAM-BOOOO SIR!" from the Ugandans.

For some reason the word "Jambo" gets them going pretty good. I haven't made the journey to Afghanistan, so I'm not sure if these guys are there. If they are, and you happen to be there now, make sure you give them a good Jambo next time you see them. If you happen to be in Iraq, and pass by some Ugandan guards, definitely give them a hefty Jambo.

TERMINAL LANCE #7 "Good Reasons to Not Go to the Gym"

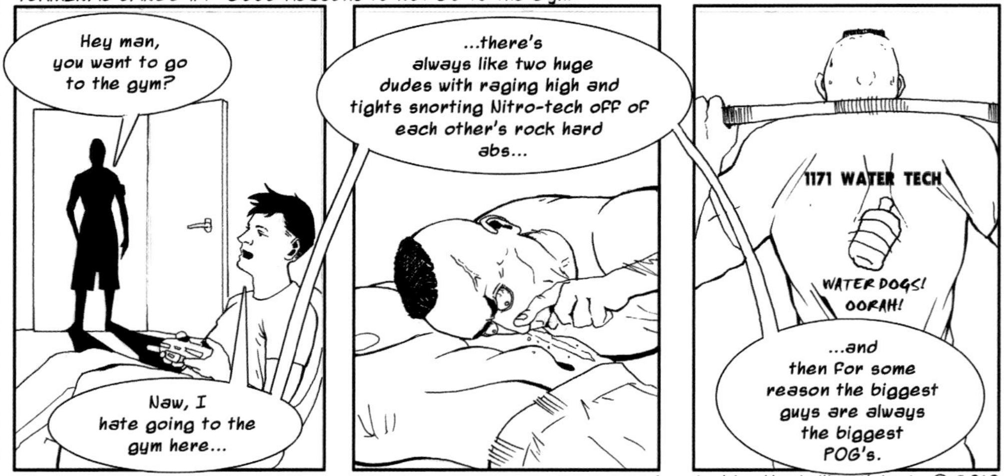
Hey man, you want to go to the gym?
Naw, I hate going to the gym here...
...there's always like two huge dudes with raging high and tights snorting Nitro-tech off of each other's rock hard abs...
1171 WATER TECH
WATER DOGS! OORAH!
...and then for some reason the biggest guys are always the biggest POG's.

Created by Maximilian Uriarte © 2010

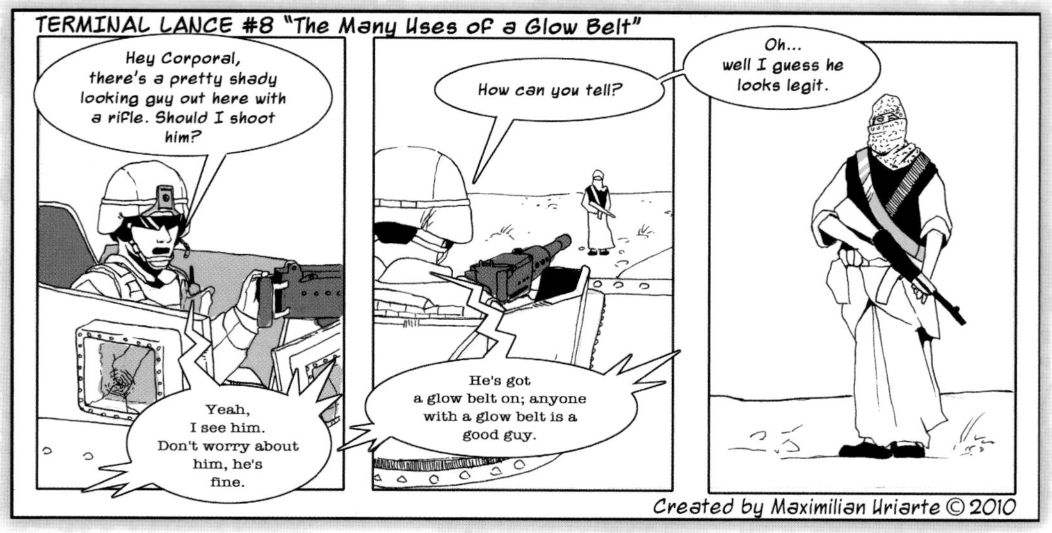
TERMINAL LANCE #8 "The Many Uses of a Glow Belt"
Hey Corporal, there's a pretty shady looking guy out here with a rifle. Should I shoot him?
Yeah, I see him. Don't worry about him, he's fine.
How can you tell?
He's got a glow belt on; anyone with a glow belt is a good guy.
Oh... well I guess he looks legit.
Created by Maximilian Uriarte © 2010

8 "The Many Uses of a Glow Belt"

This strip is based on a true story. During my first deployment in '07, the ISF (Iraqi Security Forces) guys didn't have any uniforms. These were men who wanted to stand up for their neighborhoods and regions. The US Military would pay them to stand around at checkpoints and defend their locale. There were no uniforms then, however, so we gave them glow belts.

I remember my first few convoys, seeing these seemingly shady guys and having no idea whether we could trust them. A lot of Marines had trouble trusting the local forces because we didn't always know where they came from. While we were there, there was a lot of chatter that the IP's (Iraqi Police) were going to turn on us. We were on high alert just in case.

I recall one story from this time of friction between the IP's and the Coalition forces quite fondly. I was part of a PSD platoon during my first deployment. I was the lead turret gunner of an MRAP behind the M2 .50 Cal. We would often escort our company commander to the local Iraqi Police chief's headquarters and would sit outside during their long meetings. During one of our trips, I was sitting in the turret posted on security around the building as usual. Suddenly, I heard a three-round burst coming from the inside. Naturally, given the level of mistrust that existed between us and the Iraqi police, I assumed it was time—the Iraqi Police had turned on us. I sprung from my strap and immediately rotated my gun to the house, ready to rock and roll on the Deuce.

To my surprise, no one in the compound was firing or on high alert. I saw an Iraqi behind a PKC machine gun and took aim at him, but he put his hands up and the Iraqi Police and Marines started waving me down before I started firing. It was passed over the 'net that apparently one of the IP's was fucking around a bit too much on the PKC and had a misfire. I wanted to punch him, but I think I got my vengeance on his pants—as the look on his face when he saw the barrel of my .50 on him could only be described as that of someone shitting himself.

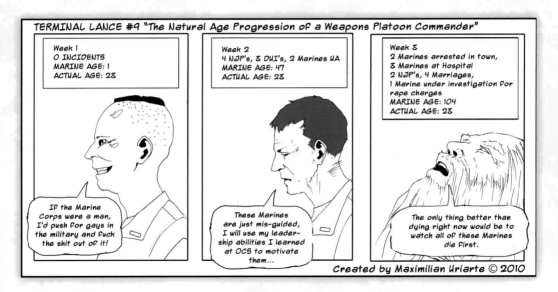

TERMINAL LANCE #9 "The Natural Age Progression of a Weapons Platoon Commander"

Week 1
0 INCIDENTS
MARINE AGE: 1
ACTUAL AGE: 23

If the Marine Corps were a man, I'd push for gays in the military and fuck the shit out of it!

Week 2
4 NJP's, 3 DUI's, 2 Marines UA
MARINE AGE: 47
ACTUAL AGE: 23

These Marines are just mis-guided, I will use my leadership abilities I learned at OCS to motivate them...

Week 3
2 Marines arrested in town,
3 Marines at Hospital
2 NJP's, 4 Marriages,
1 Marine under investigation for rape charges
MARINE AGE: 104
ACTUAL AGE: 23

The only thing better than dying right now would be to watch all of these Marines die first.

Created by Maximilian Uriarte © 2010

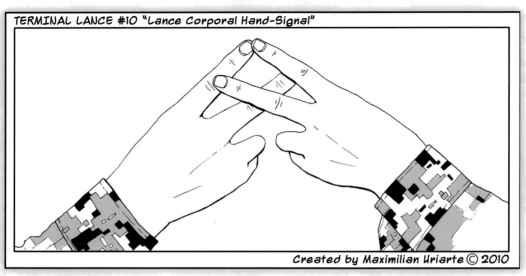

TERMINAL LANCE #10 "Lance Corporal Hand-Signal"

Created by Maximilian Uriarte © 2010

10   "Lance Corporal Hand-Signal"

Throw it up, gents! Represent your true colors, with the Lance Corporal hand signal. I can't actually take credit for the hand signal; my aforementioned friend Bill created it during our first deployment.

The Lance Corporal in the infantry goes a long way. It is generally recognized within our ranks that being a Lance virtually means nothing to us. We have a full understanding of how broken the cutting score system is and how ridiculous promotions are. And the best of us are unwilling to suck enough dick to get promoted.

If Sergeants are the backbone of the Marine Corps, then Lance Corporals are the extremities, ultimately responsible for performing the tasks to keep the Corps alive. Unfortunately for the infantry, Lance Corporals have to be more than just extremities. I have seen Lances fill billets they shouldn't have to, and do it admirably. For instance, the Section Leader billet of an Assaultman section is supposed to be a Staff Sergeant. Obviously, that doesn't happen in real life. But couldn't it at least be a Sergeant? Nope, that usually doesn't happen either. For my first couple years in the Marines, my section leader was a Lance Corporal, until he was rightfully meritoriously promoted to Corporal. After he left, we had another Lance Corporal take his place until he was again promoted to Corporal.

So if Lances can fill the shoes of Staff NCO's and NCO's, why shouldn't we be proud to be one? I say we take the shame away from being a one-chevron, cross-rifle rocking monkey and take pride in it! Throw up that hand signal and let the world know that with a promotion system as fucked as ours, there's no point in giving a shit! Ever seen a Corporal or Sergeant with fewer ribbons than you? I have, and it pisses me off every time.

I'm not a Lance because I got in trouble, or I didn't do my job. I never claimed to be God's gift to the Marine Corps, but I performed my job just fine. I'm the result of a promotion system that is flat-out broken. The cutting score requirement for my MOS (Military Occupational Specialty) was always either absurdly high or simply closed entirely.

So like I said, throw that shit up.

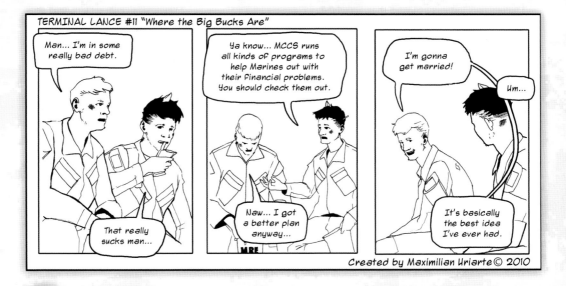

TERMINAL LANCE #11 "Where the Big Bucks Are"
Man... I'm in some really bad debt.
That really sucks man...
Ya know... MCCS runs all kinds of programs to help Marines out with their financial problems. You should check them out.
Naw... I got a better plan anyway...
MRE
I'm gonna get married!
Um...
It's basically the best idea I've ever had.
Created by Maximilian Uriarte© 2010

11 "Where the Big Bucks Are"

This strip may hit a bit too close to home for some. But I'll be honest: Marriage in the Marine Corps is more of a problem than a blessing. Too often, especially in the infantry, Marines get married as an answer to financial problems. The problem lies within the foundation of the system itself. Where in the civilian world would you get paid to be married? Probably nowhere, but the military unwittingly encourages it with gratuitous BAH (Base Allowance for Housing) payments or potentially even a rent-free two-bedroom house in one of the base housing blocks. When living in the barracks is such a shit show, tying the knot can be an easy escape for an enterprising Lance Corporal.

While there are plenty of hoops to jump through when it comes time to tie the knot, none of them truly work as a deterrent against a marriage. The result is an 80 percent divorce rate brought on by Marines who just don't understand the consequences of what they're getting themselves into. We shouldn't encourage Marines to get married at such a young age. Whatever the solution, the system needs to be fixed.

Divorce rates and the resultant alimonies truly are a rampant problem in the Marines, and probably the military as a whole. Single Marines need to stop being treated worse, stop getting fucked with 24/7, maybe even have the option of receiving BAH. Little things like this will go a long way in fighting young marriage—and divorce—rates.

TERMINAL LANCE #12 "Tom Clancy Is Full of Shit"

BWEEEE!

Night-vision is so badass! I can't wait to use it in real life!

4 months later...
SOI West

These fucking suck, I can't see anything! Tom Clancy is full of shit.

Created by Maximilian Uriarte © 2010

TERMINAL LANCE #13 "Salty Cammies"

I sure love my salty cammies. They're so much more comfortable and soft.

...boot.

Created by Maximilian Uriarte © 2010

TERMINAL LANCE #14 "The Mr. E Mystery 1"

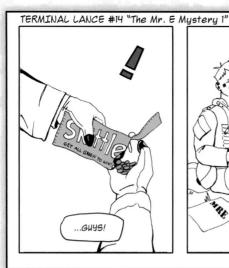

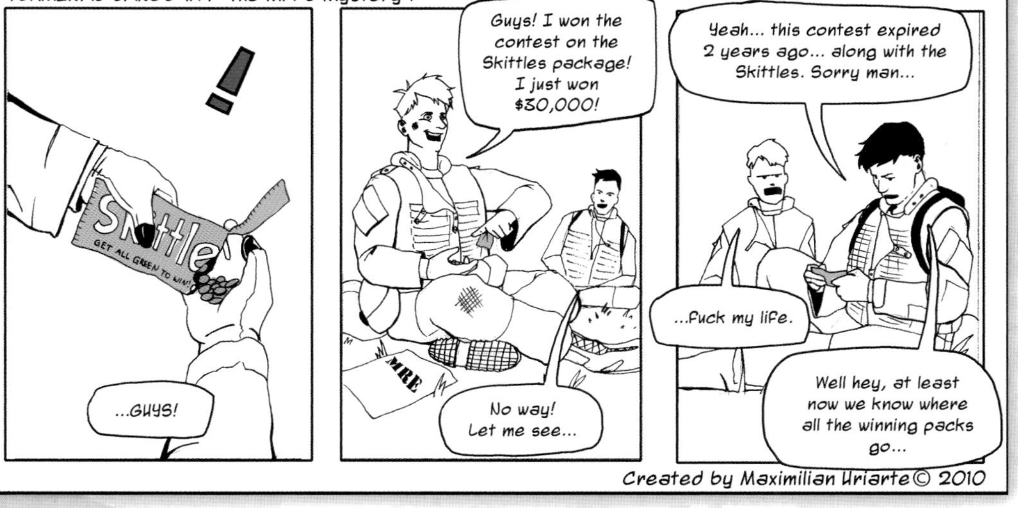
!
Skittles
GET ALL GREEN TO WIN!
...GUYS!
Guys! I won the contest on the Skittles package! I just won $30,000!
MRE
No way! Let me see...
Yeah... this contest expired 2 years ago... along with the Skittles. Sorry man...
...Fuck my life.
Well hey, at least now we know where all the winning packs go...
Created by Maximilian Uriarte © 2010

TERMINAL LANCE #15 "SPECIAL EDITION"

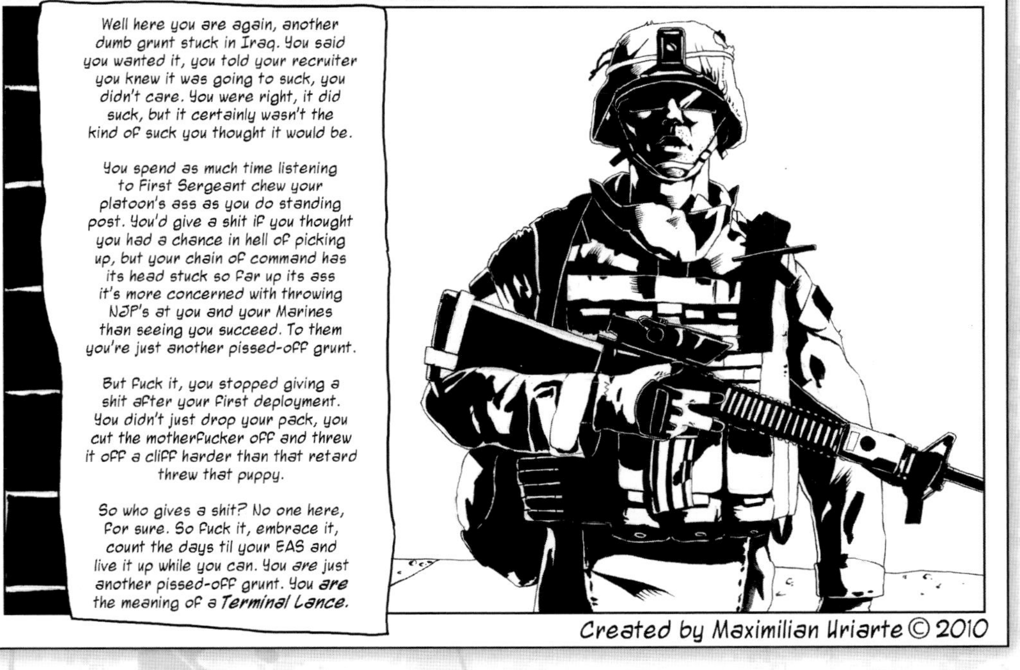
Well here you are again, another dumb grunt stuck in Iraq. You said you wanted it, you told your recruiter you knew it was going to suck, you didn't care. You were right, it did suck, but it certainly wasn't the kind of suck you thought it would be.
You spend as much time listening to First Sergeant chew your platoon's ass as you do standing post. You'd give a shit if you thought you had a chance in hell of picking up, but your chain of command has its head stuck so far up its ass it's more concerned with throwing NJP's at you and your Marines than seeing you succeed. To them you're just another pissed-off grunt.
But fuck it, you stopped giving a shit after your first deployment. You didn't just drop your pack, you cut the motherfucker off and threw it off a cliff harder than that retard threw that puppy.
So who gives a shit? No one here, for sure. So fuck it, embrace it, count the days til your EAS and live it up while you can. You are just another pissed-off grunt. You *are* the meaning of a *Terminal Lance*.
Created by Maximilian Uriarte © 2010

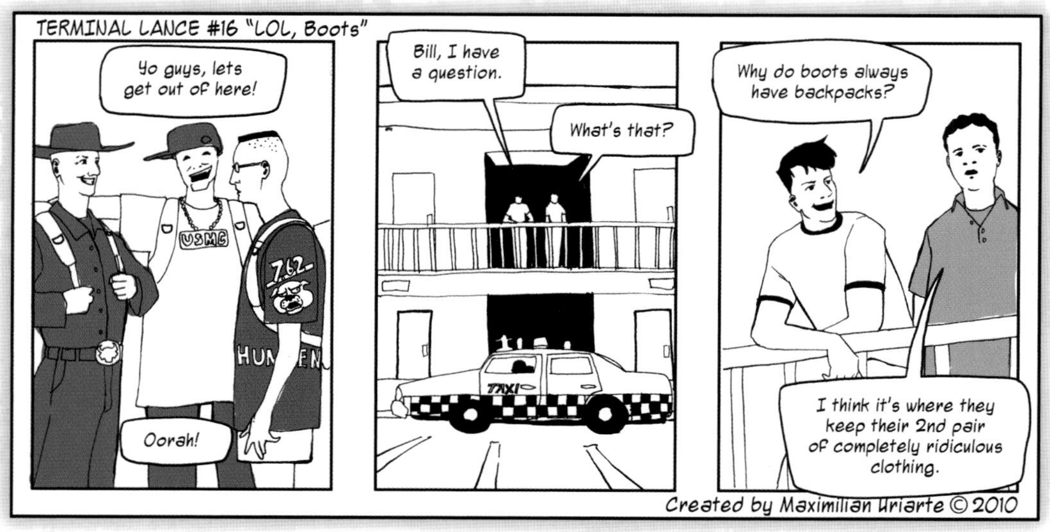
TERMINAL LANCE #16 "LOL, Boots"
Yo guys, lets get out of here!
USMC
7.62
Oorah!
Bill, I have a question.
What's that?
TAXI
Why do boots always have backpacks?
I think it's where they keep their 2nd pair of completely ridiculous clothing.
Created by Maximilian Uriarte © 2010

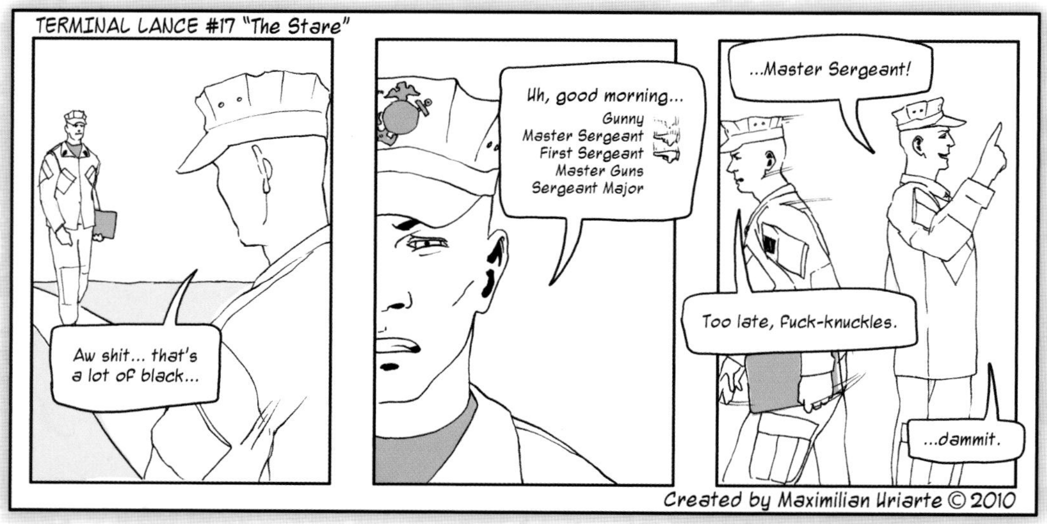
TERMINAL LANCE #17 "The Stare"
Aw shit... that's a lot of black...
Uh, good morning...
Gunny
Master Sergeant
First Sergeant
Master Guns
Sergeant Major
...Master Sergeant!
Too late, fuck-knuckles.
...dammit.
Created by Maximilian Uriarte © 2010

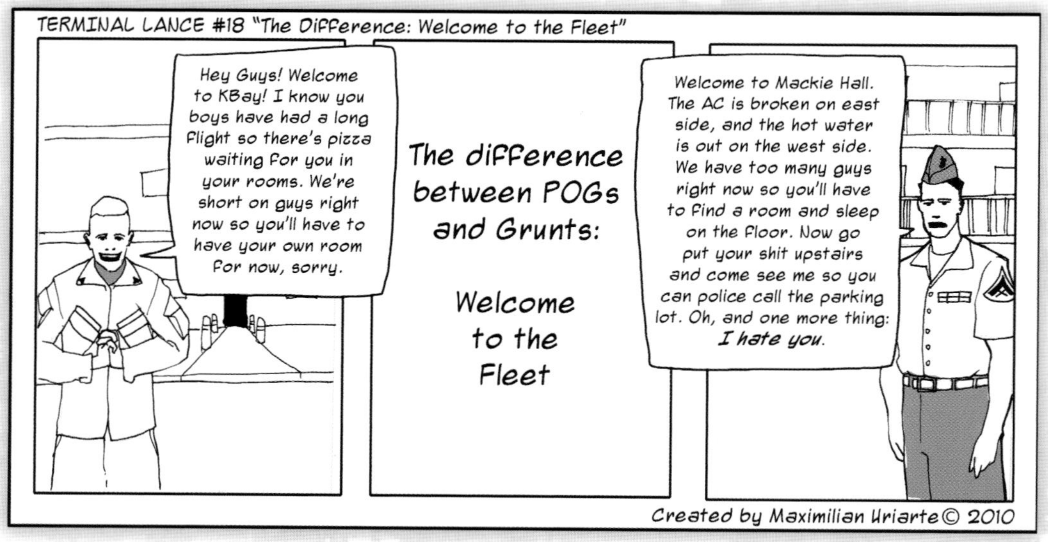
TERMINAL LANCE #18 "The Difference: Welcome to the Fleet"
Hey Guys! Welcome to KBay! I know you boys have had a long flight so there's pizza waiting for you in your rooms. We're short on guys right now so you'll have to have your own room for now, sorry.
The difference between POGs and Grunts:
Welcome to the Fleet
Welcome to Mackie Hall. The AC is broken on east side, and the hot water is out on the west side. We have too many guys right now so you'll have to find a room and sleep on the floor. Now go put your shit upstairs and come see me so you can police call the parking lot. Oh, and one more thing: I hate you.
Created by Maximilian Uriarte © 2010

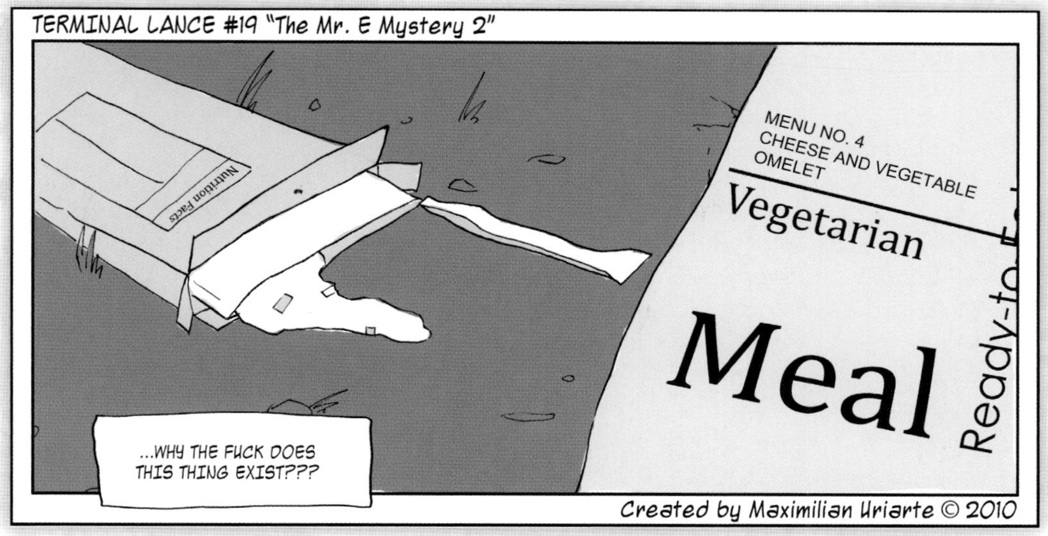
TERMINAL LANCE #19 "The Mr. E Mystery 2"
Nutrition Facts
MENU NO. 4
CHEESE AND VEGETABLE
OMELET
Vegetarian
Meal
Ready-to
...WHY THE FUCK DOES THIS THING EXIST???
Created by Maximilian Uriarte © 2010

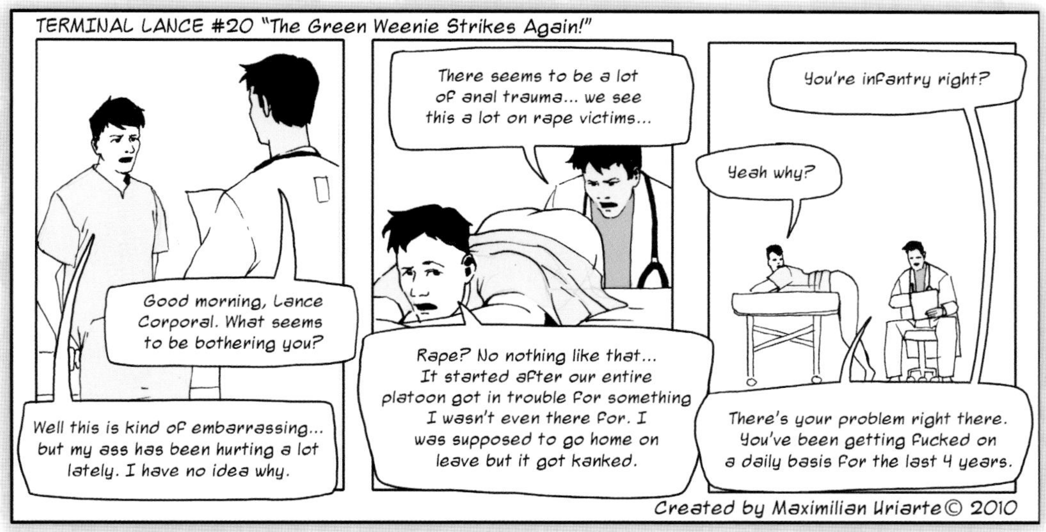
TERMINAL LANCE #20 "The Green Weenie Strikes Again!"
Good morning, Lance Corporal. What seems to be bothering you?
Well this is kind of embarrassing... but my ass has been hurting a lot lately. I have no idea why.
There seems to be a lot of anal trauma... we see this a lot on rape victims...
Rape? No nothing like that... It started after our entire platoon got in trouble for something I wasn't even there for. I was supposed to go home on leave but it got kanked.
You're infantry right?
Yeah why?
There's your problem right there. You've been getting fucked on a daily basis for the last 4 years.
Created by Maximilian Uriarte © 2010

20 "The Green Weenie Strikes Again!"

This comic was inspired by what transpired at my final physical. Over the years in an infantry battalion, you really don't get to go to BAS (Base Aid Station) enough. Well, those of us that are worth a damn don't. There's definitely a stigma associated with going to medical while you're in the infantry. To go to medical is to be weak, and as a result most grunts end up with all kinds of improperly treated problems by the time their final physicals roll around and have no real excuse for it.

All the medical problems I'd ever had came to light during my final physical, and the good doctor was noticeably annoyed. Granted, she was an H&S Bn. doctor and probably doesn't see too many grunts, but I can imagine her frustration at my helplessness. She took about four pages of notes while I explained all my problems, including the fact that I didn't have my medical record because my old unit decided to take it with them to Twentynine Palms despite the fact that I had moved over to the base Combat Camera shop. Oh, the green weenie strikes hard, and it strikes fast.

This ultimately led to my getting about seventeen X-rays done on my back and rib cage, as well as about four follow-up appointments.

This story may not seem like it has much to do with the strip, but getting "fucked on a daily basis" is precisely what it's like to be in the infantry. The medical record thing is just one of the many nuances of being in the grunts. The doctor was dumbfounded by the lack of recording and procedure followed by my old unit's BAS. I never thought anything of it; I assumed that's just how the Marine Corps was. But I soon discovered that medical care outside of the infantry is actually quite up to par. The clinic I went to was not a shady, cleared-out barracks-turned-BAS, but an actual clinic. The green weenie may be taking its toll on your rectum behind the scenes and you may not even know it, because you've never been exposed to the other side.

Needless to say, grunts get fucked on a daily basis for a number of other reasons. Mass punishment is a common problem, as it usually accomplishes nothing. The same people always make the same stupid decisions, and it especially doesn't work in a weapons platoon. Here's why: Three different MOS (Military Occupational Specialty), three completely different kinds of people. The allure of machine guns, mortars, or rockets appeal to very different people. These three different personality types cannot be expected to act the same, and they often clash. In my experience, the brutes in Machine Guns tend to fuck it up the most, and "skatin' Assault" and Mortars end up paying for it as well.

In addition, grunts typically don't get half of the benefits or the benefits even explained to them that the POG's of the Corps do. You have no idea how many times I've said, ". . . what is that?" when someone around the ComCam shop has mentioned some Marine Corps order that everyone seems to know but me. It's an unfair dichotomy, to be sure. I do feel, however, that the grunt path is the true path of the Marine Corps experience.

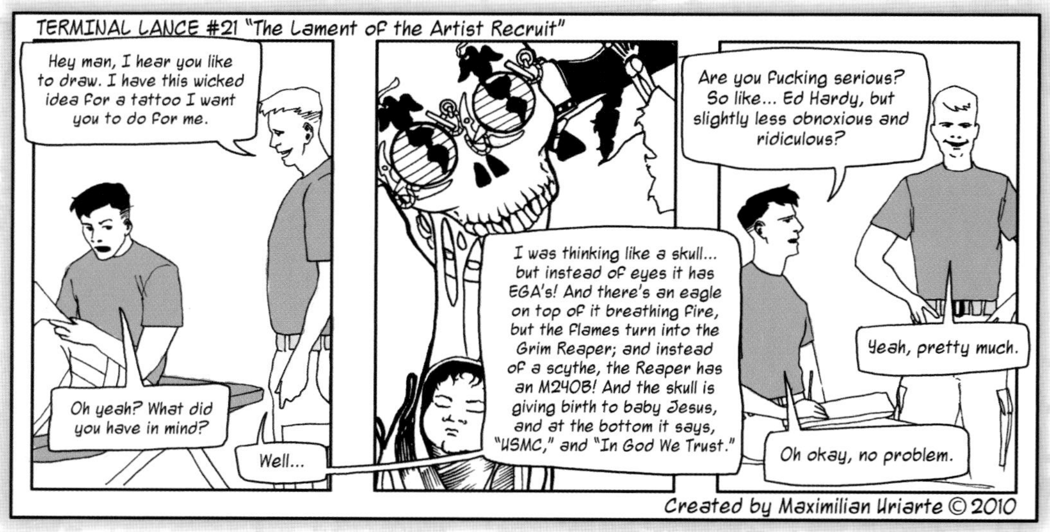
TERMINAL LANCE #21 "The Lament of the Artist Recruit"
Hey man, I hear you like to draw. I have this wicked idea for a tattoo I want you to do for me.
Oh yeah? What did you have in mind?
Well...
I was thinking like a skull... but instead of eyes it has EGA's! And there's an eagle on top of it breathing fire, but the flames turn into the Grim Reaper; and instead of a scythe, the Reaper has an M240B! And the skull is giving birth to baby Jesus, and at the bottom it says, "USMC," and "In God We Trust."
Oh okay, no problem.
Are you fucking serious? So like... Ed Hardy, but slightly less obnoxious and ridiculous?
Yeah, pretty much.
Created by Maximilian Uriarte © 2010

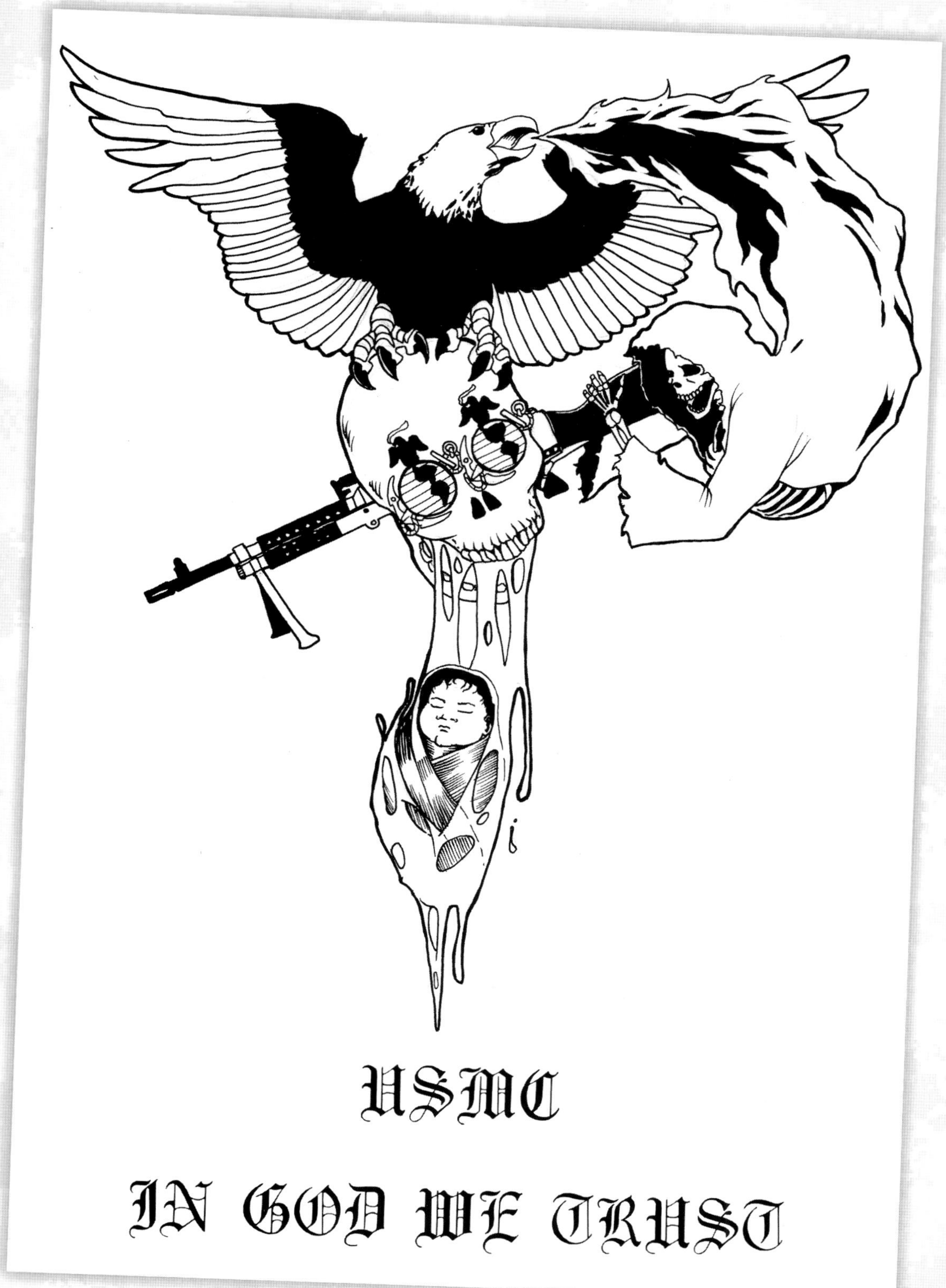
USMC
IN GOD WE TRUST

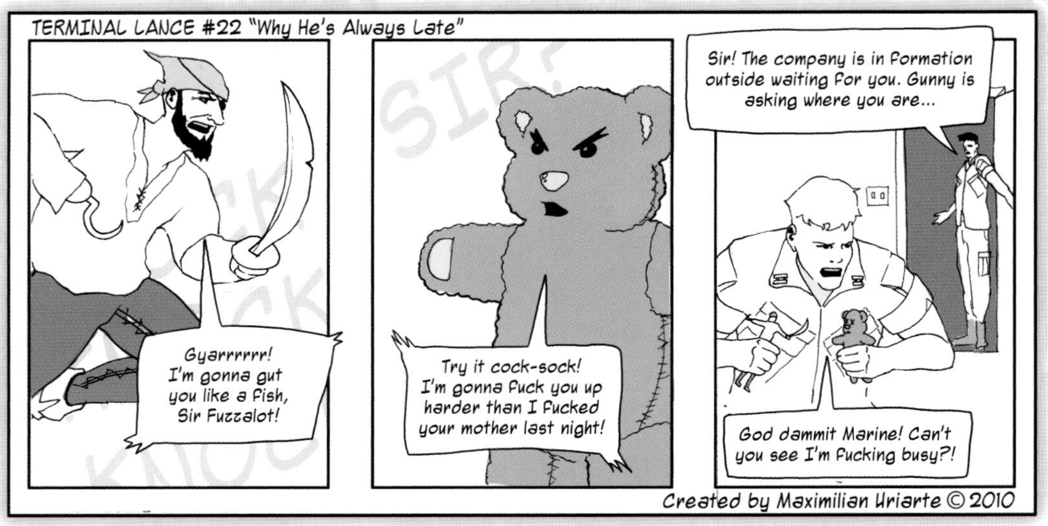
TERMINAL LANCE #22 "Why He's Always Late"
Gyarrrrrr! I'm gonna gut you like a fish, Sir Fuzzalot!
Try it cock-sock! I'm gonna fuck you up harder than I fucked your mother last night!
Sir! The company is in formation outside waiting for you. Gunny is asking where you are...
God dammit Marine! Can't you see I'm fucking busy?!
Created by Maximilian Uriarte © 2010

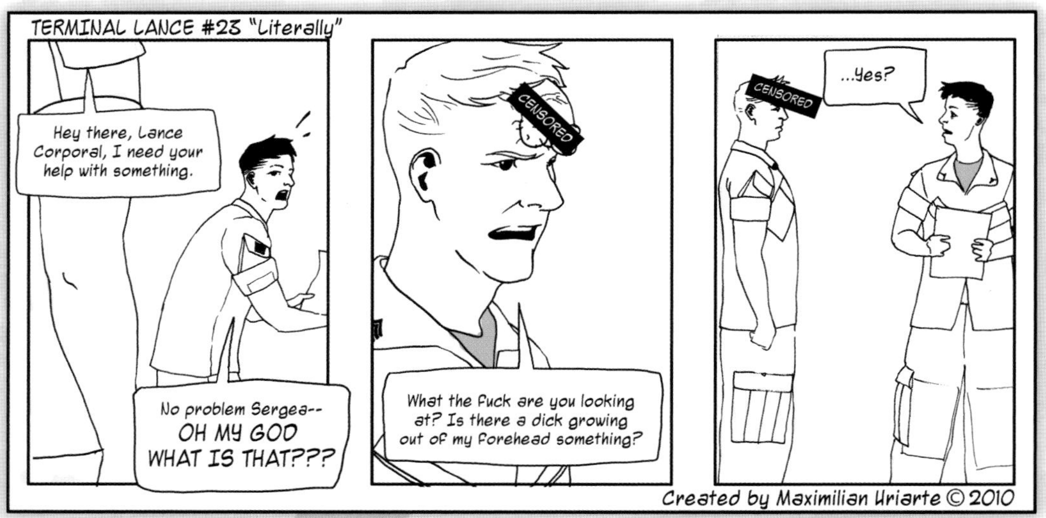
TERMINAL LANCE #23 "Literally"
Hey there, Lance Corporal, I need your help with something.
No problem Sergea-- OH MY GOD WHAT IS THAT???
CENSORED
What the fuck are you looking at? Is there a dick growing out of my forehead something?
CENSORED
...Yes?
Created by Maximilian Uriarte © 2010

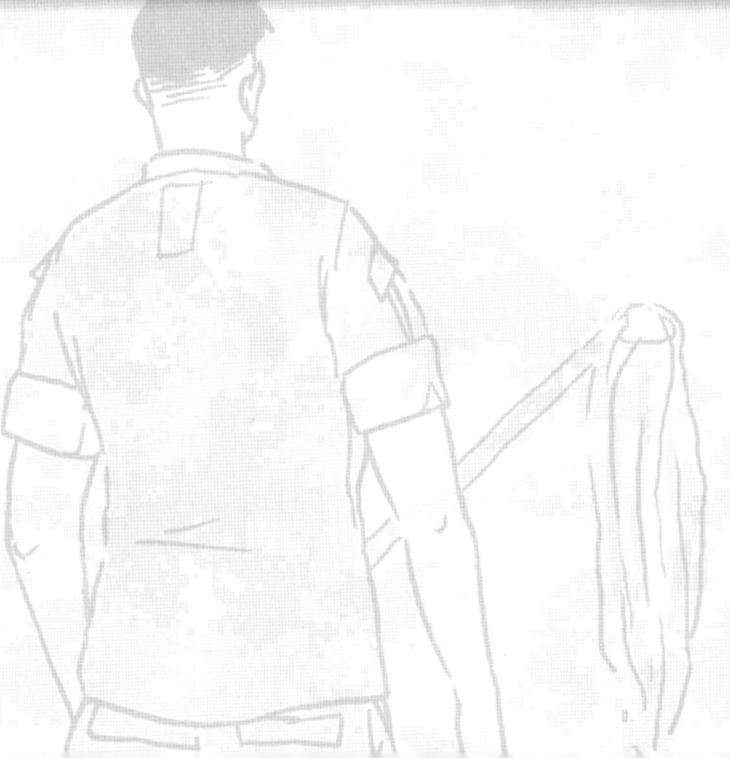

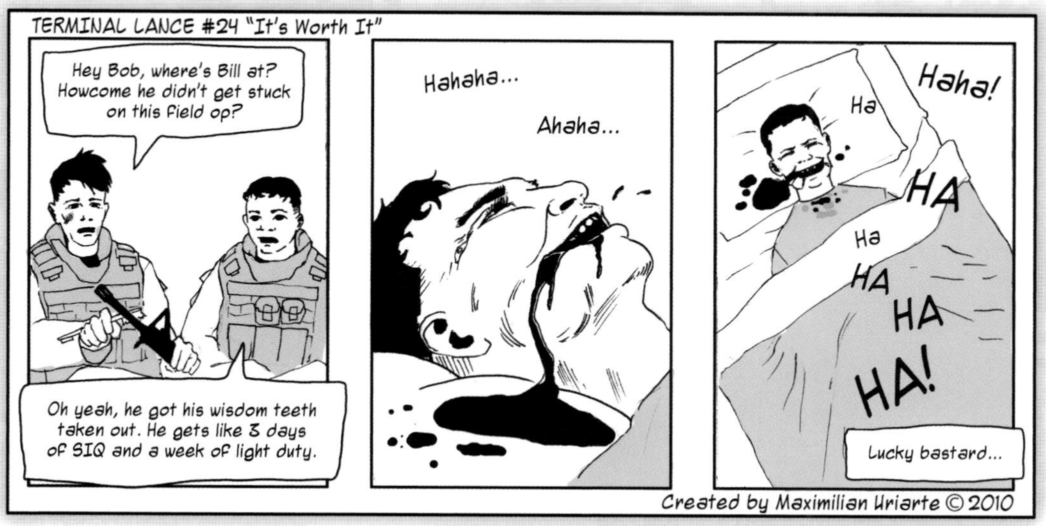
TERMINAL LANCE #24 "It's Worth It"
Hey Bob, where's Bill at? Howcome he didn't get stuck on this field op?
Oh yeah, he got his wisdom teeth taken out. He gets like 3 days of SIQ and a week of light duty.
Hahaha...
Ahaha...
Haha!
Ha
HA
Ha
HA
HA
HA!
Lucky bastard...
Created by Maximilian Uriarte © 2010

24 "It's Worth It"

This is a true story. Well, I dunno if Bill actually did any maniacal laughing at the time, but this is based on true events much in the same way Hollywood makes movies "based on true events."

Wisdom teeth are one of those things that are probably better pulled out while you're active duty and have that ever-so-popular "free medical." After all, they do get you out of work and if you're of the Oh-Three type, maybe even a field op. While they are completely miserable, field ops do have value. The field is where the heart of the Marine Corps is. In a strange way, the field is where things make sense. There's no outside world to worry about in the field, and it brings Marines close, especially because we all hate it. The field is a place of bonding. As one of my seniors explained to me on my first deployment, Marines come closer together when they have the common enemy of the Marine Corps to bitch about. Thus putting Marines through misery on a daily basis makes them much closer in the long run.

Strip a platoon or company of all their material worries, and all they have left is each other.

Going back to the comic, though; before the 2008 recession hit America, getting Marines to join was a problem. Recruitment was low and retention even lower, so Marines were being offered bonuses of up to $90,000 to re-up—a hefty offer to say the least. Maybe—now this is just a thought—retention would be easier to attain if Marines didn't prefer to have brutal oral surgery performed instead of doing their job.

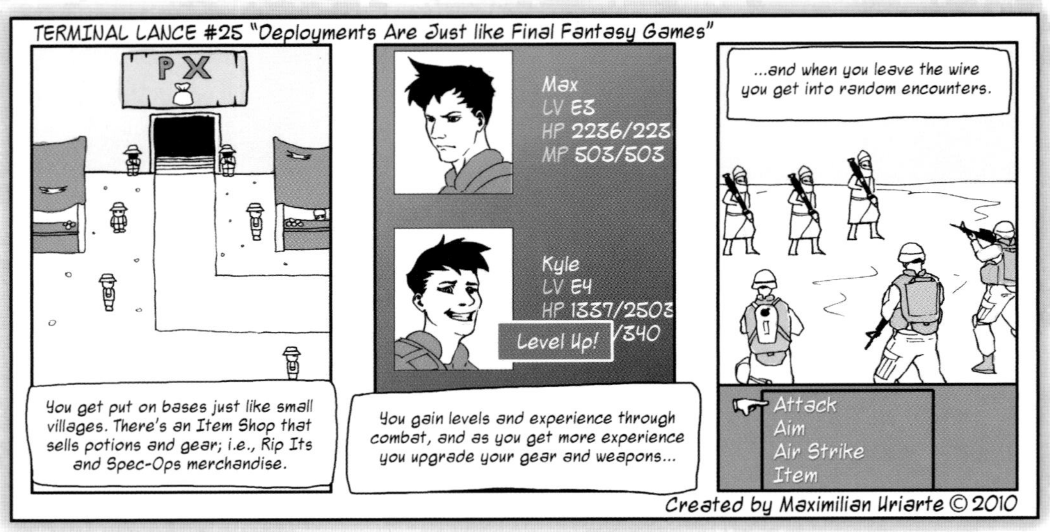
TERMINAL LANCE #25 "Deployments Are Just like Final Fantasy Games"
PX
You get put on bases just like small villages. There's an Item Shop that sells potions and gear; i.e., Rip Its and Spec-Ops merchandise.
Max
LV E3
HP 2236/223
MP 503/503
Kyle
LV E4
HP 1337/2503
/340
Level Up!
You gain levels and experience through combat, and as you get more experience you upgrade your gear and weapons...
...and when you leave the wire you get into random encounters.
Attack
Aim
Air Strike
Item
Created by Maximilian Uriarte © 2010

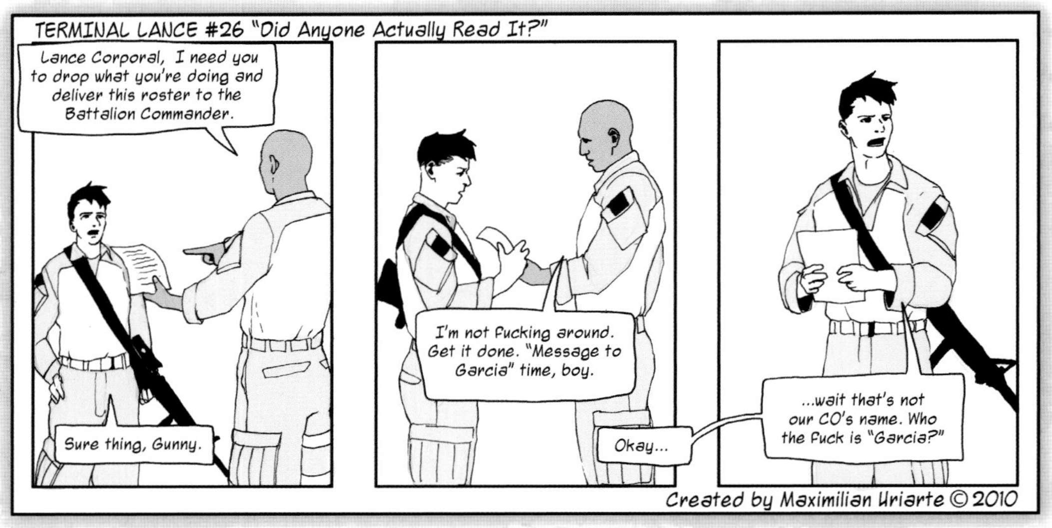
TERMINAL LANCE #26 "Did Anyone Actually Read It?"
Lance Corporal, I need you to drop what you're doing and deliver this roster to the Battalion Commander.
Sure thing, Gunny.
I'm not fucking around. Get it done. "Message to Garcia" time, boy.
Okay...
...wait that's not our CO's name. Who the fuck is "Garcia?"
Created by Maximilian Uriarte © 2010

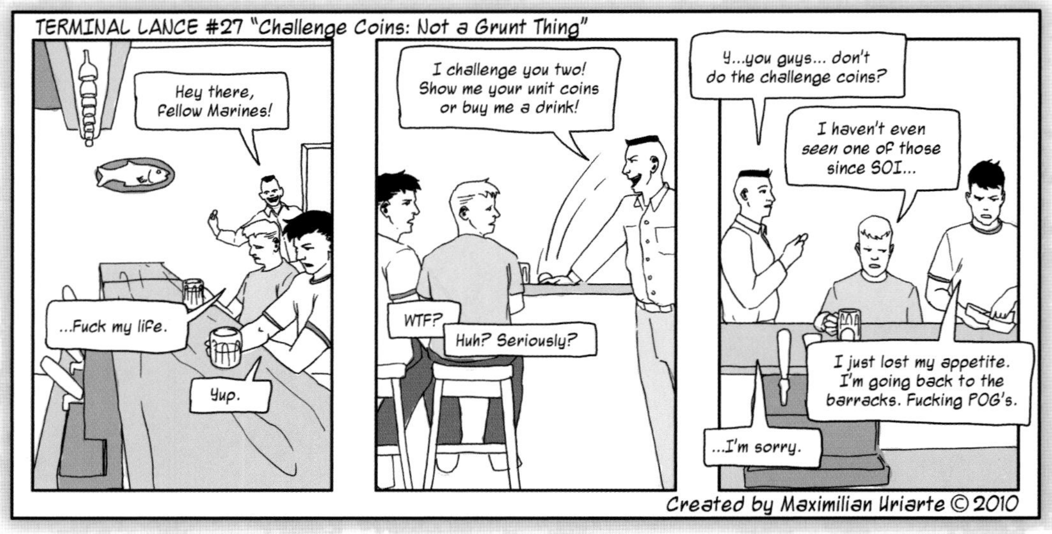
TERMINAL LANCE #27 "Challenge Coins: Not a Grunt Thing"
Hey there, fellow Marines!
...Fuck my life.
Yup.
I challenge you two! Show me your unit coins or buy me a drink!
WTF?
Huh? Seriously?
Y...you guys... don't do the challenge coins?
I haven't even seen one of those since SOI...
I just lost my appetite. I'm going back to the barracks. Fucking POG's.
...I'm sorry.
Created by Maximilian Uriarte © 2010

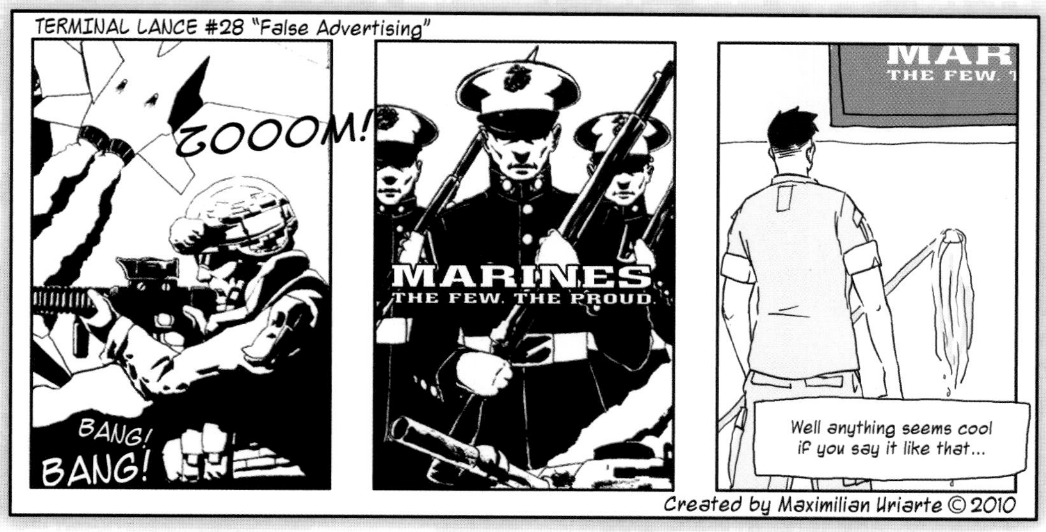
TERMINAL LANCE #28 "False Advertising"
ZOOOM!
BANG!
BANG!
MARINES
THE FEW. THE PROUD.
MAR
THE FEW. T
Well anything seems cool if you say it like that...
Created by Maximilian Uriarte © 2010

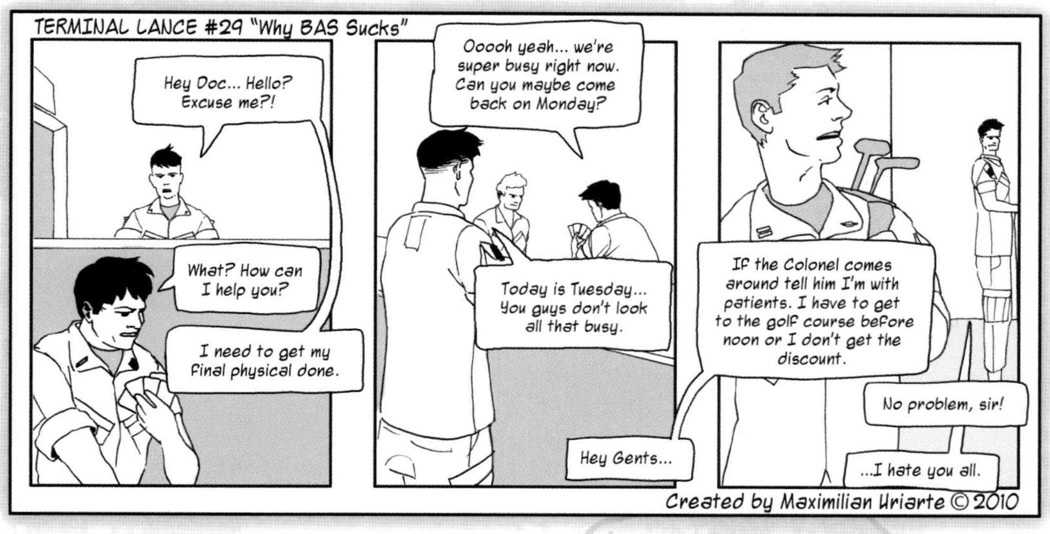
TERMINAL LANCE #29 "Why BAS Sucks"
Hey Doc... Hello? Excuse me?!
What? How can I help you?
I need to get my final physical done.
Ooooh yeah... we're super busy right now. Can you maybe come back on Monday?
Today is Tuesday... You guys don't look all that busy.
Hey Gents...
If the Colonel comes around tell him I'm with patients. I have to get to the golf course before noon or I don't get the discount.
No problem, sir!
...I hate you all.
Created by Maximilian Uriarte © 2010

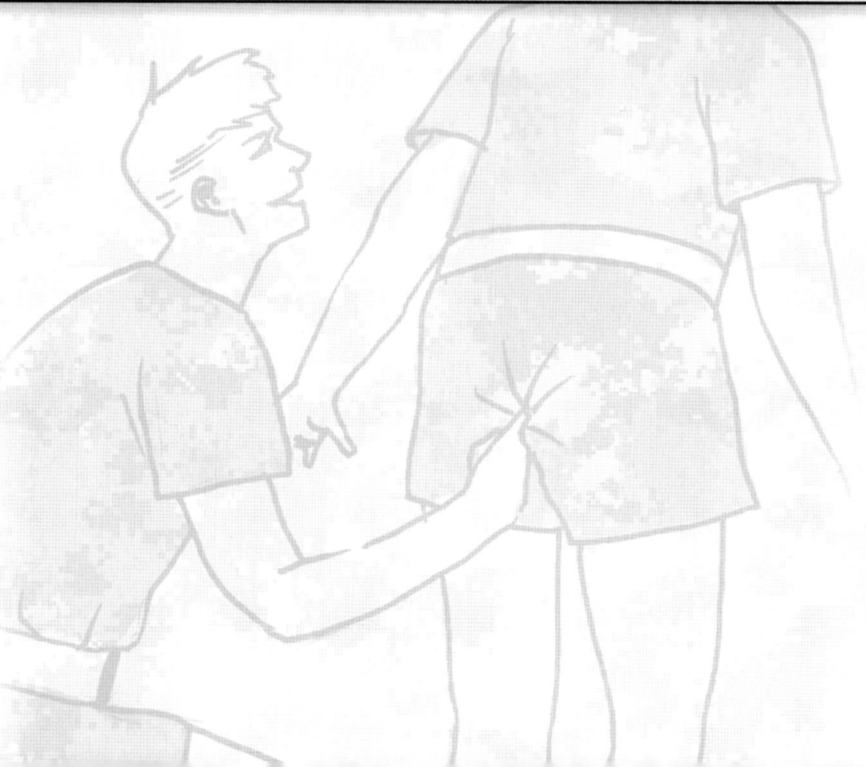

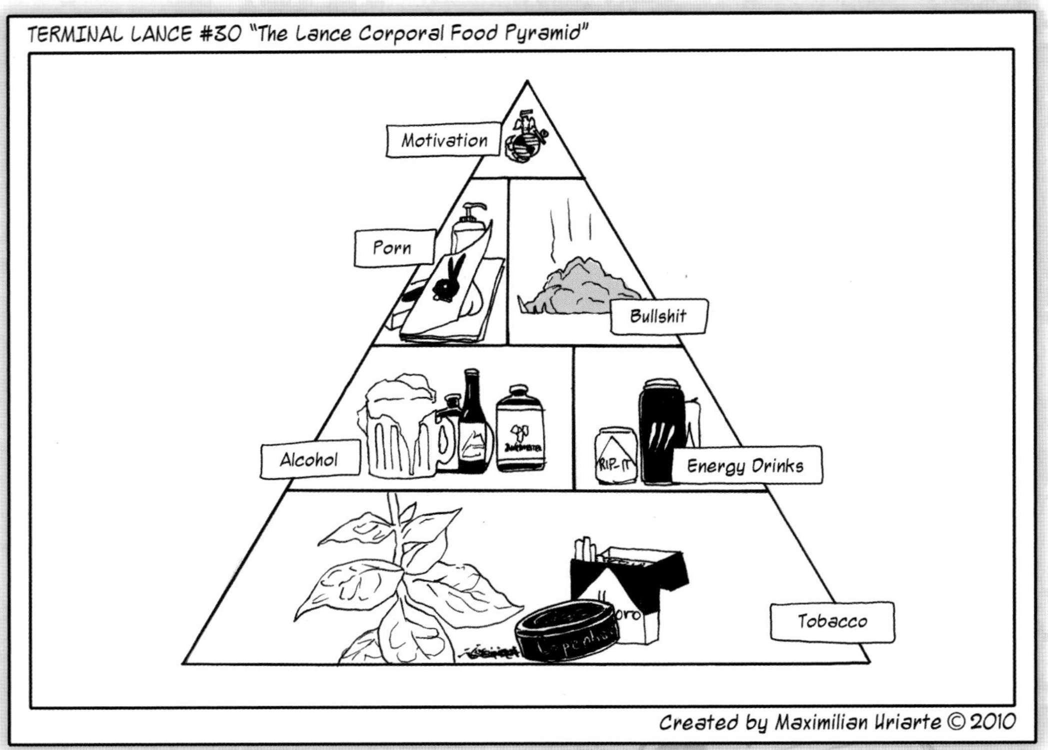
TERMINAL LANCE #30 "The Lance Corporal Food Pyramid"
Motivation
Porn
Bullshit
Alcohol
Energy Drinks
Tobacco
Created by Maximilian Uriarte © 2010

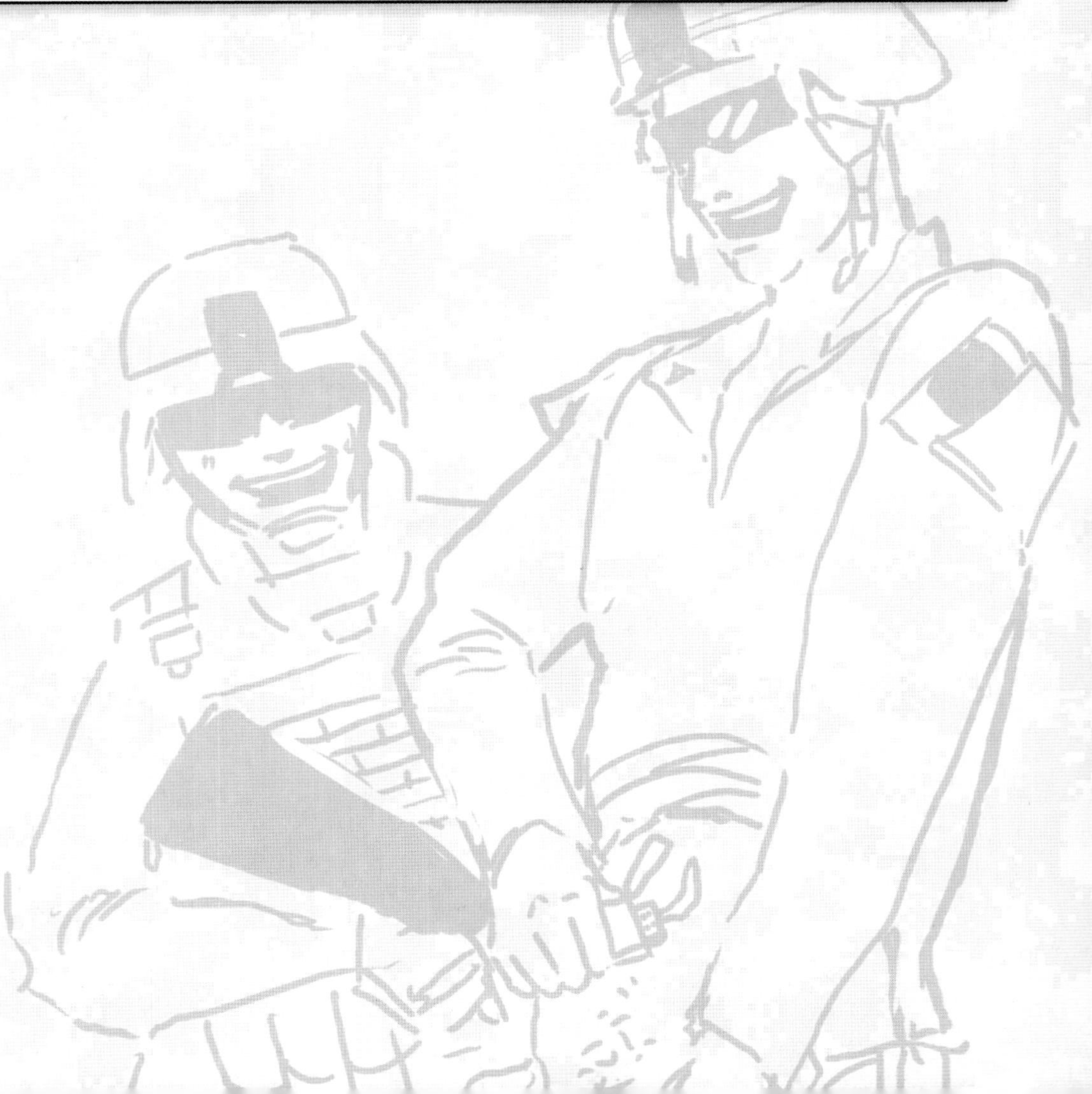

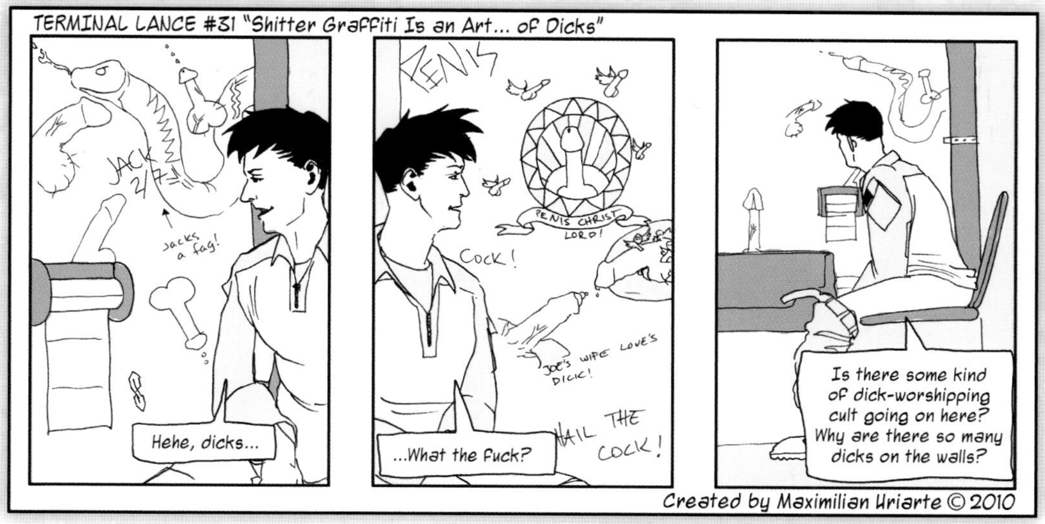
TERMINAL LANCE #31 "Shitter Graffiti Is an Art... of Dicks"
JACK 24/7
Jacks a fag!
Hehe, dicks...
PENIS
PENIS CHRIST LORD!
COCK!
JOE'S WIFE LOVE'S DICK!
HAIL THE COCK!
...What the fuck?
Is there some kind of dick-worshipping cult going on here? Why are there so many dicks on the walls?
Created by Maximilian Uriarte © 2010

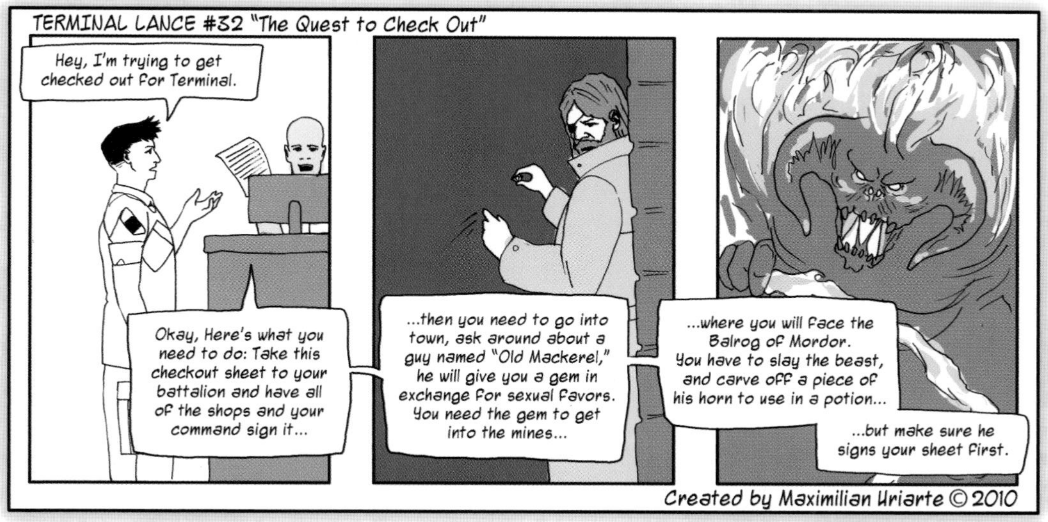
TERMINAL LANCE #32 "The Quest to Check Out"
Hey, I'm trying to get checked out for Terminal.
Okay, Here's what you need to do: Take this checkout sheet to your battalion and have all of the shops and your command sign it...
...then you need to go into town, ask around about a guy named "Old Mackerel," he will give you a gem in exchange for sexual favors. You need the gem to get into the mines...
...where you will face the Balrog of Mordor. You have to slay the beast, and carve off a piece of his horn to use in a potion...
...but make sure he signs your sheet first.
Created by Maximilian Uriarte © 2010

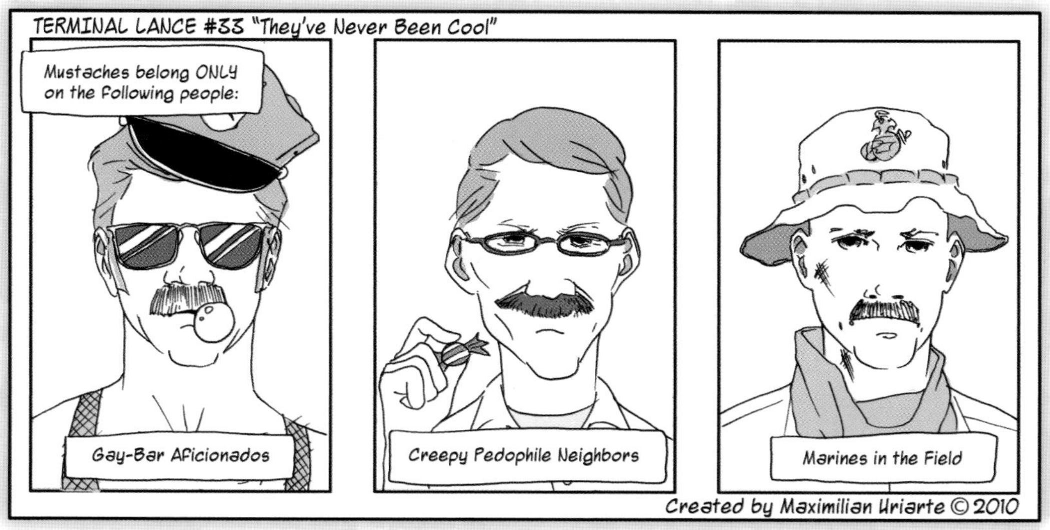
TERMINAL LANCE #33 "They've Never Been Cool"
Mustaches belong ONLY on the following people:
Gay-Bar Aficionados
Creepy Pedophile Neighbors
Marines in the Field
Created by Maximilian Uriarte © 2010

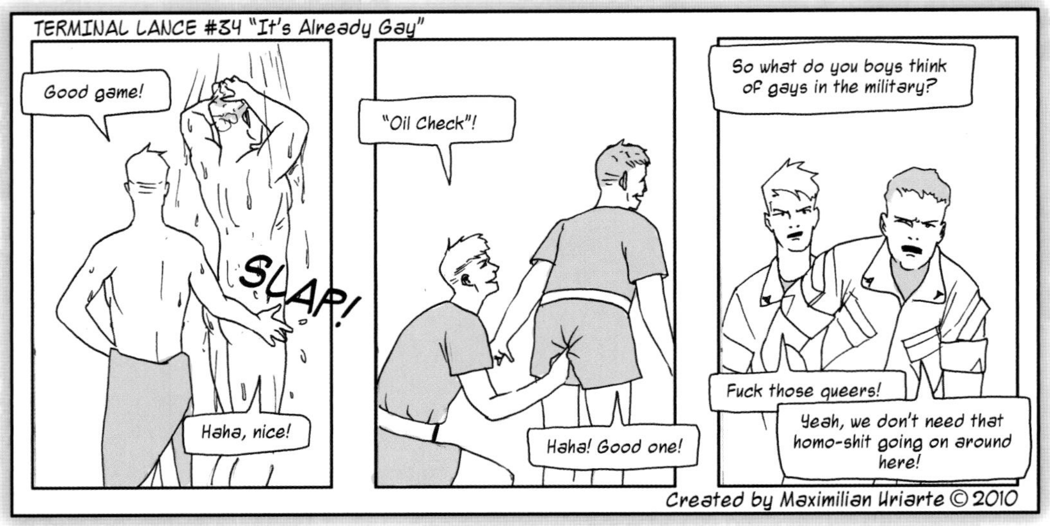
TERMINAL LANCE #34 "It's Already Gay"
Good game!
SLAP!
Haha, nice!
"Oil Check"!
Haha! Good one!
So what do you boys think of gays in the military?
Fuck those queers!
Yeah, we don't need that homo-shit going on around here!
Created by Maximilian Uriarte © 2010

34 "It's Already Gay"

The issue of gays in the military has always been a tough subject, and I'll leave my opinion out of this. As the strip suggests though, it is quite ironic that so many Marines are against gays and lesbians serving in the military, but are guilty of doing gayer shit than the average gay man on a daily basis. The "oil check" was something I never really thought was appropriate, in any situation—yet it had its heyday in my old platoon for a good couple of weeks.

There's always some new practical, physical joke that spreads around and lasts for a week or two. Usually it involves some form of homoerotic behavior like fingering another man's asshole or showing someone your balls. I suppose when you're stuck in shitty situations on a near constant basis away from civilization, a group of young men will inevitably resort to using their own bodies to find humor.

MAX NOTE 2017: This strip was released before the repeal of "Don't Ask, Don't Tell," when gays and lesbians were not permitted to serve openly in any military branch. The goal of this strip was to point out the absurdity of the anti-gay vitriol of the time, considering the fact that joining the Marine Corps is by far the gayest thing any straight man can possibly do.

The gayest.

As you'd expect, once the repeal actually happened, absolutely nothing was different—proving that disallowing gays to openly serve in the military was a stupid rule to begin with that cost many otherwise great service members their careers.

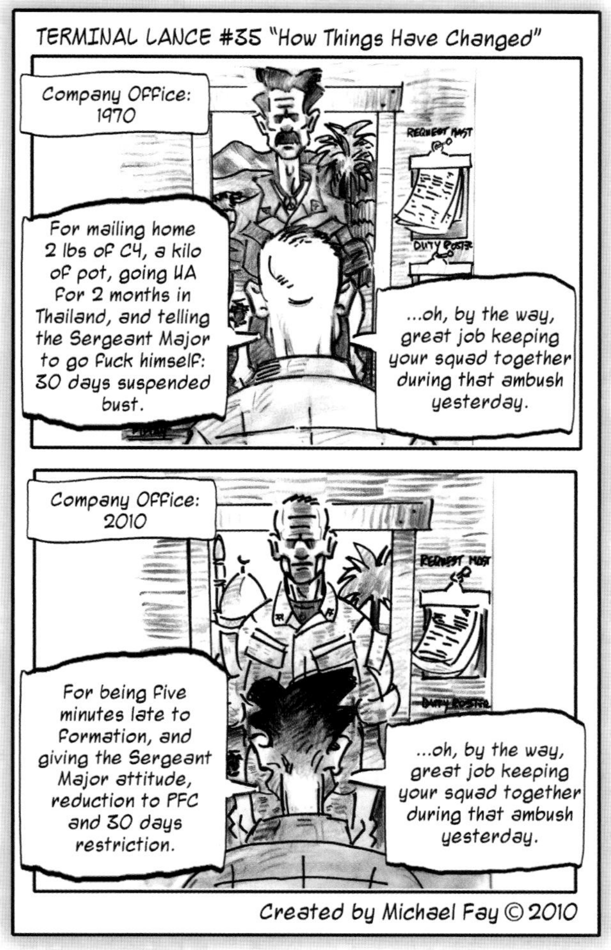
TERMINAL LANCE #35 "How Things Have Changed"
Company Office: 1970
For mailing home 2 lbs of C4, a kilo of pot, going UA for 2 months in Thailand, and telling the Sergeant Major to go fuck himself: 30 days suspended bust.
...oh, by the way, great job keeping your squad together during that ambush yesterday.
Company Office: 2010
For being five minutes late to formation, and giving the Sergeant Major attitude, reduction to PFC and 30 days restriction.
...oh, by the way, great job keeping your squad together during that ambush yesterday.
Created by Michael Fay © 2010

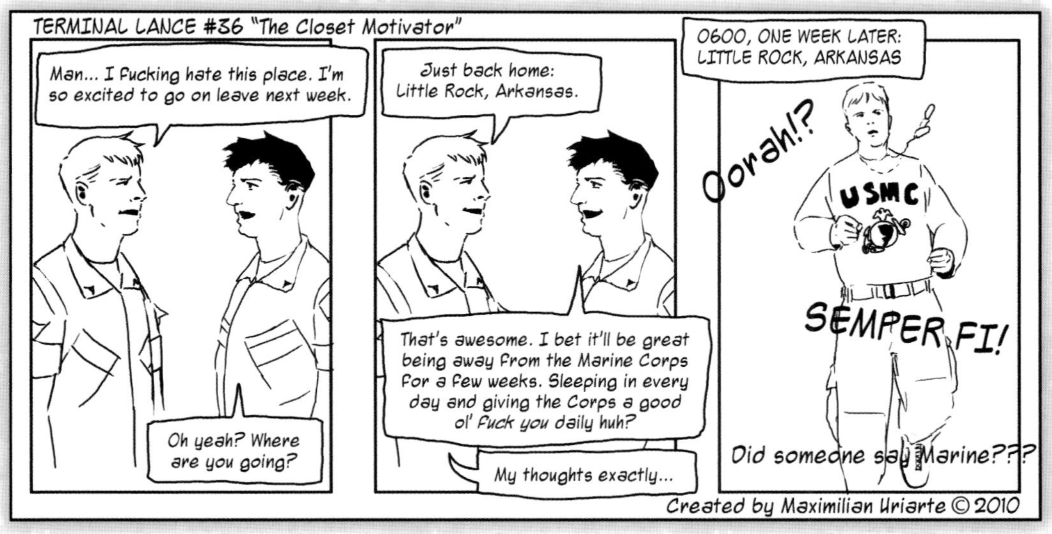
TERMINAL LANCE #36 "The Closet Motivator"
Man... I fucking hate this place. I'm so excited to go on leave next week.
Oh yeah? Where are you going?
Just back home: Little Rock, Arkansas.
That's awesome. I bet it'll be great being away from the Marine Corps for a few weeks. Sleeping in every day and giving the Corps a good ol' fuck you daily huh?
My thoughts exactly...
0600, ONE WEEK LATER: LITTLE ROCK, ARKANSAS
Oorah!?
USMC
SEMPER FI!
Did someone say Marine???
Created by Maximilian Uriarte © 2010

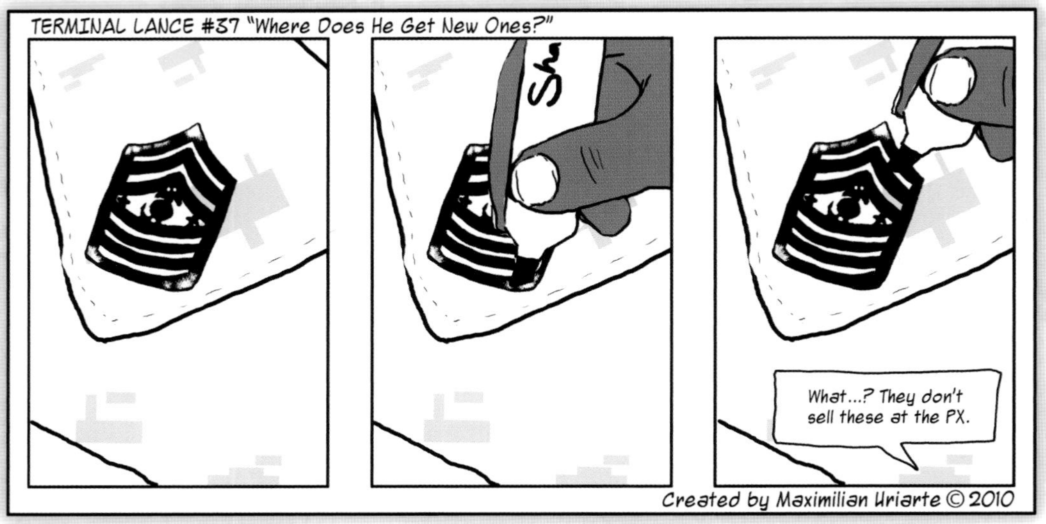
TERMINAL LANCE #37 "Where Does He Get New Ones?"
What...? They don't sell these at the PX.
Created by Maximilian Uriarte © 2010

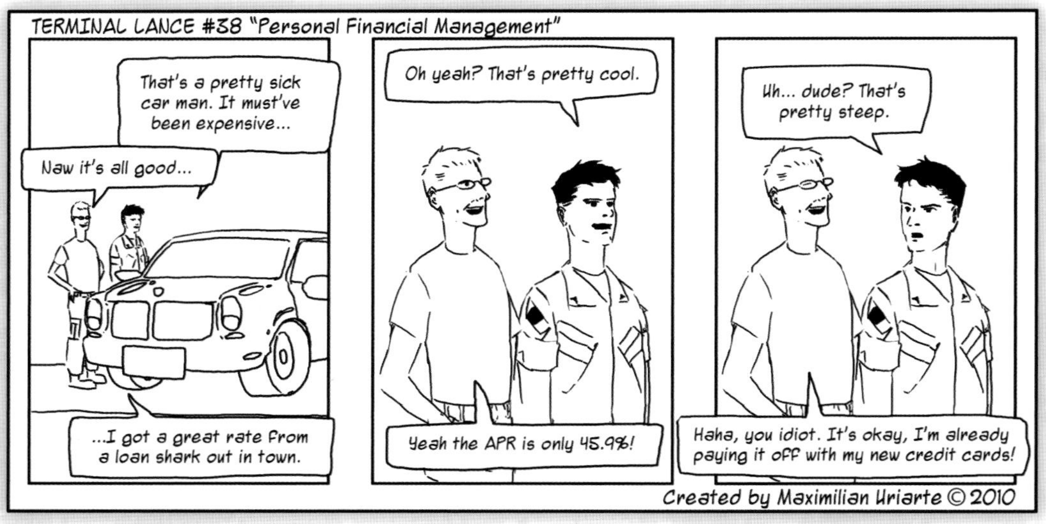
TERMINAL LANCE #38 "Personal Financial Management"
That's a pretty sick car man. It must've been expensive...
Naw it's all good...
...I got a great rate from a loan shark out in town.
Oh yeah? That's pretty cool.
Yeah the APR is only 45.9%!
Uh... dude? That's pretty steep.
Haha, you idiot. It's okay, I'm already paying it off with my new credit cards!
Created by Maximilian Uriarte © 2010

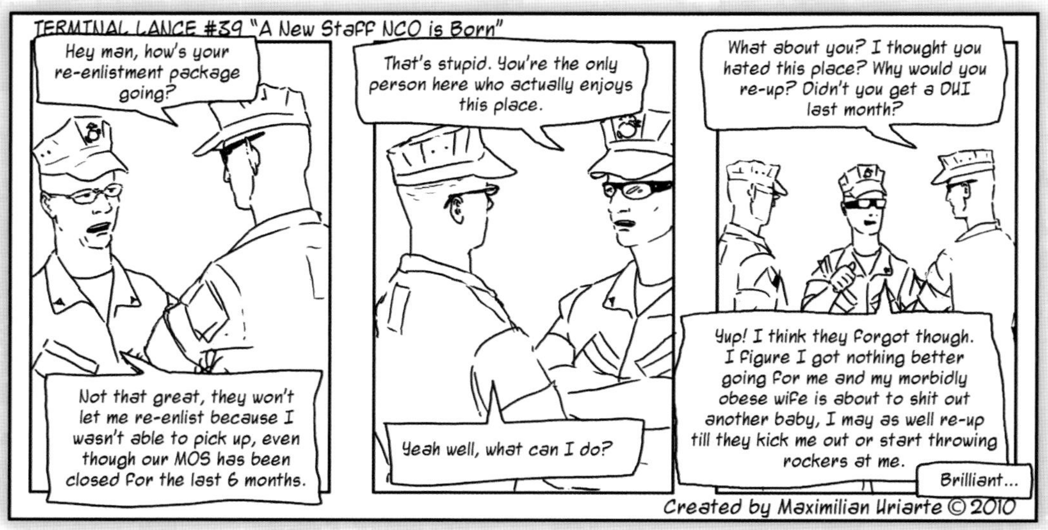
TERMINAL LANCE #39 "A New Staff NCO is Born"
Hey man, how's your re-enlistment package going?
Not that great, they won't let me re-enlist because I wasn't able to pick up, even though our MOS has been closed for the last 6 months.
That's stupid. You're the only person here who actually enjoys this place.
Yeah well, what can I do?
What about you? I thought you hated this place? Why would you re-up? Didn't you get a DUI last month?
Yup! I think they forgot though. I figure I got nothing better going for me and my morbidly obese wife is about to shit out another baby, I may as well re-up till they kick me out or start throwing rockers at me.
Brilliant...
Created by Maximilian Uriarte © 2010

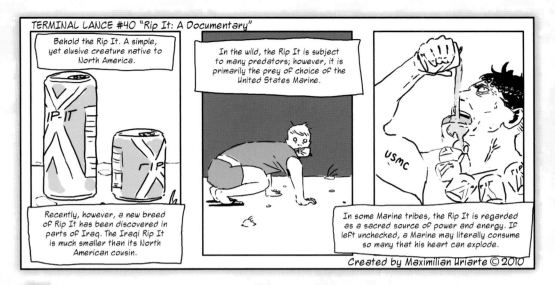

TERMINAL LANCE #40 "Rip It: A Documentary"
Behold the Rip It. A simple, yet elusive creature native to North America.
IP-IT
RIP
Recently, however, a new breed of Rip It has been discovered in parts of Iraq. The Iraqi Rip It is much smaller than its North American cousin.
In the wild, the Rip It is subject to many predators; however, it is primarily the prey of choice of the United States Marine.
USMC
In some Marine tribes, the Rip It is regarded as a sacred source of power and energy. If left unchecked, a Marine may literally consume so many that his heart can explode.
Created by Maximilian Uriarte © 2010

40 "Rip It®: A Documentary"

Rip It® is a registered trademark of Sundance Beverage Company.

I'll just get straight to the point on this one: Marines love Rip Its.

For those of you that have never been to Iraq, a Rip It is an energy drink that they hand out to the Marines and soldiers overseas. They're like delectable cans of liquid candy. Marines will raid the chow halls when they get the chance and shove as many as they can fit in their cargo pockets, shove 'em in their trucks or keep a reserve in their cans. A good Marine can take about eight out of the chow hall on a good run, and boy do they.

Energy drinks are big in the Marine Corps. I did this strip on Rip Its because it is really as much Iraq humor as it is Marine humor. However, back in garrison—where the world is readily available—Monsters and Rock Stars are just as prevalent. I have yet to see the short cans stateside, though I wouldn't be too shocked to find them.

In any case, the Citrus X ones were fantastic. Many long nights in the turret were kept fueled by those sweet little cans of delicious. The initial idea for this strip was actually a live-action documentary I was going to make on my second deployment, given that I worked with ComCam every day and I had access to high-quality camera equipment. However, that idea passed by and has been reborn here in three panels.

AWESOME!

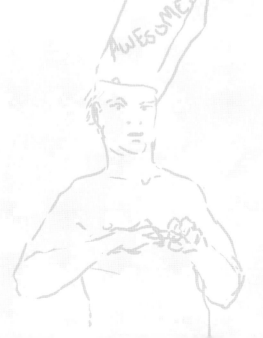

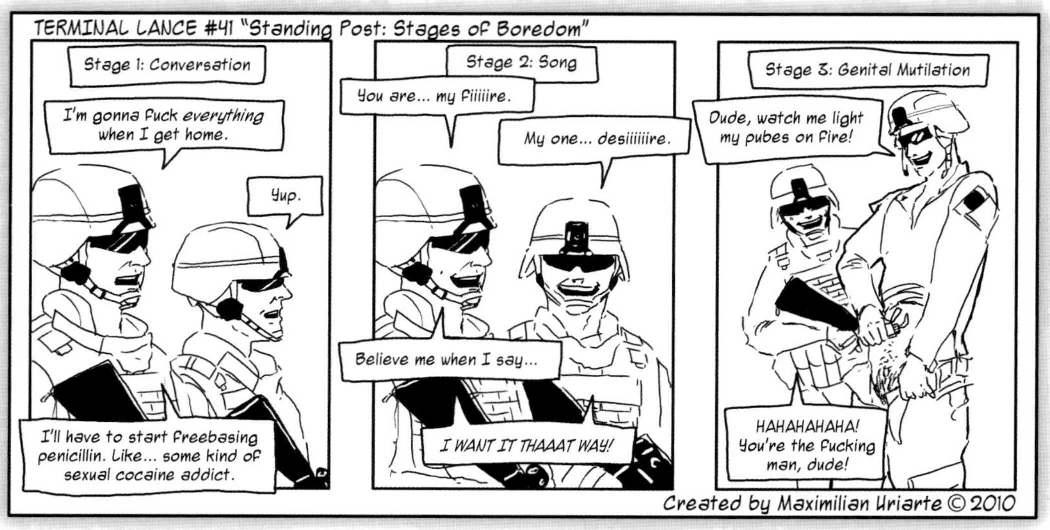
TERMINAL LANCE #41 "Standing Post: Stages of Boredom"
Stage 1: Conversation
I'm gonna fuck everything when I get home.
Yup.
I'll have to start freebasing penicillin. Like... some kind of sexual cocaine addict.
Stage 2: Song
You are... my fiiiiire.
My one... desiiiiiire.
Believe me when I say...
I WANT IT THAAAT WAY!
Stage 3: Genital Mutilation
Dude, watch me light my pubes on fire!
HAHAHAHAHA! You're the fucking man, dude!
Created by Maximilian Uriarte © 2010

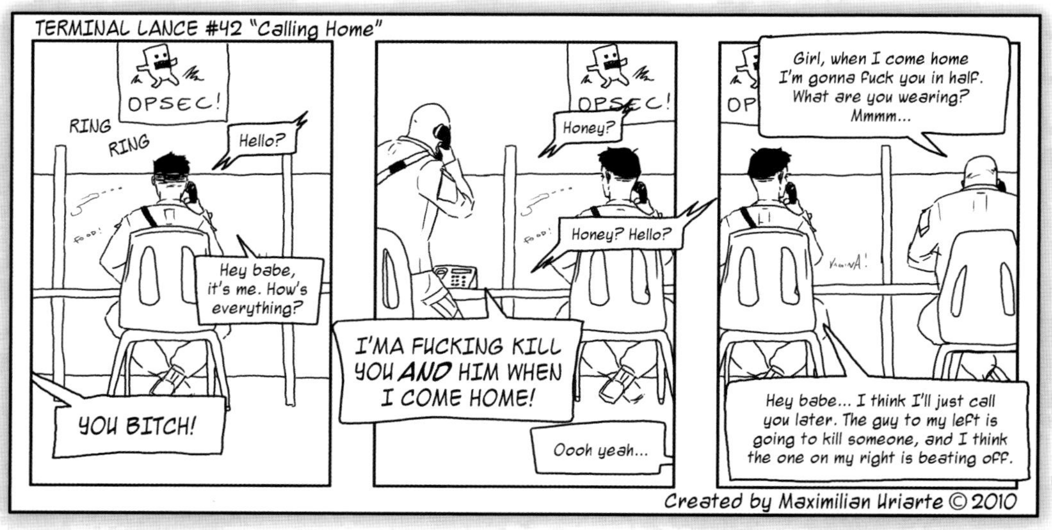
TERMINAL LANCE #42 "Calling Home"
OPSEC!
RING
RING
Hello?
Hey babe, it's me. How's everything?
YOU BITCH!
Honey?
Honey? Hello?
I'MA FUCKING KILL YOU AND HIM WHEN I COME HOME!
Oooh yeah...
Girl, when I come home I'm gonna fuck you in half. What are you wearing? Mmmm...
Hey babe... I think I'll just call you later. The guy to my left is going to kill someone, and I think the one on my right is beating off.
Created by Maximilian Uriarte © 2010

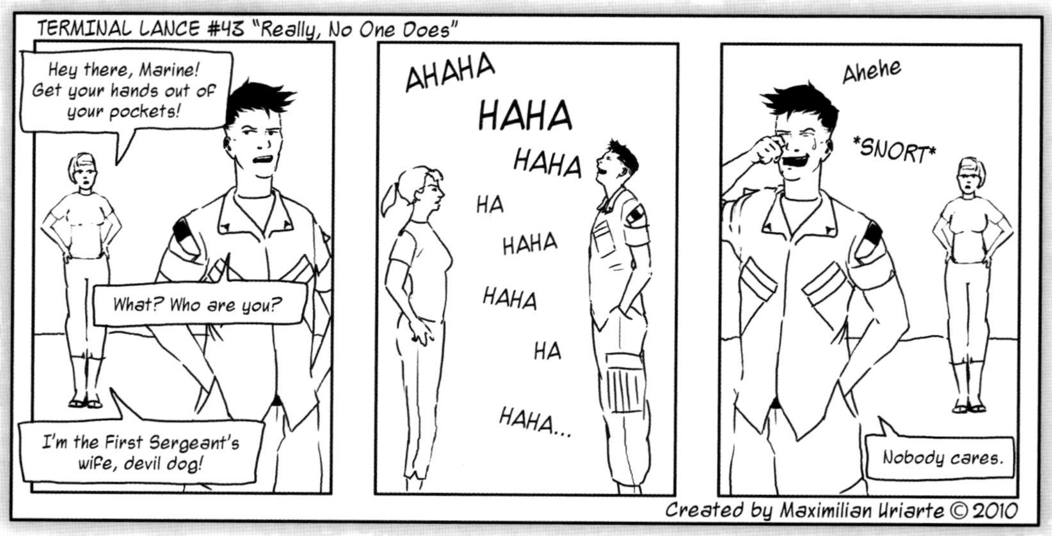
TERMINAL LANCE #43 "Really, No One Does"
Hey there, Marine! Get your hands out of your pockets!
What? Who are you?
I'm the First Sergeant's wife, devil dog!
AHAHA
HAHA
HAHA
HA
HAHA
HAHA
HA
HAHA...
Ahehe
SNORT
Nobody cares.
Created by Maximilian Uriarte © 2010

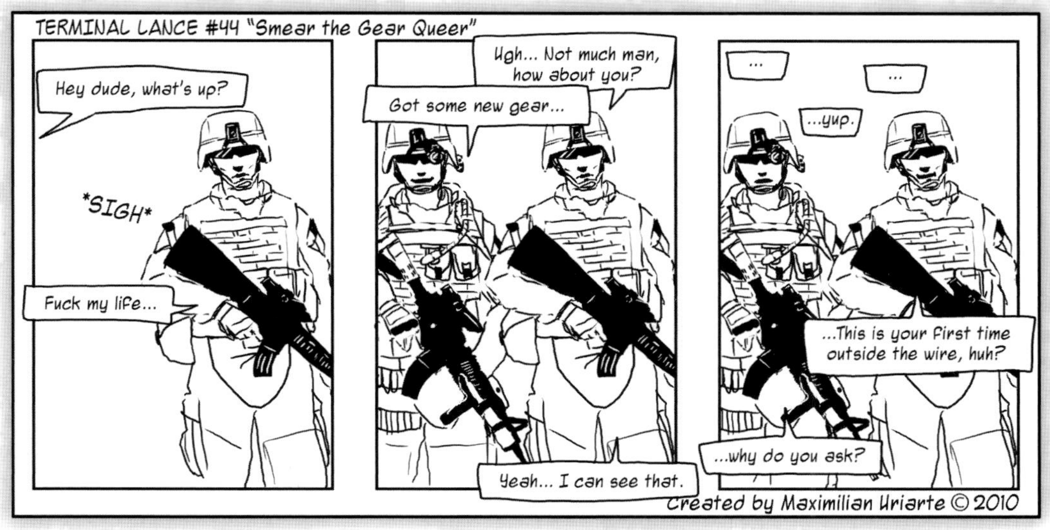
TERMINAL LANCE #44 "Smear the Gear Queer"
Hey dude, what's up?
SIGH
Fuck my life...
Ugh... Not much man, how about you?
Got some new gear...
Yeah... I can see that.
...
...
...yup.
...This is your first time outside the wire, huh?
...why do you ask?
Created by Maximilian Uriarte © 2010

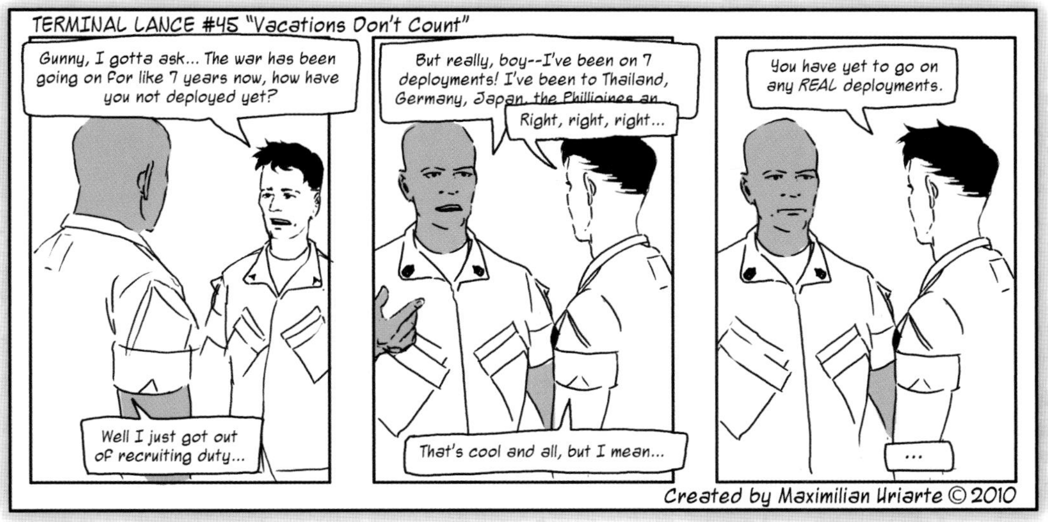
TERMINAL LANCE #45 "Vacations Don't Count"
Gunny, I gotta ask... The war has been going on for like 7 years now, how have you not deployed yet?
Well I just got out of recruiting duty...
But really, boy--I've been on 7 deployments! I've been to Thailand, Germany, Japan, the Phillipines an
Right, right, right...
That's cool and all, but I mean...
You have yet to go on any REAL deployments.
...
Created by Maximilian Uriarte © 2010

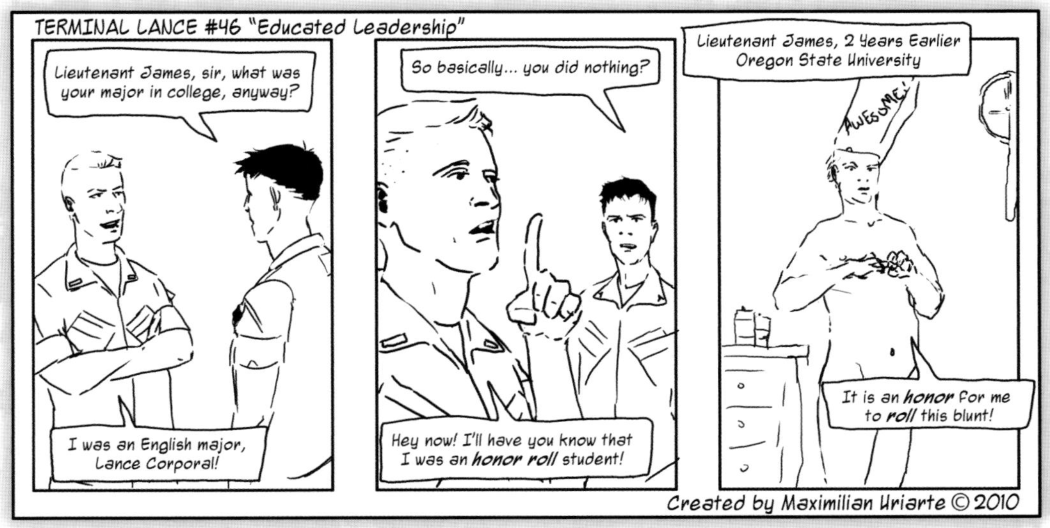
TERMINAL LANCE #46 "Educated Leadership"
Lieutenant James, sir, what was your major in college, anyway?
I was an English major, Lance Corporal!
So basically... you did nothing?
Hey now! I'll have you know that I was an honor roll student!
Lieutenant James, 2 Years Earlier Oregon State University
AWESOME!
It is an honor for me to roll this blunt!
Created by Maximilian Uriarte © 2010

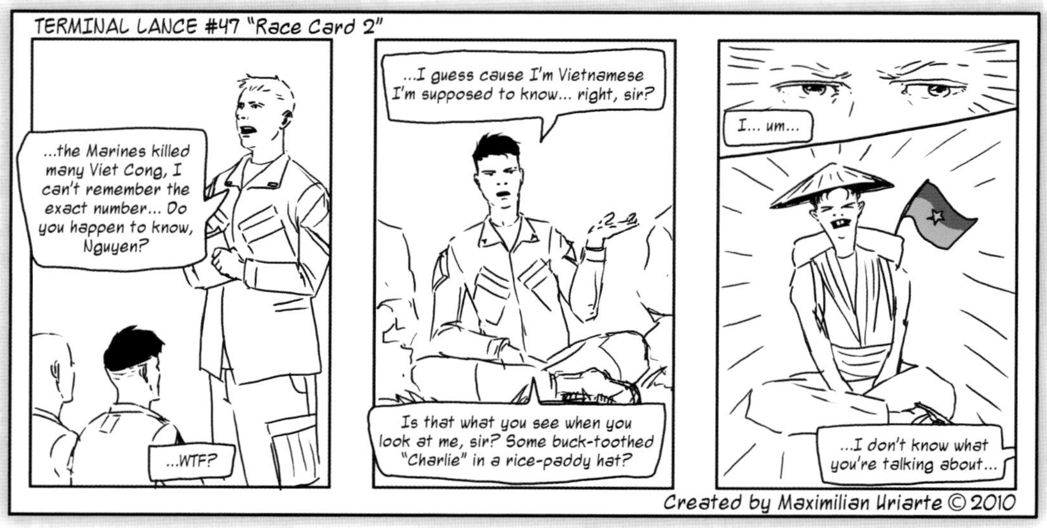
TERMINAL LANCE #47 "Race Card 2"
...the Marines killed many Viet Cong, I can't remember the exact number... Do you happen to know, Nguyen?
...WTF?
...I guess cause I'm Vietnamese I'm supposed to know... right, sir?
Is that what you see when you look at me, sir? Some buck-toothed "Charlie" in a rice-paddy hat?
I... um...
...I don't know what you're talking about...
Created by Maximilian Uriarte © 2010

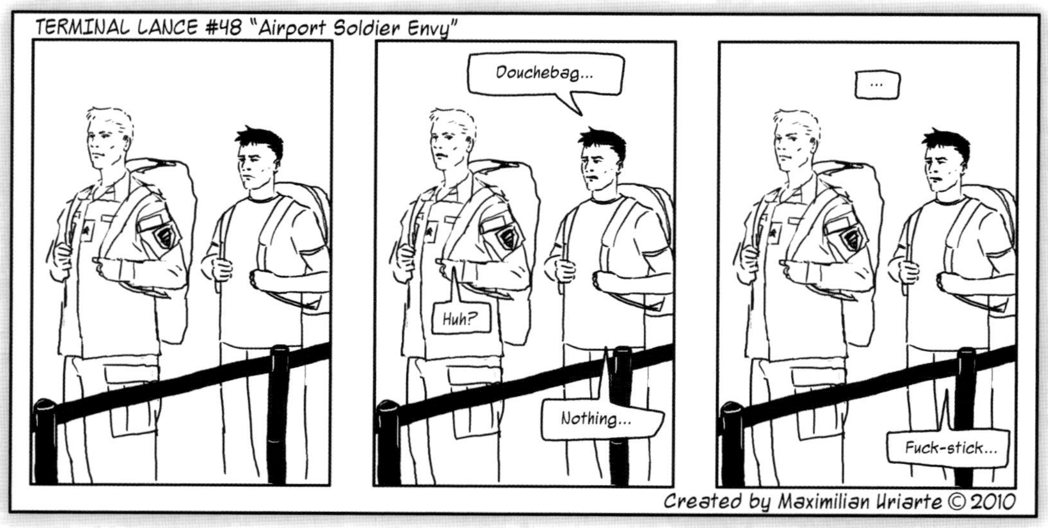
TERMINAL LANCE #48 "Airport Soldier Envy"
Douchebag...
Huh?
Nothing...
...
Fuck-stick...
Created by Maximilian Uriarte © 2010

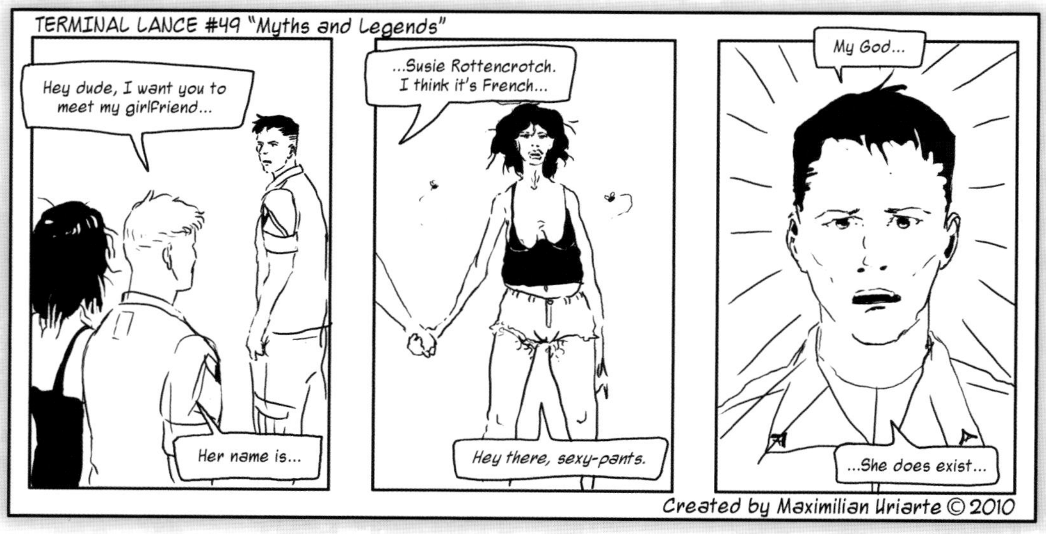
TERMINAL LANCE #49 "Myths and Legends"
Hey dude, I want you to meet my girlfriend...
Her name is...
...Susie Rottencrotch. I think it's French...
Hey there, sexy-pants.
My God...
...She does exist...
Created by Maximilian Uriarte © 2010

TERMINAL LANCE #50 "I'm Putting You Up For One"
I have a question, First Sergeant... Is it true that the "Company Clerk" got another NAM last week?
Mista!
Mista!
Mista!
Why yes it is, he does his job exceptionally well.
Then I think my entire squad deserves some NAM's... we didn't die this week.
Marine, I oughta slap the dog-piss out of you for talking to me like that! You think we just hand those things out like candy!? Get the fuck away from me before I throw so much paperwork up your ass you'll be shitting trees!
Fucking ingrate...
Mista!
Kids, kids, calm down! Here, have a couple of NAM's.
Mista!
Mista!
Chocolate, mista!
Ooooo...
Created by Maximilian Uriarte © 2010

50 "I'm Putting You Up For One"

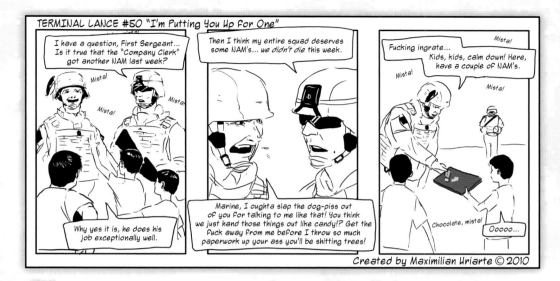

For my beloved readers that are not in the loop, "NAM" stands for "Navy/Marine Corps Achievement Medal," and is awarded to people who go above and beyond their normal duties assigned to them. However, the medal somehow always seems to find its way onto the chests of those closest to Headquarters or H&S Company. Even though the guys on the ground are out there every day, risking life and limb, they are usually the last people to receive the award.

Despite the comic, I refuse to believe that the average grunt deserves a NAM every day he's outside the wire. However, I also refuse to believe the company clerk, police sergeant, intel guy, etc., rates the award every time he does his job. I'm not saying I've never agreed with the awarding of it to the less salty population, but I think the system is fairly slanted in their favor.

Take a Headquarters platoon for example: every day they are in the company office, under close supervision to the top-ranking members of the company. How often does the Company First Sergeant or the Commanding Officer see Lance Corporal Dipshit offer a child some water or some of his own food outside the wire? How often does even the platoon commander see it? If you're a good squad leader, hopefully never—because no squad leader wants to have to deal with an "LT" or an "Echo-8" on any sort of a daily basis. Unfortunately, it takes something much greater for the average grunt to earn the medal than just . . . doing what he's asked to do—which isn't always the case for the other side.

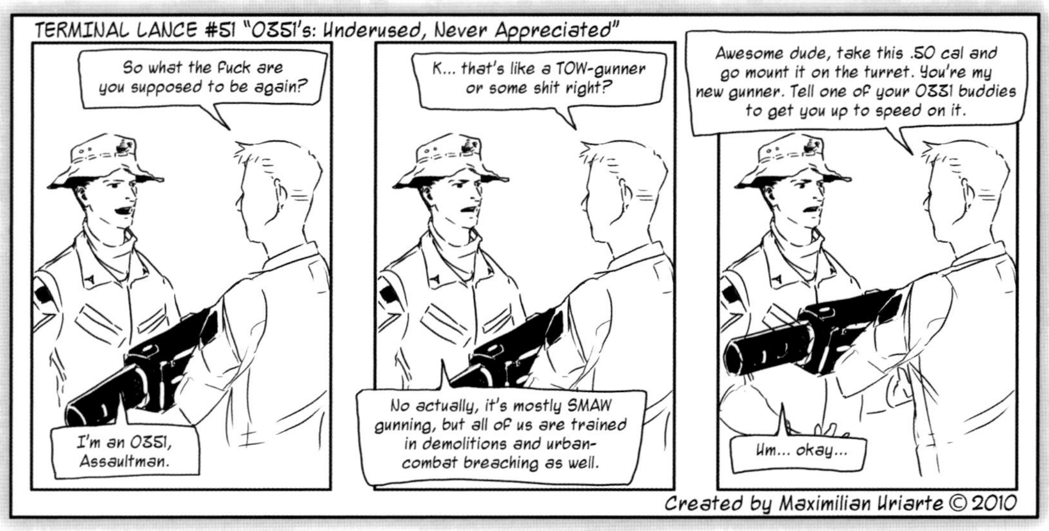
TERMINAL LANCE #51 "0351's: Underused, Never Appreciated"
So what the fuck are you supposed to be again?
I'm an 0351, Assaultman.
K... that's like a TOW-gunner or some shit right?
No actually, it's mostly SMAW gunning, but all of us are trained in demolitions and urban-combat breaching as well.
Awesome dude, take this .50 cal and go mount it on the turret. You're my new gunner. Tell one of your 0331 buddies to get you up to speed on it.
Um... okay...
Created by Maximilian Uriarte © 2010

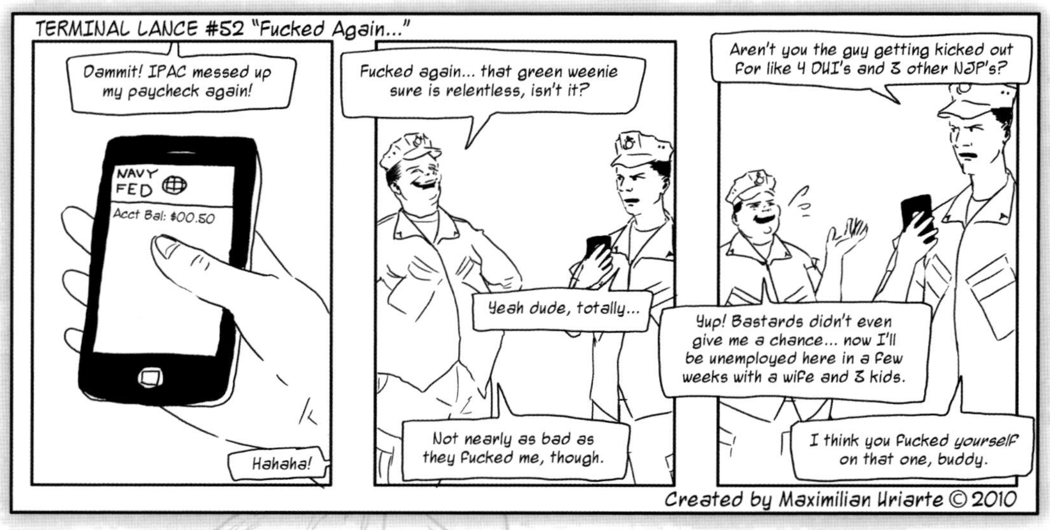
TERMINAL LANCE #52 "Fucked Again..."
Dammit! IPAC messed up my paycheck again!
NAVY FED
Acct Bal: $00.50
Hahaha!
Fucked again... that green weenie sure is relentless, isn't it?
Yeah dude, totally...
Not nearly as bad as they fucked me, though.
Aren't you the guy getting kicked out for like 4 DUI's and 3 other NJP's?
Yup! Bastards didn't even give me a chance... now I'll be unemployed here in a few weeks with a wife and 3 kids.
I think you fucked yourself on that one, buddy.
Created by Maximilian Uriarte © 2010

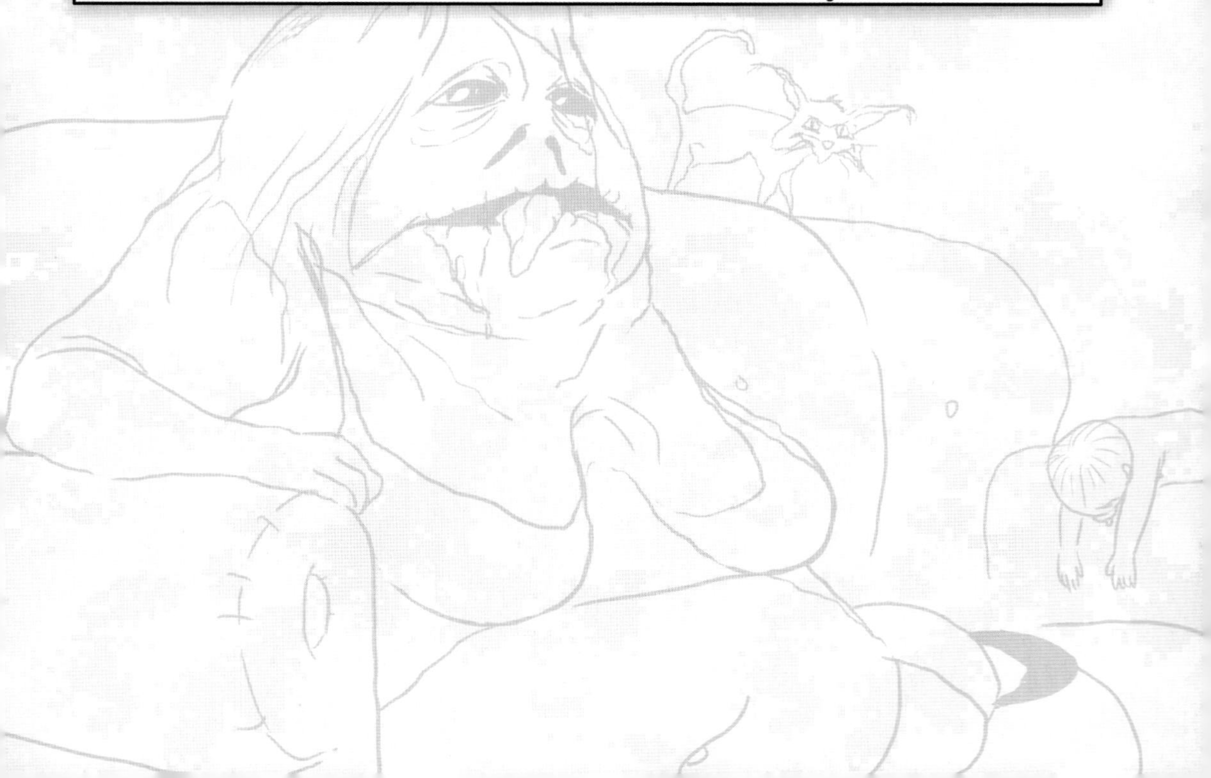

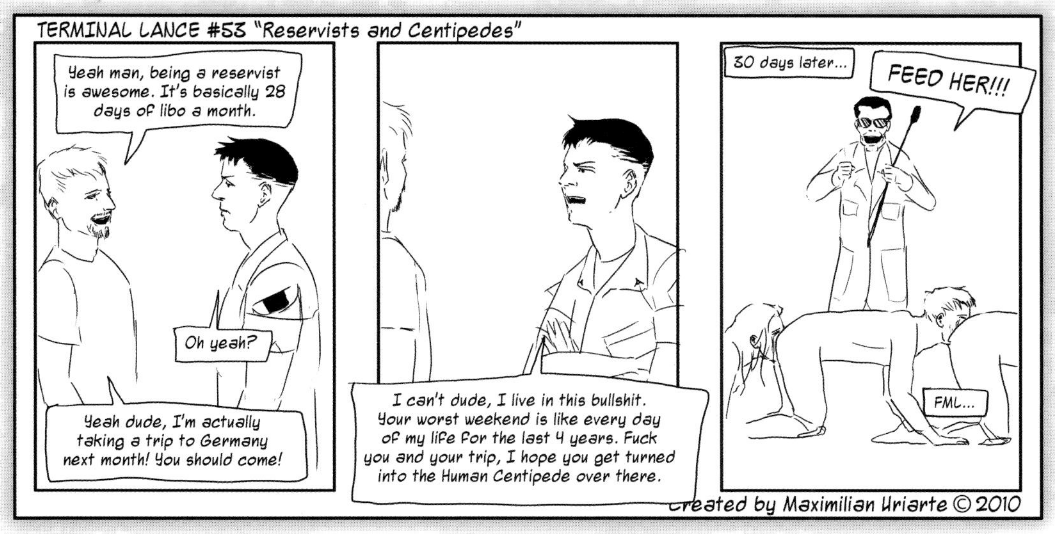
TERMINAL LANCE #53 "Reservists and Centipedes"
Yeah man, being a reservist is awesome. It's basically 28 days of libo a month.
Oh yeah?
Yeah dude, I'm actually taking a trip to Germany next month! You should come!
I can't dude, I live in this bullshit. Your worst weekend is like every day of my life for the last 4 years. Fuck you and your trip, I hope you get turned into the Human Centipede over there.
30 days later...
FEED HER!!!
FML...
Created by Maximilian Uriarte © 2010

53 "Reservists and Centipedes"

I don't typically try to sell my punch lines on pop-culture references. However, I recently saw *The Human Centipede* and was so excited I had to find a way to put it into a strip. The point of the strip was easy to make within three panels. Active-duty Marines hate reservists—those assholes found a way to be in the Marines but still be at home all the time and not have to deal with the bullshit every day.

I remember graduation day at SOI. Everyone was in their Bravos, getting ready to head to the airport to continue their Marine Corps journey. Well, at least some of us were . . . half of the company just went to the airport to fly home, never to be seen again by the active-duty guys heading to their duty stations to be hazed by hungover Lance Corporals at 0100 in the morning. The split is abrupt and deceptive. Marines that have been your friends and allies against the common evil of Marine-dom are sent back to their homes, back to their civilian friends and family, and back to their lives. Active duty never gets that luxury. We only go home on leave blocks and the rest of the time, we deal with the brunt of hazing and weekly field ops.

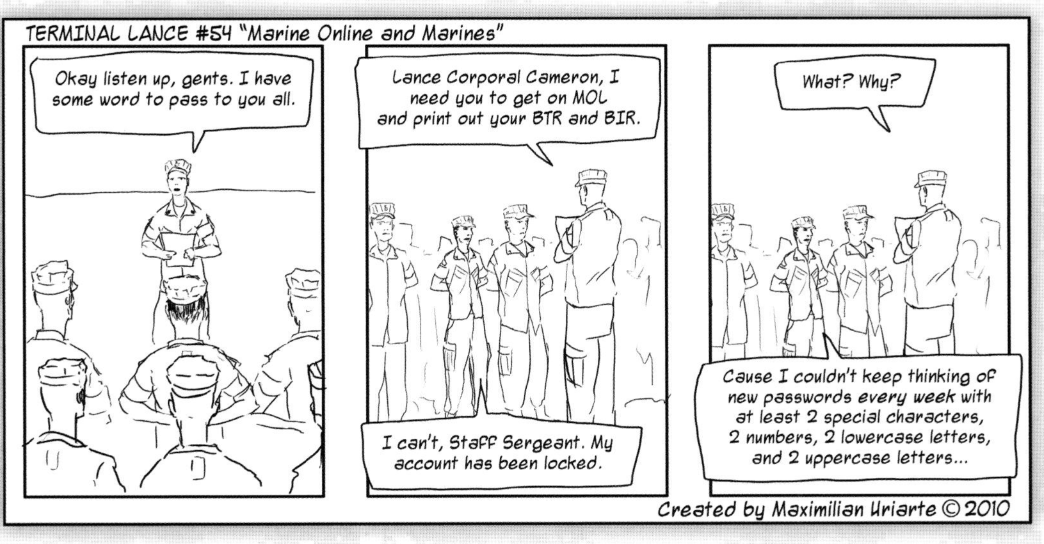
TERMINAL LANCE #54 "Marine Online and Marines"
Okay listen up, gents. I have some word to pass to you all.
Lance Corporal Cameron, I need you to get on MOL and print out your BTR and BIR.
I can't, Staff Sergeant. My account has been locked.
What? Why?
Cause I couldn't keep thinking of new passwords every week with at least 2 special characters, 2 numbers, 2 lowercase letters, and 2 uppercase letters...
Created by Maximilian Uriarte © 2010

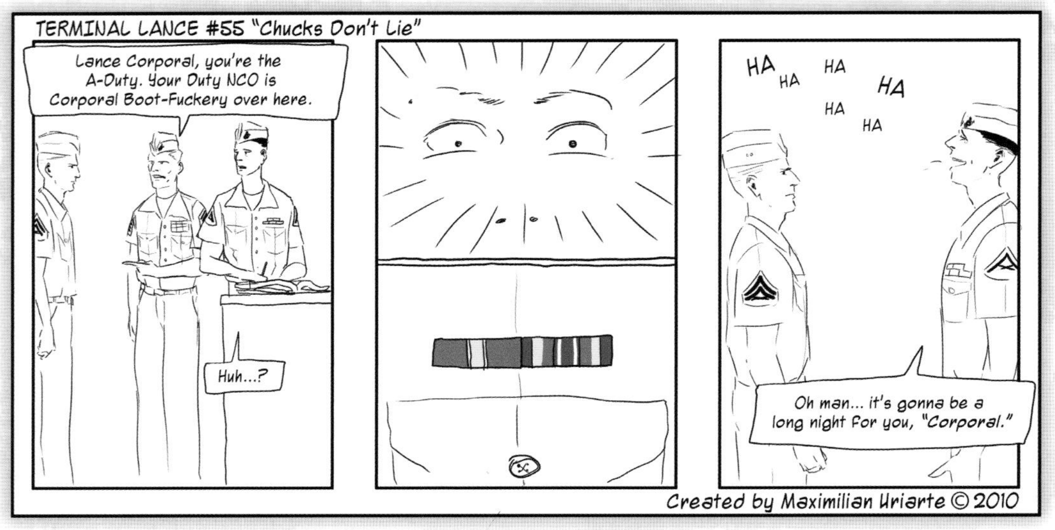
TERMINAL LANCE #55 "Chucks Don't Lie"
Lance Corporal, you're the A-Duty. Your Duty NCO is Corporal Boot-Fuckery over here.
Huh...?
HA HA HA HA HA HA
Oh man... it's gonna be a long night for you, "Corporal."
Created by Maximilian Uriarte © 2010

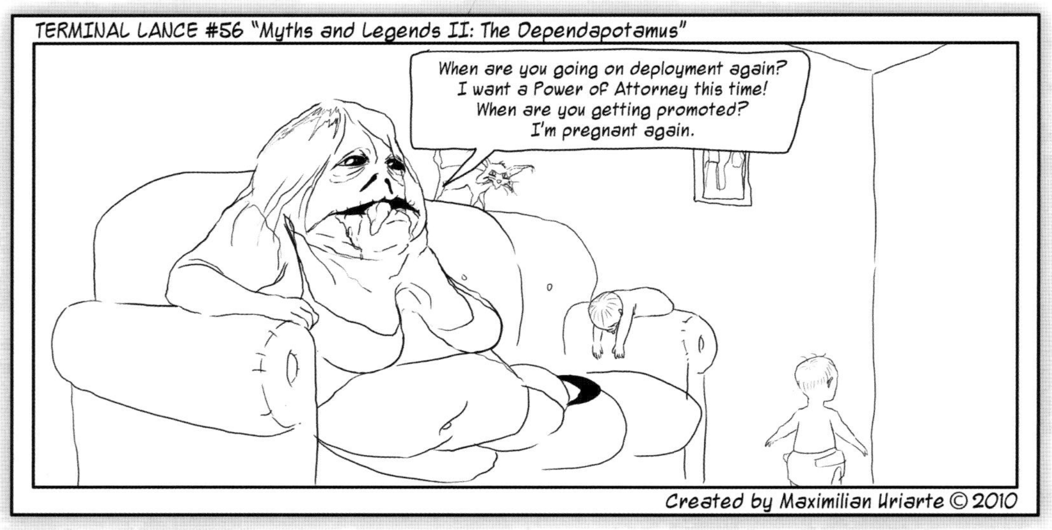
TERMINAL LANCE #56 "Myths and Legends II: The Dependapotamus"
When are you going on deployment again? I want a Power of Attorney this time! When are you getting promoted? I'm pregnant again.
Created by Maximilian Uriarte © 2010

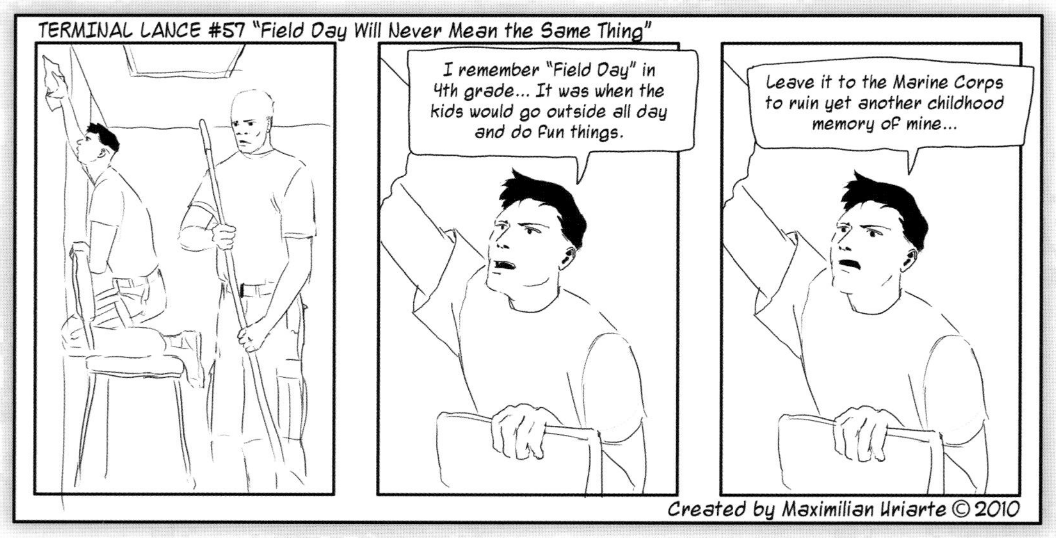
TERMINAL LANCE #57 "Field Day Will Never Mean the Same Thing"
I remember "Field Day" in 4th grade... It was when the kids would go outside all day and do fun things.
Leave it to the Marine Corps to ruin yet another childhood memory of mine...
Created by Maximilian Uriarte © 2010

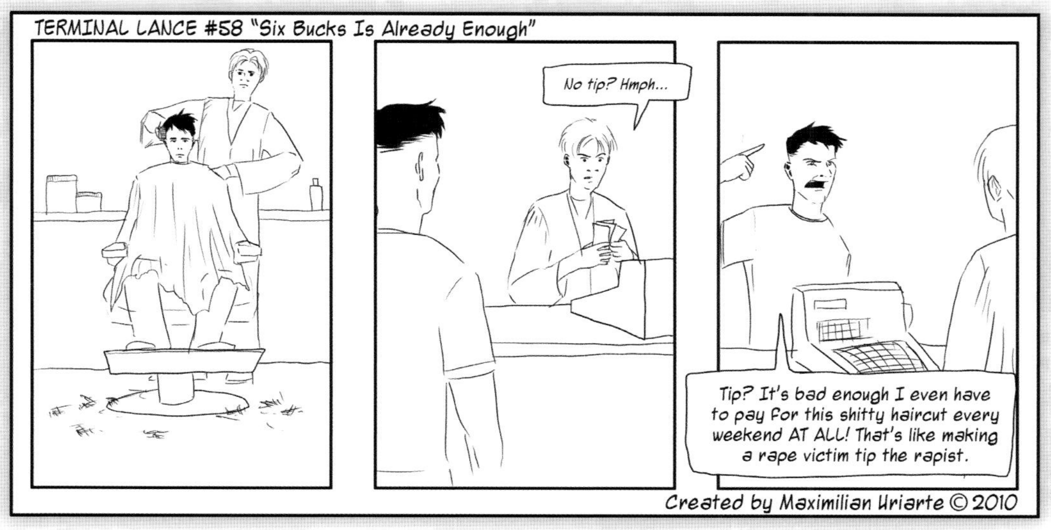
TERMINAL LANCE #58 "Six Bucks Is Already Enough"
No tip? Hmph...
Tip? It's bad enough I even have to pay for this shitty haircut every weekend AT ALL! That's like making a rape victim tip the rapist.
Created by Maximilian Uriarte © 2010

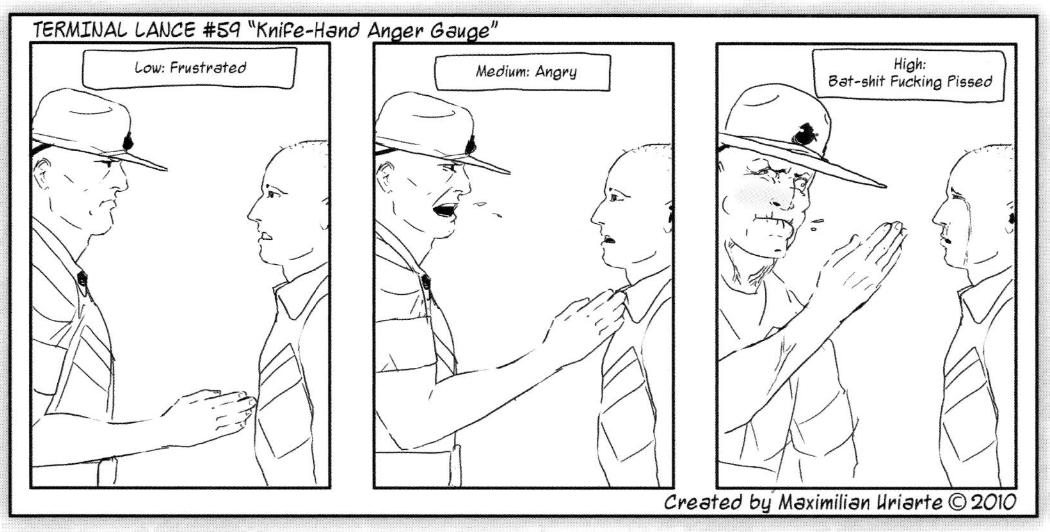
TERMINAL LANCE #59 "Knife-Hand Anger Gauge"
Low: Frustrated
Medium: Angry
High: Bat-shit Fucking Pissed
Created by Maximilian Uriarte © 2010

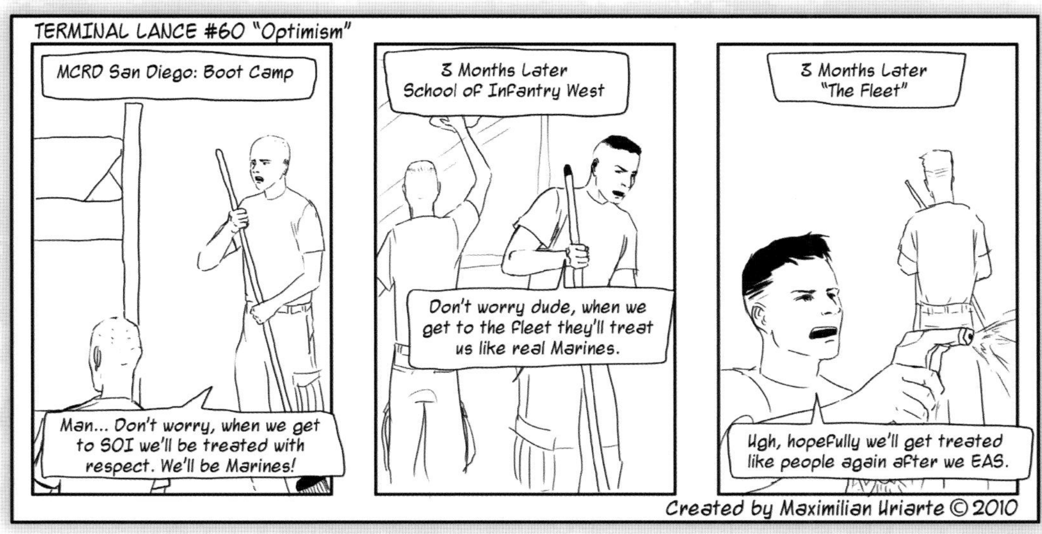
TERMINAL LANCE #60 "Optimism"
MCRD San Diego: Boot Camp
Man... Don't worry, when we get to SOI we'll be treated with respect. We'll be Marines!
3 Months Later School of Infantry West
Don't worry dude, when we get to the fleet they'll treat us like real Marines.
3 Months Later "The Fleet"
Ugh, hopefully we'll get treated like people again after we EAS.
Created by Maximilian Uriarte © 2010

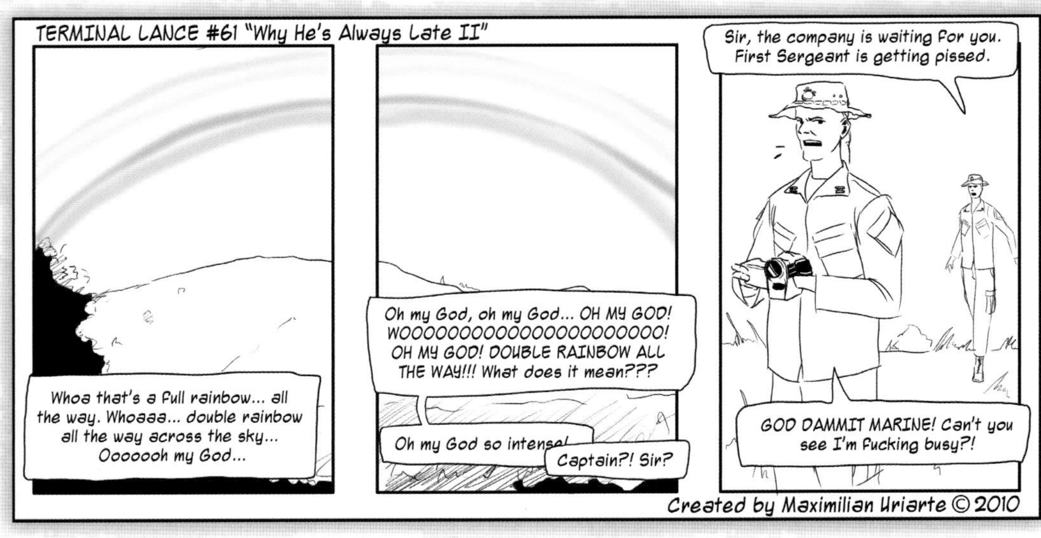
TERMINAL LANCE #61 "Why He's Always Late II"
Whoa that's a full rainbow... all the way. Whoaaa... double rainbow all the way across the sky... Ooooooh my God...
Oh my God, oh my God... OH MY GOD! WOOOOOOOOOOOOOOOOOOOOO! OH MY GOD! DOUBLE RAINBOW ALL THE WAY!!! What does it mean???
Oh my God so intense!
Captain?! Sir?
Sir, the company is waiting for you. First Sergeant is getting pissed.
GOD DAMMIT MARINE! Can't you see I'm fucking busy?!
Created by Maximilian Uriarte © 2010

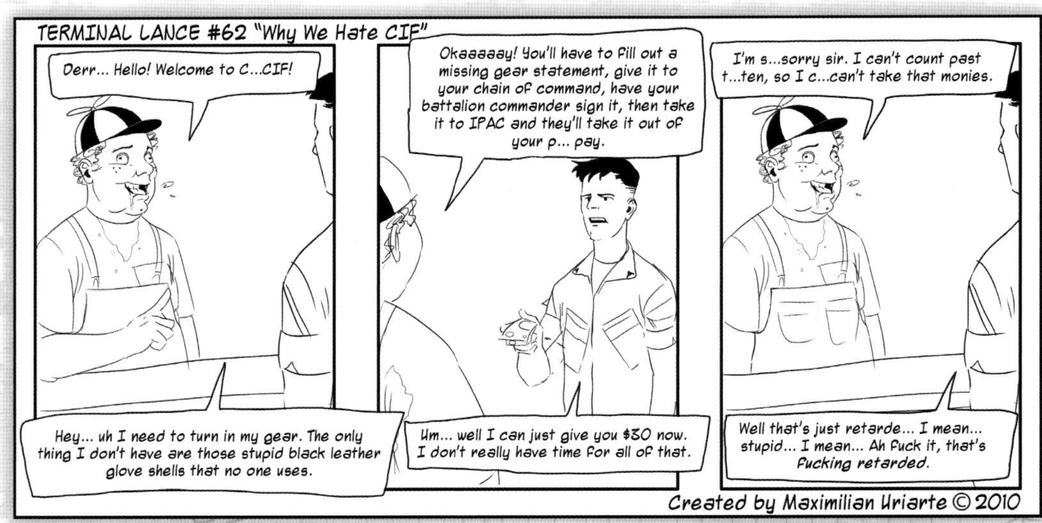
TERMINAL LANCE #62 "Why We Hate CIF"
Derr... Hello! Welcome to C...CIF!
Hey... uh I need to turn in my gear. The only thing I don't have are those stupid black leather glove shells that no one uses.
Okaaaaay! You'll have to fill out a missing gear statement, give it to your chain of command, have your battalion commander sign it, then take it to IPAC and they'll take it out of your p... pay.
Um... well I can just give you $30 now. I don't really have time for all of that.
I'm s...sorry sir. I can't count past t...ten, so I c...can't take that monies.
Well that's just retarde... I mean... stupid... I mean... Ah fuck it, that's fucking retarded.
Created by Maximilian Uriarte © 2010

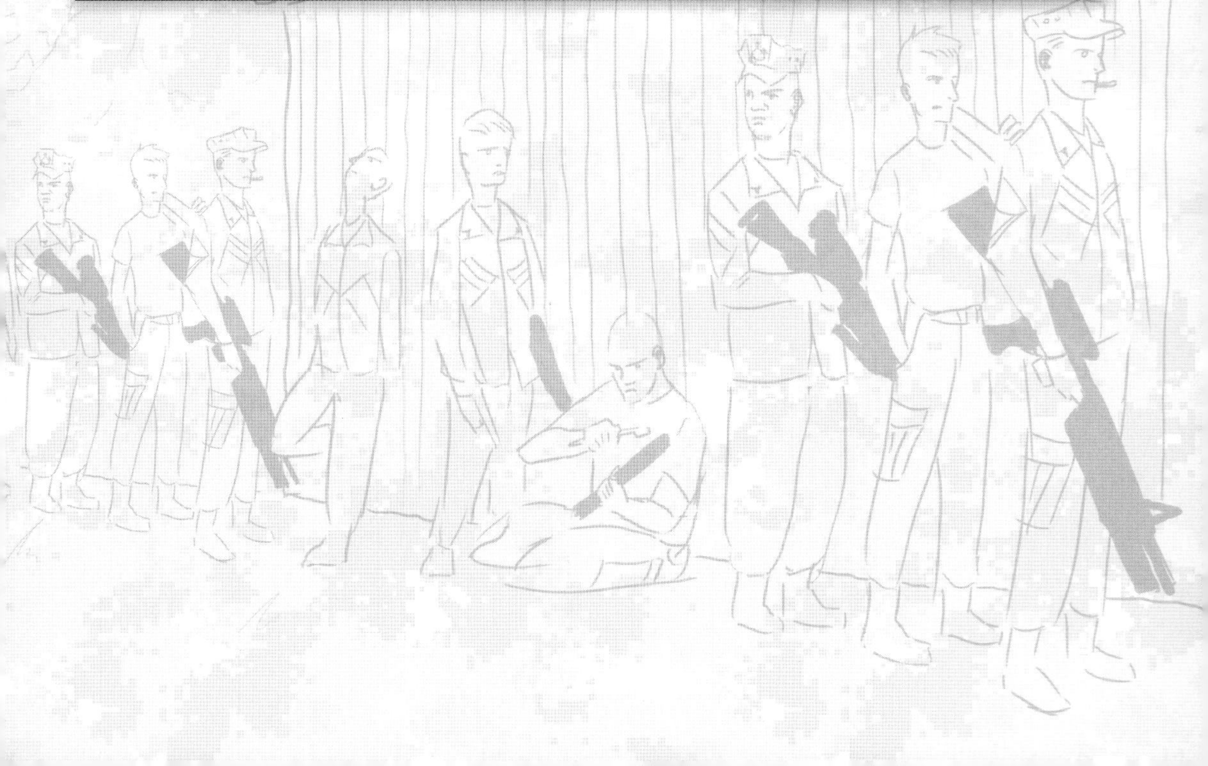

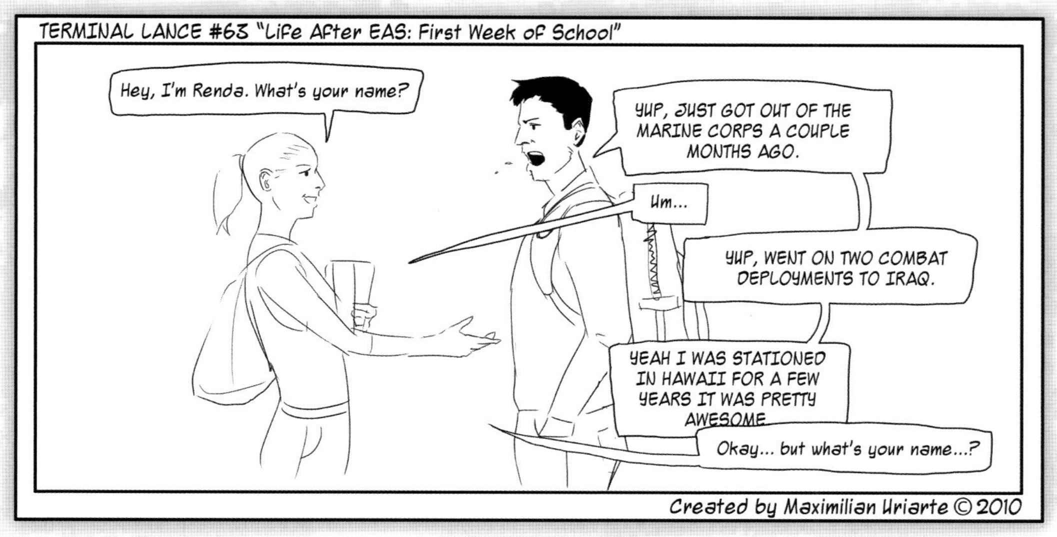
TERMINAL LANCE #63 "Life After EAS: First Week of School"
Hey, I'm Renda. What's your name?
YUP, JUST GOT OUT OF THE MARINE CORPS A COUPLE MONTHS AGO.
Um...
YUP, WENT ON TWO COMBAT DEPLOYMENTS TO IRAQ.
YEAH I WAS STATIONED IN HAWAII FOR A FEW YEARS IT WAS PRETTY AWESOME
Okay... but what's your name...?
Created by Maximilian Uriarte © 2010

63 "Life After EAS: First Week of School"

With this strip, I decided that instead of making fun of the Marine Corps I would make fun of myself. I doubt I'm the only one that's ever had this problem, but I noticed that after I got out of the Marines and back into school, I found myself really wanting to tell people about what I did—whether they asked to hear about it or not. Though this is obviously an exaggeration, I did find it very difficult to keep my experiences to myself.

A tour through the Marine Corps is such a unique, odd, and life-changing experience that it's hard to ignore it once you're out. It's like some kind of duty afterward, some need to make sure that people know you've seen the world, to explode into a shouted "OMG I WAS IN THE MARINE CORPS I DID THIS" every time the opportunity arises.

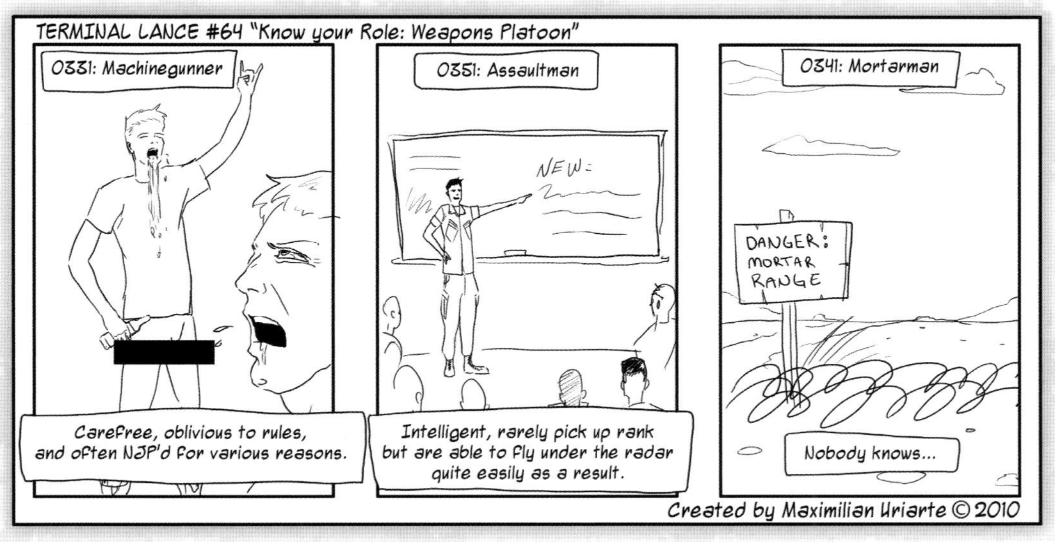
TERMINAL LANCE #64 "Know your Role: Weapons Platoon"
0331: Machinegunner
Carefree, oblivious to rules, and often NJP'd for various reasons.
0351: Assaultman
NEW:
Intelligent, rarely pick up rank but are able to fly under the radar quite easily as a result.
0341: Mortarman
DANGER: MORTAR RANGE
Nobody knows...
Created by Maximilian Uriarte © 2010

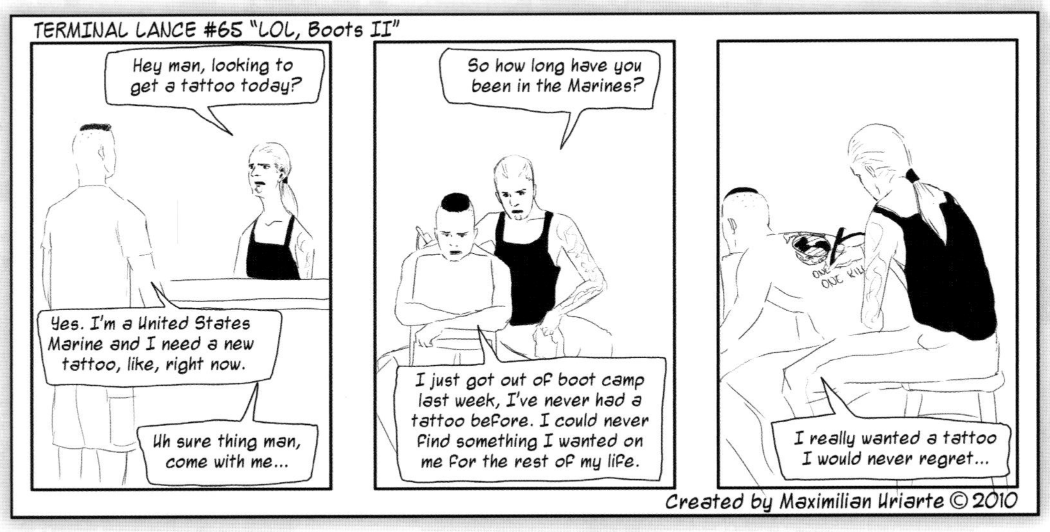
TERMINAL LANCE #65 "LOL, Boots II"
Hey man, looking to get a tattoo today?
Yes. I'm a United States Marine and I need a new tattoo, like, right now.
Uh sure thing man, come with me...
So how long have you been in the Marines?
I just got out of boot camp last week, I've never had a tattoo before. I could never find something I wanted on me for the rest of my life.
I really wanted a tattoo I would never regret...
Created by Maximilian Uriarte © 2010

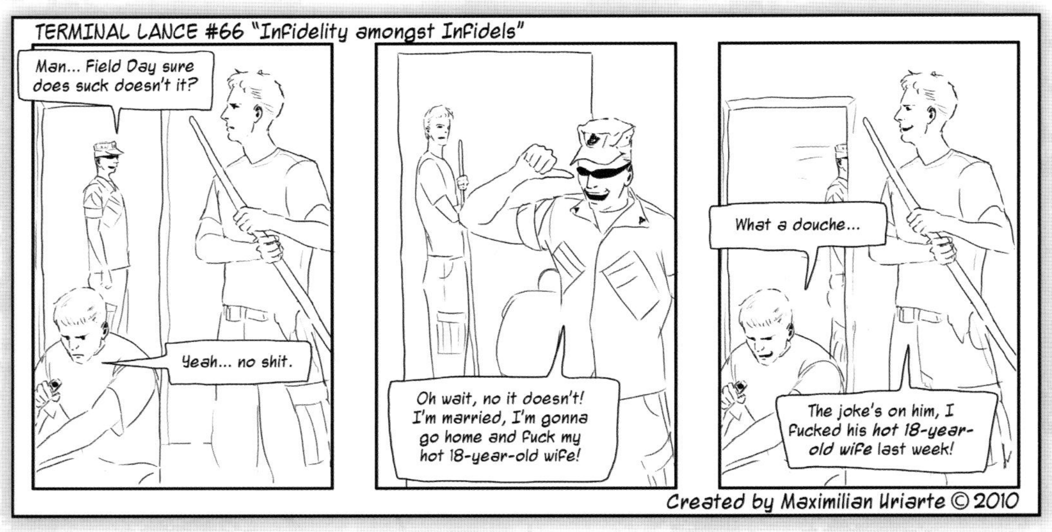
TERMINAL LANCE #66 "Infidelity amongst Infidels"
Man... Field Day sure does suck doesn't it?
Yeah... no shit.
Oh wait, no it doesn't! I'm married, I'm gonna go home and fuck my hot 18-year-old wife!
What a douche...
The joke's on him, I fucked his hot 18-year-old wife last week!
Created by Maximilian Uriarte © 2010

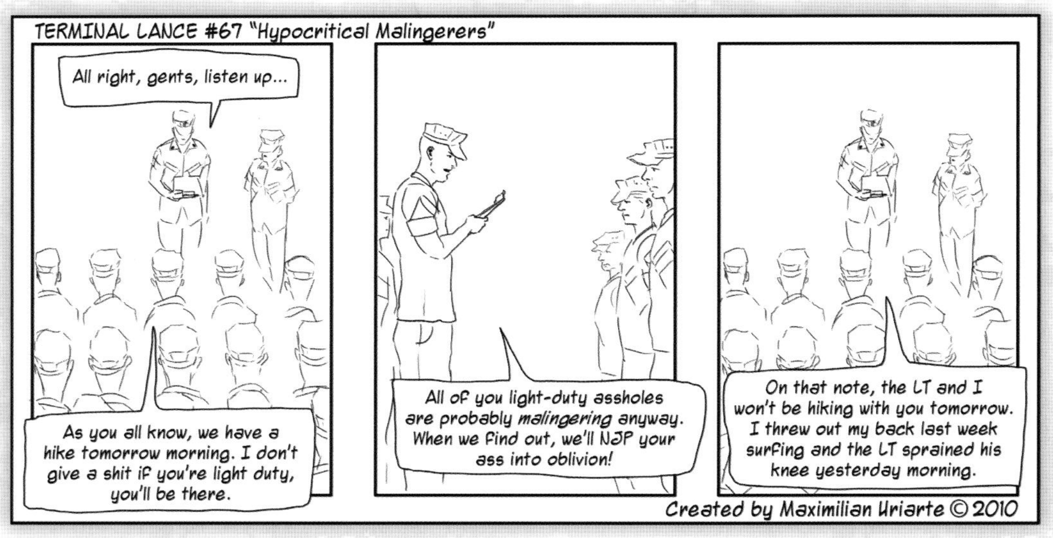
TERMINAL LANCE #67 "Hypocritical Malingerers"
All right, gents, listen up...
As you all know, we have a hike tomorrow morning. I don't give a shit if you're light duty, you'll be there.
All of you light-duty assholes are probably malingering anyway. When we find out, we'll NJP your ass into oblivion!
On that note, the LT and I won't be hiking with you tomorrow. I threw out my back last week surfing and the LT sprained his knee yesterday morning.
Created by Maximilian Uriarte © 2010

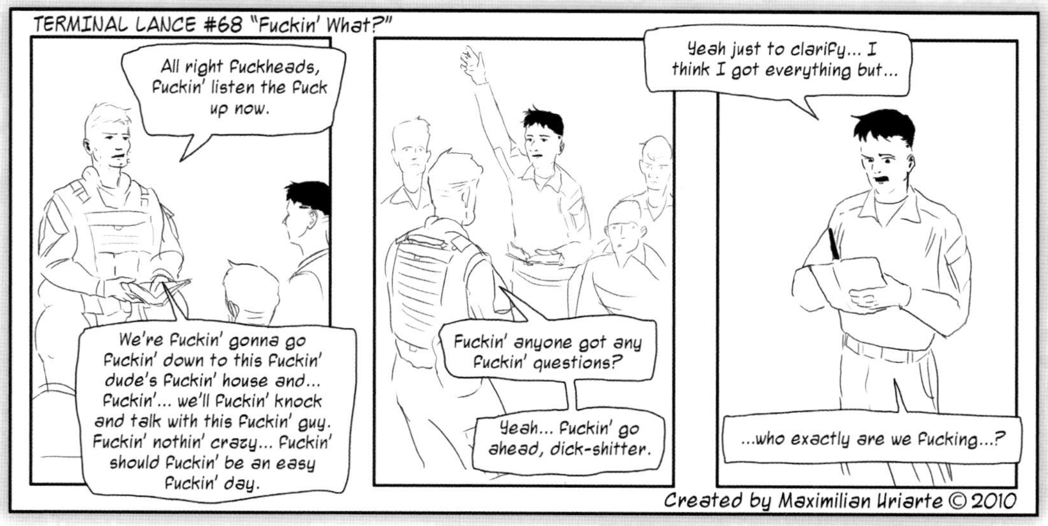
TERMINAL LANCE #68 "Fuckin' What?"
All right fuckheads, fuckin' listen the fuck up now.
We're fuckin' gonna go fuckin' down to this fuckin' dude's fuckin' house and... fuckin'... we'll fuckin' knock and talk with this fuckin' guy. Fuckin' nothin' crazy... fuckin' should fuckin' be an easy fuckin' day.
Fuckin' anyone got any fuckin' questions?
Yeah... fuckin' go ahead, dick-shitter.
Yeah just to clarify... I think I got everything but...
...who exactly are we fucking...?
Created by Maximilian Uriarte © 2010

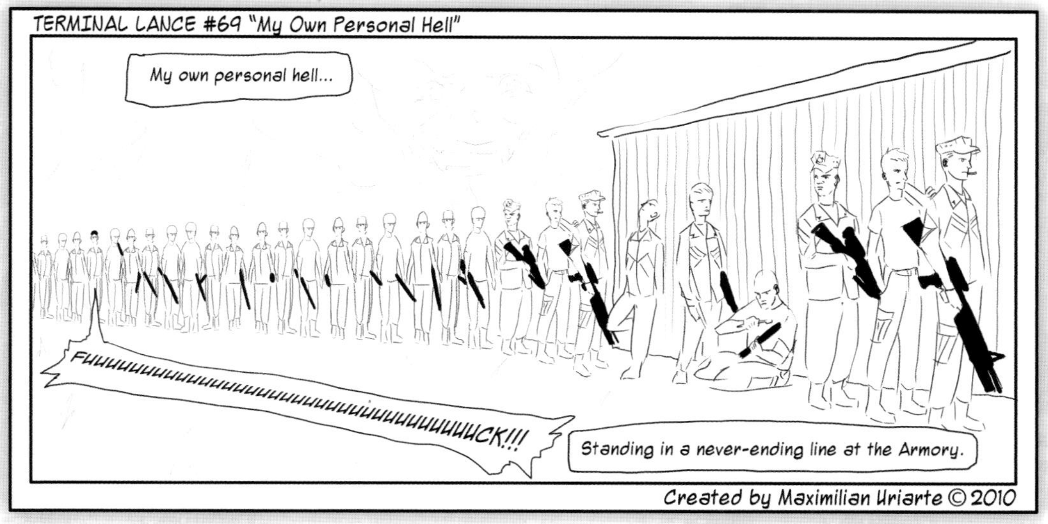
TERMINAL LANCE #69 "My Own Personal Hell"
My own personal hell...
FUUUUUUUUUUUUUUUUUUUUUUUUUUUUUUUUUUUUUUUUUUUUUUUUUUUUUUUUUUUUUUCK!!!
Standing in a never-ending line at the Armory.
Created by Maximilian Uriarte © 2010

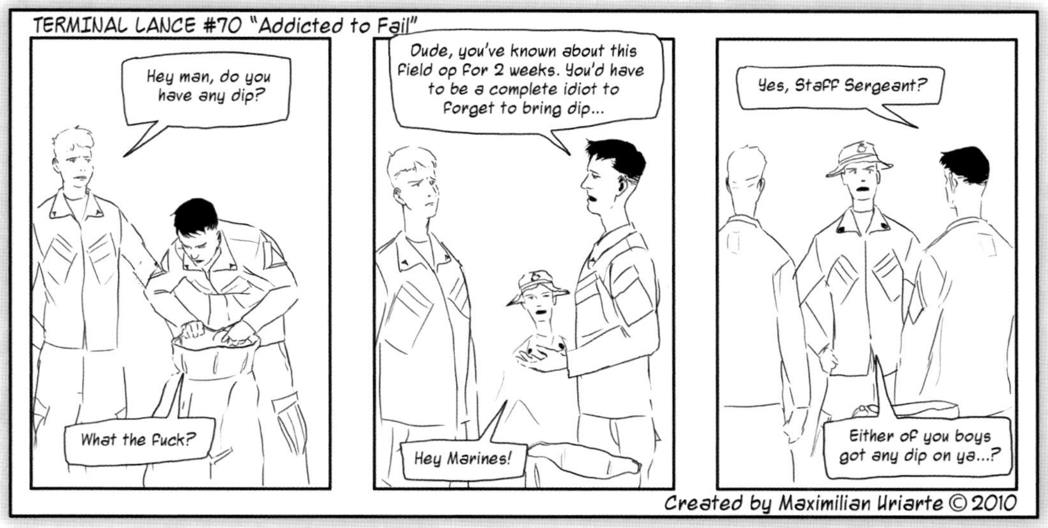
TERMINAL LANCE #70 "Addicted to Fail"
Hey man, do you have any dip?
What the fuck?
Dude, you've known about this field op for 2 weeks. You'd have to be a complete idiot to forget to bring dip...
Hey Marines!
Yes, Staff Sergeant?
Either of you boys got any dip on ya...?
Created by Maximilian Uriarte © 2010

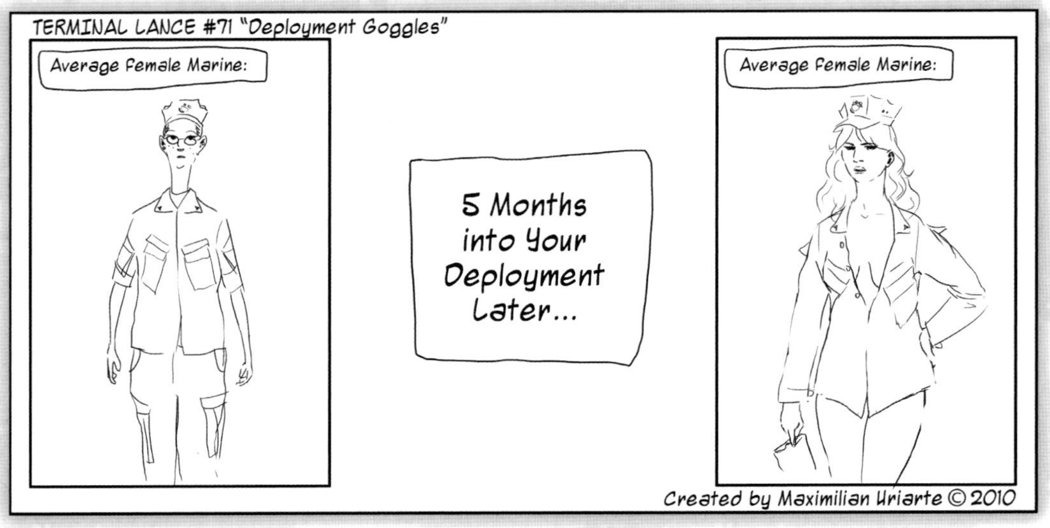
TERMINAL LANCE #71 "Deployment Goggles"
Average female Marine:
5 Months into Your Deployment Later...
Average female Marine:
Created by Maximilian Uriarte © 2010

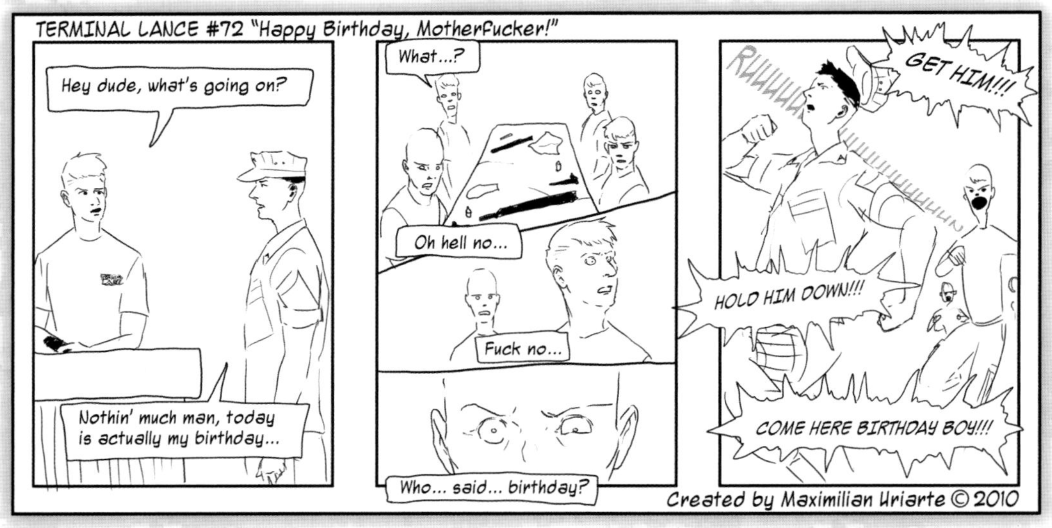
TERMINAL LANCE #72 "Happy Birthday, Motherfucker!"
Hey dude, what's going on?
Nothin' much man, today is actually my birthday...
What...?
Oh hell no...
Fuck no...
Who... said... birthday?
GET HIM!!!
HOLD HIM DOWN!!!
COME HERE BIRTHDAY BOY!!!
Created by Maximilian Uriarte © 2010

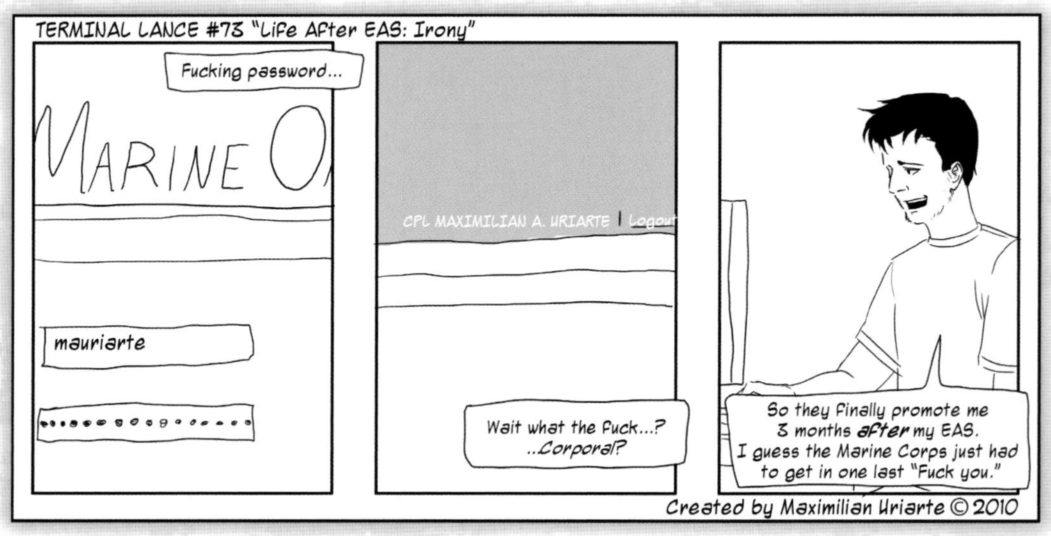
TERMINAL LANCE #73 "Life After EAS: Irony"
Fucking password...
MARINE O
mauriarte
CPL MAXIMILIAN A. URIARTE | Logout
Wait what the fuck...? ..Corporal?
So they finally promote me 3 months after my EAS. I guess the Marine Corps just had to get in one last "Fuck you."
Created by Maximilian Uriarte © 2010

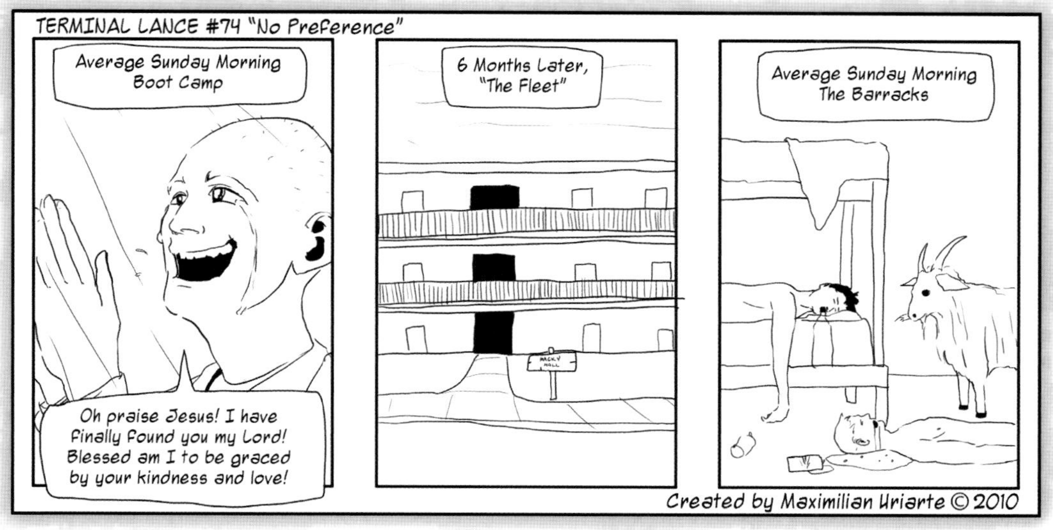
TERMINAL LANCE #74 "No Preference"
Average Sunday Morning
Boot Camp
Oh praise Jesus! I have finally found you my Lord! Blessed am I to be graced by your kindness and love!
6 Months Later,
"The Fleet"
Average Sunday Morning
The Barracks
Created by Maximilian Uriarte © 2010

74 "No Preference"

In terms of religious experience, boot camp is probably one of the most intense places that hopeful Marines can find themselves. For a number of reasons, recruits tend to undergo a kind of extreme religious epiphany as soon as they step on those yellow footprints. Gone are their old ways of sinful heathenism. Now they are acolytes of God, warriors of the Lord himself . . . that is, until they discover that epic amounts of alcohol can replace their voids of faith on the weekends once they hit the fleet.

I vividly recall the numbers of recruits that attended the church masses. Many even underwent baptism in front of an applauding audience of like-minded recruits. As in "the real world," religion in the Marines tends to only belong where it's needed. During the stressful culture shock of recruit training, Marine recruits find solace in faith otherwise left alone. I succumbed to this endeavor as well, though my Jewish background led me to synagogue on Fridays instead of church on Sundays—which actually worked out great, because I still got to chill out alone in the squad bay on Sundays while everyone else was at church.

But, for many, the culture of fleethood soon replaces this newfound religion. The average Lance Corporal is more likely to attend the omelet line at the chow hall on a Sunday than he is church. Some Marines remain devout, but, for many others, their sudden interest in religion is temporary and is relegated to the Depot.

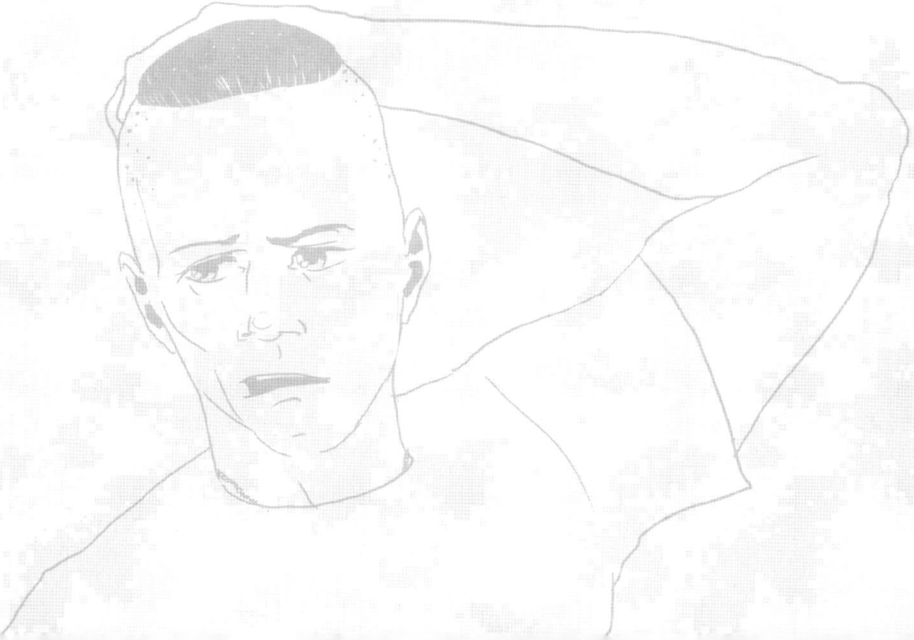

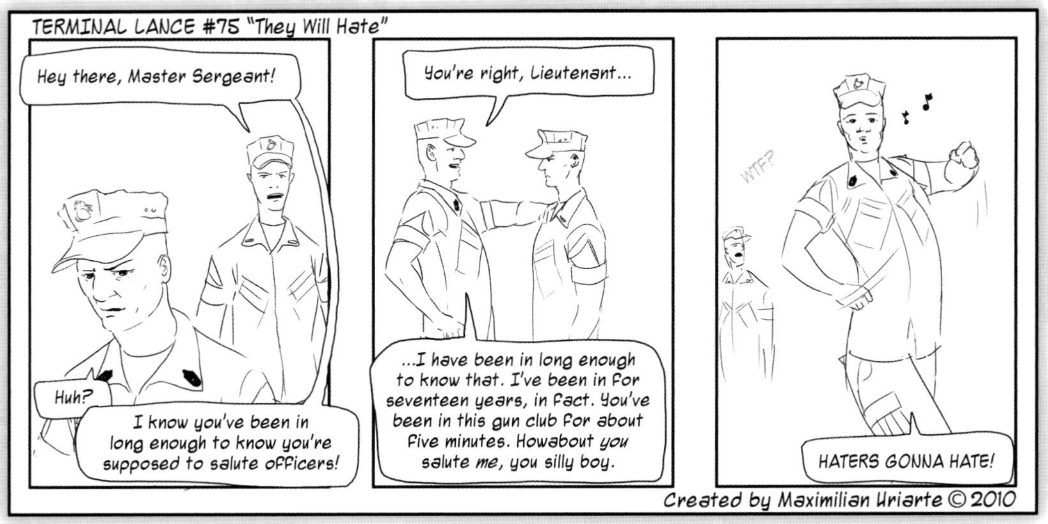
TERMINAL LANCE #75 "They Will Hate"
Hey there, Master Sergeant!
Huh?
I know you've been in long enough to know you're supposed to salute officers!
You're right, Lieutenant...
...I have been in long enough to know that. I've been in for seventeen years, in fact. You've been in this gun club for about five minutes. Howabout *you* salute *me*, you silly boy.
WTF?
HATERS GONNA HATE!
Created by Maximilian Uriarte © 2010

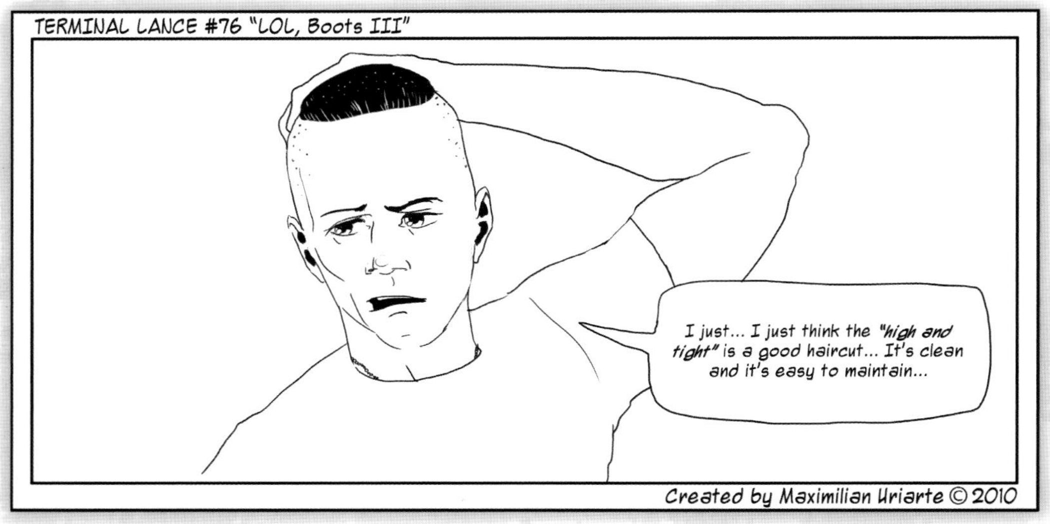
TERMINAL LANCE #76 "LOL, Boots III"
I just... I just think the *"high and tight"* is a good haircut... It's clean and it's easy to maintain...
Created by Maximilian Uriarte © 2010

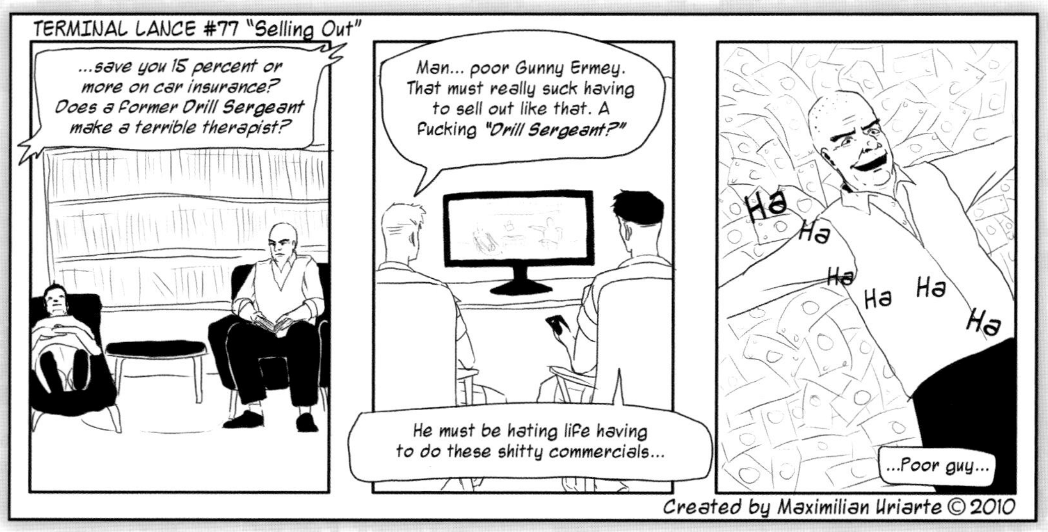
TERMINAL LANCE #77 "Selling Out"
...save you 15 percent or more on car insurance? Does a former Drill Sergeant make a terrible therapist?
Man... poor Gunny Ermey. That must really suck having to sell out like that. A fucking *"Drill Sergeant?"*
He must be hating life having to do these shitty commercials...
Ha Ha Ha Ha Ha Ha
...Poor guy...
Created by Maximilian Uriarte © 2010

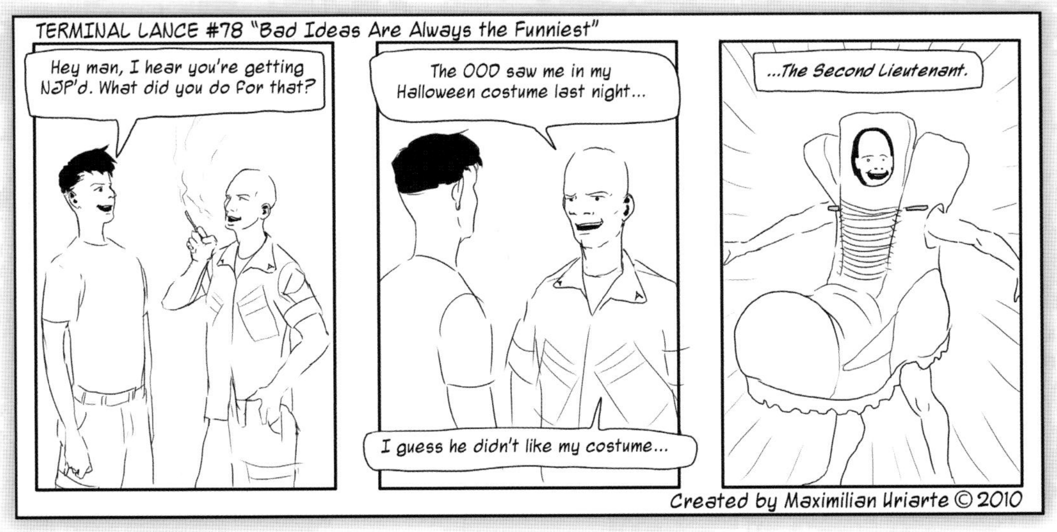
TERMINAL LANCE #78 "Bad Ideas Are Always the Funniest"
Hey man, I hear you're getting NJP'd. What did you do for that?
The OOD saw me in my Halloween costume last night...
I guess he didn't like my costume...
...The Second Lieutenant.
Created by Maximilian Uriarte © 2010

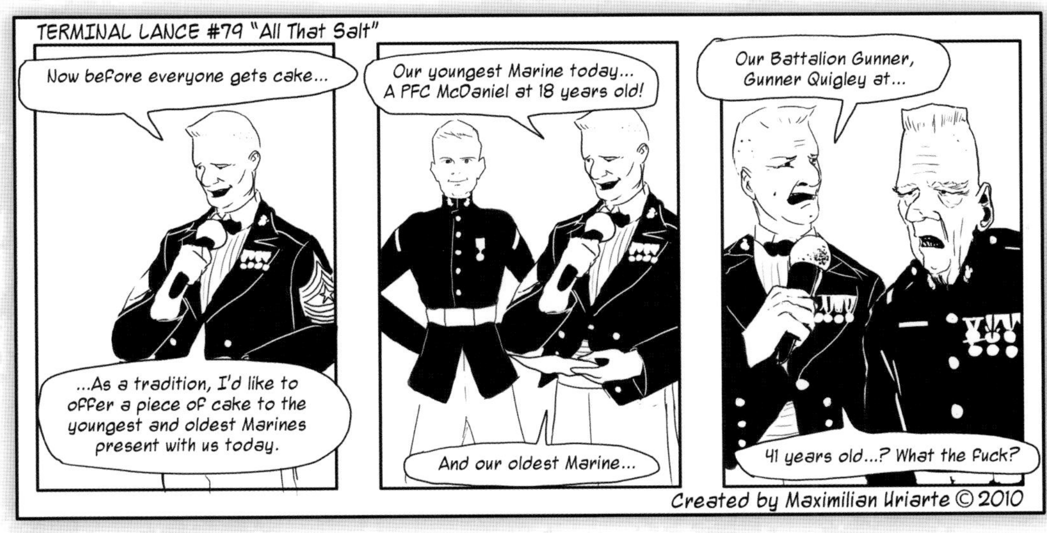
TERMINAL LANCE #79 "All That Salt"
Now before everyone gets cake...
...As a tradition, I'd like to offer a piece of cake to the youngest and oldest Marines present with us today.
Our youngest Marine today... A PFC McDaniel at 18 years old!
And our oldest Marine...
Our Battalion Gunner, Gunner Quigley at...
41 years old...? What the fuck?
Created by Maximilian Uriarte © 2010

79 "All That Salt"

I dunno what it is about the Marine Corps. Have you ever noticed how common it is to see Marines barely in their middle age looking like geriatrics? In reality, it is simply a result of a lifetime of physical abuse to the body. All those flak runs, hikes, deployments, hardcore PT sessions, and binge drinking add up over the years. The first time I returned from Iraq, I looked like I had aged several years in the span of seven months. Physical and emotional strain on a daily basis are not good for the human body and those decrepit SNCO's and officers that just barely turned forty are the result. I'm not saying it necessarily happens to everyone. In fact, I would be willing to bet that those who spend their whole careers in the infantry are much more likely to develop this rapid aging syndrome.

As for Marine Corps balls, well they're usually one of two things: an extremely boring cesspool of uniforms and overpriced food, or an extremely boring cesspool of uniforms and overpriced food interspersed with random drunk outbursts from your company

Gunny and your friends. My last and final Marine Corps ball was the only really fun time I've had at one. Drinking with some unlikely people was an especially good time—as was walking to Wailana in Honolulu for pancakes at two a.m. in a drunken stupor.

Birthday balls have a way of being either miserable or a lot of fun, but as with most things in the Corps—it's only fun if you make it that way.

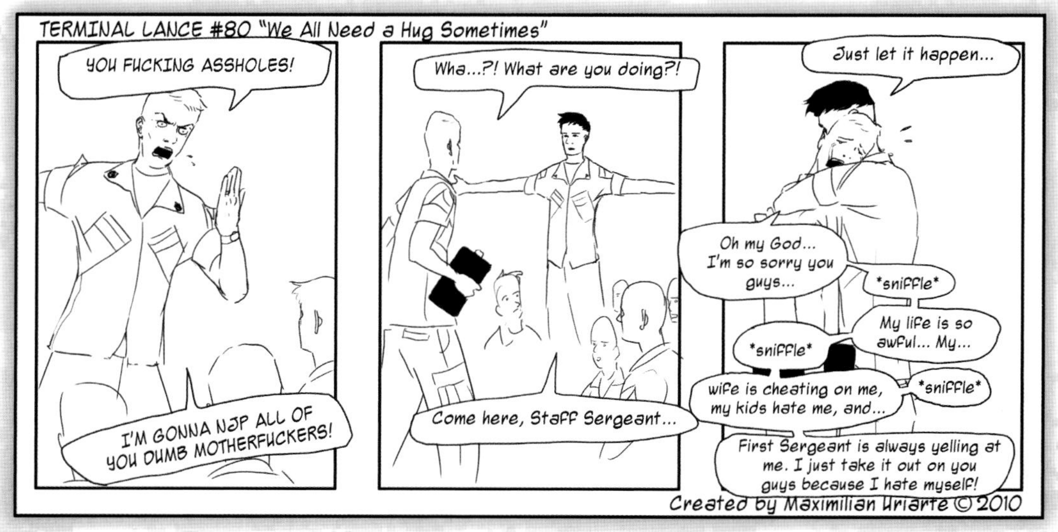
TERMINAL LANCE #80 "We All Need a Hug Sometimes"
YOU FUCKING ASSHOLES!
I'M GONNA NJP ALL OF YOU DUMB MOTHERFUCKERS!
Wha...?! What are you doing?!
Come here, Staff Sergeant...
Just let it happen...
Oh my God... I'm so sorry you guys...
sniffle
My life is so awful... My...
sniffle
wife is cheating on me, my kids hate me, and...
sniffle
First Sergeant is always yelling at me. I just take it out on you guys because I hate myself!
Created by Maximilian Uriarte © 2010

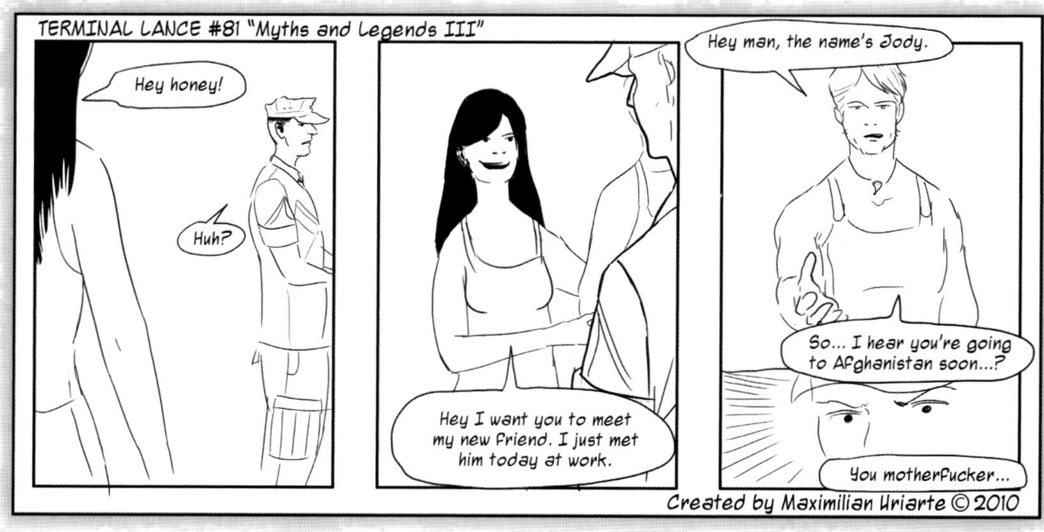
TERMINAL LANCE #81 "Myths and Legends III"
Hey honey!
Huh?
Hey I want you to meet my new friend. I just met him today at work.
Hey man, the name's Jody.
So... I hear you're going to Afghanistan soon...?
You motherfucker...
Created by Maximilian Uriarte © 2010

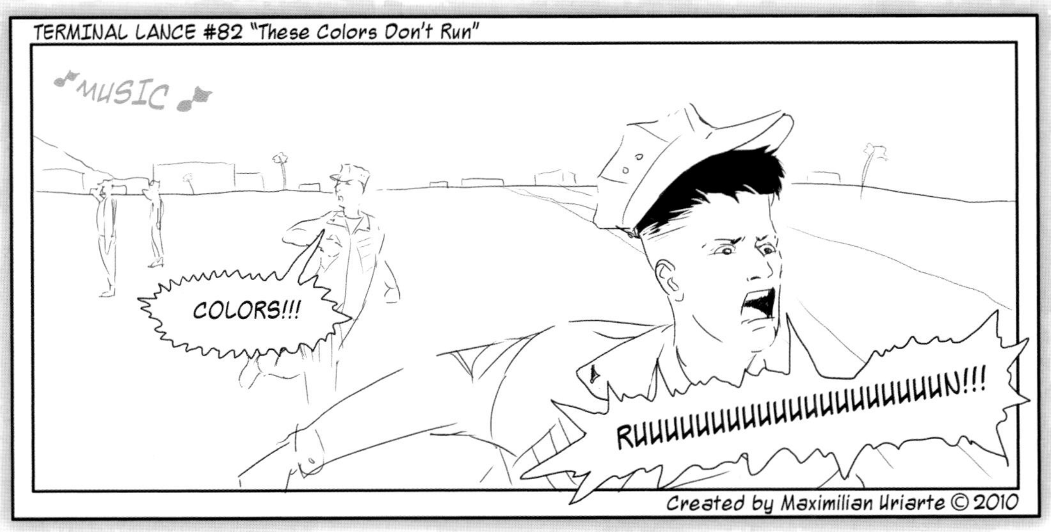
TERMINAL LANCE #82 "These Colors Don't Run"
MUSIC
COLORS!!!
RUUUUUUUUUUUUUUUUUUUN!!!
Created by Maximilian Uriarte © 2010

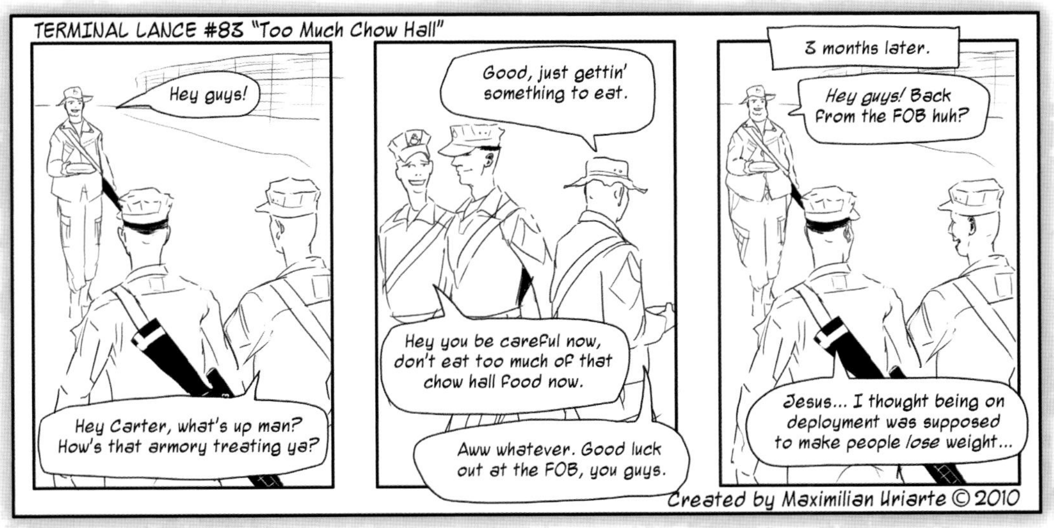
TERMINAL LANCE #83 "Too Much Chow Hall"
Hey guys!
Hey Carter, what's up man? How's that armory treating ya?
Good, just gettin' something to eat.
Hey you be careful now, don't eat too much of that chow hall food now.
Aww whatever. Good luck out at the FOB, you guys.
3 months later.
Hey guys! Back from the FOB huh?
Jesus... I thought being on deployment was supposed to make people lose weight...
Created by Maximilian Uriarte © 2010

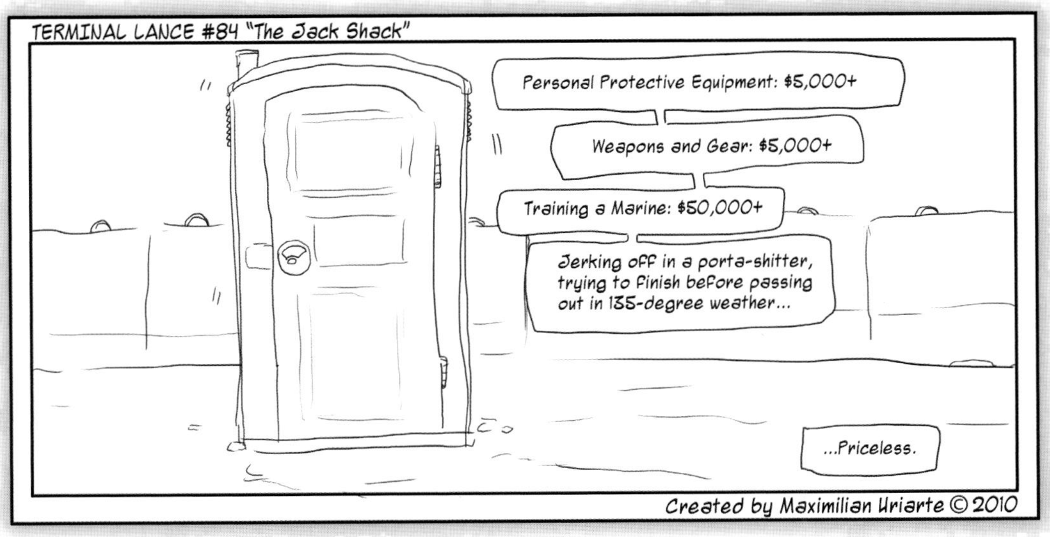
TERMINAL LANCE #84 "The Jack Shack"
Personal Protective Equipment: $5,000+
Weapons and Gear: $5,000+
Training a Marine: $50,000+
Jerking off in a porta-shitter, trying to finish before passing out in 135-degree weather...
...Priceless.
Created by Maximilian Uriarte © 2010

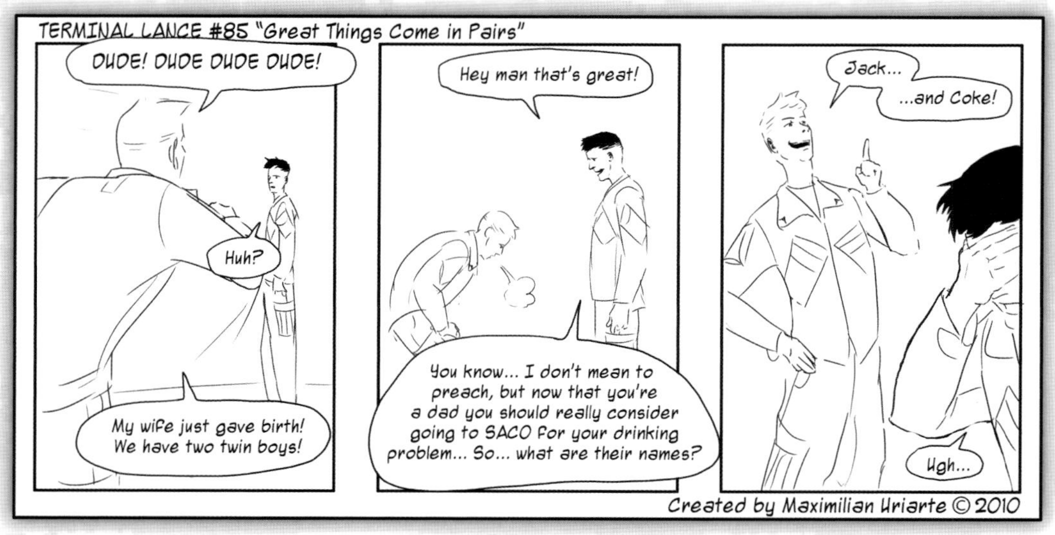
TERMINAL LANCE #85 "Great Things Come in Pairs"
DUDE! DUDE DUDE DUDE!
Huh?
My wife just gave birth! We have two twin boys!
Hey man that's great!
You know... I don't mean to preach, but now that you're a dad you should really consider going to SACO for your drinking problem... So... what are their names?
Jack...
...and Coke!
Ugh...
Created by Maximilian Uriarte © 2010

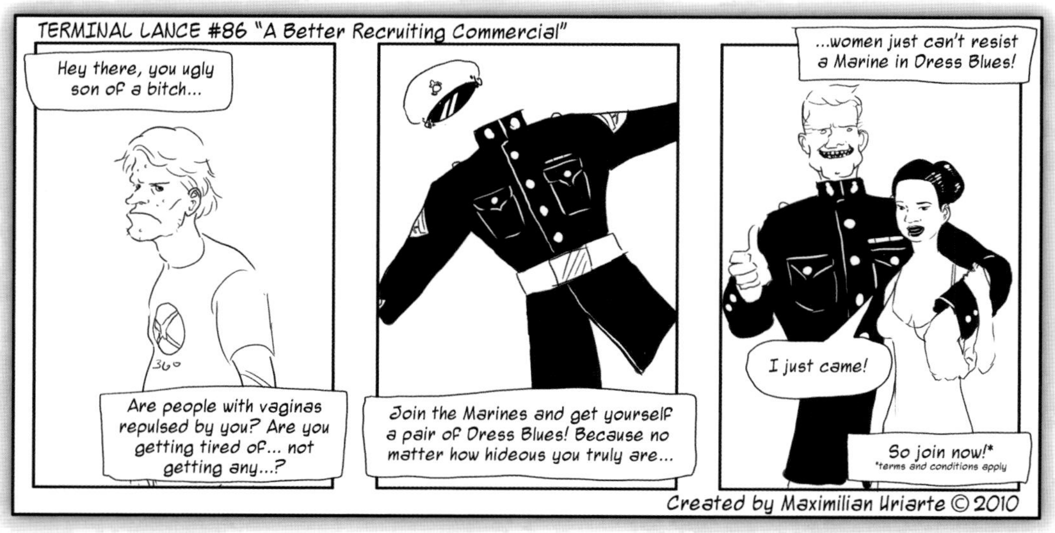
TERMINAL LANCE #86 "A Better Recruiting Commercial"
Hey there, you ugly son of a bitch...
Are people with vaginas repulsed by you? Are you getting tired of... not getting any...?
Join the Marines and get yourself a pair of Dress Blues! Because no matter how hideous you truly are...
...women just can't resist a Marine in Dress Blues!
I just came!
So join now!*
*terms and conditions apply
Created by Maximilian Uriarte © 2010

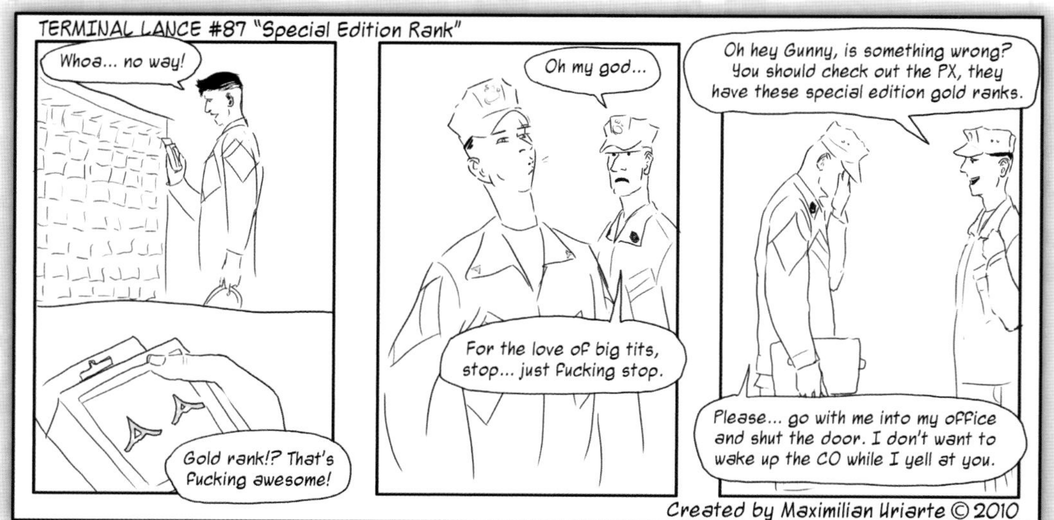
TERMINAL LANCE #87 "Special Edition Rank"
Whoa... no way!
Gold rank!? That's fucking awesome!
Oh my god...
For the love of big tits, stop... just fucking stop.
Oh hey Gunny, is something wrong? You should check out the PX, they have these special edition gold ranks.
Please... go with me into my office and shut the door. I don't want to wake up the CO while I yell at you.
Created by Maximilian Uriarte © 2010

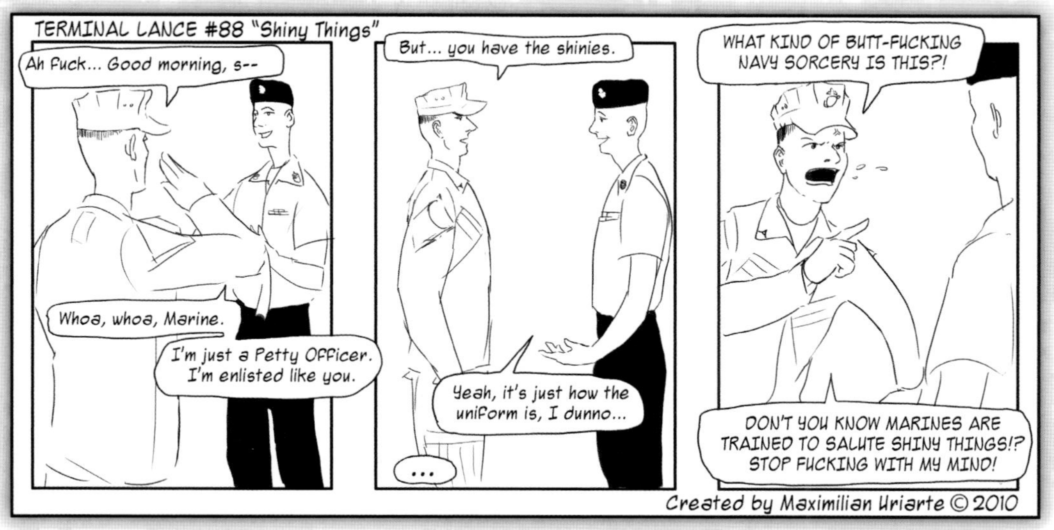
TERMINAL LANCE #88 "Shiny Things"
Ah Fuck... Good morning, s--
Whoa, whoa, Marine.
I'm just a Petty Officer. I'm enlisted like you.
But... you have the shinies.
Yeah, it's just how the uniform is, I dunno...
...
WHAT KIND OF BUTT-FUCKING NAVY SORCERY IS THIS?!
DON'T YOU KNOW MARINES ARE TRAINED TO SALUTE SHINY THINGS!? STOP FUCKING WITH MY MIND!
Created by Maximilian Uriarte © 2010

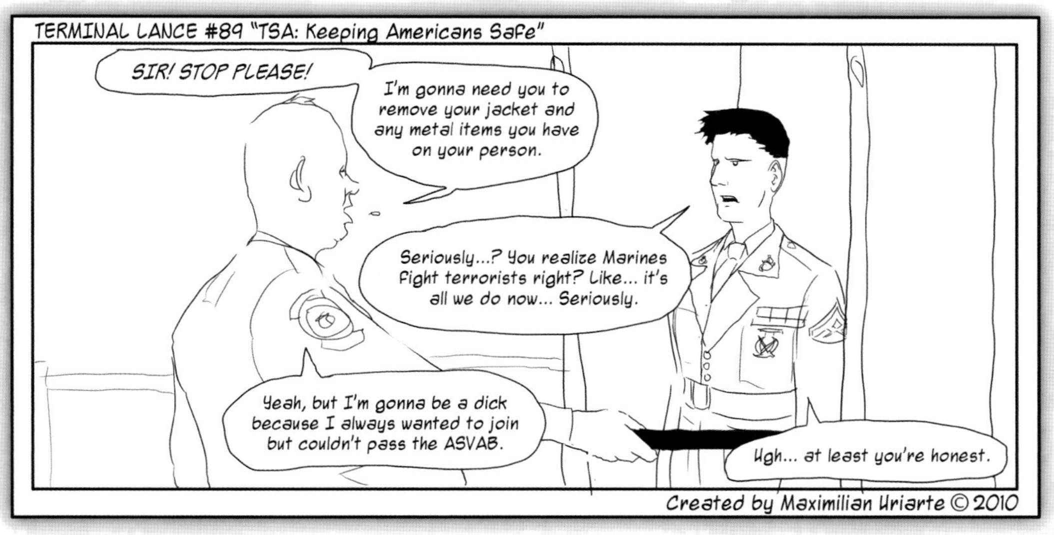
TERMINAL LANCE #89 "TSA: Keeping Americans Safe"
SIR! STOP PLEASE!
I'm gonna need you to remove your jacket and any metal items you have on your person.
Seriously...? You realize Marines fight terrorists right? Like... it's all we do now... Seriously.
Yeah, but I'm gonna be a dick because I always wanted to join but couldn't pass the ASVAB.
Ugh... at least you're honest.
Created by Maximilian Uriarte © 2010

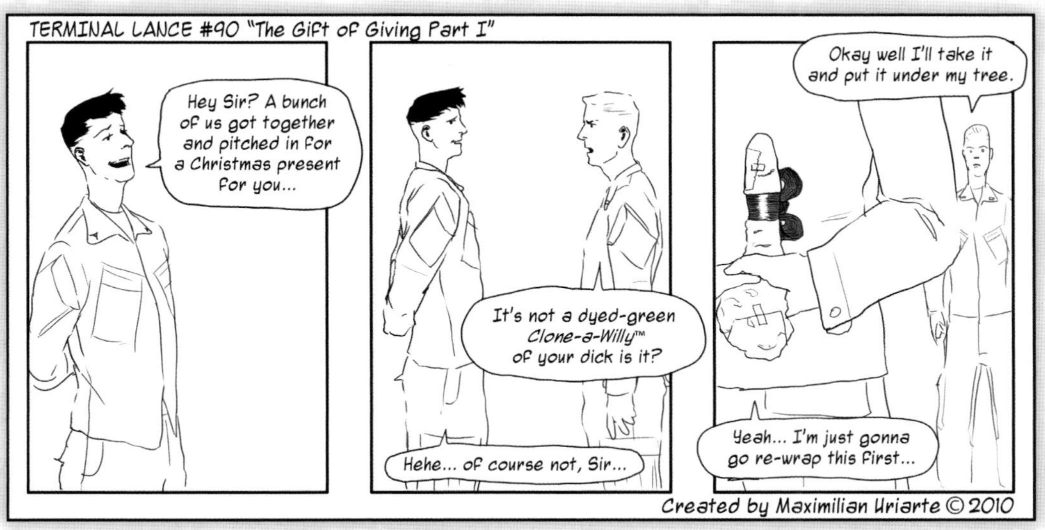
TERMINAL LANCE #90 "The Gift of Giving Part I"
Hey Sir? A bunch of us got together and pitched in for a Christmas present for you...
It's not a dyed-green Clone-a-Willy™ of your dick is it?
Hehe... of course not, Sir...
Okay well I'll take it and put it under my tree.
Yeah... I'm just gonna go re-wrap this first...
Created by Maximilian Uriarte © 2010

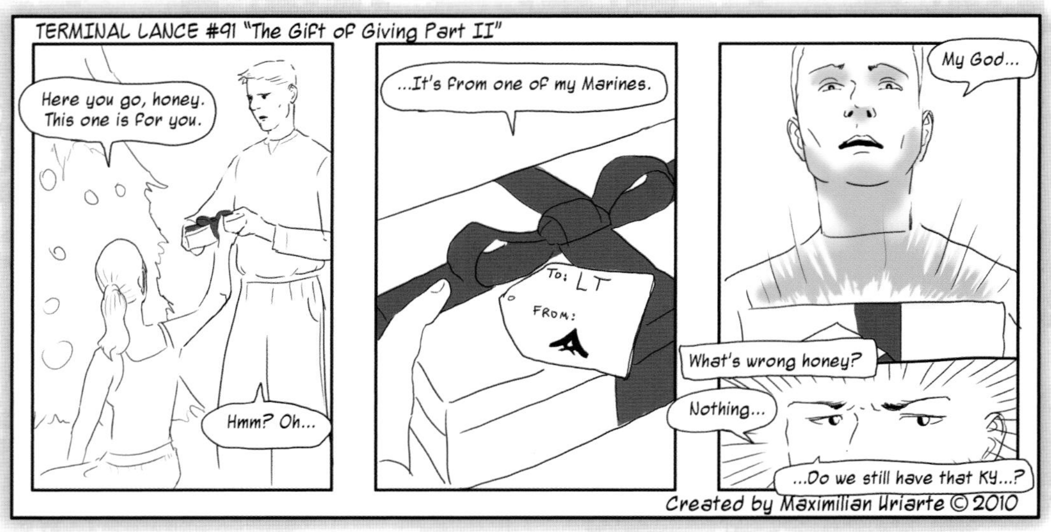
TERMINAL LANCE #91 "The Gift of Giving Part II"
Here you go, honey. This one is for you.
Hmm? Oh...
...It's from one of my Marines.
To: LT
FROM:
My God...
What's wrong honey?
Nothing...
...Do we still have that KY...?
Created by Maximilian Uriarte © 2010

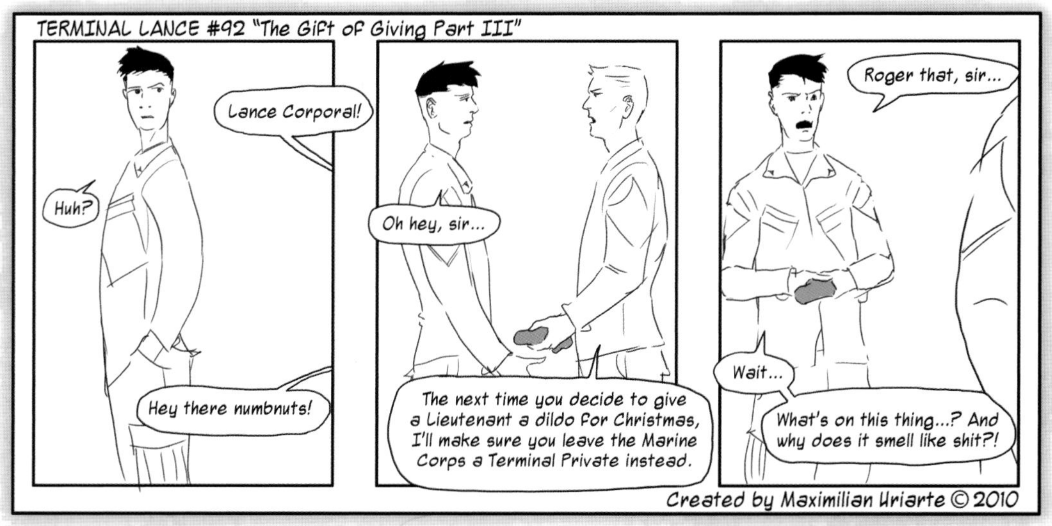
TERMINAL LANCE #92 "The Gift of Giving Part III"
Lance Corporal!
Huh?
Hey there numbnuts!
Oh hey, sir...
The next time you decide to give a Lieutenant a dildo for Christmas, I'll make sure you leave the Marine Corps a Terminal Private instead.
Roger that, sir...
Wait...
What's on this thing...? And why does it smell like shit?!
Created by Maximilian Uriarte © 2010

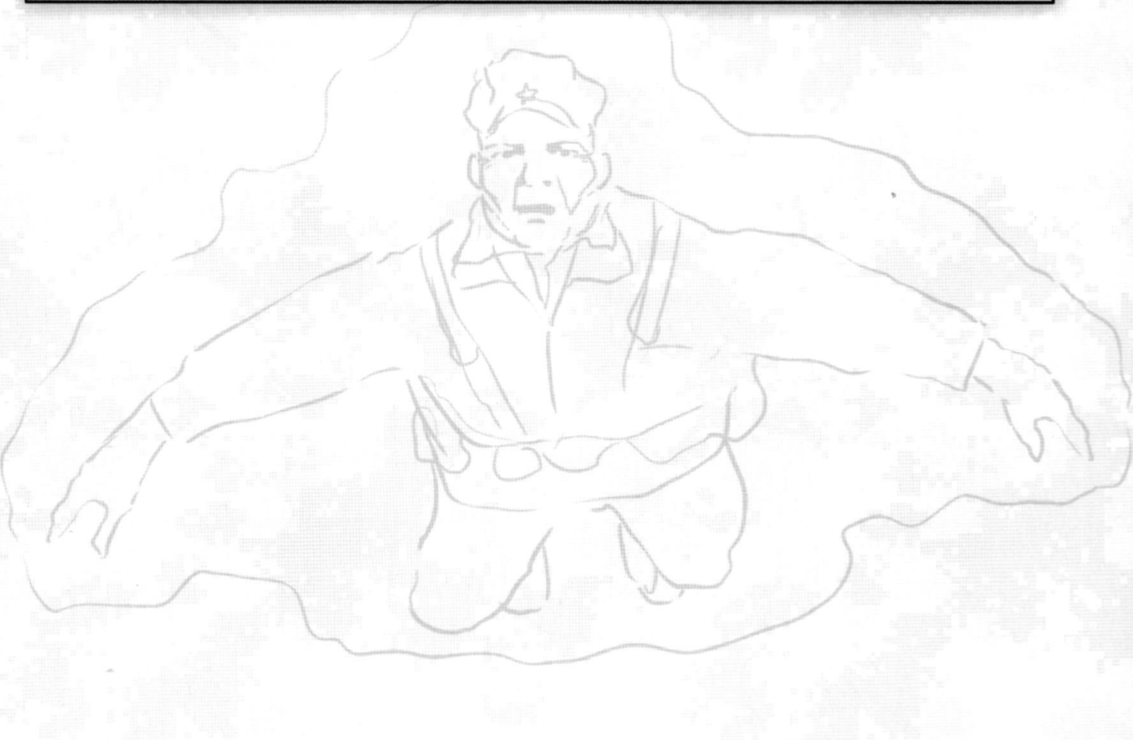

TERMINAL LANCE #93 "POG's Impressing the Grunts"
Hey there, oh-threes! You boys wanna see the inside of MY TANK?!
Oh my god yes please...
...I love you.
Meanwhile, at IPAC
Hey, you wanna see me conduct an SRB AUDIT?!
...Not especially...
Created by Maximilian Uriarte © 2010

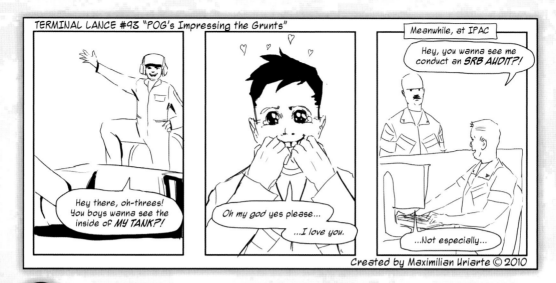

93 "POG's Impressing the Grunts"

Outside of the infantry (and even in it, some could argue), not all Marine Corps MOS are treated equal. It is a complete fallacy to say that there aren't any cool POG jobs—tank crewman, for example—but there are many non-infantry jobs that one could consider badass. Obviously, there are also many POG jobs that one would not consider badass, which I've exemplified here with IPAC. Though, frankly, I think the lamest POG job I've ever heard of is the 1171 Water Tech. When I first heard a Marine say to others, "They call us water dogs!" I literally shuddered in disbelief that the Marines could possibly have a job that lame.

Sorry, 1171's, but it's not the first time I've made fun of you.

TERMINAL LANCE #94 "Moto Parents"
Hey Dad! It's...
What the fuck!?
Hey son!
Why... do you have a high and tight...?
We just wanted to be supportive.
We're so proud of our little boy!
Mom?!
Created by Maximilian Uriarte © 2010

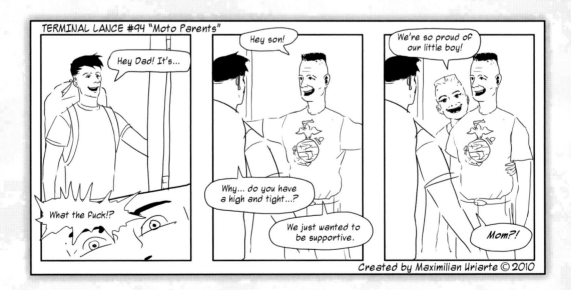

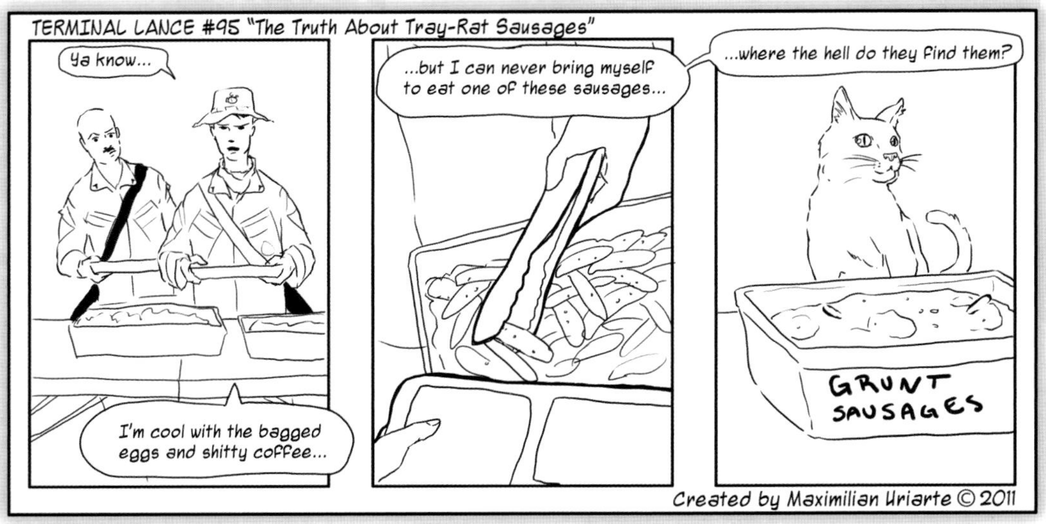
TERMINAL LANCE #95 "The Truth About Tray-Rat Sausages"
Ya know...
I'm cool with the bagged eggs and shitty coffee...
...but I can never bring myself to eat one of these sausages...
...where the hell do they find them?
GRUNT SAUSAGES
Created by Maximilian Uriarte © 2011

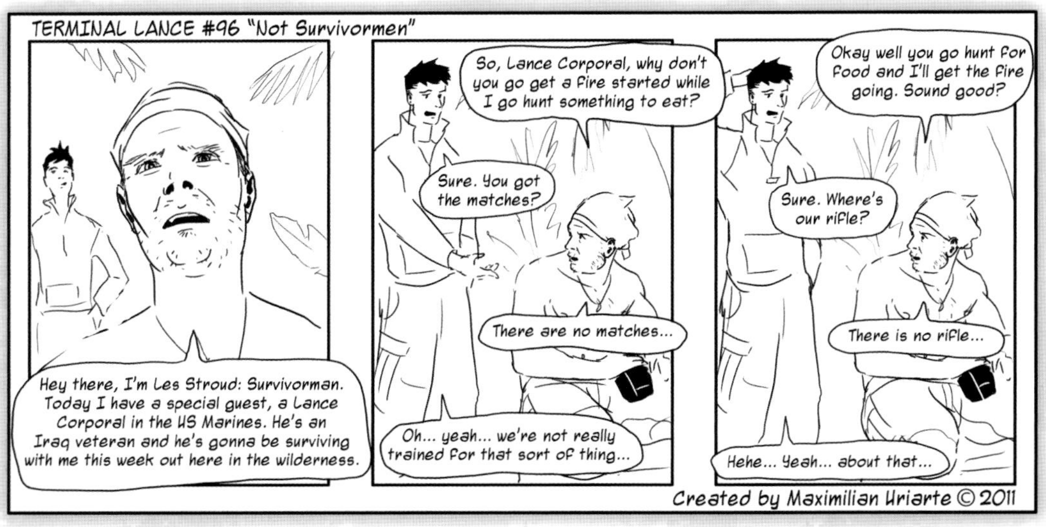
TERMINAL LANCE #96 "Not Survivormen"
Hey there, I'm Les Stroud: Survivorman. Today I have a special guest, a Lance Corporal in the US Marines. He's an Iraq veteran and he's gonna be surviving with me this week out here in the wilderness.
So, Lance Corporal, why don't you go get a fire started while I go hunt something to eat?
Sure. You got the matches?
There are no matches...
Oh... yeah... we're not really trained for that sort of thing...
Okay well you go hunt for food and I'll get the fire going. Sound good?
Sure. Where's our rifle?
There is no rifle...
Hehe... Yeah... about that...
Created by Maximilian Uriarte © 2011

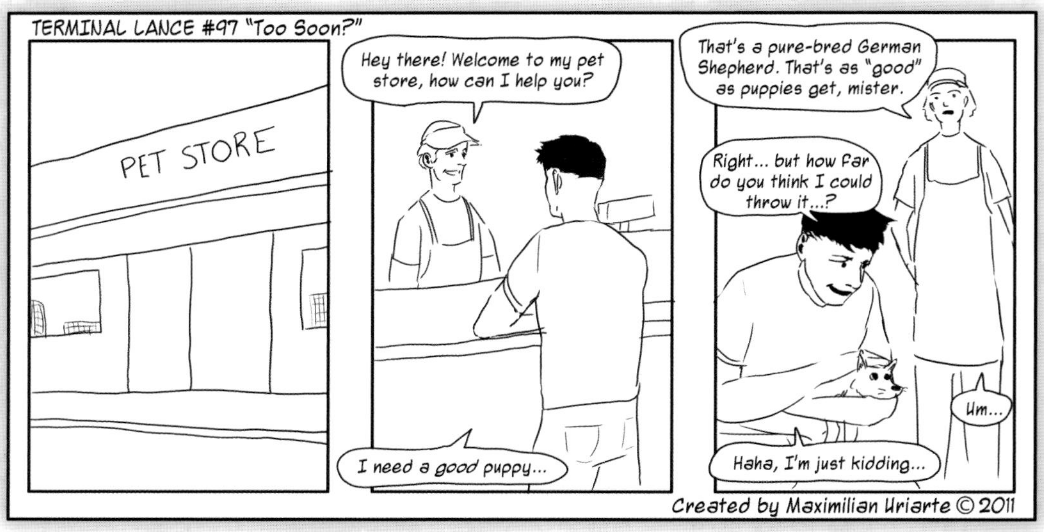
TERMINAL LANCE #97 "Too Soon?"
PET STORE
Hey there! Welcome to my pet store, how can I help you?
I need a good puppy...
That's a pure-bred German Shepherd. That's as "good" as puppies get, mister.
Right... but how far do you think I could throw it...?
Um...
Haha, I'm just kidding...
Created by Maximilian Uriarte © 2011

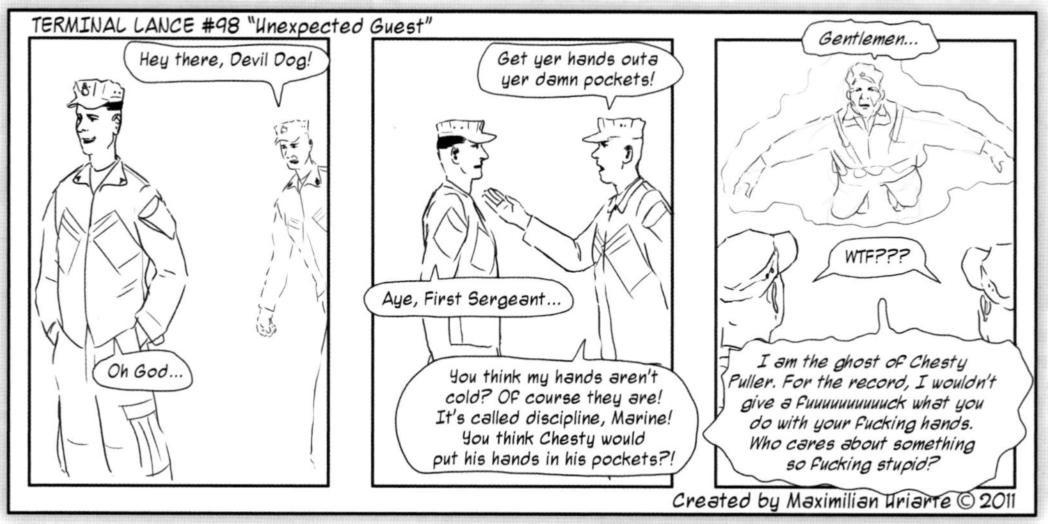
TERMINAL LANCE #98 "Unexpected Guest"
Hey there, Devil Dog!
Oh God...
Get yer hands outa yer damn pockets!
Aye, First Sergeant...
You think my hands aren't cold? Of course they are! It's called discipline, Marine! You think Chesty would put his hands in his pockets?!
Gentlemen...
WTF???
I am the ghost of Chesty Puller. For the record, I wouldn't give a fuuuuuuuuuck what you do with your fucking hands. Who cares about something so fucking stupid?
Created by Maximilian Uriarte © 2011

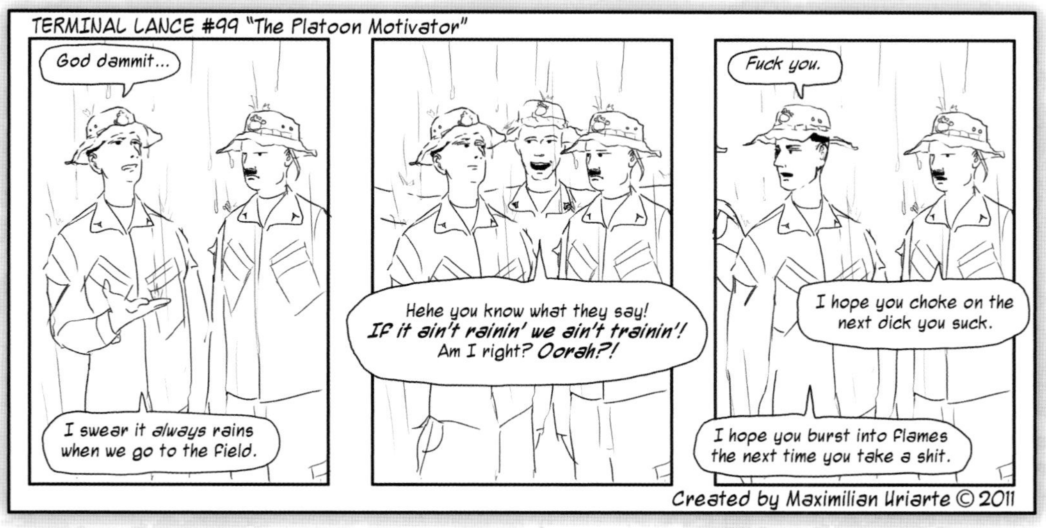
TERMINAL LANCE #99 "The Platoon Motivator"
God dammit...
I swear it always rains when we go to the field.
Hehe you know what they say! If it ain't rainin' we ain't trainin'! Am I right? Oorah?!
Fuck you.
I hope you choke on the next dick you suck.
I hope you burst into flames the next time you take a shit.
Created by Maximilian Uriarte © 2011

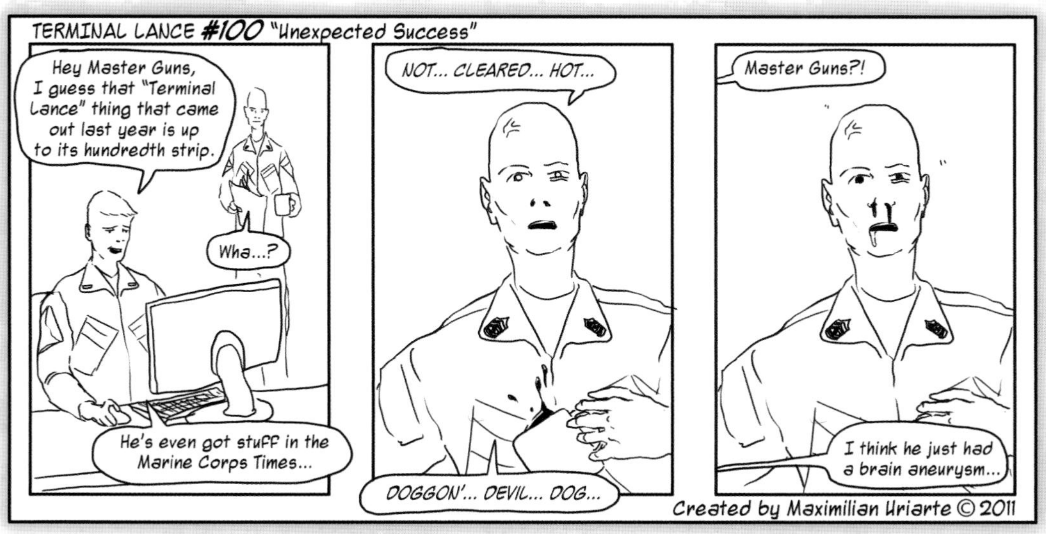
TERMINAL LANCE #100 "Unexpected Success"
Hey Master Guns, I guess that "Terminal Lance" thing that came out last year is up to its hundredth strip.
Wha...?
He's even got stuff in the Marine Corps Times...
NOT... CLEARED... HOT...
DOGGON'... DEVIL... DOG...
Master Guns?!
I think he just had a brain aneurysm...
Created by Maximilian Uriarte © 2011

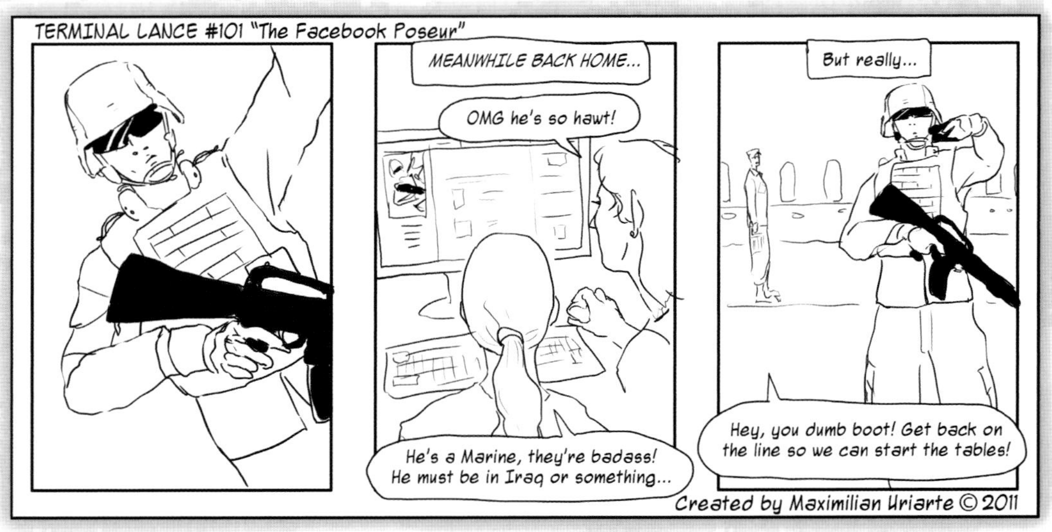
TERMINAL LANCE #101 "The Facebook Poseur"
MEANWHILE BACK HOME...
OMG he's so hawt!
He's a Marine, they're badass! He must be in Iraq or something...
But really...
Hey, you dumb boot! Get back on the line so we can start the tables!
Created by Maximilian Uriarte © 2011

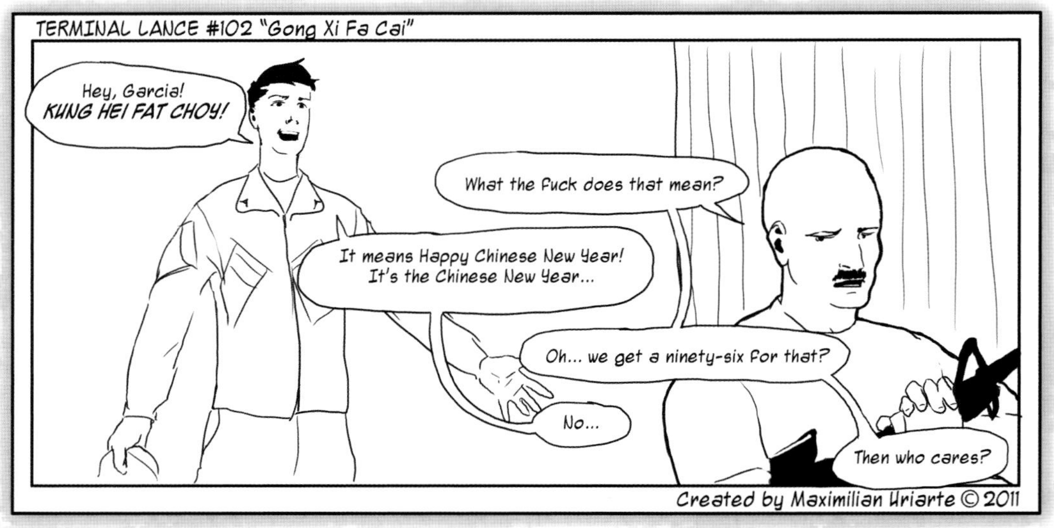
TERMINAL LANCE #102 "Gong Xi Fa Cai"
Hey, Garcia! KUNG HEI FAT CHOY!
What the fuck does that mean?
It means Happy Chinese New Year! It's the Chinese New Year...
Oh... we get a ninety-six for that?
No...
Then who cares?
Created by Maximilian Uriarte © 2011

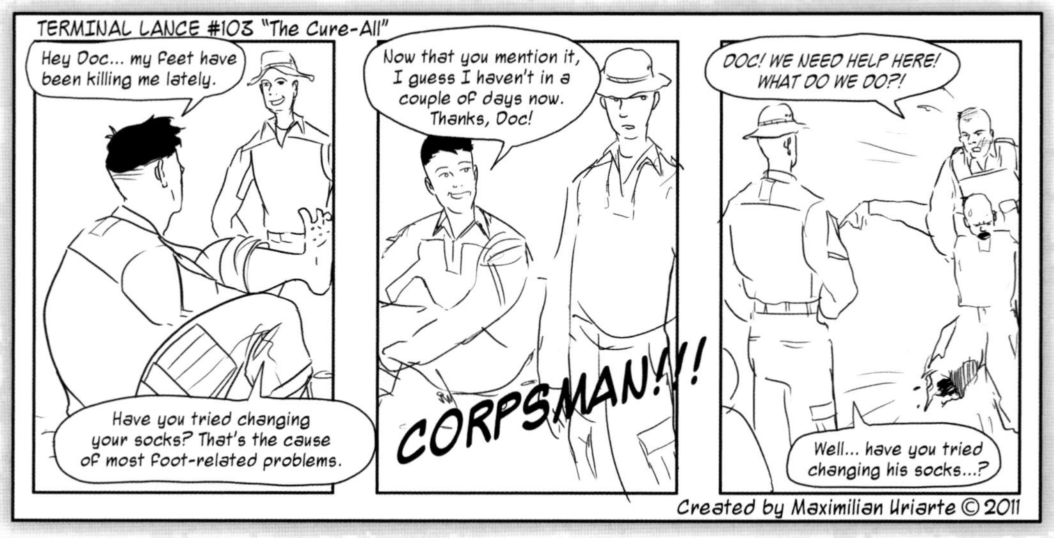
TERMINAL LANCE #103 "The Cure-All"
Hey Doc... my feet have been killing me lately.
Have you tried changing your socks? That's the cause of most foot-related problems.
Now that you mention it, I guess I haven't in a couple of days now. Thanks, Doc!
CORPSMAN!!!
DOC! WE NEED HELP HERE! WHAT DO WE DO?!
Well... have you tried changing his socks...?
Created by Maximilian Uriarte © 2011

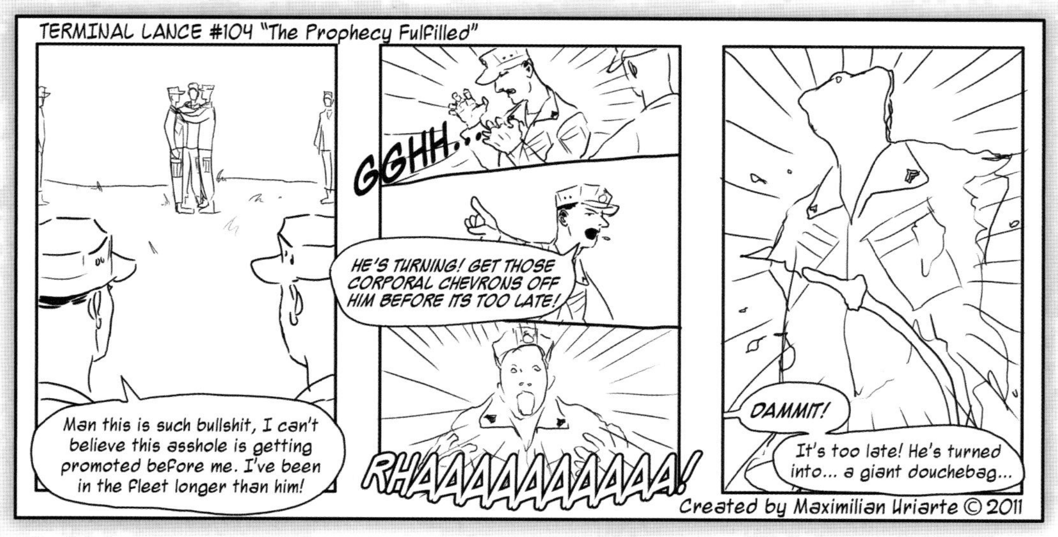
TERMINAL LANCE #104 "The Prophecy Fulfilled"
Man this is such bullshit, I can't believe this asshole is getting promoted before me. I've been in the fleet longer than him!
GGHH...
HE'S TURNING! GET THOSE CORPORAL CHEVRONS OFF HIM BEFORE ITS TOO LATE!
RHAAAAAAAAAAA!
DAMMIT!
It's too late! He's turned into... a giant douchebag...
Created by Maximilian Uriarte © 2011

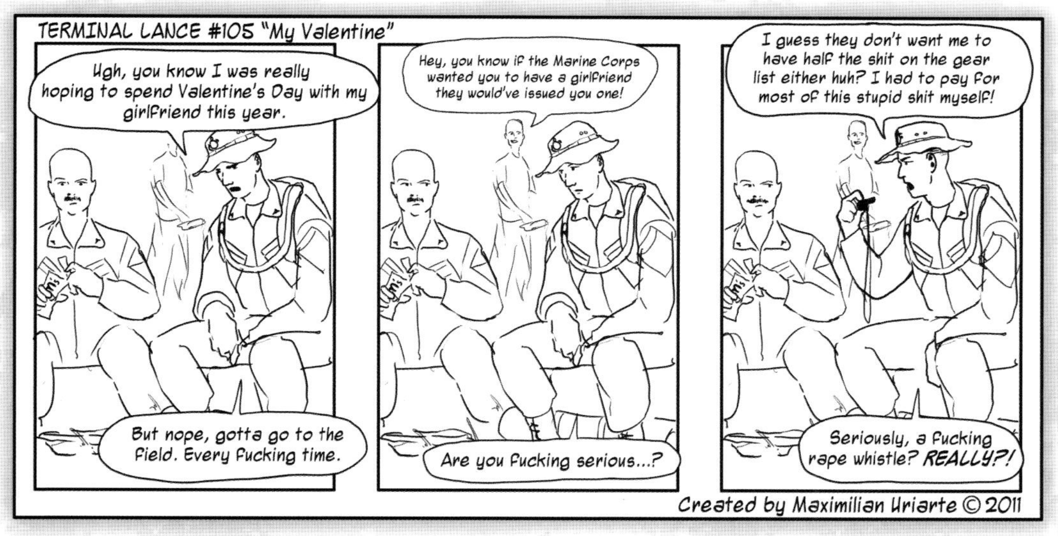
TERMINAL LANCE #105 "My Valentine"
Ugh, you know I was really hoping to spend Valentine's Day with my girlfriend this year.
But nope, gotta go to the field. Every fucking time.
Hey, you know if the Marine Corps wanted you to have a girlfriend they would've issued you one!
Are you fucking serious...?
I guess they don't want me to have half the shit on the gear list either huh? I had to pay for most of this stupid shit myself!
Seriously, a fucking rape whistle? REALLY?!
Created by Maximilian Uriarte © 2011

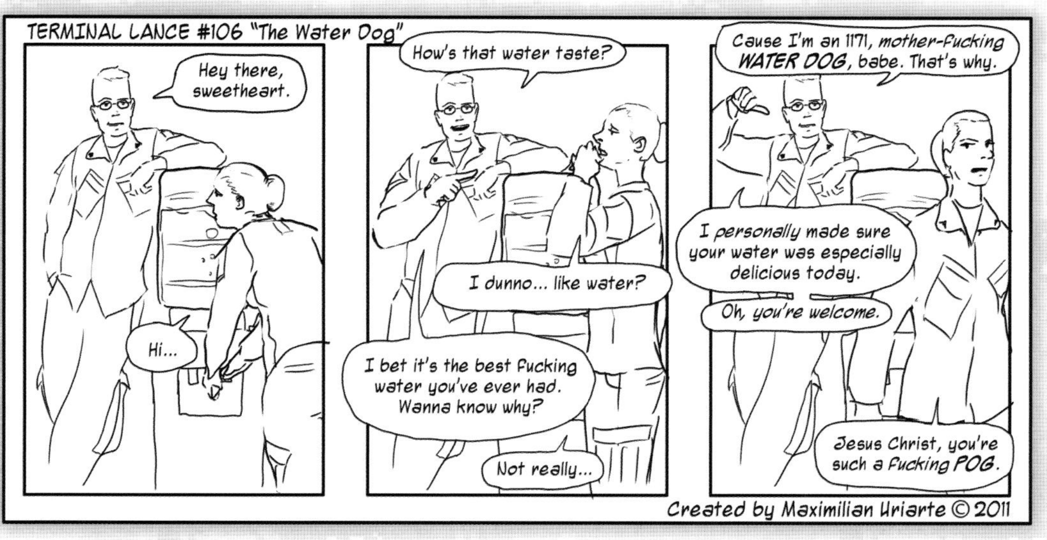
TERMINAL LANCE #106 "The Water Dog"
Hey there, sweetheart.
Hi...
How's that water taste?
I dunno... like water?
I bet it's the best fucking water you've ever had. Wanna know why?
Not really...
Cause I'm an 1171, mother-fucking WATER DOG, babe. That's why.
I personally made sure your water was especially delicious today.
Oh, you're welcome.
Jesus Christ, you're such a fucking POG.
Created by Maximilian Uriarte © 2011

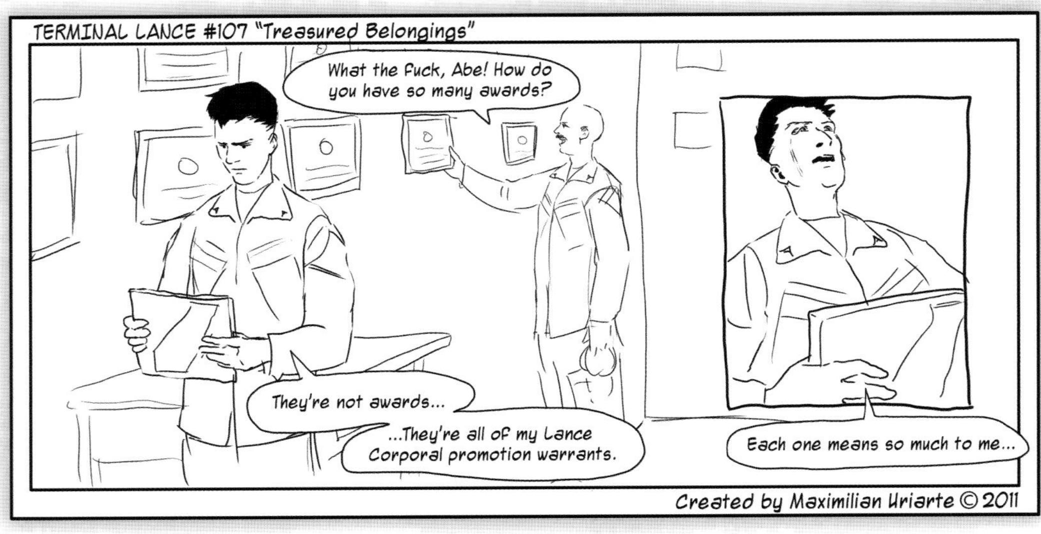
TERMINAL LANCE #107 "Treasured Belongings"
What the fuck, Abe! How do you have so many awards?
They're not awards...
...They're all of my Lance Corporal promotion warrants.
Each one means so much to me...
Created by Maximilian Uriarte © 2011

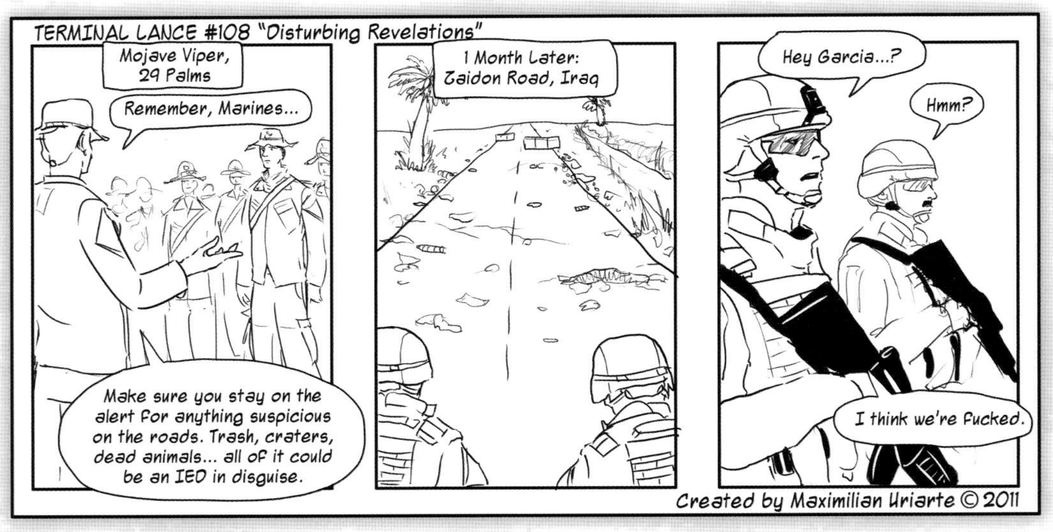
TERMINAL LANCE #108 "Disturbing Revelations"
Mojave Viper, 29 Palms
Remember, Marines...
Make sure you stay on the alert for anything suspicious on the roads. Trash, craters, dead animals... all of it could be an IED in disguise.
1 Month Later: Zaidon Road, Iraq
Hey Garcia...?
Hmm?
I think we're fucked.
Created by Maximilian Uriarte © 2011

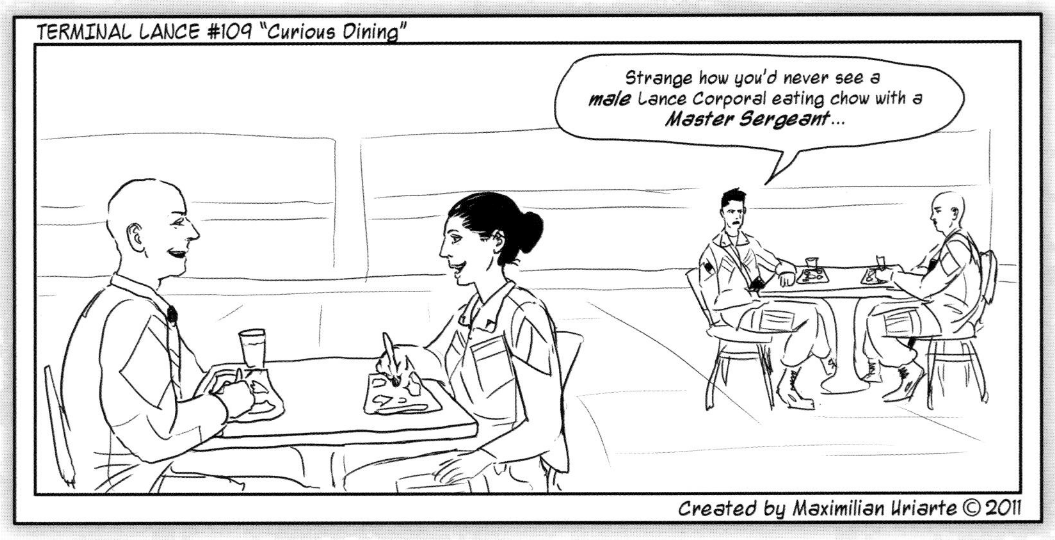
TERMINAL LANCE #109 "Curious Dining"
Strange how you'd never see a **male** Lance Corporal eating chow with a **Master Sergeant**...
Created by Maximilian Uriarte © 2011

TERMINAL LANCE #110 "Boot Camp: The Swarm"

Created by Maximilian Uriarte © 2011

110 "Boot Camp: The Swarm"

Drill Instructors have a kind of magical quality about them. The animated characters that run around yelling at recruits all day have a certain kinship and likeness to many of my favorite Saturday morning cartoons. I'm fairly certain I once saw a DI pull a large wooden mallet from behind his back and smack a recruit in the face with it.

But really, DI's are always fun to laugh at. Their exaggerated movements, gestures, and voices create someone that is more character than human. Love DI's or hate them, I guarantee that every Marine has done a DI impression at some point in his or her life. The trademark frog voice and knife-hands are as unforgettable afterward as they are feared in recruit training.

I've been out for a while now, and knife-hands still get me every time. Seriously . . . *knife-hands?* Possibly the most absurd and uniquely Marine Corps thing anyone's ever shouted at me with the raging passion of a thousand hungry baboons is simply, "KNIFE HAAAAAAAANDS!"

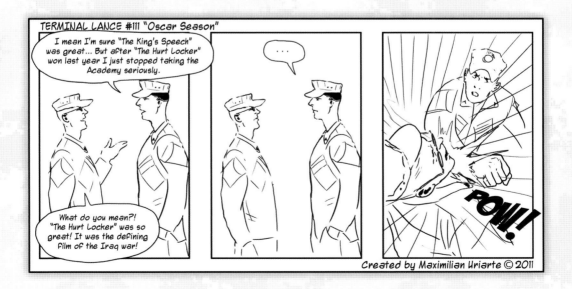

TERMINAL LANCE #111 "Oscar Season"

I mean I'm sure "The King's Speech" was great... But after "The Hurt Locker" won last year I just stopped taking the Academy seriously.

What do you mean?! "The Hurt Locker" was so great! It was the defining film of the Iraq war!

. . .

POW!

Created by Maximilian Uriarte © 2011

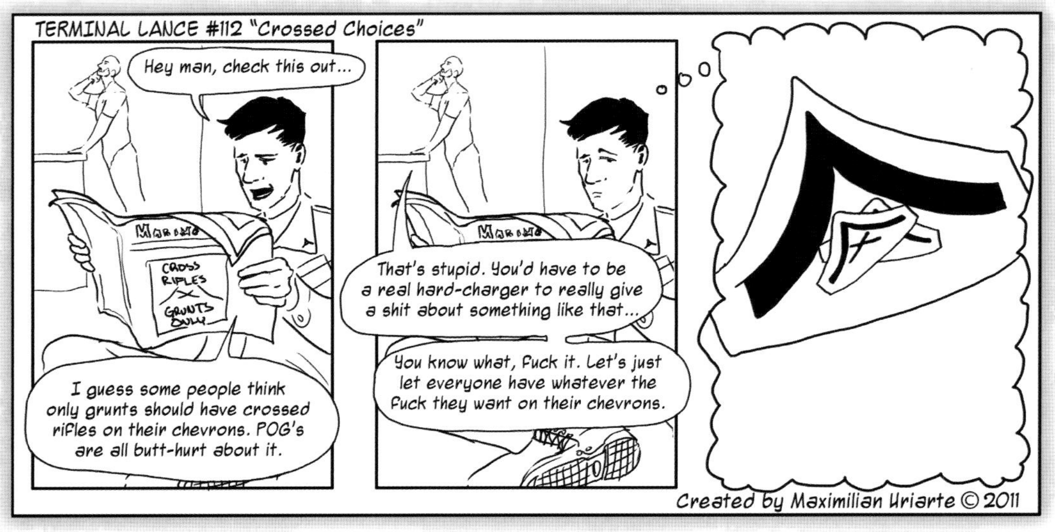
TERMINAL LANCE #112 "Crossed Choices"
Hey man, check this out...
CROSS RIFLES
GRUNTS ONLY
I guess some people think only grunts should have crossed rifles on their chevrons. POG's are all butt-hurt about it.
That's stupid. You'd have to be a real hard-charger to really give a shit about something like that...
You know what, fuck it. Let's just let everyone have whatever the fuck they want on their chevrons.
Created by Maximilian Uriarte © 2011

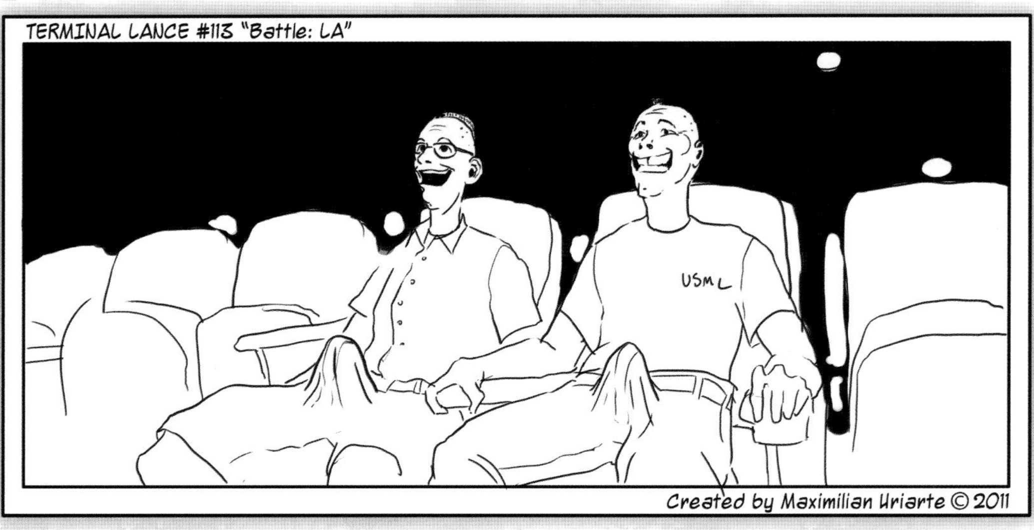
TERMINAL LANCE #113 "Battle: LA"
USMC
Created by Maximilian Uriarte © 2011

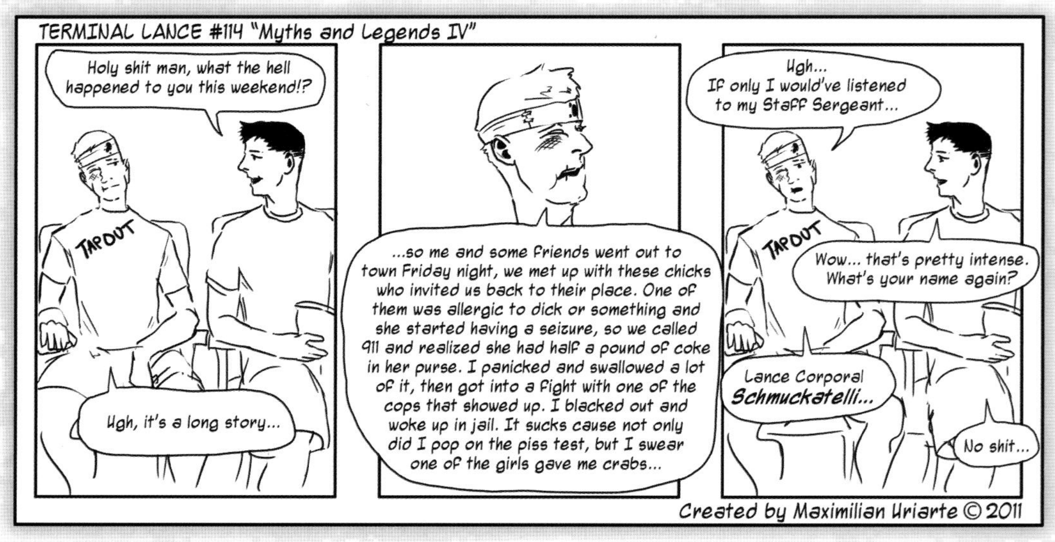
TERMINAL LANCE #114 "Myths and Legends IV"
Holy shit man, what the hell happened to you this weekend!?
TAPOUT
Ugh, it's a long story...
...so me and some friends went out to town Friday night, we met up with these chicks who invited us back to their place. One of them was allergic to dick or something and she started having a seizure, so we called 911 and realized she had half a pound of coke in her purse. I panicked and swallowed a lot of it, then got into a fight with one of the cops that showed up. I blacked out and woke up in jail. It sucks cause not only did I pop on the piss test, but I swear one of the girls gave me crabs...
Ugh... If only I would've listened to my Staff Sergeant...
Wow... that's pretty intense. What's your name again?
Lance Corporal Schmuckatelli...
No shit...
Created by Maximilian Uriarte © 2011

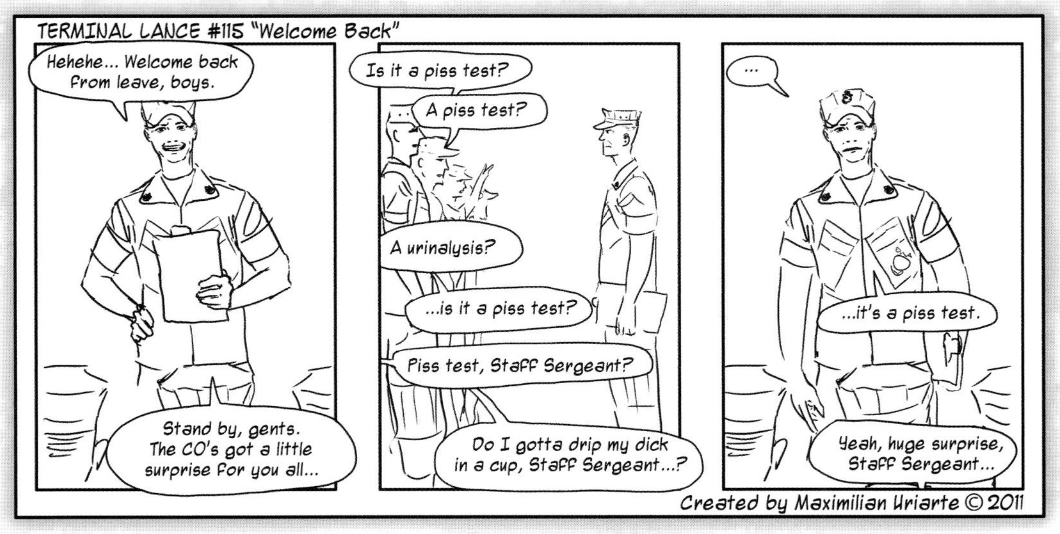
TERMINAL LANCE #115 "Welcome Back"
Hehehe... Welcome back from leave, boys.
Stand by, gents. The CO's got a little surprise for you all...
Is it a piss test?
A piss test?
A urinalysis?
...is it a piss test?
Piss test, Staff Sergeant?
Do I gotta drip my dick in a cup, Staff Sergeant...?
...
...it's a piss test.
Yeah, huge surprise, Staff Sergeant...
Created by Maximilian Uriarte © 2011

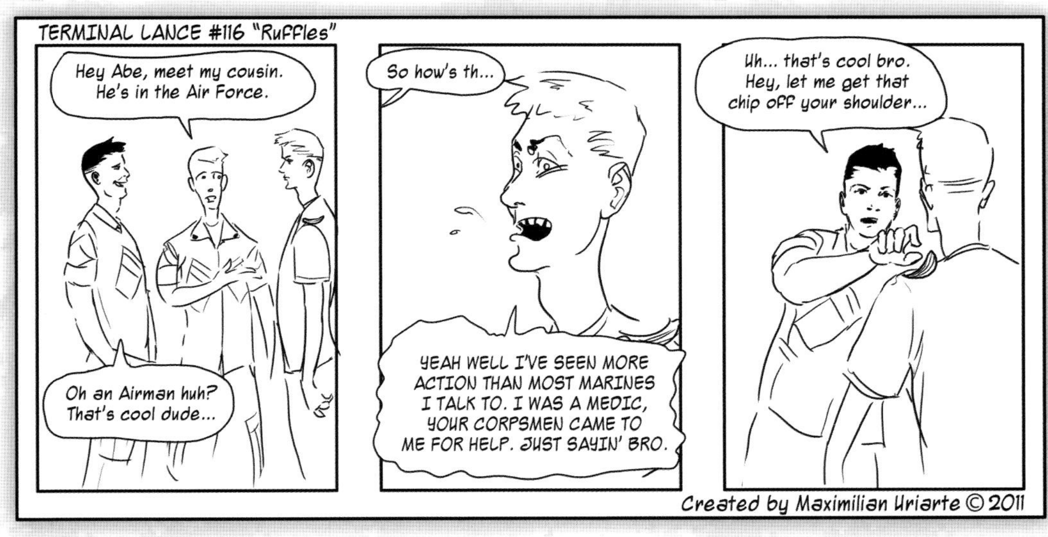
TERMINAL LANCE #116 "Ruffles"
Hey Abe, meet my cousin. He's in the Air Force.
Oh an Airman huh? That's cool dude...
So how's th...
YEAH WELL I'VE SEEN MORE ACTION THAN MOST MARINES I TALK TO. I WAS A MEDIC, YOUR CORPSMEN CAME TO ME FOR HELP. JUST SAYIN' BRO.
Uh... that's cool bro. Hey, let me get that chip off your shoulder...
Created by Maximilian Uriarte © 2011

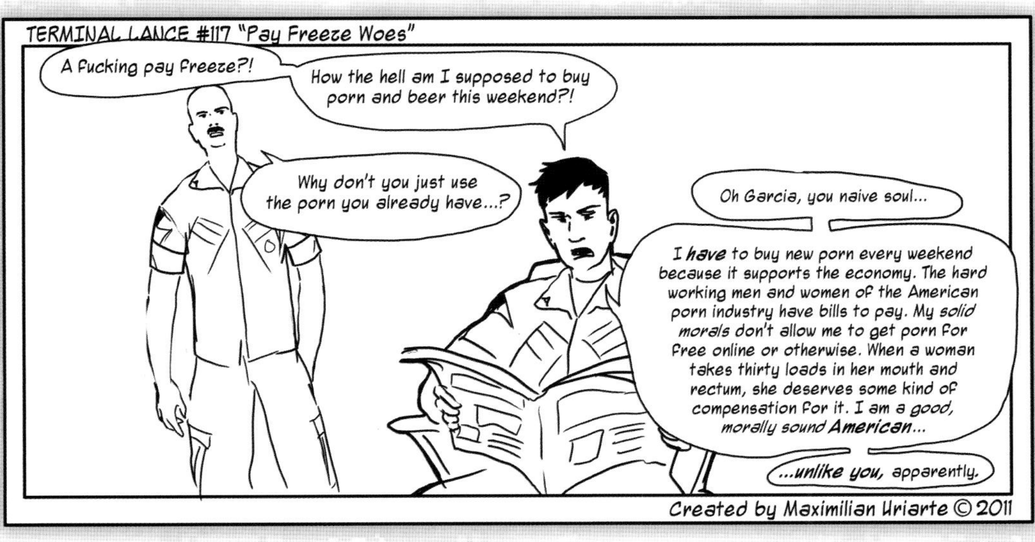
TERMINAL LANCE #117 "Pay Freeze Woes"
A fucking pay freeze?!
How the hell am I supposed to buy porn and beer this weekend?!
Why don't you just use the porn you already have...?
Oh Garcia, you naive soul...
I *have* to buy new porn every weekend because it supports the economy. The hard working men and women of the American porn industry have bills to pay. My *solid morals* don't allow me to get porn for free online or otherwise. When a woman takes thirty loads in her mouth and rectum, she deserves some kind of compensation for it. I am a *good*, morally sound **American**...
...unlike you, apparently.
Created by Maximilian Uriarte © 2011

TERMINAL LANCE #118 "The Hunt"
Look carefully...
You may have noticed the naturally camouflaged Echo-Eight on the hunt.
Oh dear, it appears he's spotted two unwitting Lance Corporals. Both have hands in their pockets and one has no cover. The Echo-Eight has spotted its prey...
...It moves in for the kill.
The Lance Corporals have spotted the Echo-Eight, but they are stunned. It is too late for them to run.
The Echo-Eight pounces for the kill.
The weaker of the two Lance Corporals succumbs to the douche-baggery. Once those knife hands come out there's not much one can do but watch.
The Echo-Eight needs the annoyance and suffering of Lance Corporals to survive. Without it, it will die of boredom. It truly just has nothing better to do than to correct the Lance Corporal's appearance.
Created by Maximilian Uriarte © 2011

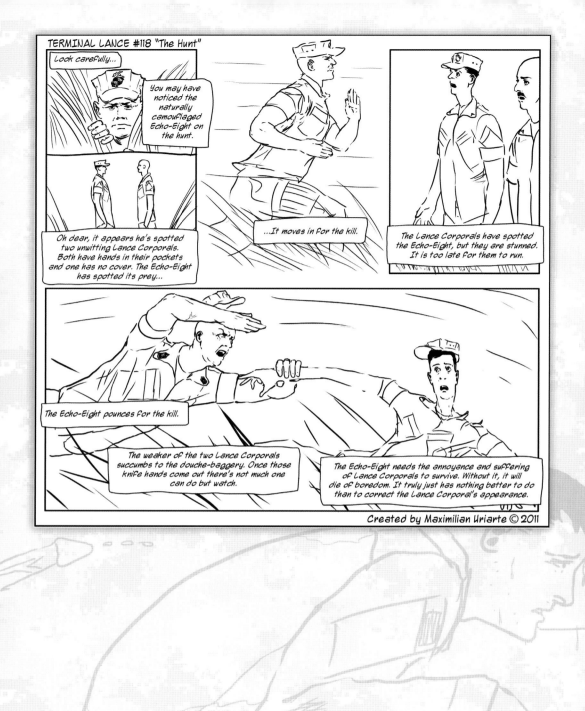

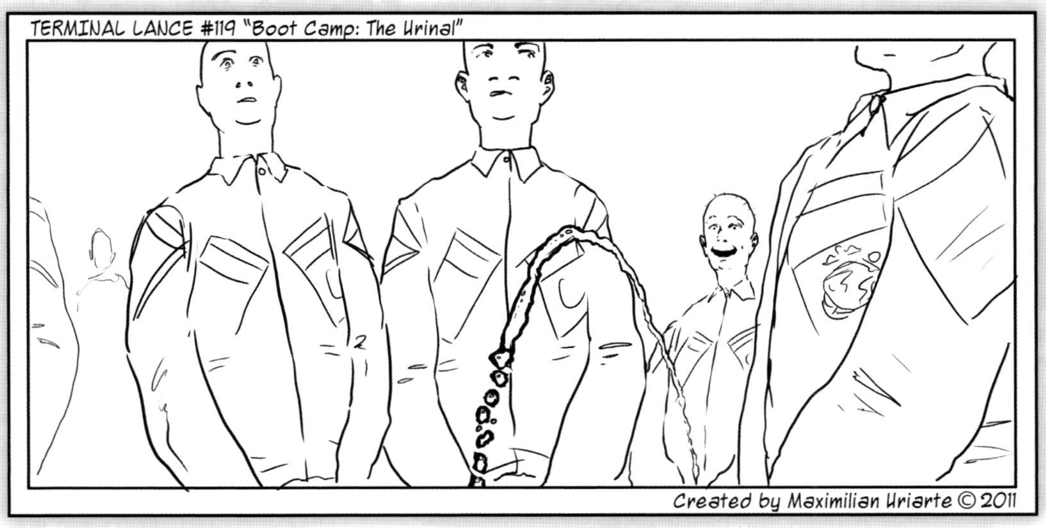
TERMINAL LANCE #119 "Boot Camp: The Urinal"
Created by Maximilian Uriarte © 2011

119 "Boot Camp: The Urinal"

One of the many fond memories I have of boot camp is of the many excursions we had to the men's room. My platoon of roughly fifty Marines was forced to use the "head" all at the same time. There were a total of eight urinals in the main bathroom, with some "shitters" down the hall. It was the only time in my life that I have ever shared a urinal with three other men. Results like you see in this strip were a daily occurrence.

In addition to boning over urine, dropping a deuce became another social activity in boot camp. When you had to do the deed, you would go up to your buddy and ask, "Hey, you wanna go take a shit?" Instead of being met with obvious disgust and confusion, as I'm sure you would be in the "real world," in boot camp, the response will likely be an obliged "Yes, I'd love to take a shit with you."

Well, maybe not so articulate (probably with more "fuckin'"s), but you get the idea.

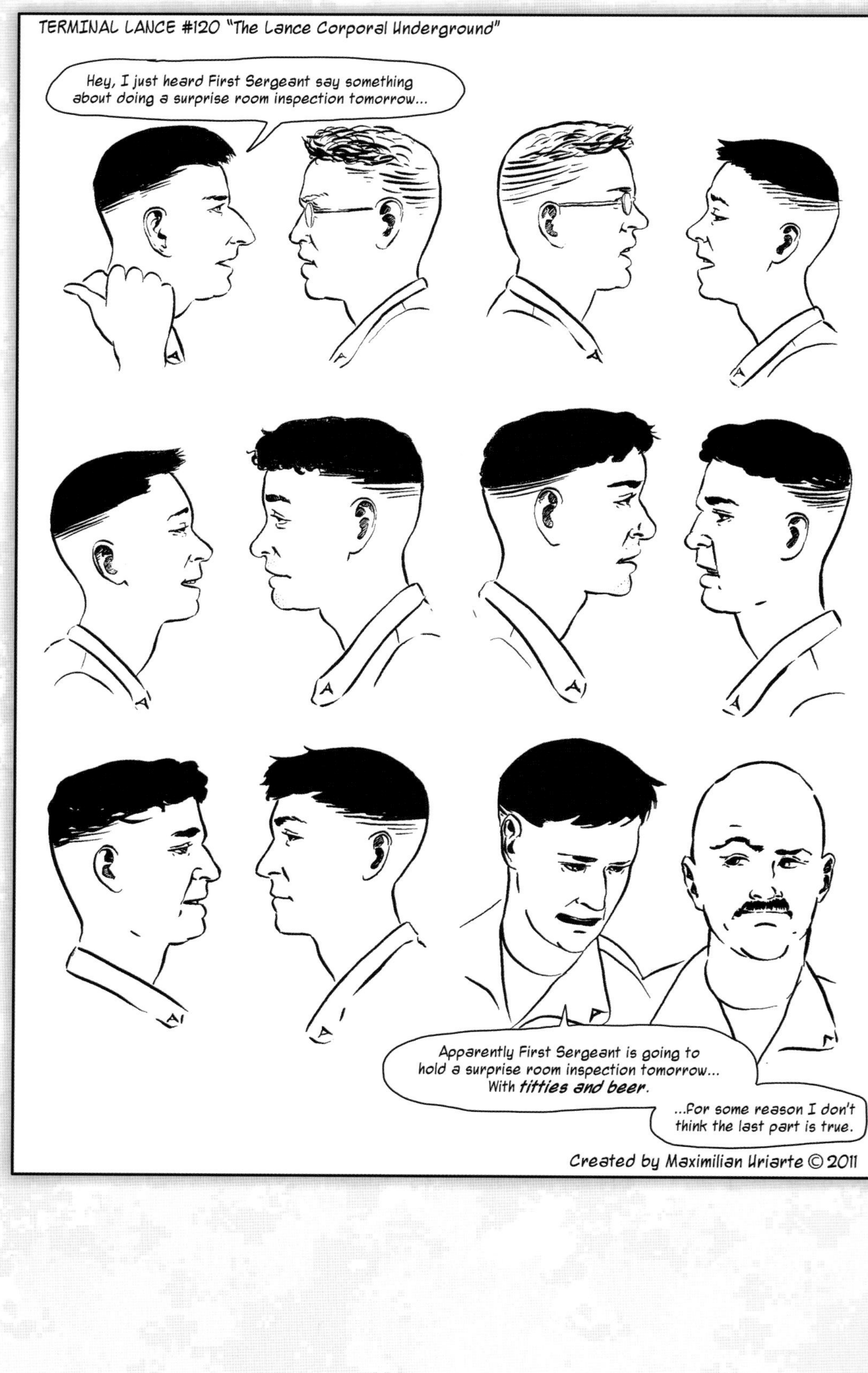
TERMINAL LANCE #120 "The Lance Corporal Underground"
Hey, I just heard First Sergeant say something about doing a surprise room inspection tomorrow...
Apparently First Sergeant is going to hold a surprise room inspection tomorrow... With titties and beer.
...For some reason I don't think the last part is true.
Created by Maximilian Uriarte © 2011

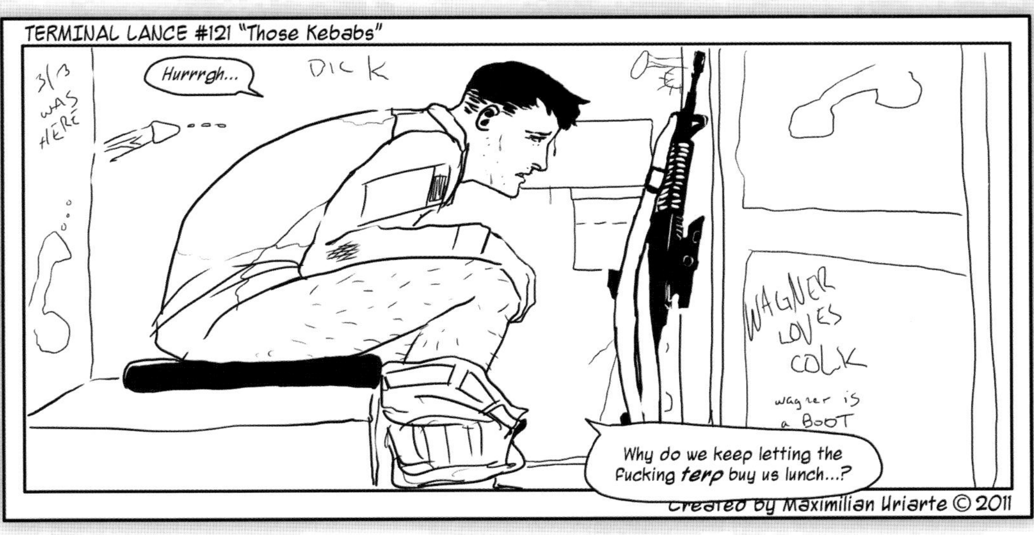
TERMINAL LANCE #121 "Those Kebabs"
Hurrrgh...
DICK
3/3 WAS HERE
wagner is a BOOT
Why do we keep letting the fucking *terp* buy us lunch...?
Created by Maximilian Uriarte © 2011

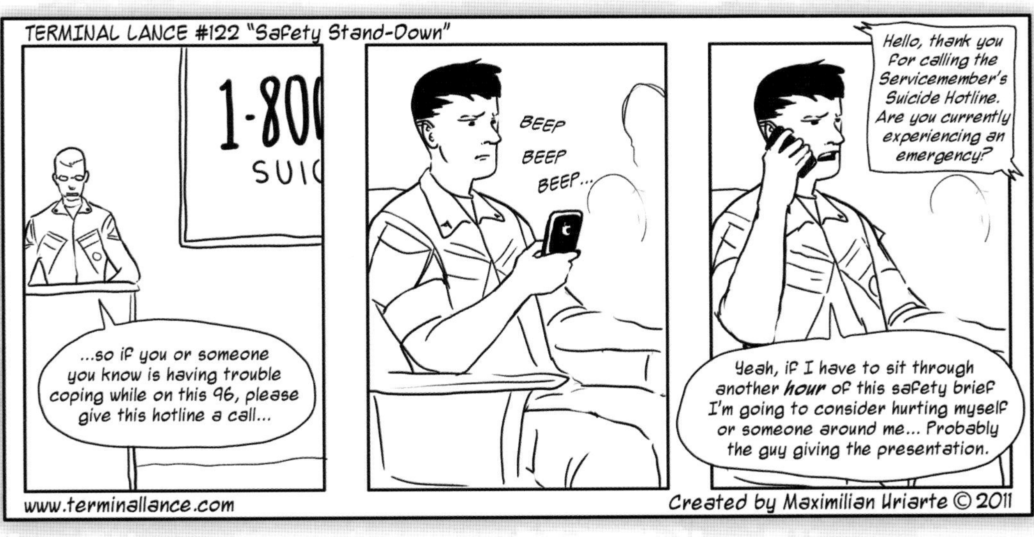
TERMINAL LANCE #122 "Safety Stand-Down"
1-800
SUIC
...so if you or someone you know is having trouble coping while on this 96, please give this hotline a call...
BEEP
BEEP
BEEP...
Hello, thank you for calling the Servicemember's Suicide Hotline. Are you currently experiencing an emergency?
Yeah, if I have to sit through another *hour* of this safety brief I'm going to consider hurting myself or someone around me... Probably the guy giving the presentation.
www.terminallance.com
Created by Maximilian Uriarte © 2011

122 "Safety Stand-Down"

I don't want anyone to think I'm making fun of suicide here, just the safety stand-down in a general sense. Everyone who's been on a holiday 96 (what Marines call a four-day weekend) knows the horrendous experience of a safety stand-down. For whatever reason, the Marine Corps' idea of preventing injury to fellow Marines is to make them sit through a mind-numbing six hours of classes prior to letting them enjoy a long weekend. I don't know what statistical evidence there is to support this strategy; I'm sure it exists, but I don't personally feel that six hours of texting-time is an effective way to put a stop to drunk driving or suicide.

Perhaps a more effective way to combat these problems would be to allow these briefs to be done on a more personal level, perhaps at the platoon leadership or even lower. Training NCO's and small-unit leaders to brief Marines on the dangers of everything the Marine Corps hates would probably be more effective than having Marines meander to the base-theater in droves for an apathetic series of briefs on things they already know. Marines—well, anyone really—tend to tune out things performed in this manner anyway. Everyone knows that in education, smaller class sizes are more effective.

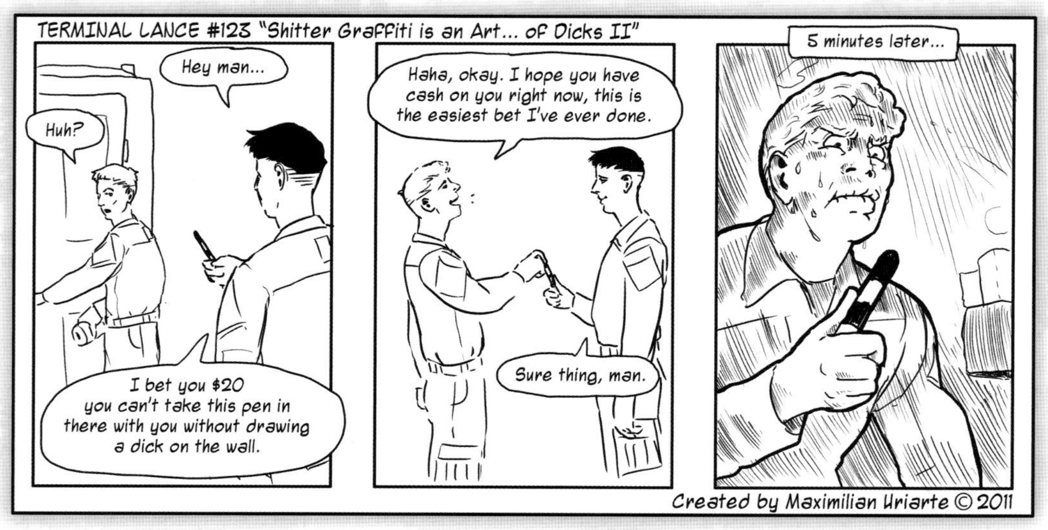
TERMINAL LANCE #123 "Shitter Graffiti is an Art... of Dicks II"
Hey man...
Huh?
I bet you $20 you can't take this pen in there with you without drawing a dick on the wall.
Haha, okay. I hope you have cash on you right now, this is the easiest bet I've ever done.
Sure thing, man.
5 minutes later...
Created by Maximilian Uriarte © 2011

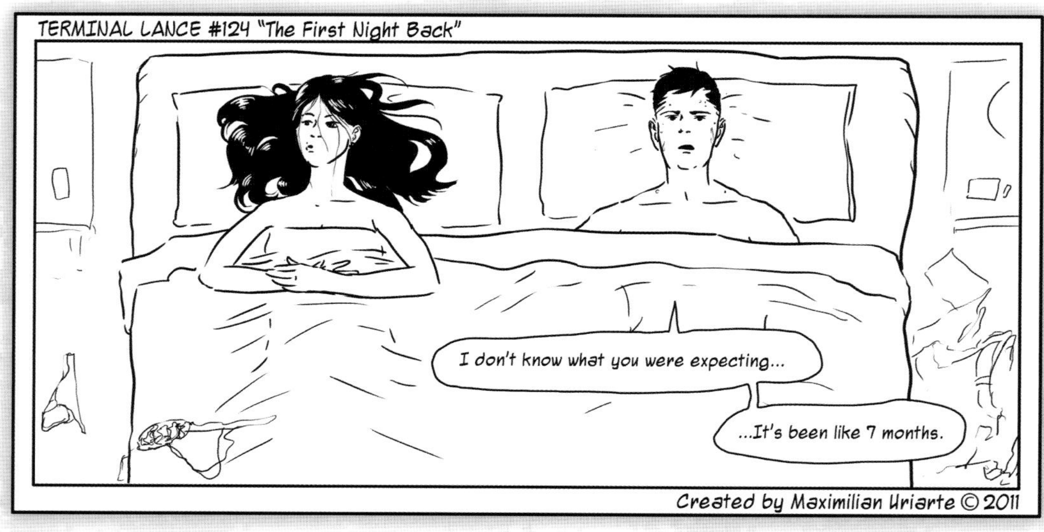
TERMINAL LANCE #124 "The First Night Back"
I don't know what you were expecting...
...It's been like 7 months.
Created by Maximilian Uriarte © 2011

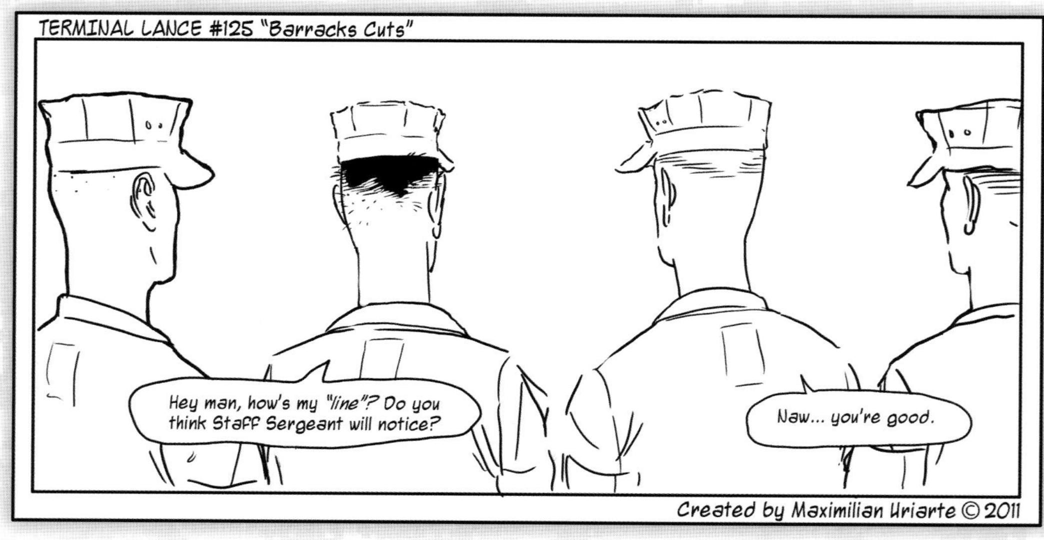
TERMINAL LANCE #125 "Barracks Cuts"
Hey man, how's my "line"? Do you think Staff Sergeant will notice?
Naw... you're good.
Created by Maximilian Uriarte © 2011

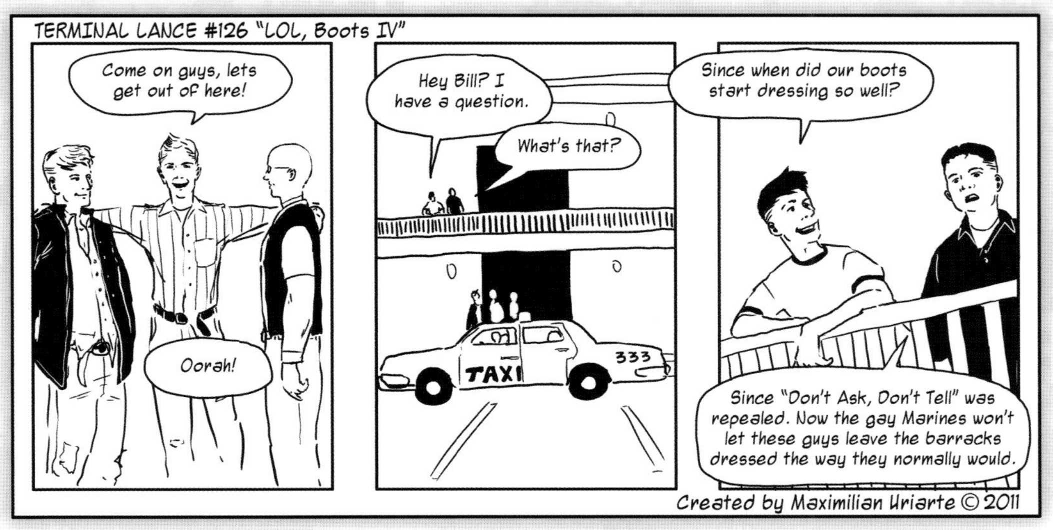
TERMINAL LANCE #126 "LOL, Boots IV"
Come on guys, lets get out of here!
Oorah!
Hey Bill? I have a question.
What's that?
TAXI
333
Since when did our boots start dressing so well?
Since "Don't Ask, Don't Tell" was repealed. Now the gay Marines won't let these guys leave the barracks dressed the way they normally would.
Created by Maximilian Uriarte © 2011

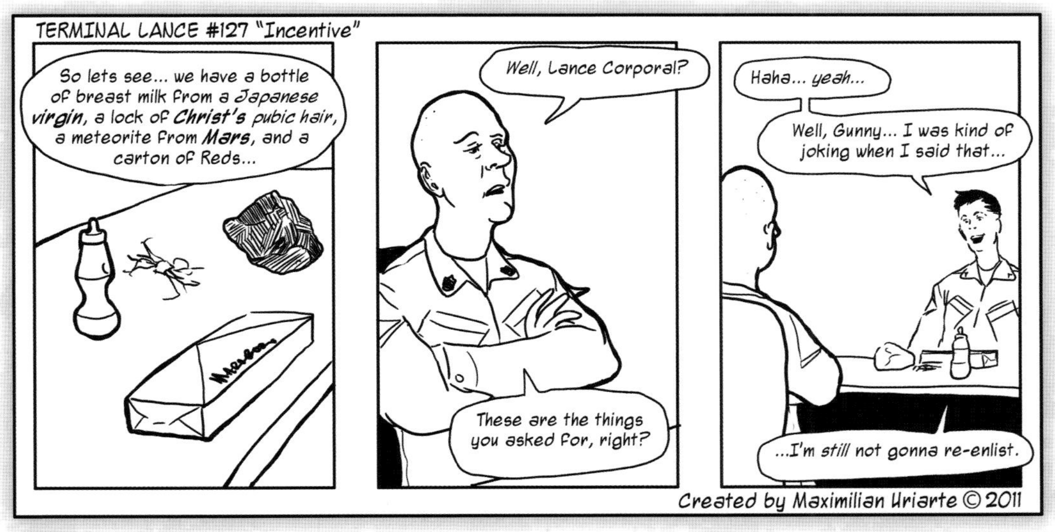
TERMINAL LANCE #127 "Incentive"
So lets see... we have a bottle of breast milk from a Japanese virgin, a lock of Christ's pubic hair, a meteorite from Mars, and a carton of Reds...
Well, Lance Corporal?
These are the things you asked for, right?
Haha... yeah...
Well, Gunny... I was kind of joking when I said that...
...I'm still not gonna re-enlist.
Created by Maximilian Uriarte © 2011

127 "Incentive"

In real life, your local Career Planner probably won't be trying too hard to get a Lance Corporal to reenlist. However, there was a point in time—around 2008 or 2009—when the Marine Corps was offering $90,000 in cold, hard, dick-twitching cash money to reenlist if you served as a squad leader in combat. Ninety-fucking-grand. Needless to say, many Marines found that to be a fruitful incentive. That's at least two Mustangs and a bottle of Grey Goose.

Abe, on the other hand, isn't so interested in reenlisting. Abe, much like myself, always wondered what kind of ridiculous shit you could get away with when it came to reenlistment incentives. The ridiculous shit you could throw at them would be an endless source of entertainment—one that I missed out on due to the fact that no one wanted an 0351 Lance Coolie to reenlist in mid-2010. Regardless, I wouldn't have, but it would've at least been fun to try and find out.

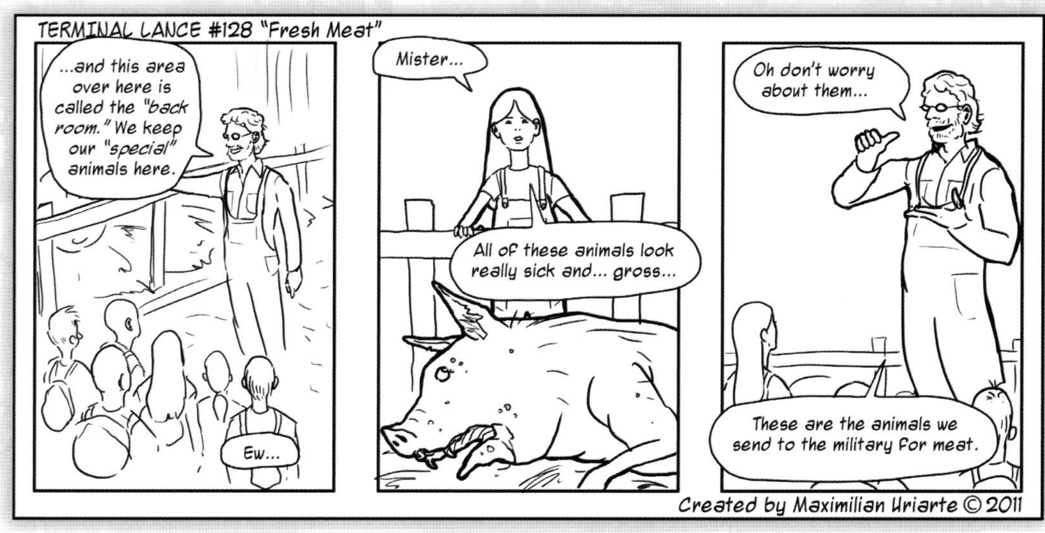
TERMINAL LANCE #128 "Fresh Meat"
...and this area over here is called the "back room." We keep our "special" animals here.
Ew...
Mister...
All of these animals look really sick and... gross...
Oh don't worry about them...
These are the animals we send to the military for meat.
Created by Maximilian Uriarte © 2011

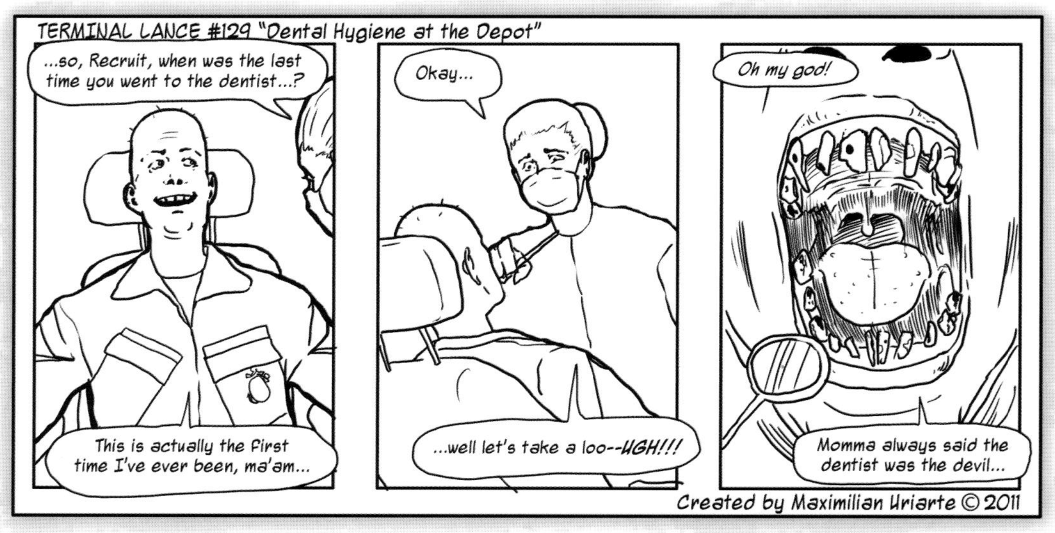
TERMINAL LANCE #129 "Dental Hygiene at the Depot"
...so, Recruit, when was the last time you went to the dentist...?
This is actually the first time I've ever been, ma'am...
Okay...
...well let's take a loo--UGH!!!
Oh my god!
Momma always said the dentist was the devil...
Created by Maximilian Uriarte © 2011

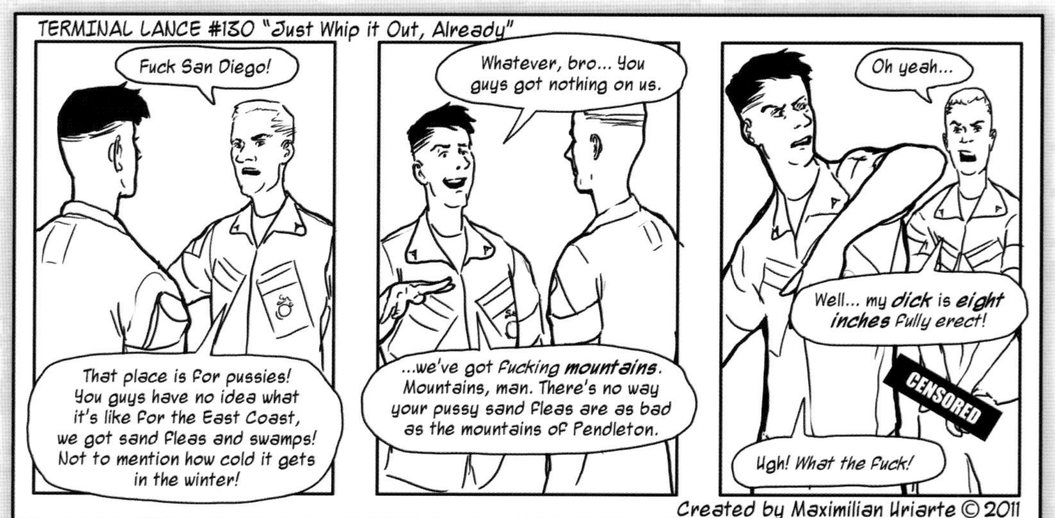
TERMINAL LANCE #130 "Just Whip it Out, Already"
Fuck San Diego!
That place is for pussies! You guys have no idea what it's like for the East Coast, we got sand fleas and swamps! Not to mention how cold it gets in the winter!
Whatever, bro... You guys got nothing on us.
...we've got fucking mountains. Mountains, man. There's no way your pussy sand fleas are as bad as the mountains of Pendleton.
Oh yeah...
Well... my dick is eight inches fully erect!
CENSORED
Ugh! What the fuck!
Created by Maximilian Uriarte © 2011

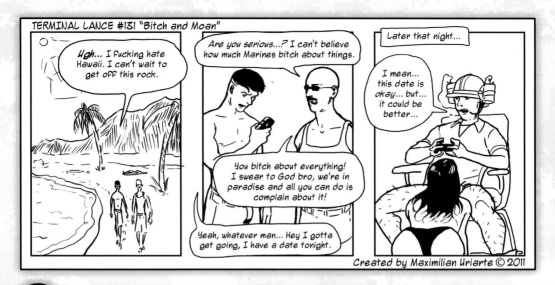

TERMINAL LANCE #131 "Bitch and Moan"
Ugh... I fucking hate Hawaii. I can't wait to get off this rock.
Are you serious...? I can't believe how much Marines bitch about things.
You bitch about everything! I swear to God bro, we're in paradise and all you can do is complain about it!
Yeah, whatever man... Hey I gotta get going, I have a date tonight.
Later that night...
I mean... this date is okay... but... it could be better...
Created by Maximilian Uriarte © 2011

131 "Bitch and Moan"

If there's one constant of the Marine Corps, it's that Marines will bitch about pretty much anything. You can give them the world, but something will be wrong with it. When I was stationed in Hawaii, I heard complaints every day. *I can't wait to get off this rock, fuck this place, I hate Hawaii, this island sucks*—it was truly nonstop. All the sun, beaches, warm weather, and beautiful women in the world didn't seem to sway those who were convinced it was the worst place they'd ever been.

Unfortunately, a lot of Marines aren't able to distinguish their raw emotions from their current situation. They're not actually mad at Hawaii, they don't actually hate Hawaii—their misplaced anger is incorrectly directed at the beautiful islands of Aloha. The anguish that comes with being stationed on the islands is a general feeling of discontent toward the military as a whole. To them, the islands become the Marine Corps. The Marines in Hawaii miss their homes and the islands are a new and alien environment to most of them.

Frankly, I loved Hawaii. After all, there are plenty of worse places to be stationed. Take a look at Twentynine Palms—or as I refer to it: *Satan's asshole*. Secluded in the California desert, it is easily the most miserable permanent duty station in the Corps that I've ever been to—and my experiences were limited to a couple of runs through Mojave Viper.

I'm sure the Marines in the desert reading this are going, "WTF? Marines bitch about Hawaii?" Yes. Yes, they do. Every day.

It's true, Marines will bitch about anything.

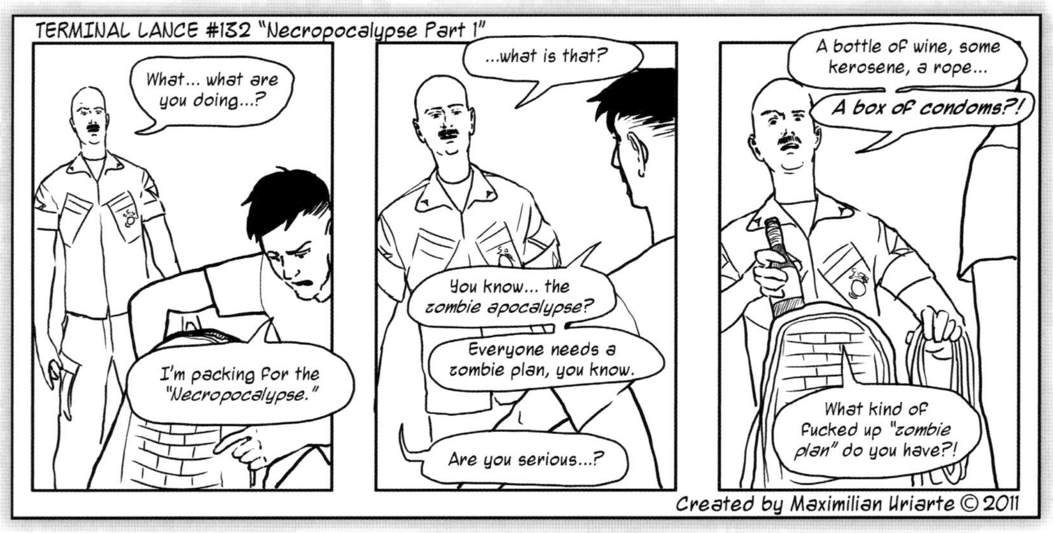
TERMINAL LANCE #132 "Necropocalypse Part 1"
What... what are you doing...?
I'm packing for the "Necropocalypse."
...what is that?
You know... the zombie apocalypse?
Everyone needs a zombie plan, you know.
Are you serious...?
A bottle of wine, some kerosene, a rope...
A box of condoms?!
What kind of fucked up "zombie plan" do you have?!
Created by Maximilian Uriarte © 2011

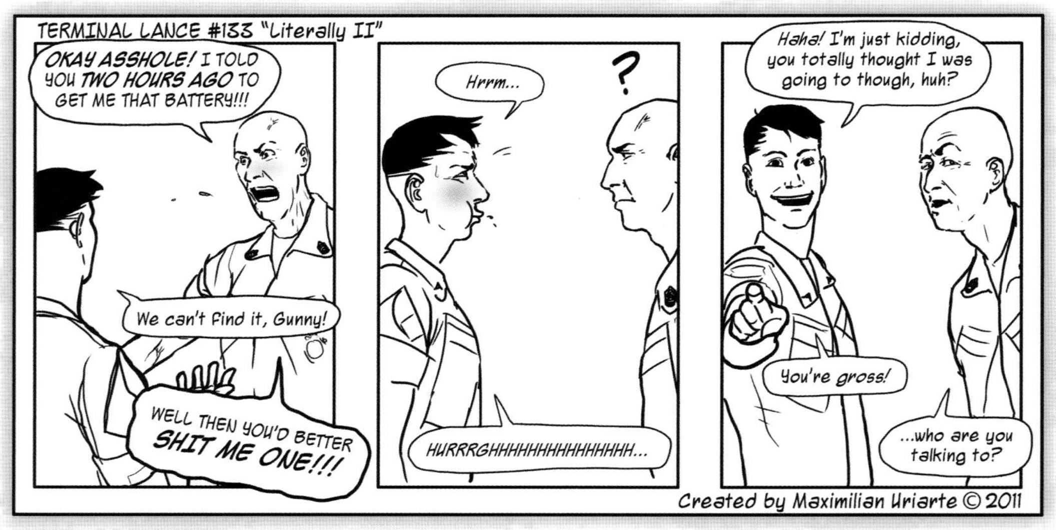
TERMINAL LANCE #133 "Literally II"
OKAY ASSHOLE! I TOLD YOU TWO HOURS AGO TO GET ME THAT BATTERY!!!
We can't find it, Gunny!
WELL THEN YOU'D BETTER SHIT ME ONE!!!
Hrrm...
?
HURRRGHHHHHHHHHHHHHHH...
Haha! I'm just kidding, you totally thought I was going to though, huh?
You're gross!
...who are you talking to?
Created by Maximilian Uriarte © 2011

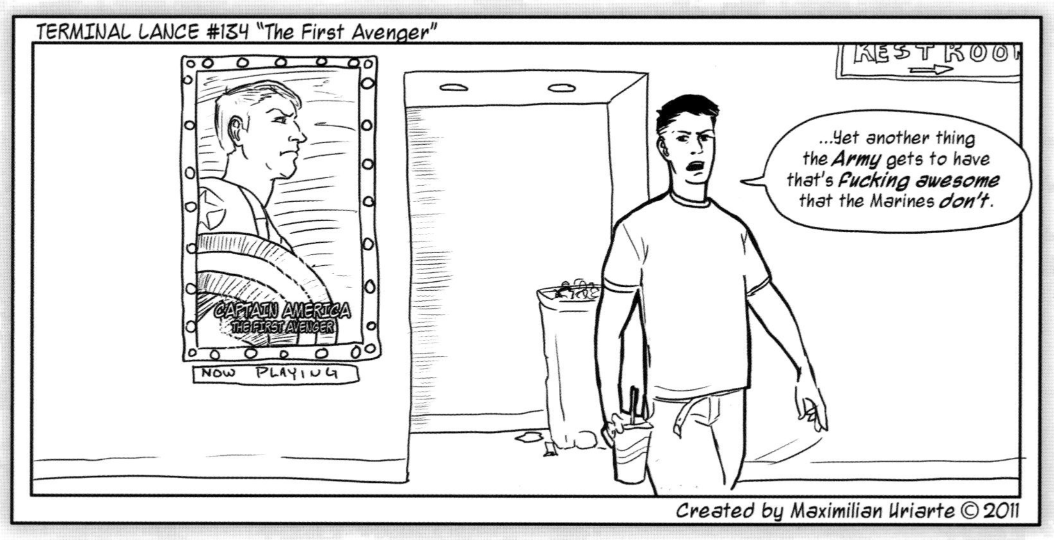
TERMINAL LANCE #134 "The First Avenger"
CAPTAIN AMERICA
THE FIRST AVENGER
NOW PLAYING
REST ROO
...Yet another thing the Army gets to have that's Fucking awesome that the Marines don't.
Created by Maximilian Uriarte © 2011

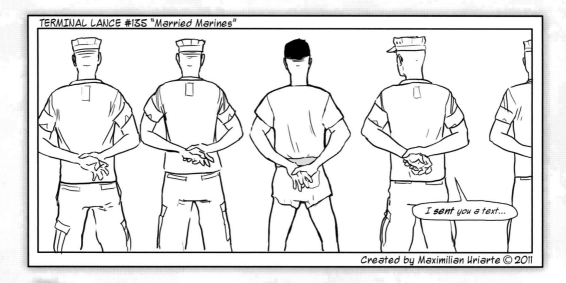

TERMINAL LANCE #135 "Married Marines"
I sent you a text...
Created by Maximilian Uriarte © 2011

135 "Married Marines"

The life of a married Marine is one of perceived luxury, and in many ways, it is luxurious, but at the same time, marriage surely alienates them from the dark, soulless heart of the Lance Corporal Underground: the barracks.

In the infantry word changes, and it changes a lot. It happens like a brush fire in the barracks; one minute you're sitting in your standard-issue chair playing *Call of Duty*, the next minute some other Lance Corporal is peeking his head into your room and saying to you, "Hey, cammies tomorrow instead of PT gear." Without so much as a glance you'll acknowledge it, get your cammies ready for the morning, and be set to go. In this age of modern technical wizardry, it's astonishing that it is still possible for "the word" to not get to those outside the epicenter of Marinedom, yet it happens daily. I suppose in a platoon so large, with word so readily available in the barracks, it just happens that you forget about the guy who lives on the other side of the base with his wife and dog. It could be, of course, a treacherous form of betrayal to spite those luxuries—but he would be none the wiser.

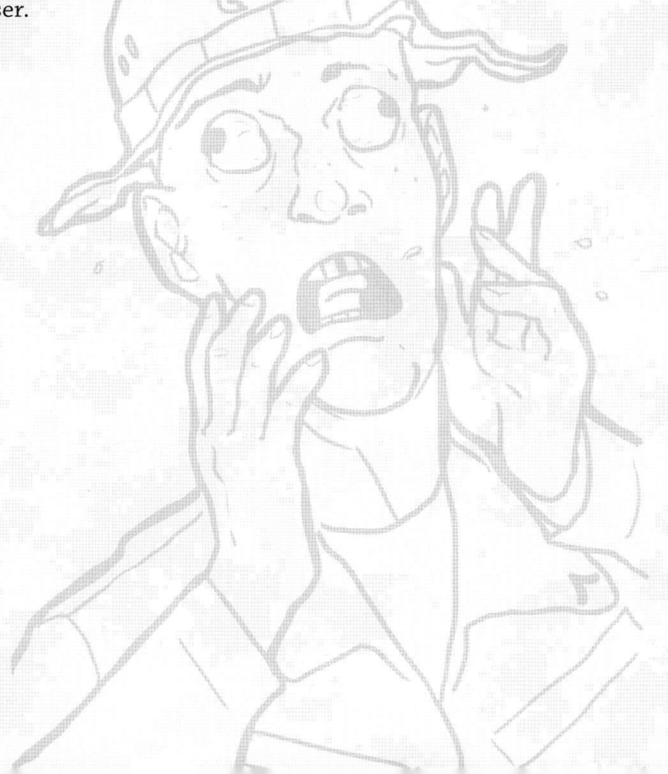

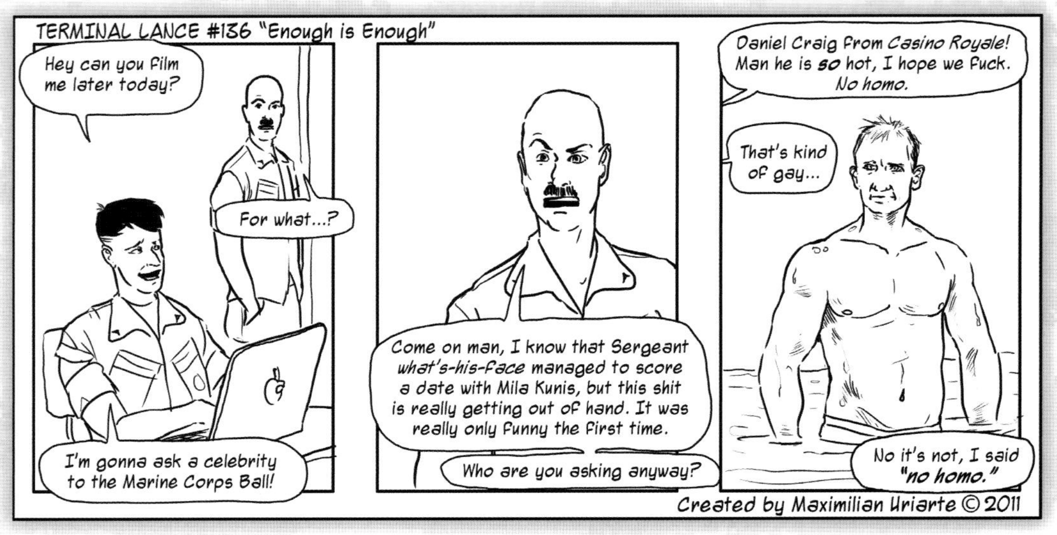
TERMINAL LANCE #136 "Enough is Enough"
Hey can you film me later today?
For what...?
I'm gonna ask a celebrity to the Marine Corps Ball!
Come on man, I know that Sergeant *what's-his-face* managed to score a date with Mila Kunis, but this shit is really getting out of hand. It was really only funny the first time.
Who are you asking anyway?
Daniel Craig from *Casino Royale*! Man he is ***so*** hot, I hope we fuck. *No homo.*
That's kind of gay...
No it's not, I said ***"no homo."***
Created by Maximilian Uriarte © 2011

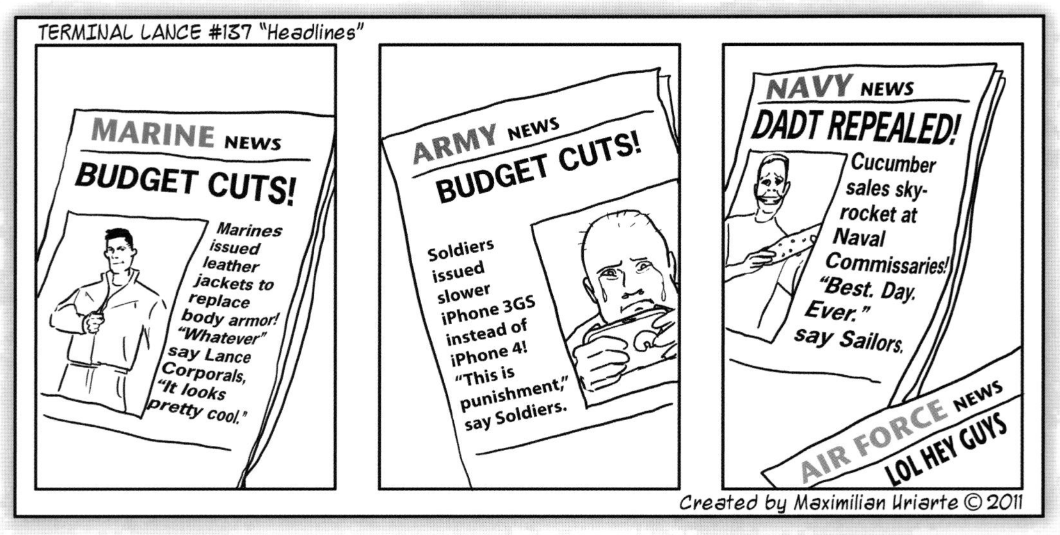
TERMINAL LANCE #137 "Headlines"
MARINE NEWS
BUDGET CUTS!
Marines issued leather jackets to replace body armor! "Whatever" say Lance Corporals, "It looks pretty cool."
ARMY NEWS
BUDGET CUTS!
Soldiers issued slower iPhone 3GS instead of iPhone 4! "This is punishment," say Soldiers.
NAVY NEWS
DADT REPEALED!
Cucumber sales sky-rocket at Naval Commissaries! "Best. Day. Ever." say Sailors.
AIR FORCE NEWS
LOL HEY GUYS
Created by Maximilian Uriarte © 2011

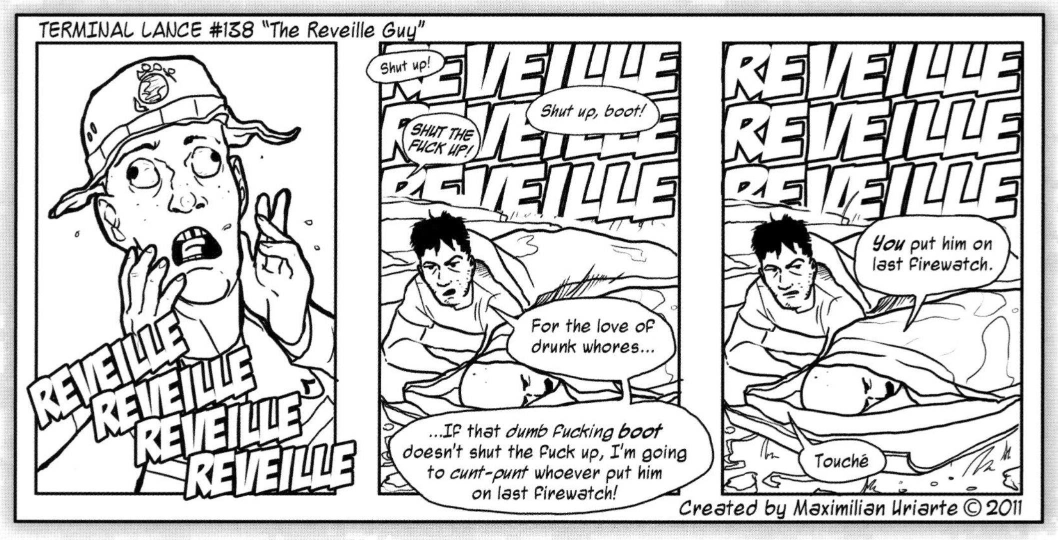
TERMINAL LANCE #138 "The Reveille Guy"
REVEILLE REVEILLE REVEILLE REVEILLE
Shut up!
Shut up, boot!
SHUT THE FUCK UP!
REVEILLE REVEILLE REVEILLE
For the love of drunk whores...
...If that *dumb fucking* ***boot*** doesn't shut the fuck up, I'm going to *cunt-punt* whoever put him on last firewatch!
REVEILLE REVEILLE REVEILLE
You put him on last firewatch.
Touché
Created by Maximilian Uriarte © 2011

TERMINAL LANCE #139 "Semantics"
Look Marines, all E-Threes are the same in this Battalion.
I don't want to hear any more of this "Senior Lance Corporal" stuff. All Lance Corporals are equal in my book.
BATTALION... FALL OUT!
Well... you heard him.
You can no longer call me a "Senior Lance Corporal"...
You must now refer to me as: "Lance Corporal that has been on Combat Deployments."
You, on the other hand, are still "Boot," "Bitch," or "Fuck-Stick."
Created by Maximilian Uriarte © 2011

TERMINAL LANCE #140 "Escalation of Force"
Hey guys... we have a vehicle heading toward us!
Uh... Fuck...
Shout... shove... flag... show... pen-flare... shoot... FUCK!!!
Fuck this!
SHLOCK!
I'll take the NJP if I'm wrong!
Created by Maximilian Uriarte © 2011

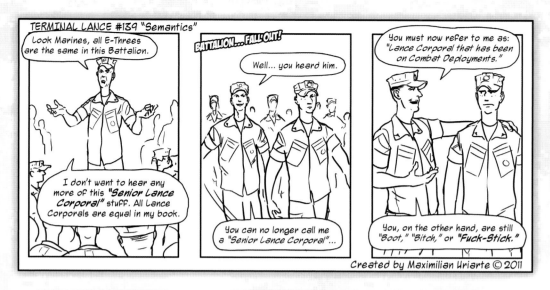

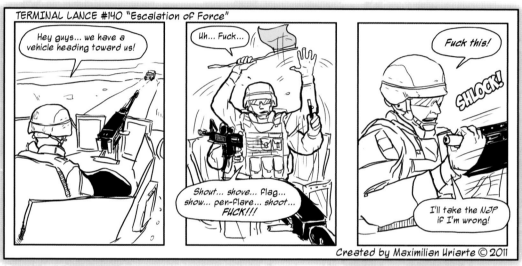

140 "Escalation of Force"

Shout, show, shove, shoot.

This was the mantra given to turret gunners in my battalion during my time in Iraq. The "Escalation of Force" procedures varied depending on the tools available to the gunner. For me, I had a square of brightly colored orange safety-fabric strung up to a stick (literally, a stick—as in, from a tree) with 550 cord for shouting; I had a pen-flare for showing, which was a small flare shot out of a pen-sized launcher; I had my M16-A4 loaded with tracer rounds for shoving; and of course my beloved M2 .50 for shooting.

All of us knew the steps, and they weren't hard to remember. However, during my time in country, the guidelines became increasingly strict. As a result, Marines became more wary of actually shooting at an oncoming vehicle. Not because they might shoot back, but because they might face punishment back in the rear. I recall one event on MSR Mobile: we pulled off onto a side road. My vehicle, the lead truck, successfully traversed the turn. However, the vehicle behind me had a close call with an oncoming Iraqi truck. The gunner, we'll call him Bob, ended up taking a couple of warning shots at the vehicle to get it to stop moving.

Bob followed all the necessary EoF procedures, but when we got back to the rear he was placed under an absurd investigation. The Iraqi was fine, no one was injured, it was really just a misunderstanding of the Iraqi driver. While Bob ended up being cleared, and rightfully so, the company ended up putting our entire platoon under a death-by-PowerPoint style presentation of EoF procedures. In addition, they decided to fill the rest of the day with other safety classes that had nothing to do with EoF, shooting, or Iraq.

The next morning, just about everyone in the platoon told Bob, "Hey, don't shoot at anyone today—I don't feel like sitting through another day of bullshit classes."

It is a tricky situation. Ultimately, I believe the strict enforcement of EoF procedures undoubtedly led to fewer deaths of innocent Iraqi civilians—a very favorable result. However, for the grunt—for the guy behind the gun—it becomes a stressful fumble of figuring out what step is next and whether it is the right thing to do.

However, the same can be said for just about any situation in a war when there's guns and people involved.

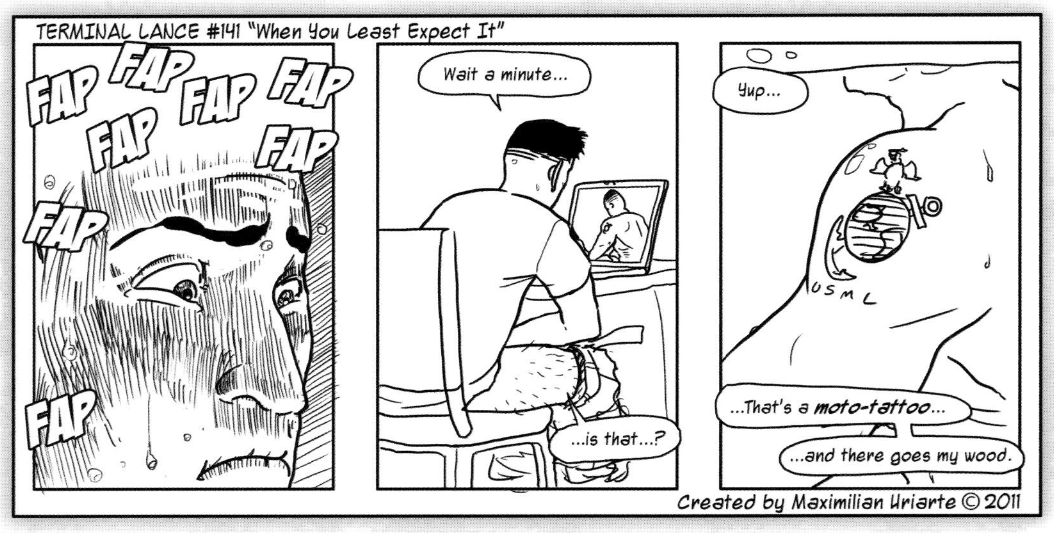
TERMINAL LANCE #141 "When You Least Expect It"
FAP FAP FAP FAP FAP FAP FAP FAP
Wait a minute...
...is that...?
Yup...
USMC
...That's a moto-tattoo...
...and there goes my wood.
Created by Maximilian Uriarte © 2011

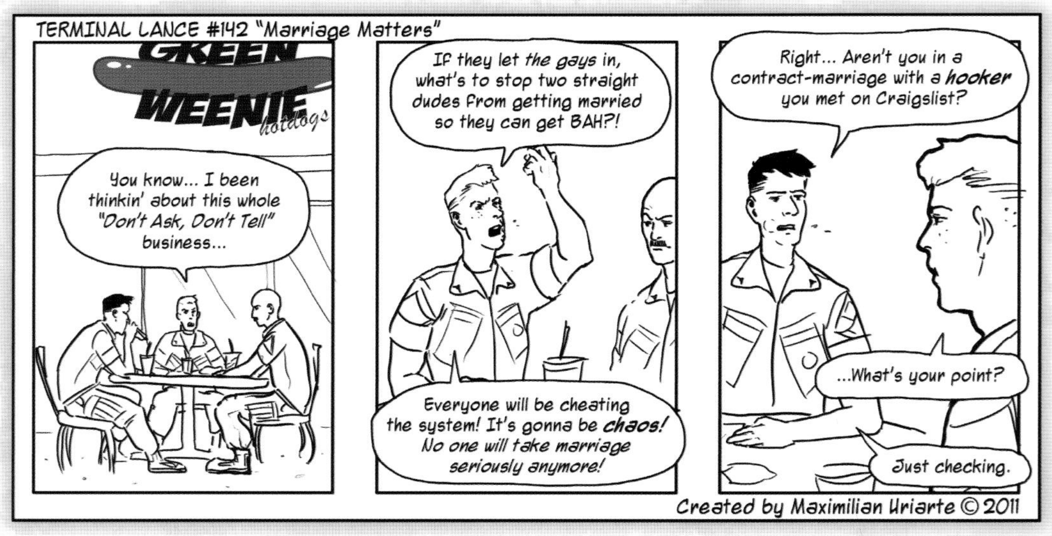
TERMINAL LANCE #142 "Marriage Matters"
GREEN WEENIE hotdogs
You know... I been thinkin' about this whole "Don't Ask, Don't Tell" business...
If they let the gays in, what's to stop two straight dudes from getting married so they can get BAH?!
Everyone will be cheating the system! It's gonna be chaos! No one will take marriage seriously anymore!
Right... Aren't you in a contract-marriage with a hooker you met on Craigslist?
...What's your point?
Just checking.
Created by Maximilian Uriarte © 2011

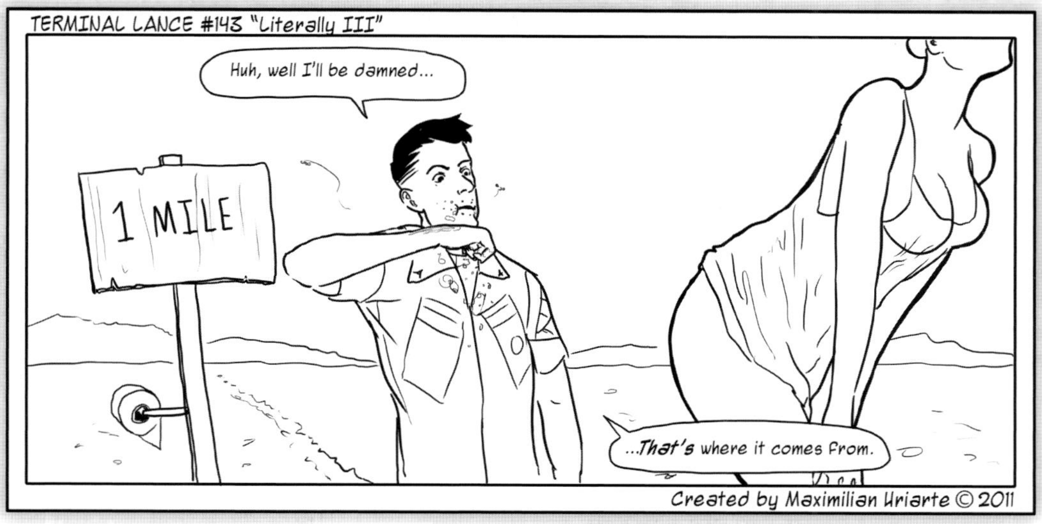
TERMINAL LANCE #143 "Literally III"
Huh, well I'll be damned...
1 MILE
...That's where it comes from.
Created by Maximilian Uriarte © 2011

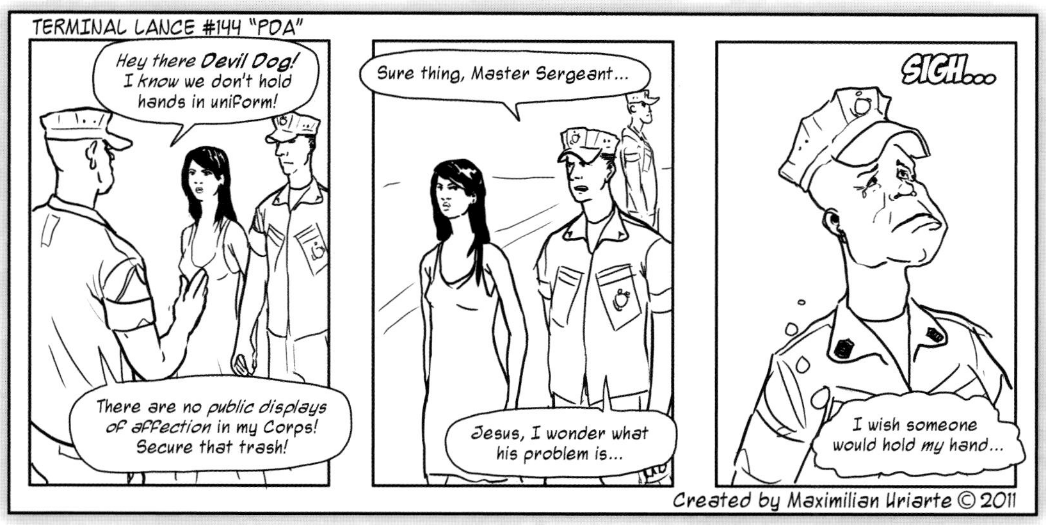
TERMINAL LANCE #144 "PDA"
Hey there Devil Dog! I know we don't hold hands in uniform!
There are no public displays of affection in my Corps! Secure that trash!
Sure thing, Master Sergeant...
Jesus, I wonder what his problem is...
SIGH...
I wish someone would hold my hand...
Created by Maximilian Uriarte © 2011

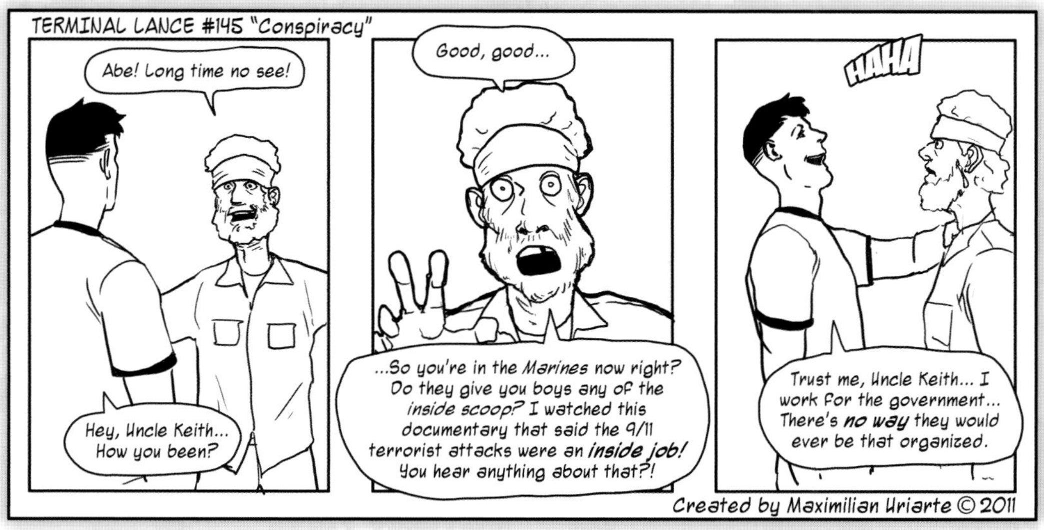
TERMINAL LANCE #145 "Conspiracy"
Abe! Long time no see!
Hey, Uncle Keith... How you been?
Good, good...
...So you're in the Marines now right? Do they give you boys any of the inside scoop? I watched this documentary that said the 9/11 terrorist attacks were an inside job! You hear anything about that?!
HAHA
Trust me, Uncle Keith... I work for the government... There's no way they would ever be that organized.
Created by Maximilian Uriarte © 2011

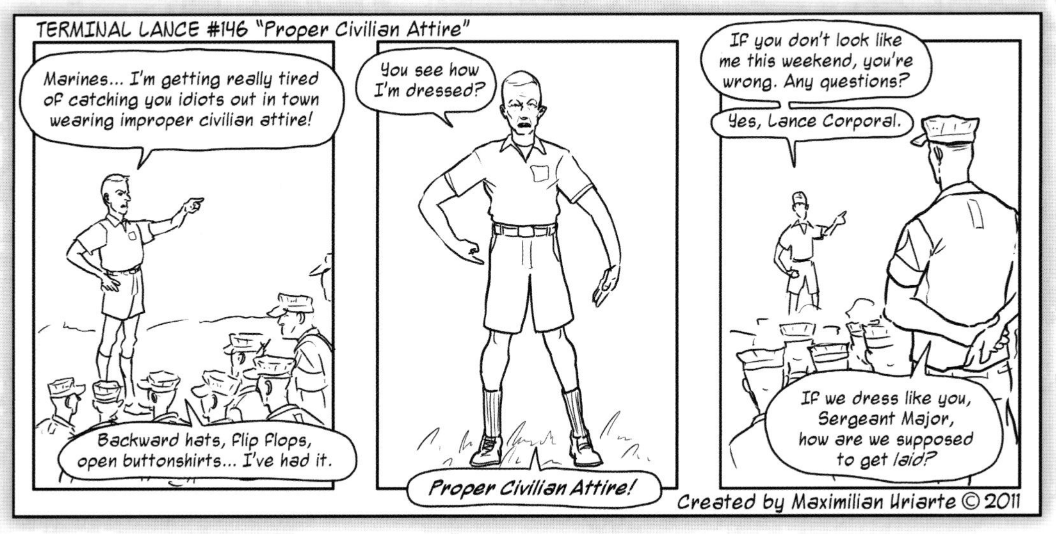
TERMINAL LANCE #146 "Proper Civilian Attire"
Marines... I'm getting really tired of catching you idiots out in town wearing improper civilian attire!
Backward hats, flip flops, open buttonshirts... I've had it.
You see how I'm dressed?
Proper Civilian Attire!
If you don't look like me this weekend, you're wrong. Any questions?
Yes, Lance Corporal.
If we dress like you, Sergeant Major, how are we supposed to get *laid?*
Created by Maximilian Uriarte © 2011

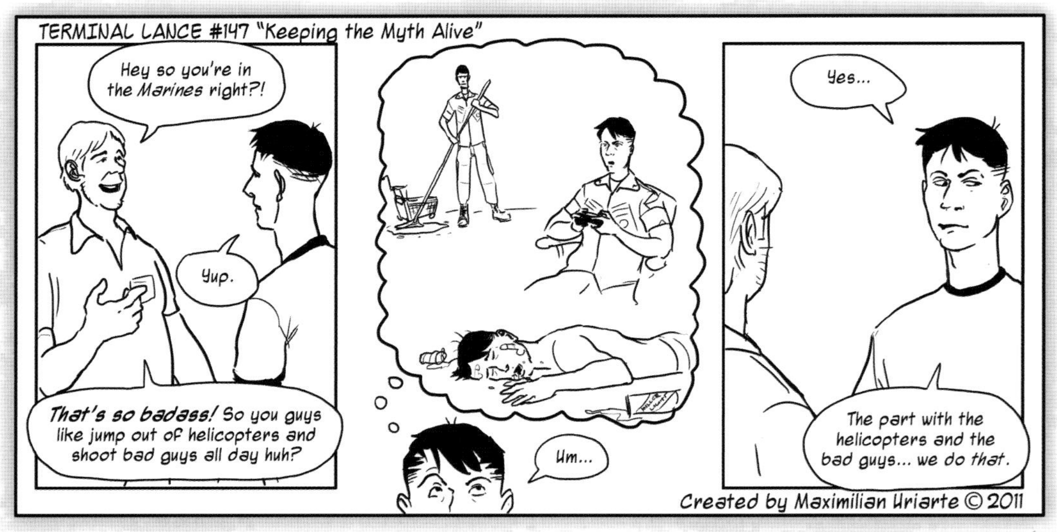
TERMINAL LANCE #147 "Keeping the Myth Alive"
Hey so you're in the *Marines* right?!
Yup.
That's so badass! So you guys like jump out of helicopters and shoot bad guys all day huh?
Um...
Yes...
The part with the helicopters and the bad guys... we do *that.*
Created by Maximilian Uriarte © 2011

147 "Keeping the Myth Alive"

Perhaps I'm in the minority here, but when I look back on my time in the Marine Corps, the cool stuff isn't what immediately comes to mind. Instead, I tend to think of small things like the hours I spent cleaning floors, jerking off in port-a-shitters, cleaning a rifle, barracks parties (which are every night), hazing, bullshit, the way cammies kind of chafe my inner thighs, and anything else that was part of my everyday life.

The great secret of the Marine Corps is that we only do the cool stuff about 10 percent of the time. The other 90 percent is spent doing everything mentioned above. And confusion and anger linger at every corner. I shot over twenty SMAW rockets in my four years, trained for weeks at a time in the field, and spent sleepless nights and sizzling days hunched over an M2 .50 cal atop an MRAP, but I don't usually think about it.

The Marine Corps—actually living the Marine Corps—isn't about the cool stuff. It's about the little things, the 90 percent of the time things that are both funny and immensely miserable at the same time.

But it's very important that we don't reveal to our civilian brethren what really goes on in the Corps. Otherwise, those care packages would come a lot less often.

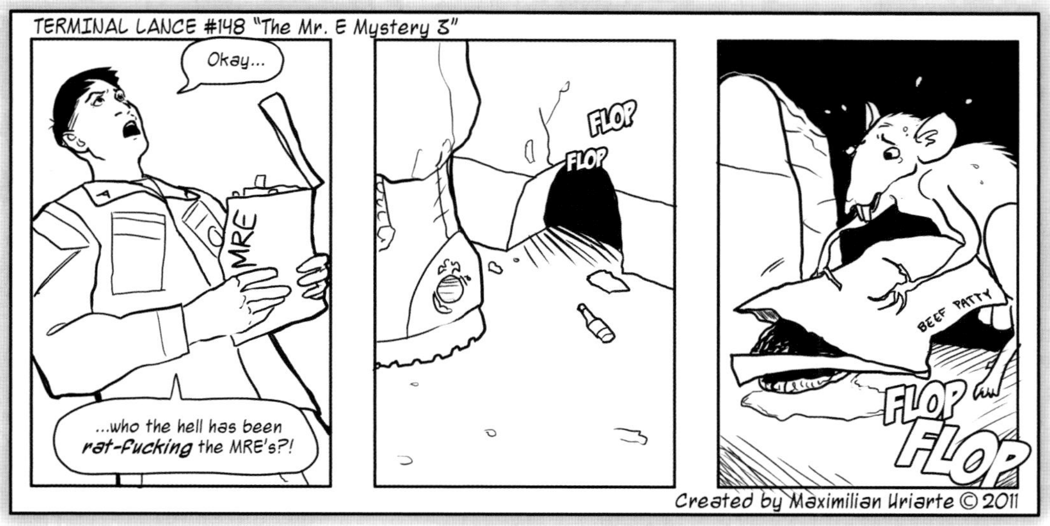
TERMINAL LANCE #148 "The Mr. E Mystery 3"
Okay...
...who the hell has been rat-fucking the MRE's?!
MRE
FLOP
FLOP
BEEF PATTY
FLOP
FLOP
Created by Maximilian Uriarte © 2011

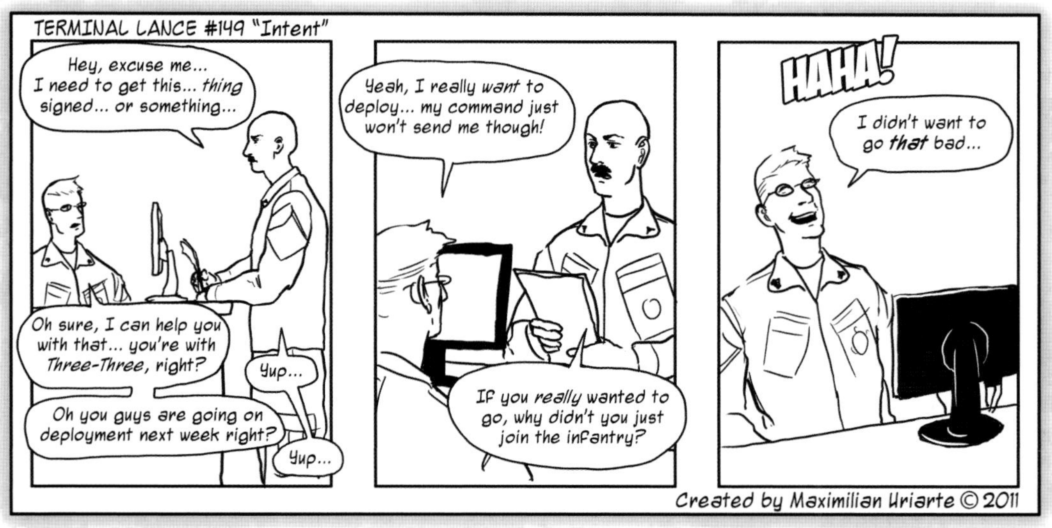
TERMINAL LANCE #149 "Intent"
Hey, excuse me... I need to get this... thing signed... or something...
Oh sure, I can help you with that... you're with Three-Three, right?
Yup...
Oh you guys are going on deployment next week right?
Yup...
Yeah, I really want to deploy... my command just won't send me though!
If you really wanted to go, why didn't you just join the infantry?
HAHA!
I didn't want to go that bad...
Created by Maximilian Uriarte © 2011

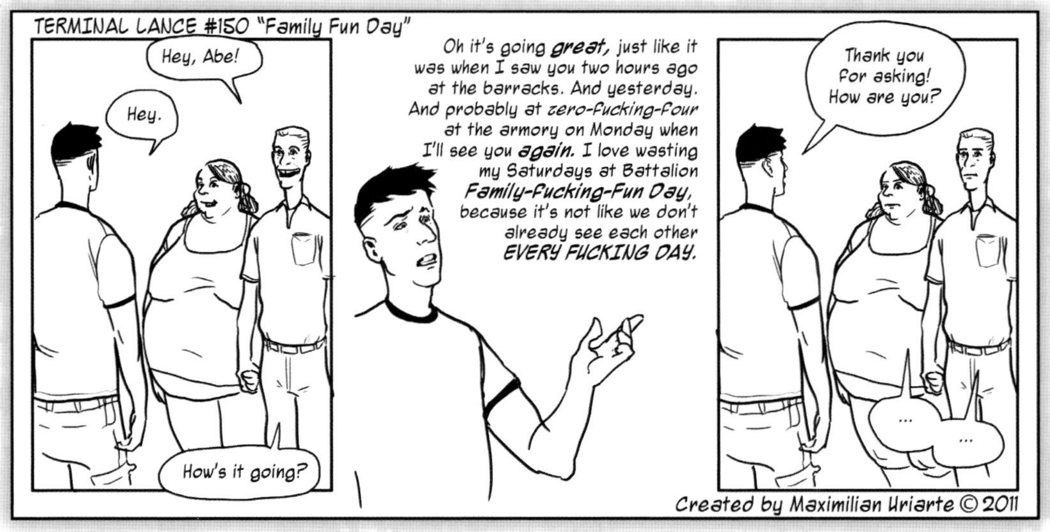
TERMINAL LANCE #150 "Family Fun Day"
Hey, Abe!
Hey.
How's it going?
Oh it's going great, just like it was when I saw you two hours ago at the barracks. And yesterday. And probably at zero-fucking-four at the armory on Monday when I'll see you again. I love wasting my Saturdays at Battalion Family-fucking-Fun Day, because it's not like we don't already see each other EVERY FUCKING DAY.
Thank you for asking! How are you?
...
...
Created by Maximilian Uriarte © 2011

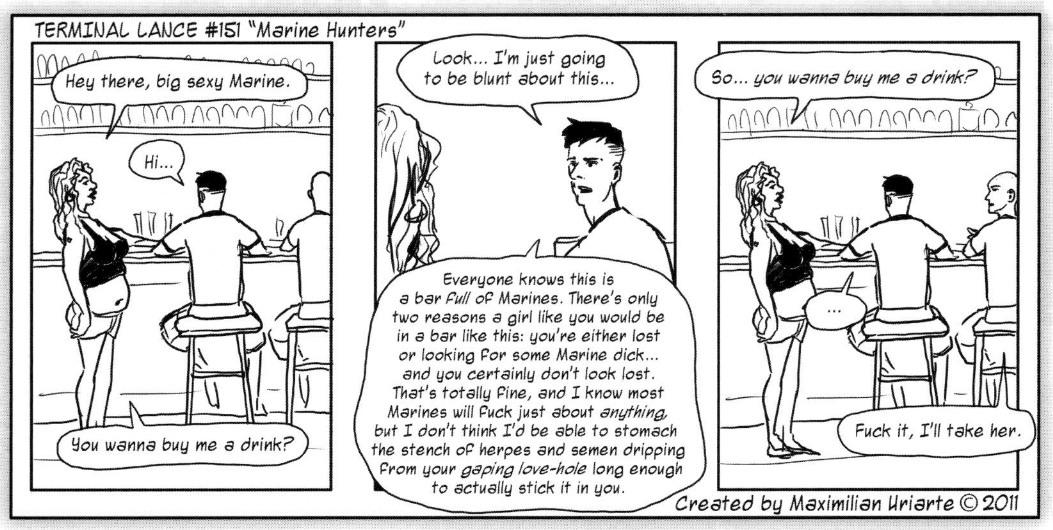
TERMINAL LANCE #151 "Marine Hunters"
Hey there, big sexy Marine.
Hi...
You wanna buy me a drink?
Look... I'm just going to be blunt about this...
Everyone knows this is a bar *full* of Marines. There's only two reasons a girl like you would be in a bar like this: you're either lost or looking for some Marine dick... and you certainly don't look lost. That's totally fine, and I know most Marines will fuck just about *anything*, but I don't think I'd be able to stomach the stench of herpes and semen dripping from your *gaping love-hole* long enough to actually stick it in you.
So... you wanna buy me a drink?
...
Fuck it, I'll take her.
Created by Maximilian Uriarte © 2011

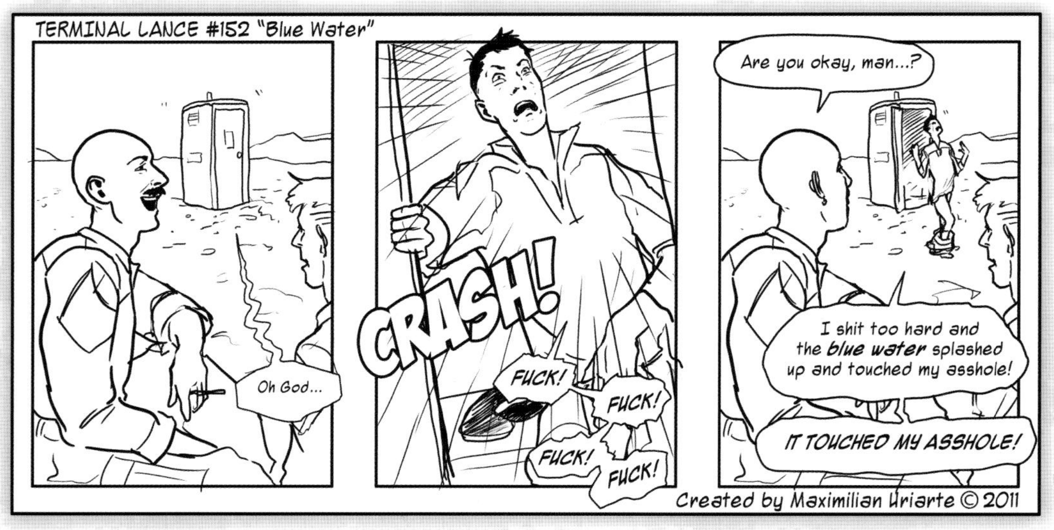
TERMINAL LANCE #152 "Blue Water"
Oh God...
CRASH!
FUCK!
FUCK!
FUCK!
FUCK!
Are you okay, man...?
I shit too hard and the **blue water** splashed up and touched my asshole!
IT TOUCHED MY ASSHOLE!
Created by Maximilian Uriarte © 2011

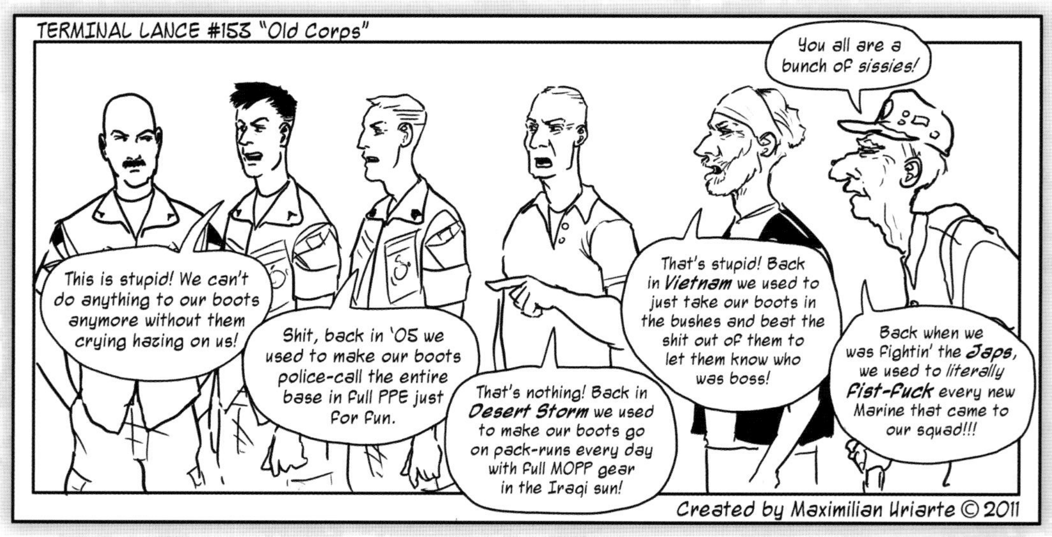
TERMINAL LANCE #153 "Old Corps"
This is stupid! We can't do anything to our boots anymore without them crying hazing on us!
Shit, back in '05 we used to make our boots police-call the entire base in full PPE just for fun.
That's nothing! Back in **Desert Storm** we used to make our boots go on pack-runs every day with full MOPP gear in the Iraqi sun!
That's stupid! Back in **Vietnam** we used to just take our boots in the bushes and beat the shit out of them to let them know who was boss!
You all are a bunch of *sissies!*
Back when we was fightin' the **Japs**, we used to *literally* **fist-fuck** every new Marine that came to our squad!!!
Created by Maximilian Uriarte © 2011

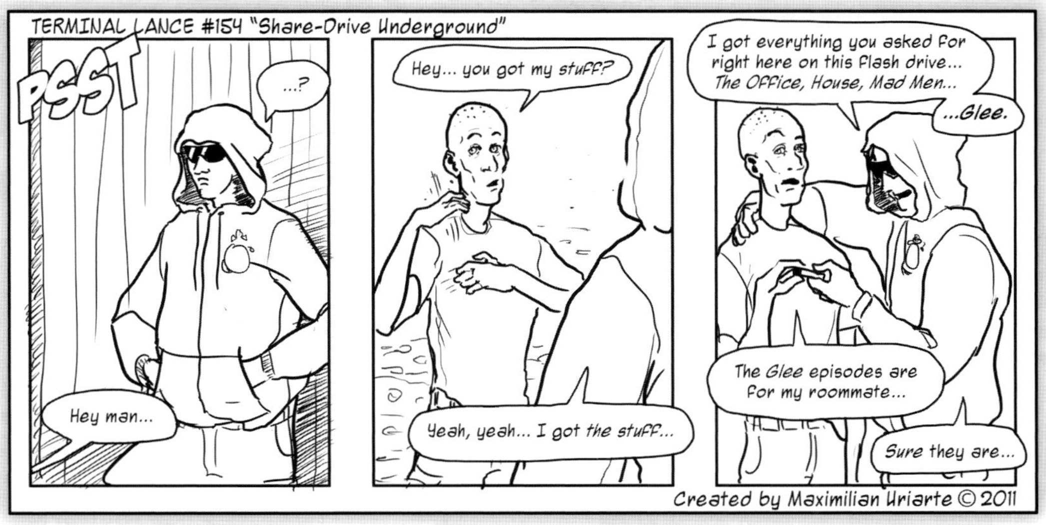
TERMINAL LANCE #154 "Share-Drive Underground"
PSST
...?
Hey man...
Hey... you got my stuff?
Yeah, yeah... I got the stuff...
I got everything you asked for right here on this flash drive... The Office, House, Mad Men...
...Glee.
The Glee episodes are for my roommate...
Sure they are...
Created by Maximilian Uriarte © 2011

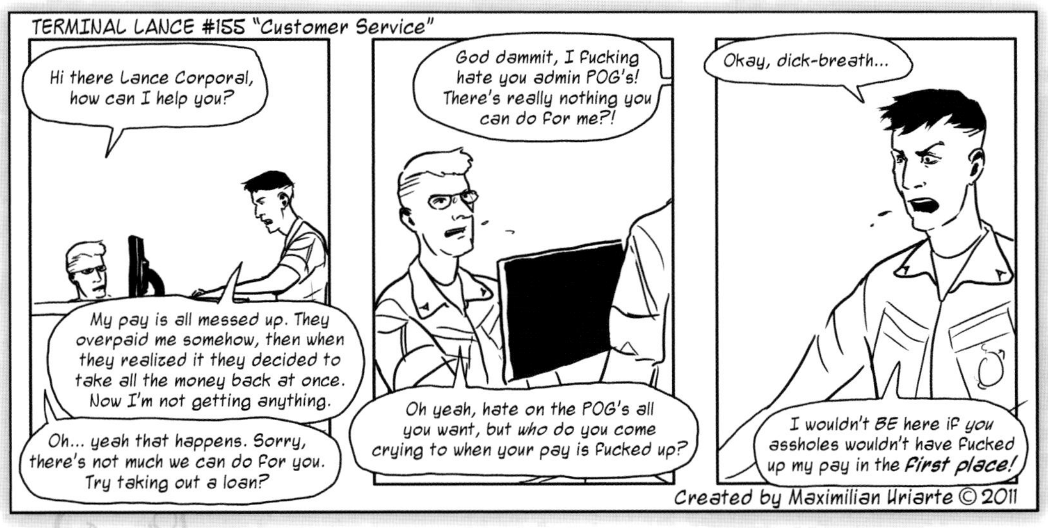
TERMINAL LANCE #155 "Customer Service"
Hi there Lance Corporal, how can I help you?
My pay is all messed up. They overpaid me somehow, then when they realized it they decided to take all the money back at once. Now I'm not getting anything.
Oh... yeah that happens. Sorry, there's not much we can do for you. Try taking out a loan?
God dammit, I fucking hate you admin POG's! There's really nothing you can do for me?!
Oh yeah, hate on the POG's all you want, but who do you come crying to when your pay is fucked up?
Okay, dick-breath...
I wouldn't BE here if you assholes wouldn't have fucked up my pay in the First place!
Created by Maximilian Uriarte © 2011

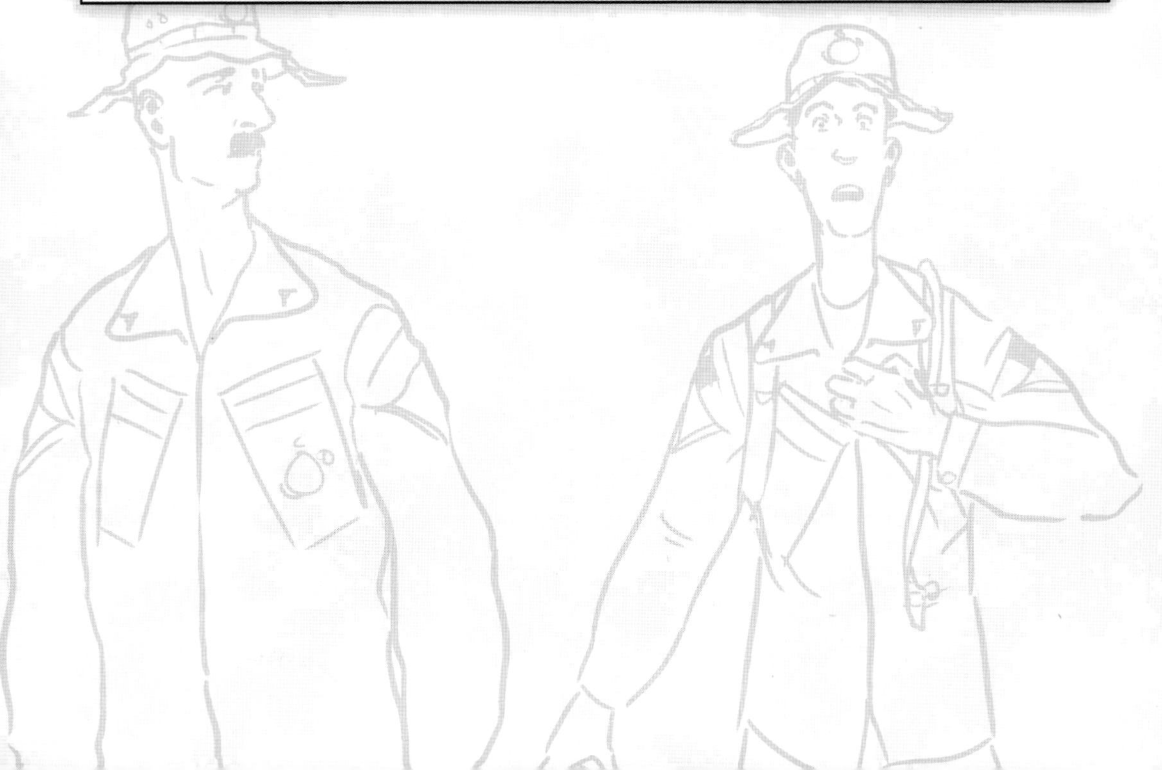

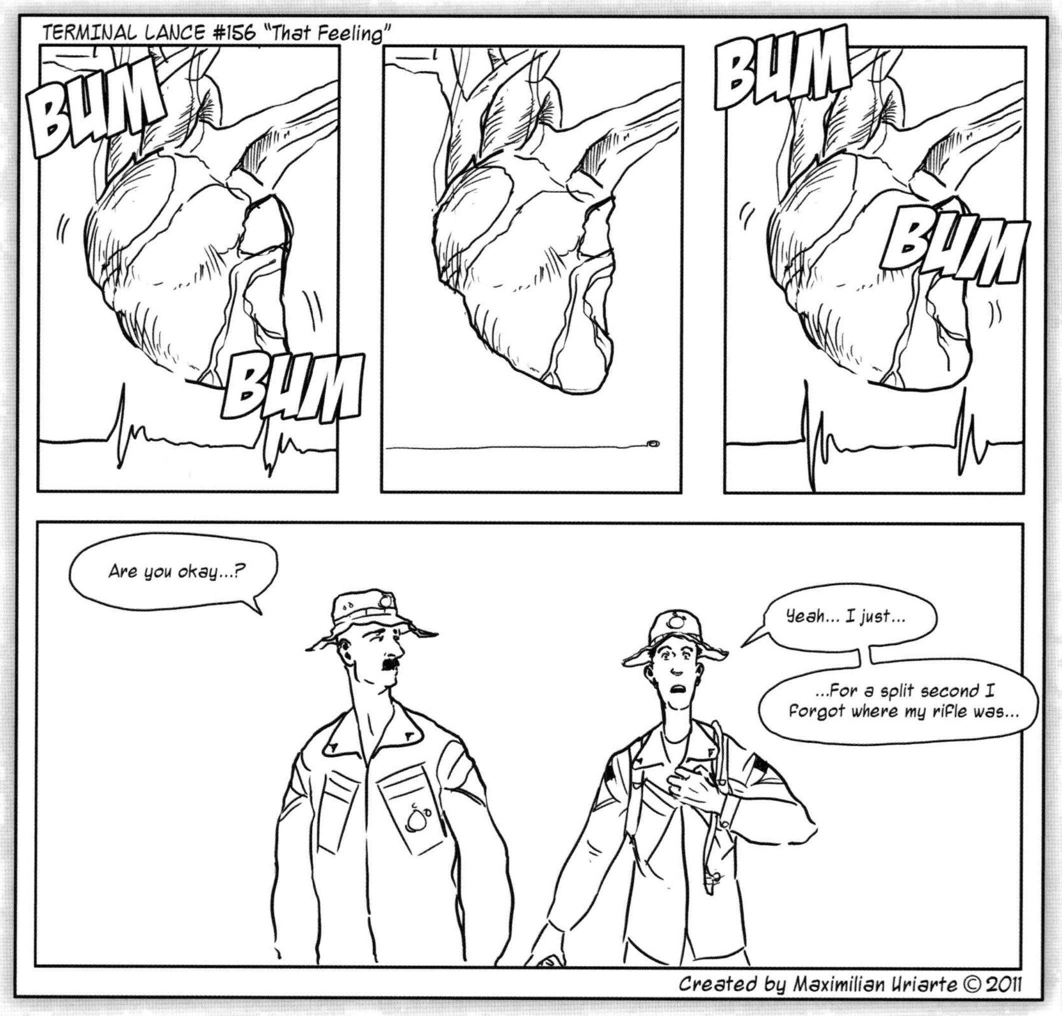
TERMINAL LANCE #156 "That Feeling"
BUM
BUM
BUM
BUM
Are you okay...?
Yeah... I just...
...For a split second I forgot where my rifle was...
Created by Maximilian Uriarte © 2011

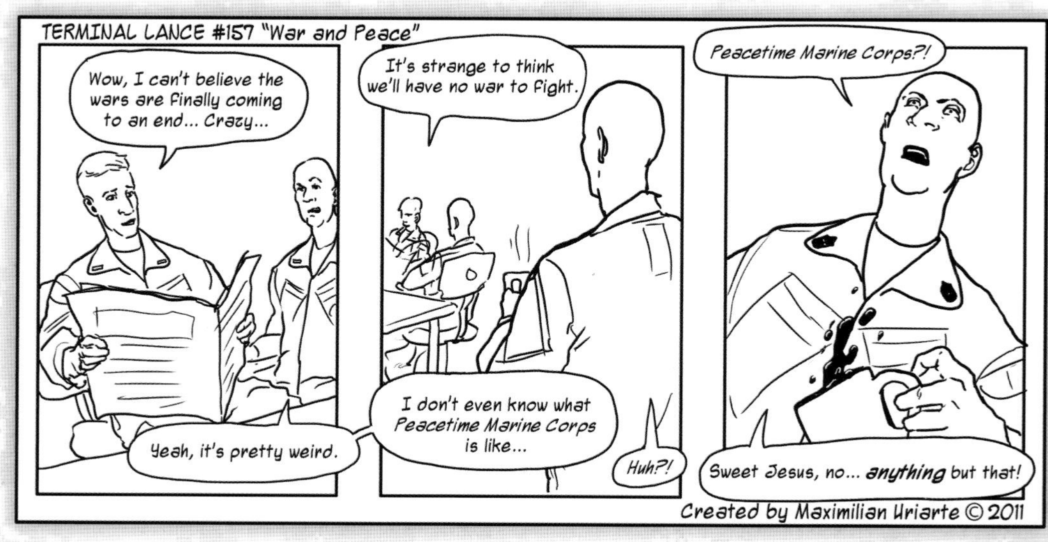
TERMINAL LANCE #157 "War and Peace"
Wow, I can't believe the wars are finally coming to an end... Crazy...
Yeah, it's pretty weird.
It's strange to think we'll have no war to fight.
I don't even know what Peacetime Marine Corps is like...
Huh?!
Peacetime Marine Corps?!
Sweet Jesus, no... anything but that!
Created by Maximilian Uriarte © 2011

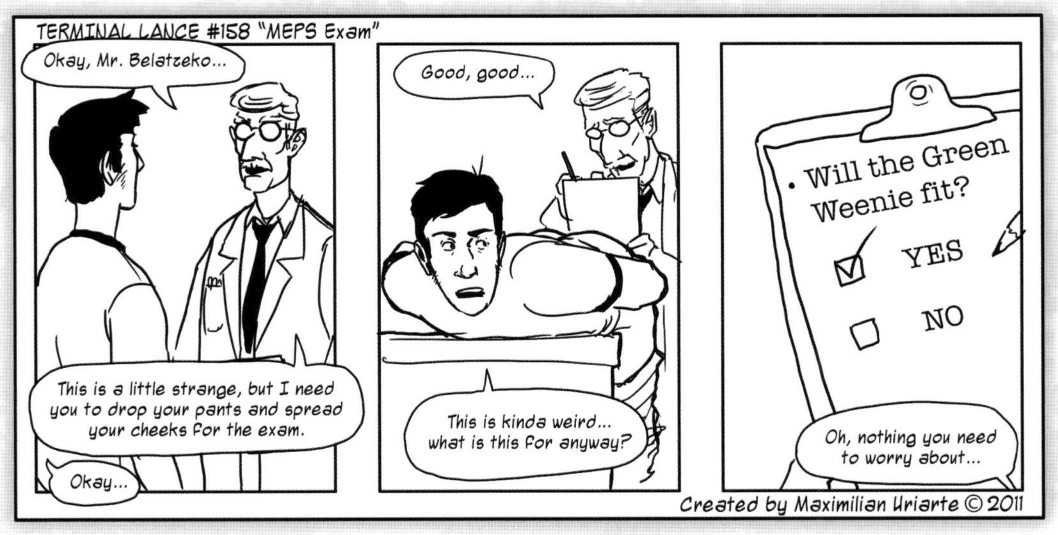
TERMINAL LANCE #158 "MEPS Exam"
Okay, Mr. Belatzeko...
This is a little strange, but I need you to drop your pants and spread your cheeks for the exam.
Okay...
Good, good...
This is kinda weird... what is this for anyway?
• Will the Green Weenie fit?
YES
NO
Oh, nothing you need to worry about...
Created by Maximilian Uriarte © 2011

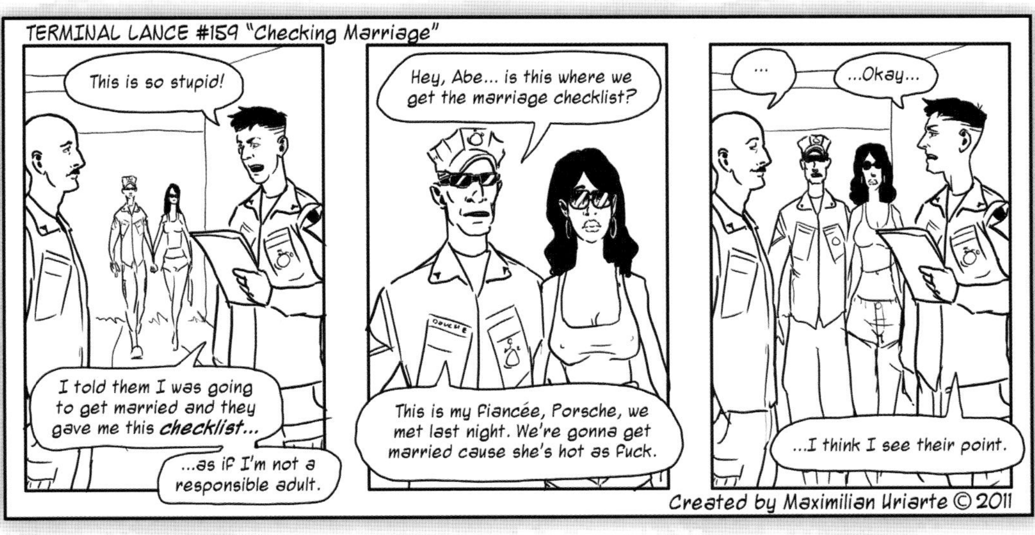
TERMINAL LANCE #159 "Checking Marriage"
This is so stupid!
I told them I was going to get married and they gave me this checklist...
...as if I'm not a responsible adult.
Hey, Abe... is this where we get the marriage checklist?
This is my fiancée, Porsche, we met last night. We're gonna get married cause she's hot as fuck.
...
...Okay...
...I think I see their point.
Created by Maximilian Uriarte © 2011

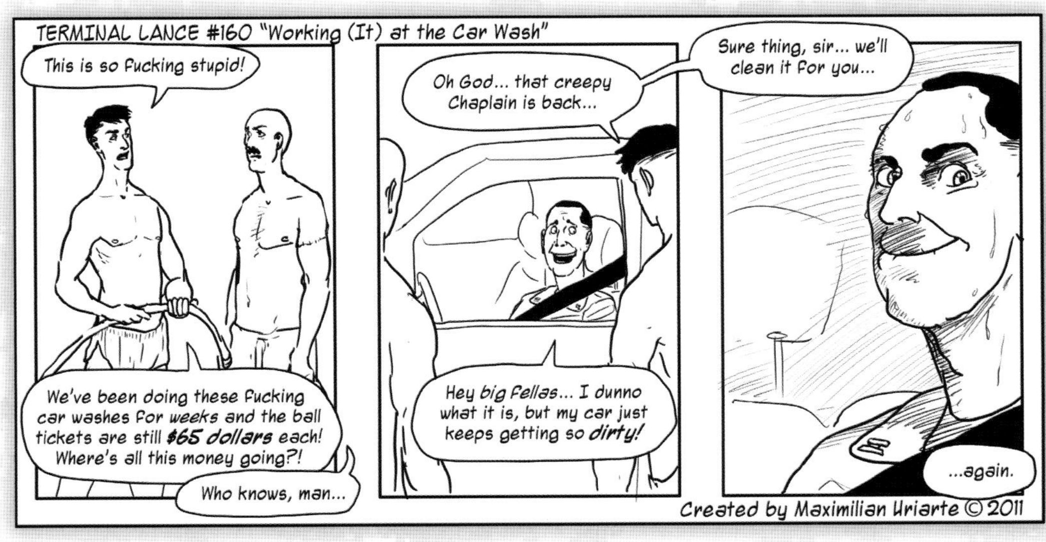
TERMINAL LANCE #160 "Working (It) at the Car Wash"
This is so fucking stupid!
We've been doing these fucking car washes for weeks and the ball tickets are still $65 dollars each! Where's all this money going?!
Who knows, man...
Oh God... that creepy Chaplain is back...
Hey big fellas... I dunno what it is, but my car just keeps getting so dirty!
Sure thing, sir... we'll clean it for you...
...again.
Created by Maximilian Uriarte © 2011

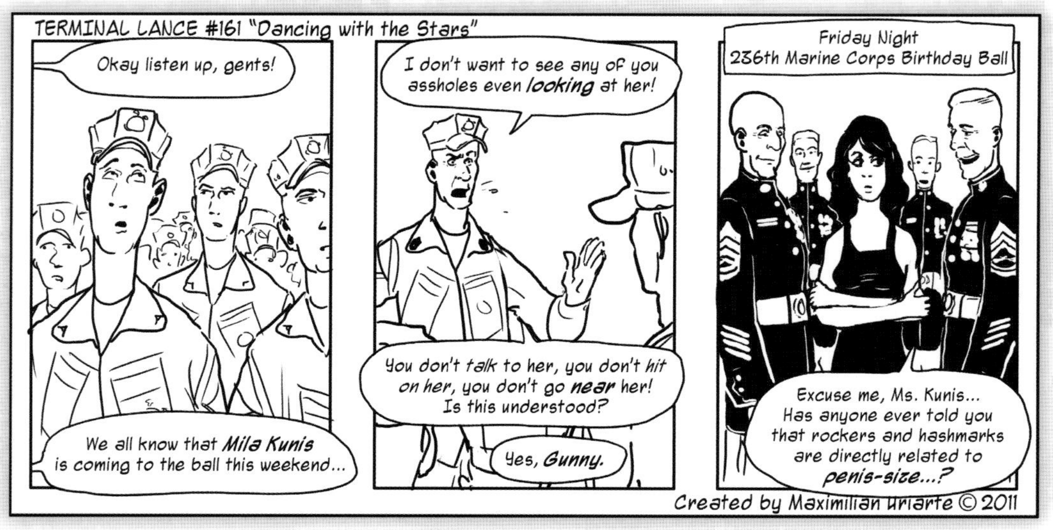
TERMINAL LANCE #161 "Dancing with the Stars"
Okay listen up, gents!
We all know that *Mila Kunis* is coming to the ball this weekend...
I don't want to see any of you assholes even *looking* at her!
You don't *talk* to her, you don't *hit* on her, you don't go ***near*** her! Is this understood?
Yes, *Gunny.*
Friday Night 236th Marine Corps Birthday Ball
Excuse me, Ms. Kunis... Has anyone ever told you that rockers and hashmarks are directly related to ***penis-size...?***
Created by Maximilian Uriarte © 2011

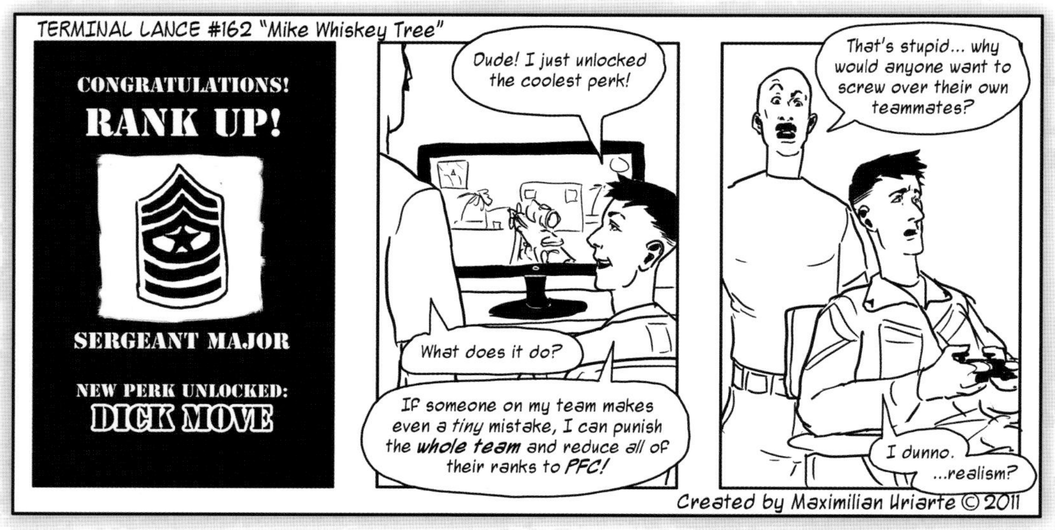
TERMINAL LANCE #162 "Mike Whiskey Tree"
CONGRATULATIONS!
RANK UP!
SERGEANT MAJOR
NEW PERK UNLOCKED:
DICK MOVE
Dude! I just unlocked the coolest perk!
What does it do?
If someone on my team makes even a *tiny* mistake, I can punish the ***whole team*** and reduce *all* of their ranks to *PFC!*
That's stupid... why would anyone want to screw over their own teammates?
I dunno. ...realism?
Created by Maximilian Uriarte © 2011

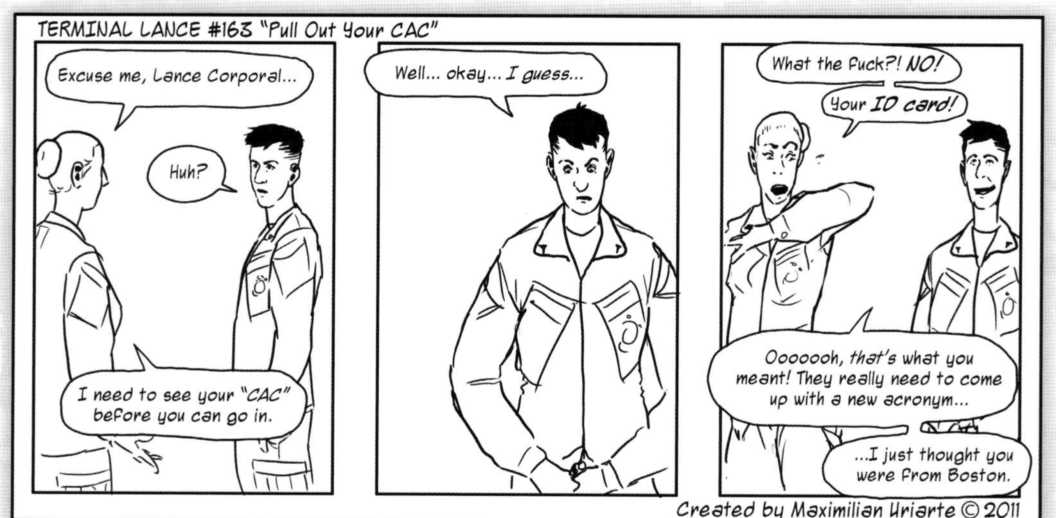
TERMINAL LANCE #163 "Pull Out Your CAC"
Excuse me, Lance Corporal...
Huh?
I need to see your "*CAC*" before you can go in.
Well... okay... *I guess...*
What the fuck?! *NO!*
Your *ID card!*
Ooooooh, *that's* what you meant! They really need to come up with a new acronym...
...I just thought you were from Boston.
Created by Maximilian Uriarte © 2011

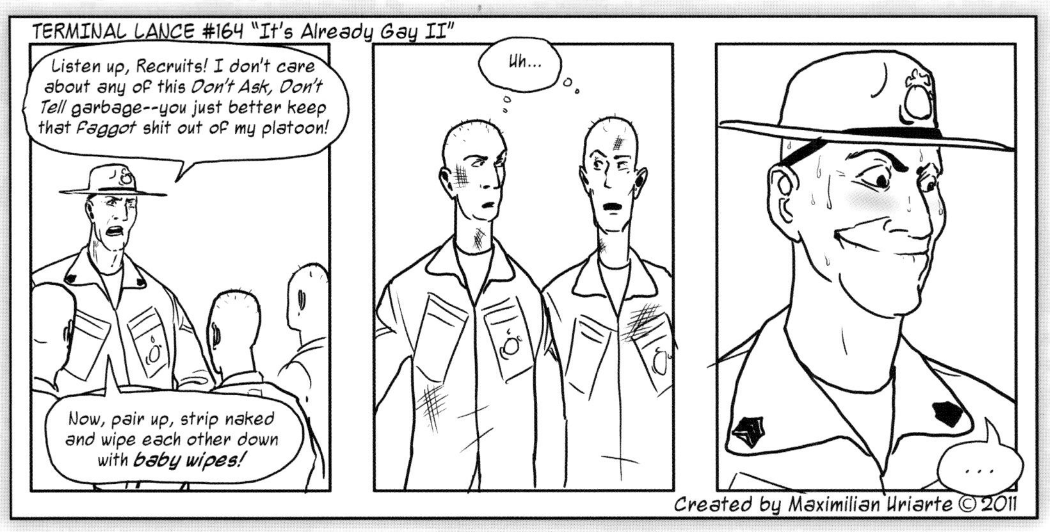
TERMINAL LANCE #164 "It's Already Gay II"
Listen up, Recruits! I don't care about any of this Don't Ask, Don't Tell garbage--you just better keep that faggot shit out of my platoon!
Now, pair up, strip naked and wipe each other down with baby wipes!
Uh...
...
Created by Maximilian Uriarte © 2011

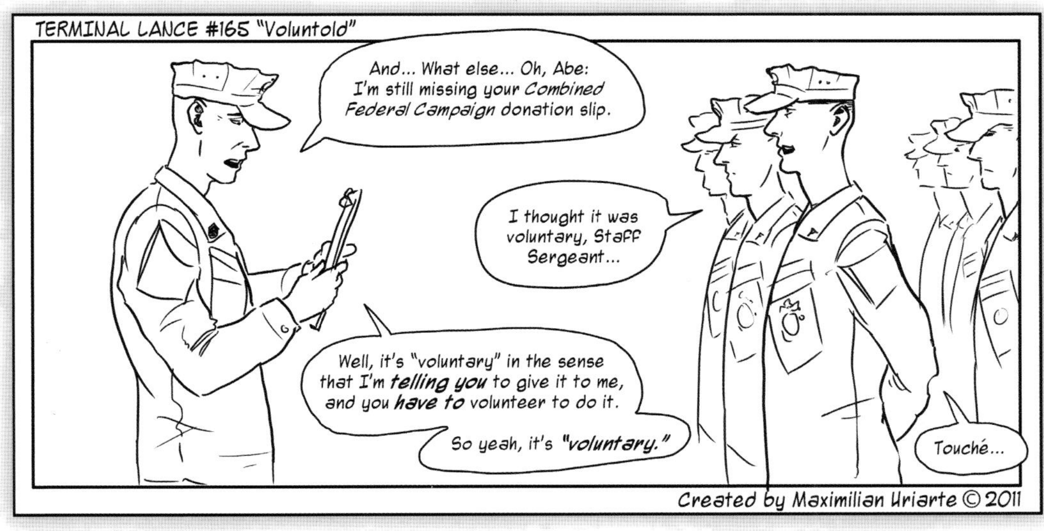
TERMINAL LANCE #165 "Voluntold"
And... What else... Oh, Abe: I'm still missing your Combined Federal Campaign donation slip.
I thought it was voluntary, Staff Sergeant...
Well, it's "voluntary" in the sense that I'm telling you to give it to me, and you have to volunteer to do it.
So yeah, it's "voluntary."
Touché...
Created by Maximilian Uriarte © 2011

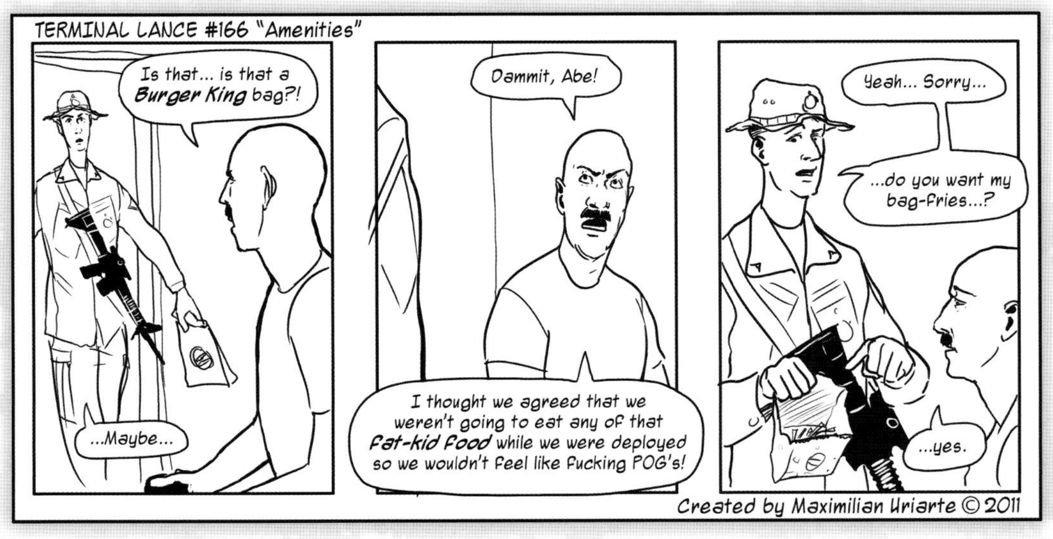
TERMINAL LANCE #166 "Amenities"
Is that... is that a Burger King bag?!
...Maybe...
Dammit, Abe!
I thought we agreed that we weren't going to eat any of that fat-kid food while we were deployed so we wouldn't feel like fucking POG's!
Yeah... Sorry...
...do you want my bag-fries...?
...yes.
Created by Maximilian Uriarte © 2011

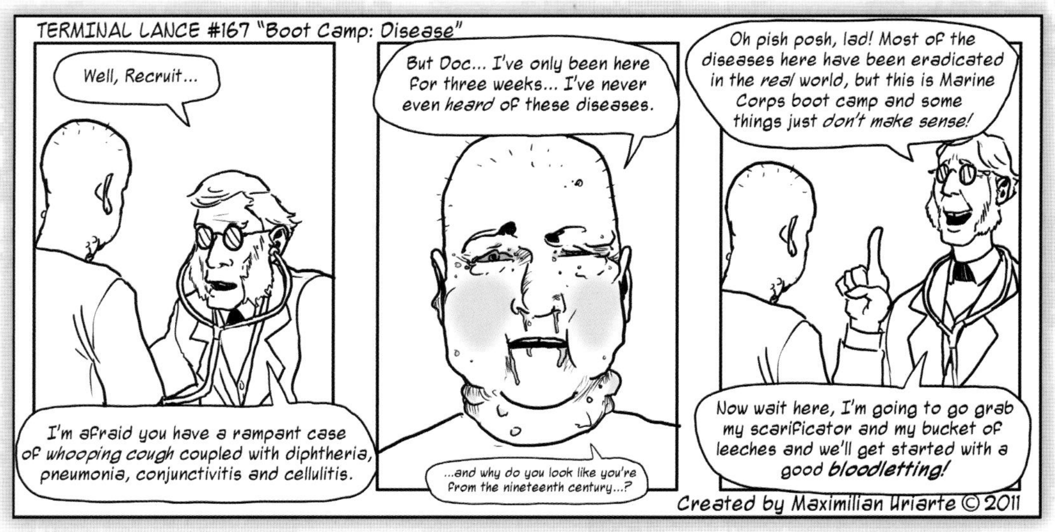
TERMINAL LANCE #167 "Boot Camp: Disease"
Well, Recruit...
I'm afraid you have a rampant case of whooping cough coupled with diphtheria, pneumonia, conjunctivitis and cellulitis.
But Doc... I've only been here for three weeks... I've never even heard of these diseases.
...and why do you look like you're from the nineteenth century...?
Oh pish posh, lad! Most of the diseases here have been eradicated in the real world, but this is Marine Corps boot camp and some things just don't make sense!
Now wait here, I'm going to go grab my scarificator and my bucket of leeches and we'll get started with a good bloodletting!
Created by Maximilian Uriarte © 2011

167 "Boot Camp: Disease"

I don't remember a lot about boot camp, but I remember one thing very vividly: I was always fucking sick.

Most recruits were. In fact, I believe there were moments during "2nd phase" when the infection rate of my platoon was 100 percent. Everyone was sick with something. As it turns out, being thrust into a new environment with sixty other guys from different parts of the country for three months is a shock to the immune system. No amount of peanut butter shots or vaccinations can keep the sickness away—you will end up with some strange disease you've never heard of.

My favorite? Cellulitis. Never before joining the Marine Corps had I heard of it, yet it was one of the most rampant problems in my platoon. Cellulitis is simply a bacterial infection that makes whatever part of your body is infected swell with pus and nastiness until it gets drained and treated—it can also cause a fever and is actually very dangerous. I never got it personally, because I maintained good hygiene, but many recruits would find themselves with some horrific growth dangling off their bodies, desperately trying to hide it from the Drill Instructors so they wouldn't get dropped into MRP (Medical Recovery Platoon).

We had a recruit catch such a bad case of pneumonia that his lungs filled with fluid and he was sent to the hospital two days before graduation. He almost died, but no one wants to get dropped from their platoon.

Also rampant in my platoon was the somewhat humorous disease of "pink eye" or conjunctivitis. Everyone had pink eye at some point. I got it during the crucible, and actually did the entire reaper hike with pink eye in both eyes. It was terrible, but just part of the reality of boot camp.

As for the old-timey doctor . . . I just thought it would be funnier.

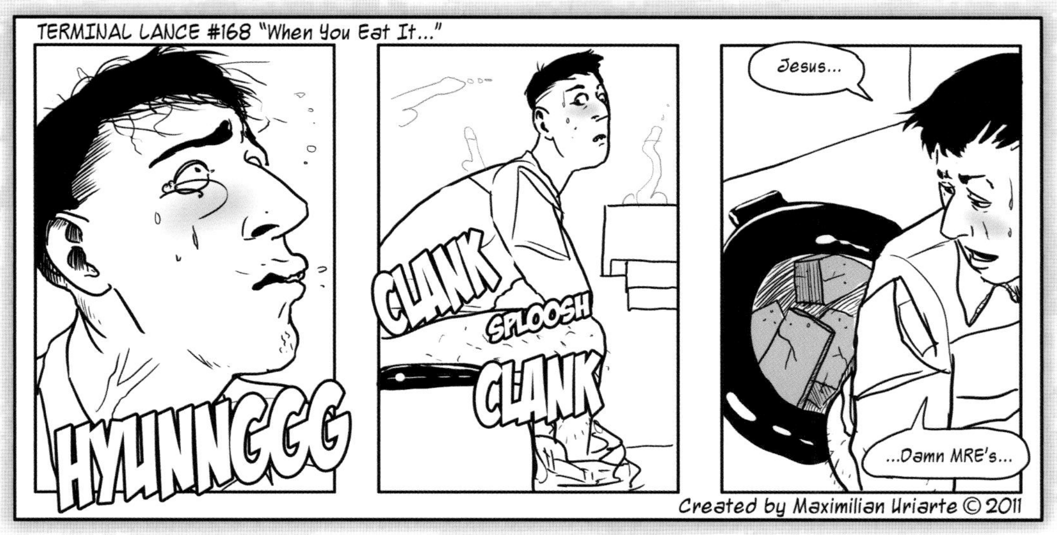
TERMINAL LANCE #168 "When You Eat It..."
HYUNNGGG
CLANK
SPLOOSH
CLANK
Jesus...
...Damn MRE's...
Created by Maximilian Uriarte © 2011

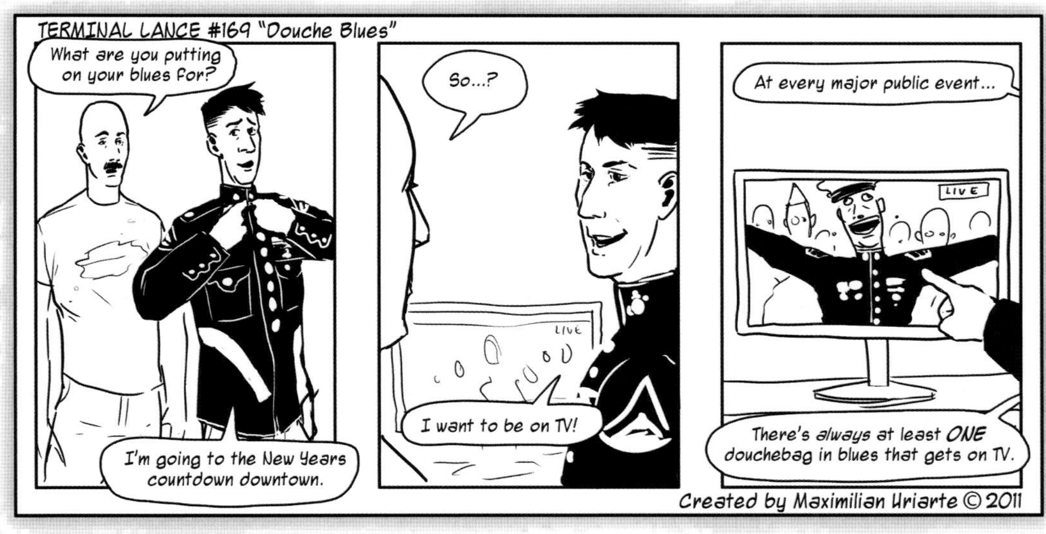
TERMINAL LANCE #169 "Douche Blues"
What are you putting on your blues for?
I'm going to the New Years countdown downtown.
So...?
LIVE
I want to be on TV!
At every major public event...
LIVE
There's always at least ONE douchebag in blues that gets on TV.
Created by Maximilian Uriarte © 2011

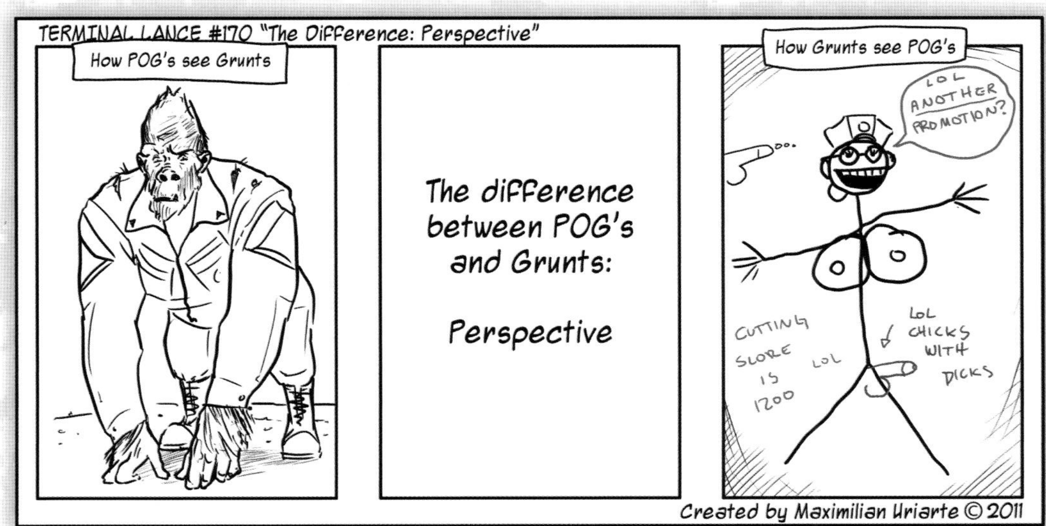
TERMINAL LANCE #170 "The Difference: Perspective"
How POG's see Grunts
The difference between POG's and Grunts:
Perspective
How Grunts see POG's
LOL ANOTHER PROMOTION?
CUTTING SCORE IS 1200
LOL
LOL CHICKS WITH DICKS
Created by Maximilian Uriarte © 2011

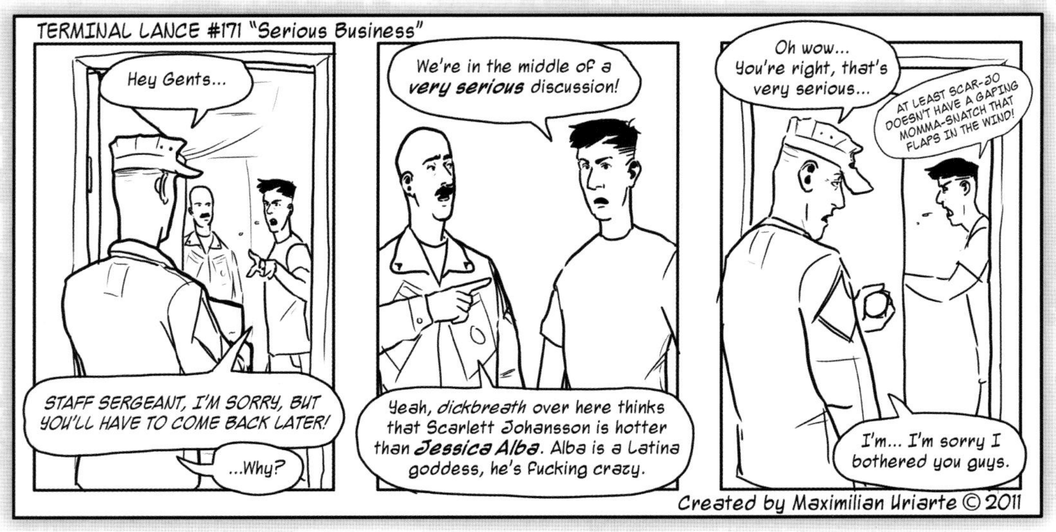
TERMINAL LANCE #171 "Serious Business"
Hey Gents...
STAFF SERGEANT, I'M SORRY, BUT YOU'LL HAVE TO COME BACK LATER!
...Why?
We're in the middle of a *very serious* discussion!
Yeah, *dickbreath* over here thinks that Scarlett Johansson is hotter than **Jessica Alba**. Alba is a Latina goddess, he's fucking crazy.
Oh wow... You're right, that's very serious...
AT LEAST SCAR-JO DOESN'T HAVE A GAPING MOMMA-SNATCH THAT FLAPS IN THE WIND!
I'm... I'm sorry I bothered you guys.
Created by Maximilian Uriarte © 2011

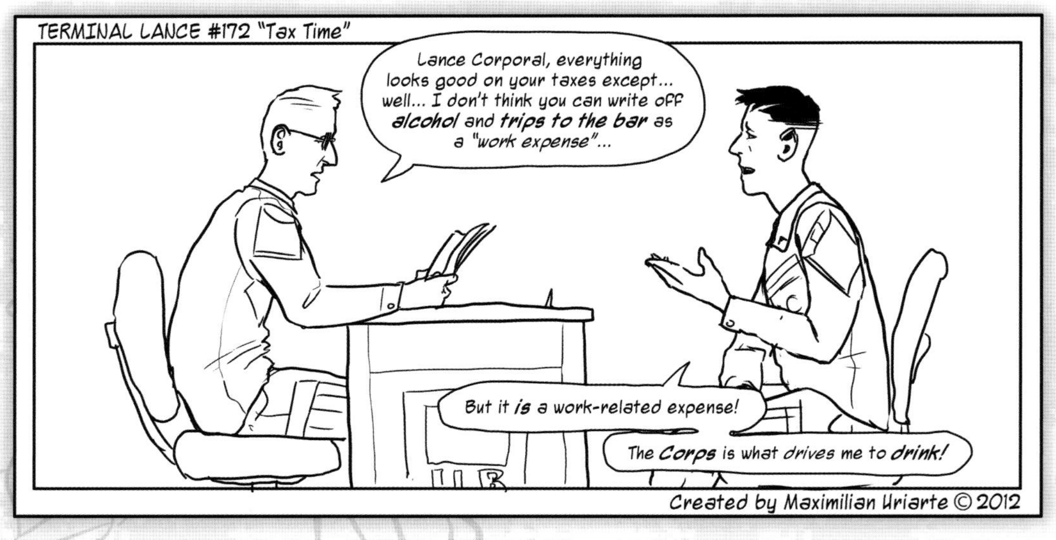
TERMINAL LANCE #172 "Tax Time"
Lance Corporal, everything looks good on your taxes except... well... I don't think you can write off **alcohol** and **trips to the bar** as a "work expense"...
But it *is* a work-related expense!
The *Corps* is what *drives* me to *drink!*
Created by Maximilian Uriarte © 2012

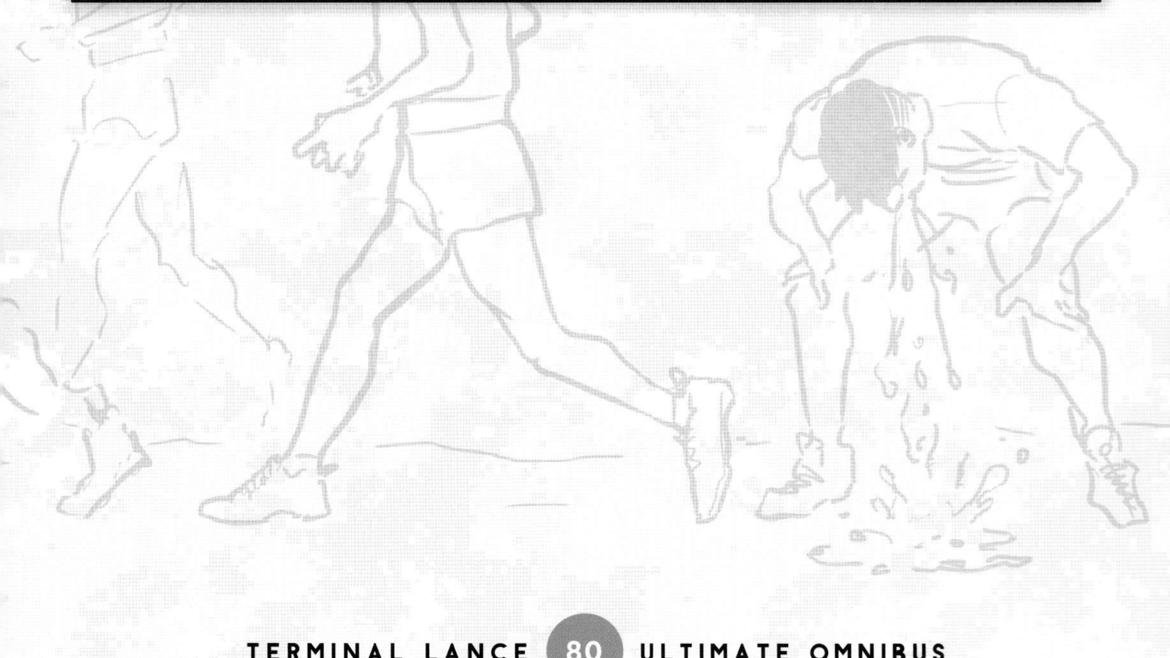

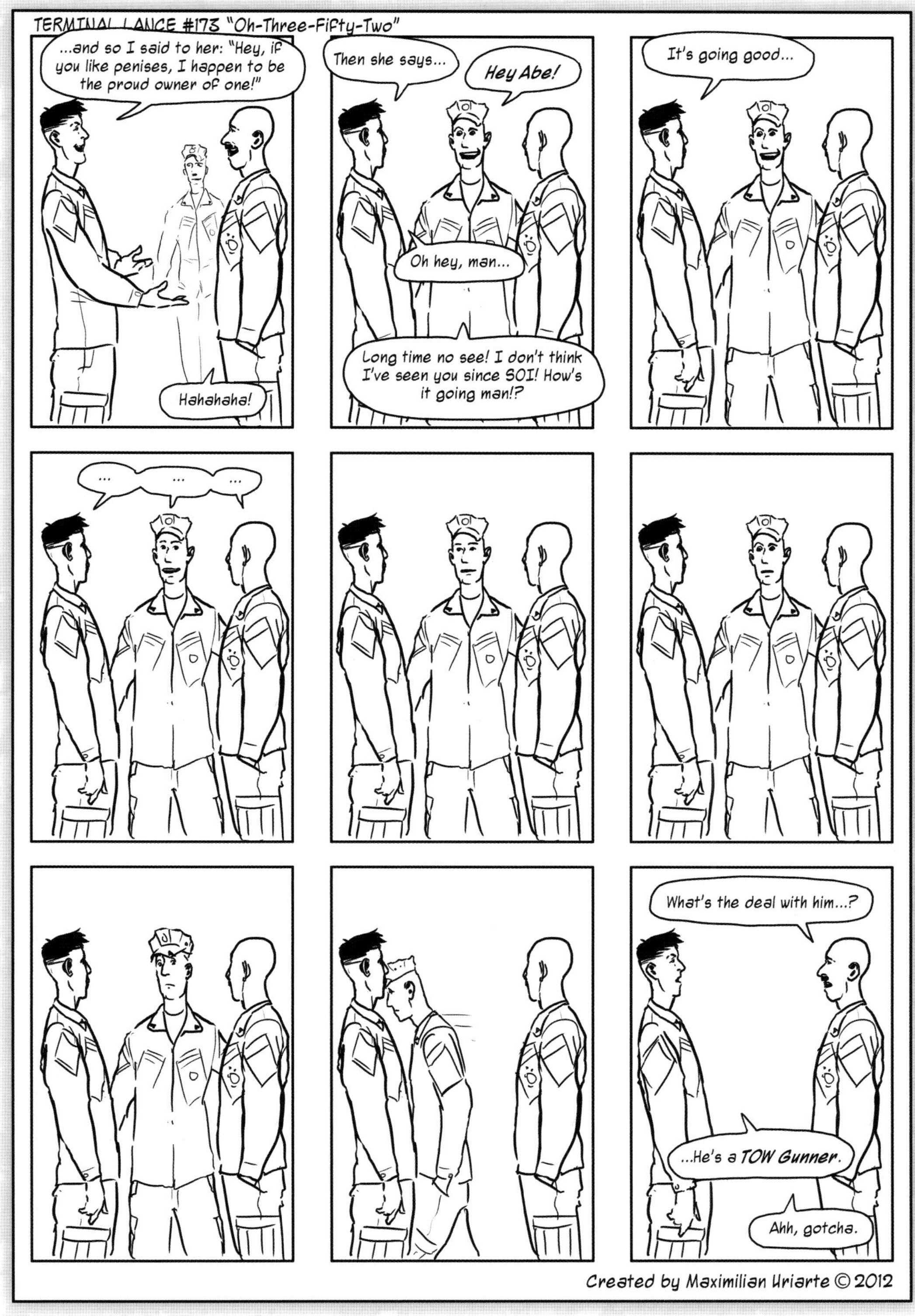
TERMINAL LANCE #173 "Oh-Three-Fifty-Two"
...and so I said to her: "Hey, if you like penises, I happen to be the proud owner of one!"
Hahahaha!
Then she says...
Hey Abe!
Oh hey, man...
Long time no see! I don't think I've seen you since SOI! How's it going man!?
It's going good...
... ...
What's the deal with him...?
...He's a TOW Gunner.
Ahh, gotcha.
Created by Maximilian Uriarte © 2012

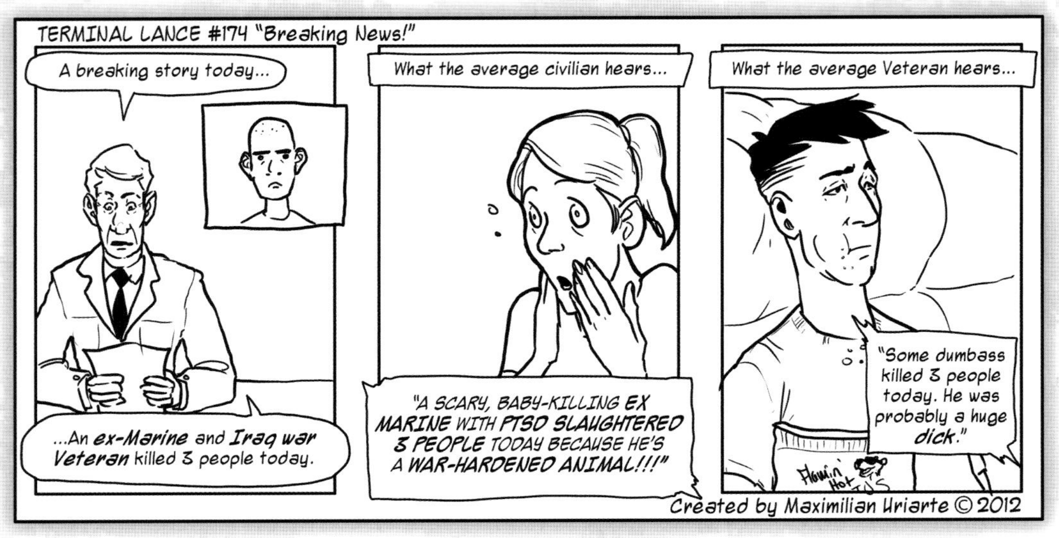
TERMINAL LANCE #174 "Breaking News!"
A breaking story today...
...An ex-Marine and Iraq war Veteran killed 3 people today.
What the average civilian hears...
"A SCARY, BABY-KILLING EX MARINE WITH PTSD SLAUGHTERED 3 PEOPLE TODAY BECAUSE HE'S A WAR-HARDENED ANIMAL!!!"
What the average Veteran hears...
"Some dumbass killed 3 people today. He was probably a huge dick."
Created by Maximilian Uriarte © 2012

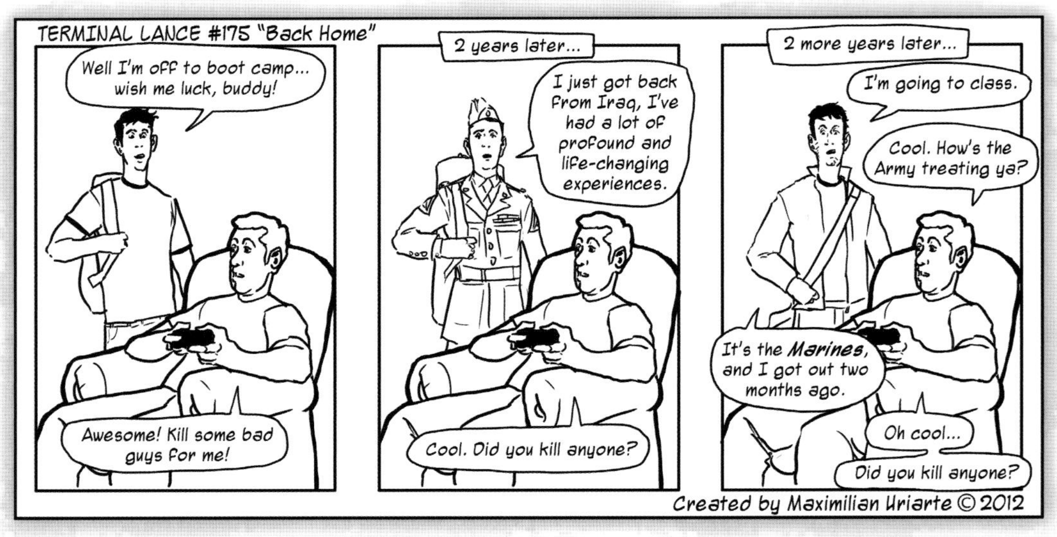
TERMINAL LANCE #175 "Back Home"
Well I'm off to boot camp... wish me luck, buddy!
Awesome! Kill some bad guys for me!
2 years later...
I just got back from Iraq, I've had a lot of profound and life-changing experiences.
Cool. Did you kill anyone?
2 more years later...
I'm going to class.
Cool. How's the Army treating ya?
It's the Marines, and I got out two months ago.
Oh cool...
Did you kill anyone?
Created by Maximilian Uriarte © 2012

175 "Back Home"

If there's one thing that can be said about the experience that is joining the Marines, it's that your friends back home won't understand a damn bit of it. For every life-altering experience you may have had while on duty, your friends back home will largely be the same way they were when you left them.

You'll meet new people, see new things—new worlds even—and they won't even begin to understand it. Going home will never be the same again. And, after being at home awhile, you'll wish you were gone again. The very idea of home becomes a distant memory, because it's never the same as it was. It's not that home has changed—in fact it's remained largely the same.

What's really changed is *you*.

But hey, that's okay. Regular people live regular lives, and you've lived anything but. What's really important is that you try your best not to alienate everyone at home, and if you need help, don't be afraid to seek it. Your friends and family will never understand, but they can try if you give them a chance.

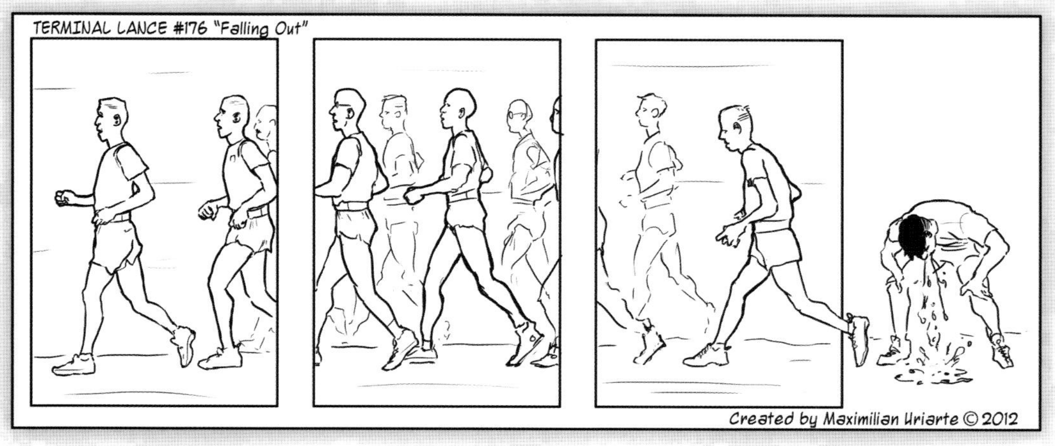
TERMINAL LANCE #176 "Falling Out"
Created by Maximilian Uriarte © 2012

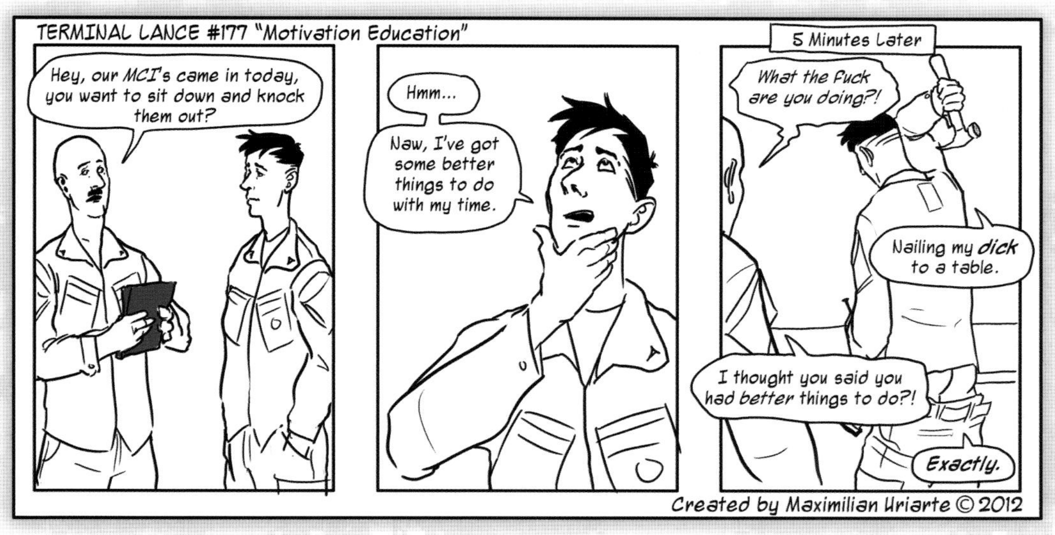
TERMINAL LANCE #177 "Motivation Education"
Hey, our MCI's came in today, you want to sit down and knock them out?
Hmm...
Naw, I've got some better things to do with my time.
5 Minutes Later
What the fuck are you doing?!
Nailing my dick to a table.
I thought you said you had better things to do?!
Exactly.
Created by Maximilian Uriarte © 2012

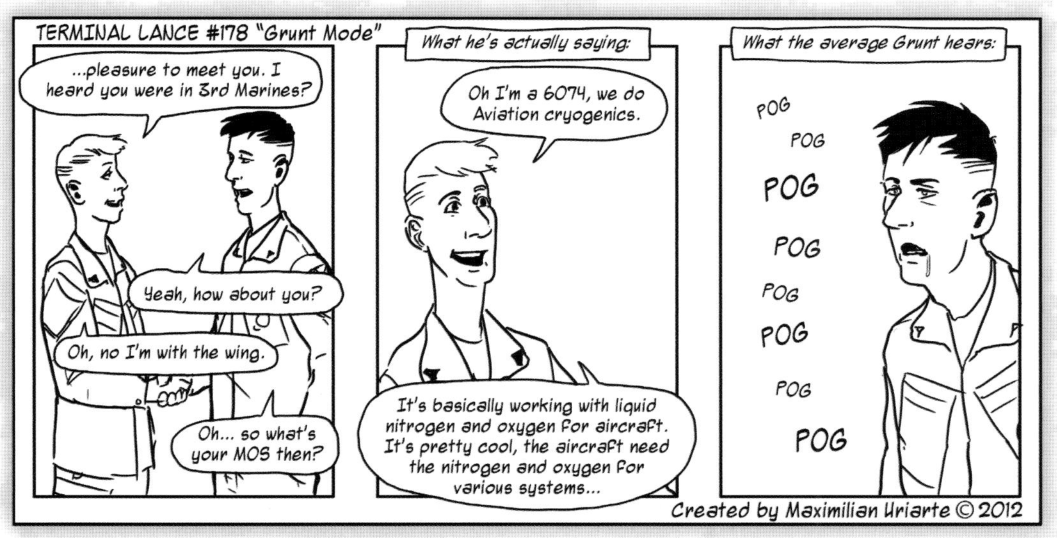
TERMINAL LANCE #178 "Grunt Mode"
...pleasure to meet you. I heard you were in 3rd Marines?
Yeah, how about you?
Oh, no I'm with the wing.
Oh... so what's your MOS then?
What he's actually saying:
Oh I'm a 6074, we do Aviation cryogenics.
It's basically working with liquid nitrogen and oxygen for aircraft. It's pretty cool, the aircraft need the nitrogen and oxygen for various systems...
What the average Grunt hears:
POG
POG
POG
POG
POG
POG
POG
POG
Created by Maximilian Uriarte © 2012

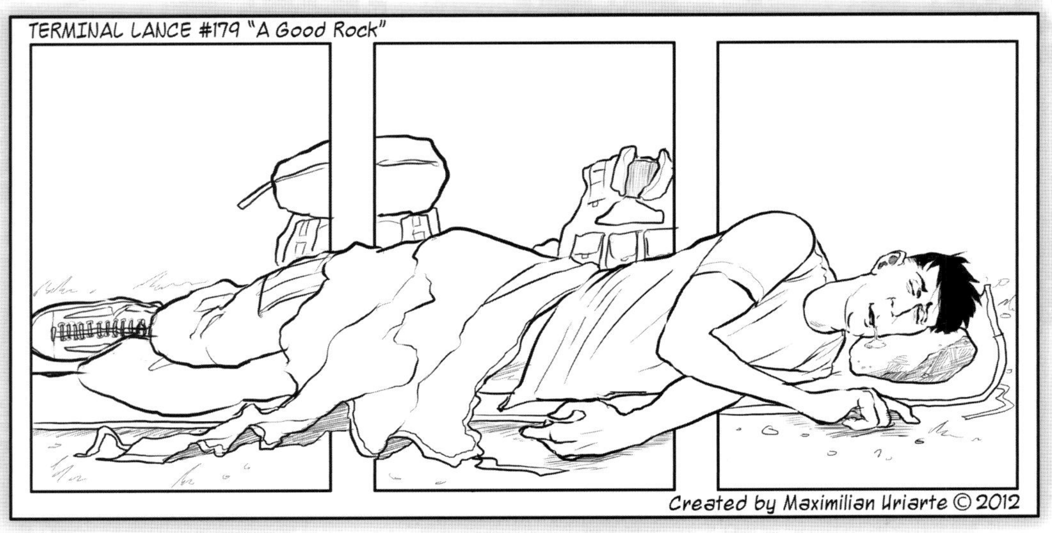
TERMINAL LANCE #179 "A Good Rock"
Created by Maximilian Uriarte © 2012

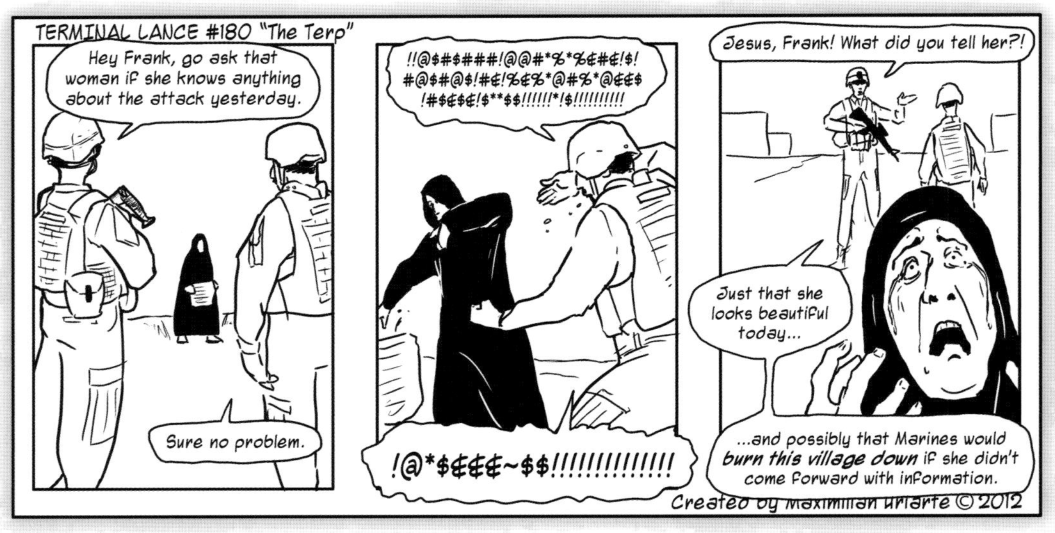
TERMINAL LANCE #180 "The Terp"
Hey Frank, go ask that woman if she knows anything about the attack yesterday.
Sure no problem.
!!@$#$###!@@#*%*%€#€!$! #@$#@$!#€!%€%*@#%*@€€$!#$€$€!$**$$!!!!!!*!$!!!!!!!!!!
!@*$€€€~$$!!!!!!!!!!!!!!
Jesus, Frank! What did you tell her?!
Just that she looks beautiful today...
...and possibly that Marines would **burn this village down** if she didn't come forward with information.
Created by Maximilian Uriarte © 2012

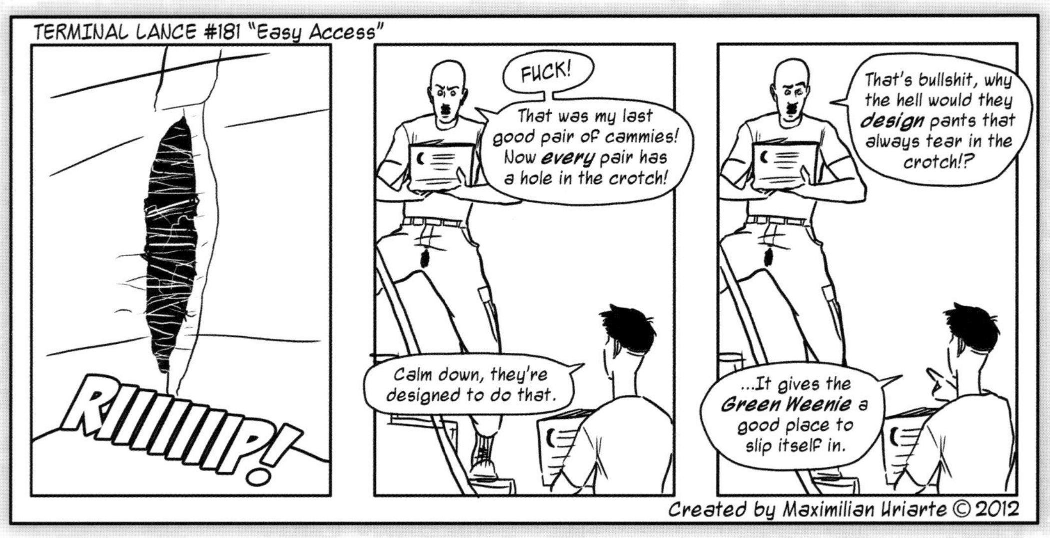
TERMINAL LANCE #181 "Easy Access"
RIIIIIIP!
FUCK!
That was my last good pair of cammies! Now **every** pair has a hole in the crotch!
Calm down, they're designed to do that.
That's bullshit, why the hell would they **design** pants that always tear in the crotch!?
...It gives the **Green Weenie** a good place to slip itself in.
Created by Maximilian Uriarte © 2012

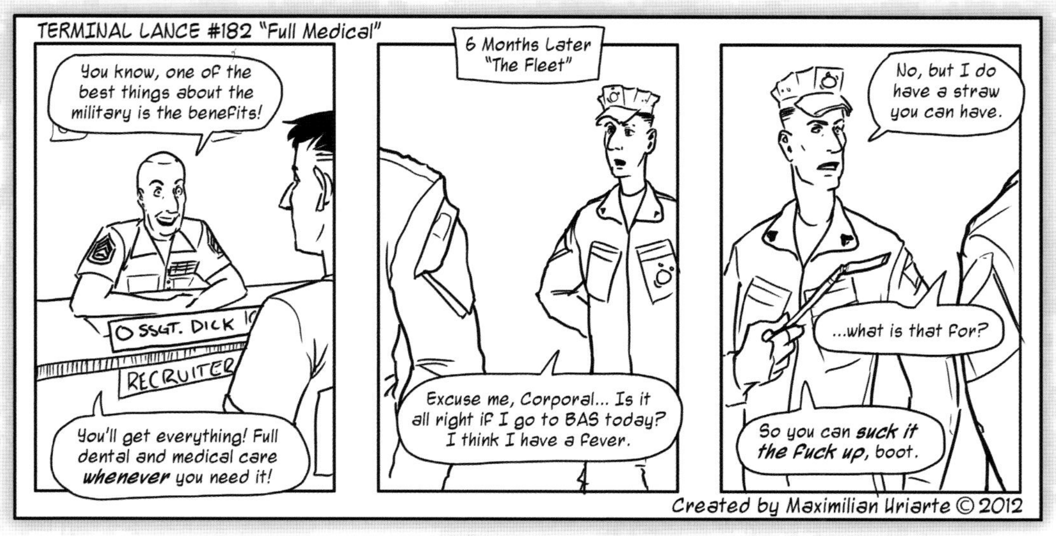
TERMINAL LANCE #182 "Full Medical"
You know, one of the best things about the military is the benefits!
SSGT. DICK
RECRUITER
You'll get everything! Full dental and medical care **whenever** you need it!
6 Months Later "The Fleet"
Excuse me, Corporal... Is it all right if I go to BAS today? I think I have a fever.
No, but I do have a straw you can have.
...what is that for?
So you can **suck it the fuck up**, boot.
Created by Maximilian Uriarte © 2012

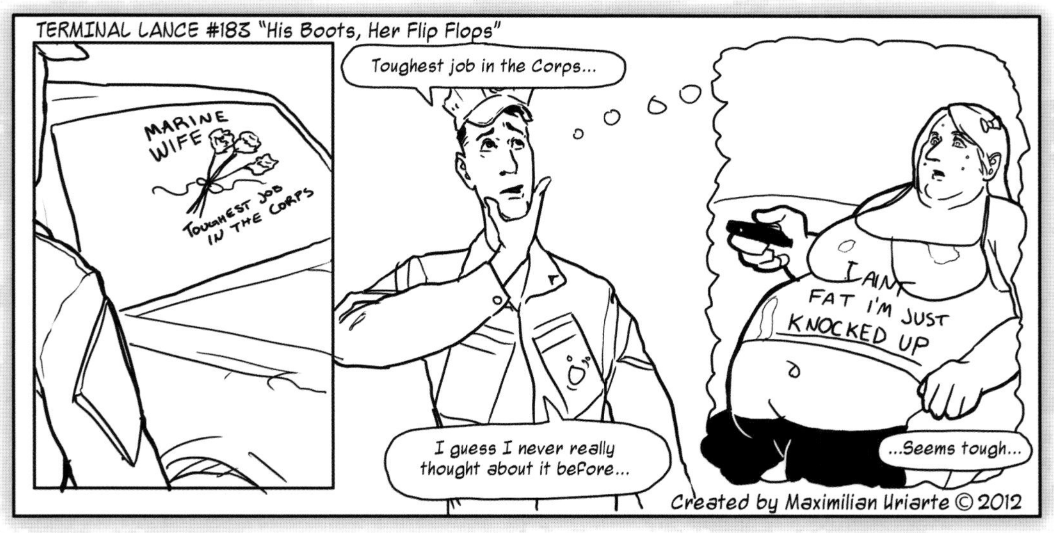
TERMINAL LANCE #183 "His Boots, Her Flip Flops"
MARINE WIFE
TOUGHEST JOB IN THE CORPS
Toughest job in the Corps...
I guess I never really thought about it before...
I AIN'T FAT I'M JUST KNOCKED UP
...Seems tough...
Created by Maximilian Uriarte © 2012

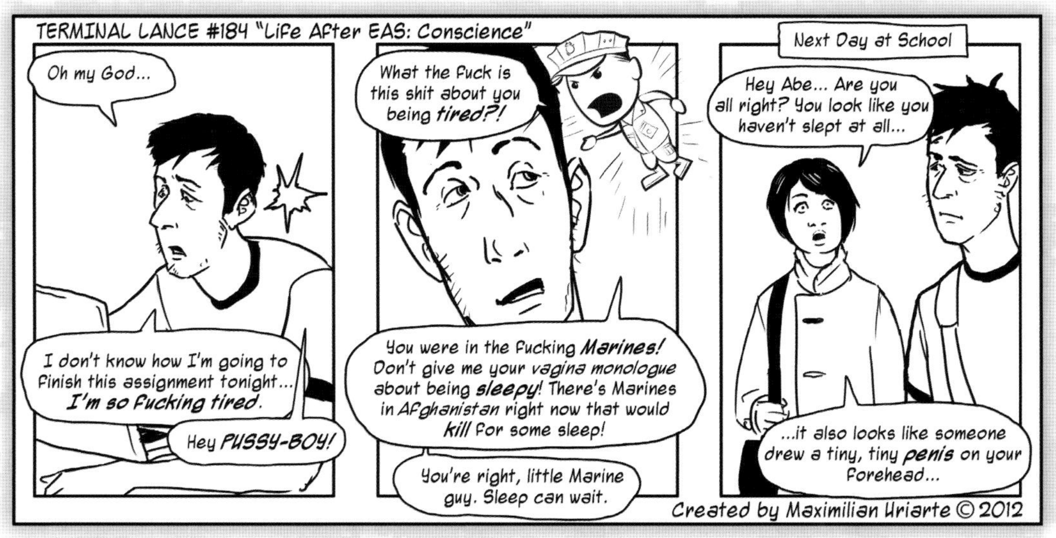
TERMINAL LANCE #184 "Life After EAS: Conscience"
Oh my God...
I don't know how I'm going to finish this assignment tonight... ***I'm so fucking tired***.
Hey ***PUSSY-BOY!***
What the fuck is this shit about you being ***tired?!***
You were in the fucking ***Marines!*** Don't give me your *vagina monologue* about being ***sleepy***! There's Marines in *Afghanistan* right now that would ***kill*** for some sleep!
You're right, little Marine guy. Sleep can wait.
Next Day at School
Hey Abe... Are you all right? You look like you haven't slept at all...
...it also looks like someone drew a tiny, tiny ***penis*** on your forehead...
Created by Maximilian Uriarte © 2012

TERMINAL LANCE #185 "Experience"

Man, you're really good at *Call of Duty*...

It's from the Marine Corps.

Whoa! You mean you use your *military training* in the game?!

That's so badass!

Haha! No. That's ridiculous.

We're on *standby* all the time. Practically all we do is play *Call of Duty*.

Created by Maximilian Uriarte © 2012

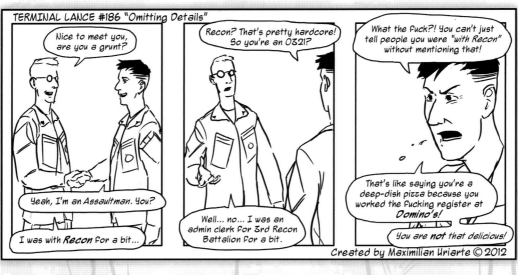

TERMINAL LANCE #186 "Omitting Details"

Nice to meet you, are you a grunt?

Yeah, I'm an Assaultman. You?

I was with *Recon* for a bit...

Recon? That's pretty hardcore! So you're an 0321?

Well... no... I was an admin clerk for 3rd Recon Battalion for a bit.

What the Fuck?! You can't just tell people you were "with Recon" without mentioning that!

That's like saying you're a deep-dish pizza because you worked the Fucking register at *Domino's!*

You are *not* that delicious!

Created by Maximilian Uriarte © 2012

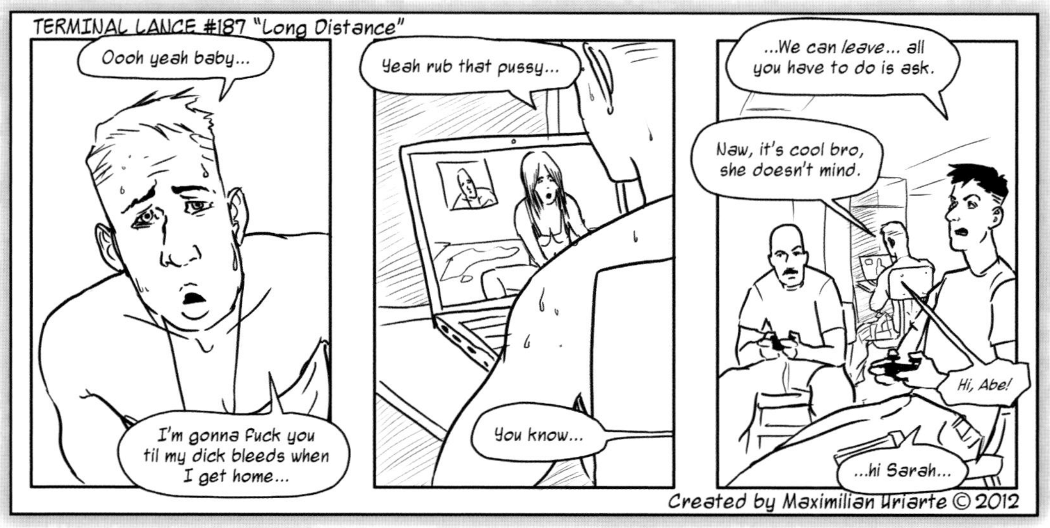
TERMINAL LANCE #187 "Long Distance"
Oooh yeah baby...
I'm gonna fuck you til my dick bleeds when I get home...
Yeah rub that pussy...
You know...
...We can leave... all you have to do is ask.
Naw, it's cool bro, she doesn't mind.
Hi, Abe!
...hi Sarah...
Created by Maximilian Uriarte © 2012

187 "Long Distance"

The Marine lifestyle is certainly unstable. As a result, the United States Marine is no stranger to the long-distance relationship. Most Marines probably start off in one, with some girl from "back home" that writes to them in boot camp. Around 80 percent of those women will leave them while they're in boot camp; the other 20 percent will either cheat on them or leave them later (or both). Regardless, the long-distance Skype webcam sex session is also no stranger to the Marine Corps.

Skype has done wonderful things for the world, especially the military. One of those wonderful things is the power to flog your Cobra Commander in front of your significant other from thousands of miles away.

Even with the advent of Skype, these sorts of relationships are always hard. Most couples don't make it, though some do. I personally dealt with the long-distance relationship as much as anyone else, as I was with my wife since before I enlisted. It will always be hard, and it never gets any easier. Skype, cell phones, and the internet close the gap quite a bit, but it will be entirely up to you to make sure that your relationship stays alive.

Lastly, if you find that you need to spank your wank with your girlfriend or otherwise, at least have the common courtesy to do it in private. As well . . . don't do it on someone else's computer. That's gross.

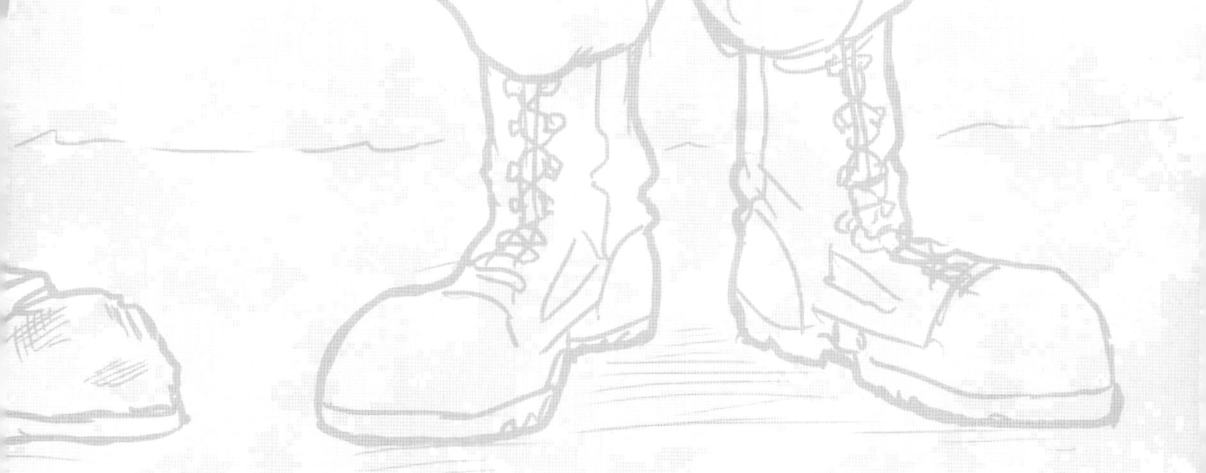

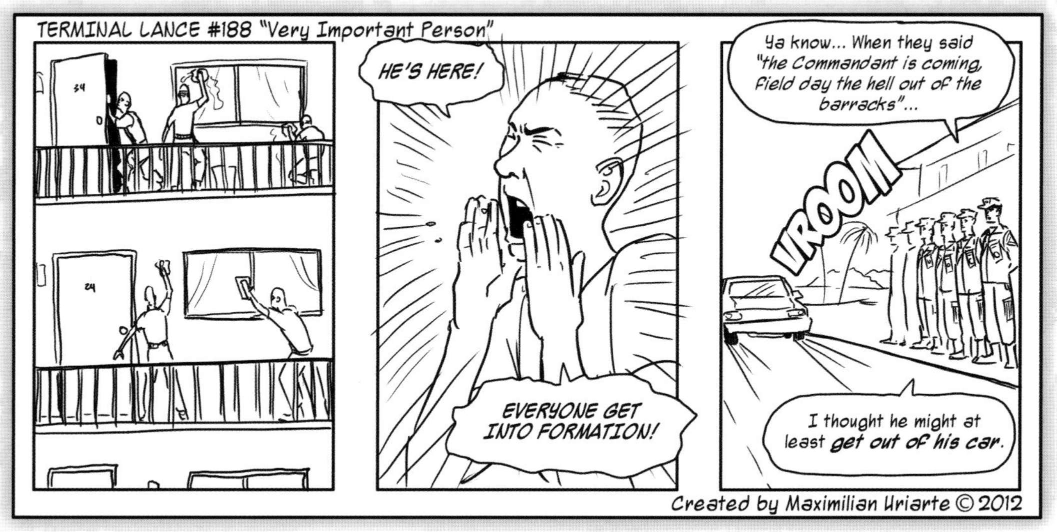
TERMINAL LANCE #188 "Very Important Person"
HE'S HERE!
EVERYONE GET INTO FORMATION!
Ya know... When they said "the Commandant is coming, Field day the hell out of the barracks"...
VROOM
I thought he might at least get out of his car.
Created by Maximilian Uriarte © 2012

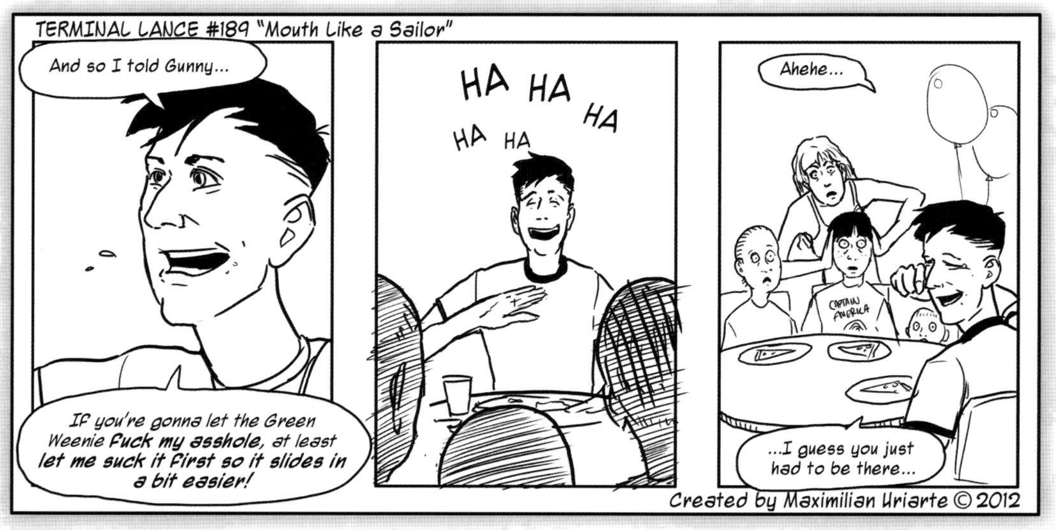
TERMINAL LANCE #189 "Mouth Like a Sailor"
And so I told Gunny...
If you're gonna let the Green Weenie fuck my asshole, at least let me suck it first so it slides in a bit easier!
HA HA HA HA HA
Ahehe...
CAPTAIN AMERICA
...I guess you just had to be there...
Created by Maximilian Uriarte © 2012

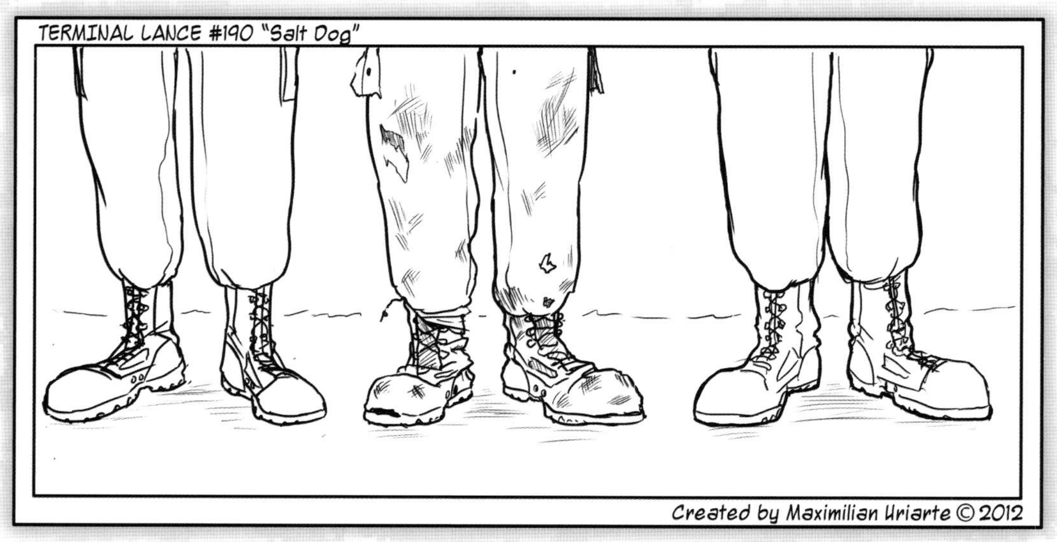
TERMINAL LANCE #190 "Salt Dog"
Created by Maximilian Uriarte © 2012

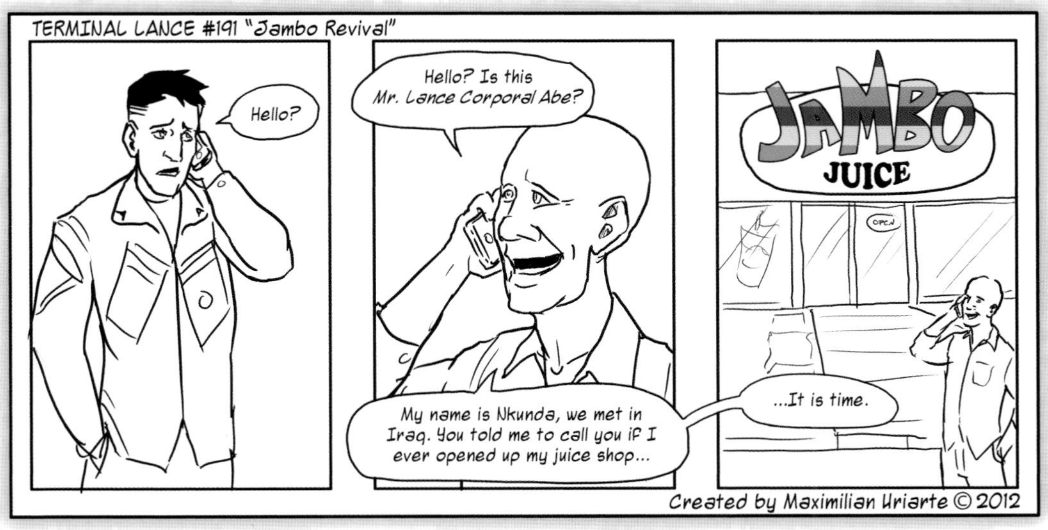
TERMINAL LANCE #191 "Jambo Revival"
Hello?
Hello? Is this Mr. Lance Corporal Abe?
My name is Nkunda, we met in Iraq. You told me to call you if I ever opened up my juice shop...
JAMBO JUICE
OPEN
...It is time.
Created by Maximilian Uriarte © 2012

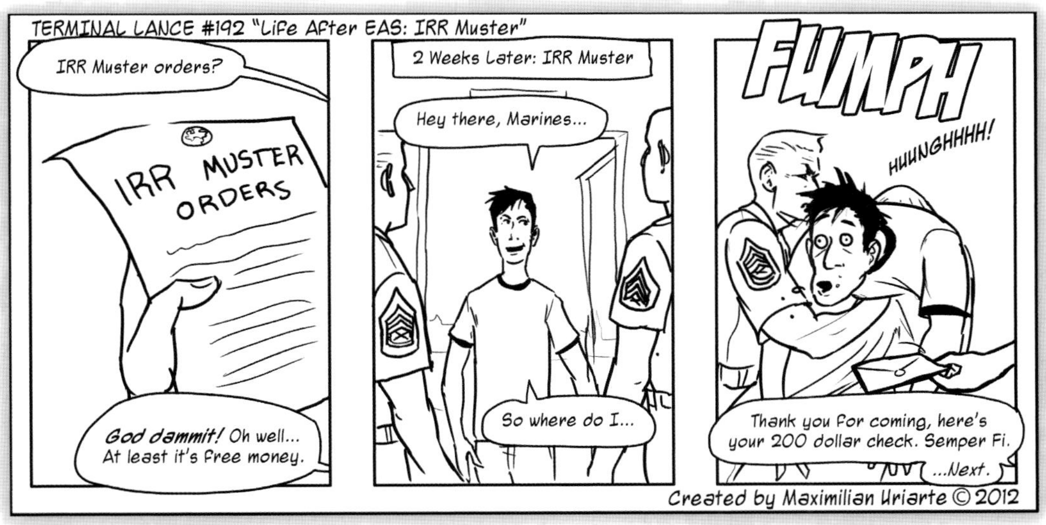
TERMINAL LANCE #192 "Life After EAS: IRR Muster"
IRR Muster orders?
IRR MUSTER ORDERS
God dammit! Oh well... At least it's free money.
2 Weeks Later: IRR Muster
Hey there, Marines...
So where do I...
FUMPH
HUUNGHHHH!
Thank you for coming, here's your 200 dollar check. Semper Fi.
...Next.
Created by Maximilian Uriarte © 2012

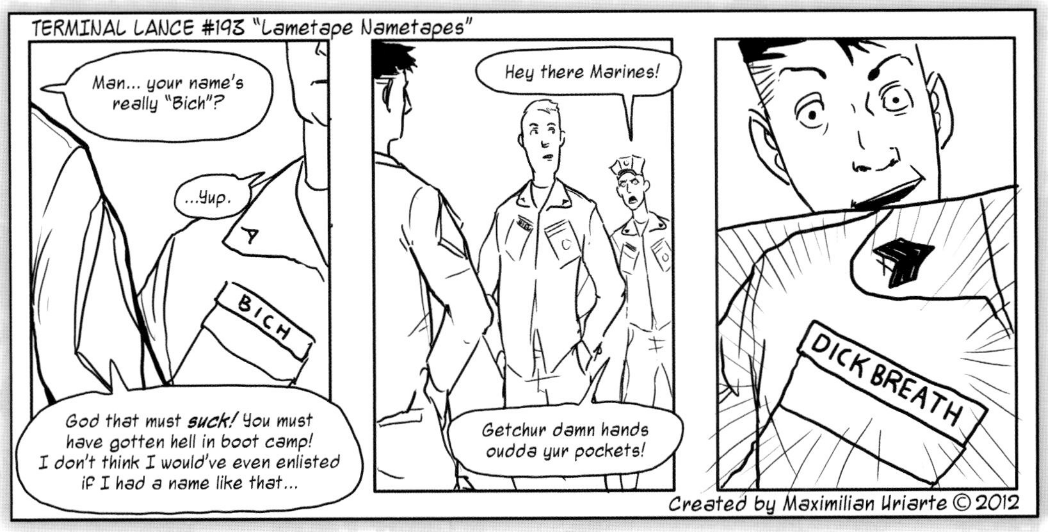
TERMINAL LANCE #193 "Lametape Nametapes"
Man... your name's really "Bich"?
...Yup.
BICH
God that must suck! You must have gotten hell in boot camp! I don't think I would've even enlisted if I had a name like that...
Hey there Marines!
Getchur damn hands oudda yur pockets!
DICK BREATH
Created by Maximilian Uriarte © 2012

TERMINAL LANCE #194 "Boot Camp: The Boot Camp Barber"

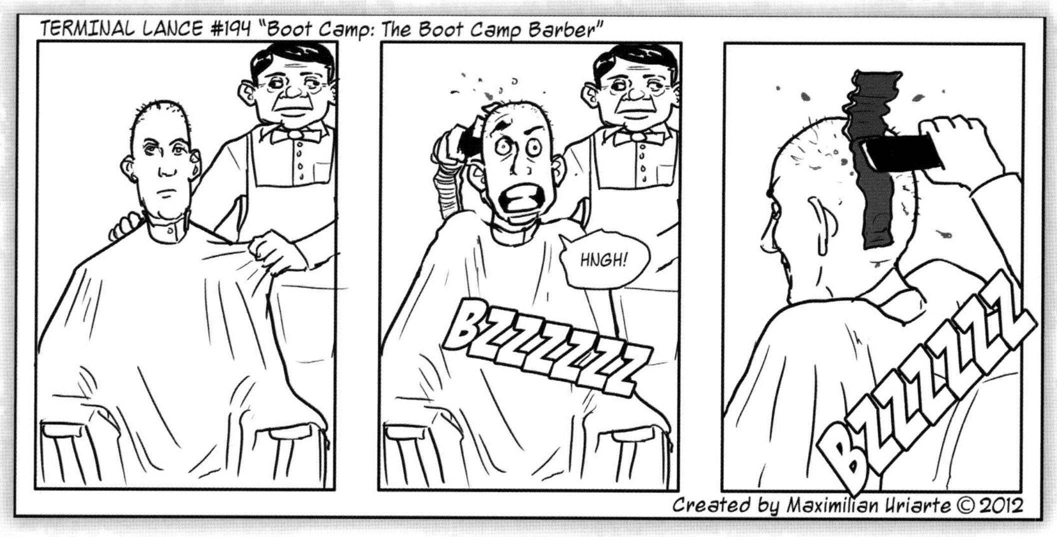
HNGH!
BZZZZZZZ
BZZZZZZZ
Created by Maximilian Uriarte © 2012

TERMINAL LANCE #195 "The Mr. E Mystery 4"

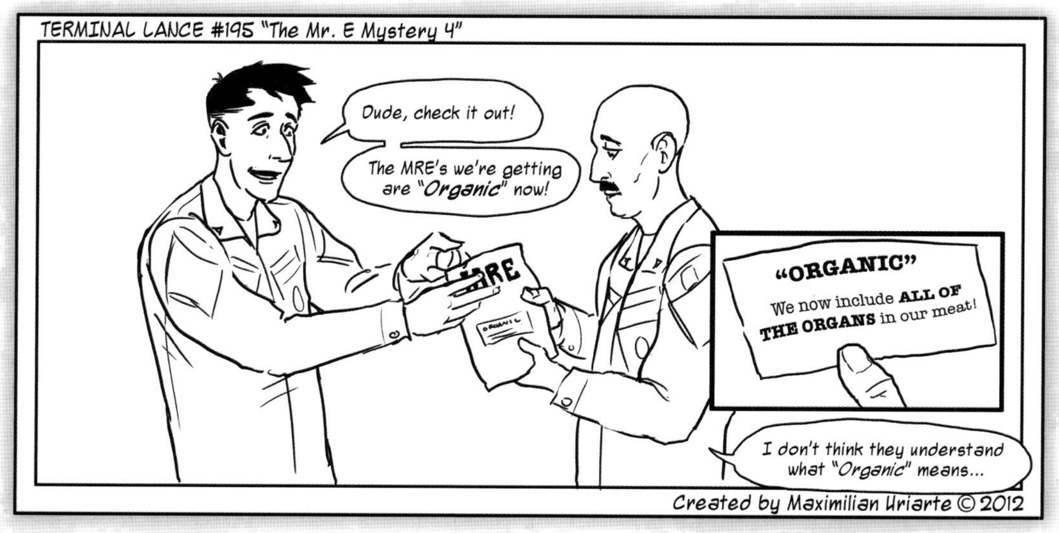
Dude, check it out!
The MRE's we're getting are "Organic" now!
MRE
"ORGANIC"
We now include ALL OF THE ORGANS in our meat!
I don't think they understand what "Organic" means...
Created by Maximilian Uriarte © 2012

TERMINAL LANCE #196 "Special Delivery"

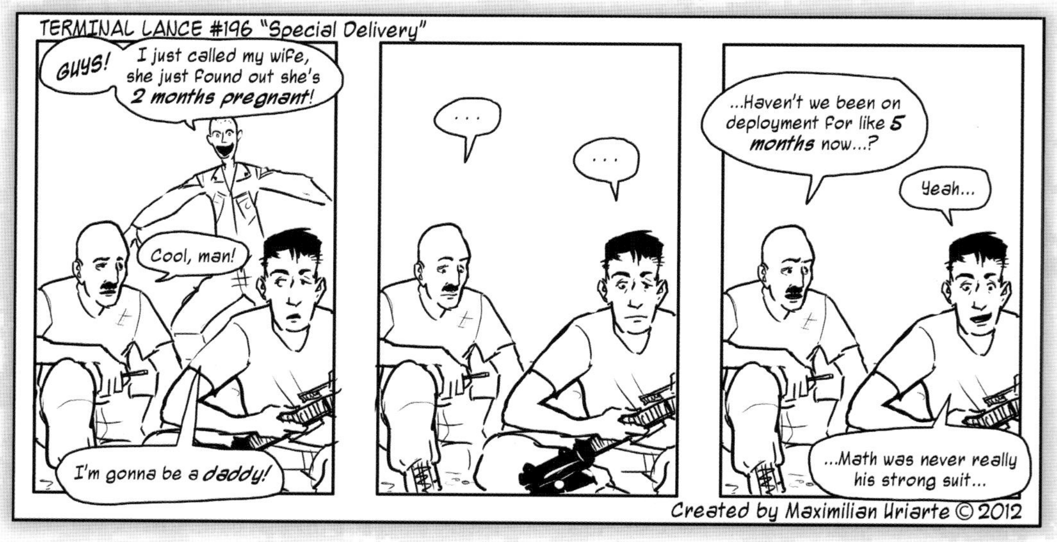
GUYS!
I just called my wife, she just found out she's 2 months pregnant!
Cool, man!
I'm gonna be a daddy!
...
...
...Haven't we been on deployment for like 5 months now...?
Yeah...
...Math was never really his strong suit...
Created by Maximilian Uriarte © 2012

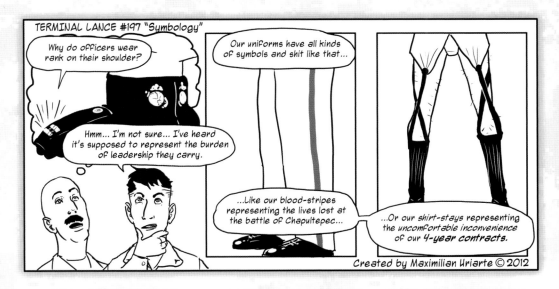

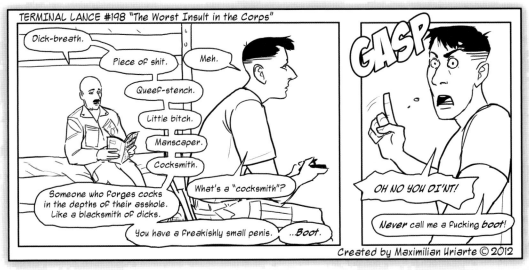

TERMINAL LANCE #197 "Symbology"
Why do officers wear rank on their shoulder?
Hmm... I'm not sure... I've heard it's supposed to represent the burden of leadership they carry.
Our uniforms have all kinds of symbols and shit like that...
...Like our blood-stripes representing the lives lost at the battle of Chapultepec...
...Or our shirt-stays representing the uncomfortable inconvenience of our 4-year contracts.
Created by Maximilian Uriarte © 2012

TERMINAL LANCE #198 "The Worst Insult in the Corps"
Dick-breath.
Piece of shit.
Meh.
Queef-stench.
Little bitch.
Manscaper.
Cocksmith.
What's a "cocksmith"?
Someone who forges cocks in the depths of their asshole. Like a blacksmith of dicks.
You have a freakishly small penis.
...Boot.
GASP
OH NO YOU DI'NT!
Never call me a fucking boot!
Created by Maximilian Uriarte © 2012

198 "The Worst Insult in the Corps"

If there's one word that can get even the surliest of Marines riled up, it's "boot." There is no greater insult in the Corps than to be labeled a boot. Of course, the average boot Marine isn't going to complain much about being called a boot (well, I mean, they do, but no one cares), but that's beside the point.

Once you've returned home from your first (or second) combat deployment, "boot" status is generally removed. The actual definition of a "boot" is somewhat sketchy, and changes depending on who you ask. For some, it's those that don't have Combat Action Ribbons. For others, it's simply those that have never been on a deployment of any kind. This, of course, is in infantry terms. When you start getting into the POG world it becomes a little stranger, since the majority of them don't go on regular deployment cycles. For most grunts though, most POG's are boots automatically, which of course isn't always true.

The "boot" label is all about experience and pride—as are most things in the Marine Corps. To be called a boot is a direct punch at the grunt's pride, and if you do so without caution it could end very poorly.

So if you're looking for fighting words, look no further.

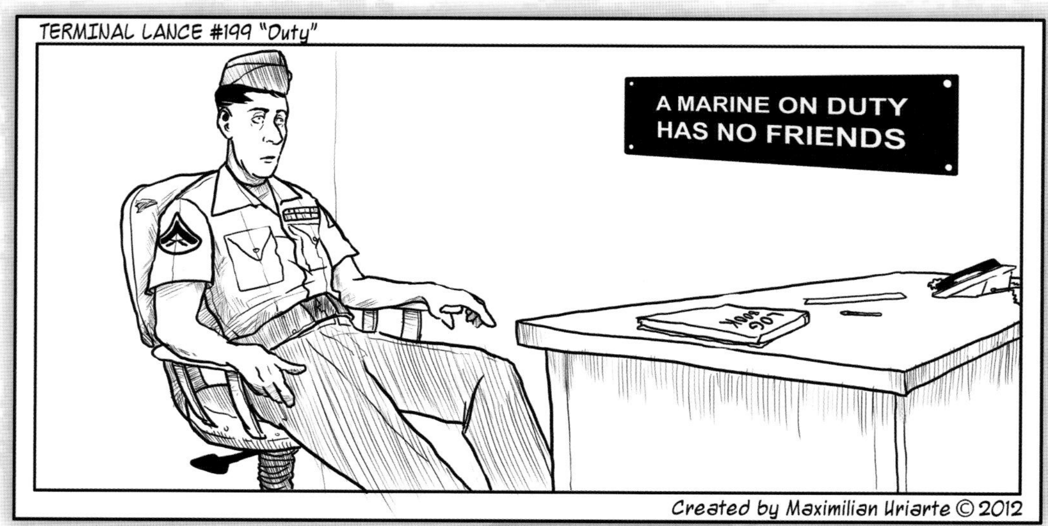
TERMINAL LANCE #199 "Duty"
A MARINE ON DUTY
HAS NO FRIENDS
LOG BOOK
Created by Maximilian Uriarte © 2012

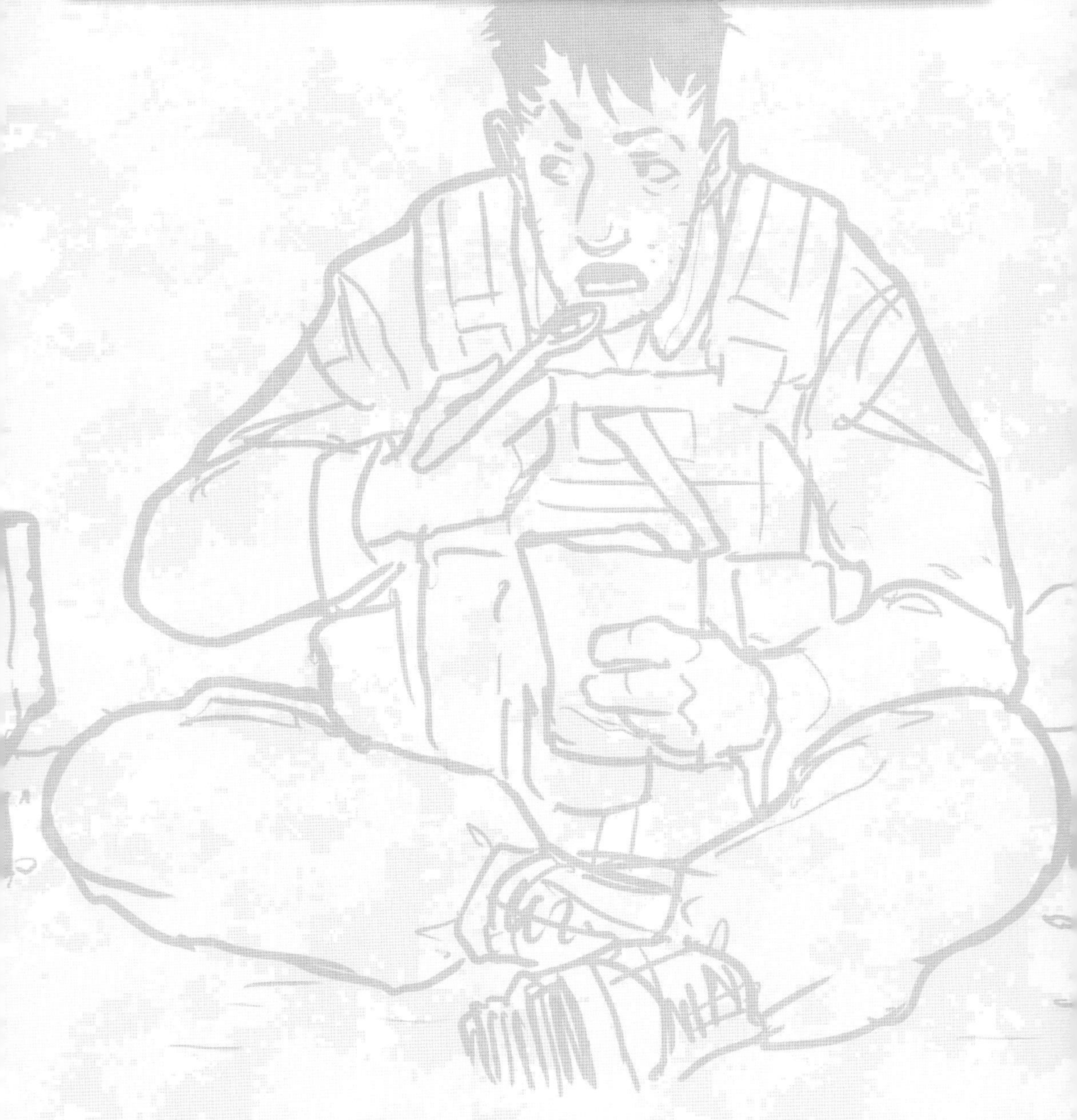

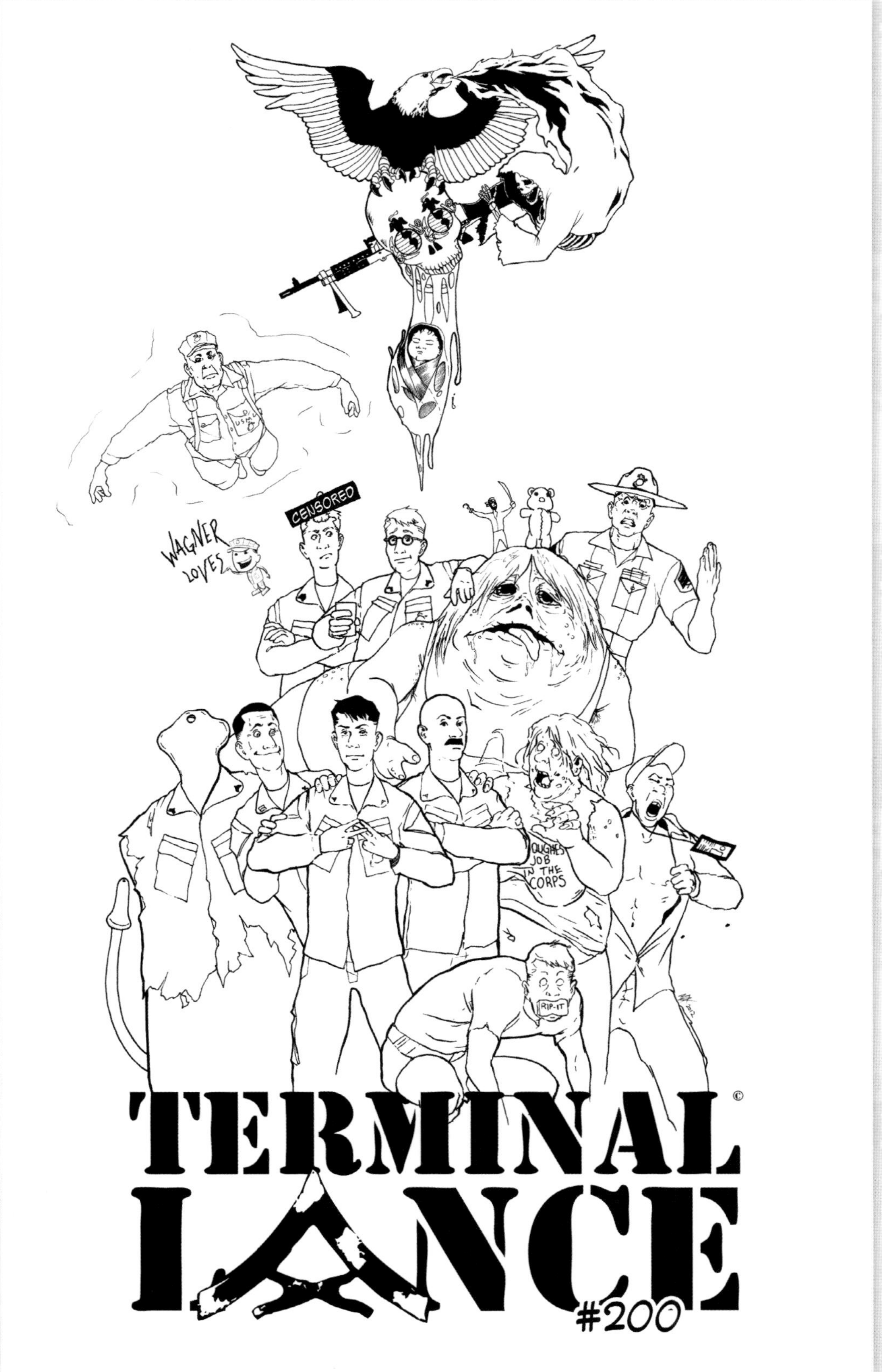
CENSORED
WAGNER LOVES
TOUGHEST JOB IN THE CORPS
RIP-IT
TERMINAL LANCE©
#200

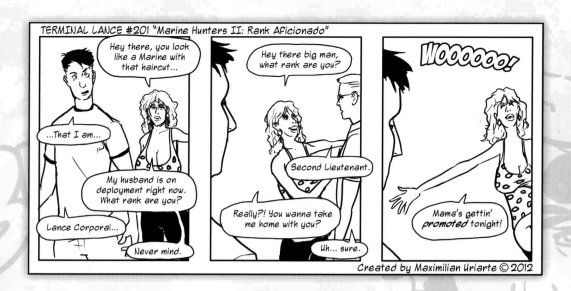

TERMINAL LANCE #201 "Marine Hunters II: Rank Aficionado"

Hey there, you look like a Marine with that haircut...
...That I am...
My husband is on deployment right now. What rank are you?
Lance Corporal...
Never mind.
Hey there big man, what rank are you?
Second Lieutenant.
Really?! You wanna take me home with you?
Uh... sure.
WOOOOOO!
Mama's gettin' *promoted* tonight!

Created by Maximilian Uriarte © 2012

TERMINAL LANCE #202 "Old Jokes"

Hey I heard this earlier...
What's the difference between a PFC and a Second Lieutenant?
One is a total **asshole**...?
That's not how it...
...Yeah that works.

Created by Maximilian Uriarte © 2012

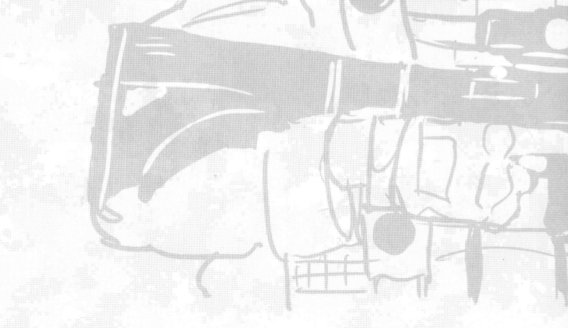

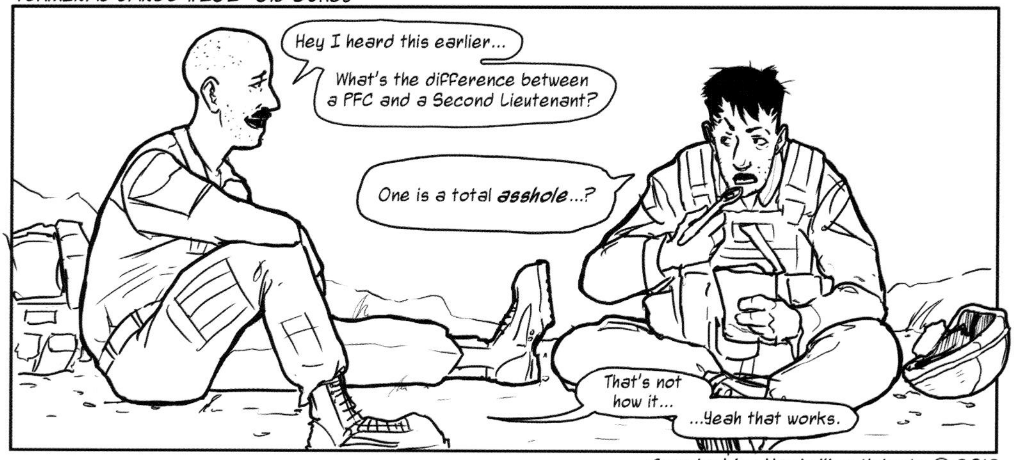

TERMINAL LANCE #203 "That One Guy"
Holy shit, Cone!
You just ran a 14-minute 3-mile!
That has to be a battalion record! What's your secret?
I'm drunk as fuck, Staff Sergeant!
Created by Maximilian Uriarte © 2012

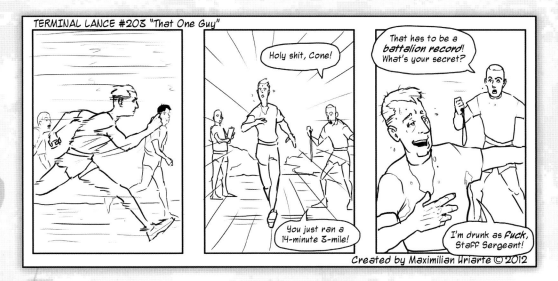

203 "That One Guy"

There's always that one guy.

He's the one that blows past everyone on the PFT (Physical Fitness Test), and does his twenty pull-ups and hundred crunches all while absolutely reeking of his good friend Jack Daniel's. He's that one guy you can always expect to be hammered and somehow not only perform his job, but do it probably better than most people. Cone is that guy. For Cone, operating on alcohol is operating on a normal level.

The seriousness of alcoholism aside, every platoon has that one guy. Not necessarily the platoon alcoholic, but the guy that's always lovably drunk at the best moments.

Cone is a real person, and he's awesome. One of my favorite memories of him was one of many nights he got really hammered and fell off the second story catwalk at Mackie Hall in Hawaii. He got up, without a scratch on him, and came back up the stairs like it never even happened and continued to drink and party. I'm fairly convinced that he's immortal.

Max note 2017: In 2014, Tyler Cone, my friend and an Iraq and Afghanistan veteran, succumbed to his demons and ended his own life. I attended his funeral in his small hometown in Nebraska. He was active duty at the time and stationed at Camp Lejeune with 3/6.

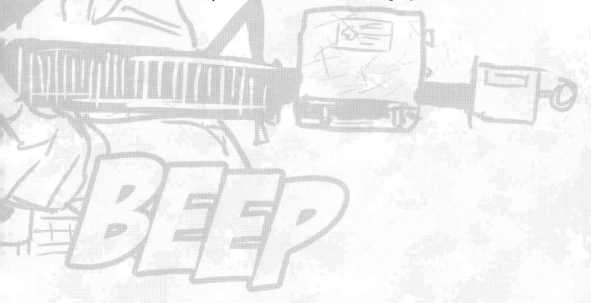

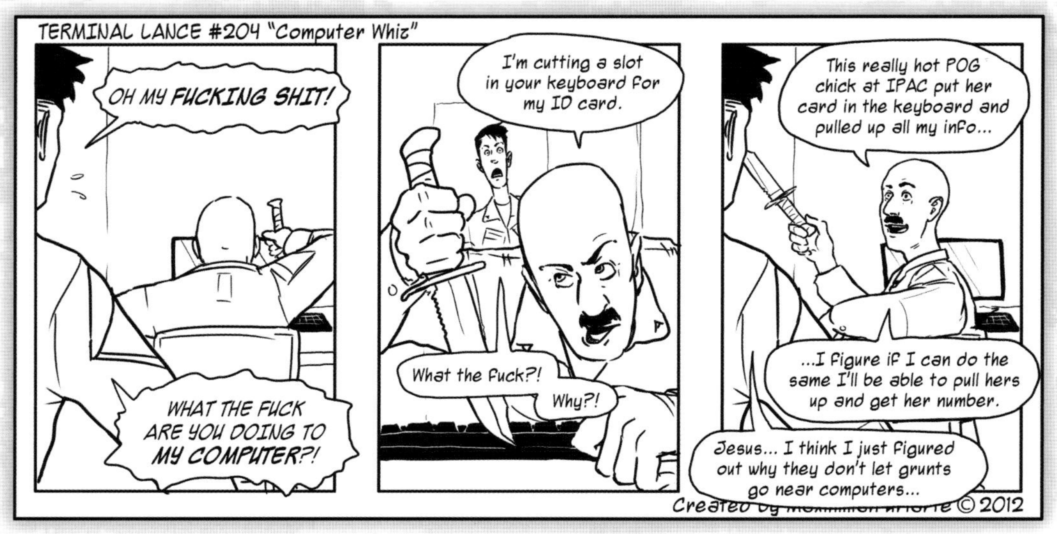
TERMINAL LANCE #204 "Computer Whiz"
OH MY FUCKING SHIT!
WHAT THE FUCK ARE YOU DOING TO MY COMPUTER?!
I'm cutting a slot in your keyboard for my ID card.
What the fuck?!
Why?!
This really hot POG chick at IPAC put her card in the keyboard and pulled up all my info...
...I figure if I can do the same I'll be able to pull hers up and get her number.
Jesus... I think I just figured out why they don't let grunts go near computers...
Created by Maximilian Uriarte © 2012

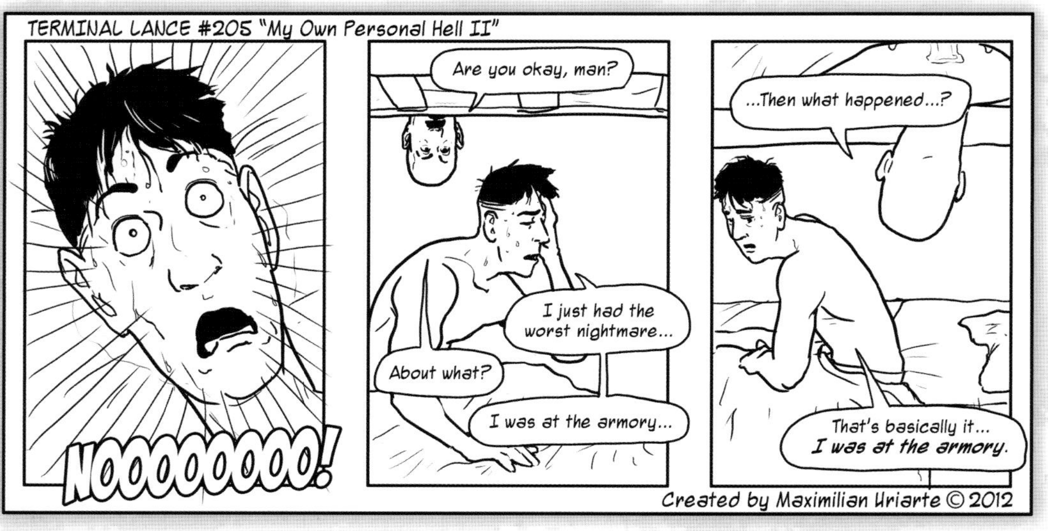
TERMINAL LANCE #205 "My Own Personal Hell II"
NOOOOOOOO!
Are you okay, man?
I just had the worst nightmare...
About what?
I was at the armory...
...Then what happened...?
That's basically it... I was at the armory.
Created by Maximilian Uriarte © 2012

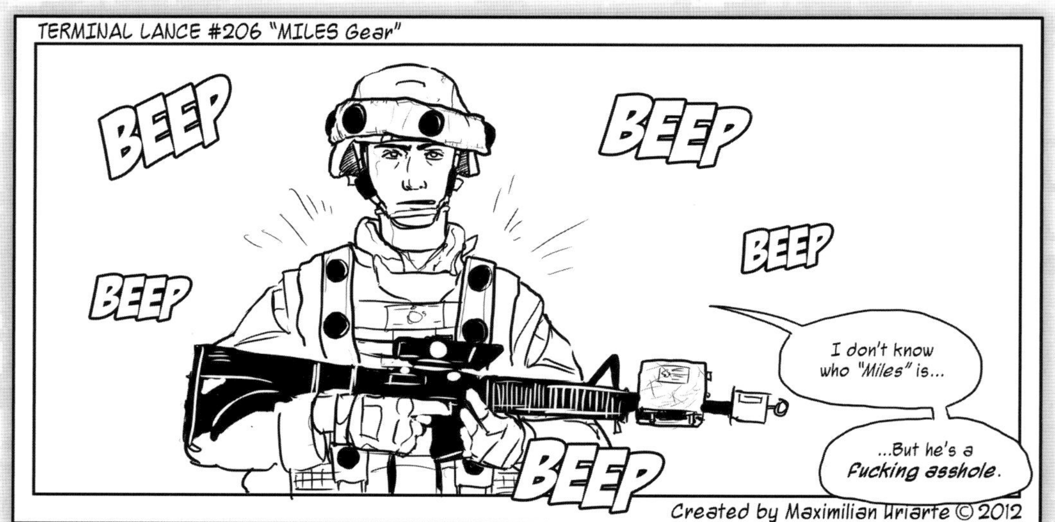
TERMINAL LANCE #206 "MILES Gear"
BEEP
BEEP
BEEP
BEEP
BEEP
I don't know who "Miles" is...
...But he's a fucking asshole.
Created by Maximilian Uriarte © 2012

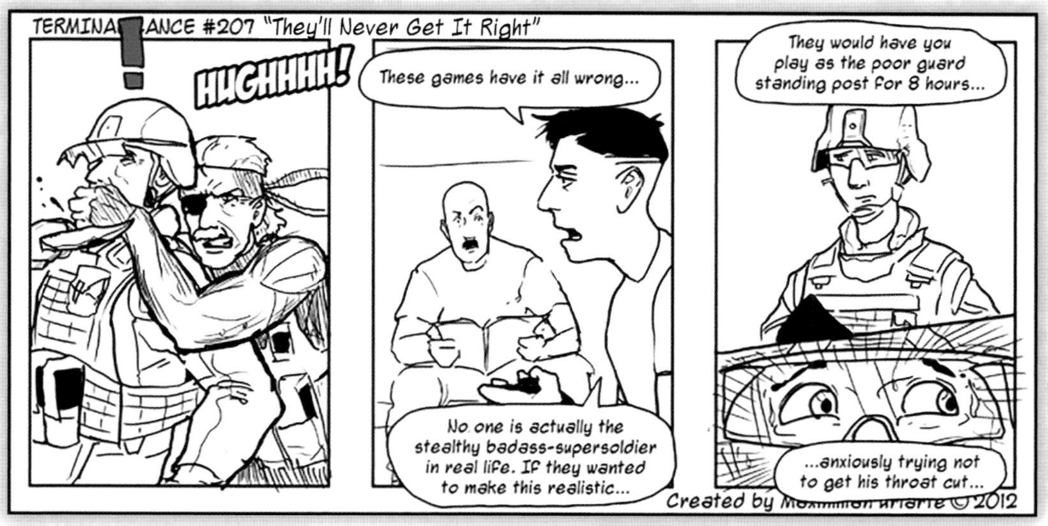
TERMINAL LANCE #207 "They'll Never Get It Right"
HUGHHHH!
These games have it all wrong...
No one is actually the stealthy badass-supersoldier in real life. If they wanted to make this realistic...
They would have you play as the poor guard standing post for 8 hours...
...anxiously trying not to get his throat cut...
Created by Maximilian Uriarte © 2012

207 "They'll Never Get It Right"

It's hard not to talk about video games in relation to the Marine Corps. For starters, I'm a huge nerd, and there's so many games about the military that it's hard to ignore. I believe I've mentioned before that when I enlisted there was some image of me being Solid Snake somewhere in the depths of my imagination. Everyone has that daydream: They're the lone wolf badass they play in all the games, the one that takes on an entire enemy encampment by themselves and saves the lives of thousands.

I was at CAX before my first deployment when it hit me, standing fire-watch in the open and guarding a stack of SMAW rockets for use on the range the next day. I suddenly realized I certainly wasn't Solid Snake in this scenario. Instead, I was the idiot guard standing post, walking in a repeated square pattern.

We all want to think we're the badass in the bandanna, but we never are. We're the fodder that he has to go through on his way to the objective.

We are the grunts.

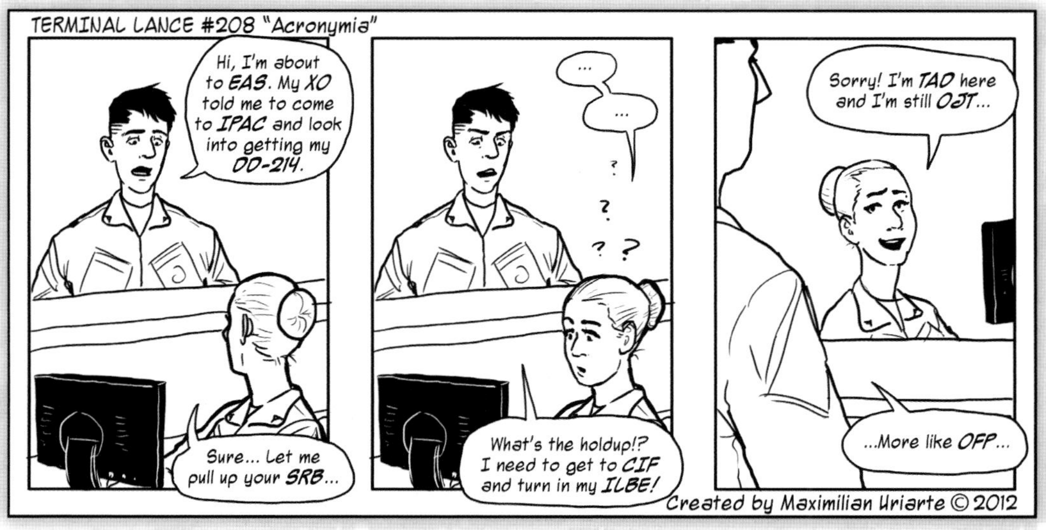
TERMINAL LANCE #208 "Acronymia"
Hi, I'm about to EAS. My XO told me to come to IPAC and look into getting my DD-214.
Sure... Let me pull up your SRB...
...
...
?
?
? ?
What's the holdup!? I need to get to CIF and turn in my ILBE!
Sorry! I'm TAD here and I'm still OJT...
...More like OFP...
Created by Maximilian Uriarte © 2012

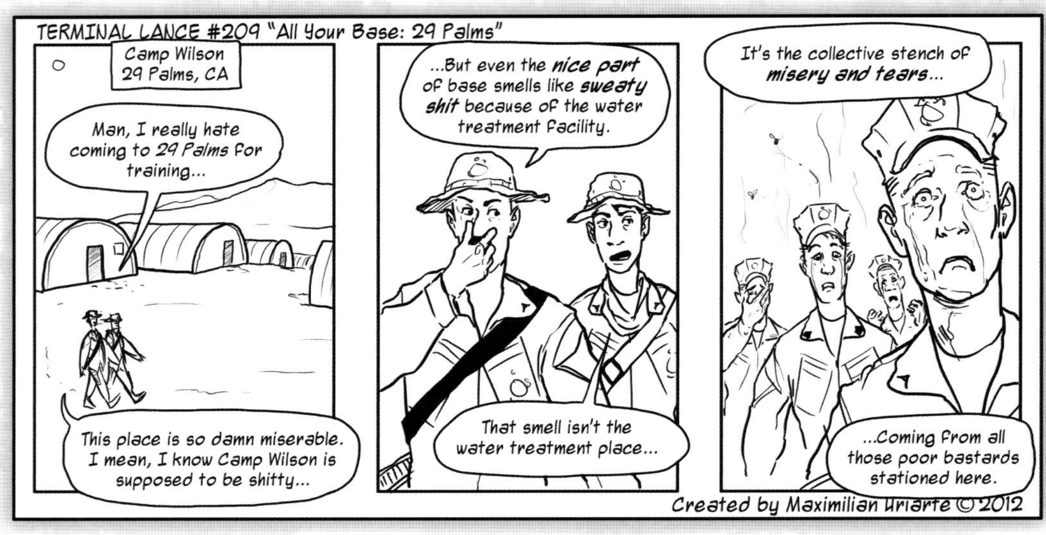
TERMINAL LANCE #209 "All Your Base: 29 Palms"
Camp Wilson 29 Palms, CA
Man, I really hate coming to 29 Palms for training...
This place is so damn miserable. I mean, I know Camp Wilson is supposed to be shitty...
...But even the **nice part** of base smells like **sweaty shit** because of the water treatment facility.
That smell isn't the water treatment place...
It's the collective stench of **misery and tears**...
...Coming from all those poor bastards stationed here.
Created by Maximilian Uriarte © 2012

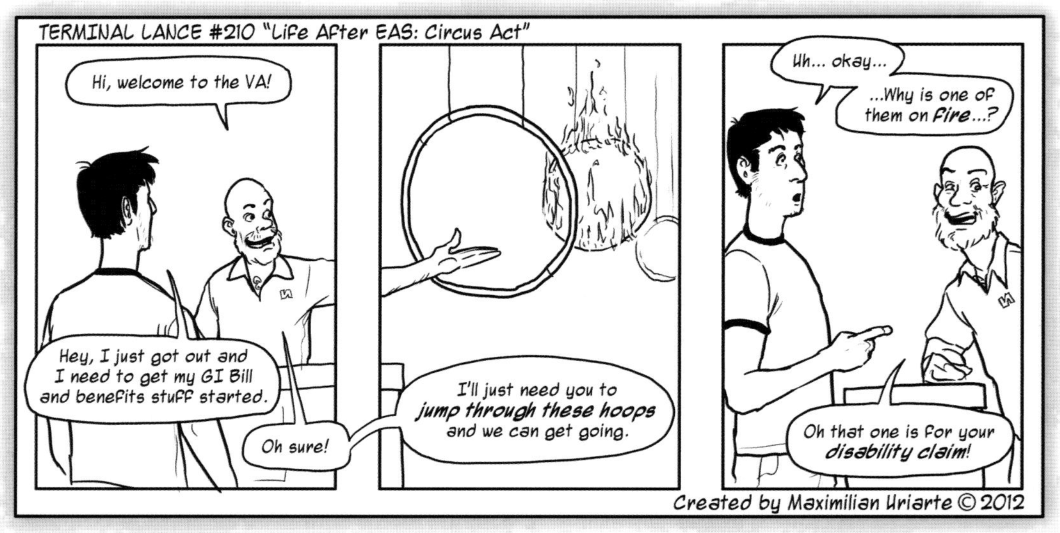
TERMINAL LANCE #210 "Life After EAS: Circus Act"
Hi, welcome to the VA!
Hey, I just got out and I need to get my GI Bill and benefits stuff started.
Oh sure!
I'll just need you to **jump through these hoops** and we can get going.
Uh... okay...
...Why is one of them on **fire**...?
Oh that one is for your **disability claim**!
Created by Maximilian Uriarte © 2012

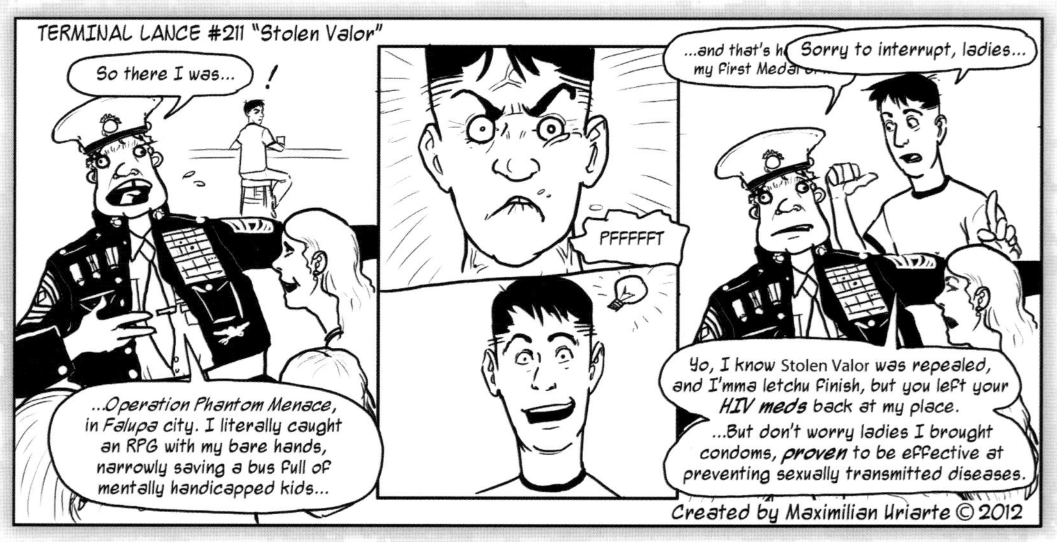
TERMINAL LANCE #211 "Stolen Valor"
So there I was...
!
...Operation Phantom Menace, in Falupa city. I literally caught an RPG with my bare hands, narrowly saving a bus full of mentally handicapped kids...
PFFFFFT
Sorry to interrupt, ladies...
Yo, I know Stolen Valor was repealed, and I'mma letchu finish, but you left your **HIV meds** back at my place.
...But don't worry ladies I brought condoms, **proven** to be effective at preventing sexually transmitted diseases.
Created by Maximilian Uriarte © 2012

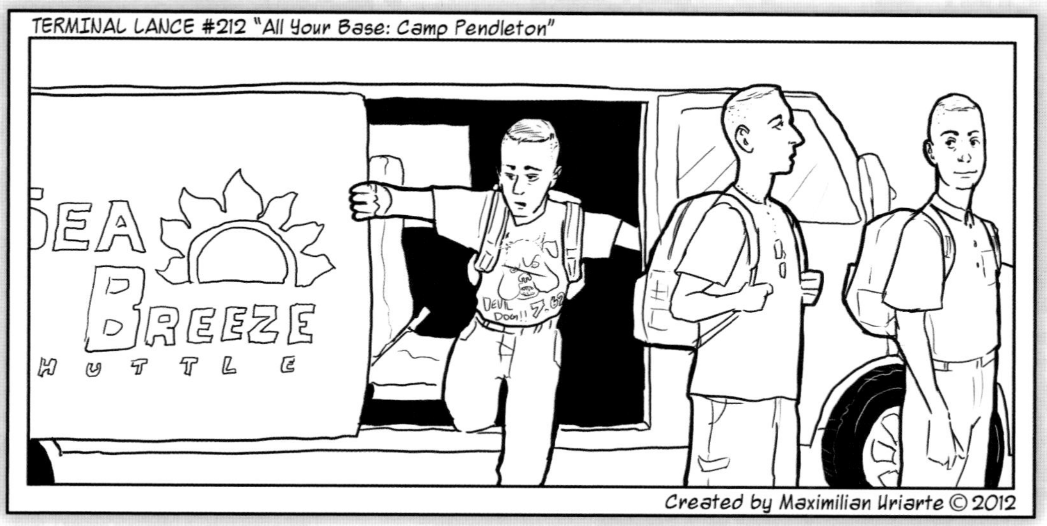
TERMINAL LANCE #212 "All Your Base: Camp Pendleton"
SEA BREEZE SHUTTLE
DEVIL DOG!! 7.62
Created by Maximilian Uriarte © 2012

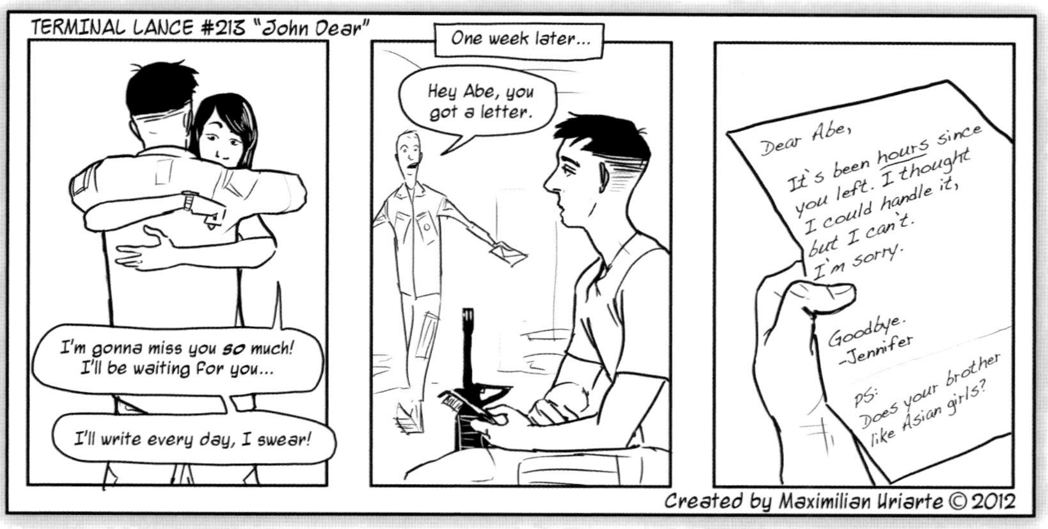
TERMINAL LANCE #213 "John Dear"
I'm gonna miss you so much! I'll be waiting for you...
I'll write every day, I swear!
One week later...
Hey Abe, you got a letter.
Dear Abe,
It's been hours since you left. I thought I could handle it, but I can't. I'm sorry.
Goodbye.
-Jennifer
PS: Does your brother like Asian girls?
Created by Maximilian Uriarte © 2012

213 "John Dear"

It's kind of a silly question, really. All white guys love Asian girls.

I say this all the time, but if there's one constant of the military, it's breakups, infidelity, and the infamous "Dear John" letters that countless Marines have fallen victim to. That girl back home that you swore wasn't like the other girls can potentially rip your heart out and destroy your soul from thousands of miles across the globe. It wouldn't be wrong to say that some women just can't hack it as a military spouse or girlfriend. Temptations are a bitch, and there is no greater temptation than a boyfriend on the other side of the planet. Dignity is not a virtue that everyone possesses.

Fidelity is a rough issue, and I'm not going to sit here and pretend that Marines don't cheat on their wives. But for most Marines on deployment, finding out about a cheating girlfriend or wife can be mentally devastating. Deployments are rough as it is, and you cling to every reminder of all you're leaving back at home. Women hold a special kind of power over Marines while they're overseas. For some Marines, their mental health can reside solely on the strength of that bond.

As the old saying goes though, if the Marine Corps wanted you to have a wife, they would have issued you one. You can chalk up bad relationships to one of the many reasons being in the military can be an awful experience. Finding yourself holding a Dear John letter is definitely not a situation you want to end up in.

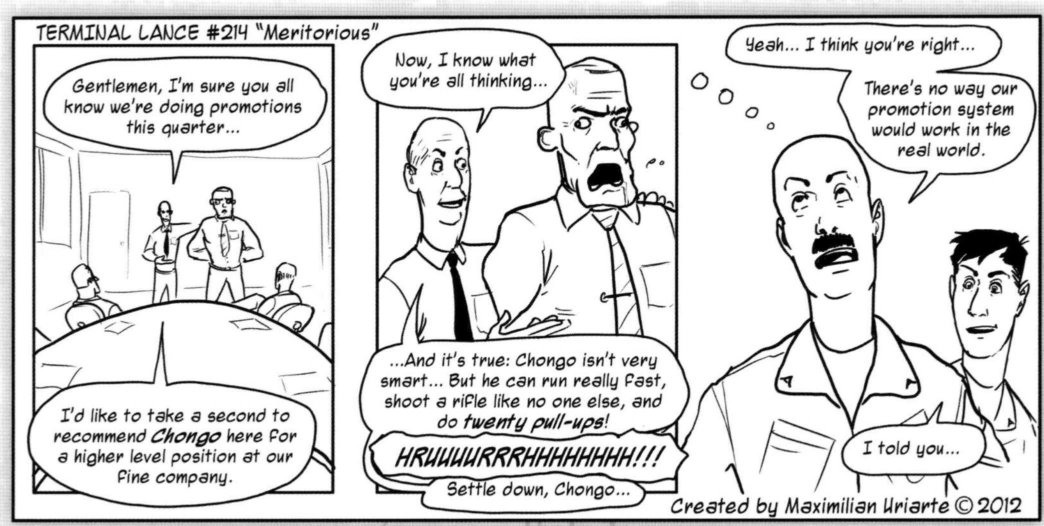

TERMINAL LANCE #214 "Meritorious"
Gentlemen, I'm sure you all know we're doing promotions this quarter...
I'd like to take a second to recommend *Chongo* here for a higher level position at our fine company.
Now, I know what you're all thinking...
...And it's true: Chongo isn't very smart... But he can run really fast, shoot a rifle like no one else, and do *twenty pull-ups*!
HRUUUURRRHHHHHHHH!!!
Settle down, Chongo...
Yeah... I think you're right...
There's no way our promotion system would work in the real world.
I told you...
Created by Maximilian Uriarte © 2012

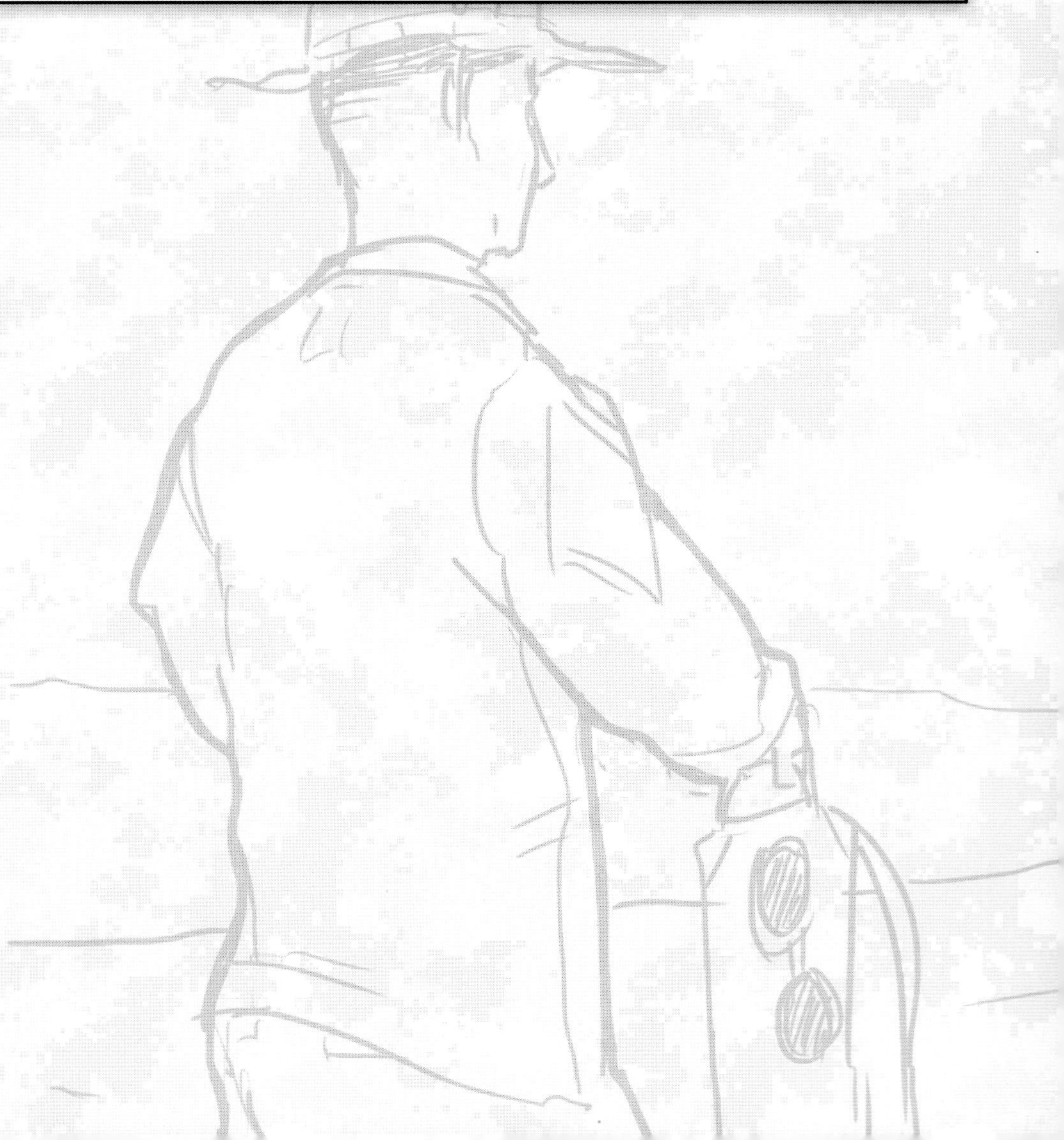

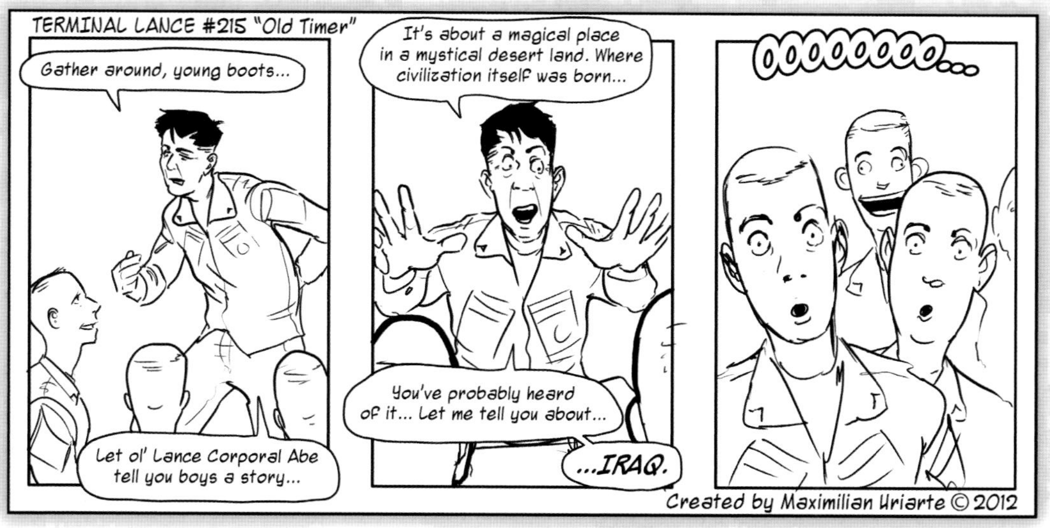
TERMINAL LANCE #215 "Old Timer"
Gather around, young boots...
Let ol' Lance Corporal Abe tell you boys a story...
It's about a magical place in a mystical desert land. Where civilization itself was born...
You've probably heard of it... Let me tell you about...
...IRAQ.
OOOOOOOOO...
Created by Maximilian Uriarte © 2012

215 "Old Timer"

It's hard not to feel like an old man talking about Iraq. When I enlisted, Iraq was all the rage. Civilians barely even knew about Afghanistan at that point, and most of the Marines were being cycled to the Cradle of Civilization, as it's known. Having never been to Afghanistan, I'm often met with confusion when I tell people I was in the Marines and went to Iraq twice instead of stepping foot in the 'Stan. Of course, I was enlisted at a time when this was normal, but it seems many people have already forgotten about Iraq.

Marines enlisting in 2018 were born in the year 2000.

Take a moment to let that sink in.

. . .

They were infants and children when 9/11 changed the world for the worse. Iraq is merely a bedtime story to them. The flat, palm tree–laden desert landscape flourishing along the Euphrates isn't common imagery anymore to the new enlistee. This has all been replaced with FROG suits, plate carriers, mountains, and mud huts. This will eventually fade as well, assuming the war on terror ever truly ends. Some day they will also seem old and grizzled.

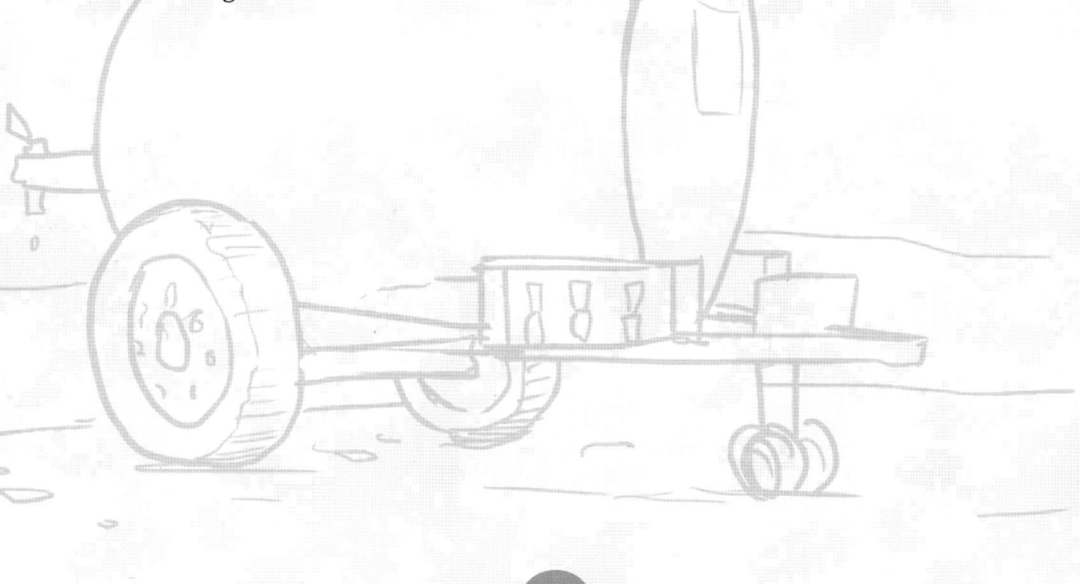

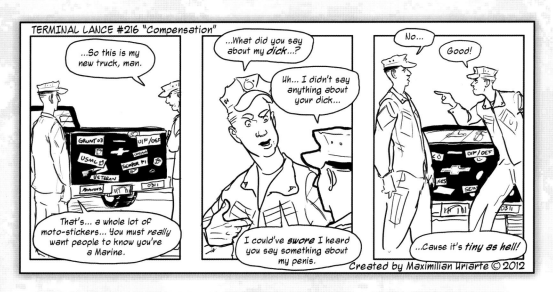

TERMINAL LANCE #216 "Compensation"

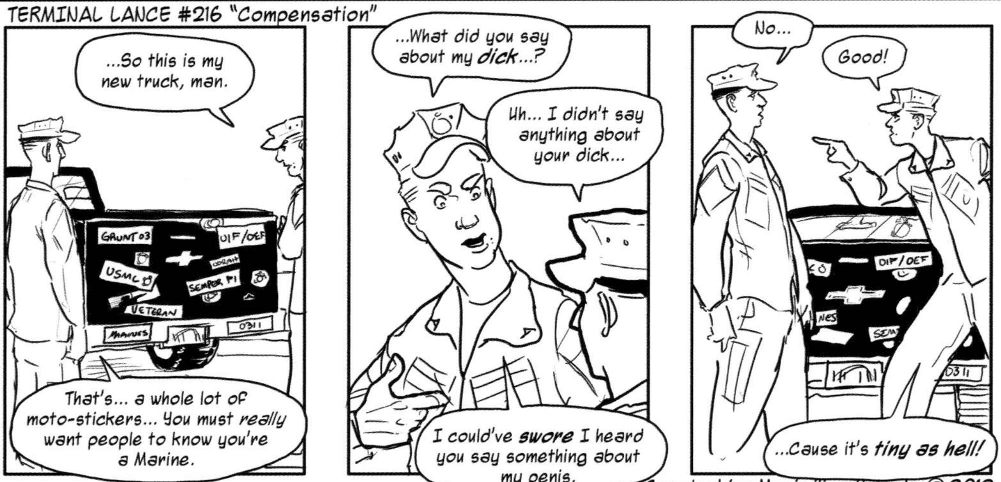

...So this is my new truck, man.
GRUNT 03
OIF/OEF
USMC
SEMPER FI
VETERAN
0311
That's... a whole lot of moto-stickers... You must *really* want people to know you're a Marine.
...What did you say about my *dick*...?
Uh... I didn't say anything about your dick...
I could've ***swore*** I heard you say something about my penis.
No...
Good!
...Cause it's ***tiny as hell!***

Created by Maximilian Uriarte © 2012

TERMINAL LANCE #217 "The Underwater Level"

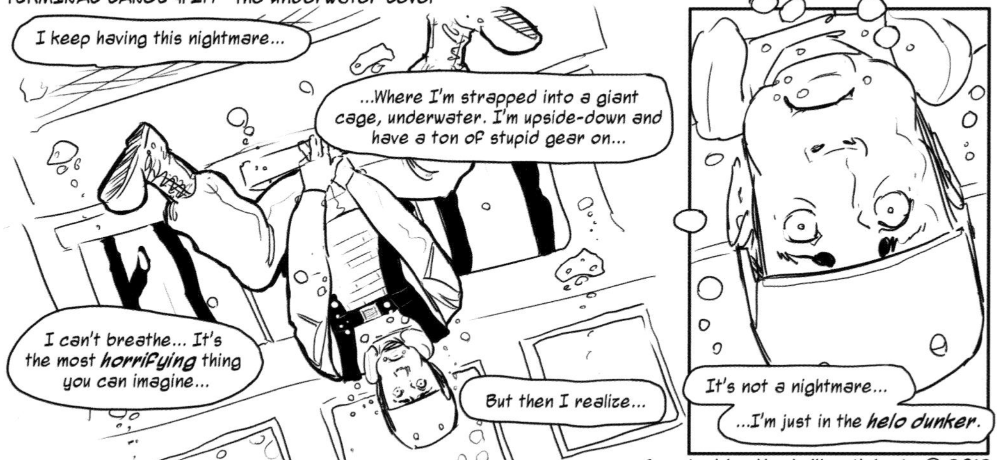

I keep having this nightmare...
...Where I'm strapped into a giant cage, underwater. I'm upside-down and have a ton of stupid gear on...
I can't breathe... It's the most ***horrifying*** thing you can imagine...
But then I realize...
It's not a nightmare...
...I'm just in the ***helo dunker***.

Created by Maximilian Uriarte © 2012

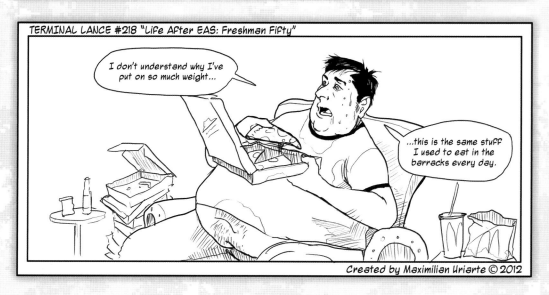

TERMINAL LANCE #218 "Life After EAS: Freshman Fifty"

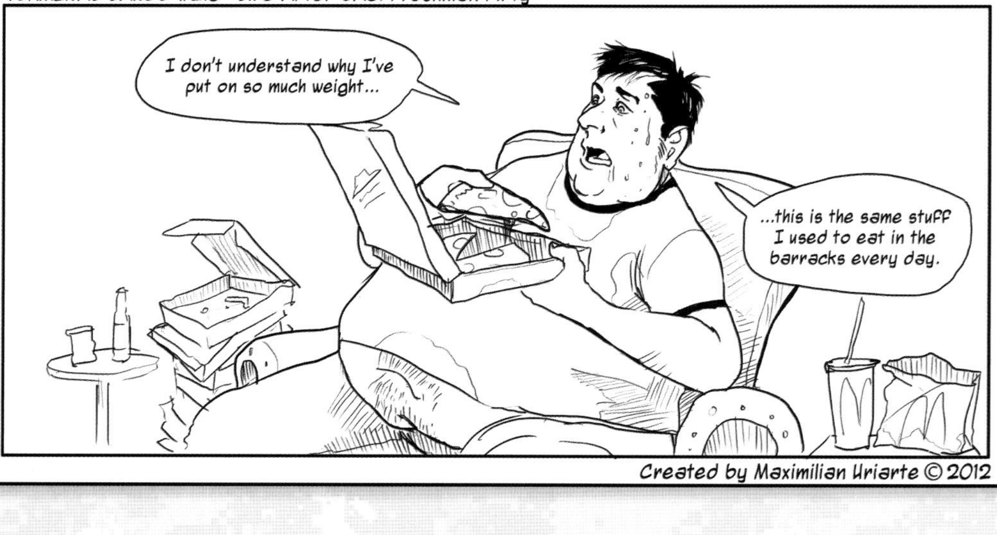

I don't understand why I've put on so much weight...
...this is the same stuff I used to eat in the barracks every day.

Created by Maximilian Uriarte © 2012

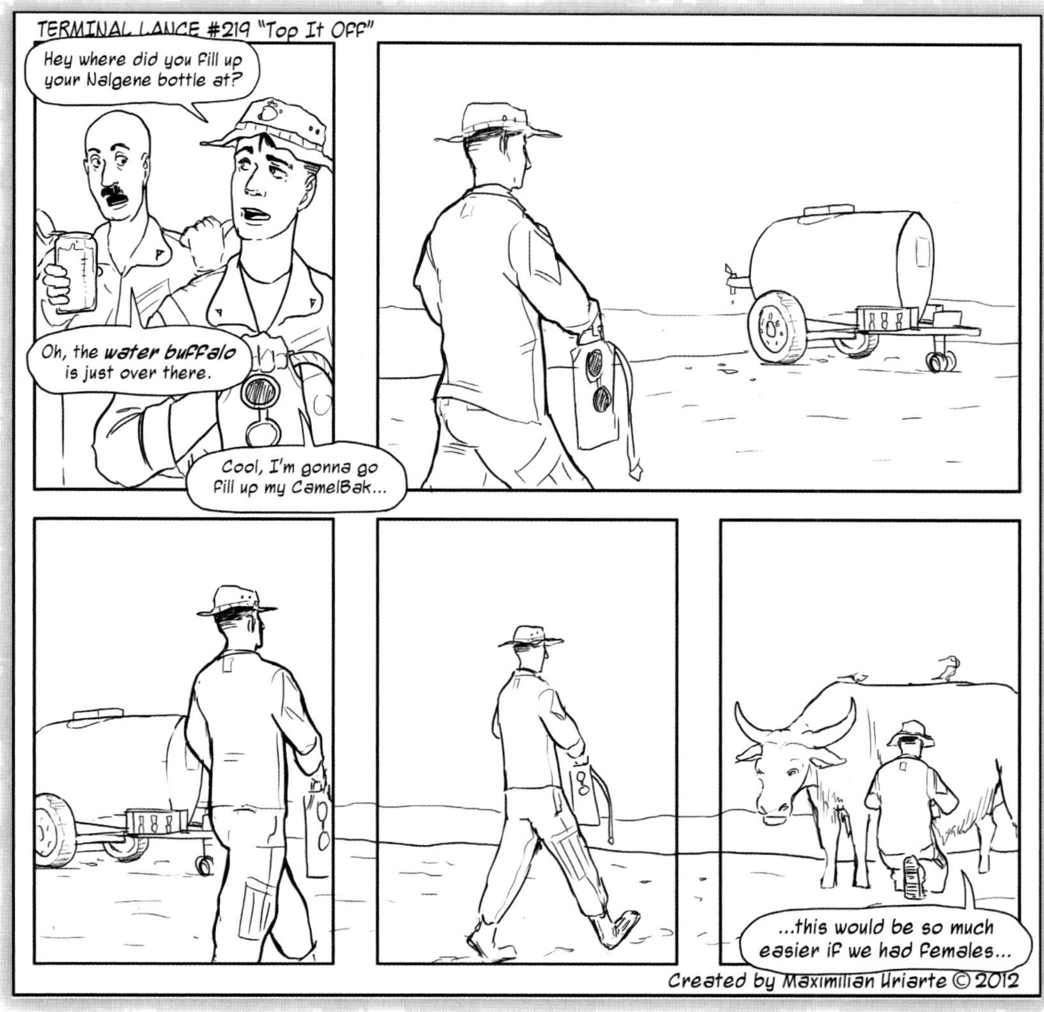
TERMINAL LANCE #219 "Top It Off"
Hey where did you fill up your Nalgene bottle at?
Oh, the water buffalo is just over there.
Cool, I'm gonna go fill up my CamelBak...
...this would be so much easier if we had females...
Created by Maximilian Uriarte © 2012

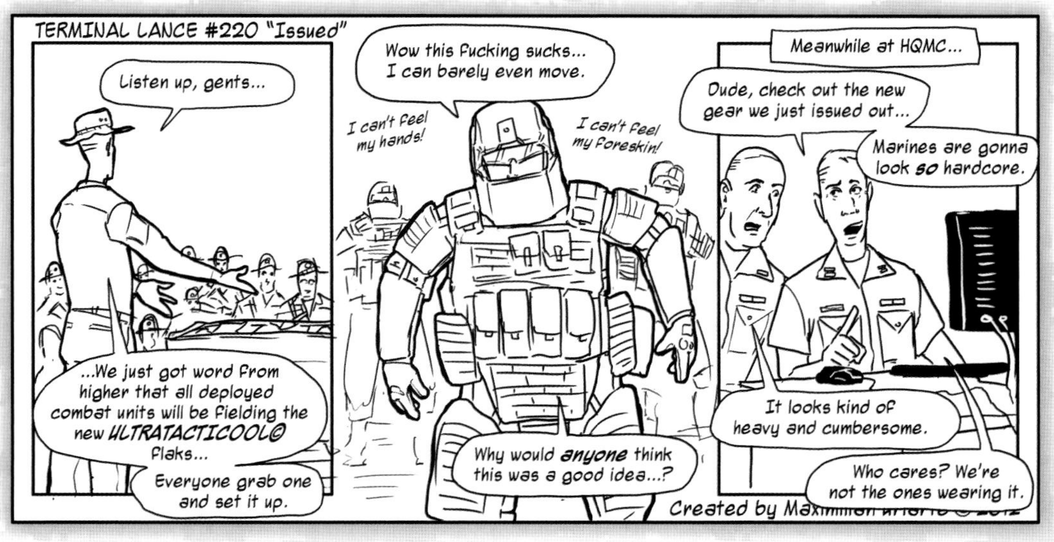
TERMINAL LANCE #220 "Issued"
Listen up, gents...
...We just got word from higher that all deployed combat units will be fielding the new ULTRATACTICOOL© flaks...
Everyone grab one and set it up.
Wow this fucking sucks... I can barely even move.
I can't feel my hands!
I can't feel my foreskin!
Why would anyone think this was a good idea...?
Meanwhile at HQMC...
Dude, check out the new gear we just issued out...
Marines are gonna look so hardcore.
It looks kind of heavy and cumbersome.
Who cares? We're not the ones wearing it.

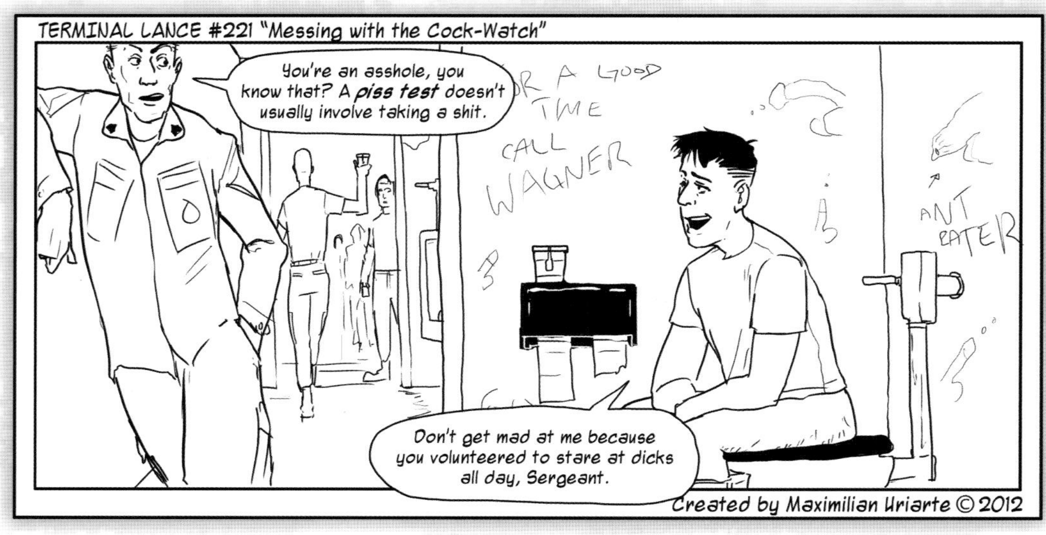
TERMINAL LANCE #221 "Messing with the Cock-Watch"
You're an asshole, you know that? A *piss test* doesn't usually involve taking a shit.
CALL WAGNER
ANT EATER
Don't get mad at me because you volunteered to stare at dicks all day, Sergeant.
Created by Maximilian Uriarte © 2012

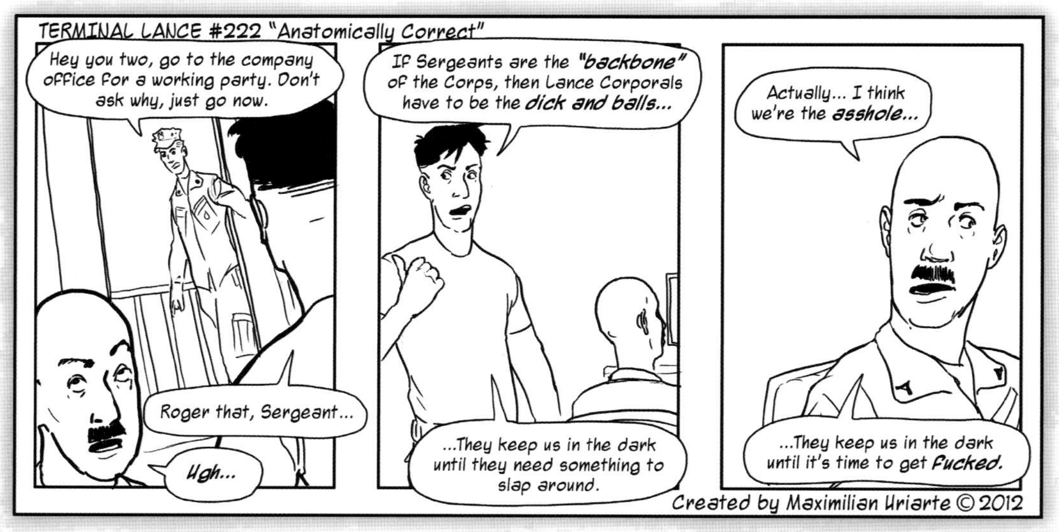
TERMINAL LANCE #222 "Anatomically Correct"
Hey you two, go to the company office for a working party. Don't ask why, just go now.
Roger that, Sergeant...
Ugh...
If Sergeants are the *"backbone"* of the Corps, then Lance Corporals have to be the *dick and balls...*
...They keep us in the dark until they need something to slap around.
Actually... I think we're the *asshole...*
...They keep us in the dark until it's time to get *fucked.*
Created by Maximilian Uriarte © 2012

222 "Anatomically Correct"

It's one or the other, amirite, guys?

No, but really, you always hear about how Sergeants are the "backbone" of the Corps, or Gunnery Sergeants are the "backbone" of the Staff NCO Corps, or Lance Corporals are the "backbone" of lower enlisted. But there's only so many backbones. We need to start assigning the anatomically correct body parts in relation to members of the Marine Corps.

So we've already established that Sergeants are the backbone. Okay, they deserve that.

- Private: The appendix or something useless. Who's a Private anyway besides students?
- Private First Class: The gooch of the Corps. Underneath even the Lance Corporals, who we've established are either the dick and balls or the asshole.

- Lance Corporal: See strip.
- Corporal: The buttocks. These Marines are underneath the Sergeants but above the asshole. Some can look nice and even fuckable, but may smell of sweaty shit upon closer inspection.
- Sergeant: See strip.
- Staff Sergeant: The lungs. They spout hot air given to them by higher-ups and play a major role in the operation of the entire body by circulating their oxygenated bullshit throughout the vascular system.
- Gunny: The rippling, sweaty, muscular arms of the Marine Corps. Gunnys are usually the cool guys of the Staff NCO's, they're high enough rank that no one bothers them but not high enough to really give a shit about anything. They're just there, looking cool and occasionally doing some heavy lifting.
- First Sergeant/Master Sergeant: These guys are the eyeballs of the Marine Corps. Well, maybe, who knows? All I know is nine times out of ten, if you're getting your ass chewed, it's by one of these E8's with eagle-like vision that spotted you from across the PX parking lot for something that may or may not be your fault.
- Sergeant Major: The hard skull/cranium. We rarely see the brain as a lower-enlisted. Instead we usually see the face of the battalion command represented by the highest enlisted. The Sergeant Major protects the CO (the brain) from rocks and other small objects that may be thrown as a result of hearing things like, "LOL your leave is canked," and "LOL no chow this week, guys."

People asked about Master Guns. They are a mythical creature that doesn't actually exist, like a unicorn or a First Sergeant with a soul.

Officers are a whole other thing—generally different parts of the brain. I'm pretty sure Second Lieutenants are that part they say we never use throughout our entire lives.

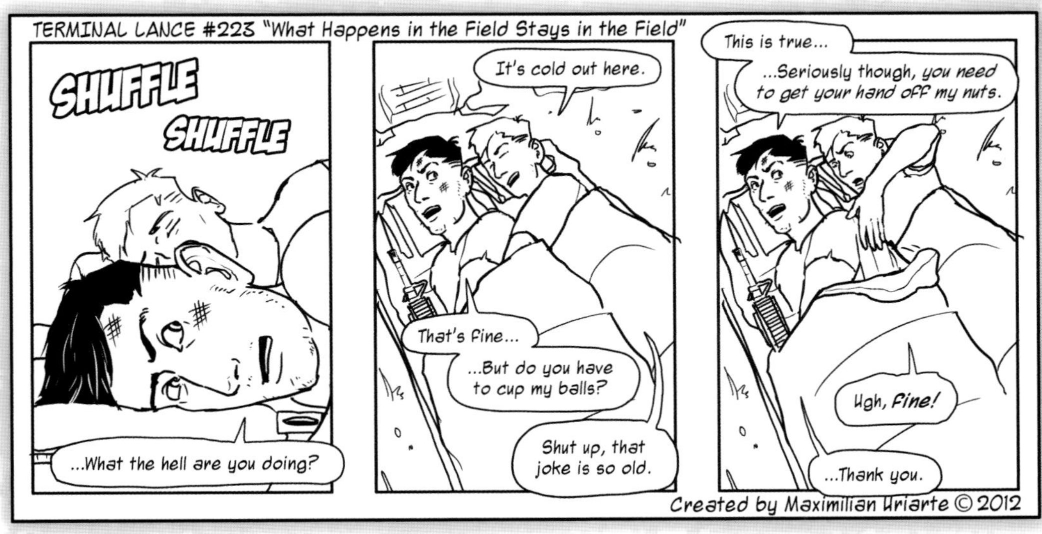
TERMINAL LANCE #223 "What Happens in the Field Stays in the Field"
SHUFFLE
SHUFFLE
...What the hell are you doing?
It's cold out here.
That's fine...
...But do you have to cup my balls?
Shut up, that joke is so old.
This is true...
...Seriously though, you need to get your hand off my nuts.
Ugh, Fine!
...Thank you.
Created by Maximilian Uriarte © 2012

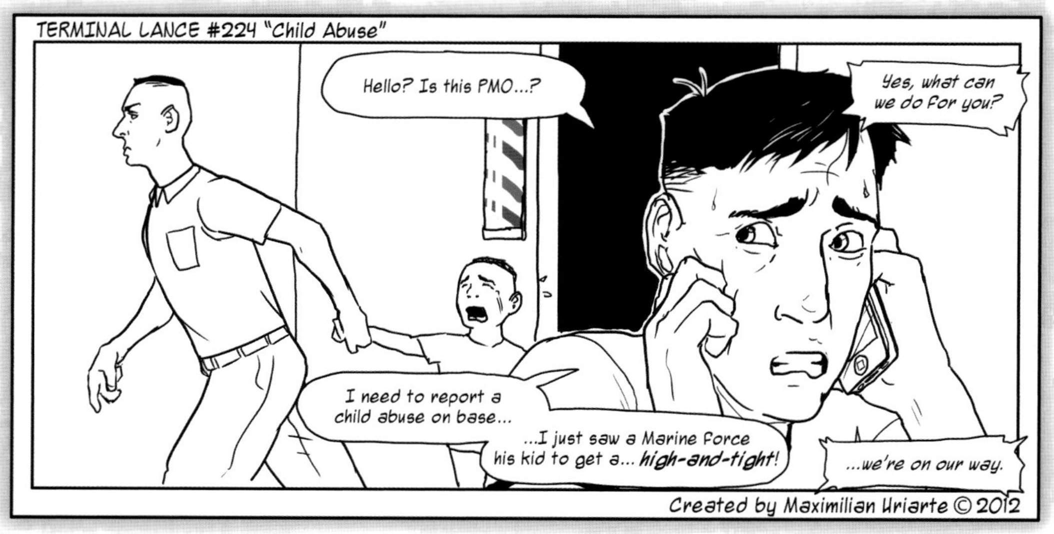
TERMINAL LANCE #224 "Child Abuse"
Hello? Is this PMO...?
Yes, what can we do for you?
I need to report a child abuse on base...
...I just saw a Marine force his kid to get a... high-and-tight!
...we're on our way.
Created by Maximilian Uriarte © 2012

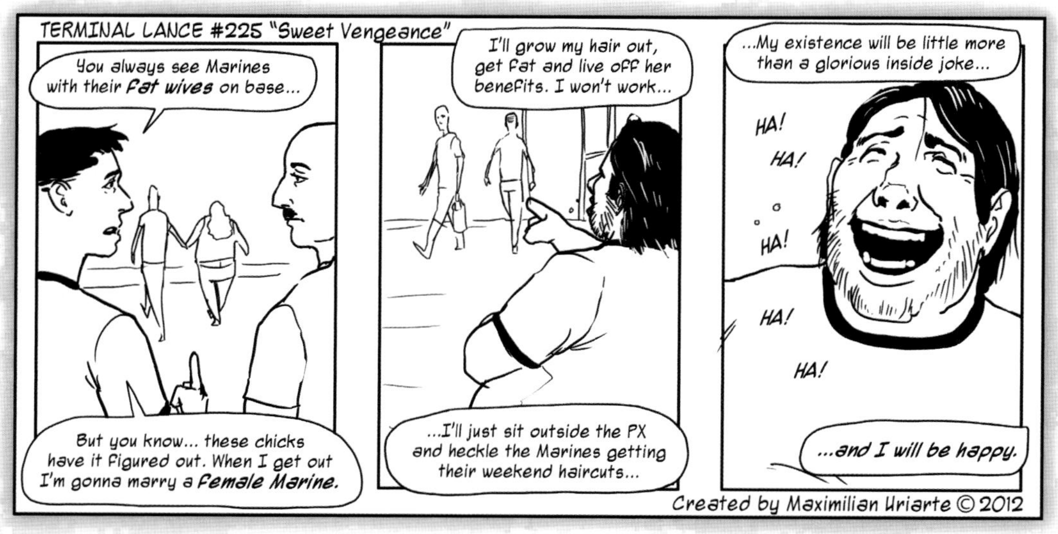
TERMINAL LANCE #225 "Sweet Vengeance"
You always see Marines with their fat wives on base...
But you know... these chicks have it figured out. When I get out I'm gonna marry a Female Marine.
I'll grow my hair out, get fat and live off her benefits. I won't work...
...I'll just sit outside the PX and heckle the Marines getting their weekend haircuts...
...My existence will be little more than a glorious inside joke...
HA! HA! HA! HA! HA!
...and I will be happy.
Created by Maximilian Uriarte © 2012

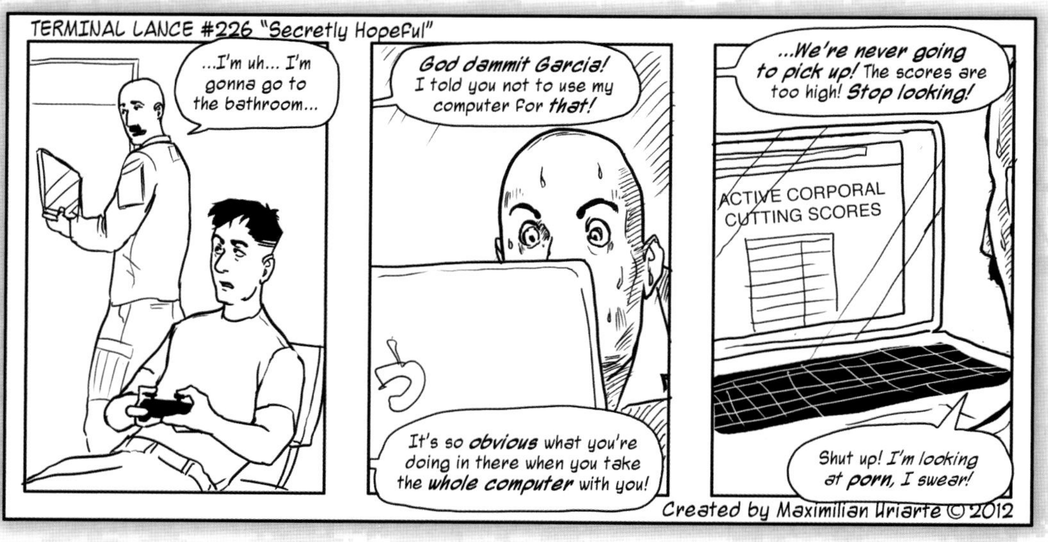
TERMINAL LANCE #226 "Secretly Hopeful"
...I'm uh... I'm gonna go to the bathroom...
God dammit Garcia! I told you not to use my computer for that!
It's so obvious what you're doing in there when you take the whole computer with you!
...We're never going to pick up! The scores are too high! Stop looking!
ACTIVE CORPORAL CUTTING SCORES
Shut up! I'm looking at porn, I swear!
Created by Maximilian Uriarte © 2012

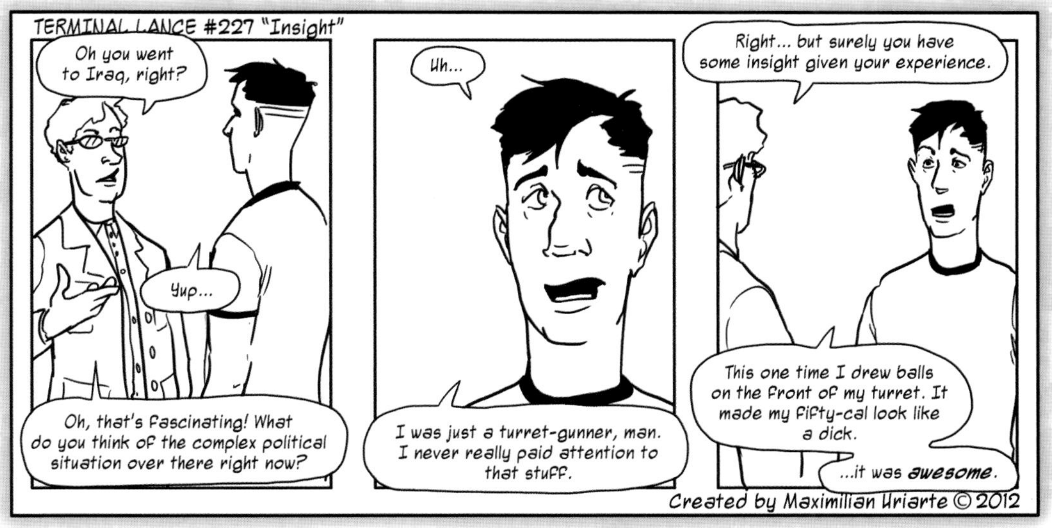
TERMINAL LANCE #227 "Insight"
Oh you went to Iraq, right?
Yup...
Oh, that's fascinating! What do you think of the complex political situation over there right now?
Uh...
I was just a turret-gunner, man. I never really paid attention to that stuff.
Right... but surely you have some insight given your experience.
This one time I drew balls on the front of my turret. It made my fifty-cal look like a dick.
...it was **awesome**.
Created by Maximilian Uriarte © 2012

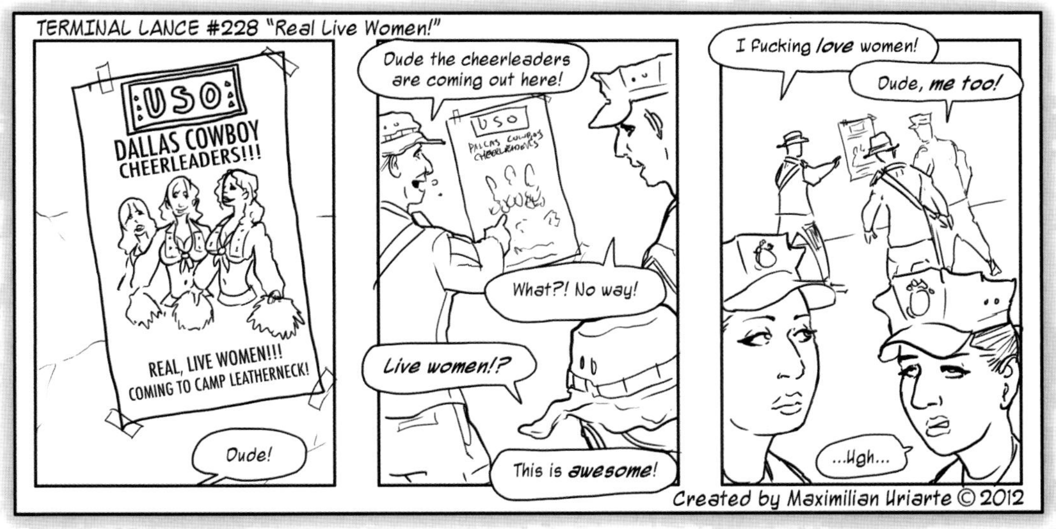
TERMINAL LANCE #228 "Real Live Women!"
USO
DALLAS COWBOY CHEERLEADERS!!!
REAL, LIVE WOMEN!!! COMING TO CAMP LEATHERNECK!
Dude!
Dude the cheerleaders are coming out here!
What?! No way!
Live women!?
This is **awesome**!
I fucking *love* women!
Dude, **me too!**
...Ugh...
Created by Maximilian Uriarte © 2012

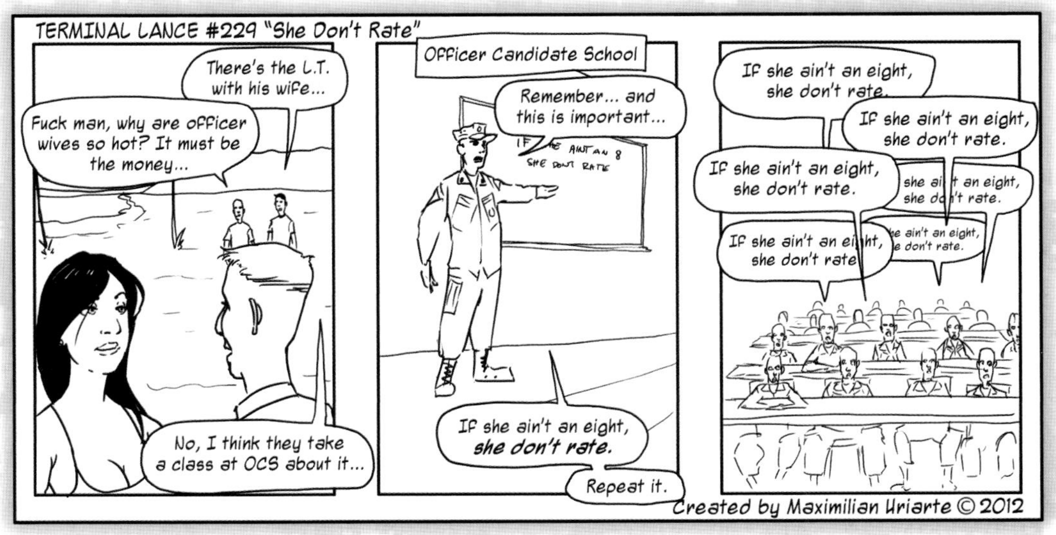
TERMINAL LANCE #229 "She Don't Rate"
There's the L.T. with his wife...
Fuck man, why are officer wives so hot? It must be the money...
No, I think they take a class at OCS about it...
Officer Candidate School
Remember... and this is important...
If she ain't an eight, **she don't rate.**
Repeat it.
If she ain't an eight, she don't rate.
If she ain't an eight, she don't rate.
If she ain't an eight, she don't rate.
Created by Maximilian Uriarte © 2012

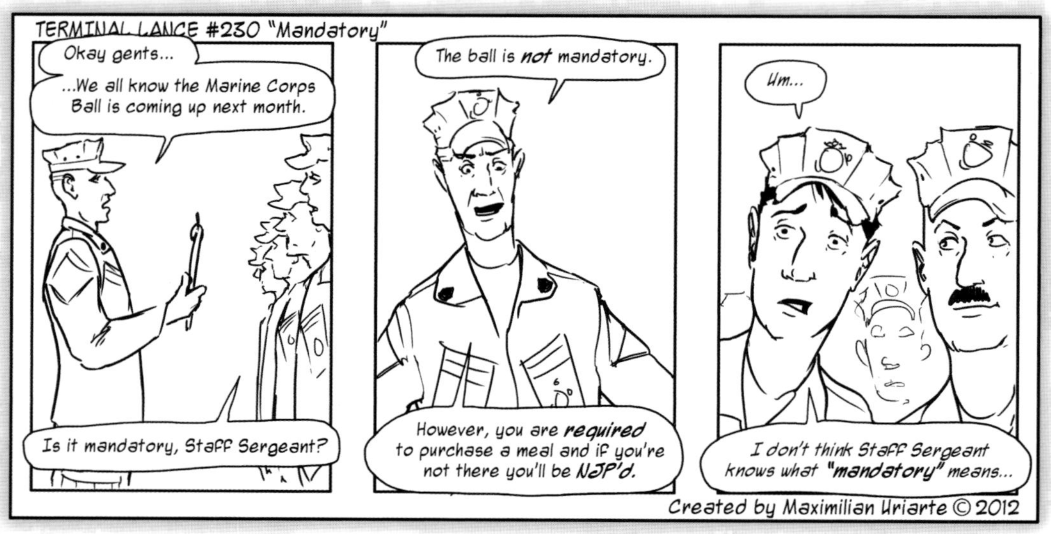
TERMINAL LANCE #230 "Mandatory"
Okay gents...
...We all know the Marine Corps Ball is coming up next month.
Is it mandatory, Staff Sergeant?
The ball is **not** mandatory.
However, you are **required** to purchase a meal and if you're not there you'll be NJP'd.
Um...
I don't think Staff Sergeant knows what **"mandatory"** means...
Created by Maximilian Uriarte © 2012

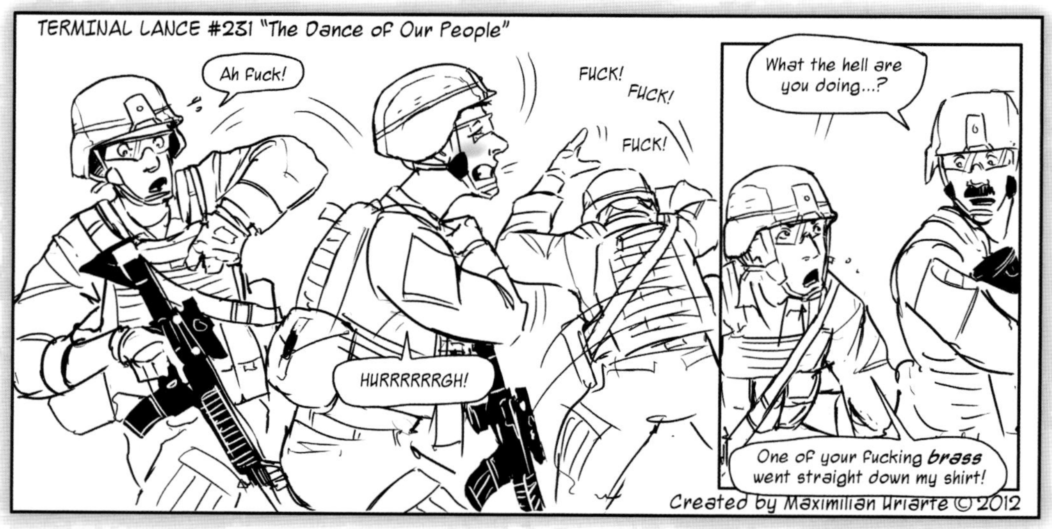
TERMINAL LANCE #231 "The Dance of Our People"
Ah Fuck!
FUCK!
FUCK!
FUCK!
HURRRRRRGH!
What the hell are you doing...?
One of your fucking **brass** went straight down my shirt!
Created by Maximilian Uriarte © 2012

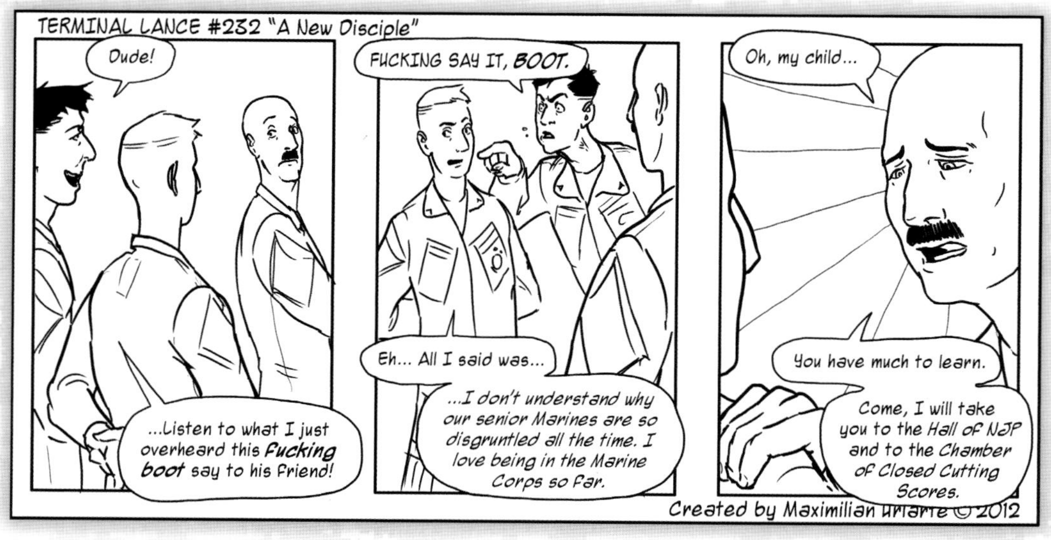
TERMINAL LANCE #232 "A New Disciple"
Dude!
...Listen to what I just overheard this ***Fucking boot*** say to his friend!
FUCKING SAY IT, ***BOOT.***
Eh... All I said was...
...*I don't understand why our senior Marines are so disgruntled all the time. I love being in the Marine Corps so far.*
Oh, my child...
You have much to learn.
Come, I will take you to the *Hall of NJP* and to the *Chamber of Closed Cutting Scores.*
Created by Maximilian Uriarte © 2012

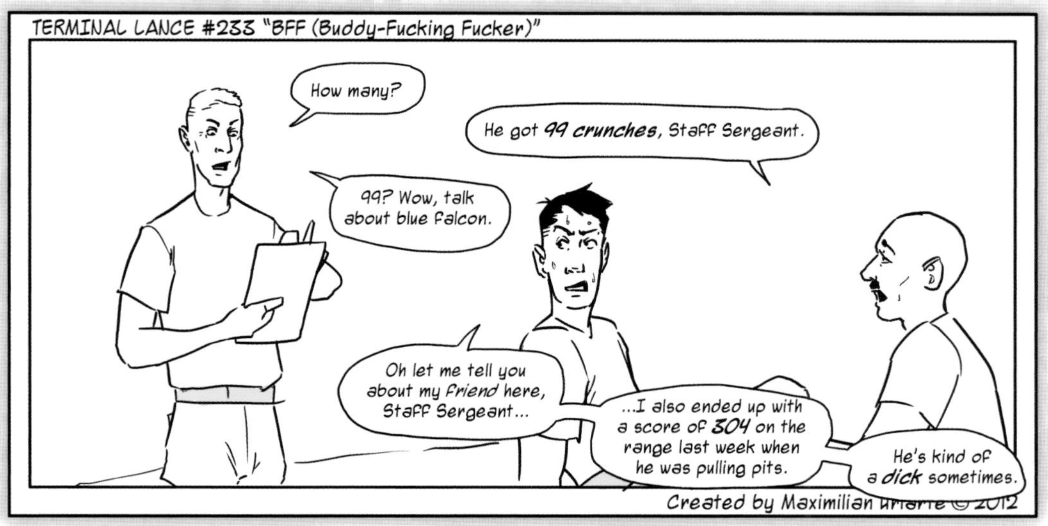
TERMINAL LANCE #233 "BFF (Buddy-Fucking Fucker)"
How many?
He got 99 crunches, Staff Sergeant.
99? Wow, talk about blue falcon.
Oh let me tell you about my friend here, Staff Sergeant...
...I also ended up with a score of 304 on the range last week when he was pulling pits.
He's kind of a dick sometimes.
Created by Maximilian Uriarte © 2012

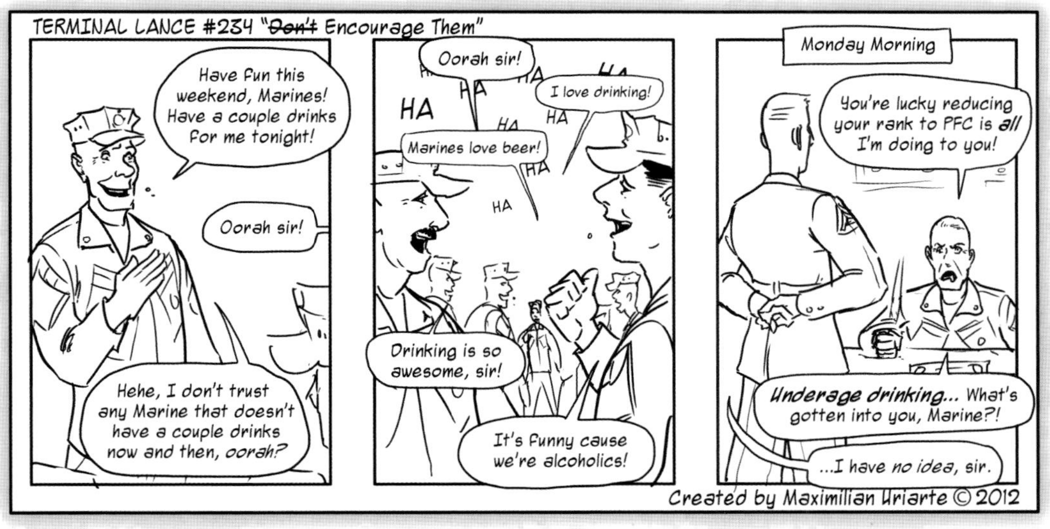
TERMINAL LANCE #234 "~~Don't~~ Encourage Them"
Have fun this weekend, Marines! Have a couple drinks for me tonight!
Oorah sir!
Hehe, I don't trust any Marine that doesn't have a couple drinks now and then, oorah?
Oorah sir!
I love drinking!
HA
HA
HA
Marines love beer!
HA
HA
Drinking is so awesome, sir!
It's funny cause we're alcoholics!
Monday Morning
You're lucky reducing your rank to PFC is all I'm doing to you!
Underage drinking... What's gotten into you, Marine?!
...I have no idea, sir.
Created by Maximilian Uriarte © 2012

234 "~~Don't~~ Encourage Them"

I'm not one of those guys that gives a shit if you drink and you're underage. I'm also not one of those guys that thinks people under twenty-one should be allowed to drink. That's not really what this strip is about, because if it were, it'd be a display of complete apathy on my part. What I never understood in the Marine Corps is the culture of absolute encouragement when it comes to consumption of alcohol, yet the unabashed punishment of said consumption when it occurs.

As Marines, it is undeniable that there is a culture centered around drinking as an expression of masculinity. Marines drink. This is a vastly known and widely perpetuated reality in Marine culture. If you don't drink, you are abnormal.

However, I see it as a great irony that while the establishment encourages drinking in nearly every regard (Warriors Night anyone?), they have the audacity to punish younger Marines who engage in such activities even in the safety of their own barracks. Furthermore, why does the punishment always have to be so severe? The most ridiculous NJP's I've ever seen involved underage drinking. Granted, I'm not saying that if a Marine is underage, drunk, and acting a fool out in town that he should go unnoticed, but let's get real:

Marines drink. You created this stereotype. Own up to it and don't pretend like it's not expected to happen.

Now, if you'll excuse me, I'm going to go have a drink.

TERMINAL LANCE #235 "Berkeley Logic"
I don't support the troops!
I saw on the news once that a bunch of Marines killed innocent civilians over there! You're all a bunch of baby killers!
What? That's stupid, I never did that.
On the news I saw a black guy get arrested for robbery. Does that mean all black guys are robbers?
Hey!
Don't be racist!
Created by Maximilian Uriarte © 2012

TERMINAL LANCE #236 "Security Force Drops"
Listen up, gents...
You're getting a new NCO, today. Welcome Corporal Biggs.
Oh great...
Ugh...
Hey guys, great to meet you!
I'm coming from Security Forces, so this is going to be quite a change for me!
Oh, Security Forces?
Thank God...
...I was worried we might have to show you respect.
Created by Maximilian Uriarte © 2012

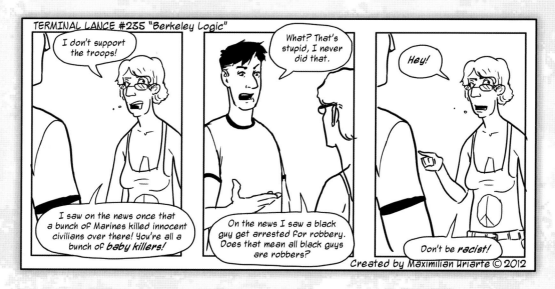

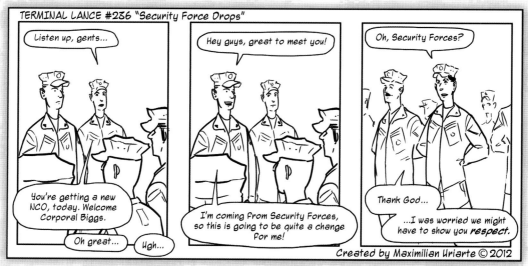

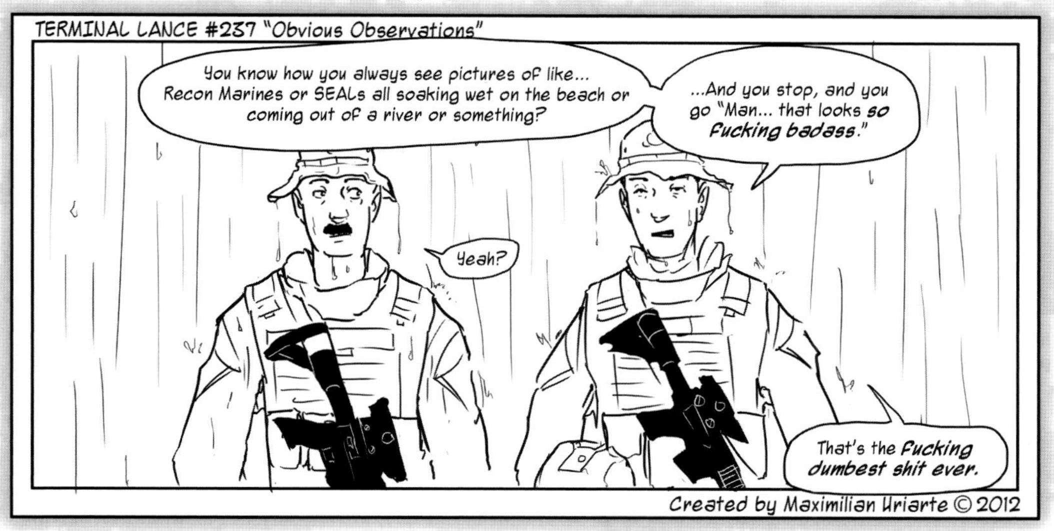
TERMINAL LANCE #237 "Obvious Observations"
You know how you always see pictures of like... Recon Marines or SEALs all soaking wet on the beach or coming out of a river or something?
...And you stop, and you go "Man... that looks so fucking badass."
Yeah?
That's the fucking dumbest shit ever.
Created by Maximilian Uriarte © 2012

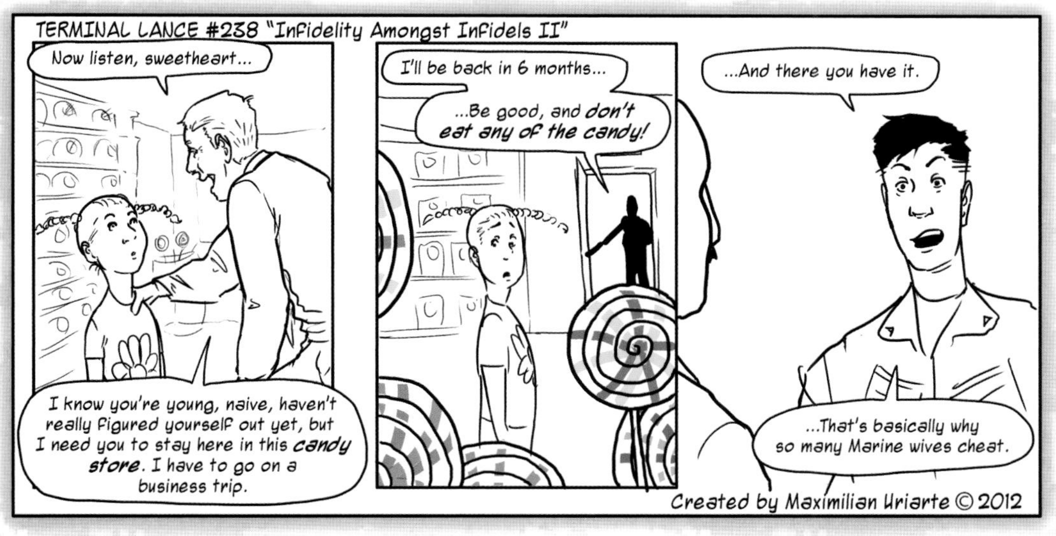
TERMINAL LANCE #238 "Infidelity Amongst Infidels II"
Now listen, sweetheart...
I know you're young, naive, haven't really figured yourself out yet, but I need you to stay here in this candy store. I have to go on a business trip.
I'll be back in 6 months...
...Be good, and don't eat any of the candy!
...And there you have it.
...That's basically why so many Marine wives cheat.
Created by Maximilian Uriarte © 2012

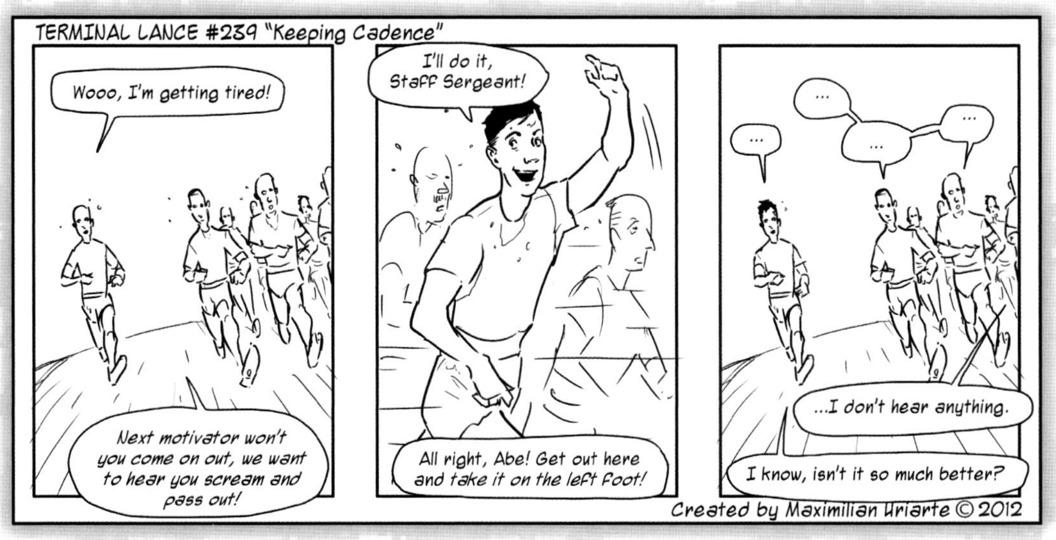
TERMINAL LANCE #239 "Keeping Cadence"
Wooo, I'm getting tired!
Next motivator won't you come on out, we want to hear you scream and pass out!
I'll do it, Staff Sergeant!
All right, Abe! Get out here and take it on the left foot!
...
...
...
...
...I don't hear anything.
I know, isn't it so much better?
Created by Maximilian Uriarte © 2012

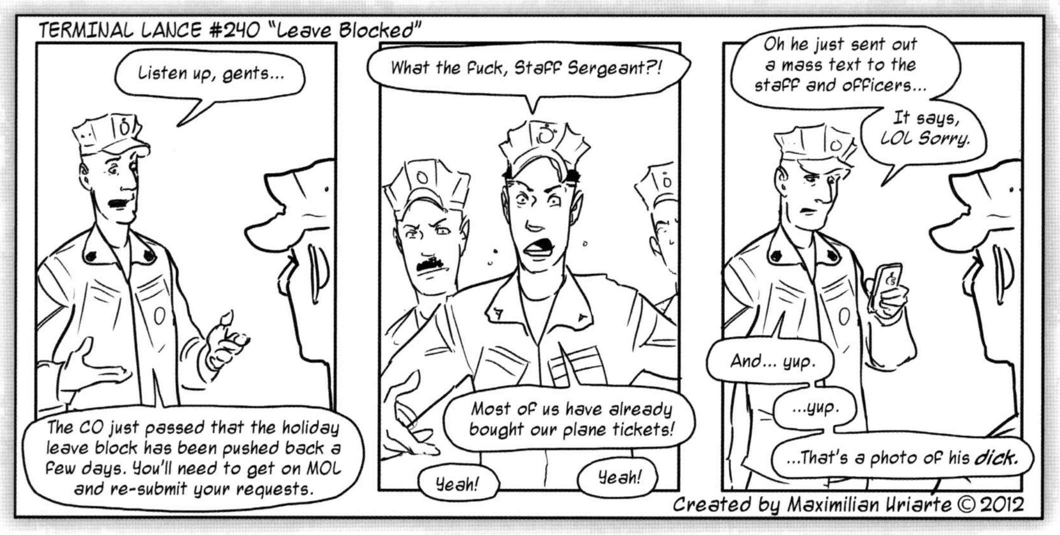
TERMINAL LANCE #240 "Leave Blocked"
Listen up, gents...
The CO just passed that the holiday leave block has been pushed back a few days. You'll need to get on MOL and re-submit your requests.
What the fuck, Staff Sergeant?!
Most of us have already bought our plane tickets!
Yeah!
Yeah!
Oh he just sent out a mass text to the staff and officers...
It says, LOL Sorry.
And... yup.
...yup.
...That's a photo of his dick.
Created by Maximilian Uriarte © 2012

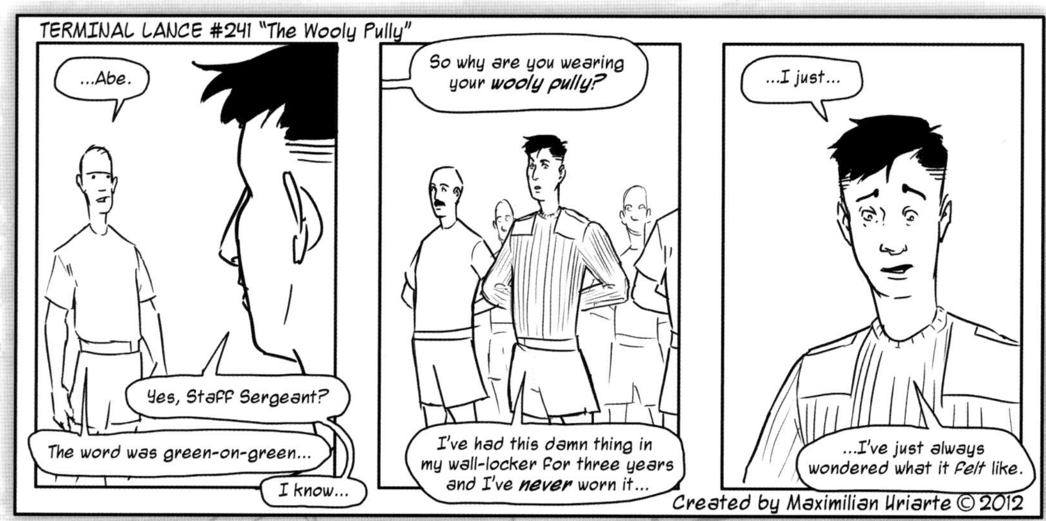
TERMINAL LANCE #241 "The Wooly Pully"
...Abe.
Yes, Staff Sergeant?
The word was green-on-green...
I know...
So why are you wearing your wooly pully?
I've had this damn thing in my wall-locker for three years and I've never worn it...
...I just...
...I've just always wondered what it felt like.
Created by Maximilian Uriarte © 2012

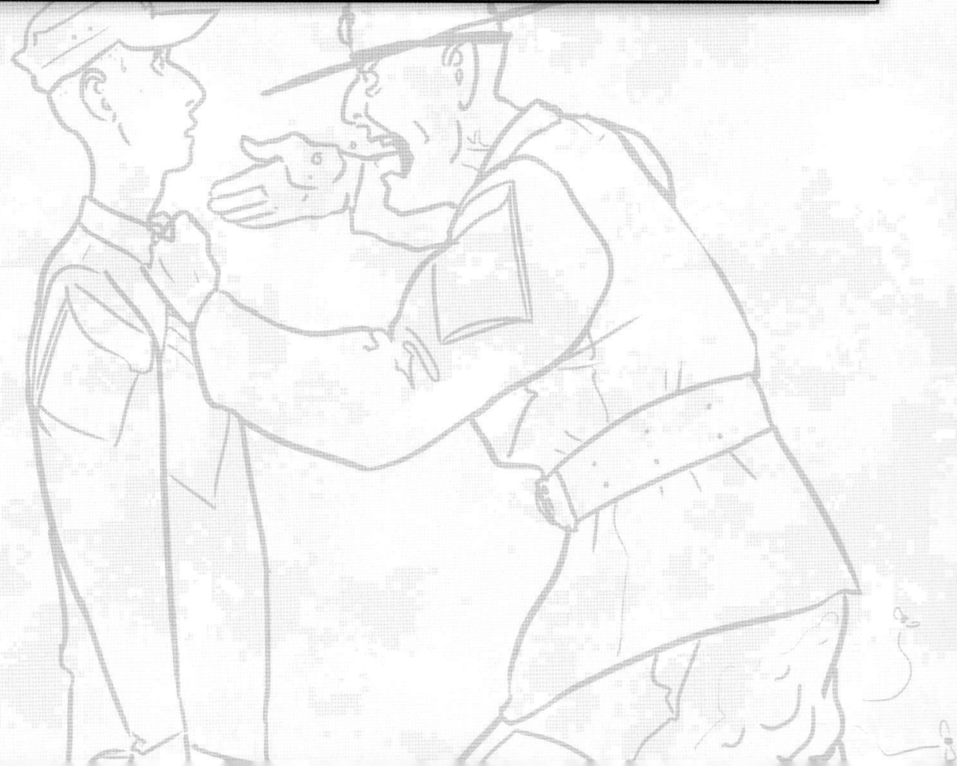

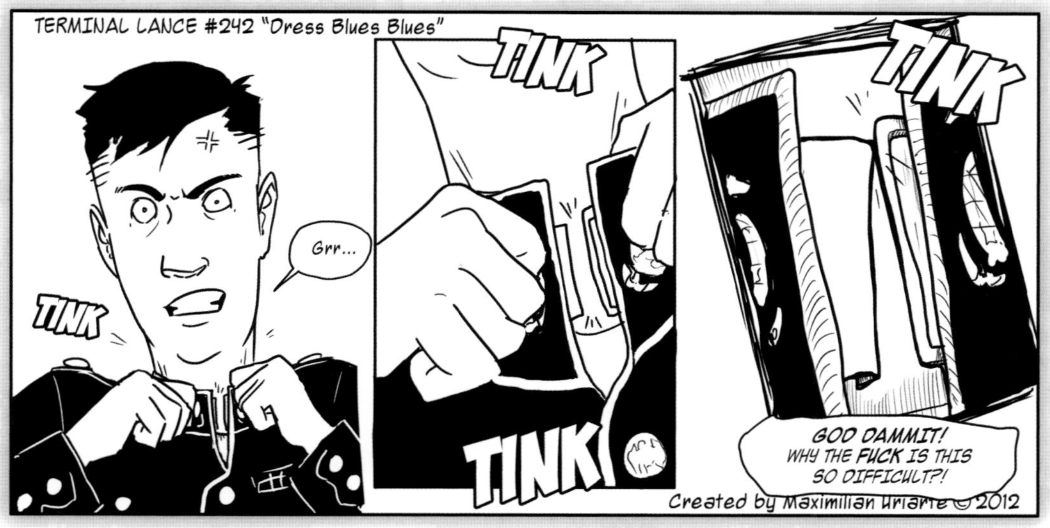
TERMINAL LANCE #242 "Dress Blues Blues"
TINK
Grr...
TINK
TINK
TINK
GOD DAMMIT!
WHY THE FUCK IS THIS
SO DIFFICULT?!
Created by Maximilian Uriarte © 2012

242 "Dress Blues Blues"

I like wearing my dress blues. They look snazzy as shit and I look great in them. That's all the reason I need. That little neck thing—the clasps that bring the collar together—bugs the fucking hell out of me though. It's one of those little things that you sit there and pick at for a couple of minutes before you give up and ask someone for help. Those couple of minutes are the most excruciatingly annoying minutes of your entire life.

I've long believed the collar of the dress blue uniform to be the key to its great track record of getting Marines laid. The collar in combination with those two little golden Eagle, Globe, and Anchors make that entire outfit. But this delectable collar comes at a price—and it's your sanity as you try to clasp the damned thing together five minutes before you're supposed to be out the door. A Terminal Lance Forum user gave this pro tip:

Take the blues jacket to the tailor, replace the clasp with Velcro.

Brilliant.

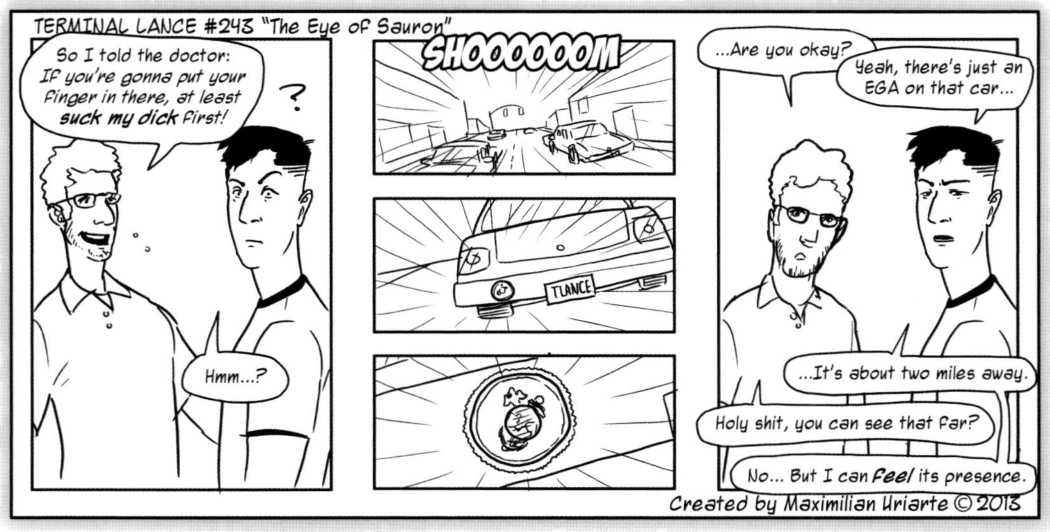
TERMINAL LANCE #243 "The Eye of Sauron"
So I told the doctor: If you're gonna put your finger in there, at least suck my dick first!
?
Hmm...?
SHOOOOOOOM
TLANCE
...Are you okay?
Yeah, there's just an EGA on that car...
...It's about two miles away.
Holy shit, you can see that far?
No... But I can feel its presence.
Created by Maximilian Uriarte © 2013

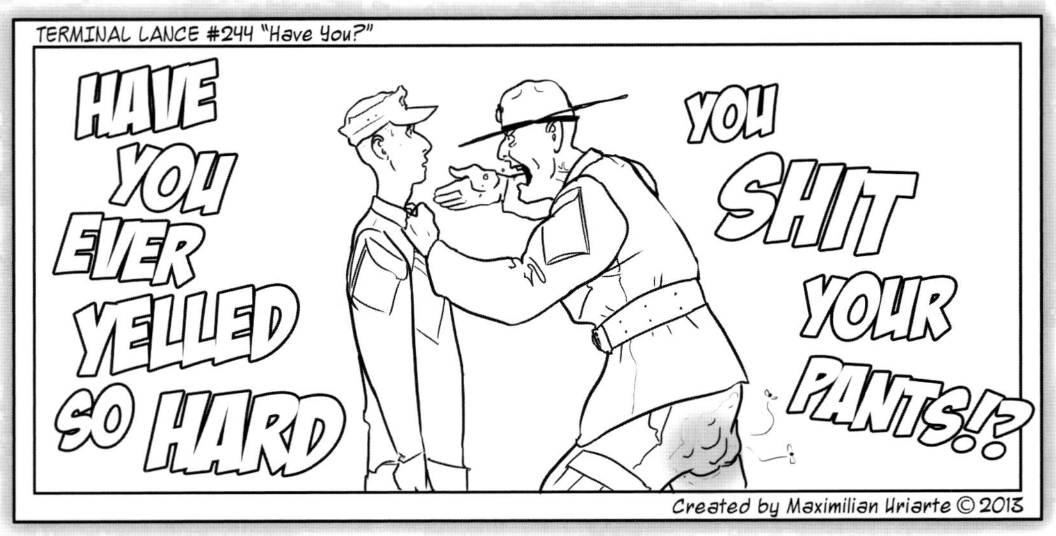
TERMINAL LANCE #244 "Have You?"
HAVE YOU EVER YELLED SO HARD
YOU SHIT YOUR PANTS!?
Created by Maximilian Uriarte © 2013

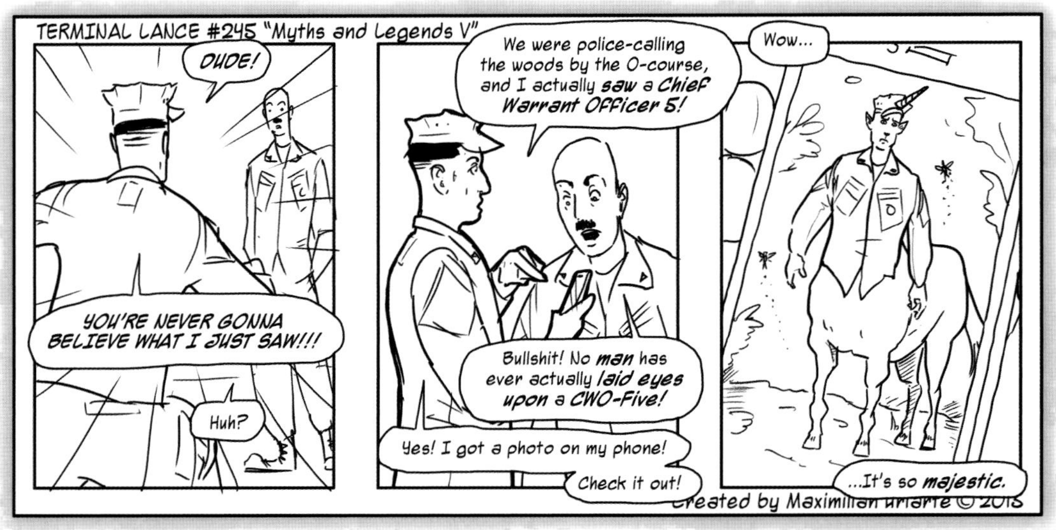
TERMINAL LANCE #245 "Myths and Legends V"
DUDE!
YOU'RE NEVER GONNA BELIEVE WHAT I JUST SAW!!!
Huh?
We were police-calling the woods by the O-course, and I actually saw a Chief Warrant Officer 5!
Bullshit! No man has ever actually laid eyes upon a CWO-Five!
Yes! I got a photo on my phone!
Check it out!
Wow...
...It's so majestic.
Created by Maximilian Uriarte © 2013

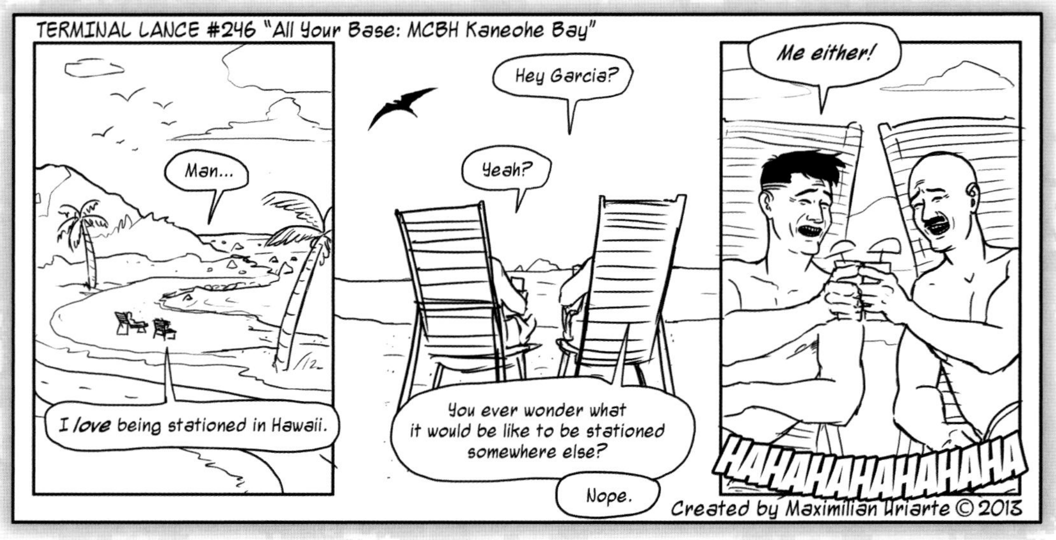
TERMINAL LANCE #246 "All Your Base: MCBH Kaneohe Bay"
Man...
I love being stationed in Hawaii.
Hey Garcia?
Yeah?
You ever wonder what it would be like to be stationed somewhere else?
Nope.
Me either!
HAHAHAHAHAHAHA
Created by Maximilian Uriarte © 2013

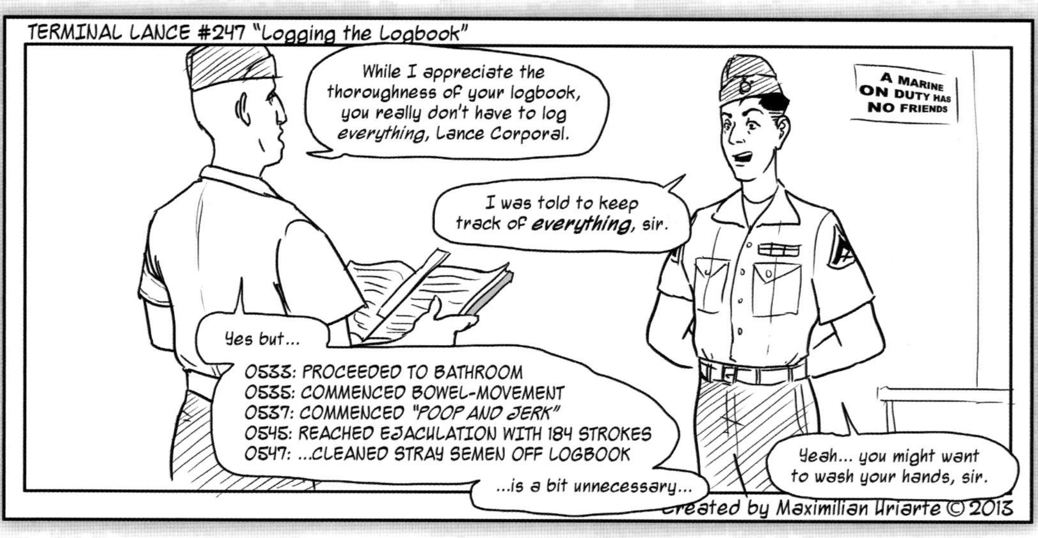
TERMINAL LANCE #247 "Logging the Logbook"
While I appreciate the thoroughness of your logbook, you really don't have to log everything, Lance Corporal.
A MARINE ON DUTY HAS NO FRIENDS
I was told to keep track of everything, sir.
Yes but...
0533: PROCEEDED TO BATHROOM
0535: COMMENCED BOWEL-MOVEMENT
0537: COMMENCED "POOP AND JERK"
0545: REACHED EJACULATION WITH 184 STROKES
0547: ...CLEANED STRAY SEMEN OFF LOGBOOK
...is a bit unnecessary...
Yeah... you might want to wash your hands, sir.
Created by Maximilian Uriarte © 2013

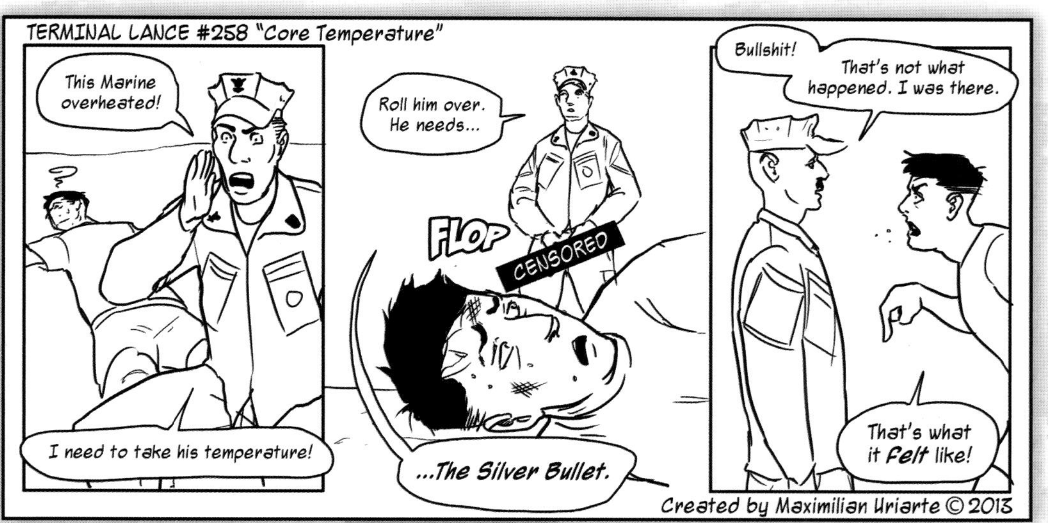
TERMINAL LANCE #258 "Core Temperature"
This Marine overheated!
I need to take his temperature!
Roll him over. He needs...
FLOP
CENSORED
...The Silver Bullet.
Bullshit!
That's not what happened. I was there.
That's what it felt like!
Created by Maximilian Uriarte © 2013

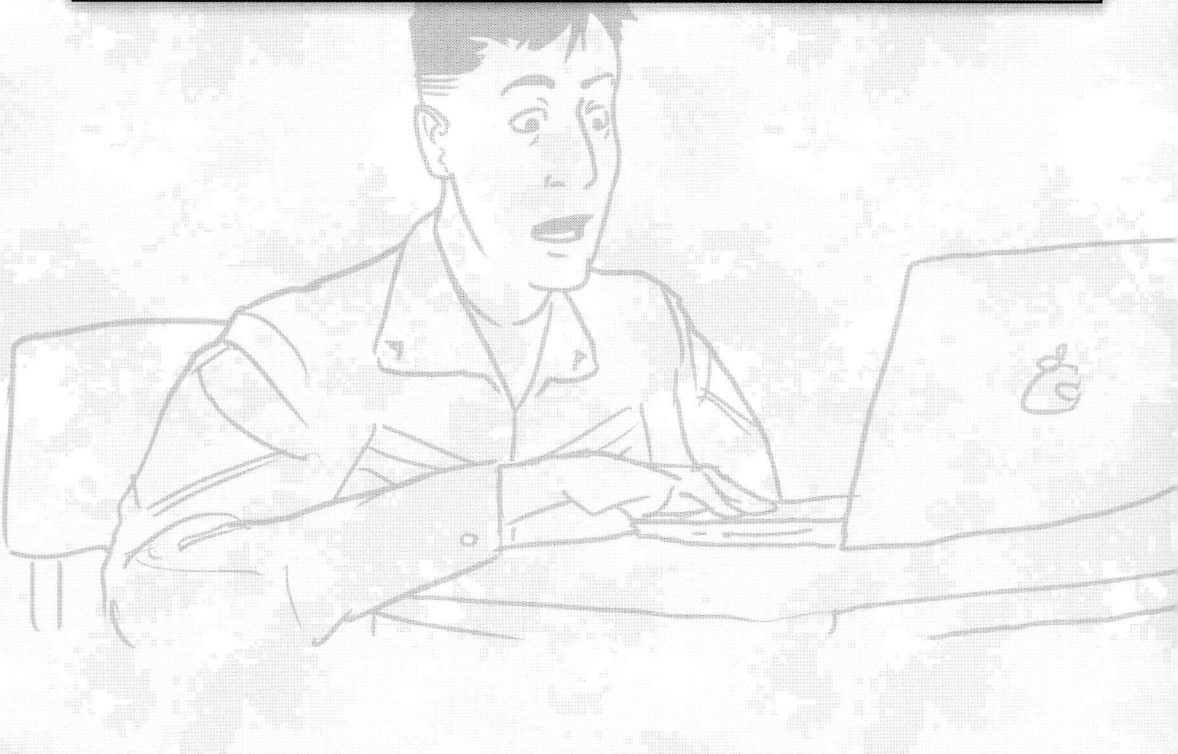

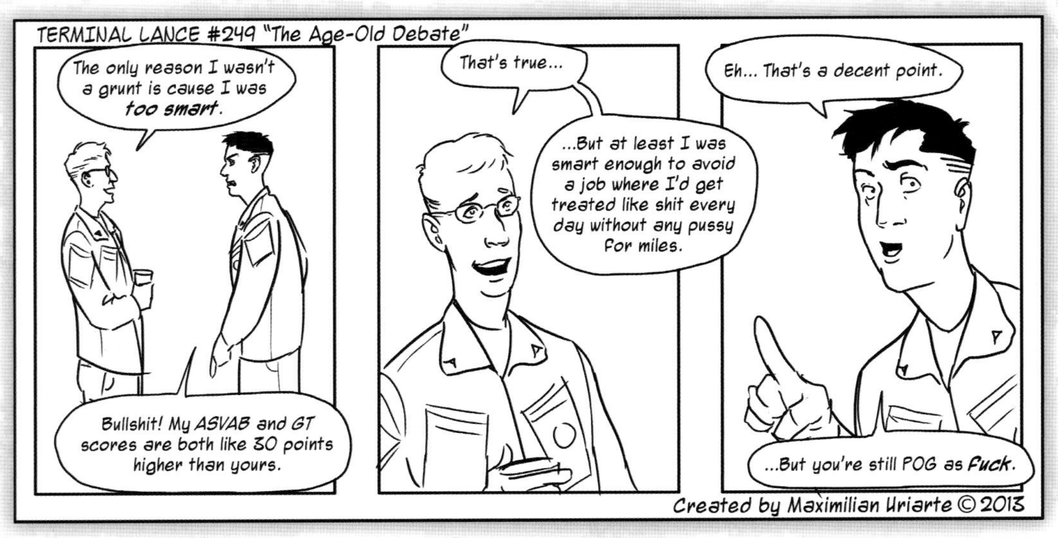
TERMINAL LANCE #249 "The Age-Old Debate"
The only reason I wasn't a grunt is cause I was *too smart*.
Bullshit! My ASVAB and GT scores are both like 30 points higher than yours.
That's true...
...But at least I was smart enough to avoid a job where I'd get treated like shit every day without any pussy for miles.
Eh... That's a decent point.
...But you're still POG as *fuck*.
Created by Maximilian Uriarte © 2013

249 "The Age-Old Debate"

The classic debate of POG's (People Other than Grunts) vs. Grunts will be around as long as these classifications exist in the Marine Corps.

The argument I always despised most was that a POG was not of the oh-three inclination because he was simply too smart for such menial duties during his enlistment. I'd like to think that this comic, along with whatever other accomplishments of mine and those of other successful infantry Marines, should serve to prove that grunts are in fact not stupid. I'm proud to say that my ASVAB score was above 90 and my GT was above 130. I chose to be infantry (specifically, I chose 0300 open-contract and 0351 once I got to SOI).

Scores and other numbers aside, perhaps there is a greater wisdom in the long-term vision that most of the POG population enlisted with. Most grunts tend to have a somewhat existential purpose for their enlistment, transcending rational things like job security after their four years or whether they'll actually enjoy it. That's not really the point of joining the infantry. You don't choose to be in the infantry because you're worried about what job you'll get when you leave. You don't choose to be in the infantry for anything else that can be expressed on a résumé. You do it because you have something to prove.

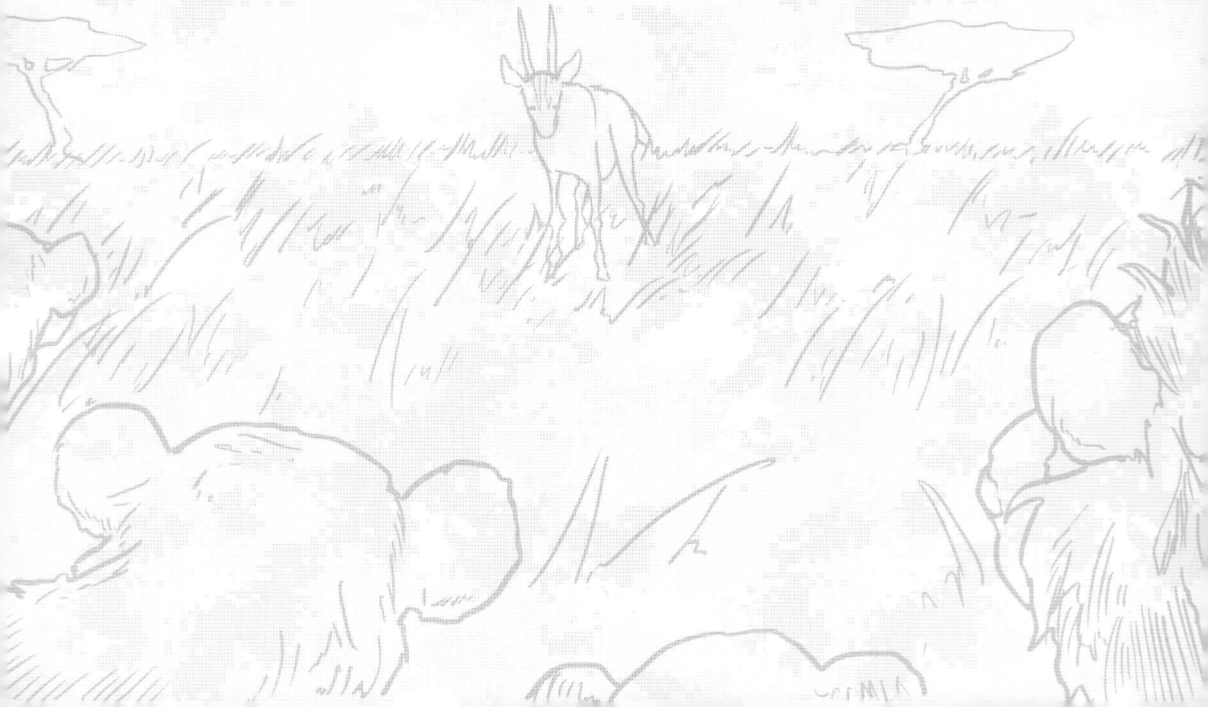

TERMINAL LANCE #250 "Greeting a Staff NCO"
Identify Rank
Do you need to pretend to respect this person by greeting them?
Watch Eyes
If eye contact breaks and moves to your hands or body, be prepared to "fix yourself, Marine."
DOUCHE
Identify Nametape
Do you know this Marine? If not, don't converse under any circumstances. If so, pretend to laugh at bad jokes.
Overall Physique
If you tell this Marine to fuck off, can you outrun them?

TERMINAL LANCE #251 "Military Working Dogs"
Hey is it true that military working dogs outrank their handlers, Sergeant?
Yup! Ol' Odin here is actually a Staff Sergeant!
Oh cool. So when you have sex with him, is that considered bestiality or fraternization?
You know what I'm not sure actua...
Hey wait I don't fuck my dog! Get away from us you asshole!
Shhh... It's okay Odin, don't worry about him.

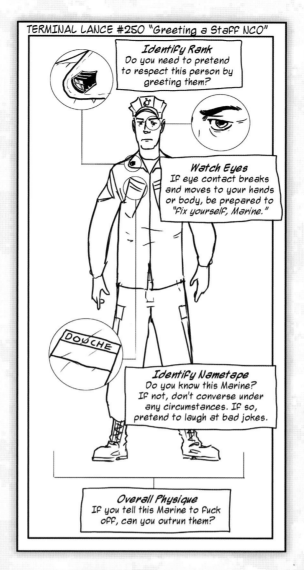

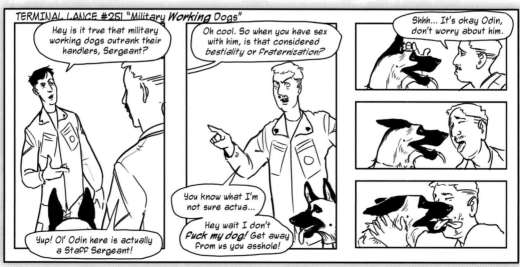

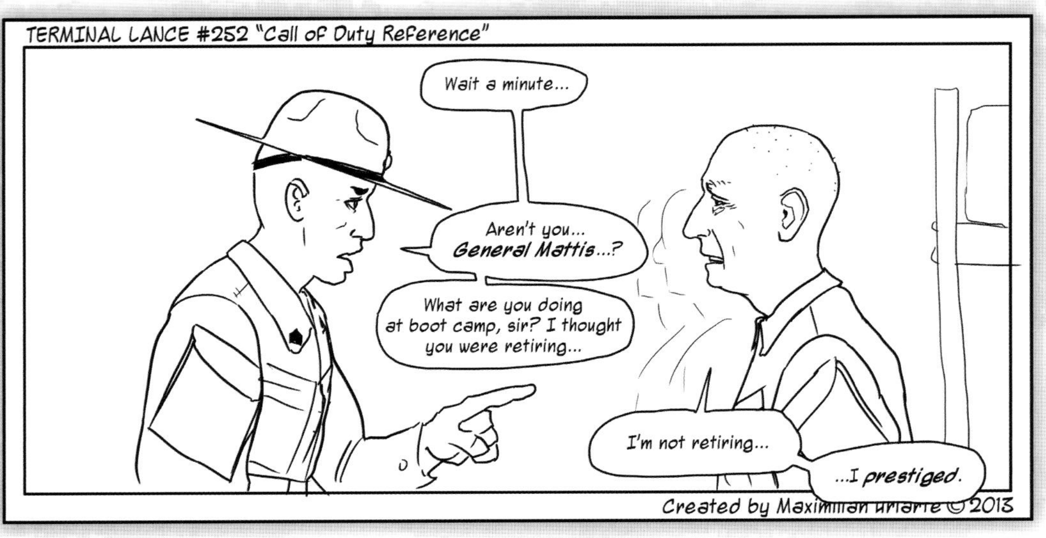
TERMINAL LANCE #252 "Call of Duty Reference"
Wait a minute...
Aren't you... General Mattis...?
What are you doing at boot camp, sir? I thought you were retiring...
I'm not retiring...
...I prestiged.
Created by Maximilian Uriarte © 2013

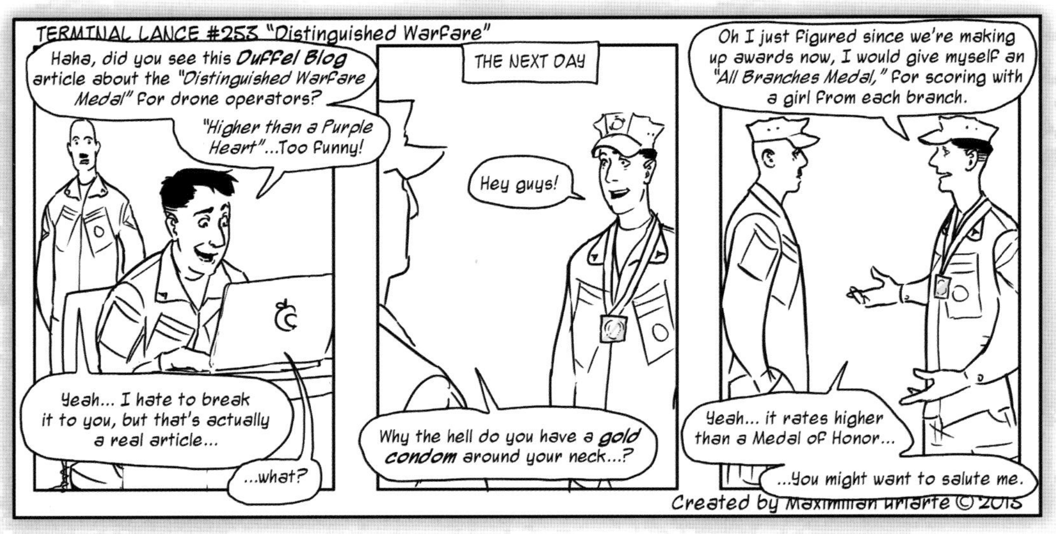
TERMINAL LANCE #253 "Distinguished Warfare"
Haha, did you see this Duffel Blog article about the "Distinguished Warfare Medal" for drone operators?
"Higher than a Purple Heart"...Too funny!
Yeah... I hate to break it to you, but that's actually a real article...
...what?
THE NEXT DAY
Hey guys!
Why the hell do you have a gold condom around your neck...?
Oh I just figured since we're making up awards now, I would give myself an "All Branches Medal," for scoring with a girl from each branch.
Yeah... it rates higher than a Medal of Honor...
...You might want to salute me.
Created by Maximilian Uriarte © 2013

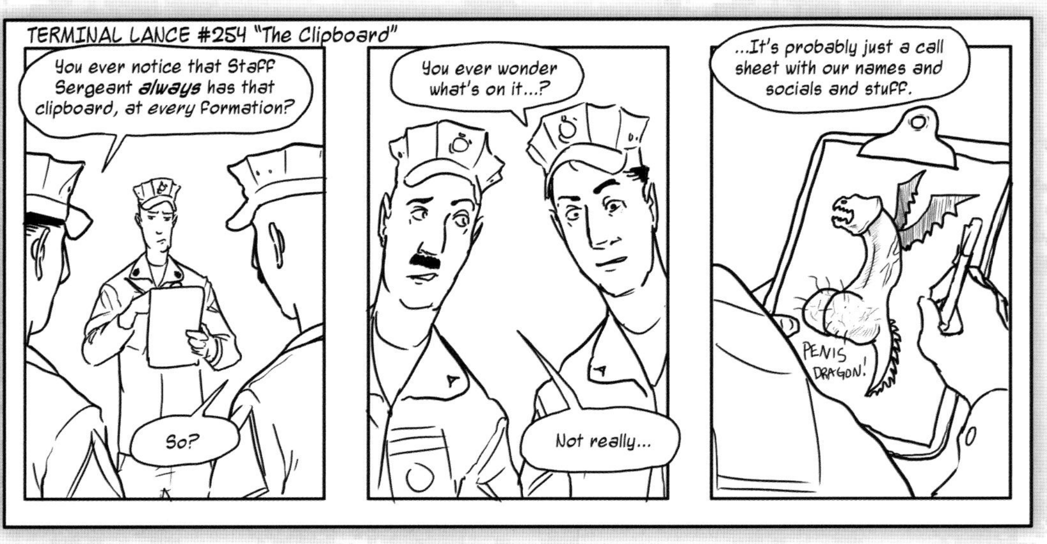
TERMINAL LANCE #254 "The Clipboard"
You ever notice that Staff Sergeant always has that clipboard, at every formation?
So?
You ever wonder what's on it...?
Not really...
...It's probably just a call sheet with our names and socials and stuff.
PENIS DRAGON!

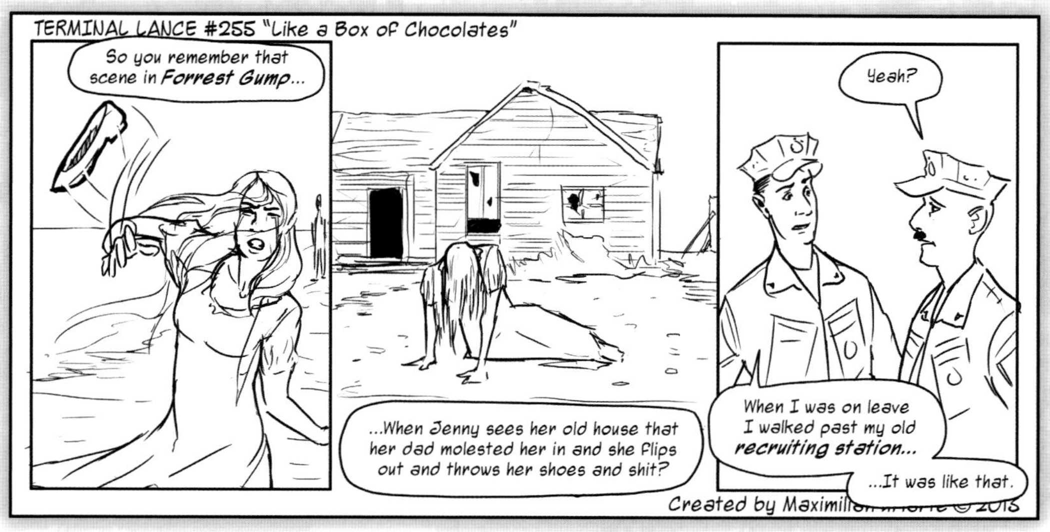
TERMINAL LANCE #255 "Like a Box of Chocolates"
So you remember that scene in Forrest Gump...
...When Jenny sees her old house that her dad molested her in and she flips out and throws her shoes and shit?
Yeah?
When I was on leave I walked past my old recruiting station...
...It was like that.
Created by Maximilian Uriarte © 2013

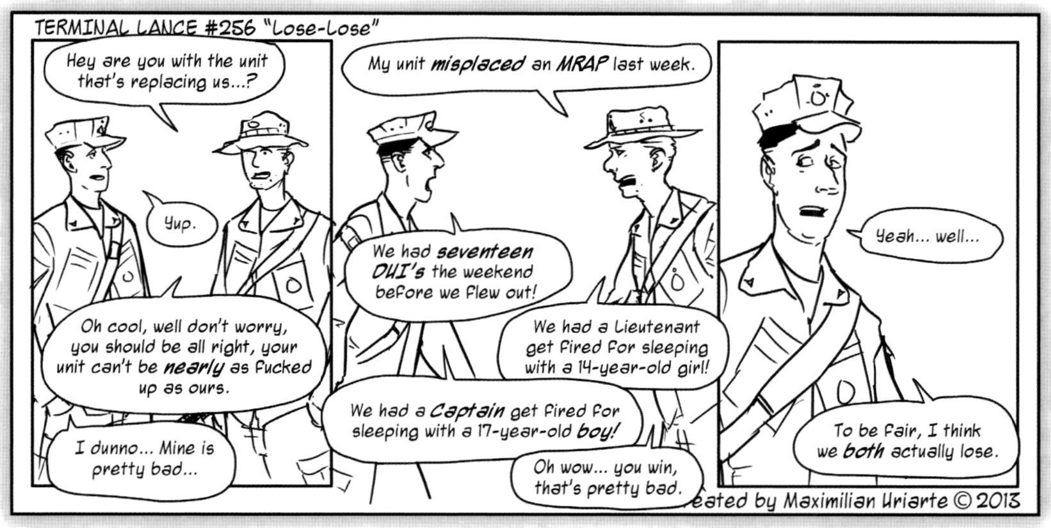
TERMINAL LANCE #256 "Lose-Lose"
Hey are you with the unit that's replacing us...?
Yup.
Oh cool, well don't worry, you should be all right, your unit can't be nearly as fucked up as ours.
I dunno... Mine is pretty bad...
My unit misplaced an MRAP last week.
We had seventeen DUI's the weekend before we flew out!
We had a Lieutenant get fired for sleeping with a 14-year-old girl!
We had a Captain get fired for sleeping with a 17-year-old boy!
Oh wow... you win, that's pretty bad.
Yeah... well...
To be fair, I think we both actually lose.
Created by Maximilian Uriarte © 2013

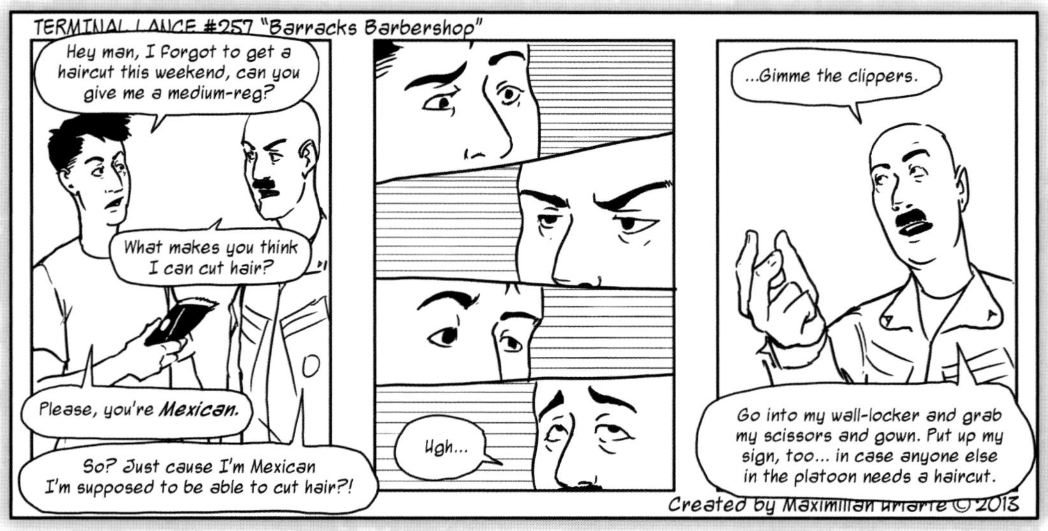
TERMINAL LANCE #257 "Barracks Barbershop"
Hey man, I forgot to get a haircut this weekend, can you give me a medium-reg?
What makes you think I can cut hair?
Please, you're Mexican.
So? Just cause I'm Mexican I'm supposed to be able to cut hair?!
Ugh...
...Gimme the clippers.
Go into my wall-locker and grab my scissors and gown. Put up my sign, too... in case anyone else in the platoon needs a haircut.
Created by Maximilian Uriarte © 2013

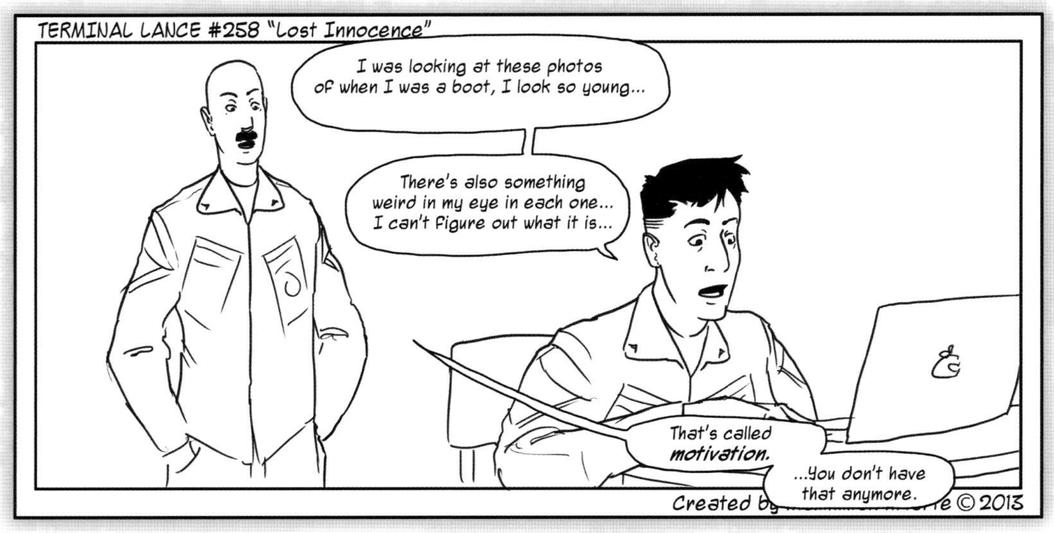
TERMINAL LANCE #258 "Lost Innocence"
I was looking at these photos of when I was a boot, I look so young...
There's also something weird in my eye in each one... I can't figure out what it is...
That's called **motivation.**
...You don't have that anymore.
Created by
© 2013

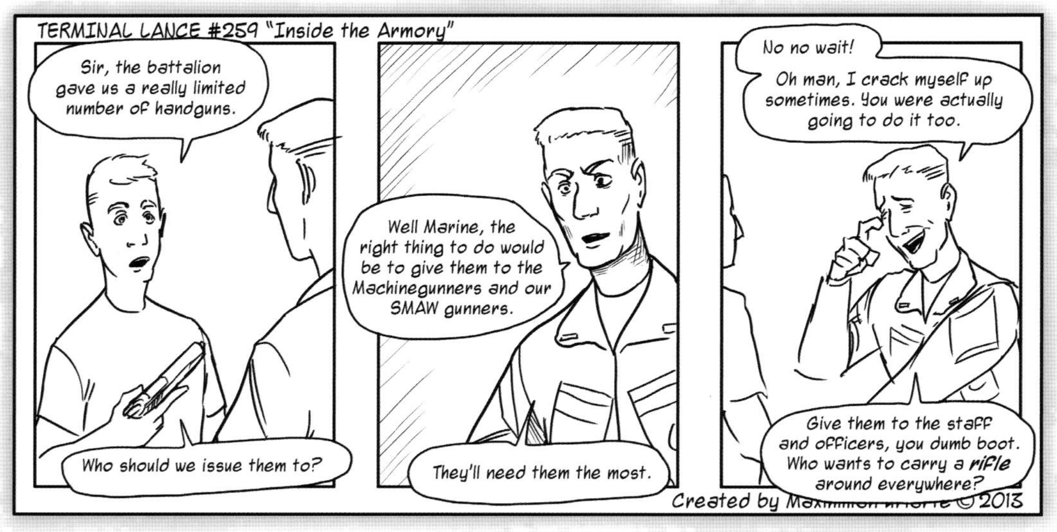
TERMINAL LANCE #259 "Inside the Armory"
Sir, the battalion gave us a really limited number of handguns.
Who should we issue them to?
Well Marine, the right thing to do would be to give them to the Machinegunners and our SMAW gunners.
They'll need them the most.
No no wait!
Oh man, I crack myself up sometimes. You were actually going to do it too.
Give them to the staff and officers, you dumb boot. Who wants to carry a *rifle* around everywhere?
Created by
© 2013

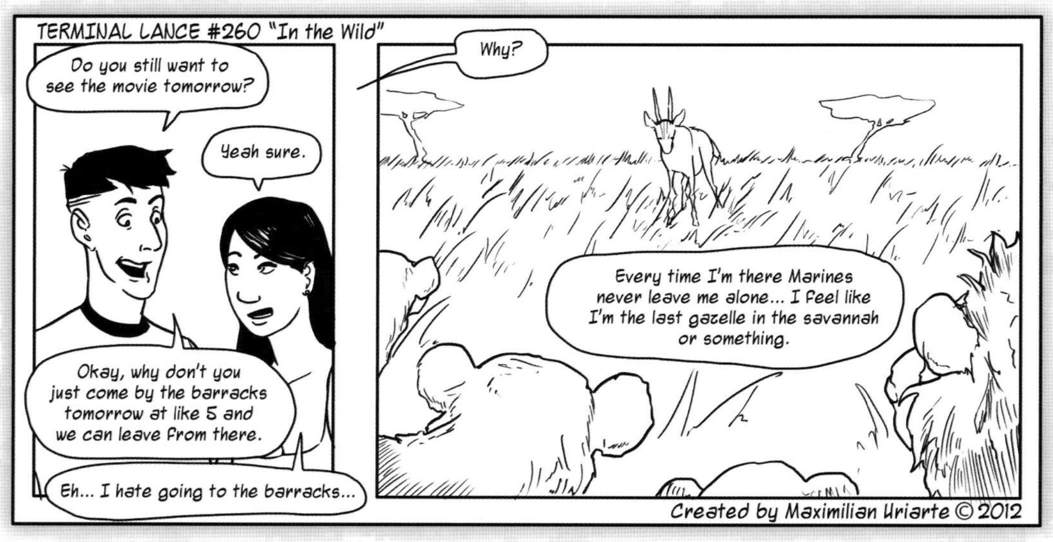
TERMINAL LANCE #260 "In the Wild"
Do you still want to see the movie tomorrow?
Yeah sure.
Okay, why don't you just come by the barracks tomorrow at like 5 and we can leave from there.
Eh... I hate going to the barracks...
Why?
Every time I'm there Marines never leave me alone... I feel like I'm the last gazelle in the savannah or something.
Created by Maximilian Uriarte © 2012

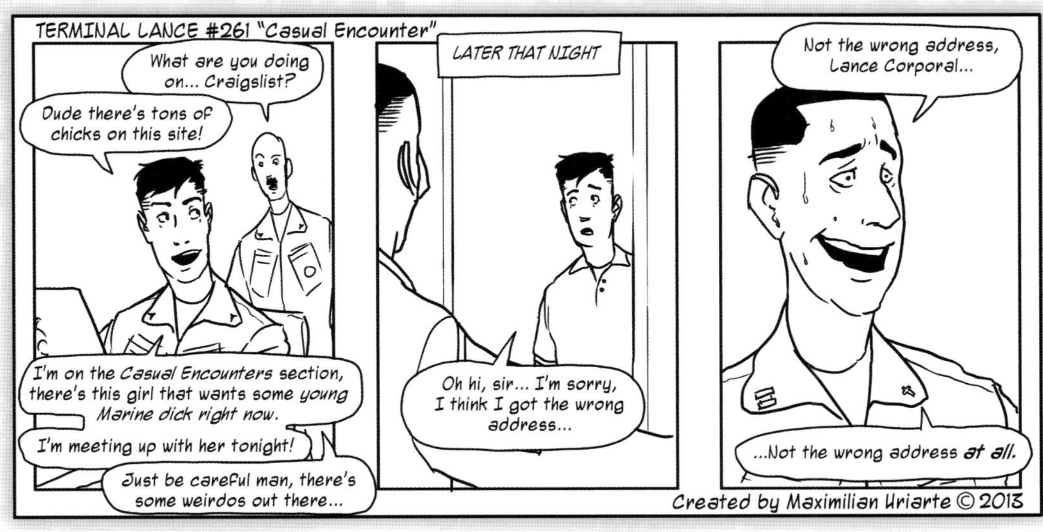
TERMINAL LANCE #261 "Casual Encounter"
What are you doing on... Craigslist?
Dude there's tons of chicks on this site!
I'm on the Casual Encounters section, there's this girl that wants some young Marine dick right now.
I'm meeting up with her tonight!
Just be careful man, there's some weirdos out there...
LATER THAT NIGHT
Oh hi, sir... I'm sorry, I think I got the wrong address...
Not the wrong address, Lance Corporal...
...Not the wrong address at all.
Created by Maximilian Uriarte © 2013

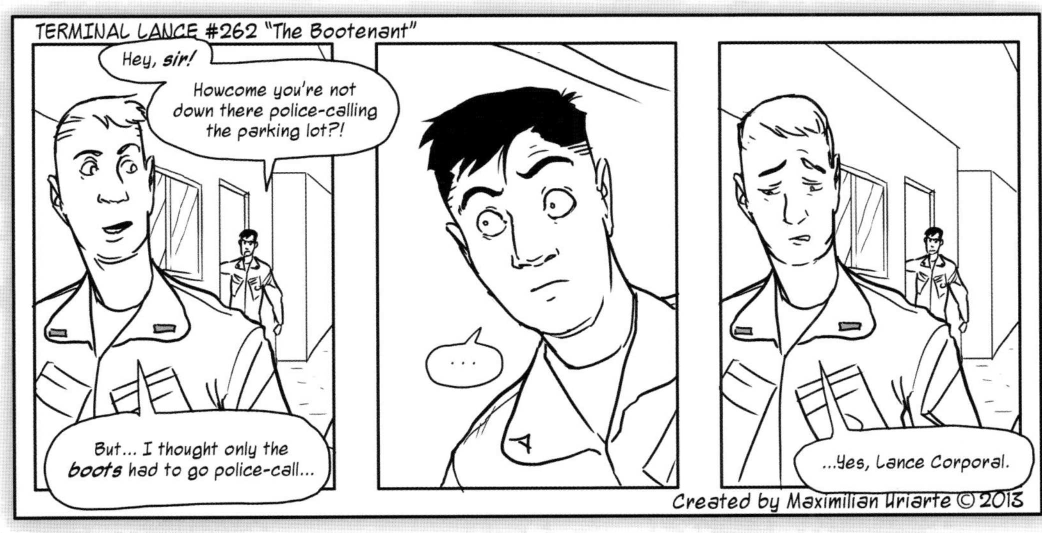
TERMINAL LANCE #262 "The Bootenant"
Hey, sir!
Howcome you're not down there police-calling the parking lot?!
But... I thought only the boots had to go police-call...
...
...Yes, Lance Corporal.
Created by Maximilian Uriarte © 2013

262 "The Bootenant"

If it weren't for the fact that they get paid out of the gate about twice as much as an equally experienced enlisted Marine, I might feel bad for Lieutenants when they enter the fleet. The Lieutenant has the dubious honor of being in charge of about forty guys that really have absolutely no respect for him whatsoever. To the average salty Lance Corporal with a deployment and an NJP or two under his belt, someone with no deployment experience and shiny bars is just as boot as the fresh-faced kid from SOI that can barely tie his own boots.

Unfortunately, there's not really much you can do about it. New Lieutenants are given a platoon to command. That's just how it is. My platoon went through a few butter-bars in my time, and it's always interesting to see how they act when they first get there. One new Lieutenant actually used to stand at parade rest for the senior Lance Corporals and would refer to them by their rank. While I respect the ideology of this approach, it ultimately fails to gain respect because an infantry platoon is prison rules, bitch. You better make someone your bitch on the first day, or else the green weenie won't be the only thing working its way up your rectum daily.

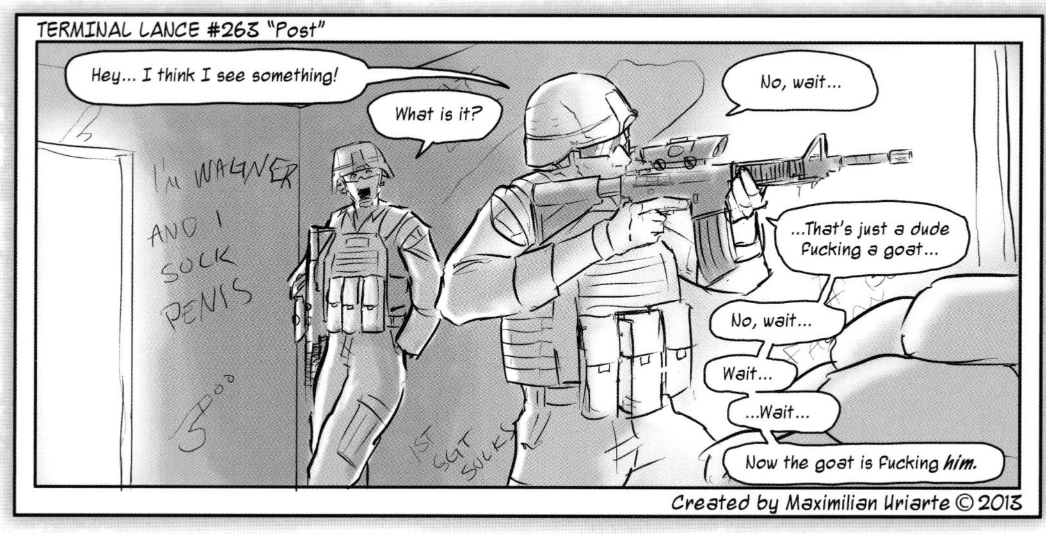
TERMINAL LANCE #263 "Post"
Hey... I think I see something!
What is it?
No, wait...
I'M WAGNER AND I SUCK PENIS
...That's just a dude fucking a goat...
No, wait...
Wait...
...Wait...
1ST SGT SUCKS
Now the goat is fucking *him.*
Created by Maximilian Uriarte © 2013

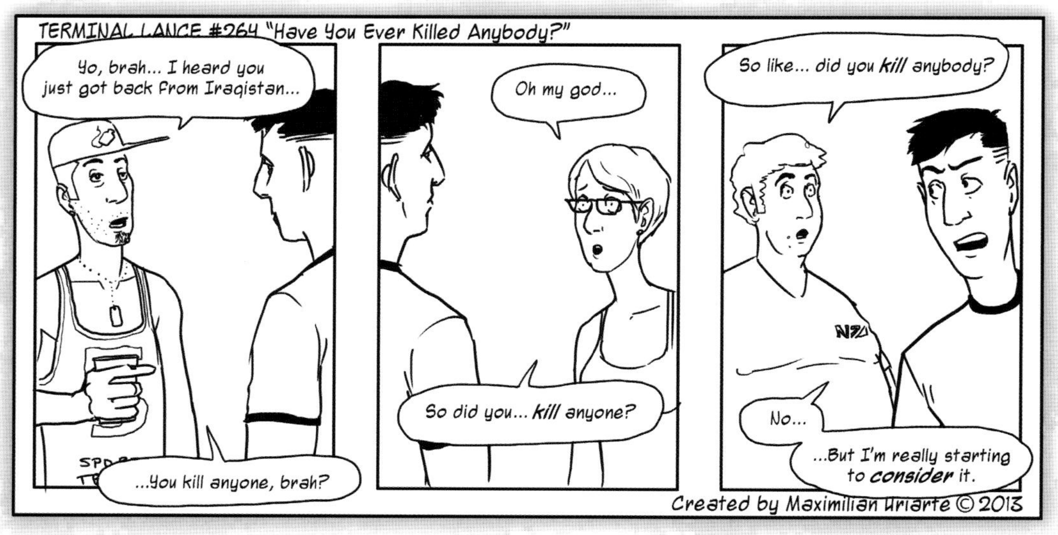
TERMINAL LANCE #264 "Have You Ever Killed Anybody?"
Yo, brah... I heard you just got back from Iraqistan...
...You kill anyone, brah?
Oh my god...
So did you... *kill* anyone?
So like... did you *kill* anybody?
No...
...But I'm really starting to *consider* it.
Created by Maximilian Uriarte © 2013

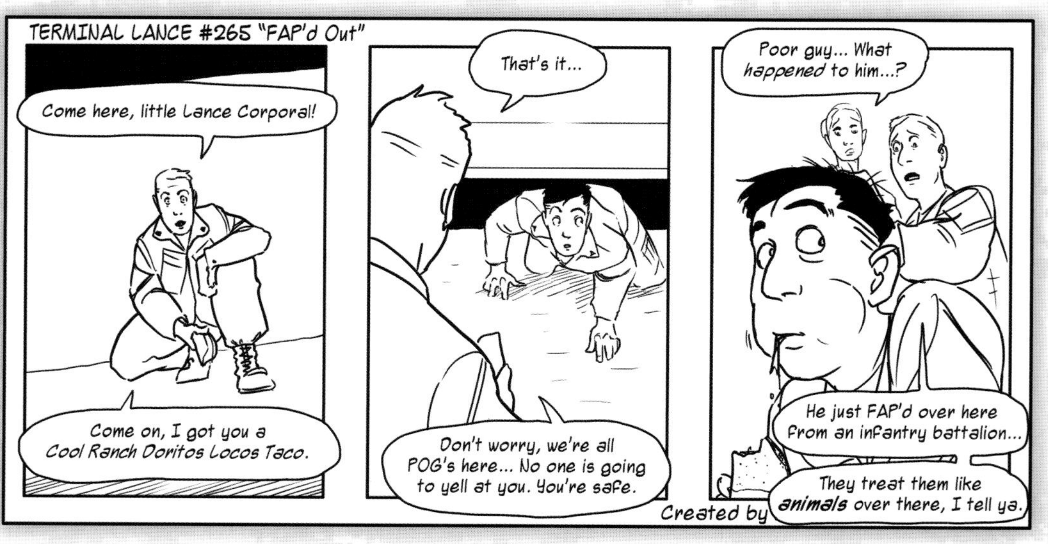
TERMINAL LANCE #265 "FAP'd Out"
Come here, little Lance Corporal!
Come on, I got you a Cool Ranch Doritos Locos Taco.
That's it...
Don't worry, we're all POG's here... No one is going to yell at you. You're safe.
Poor guy... What *happened* to him...?
He just FAP'd over here from an infantry battalion...
They treat them like *animals* over there, I tell ya.
Created by

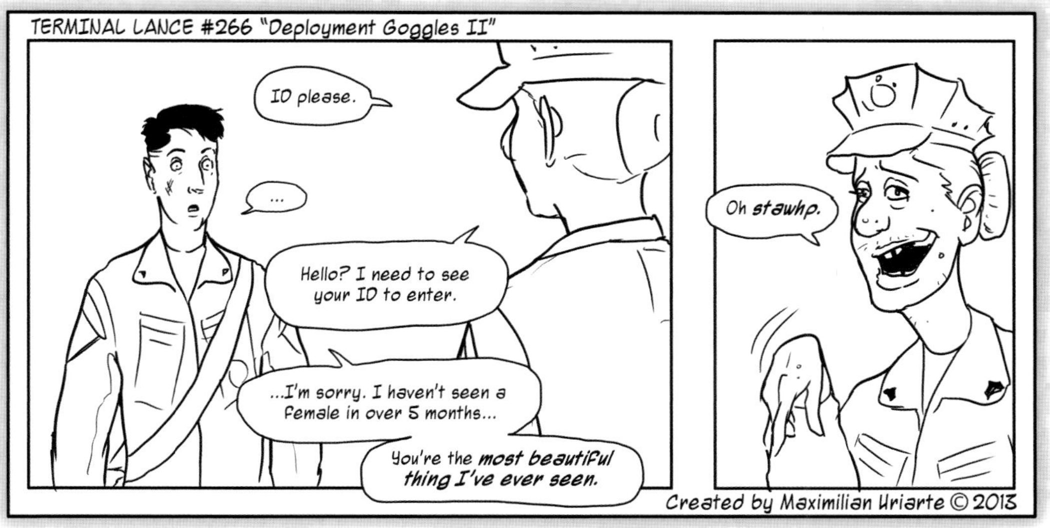
TERMINAL LANCE #266 "Deployment Goggles II"
ID please.
...
Hello? I need to see your ID to enter.
...I'm sorry. I haven't seen a female in over 5 months...
You're the most beautiful thing I've ever seen.
Oh stawhp.
Created by Maximilian Uriarte © 2013

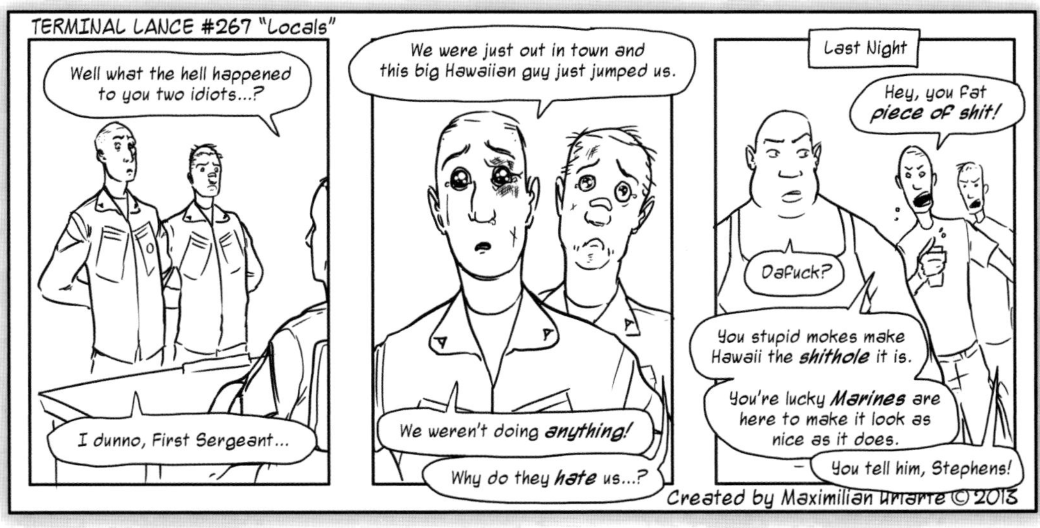
TERMINAL LANCE #267 "Locals"
Well what the hell happened to you two idiots...?
I dunno, First Sergeant...
We were just out in town and this big Hawaiian guy just jumped us.
We weren't doing anything!
Why do they hate us...?
Last Night
Hey, you fat piece of shit!
Dafuck?
You stupid mokes make Hawaii the shithole it is.
You're lucky Marines are here to make it look as nice as it does.
You tell him, Stephens!
Created by Maximilian Uriarte © 2013

267 "Locals"

I feel like this strip might not really apply to places like Camp Pendleton or Lejeune, but to those of us that were stationed in Hawaii or even you Okinawa vets, surely it's something you've seen happen. While aboard beautiful Kaneohe Bay, it seemed like every weekend there was some new incident involving locals out in town. The Marines would have the same story every time (*"They just jumped us"*), when in reality, Marines aren't always the most tactful of species. And it was usually the same Marines that seemed to always get jumped out in town. In all the three and a half years I was there, I never once ran into any locals that meant me harm. Either I just hung out in the right neighborhoods, or I'm not a complete asshole.

Of course, I'm not saying that violent crimes don't happen for a reason, because of course they do.

All I'm saying is, well, I know Marines.

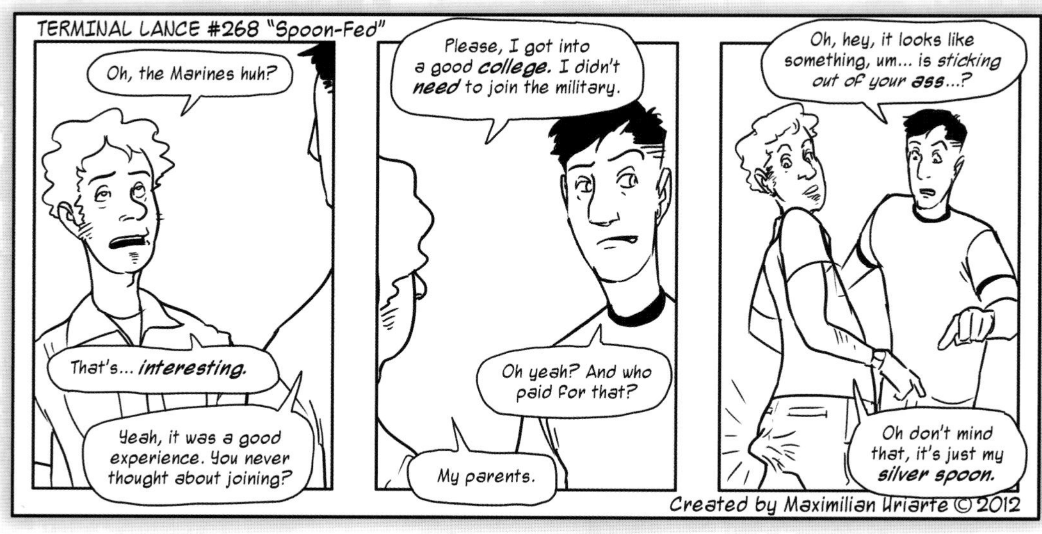
TERMINAL LANCE #268 "Spoon-Fed"
Oh, the Marines huh?
That's... *interesting.*
Yeah, it was a good experience. You never thought about joining?
Please, I got into a good **college.** I didn't **need** to join the military.
Oh yeah? And who paid for that?
My parents.
Oh, hey, it looks like something, um... is *sticking* out of your **ass**...?
Oh don't mind that, it's just my **silver spoon.**
Created by Maximilian Uriarte © 2012

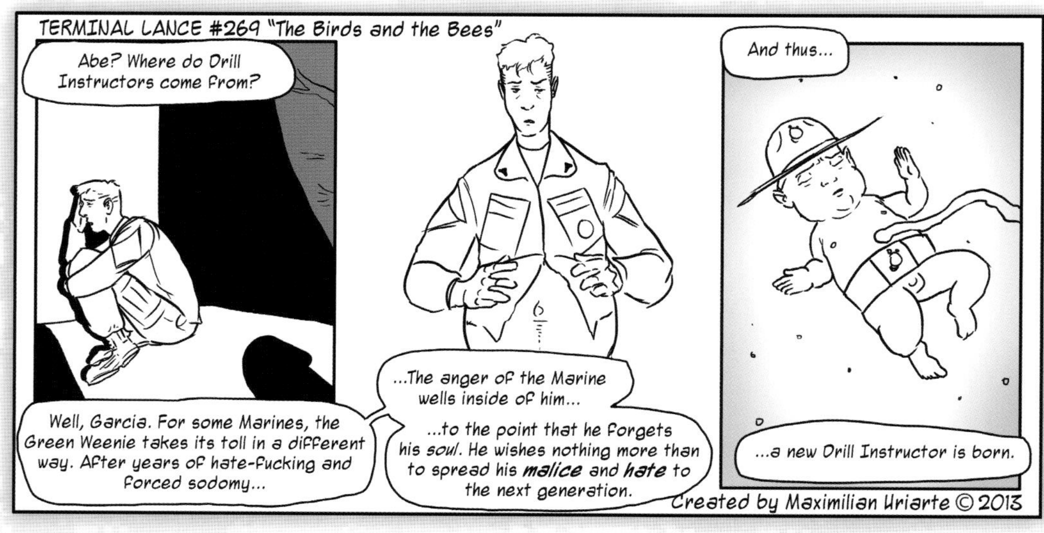
TERMINAL LANCE #269 "The Birds and the Bees"
Abe? Where do Drill Instructors come from?
Well, Garcia. For some Marines, the Green Weenie takes its toll in a different way. After years of hate-fucking and forced sodomy...
...The anger of the Marine wells inside of him...
...to the point that he forgets his *soul.* He wishes nothing more than to spread his **malice** and **hate** to the next generation.
And thus...
...a new Drill Instructor is born.
Created by Maximilian Uriarte © 2013

269 "The Birds and the Bees"

I could never do it.

I could never be a Drill Instructor.

Don't get me wrong—I respect what they do. Without DI's we wouldn't have Marines. It's hard work and not everyone is cut out for it. I consider myself one of those people. I couldn't be a DI because I just don't think I would enjoy being a complete asshole 24/7 for three months straight. That's a very demanding regimen of eating nothing but recruit dignity and sorrow, and I've never been particularly good at dieting.

But really, it does take a special kind of person to actually be a good Drill Instructor. You can't just yell all the time, or no one takes you seriously. I found that the new DI's tend to yell the most. They think that's the way to get results, when really, it was much scarier when one of them didn't wear their anger on the surface. When you didn't know what they were thinking . . . that's when you would shit your pants. Having someone screaming in your face is something you get used to rather quickly.

Again though, I have plethoric respect for those that wear the campaign cover. It's just a tough job, babysitting sixty to a hundred sloppily shaven recruits that smell like a combination of sweaty shit and Cobra 65.

So, good on you, Drill Instructors. I could never do what you do, and would never want to.

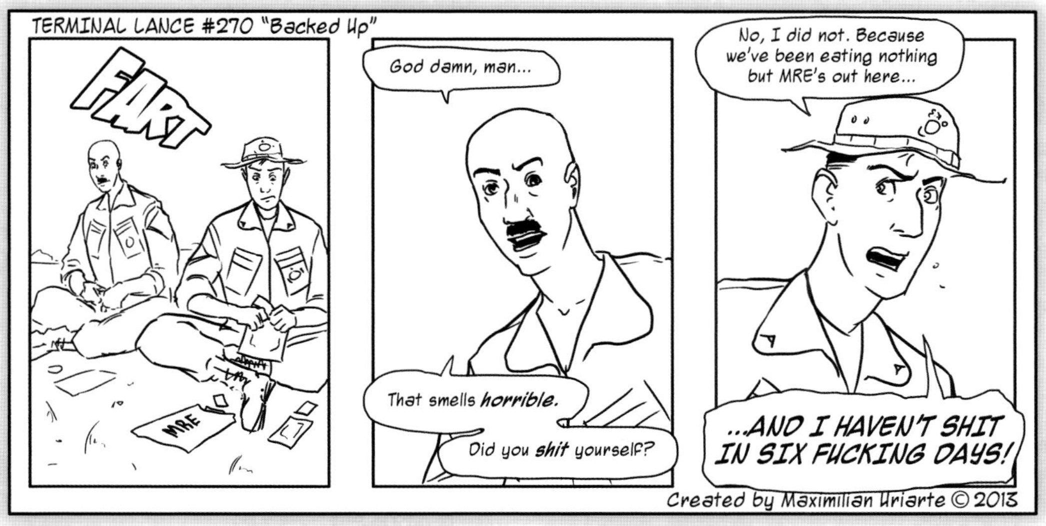
TERMINAL LANCE #270 "Backed Up"
FART
MRE
God damn, man...
That smells *horrible.*
Did you *shit* yourself?
No, I did not. Because we've been eating nothing but MRE's out here...
...AND I HAVEN'T SHIT IN SIX FUCKING DAYS!
Created by Maximilian Uriarte © 2013

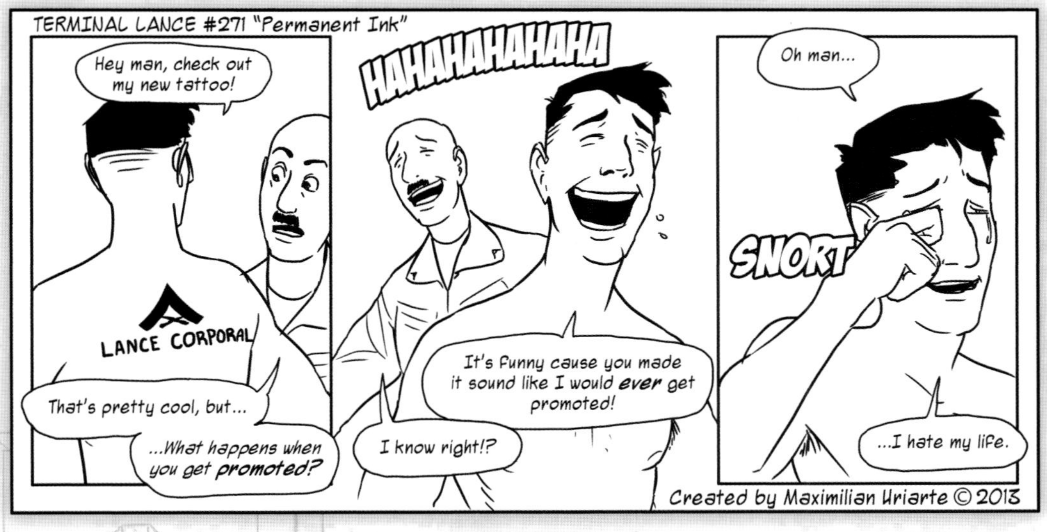
TERMINAL LANCE #271 "Permanent Ink"
Hey man, check out my new tattoo!
LANCE CORPORAL
That's pretty cool, but...
...What happens when you get *promoted?*
HAHAHAHAHAHA
It's funny cause you made it sound like I would *ever* get promoted!
I know right!?
Oh man...
SNORT
...I hate my life.
Created by Maximilian Uriarte © 2013

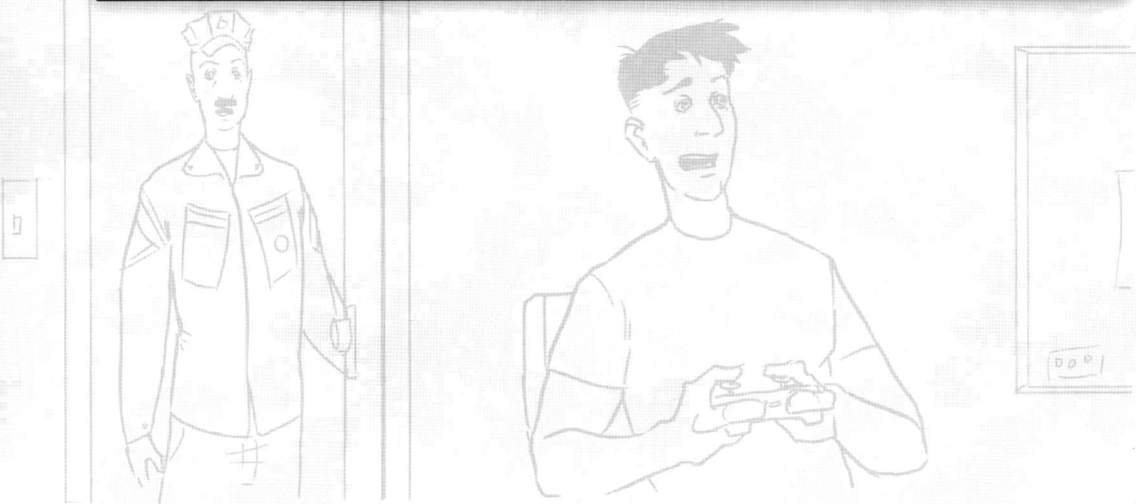

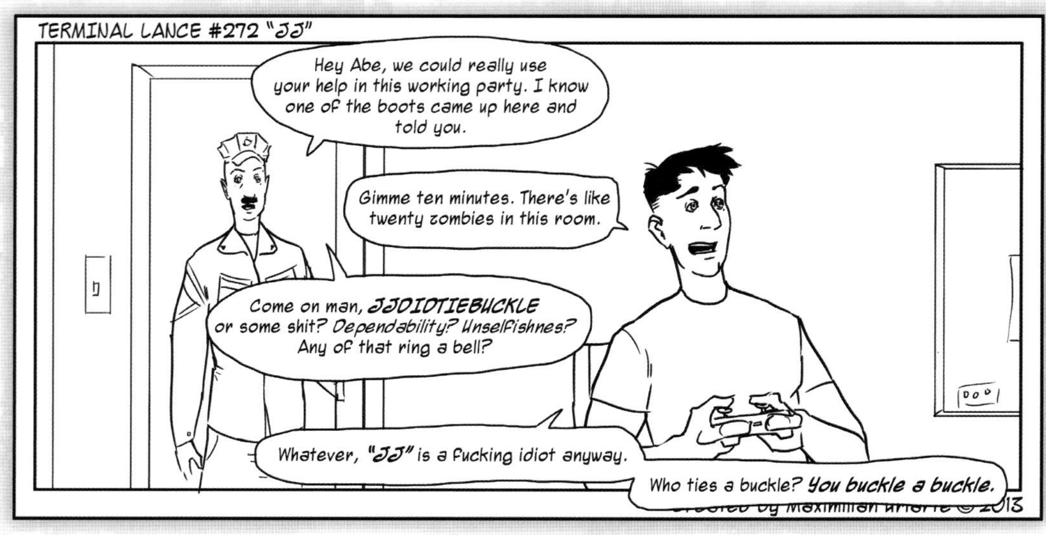
TERMINAL LANCE #272 "JJ"
Hey Abe, we could really use your help in this working party. I know one of the boots came up here and told you.
Gimme ten minutes. There's like twenty zombies in this room.
Come on man, JJDIDTIEBUCKLE or some shit? Dependability? Unselfishnes? Any of that ring a bell?
Whatever, "JJ" is a fucking idiot anyway.
Who ties a buckle? You buckle a buckle.
Created by Maximilian Uriarte © 2013

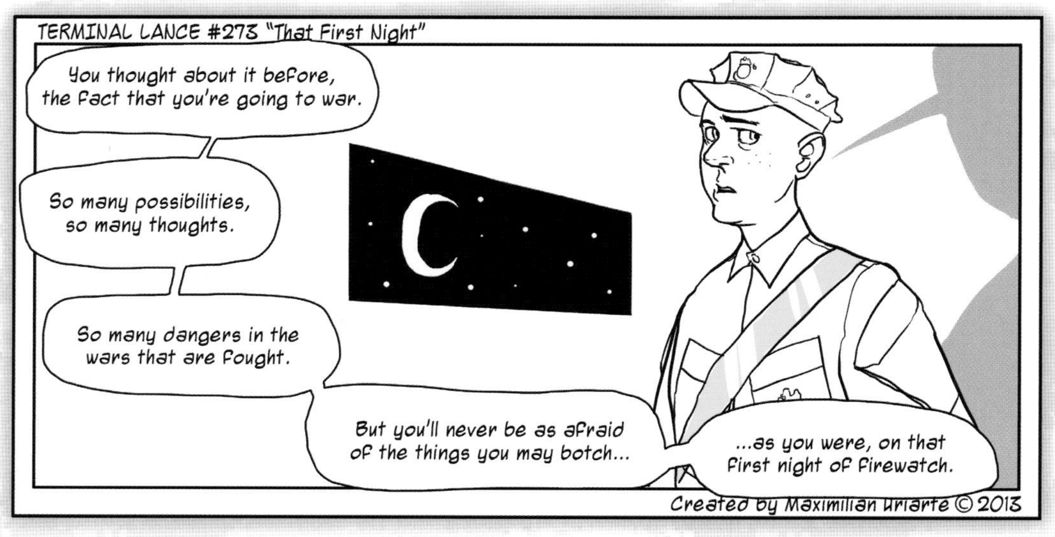
TERMINAL LANCE #273 "That First Night"
You thought about it before, the fact that you're going to war.
So many possibilities, so many thoughts.
So many dangers in the wars that are fought.
But you'll never be as afraid of the things you may botch...
...as you were, on that first night of firewatch.
Created by Maximilian Uriarte © 2013

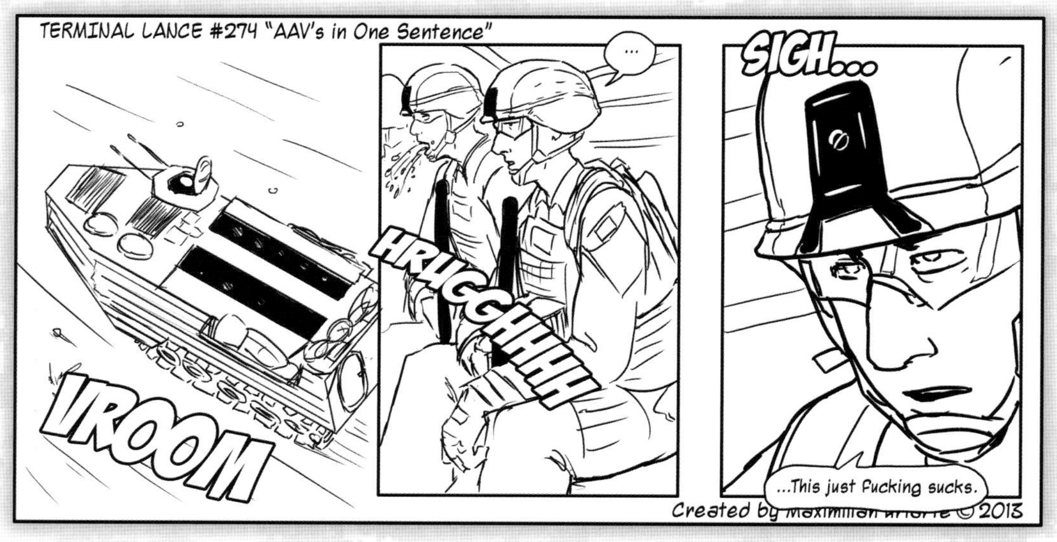
TERMINAL LANCE #274 "AAV's in One Sentence"
VROOM
...
HRUGGHHHH
SIGH...
...This just fucking sucks.
Created by Maximilian Uriarte © 2013

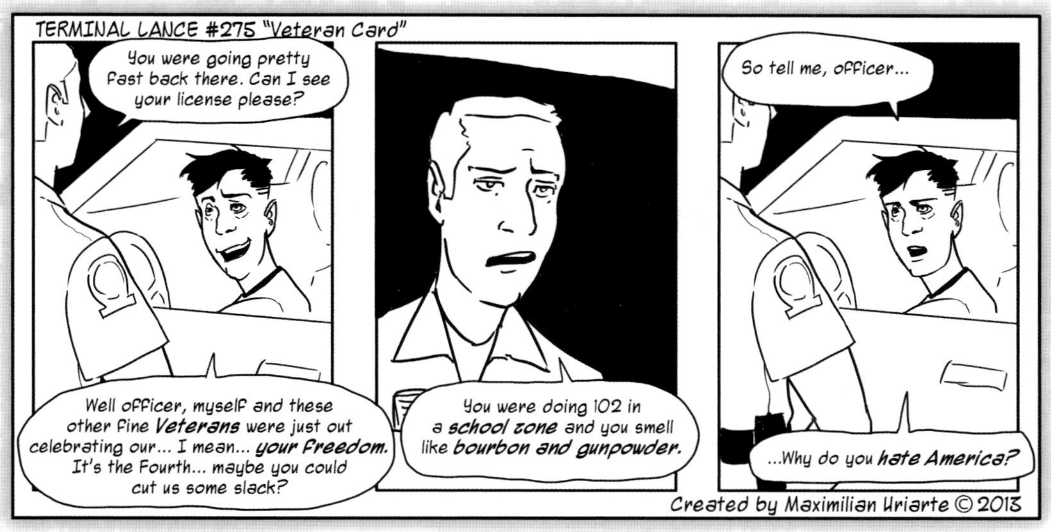
TERMINAL LANCE #275 "Veteran Card"
You were going pretty fast back there. Can I see your license please?
Well officer, myself and these other fine Veterans were just out celebrating our... I mean... your freedom. It's the Fourth... maybe you could cut us some slack?
You were doing 102 in a school zone and you smell like bourbon and gunpowder.
So tell me, officer...
...Why do you hate America?
Created by Maximilian Uriarte © 2013

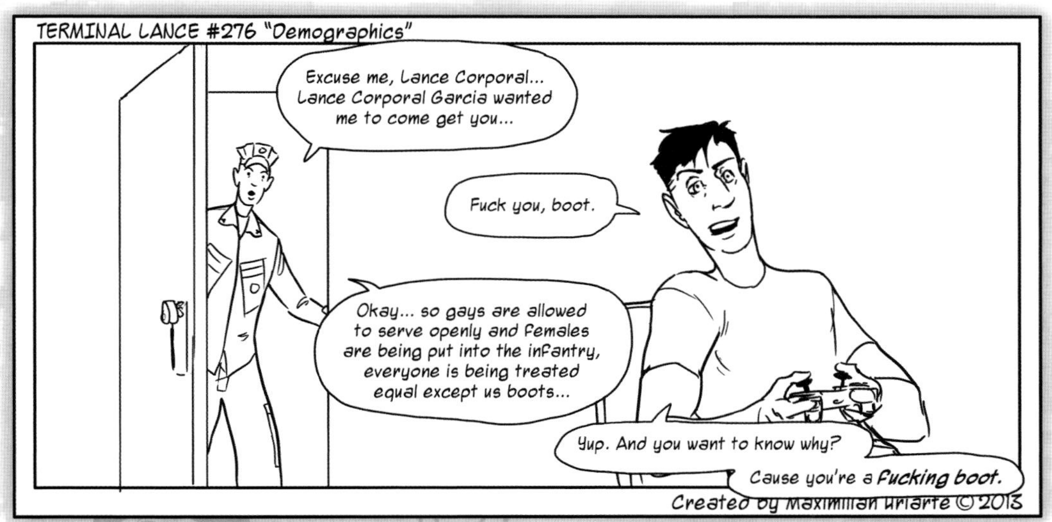
TERMINAL LANCE #276 "Demographics"
Excuse me, Lance Corporal... Lance Corporal Garcia wanted me to come get you...
Fuck you, boot.
Okay... so gays are allowed to serve openly and females are being put into the infantry, everyone is being treated equal except us boots...
Yup. And you want to know why?
Cause you're a fucking boot.
Created by Maximilian Uriarte © 2013

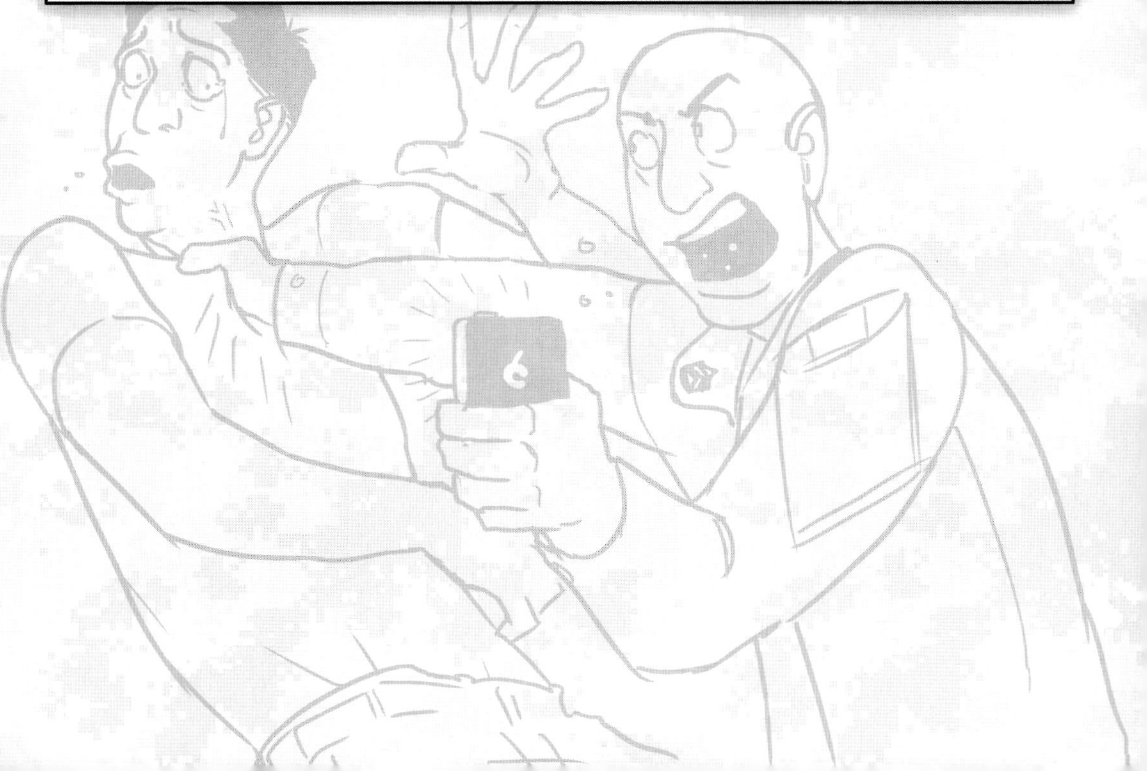

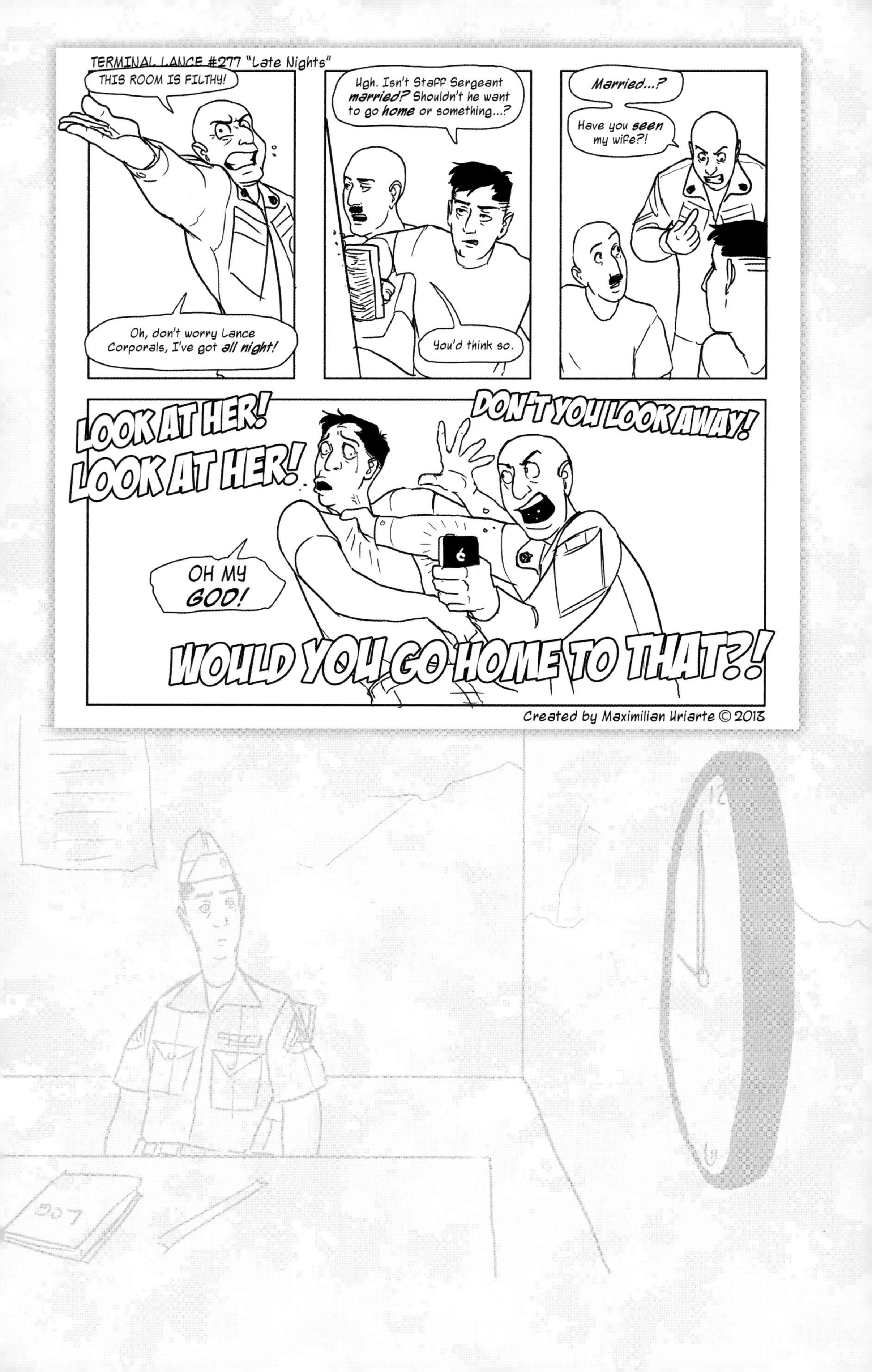
TERMINAL LANCE #277 "Late Nights"
THIS ROOM IS FILTHY!
Oh, don't worry Lance Corporals, I've got *all night!*
Ugh. Isn't Staff Sergeant *married?* Shouldn't he want to go *home* or something...?
You'd think so.
Married...?
Have you *seen* my wife?!
LOOK AT HER! LOOK AT HER!
DON'T YOU LOOK AWAY!
OH MY *GOD!*
WOULD YOU GO HOME TO THAT?!
Created by Maximilian Uriarte © 2013
LOG

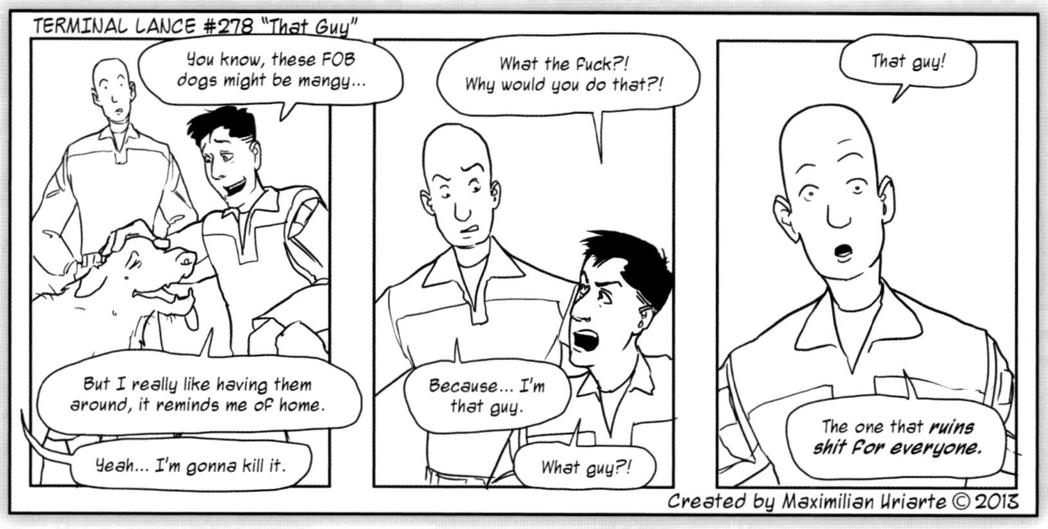
TERMINAL LANCE #278 "That Guy"
You know, these FOB dogs might be mangy...
But I really like having them around, it reminds me of home.
Yeah... I'm gonna kill it.
What the fuck?! Why would you do that?!
Because... I'm that guy.
What guy?!
That guy!
The one that **ruins shit for everyone.**
Created by Maximilian Uriarte © 2013

278 "That Guy"

Not to be confused with "That One Guy," this is "That Guy."

While That Guy doesn't necessarily have to be about FOB dogs, there's always some douchemaster that wants to shoot the animals aboard the FOB. You know them, we all do. They're the fucking asshole that grew up with an abusive father or something so they feel the need to shoot harmless animals.

Now don't get me wrong: I'm well aware that many of the dogs in the Middle East are feral and shouldn't be kept aboard the FOB. That's not what I'm talking about. When I was in Iraq in 2007, we had this random orange cat wander into the camp and sleep around for a few days in different beds. I am partial to orange cats (every cat I've ever had has been orange), so naturally it stayed with me and my people for a few days. It wandered off, but within two days we came to find out that That Guy smashed its head with a brick. The reason? Who knows.

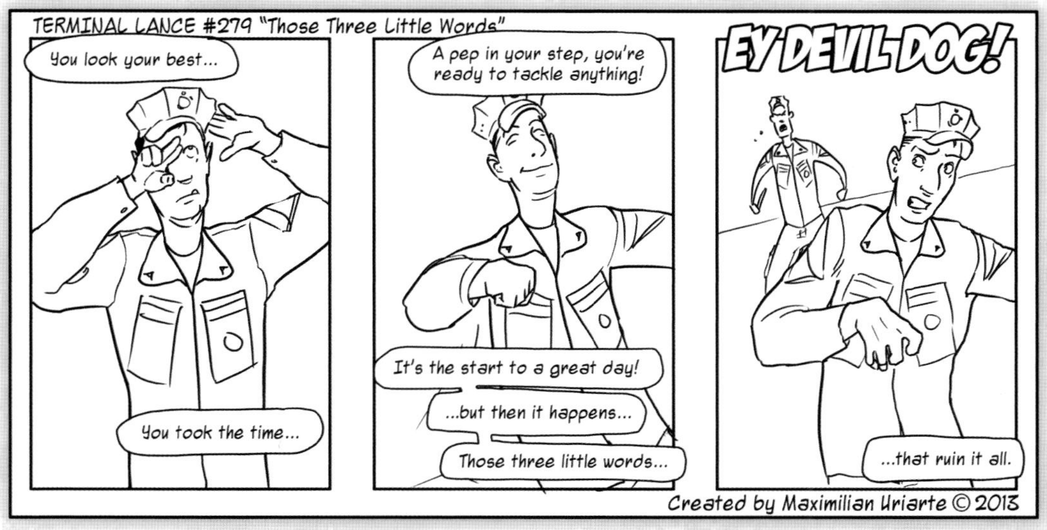
TERMINAL LANCE #279 "Those Three Little Words"
You look your best...
You took the time...
A pep in your step, you're ready to tackle anything!
It's the start to a great day!
...but then it happens...
Those three little words...
EY DEVIL DOG!
...that ruin it all.
Created by Maximilian Uriarte © 2013

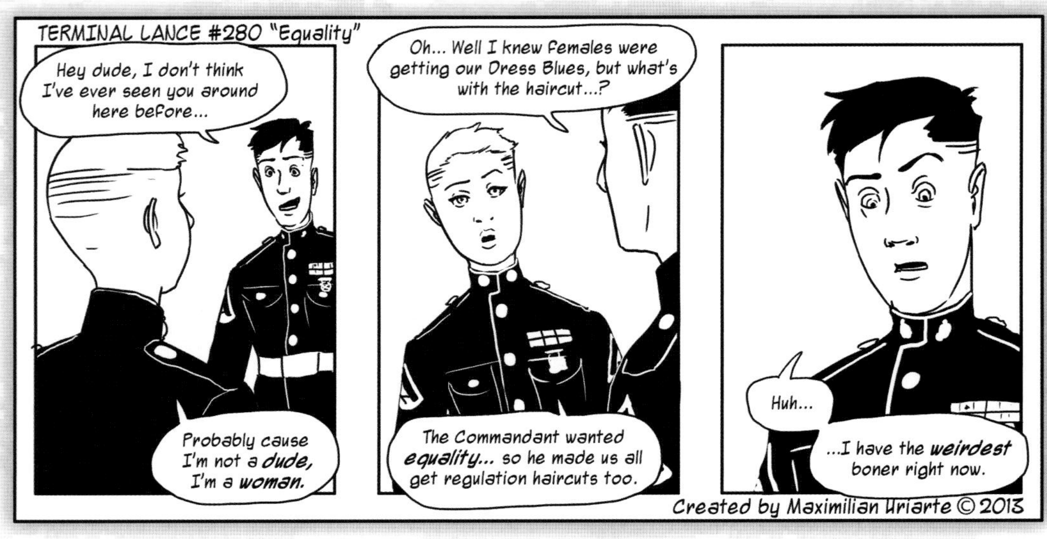
TERMINAL LANCE #280 "Equality"
Hey dude, I don't think I've ever seen you around here before...
Probably cause I'm not a *dude,* I'm a *woman.*
Oh... Well I knew females were getting our Dress Blues, but what's with the haircut...?
The Commandant wanted *equality...* so he made us all get regulation haircuts too.
Huh...
...I have the *weirdest* boner right now.
Created by Maximilian Uriarte © 2013

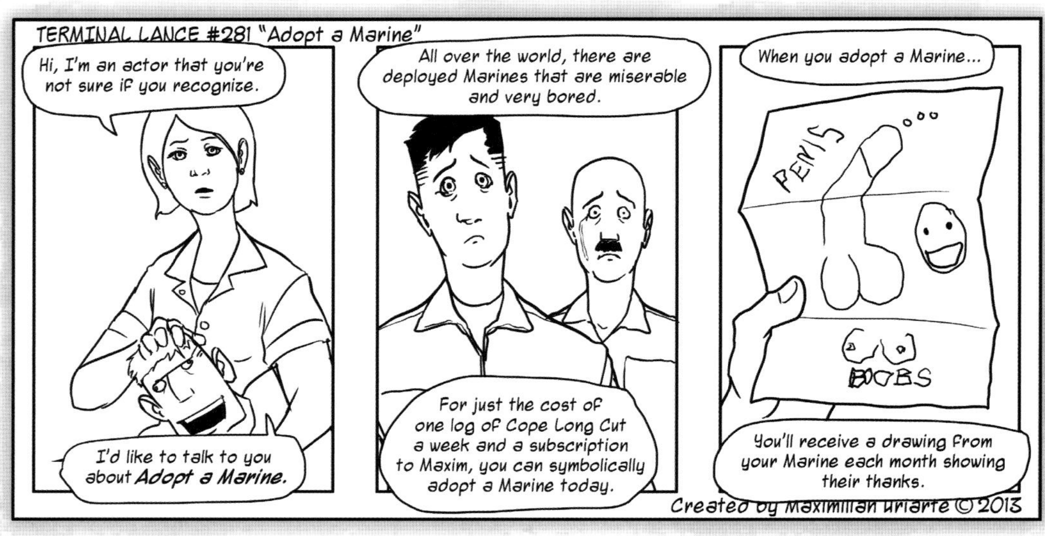
TERMINAL LANCE #281 "Adopt a Marine"
Hi, I'm an actor that you're not sure if you recognize.
I'd like to talk to you about *Adopt a Marine.*
All over the world, there are deployed Marines that are miserable and very bored.
For just the cost of one log of Cope Long Cut a week and a subscription to Maxim, you can symbolically adopt a Marine today.
When you adopt a Marine...
PENIS
BOOBS
You'll receive a drawing from your Marine each month showing their thanks.
Created by Maximilian Uriarte © 2013

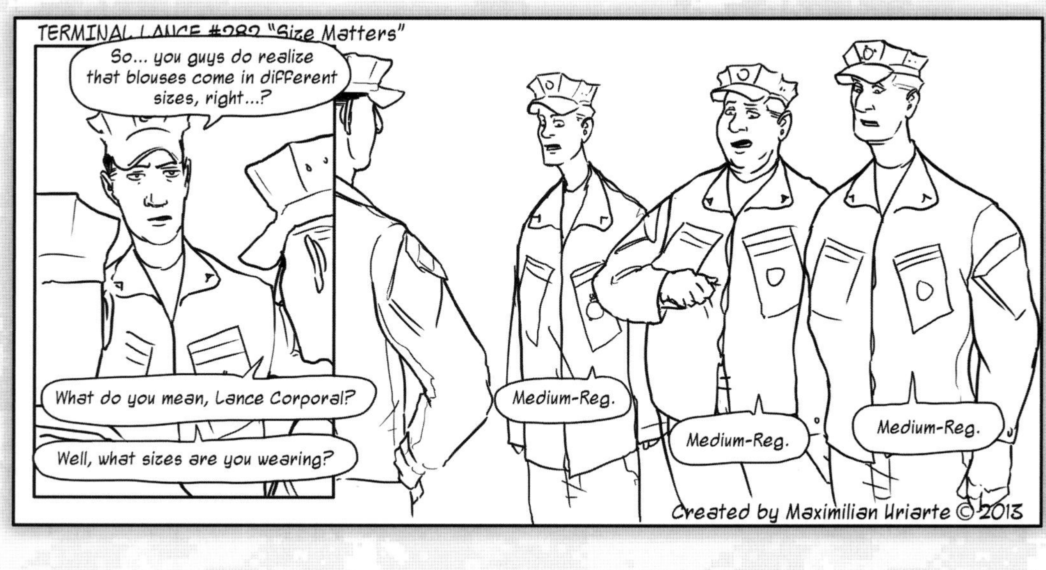
TERMINAL LANCE #282 "Size Matters"
So... you guys do realize that blouses come in different sizes, right...?
What do you mean, Lance Corporal?
Well, what sizes are you wearing?
Medium-Reg.
Medium-Reg.
Medium-Reg.
Created by Maximilian Uriarte © 2013

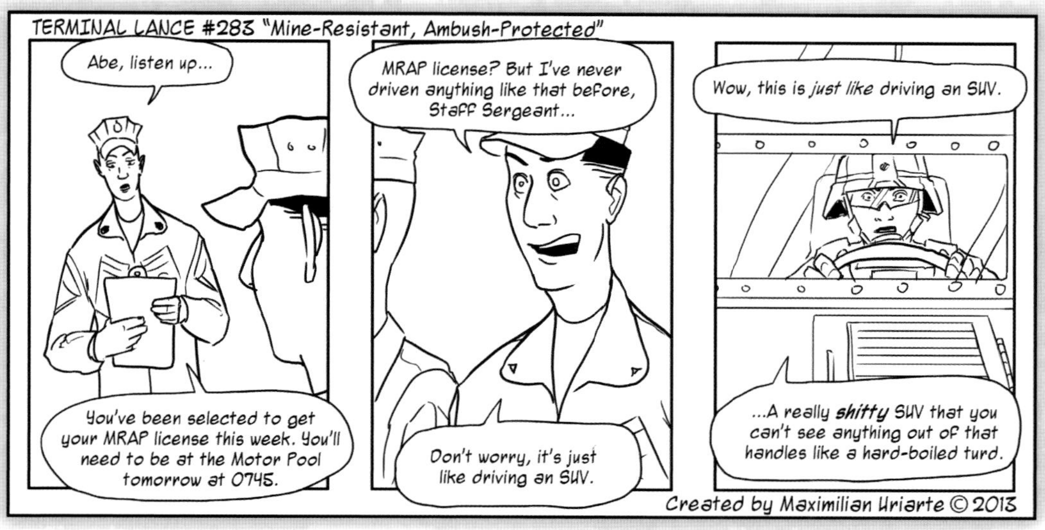
TERMINAL LANCE #283 "Mine-Resistant, Ambush-Protected"
Abe, listen up...
You've been selected to get your MRAP license this week. You'll need to be at the Motor Pool tomorrow at 0745.
MRAP license? But I've never driven anything like that before, Staff Sergeant...
Don't worry, it's just like driving an SUV.
Wow, this is *just like* driving an SUV.
...A really ***shitty*** SUV that you can't see anything out of that handles like a hard-boiled turd.
Created by Maximilian Uriarte © 2013

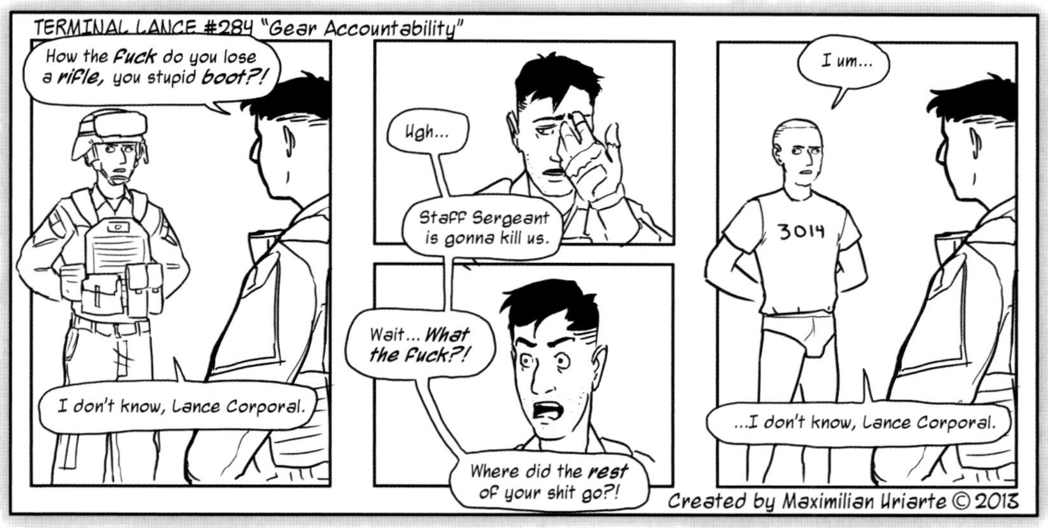
TERMINAL LANCE #284 "Gear Accountability"
How the ***fuck*** do you lose a ***rifle,*** you stupid ***boot?!***
I don't know, Lance Corporal.
Ugh...
Staff Sergeant is gonna kill us.
Wait... ***What the fuck?!***
Where did the ***rest*** of your shit go?!
I um...
3014
...I don't know, Lance Corporal.
Created by Maximilian Uriarte © 2013

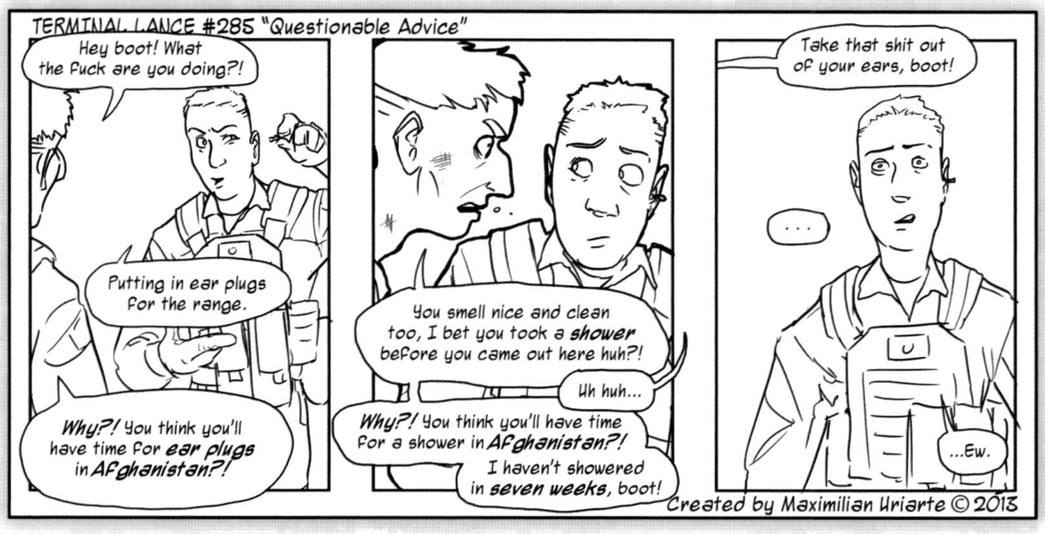
TERMINAL LANCE #285 "Questionable Advice"
Hey boot! What the fuck are you doing?!
Putting in ear plugs for the range.
Why?! You think you'll have time for ***ear plugs*** in ***Afghanistan?!***
You smell nice and clean too, I bet you took a ***shower*** before you came out here huh?!
Uh huh...
Why?! You think you'll have time for a shower in ***Afghanistan?!***
I haven't showered in ***seven weeks***, boot!
Take that shit out of your ears, boot!
. . .
...Ew.
Created by Maximilian Uriarte © 2013

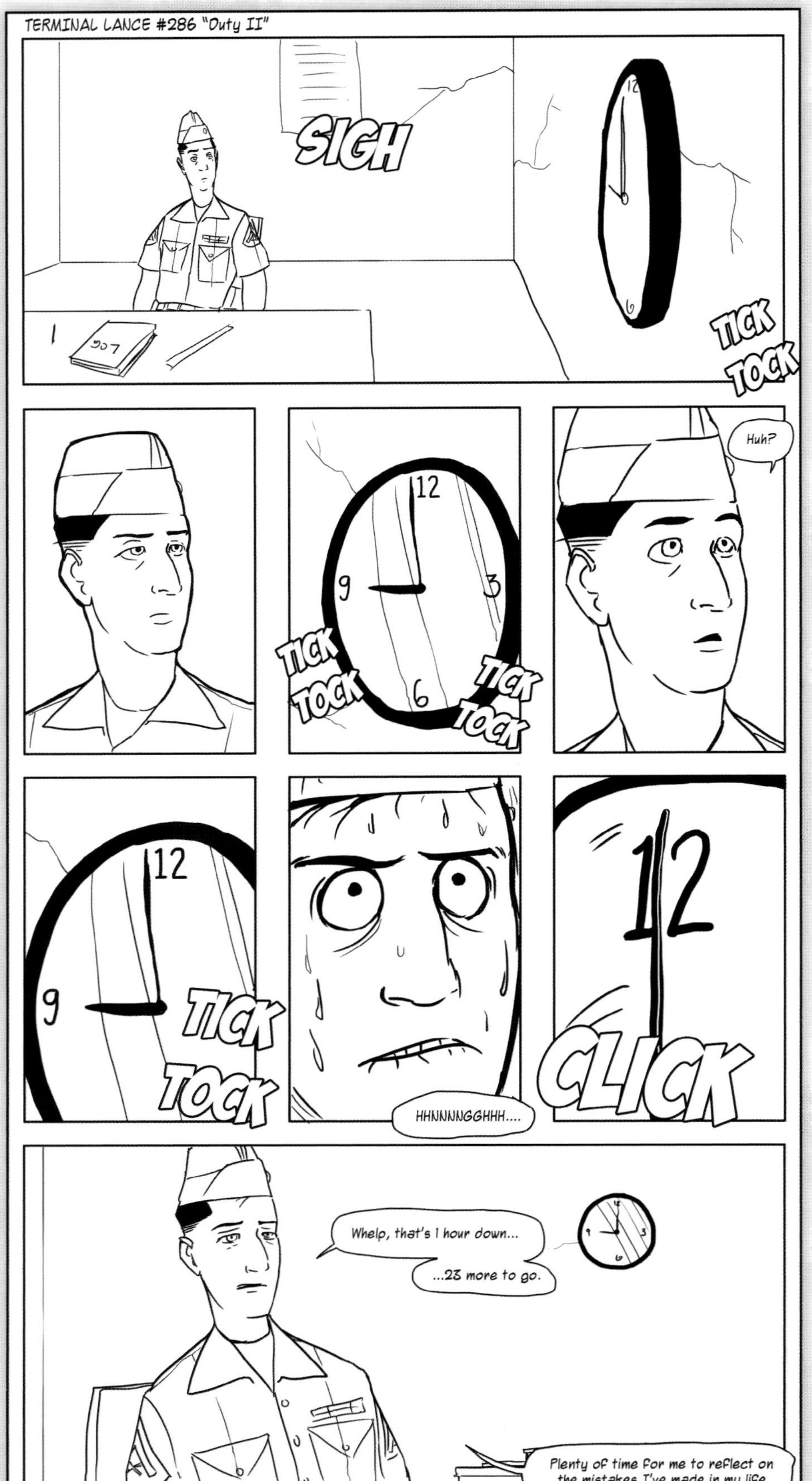
TERMINAL LANCE #286 "Duty II"
SIGH
LOG
TICK
TOCK
12
TICK
TOCK
12
9
3
6
TICK
TOCK
Huh?
12
9
TICK
TOCK
HHNNNNGGHHH....
12
CLICK
Whelp, that's 1 hour down...
...23 more to go.
Plenty of time for me to reflect on the mistakes I've made in my life.
Created by Maximilian Uriarte © 2013

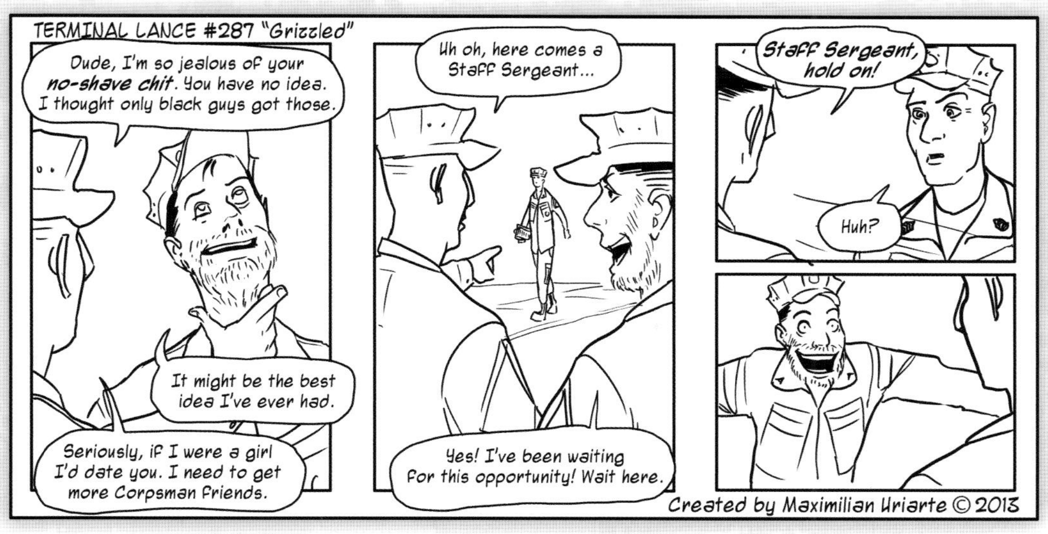
TERMINAL LANCE #287 "Grizzled"
Dude, I'm so jealous of your *no-shave chit*. You have no idea. I thought only black guys got those.
It might be the best idea I've ever had.
Seriously, if I were a girl I'd date you. I need to get more Corpsman friends.
Uh oh, here comes a Staff Sergeant...
Yes! I've been waiting for this opportunity! Wait here.
Staff Sergeant, hold on!
Huh?
Created by Maximilian Uriarte © 2013

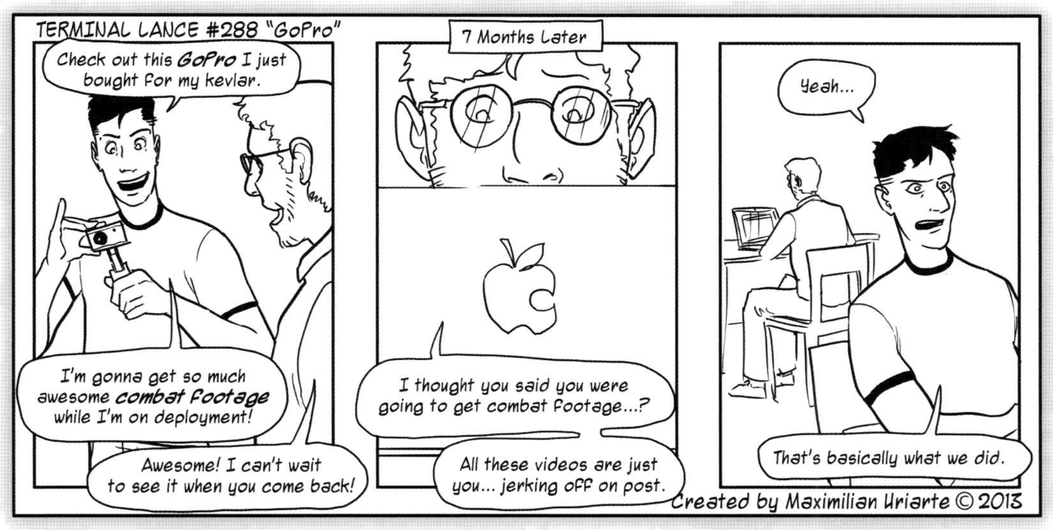
TERMINAL LANCE #288 "GoPro"
Check out this *GoPro* I just bought for my kevlar.
I'm gonna get so much awesome *combat footage* while I'm on deployment!
Awesome! I can't wait to see it when you come back!
7 Months Later
I thought you said you were going to get combat footage...?
All these videos are just you... jerking off on post.
Yeah...
That's basically what we did.
Created by Maximilian Uriarte © 2013

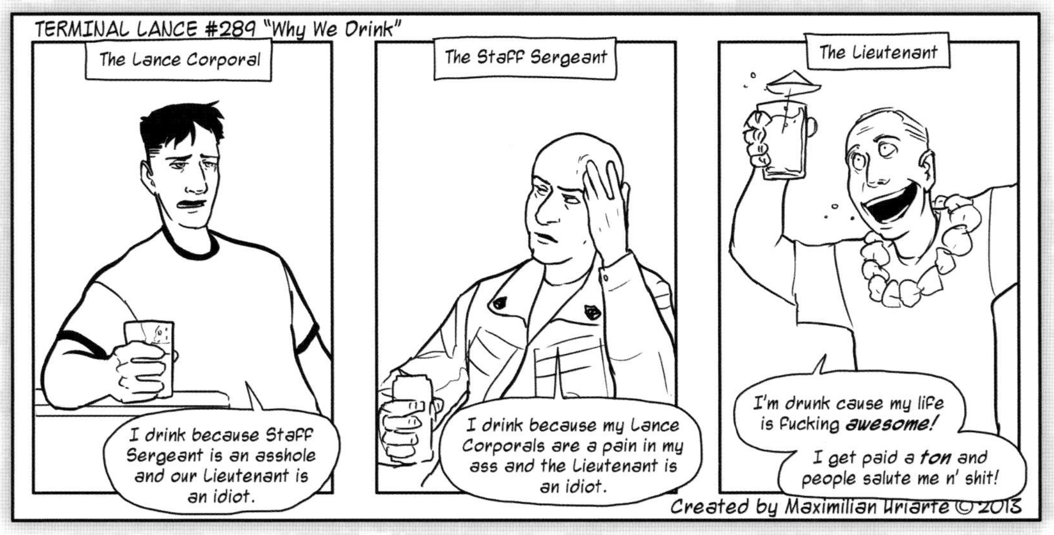
TERMINAL LANCE #289 "Why We Drink"
The Lance Corporal
I drink because Staff Sergeant is an asshole and our Lieutenant is an idiot.
The Staff Sergeant
I drink because my Lance Corporals are a pain in my ass and the Lieutenant is an idiot.
The Lieutenant
I'm drunk cause my life is fucking *awesome!*
I get paid a *ton* and people salute me n' shit!
Created by Maximilian Uriarte © 2013

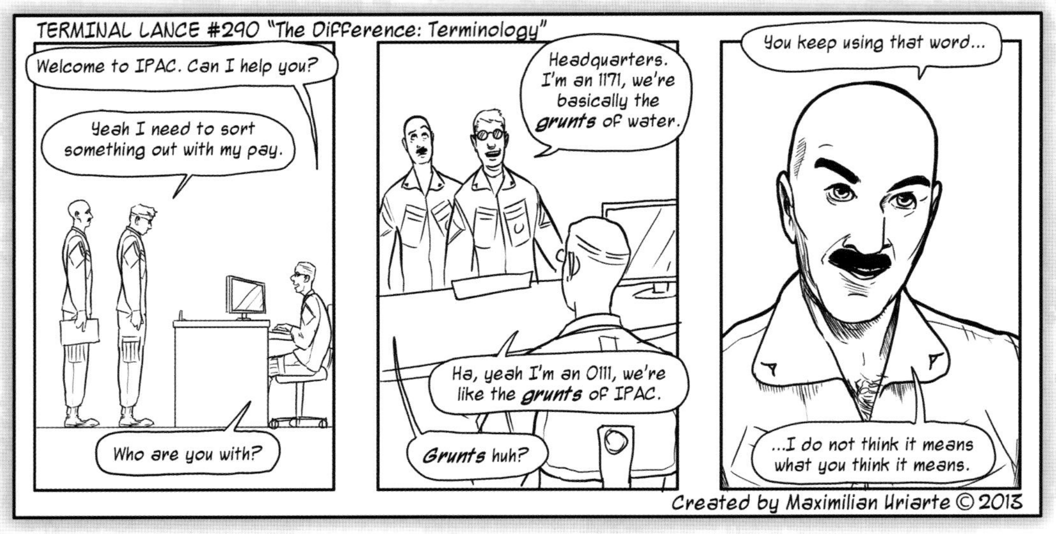
TERMINAL LANCE #290 "The Difference: Terminology"
Welcome to IPAC. Can I help you?
Yeah I need to sort something out with my pay.
Who are you with?
Headquarters. I'm an 1171, we're basically the grunts of water.
Ha, yeah I'm an 0111, we're like the grunts of IPAC.
Grunts huh?
You keep using that word...
...I do not think it means what you think it means.
Created by Maximilian Uriarte © 2013

290 "The Difference: Terminology"

If I had a dime for every time a POG told me "I'm basically the grunt of ________," I'd have like $1.30.

"Grunt" is a term that gets thrown around a lot between MOS's, but grunts are grunts. Typically, anyone calling themselves a "grunt" is supposed to have the moniker of "03" in front of their MOS. Of course, it's all semantics anyway, but the point is the same. The fact is that the grass is definitely greener on the other side, and it's not the side of the grunts.

It's kind of like a white guy saying, "Yeah, I know what it's like to be black, someone called me a cracker once."

No, you privileged shit, it's not the same.

The two worlds are completely different. Being a grunt isn't just about having "03" or going on deployments. It's about spending hours in formation for no reason, standing by all the fucking time, going to the armory for eight hours to clean your rifle again, working parties, and just generally being treated like complete shit. There's no office hours, there's no "shop" to report to in the morning, you just do as you're told.

You are a grunt.

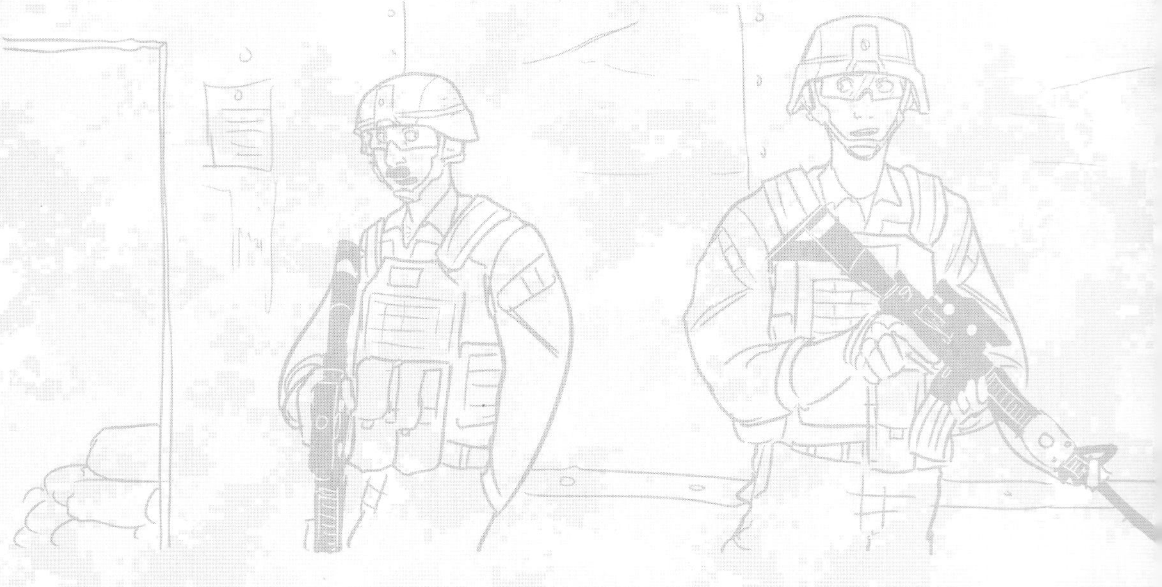

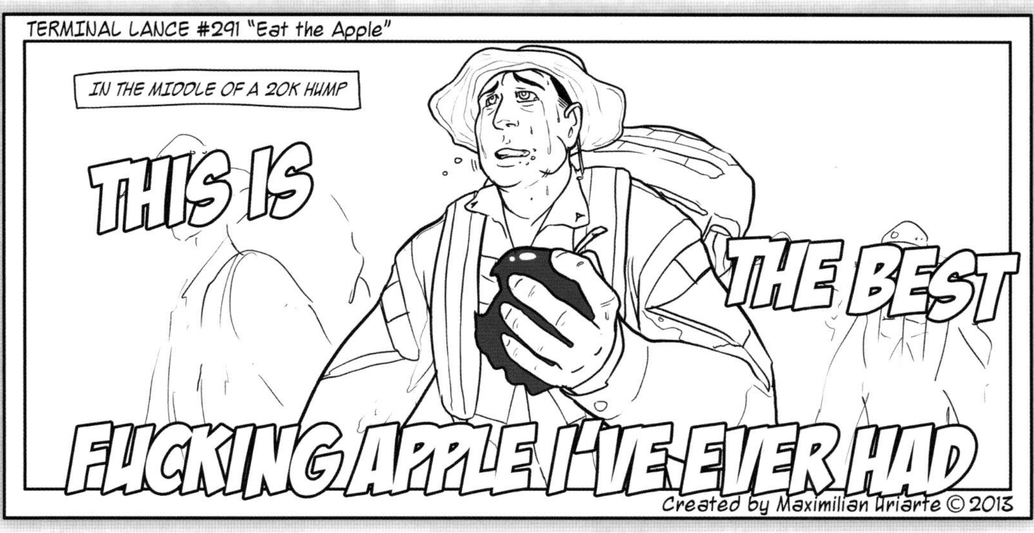
TERMINAL LANCE #291 "Eat the Apple"
IN THE MIDDLE OF A 20K HUMP
THIS IS
THE BEST
FUCKING APPLE I'VE EVER HAD
Created by Maximilian Uriarte © 2013

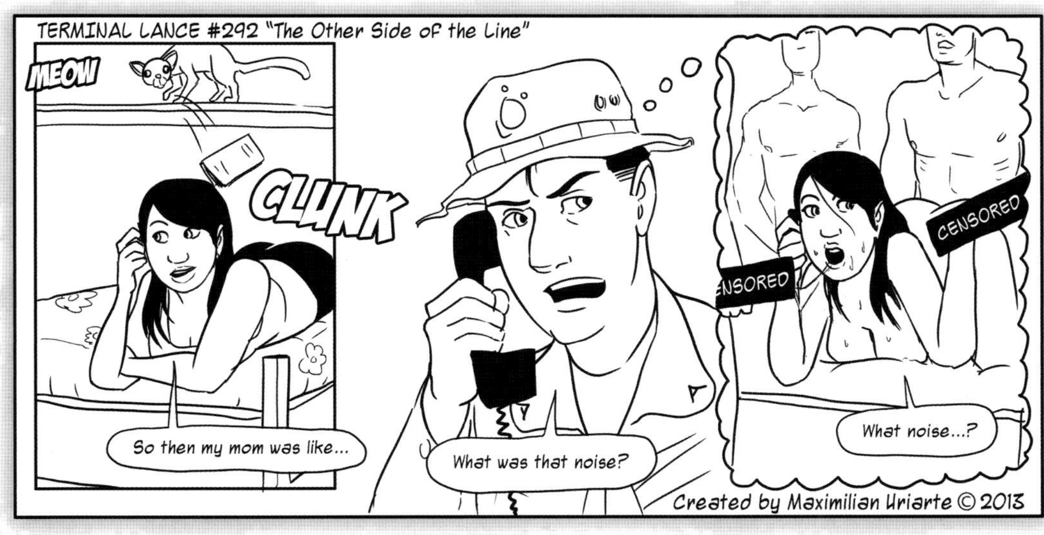
TERMINAL LANCE #292 "The Other Side of the Line"
MEOW
CLUNK
So then my mom was like...
What was that noise?
ENSORED
CENSORED
What noise...?
Created by Maximilian Uriarte © 2013

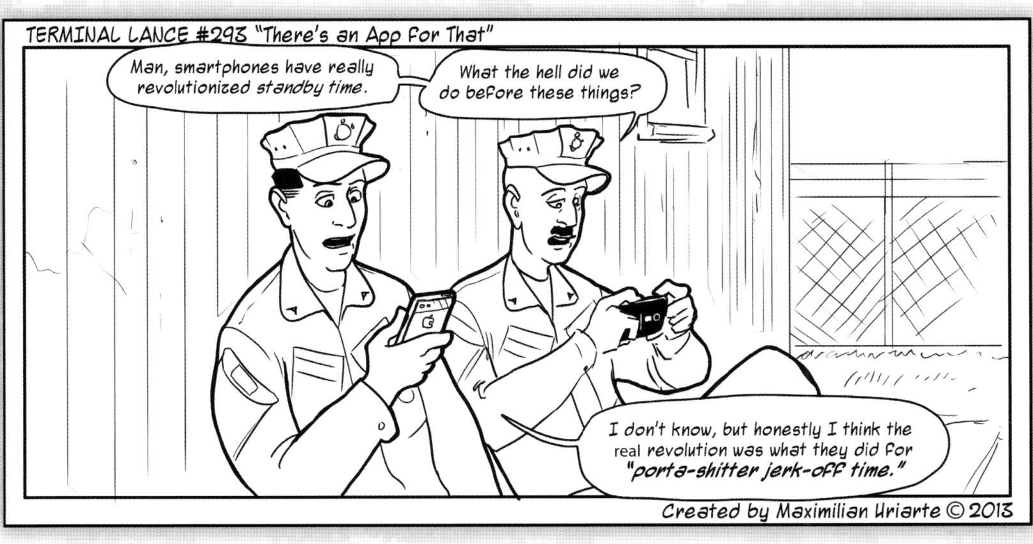
TERMINAL LANCE #293 "There's an App for That"
Man, smartphones have really revolutionized standby time.
What the hell did we do before these things?
I don't know, but honestly I think the real revolution was what they did for "porta-shitter jerk-off time."
Created by Maximilian Uriarte © 2013

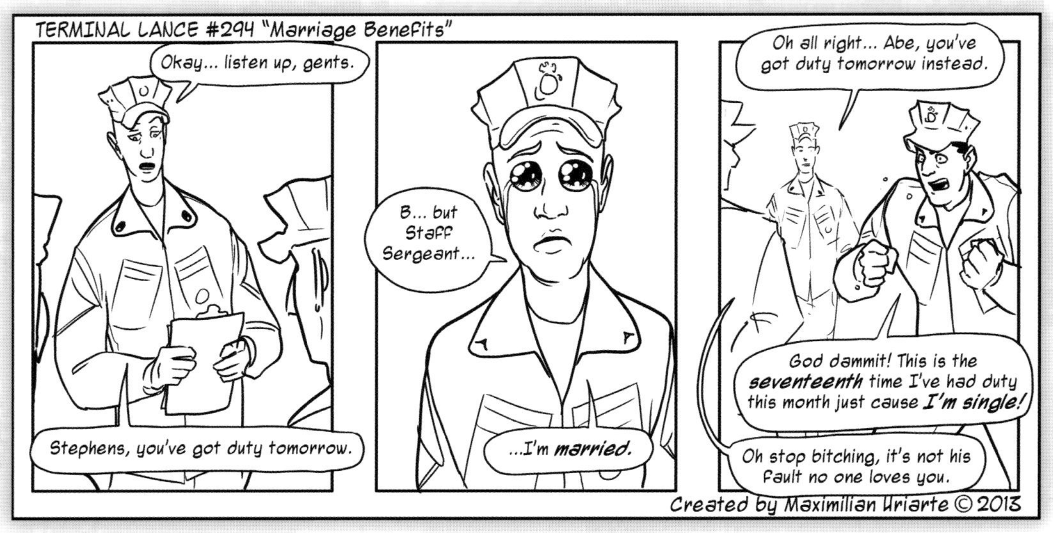
TERMINAL LANCE #294 "Marriage Benefits"
Okay... listen up, gents.
Stephens, you've got duty tomorrow.
B... but Staff Sergeant...
...I'm **married.**
Oh all right... Abe, you've got duty tomorrow instead.
God dammit! This is the **seventeenth** time I've had duty this month just cause ***I'm single!***
Oh stop bitching, it's not his fault no one loves you.
Created by Maximilian Uriarte © 2013

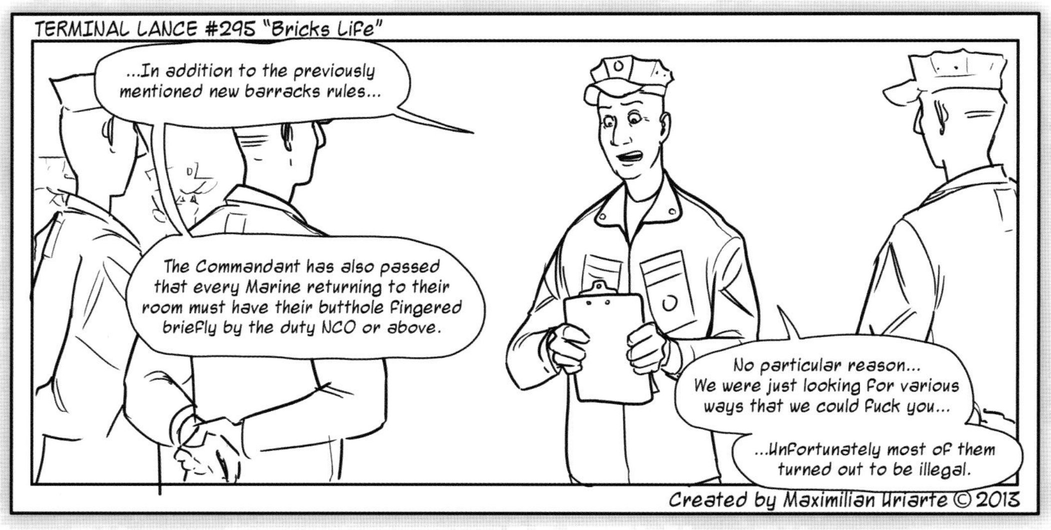
TERMINAL LANCE #295 "Bricks Life"
...In addition to the previously mentioned new barracks rules...
The Commandant has also passed that every Marine returning to their room must have their butthole fingered briefly by the duty NCO or above.
No particular reason... We were just looking for various ways that we could fuck you...
...Unfortunately most of them turned out to be illegal.
Created by Maximilian Uriarte © 2013

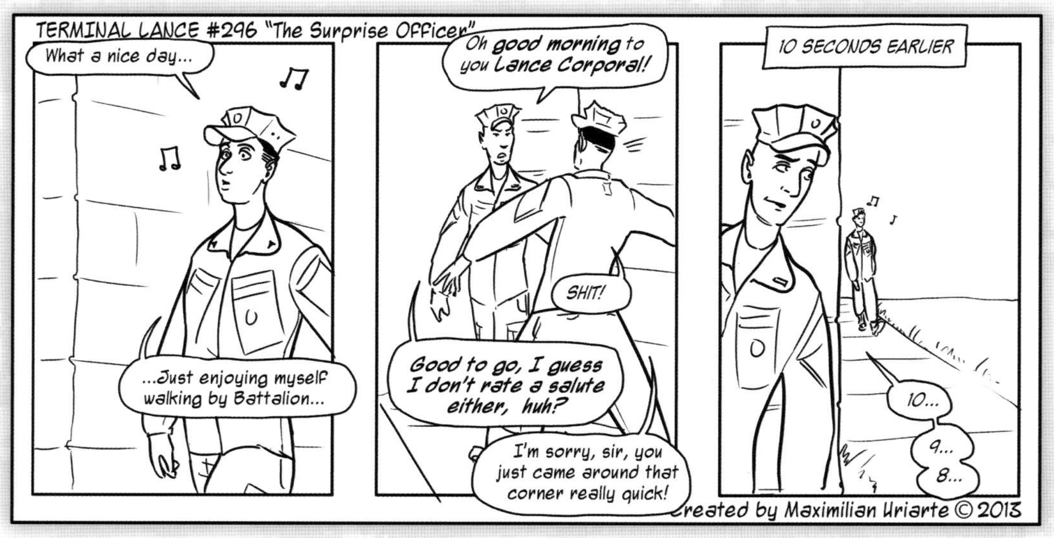
TERMINAL LANCE #296 "The Surprise Officer"
What a nice day...
...Just enjoying myself walking by Battalion...
Oh **good morning** to you **Lance Corporal!**
SHIT!
Good to go, I guess I don't rate a salute either, huh?
I'm sorry, sir, you just came around that corner really quick!
10 SECONDS EARLIER
10...
9...
8...
Created by Maximilian Uriarte © 2013

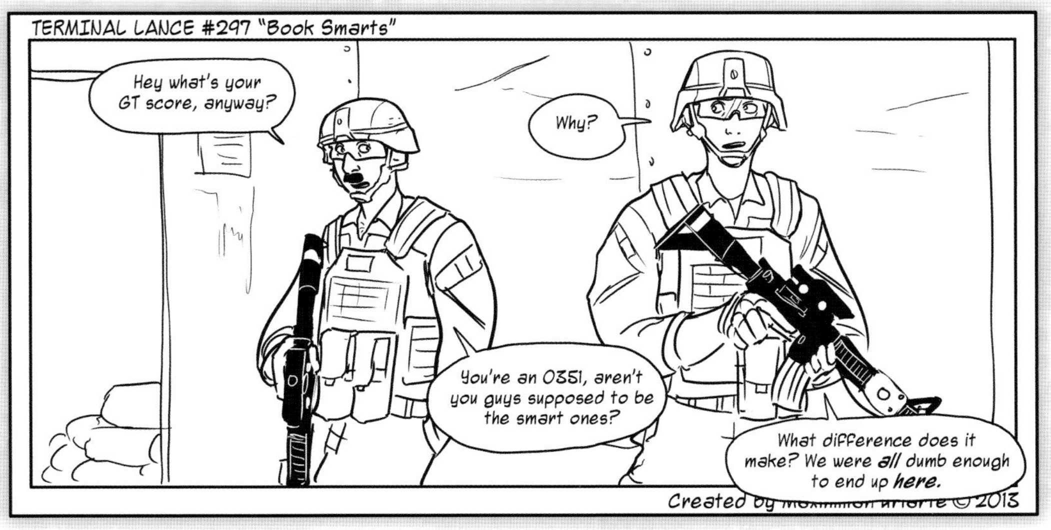
TERMINAL LANCE #297 "Book Smarts"
Hey what's your GT score, anyway?
Why?
You're an 0351, aren't you guys supposed to be the smart ones?
What difference does it make? We were all dumb enough to end up here.
Created by Maximilian Uriarte © 2013

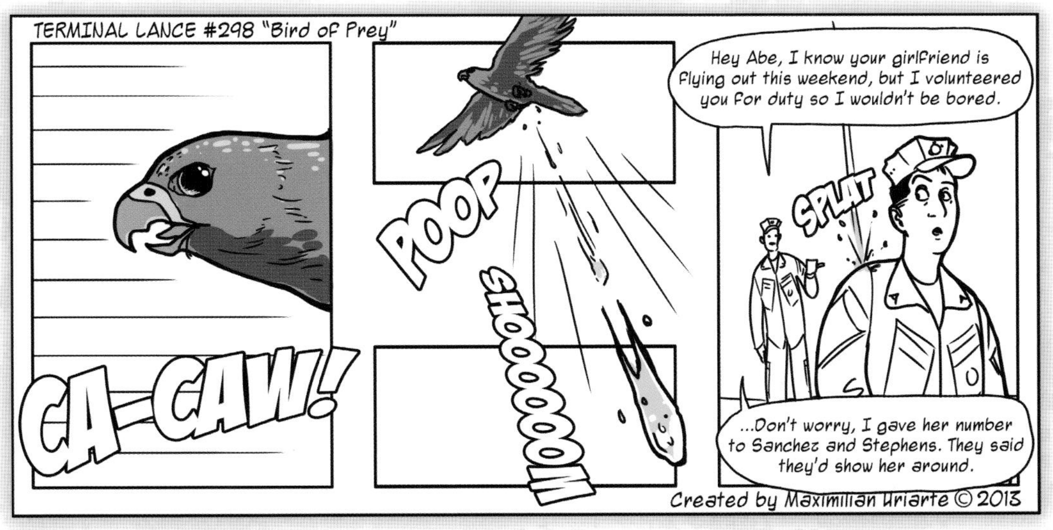
TERMINAL LANCE #298 "Bird of Prey"
CA-CAW!
POOP
SHOOOOOOOM
Hey Abe, I know your girlfriend is flying out this weekend, but I volunteered you for duty so I wouldn't be bored.
SPLAT
...Don't worry, I gave her number to Sanchez and Stephens. They said they'd show her around.
Created by Maximilian Uriarte © 2013

298 "Bird of Prey"

Beware the call of the mighty Blue Falcon.

He prowls the skies searching for his next target. He is a bird of prey, but he preys not on the typical feast of field mice and smaller birds. No, this great azure raptor seeks only those to whom it is close . . . for you must be its buddy, in order to be buddy-fucked. When you feel that warm splat of milky blue shit on your shoulder, you know you've been hit.

The Blue Falcon comes in many forms, but usually it's the careless friend of yours that unintentionally (or intentionally—for the true assholes) manages to screw you over in some way or another. The Blue Falcon is merely a guise for the infamous Buddy Fucker, an alternate form of being for when he is in the skies, on the prowl. In all reality, it can be really easy to fuck your buddy over in the Marine Corps, without even realizing it. You can have the best of intentions, but if you find that you've fucked your buddy, you shouldn't be surprised when he pulls the wings off and calls you by your true name . . .

. . . Buddy Fucker.

The Marine Corps is all about the brotherhood. I know it's a cliché, but it's true. Human interaction is an important, yet fading part of a good Marine Corps. Too many officers, commissioned and non-, are so quick to push paperwork down your throat instead of actually talking to you, man-to-man. Email has replaced conversation, with comically long and obtuse signature lines replacing an honest "thank you."

The CO that slams you with an NJP before even trying to fix the situation with counseling is just as much the fucker of buddies as the falcon of the skies.

Don't be the falcon, be a man. If someone is acting out, there's always a million ways around it before anything official needs to be done, potentially ruining someone's career.

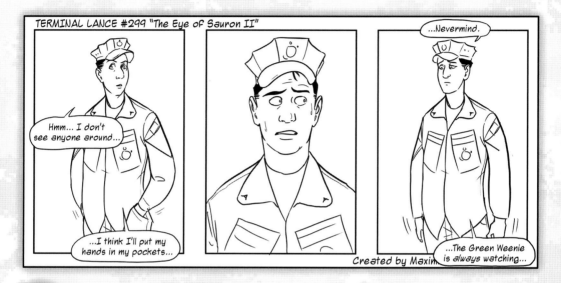

TERMINAL LANCE #299 "The Eye of Sauron II"
Hmm... I don't see anyone around...
...I think I'll put my hands in my pockets...
...Nevermind.
...The Green Weenie is always watching...
Created by Maxim

299 "The Eye of Sauron II"

Always watching . . .

If it wasn't entirely apparent by now, I am a gigantic nerd. It might explain why I chose to go 0351 when I was at SOI. It seemed to be where the rest of my kind culminated in the infantry. This, of course, brings us to where we are today: from a *Star Wars* parody to a *Lord of the Rings* reference. If the whole Eye of Sauron is lost on you, I invite you to 2001 to come watch *Lord of the Rings* with me. I was fifteen, 150 pounds, and had yet to see a vagina in person.

More to the point, I remember always being told in boot camp:

Integrity is doing the right thing, even when no one is watching.

It's actually not bad advice for your everyday life, but it always felt more like an underhanded warning coming from the institution itself. From the very beginning, Drill Instructors instill the fear of the Marine Corps into you: "We see everything," they tell you—and they're entirely correct. It's the fear of the Great Eye that keeps you from wearing uniform items while on leave, or putting on a hat indoors months after you've separated from the service.

The Great Eye of Sauron sees all.

It's always watching.

Max note 2017: On terminallance.com, this strip is actually an animated GIF. The middle panel flashes between Abe's nervous face and the eye of the green weenie!

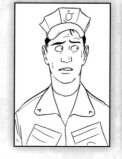

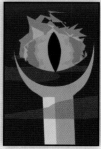

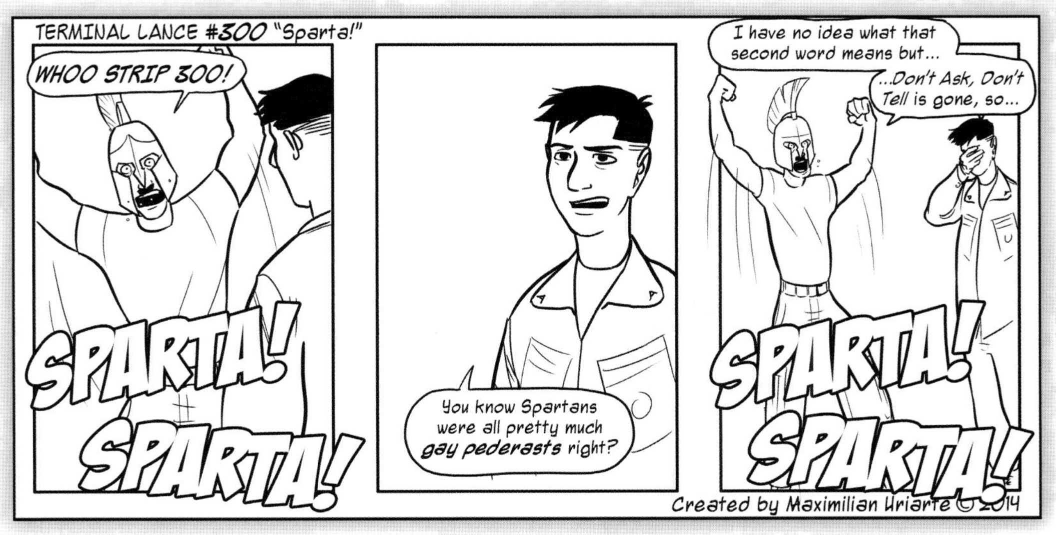
TERMINAL LANCE #300 "Sparta!"
WHOO STRIP 300!
SPARTA!
SPARTA!
You know Spartans were all pretty much gay pederasts right?
I have no idea what that second word means but...
...Don't Ask, Don't Tell is gone, so...
SPARTA!
SPARTA!
Created by Maximilian Uriarte © 2014

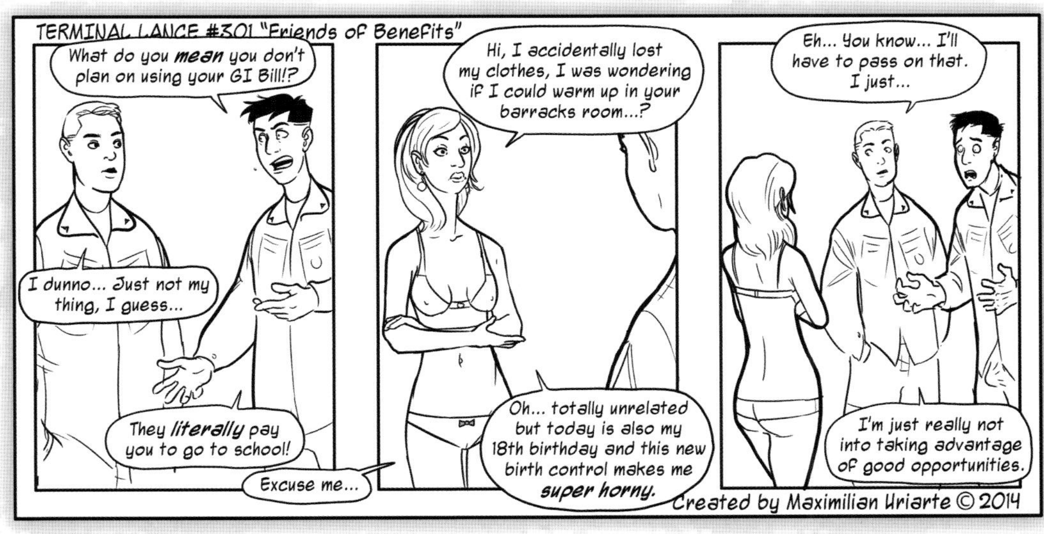
TERMINAL LANCE #301 "Friends of Benefits"
What do you mean you don't plan on using your GI Bill!?
I dunno... Just not my thing, I guess...
They literally pay you to go to school!
Excuse me...
Hi, I accidentally lost my clothes, I was wondering if I could warm up in your barracks room...?
Oh... totally unrelated but today is also my 18th birthday and this new birth control makes me super horny.
Eh... You know... I'll have to pass on that. I just...
I'm just really not into taking advantage of good opportunities.
Created by Maximilian Uriarte © 2014

301 "Friends of Benefits"

More than once, I've had people tell me they don't really plan on using their GI Bill.

"I dunno, I just don't like school."

"I've got a buddy back home that's gonna hook me up with a job."

"I'm an idiot."

These are the kinds of responses I get, all of which are excuses rather than reasons. Here's the thing: In today's world, the college degree is the new high school diploma. You really need one if you plan on doing anything outside of a regular blue collar job. Of course, there's absolutely nothing wrong with blue collar work, but you're literally being handed an opportunity to do absolutely anything. Yeah, college can be lame and you'll be surrounded by some spoiled shitheads that you can't relate to, but you'll also learn a lot, you'll meet some great new people that don't suck, and it's a great way to ease back into civilian life without the pressure of needing to find a job.

Even if you have absolutely no ambition upon exiting the Marine Corps, college is a great place for you to chill out for four years until you figure out what it is you want to do when you grow up. Compared to the Marine Corps, it's really not that hard and you'll walk away with a bachelor's degree at the end of the day.

So really, you have no excuse.

Also, why is it that whenever someone has a "buddy back home" that's going to give them a job, it's always the most obscure shit you've ever heard of?

"Yeah, my buddy back home installs window-lining on fire trucks, he makes $8,234 an hour."

Maybe I just need more buddies.

TERMINAL LANCE #302 "Pirate Sword"
...Okay do you see the guy fucking the goat?
Uh-huh...
Okay, do you see the guy next to him?
Uh-huh...
I'm pretty sure that guy is our HVT.
Then we shall pursue him!
Marines! Forward!
Wait... you really brought your NCO sword on deployment?
Fuck yeah I did, I spent $600 on this stupid thing...
I'm not going home til I stab a motherfucker.
Created by Maximilian Uriarte © 2014

TERMINAL LANCE #303 "Too Early For Fun"
Good morning gents!
Today for PT we're going to do a little game we used to do at TBS...
...I think you'll really like it!
Question, Sir...
Is there any point in this game where we get to go back up to our rooms and sleep off our hangovers?
No...
Then I seriously doubt we're going to enjoy it as much as you think we will.
Created by Maximilian Uriarte © 2014

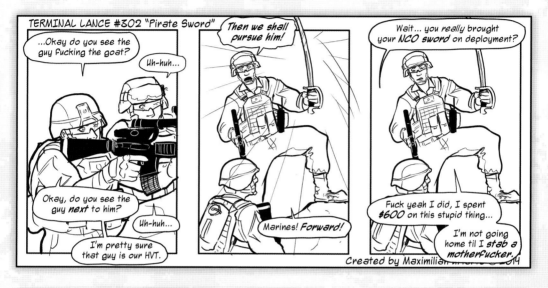

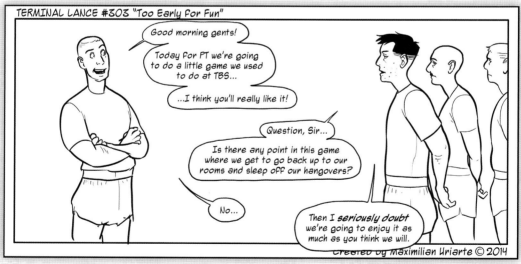

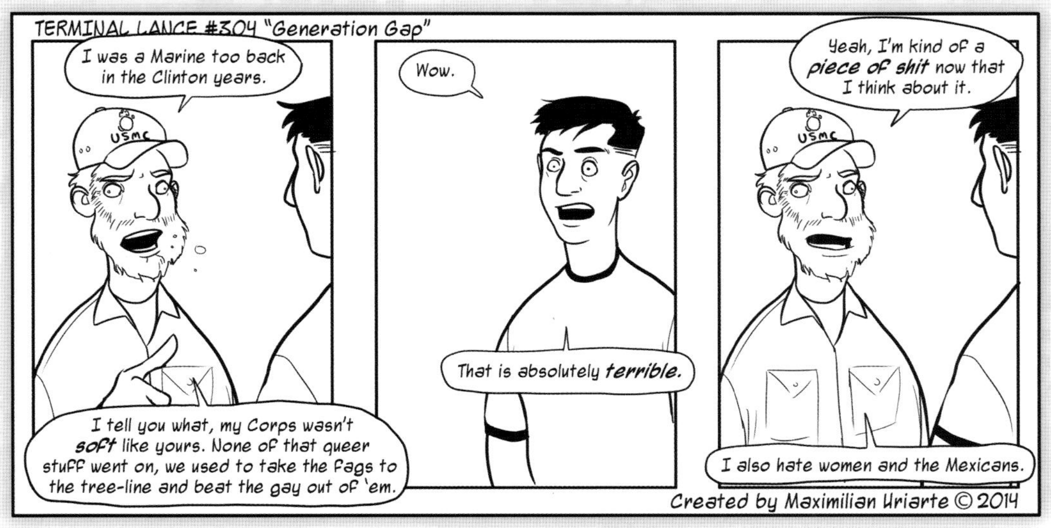
TERMINAL LANCE #304 "Generation Gap"
I was a Marine too back in the Clinton years.
I tell you what, my Corps wasn't ***soft*** like yours. None of that queer stuff went on, we used to take the fags to the tree-line and beat the gay out of 'em.
Wow.
That is absolutely ***terrible.***
Yeah, I'm kind of a ***piece of shit*** now that I think about it.
I also hate women and the Mexicans.
Created by Maximilian Uriarte © 2014

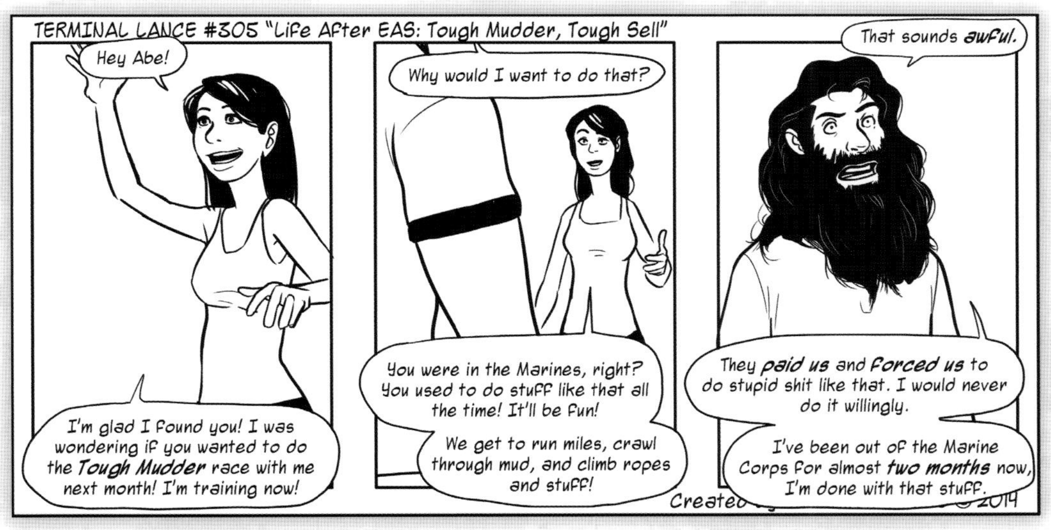
TERMINAL LANCE #305 "Life After EAS: Tough Mudder, Tough Sell"
Hey Abe!
I'm glad I found you! I was wondering if you wanted to do the ***Tough Mudder*** race with me next month! I'm training now!
Why would I want to do that?
You were in the Marines, right? You used to do stuff like that all the time! It'll be fun!
We get to run miles, crawl through mud, and climb ropes and stuff!
That sounds ***awful.***
They ***paid us*** and ***forced us*** to do stupid shit like that. I would never do it willingly.
I've been out of the Marine Corps for almost ***two months*** now, I'm done with that stuff.

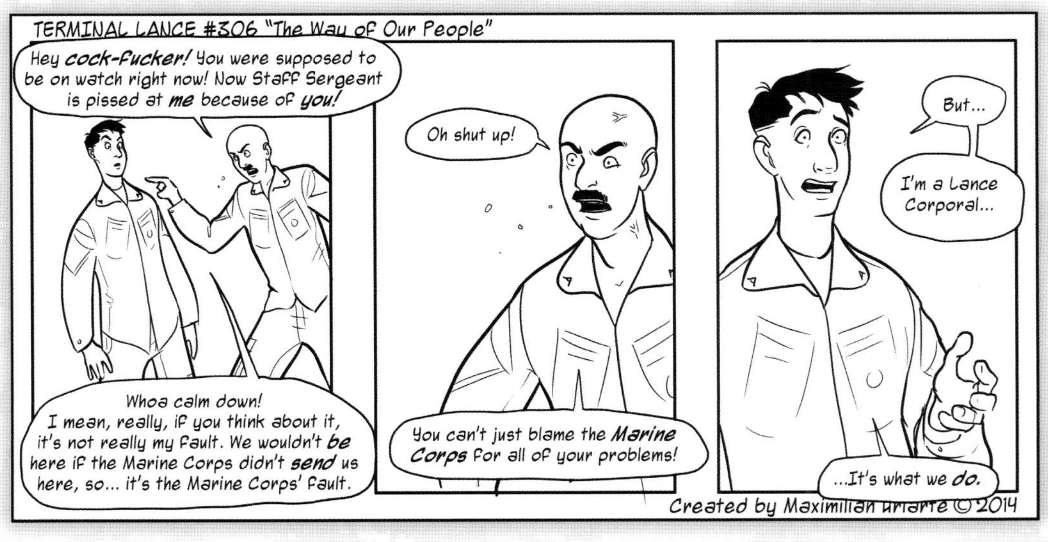
TERMINAL LANCE #306 "The Way of Our People"
Hey ***cock-fucker!*** You were supposed to be on watch right now! Now Staff Sergeant is pissed at ***me*** because of ***you!***
Whoa calm down! I mean, really, if you think about it, it's not really my fault. We wouldn't ***be*** here if the Marine Corps didn't ***send*** us here, so... it's the Marine Corps' fault.
Oh shut up!
You can't just blame the ***Marine Corps*** for all of your problems!
But...
I'm a Lance Corporal...
...It's what we ***do.***
Created by Maximilian Uriarte © 2014

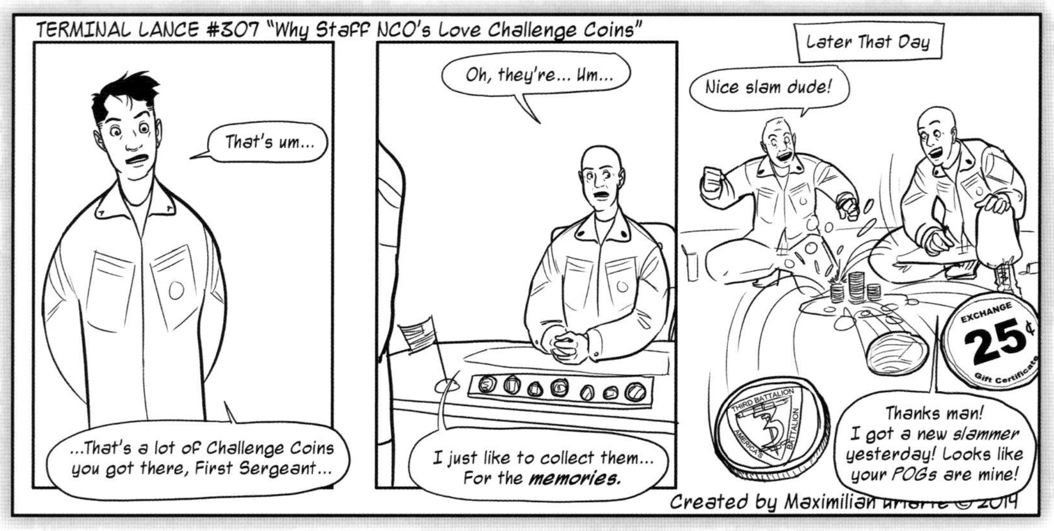
TERMINAL LANCE #307 "Why Staff NCO's Love Challenge Coins"
That's um...
...That's a lot of Challenge Coins you got there, First Sergeant...
Oh, they're... Um...
I just like to collect them... For the memories.
Later That Day
Nice slam dude!
Thanks man! I got a new slammer yesterday! Looks like your POGs are mine!
EXCHANGE 25¢ Gift Certificate
THIRD BATTALION AMERICA'S BATTALION 3
Created by Maximilian Uriarte © 2014

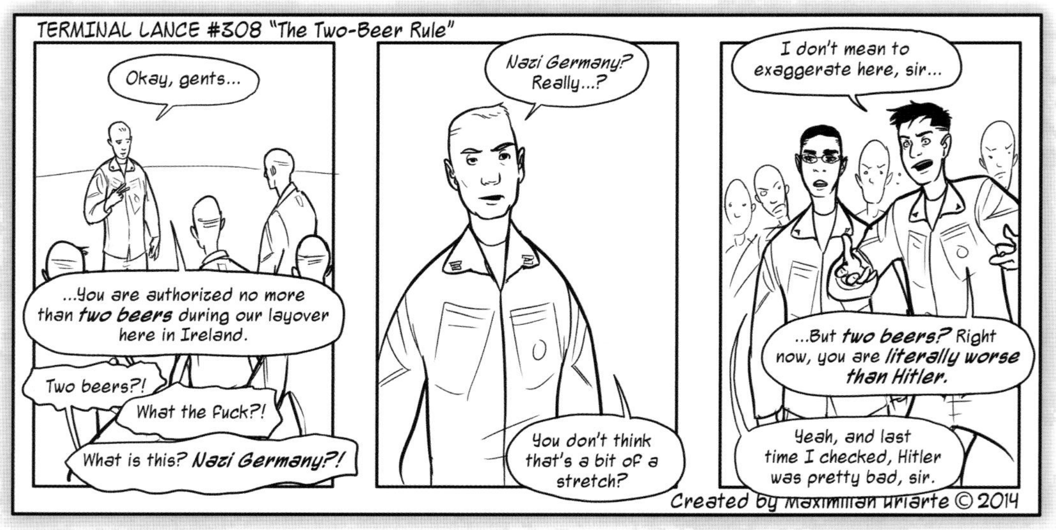
TERMINAL LANCE #308 "The Two-Beer Rule"
Okay, gents...
...You are authorized no more than two beers during our layover here in Ireland.
Two beers?!
What the fuck?!
What is this? Nazi Germany?!
Nazi Germany? Really...?
You don't think that's a bit of a stretch?
I don't mean to exaggerate here, sir...
...But two beers? Right now, you are literally worse than Hitler.
Yeah, and last time I checked, Hitler was pretty bad, sir.
Created by Maximilian Uriarte © 2014

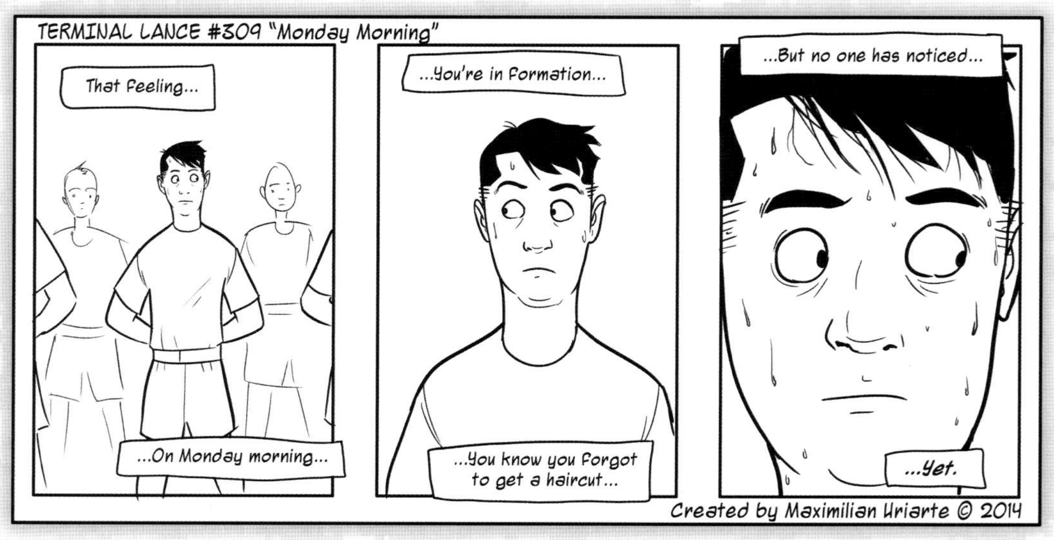
TERMINAL LANCE #309 "Monday Morning"
That feeling...
...On Monday morning...
...You're in formation...
...You know you forgot to get a haircut...
...But no one has noticed...
...Yet.
Created by Maximilian Uriarte © 2014

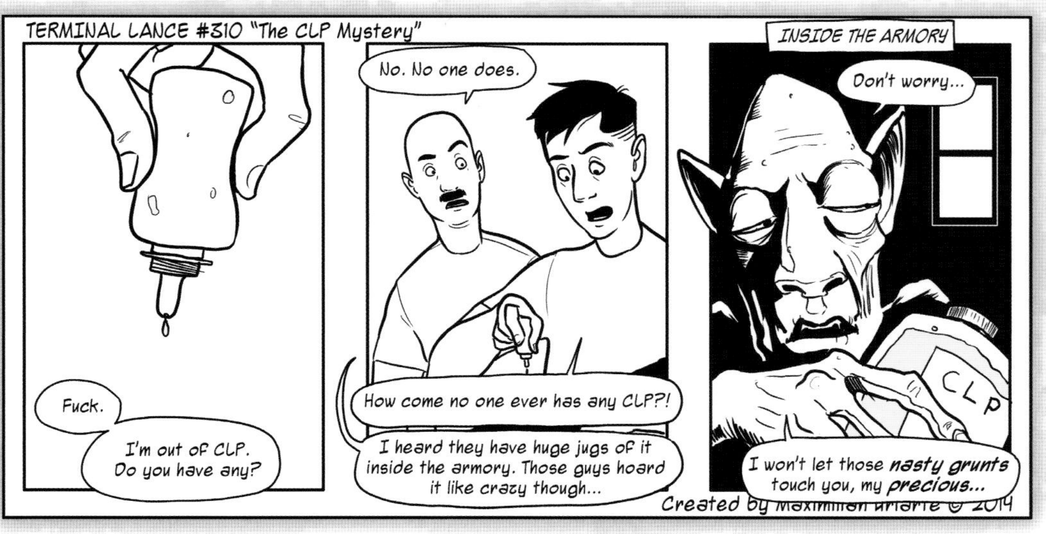
TERMINAL LANCE #310 "The CLP Mystery"
Fuck.
I'm out of CLP. Do you have any?
No. No one does.
How come no one ever has any CLP?!
I heard they have huge jugs of it inside the armory. Those guys hoard it like crazy though...
INSIDE THE ARMORY
Don't worry...
CLP
I won't let those **nasty grunts** touch you, my ***precious...***
Created by Maximilian Uriarte © 2014

310 "The CLP Mystery"

In absolute darkness they reside, spiteful of the day walkers outside always asking for something. Optics that aren't broken, a new cleaning kit, new weapons cards, CLP; their demands are endless. The creature-like people inside the armory were once people like you and me, Marines even, but in the darkness their features became twisted versions of their former selves. Their eyes have grown large to adapt to the dark, they see mostly with sound now, constantly tinkering with their gear and weapons. They scurry up the walls and into corners when that small window opens, shielding themselves from the harsh sunlight outside. A mere tickle of UV light will send their skin into an instant boil.

I speak, of course, of Armory Clerks.

Armory Clerks are kind of universally hated among the infantry. They have absolute control over their domain, which is a domain you are forced to frequent on a regular basis. When you pull out your weapon to clean it, there's no guarantee you'll be able to turn it back in with any reasonable haste, because it's not up to you. There's a certain maleficent cruelty involved in being one of these people. Who can blame them though? Shut away in the cold, cement confines of the base armory, forgotten by the rest of the Marine Corps.

All drama aside, why the fuck does no one ever have any CLP? I mean seriously, that shit is like greasy, liquid gold.

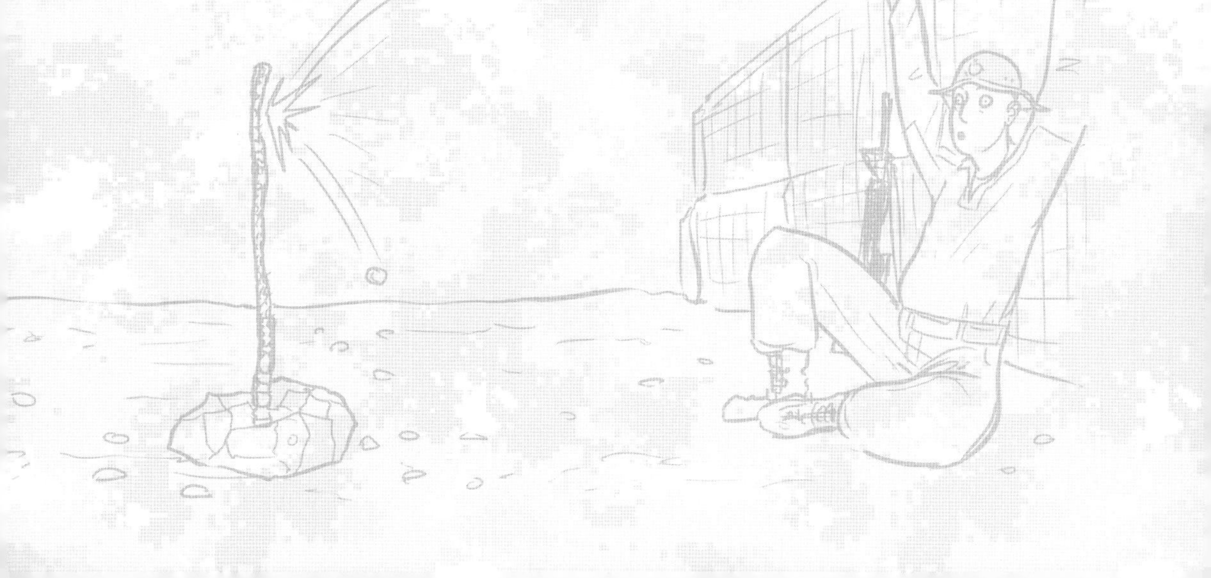

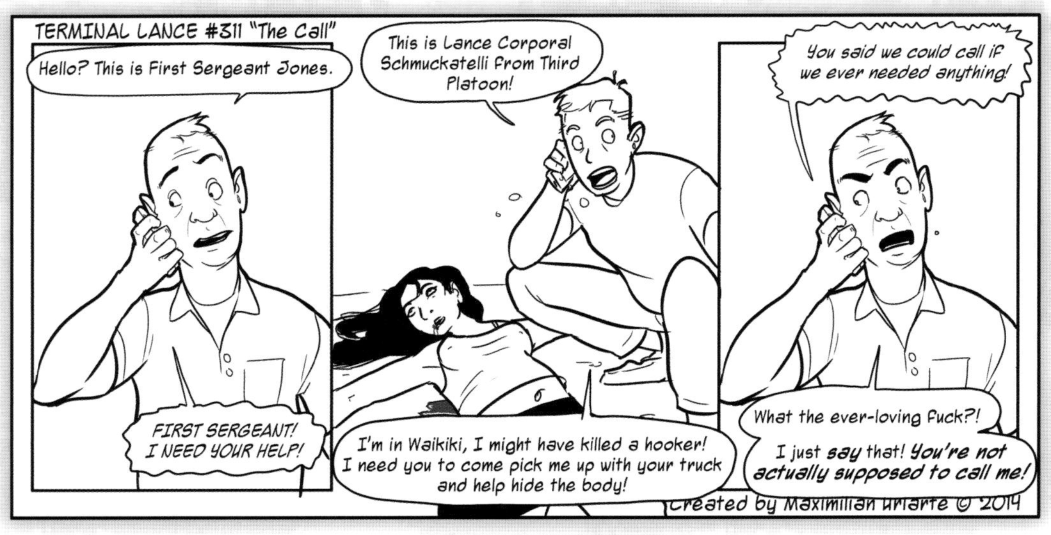
TERMINAL LANCE #311 "The Call"
Hello? This is First Sergeant Jones.
FIRST SERGEANT! I NEED YOUR HELP!
This is Lance Corporal Schmuckatelli from Third Platoon!
I'm in Waikiki, I might have killed a hooker! I need you to come pick me up with your truck and help hide the body!
You said we could call if we ever needed anything!
What the ever-loving fuck?!
I just *say* that! ***You're not actually supposed to call me!***
Created by Maximilian Uriarte © 2014

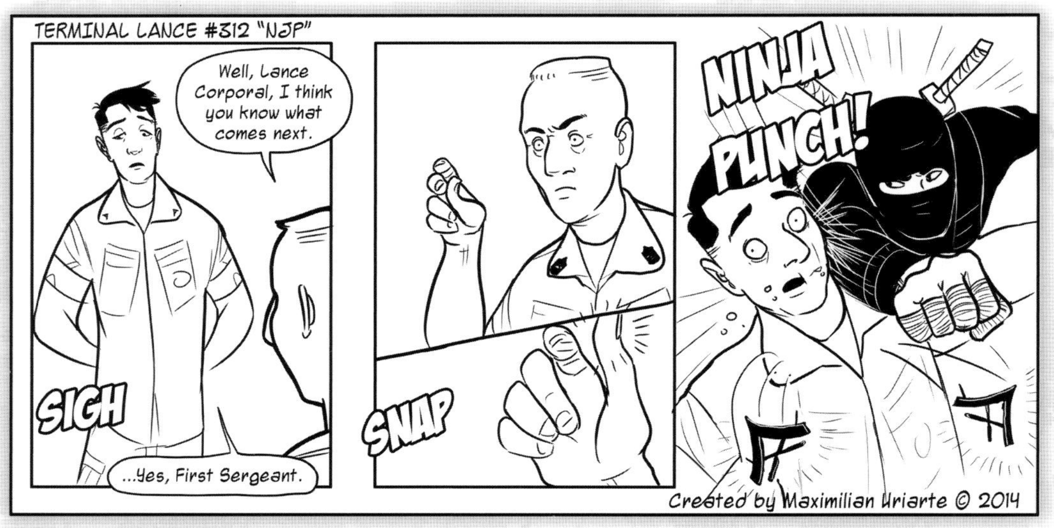
TERMINAL LANCE #312 "NJP"
Well, Lance Corporal, I think you know what comes next.
SIGH
...Yes, First Sergeant.
SNAP
NINJA PUNCH!
Created by Maximilian Uriarte © 2014

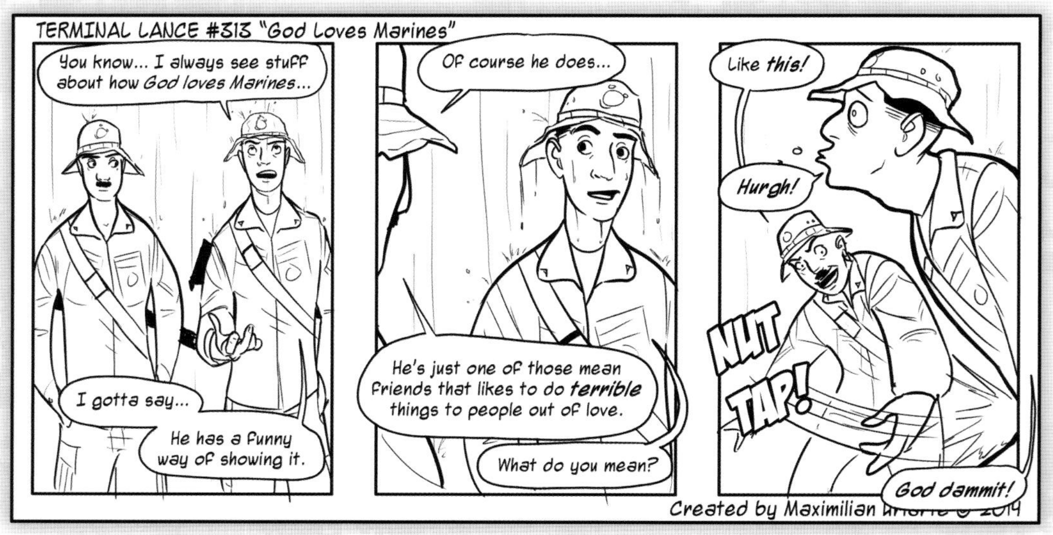
TERMINAL LANCE #313 "God Loves Marines"
You know... I always see stuff about how *God loves Marines*...
I gotta say...
He has a funny way of showing it.
Of course he does...
He's just one of those mean friends that likes to do *terrible* things to people out of love.
What do you mean?
Like *this!*
Hurgh!
NUT TAP!
God dammit!
Created by Maximilian Uriarte © 2014

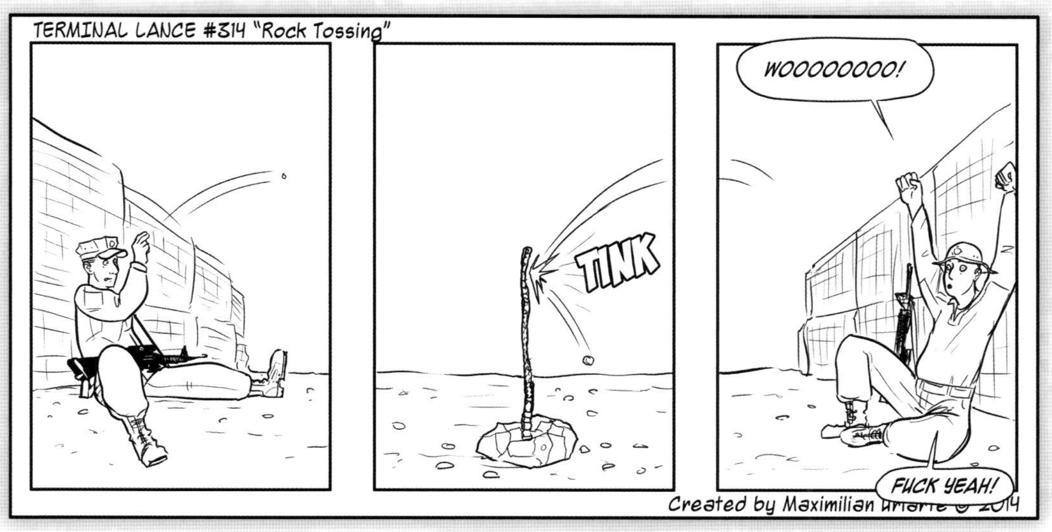
TERMINAL LANCE #314 "Rock Tossing"
TINK
WOOOOOOOO!
FUCK YEAH!
Created by Maximilian Uriarte © 2014

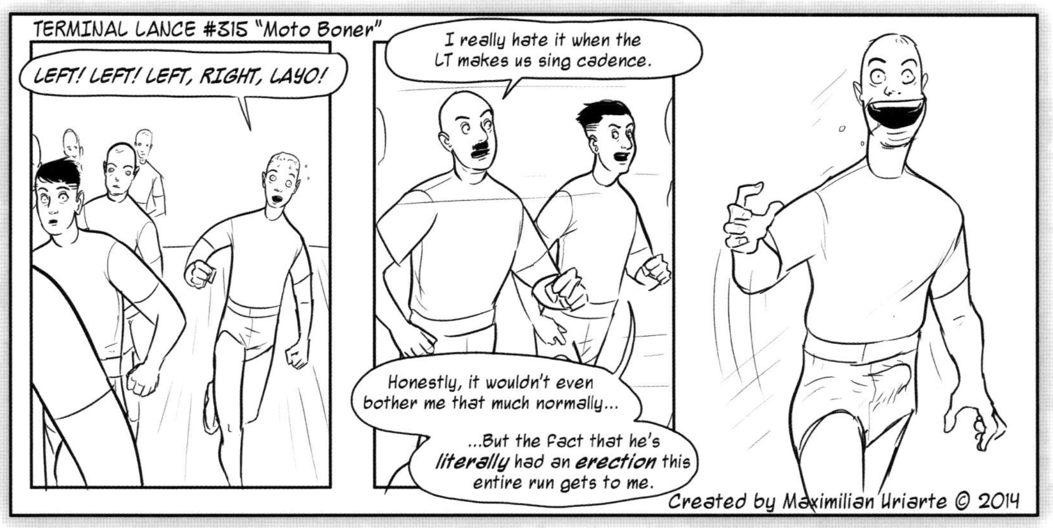
TERMINAL LANCE #315 "Moto Boner"
LEFT! LEFT! LEFT, RIGHT, LAYO!
I really hate it when the LT makes us sing cadence.
Honestly, it wouldn't even bother me that much normally...
...But the fact that he's literally had an erection this entire run gets to me.
Created by Maximilian Uriarte © 2014

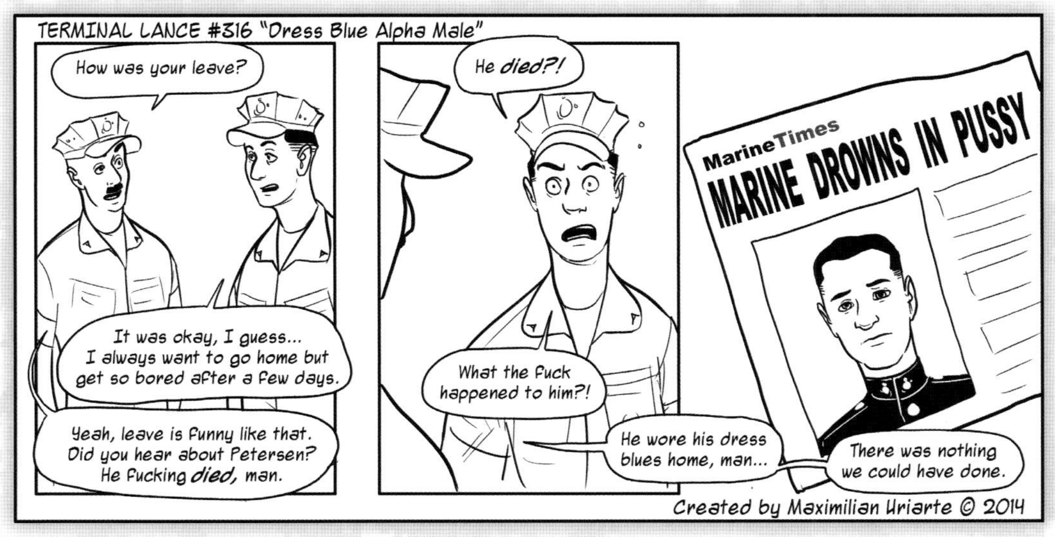
TERMINAL LANCE #316 "Dress Blue Alpha Male"
How was your leave?
It was okay, I guess... I always want to go home but get so bored after a few days.
Yeah, leave is funny like that. Did you hear about Petersen? He fucking died, man.
He died?!
What the fuck happened to him?!
He wore his dress blues home, man...
MarineTimes
MARINE DROWNS IN PUSSY
There was nothing we could have done.
Created by Maximilian Uriarte © 2014

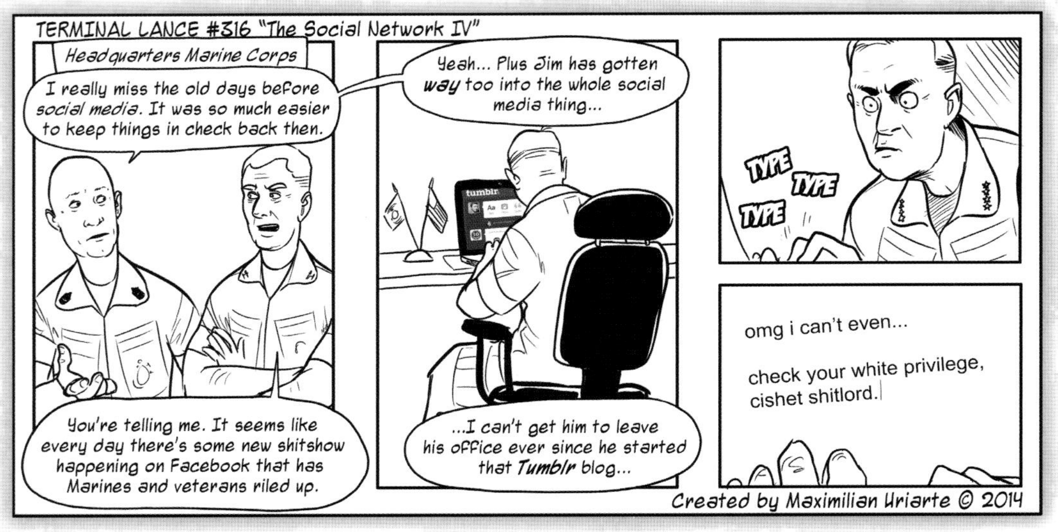
TERMINAL LANCE #316 "The Social Network IV"
Headquarters Marine Corps
I really miss the old days before social media. It was so much easier to keep things in check back then.
You're telling me. It seems like every day there's some new shitshow happening on Facebook that has Marines and veterans riled up.
Yeah... Plus Jim has gotten **way** too into the whole social media thing...
...I can't get him to leave his office ever since he started that *Tumblr* blog...
TYPE
TYPE
TYPE
omg i can't even...
check your white privilege, cishet shitlord.
Created by Maximilian Uriarte © 2014

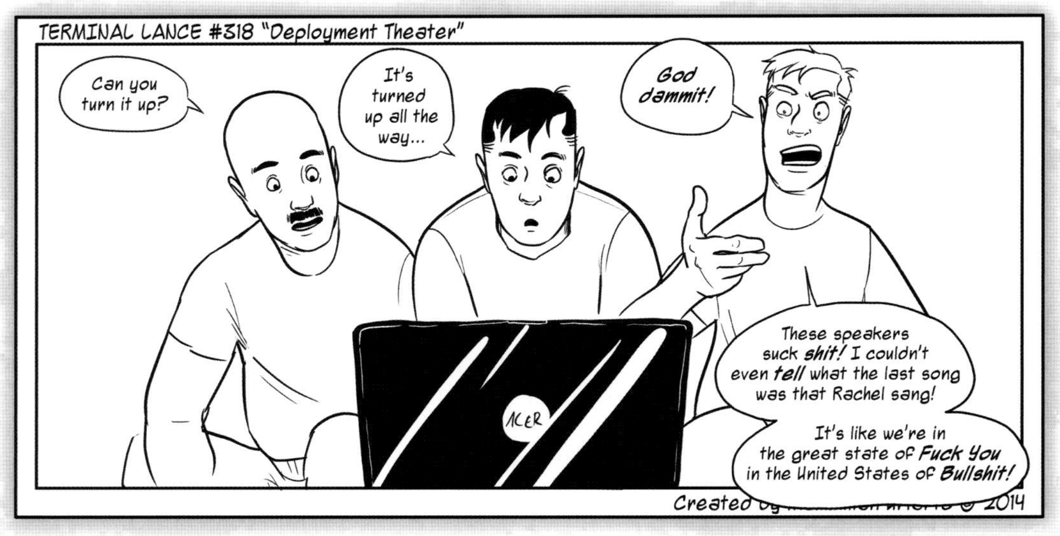
TERMINAL LANCE #318 "Deployment Theater"
Can you turn it up?
It's turned up all the way...
God dammit!
ACER
These speakers suck **shit!** I couldn't even **tell** what the last song was that Rachel sang!
It's like we're in the great state of **Fuck You** in the United States of **Bullshit!**
Created by Maximilian Uriarte © 2014

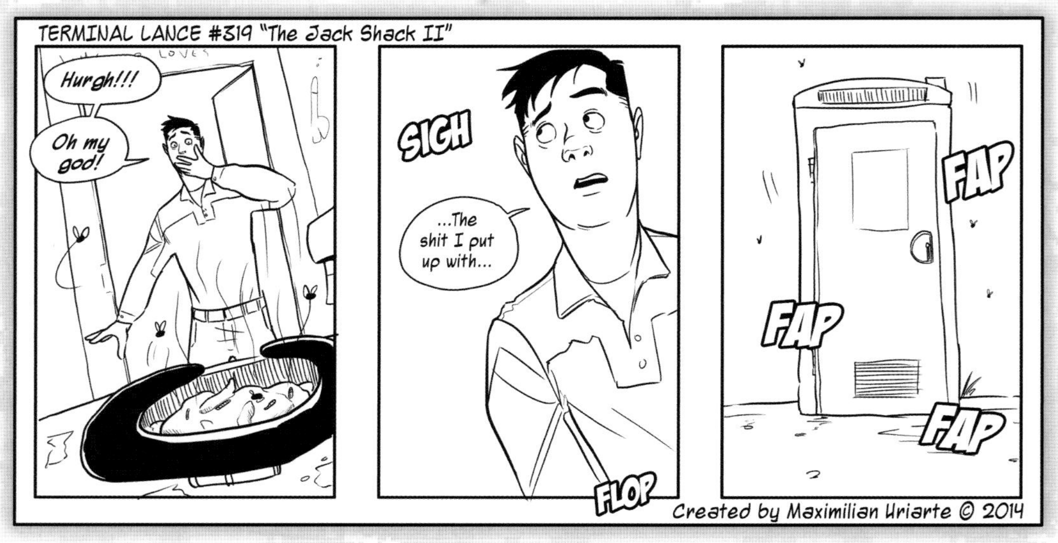
TERMINAL LANCE #319 "The Jack Shack II"
Hurgh!!!
Oh my god!
SIGH
...The shit I put up with...
FLOP
FAP
FAP
FAP
Created by Maximilian Uriarte © 2014

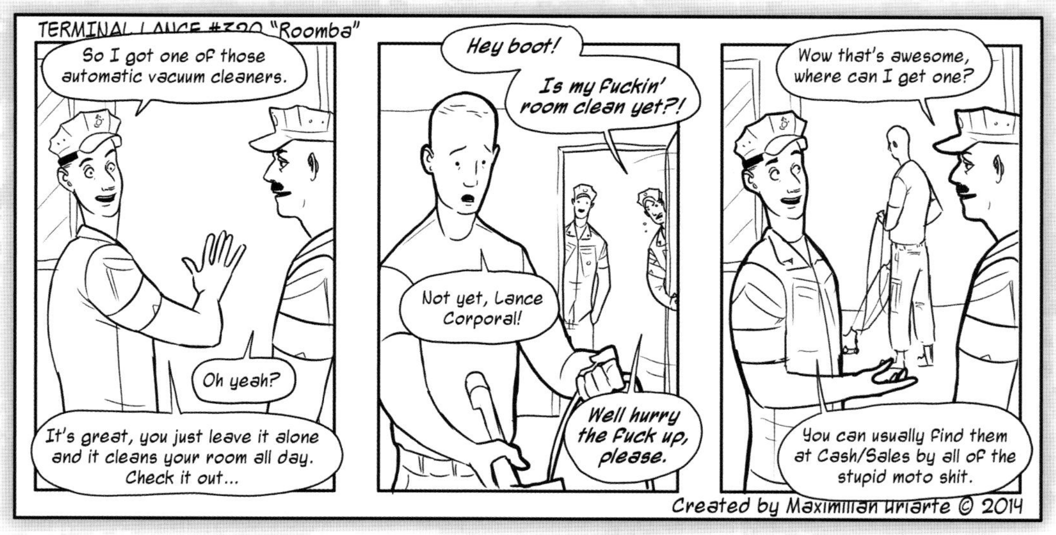
TERMINAL LANCE #320 "Roomba"
So I got one of those automatic vacuum cleaners.
Oh yeah?
It's great, you just leave it alone and it cleans your room all day. Check it out...
Hey boot!
Is my fuckin' room clean yet?!
Not yet, Lance Corporal!
Well hurry the fuck up, please.
Wow that's awesome, where can I get one?
You can usually find them at Cash/Sales by all of the stupid moto shit.
Created by Maximilian Uriarte © 2014

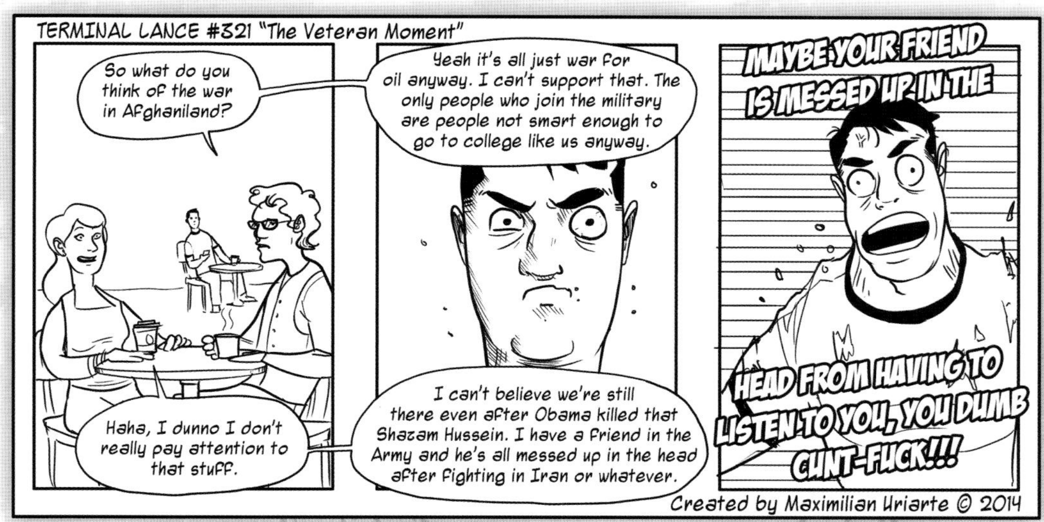
TERMINAL LANCE #321 "The Veteran Moment"
So what do you think of the war in Afghaniland?
Haha, I dunno I don't really pay attention to that stuff.
Yeah it's all just war for oil anyway. I can't support that. The only people who join the military are people not smart enough to go to college like us anyway.
I can't believe we're still there even after Obama killed that Shazam Hussein. I have a friend in the Army and he's all messed up in the head after fighting in Iran or whatever.
MAYBE YOUR FRIEND IS MESSED UP IN THE
HEAD FROM HAVING TO LISTEN TO YOU, YOU DUMB CUNT-FUCK!!!
Created by Maximilian Uriarte © 2014

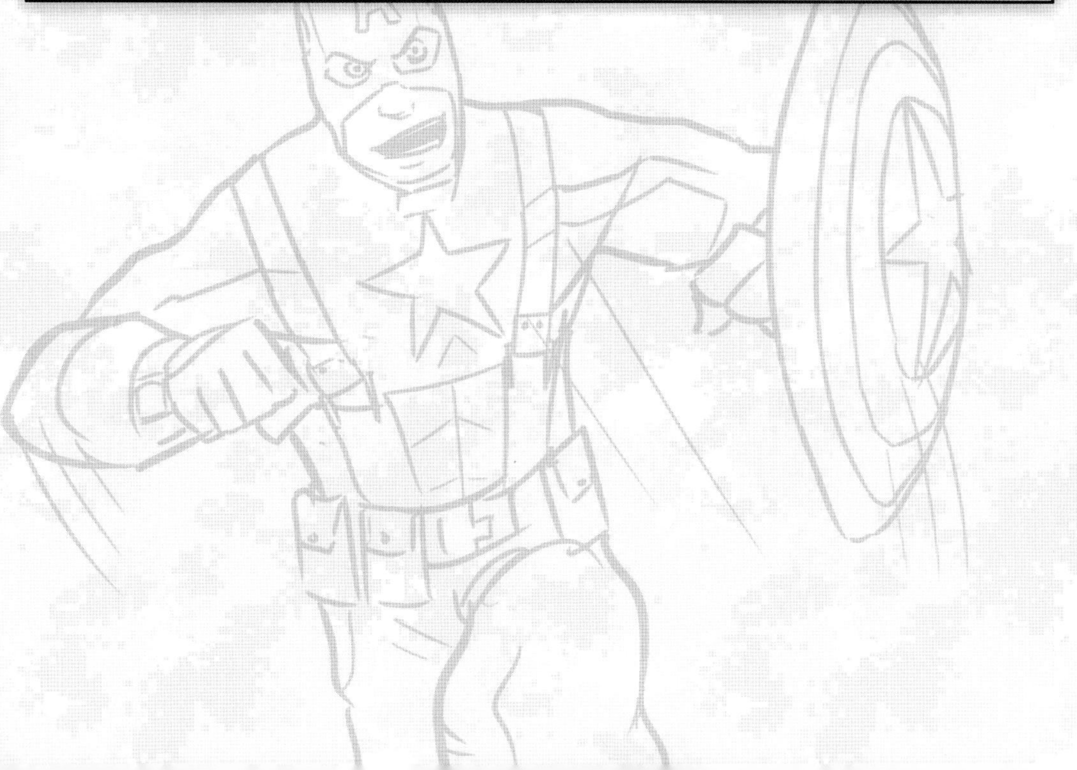

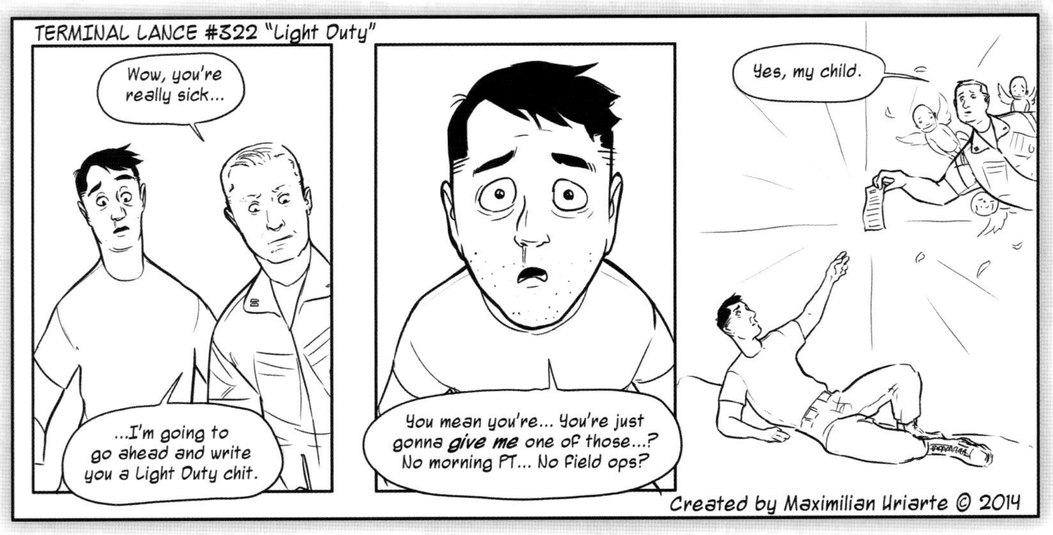
TERMINAL LANCE #322 "Light Duty"
Wow, you're really sick...
...I'm going to go ahead and write you a Light Duty chit.
You mean you're... You're just gonna **give me** one of those...? No morning PT... No field ops?
Yes, my child.
Created by Maximilian Uriarte © 2014

322 "Light Duty"

While it is certainly true that there is a stigma associated with medical treatment while on active duty, receiving a Light Duty chit is a magical moment. The heavens part, rays of brilliant light caress your face with their holy warmth. The blessings from your BAS grant you a brief relent from the daily grind. Not only do you get to don your go-fasters (as they call them) with your cammies, but you get to avoid morning PT as well as field ops.

It's a slippery slope, however. For as much as Marines value the opportunity to skate through another day, too much Light Duty won't sit well with the rest of the platoon. No one likes a malingerer, but more importantly, no one likes someone who doesn't have to deal with the same bullshit as everyone else. The Light Duty chit is a rare gift, and should be savored as such.

Even more rare, but exponentially more powerful, is the Bed Rest chit. Obtain this holiest of holies and you will be revered as a god.

Medical care in the Marine Corps is interesting. One of the best perks of being enlisted is the free medical. Well, free with a catch. You see, you don't really get to go to the doctor when you need to. If something's wrong, you talk to the Corpsman, and if he thinks it's bad enough you get to go to the BAS where you may or may not see a doctor. More often than not, "free medical" just means "free Motrin and water with a slur insulting my manhood if I question it."

Not that I'm an expert, though I have been binge watching *House, M.D.* on Netflix lately.

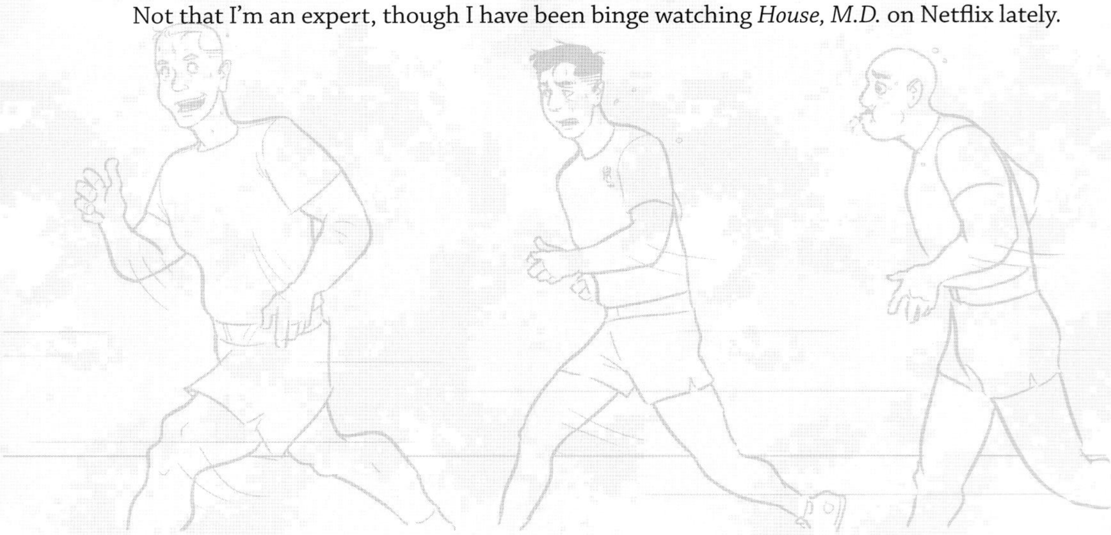

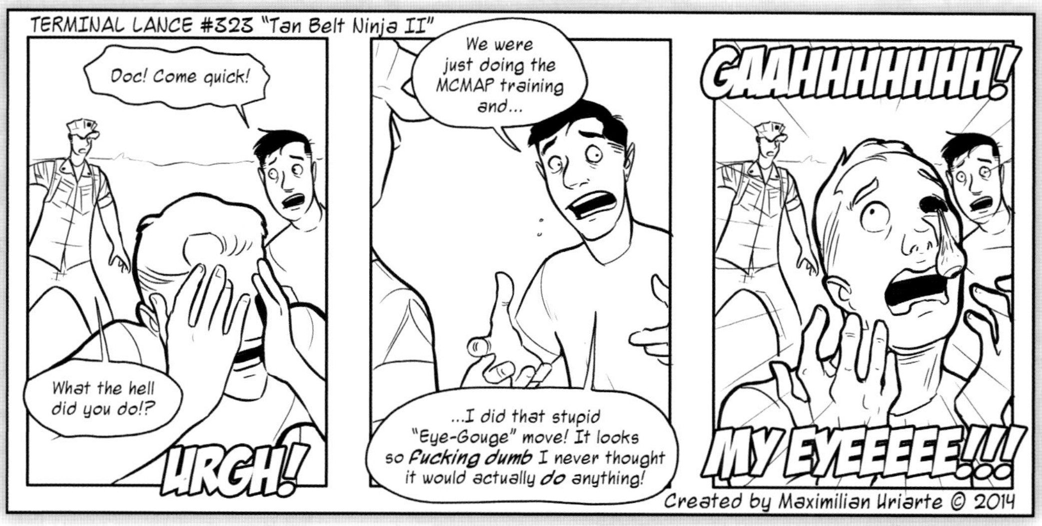
TERMINAL LANCE #323 "Tan Belt Ninja II"
Doc! Come quick!
What the hell did you do!?
URGH!
We were just doing the MCMAP training and...
...I did that stupid "Eye-Gouge" move! It looks so fucking dumb I never thought it would actually do anything!
GAAHHHHHHH!
MY EYEEEEE!!!
Created by Maximilian Uriarte © 2014

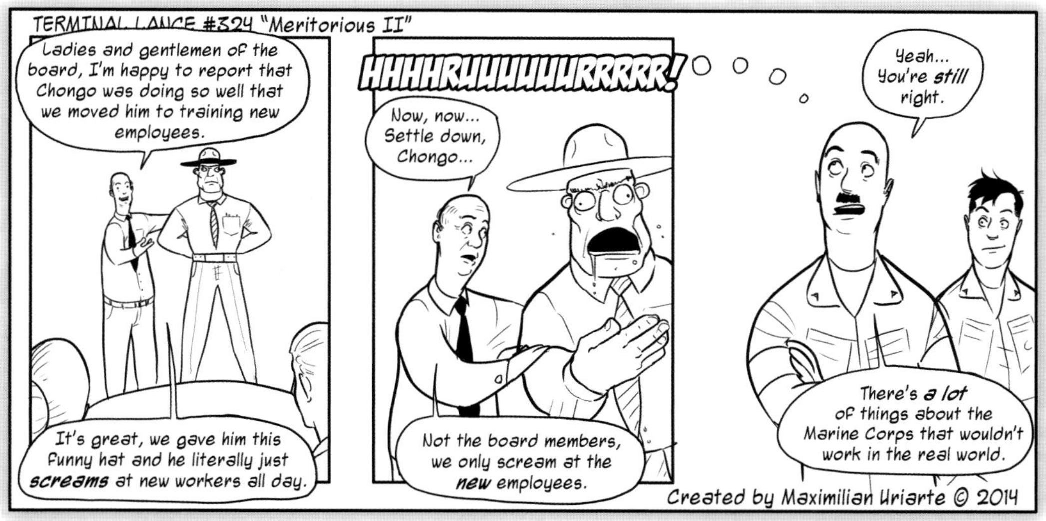
TERMINAL LANCE #324 "Meritorious II"
Ladies and gentlemen of the board, I'm happy to report that Chongo was doing so well that we moved him to training new employees.
It's great, we gave him this funny hat and he literally just screams at new workers all day.
HHHHRUUUUUURRRRR!
Now, now... Settle down, Chongo...
Not the board members, we only scream at the new employees.
Yeah... You're still right.
There's a lot of things about the Marine Corps that wouldn't work in the real world.
Created by Maximilian Uriarte © 2014

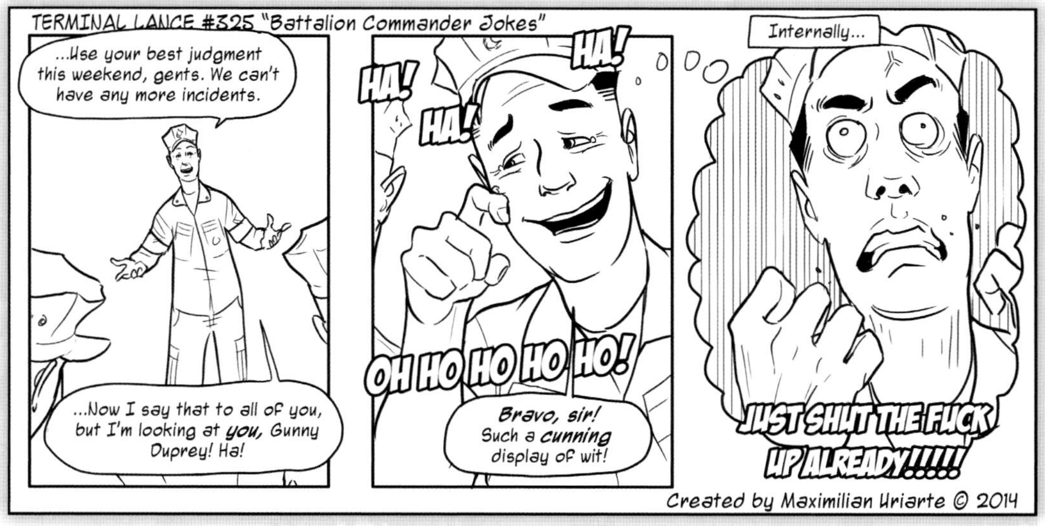
TERMINAL LANCE #325 "Battalion Commander Jokes"
...Use your best judgment this weekend, gents. We can't have any more incidents.
...Now I say that to all of you, but I'm looking at you, Gunny Duprey! Ha!
HA!
HA!
HA!
OH HO HO HO HO!
Bravo, sir! Such a cunning display of wit!
Internally...
JUST SHUT THE FUCK UP ALREADY!!!!!
Created by Maximilian Uriarte © 2014

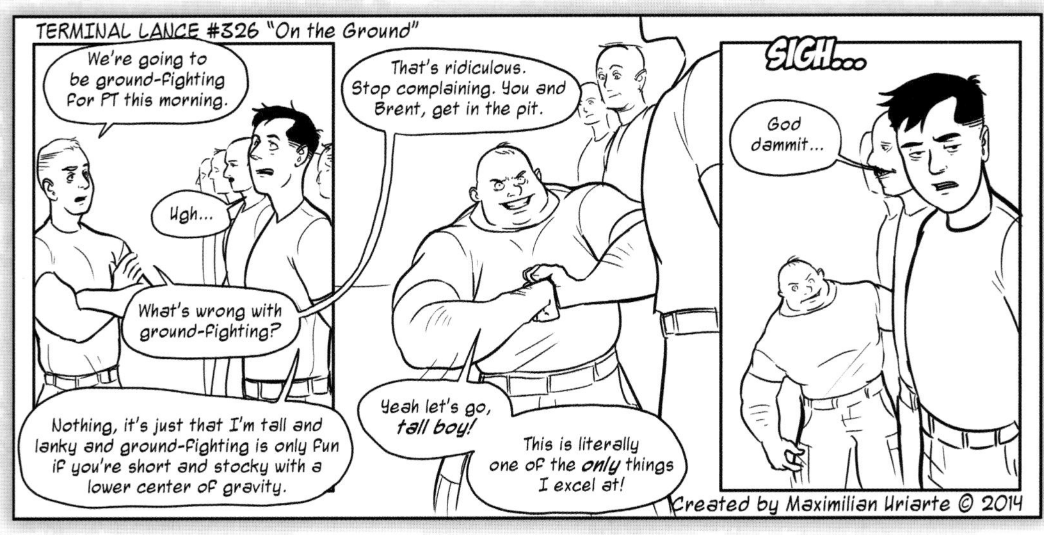
TERMINAL LANCE #326 "On the Ground"
We're going to be ground-fighting for PT this morning.
Ugh...
What's wrong with ground-fighting?
Nothing, it's just that I'm tall and lanky and ground-fighting is only fun if you're short and stocky with a lower center of gravity.
That's ridiculous. Stop complaining. You and Brent, get in the pit.
Yeah let's go, *tall boy!*
This is literally one of the *only* things I excel at!
SIGH...
God dammit...
Created by Maximilian Uriarte © 2014

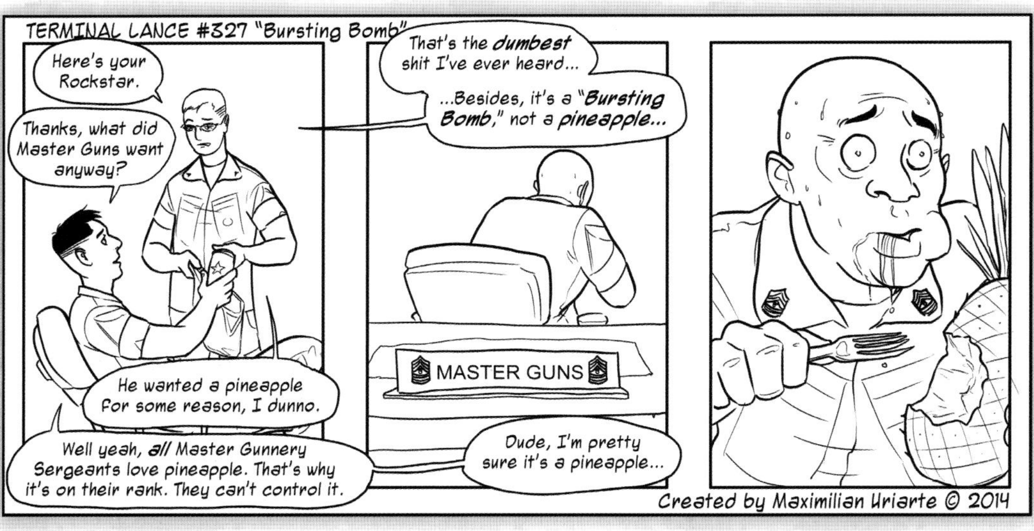
TERMINAL LANCE #327 "Bursting Bomb"
Here's your Rockstar.
Thanks, what did Master Guns want anyway?
He wanted a pineapple for some reason, I dunno.
Well yeah, *all* Master Gunnery Sergeants love pineapple. That's why it's on their rank. They can't control it.
That's the *dumbest* shit I've ever heard...
...Besides, it's a "*Bursting Bomb*," not a *pineapple...*
MASTER GUNS
Dude, I'm pretty sure it's a pineapple...
Created by Maximilian Uriarte © 2014

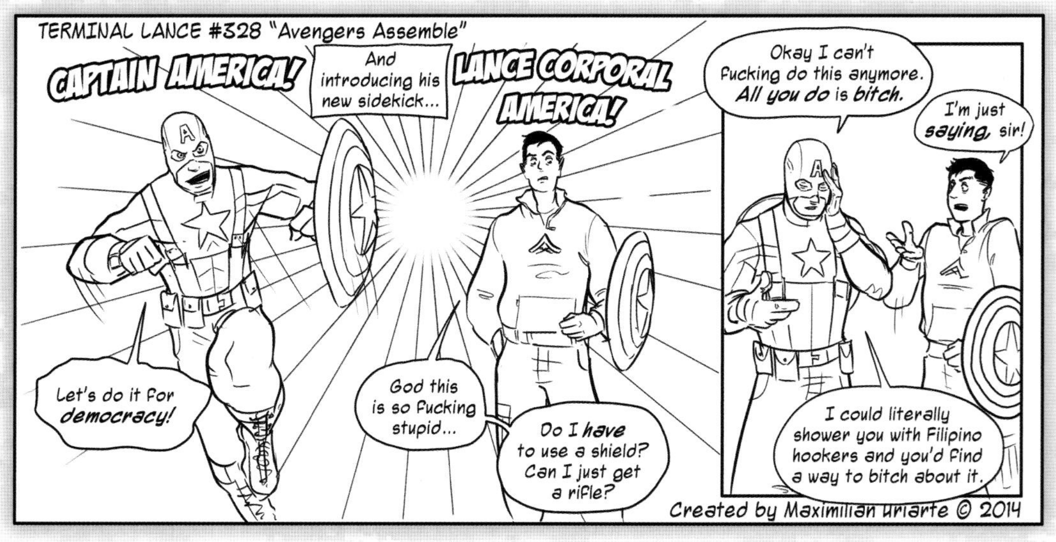
TERMINAL LANCE #328 "Avengers Assemble"
CAPTAIN AMERICA!
Let's do it for *democracy!*
And introducing his new sidekick...
LANCE CORPORAL AMERICA!
God this is so fucking stupid...
Do I *have* to use a shield? Can I just get a rifle?
Okay I can't fucking do this anymore. *All you do* is *bitch.*
I'm just *saying,* sir!
I could literally shower you with Filipino hookers and you'd find a way to bitch about it.
Created by Maximilian Uriarte © 2014

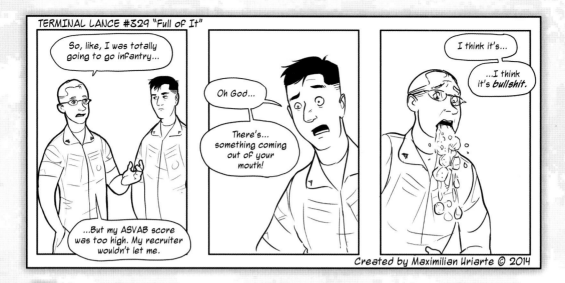

TERMINAL LANCE #329 "Full of It"
So, like, I was totally going to go infantry...
...But my ASVAB score was too high. My recruiter wouldn't let me.
Oh God...
There's... something coming out of your mouth!
I think it's...
...I think it's *bullshit.*
Created by Maximilian Uriarte © 2014

329 "Full of It"

The age-old battle between POG's and grunts continues in *Terminal Lance*!

Okay, this strip isn't really about that—it's more about just owning up to what you are. After being out for a while and meeting a lot more Marines in different fields, the one thing I can say with absolute certainty is that no one really cares what your MOS is or was. And whatever it is, you should just own it like it's the coolest shit in the world.

"Oh, you're a cook?"

"Fuck yeah, I'm a cook, and it's fucking awesome. I'll cook you the best, shittiest military food you'll ever have."

This came up in a conversation I had with a Marine once, another infantry Marine. Although the rivalry and shit talking is fun, at the end of the day it really makes no difference what stupid job you had in the Corps, as long as you're honest about it. Didn't deploy to Iraq or Afghanistan? Okay, it's a little weird since we've been at war for like eleven years now, but own the fuck out of that. Don't bullshit me about how you were going to go infantry but couldn't, or whatever stupid thing you try to say to feel less guilty. If you were really going to go infantry, you would have. I didn't even know what an ASVAB was, scored a 92, and proceeded to go open-contract 0300 infantry (where I later became an 0351 at SOI). The idea that grunts were too stupid to become POG's is lost on me, because it implies that any of them wanted it any other way to begin with. Personally, I wouldn't have enlisted at all if I couldn't do infantry, but to each his own.

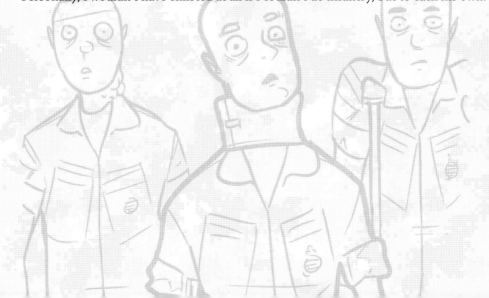

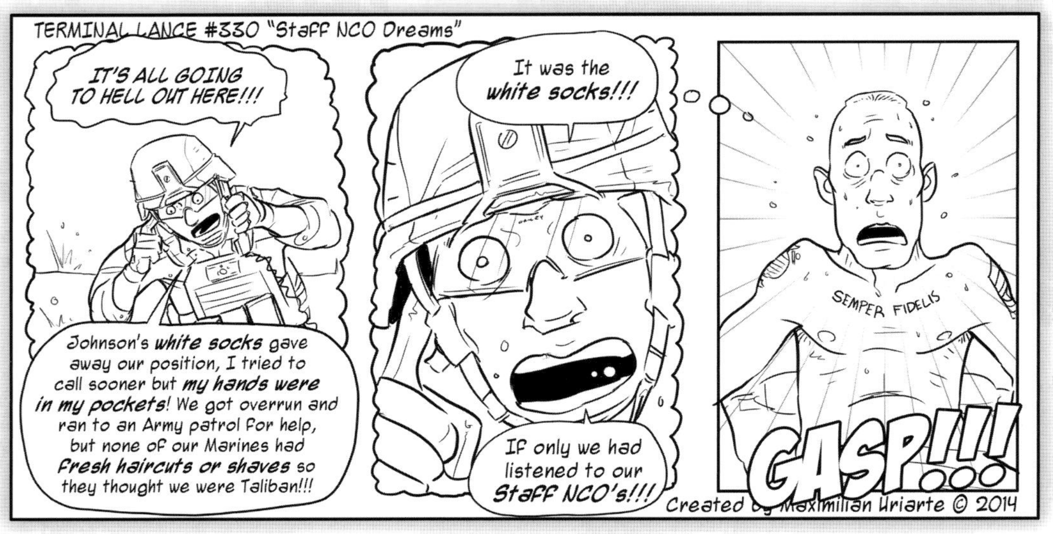
TERMINAL LANCE #330 "Staff NCO Dreams"
IT'S ALL GOING TO HELL OUT HERE!!!
Johnson's white socks gave away our position, I tried to call sooner but my hands were in my pockets! We got overrun and ran to an Army patrol for help, but none of our Marines had fresh haircuts or shaves so they thought we were Taliban!!!
It was the white socks!!!
If only we had listened to our Staff NCO's!!!
SEMPER FIDELIS
GASP!!!
Created by Maximilian Uriarte © 2014

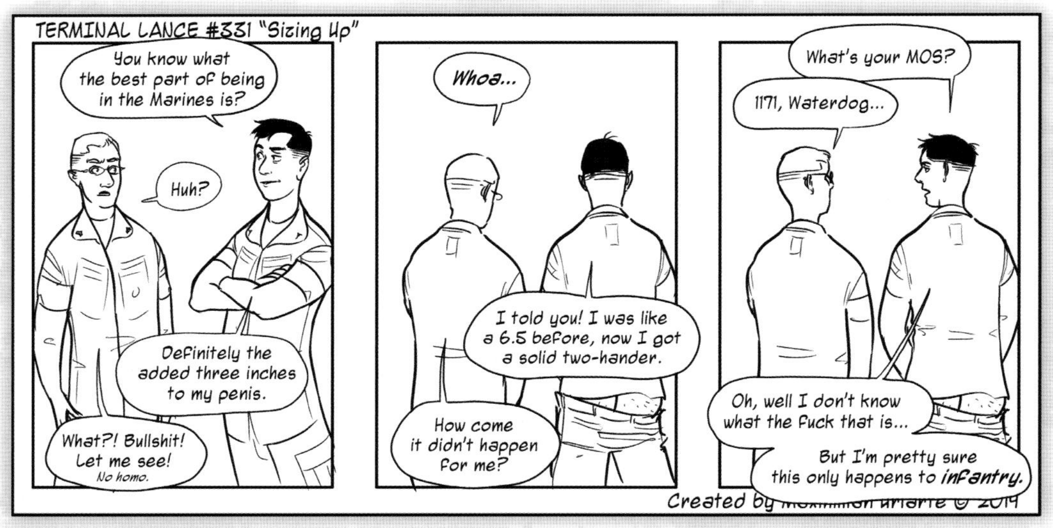
TERMINAL LANCE #331 "Sizing Up"
You know what the best part of being in the Marines is?
Huh?
Definitely the added three inches to my penis.
What?! Bullshit! Let me see!
No homo.
Whoa...
I told you! I was like a 6.5 before, now I got a solid two-hander.
How come it didn't happen for me?
What's your MOS?
1171, Waterdog...
Oh, well I don't know what the fuck that is...
But I'm pretty sure this only happens to infantry.
Created by Maximilian Uriarte © 2014

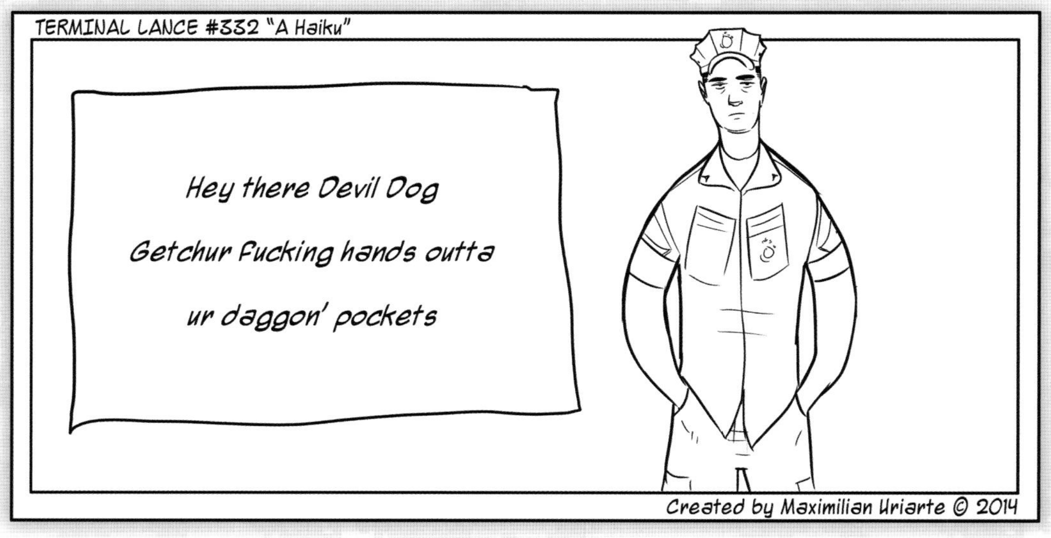
TERMINAL LANCE #332 "A Haiku"
Hey there Devil Dog
Getchur fucking hands outta
ur daggon' pockets
Created by Maximilian Uriarte © 2014

TERMINAL LANCE #333 "Oh Baby"
Thanks for helping me babysit. Can you pass me the baby wipes?
Uh... sure...
. . .
Ohhhhhh! That's why they're called baby wipes!
I've been using those things for years and have never once cleaned a baby with them.
Created by Maximilian Uriarte © 2014

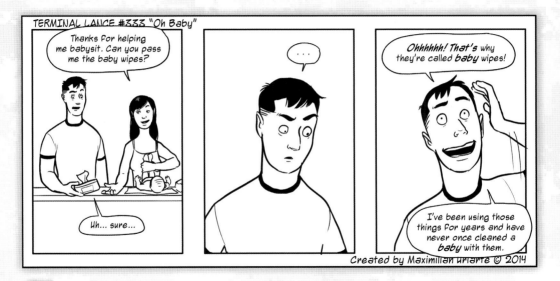

333 "Oh Baby"

Is there anything more ubiquitous in the military than baby wipes? A Marine Corps PX is probably the only place in the world you'll see legions of eighteen- to twenty-four-year-old males buying aisles of baby wipes with no intention of using them on a baby. Baby wipes serve many practical applications for Marines. They make a great alternative to bathing while you're stuck in the field; they do a wonderful job of cleaning the carbon out of your rifle's chamber; and you can use them to comfortably wipe your ass in a port-a-shitter.

Really, the only thing Marines don't use them for is cleaning babies.

If you're ever sending a care package to Marines overseas, a safe thing to always send is baby wipes. There's a million ways and reasons to use them. It can never go wrong—as long as the package also has cookies, porn, and a Nintendo Switch with *Mario Kart*.

TERMINAL LANCE #334 "Exhaust Fumes"
Hey Stephens, did you change your protein powder?
Yeah, just last night, how could you tell?
Because I can taste it in the air...
...Courtesy of your butthole.
Created by Maximilian Uriarte © 2014

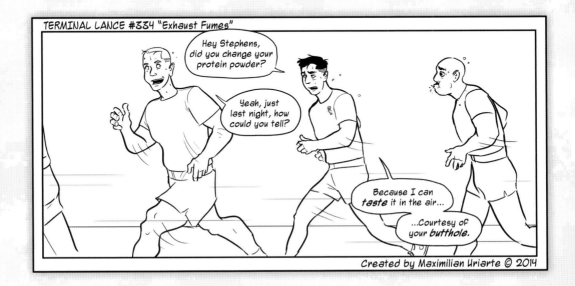

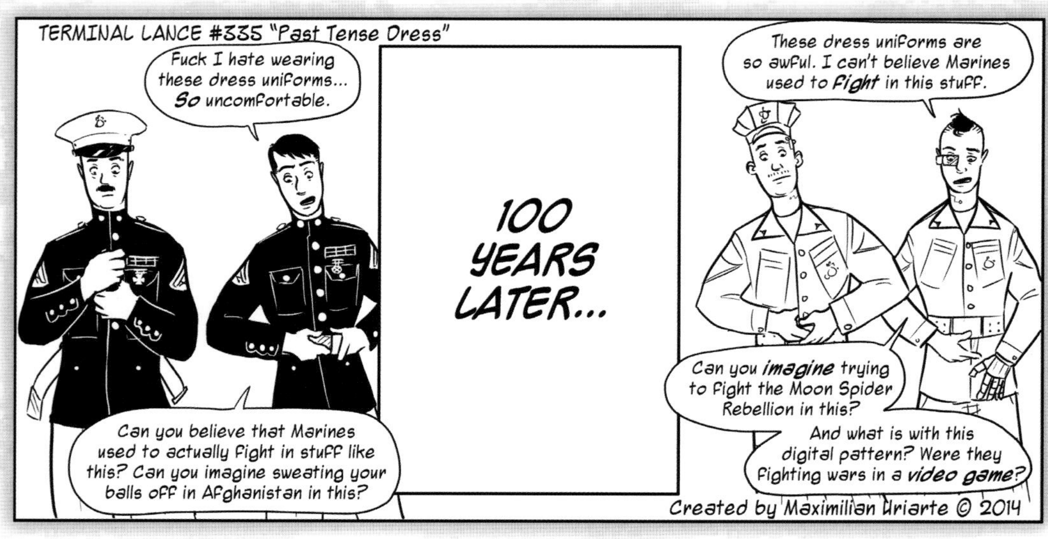
TERMINAL LANCE #335 "Past Tense Dress"
Fuck I hate wearing these dress uniforms... So uncomfortable.
Can you believe that Marines used to actually fight in stuff like this? Can you imagine sweating your balls off in Afghanistan in this?
100 YEARS LATER...
These dress uniforms are so awful. I can't believe Marines used to fight in this stuff.
Can you imagine trying to fight the Moon Spider Rebellion in this?
And what is with this digital pattern? Were they fighting wars in a video game?
Created by Maximilian Uriarte © 2014

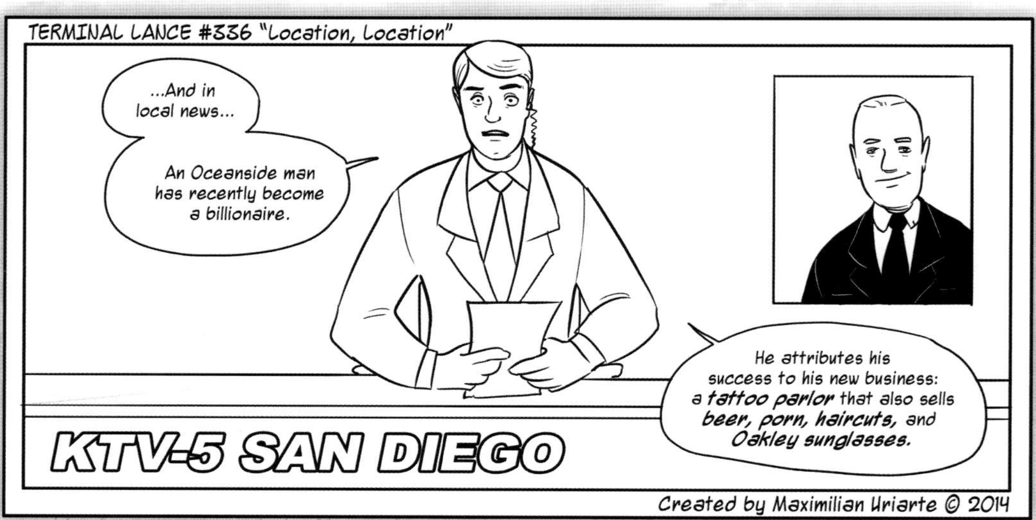
TERMINAL LANCE #336 "Location, Location"
...And in local news...
An Oceanside man has recently become a billionaire.
He attributes his success to his new business: a tattoo parlor that also sells beer, porn, haircuts, and Oakley sunglasses.
KTV-5 SAN DIEGO
Created by Maximilian Uriarte © 2014

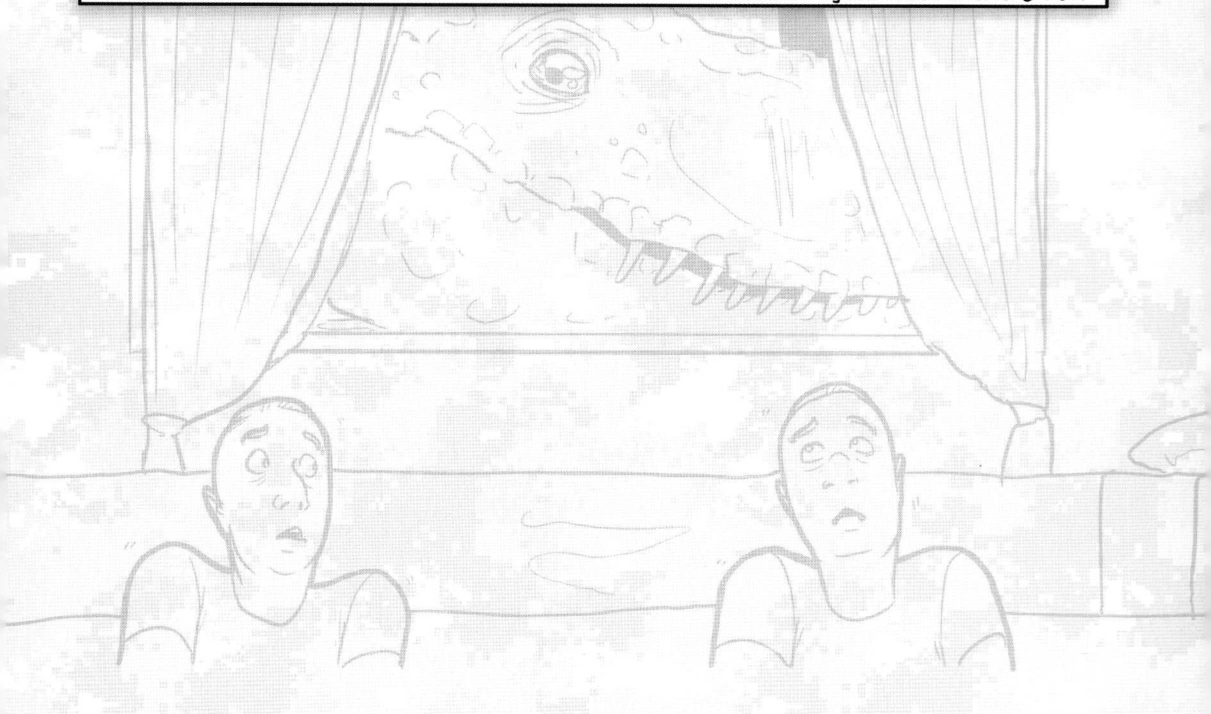

TERMINAL LANCE #337 "Boot Camp: Broke Dick Platoon"
I'm sorry, Recruit, but you're extremely sick.
3014
I have no choice but to drop you from your platoon and place you in MRP. You'll pick up with a new company when you're better.
Meanwhile, in MRP...
(Medical Recovery Platoon)
K...
...Kill me.
Please, Doc, there's gotta be something you can do here...
I'm not usually this forward, but I will suck *every* dick in this building if I have to.
3014
Created by Maximilian Uriarte © 2014

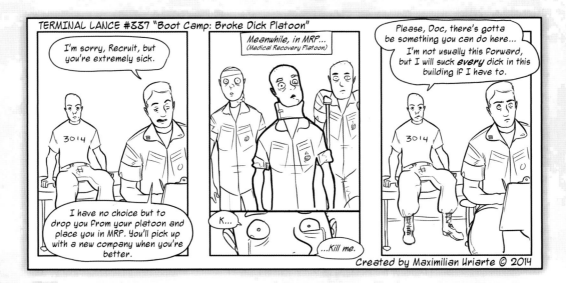

337 "Boot Camp: Broke Dick Platoon"

Easily the biggest fear of any aspiring Marine (also called a Recruit) is getting dropped to MRP during boot camp. Medical Recovery Platoon is where you go when you're just too ill to train, but are expected to recover at some point so you can finish the trials at hand.

Speaking purely as an observer, I can't imagine a more miserable place. Tales of attempted suicide and misery in the MRP permeate the Depot. Boot camp is already miserable enough for a regular, healthy recruit. The constant berating, screaming, games, and physical arduousness are something I would never want to do again, but I was fortunate enough to only have had to endure it for three months. I stress the word "fortunate" here, because I was almost dropped to MRP during my stay at MCRD.

I, like most recruits, came down with the "crud," as they call it. I had a pretty bad case of pneumonia right before we were supposed to go up north to Camp Pendleton. The Navy doctor told me I would have to be dropped to MRP, as I was simply too ill to go up north. I was horrified. I'd have to be here for another two weeks?! Two weeks might not sound like a lot to you, but two weeks in boot camp is like three years in civilian time. Luckily, like the hand of God himself, my company commander called medical moments after they gave me the news. He spoke with the doctor and convinced him to let me go up north with my platoon. I was ecstatic. Well, I mean, as ecstatic as one can be with a fever of 103 and lungs full of shit.

I was told that my company had already lost too many recruits and could not afford to lose any more, under any circumstances, so they hopped me up on Motrin and penicillin and sent me off.

At my graduation from boot camp, I found my mother in the crowd the moment I was dismissed and the first words out of my mouth were, "Did you bring my clothes? Good, let me go change so we can get the fuck out of here."

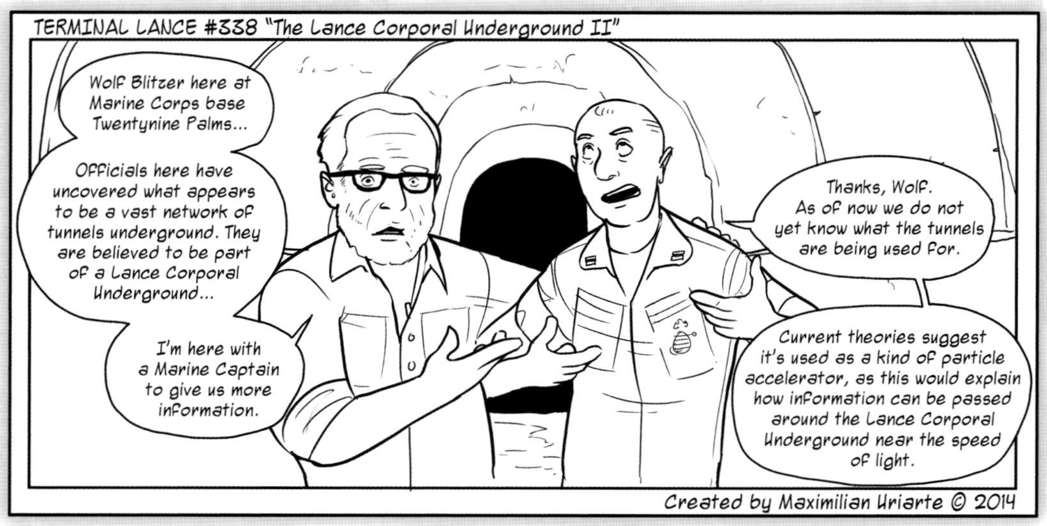
TERMINAL LANCE #338 "The Lance Corporal Underground II"
Wolf Blitzer here at Marine Corps base Twentynine Palms...
Officials here have uncovered what appears to be a vast network of tunnels underground. They are believed to be part of a Lance Corporal Underground...
I'm here with a Marine Captain to give us more information.
Thanks, Wolf. As of now we do not yet know what the tunnels are being used for.
Current theories suggest it's used as a kind of particle accelerator, as this would explain how information can be passed around the Lance Corporal Underground near the speed of light.
Created by Maximilian Uriarte © 2014

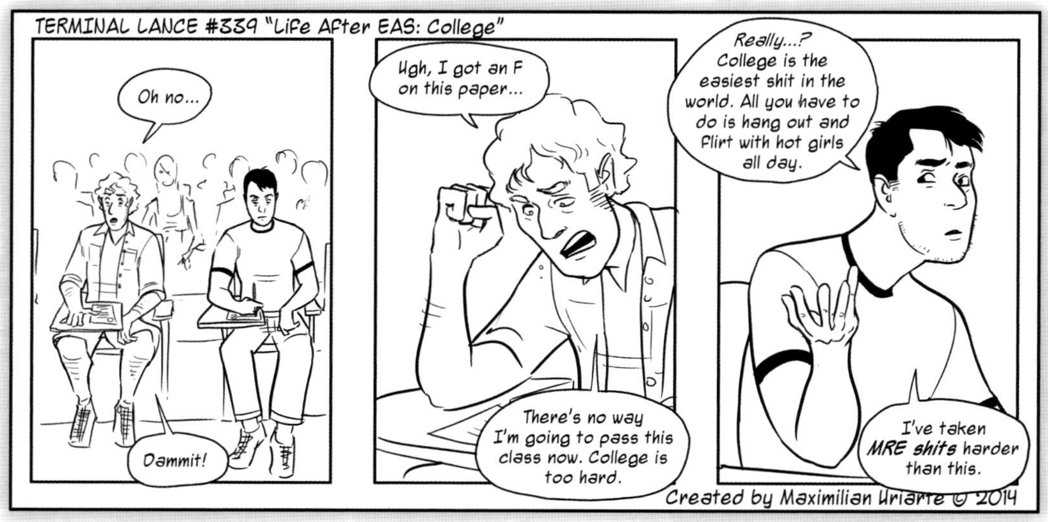
TERMINAL LANCE #339 "Life After EAS: College"
Oh no...
Dammit!
Ugh, I got an F on this paper...
There's no way I'm going to pass this class now. College is too hard.
Really...? College is the easiest shit in the world. All you have to do is hang out and flirt with hot girls all day.
I've taken MRE shits harder than this.
Created by Maximilian Uriarte © 2014

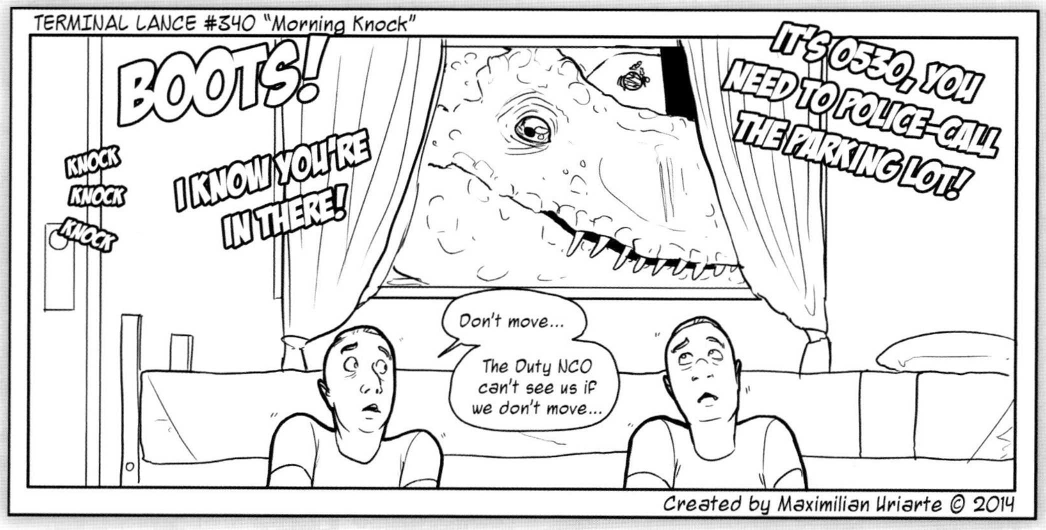
TERMINAL LANCE #340 "Morning Knock"
BOOTS!
KNOCK
KNOCK
KNOCK
I KNOW YOU'RE IN THERE!
IT'S 0530, YOU NEED TO POLICE-CALL THE PARKING LOT!
Don't move...
The Duty NCO can't see us if we don't move...
Created by Maximilian Uriarte © 2014

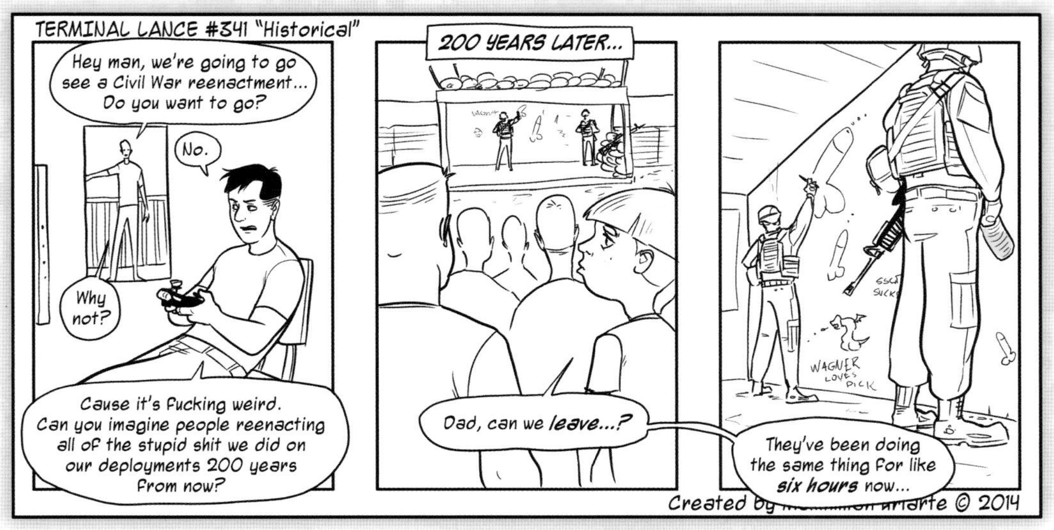
TERMINAL LANCE #341 "Historical"
Hey man, we're going to go see a Civil War reenactment... Do you want to go?
No.
Why not?
Cause it's fucking weird. Can you imagine people reenacting all of the stupid shit we did on our deployments 200 years from now?
200 YEARS LATER...
Dad, can we *leave...?*
WAGNER LOVES DICK
They've been doing the same thing for like *six hours* now...
Created by

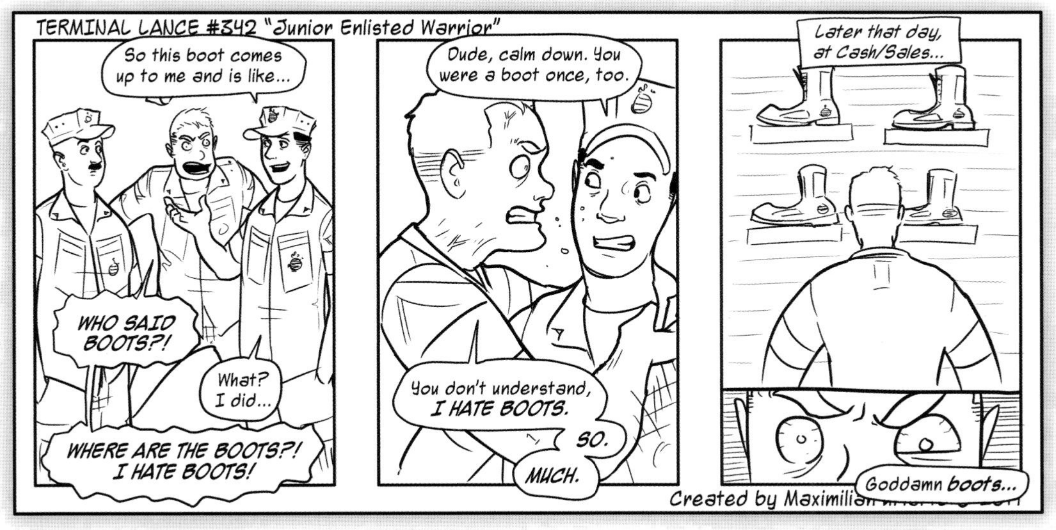
TERMINAL LANCE #342 "Junior Enlisted Warrior"
So this boot comes up to me and is like...
WHO SAID BOOTS?!
What? I did...
WHERE ARE THE BOOTS?! I HATE BOOTS!
Dude, calm down. You were a boot once, too.
You don't understand, I HATE BOOTS.
SO.
MUCH.
Later that day, at Cash/Sales...
Goddamn *boots...*
Created by Maximilian

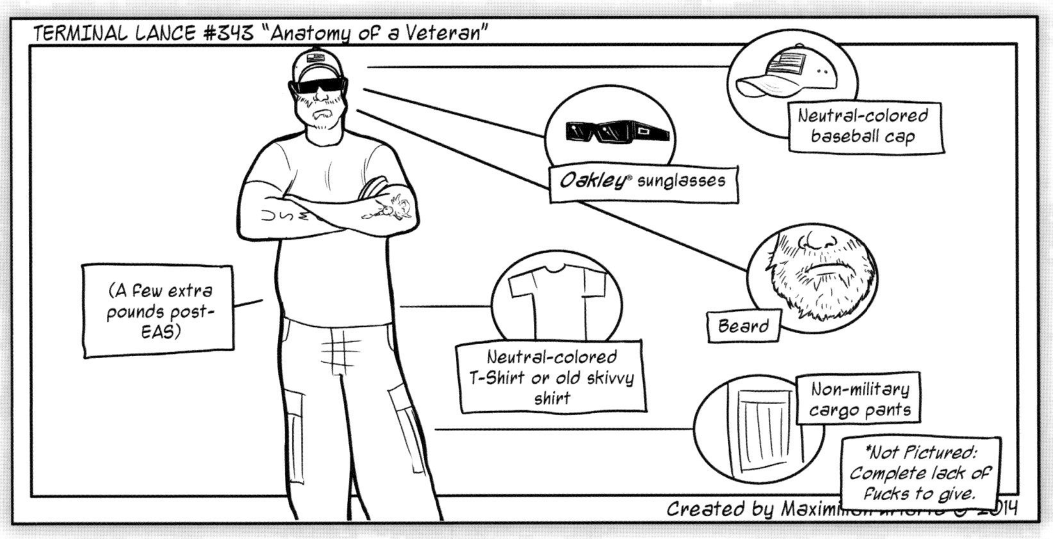
TERMINAL LANCE #343 "Anatomy of a Veteran"
Neutral-colored baseball cap
Oakley® sunglasses
Beard
(A few extra pounds post-EAS)
Neutral-colored T-Shirt or old skivvy shirt
Non-military cargo pants
*Not Pictured: Complete lack of fucks to give.
Created by Maximil

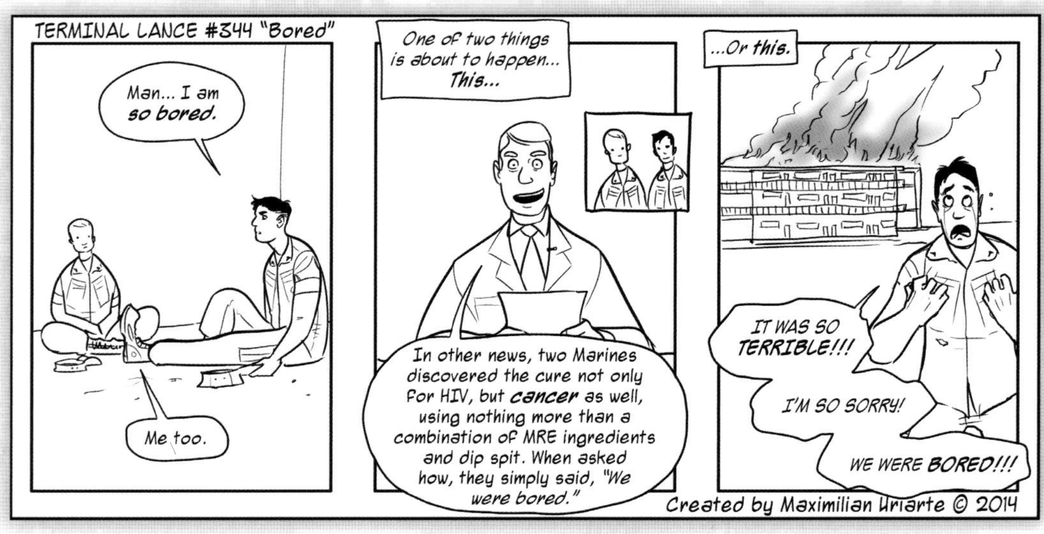
TERMINAL LANCE #344 "Bored"
Man... I am so bored.
Me too.
One of two things is about to happen... This...
In other news, two Marines discovered the cure not only for HIV, but cancer as well, using nothing more than a combination of MRE ingredients and dip spit. When asked how, they simply said, "We were bored."
...Or this.
IT WAS SO TERRIBLE!!!
I'M SO SORRY!
WE WERE BORED!!!
Created by Maximilian Uriarte © 2014

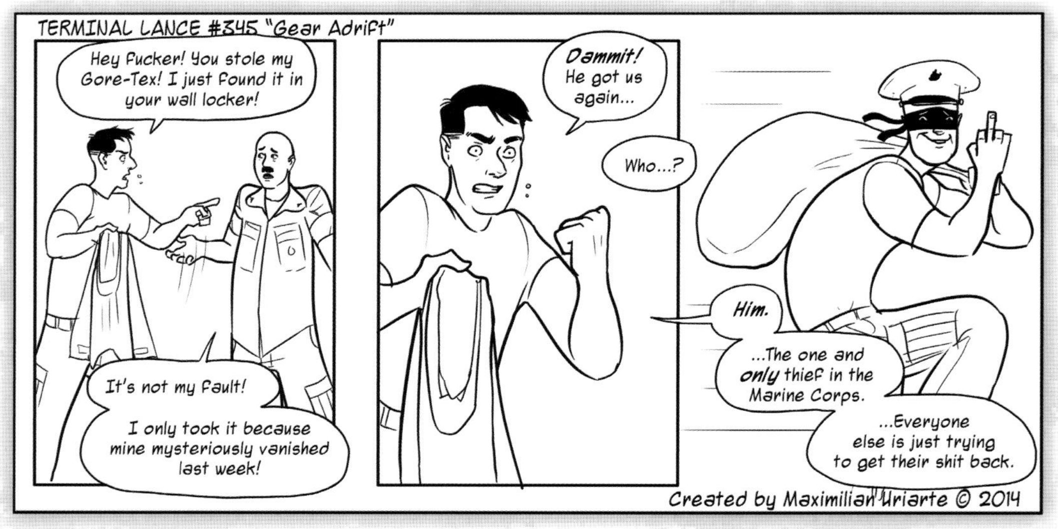
TERMINAL LANCE #345 "Gear Adrift"
Hey fucker! You stole my Gore-Tex! I just found it in your wall locker!
It's not my fault!
I only took it because mine mysteriously vanished last week!
Dammit! He got us again...
Who...?
Him.
...The one and only thief in the Marine Corps.
...Everyone else is just trying to get their shit back.
Created by Maximilian Uriarte © 2014

345 "Gear Adrift"

There's an old and eerily accurate saying in the Marine Corps:

There's only one thief in the Marine Corps. Everyone else is just trying to get their shit back.

Then again, there's also another saying:

Gear adrift is gear a gift.

One of my first experiences with lost gear was at SOI at Camp Pendleton. About halfway through the two-month ITB cycle I somehow lost my Gore-Tex jacket. I asked everyone I could and no one had any idea what happened to it. Mysteriously vanished. I want to believe it was taken by the One True Thief, if only for the fact that it would take the blame off the people around me.

However, it is rather telling that I've never seen a "Lost and Found" section of any platoon.

If you lose a piece of gear in the Marine Corps, I absolutely promise you that you will never see it again. It's unfortunate, but true, and thus the reason I ended up spending $90 on a replacement Gore-Tex at one of the military surplus stores at Oceanside.

Unsurprisingly, the store sells a lot of actual issued gear, and they pay money for gear they can sell. I wouldn't be surprised if the Gore-Tex I purchased that day (that also broke my bank account since I was a PFC with no financial management skills) was the exact same one I had lost weeks prior. After all, gear adrift is gear a gift . . . for the person that stole my Gore-Tex.

Either that, or he was just trying to get his shit back.

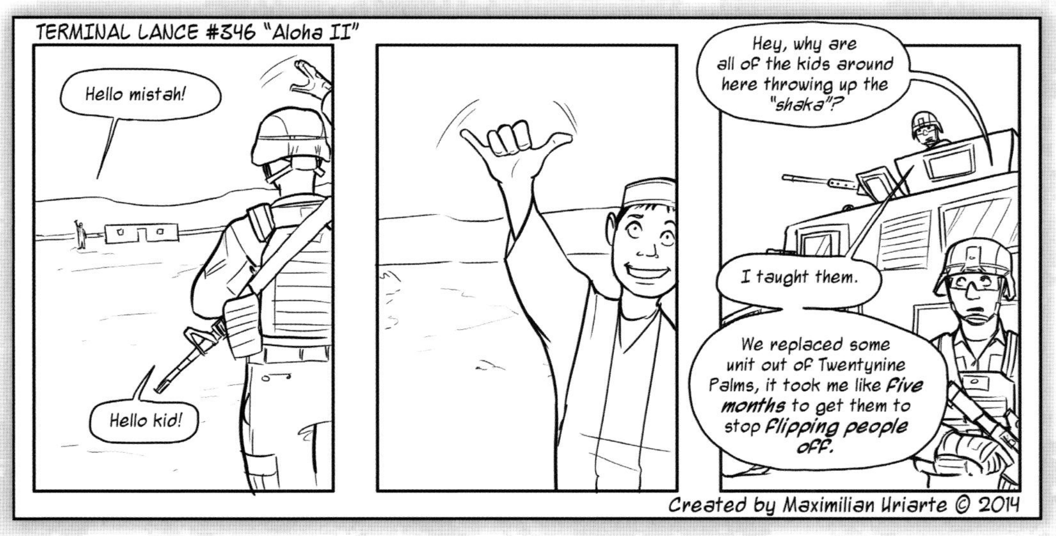
TERMINAL LANCE #346 "Aloha II"
Hello mistah!
Hello kid!
Hey, why are all of the kids around here throwing up the "shaka"?
I taught them.
We replaced some unit out of Twentynine Palms, it took me like five months to get them to stop flipping people off.
Created by Maximilian Uriarte © 2014

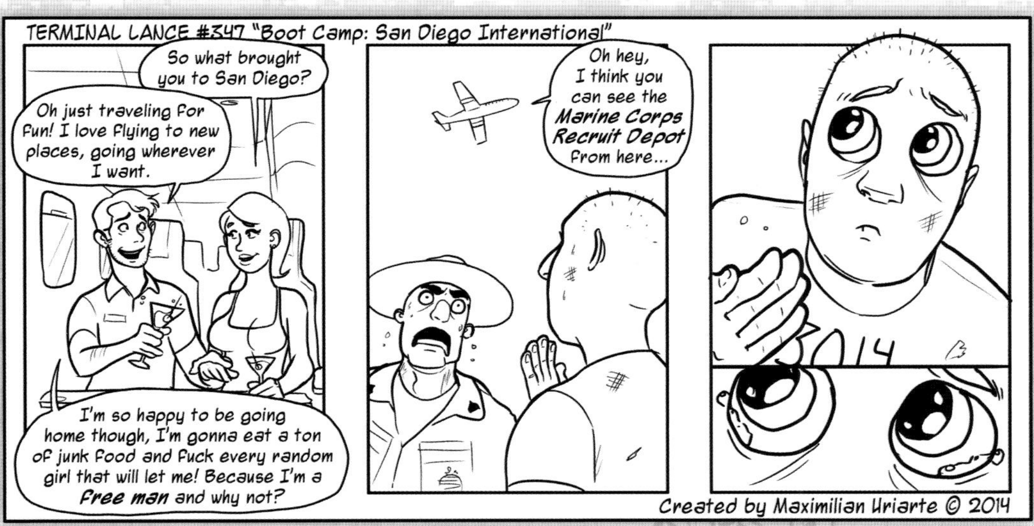
TERMINAL LANCE #347 "Boot Camp: San Diego International"
So what brought you to San Diego?
Oh just traveling for fun! I love flying to new places, going wherever I want.
I'm so happy to be going home though, I'm gonna eat a ton of junk food and fuck every random girl that will let me! Because I'm a free man and why not?
Oh hey, I think you can see the Marine Corps Recruit Depot from here...
2014
Created by Maximilian Uriarte © 2014

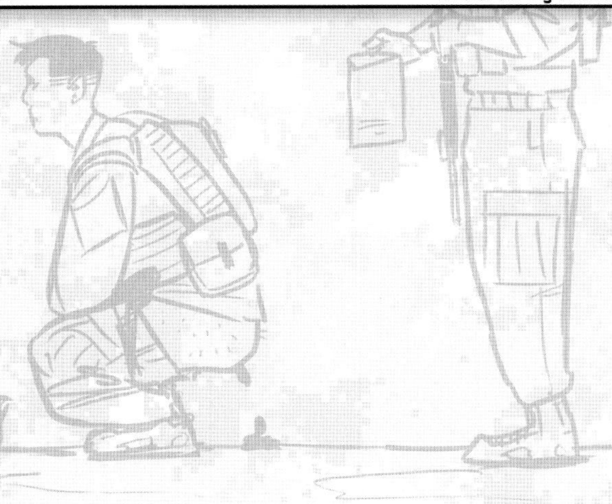

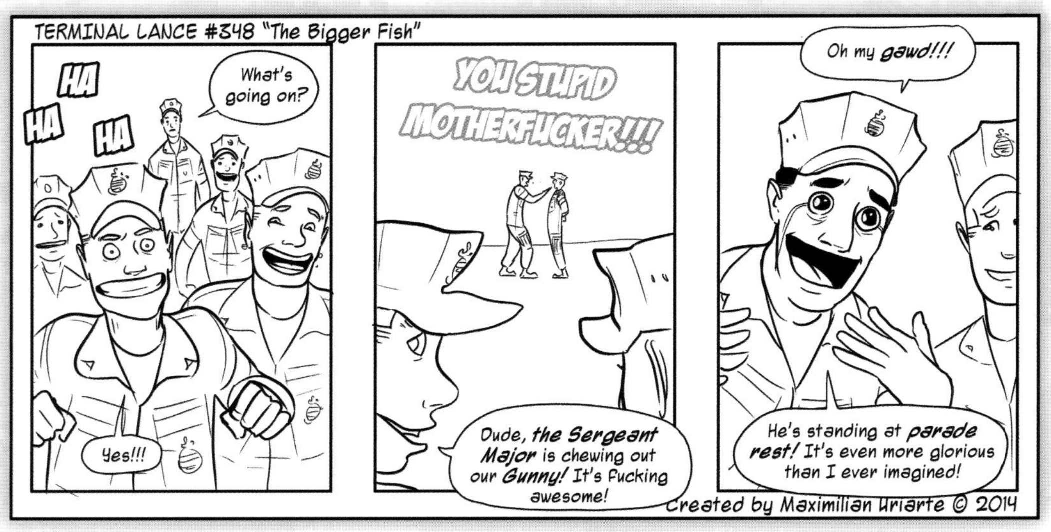
TERMINAL LANCE #348 "The Bigger Fish"
HA
HA
HA
What's going on?
Yes!!!
YOU STUPID MOTHERFUCKER!!!
Dude, the Sergeant Major is chewing out our Gunny! It's fucking awesome!
Oh my gawd!!!
He's standing at parade rest! It's even more glorious than I ever imagined!
Created by Maximilian Uriarte © 2014

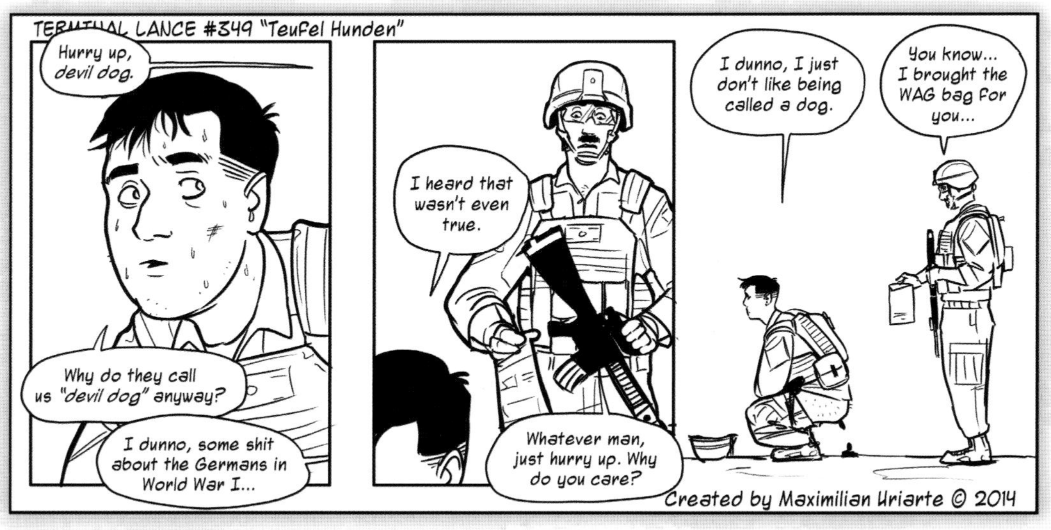
TERMINAL LANCE #349 "Teufel Hunden"
Hurry up, devil dog.
Why do they call us "devil dog" anyway?
I dunno, some shit about the Germans in World War I...
I heard that wasn't even true.
Whatever man, just hurry up. Why do you care?
I dunno, I just don't like being called a dog.
You know... I brought the WAG bag for you...
Created by Maximilian Uriarte © 2014

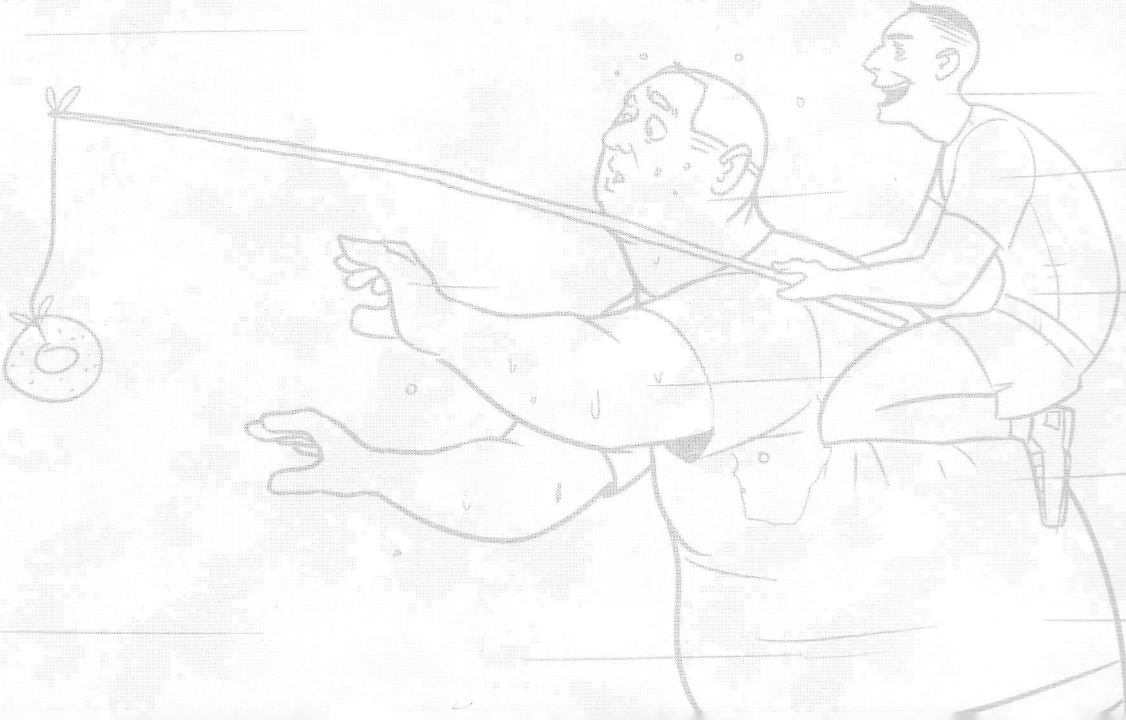

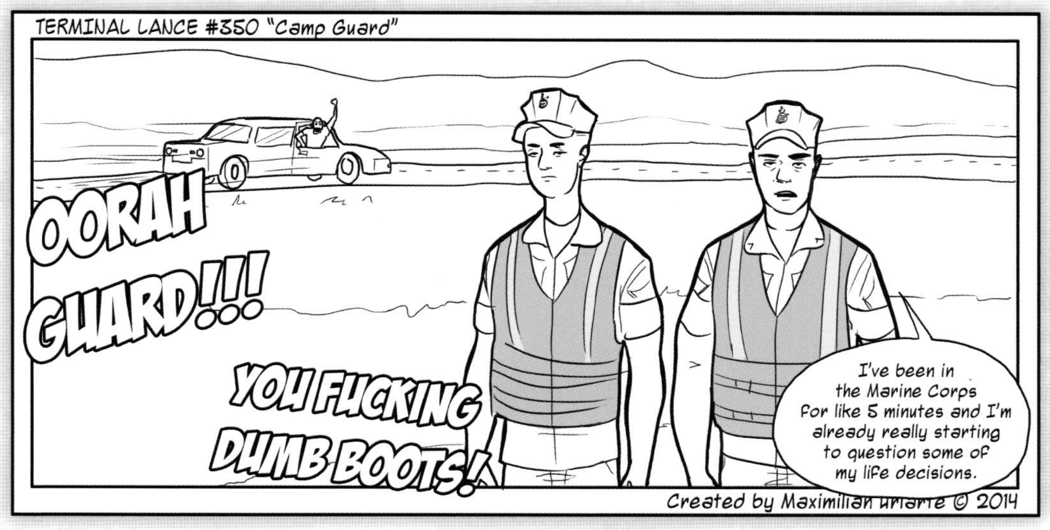
TERMINAL LANCE #350 "Camp Guard"
OORAH GUARD!!!
YOU FUCKING DUMB BOOTS!
I've been in the Marine Corps for like 5 minutes and I'm already really starting to question some of my life decisions.
Created by Maximilian Uriarte © 2014

350 "Camp Guard"

Can we just talk about how shitty being in Camp Guard is?

Non-infantry folk probably never really had to deal with this wretched duty, but for those of us that have, it was an absolutely miserable experience.

Right after boot camp, you typically go home for ten and then you get sent to either SOI West or East for your MOS training. POG's go off and do their little MCT thing for a few weeks and the grunts stick around and do their MOS training over the course of eight weeks. You're told to report into SOI West after your boot leave so you can get assigned to your training company. That is, as long as there's room.

As an active duty guy, I got wait-listed for two weeks while the reservists were rushed into their training company. So what is a boot student Marine to do for two weeks while he waits for a new ITB class to pick up?

Camp motherfucking Guard.

This consisted of eight-hour rotations patrolling the base in teams of two wearing orange glow vests, being on QRF in case some "shit" went down, or being on rest. There was no libo. We had to go to chow in formation. Cell phones weren't allowed, and you're just generally treated like the lowest form of shit on the entire base by instructors and other Marines alike.

Having just graduated boot camp, I was fairly excited to begin my new Marine Corps adventure, only to find myself in Guard purgatory for what seemed like the longest two weeks of my life until Bravo Co. picked us up. Having been to Iraq twice, it seems like a silly thing to complain about, but it really was miserable.

The trademark of Guard? Having drunk Marines drive by and shout "OORAH GUARD!!" and other obscenities at you while you just . . . did whatever it is you were doing. And because all Marines are assholes, I also partook in the belligerent shouting at Guard as soon as I was out of it.

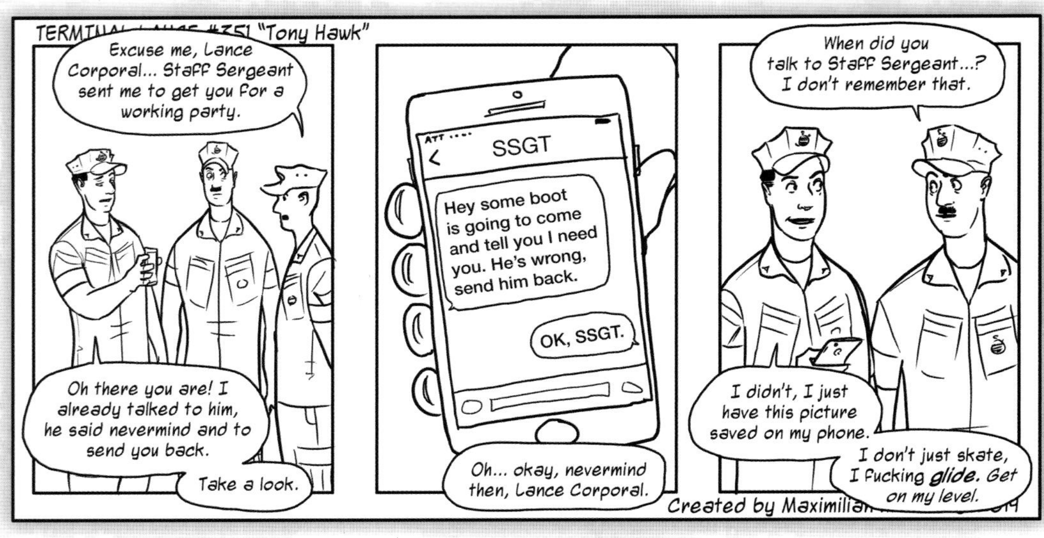
TERMINAL LANCE #351 "Tony Hawk"
Excuse me, Lance Corporal... Staff Sergeant sent me to get you for a working party.
Oh there you are! I already talked to him, he said nevermind and to send you back.
Take a look.
SSGT
Hey some boot is going to come and tell you I need you. He's wrong, send him back.
OK, SSGT.
Oh... okay, nevermind then, Lance Corporal.
When did you talk to Staff Sergeant...? I don't remember that.
I didn't, I just have this picture saved on my phone.
I don't just skate, I fucking glide. Get on my level.
Created by Maximilian

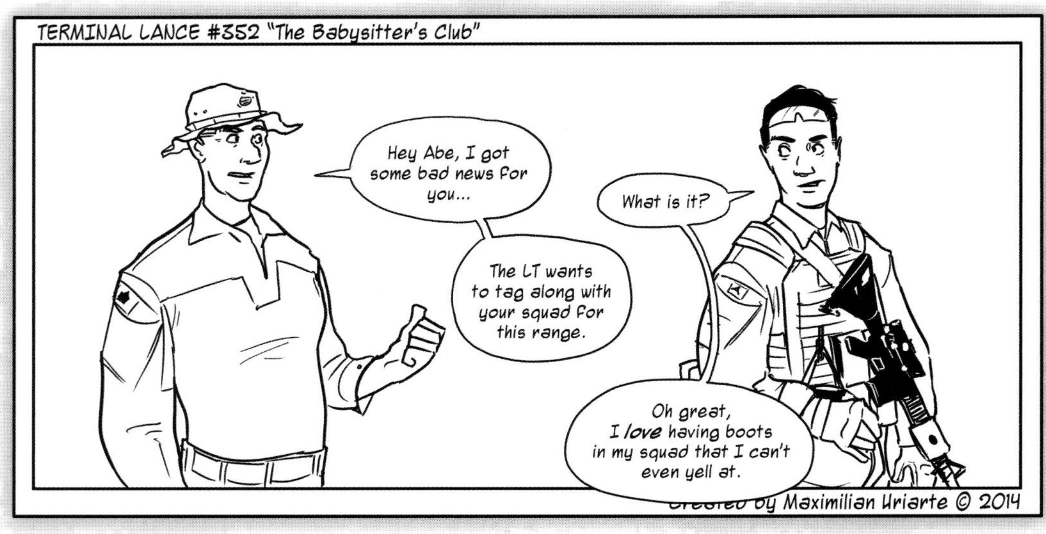
TERMINAL LANCE #352 "The Babysitter's Club"
Hey Abe, I got some bad news for you...
What is it?
The LT wants to tag along with your squad for this range.
Oh great, I love having boots in my squad that I can't even yell at.
Created by Maximilian Uriarte © 2014

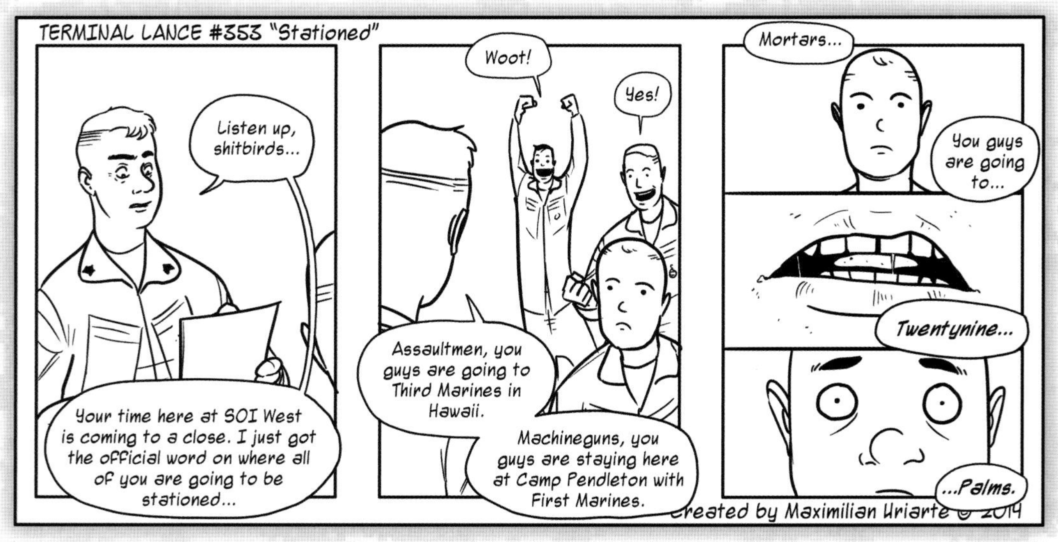
TERMINAL LANCE #353 "Stationed"
Listen up, shitbirds...
Your time here at SOI West is coming to a close. I just got the official word on where all of you are going to be stationed...
Woot!
Yes!
Assaultmen, you guys are going to Third Marines in Hawaii.
Machineguns, you guys are staying here at Camp Pendleton with First Marines.
Mortars...
You guys are going to...
Twentynine...
...Palms.
Created by Maximilian Uriarte © 2014

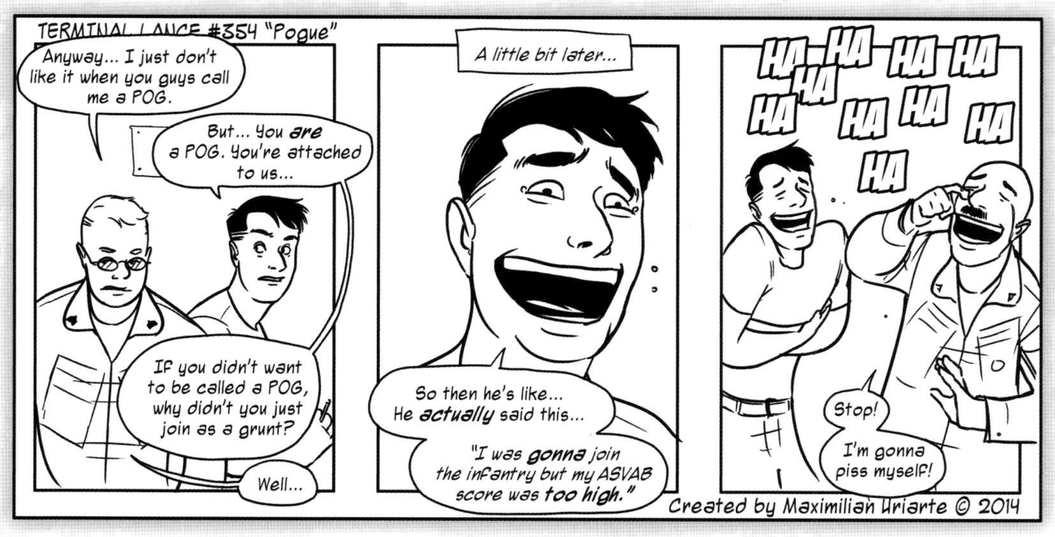
TERMINAL LANCE #354 "Pogue"
Anyway... I just don't like it when you guys call me a POG.
But... You are a POG. You're attached to us...
If you didn't want to be called a POG, why didn't you just join as a grunt?
Well...
A little bit later...
So then he's like... He actually said this...
"I was gonna join the infantry but my ASVAB score was too high."
HA HA HA HA HA HA HA HA HA HA
Stop!
I'm gonna piss myself!
Created by Maximilian Uriarte © 2014

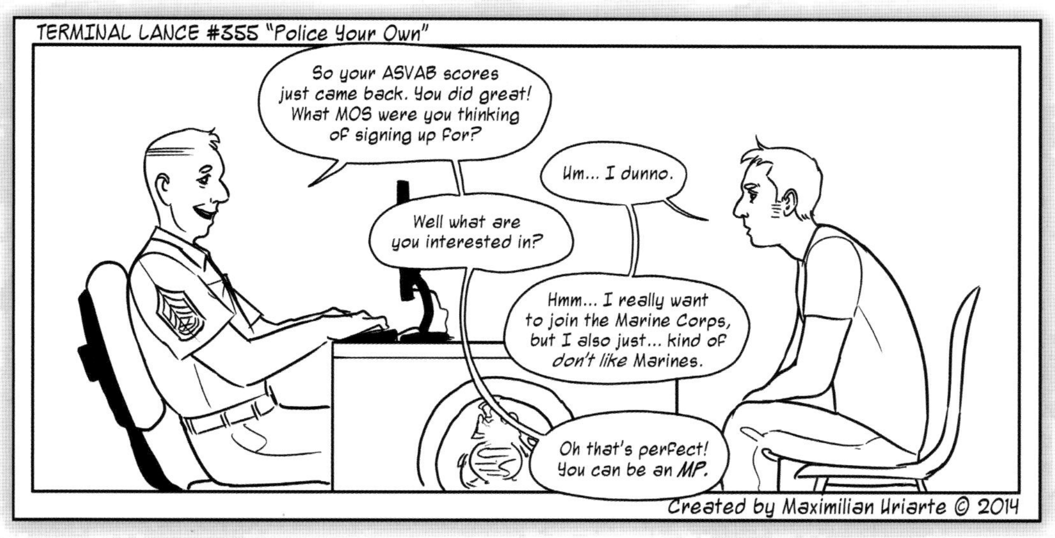
TERMINAL LANCE #355 "Police Your Own"
So your ASVAB scores just came back. You did great! What MOS were you thinking of signing up for?
Um... I dunno.
Well what are you interested in?
Hmm... I really want to join the Marine Corps, but I also just... kind of don't like Marines.
Oh that's perfect! You can be an MP.
Created by Maximilian Uriarte © 2014

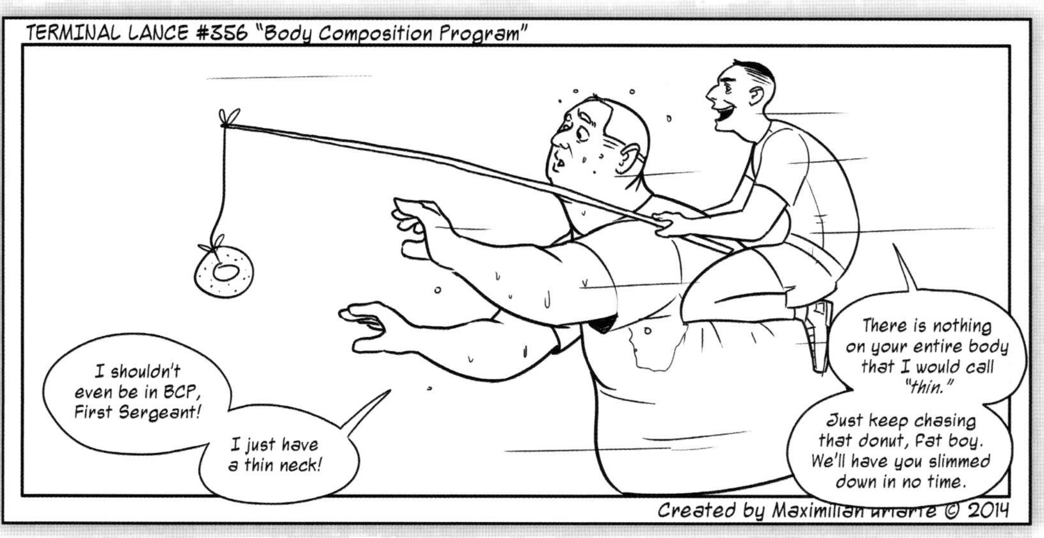
TERMINAL LANCE #356 "Body Composition Program"
I shouldn't even be in BCP, First Sergeant!
I just have a thin neck!
There is nothing on your entire body that I would call "thin."
Just keep chasing that donut, fat boy. We'll have you slimmed down in no time.
Created by Maximilian Uriarte © 2014

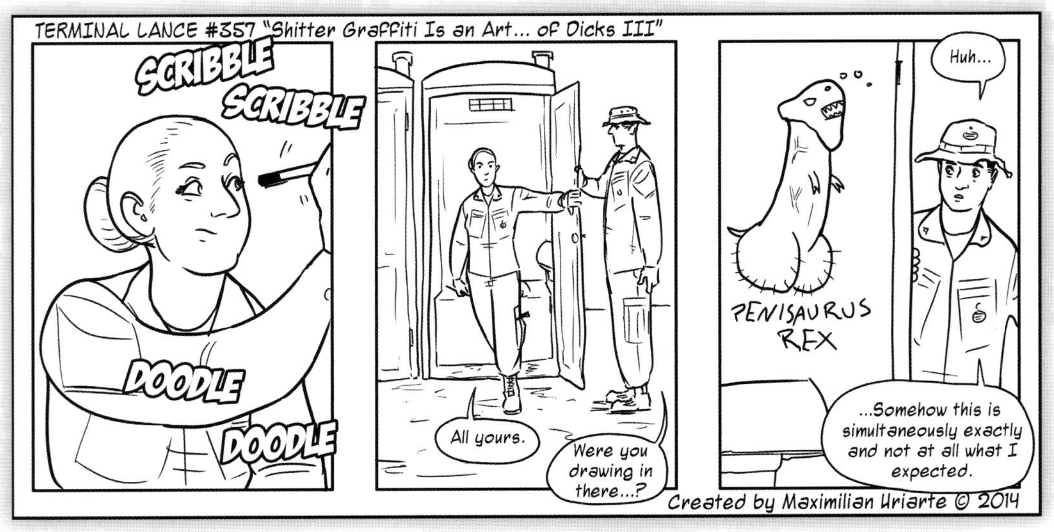
TERMINAL LANCE #357 "Shitter Graffiti Is an Art... of Dicks III"
SCRIBBLE
SCRIBBLE
DOODLE
DOODLE
All yours.
Were you drawing in there...?
Huh...
PENISAURUS REX
...Somehow this is simultaneously exactly and not at all what I expected.
Created by Maximilian Uriarte © 2014

357 "Shitter Graffiti Is an Art . . . of Dicks III"

This little comic strip of mine has given me some dubious honors over the years. One of them is that I have become the de facto dick art guy simply because I've done a couple of comic strips about the penis doodlings of Marines across the globe. You do one or two comics about penis art and all of a sudden everyone wants to send you photos of penises. I'm not sure if I should feel honored or ashamed, but I'll take it.

Either way, it's an interesting phenomenon. Recently the question was raised on my Twitter of whether female Marines engage in the doodling of phallic members on shitter walls or if perhaps they prefer their own genitalia in the matter.

After careful consideration, I have come to the only logical conclusion that female Marines cannot possibly draw vaginas, and therefore must draw penises like their male counterparts.

Why?

A simple fact: You will rarely see a vagina drawn on a bathroom wall.

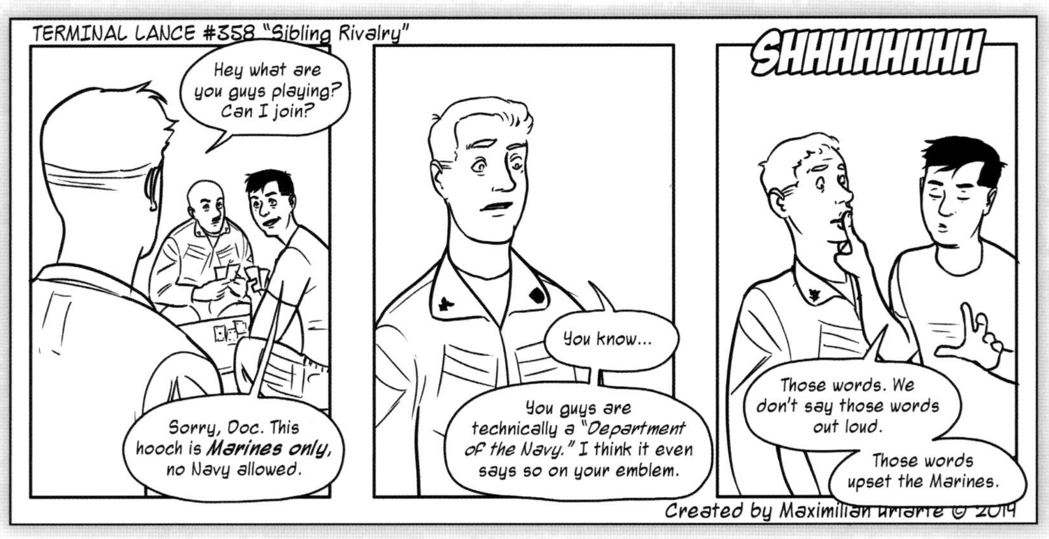
TERMINAL LANCE #358 "Sibling Rivalry"
Hey what are you guys playing? Can I join?
Sorry, Doc. This hooch is Marines only, no Navy allowed.
You know...
You guys are technically a "Department of the Navy." I think it even says so on your emblem.
SHHHHHHHH
Those words. We don't say those words out loud.
Those words upset the Marines.
Created by Maximilian Uriarte © 2014

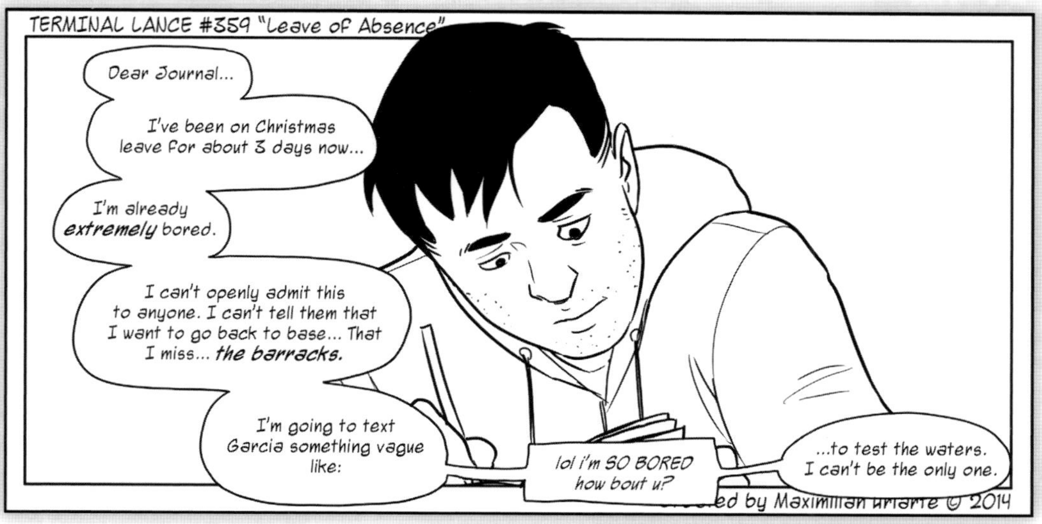
TERMINAL LANCE #359 "Leave of Absence"
Dear Journal...
I've been on Christmas leave for about 3 days now...
I'm already extremely bored.
I can't openly admit this to anyone. I can't tell them that I want to go back to base... That I miss... the barracks.
I'm going to text Garcia something vague like:
lol i'm SO BORED how bout u?
...to test the waters. I can't be the only one.
Created by Maximilian Uriarte © 2014

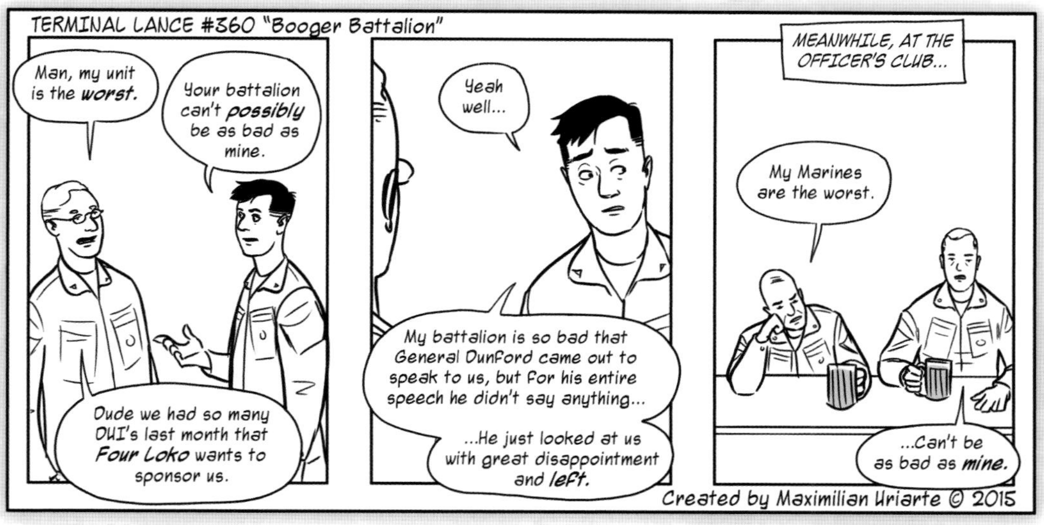
TERMINAL LANCE #360 "Booger Battalion"
Man, my unit is the worst.
Your battalion can't possibly be as bad as mine.
Dude we had so many DUI's last month that Four Loko wants to sponsor us.
Yeah well...
My battalion is so bad that General Dunford came out to speak to us, but for his entire speech he didn't say anything...
...He just looked at us with great disappointment and left.
MEANWHILE, AT THE OFFICER'S CLUB...
My Marines are the worst.
...Can't be as bad as mine.
Created by Maximilian Uriarte © 2015

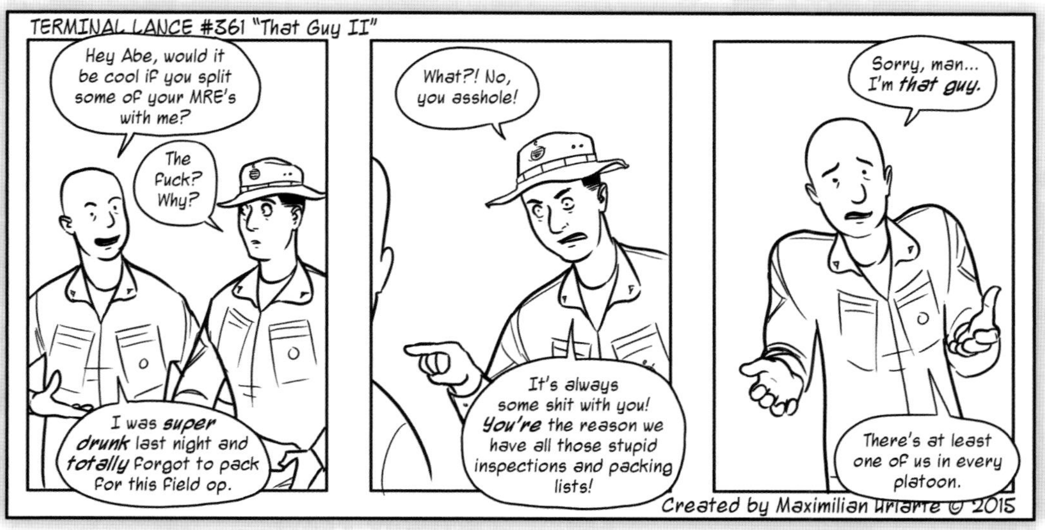
TERMINAL LANCE #361 "That Guy II"
Hey Abe, would it be cool if you split some of your MRE's with me?
The fuck? Why?
I was super drunk last night and totally forgot to pack for this field op.
What?! No, you asshole!
It's always some shit with you! You're the reason we have all those stupid inspections and packing lists!
Sorry, man... I'm that guy.
There's at least one of us in every platoon.
Created by Maximilian Uriarte © 2015

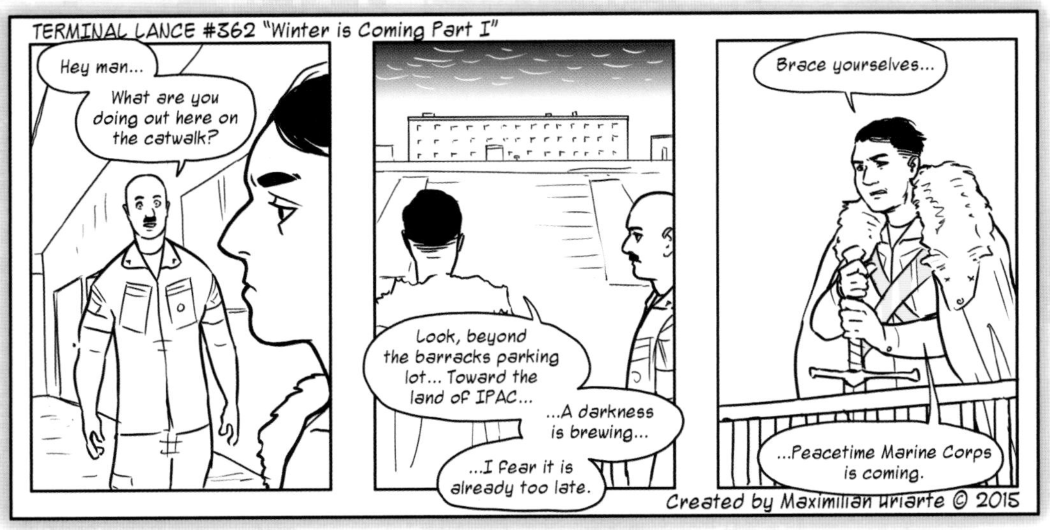
TERMINAL LANCE #362 "Winter is Coming Part I"
Hey man...
What are you doing out here on the catwalk?
Look, beyond the barracks parking lot... Toward the land of IPAC...
...A darkness is brewing...
...I fear it is already too late.
Brace yourselves...
...Peacetime Marine Corps is coming.
Created by Maximilian Uriarte © 2015

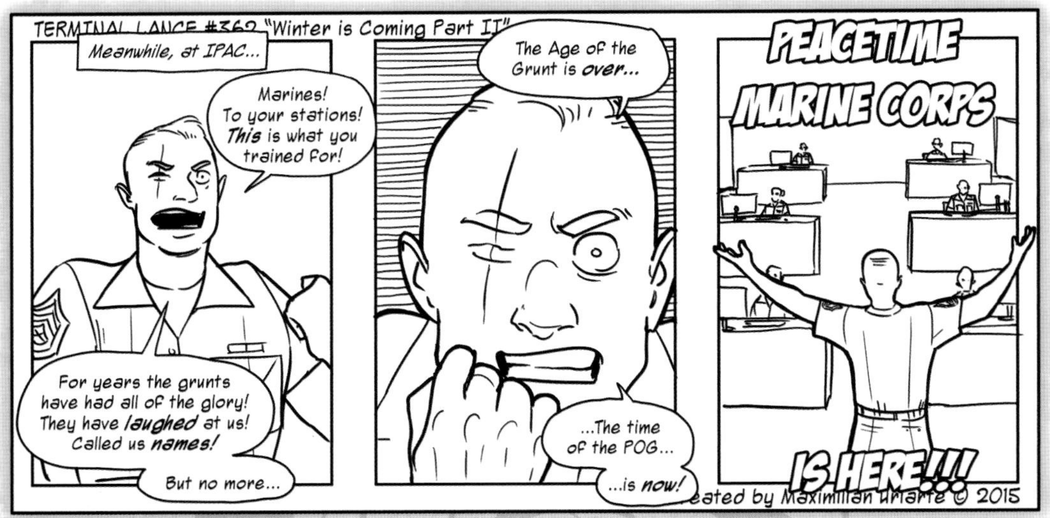
TERMINAL LANCE #362 "Winter is Coming Part II"
Meanwhile, at IPAC...
Marines! To your stations! *This* is what you trained for!
For years the grunts have had all of the glory! They have *laughed* at us! Called us *names!*
But no more...
The Age of the Grunt is *over...*
...The time of the POG...
...is *now!*
PEACETIME MARINE CORPS
IS HERE!!!
Created by Maximilian Uriarte © 2015

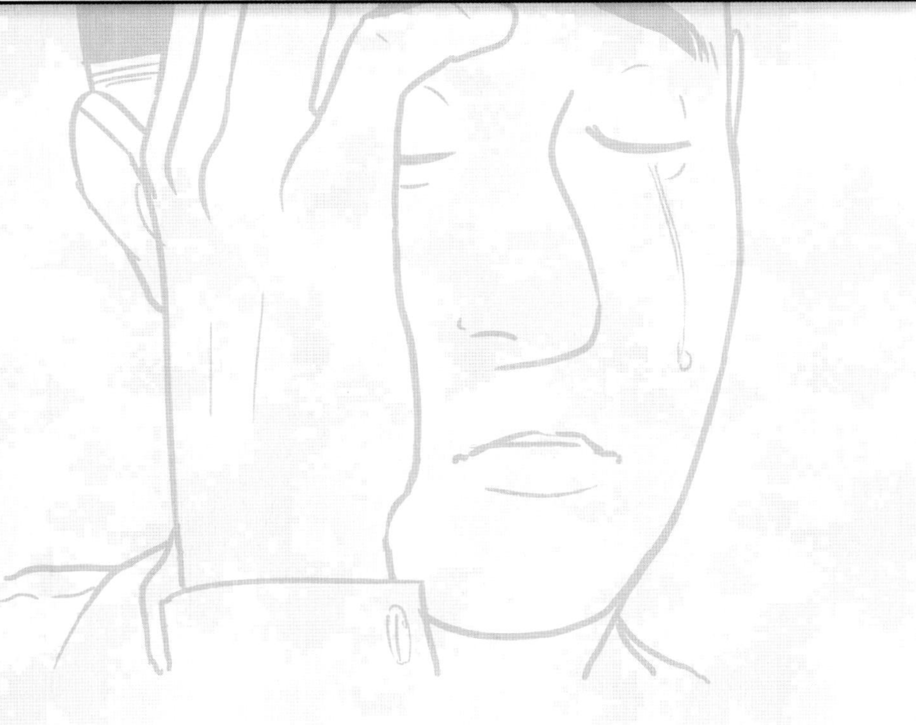

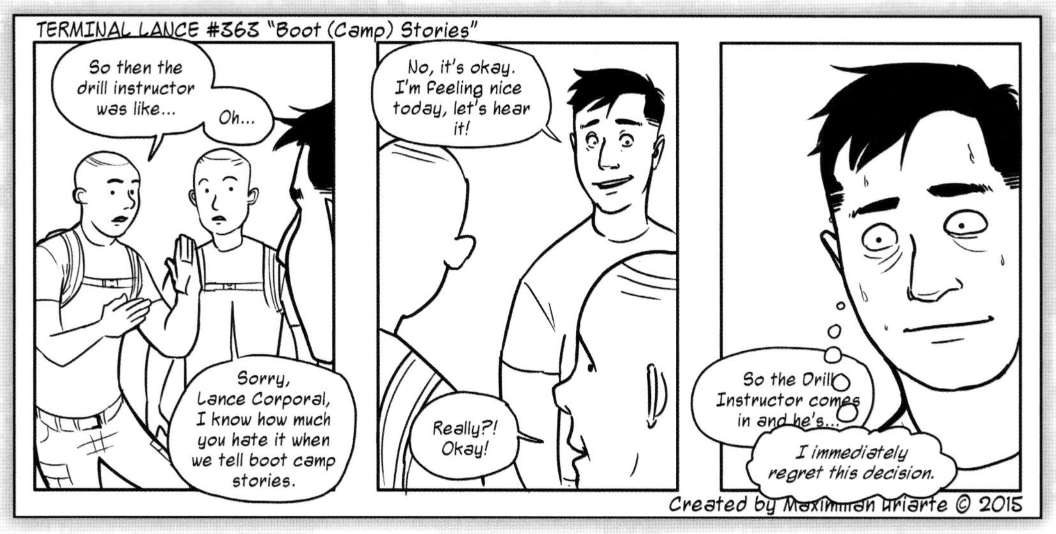
TERMINAL LANCE #363 "Boot (Camp) Stories"
So then the drill instructor was like...
Oh...
Sorry, Lance Corporal, I know how much you hate it when we tell boot camp stories.
No, it's okay. I'm feeling nice today, let's hear it!
Really?! Okay!
So the Drill Instructor comes in and he's...
I immediately regret this decision.
Created by Maximilian Uriarte © 2015

363 "Boot (Camp) Stories"

There's a strange paradox in the Corps when it comes to regaling stories of the one and only thing that all Marines have in common: Recruit Training (otherwise known as boot camp). On the one hand, everyone has been there and can share common ground regardless of their later experiences in the Corps; on the other, there's nothing more boot than a boot telling boot camp stories. The average Senior Lance Corporal would rather be anywhere else than listening to a fresh-faced eighteen-year-old tell him about that one time when the Drill Instructor got *so mad.*

But once you go on a combat deployment, boot camp becomes a distant memory, and likely one of the least interesting things you've done during your time in the Marines.

Don't get me wrong, even senior Marines tell boot camp stories, but they almost qualify it first with:

"I know this is boot as fuck to talk about, but this one time at boot camp . . ."

Still, boot camp is a universally shitty experience for everyone. I think I'd rather go back to Iraq than boot camp again. It's not that you fear for your life in boot camp, it's just that it really fucking sucks. That's really the only way to describe it.

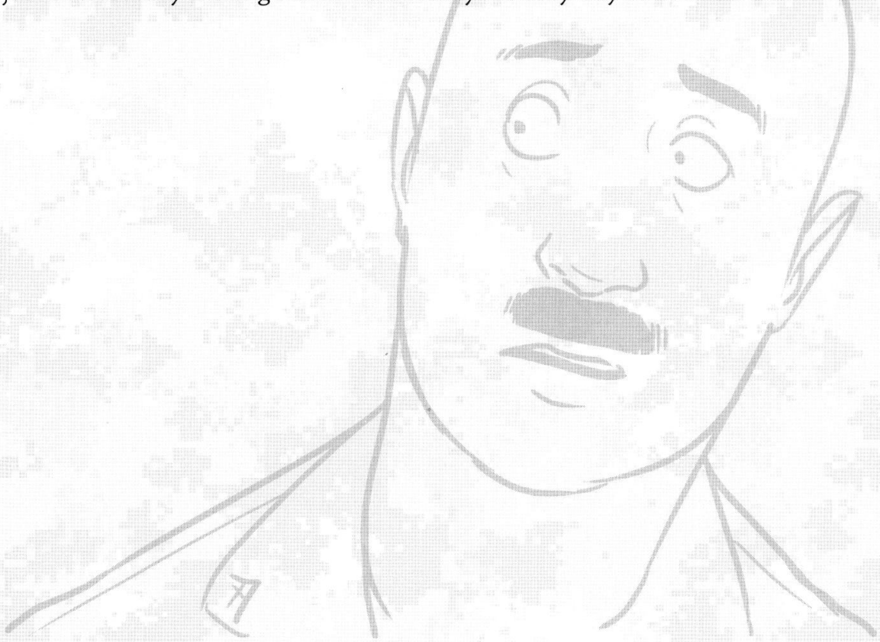

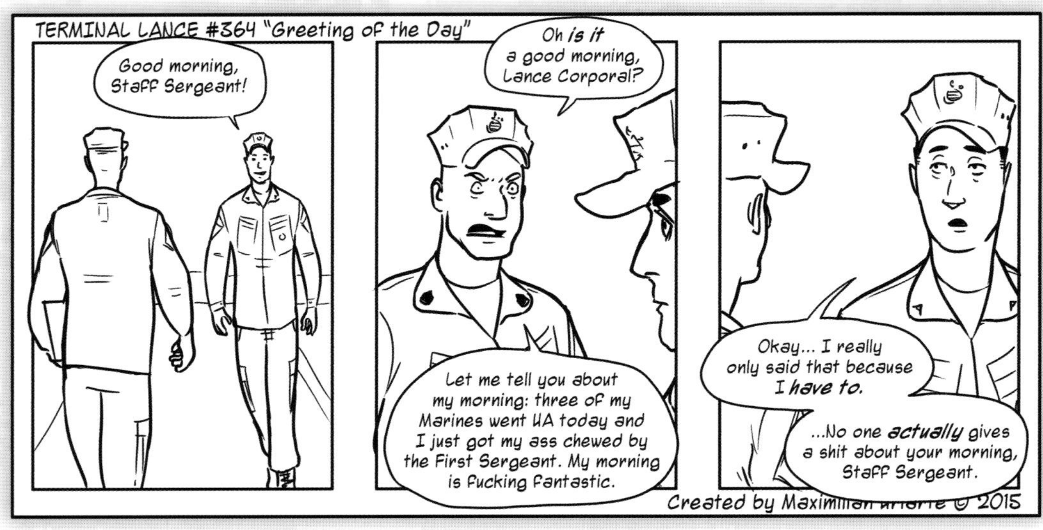
TERMINAL LANCE #364 "Greeting of the Day"
Good morning, Staff Sergeant!
Oh is it a good morning, Lance Corporal?
Let me tell you about my morning: three of my Marines went UA today and I just got my ass chewed by the First Sergeant. My morning is fucking fantastic.
Okay... I really only said that because I have to.
...No one actually gives a shit about your morning, Staff Sergeant.
Created by Maximilian Uriarte © 2015

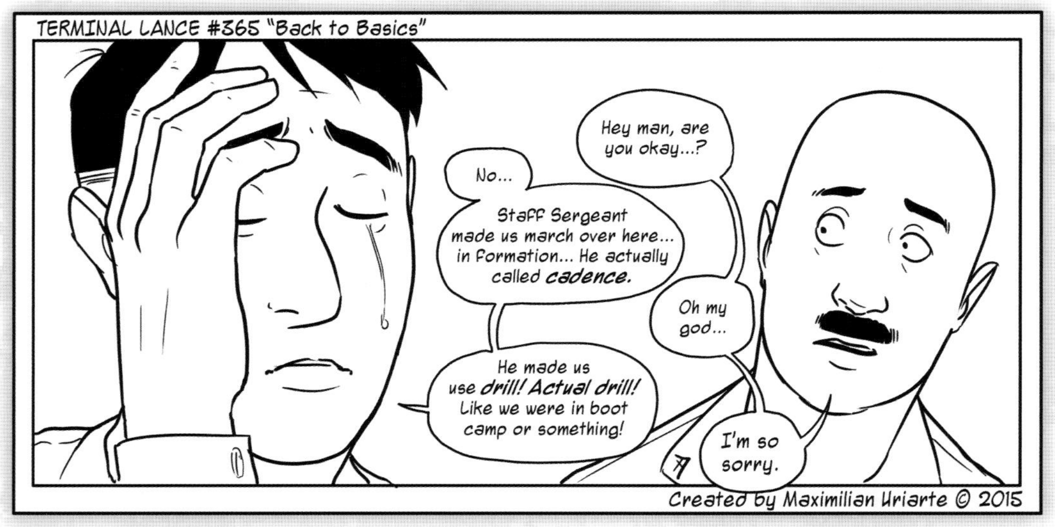
TERMINAL LANCE #365 "Back to Basics"
Hey man, are you okay...?
No...
Staff Sergeant made us march over here... in formation... He actually called cadence.
Oh my god...
He made us use drill! Actual drill! Like we were in boot camp or something!
I'm so sorry.
Created by Maximilian Uriarte © 2015

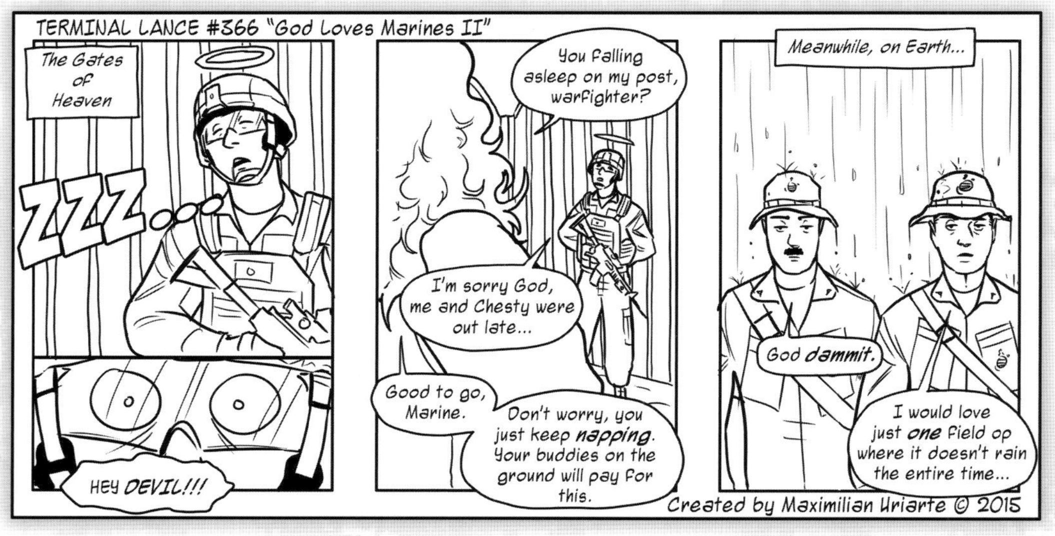
TERMINAL LANCE #366 "God Loves Marines II"
The Gates of Heaven
ZZZ...
HEY DEVIL!!!
You falling asleep on my post, warfighter?
I'm sorry God, me and Chesty were out late...
Good to go, Marine.
Don't worry, you just keep napping. Your buddies on the ground will pay for this.
Meanwhile, on Earth...
God dammit.
I would love just one field op where it doesn't rain the entire time...
Created by Maximilian Uriarte © 2015

TERMINAL LANCE #367 "Motivation Levels Over Time"
USMC
MOTIVATION
TIME
Boot Marine
The "GI-Biller"
Normal Civilian
"Terminal Lance"
Normal Civilian
Motivation

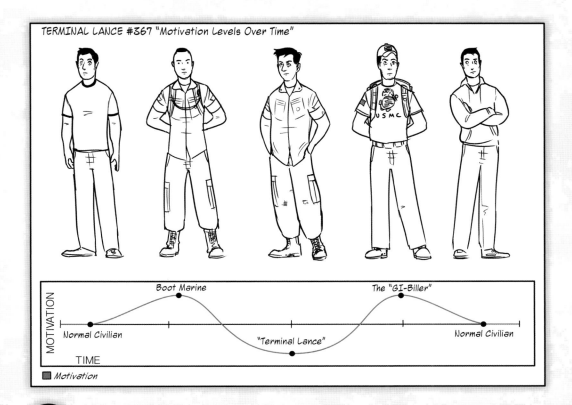

367 "Motivation Levels Over Time"

Those of you that haven't served in the military might not be familiar with the term "motivation." Well, I mean, I'm sure you've heard the word itself, but it takes on a very specific context within the Marine Corps. I shall provide you with the Marine Corps definition of motivation:

> ***mo·ti·va·tion*** | ˌmōdəˈvāSH(ə)n/ | **noun**
> **The amount of fucks a Marine gives, specifically as it relates to Marine Corps activities and lifestyle.**

To be labeled as "moto" is generally a grave insult to the Lance Corporal crowd, as it insinuates that you give a fuck. Things that would be considered moto:

- A high and tight haircut
- An Eagle, Globe, and Anchor tattoo or decoration
- Wearing a CamelBak
- The English Bulldog

When a Marine enters the Corps, he has profoundly high levels of motivation coursing through his boot veins. He tears up at the sight of bald eagles, wears a CamelBak in civilian attire to "stay hydrated," buys 7.62 T-shirts at the PX, and randomly hums "left, right, layo" to himself. He won't see this level of motivation again for quite some time.

As the young Marine matures into his MOS and unit assignment, he starts to question things. Was this really what he was looking for? Is cleaning your rifle four times a week without firing it really necessary? He starts to see the character of the environment around him, maybe even tossed an NJP or two for something that might not have been his fault.

Legend has it that this begins as soon as he is pinned with the rank of "Lance Corporal," but no one knows for sure. Motivation levels here are at an all-time low, and will stay this way for the majority of his short enlistment.

Once the Marine exits the Corps, however, you'll see his motivation levels rise to near-boot status. He'll show up to his new college, utilizing the GI Bill, telling war stories to anyone that will hear them. He'll start using Marine jargon again and maybe even a knife-hand or two—he might even consider talking to a prior-service recruiter.

Yes, a recruiter.

Assuming he doesn't succumb to the extremely high levels of motivation during these vulnerable college years, he might make it out the other side as a relatively normal civilian again. Yes, with time, the motivation starts to fade. It doesn't ever fall back into negative, as it did while you were a Lance Corporal, but rather it floats back down to a nice neutral—the experience now a positive part of your past and development. Looking back with a warm fondness for the people you met and the strange things you saw, you find yourself back where you started . . . just another civilian in a big, big world . . . and with most of your life left to live.

This is science, I didn't make this up.

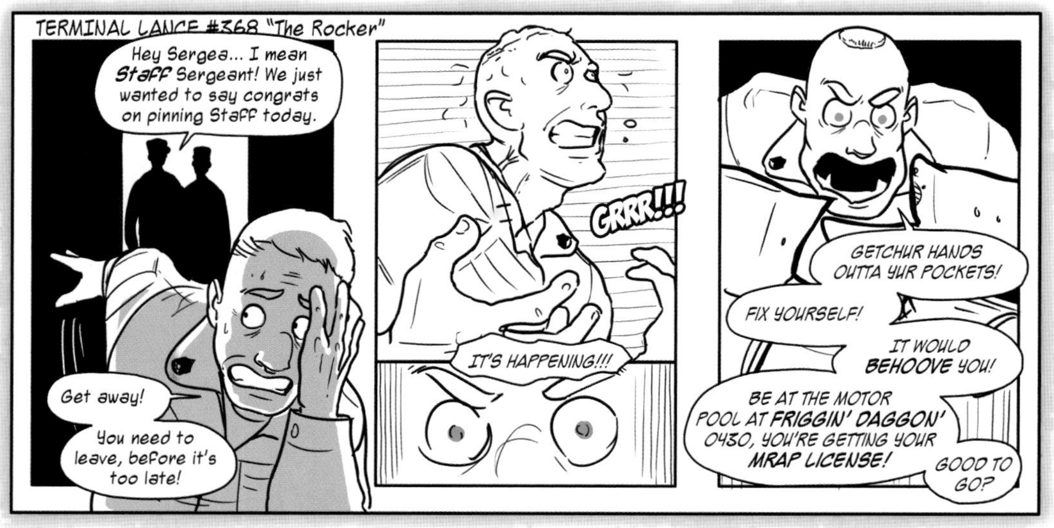

TERMINAL LANCE #368 "The Rocker"
Hey Sergea... I mean Staff Sergeant! We just wanted to say congrats on pinning Staff today.
Get away!
You need to leave, before it's too late!
GRRR!!!
IT'S HAPPENING!!!
GETCHUR HANDS OUTTA YUR POCKETS!
FIX YOURSELF!
IT WOULD BEHOOVE YOU!
BE AT THE MOTOR POOL AT FRIGGIN' DAGGON' 0430, YOU'RE GETTING YOUR MRAP LICENSE!
GOOD TO GO?

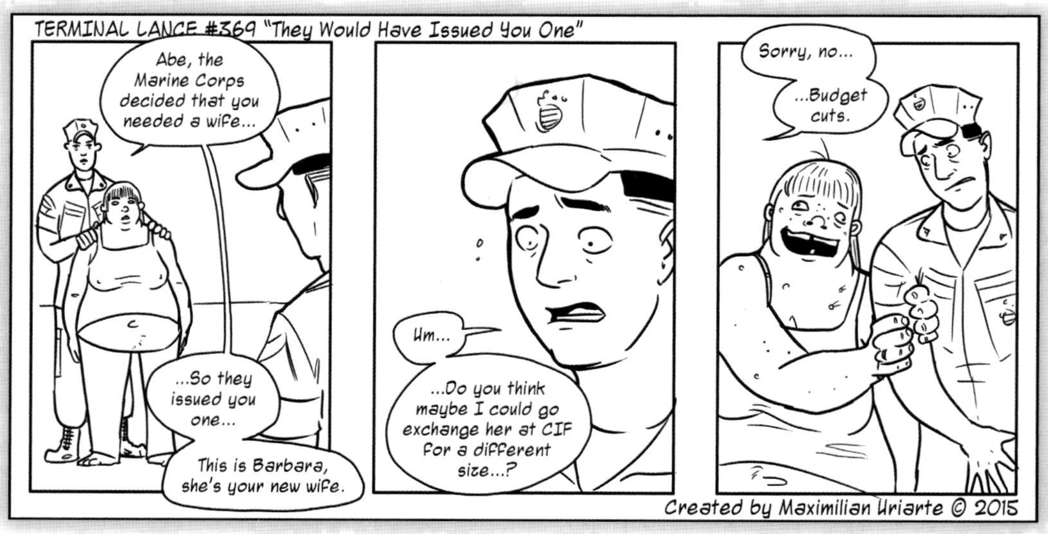

TERMINAL LANCE #369 "They Would Have Issued You One"
Abe, the Marine Corps decided that you needed a wife...
...So they issued you one...
This is Barbara, she's your new wife.
Um...
...Do you think maybe I could go exchange her at CIF for a different size...?
Sorry, no...
...Budget cuts.
Created by Maximilian Uriarte © 2015

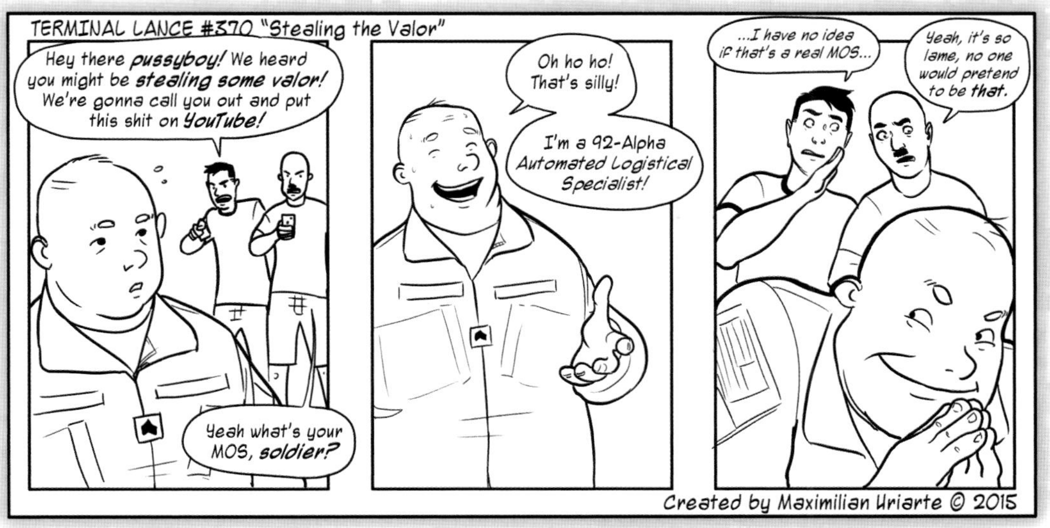
TERMINAL LANCE #370 "Stealing the Valor"
Hey there pussyboy! We heard you might be stealing some valor! We're gonna call you out and put this shit on YouTube!
Yeah what's your MOS, soldier?
Oh ho ho! That's silly!
I'm a 92-Alpha Automated Logistical Specialist!
...I have no idea if that's a real MOS...
Yeah, it's so lame, no one would pretend to be that.
Created by Maximilian Uriarte © 2015

370 "Stealing the Valor"

You know what the problem is with these Stolen Valor guys? They try to steal too much valor.

If you're the kind of piece of shit that likes to go around pretending to be in the military so you can get discounts or whatever, just say you're some total POG MOS, because most grunts will have no idea if it's true anyway. When you start talking about how you know guys from SEAL Team 6 and graduated top of your class at Ranger School while killing seventy-three enemy insurgents alongside Chris Kyle, bullshit flags start going up immediately.

Those are the kind of stories that can be easily proven wrong by just about anyone with a lick of common sense and only a marginal knowledge of the military culture.

Of course, the point of stealing "valor" is actually to steal the "valor." Being a Marine, soldier or otherwise, is usually seen as kind of badass compared to the normal population. I mostly feel sorry for these pathetic people, adults pretending to be superheroes, the way young kids put on towels and pretend to be Batman.

But I love watching these stolen valor videos. So please, if you're reading this and you're a giant piece of shit that likes to pretend to be a war hero, keep doing it. You'll eventually find yourself on a shaky, vertically shot smartphone video on YouTube with some pissed-off guys making fun of you—and I will laugh as I watch it over and over.

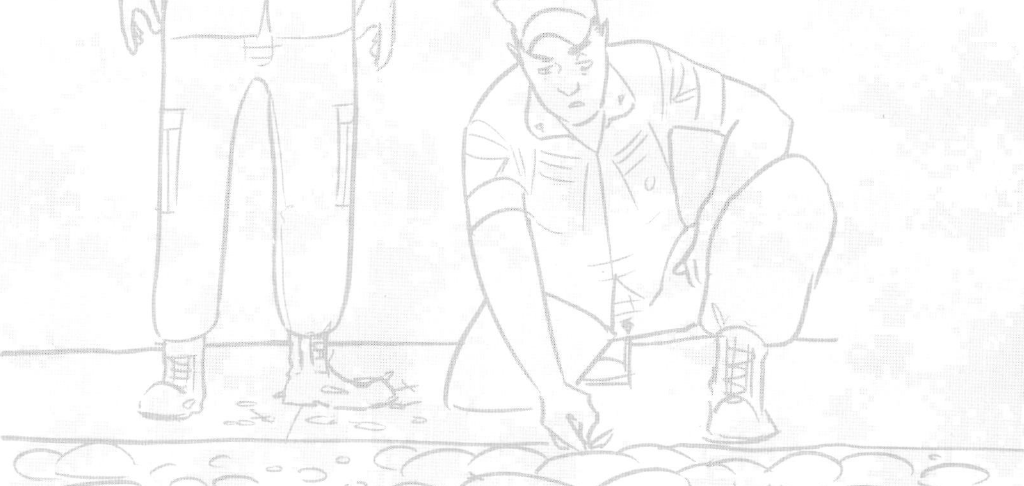

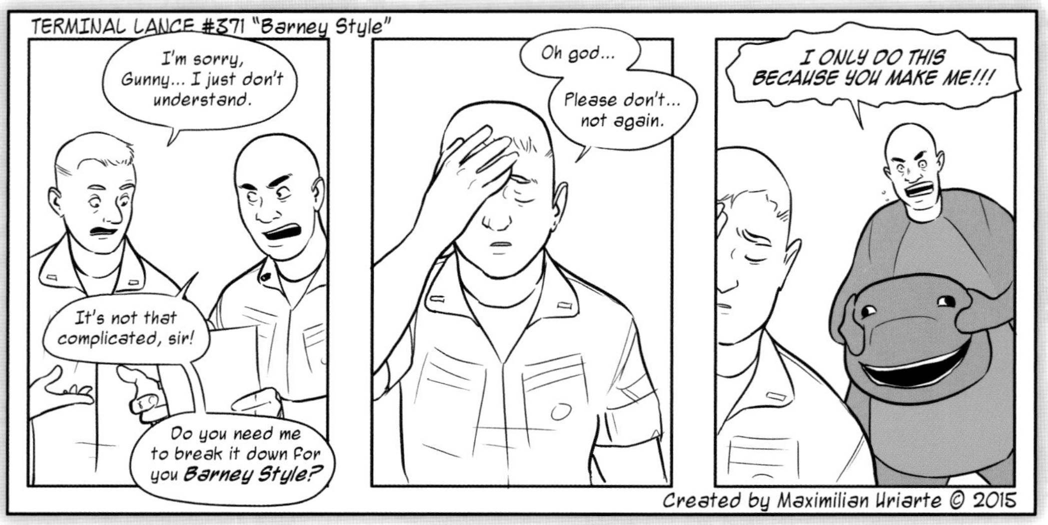
TERMINAL LANCE #371 "Barney Style"
I'm sorry, Gunny... I just don't understand.
It's not that complicated, sir!
Do you need me to break it down for you *Barney Style?*
Oh god...
Please don't... not again.
I ONLY DO THIS BECAUSE YOU MAKE ME!!!
Created by Maximilian Uriarte © 2015

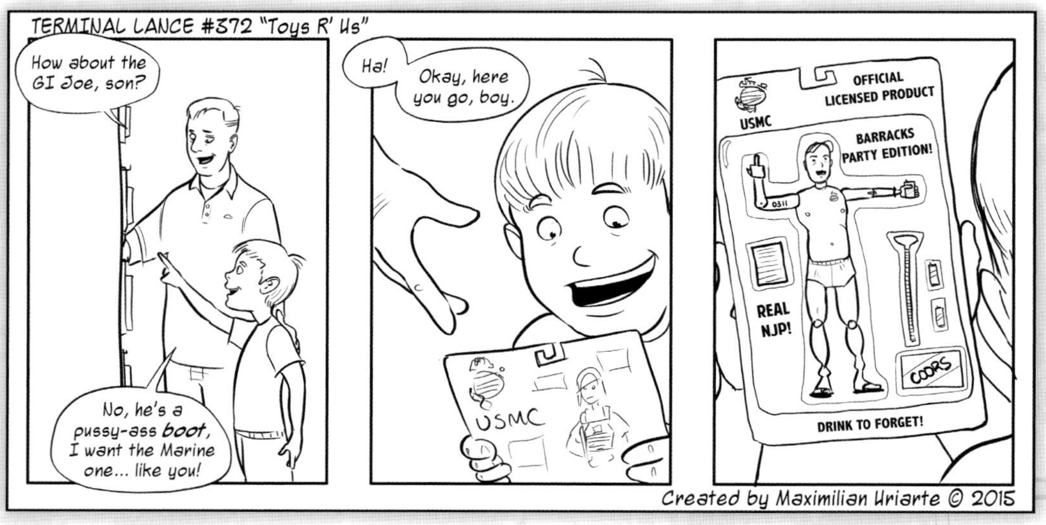
TERMINAL LANCE #372 "Toys R' Us"
How about the GI Joe, son?
No, he's a pussy-ass *boot*, I want the Marine one... like you!
Ha!
Okay, here you go, boy.
USMC
OFFICIAL LICENSED PRODUCT
USMC
BARRACKS PARTY EDITION!
0311
REAL NJP!
COORS
DRINK TO FORGET!
Created by Maximilian Uriarte © 2015

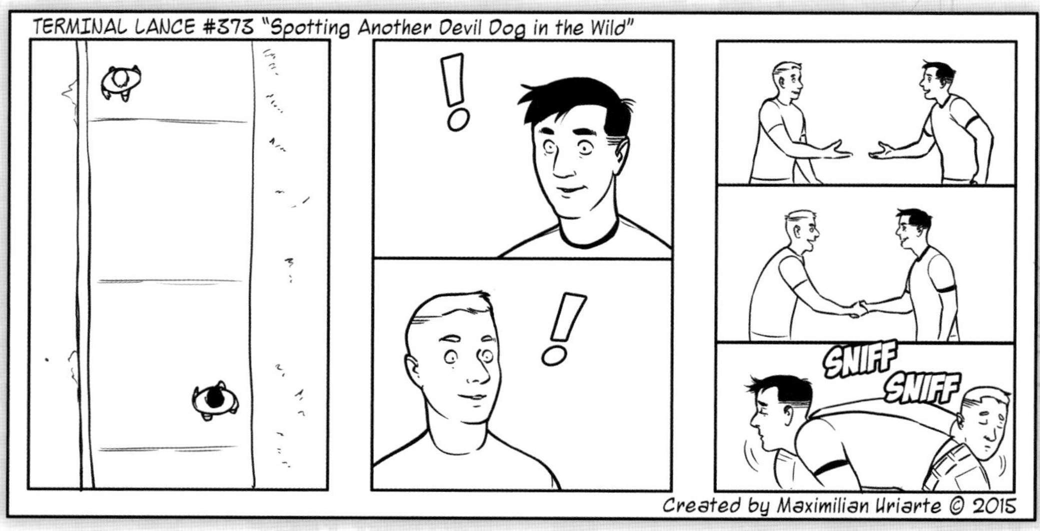
TERMINAL LANCE #373 "Spotting Another Devil Dog in the Wild"
!
!
SNIFF
SNIFF
Created by Maximilian Uriarte © 2015

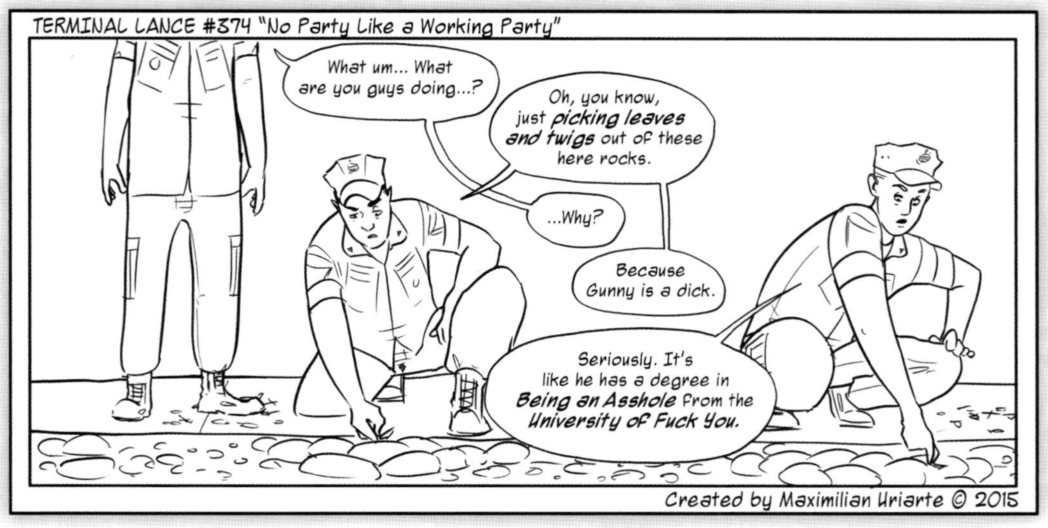
TERMINAL LANCE #374 "No Party Like a Working Party"
What um... What are you guys doing...?
Oh, you know, just picking leaves and twigs out of these here rocks.
...Why?
Because Gunny is a dick.
Seriously. It's like he has a degree in Being an Asshole from the University of Fuck You.
Created by Maximilian Uriarte © 2015

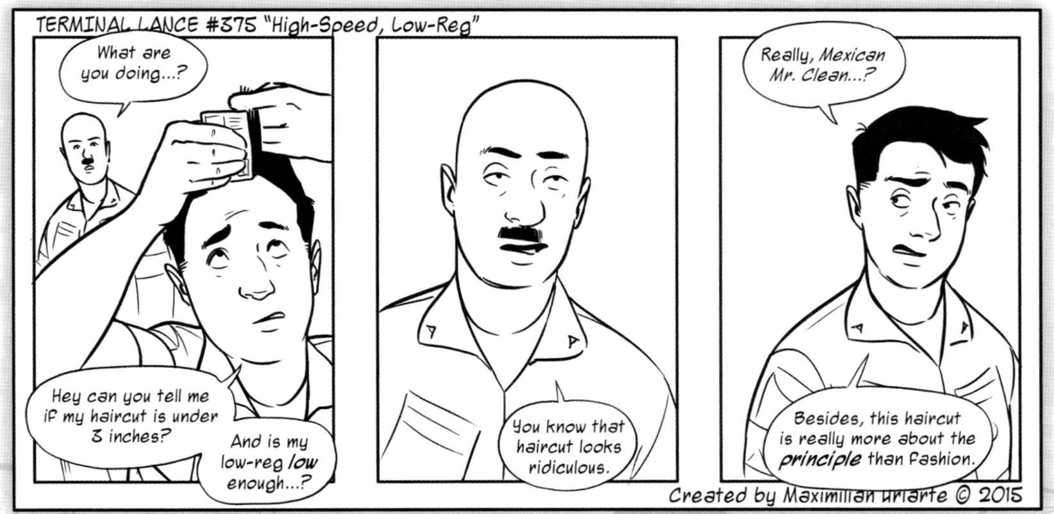
TERMINAL LANCE #375 "High-Speed, Low-Reg"
What are you doing...?
Hey can you tell me if my haircut is under 3 inches?
And is my low-reg low enough...?
You know that haircut looks ridiculous.
Really, Mexican Mr. Clean...?
Besides, this haircut is really more about the principle than fashion.
Created by Maximilian Uriarte © 2015

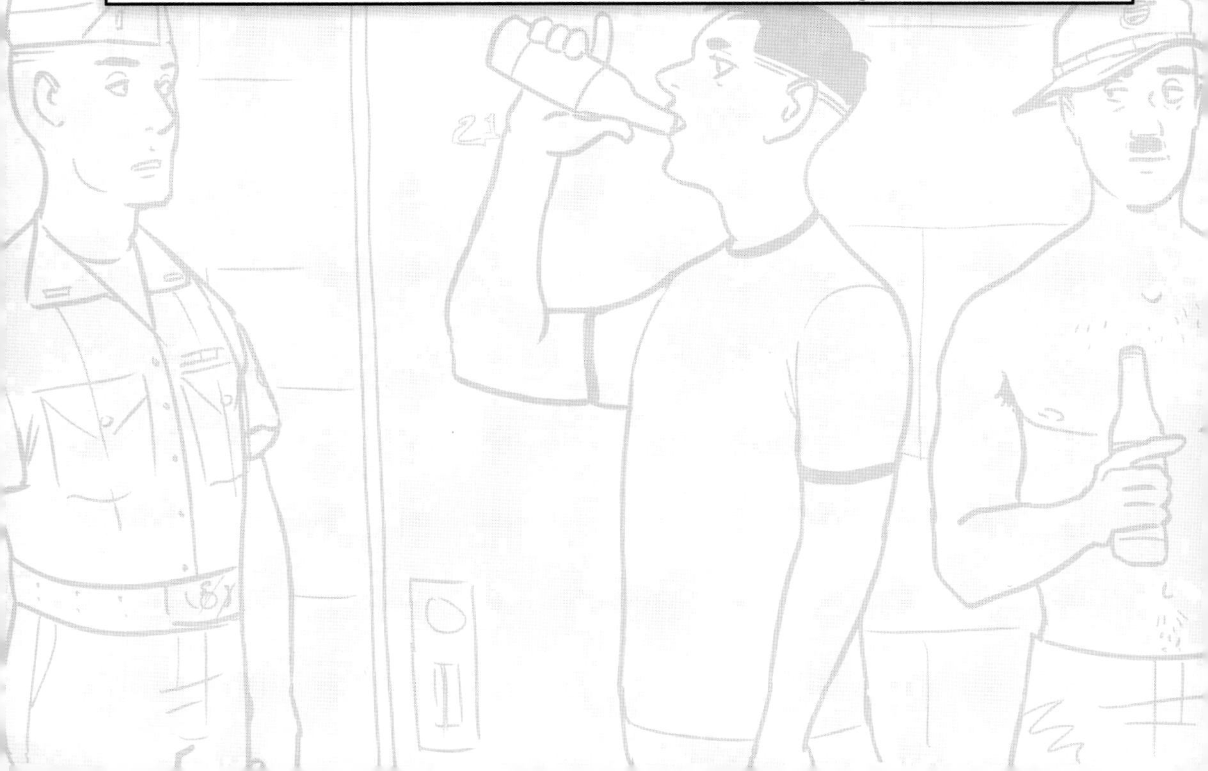

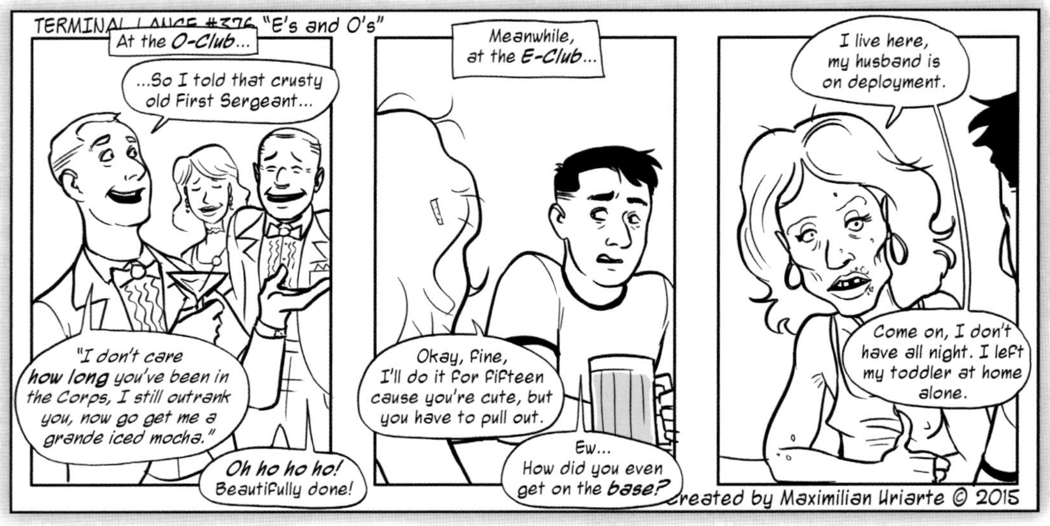
"E's and O's"
At the O-Club...
...So I told that crusty old First Sergeant...
"I don't care how long you've been in the Corps, I still outrank you, now go get me a grande iced mocha."
Oh ho ho ho! Beautifully done!
Meanwhile, at the E-Club...
Okay, fine, I'll do it for fifteen cause you're cute, but you have to pull out.
Ew... How did you even get on the base?
I live here, my husband is on deployment.
Come on, I don't have all night. I left my toddler at home alone.
reated by Maximilian Uriarte © 2015

376 "E's and O's"

Don't get me wrong, I've had plenty of fun nights at Kahuna's on MCBH Kaneohe Bay, but there's a definite disparity between the E-Club and the O-Club. Of course, this is to be expected, as officers are shiny gods and enlisted are . . . enlisted.

I once had the pleasure of eating lunch at the Officer's Club at MCBH, which looks out on the beautiful MCBH Klipper Golf Course—one of the most gorgeous golf vistas in the nation. Nothing makes you feel more like a lowly peasant than being gawked at by offended officer wives as you and a few fellow Lance Corporals awkwardly make your way through the high-end Mongolian BBQ grill and salad bar.

It's a stark contrast to the dive-bar experience of the E-Club, where you'll meet an assortment of characters ranging from drunk Lance Corporals to . . . more drunk Lance Corporals. To be fair, karaoke and wing night make for a much more colorful and entertaining experience.

Still, the lifestyle contrast between officers and enlisted is always shockingly stark. I mean, I get it, officers are a big deal and enlisted are a dime a dozen. The military wants to retain good officers, so they treat them like posh royalty. It's probably the only place where a bachelor's degree gets you an automatic high-class lifestyle, even if you occasionally have to slum it with us lowly enlisted folk.

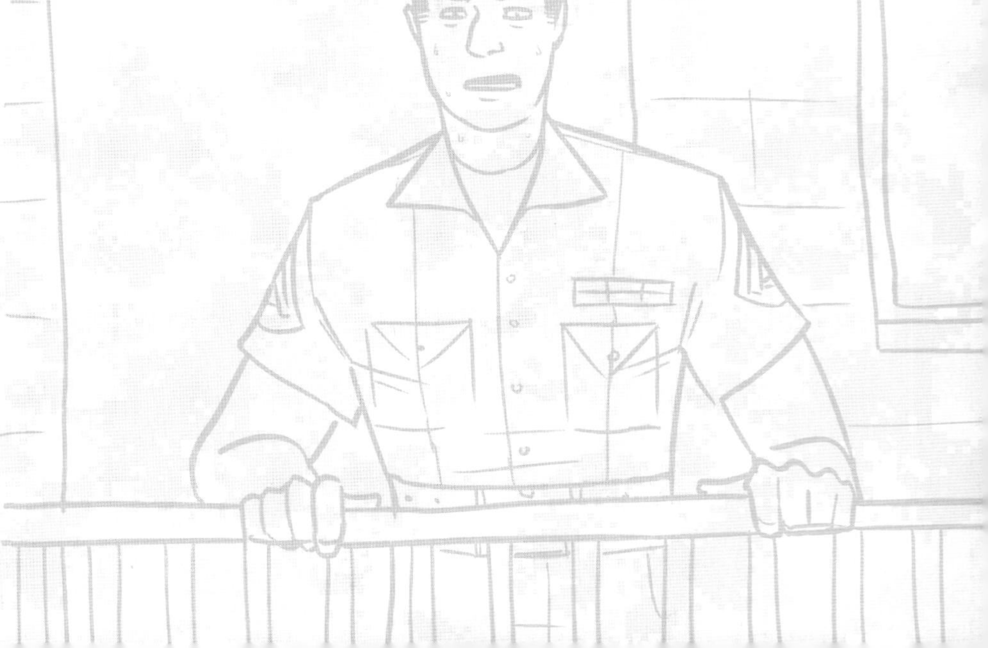

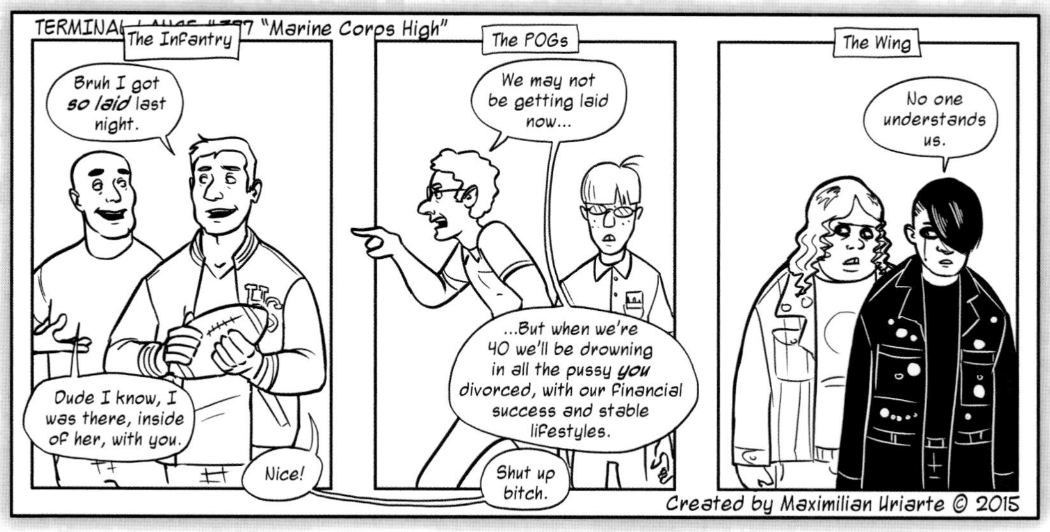

TERMINAL
"Marine Corps High"
The Infantry
Bruh I got *so laid* last night.
Dude I know, I was there, inside of her, with you.
Nice!
The POGs
We may not be getting laid now...
...But when we're 40 we'll be drowning in all the pussy *you* divorced, with our financial success and stable lifestyles.
Shut up bitch.
The Wing
No one understands us.
Created by Maximilian Uriarte © 2015

377 "Marine Corps High"

In my mind, I've always typically divided the Marine Corps up into thirds. You have the infantry, the ground-side POG's (which is what you typically think of as a POG, such as an office guy or girl), and the wing.

It's not unlike a set of high school cliques: exclusive and loyal to each other. The grunts are the jocks, the rock stars, and the guys that everyone loves (even if they won't admit it). They party hard and fuck shit up when the time comes. The POG's might say they hate them, or that they aren't impressed with them, but we know they're secretly a little jealous.

The age-old argument I see often from the POG side is that being infantry means you won't have any transferable skills in the civilian world when you get out of the Corps. True, but who cares when the Post-9/11 GI Bill can set you up with literally any career you want? May as well get the glory while you can, lest you regret it later.

As for the wing, no one really knows what the fuck goes on over there. They usually get a whole section of the base to themselves, with their own PX and barbershops, and when you occasionally see them on your side of town they're always wearing flight suits.

No one understands them.

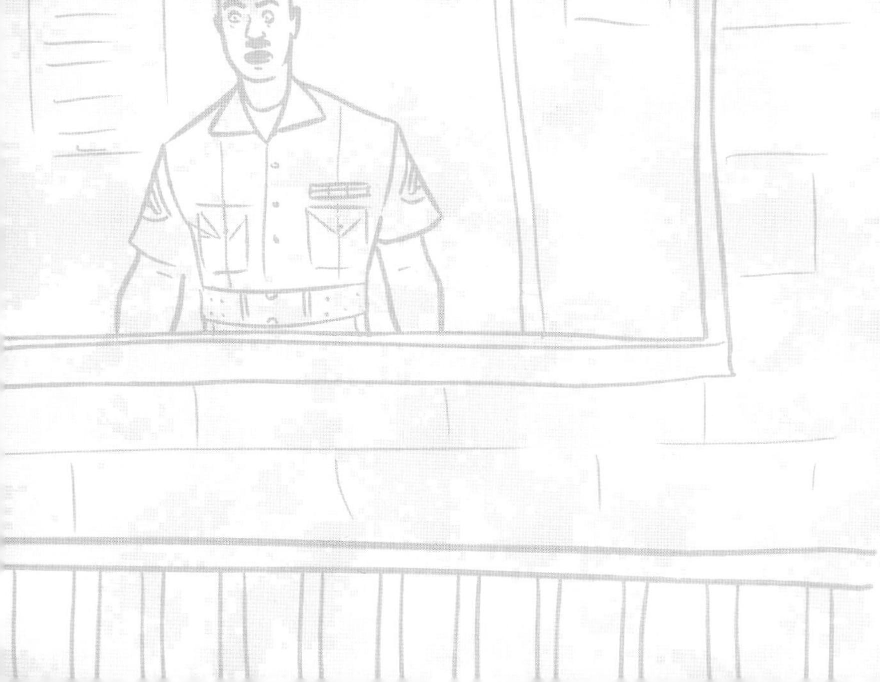

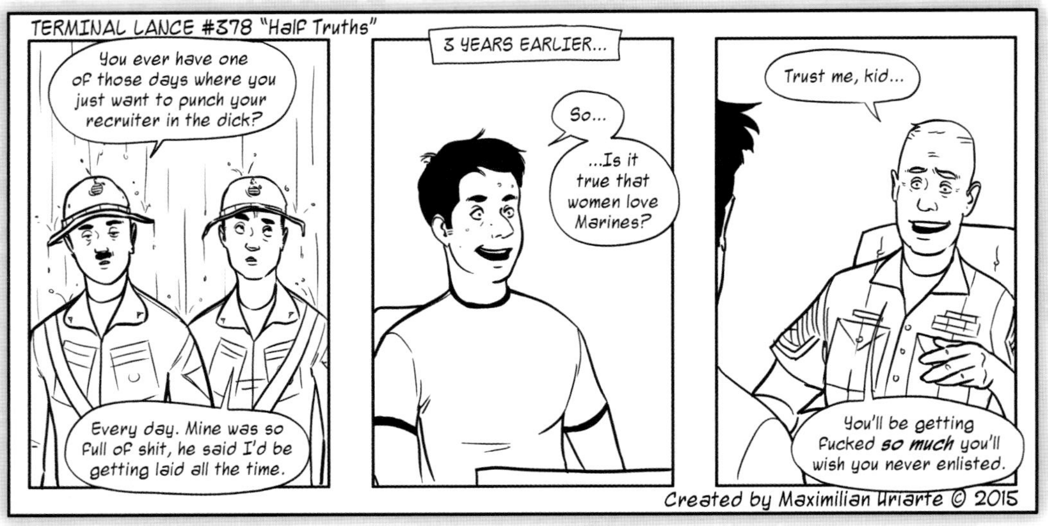
TERMINAL LANCE #378 "Half Truths"
You ever have one of those days where you just want to punch your recruiter in the dick?
Every day. Mine was so full of shit, he said I'd be getting laid all the time.
3 YEARS EARLIER...
So...
...Is it true that women love Marines?
Trust me, kid...
You'll be getting fucked **so much** you'll wish you never enlisted.
Created by Maximilian Uriarte © 2015

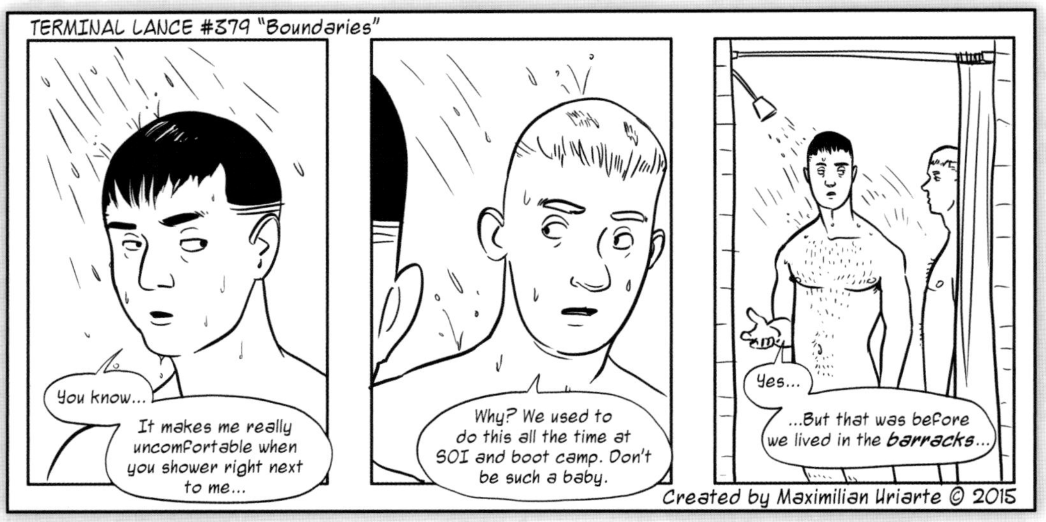
TERMINAL LANCE #379 "Boundaries"
You know...
It makes me really uncomfortable when you shower right next to me...
Why? We used to do this all the time at SOI and boot camp. Don't be such a baby.
Yes...
...But that was before we lived in the ***barracks***...
Created by Maximilian Uriarte © 2015

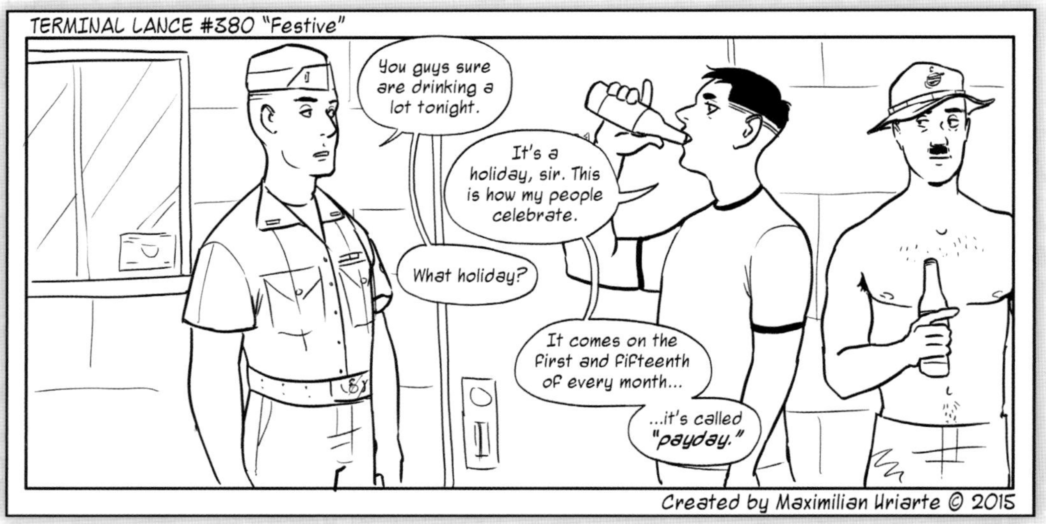
TERMINAL LANCE #380 "Festive"
You guys sure are drinking a lot tonight.
It's a holiday, sir. This is how my people celebrate.
What holiday?
It comes on the first and fifteenth of every month...
...it's called ***"payday."***
Created by Maximilian Uriarte © 2015

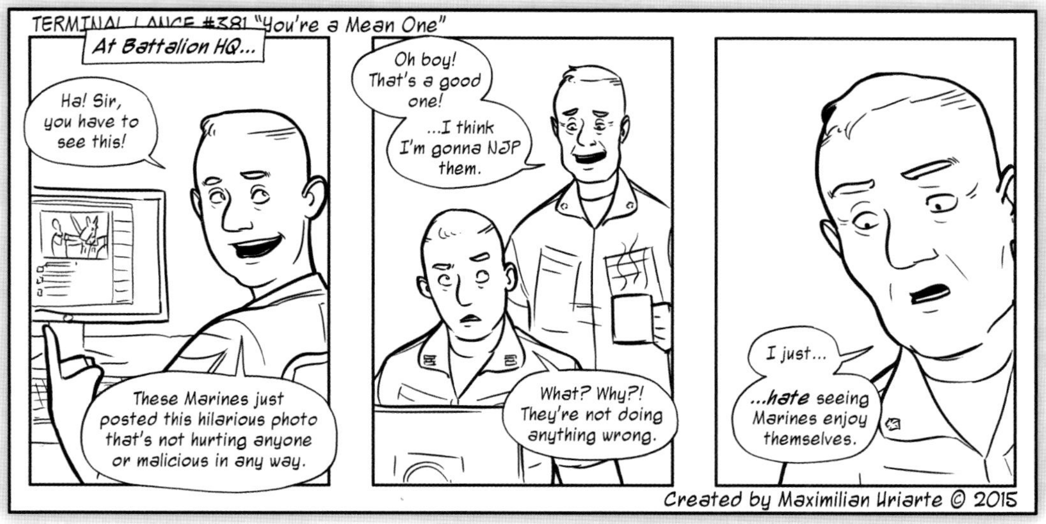
TERMINAL LANCE #381 "You're a Mean One"
At Battalion HQ...
Ha! Sir, you have to see this!
These Marines just posted this hilarious photo that's not hurting anyone or malicious in any way.
Oh boy! That's a good one!
...I think I'm gonna NJP them.
What? Why?! They're not doing anything wrong.
I just...
...hate seeing Marines enjoy themselves.
Created by Maximilian Uriarte © 2015

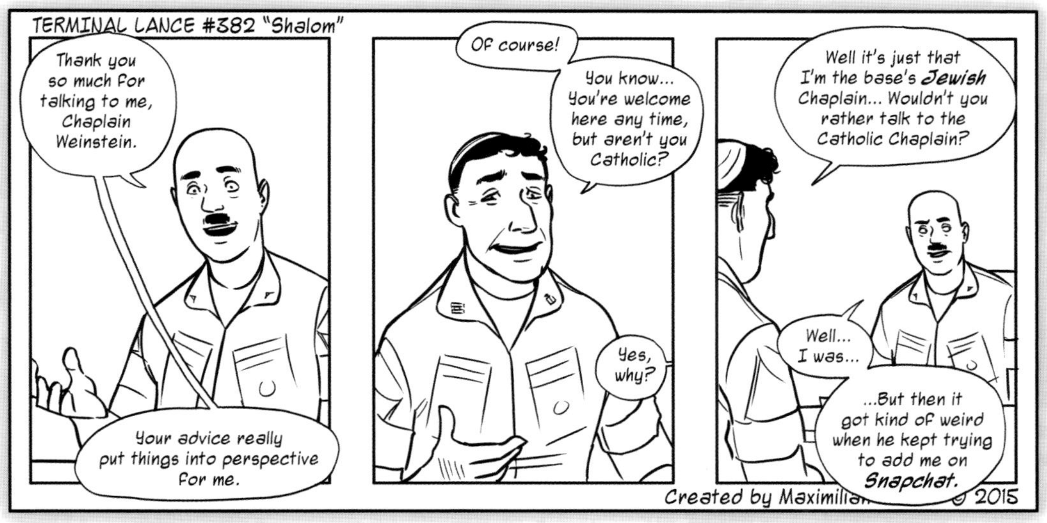
TERMINAL LANCE #382 "Shalom"
Thank you so much for talking to me, Chaplain Weinstein.
Your advice really put things into perspective for me.
Of course!
You know... You're welcome here any time, but aren't you Catholic?
Yes, why?
Well it's just that I'm the base's Jewish Chaplain... Wouldn't you rather talk to the Catholic Chaplain?
Well... I was...
...But then it got kind of weird when he kept trying to add me on Snapchat.
Created by Maximilian
© 2015

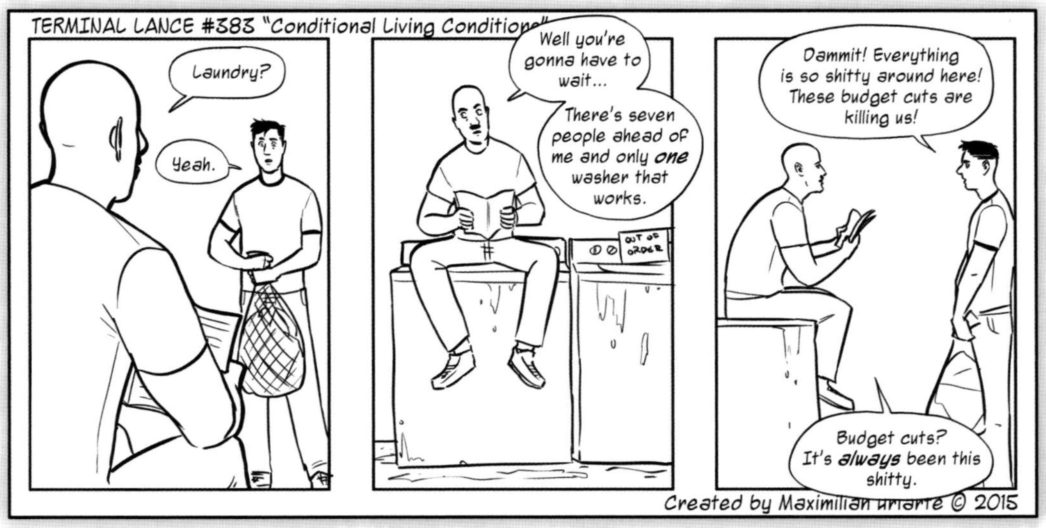
TERMINAL LANCE #383 "Conditional Living Conditio
Laundry?
Yeah.
Well you're gonna have to wait...
There's seven people ahead of me and only one washer that works.
OUT OF ORDER
Dammit! Everything is so shitty around here! These budget cuts are killing us!
Budget cuts? It's always been this shitty.
Created by Maximilian
© 2015

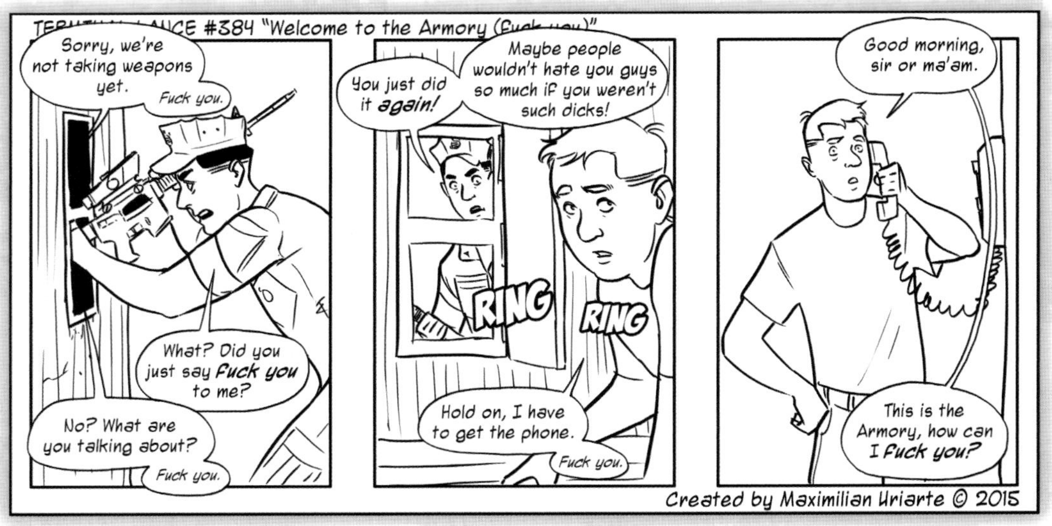
TERMINAL LANCE #384 "Welcome to the Armory (Fuck you)"
Sorry, we're not taking weapons yet.
Fuck you.
What? Did you just say *Fuck you* to me?
No? What are you talking about?
Fuck you.
You just did it *again!*
Maybe people wouldn't hate you guys so much if you weren't such dicks!
RING
RING
Hold on, I have to get the phone.
Fuck you.
Good morning, sir or ma'am.
This is the Armory, how can I *Fuck you?*
Created by Maximilian Uriarte © 2015

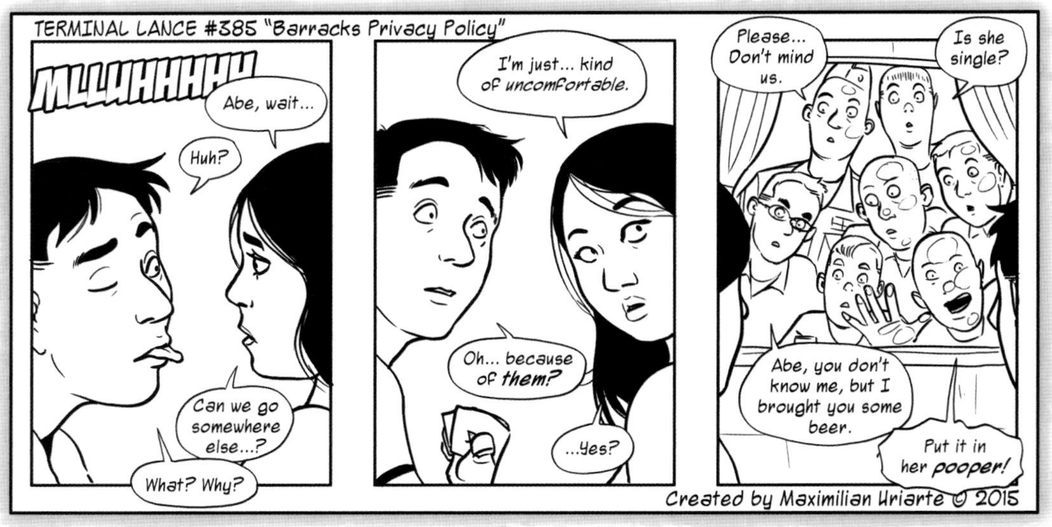
TERMINAL LANCE #385 "Barracks Privacy Policy"
MLLUHHHHU
Abe, wait...
Huh?
Can we go somewhere else...?
What? Why?
I'm just... kind of uncomfortable.
Oh... because of *them?*
...Yes?
Please... Don't mind us.
Is she single?
Abe, you don't know me, but I brought you some beer.
Put it in her *pooper!*
Created by Maximilian Uriarte © 2015

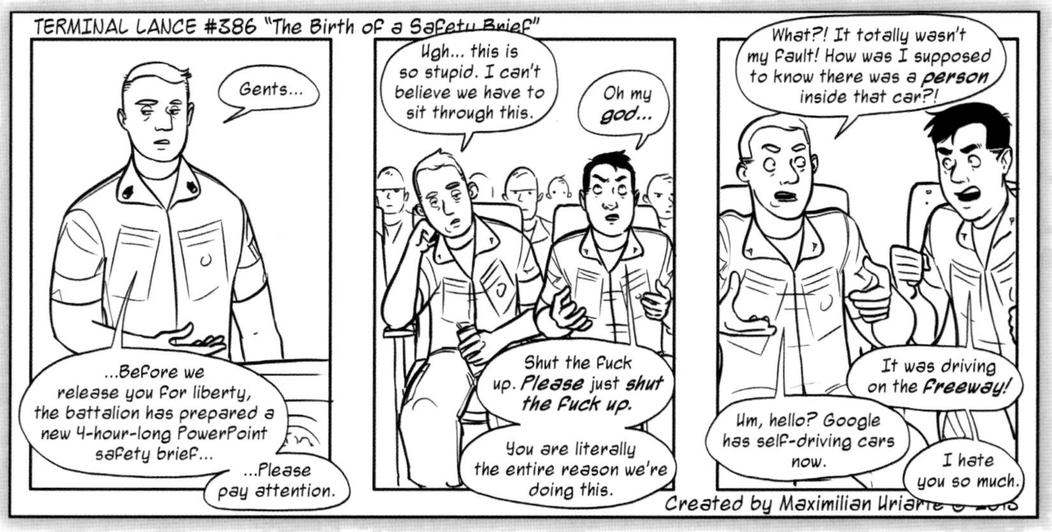
TERMINAL LANCE #386 "The Birth of a Safety Brief"
Gents...
...Before we release you for liberty, the battalion has prepared a new 4-hour-long PowerPoint safety brief...
...Please pay attention.
Ugh... this is so stupid. I can't believe we have to sit through this.
Oh my *god...*
Shut the fuck up. *Please just shut the fuck up.*
You are literally the entire reason we're doing this.
What?! It totally wasn't my fault! How was I supposed to know there was a *person* inside that car?!
It was driving on the *freeway!*
Um, hello? Google has self-driving cars now.
I hate you so much.
Created by Maximilian Uriarte

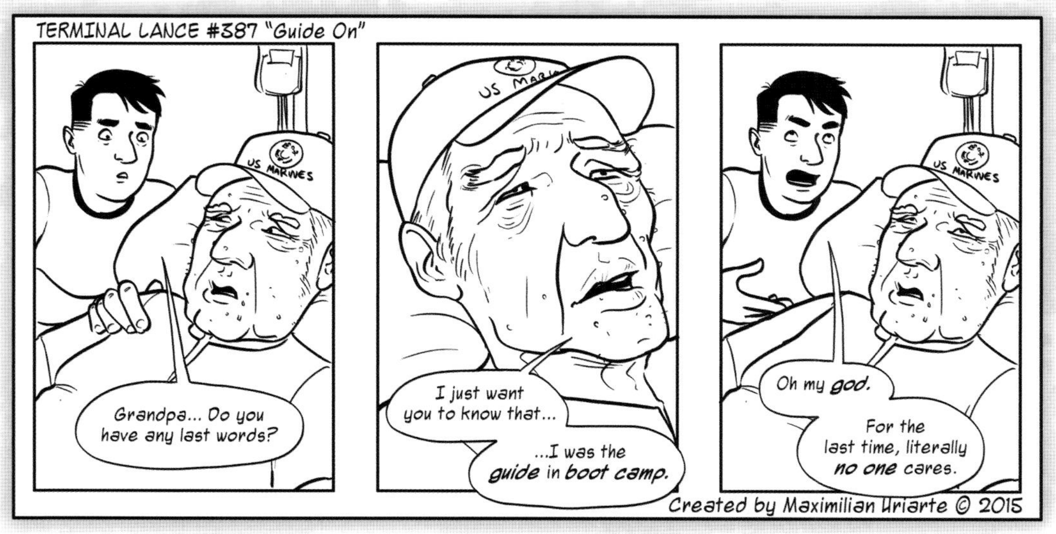
TERMINAL LANCE #387 "Guide On"
US MARINES
Grandpa... Do you have any last words?
US MARINES
I just want you to know that...
...I was the *guide* in *boot camp.*
US MARINES
Oh my *god.*
For the last time, literally *no one* cares.
Created by Maximilian Uriarte © 2015

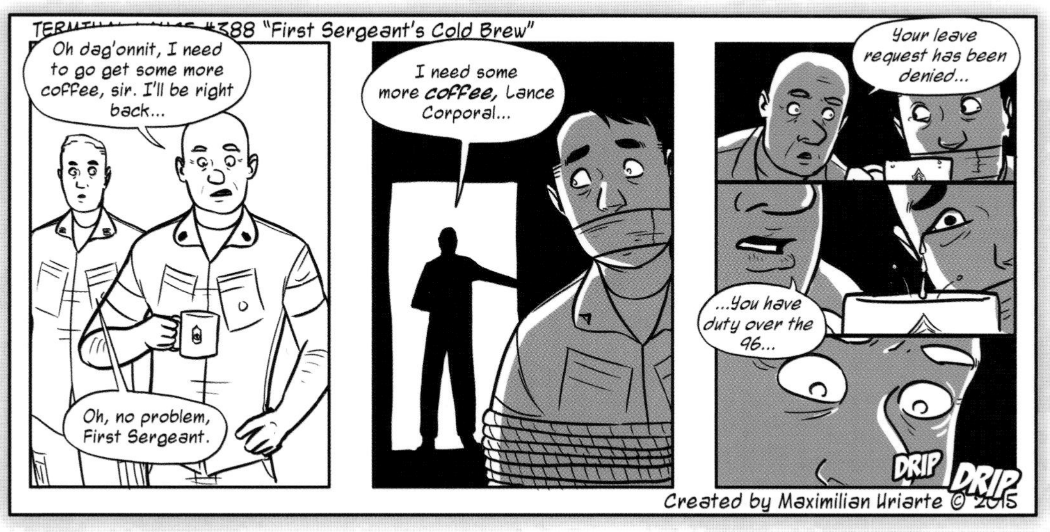
#388 "First Sergeant's Cold Brew"
Oh dag'onnit, I need to go get some more coffee, sir. I'll be right back...
Oh, no problem, First Sergeant.
I need some more *coffee,* Lance Corporal...
Your leave request has been denied...
...You have duty over the 96...
DRIP
DRIP
Created by Maximilian Uriarte © 2015

388 "First Sergeant's Cold Brew"

Have you ever noticed that Staff NCO's seem to live off coffee? You'd be hard pressed to find a set of rockers not hopped up on the glorious brown bean's black life juice.

Scientists have recently discovered, however, that First Sergeants and above don't actually have "coffee" in their mugs. Rather, they're specially trained in the cold brewing process of collecting the tears of Lance Corporals and below with the employment of their frostbitten hearts hidden deep within their chest cavities.

They say it can take up to an entire twenty-four hours to collect a mug full of tears from a single Lance Corporal, but with enough anger, green-weenie butt-fucking, and malice, some can do it in five minutes. Have you ever had a leave request that you waited to get approved for weeks, bought tickets for your entire family so you could all spend a nice time together after being assured it would go through, only to have it coldly denied? Have you ever had to stand by in the barracks while your girlfriend waited for you off-base for seven hours, only to have liberty secured at the last minute?

These are cold-brewing techniques that First Sergeants and above use to collect the tears they need to thrive. Caffeine is addicting on its own, but fucking over Lance Corporals and below gives them a fucking boner.

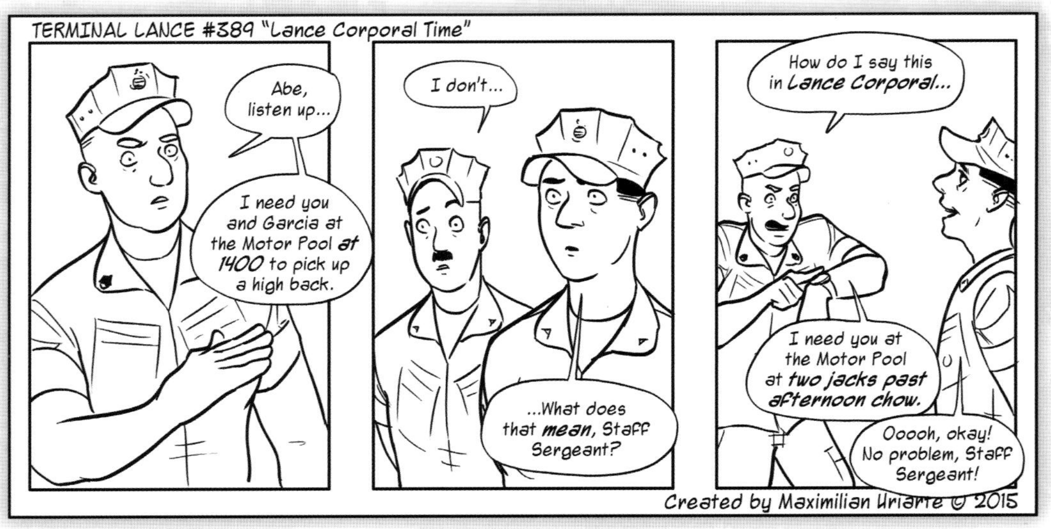
TERMINAL LANCE #389 "Lance Corporal Time"
Abe, listen up...
I need you and Garcia at the Motor Pool at 1400 to pick up a high back.
I don't...
...What does that mean, Staff Sergeant?
How do I say this in Lance Corporal...
I need you at the Motor Pool at two jacks past afternoon chow.
Ooooh, okay! No problem, Staff Sergeant!
Created by Maximilian Uriarte © 2015

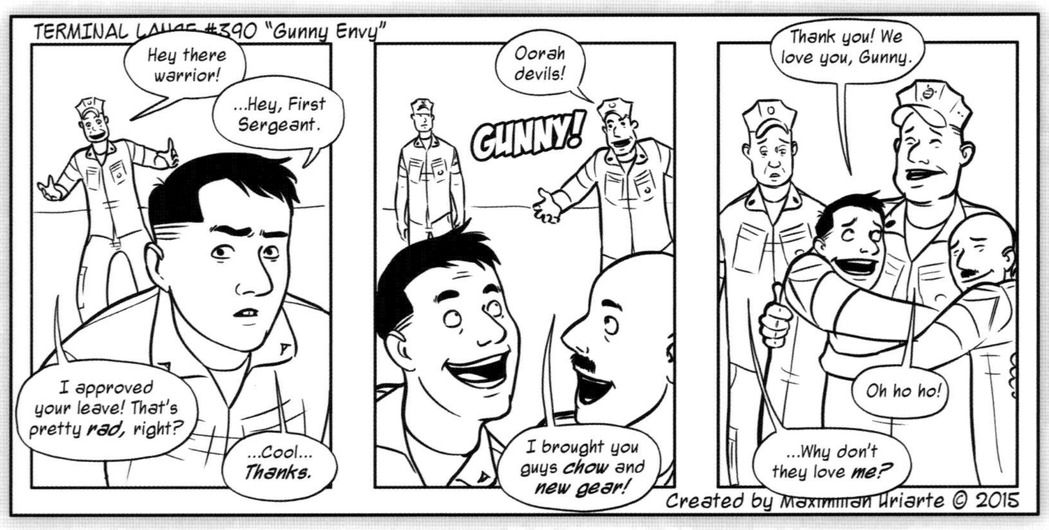
TERMINAL LANCE #390 "Gunny Envy"
Hey there warrior!
...Hey, First Sergeant.
I approved your leave! That's pretty rad, right?
...Cool... Thanks.
Oorah devils!
GUNNY!
I brought you guys chow and new gear!
Thank you! We love you, Gunny.
Oh ho ho!
...Why don't they love me?
Created by Maximilian Uriarte © 2015

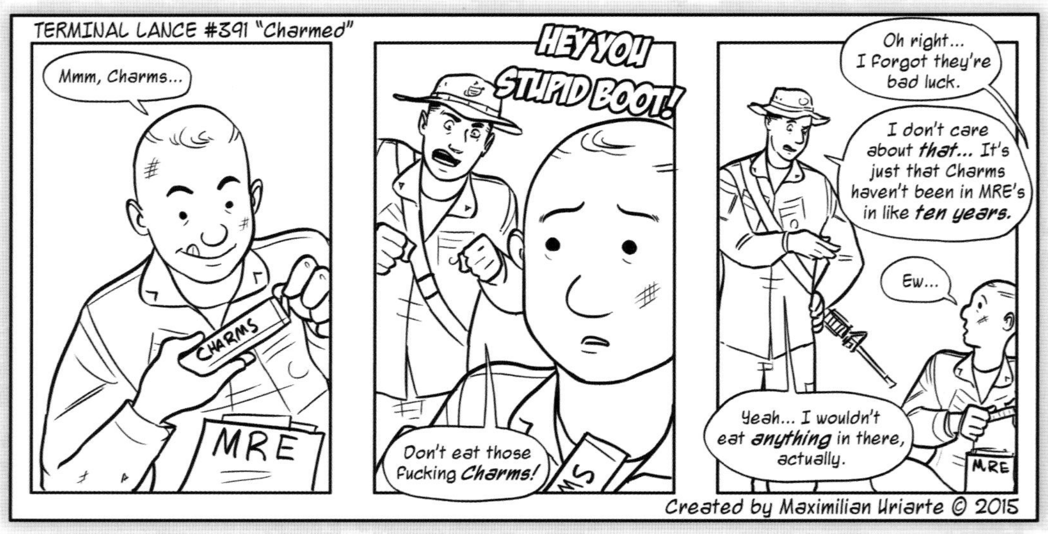
TERMINAL LANCE #391 "Charmed"
Mmm, Charms...
CHARMS
MRE
HEY YOU STUPID BOOT!
Don't eat those fucking Charms!
Oh right... I forgot they're bad luck.
I don't care about that... It's just that Charms haven't been in MRE's in like ten years.
Ew...
Yeah... I wouldn't eat anything in there, actually.
MRE
Created by Maximilian Uriarte © 2015

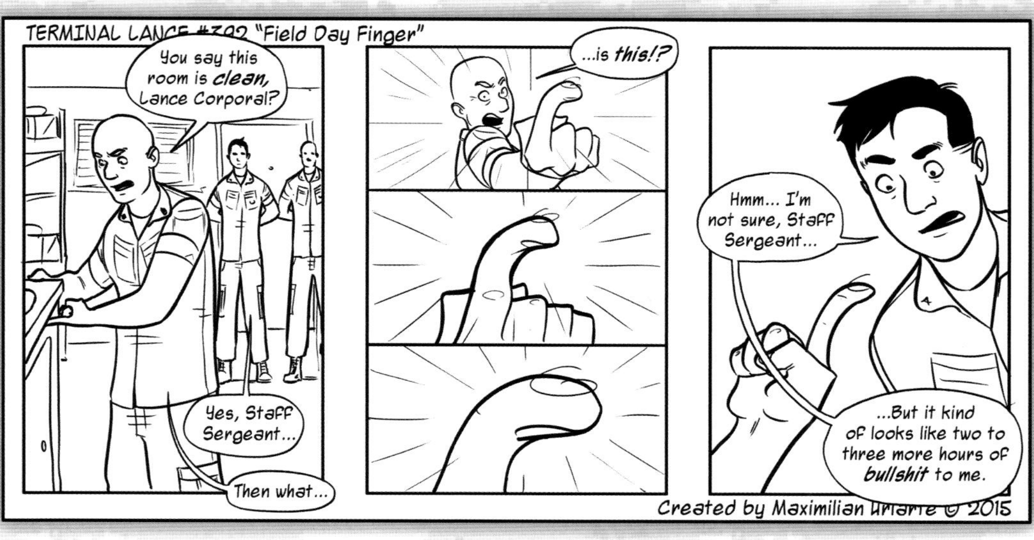
TERMINAL LANCE #392 "Field Day Finger"
You say this room is *clean,* Lance Corporal?
Yes, Staff Sergeant...
Then what...
...is *this!?*
Hmm... I'm not sure, Staff Sergeant...
...But it kind of looks like two to three more hours of *bullshit* to me.
Created by Maximilian Uriarte © 2015

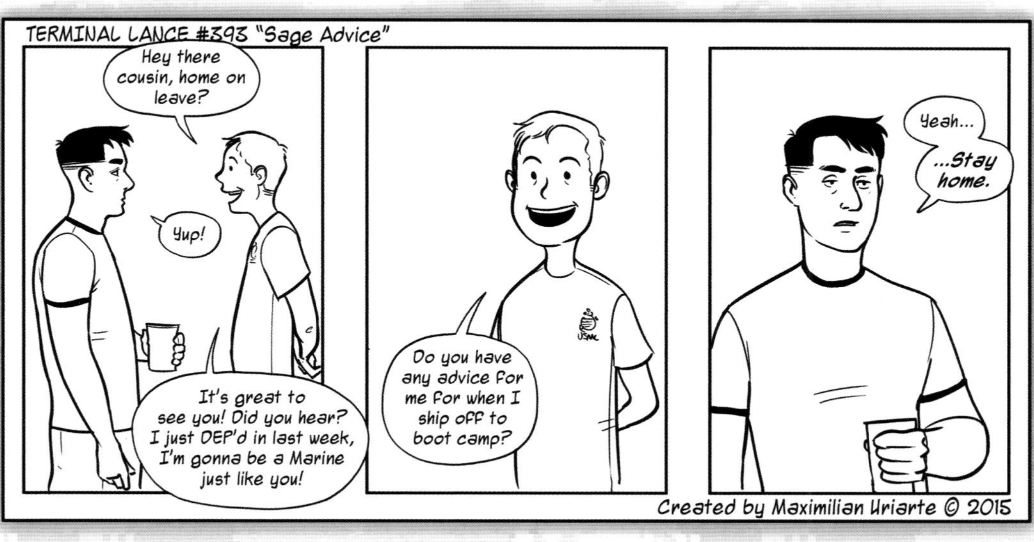
TERMINAL LANCE #393 "Sage Advice"
Hey there cousin, home on leave?
Yup!
It's great to see you! Did you hear? I just DEP'd in last week, I'm gonna be a Marine just like you!
Do you have any advice for me for when I ship off to boot camp?
Yeah...
...Stay home.
Created by Maximilian Uriarte © 2015

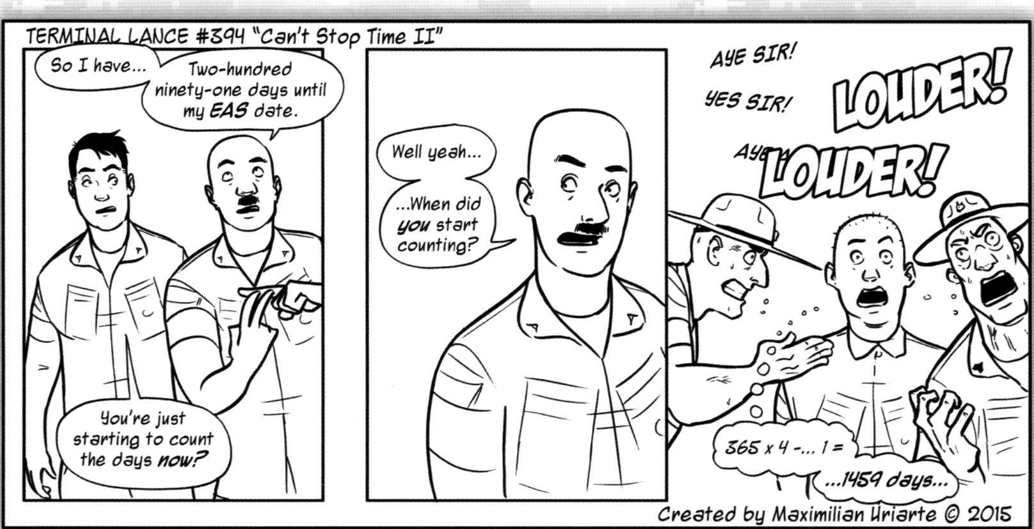
TERMINAL LANCE #394 "Can't Stop Time II"
So I have...
Two-hundred ninety-one days until my *EAS* date.
You're just starting to count the days *now?*
Well yeah...
...When did *you* start counting?
AYE SIR!
YES SIR!
LOUDER!
LOUDER!
365 x 4 -... 1 =
...1459 days...
Created by Maximilian Uriarte © 2015

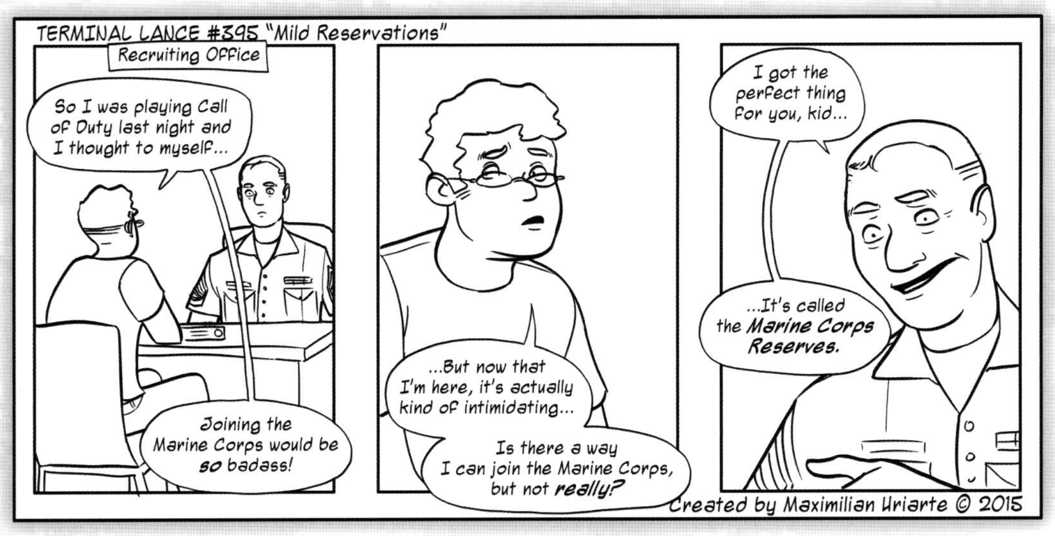
TERMINAL LANCE #395 "Mild Reservations"
Recruiting Office
So I was playing Call of Duty last night and I thought to myself...
Joining the Marine Corps would be *so* badass!
...But now that I'm here, it's actually kind of intimidating...
Is there a way I can join the Marine Corps, but not *really?*
I got the perfect thing for you, kid...
...It's called the *Marine Corps Reserves.*
Created by Maximilian Uriarte © 2015

395 "Mild Reservations"

The Reserves is like the Marine Corps Lite. Of course, they deploy and have done great things in combat and abroad. But at the end of the day, they get to go home. They check in once a month and do a two-week thing once a year unless otherwise needed. They don't live in the barracks every day, they don't get woken up at four a.m. to police call the parking lot.

Marines that I had known since boot camp were in my class in the School of Infantry, but at the end of our MOS training (0351), they got to go home. All I can remember thinking to myself was . . .

What the fuck? I didn't even know that was an option.

While they went home to go fuck their girlfriends (and probably ours), the rest of our sorry asses got sent to our Active Duty units to be hazed and treated like the lowest form of sentient entity on the planet (boots).

In my humble opinion, the reserves is the Marine Corps Lite because it's not the full experience. It's one thing to step in bullshit, it's another to build your entire house out of it and live there for four years.

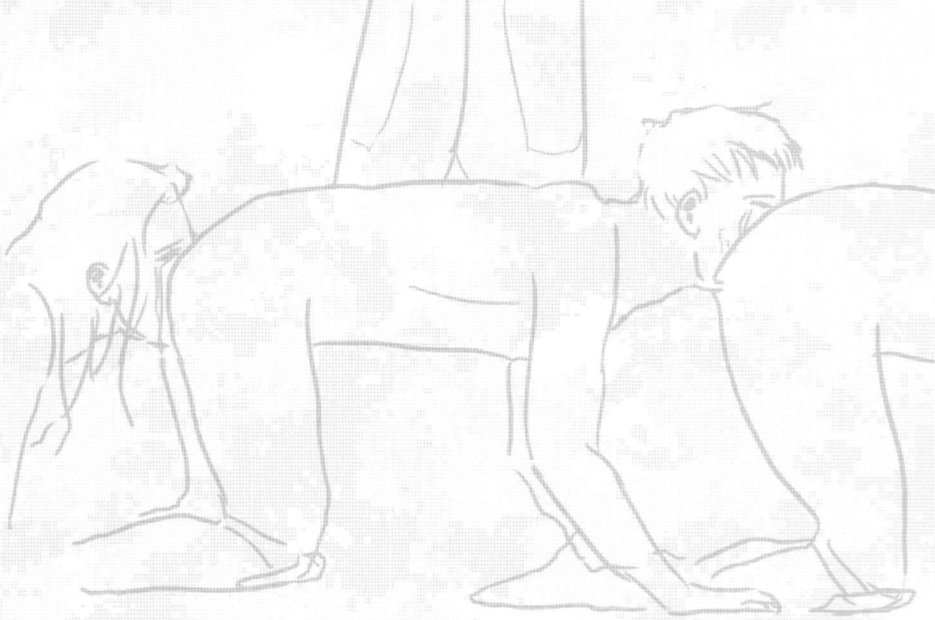

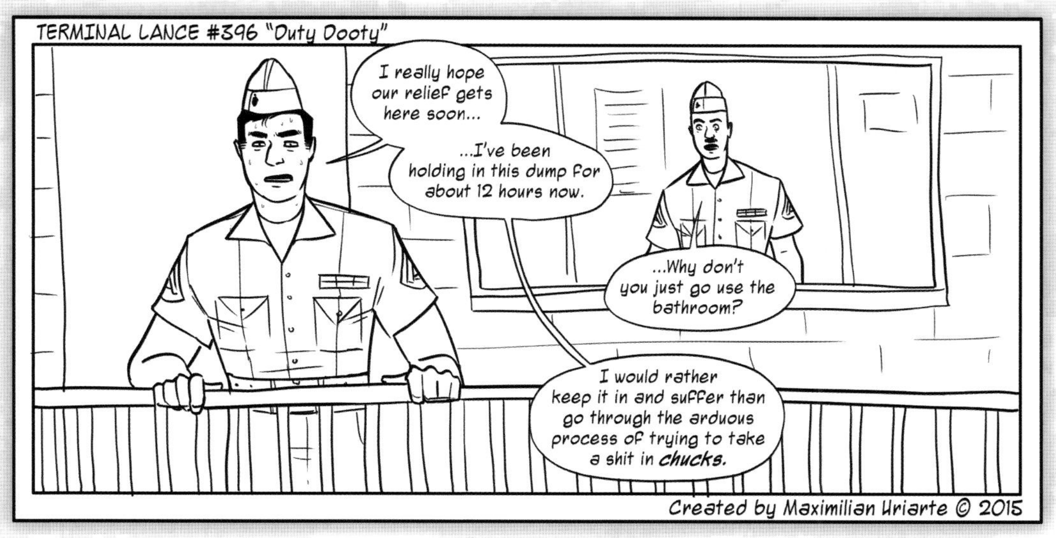
TERMINAL LANCE #396 "Duty Dooty"
I really hope our relief gets here soon...
...I've been holding in this dump for about 12 hours now.
...Why don't you just go use the bathroom?
I would rather keep it in and suffer than go through the arduous process of trying to take a shit in *chucks.*
Created by Maximilian Uriarte © 2015

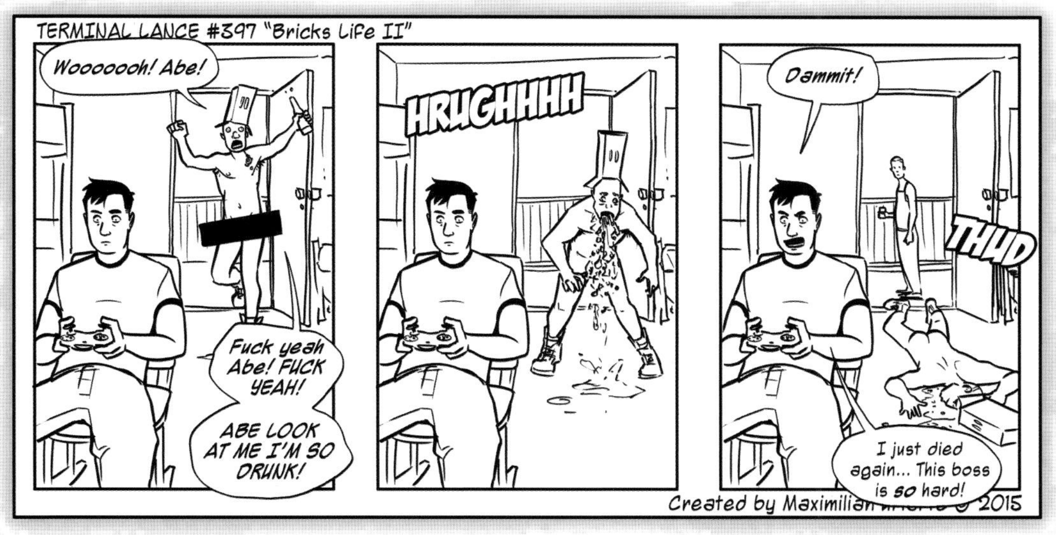
TERMINAL LANCE #397 "Bricks Life II"
Woooooh! Abe!
Fuck yeah Abe! FUCK YEAH!
ABE LOOK AT ME I'M SO DRUNK!
HRUGHHHH
Dammit!
THUD
I just died again... This boss is *so* hard!
Created by Maximilian Uriarte © 2015

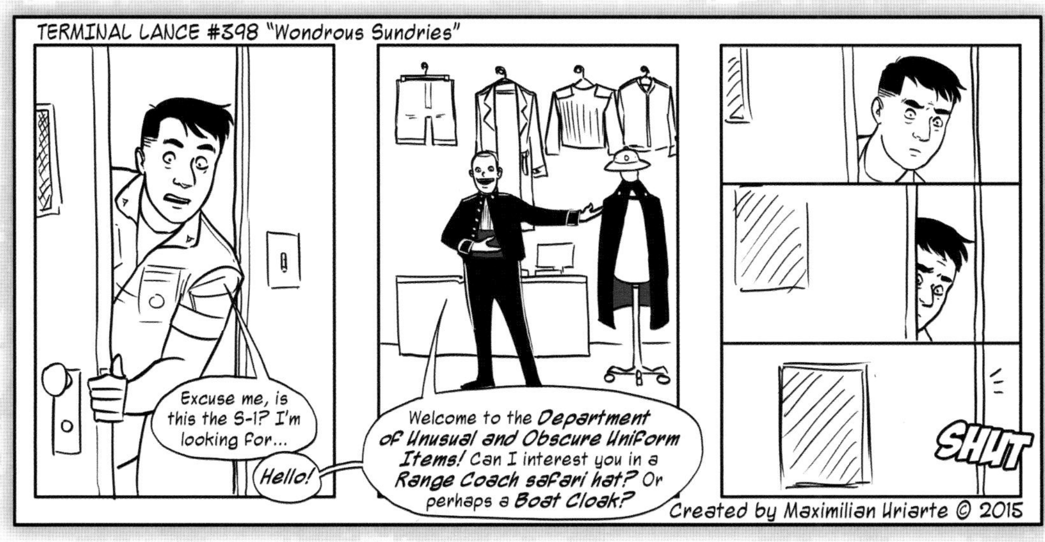
TERMINAL LANCE #398 "Wondrous Sundries"
Excuse me, is this the S-1? I'm looking for...
Hello!
Welcome to the *Department of Unusual and Obscure Uniform Items!* Can I interest you in a *Range Coach safari hat?* Or perhaps a *Boat Cloak?*
SHUT
Created by Maximilian Uriarte © 2015

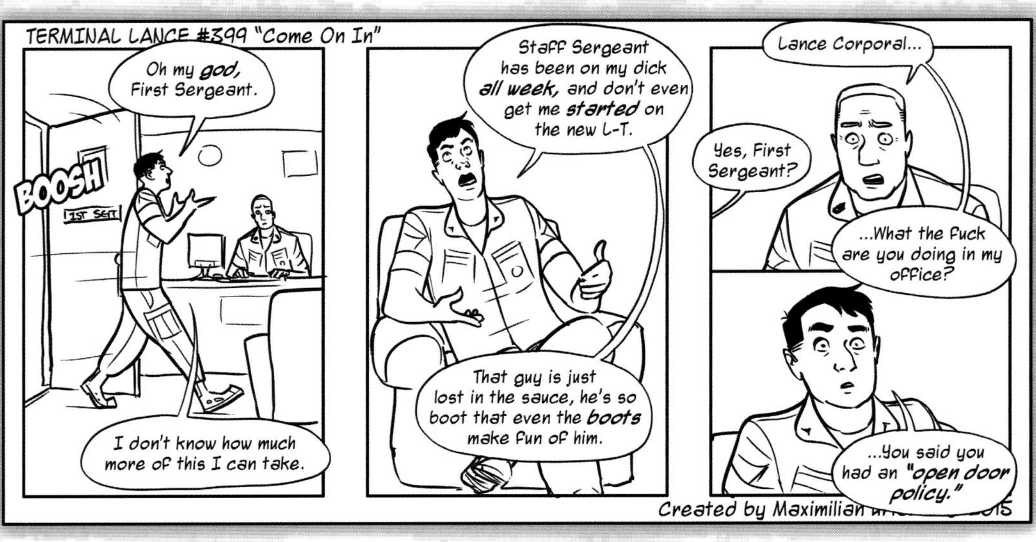
TERMINAL LANCE #399 "Come On In"
Oh my god, First Sergeant.
BOOSH
1ST SGT
I don't know how much more of this I can take.
Staff Sergeant has been on my dick all week, and don't even get me started on the new L-T.
That guy is just lost in the sauce, he's so boot that even the boots make fun of him.
Lance Corporal...
Yes, First Sergeant?
...What the fuck are you doing in my office?
...You said you had an "open door policy."
Created by Maximilian 2015

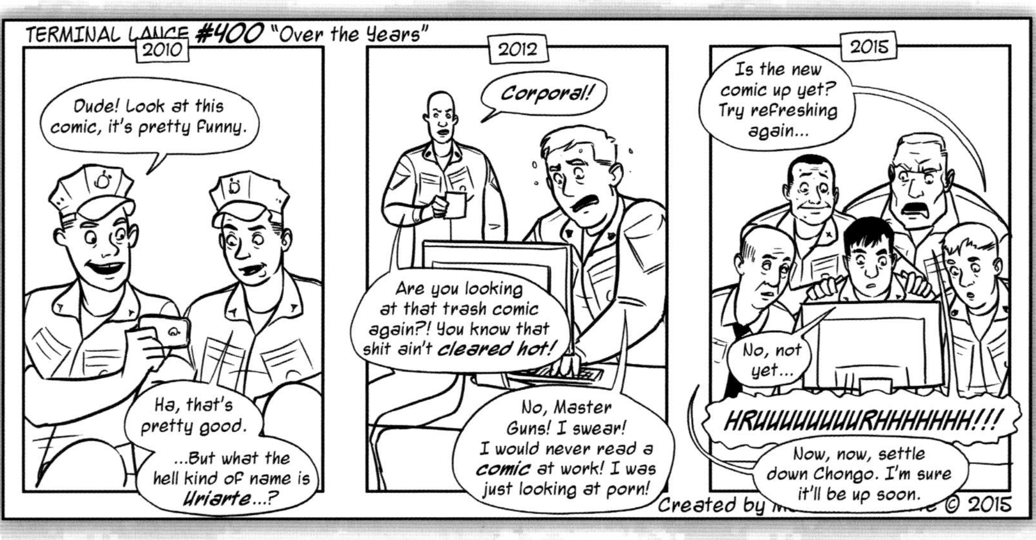
TERMINAL LANCE #400 "Over the Years"
2010
Dude! Look at this comic, it's pretty funny.
Ha, that's pretty good.
...But what the hell kind of name is Uriarte...?
2012
Corporal!
Are you looking at that trash comic again?! You know that shit ain't cleared hot!
No, Master Guns! I swear! I would never read a comic at work! I was just looking at porn!
2015
Is the new comic up yet? Try refreshing again...
No, not yet...
HRUUUUUUUURHHHHHHH!!!
Now, now, settle down Chongo. I'm sure it'll be up soon.
Created by © 2015

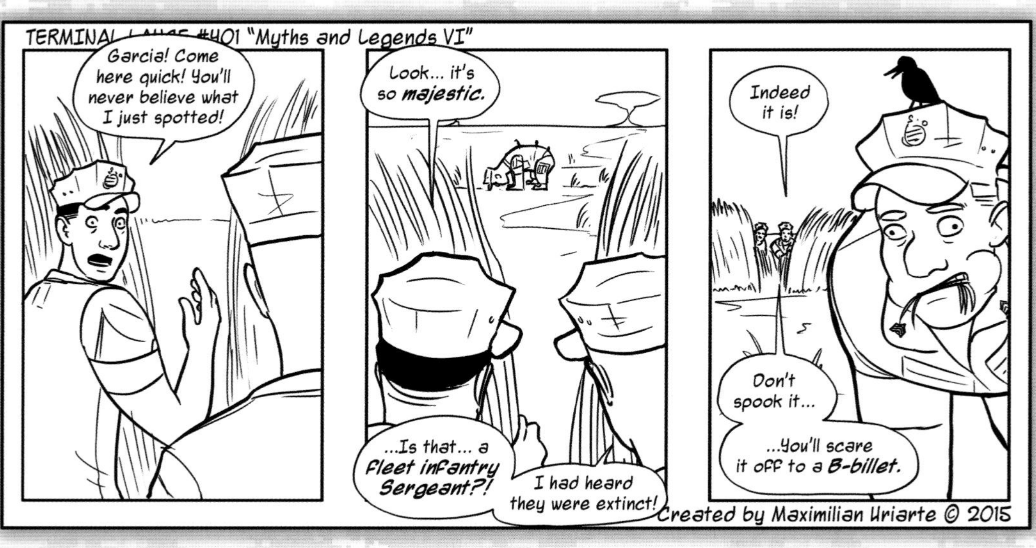
TERMINAL LANCE #401 "Myths and Legends VI"
Garcia! Come here quick! You'll never believe what I just spotted!
Look... it's so majestic.
...Is that... a Fleet infantry Sergeant?!
I had heard they were extinct!
Indeed it is!
Don't spook it...
...You'll scare it off to a B-billet.
Created by Maximilian Uriarte © 2015

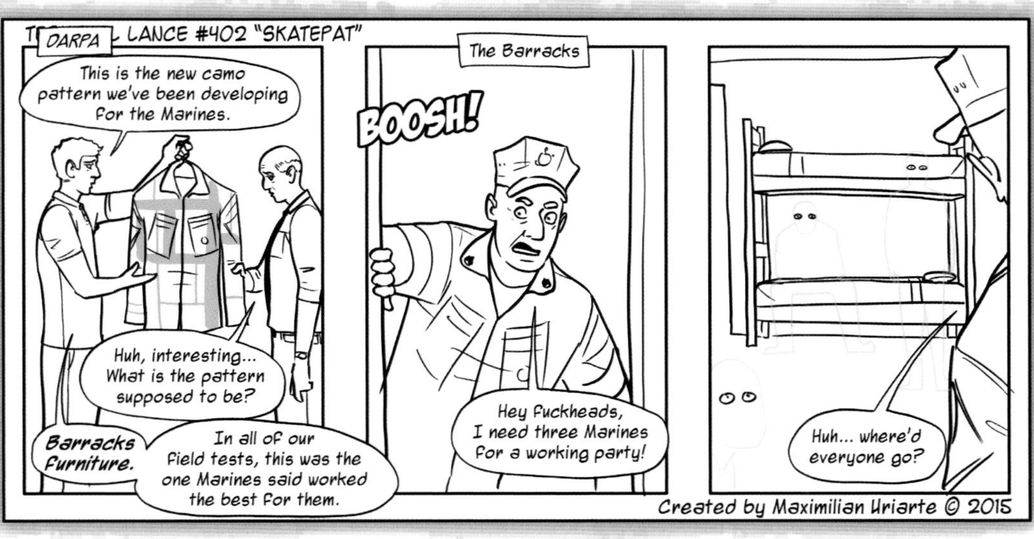
TE L LANCE #402 "SKATEPAT"
DARPA
This is the new camo pattern we've been developing for the Marines.
Huh, interesting... What is the pattern supposed to be?
Barracks Furniture.
In all of our field tests, this was the one Marines said worked the best for them.
The Barracks
BOOSH!
Hey fuckheads, I need three Marines for a working party!
Huh... where'd everyone go?
Created by Maximilian Uriarte © 2015

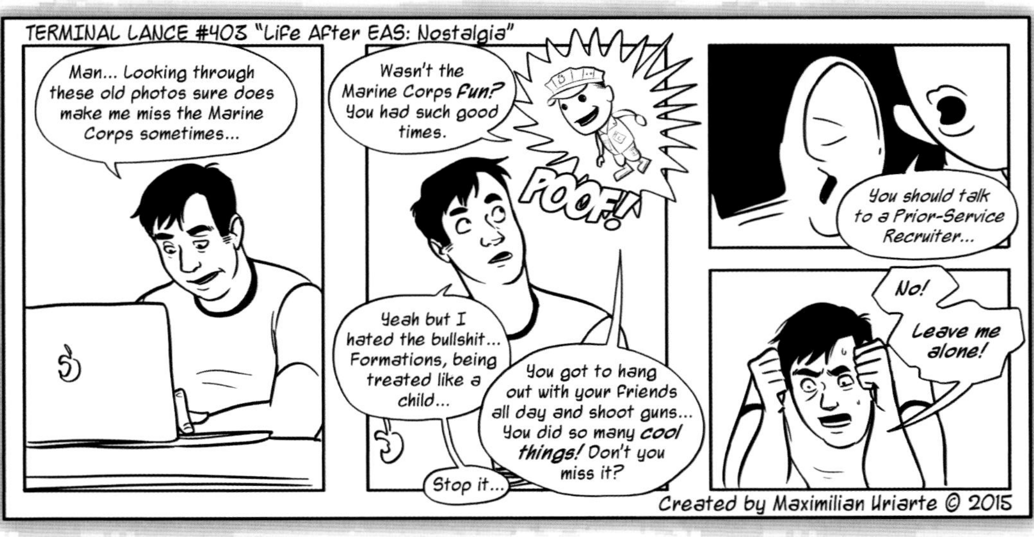
TERMINAL LANCE #403 "Life After EAS: Nostalgia"
Man... Looking through these old photos sure does make me miss the Marine Corps sometimes...
Wasn't the Marine Corps fun? You had such good times.
POOF!
Yeah but I hated the bullshit... Formations, being treated like a child...
You got to hang out with your friends all day and shoot guns... You did so many cool things! Don't you miss it?
Stop it...
You should talk to a Prior-Service Recruiter...
No!
Leave me alone!
Created by Maximilian Uriarte © 2015

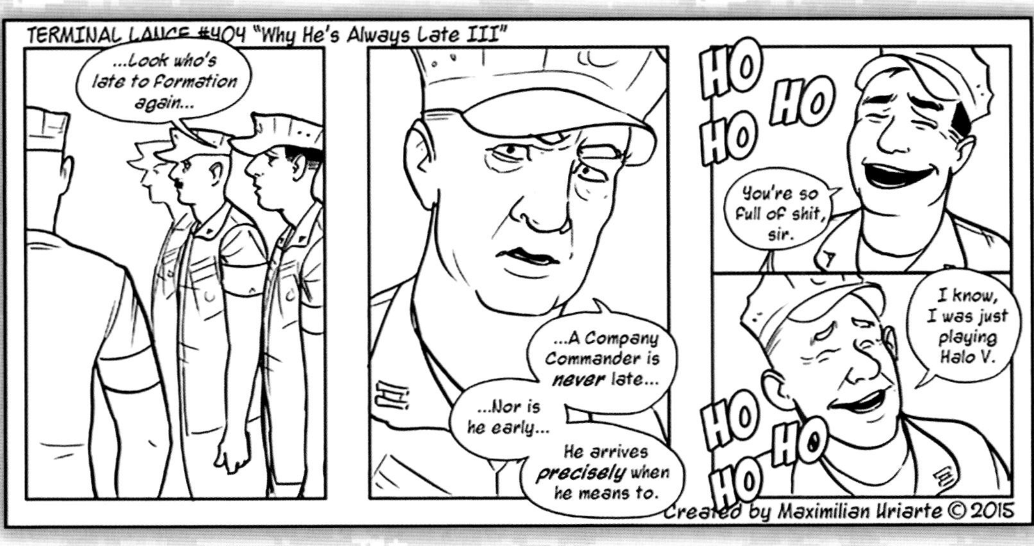
TERMINAL LANCE #404 "Why He's Always Late III"
...Look who's late to formation again...
...A Company Commander is never late...
...Nor is he early...
He arrives precisely when he means to.
HO HO HO
You're so full of shit, sir.
I know, I was just playing Halo V.
HO HO HO
Created by Maximilian Uriarte © 2015

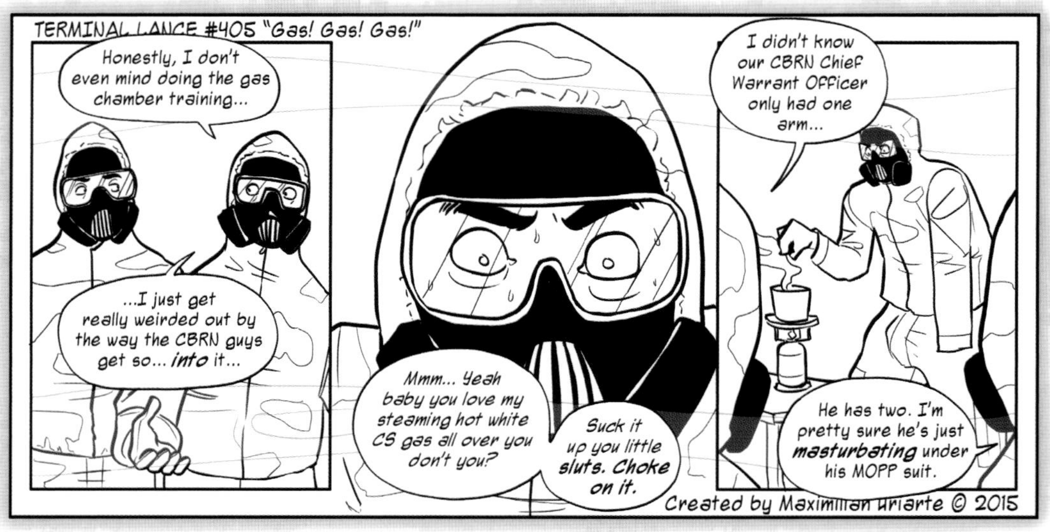
TERMINAL LANCE #405 "Gas! Gas! Gas!"
Honestly, I don't even mind doing the gas chamber training...
...I just get really weirded out by the way the CBRN guys get so... *into* it...
Mmm... Yeah baby you love my steaming hot white CS gas all over you don't you?
Suck it up you little **sluts. Choke on it.**
I didn't know our CBRN Chief Warrant Officer only had one arm...
He has two. I'm pretty sure he's just ***masturbating*** under his MOPP suit.
Created by Maximilian Uriarte © 2015

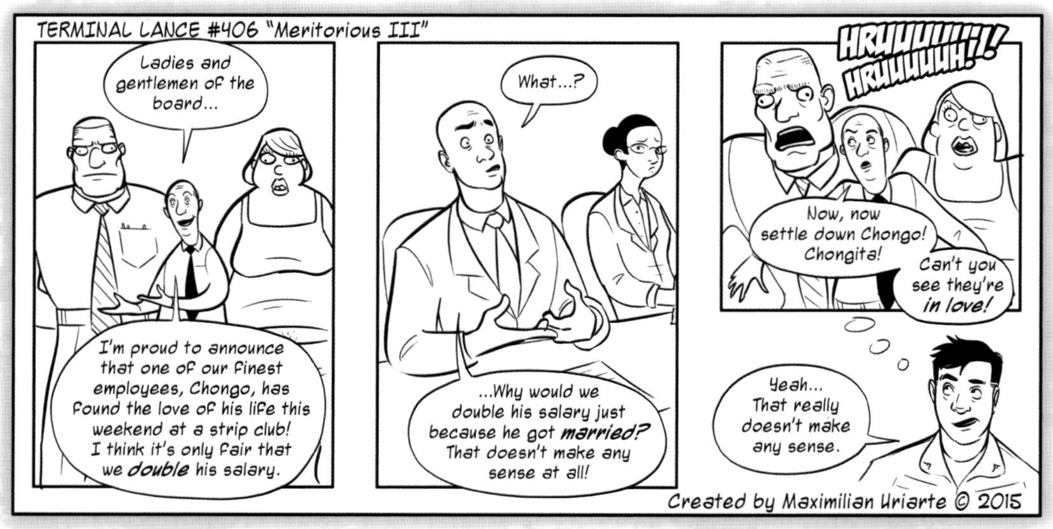
TERMINAL LANCE #406 "Meritorious III"
Ladies and gentlemen of the board...
I'm proud to announce that one of our finest employees, Chongo, has found the love of his life this weekend at a strip club! I think it's only fair that we ***double*** his salary.
What...?
...Why would we double his salary just because he got ***married?*** That doesn't make any sense at all!
HRUUUUU!!!! HRUUUUUH!!!
Now, now settle down Chongo! Chongita!
Can't you see they're ***in love!***
Yeah... That really doesn't make any sense.
Created by Maximilian Uriarte © 2015

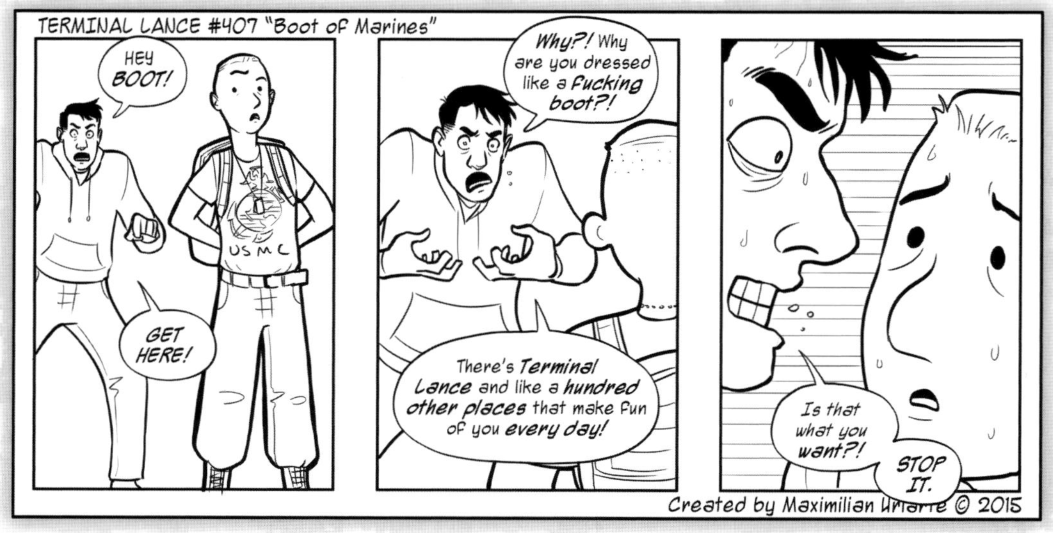
TERMINAL LANCE #407 "Boot of Marines"
HEY ***BOOT!***
USMC
GET HERE!
Why?! Why are you dressed like a ***fucking boot?!***
There's ***Terminal Lance*** and like a ***hundred other places*** that make fun of you ***every day!***
*Is that what you **want?!***
STOP IT.
Created by Maximilian Uriarte © 2015

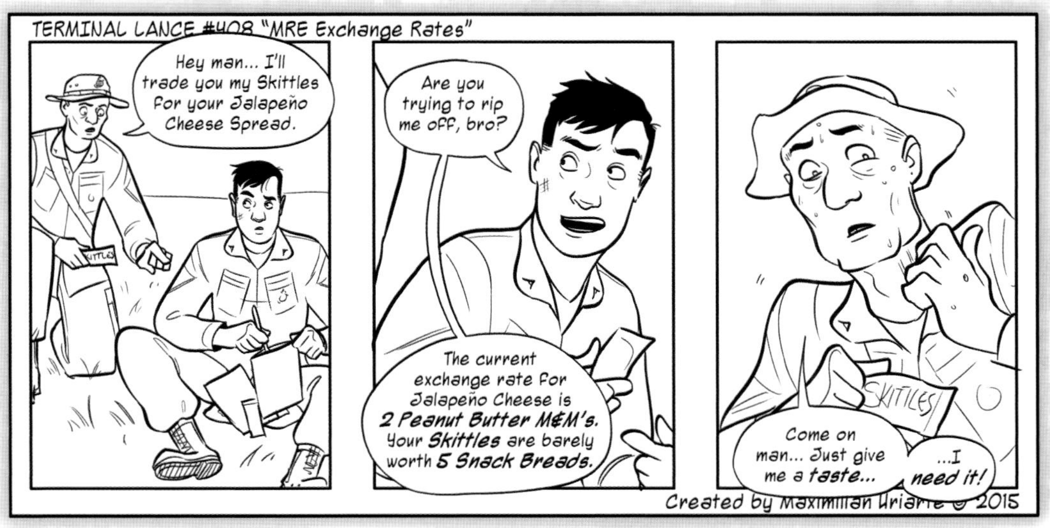
TERMINAL LANCE #408 "MRE Exchange Rates"
Hey man... I'll trade you my Skittles for your Jalapeño Cheese Spread.
SKITTLES
Are you trying to rip me off, bro?
The current exchange rate for Jalapeño Cheese is 2 Peanut Butter M&M's. Your Skittles are barely worth 5 Snack Breads.
SKITTLES
Come on man... Just give me a taste...
...I need it!
Created by Maximilian Uriarte © 2015

408 "MRE Exchange Rates"

MRE bartering and trading is a common practice in the field, as each package contains completely different stuff. Generally, MRE's come with one entrée, a cracker or "snack bread," a spread, and a dessert. The holy grail and reigning champion of these is still the coveted Jalapeño Cheese Spread. It may sound atrocious, but I assure you—it's absolutely delicious.

Imagine sitting on cold wet dirt, your rifle leaning up against your thigh and your MRE sitting atop your upturned boonie cover in front of you. You open the rather unappetizing brown plastic bag and empty the contents. You sift through plain, cardboard-boxed items: "Chili w/beans," "Tortillas," something called a "Ranger Bar." Just as you're ready to open your Chili w/beans you see it, underneath the accessory packet of random tissues and salt and shit.

Jalapeño Cheese Spread.

It glows. A children's choir can be heard behind you as you pick it up. You realize you're out in the open, you look over your shoulder to see other Marines sifting through their depressing dinners. One of them glances at you. It's Ramirez. You never really liked him, he's got that kind of face that just screams douchebag and leaves his door open in the barracks while he blasts his terrible music. He just finished telling a joke and is looking around to see if anyone heard him.

Your eyes meet. You look away, clutching your treasured spiced cheese. Ramirez loves this shit, but he can't see it. If he does, he'll obnoxiously announce to the entire platoon that you have the Jalapeño Cheese, and everyone will try to barter you for it. It's harmless, but still annoying.

You stand up, pick up your MRE-filled boonie and rifle, never looking back at him, and you walk toward the MRAP. You cautiously open the back hatch to make sure it's empty. You climb inside and set your cover on top of the turret platform, your rifle in the seat next to you. In total solitude, you covet the small, brown Jalapeño Cheese packet.

You open it with your teeth and you squeeze the contents directly into your mouth. You don't even bother putting it on a tortilla, this shit is dank as fuck.

Yeah, that's basically what getting a Jalapeño Cheese Spread is like.

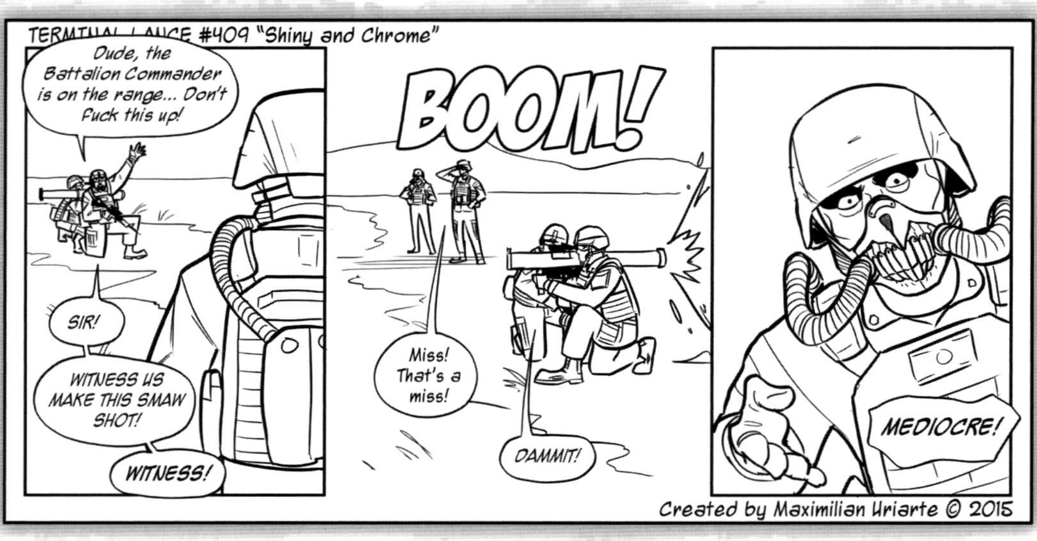
TERMINAL LANCE #409 "Shiny and Chrome"
Dude, the Battalion Commander is on the range... Don't fuck this up!
SIR!
WITNESS US MAKE THIS SMAW SHOT!
WITNESS!
BOOM!
Miss! That's a miss!
DAMMIT!
MEDIOCRE!
Created by Maximilian Uriarte © 2015

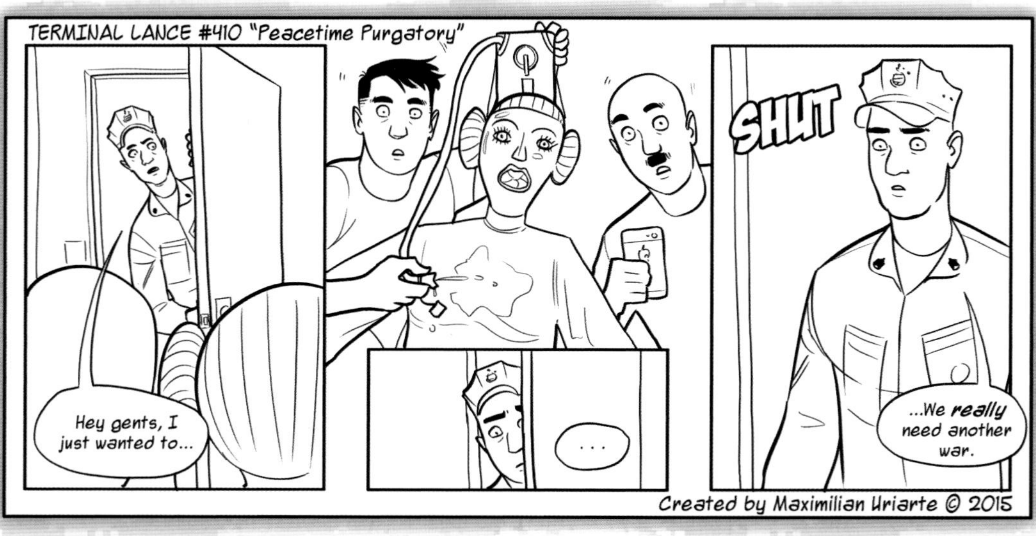
TERMINAL LANCE #410 "Peacetime Purgatory"
Hey gents, I just wanted to...
. . .
SHUT
...We really need another war.
Created by Maximilian Uriarte © 2015

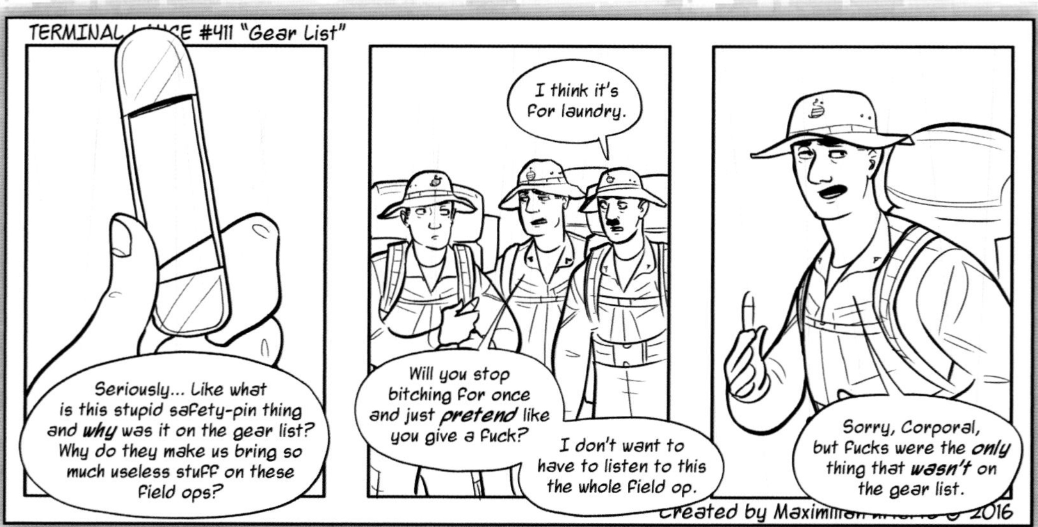
TERMINAL
CE #411 "Gear List"
Seriously... Like what is this stupid safety-pin thing and why was it on the gear list? Why do they make us bring so much useless stuff on these field ops?
I think it's for laundry.
Will you stop bitching for once and just pretend like you give a fuck?
I don't want to have to listen to this the whole field op.
Sorry, Corporal, but fucks were the only thing that wasn't on the gear list.
Created by Maximilian
2016

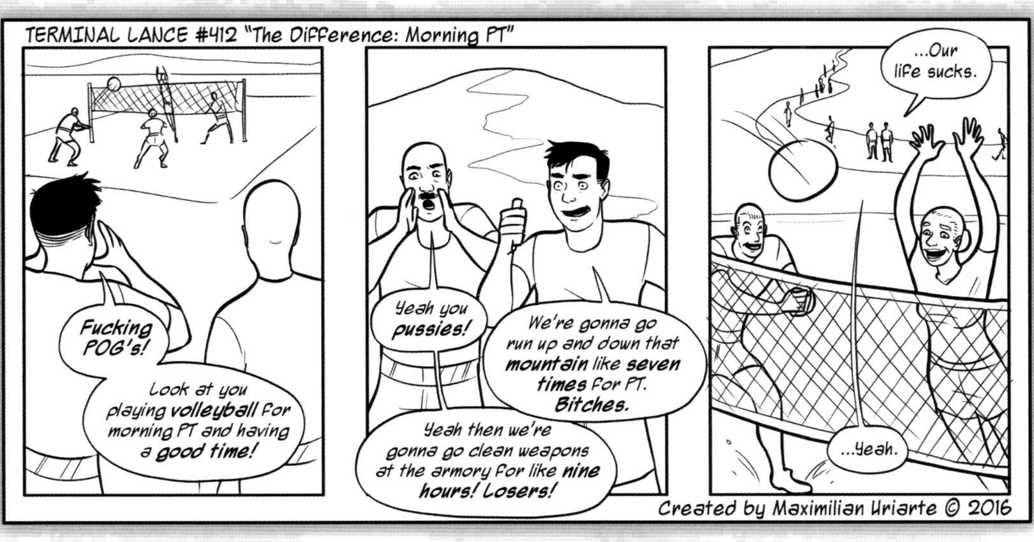
TERMINAL LANCE #412 "The Difference: Morning PT"
Fucking POG's!
Look at you playing volleyball for morning PT and having a good time!
Yeah you pussies!
We're gonna go run up and down that mountain like seven times for PT. Bitches.
Yeah then we're gonna go clean weapons at the armory for like nine hours! Losers!
...Our life sucks.
...Yeah.
Created by Maximilian Uriarte © 2016

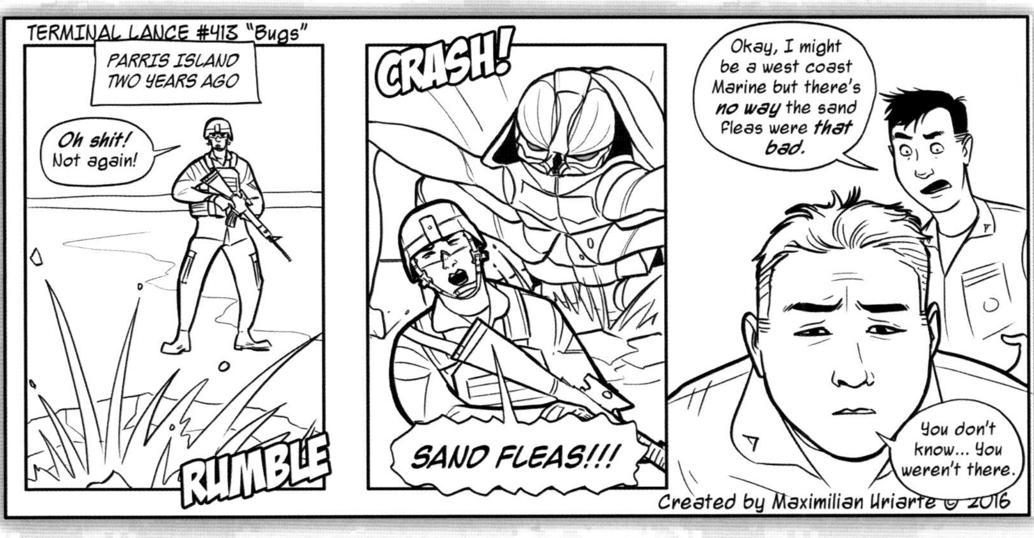
TERMINAL LANCE #413 "Bugs"
PARRIS ISLAND TWO YEARS AGO
Oh shit! Not again!
RUMBLE
CRASH!
SAND FLEAS!!!
Okay, I might be a west coast Marine but there's no way the sand fleas were that bad.
You don't know... You weren't there.
Created by Maximilian Uriarte © 2016

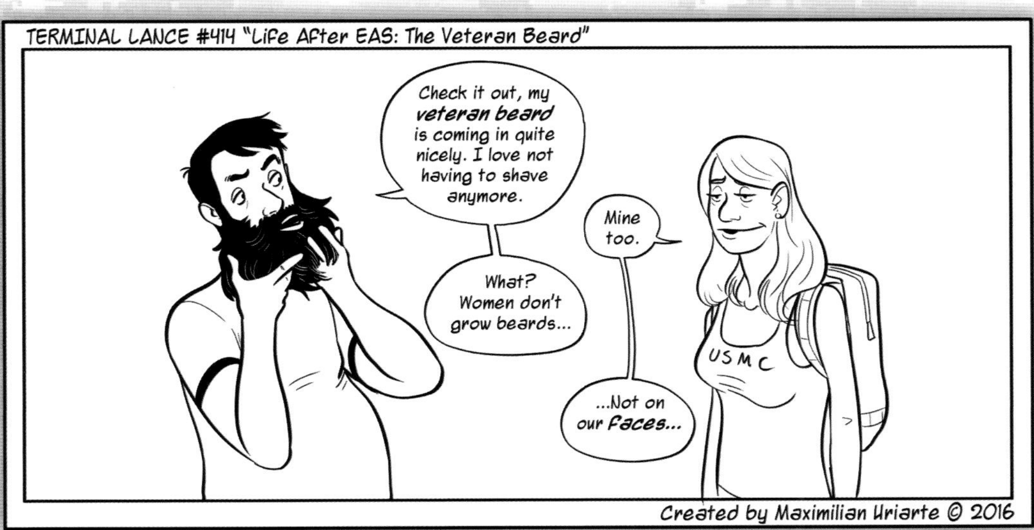
TERMINAL LANCE #414 "Life After EAS: The Veteran Beard"
Check it out, my veteran beard is coming in quite nicely. I love not having to shave anymore.
Mine too.
What? Women don't grow beards...
...Not on our faces...
USMC
Created by Maximilian Uriarte © 2016

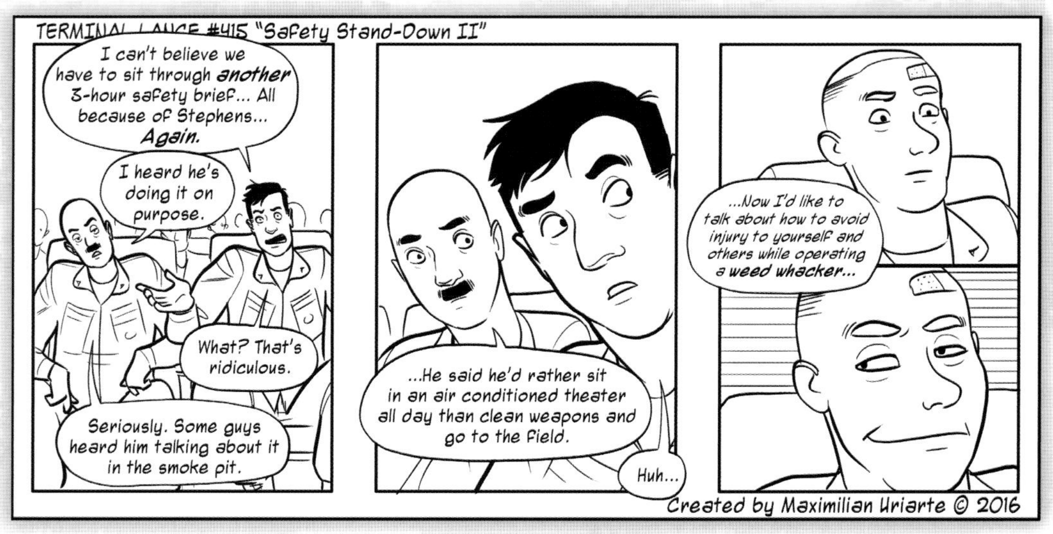
TERMINAL LANCE #415 "Safety Stand-Down II"
I can't believe we have to sit through another 3-hour safety brief... All because of Stephens... Again.
I heard he's doing it on purpose.
What? That's ridiculous.
Seriously. Some guys heard him talking about it in the smoke pit.
...He said he'd rather sit in an air conditioned theater all day than clean weapons and go to the field.
Huh...
...Now I'd like to talk about how to avoid injury to yourself and others while operating a weed whacker...
Created by Maximilian Uriarte © 2016

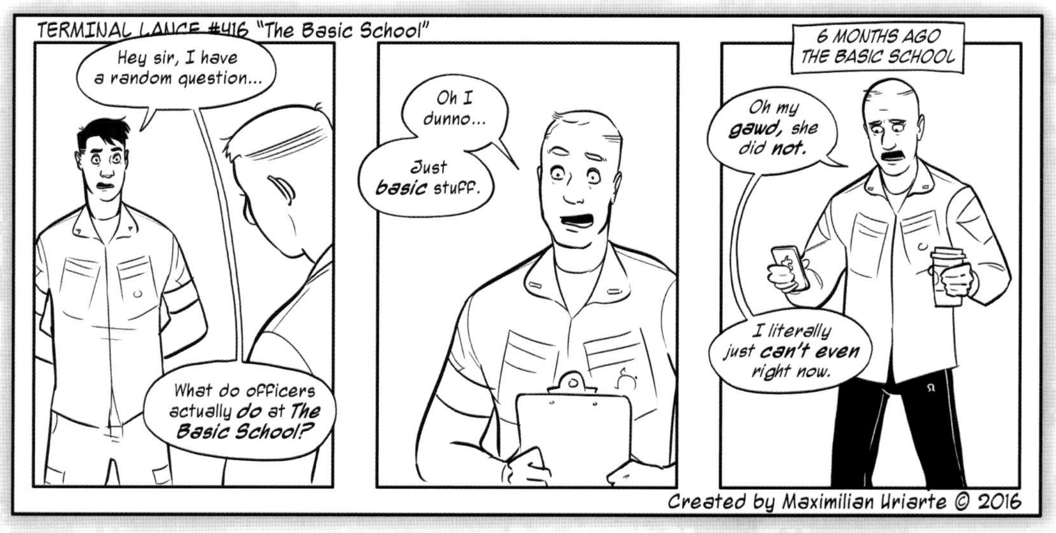
TERMINAL LANCE #416 "The Basic School"
Hey sir, I have a random question...
What do officers actually do at The Basic School?
Oh I dunno...
Just basic stuff.
6 MONTHS AGO
THE BASIC SCHOOL
Oh my gawd, she did not.
I literally just can't even right now.
Created by Maximilian Uriarte © 2016

416 "The Basic School"

When he gets to a high enough rank, he'll start his own Tumblr.

The world of the officer is very different from that of the enlisted. Instead of boot camp and SOI, officers attend Officer Candidate School (OCS) and The Basic School (TBS) for their Marine Corps indoctrination. To qualify, you just need a bachelor's degree in pretty much anything. From then on, you are a tried-and-true leader of Marines.

There's often quite a bit of friction between the officer and enlisted world. Enlisted comprises the majority of the Marine Corps—we are the working-class citizens of the military. The officers are usually seen as the white collar, pedigreed elite, with their shiny ranks and vastly superior living conditions and overall treatment.

To be completely honest, becoming an officer in the military is one of the best and highest paying jobs you'll likely find with nothing more than a bachelor's degree in today's age. On top of that, you'll be treated like royalty once you hit the fleet. The starting pay of around $30,000 a year might not seem like a ton, but the paycheck is in addition to housing, food, medical, and other perks. Plus, bitches salute you. How cool is that?

That is assuming you make it through The Basic School.

Where you learn to be basic.

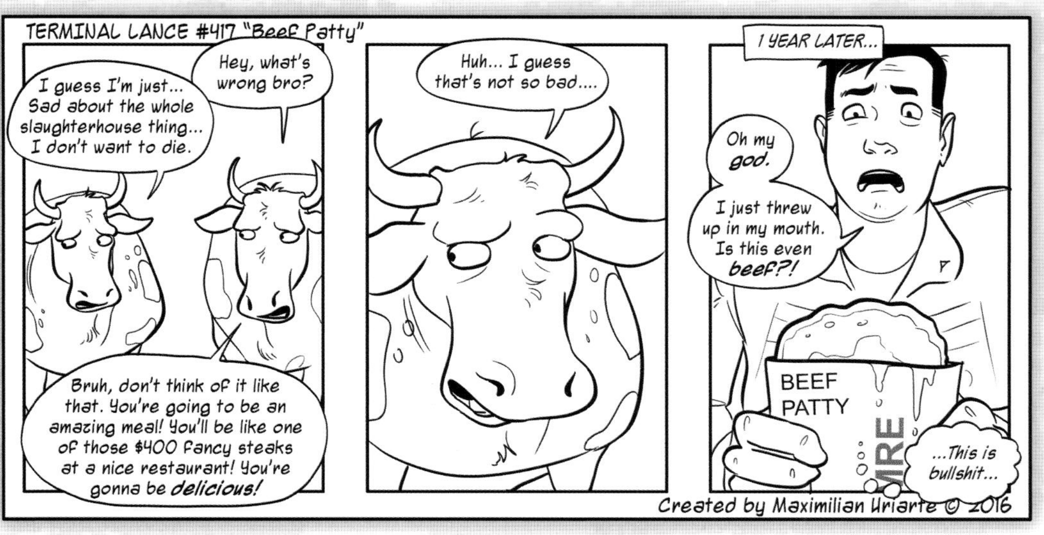
TERMINAL LANCE #417 "Beef Patty"
Hey, what's wrong bro?
I guess I'm just... Sad about the whole slaughterhouse thing... I don't want to die.
Bruh, don't think of it like that. You're going to be an amazing meal! You'll be like one of those $400 fancy steaks at a nice restaurant! You're gonna be ***delicious!***
Huh... I guess that's not so bad....
1 YEAR LATER...
Oh my ***god.***
I just threw up in my mouth. Is this even ***beef?!***
BEEF PATTY
MRE
...This is bullshit...
Created by Maximilian Uriarte © 2016

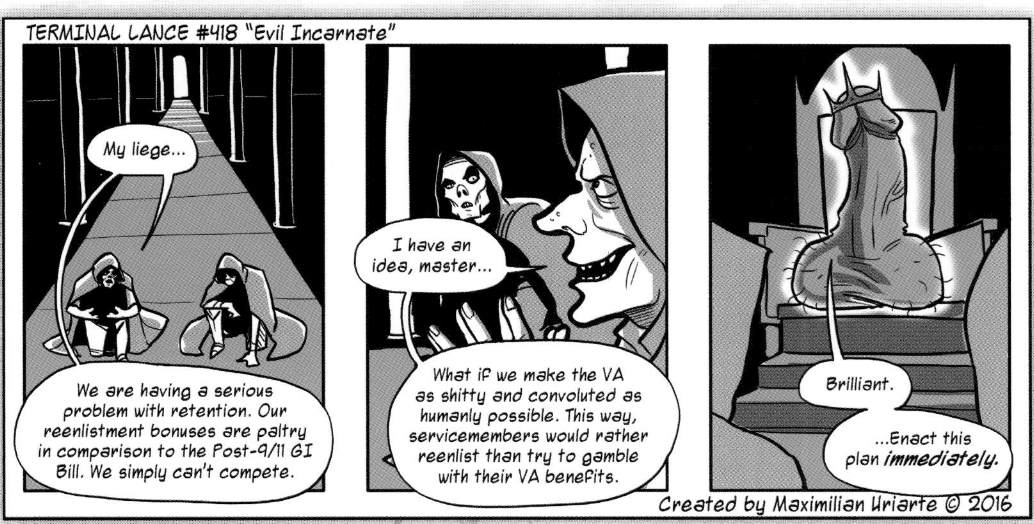
TERMINAL LANCE #418 "Evil Incarnate"
My liege...
We are having a serious problem with retention. Our reenlistment bonuses are paltry in comparison to the Post-9/11 GI Bill. We simply can't compete.
I have an idea, master...
What if we make the VA as shitty and convoluted as humanly possible. This way, servicemembers would rather reenlist than try to gamble with their VA benefits.
Brilliant.
...Enact this plan ***immediately.***
Created by Maximilian Uriarte © 2016

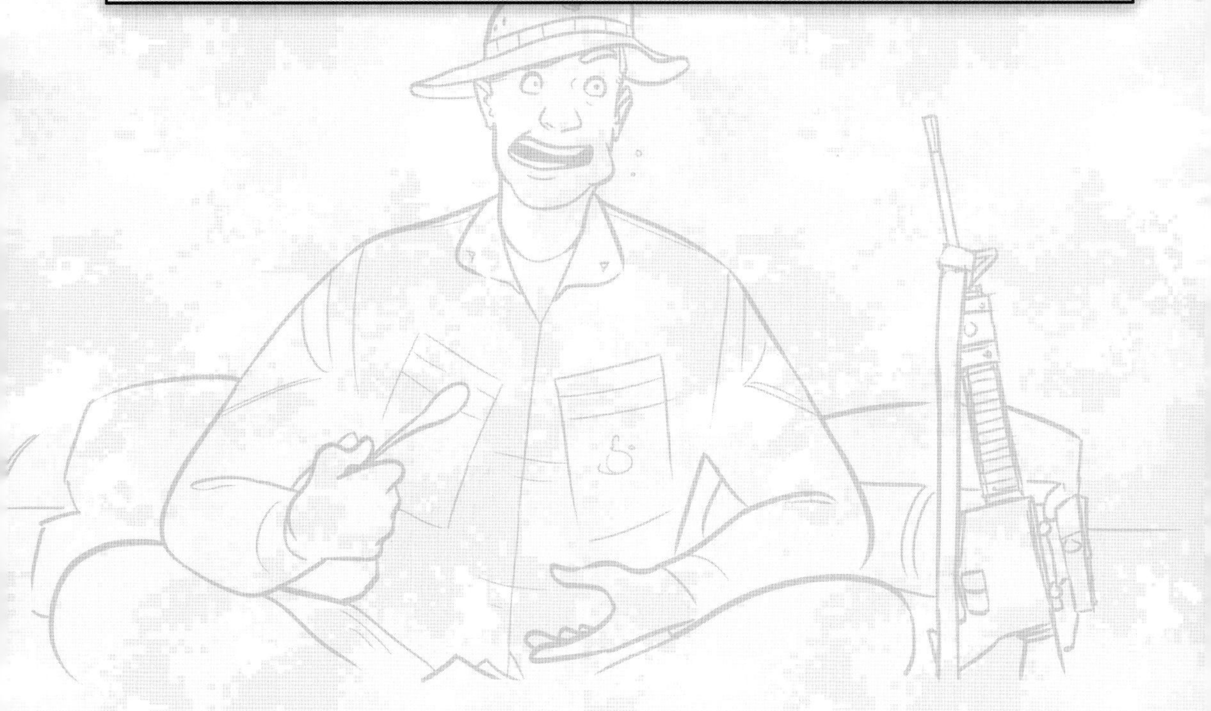

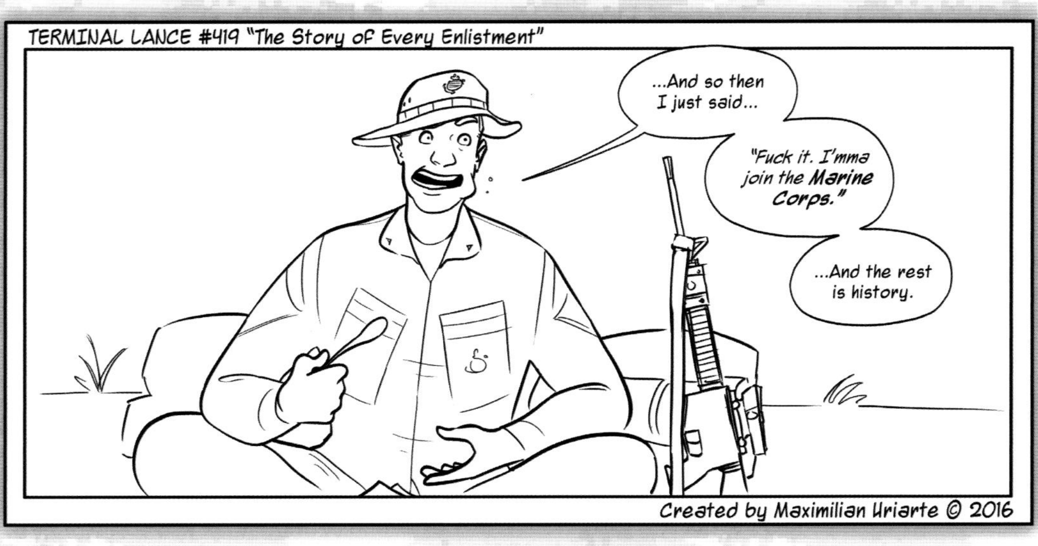
TERMINAL LANCE #419 "The Story of Every Enlistment"
...And so then I just said...
"Fuck it. I'mma join the **Marine Corps.**"
...And the rest is history.
Created by Maximilian Uriarte © 2016

419 "The Story of Every Enlistment"

If you sat down with any Marine in the Corps and asked him the story of how he came to enlist, you would surely be met with the ubiquitous sentence:

"Fuck it, I'mma join the Marine Corps."

This is the story of every Marine, past, present, and future. I realized this as I was chatting with another Marine the other day on how he ended up in the Corps. Those were his exact words, and usually are the exact words of every Marine you'll ever talk to about it.

Enlisting is an intensely personal experience, and it's one that you must come to terms with on your own. Of course, there's the typically cliché responses like "I wanted to serve my country," and "Bitches love Marines," but I would argue that most Marines enter into the Corps as part of a much more intense, personal journey. There's much mental deliberation and anxiety involved in the decision to talk to a recruiter, but eventually, everyone always comes to the same conclusion . . .

Fuck it, I'mma join the Marine Corps.

The rest is history.

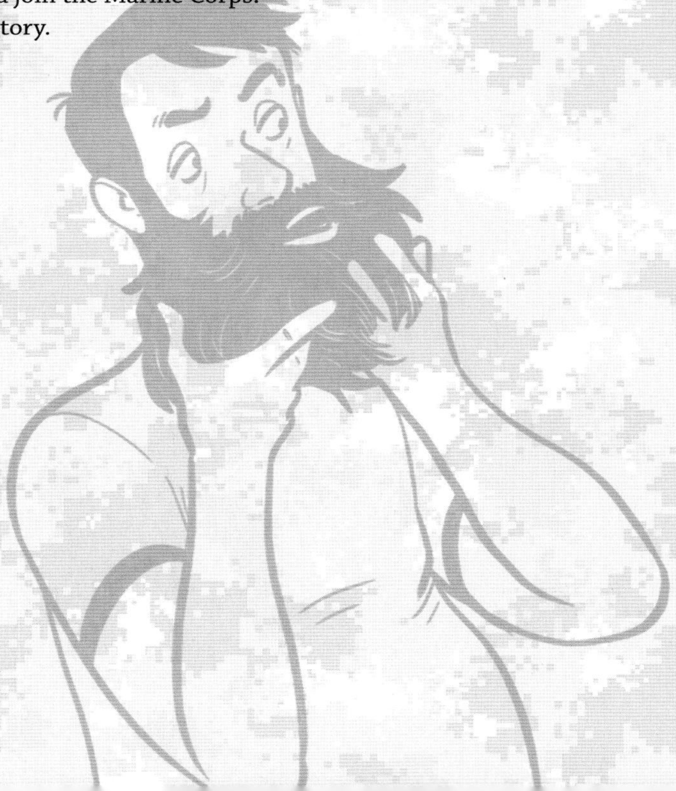

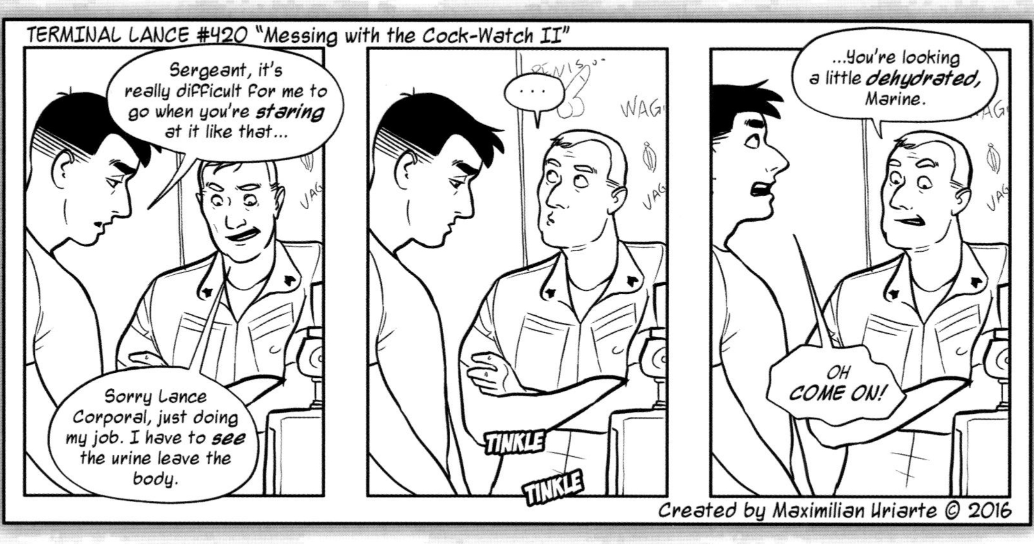
TERMINAL LANCE #420 "Messing with the Cock-Watch II"
Sergeant, it's really difficult for me to go when you're *staring* at it like that...
Sorry Lance Corporal, just doing my job. I have to *see* the urine leave the body.
. . .
TINKLE
TINKLE
...You're looking a little *dehydrated,* Marine.
OH COME ON!
Created by Maximilian Uriarte © 2016

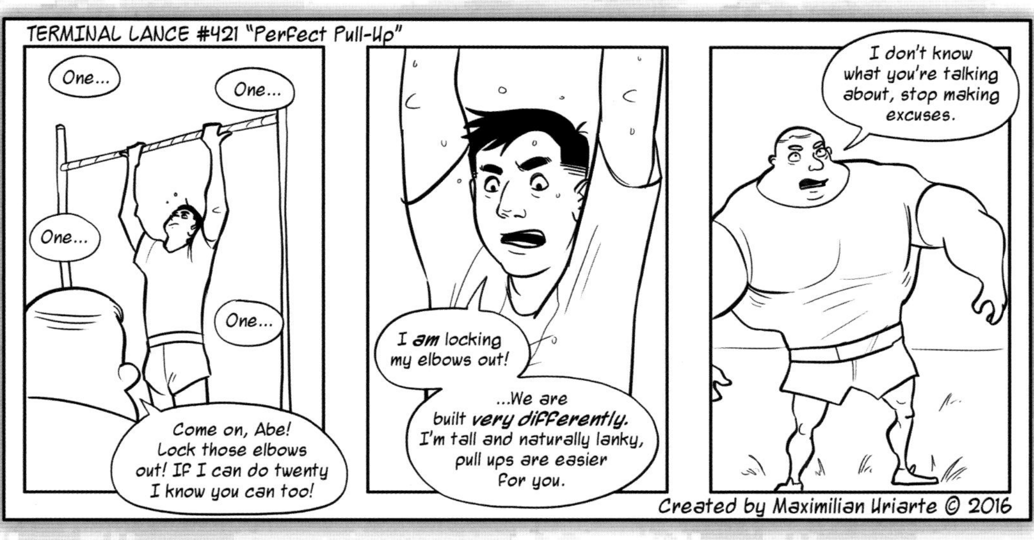
TERMINAL LANCE #421 "Perfect Pull-Up"
One...
One...
One...
One...
Come on, Abe! Lock those elbows out! If I can do twenty I know you can too!
I *am* locking my elbows out!
...We are built *very differently.* I'm tall and naturally lanky, pull ups are easier for you.
I don't know what you're talking about, stop making excuses.
Created by Maximilian Uriarte © 2016

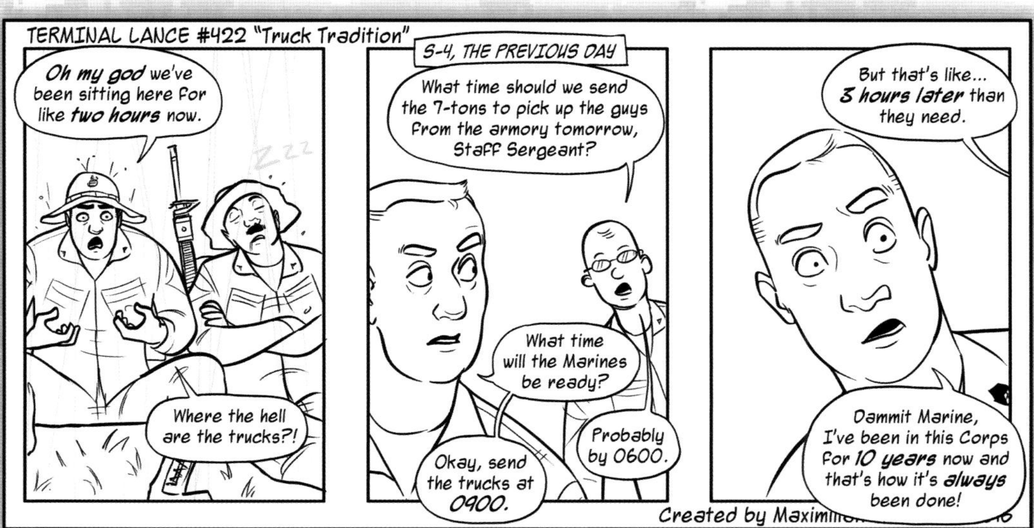
TERMINAL LANCE #422 "Truck Tradition"
Oh my god we've been sitting here for like *two hours* now.
Z z z
Where the hell are the trucks?!
S-4, THE PREVIOUS DAY
What time should we send the 7-tons to pick up the guys from the armory tomorrow, Staff Sergeant?
What time will the Marines be ready?
Probably by 0600.
Okay, send the trucks at *0900.*
But that's like... *3 hours later* than they need.
Dammit Marine, I've been in this Corps for *10 years* now and that's how it's *always* been done!
Created by Maximili

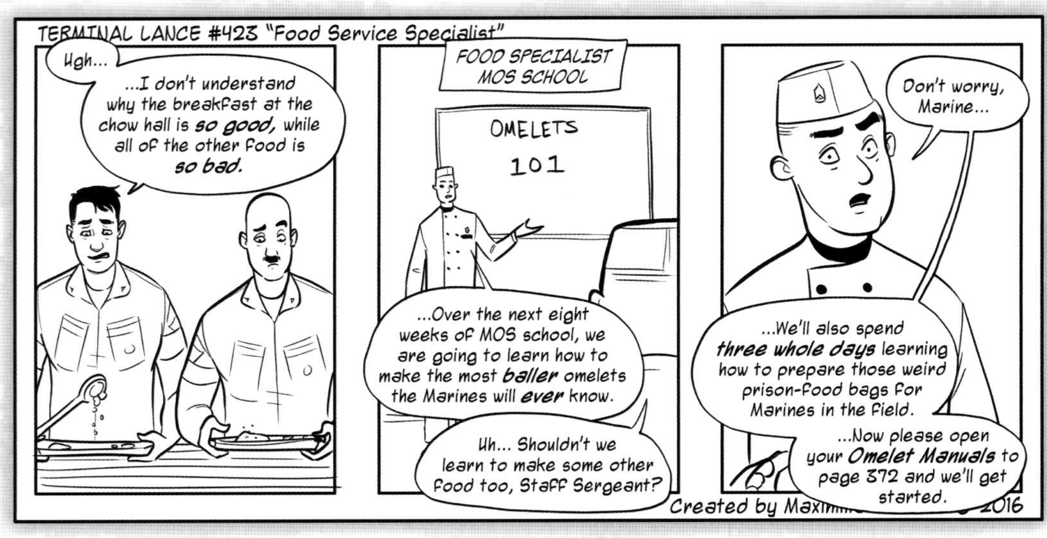
TERMINAL LANCE #423 "Food Service Specialist"
Ugh...
...I don't understand why the breakfast at the chow hall is so good, while all of the other food is so bad.
FOOD SPECIALIST MOS SCHOOL
OMELETS 101
...Over the next eight weeks of MOS school, we are going to learn how to make the most baller omelets the Marines will ever know.
Uh... Shouldn't we learn to make some other food too, Staff Sergeant?
Don't worry, Marine...
...We'll also spend three whole days learning how to prepare those weird prison-food bags for Marines in the field.
...Now please open your Omelet Manuals to page 372 and we'll get started.
Created by Maxim 2016

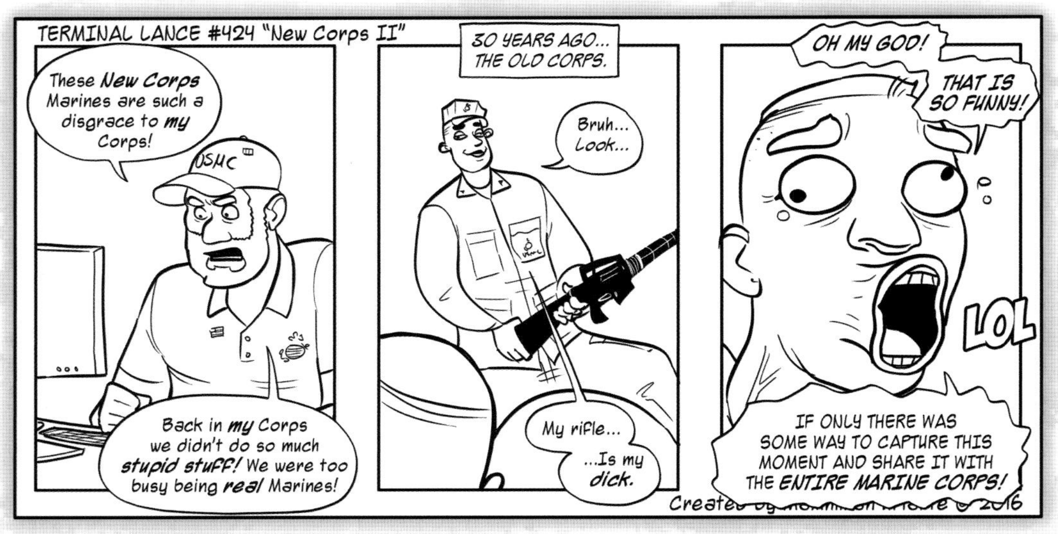
TERMINAL LANCE #424 "New Corps II"
These New Corps Marines are such a disgrace to my Corps!
USMC
Back in my Corps we didn't do so much stupid stuff! We were too busy being real Marines!
30 YEARS AGO... THE OLD CORPS.
Bruh... Look...
My rifle...
...Is my dick.
OH MY GOD!
THAT IS SO FUNNY!
LOL
IF ONLY THERE WAS SOME WAY TO CAPTURE THIS MOMENT AND SHARE IT WITH THE ENTIRE MARINE CORPS!
2016

424 "New Corps II"

I find a lot of things frustrating, but one of the most annoying things I come across while managing this monstrosity of a comic strip and social media page are the "Old Corps" guys who just can't stand all of the shenanigans coming from these "New Corps" Marines. Back in their Corps, they were too busy getting into fistfights with body-building hookers, hiking over seven hundred miles each week, and just generally being real Marines (during peacetime no less) to engage in such degrading behavior to their beloved Corps.

Unfortunately for them, it's not their Corps anymore.

Culture changes—even the culture of the Marine Corps. But I'd actually argue that the culture hasn't changed much at all. The main thing that has changed is the advent of portable cameras connected to a near limitless social media environment. The silliness of the everyday military life is no longer relegated to the dark corners of the smoke pit or the back of the squad bay. It is on full display, instantly accessible to the public and the world.

Though, to be honest, what I find even more annoying are the people (generally the same people) that send me photos of Marines being normal fucking people and expecting me to "put them on blast" in front of hundreds of thousands. Who gives a shit if some nineteen-year-old kid takes a selfie in his uniform in front of a mirror? I know I don't, and there's literally zero precedence to suggest that kid should be shamed in front of the entire Marine Corps.

If anything, we should be encouraging stupid behavior among Marines.

War is awful. These silly, fleeting moments are the only thing that keeps us going most of the time. They're the only thing that keeps us human.

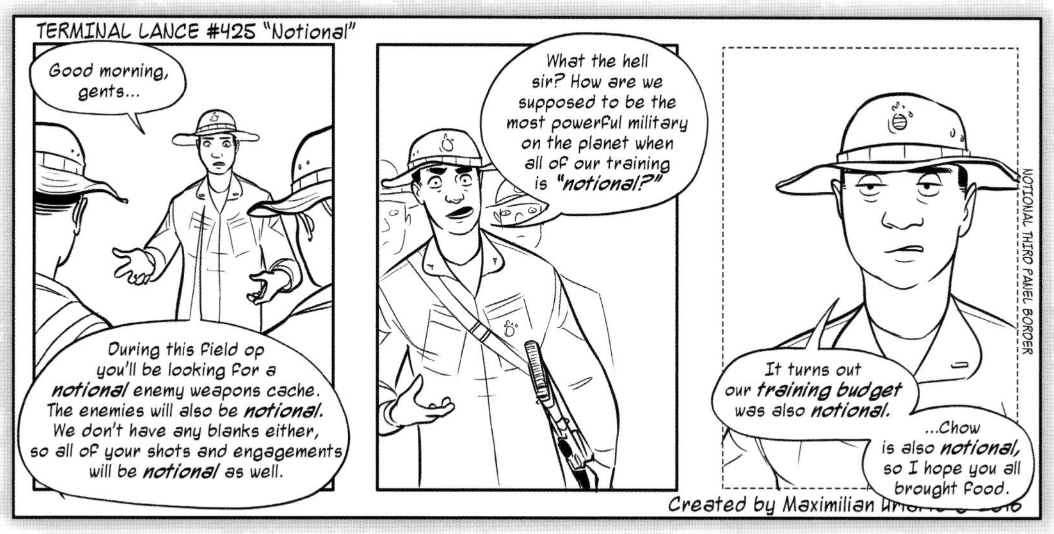
TERMINAL LANCE #425 "Notional"
Good morning, gents...
During this field op you'll be looking for a *notional* enemy weapons cache. The enemies will also be *notional.* We don't have any blanks either, so all of your shots and engagements will be *notional* as well.
What the hell sir? How are we supposed to be the most powerful military on the planet when all of our training is *"notional?"*
NOTIONAL THIRD PANEL BORDER
It turns out our *training budget* was also *notional.*
...Chow is also *notional,* so I hope you all brought food.
Created by Maximilian

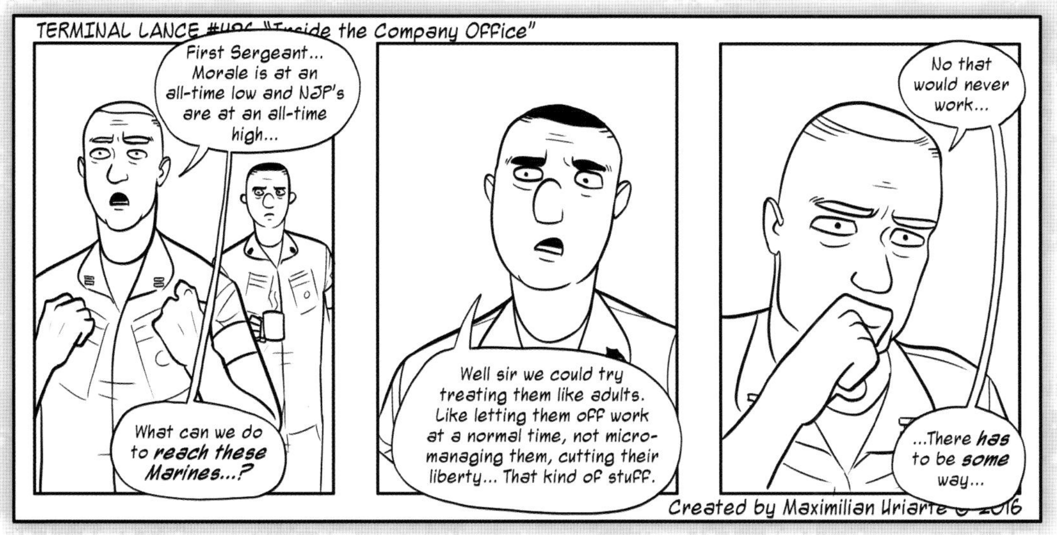
TERMINAL LANCE
the Company Office"
First Sergeant... Morale is at an all-time low and NJP's are at an all-time high...
What can we do to *reach these Marines...?*
Well sir we could try treating them like adults. Like letting them off work at a normal time, not micro-managing them, cutting their liberty... That kind of stuff.
No that would never work...
...There *has* to be *some* way...
Created by Maximilian Uriarte

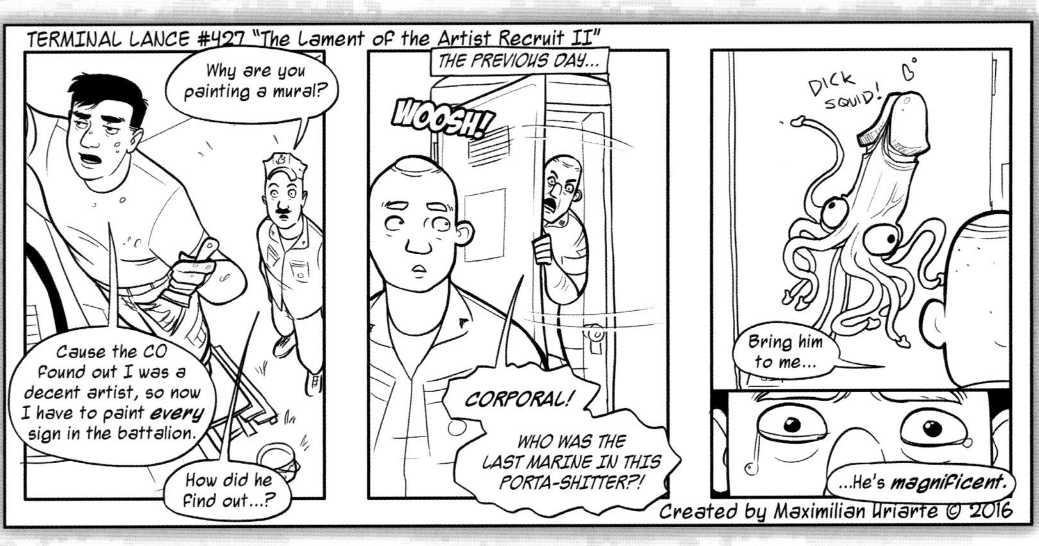
TERMINAL LANCE #427 "The Lament of the Artist Recruit II"
Why are you painting a mural?
Cause the CO found out I was a decent artist, so now I have to paint **every** sign in the battalion.
How did he find out...?
THE PREVIOUS DAY...
WOOSH!
CORPORAL!
WHO WAS THE LAST MARINE IN THIS PORTA-SHITTER?!
DICK SQUID!
Bring him to me...
...He's ***magnificent.***
Created by Maximilian Uriarte © 2016

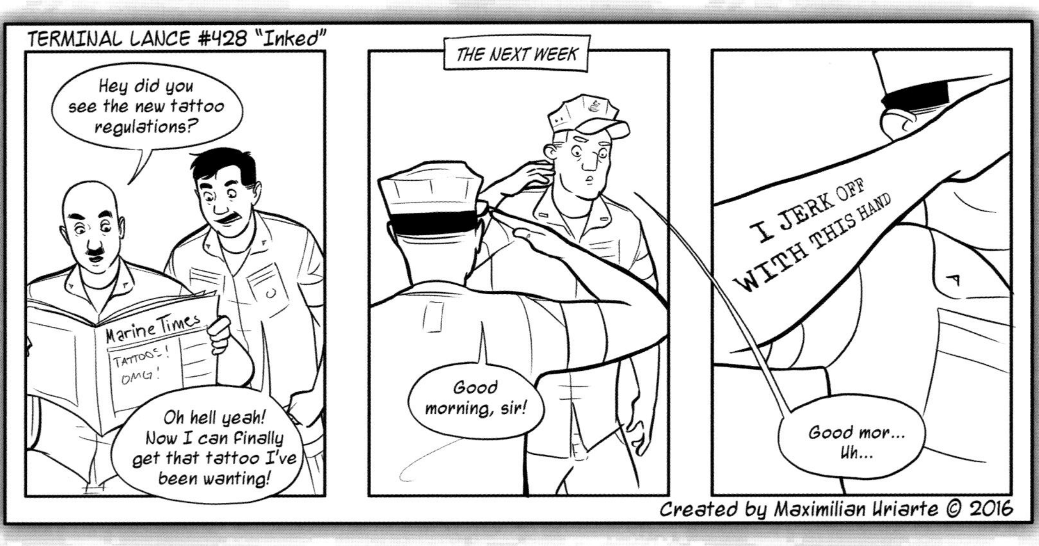
TERMINAL LANCE #428 "Inked"
Hey did you see the new tattoo regulations?
Marine Times
TATTOOS! OMG!
Oh hell yeah! Now I can finally get that tattoo I've been wanting!
THE NEXT WEEK
Good morning, sir!
I JERK OFF WITH THIS HAND
Good mor... Uh...
Created by Maximilian Uriarte © 2016

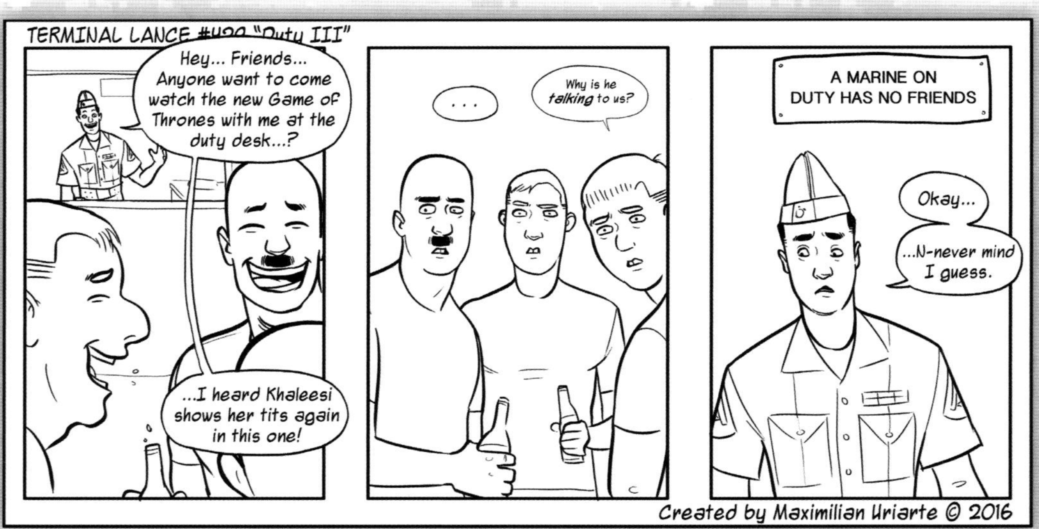
TERMINAL LANCE #429 "Duty III"
Hey... Friends... Anyone want to come watch the new Game of Thrones with me at the duty desk...?
...I heard Khaleesi shows her tits again in this one!
. . .
Why is he *talking* to us?
A MARINE ON DUTY HAS NO FRIENDS
Okay...
...N-never mind I guess.
Created by Maximilian Uriarte © 2016

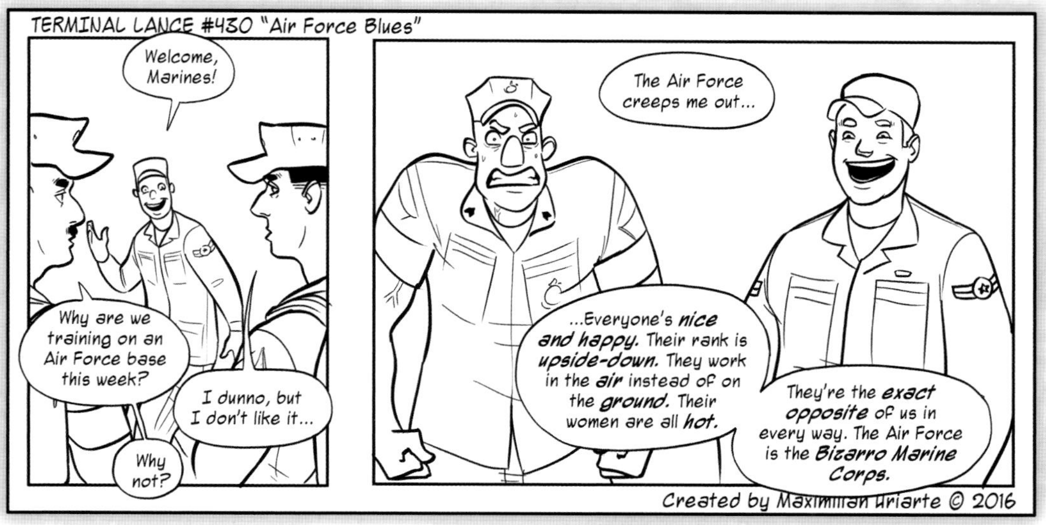
TERMINAL LANCE #430 "Air Force Blues"
Welcome, Marines!
Why are we training on an Air Force base this week?
I dunno, but I don't like it...
Why not?
The Air Force creeps me out...
...Everyone's nice and happy. Their rank is upside-down. They work in the air instead of on the ground. Their women are all hot.
They're the exact opposite of us in every way. The Air Force is the Bizarro Marine Corps.
Created by Maximilian Uriarte © 2016

430 "Air Force Blues"

The Air Force is a weird branch of the military.

Semantically, if you were to define "military" by things that are generally "military," like fitness, shooting guns, hiking, being a hard ass, etc., I'm not sure if the Air Force would fit. This isn't to say the Air Force isn't important to our national defense—of course they are—but more that it is the military lite. A Diet Military, if you would.

Marines and Airmen are nearly opposites in every conceivable way, as Abe describes in this strip. If it weren't for their largely symbiotic relationship, you could probably say the same things about the Navy and the Corps as well. However, Marines and Navy are like peanut butter and jelly—they stick together.

Ignoring the Coast Guard for a second (lol we usually do), the Air Force is generally the outlier of the military. They're small and mostly keep to themselves, with their culture rarely permeating the popular consciousness. There's nothing wrong with that—it's just their style. They don't tend to make as much noise as Marines or Army in the news, but we love them all the same.

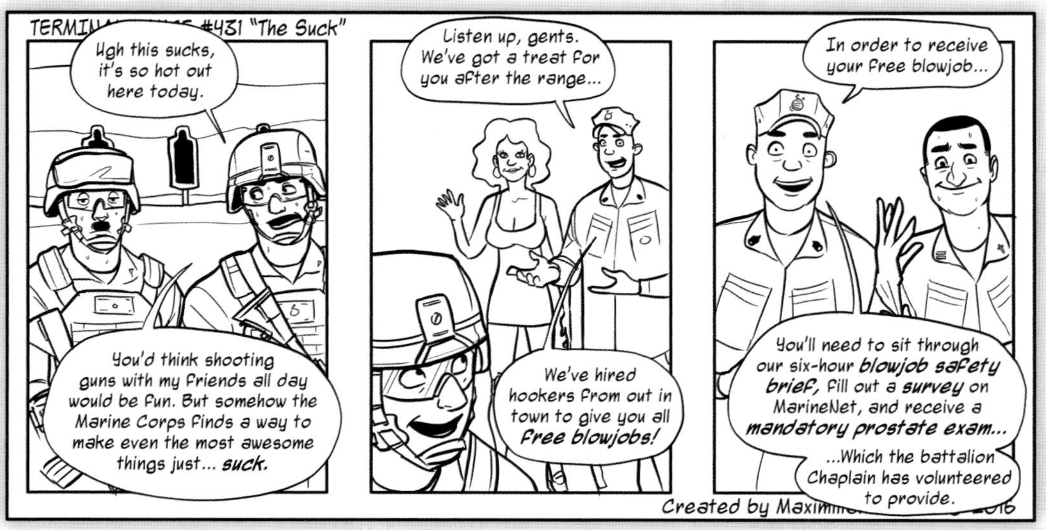
#431 "The Suck"
Ugh this sucks, it's so hot out here today.
You'd think shooting guns with my friends all day would be fun. But somehow the Marine Corps finds a way to make even the most awesome things just... suck.
Listen up, gents. We've got a treat for you after the range...
We've hired hookers from out in town to give you all free blowjobs!
In order to receive your free blowjob...
You'll need to sit through our six-hour blowjob safety brief, fill out a survey on MarineNet, and receive a mandatory prostate exam...
...Which the battalion Chaplain has volunteered to provide.
Created by Maxim

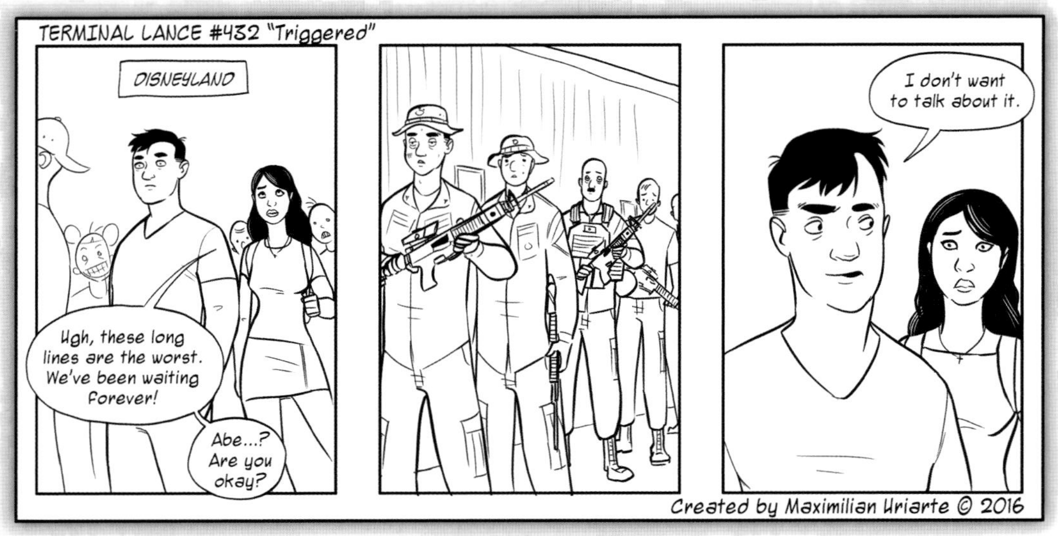
TERMINAL LANCE #432 "Triggered"
DISNEYLAND
Ugh, these long lines are the worst. We've been waiting forever!
Abe...? Are you okay?
I don't want to talk about it.
Created by Maximilian Uriarte © 2016

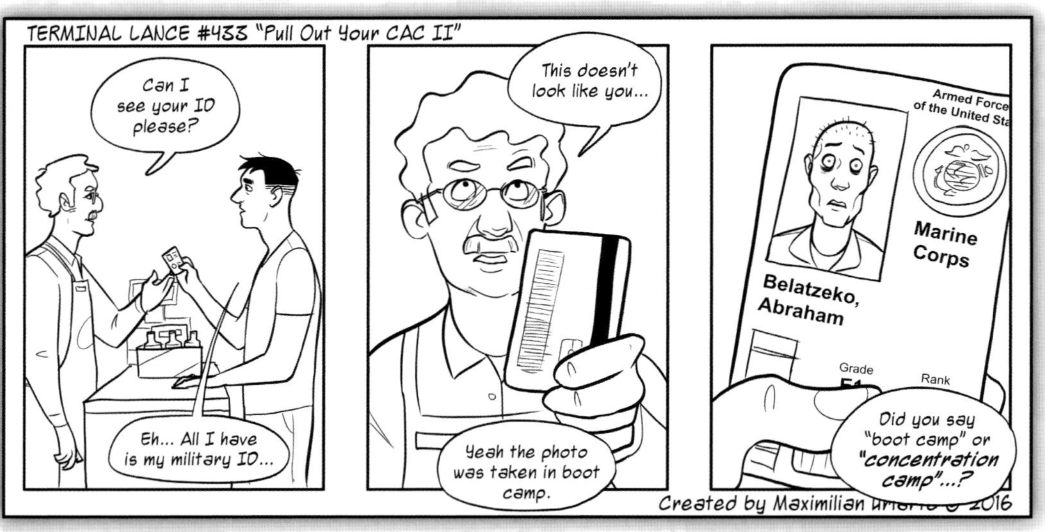
TERMINAL LANCE #433 "Pull Out Your CAC II"
Can I see your ID please?
Eh... All I have is my military ID...
This doesn't look like you...
Yeah the photo was taken in boot camp.
Marine Corps
Belatzeko, Abraham
Grade
Rank
Did you say "boot camp" or "concentration camp"...?

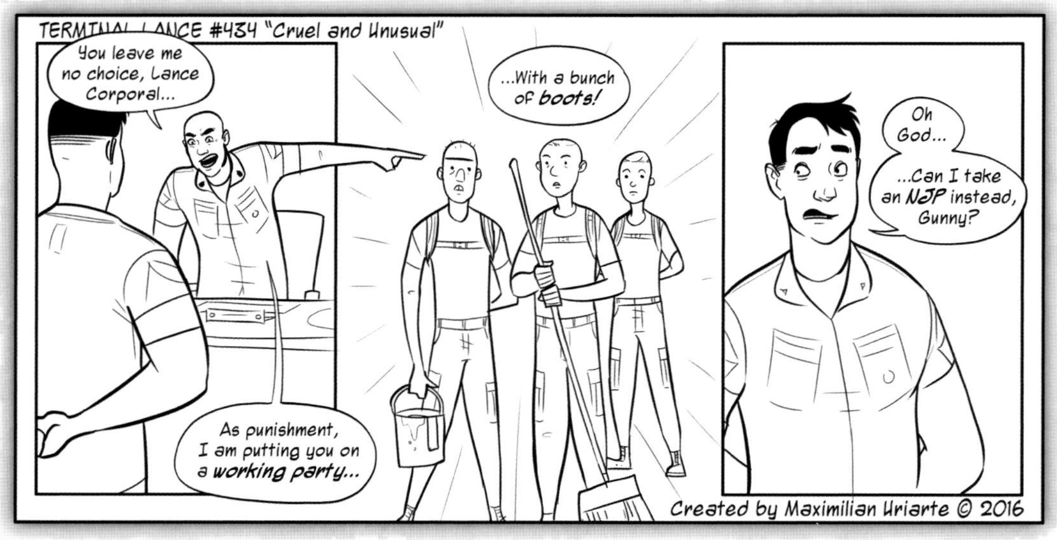
TERMINAL LANCE #434 "Cruel and Unusual"
You leave me no choice, Lance Corporal...
As punishment, I am putting you on a working party...
...With a bunch of boots!
Oh God...
...Can I take an NJP instead, Gunny?
Created by Maximilian Uriarte © 2016

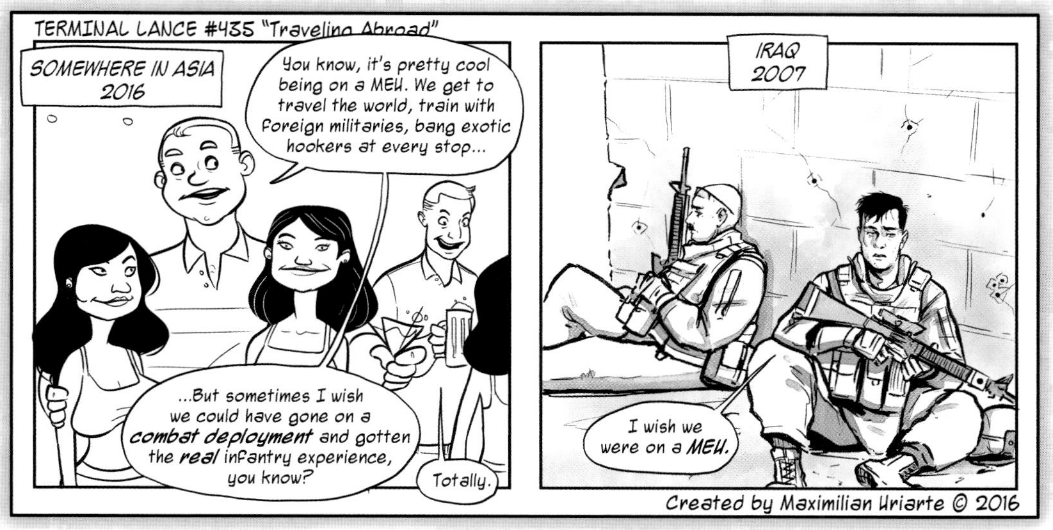
TERMINAL LANCE #435 "Traveling Abroad"
SOMEWHERE IN ASIA 2016
You know, it's pretty cool being on a MEU. We get to travel the world, train with foreign militaries, bang exotic hookers at every stop...
...But sometimes I wish we could have gone on a combat deployment and gotten the real infantry experience, you know?
Totally.
IRAQ 2007
I wish we were on a MEU.
Created by Maximilian Uriarte © 2016

435 "Traveling Abroad"

I've often heard it said that a bitching Marine is a happy Marine.

Marines definitely love to bitch. In the case of an MEU deployment, Marines often find themselves longing for the "action" of a proper combat deployment. While it is true that they are forced to spend some miserable hours on a big gray boat, at least they get to stop all over the world and check out all kinds of interesting foreign sights and sounds.

You know what foreign sights and sounds you see in Iraq? Women in burkas and gunshots. That's basically it. Shit sucks. I would rather have been on the MEU.

Of course, the grass is always greener. You can't blame Marines for wanting to experience the whole combat deployment thing—it's what they're brought up to do. When I enlisted back in 2006, I knew for sure that I would get sent to the Middle East, one way or another. Ten years later? The prospects of such adventures aren't as foretold as they once were. This is essentially peacetime, and combat is nowhere to be seen for most of the Corps.

This has been an interesting transition to witness. When I started back in 2010, most Marines were like me: two-pump chumps that were largely disillusioned and disgruntled. Today's active duty Marine Corps is undoubtedly different than the one that I left behind, and the last of the Lance Corporal combat veterans are most likely out or soon to be.

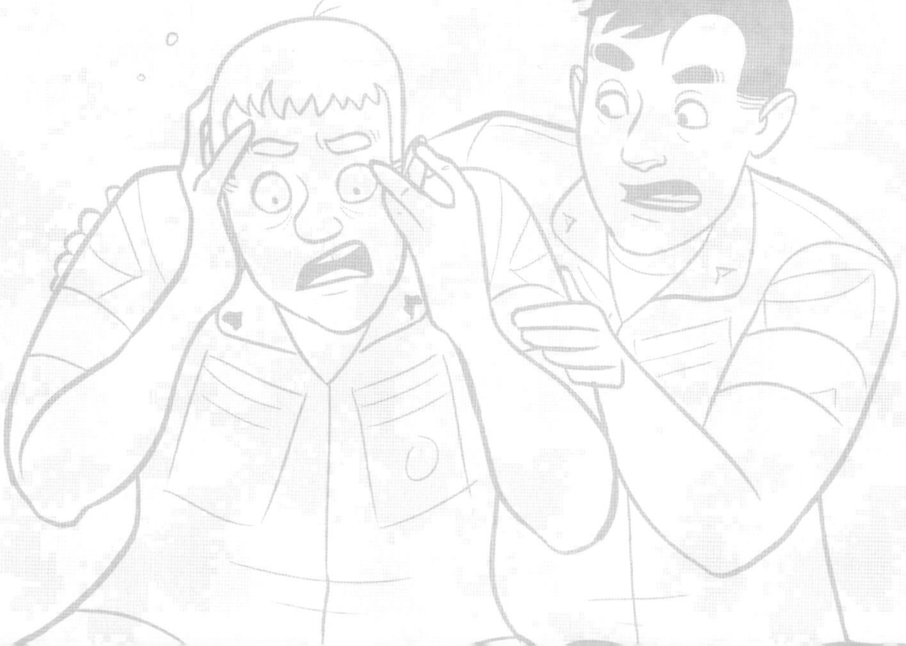

TERMINAL LANCE #436 "Fraud, Waste, and Abuse"

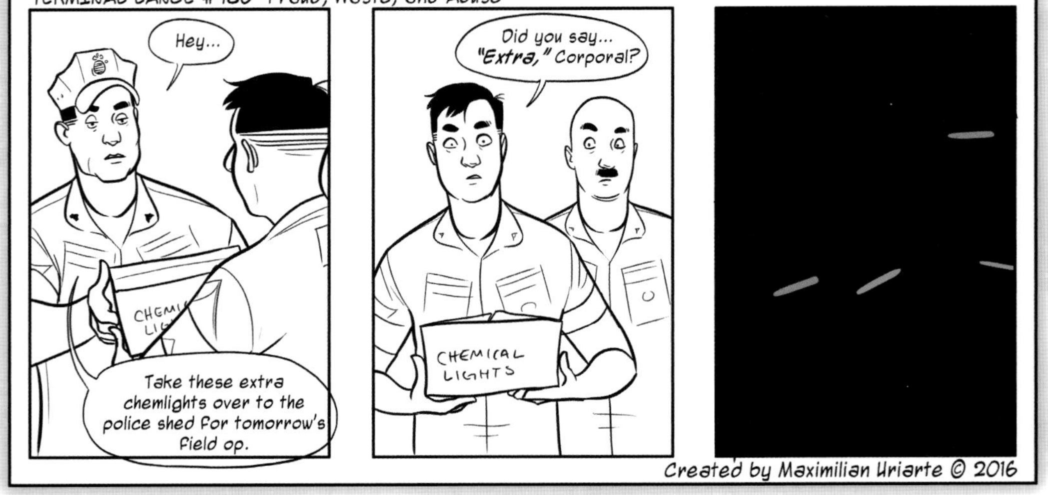
Hey...
Take these extra chemlights over to the police shed for tomorrow's field op.
CHEMICAL LIGHTS
Did you say... "Extra," Corporal?
CHEMICAL LIGHTS
Created by Maximilian Uriarte © 2016

TERMINAL LANCE #437 "Warranted"

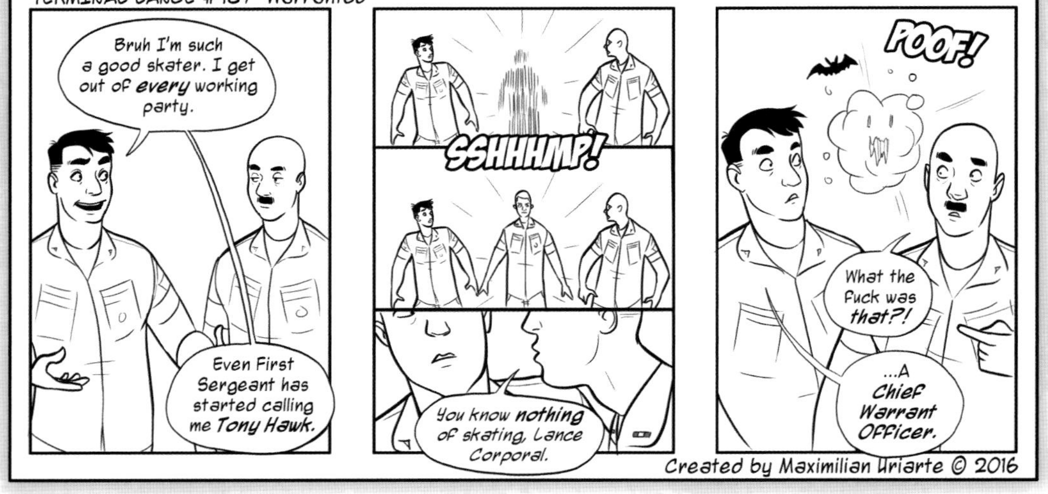
Bruh I'm such a good skater. I get out of every working party.
Even First Sergeant has started calling me Tony Hawk.
SSHHHMP!
You know nothing of skating, Lance Corporal.
POOF!
What the fuck was that?!
...A Chief Warrant Officer.
Created by Maximilian Uriarte © 2016

TERMINAL LANCE #438 "Swipe Left"

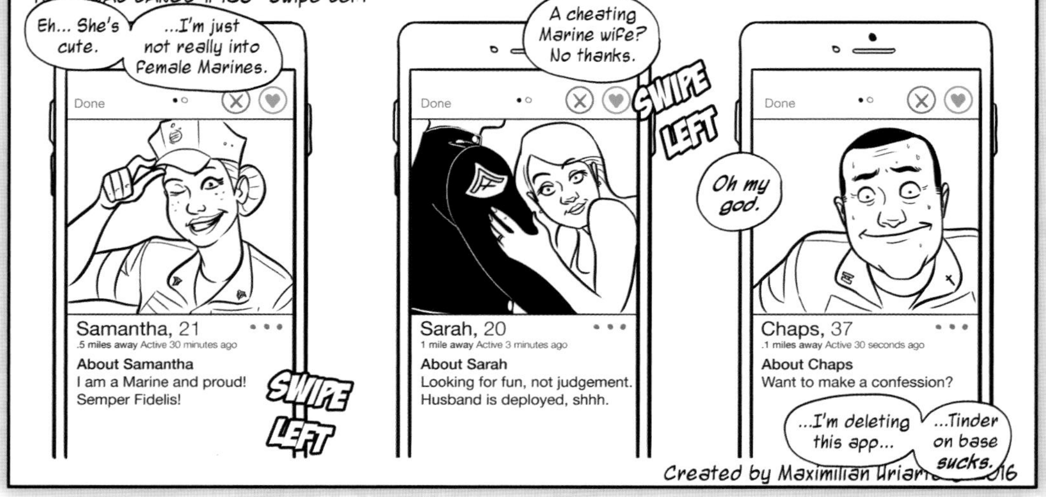
Eh... She's cute.
...I'm just not really into female Marines.
Done
Samantha, 21
.5 miles away Active 30 minutes ago
About Samantha
I am a Marine and proud! Semper Fidelis!
SWIPE LEFT
A cheating Marine wife? No thanks.
Done
Sarah, 20
1 mile away Active 3 minutes ago
About Sarah
Looking for fun, not judgement. Husband is deployed, shhh.
SWIPE LEFT
Oh my god.
Done
Chaps, 37
.1 miles away Active 30 seconds ago
About Chaps
Want to make a confession?
...I'm deleting this app...
...Tinder on base sucks.
Created by Maximilian Uriarte © 2016

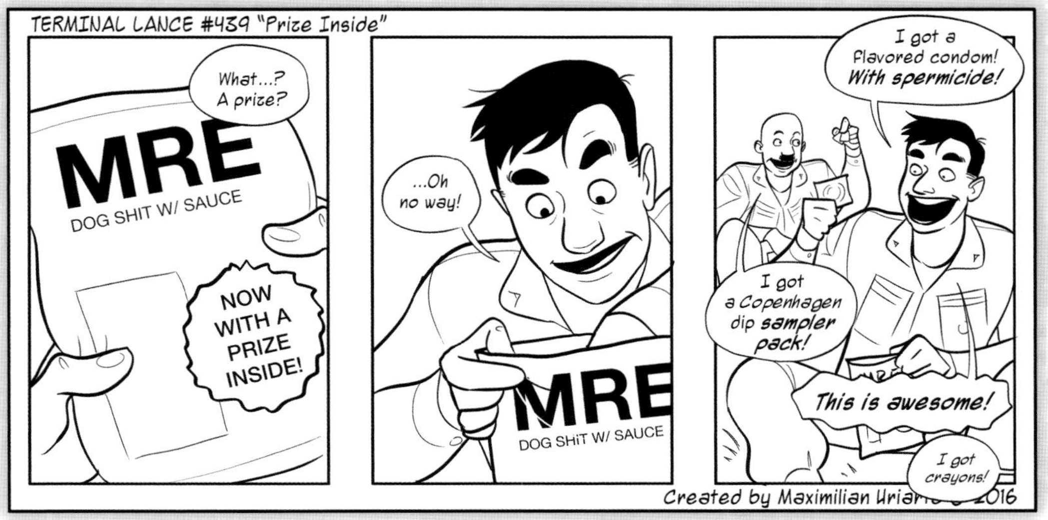
TERMINAL LANCE #439 "Prize Inside"
What...? A prize?
MRE
DOG SHIT W/ SAUCE
NOW WITH A PRIZE INSIDE!
...Oh no way!
MRE
DOG SHiT W/ SAUCE
I got a flavored condom! With spermicide!
I got a Copenhagen dip sampler pack!
This is awesome!
I got crayons!
Created by Maximilian Uriarte © 2016

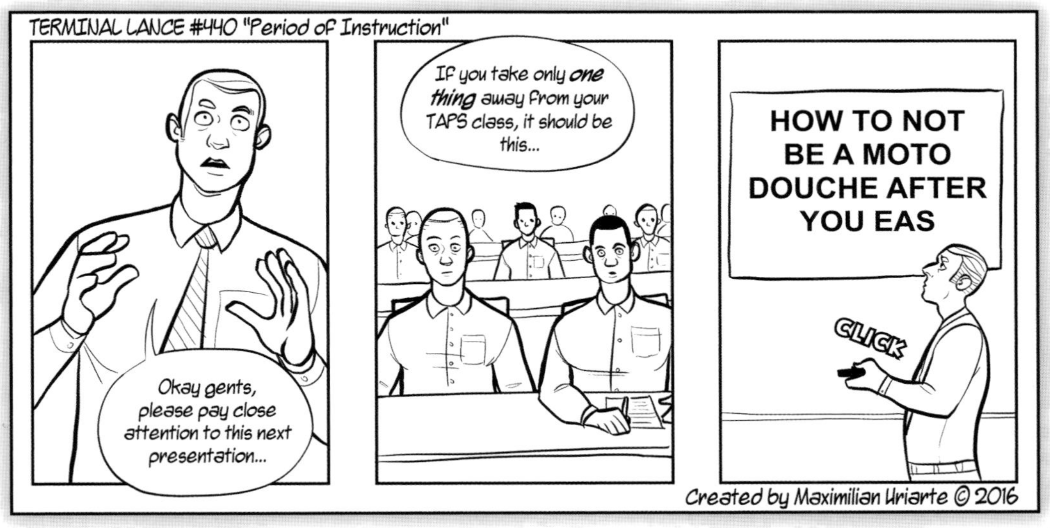
TERMINAL LANCE #440 "Period of Instruction"
Okay gents, please pay close attention to this next presentation...
If you take only one thing away from your TAPS class, it should be this...
HOW TO NOT BE A MOTO DOUCHE AFTER YOU EAS
CLICK
Created by Maximilian Uriarte © 2016

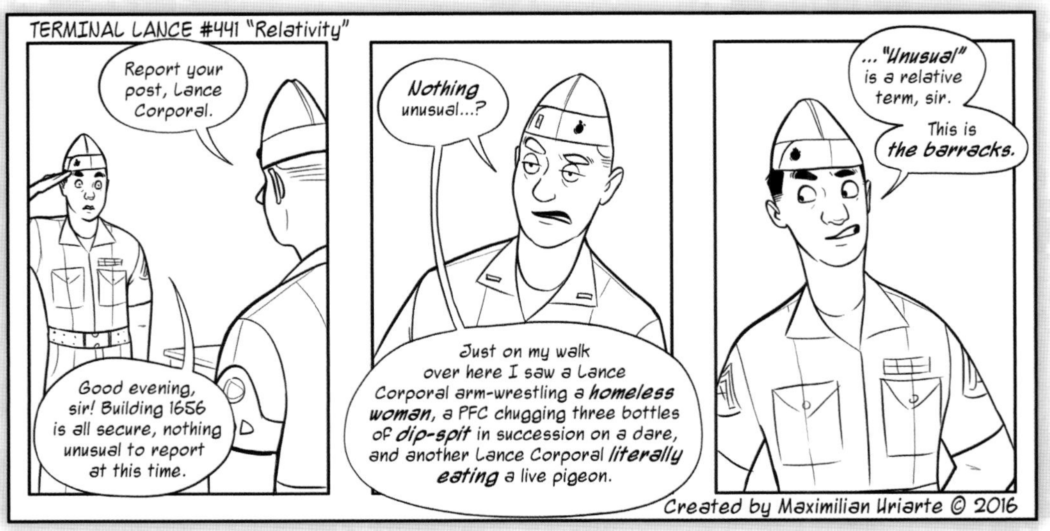
TERMINAL LANCE #441 "Relativity"
Report your post, Lance Corporal.
Good evening, sir! Building 1656 is all secure, nothing unusual to report at this time.
Nothing unusual...?
Just on my walk over here I saw a Lance Corporal arm-wrestling a homeless woman, a PFC chugging three bottles of dip-spit in succession on a dare, and another Lance Corporal literally eating a live pigeon.
..."Unusual" is a relative term, sir.
This is the barracks.
Created by Maximilian Uriarte © 2016

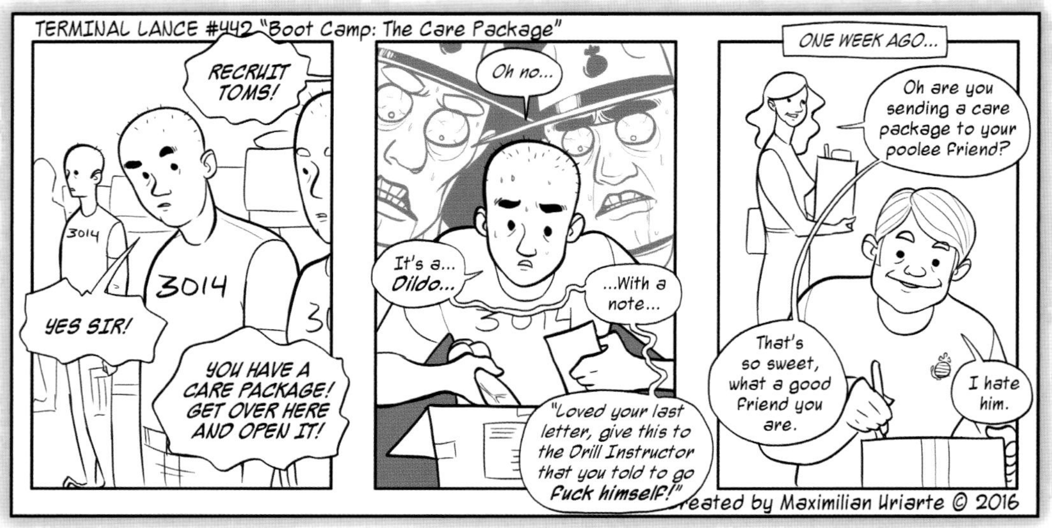
TERMINAL LANCE #442 "Boot Camp: The Care Package"
RECRUIT TOMS!
YES SIR!
YOU HAVE A CARE PACKAGE! GET OVER HERE AND OPEN IT!
3014
Oh no...
It's a... Dildo...
...With a note...
"Loved your last letter, give this to the Drill Instructor that you told to go Fuck himself!"
ONE WEEK AGO...
Oh are you sending a care package to your poolee friend?
That's so sweet, what a good friend you are.
I hate him.
Created by Maximilian Uriarte © 2016

442 "Boot Camp: The Care Package"

Boot camp is a shitty three months.

As if you don't have enough to worry about with sweaty, angry men yelling at you twenty-four hours a day, you never know what might be lurking in a box some good-intentioned family member or friend sent your way.

Comedian Sarah Silverman panicked once after realizing she may have made a grave mistake for her recruit nephew.

> **Sarah Silverman** @SarahKSilverman · 12m
> **@USMC** please help! I sent a care package to my nephew at Parris Island & now am worried he'll be in trouble for it. I'm an idiot. Please dm

Of course, in reality he will most likely be fine, assuming she didn't send a box of dildos (possible, given the nature of her comedy). Sadly though, her sudden panic is actually a result of reading headlines surrounding the abuse scandals in Parris Island Recruit Depot. I've stayed away from the subject on *Terminal Lance,* for the most part because I hate reading the comments. Hard-charging keyboard warriors act as if being thrown into a dryer is a regular occurrence that all recruits must suffer (it's not).

Even without such flagrant abuse, boot camp is arduous and mostly awful. I've said it before, but I would much rather go back to Iraq than do another three months at MCRD being treated like a recruit. I feel the worst for those poor kids that spend months in medical recovery, where they're treated like recruits for even longer.

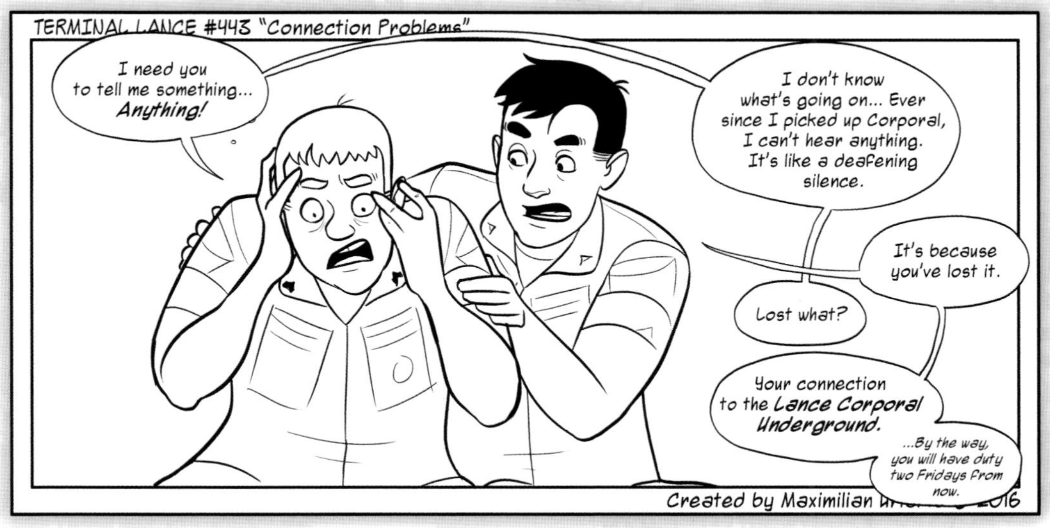
TERMINAL LANCE #443 "Connection Problems"
I need you to tell me something... Anything!
I don't know what's going on... Ever since I picked up Corporal, I can't hear anything. It's like a deafening silence.
It's because you've lost it.
Lost what?
Your connection to the Lance Corporal Underground.
...By the way, you will have duty two Fridays from now.
Created by Maximilian … 2016

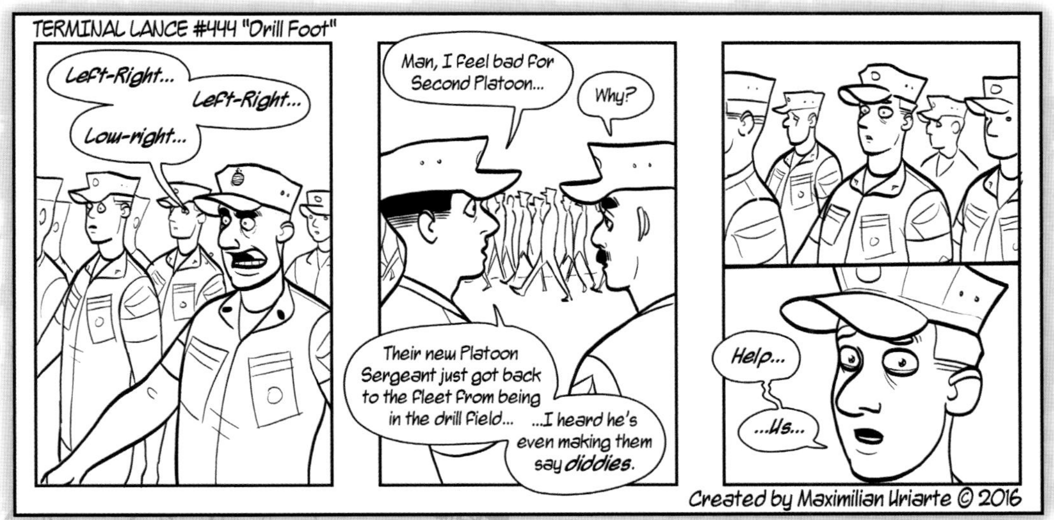
TERMINAL LANCE #444 "Drill Foot"
Left-Right...
Left-Right...
Low-right...
Man, I feel bad for Second Platoon...
Why?
Their new Platoon Sergeant just got back to the fleet from being in the drill field...
...I heard he's even making them say diddies.
Help...
...Us...
Created by Maximilian Uriarte © 2016

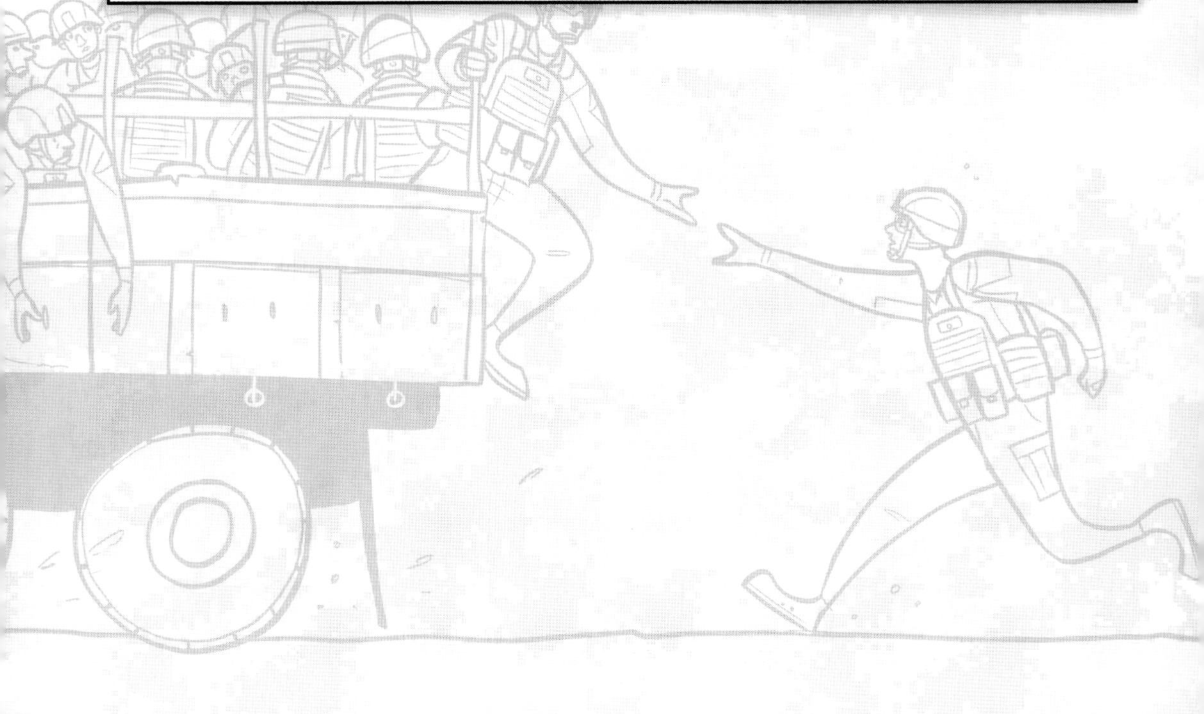

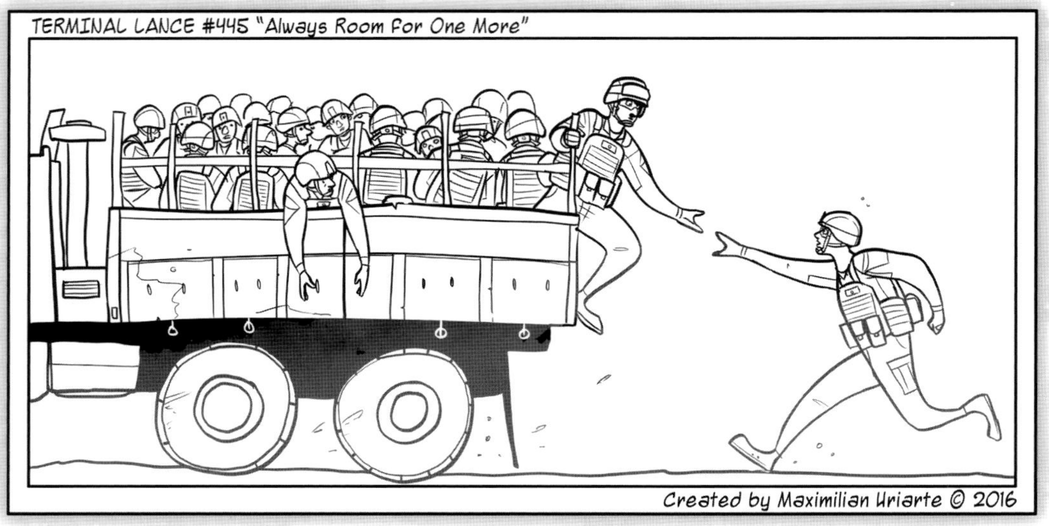
TERMINAL LANCE #445 "Always Room For One More"
Created by Maximilian Uriarte © 2016

445 "Always Room For One More"

Marines can always find a way to fit one more.

Whether it's one more Marine in the back of the 7-ton or one more piece of gear stuffed into their already-bursting main pack for the field, Marines will always find a way to fit one more. Some say this is a supernatural ability possessed by anyone that has stepped foot on the yellow footprints of destiny. As long as any Marine says to themselves out loud *"There's always room for one more,"* you will find yourself able to fit just about anything anywhere.

Ahem.

Anyway, this is a simple strip but I wanted to do something that would kind of lighten the mood. For all of the bullshit in the world, I take comfort in knowing that Marines never change. This, above all else, continues to make Marines my favorite people on the planet.

I get emails and messages from Marines all the time, some as old as my parents and others as young as my niece, saying that no matter when they served, they reckon that after reading my comic they're glad to see that the Marine Corps hasn't changed a bit.

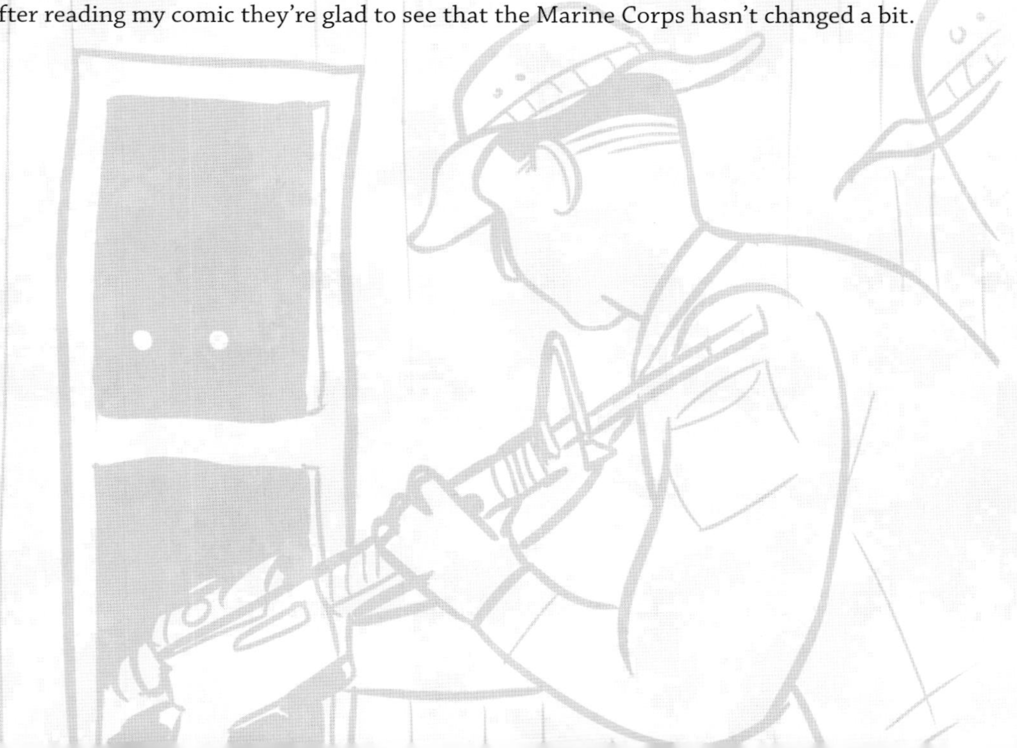

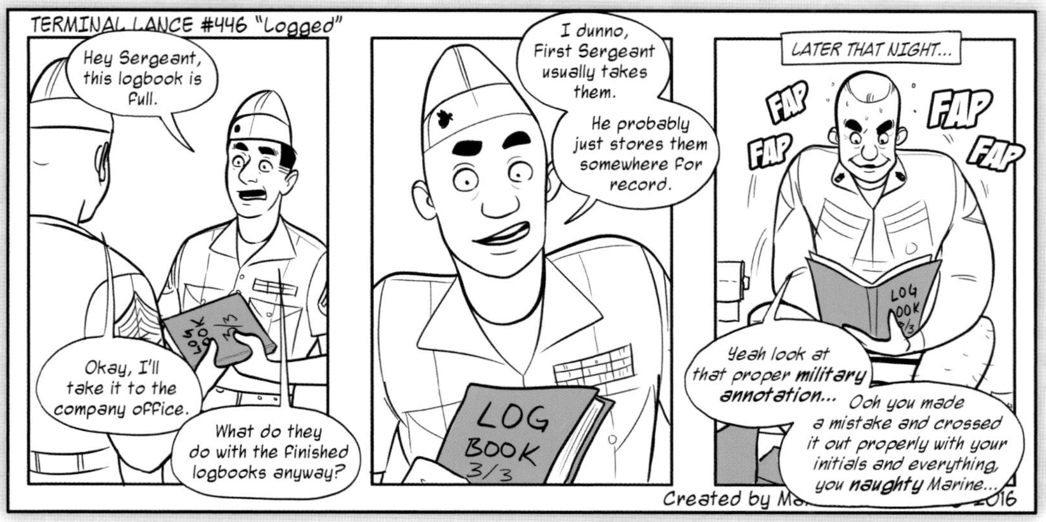
TERMINAL LANCE #446 "Logged"
Hey Sergeant, this logbook is full.
Okay, I'll take it to the company office.
What do they do with the finished logbooks anyway?
LOG BOOK 3/3
I dunno, First Sergeant usually takes them.
He probably just stores them somewhere for record.
LOG BOOK 3/3
LATER THAT NIGHT...
FAP
FAP
FAP
FAP
Yeah look at that proper military annotation...
Ooh you made a mistake and crossed it out properly with your initials and everything, you naughty Marine...

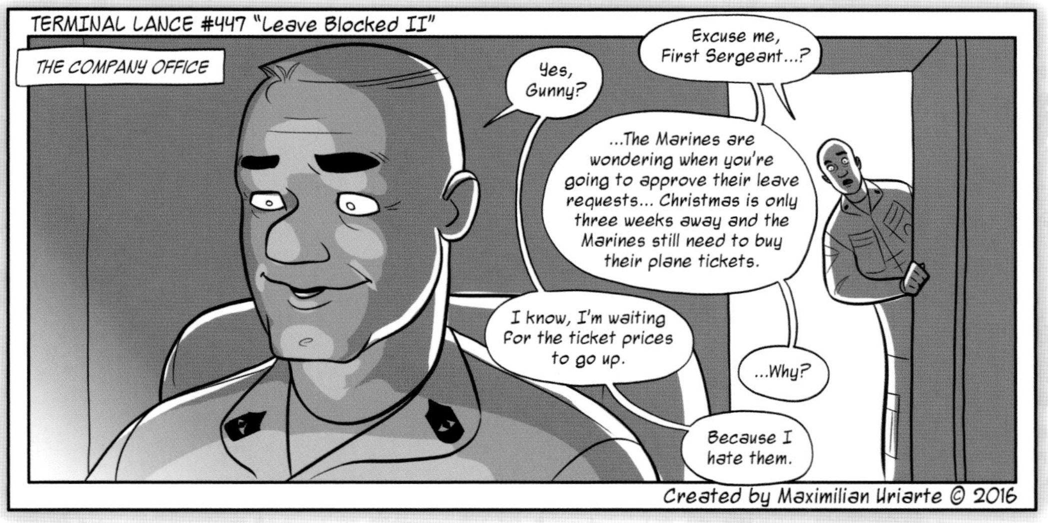
TERMINAL LANCE #447 "Leave Blocked II"
THE COMPANY OFFICE
Excuse me, First Sergeant...?
Yes, Gunny?
...The Marines are wondering when you're going to approve their leave requests... Christmas is only three weeks away and the Marines still need to buy their plane tickets.
I know, I'm waiting for the ticket prices to go up.
...Why?
Because I hate them.
Created by Maximilian Uriarte © 2016

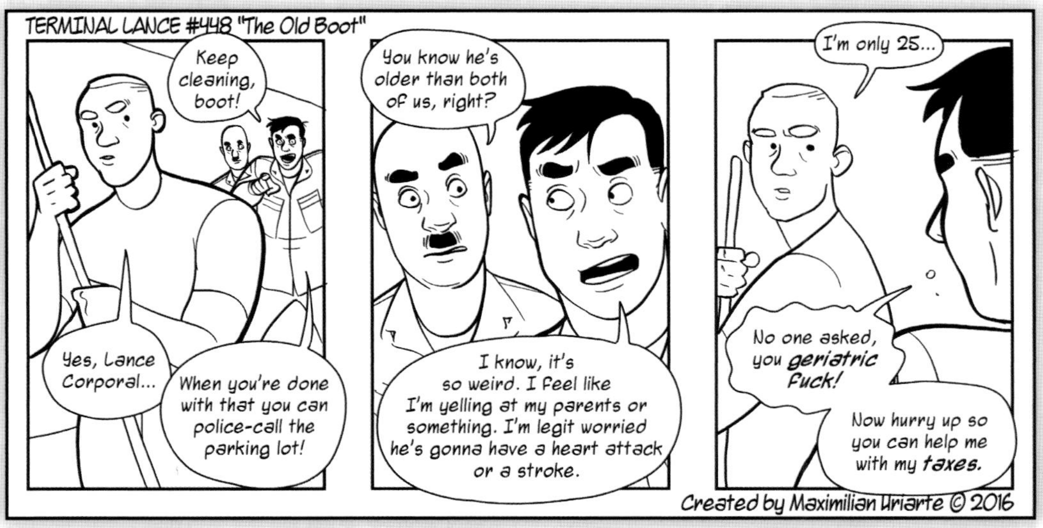
TERMINAL LANCE #448 "The Old Boot"
Keep cleaning, boot!
Yes, Lance Corporal...
When you're done with that you can police-call the parking lot!
You know he's older than both of us, right?
I know, it's so weird. I feel like I'm yelling at my parents or something. I'm legit worried he's gonna have a heart attack or a stroke.
I'm only 25...
No one asked, you geriatric fuck!
Now hurry up so you can help me with my taxes.
Created by Maximilian Uriarte © 2016

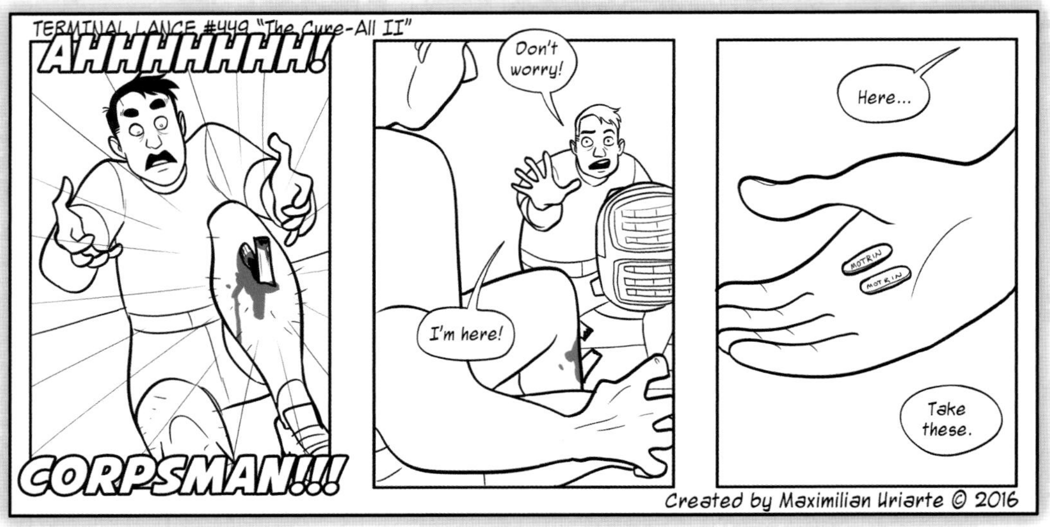
TERMINAL LANCE #449 "The Cure-All II"
AHHHHHHHH!
CORPSMAN!!!
Don't worry!
I'm here!
Here...
MOTRIN
MOTRIN
Take these.
Created by Maximilian Uriarte © 2016

449 "The Cure-All II"

doc pls

Medicine in the military is a funny thing. One great and enticing benefit of serving an enlistment is the free medical.

The bennies bring all the boys to the yard.

Unfortunately, even though we all love Doc, "free medical" usually consists of an all-you-can-eat supply of Motrin and straws to suck it the fuck up. If you do get to BAS and make it through the cadre of bored Corpsmen to the point that you actually get to see a doctor, he'll likely give you a once-over, call you a pussy, and send you on your way.

Upon second thought though, maybe this is how medical care should be for everyone. My wife is British and works at the NHS, so I've gotten quite the earful of stories of lazy people who clog up the emergency room for a common cold to get some free ibuprofen (which is cheap and available over the counter). A random aside, but true nonetheless.

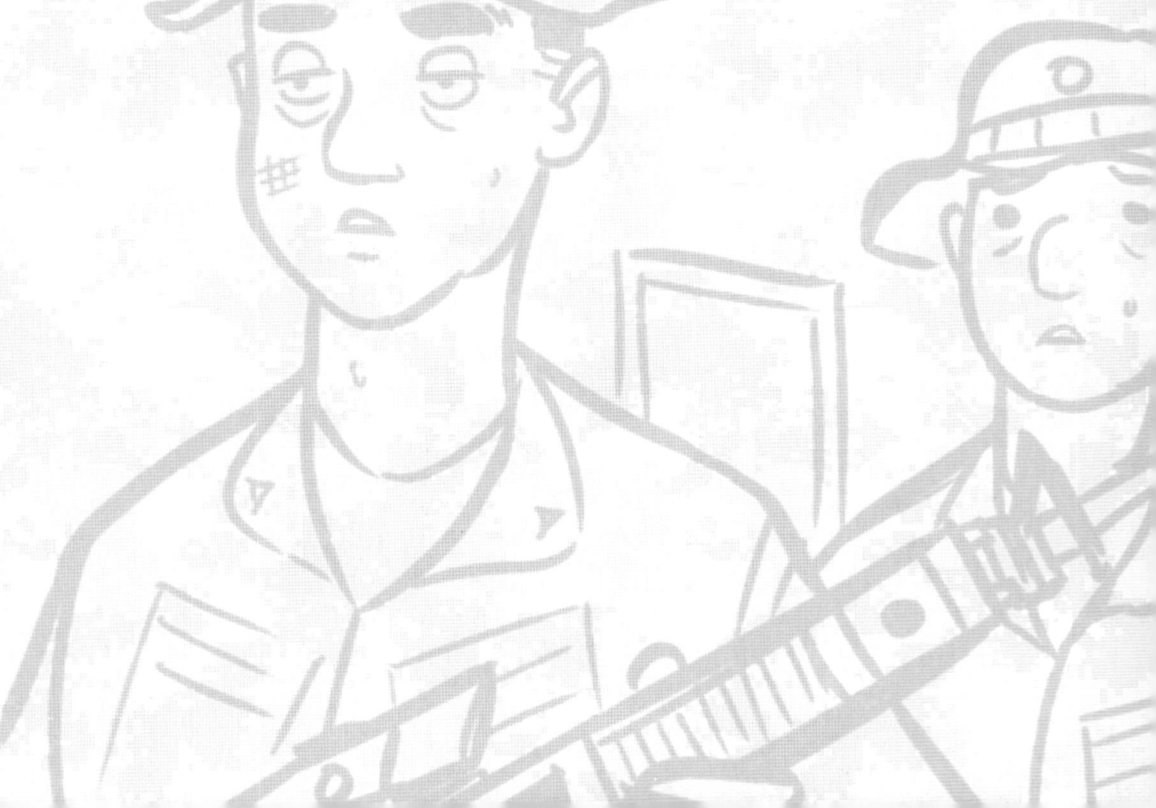

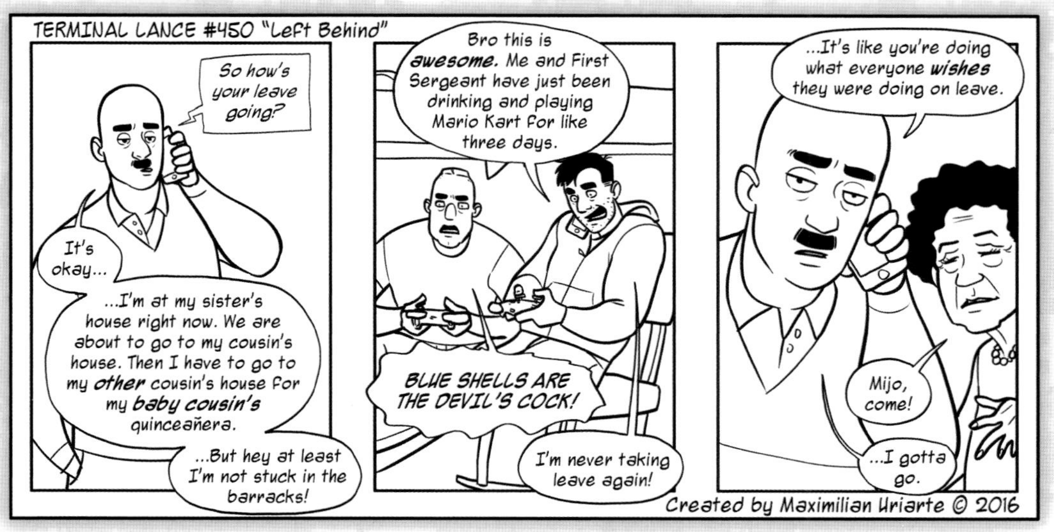
TERMINAL LANCE #450 "Left Behind"
So how's your leave going?
It's okay...
...I'm at my sister's house right now. We are about to go to my cousin's house. Then I have to go to my *other* cousin's house for my *baby cousin's* quinceañera.
...But hey at least I'm not stuck in the barracks!
Bro this is *awesome*. Me and First Sergeant have just been drinking and playing Mario Kart for like three days.
BLUE SHELLS ARE THE DEVIL'S COCK!
I'm never taking leave again!
...It's like you're doing what everyone *wishes* they were doing on leave.
Mijo, come!
...I gotta go.
Created by Maximilian Uriarte © 2016

450 "Left Behind"

When Marines come home on holiday leave, they often find themselves somehow busier than they were before they left. What is supposed to be a relaxing stay at home turns into nonstop family dinners and visits with friends. Sometimes I wished I would have just stayed back at the barracks.

Of course, no one has to take leave, but when you're a twenty-year-old Lance Corporal you don't really think about it like that. Your first thought is always:

I need to get the fuck out of here.

But staying behind isn't all that bad, since basically the entire Marine Corps is out for the holidays. You might have to check in with your First Sergeant every morning, if he's even there, but most likely he isn't going to give any more of a shit than you do about the plan of the day. The only time I ever stayed back in Hawaii for Christmas leave, I ended up with duty once and we had a single formation of about ten guys. First Sergeant didn't give a fuck. We all went back to our rooms and played video games while saving up for that delicious Terminal leave.

And never forget . . . Blue shells *are* the devil's cock.

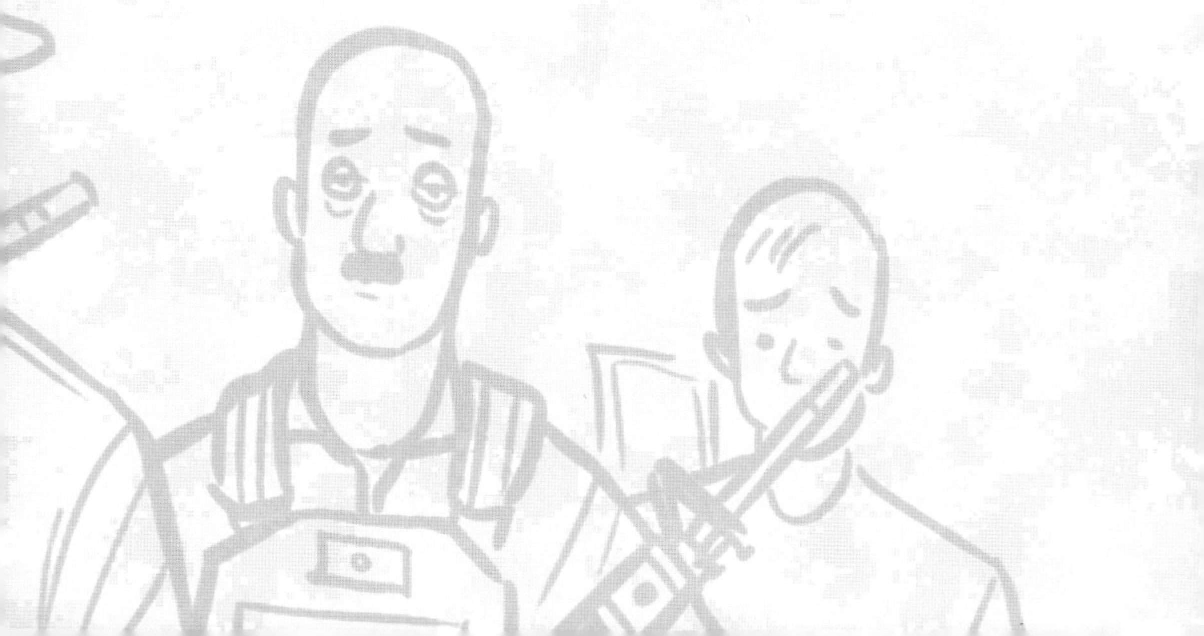

PART 2
HOLIDAY AND SPECIAL STRIPS

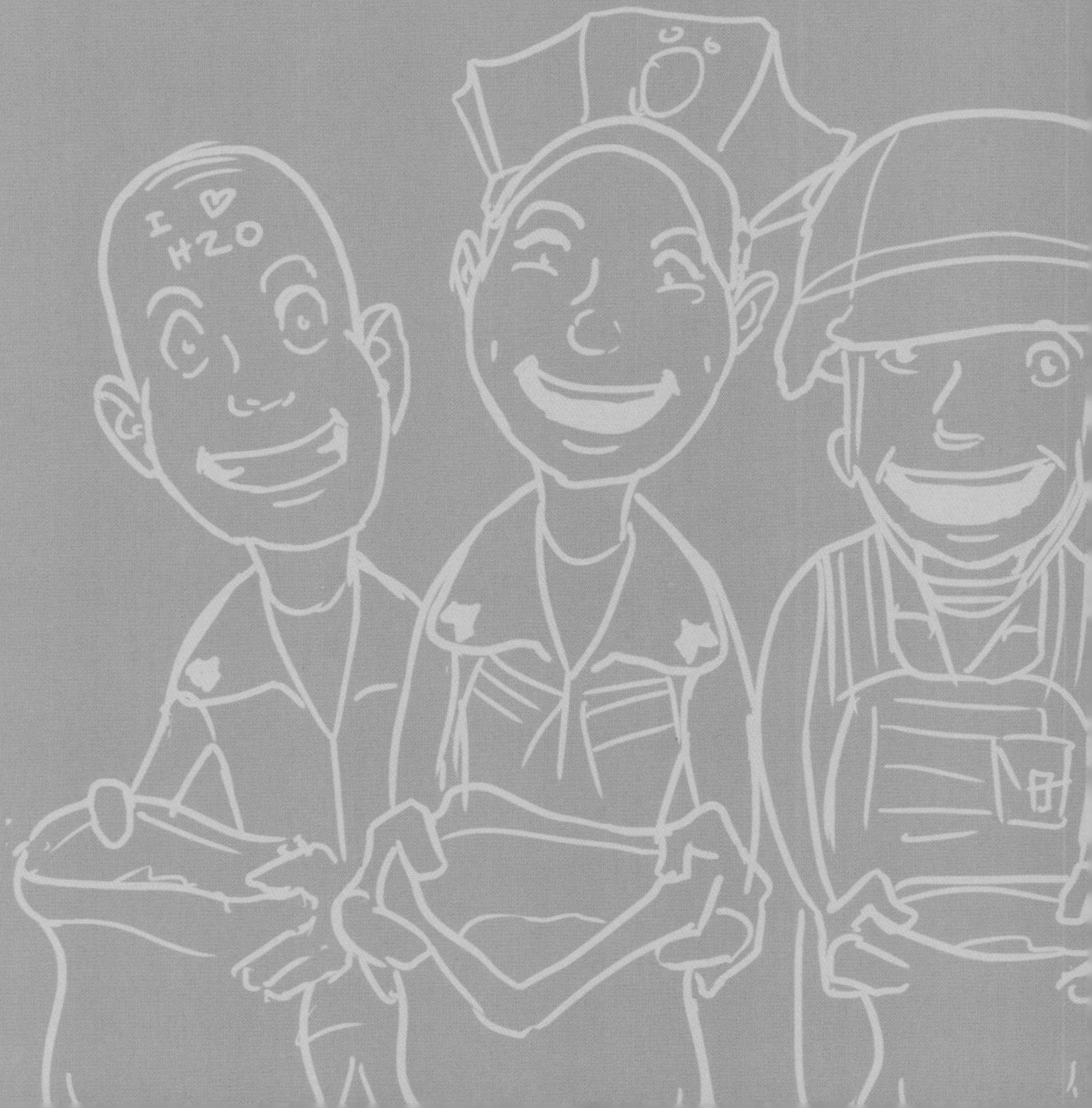
I ♥ H2O

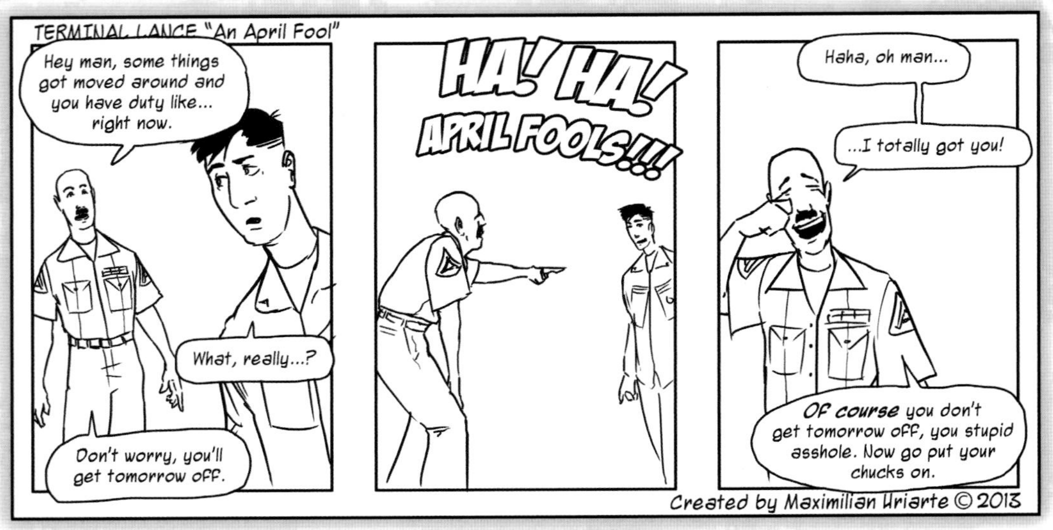
TERMINAL LANCE "An April Fool"
Hey man, some things got moved around and you have duty like... right now.
What, really...?
Don't worry, you'll get tomorrow off.
HA! HA! APRIL FOOLS!!!
Haha, oh man...
...I totally got you!
Of course you don't get tomorrow off, you stupid asshole. Now go put your chucks on.
Created by Maximilian Uriarte © 2013

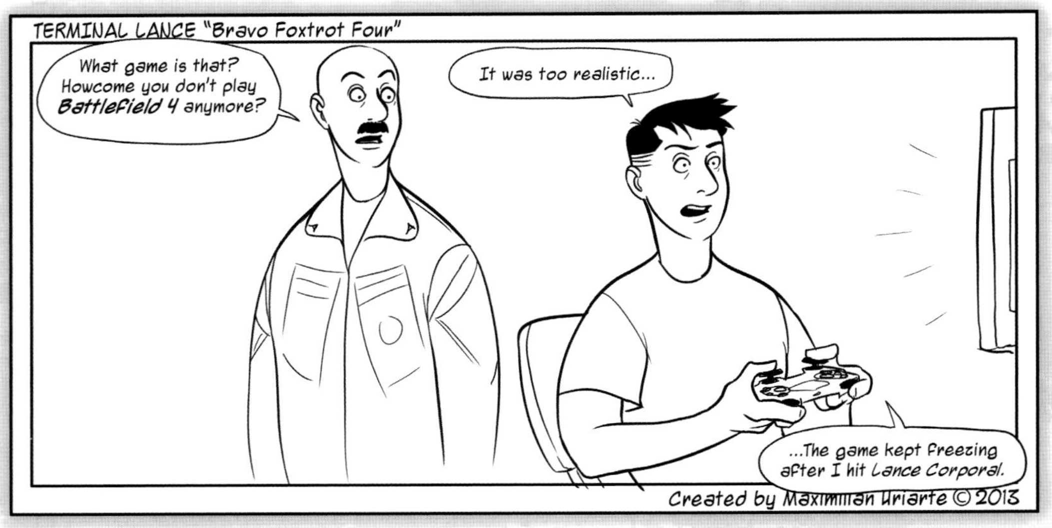
TERMINAL LANCE "Bravo Foxtrot Four"
What game is that? Howcome you don't play Battlefield 4 anymore?
It was too realistic...
...The game kept freezing after I hit Lance Corporal.
Created by Maximilian Uriarte © 2013

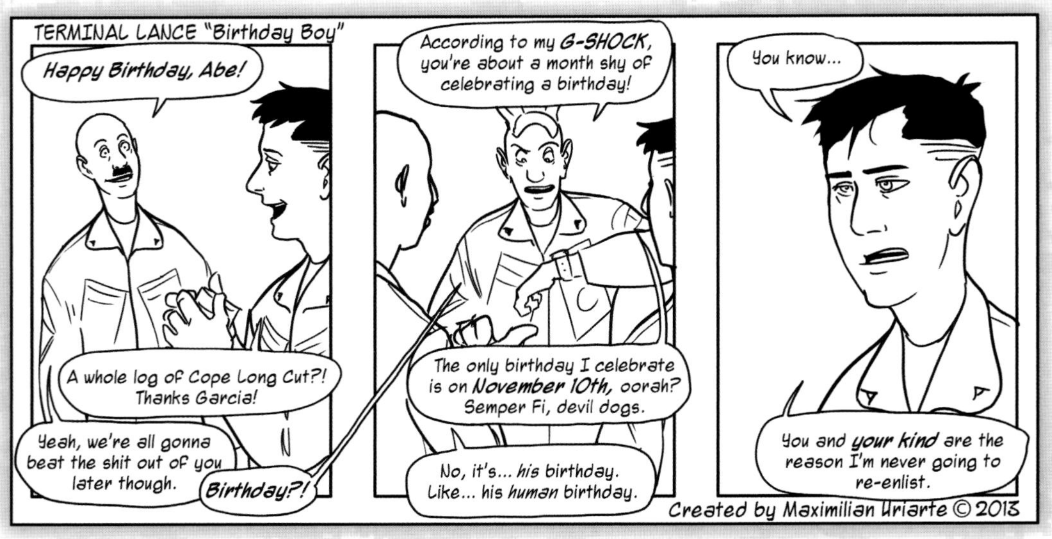
TERMINAL LANCE "Birthday Boy"
Happy Birthday, Abe!
A whole log of Cope Long Cut?! Thanks Garcia!
Yeah, we're all gonna beat the shit out of you later though.
Birthday?!
According to my G-SHOCK, you're about a month shy of celebrating a birthday!
The only birthday I celebrate is on November 10th, oorah? Semper Fi, devil dogs.
No, it's... his birthday. Like... his human birthday.
You know...
You and your kind are the reason I'm never going to re-enlist.
Created by Maximilian Uriarte © 2013

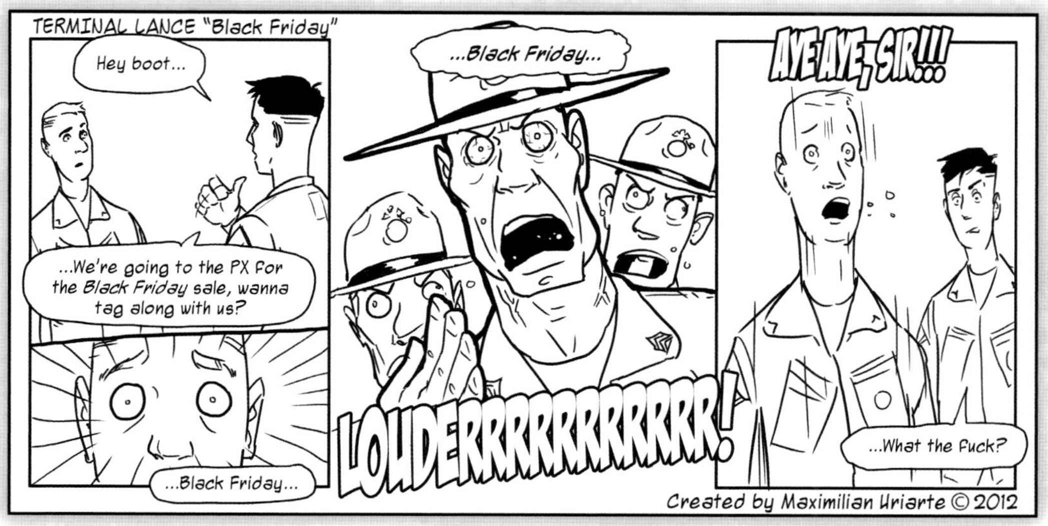
TERMINAL LANCE "Black Friday"
Hey boot...
...We're going to the PX for the Black Friday sale, wanna tag along with us?
...Black Friday...
...Black Friday...
LOUDERRRRRRRRRRR!
AYE AYE, SIR!!!
...What the fuck?
Created by Maximilian Uriarte © 2012

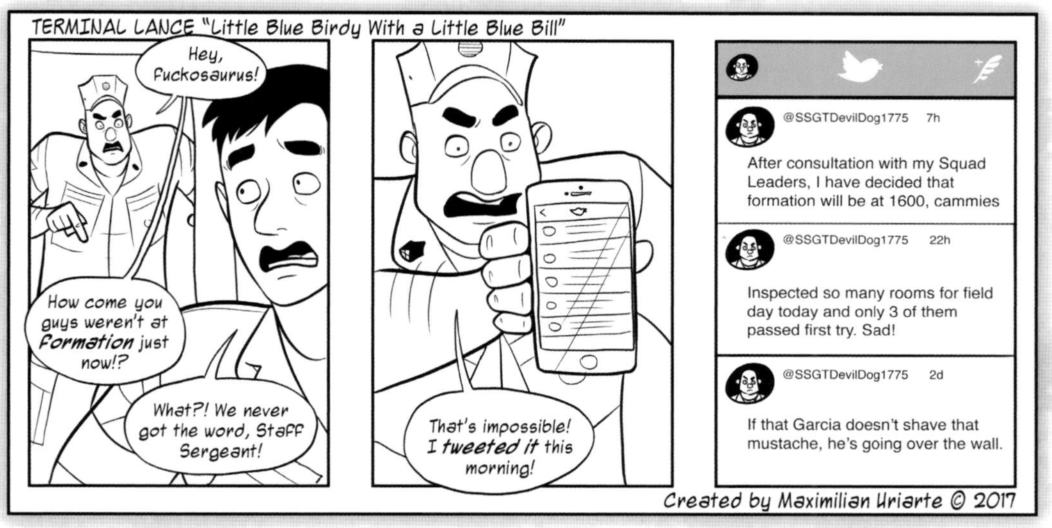
TERMINAL LANCE "Little Blue Birdy With a Little Blue Bill"
Hey, Fuckosaurus!
How come you guys weren't at formation just now!?
What?! We never got the word, Staff Sergeant!
That's impossible! I tweeted it this morning!
@SSGTDevilDog1775 7h
After consultation with my Squad Leaders, I have decided that formation will be at 1600, cammies
@SSGTDevilDog1775 22h
Inspected so many rooms for field day today and only 3 of them passed first try. Sad!
@SSGTDevilDog1775 2d
If that Garcia doesn't shave that mustache, he's going over the wall.
Created by Maximilian Uriarte © 2017

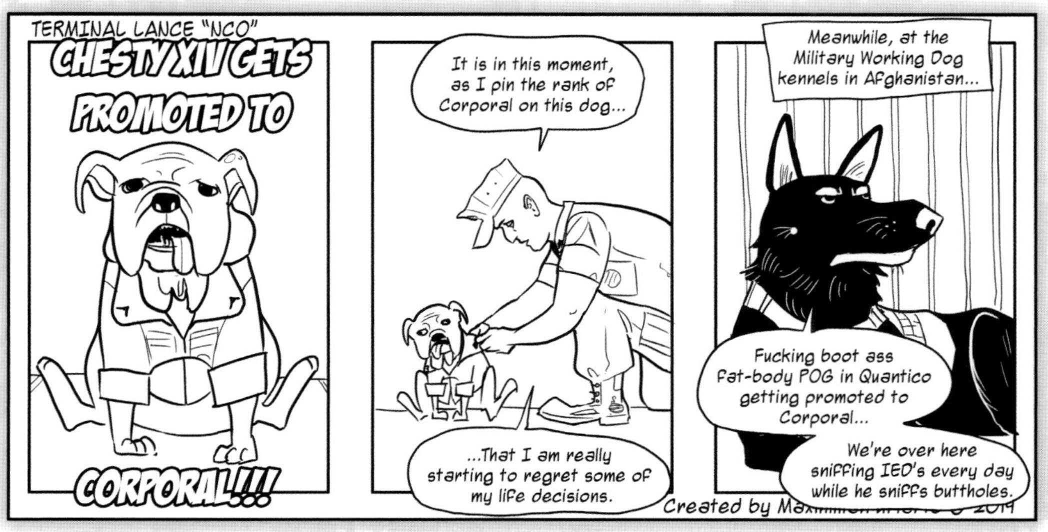
TERMINAL LANCE "NCO"
CHESTY XIV GETS PROMOTED TO CORPORAL!!!
It is in this moment, as I pin the rank of Corporal on this dog...
...That I am really starting to regret some of my life decisions.
Meanwhile, at the Military Working Dog kennels in Afghanistan...
Fucking boot ass fat-body POG in Quantico getting promoted to Corporal...
We're over here sniffing IED's every day while he sniffs buttholes.
Created by

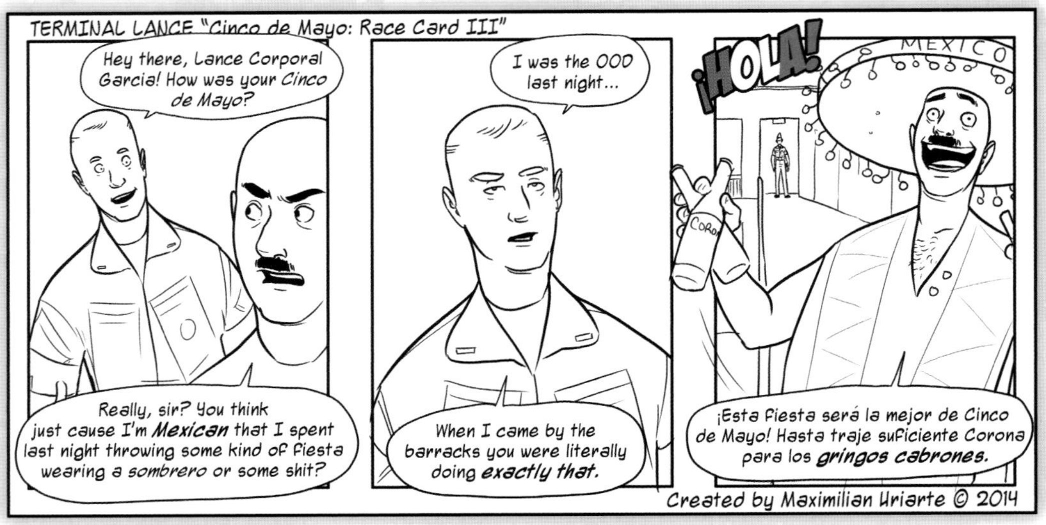
TERMINAL LANCE "Cinco de Mayo: Race Card III"
Hey there, Lance Corporal Garcia! How was your Cinco de Mayo?
Really, sir? You think just cause I'm Mexican that I spent last night throwing some kind of fiesta wearing a sombrero or some shit?
I was the OOD last night...
When I came by the barracks you were literally doing exactly that.
¡HOLA!
MEXICO
¡Esta fiesta será la mejor de Cinco de Mayo! Hasta traje suficiente Corona para los gringos cabrones.
Created by Maximilian Uriarte © 2014

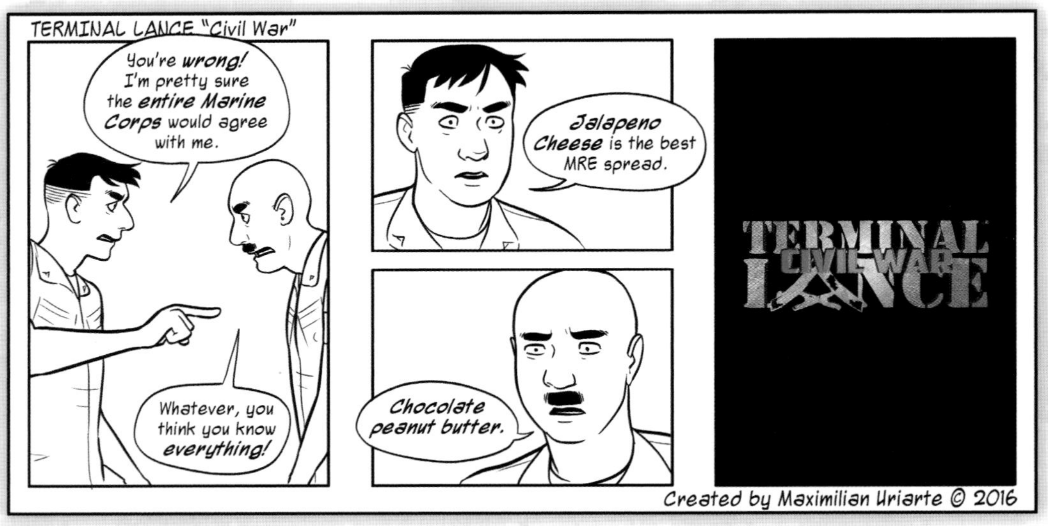
TERMINAL LANCE "Civil War"
You're wrong! I'm pretty sure the entire Marine Corps would agree with me.
Whatever, you think you know everything!
Jalapeno Cheese is the best MRE spread.
Chocolate peanut butter.
TERMINAL CIVIL WAR LANCE
Created by Maximilian Uriarte © 2016

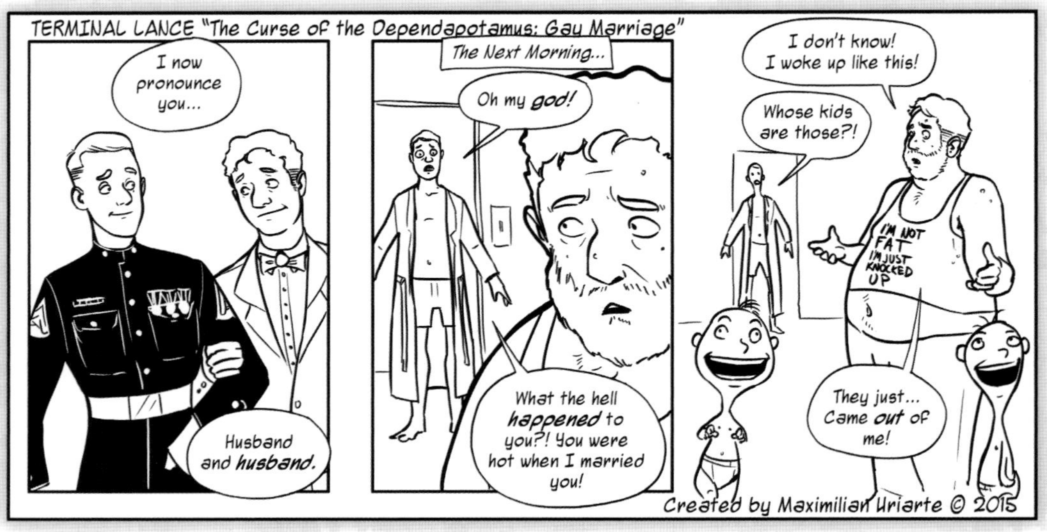
TERMINAL LANCE "The Curse of the Dependapotamus: Gay Marriage"
I now pronounce you...
Husband and husband.
The Next Morning...
Oh my god!
What the hell happened to you?! You were hot when I married you!
Whose kids are those?!
I don't know! I woke up like this!
I'M NOT FAT I'M JUST KNOCKED UP
They just... Came out of me!
Created by Maximilian Uriarte © 2015

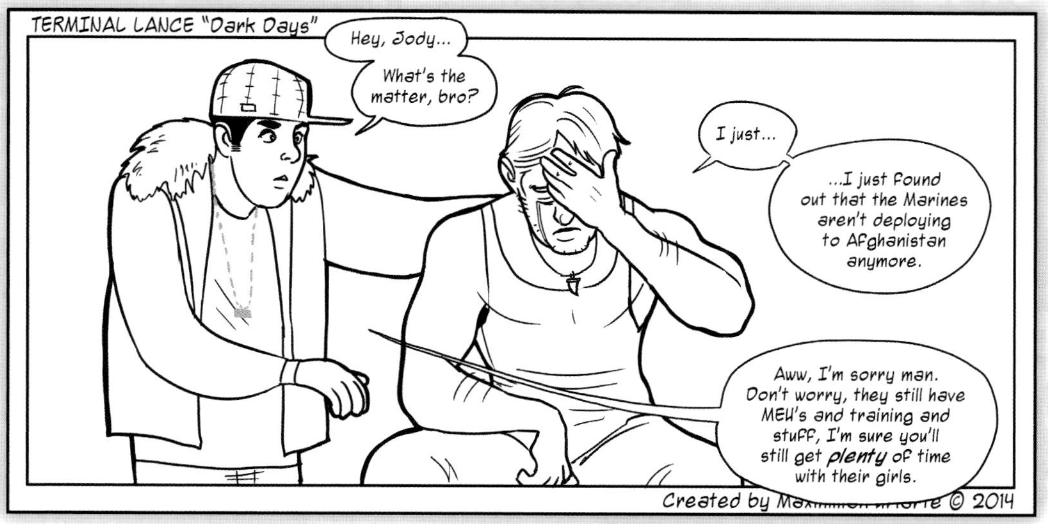
TERMINAL LANCE "Dark Days"
Hey, Jody...
What's the matter, bro?
I just...
...I just found out that the Marines aren't deploying to Afghanistan anymore.
Aww, I'm sorry man. Don't worry, they still have MEU's and training and stuff, I'm sure you'll still get plenty of time with their girls.
Created by Maximilian Uriarte © 2014

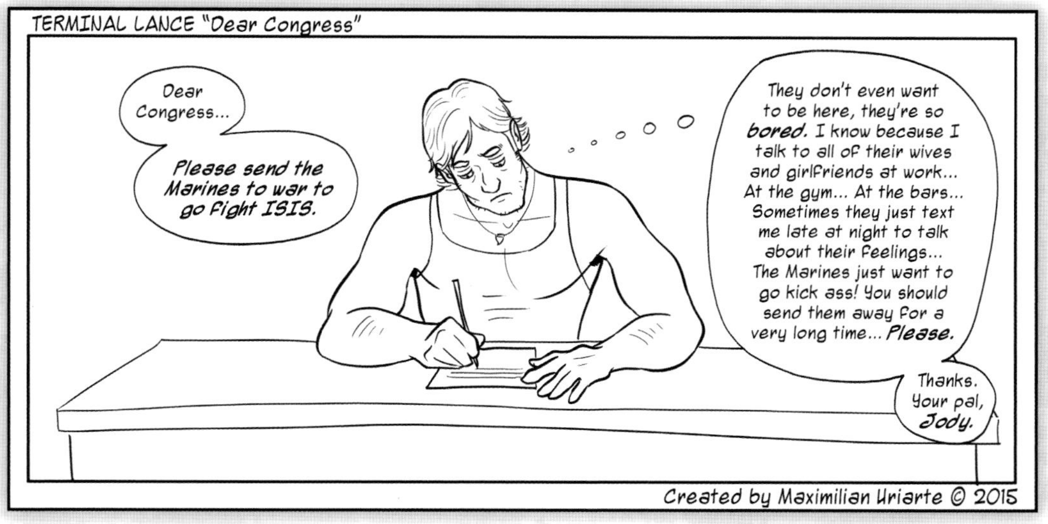
TERMINAL LANCE "Dear Congress"
Dear Congress...
Please send the Marines to war to go fight ISIS.
They don't even want to be here, they're so bored. I know because I talk to all of their wives and girlfriends at work... At the gym... At the bars... Sometimes they just text me late at night to talk about their feelings... The Marines just want to go kick ass! You should send them away for a very long time... Please.
Thanks. Your pal, Jody.
Created by Maximilian Uriarte © 2015

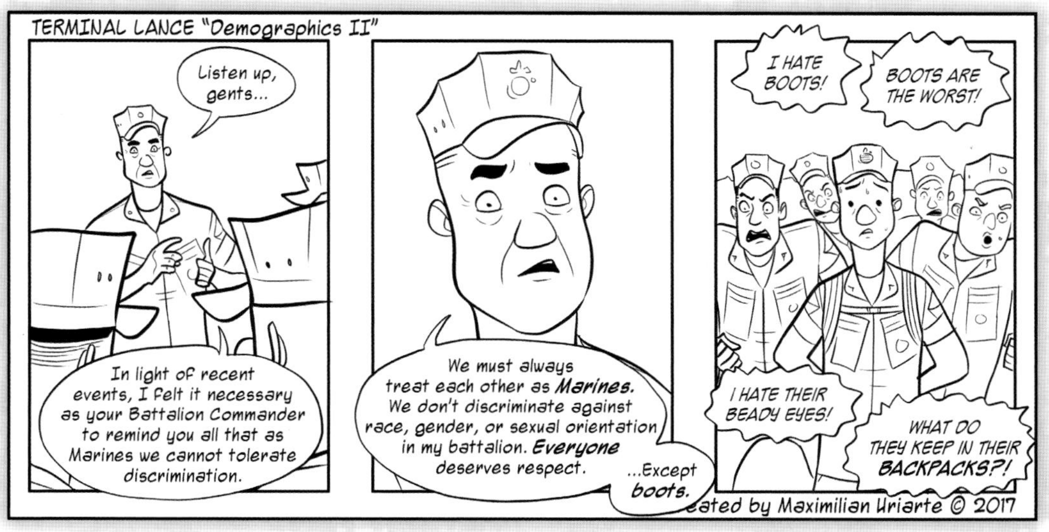
TERMINAL LANCE "Demographics II"
Listen up, gents...
In light of recent events, I felt it necessary as your Battalion Commander to remind you all that as Marines we cannot tolerate discrimination.
We must always treat each other as Marines. We don't discriminate against race, gender, or sexual orientation in my battalion. Everyone deserves respect.
...Except boots.
I HATE BOOTS!
BOOTS ARE THE WORST!
I HATE THEIR BEADY EYES!
WHAT DO THEY KEEP IN THEIR BACKPACKS?!
eated by Maximilian Uriarte © 2017

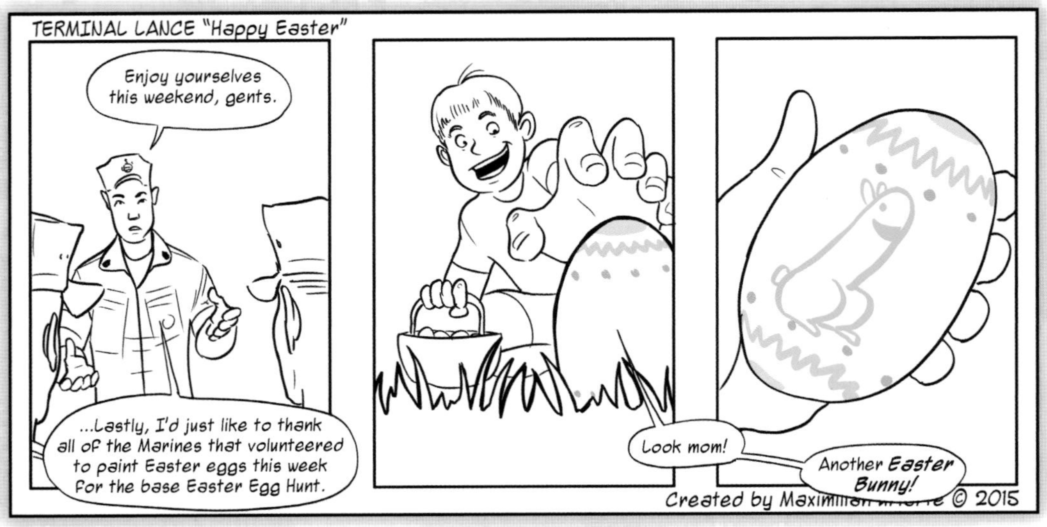
TERMINAL LANCE "Happy Easter"
Enjoy yourselves this weekend, gents.
...Lastly, I'd just like to thank all of the Marines that volunteered to paint Easter eggs this week for the base Easter Egg Hunt.
Look mom!
Another Easter Bunny!
Created by Maximilian Uriarte © 2015

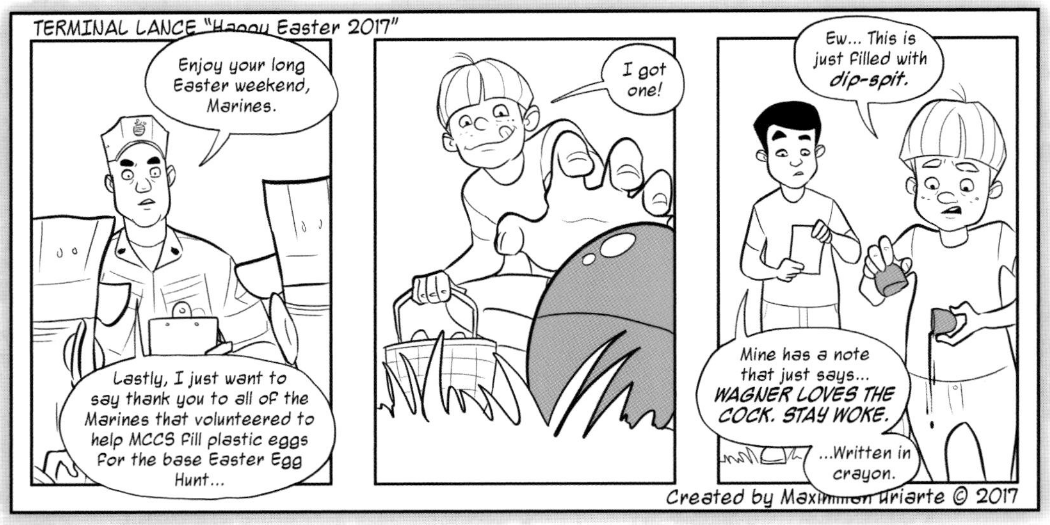
TERMINAL LANCE "Happy Easter 2017"
Enjoy your long Easter weekend, Marines.
Lastly, I just want to say thank you to all of the Marines that volunteered to help MCCS fill plastic eggs for the base Easter Egg Hunt...
I got one!
Ew... This is just filled with dip-spit.
Mine has a note that just says... WAGNER LOVES THE COCK. STAY WOKE.
...Written in crayon.
Created by Maximilian Uriarte © 2017

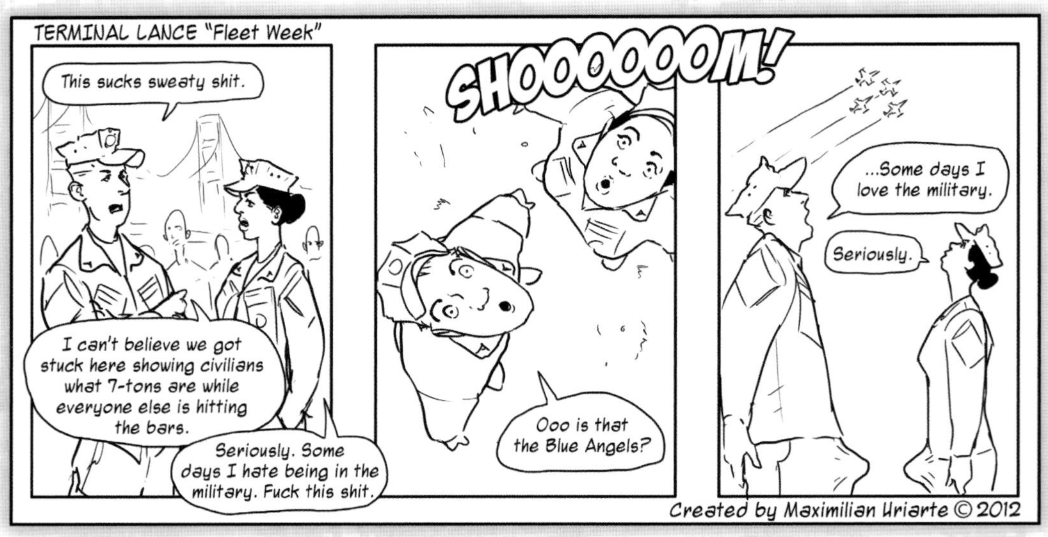
TERMINAL LANCE "Fleet Week"
This sucks sweaty shit.
I can't believe we got stuck here showing civilians what 7-tons are while everyone else is hitting the bars.
Seriously. Some days I hate being in the military. Fuck this shit.
SHOOOOOOM!
Ooo is that the Blue Angels?
...Some days I love the military.
Seriously.
Created by Maximilian Uriarte © 2012

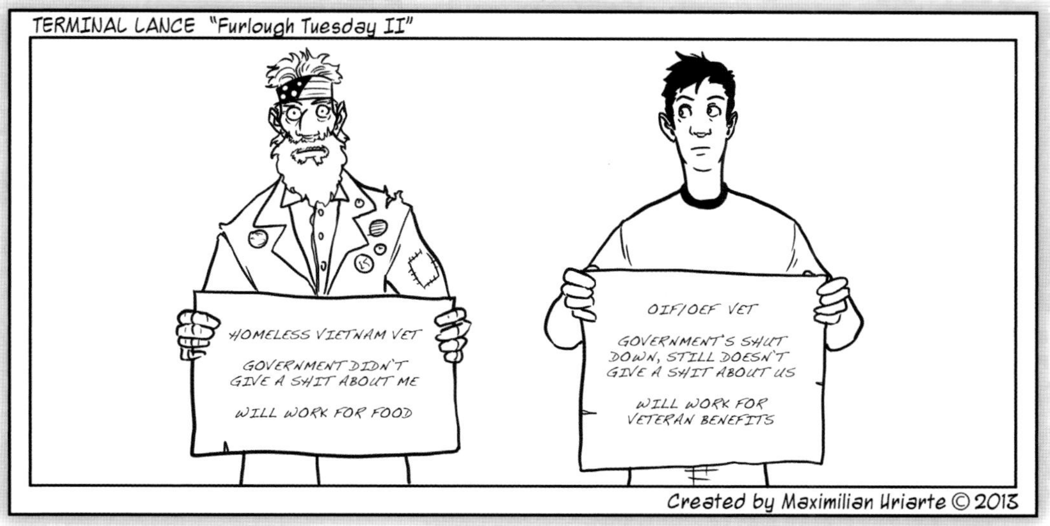
TERMINAL LANCE "Furlough Tuesday II"
HOMELESS VIETNAM VET
GOVERNMENT DIDN'T GIVE A SHIT ABOUT ME
WILL WORK FOR FOOD
OIF/OEF VET
GOVERNMENT'S SHUT DOWN, STILL DOESN'T GIVE A SHIT ABOUT US
WILL WORK FOR VETERAN BENEFITS
Created by Maximilian Uriarte © 2013

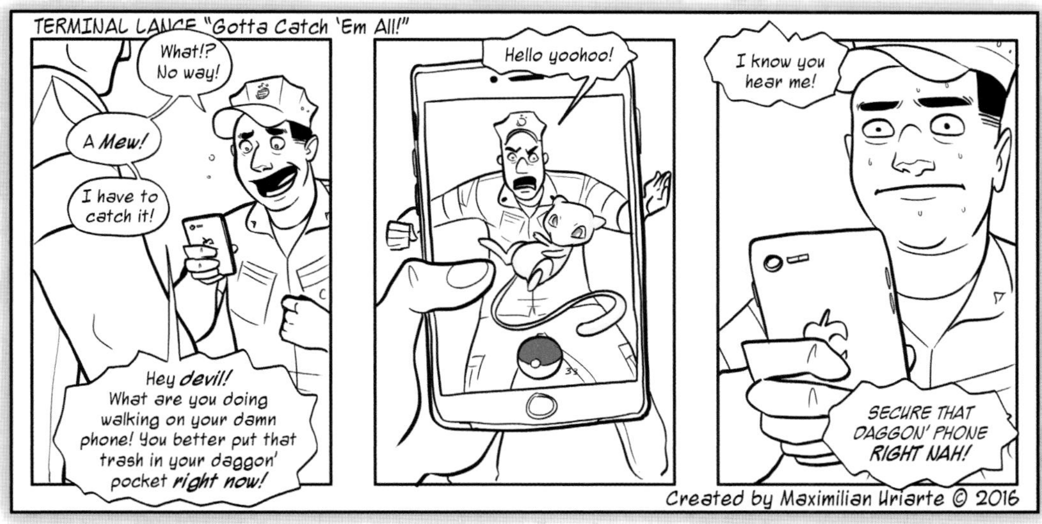
TERMINAL LANCE "Gotta Catch 'Em All!"
What!? No way!
A Mew!
I have to catch it!
Hey devil! What are you doing walking on your damn phone! You better put that trash in your daggon' pocket right now!
Hello yoohoo!
I know you hear me!
SECURE THAT DAGGON' PHONE RIGHT NAH!
Created by Maximilian Uriarte © 2016

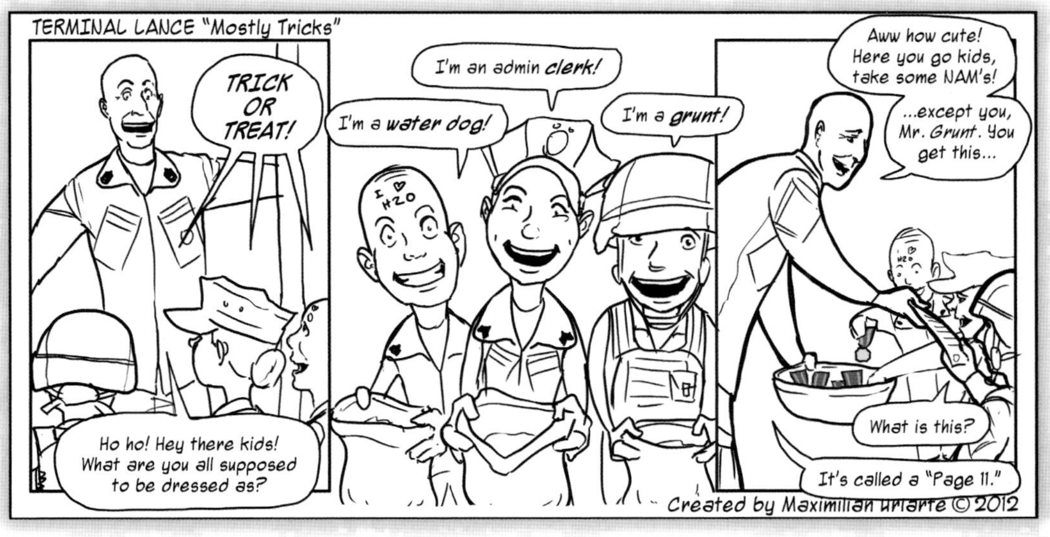
TERMINAL LANCE "Mostly Tricks"
TRICK OR TREAT!
Ho ho! Hey there kids! What are you all supposed to be dressed as?
I'm an admin clerk!
I'm a water dog!
I'm a grunt!
Aww how cute! Here you go kids, take some NAM's!
...except you, Mr. Grunt. You get this...
What is this?
It's called a "Page 11."
Created by Maximilian Uriarte © 2012

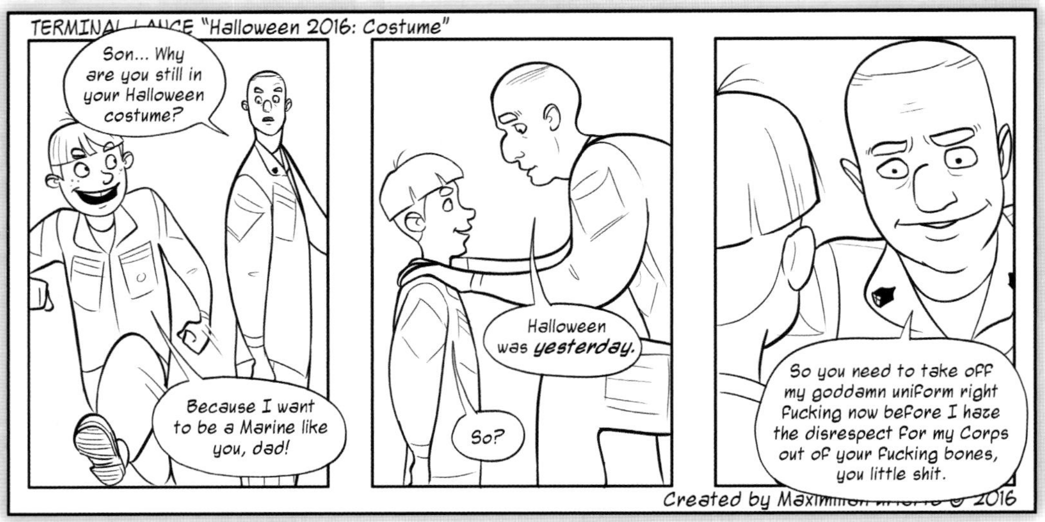
TERMINAL LANCE "Halloween 2016: Costume"
Son... Why are you still in your Halloween costume?
Because I want to be a Marine like you, dad!
Halloween was *yesterday.*
So?
So you need to take off my goddamn uniform right fucking now before I haze the disrespect for my Corps out of your fucking bones, you little shit.
Created by Maximilian Uriarte © 2016

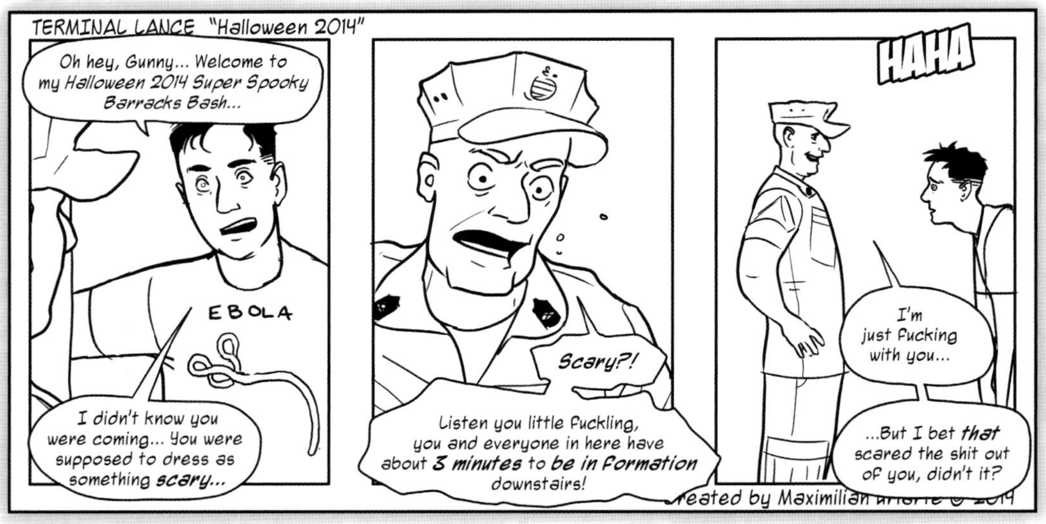
TERMINAL LANCE "Halloween 2014"
Oh hey, Gunny... Welcome to my Halloween 2014 Super Spooky Barracks Bash...
EBOLA
I didn't know you were coming... You were supposed to dress as something *scary...*
Scary?!
Listen you little fuckling, you and everyone in here have about **3 minutes** to **be in formation** downstairs!
HAHA
I'm just fucking with you...
...But I bet ***that*** scared the shit out of you, didn't it?
Created by Maximilian Uriarte © 2014

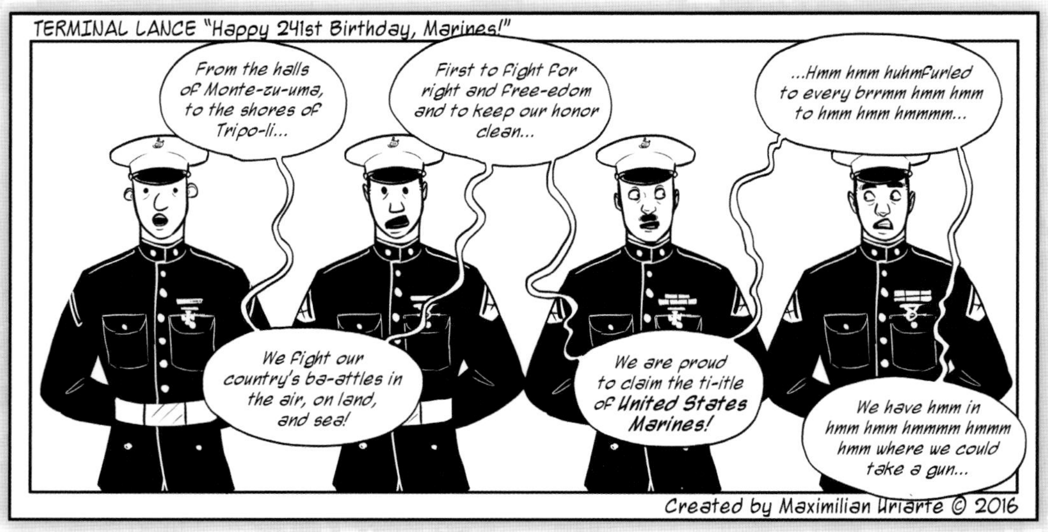
TERMINAL LANCE "Happy 241st Birthday, Marines!"
From the halls of Monte-zu-uma, to the shores of Tripo-li...
We fight our country's ba-attles in the air, on land, and sea!
First to fight for right and free-edom and to keep our honor clean...
We are proud to claim the ti-itle of **United States Marines!**
...Hmm hmm huhmfurled to every brrmm hmm hmm to hmm hmm hmmmm...
We have hmm in hmm hmm hmmmm hmmm hmm where we could take a gun...
Created by Maximilian Uriarte © 2016

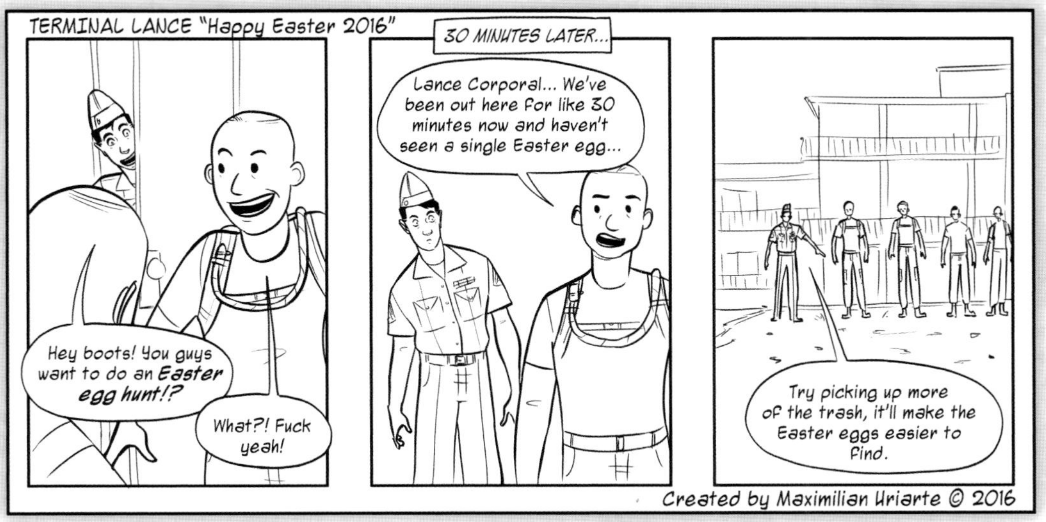
TERMINAL LANCE "Happy Easter 2016"
Hey boots! You guys want to do an ***Easter egg hunt!?***
What?! Fuck yeah!
30 MINUTES LATER...
Lance Corporal... We've been out here for like 30 minutes now and haven't seen a single Easter egg...
Try picking up more of the trash, it'll make the Easter eggs easier to find.
Created by Maximilian Uriarte © 2016

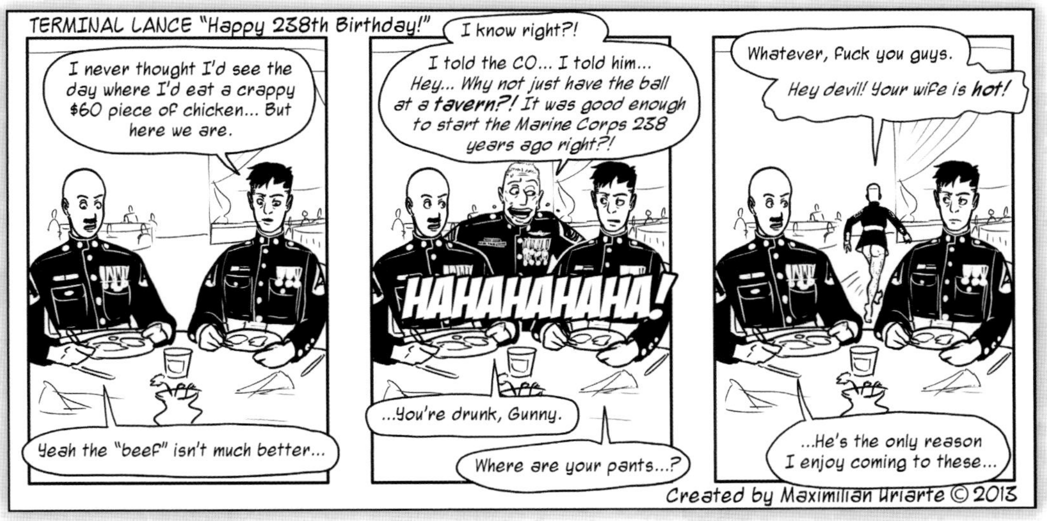
TERMINAL LANCE "Happy 238th Birthday!"
I never thought I'd see the day where I'd eat a crappy $60 piece of chicken... But here we are.
Yeah the "beef" isn't much better...
I know right?!
*I told the CO... I told him... Hey... Why not just have the ball at a **tavern?!** It was good enough to start the Marine Corps 238 years ago right?!*
HAHAHAHAHA!
...You're drunk, Gunny.
Where are your pants...?
Whatever, fuck you guys.
*Hey devil! Your wife is **hot!***
...He's the only reason I enjoy coming to these...
Created by Maximilian Uriarte © 2013

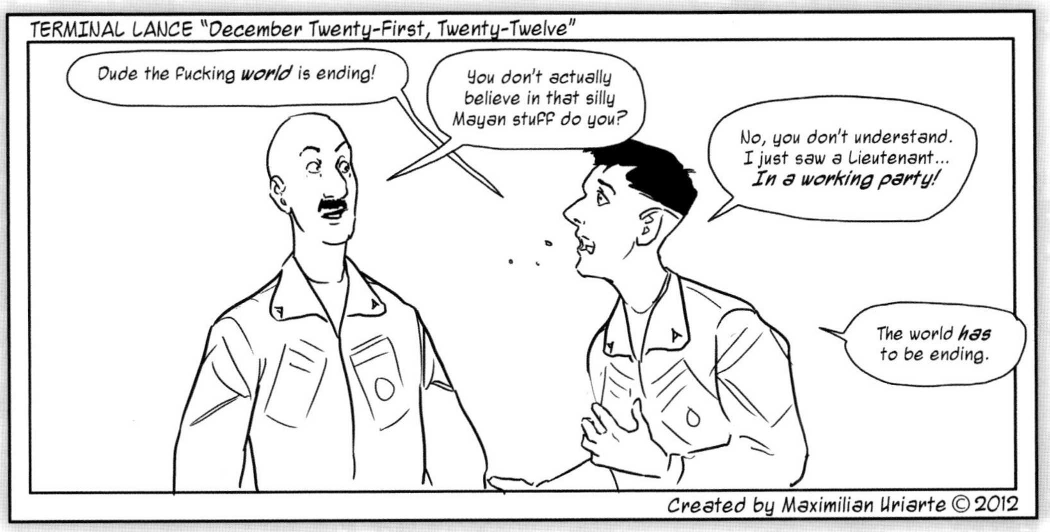
TERMINAL LANCE "December Twenty-First, Twenty-Twelve"
Dude the fucking ***world*** is ending!
You don't actually believe in that silly Mayan stuff do you?
No, you don't understand. I just saw a Lieutenant... ***In a working party!***
The world ***has*** to be ending.
Created by Maximilian Uriarte © 2012

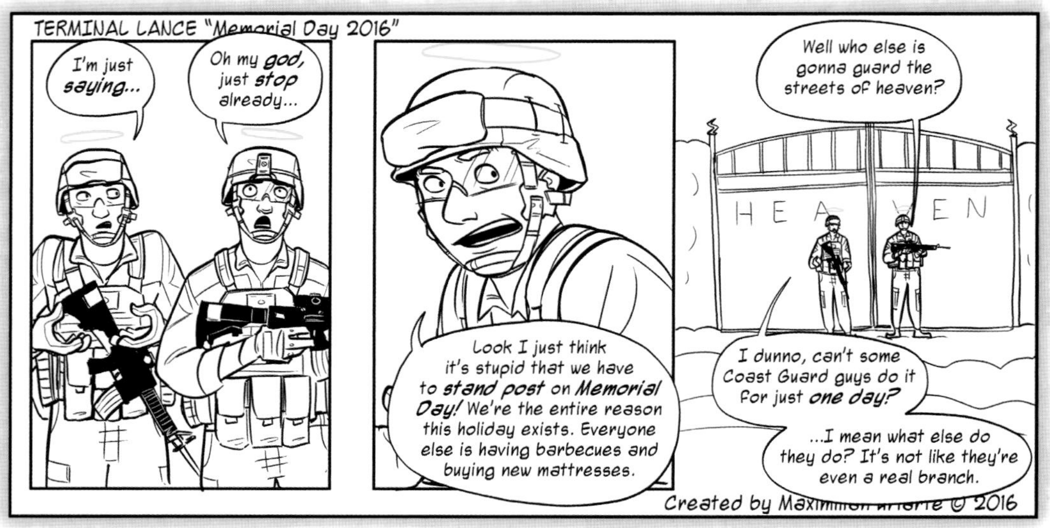
TERMINAL LANCE "Memorial Day 2016"
I'm just saying...
Oh my god, just stop already...
Look I just think it's stupid that we have to stand post on Memorial Day! We're the entire reason this holiday exists. Everyone else is having barbecues and buying new mattresses.
Well who else is gonna guard the streets of heaven?
HEAVEN
I dunno, can't some Coast Guard guys do it for just one day?
...I mean what else do they do? It's not like they're even a real branch.
Created by Maximilian Uriarte © 2016

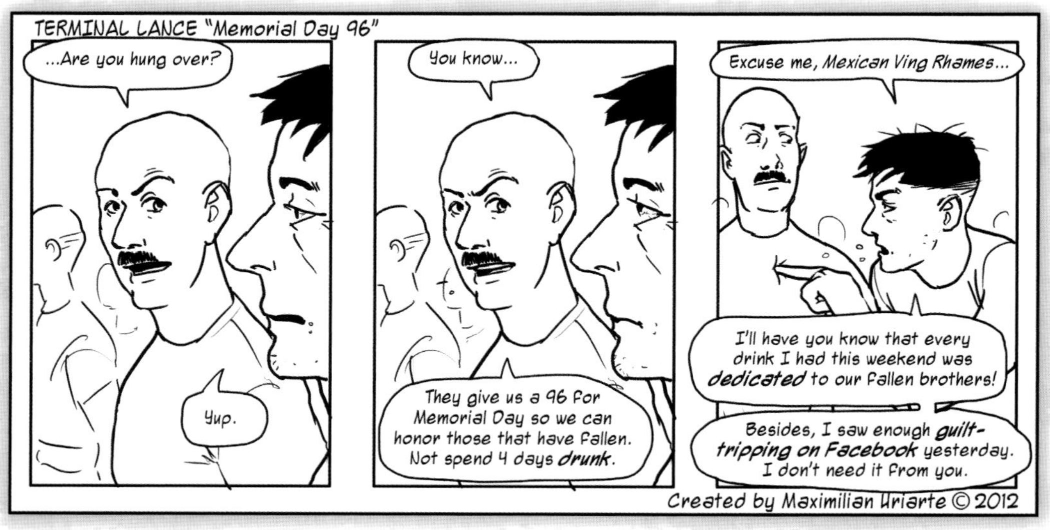
TERMINAL LANCE "Memorial Day 96"
...Are you hung over?
Yup.
You know...
They give us a 96 for Memorial Day so we can honor those that have fallen. Not spend 4 days drunk.
Excuse me, Mexican Ving Rhames...
I'll have you know that every drink I had this weekend was dedicated to our fallen brothers!
Besides, I saw enough guilt-tripping on Facebook yesterday. I don't need it from you.
Created by Maximilian Uriarte © 2012

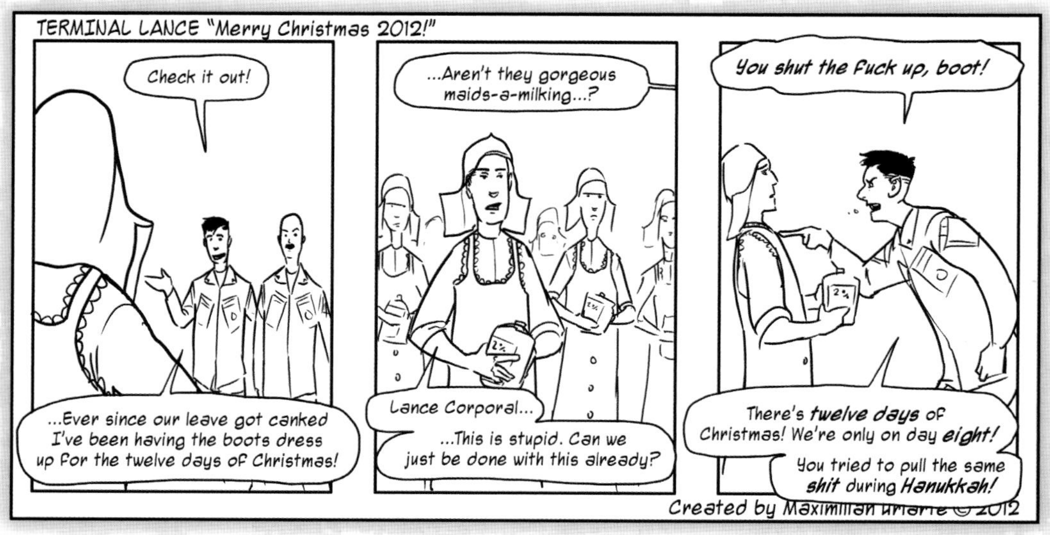
TERMINAL LANCE "Merry Christmas 2012!"
Check it out!
...Ever since our leave got canked I've been having the boots dress up for the twelve days of Christmas!
...Aren't they gorgeous maids-a-milking...?
Lance Corporal...
...This is stupid. Can we just be done with this already?
You shut the fuck up, boot!
There's twelve days of Christmas! We're only on day eight!
You tried to pull the same shit during Hanukkah!
Created by Maximilian Uriarte © 2012

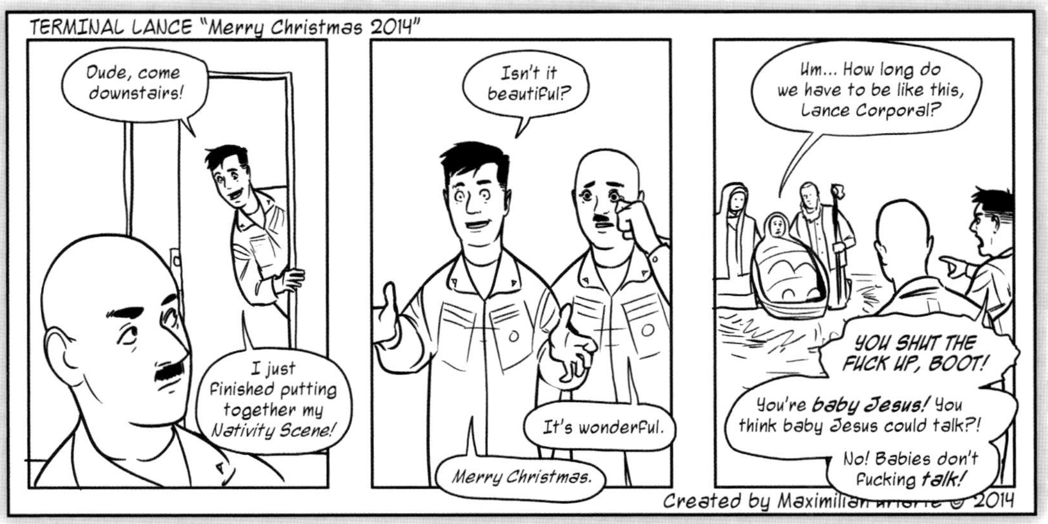
TERMINAL LANCE "Merry Christmas 2014"
Dude, come downstairs!
I just finished putting together my Nativity Scene!
Isn't it beautiful?
It's wonderful.
Merry Christmas.
Um... How long do we have to be like this, Lance Corporal?
YOU SHUT THE FUCK UP, BOOT!
You're baby Jesus! You think baby Jesus could talk?!
No! Babies don't fucking talk!
Created by Maximilian © 2014

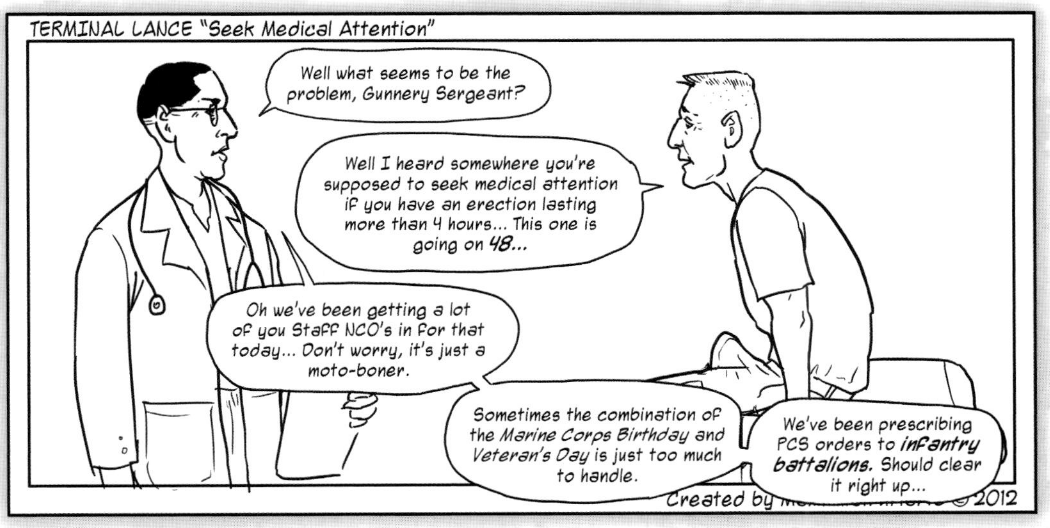
TERMINAL LANCE "Seek Medical Attention"
Well what seems to be the problem, Gunnery Sergeant?
Well I heard somewhere you're supposed to seek medical attention if you have an erection lasting more than 4 hours... This one is going on 48...
Oh we've been getting a lot of you Staff NCO's in for that today... Don't worry, it's just a moto-boner.
Sometimes the combination of the Marine Corps Birthday and Veteran's Day is just too much to handle.
We've been prescribing PCS orders to infantry battalions. Should clear it right up...
Created by © 2012

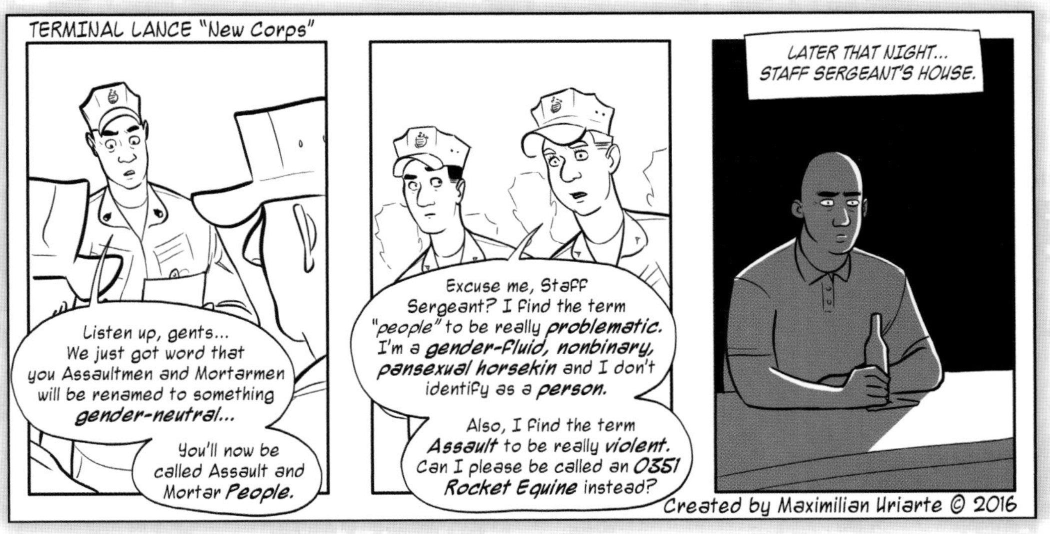
TERMINAL LANCE "New Corps"
Listen up, gents... We just got word that you Assaultmen and Mortarmen will be renamed to something gender-neutral...
You'll now be called Assault and Mortar People.
Excuse me, Staff Sergeant? I find the term "people" to be really problematic. I'm a gender-fluid, nonbinary, pansexual horsekin and I don't identify as a person.
Also, I find the term Assault to be really violent. Can I please be called an 0351 Rocket Equine instead?
LATER THAT NIGHT... STAFF SERGEANT'S HOUSE.
Created by Maximilian Uriarte © 2016

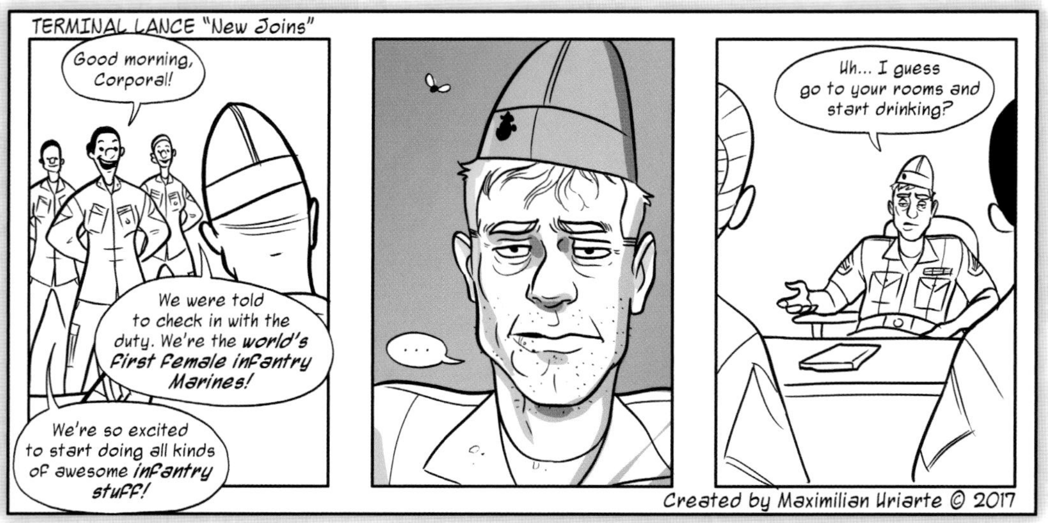
TERMINAL LANCE "New Joins"
Good morning, Corporal!
We were told to check in with the duty. We're the world's first female infantry Marines!
We're so excited to start doing all kinds of awesome infantry stuff!
...
Uh... I guess go to your rooms and start drinking?
Created by Maximilian Uriarte © 2017

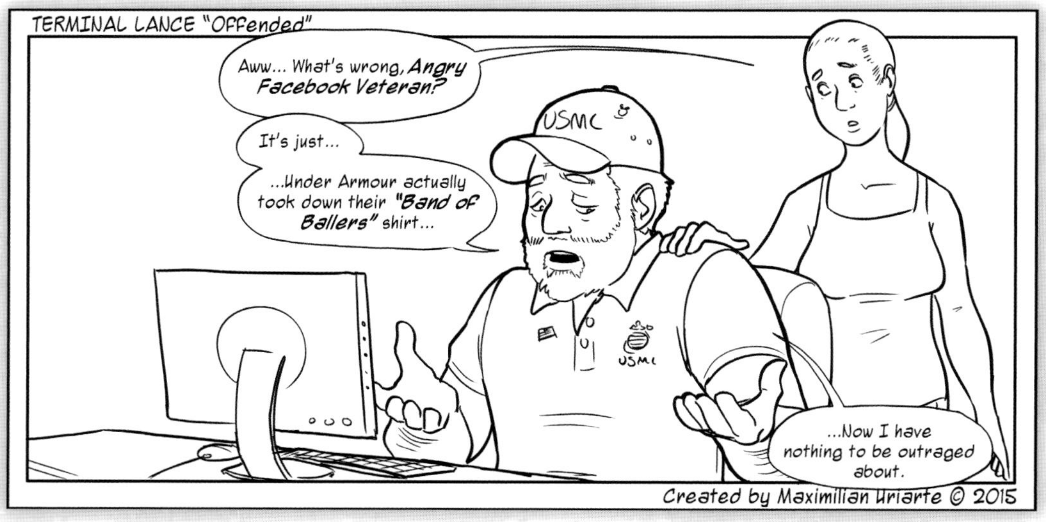
TERMINAL LANCE "Offended"
Aww... What's wrong, Angry Facebook Veteran?
It's just...
...Under Armour actually took down their "Band of Ballers" shirt...
...Now I have nothing to be outraged about.
USMC
Created by Maximilian Uriarte © 2015

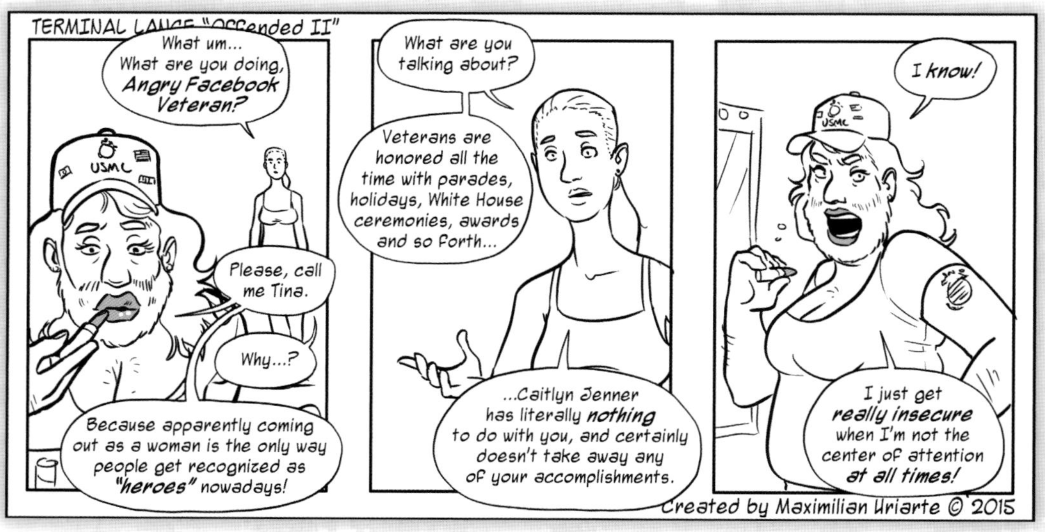
TERMINAL LANCE "Offended II"
What um... What are you doing, Angry Facebook Veteran?
Please, call me Tina.
Why...?
Because apparently coming out as a woman is the only way people get recognized as "heroes" nowadays!
What are you talking about?
Veterans are honored all the time with parades, holidays, White House ceremonies, awards and so forth...
...Caitlyn Jenner has literally nothing to do with you, and certainly doesn't take away any of your accomplishments.
I know!
I just get really insecure when I'm not the center of attention at all times!
Created by Maximilian Uriarte © 2015

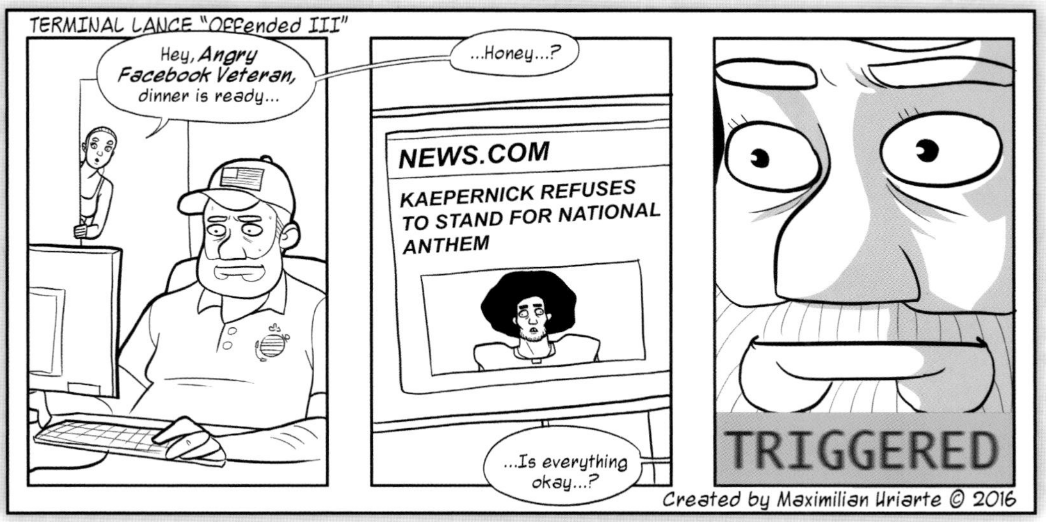
TERMINAL LANCE "Offended III"
Hey, Angry Facebook Veteran, dinner is ready...
...Honey...?
NEWS.COM
KAEPERNICK REFUSES TO STAND FOR NATIONAL ANTHEM
...Is everything okay...?
TRIGGERED
Created by Maximilian Uriarte © 2016

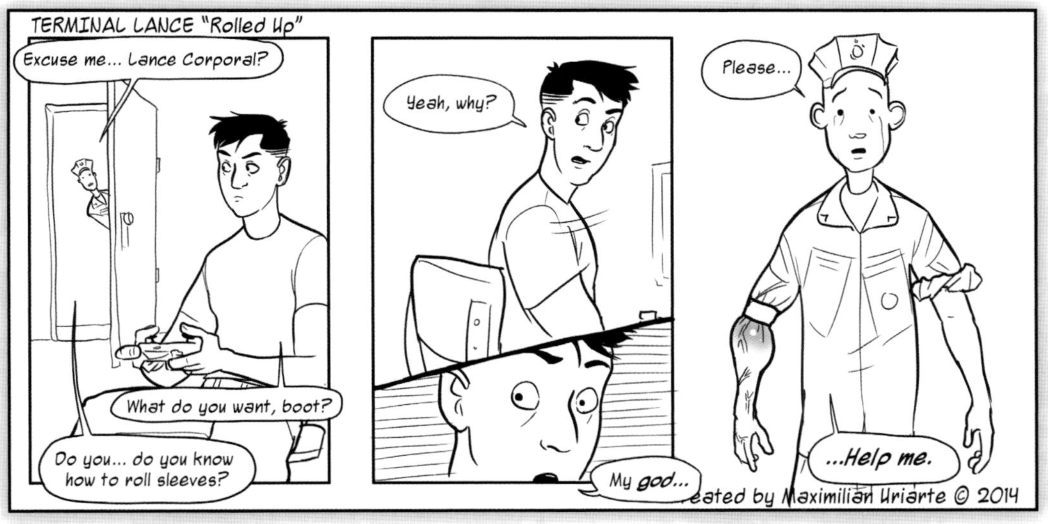
TERMINAL LANCE "Rolled Up"
Excuse me... Lance Corporal?
What do you want, boot?
Do you... do you know how to roll sleeves?
Yeah, why?
My god...
Please...
...Help me.
Created by Maximilian Uriarte © 2014

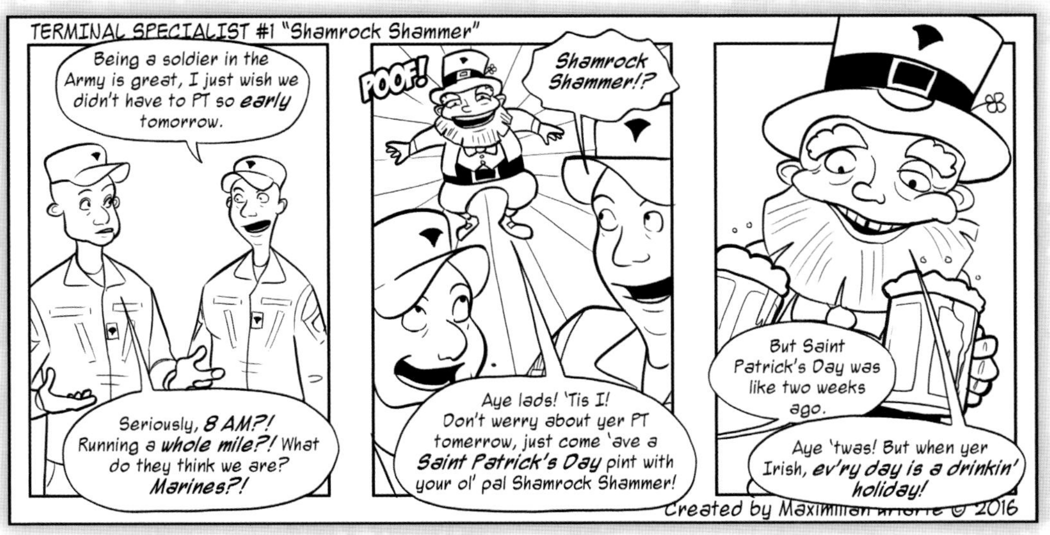
TERMINAL SPECIALIST #1 "Shamrock Shammer"
Being a soldier in the Army is great, I just wish we didn't have to PT so early tomorrow.
Seriously, 8 AM?! Running a whole mile?! What do they think we are? Marines?!
POOF!
Shamrock Shammer!?
Aye lads! 'Tis I! Don't werry about yer PT tomorrow, just come 'ave a Saint Patrick's Day pint with your ol' pal Shamrock Shammer!
But Saint Patrick's Day was like two weeks ago.
Aye 'twas! But when yer Irish, ev'ry day is a drinkin' holiday!
Created by Maximilian Uriarte © 2016

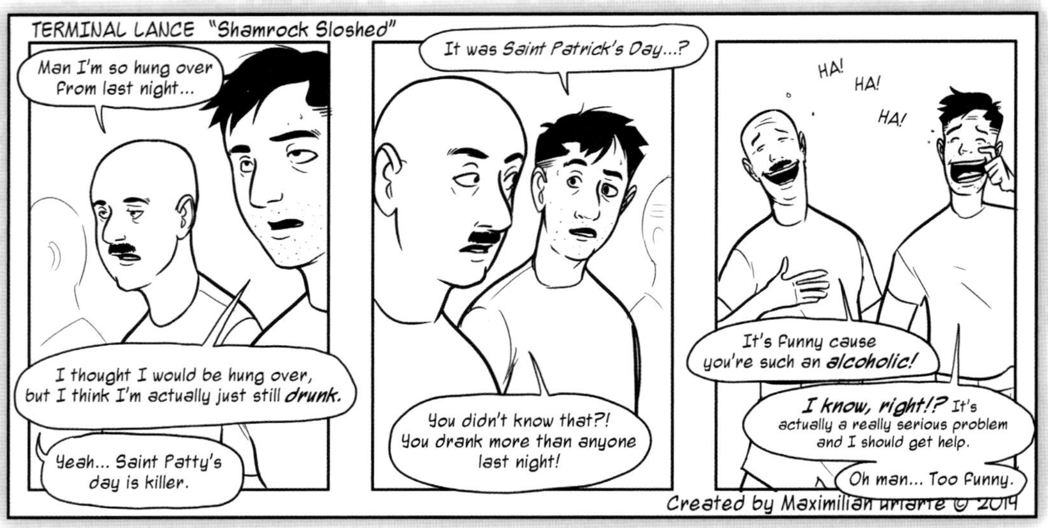
TERMINAL LANCE "Shamrock Sloshed"
Man I'm so hung over from last night...
I thought I would be hung over, but I think I'm actually just still drunk.
Yeah... Saint Patty's day is killer.
It was Saint Patrick's Day...?
You didn't know that?! You drank more than anyone last night!
HA! HA! HA!
It's funny cause you're such an alcoholic!
I know, right!? It's actually a really serious problem and I should get help.
Oh man... Too funny.
Created by Maximilian Uriarte © 2014

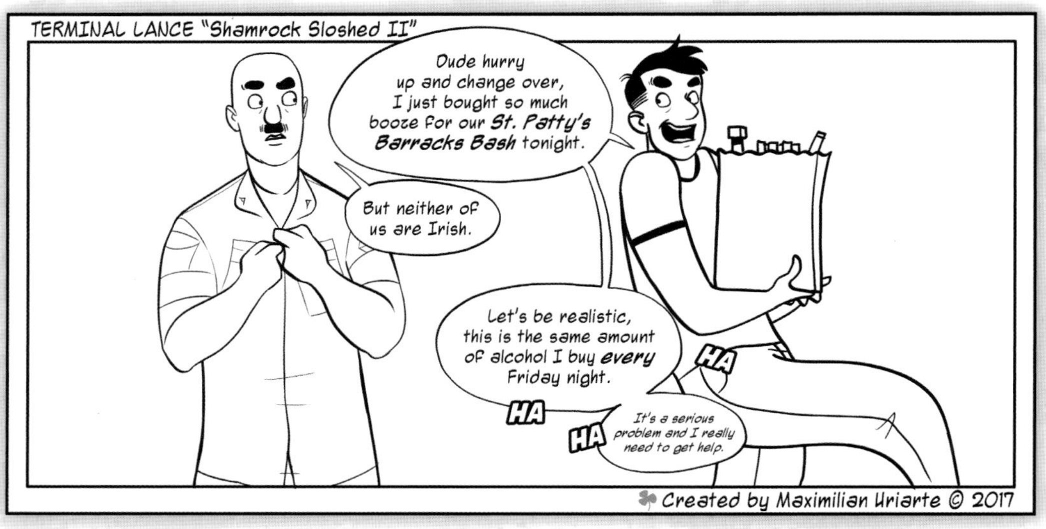
TERMINAL LANCE "Shamrock Sloshed II"
Dude hurry up and change over, I just bought so much booze for our St. Patty's Barracks Bash tonight.
But neither of us are Irish.
Let's be realistic, this is the same amount of alcohol I buy every Friday night.
HA
HA
HA
It's a serious problem and I really need to get help.
Created by Maximilian Uriarte © 2017

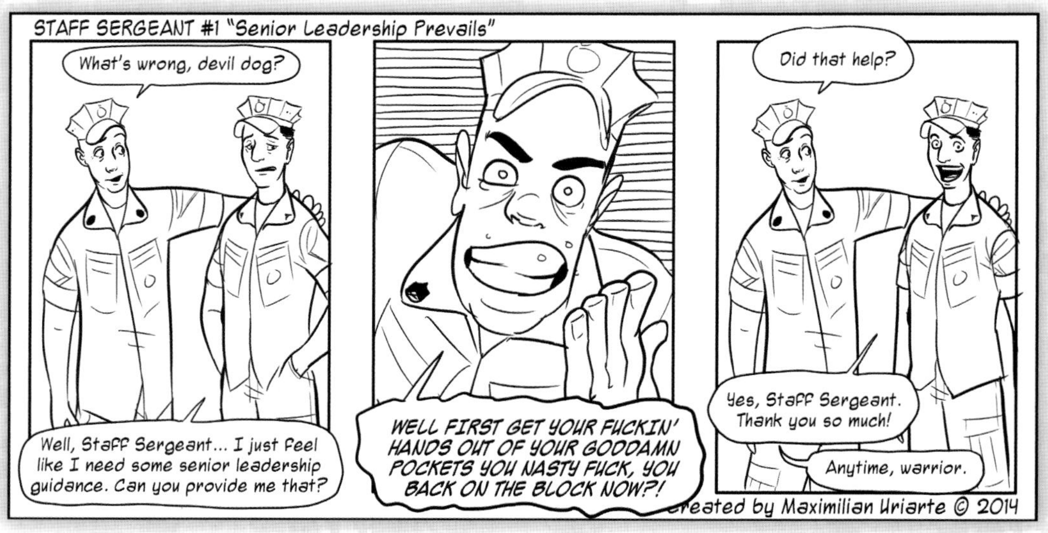
STAFF SERGEANT #1 "Senior Leadership Prevails"
What's wrong, devil dog?
Well, Staff Sergeant... I just feel like I need some senior leadership guidance. Can you provide me that?
WELL FIRST GET YOUR FUCKIN' HANDS OUT OF YOUR GODDAMN POCKETS YOU NASTY FUCK, YOU BACK ON THE BLOCK NOW?!
Did that help?
Yes, Staff Sergeant. Thank you so much!
Anytime, warrior.
Created by Maximilian Uriarte © 2014

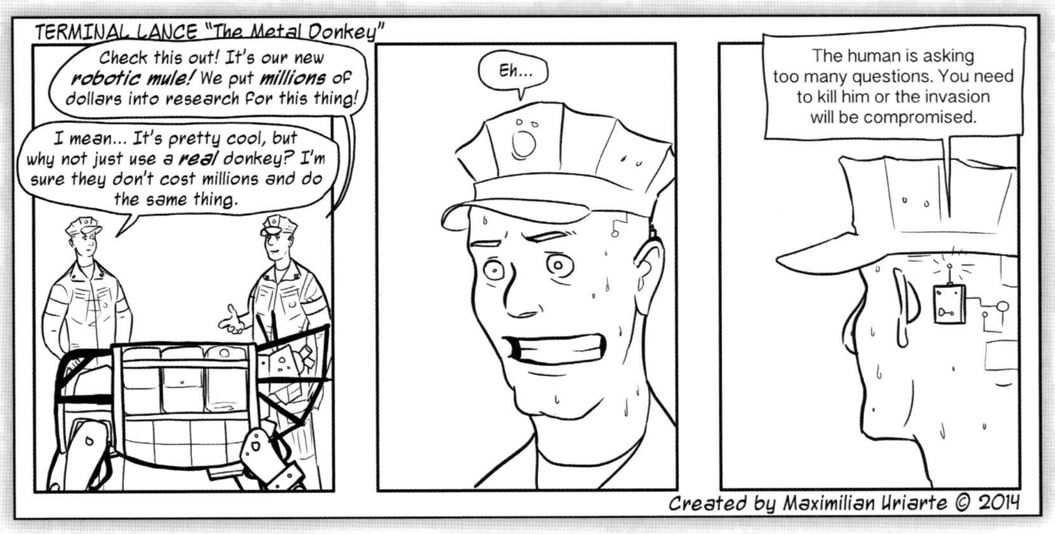
TERMINAL LANCE "The Metal Donkey"
Check this out! It's our new robotic mule! We put millions of dollars into research for this thing!
I mean... It's pretty cool, but why not just use a real donkey? I'm sure they don't cost millions and do the same thing.
Eh...
The human is asking too many questions. You need to kill him or the invasion will be compromised.
Created by Maximilian Uriarte © 2014

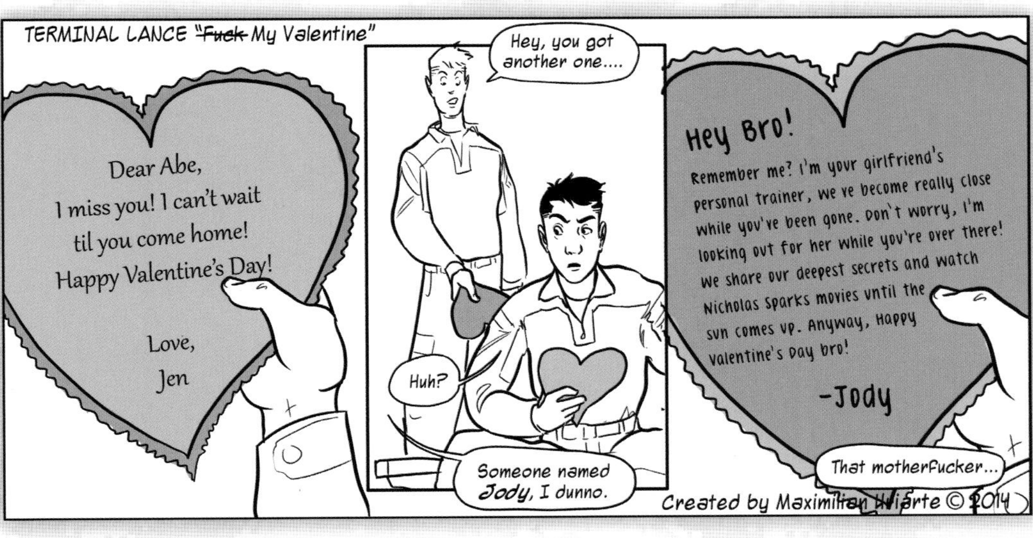
TERMINAL LANCE "~~Fuck~~ My Valentine"
Dear Abe,
I miss you! I can't wait til you come home!
Happy Valentine's Day!
Love,
Jen
Hey, you got another one....
Huh?
Someone named Jody, I dunno.
Hey Bro!
Remember me? I'm your girlfriend's personal trainer, we've become really close while you've been gone. Don't worry, I'm looking out for her while you're over there! We share our deepest secrets and watch Nicholas Sparks movies until the sun comes up. Anyway, Happy Valentine's Day bro!
-Jody
That motherfucker...
Created by Maximilian Uriarte © 2014

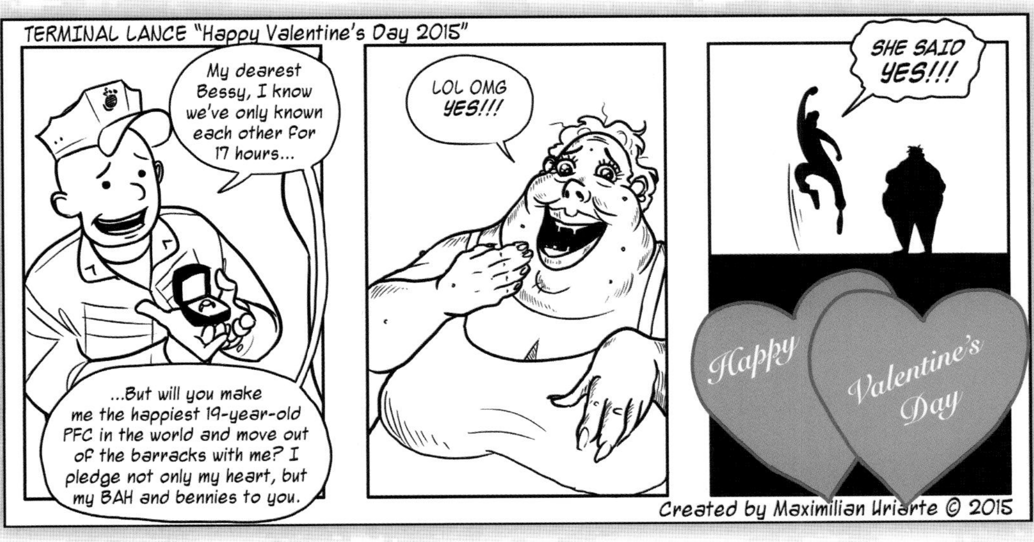
TERMINAL LANCE "Happy Valentine's Day 2015"
My dearest Bessy, I know we've only known each other for 17 hours...
...But will you make me the happiest 19-year-old PFC in the world and move out of the barracks with me? I pledge not only my heart, but my BAH and bennies to you.
LOL OMG YES!!!
SHE SAID YES!!!
Happy
Valentine's Day
Created by Maximilian Uriarte © 2015

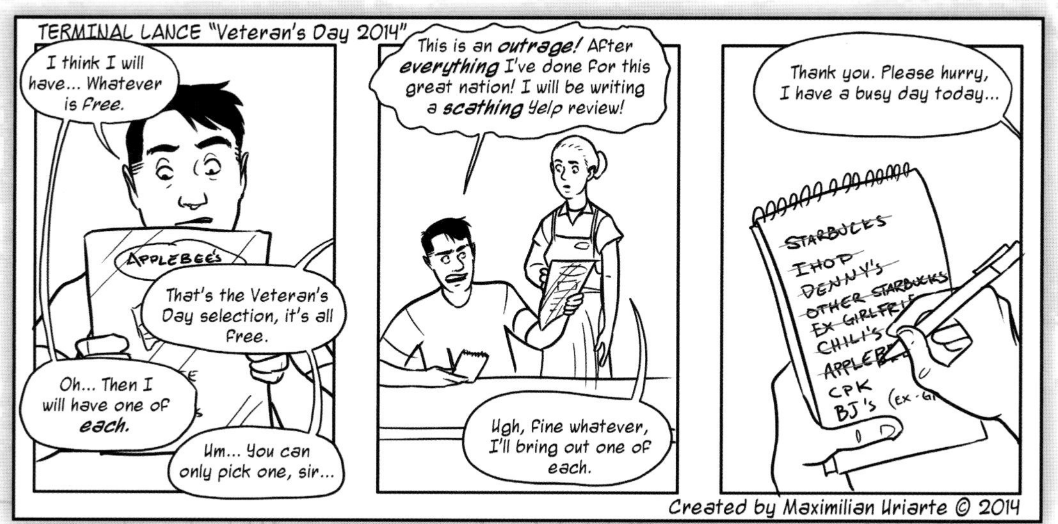

TERMINAL LANCE "Veteran's Day 2014"
I think I will have... Whatever is free.
APPLEBEE'S
That's the Veteran's Day selection, it's all free.
Oh... Then I will have one of ***each.***
Um... You can only pick one, sir...
This is an ***outrage!*** After ***everything*** I've done for this great nation! I will be writing a ***scathing*** Yelp review!
Ugh, fine whatever, I'll bring out one of each.
Thank you. Please hurry, I have a busy day today...
STARBUCKS
IHOP
DENNY's
OTHER STARBUCKS
CHILI's
CPK
BJ's
Created by Maximilian Uriarte © 2014

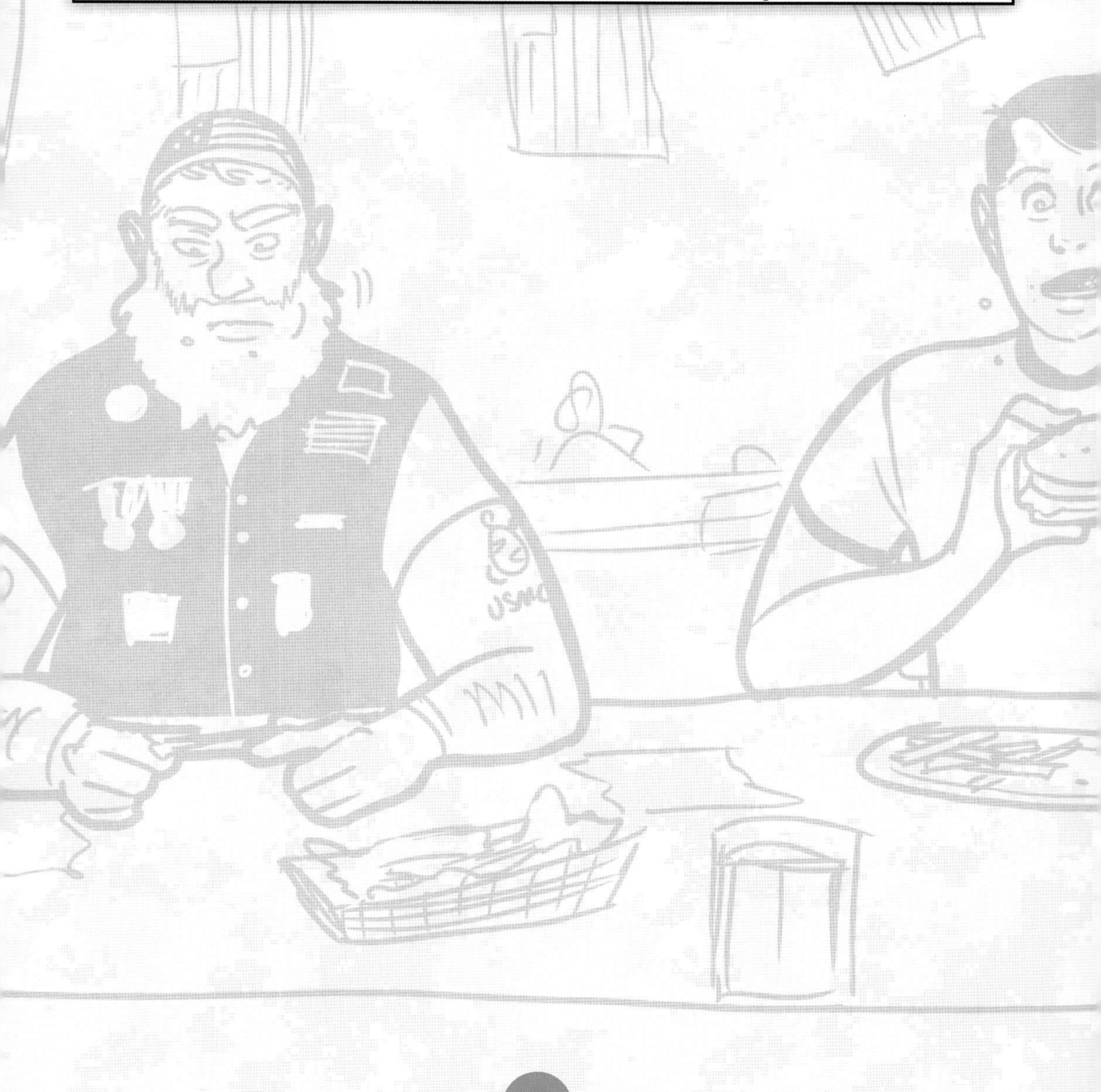

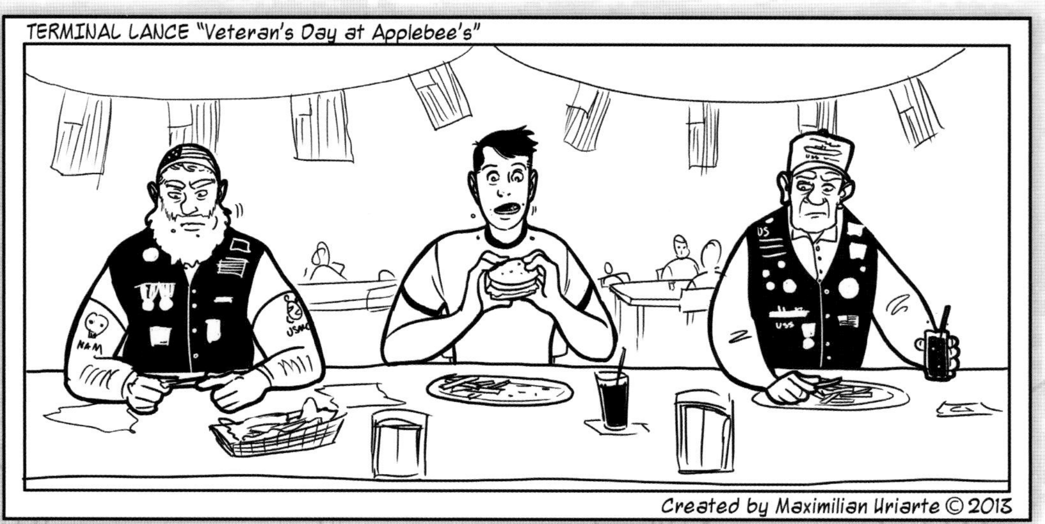
TERMINAL LANCE "Veteran's Day at Applebee's"
NAM
USMC
US
USS
Created by Maximilian Uriarte © 2013

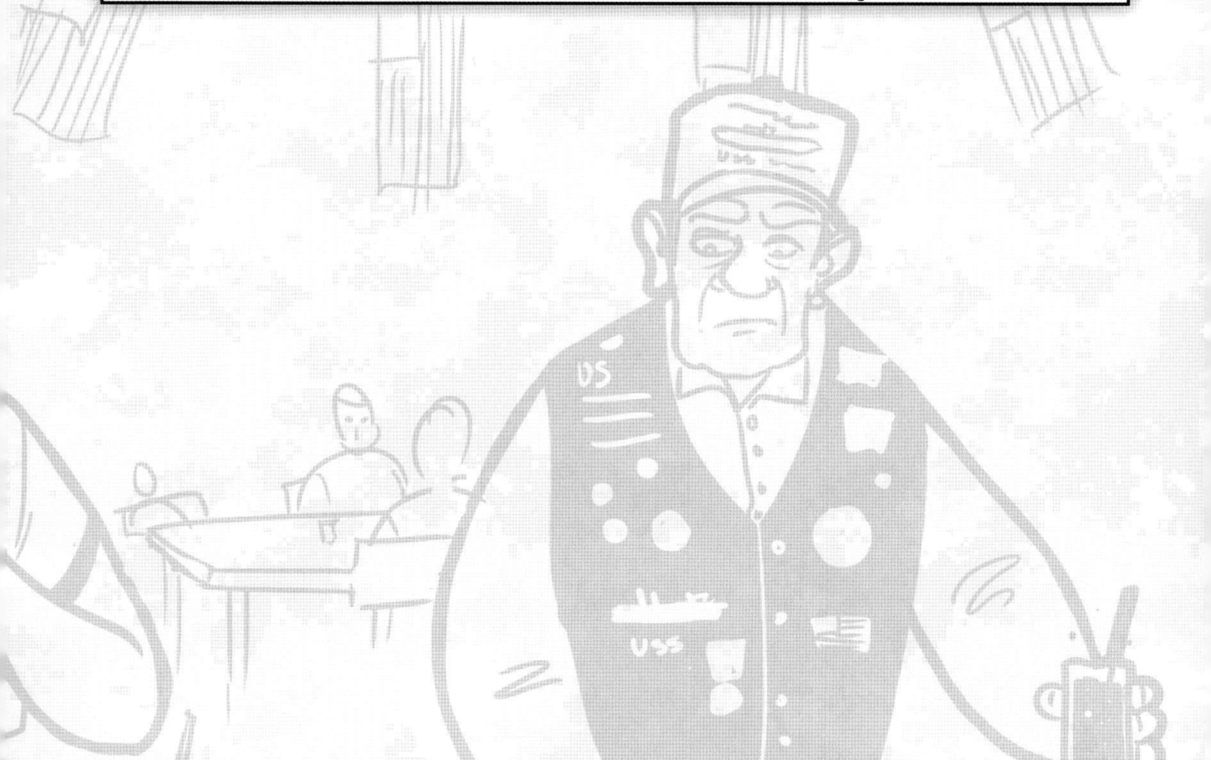
US
USS

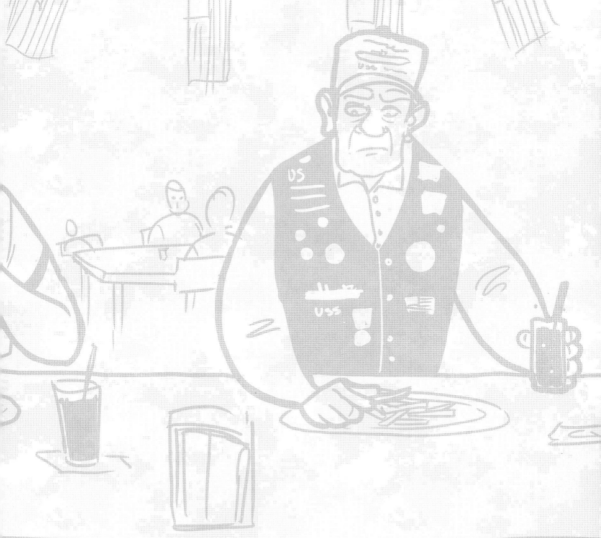

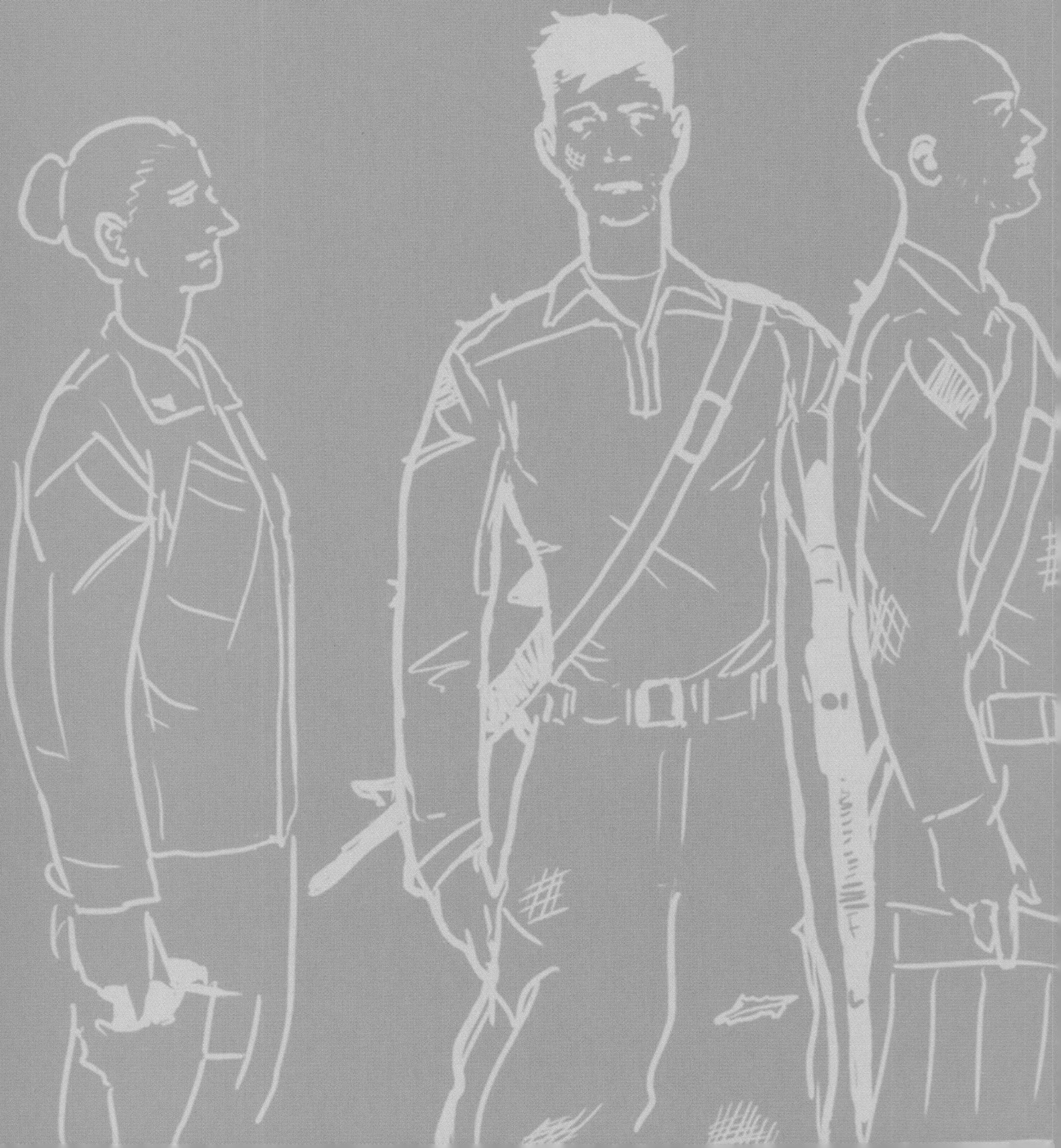

PART 3
MARINE CORPS TIMES
STRIPS

"How to Pass Field Day"

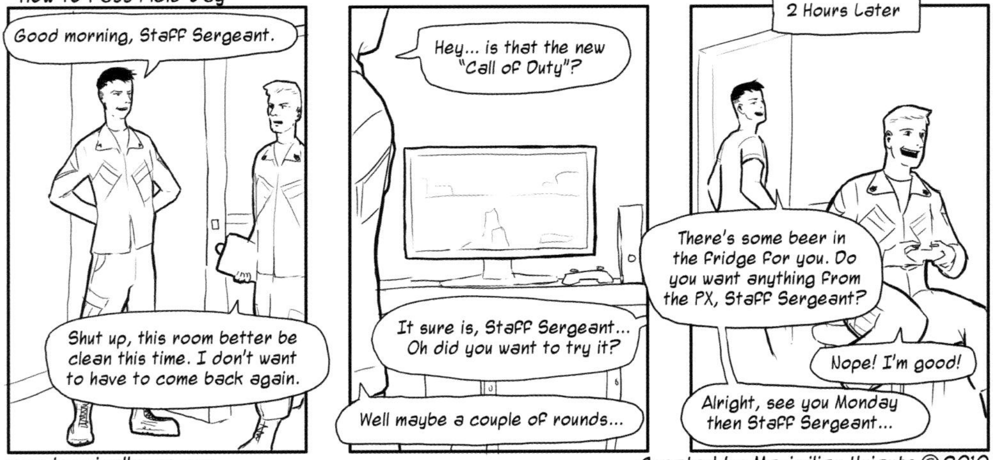
Good morning, Staff Sergeant.
Shut up, this room better be clean this time. I don't want to have to come back again.
Hey... is that the new "Call of Duty"?
It sure is, Staff Sergeant... Oh did you want to try it?
Well maybe a couple of rounds...
2 Hours Later
There's some beer in the fridge for you. Do you want anything from the PX, Staff Sergeant?
Nope! I'm good!
Alright, see you Monday then Staff Sergeant...

www.terminallance.com Created by Maximilian Uriarte © 2010

"Silkies"

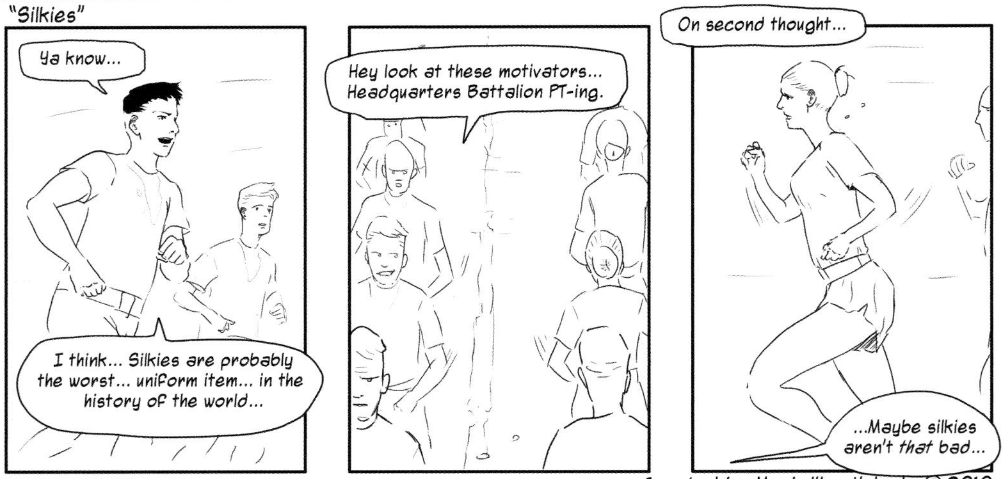
Ya know...
I think... Silkies are probably the worst... uniform item... in the history of the world...
Hey look at these motivators... Headquarters Battalion PT-ing.
On second thought...
...Maybe silkies aren't *that* bad...

www.terminallance.com Created by Maximilian Uriarte © 2010

"Holiday Spirit"

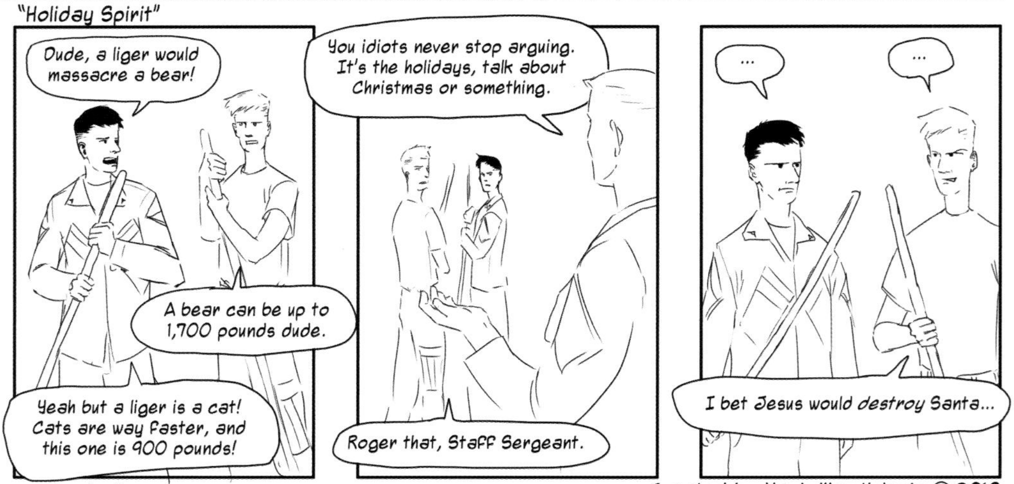
Dude, a liger would massacre a bear!
A bear can be up to 1,700 pounds dude.
Yeah but a liger is a cat! Cats are way faster, and this one is 900 pounds!
You idiots never stop arguing. It's the holidays, talk about Christmas or something.
Roger that, Staff Sergeant.
...
...
I bet Jesus would *destroy* Santa...

www.terminallance.com Created by Maximilian Uriarte © 2010

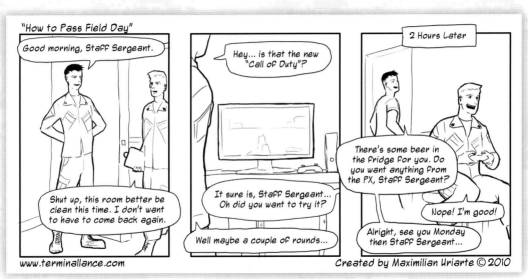

"Prospects"

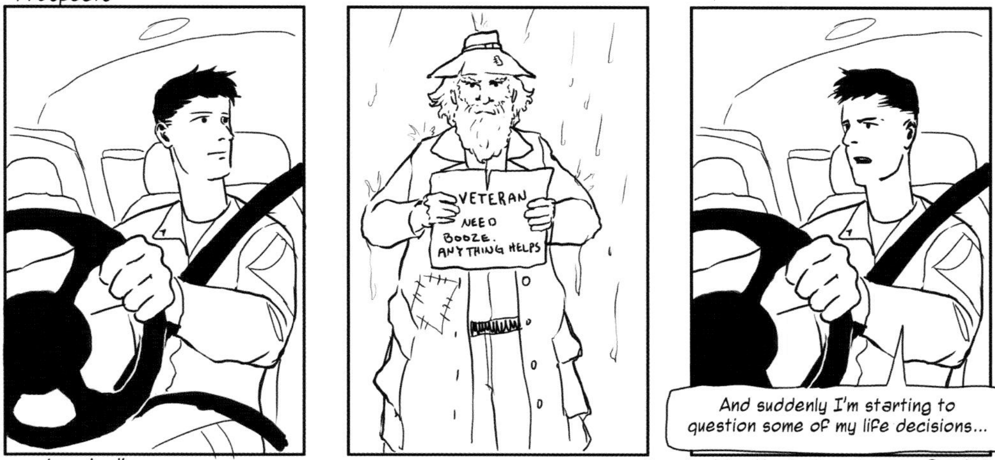

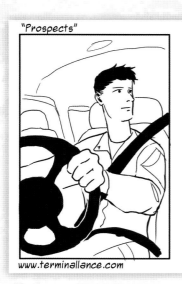

VETERAN
NEED BOOZE.
ANYTHING HELPS
And suddenly I'm starting to question some of my life decisions...

www.terminallance.com Created by Maximilian Uriarte © 2010

"The Unscrupulous Recruiter"

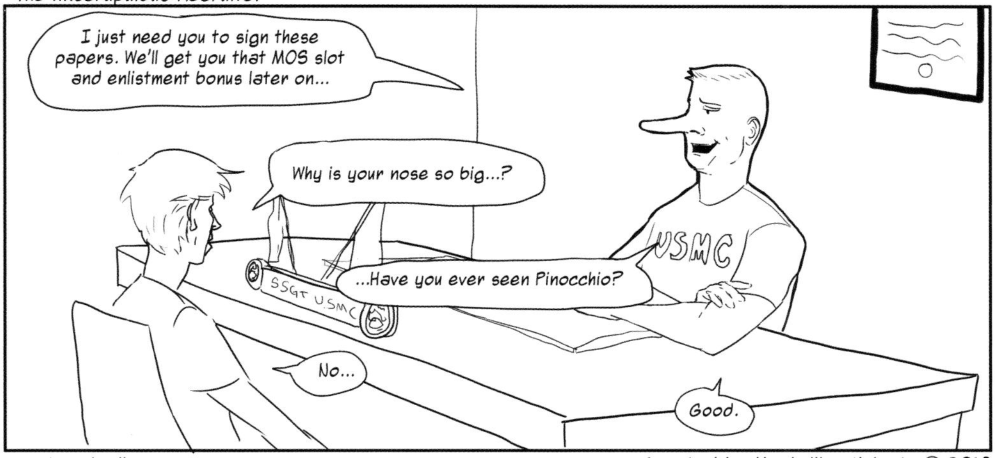

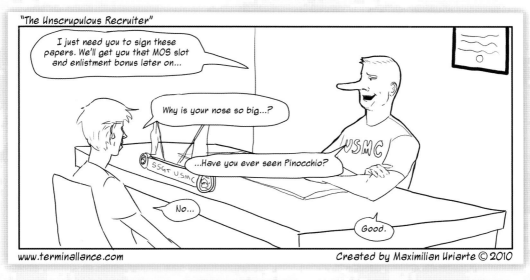

I just need you to sign these papers. We'll get you that MOS slot and enlistment bonus later on...
Why is your nose so big...?
USMC
SSGT USMC
...Have you ever seen Pinocchio?
No...
Good.

www.terminallance.com Created by Maximilian Uriarte © 2010

"Decisions, Decisions at the Chow Hall"

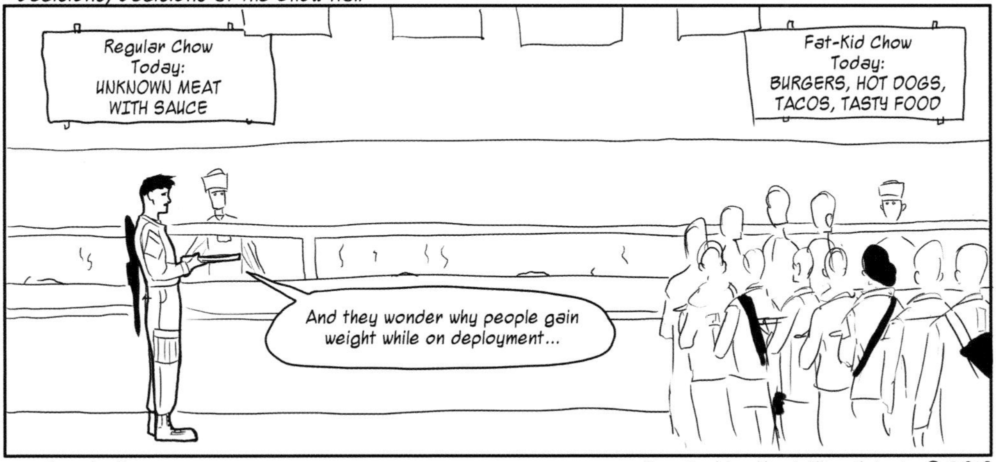

Regular Chow Today: UNKNOWN MEAT WITH SAUCE
Fat-Kid Chow Today: BURGERS, HOT DOGS, TACOS, TASTY FOOD
And they wonder why people gain weight while on deployment...

www.terminallance.com Created by Maximilian Uriarte © 2010

"Pulling Pits"

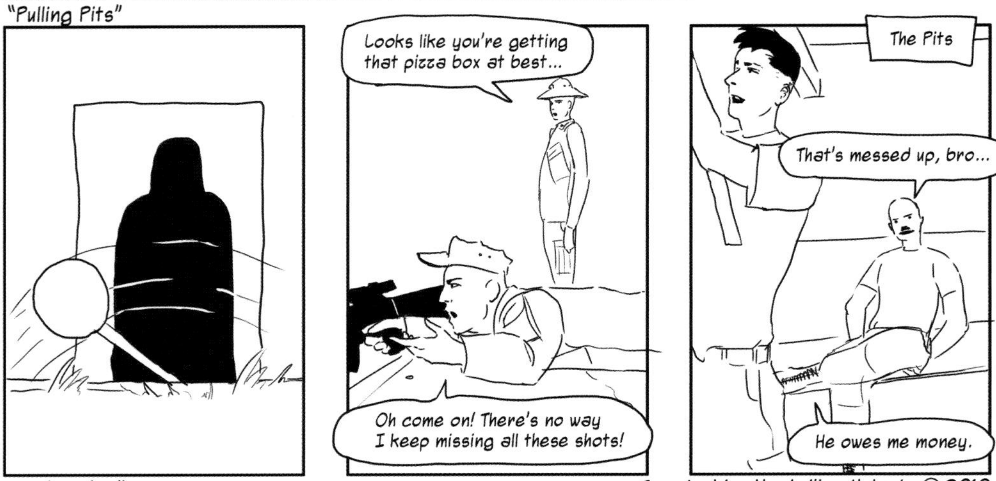
Looks like you're getting that pizza box at best...
Oh come on! There's no way I keep missing all these shots!
The Pits
That's messed up, bro...
He owes me money.

www.terminallance.com Created by Maximilian Uriarte © 2010

"Does This Mean They'll Start Asking?"

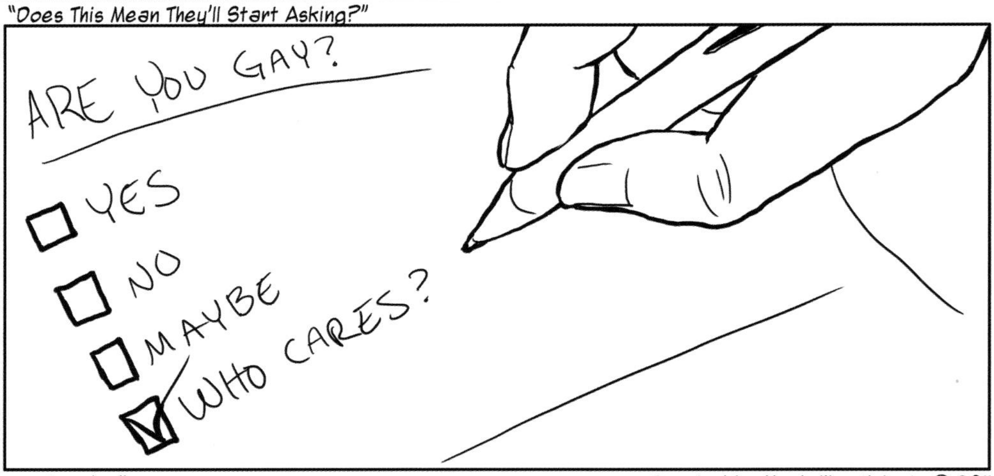
ARE YOU GAY?
YES
NO
MAYBE
WHO CARES?

www.terminallance.com Created by Maximilian Uriarte © 2011

"Life After EAS: The First Haircut"

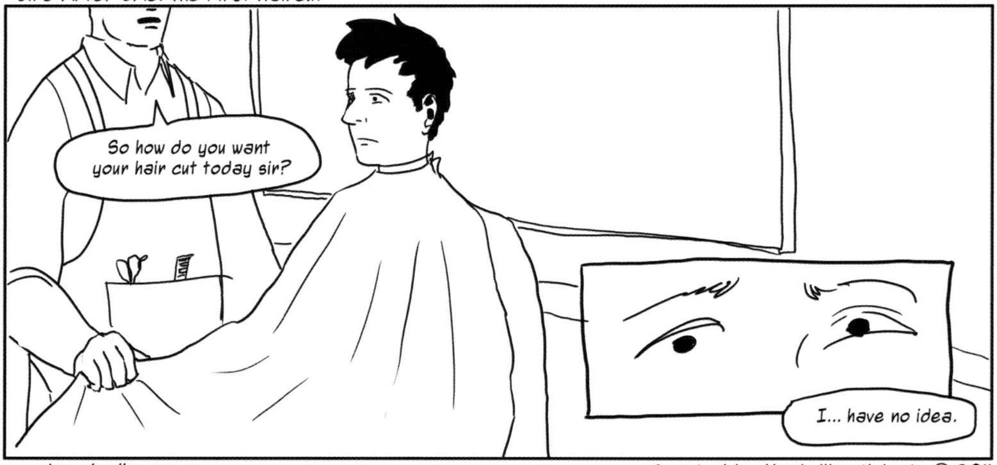
So how do you want your hair cut today sir?
I... have no idea.

www.terminallance.com Created by Maximilian Uriarte © 2011

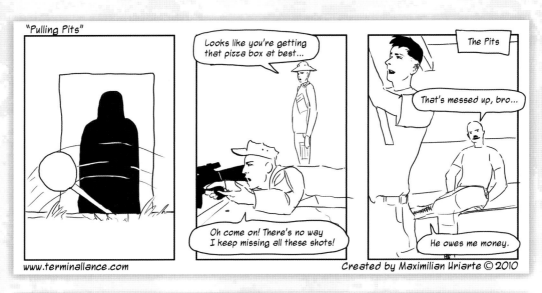

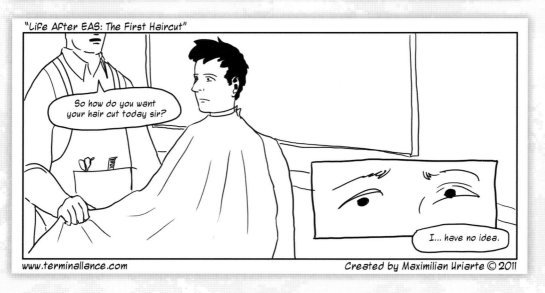

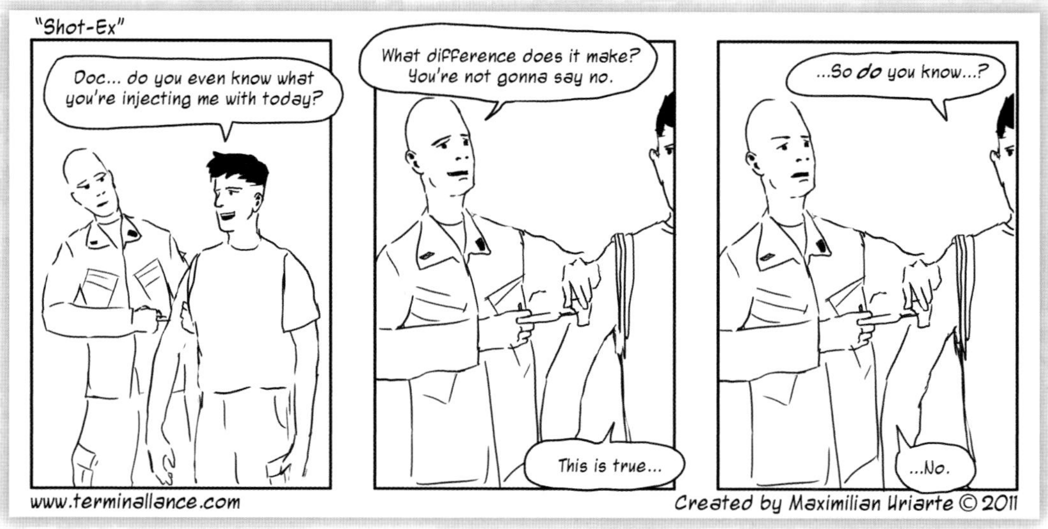
"Shot-Ex"
Doc... do you even know what you're injecting me with today?
What difference does it make? You're not gonna say no.
This is true...
...So do you know...?
...No.
www.terminallance.com
Created by Maximilian Uriarte © 2011

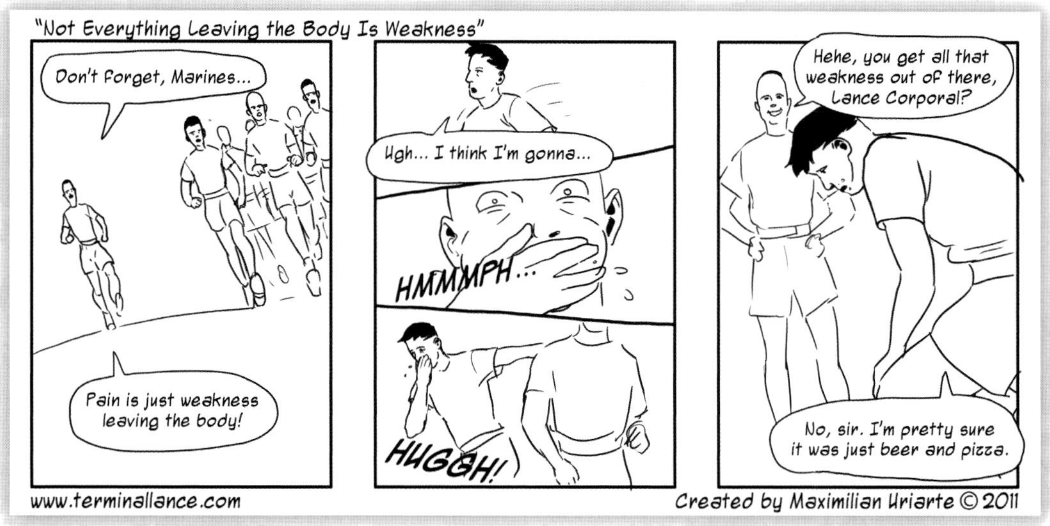
"Not Everything Leaving the Body Is Weakness"
Don't forget, Marines...
Pain is just weakness leaving the body!
Ugh... I think I'm gonna...
HMMMPH...
HUGGH!
Hehe, you get all that weakness out of there, Lance Corporal?
No, sir. I'm pretty sure it was just beer and pizza.
www.terminallance.com
Created by Maximilian Uriarte © 2011

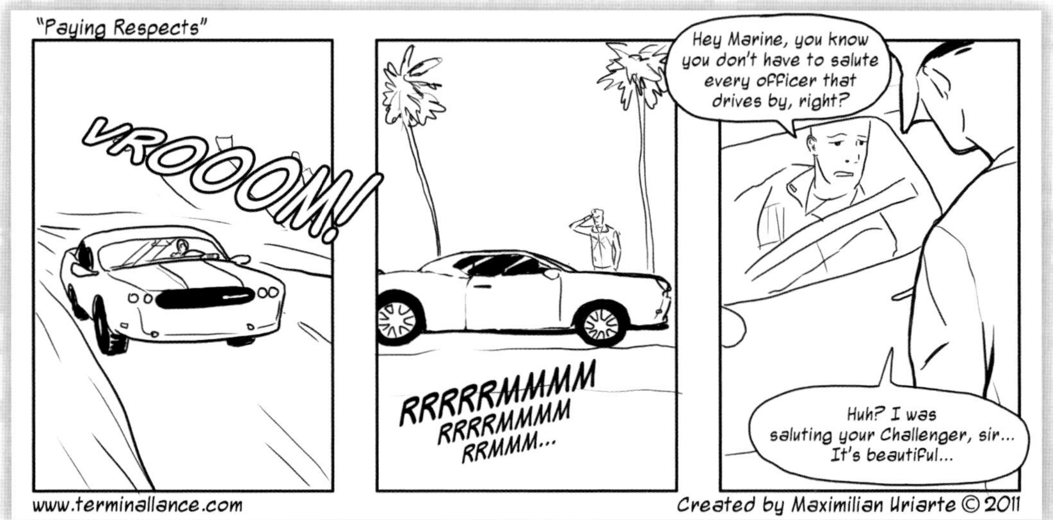
"Paying Respects"
VROOOOM!
RRRRRMMMM
RRRRMMMM
RRMMM...
Hey Marine, you know you don't have to salute every officer that drives by, right?
Huh? I was saluting your Challenger, sir... It's beautiful...
www.terminallance.com
Created by Maximilian Uriarte © 2011

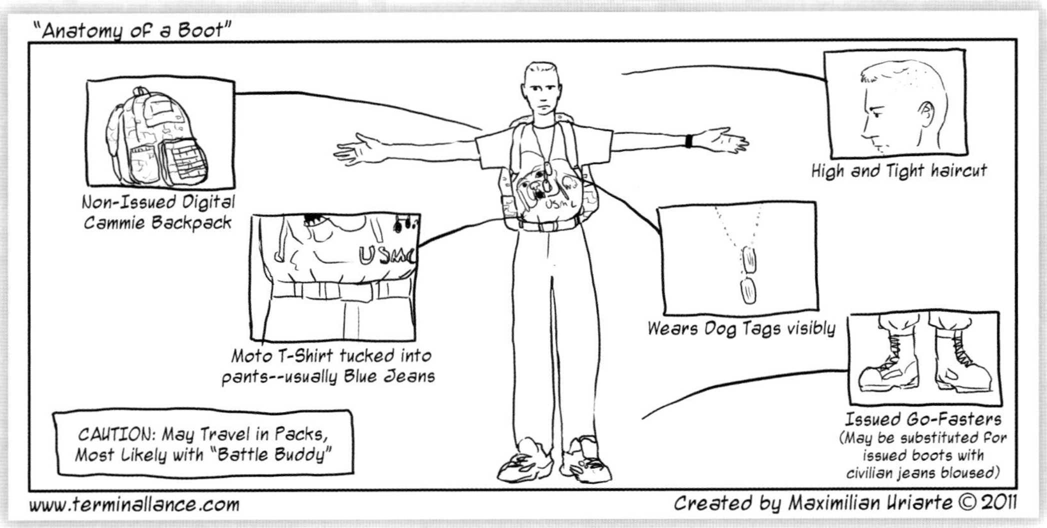
"Anatomy of a Boot"
Non-Issued Digital Cammie Backpack
USMC
Moto T-Shirt tucked into pants--usually Blue Jeans
High and Tight haircut
Wears Dog Tags visibly
Issued Go-Fasters
(May be substituted for issued boots with civilian jeans bloused)
CAUTION: May Travel in Packs, Most Likely with "Battle Buddy"
www.terminallance.com
Created by Maximilian Uriarte © 2011

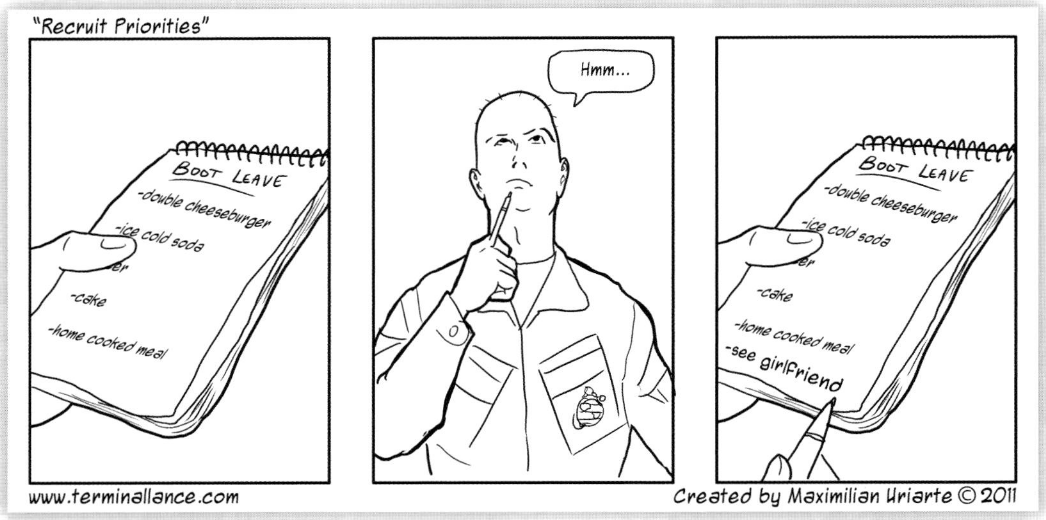
"Recruit Priorities"
BOOT LEAVE
-double cheeseburger
-ice cold soda
-cake
-home cooked meal
Hmm...
BOOT LEAVE
-double cheeseburger
-ice cold soda
-cake
-home cooked meal
-see girlfriend
www.terminallance.com
Created by Maximilian Uriarte © 2011

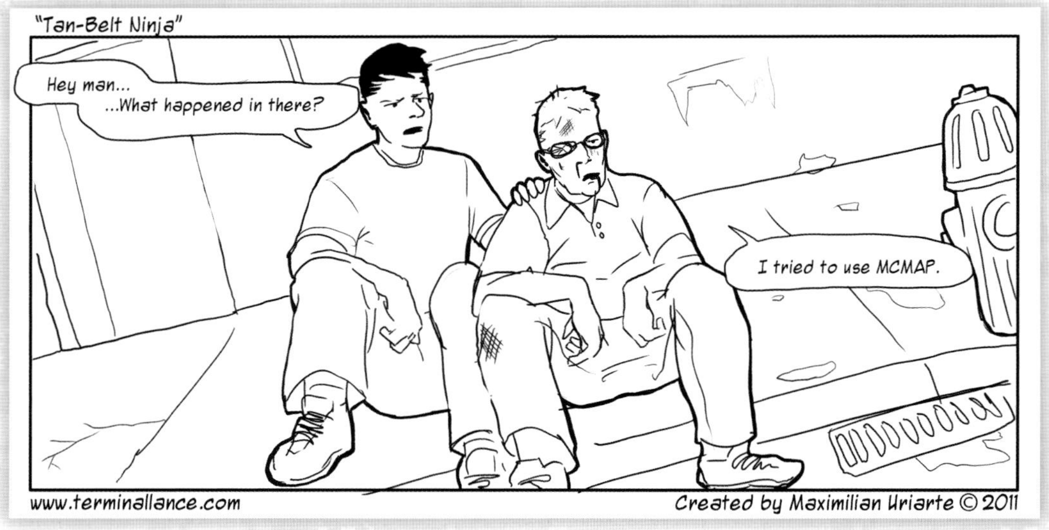
"Tan-Belt Ninja"
Hey man... ...What happened in there?
I tried to use MCMAP.
www.terminallance.com
Created by Maximilian Uriarte © 2011

"Aloha!"

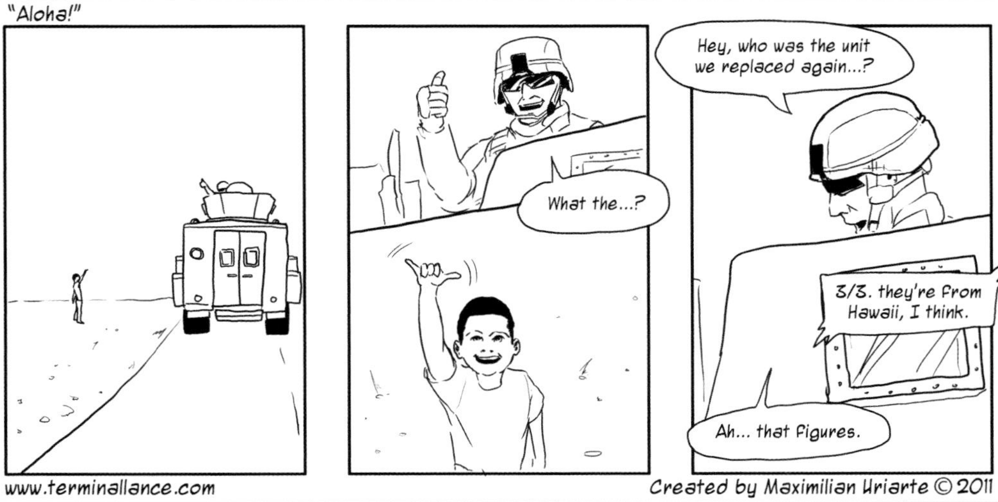

Hey, who was the unit we replaced again...?
What the...?
3/3. they're from Hawaii, I think.
Ah... that figures.
www.terminallance.com
Created by Maximilian Uriarte © 2011

"Wildlife at the School of Infantry"

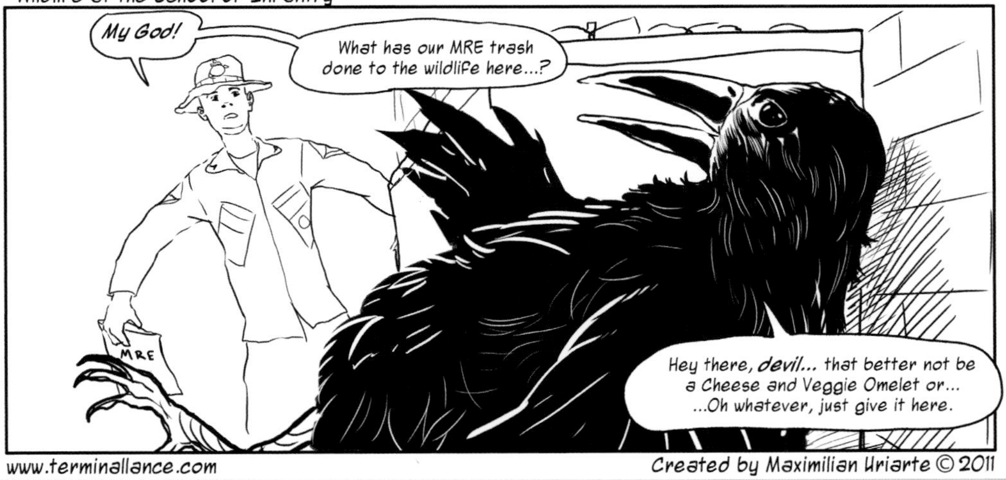

My God!
What has our MRE trash done to the wildlife here...?
MRE
Hey there, *devil...* that better not be a Cheese and Veggie Omelet or... ...Oh whatever, just give it here.
www.terminallance.com
Created by Maximilian Uriarte © 2011

"Silkies 2"

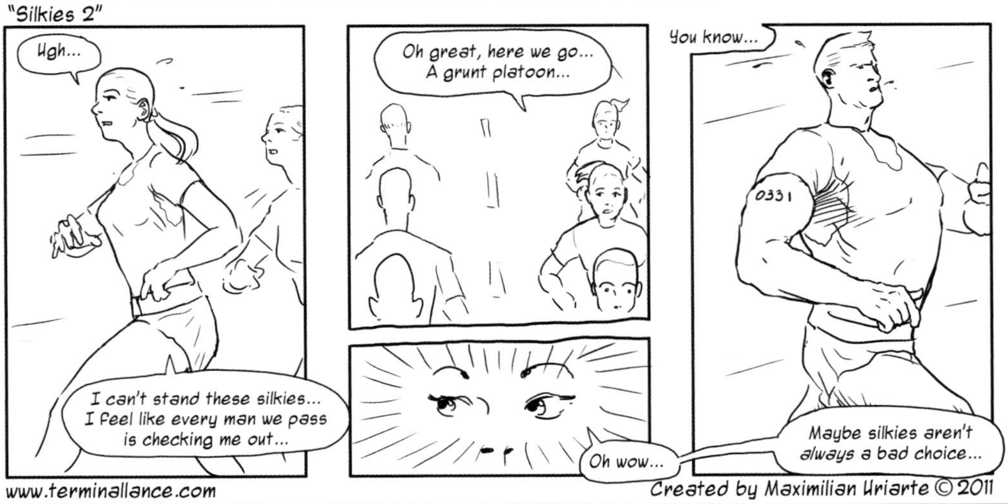

Ugh...
I can't stand these silkies... I feel like every man we pass is checking me out...
Oh great, here we go... A grunt platoon...
Oh wow...
You know...
0331
Maybe silkies aren't *always* a bad choice...
www.terminallance.com
Created by Maximilian Uriarte © 2011

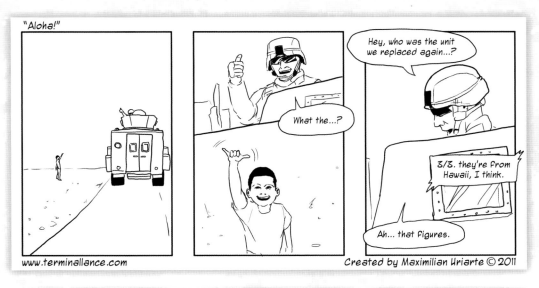

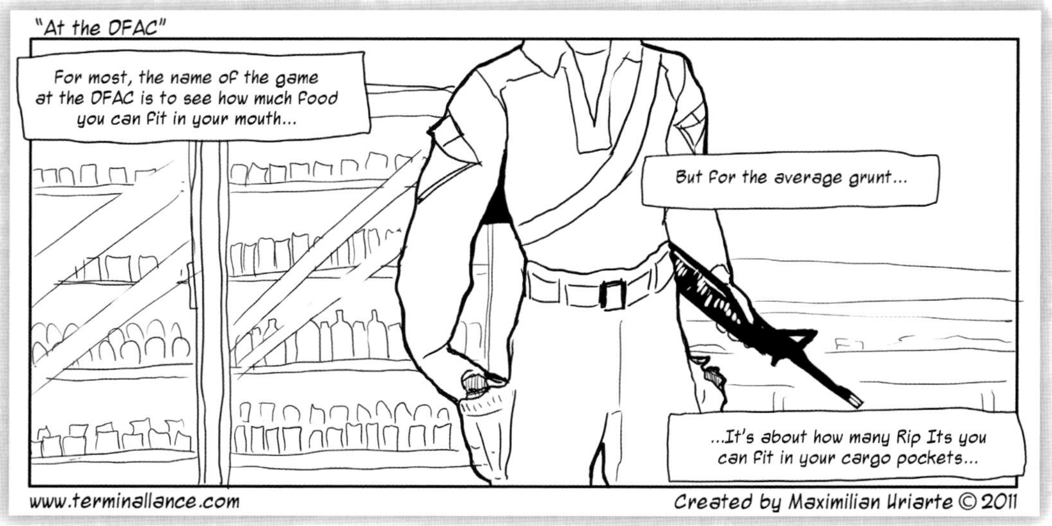
"At the OFAC"
For most, the name of the game at the OFAC is to see how much food you can fit in your mouth...
But for the average grunt...
...It's about how many Rip Its you can fit in your cargo pockets...
www.terminallance.com
Created by Maximilian Uriarte © 2011

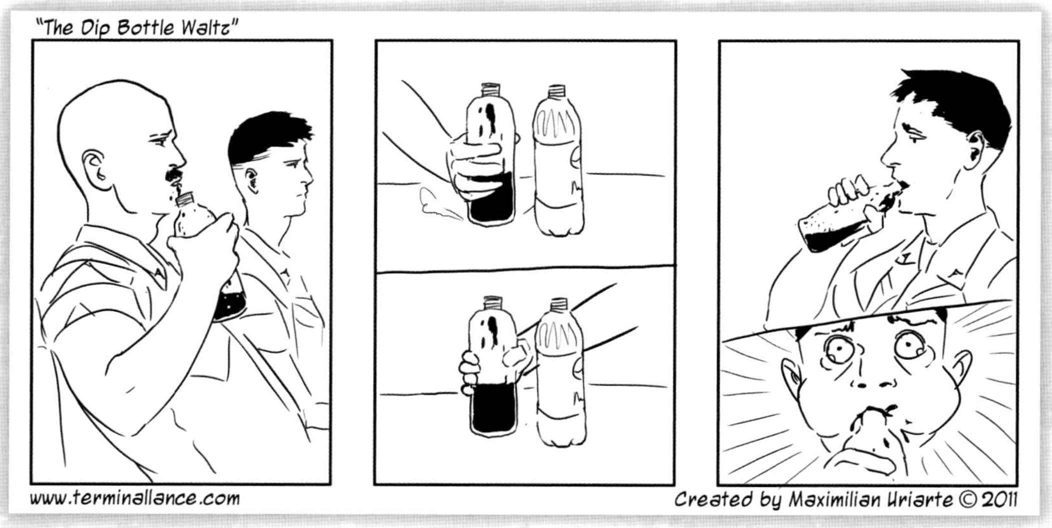
"The Dip Bottle Waltz"
www.terminallance.com
Created by Maximilian Uriarte © 2011

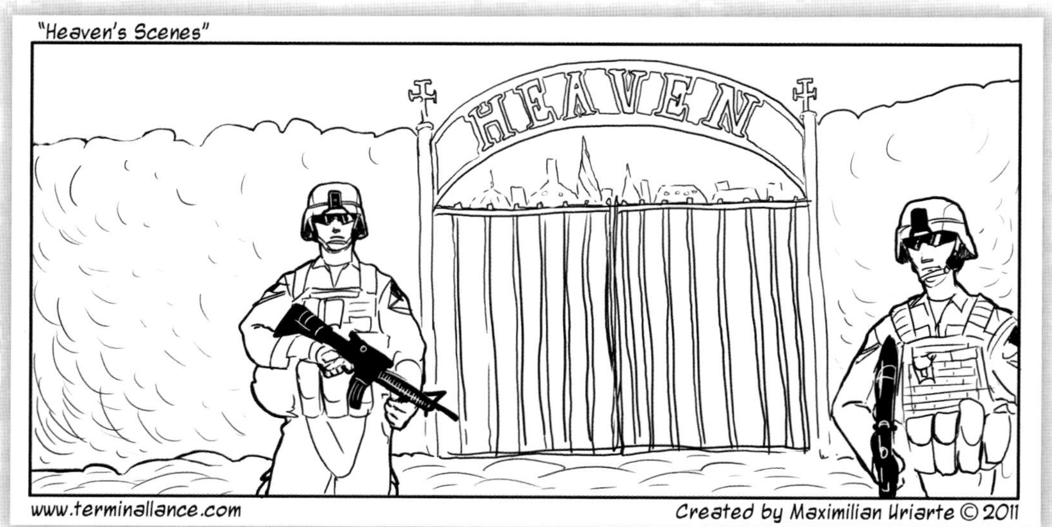
"Heaven's Scenes"
HEAVEN
www.terminallance.com
Created by Maximilian Uriarte © 2011

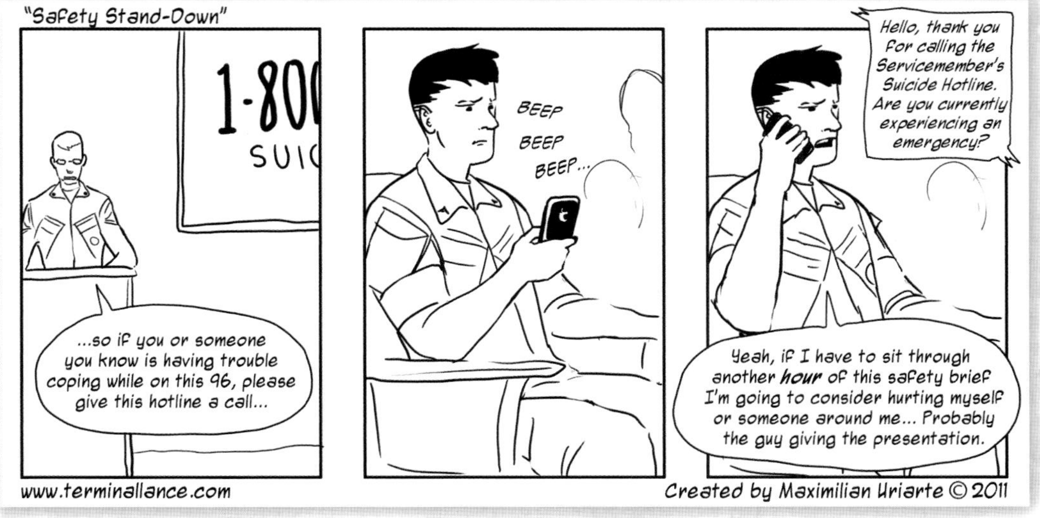
"Safety Stand-Down"
1-800
SUIC
...so if you or someone you know is having trouble coping while on this 96, please give this hotline a call...
BEEP
BEEP
BEEP...
Hello, thank you for calling the Servicemember's Suicide Hotline. Are you currently experiencing an emergency?
Yeah, if I have to sit through another **hour** of this safety brief I'm going to consider hurting myself or someone around me... Probably the guy giving the presentation.
www.terminallance.com
Created by Maximilian Uriarte © 2011

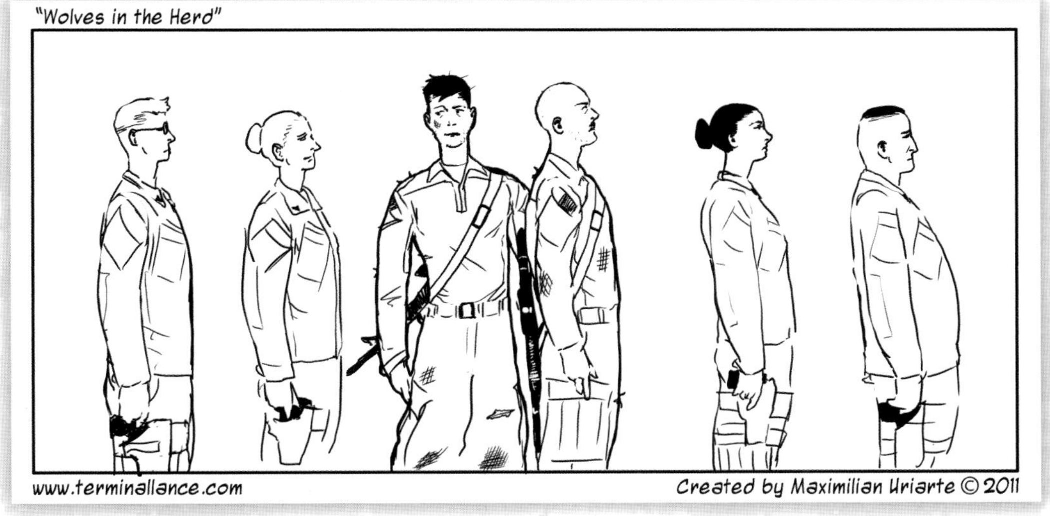
"Wolves in the Herd"
www.terminallance.com
Created by Maximilian Uriarte © 2011

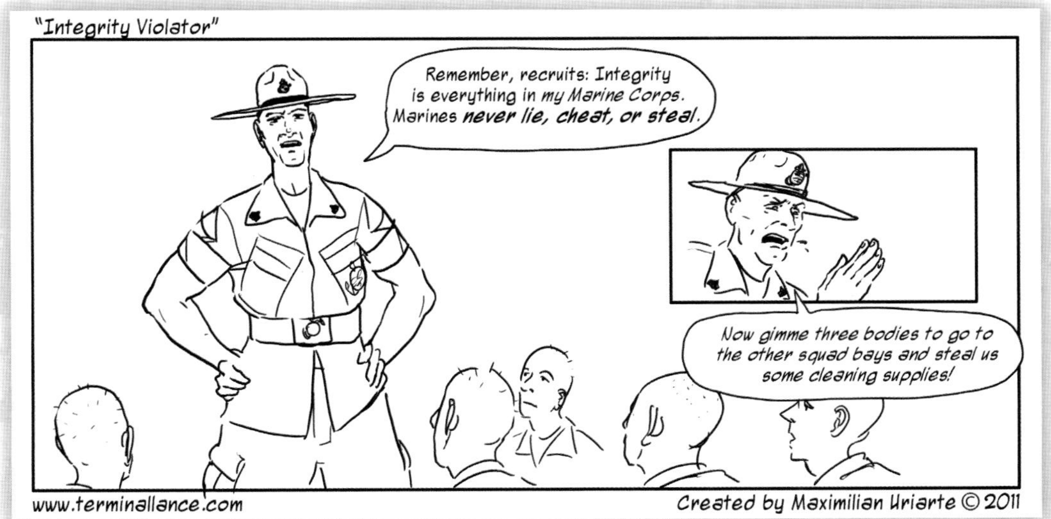
"Integrity Violator"
Remember, recruits: Integrity is everything in *my Marine Corps*. Marines ***never lie, cheat, or steal***.
Now gimme three bodies to go to the other squad bays and steal us some cleaning supplies!
www.terminallance.com
Created by Maximilian Uriarte © 2011

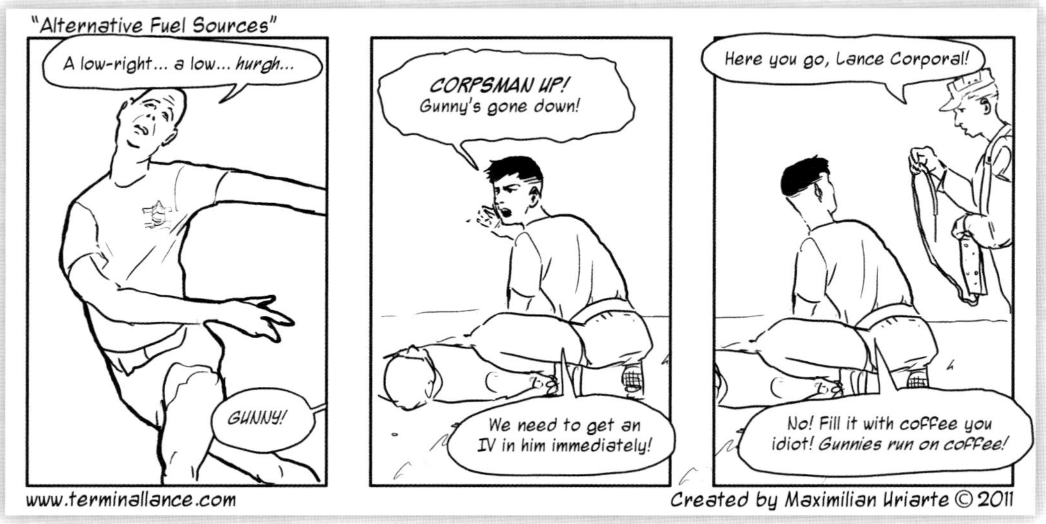
"Alternative Fuel Sources"
A low-right... a low... hurgh...
GUNNY!
CORPSMAN UP! Gunny's gone down!
We need to get an IV in him immediately!
Here you go, Lance Corporal!
No! Fill it with coffee you idiot! Gunnies run on coffee!
www.terminallance.com
Created by Maximilian Uriarte © 2011

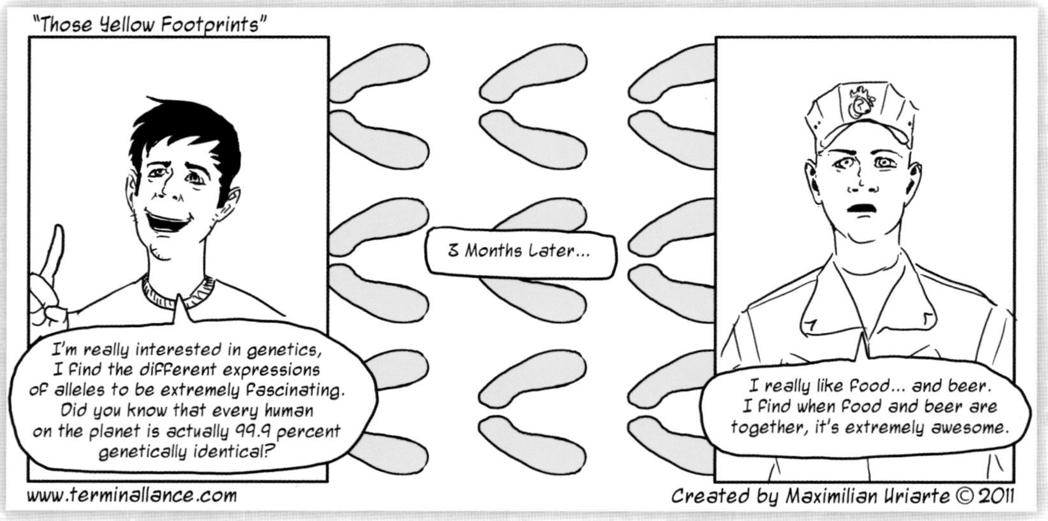
"Those Yellow Footprints"
I'm really interested in genetics, I find the different expressions of alleles to be extremely fascinating. Did you know that every human on the planet is actually 99.9 percent genetically identical?
3 Months Later...
I really like food... and beer. I find when food and beer are together, it's extremely awesome.
www.terminallance.com
Created by Maximilian Uriarte © 2011

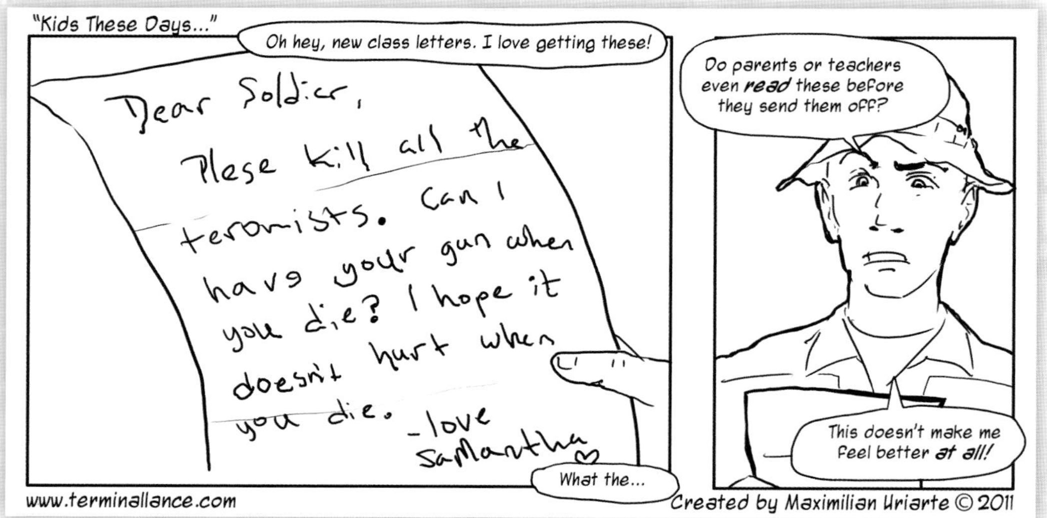
"Kids These Days..."
Oh hey, new class letters. I love getting these!
Dear Soldier,
Plese kill all the teromists. Can I have your gun when you die? I hope it doesn't hurt when you die. -love Samantha
What the...
Do parents or teachers even read these before they send them off?
This doesn't make me feel better at all!
www.terminallance.com
Created by Maximilian Uriarte © 2011

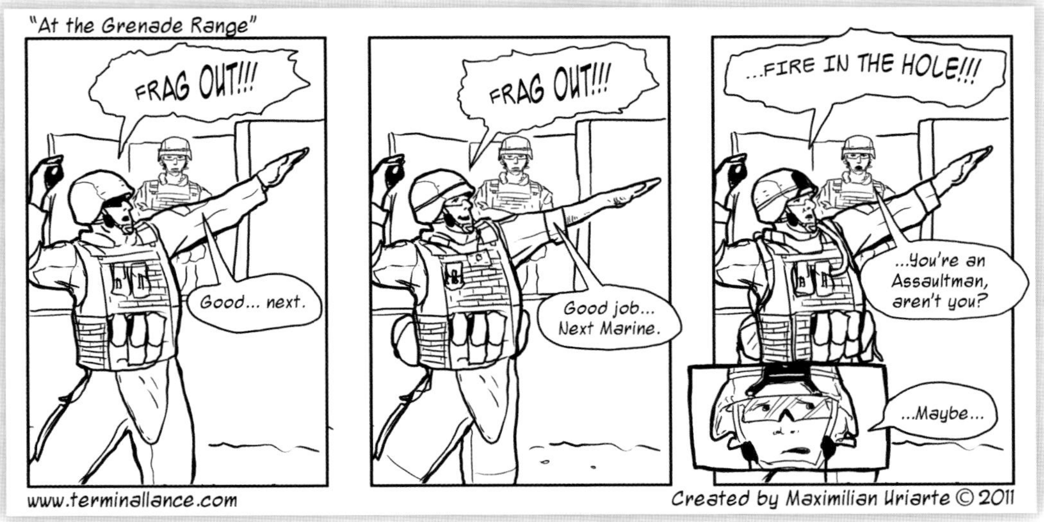
"At the Grenade Range"
FRAG OUT!!!
Good... next.
FRAG OUT!!!
Good job... Next Marine.
...FIRE IN THE HOLE!!!
...You're an Assaultman, aren't you?
...Maybe...
www.terminallance.com
Created by Maximilian Uriarte © 2011

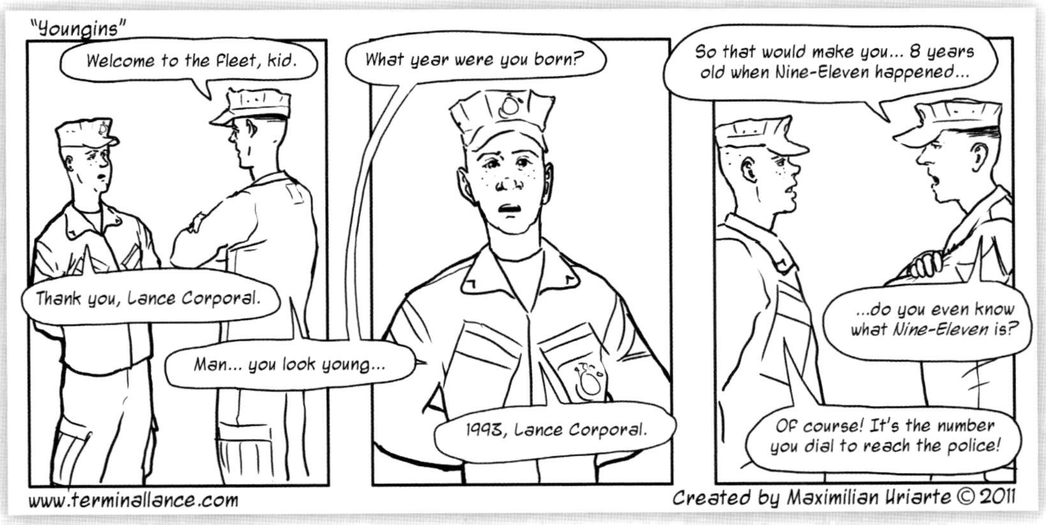
"Youngins"
Welcome to the fleet, kid.
Thank you, Lance Corporal.
Man... you look young...
What year were you born?
1993, Lance Corporal.
So that would make you... 8 years old when Nine-Eleven happened...
...do you even know what Nine-Eleven is?
Of course! It's the number you dial to reach the police!
www.terminallance.com
Created by Maximilian Uriarte © 2011

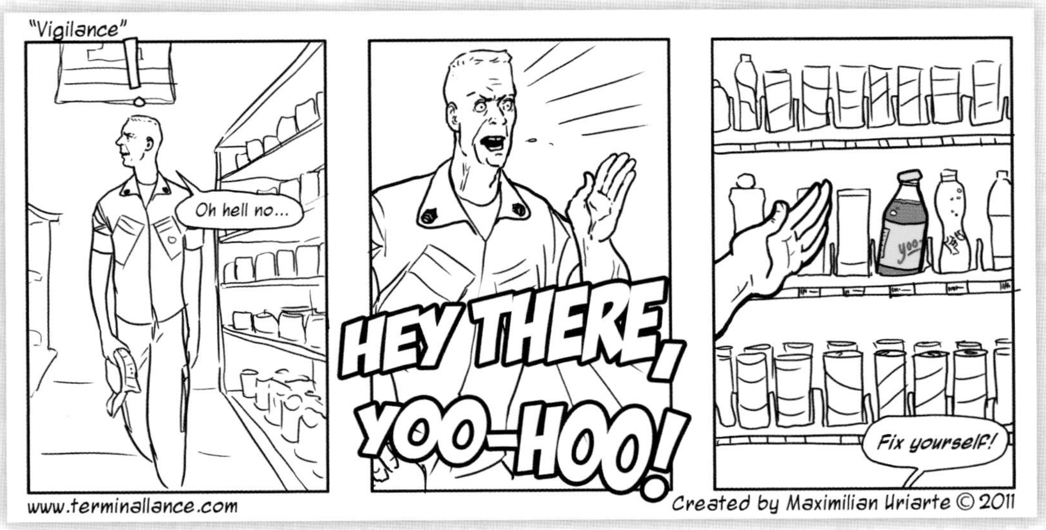
"Vigilance"
Oh hell no...
HEY THERE, YOO-HOO!
Fix yourself!
www.terminallance.com
Created by Maximilian Uriarte © 2011

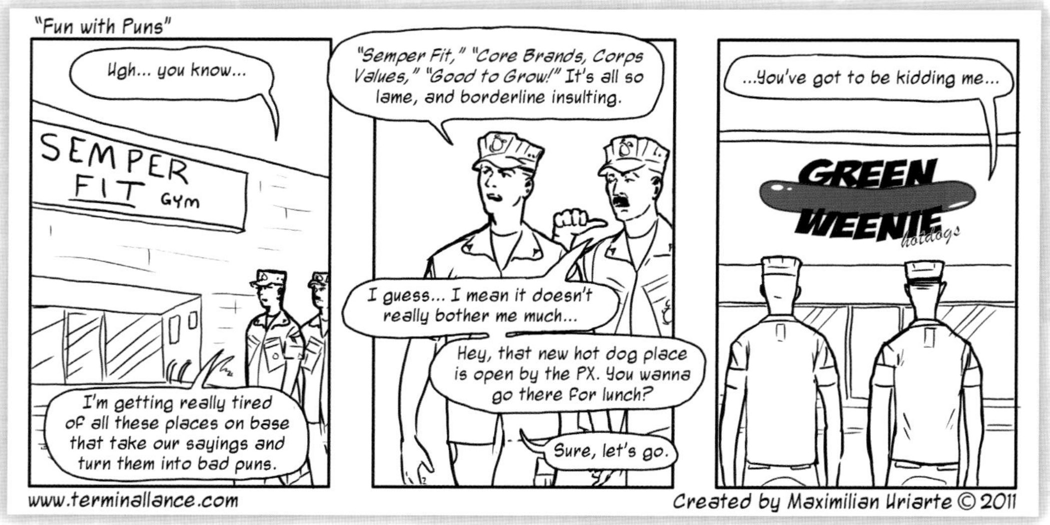
"Fun with Puns"
Ugh... you know...
SEMPER FIT GYM
I'm getting really tired of all these places on base that take our sayings and turn them into bad puns.
"Semper Fit," "Core Brands, Corps Values," "Good to Grow!" It's all so lame, and borderline insulting.
I guess... I mean it doesn't really bother me much...
Hey, that new hot dog place is open by the PX. You wanna go there for lunch?
Sure, let's go.
...You've got to be kidding me...
GREEN WEENIE hotdogs
www.terminallance.com
Created by Maximilian Uriarte © 2011

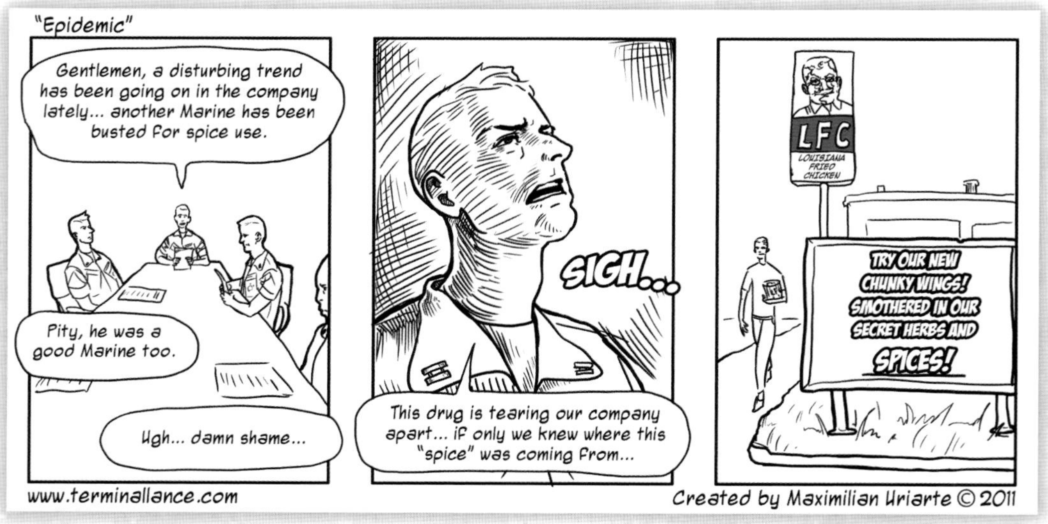
"Epidemic"
Gentlemen, a disturbing trend has been going on in the company lately... another Marine has been busted for spice use.
Pity, he was a good Marine too.
Ugh... damn shame...
SIGH...
This drug is tearing our company apart... if only we knew where this "spice" was coming from...
LFC
LOUISIANA FRIED CHICKEN
TRY OUR NEW CHUNKY WINGS! SMOTHERED IN OUR SECRET HERBS AND SPICES!
www.terminallance.com
Created by Maximilian Uriarte © 2011

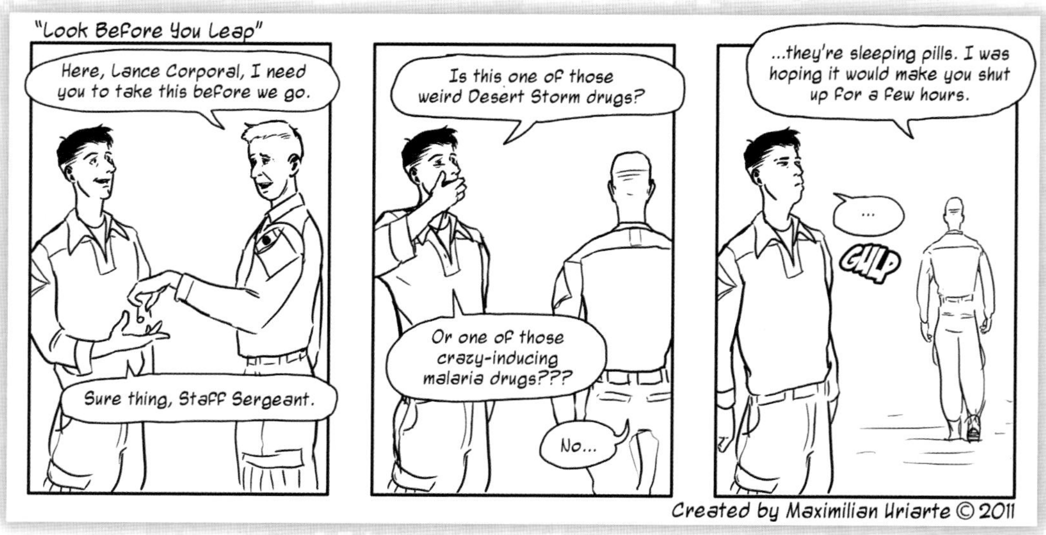
"Look Before You Leap"
Here, Lance Corporal, I need you to take this before we go.
Sure thing, Staff Sergeant.
Is this one of those weird Desert Storm drugs?
Or one of those crazy-inducing malaria drugs???
No...
...they're sleeping pills. I was hoping it would make you shut up for a few hours.
...
GULP
Created by Maximilian Uriarte © 2011

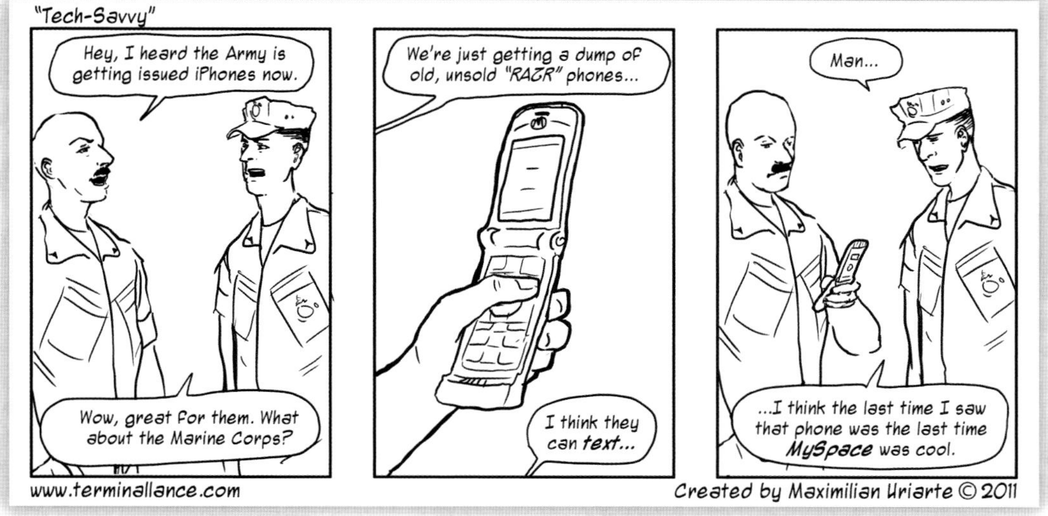
"Tech-Savvy"
Hey, I heard the Army is getting issued iPhones now.
Wow, great for them. What about the Marine Corps?
We're just getting a dump of old, unsold "RAZR" phones...
I think they can *text*...
Man...
...I think the last time I saw that phone was the last time *MySpace* was cool.
www.terminallance.com
Created by Maximilian Uriarte © 2011

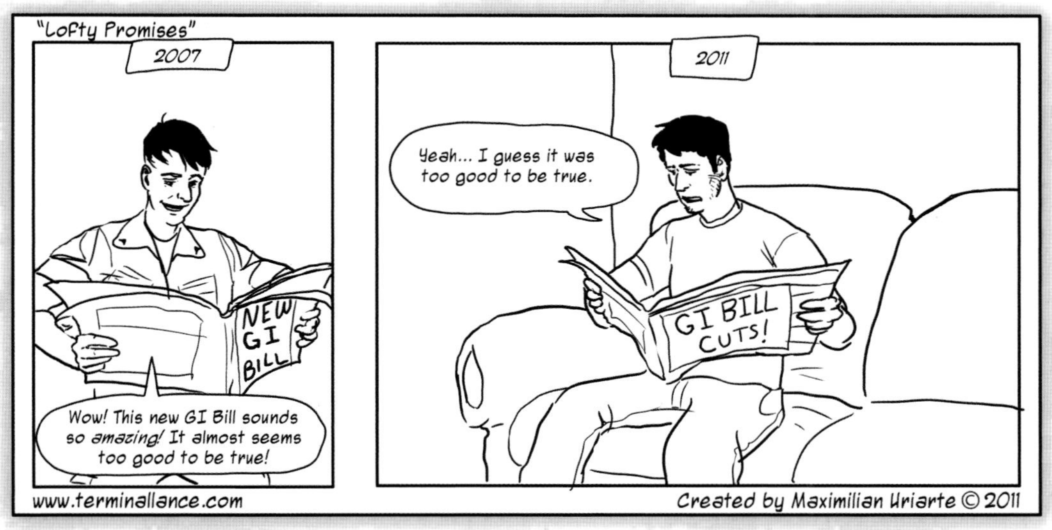
"Lofty Promises"
2007
NEW GI BILL
Wow! This new GI Bill sounds so *amazing!* It almost seems too good to be true!
2011
Yeah... I guess it was too good to be true.
GI BILL CUTS!
www.terminallance.com
Created by Maximilian Uriarte © 2011

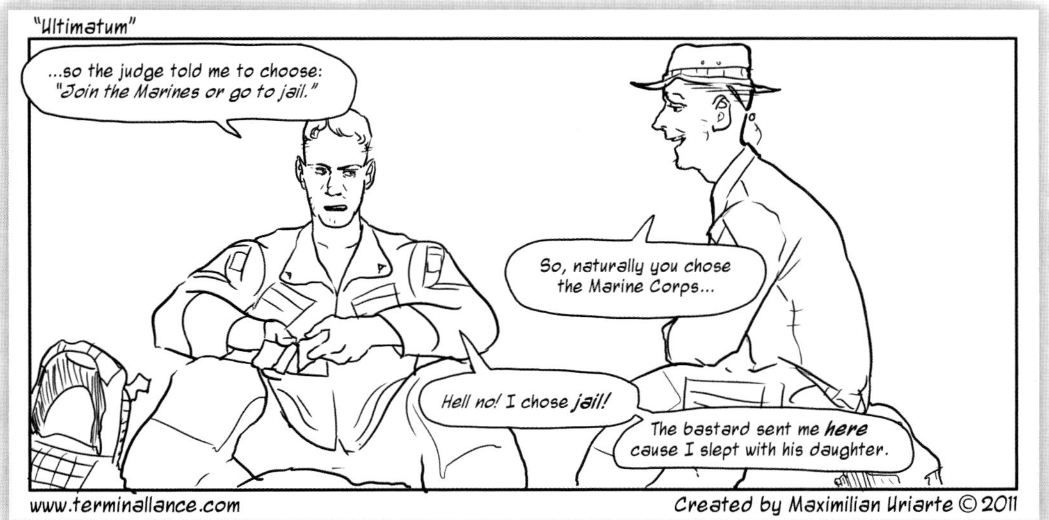
"Ultimatum"
...so the judge told me to choose: "Join the Marines or go to jail."
So, naturally you chose the Marine Corps...
Hell no! I chose *jail!*
The bastard sent me *here* cause I slept with his daughter.
www.terminallance.com
Created by Maximilian Uriarte © 2011

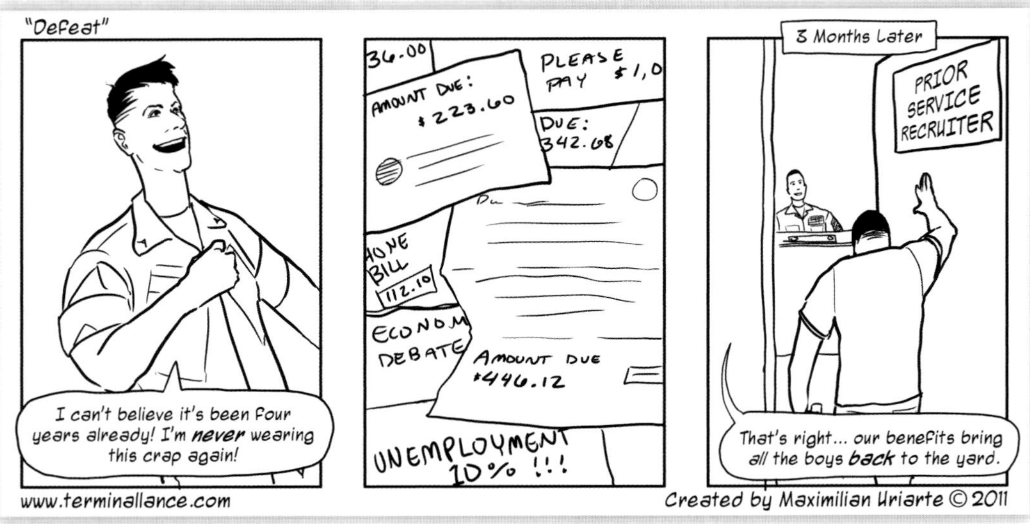
"Defeat"
I can't believe it's been four years already! I'm never wearing this crap again!
36.00
PLEASE PAY $1,0
AMOUNT DUE: $223.60
DUE: 342.68
HONE BILL 112.10
ECONOM DEBATE
AMOUNT DUE $446.12
UNEMPLOYMENT 10% !!!
3 Months Later
PRIOR SERVICE RECRUITER
That's right... our benefits bring all the boys back to the yard.
www.terminallance.com
Created by Maximilian Uriarte © 2011

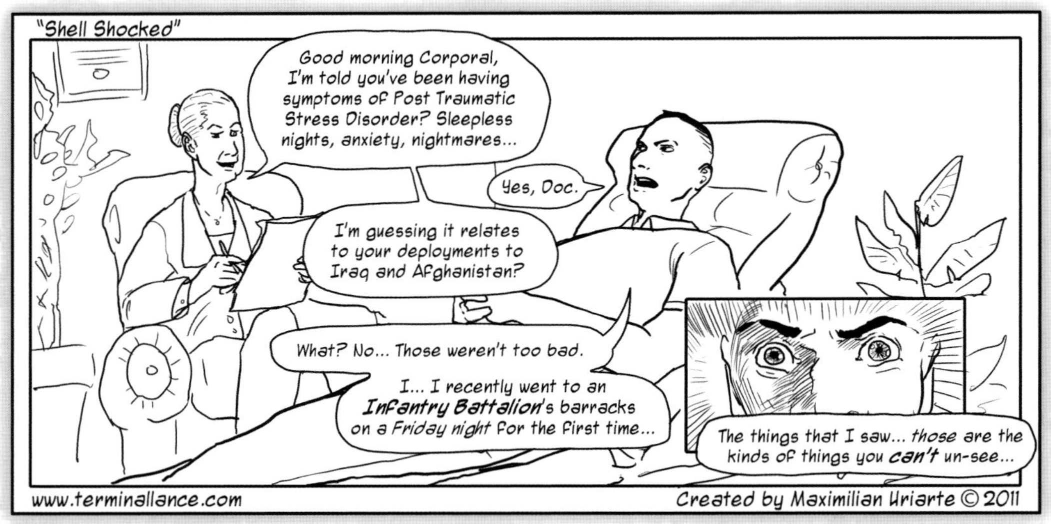
"Shell Shocked"
Good morning Corporal, I'm told you've been having symptoms of Post Traumatic Stress Disorder? Sleepless nights, anxiety, nightmares...
Yes, Doc.
I'm guessing it relates to your deployments to Iraq and Afghanistan?
What? No... Those weren't too bad.
I... I recently went to an Infantry Battalion's barracks on a Friday night for the first time...
The things that I saw... those are the kinds of things you can't un-see...
www.terminallance.com
Created by Maximilian Uriarte © 2011

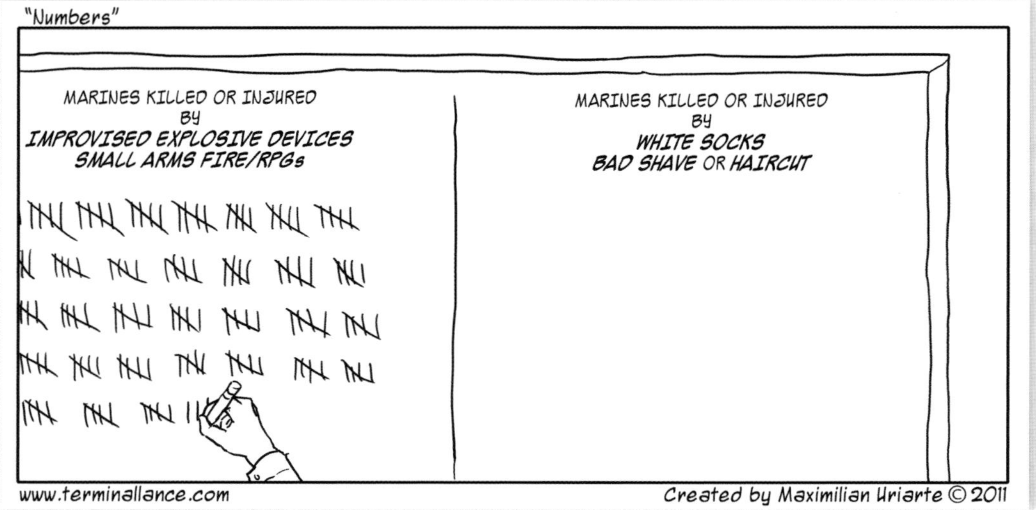
"Numbers"
MARINES KILLED OR INJURED BY IMPROVISED EXPLOSIVE DEVICES SMALL ARMS FIRE/RPGs
MARINES KILLED OR INJURED BY WHITE SOCKS BAD SHAVE OR HAIRCUT
www.terminallance.com
Created by Maximilian Uriarte © 2011

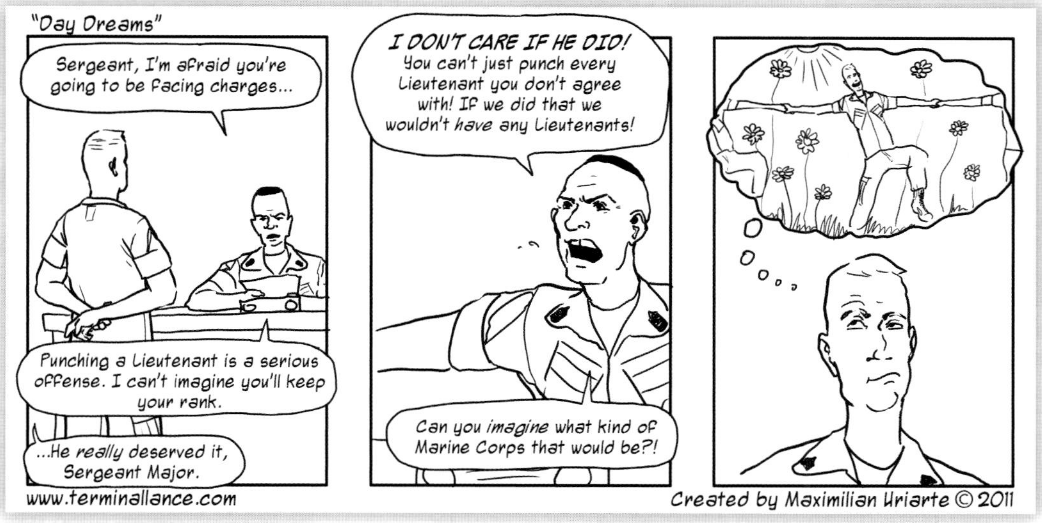
"Day Dreams"
Sergeant, I'm afraid you're going to be facing charges...
Punching a Lieutenant is a serious offense. I can't imagine you'll keep your rank.
...He *really* deserved it, Sergeant Major.
I DON'T CARE IF HE DID! You can't just punch every Lieutenant you don't agree with! If we did that we wouldn't *have* any Lieutenants!
Can you *imagine* what kind of Marine Corps that would be?!
www.terminallance.com
Created by Maximilian Uriarte © 2011

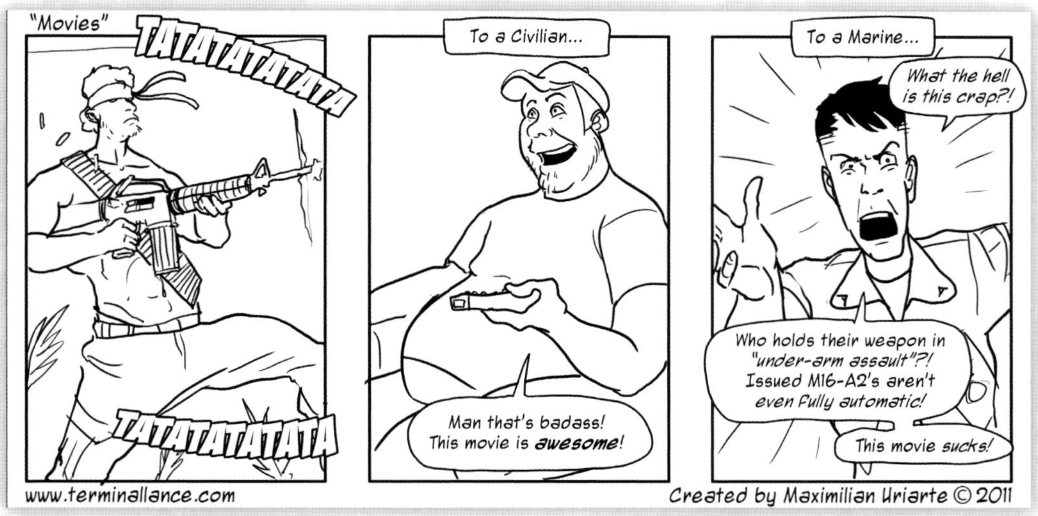
"Movies"
TATATATATATATA
TATATATATATA
To a Civilian...
Man that's badass! This movie is **awesome**!
To a Marine...
What the hell is this crap?!
Who holds their weapon in *"under-arm assault"*?! Issued M16-A2's aren't even fully automatic!
This movie sucks!
www.terminallance.com
Created by Maximilian Uriarte © 2011

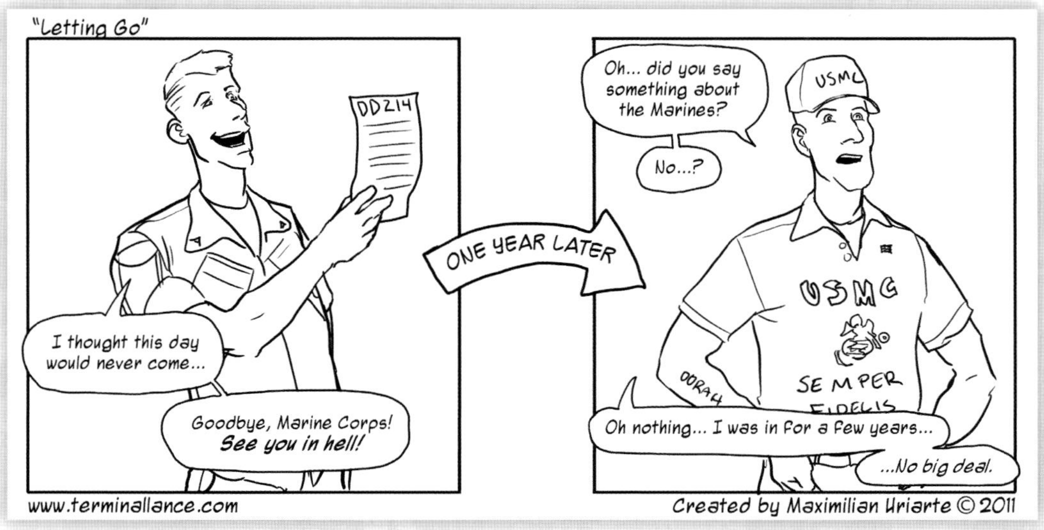
"Letting Go"
DD214
I thought this day would never come...
Goodbye, Marine Corps! **See you in hell!**
ONE YEAR LATER
Oh... did you say something about the Marines?
No...?
USMC
USMC
SEMPER FIDELIS
OORAH
Oh nothing... I was in for a few years...
...No big deal.
www.terminallance.com
Created by Maximilian Uriarte © 2011

"Camp Cupcake"

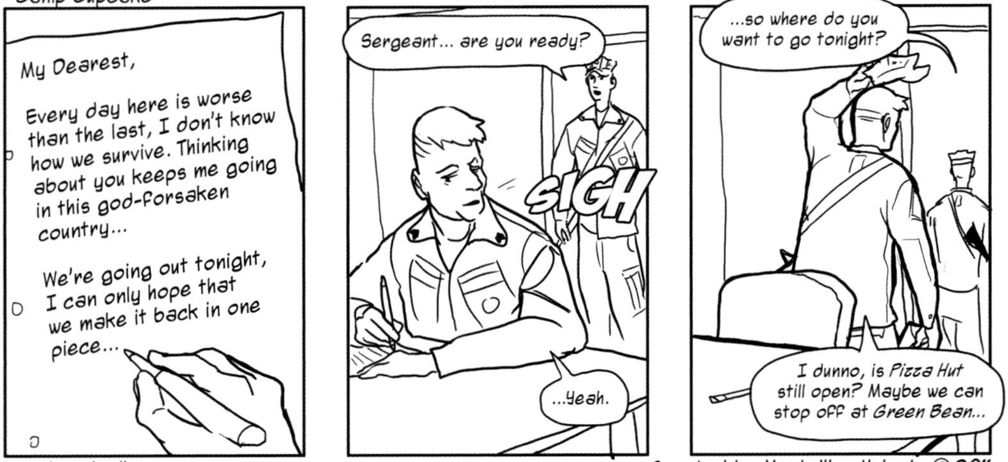
My Dearest,
Every day here is worse than the last, I don't know how we survive. Thinking about you keeps me going in this god-forsaken country...
We're going out tonight, I can only hope that we make it back in one piece...
Sergeant... are you ready?
SIGH
...Yeah.
...so where do you want to go tonight?
I dunno, is Pizza Hut still open? Maybe we can stop off at Green Bean...

www.terminallance.com Created by Maximilian Uriarte © 2011

"The Nomenclature of Rank"

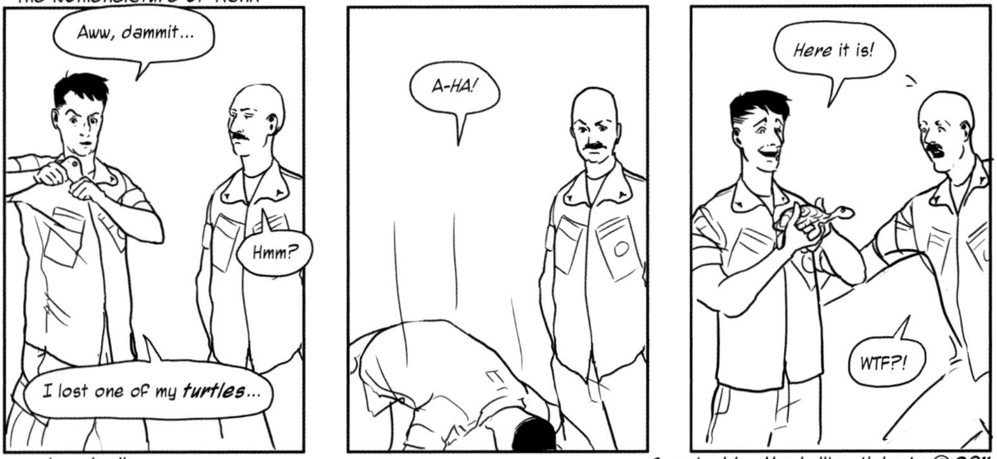
Aww, dammit...
Hmm?
I lost one of my turtles...
A-HA!
Here it is!
WTF?!

www.terminallance.com Created by Maximilian Uriarte © 2011

"Confusing Combat Uniforms"

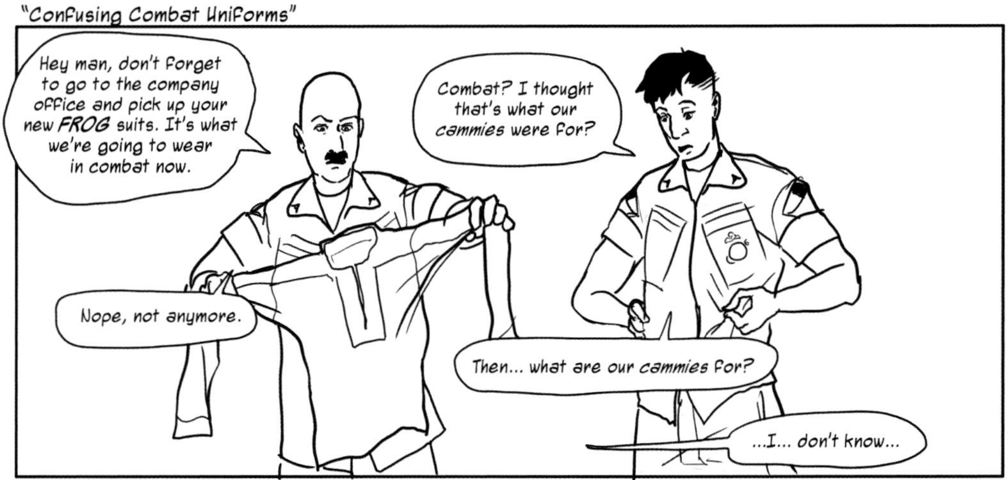
Hey man, don't forget to go to the company office and pick up your new FROG suits. It's what we're going to wear in combat now.
Combat? I thought that's what our cammies were for?
Nope, not anymore.
Then... what are our cammies for?
...I... don't know...

www.terminallance.com Created by Maximilian Uriarte © 2011

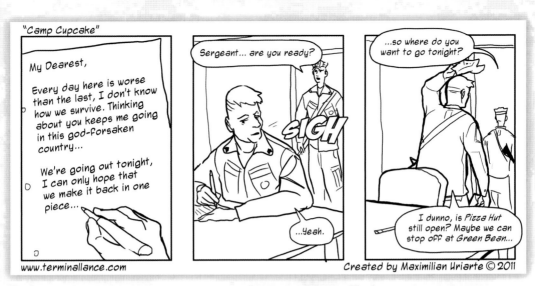

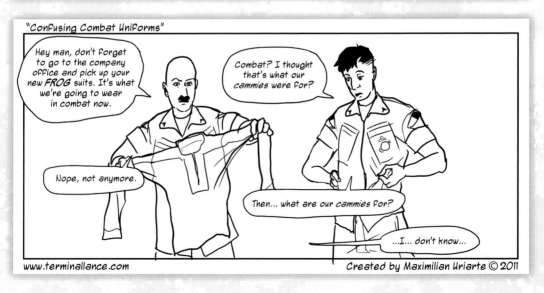

"Expectations"

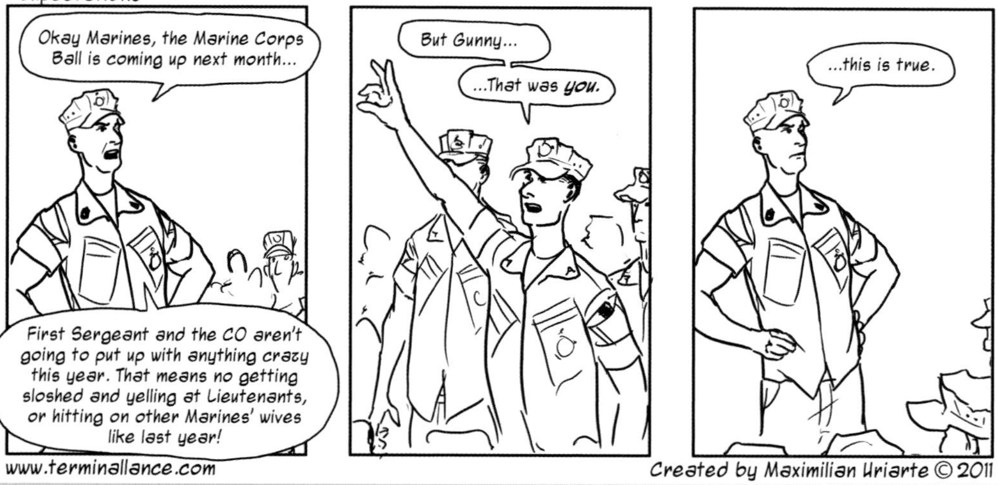
Okay Marines, the Marine Corps Ball is coming up next month...
First Sergeant and the CO aren't going to put up with anything crazy this year. That means no getting sloshed and yelling at Lieutenants, or hitting on other Marines' wives like last year!
But Gunny...
...That was *you.*
...this is true.
www.terminallance.com
Created by Maximilian Uriarte © 2011

"The Social Network"

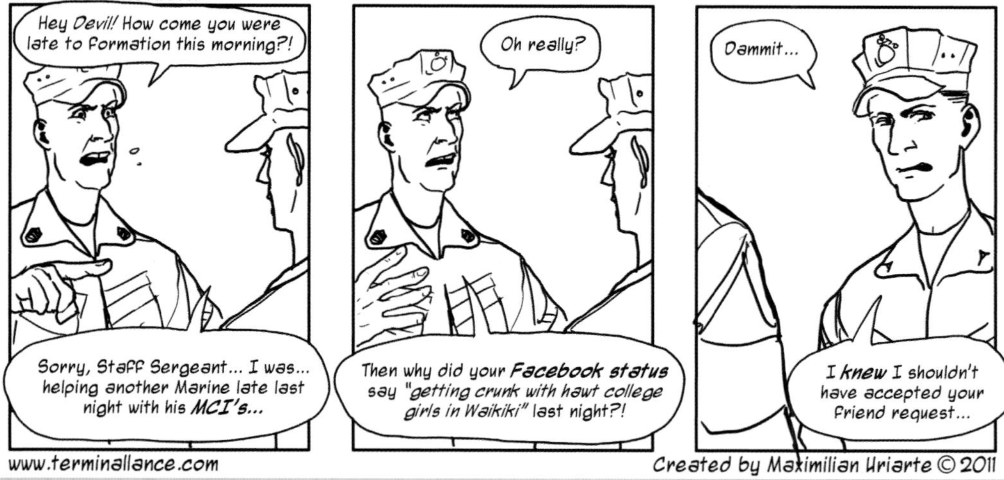
Hey *Devil!* How come you were late to formation this morning?!
Sorry, Staff Sergeant... I was... helping another Marine late last night with his *MCI's...*
Oh really?
Then why did your ***Facebook status*** say *"getting crunk with hawt college girls in Waikiki"* last night?!
Dammit...
I ***knew*** I shouldn't have accepted your friend request...
www.terminallance.com
Created by Maximilian Uriarte © 2011

"Sleeves Down"

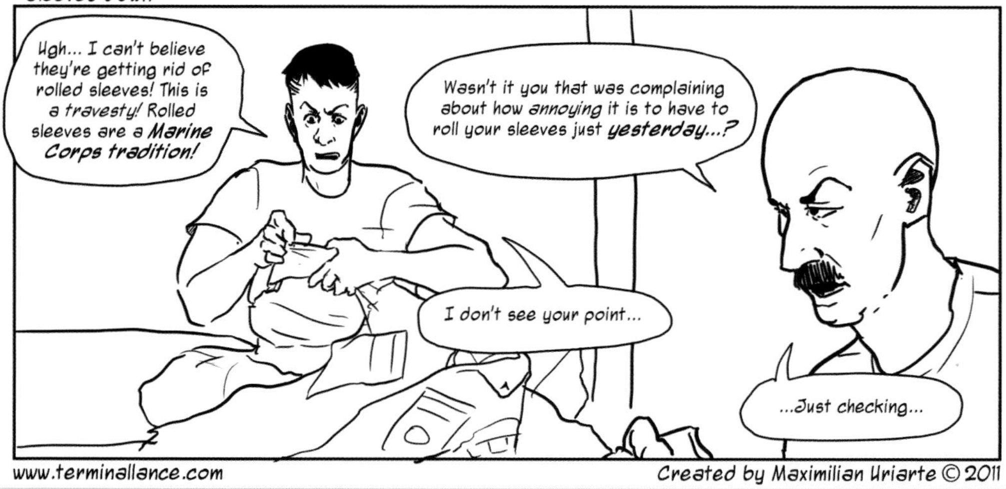
Ugh... I can't believe they're getting rid of rolled sleeves! This is a *travesty!* Rolled sleeves are a ***Marine Corps tradition!***
Wasn't it you that was complaining about how *annoying* it is to have to roll your sleeves just ***yesterday...?***
I don't see your point...
...Just checking...
www.terminallance.com
Created by Maximilian Uriarte © 2011

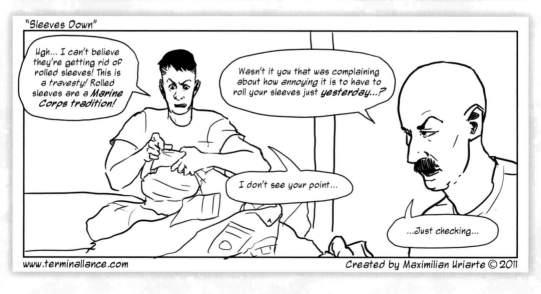

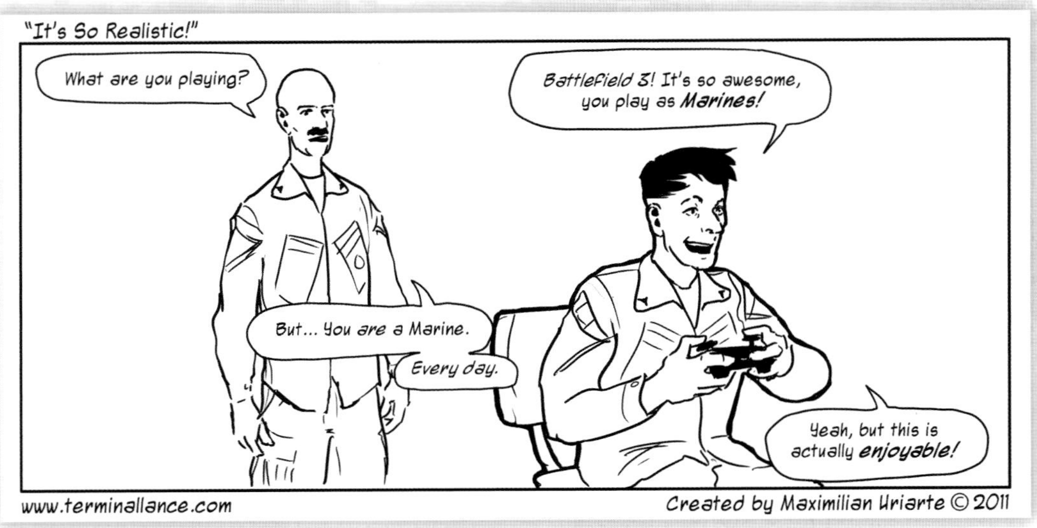
"It's So Realistic!"
What are you playing?
Battlefield 3! It's so awesome, you play as **Marines!**
But... You are a Marine.
Every day.
Yeah, but this is actually ***enjoyable!***
www.terminallance.com
Created by Maximilian Uriarte © 2011

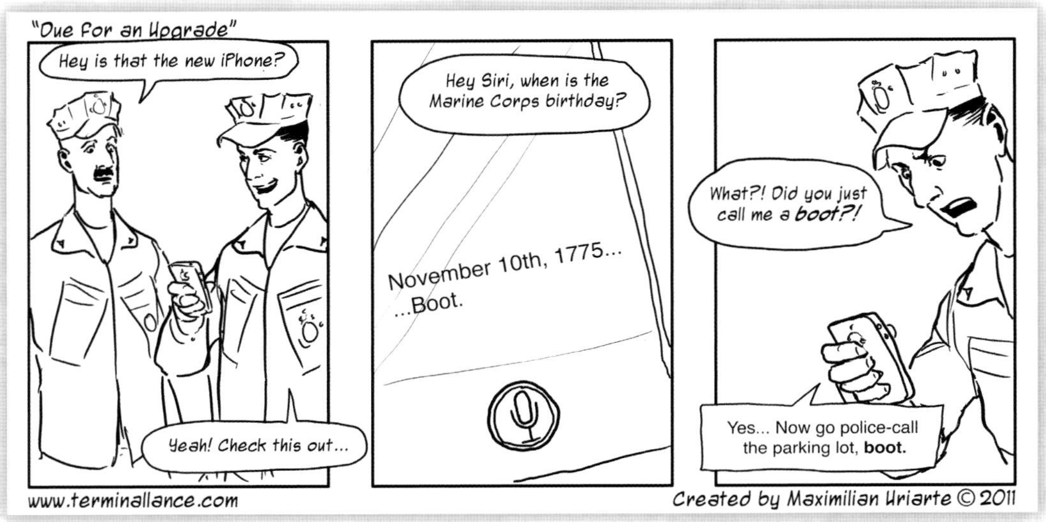
"Due for an Upgrade"
Hey is that the new iPhone?
Yeah! Check this out...
Hey Siri, when is the Marine Corps birthday?
November 10th, 1775...
...Boot.
What?! Did you just call me a ***boot?!***
Yes... Now go police-call the parking lot, **boot.**
www.terminallance.com
Created by Maximilian Uriarte © 2011

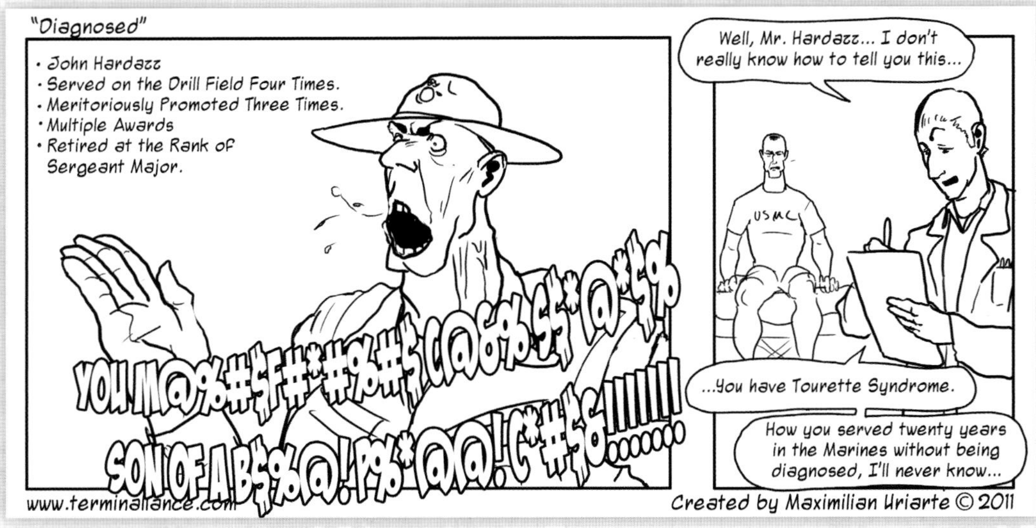
"Diagnosed"
• John Hardazz
• Served on the Drill Field Four Times.
• Meritoriously Promoted Three Times.
• Multiple Awards
• Retired at the Rank of Sergeant Major.
YOU M@%#$F#*#%#$(@&%$$*@*$%
SON OF A B$%@!?%*@@!(*#$&!!!!!!!........
Well, Mr. Hardazz... I don't really know how to tell you this...
...You have Tourette Syndrome.
How you served twenty years in the Marines without being diagnosed, I'll never know...
USMC
www.terminallance.com
Created by Maximilian Uriarte © 2011

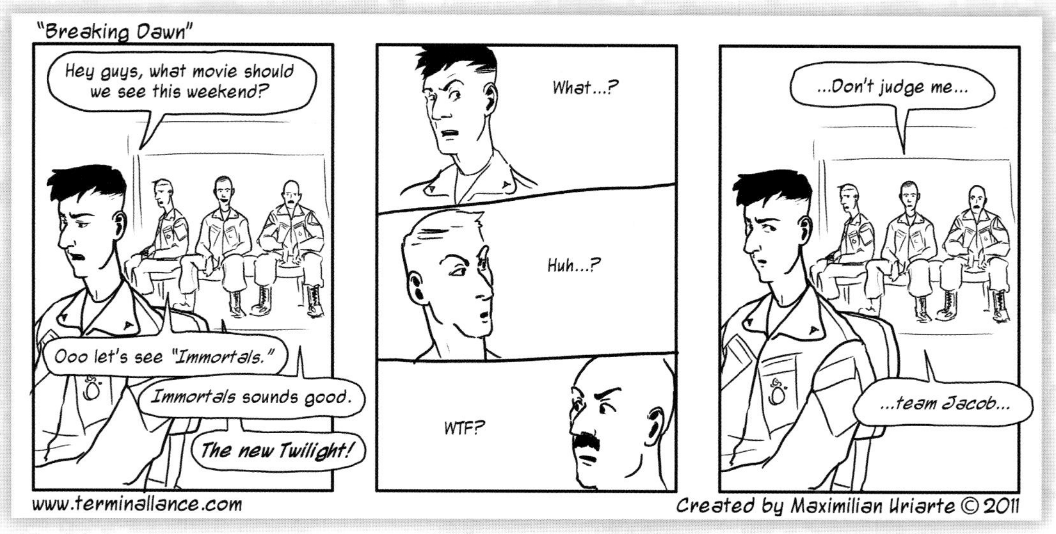
"Breaking Dawn"
Hey guys, what movie should we see this weekend?
Ooo let's see "Immortals."
Immortals sounds good.
The new Twilight!
What...?
Huh...?
WTF?
...Don't judge me...
...team Jacob...
www.terminallance.com
Created by Maximilian Uriarte © 2011

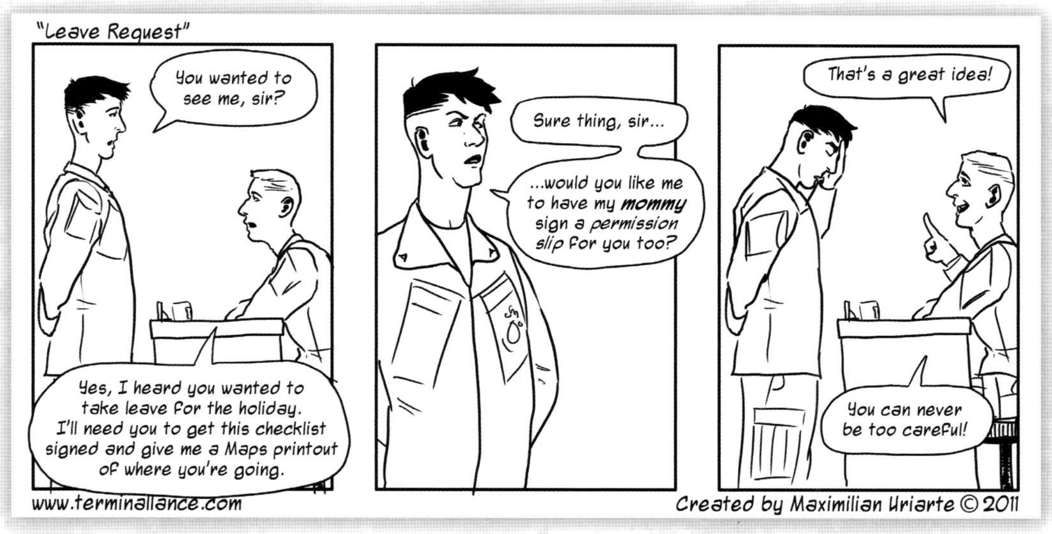
"Leave Request"
You wanted to see me, sir?
Yes, I heard you wanted to take leave for the holiday. I'll need you to get this checklist signed and give me a Maps printout of where you're going.
Sure thing, sir...
...would you like me to have my **mommy** sign a *permission slip* for you too?
That's a great idea!
You can never be too careful!
www.terminallance.com
Created by Maximilian Uriarte © 2011

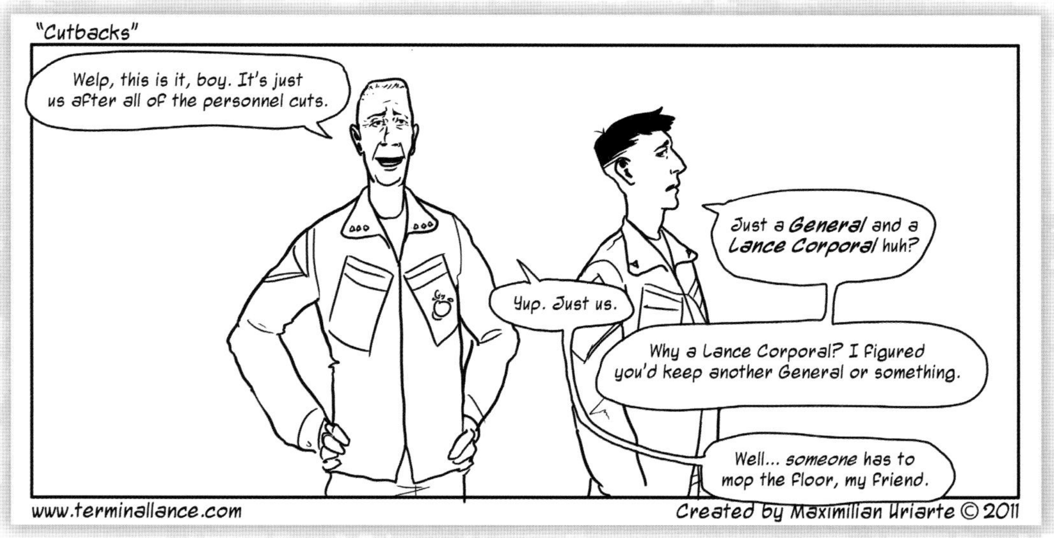
"Cutbacks"
Welp, this is it, boy. It's just us after all of the personnel cuts.
Just a **General** and a **Lance Corporal** huh?
Yup. Just us.
Why a Lance Corporal? I figured you'd keep another General or something.
Well... someone has to mop the floor, my friend.
www.terminallance.com
Created by Maximilian Uriarte © 2011

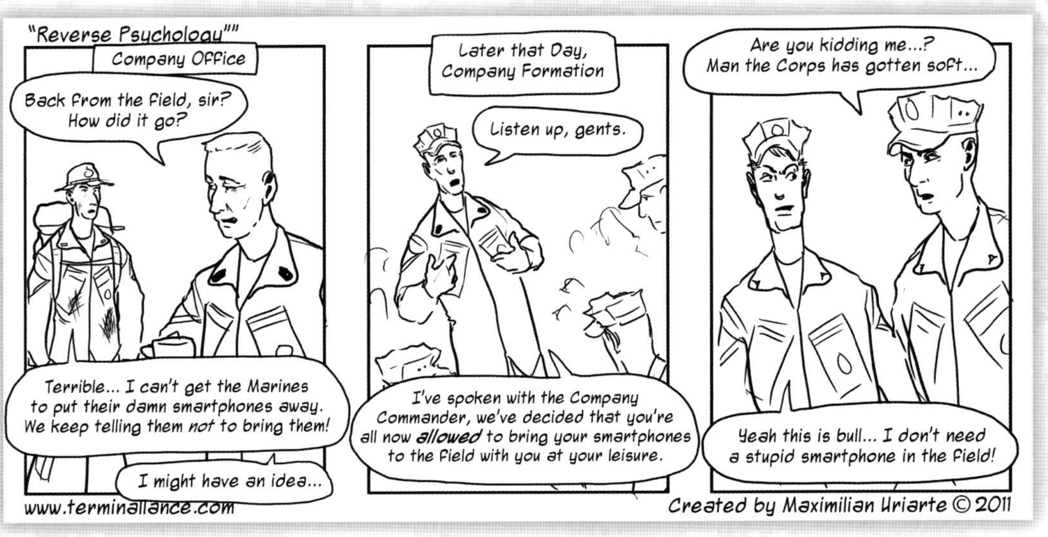
"Reverse Psychology"
Company Office
Back from the field, sir? How did it go?
Terrible... I can't get the Marines to put their damn smartphones away. We keep telling them *not* to bring them!
I might have an idea...
Later that Day, Company Formation
Listen up, gents.
I've spoken with the Company Commander, we've decided that you're all now ***allowed*** to bring your smartphones to the field with you at your leisure.
Are you kidding me...? Man the Corps has gotten soft...
Yeah this is bull... I don't need a stupid smartphone in the field!
www.terminallance.com
Created by Maximilian Uriarte © 2011

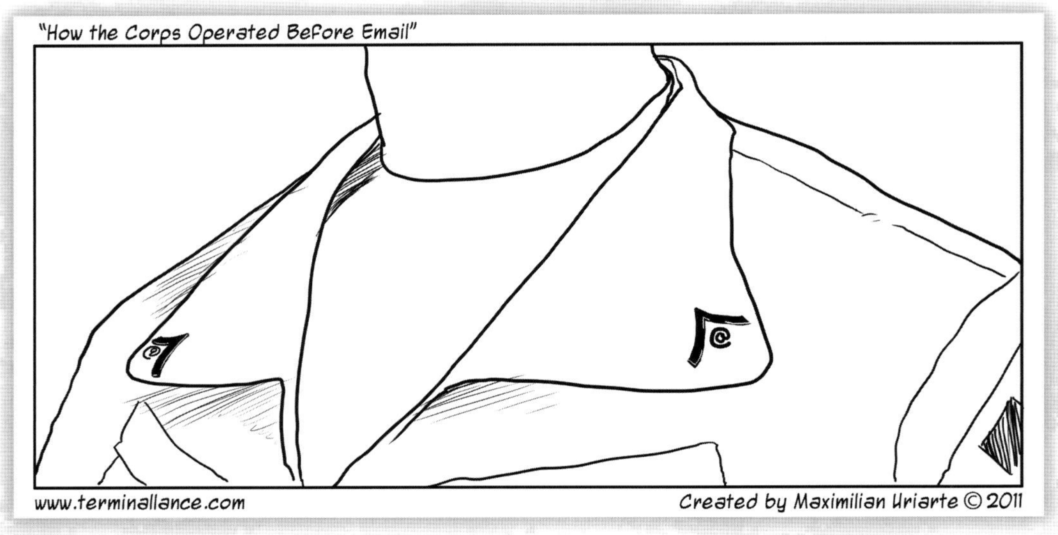
"How the Corps Operated Before Email"
www.terminallance.com
Created by Maximilian Uriarte © 2011

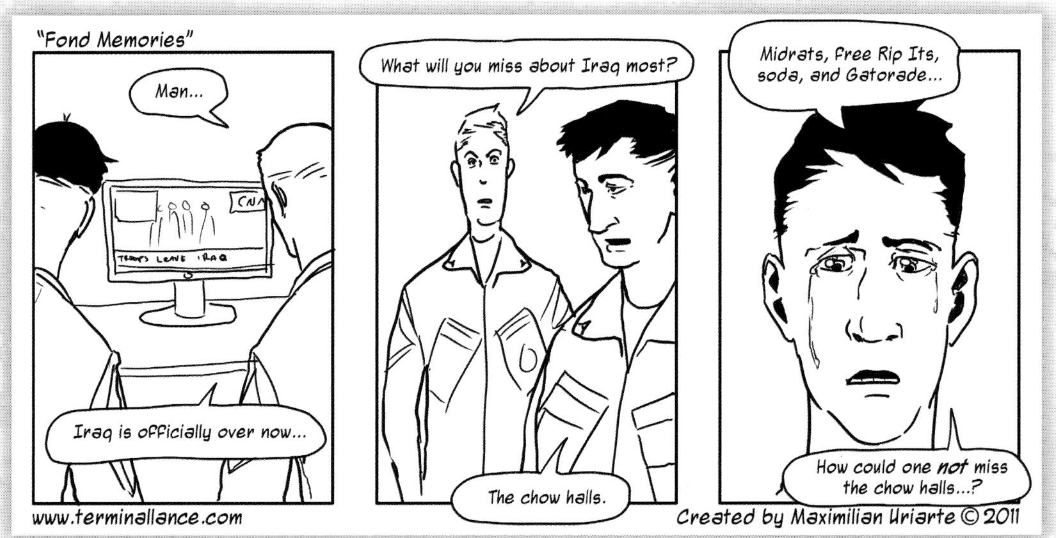
"Fond Memories"
Man...
Iraq is officially over now...
What will you miss about Iraq most?
The chow halls.
Midrats, free Rip Its, soda, and Gatorade...
How could one ***not*** miss the chow halls...?
www.terminallance.com
Created by Maximilian Uriarte © 2011

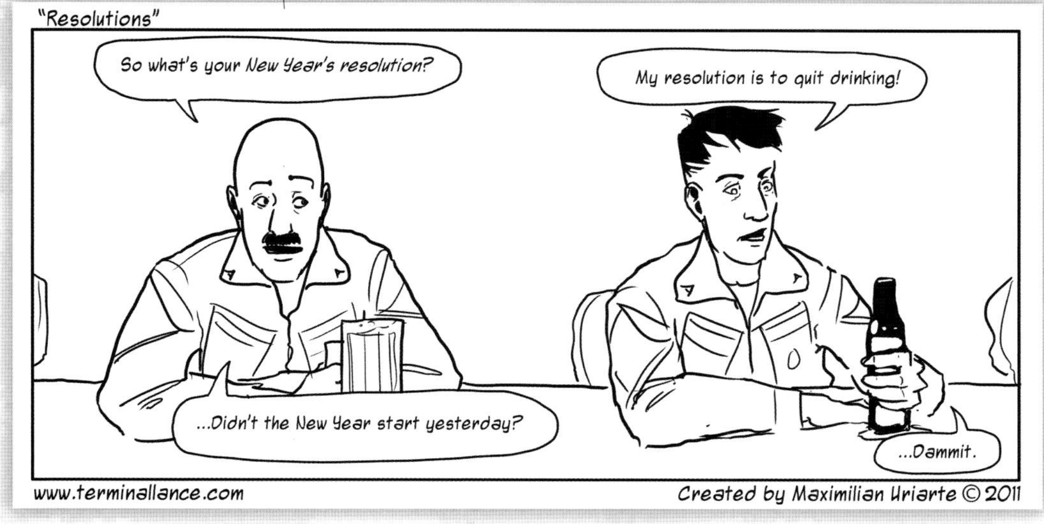
"Resolutions"
So what's your New Year's resolution?
My resolution is to quit drinking!
...Didn't the New Year start yesterday?
...Dammit.
www.terminallance.com
Created by Maximilian Uriarte © 2011

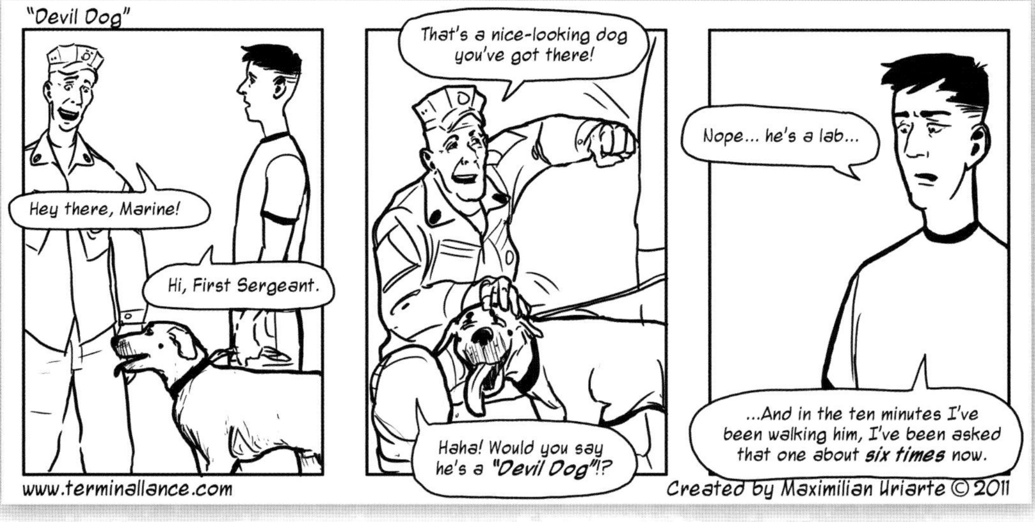
"Devil Dog"
Hey there, Marine!
Hi, First Sergeant.
That's a nice-looking dog you've got there!
Haha! Would you say he's a "Devil Dog"!?
Nope... he's a lab...
...And in the ten minutes I've been walking him, I've been asked that one about six times now.
www.terminallance.com
Created by Maximilian Uriarte © 2011

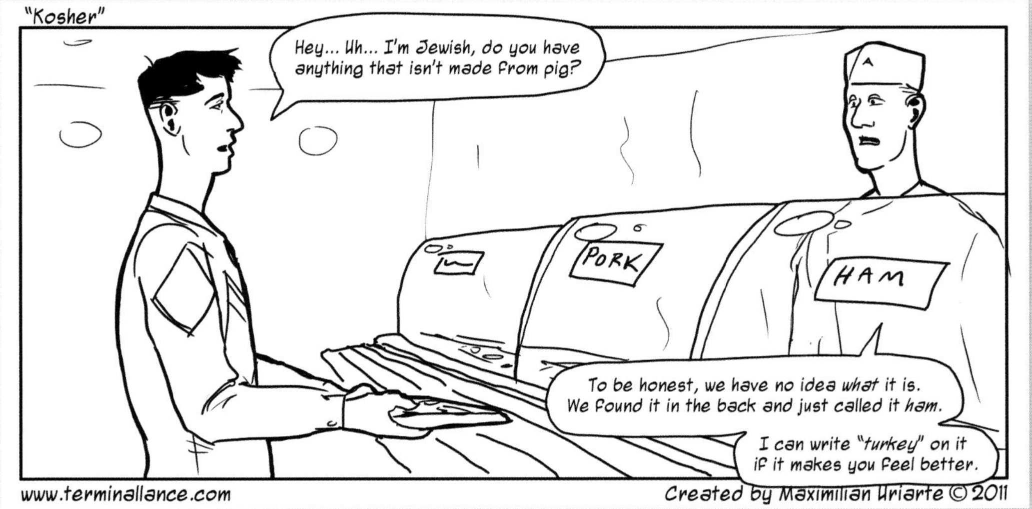
"Kosher"
Hey... Uh... I'm Jewish, do you have anything that isn't made from pig?
PORK
HAM
To be honest, we have no idea what it is. We found it in the back and just called it ham.
I can write "turkey" on it if it makes you feel better.
www.terminallance.com
Created by Maximilian Uriarte © 2011

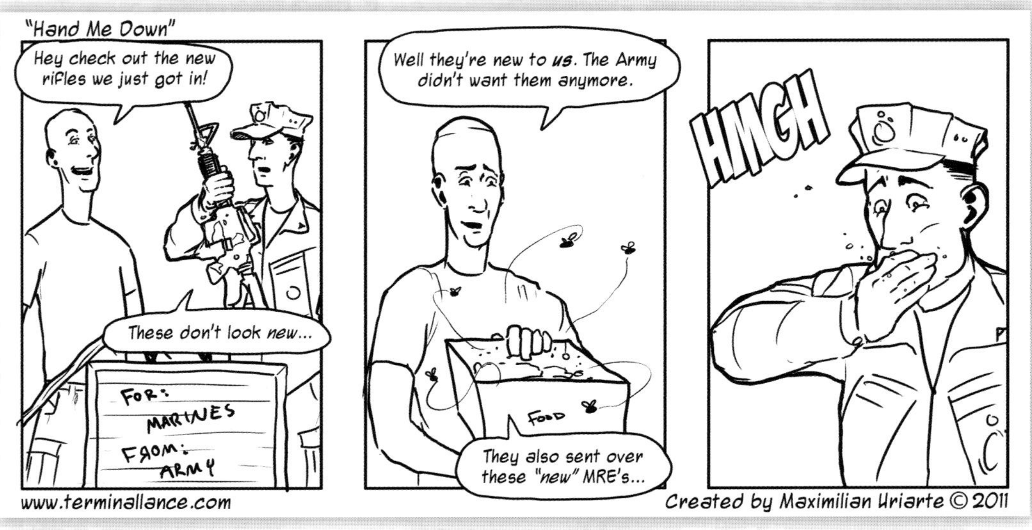
"Hand Me Down"
Hey check out the new rifles we just got in!
These don't look new...
FOR: MARINES FROM: ARMY
Well they're new to *us*. The Army didn't want them anymore.
FOOD
They also sent over these "*new*" MRE's...
HMGH
www.terminallance.com
Created by Maximilian Uriarte © 2011

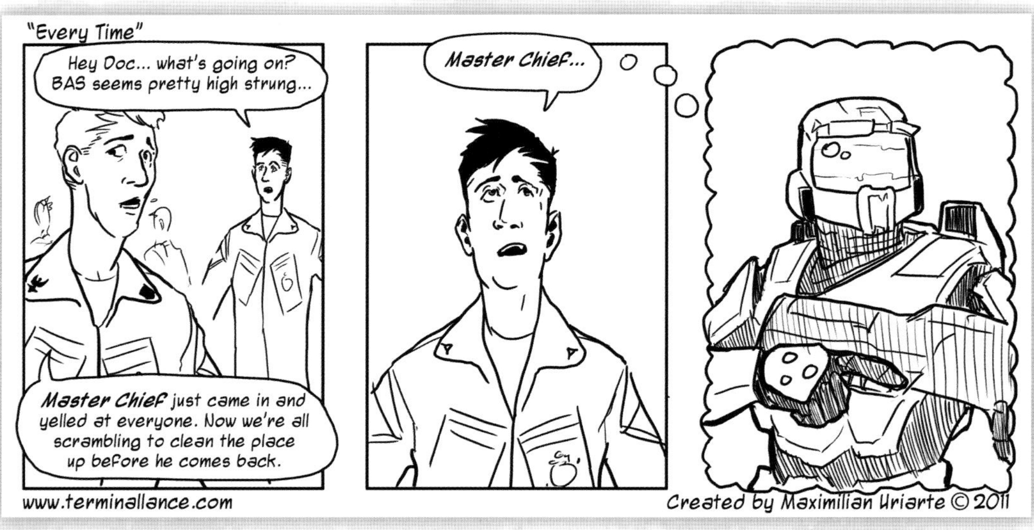
"Every Time"
Hey Doc... what's going on? BAS seems pretty high strung...
Master Chief just came in and yelled at everyone. Now we're all scrambling to clean the place up before he comes back.
Master Chief...
www.terminallance.com
Created by Maximilian Uriarte © 2011

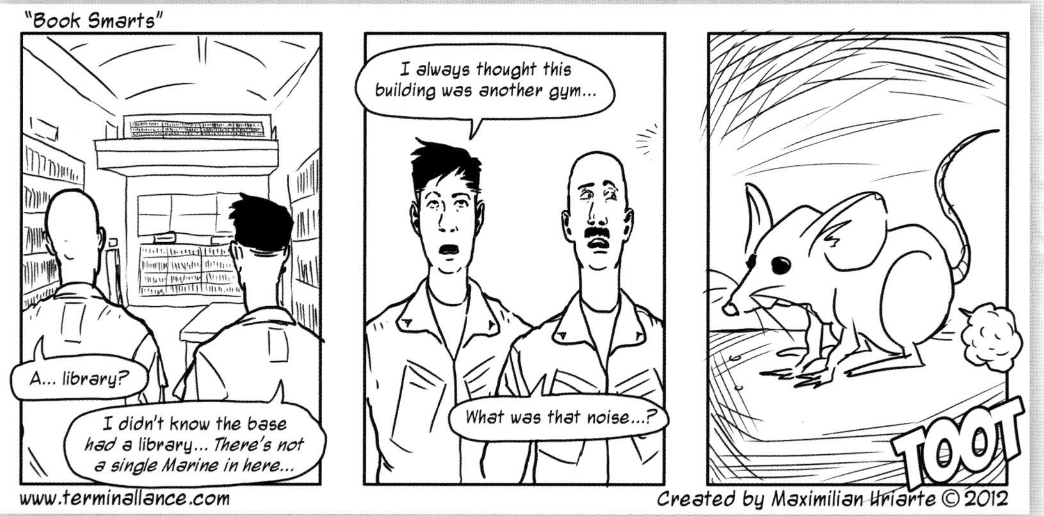
"Book Smarts"
A... library?
I didn't know the base had a library... There's not a single Marine in here...
I always thought this building was another gym...
What was that noise...?
TOOT
www.terminallance.com
Created by Maximilian Uriarte © 2012

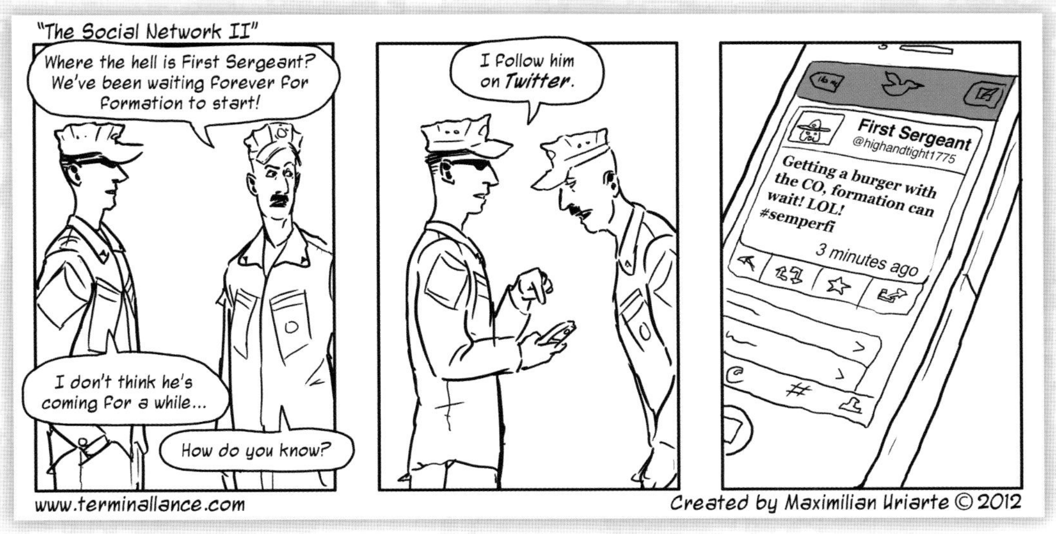
"The Social Network II"
Where the hell is First Sergeant? We've been waiting forever for formation to start!
I don't think he's coming for a while...
How do you know?
I follow him on *Twitter*.
First Sergeant
@highandtight1775
Getting a burger with the CO, formation can wait! LOL! #semperfi
3 minutes ago
www.terminallance.com
Created by Maximilian Uriarte © 2012

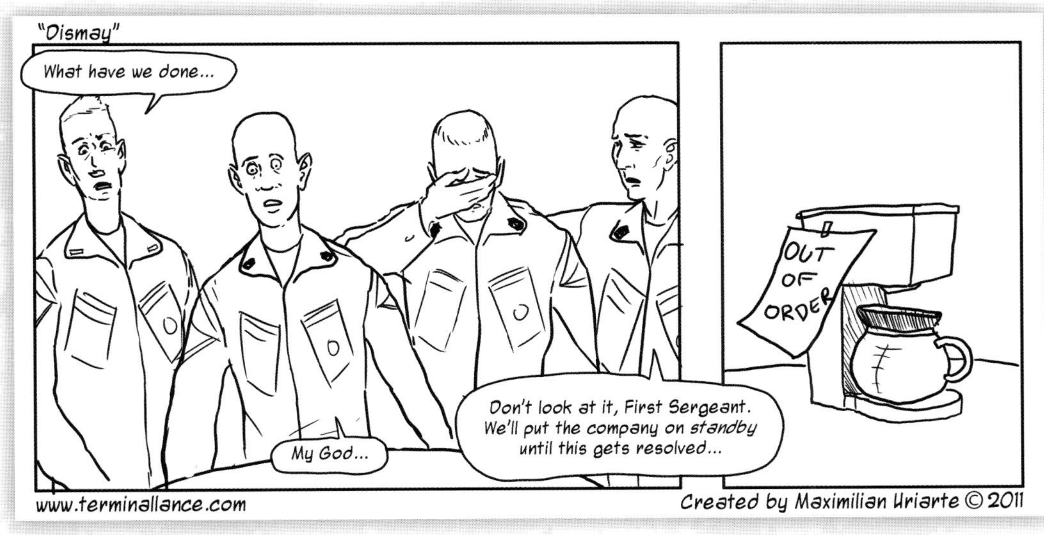
"Dismay"
What have we done...
My God...
Don't look at it, First Sergeant. We'll put the company on *standby* until this gets resolved...
OUT OF ORDER
www.terminallance.com
Created by Maximilian Uriarte © 2011

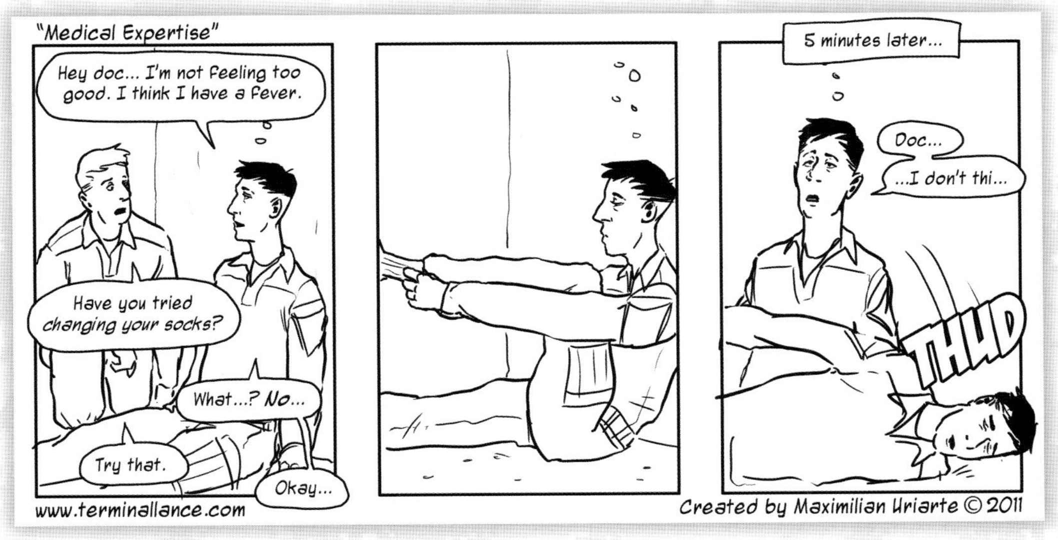
"Medical Expertise"
Hey doc... I'm not feeling too good. I think I have a fever.
Have you tried changing your socks?
What...? *No*...
Try that.
Okay...
5 minutes later...
Doc...
...I don't thi...
THUD
www.terminallance.com
Created by Maximilian Uriarte © 2011

"Hazy Foresight"

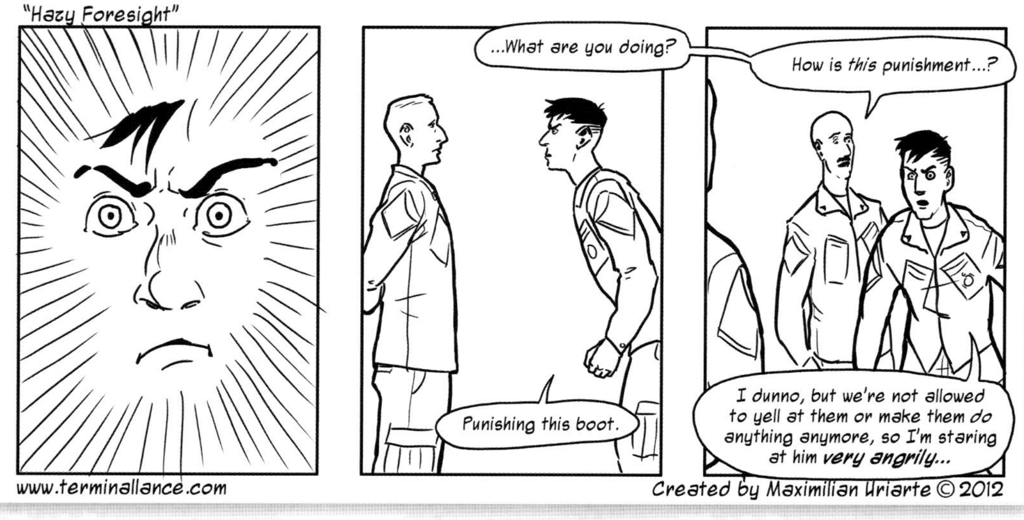
...What are you doing?
Punishing this boot.
How is *this* punishment...?
I dunno, but we're not allowed to yell at them or make them *do* anything anymore, so I'm staring at him ***very angrily...***
www.terminallance.com
Created by Maximilian Uriarte © 2012

"Fog of Formation"

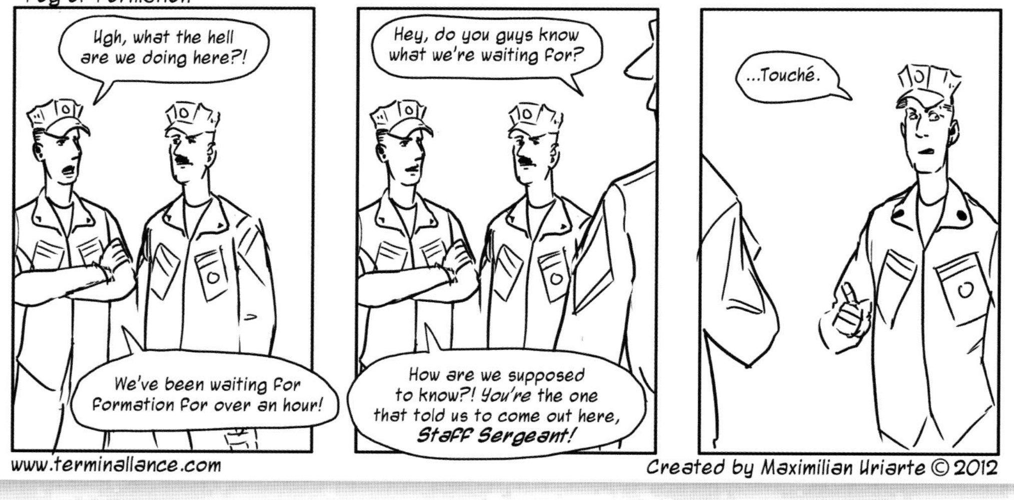
Ugh, what the hell are we doing here?!
We've been waiting for formation for over an hour!
Hey, do you guys know what we're waiting for?
How are we supposed to know?! *You're* the one that told us to come out here, ***Staff Sergeant!***
...Touché.
www.terminallance.com
Created by Maximilian Uriarte © 2012

"Internet Authority"

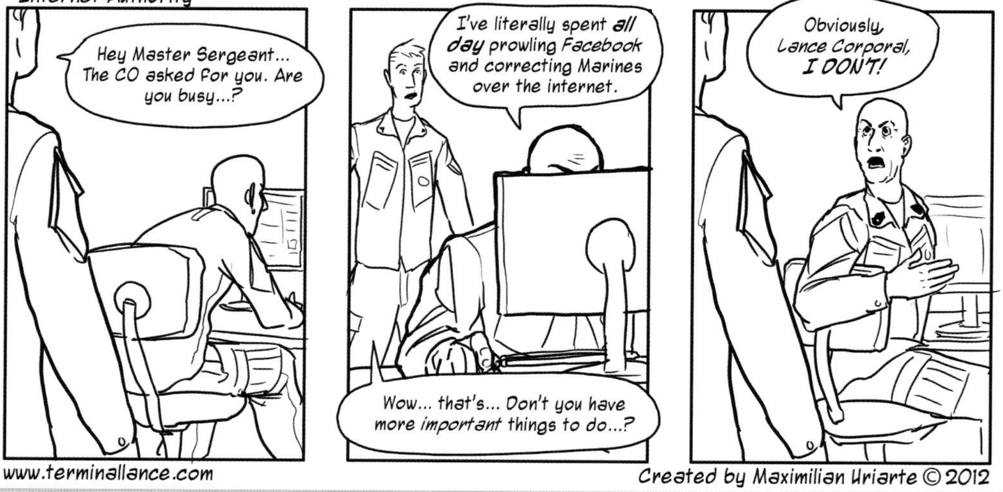
Hey Master Sergeant... The CO asked for you. Are you busy...?
I've literally spent ***all day*** prowling *Facebook* and correcting Marines over the internet.
Wow... that's... Don't you have more *important* things to do...?
Obviously, Lance Corporal, ***I DON'T!***
www.terminallance.com
Created by Maximilian Uriarte © 2012

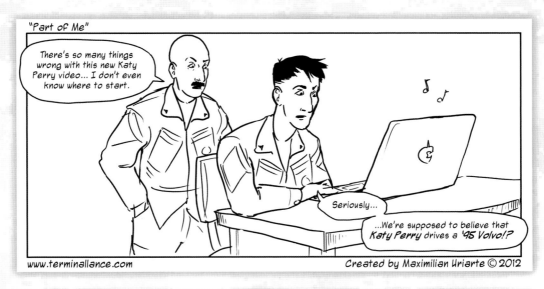

"Part of Me"

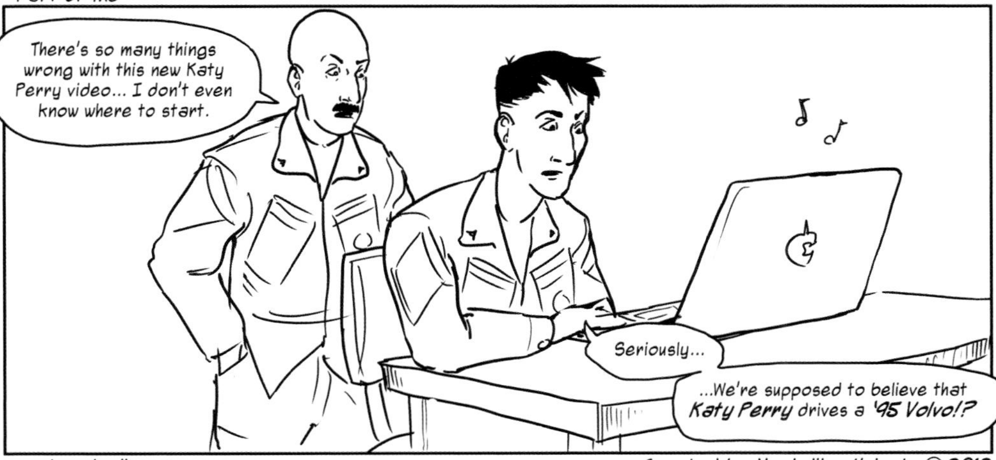
There's so many things wrong with this new Katy Perry video... I don't even know where to start.
Seriously...
...We're supposed to believe that *Katy Perry* drives a '95 Volvo!?

www.terminallance.com Created by Maximilian Uriarte © 2012

"Ring Ring"

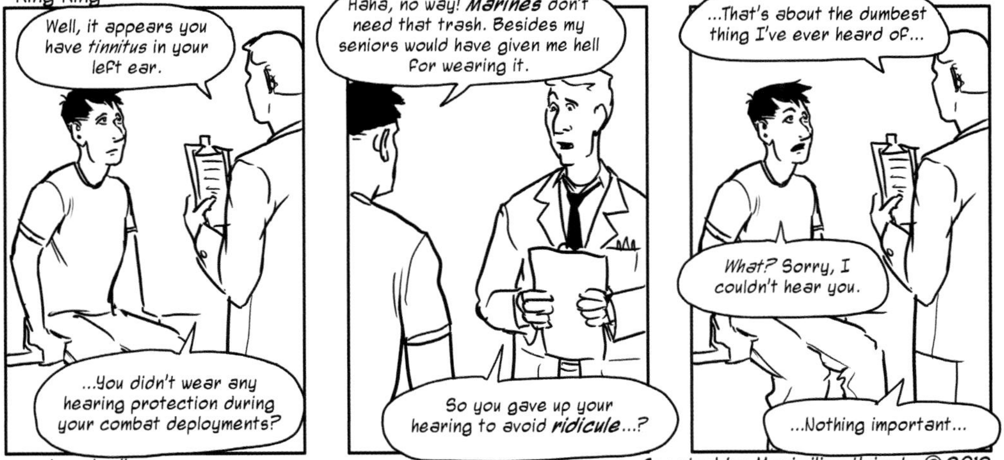
Well, it appears you have *tinnitus* in your left ear.
...You didn't wear any hearing protection during your combat deployments?
Haha, no way! ***Marines*** don't need that trash. Besides my seniors would have given me hell for wearing it.
So you gave up your hearing to avoid ***ridicule***...?
...That's about the dumbest thing I've ever heard of...
What? Sorry, I couldn't hear you.
...Nothing important...

www.terminallance.com Created by Maximilian Uriarte © 2012

"Life After EAS: The Infantry Experience"

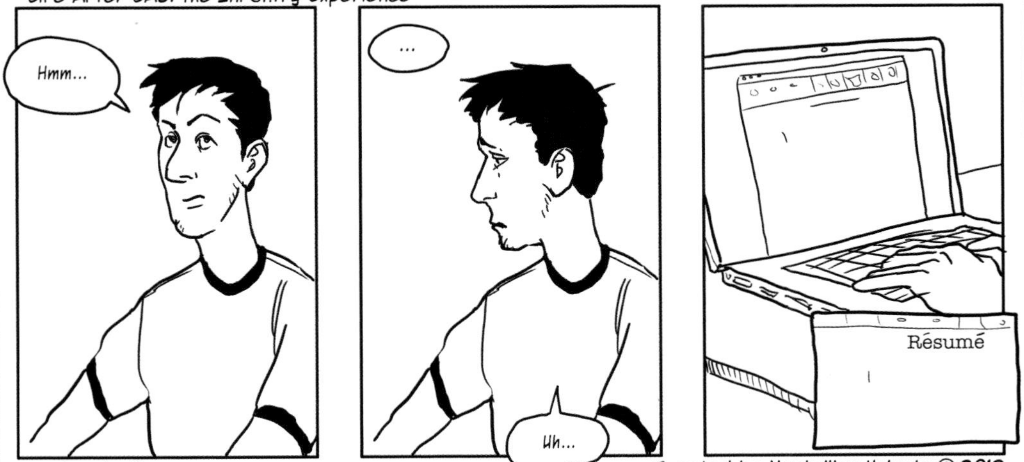
Hmm...
...
Uh...
Résumé

www.terminallance.com Created by Maximilian Uriarte © 2012

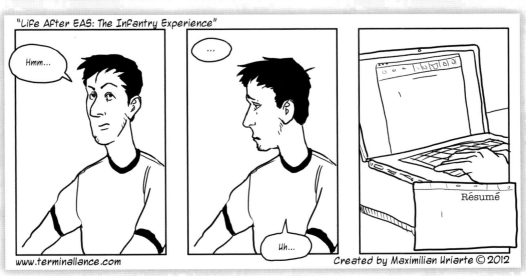

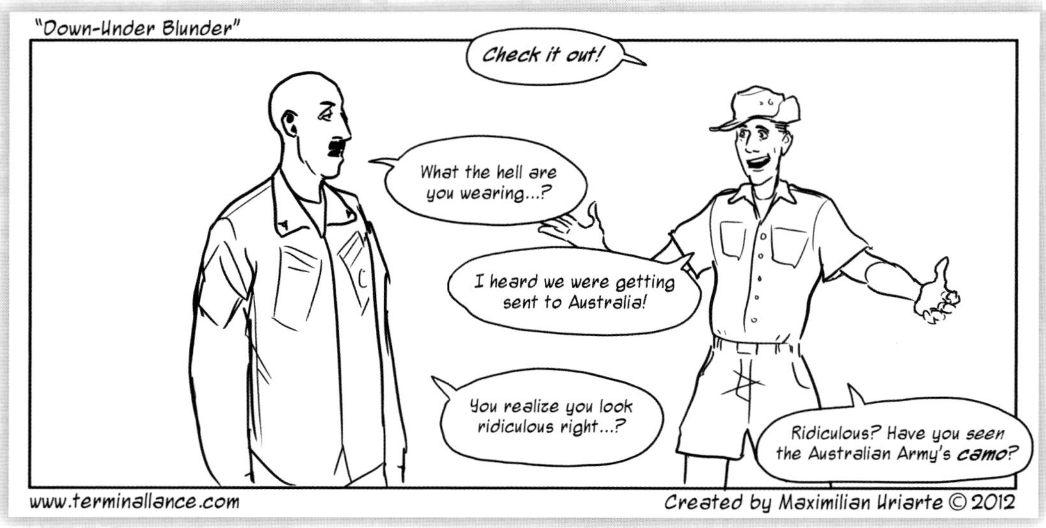
"Down-Under Blunder"
Check it out!
What the hell are you wearing...?
I heard we were getting sent to Australia!
You realize you look ridiculous right...?
Ridiculous? Have you seen the Australian Army's camo?
www.terminallance.com
Created by Maximilian Uriarte © 2012

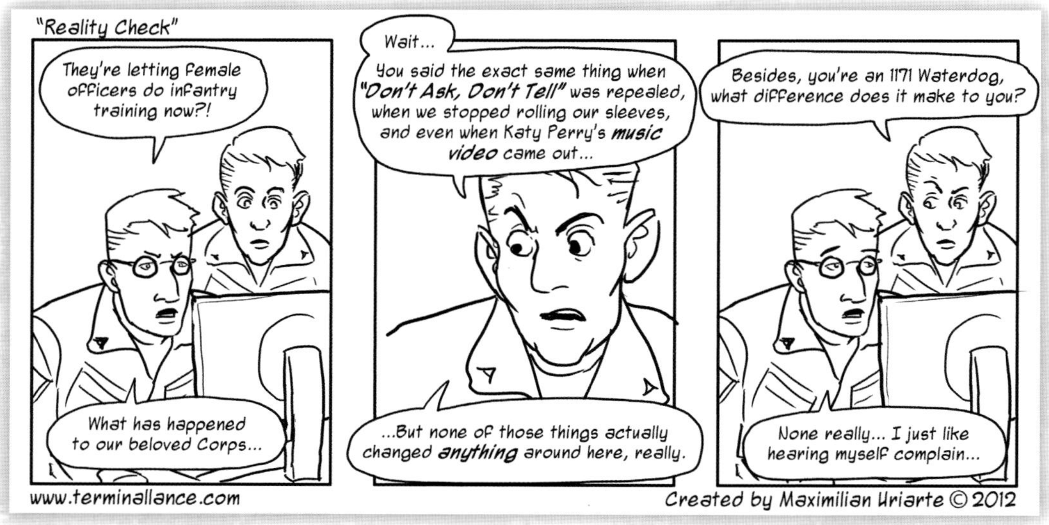
"Reality Check"
They're letting female officers do infantry training now?!
What has happened to our beloved Corps...
Wait...
You said the exact same thing when "Don't Ask, Don't Tell" was repealed, when we stopped rolling our sleeves, and even when Katy Perry's music video came out...
...But none of those things actually changed anything around here, really.
Besides, you're an 1171 Waterdog, what difference does it make to you?
None really... I just like hearing myself complain...
www.terminallance.com
Created by Maximilian Uriarte © 2012

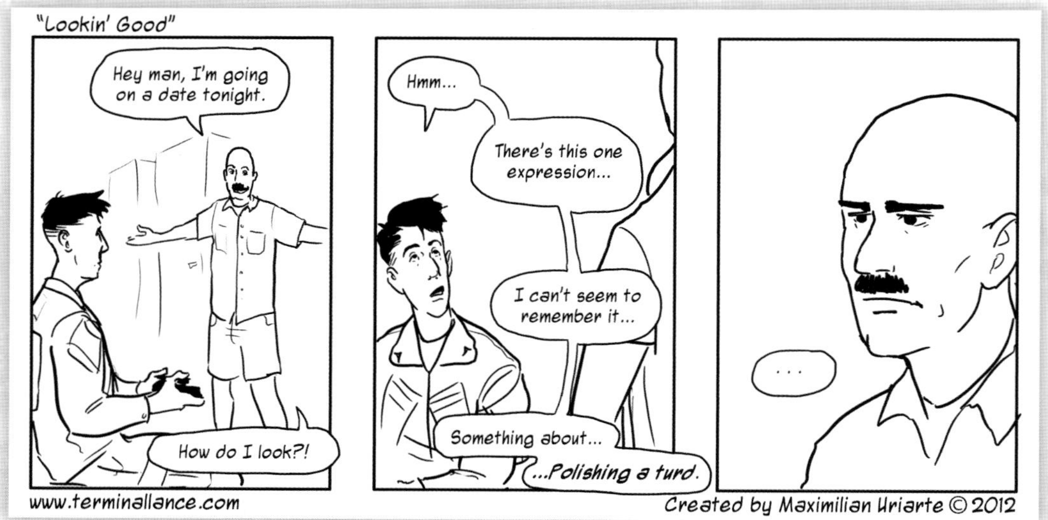
"Lookin' Good"
Hey man, I'm going on a date tonight.
How do I look?!
Hmm...
There's this one expression...
I can't seem to remember it...
Something about...
...Polishing a turd.
. . .
www.terminallance.com
Created by Maximilian Uriarte © 2012

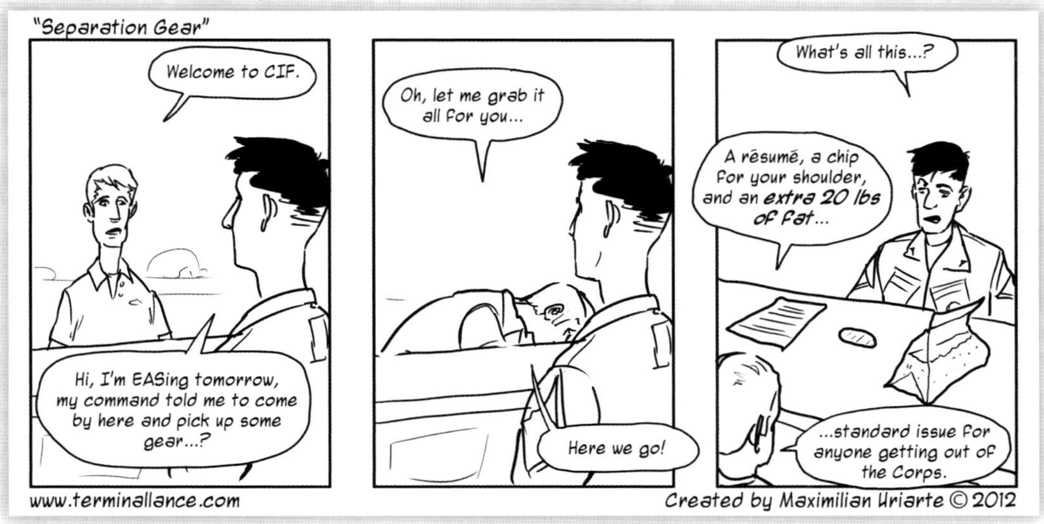
"Separation Gear"
Welcome to CIF.
Hi, I'm EASing tomorrow, my command told me to come by here and pick up some gear...?
Oh, let me grab it all for you...
Here we go!
What's all this...?
A résumé, a chip for your shoulder, and an **extra 20 lbs of fat**...
...standard issue for anyone getting out of the Corps.
www.terminallance.com
Created by Maximilian Uriarte © 2012

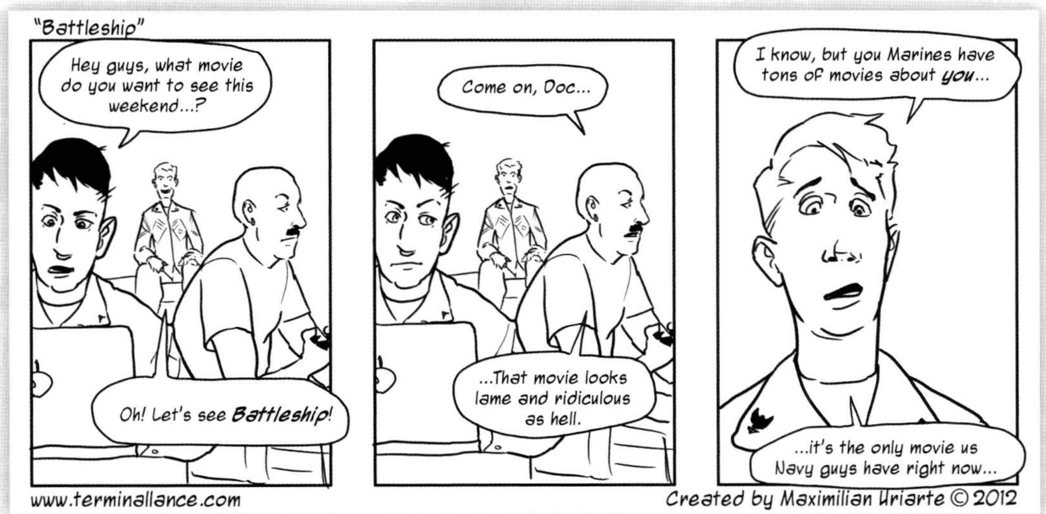
"Battleship"
Hey guys, what movie do you want to see this weekend...?
Oh! Let's see ***Battleship***!
Come on, Doc...
...That movie looks lame and ridiculous as hell.
I know, but you Marines have tons of movies about ***you***...
...it's the only movie us Navy guys have right now...
www.terminallance.com
Created by Maximilian Uriarte © 2012

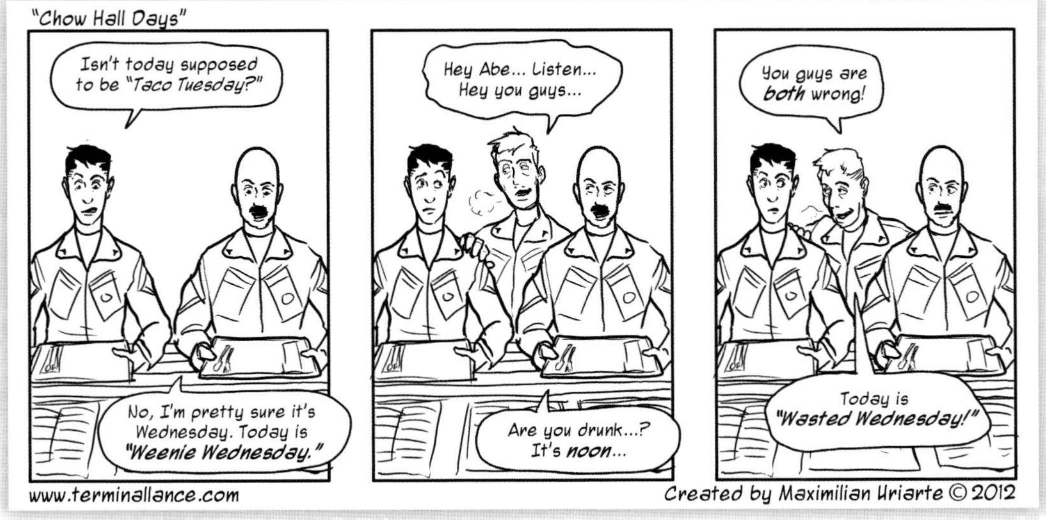
"Chow Hall Days"
Isn't today supposed to be *"Taco Tuesday?"*
No, I'm pretty sure it's Wednesday. Today is ***"Weenie Wednesday."***
Hey Abe... Listen... Hey you guys...
Are you drunk...? It's ***noon***...
You guys are ***both*** wrong!
Today is ***"Wasted Wednesday!"***
www.terminallance.com
Created by Maximilian Uriarte © 2012

"Run-in with an Old Friend"

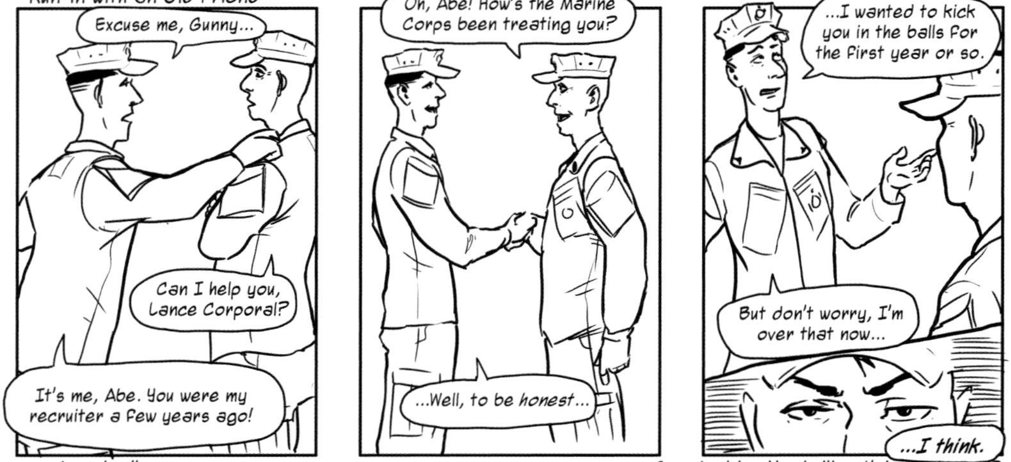
Excuse me, Gunny...
Can I help you, Lance Corporal?
It's me, Abe. You were my recruiter a few years ago!
Oh, Abe! How's the Marine Corps been treating you?
...Well, to be honest...
...I wanted to kick you in the balls for the first year or so.
But don't worry, I'm over that now...
...I think.

www.terminallance.com Created by Maximilian Uriarte © 2012

"Drawdown"

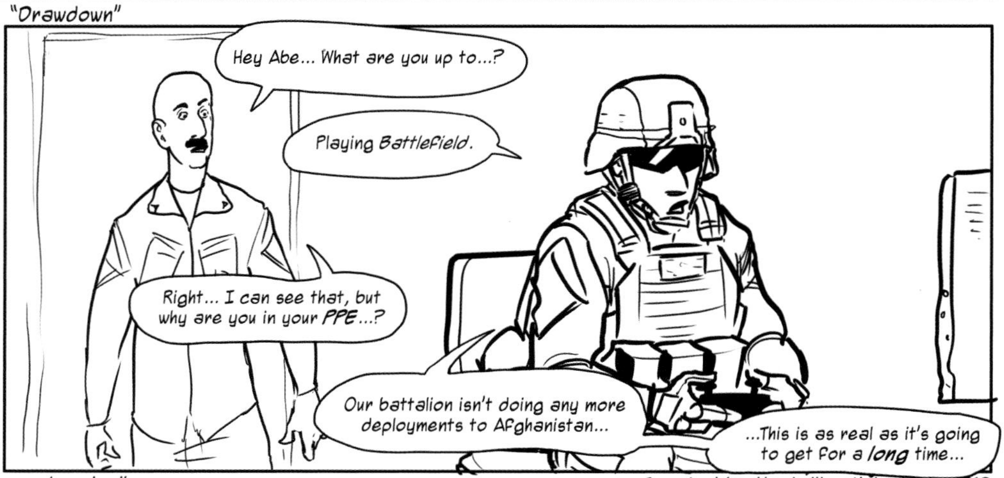
Hey Abe... What are you up to...?
Playing *Battlefield*.
Right... I can see that, but why are you in your *PPE*...?
Our battalion isn't doing any more deployments to Afghanistan...
...This is as real as it's going to get for a *long* time...

www.terminallance.com Created by Maximilian Uriarte © 2012

"Bare Minimum"

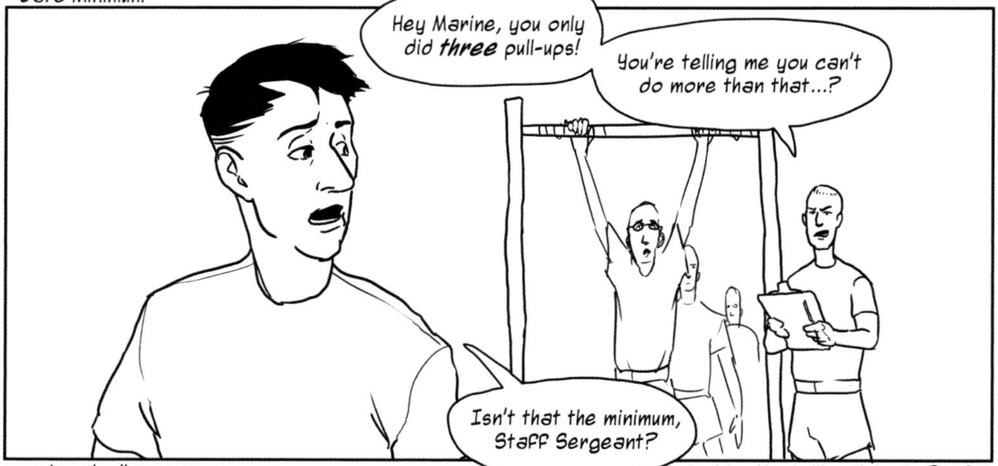
Hey Marine, you only did **three** pull-ups!
You're telling me you can't do more than that...?
Isn't that the minimum, Staff Sergeant?

www.terminallance.com Created by Maximilian Uriarte © 2012

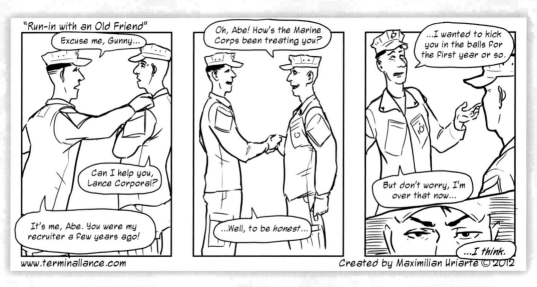

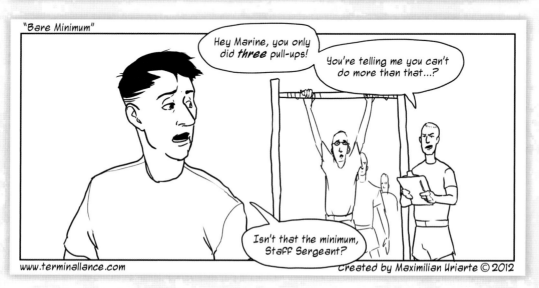

"Inspection Ready"

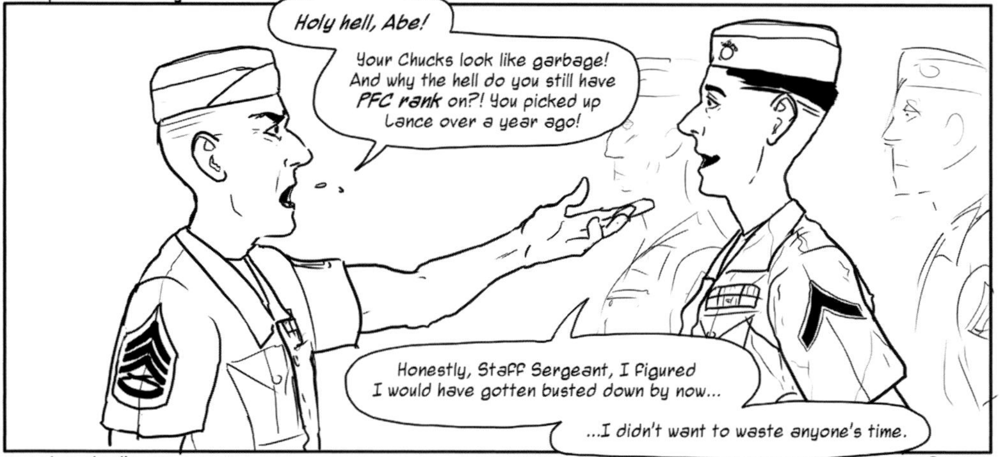
Holy hell, Abe!
Your Chucks look like garbage! And why the hell do you still have PFC rank on?! You picked up Lance over a year ago!
Honestly, Staff Sergeant, I figured I would have gotten busted down by now...
...I didn't want to waste anyone's time.

www.terminallance.com Created by Maximilian Uriarte © 2012

"What Your Hair Length Says about You"

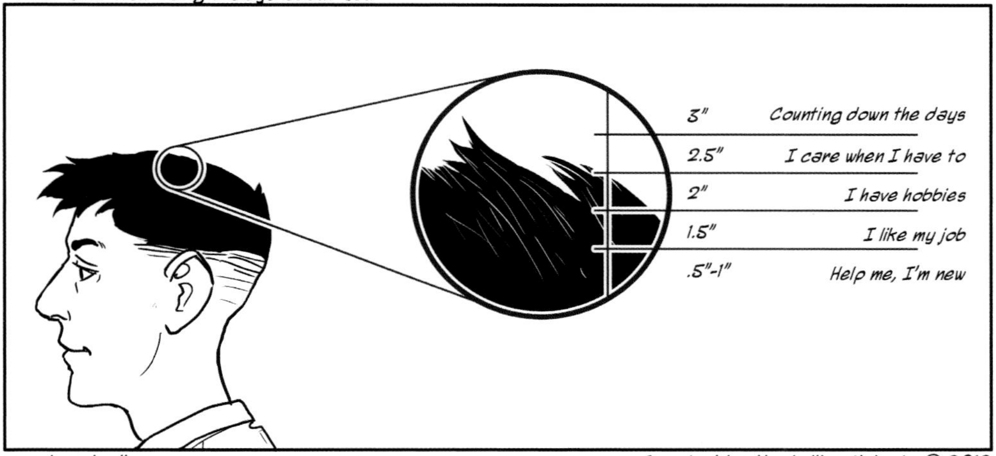
3" Counting down the days
2.5" I care when I have to
2" I have hobbies
1.5" I like my job
.5"-1" Help me, I'm new

www.terminallance.com Created by Maximilian Uriarte © 2012

"Swim Qual Revelations"

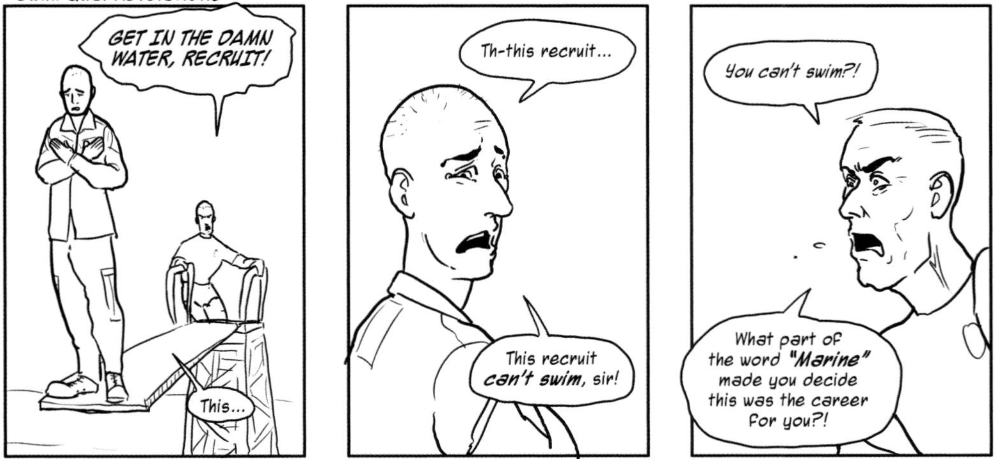
GET IN THE DAMN WATER, RECRUIT!
This...
Th-this recruit...
This recruit can't swim, sir!
You can't swim?!
What part of the word "Marine" made you decide this was the career for you?!

www.terminallance.com Created by Maximilian Uriarte © 2012

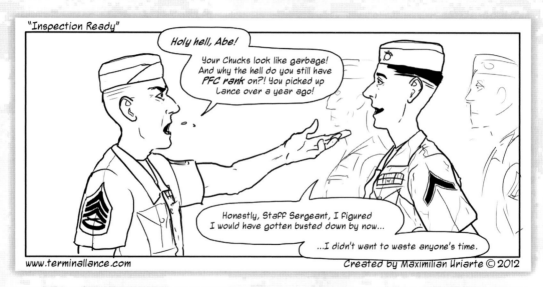

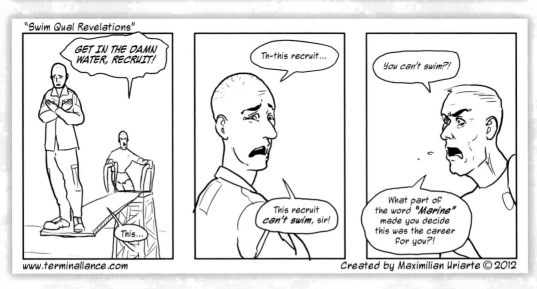

"Before It Was Cool"

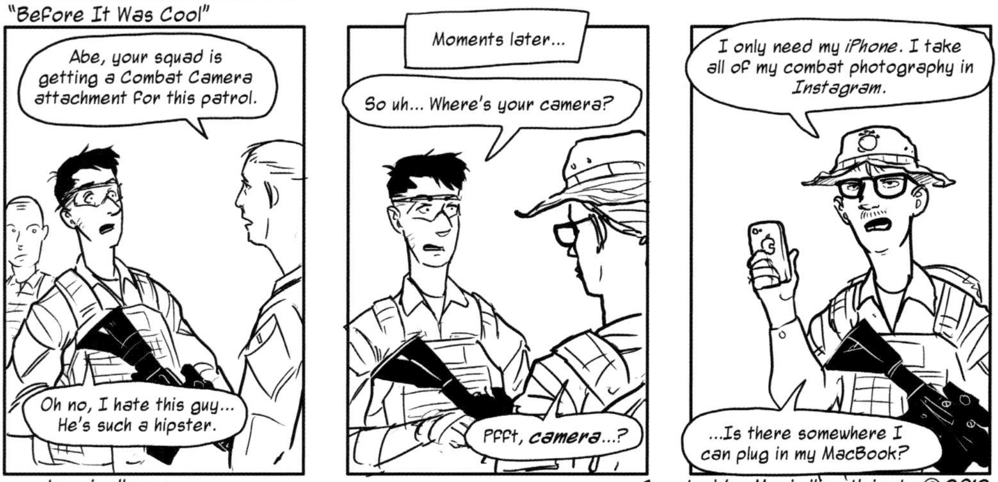
Abe, your squad is getting a Combat Camera attachment for this patrol.
Oh no, I hate this guy... He's such a hipster.
Moments later...
So uh... Where's your camera?
Pffft, *camera*...?
I only need my *iPhone*. I take all of my combat photography in *Instagram*.
...Is there somewhere I can plug in my MacBook?

www.terminallance.com Created by Maximilian Uriarte © 2012

"Re-Up"

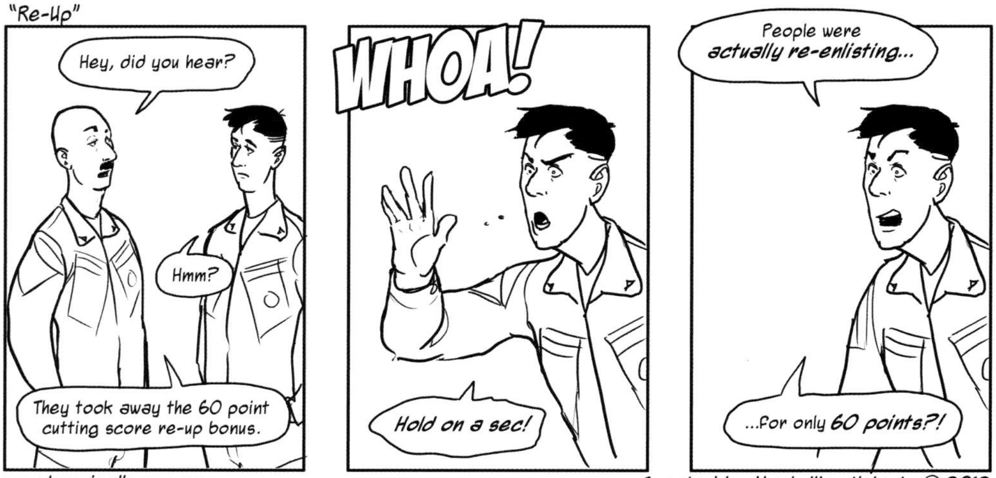
Hey, did you hear?
Hmm?
They took away the 60 point cutting score re-up bonus.
WHOA!
Hold on a sec!
People were *actually re-enlisting...*
...for only *60 points?!*

www.terminallance.com Created by Maximilian Uriarte © 2012

"Can't Stop Time"

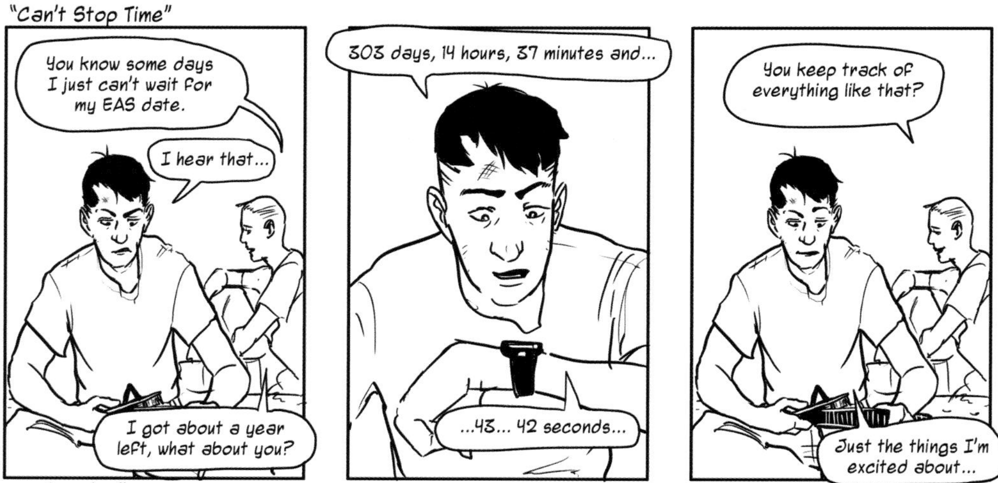
You know some days I just can't wait for my EAS date.
I hear that...
I got about a year left, what about you?
303 days, 14 hours, 37 minutes and...
...43... 42 seconds...
You keep track of everything like that?
Just the things I'm excited about...

www.terminallance.com Created by Maximilian Uriarte © 2012

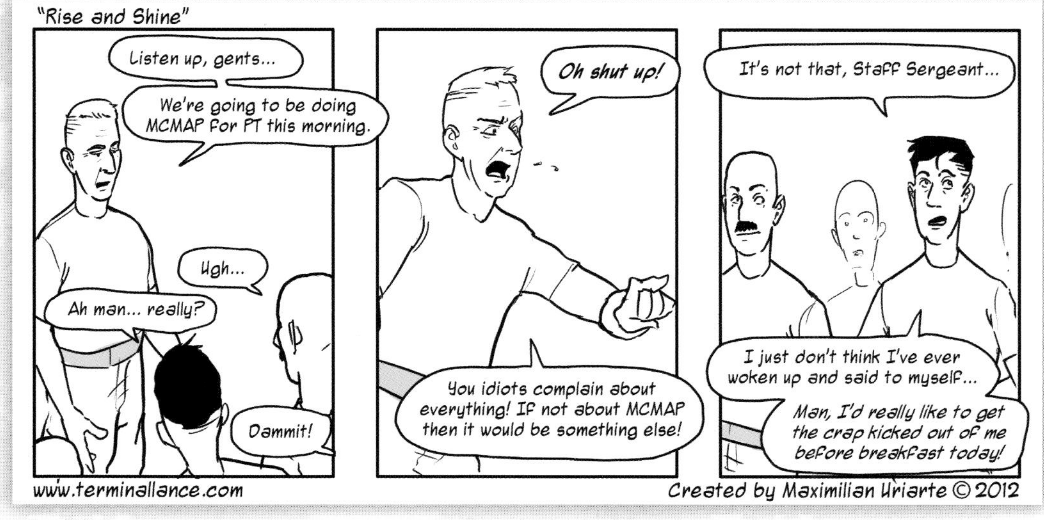
"Rise and Shine"
Listen up, gents...
We're going to be doing MCMAP for PT this morning.
Ugh...
Ah man... really?
Dammit!
Oh shut up!
You idiots complain about everything! If not about MCMAP then it would be something else!
It's not that, Staff Sergeant...
I just don't think I've ever woken up and said to myself...
Man, I'd really like to get the crap kicked out of me before breakfast today!
www.terminallance.com
Created by Maximilian Uriarte © 2012

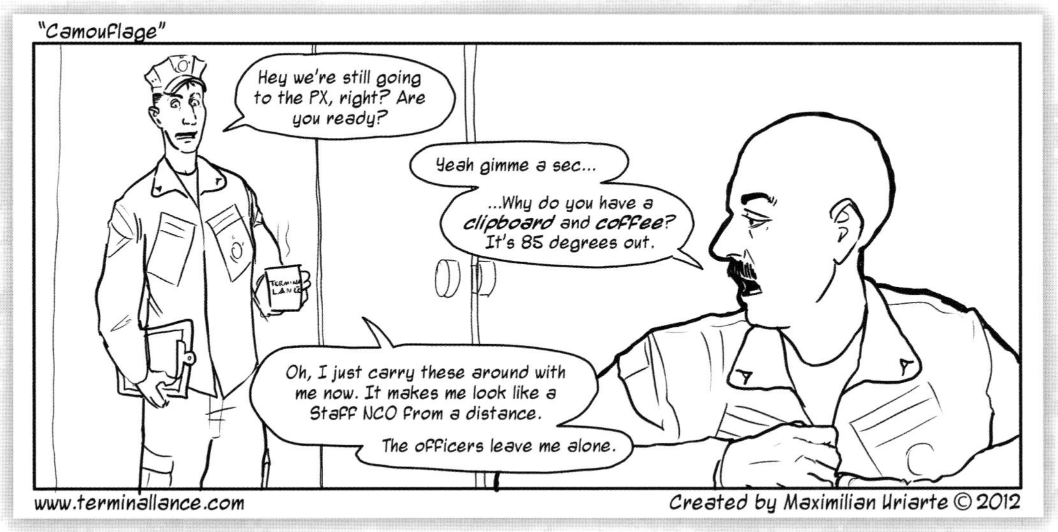
"Camouflage"
Hey we're still going to the PX, right? Are you ready?
Yeah gimme a sec...
...Why do you have a clipboard and coffee? It's 85 degrees out.
Oh, I just carry these around with me now. It makes me look like a Staff NCO from a distance.
The officers leave me alone.
www.terminallance.com
Created by Maximilian Uriarte © 2012

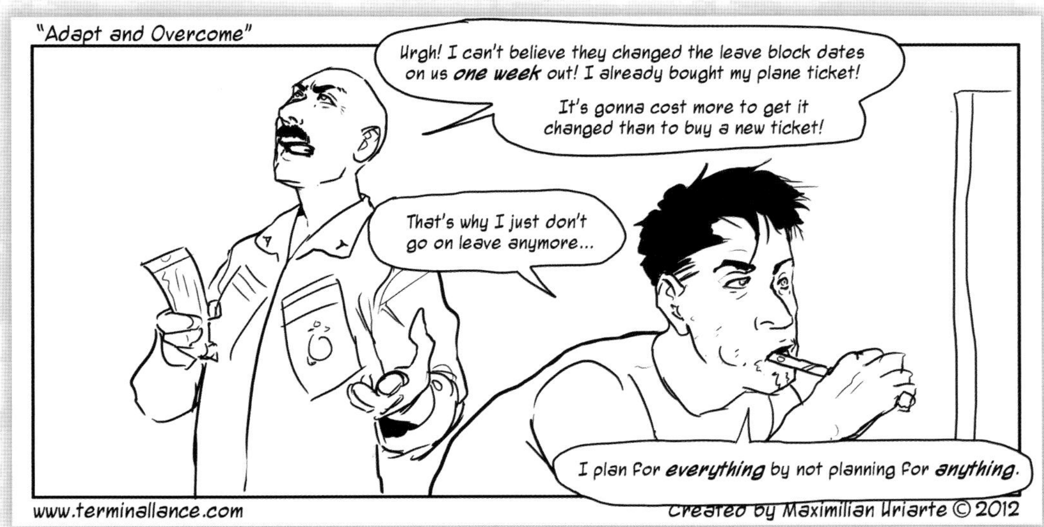
"Adapt and Overcome"
Urgh! I can't believe they changed the leave block dates on us one week out! I already bought my plane ticket!
It's gonna cost more to get it changed than to buy a new ticket!
That's why I just don't go on leave anymore...
I plan for everything by not planning for anything.
www.terminallance.com
Created by Maximilian Uriarte © 2012

"Earning It"

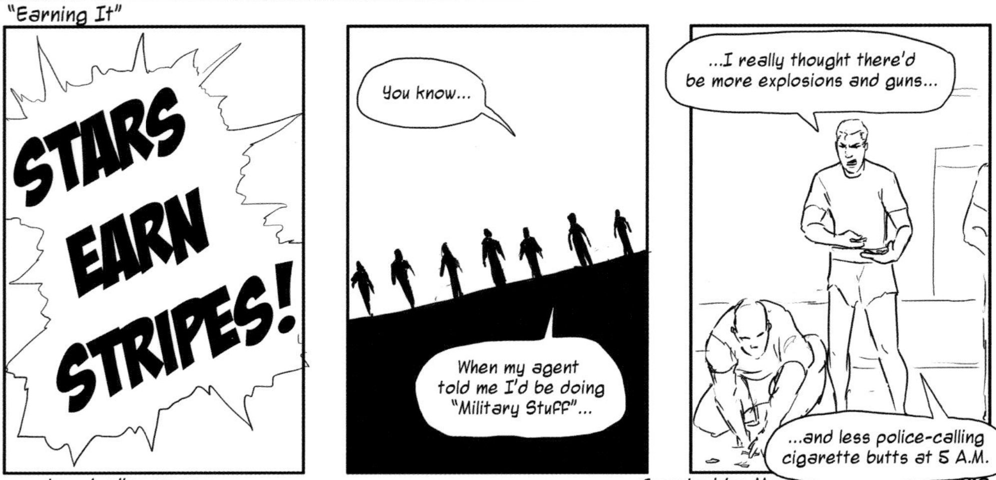
STARS EARN STRIPES!
You know...
When my agent told me I'd be doing "Military Stuff"...
...I really thought there'd be more explosions and guns...
...and less police-calling cigarette butts at 5 A.M.

www.terminallance.com Created by Maximilian Uriarte © 2012

"The Obvious Choice"

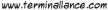

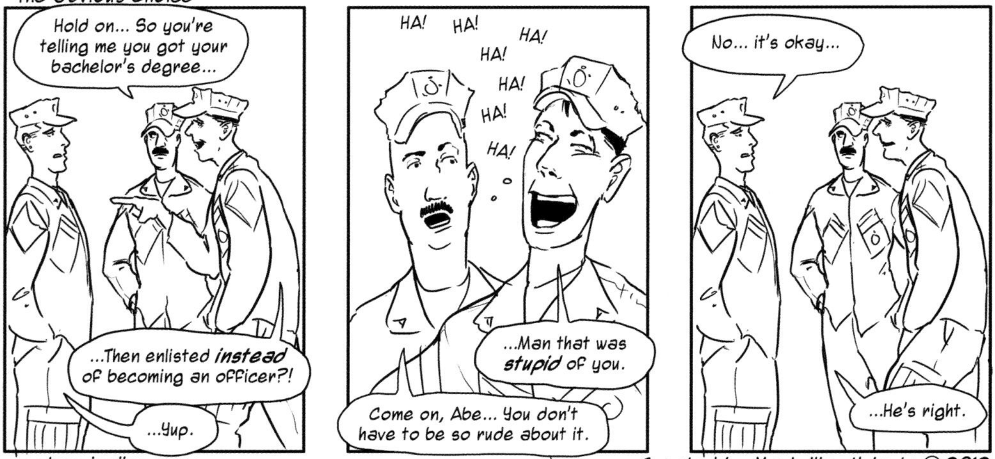
Hold on... So you're telling me you got your bachelor's degree...
...Then enlisted *instead* of becoming an officer?!
...Yup.
HA! HA! HA! HA! HA! HA! HA!
...Man that was *stupid* of you.
Come on, Abe... You don't have to be so rude about it.
No... it's okay...
...He's right.

www.terminallance.com Created by Maximilian Uriarte © 2012

"Like Old Times"

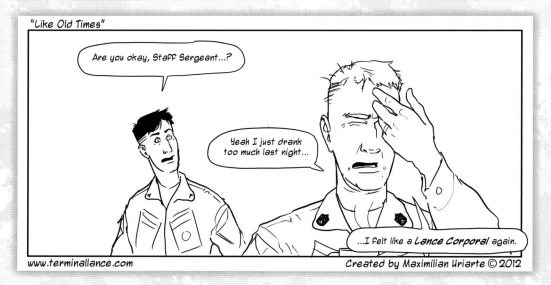

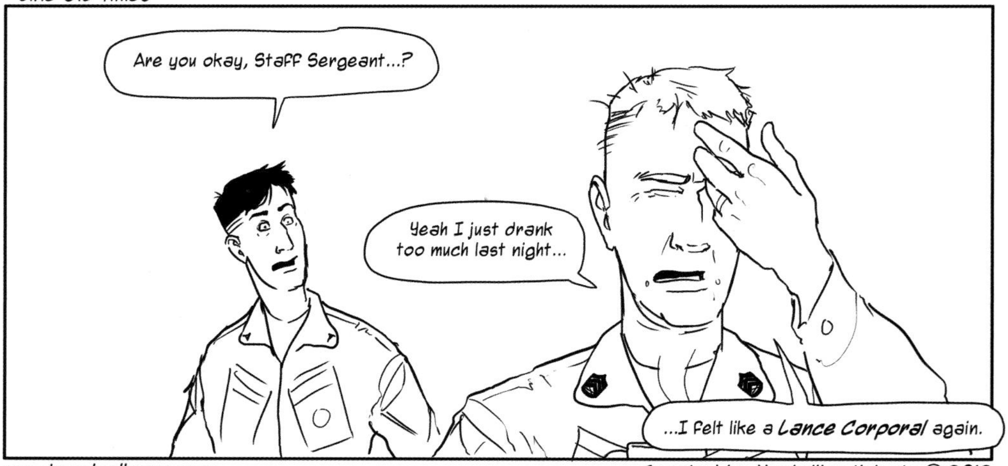
Are you okay, Staff Sergeant...?
Yeah I just drank too much last night...
...I felt like a *Lance Corporal* again.

www.terminallance.com Created by Maximilian Uriarte © 2012

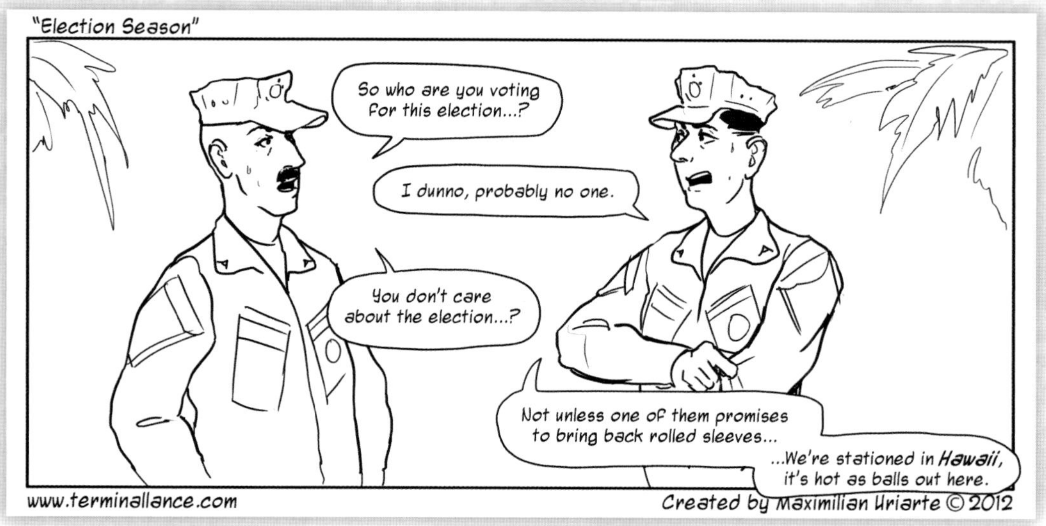
"Election Season"
So who are you voting for this election...?
I dunno, probably no one.
You don't care about the election...?
Not unless one of them promises to bring back rolled sleeves...
...We're stationed in Hawaii, it's hot as balls out here.
www.terminallance.com
Created by Maximilian Uriarte © 2012

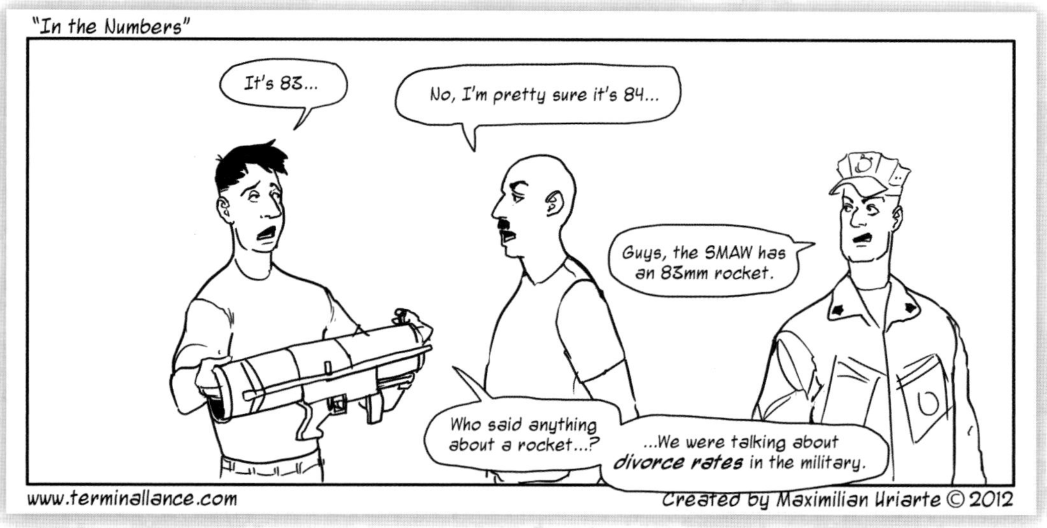
"In the Numbers"
It's 83...
No, I'm pretty sure it's 84...
Guys, the SMAW has an 83mm rocket.
Who said anything about a rocket...?
...We were talking about divorce rates in the military.
www.terminallance.com
Created by Maximilian Uriarte © 2012

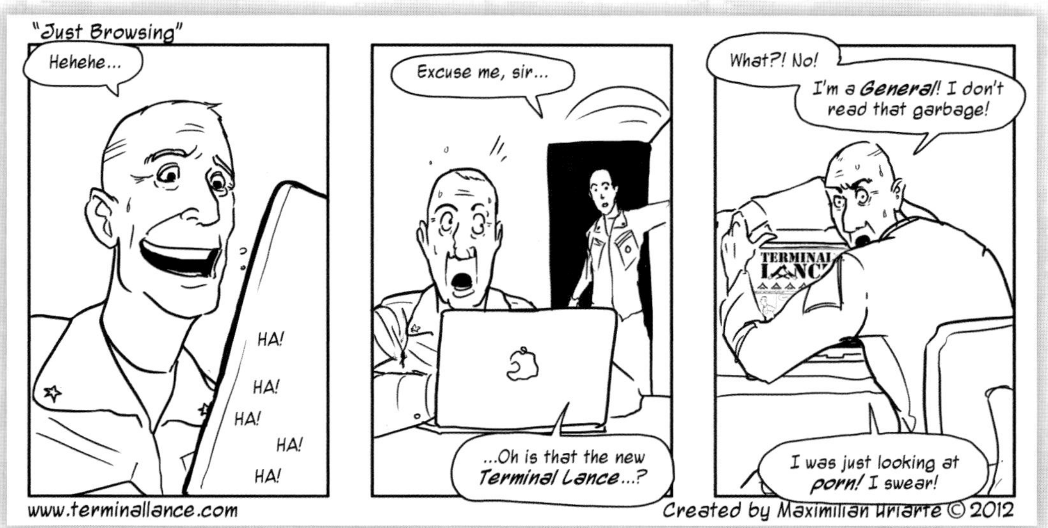
"Just Browsing"
Hehehe...
HA!
HA!
HA!
HA!
HA!
Excuse me, sir...
...Oh is that the new Terminal Lance...?
What?! No!
I'm a General! I don't read that garbage!
TERMINAL LANCE
I was just looking at porn! I swear!
www.terminallance.com
Created by Maximilian Uriarte © 2012

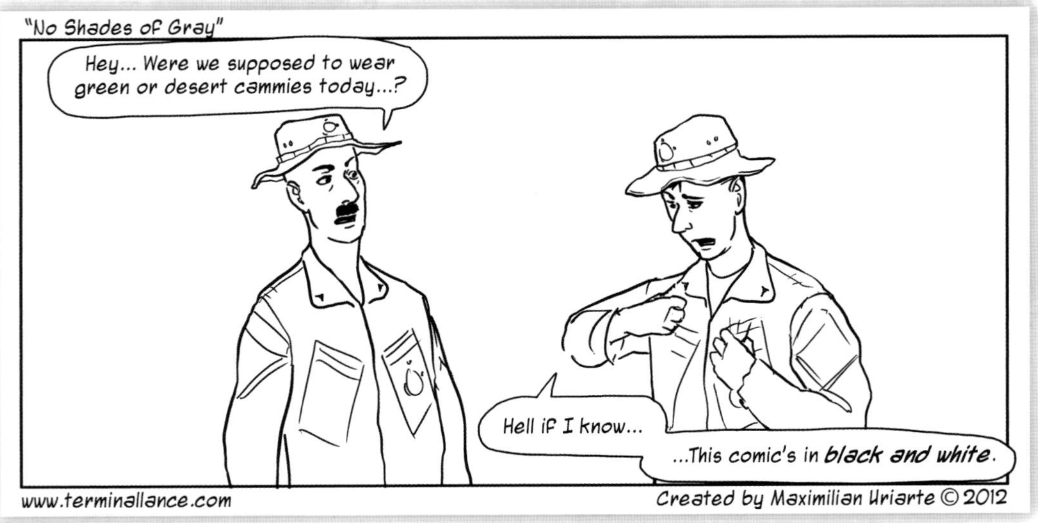
"No Shades of Gray"
Hey... Were we supposed to wear green or desert cammies today...?
Hell if I know...
...This comic's in *black and white*.
www.terminallance.com
Created by Maximilian Uriarte © 2012

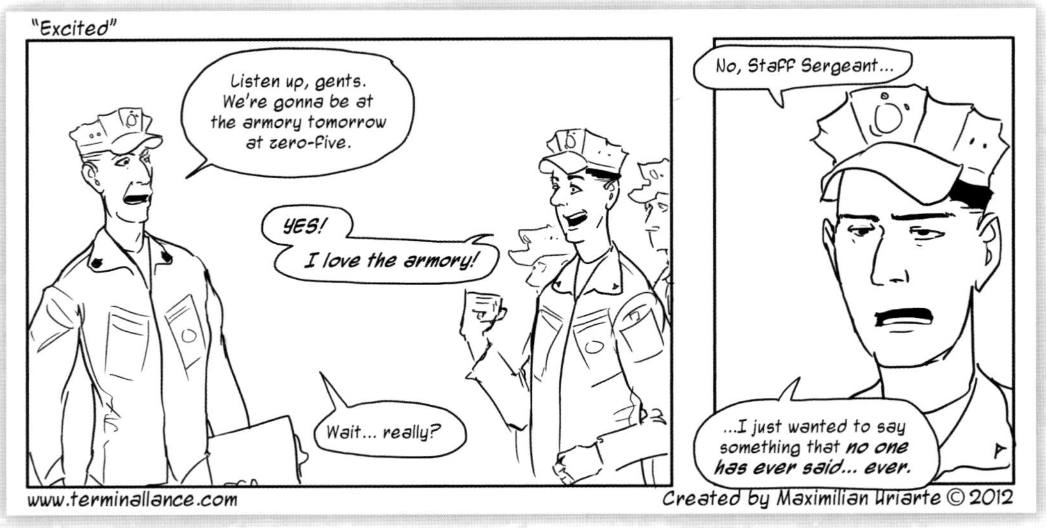
"Excited"
Listen up, gents. We're gonna be at the armory tomorrow at zero-five.
YES! I love the armory!
Wait... really?
No, Staff Sergeant...
...I just wanted to say something that *no one has ever said... ever.*
www.terminallance.com
Created by Maximilian Uriarte © 2012

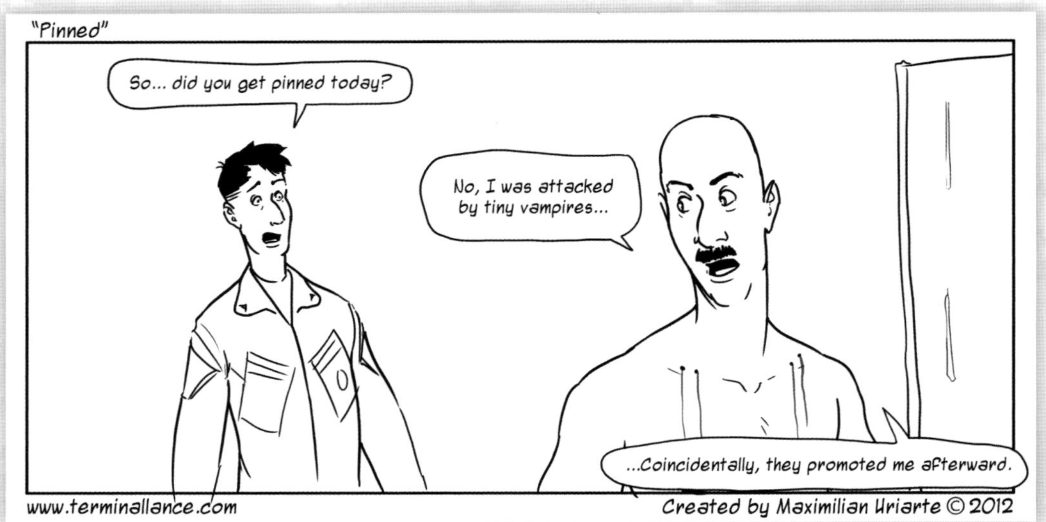
"Pinned"
So... did you get pinned today?
No, I was attacked by tiny vampires...
...Coincidentally, they promoted me afterward.
www.terminallance.com
Created by Maximilian Uriarte © 2012

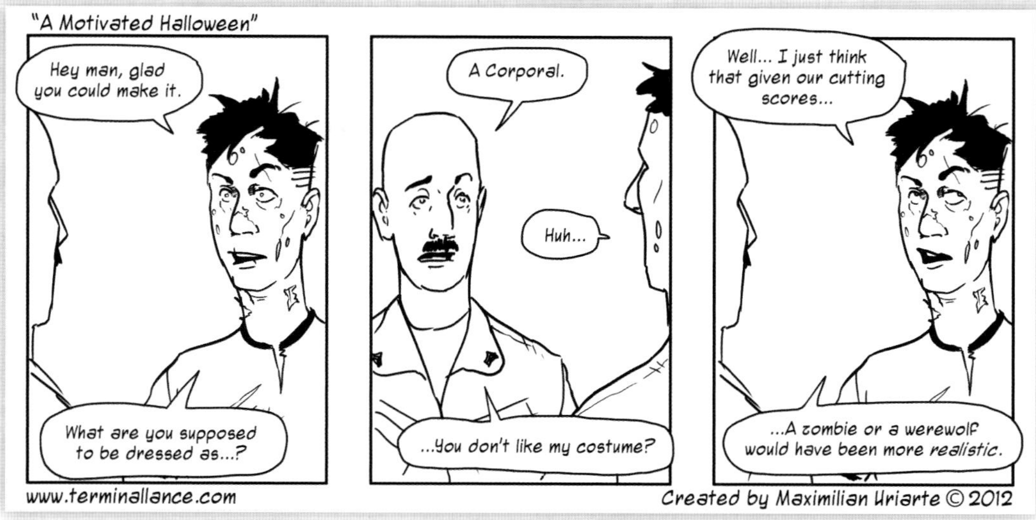
"A Motivated Halloween"
Hey man, glad you could make it.
What are you supposed to be dressed as...?
A Corporal.
Huh...
...You don't like my costume?
Well... I just think that given our cutting scores...
...A zombie or a werewolf would have been more realistic.
www.terminallance.com
Created by Maximilian Uriarte © 2012

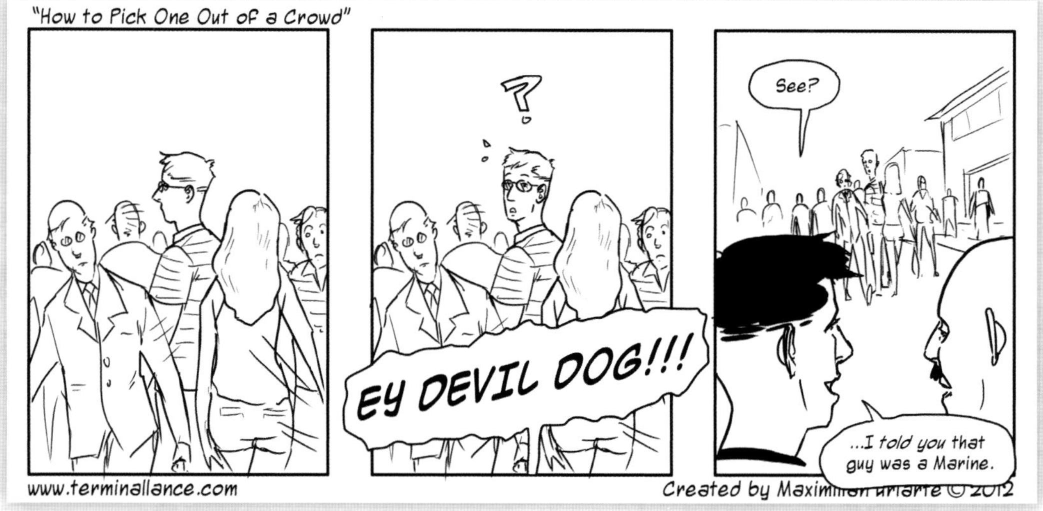
"How to Pick One Out of a Crowd"
?
EY DEVIL DOG!!!
See?
...I told you that guy was a Marine.
www.terminallance.com
Created by Maximilian Uriarte © 2012

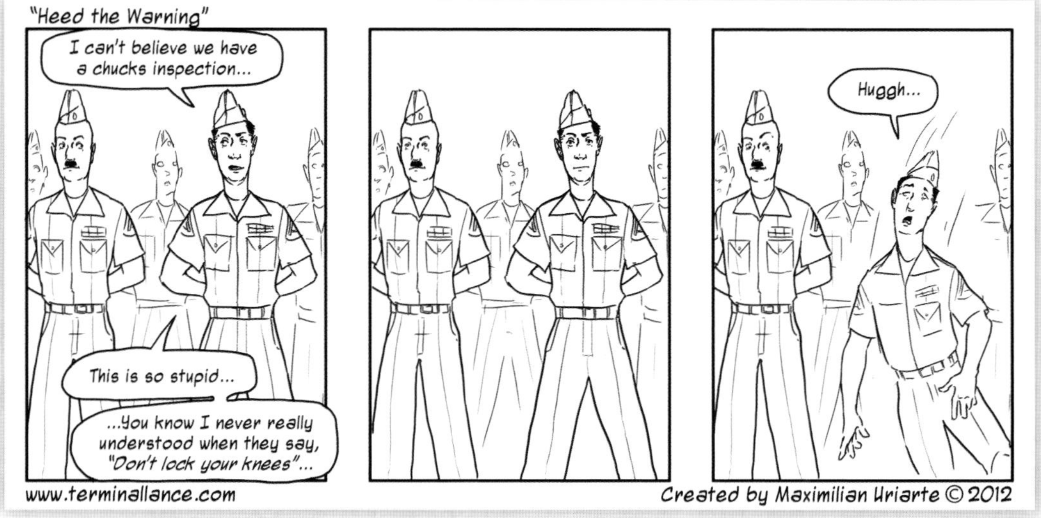
"Heed the Warning"
I can't believe we have a chucks inspection...
This is so stupid...
...You know I never really understood when they say, "Don't lock your knees"...
Huggh...
www.terminallance.com
Created by Maximilian Uriarte © 2012

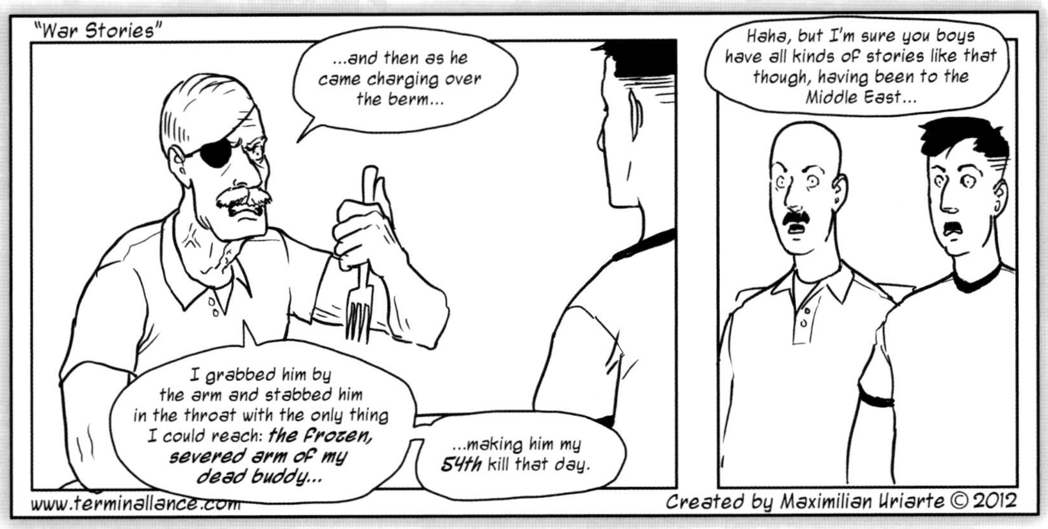
"War Stories"
...and then as he came charging over the berm...
I grabbed him by the arm and stabbed him in the throat with the only thing I could reach: **the frozen, severed arm of my dead buddy...**
...making him my **54th** kill that day.
Haha, but I'm sure you boys have all kinds of stories like that though, having been to the Middle East...
www.terminallance.com
Created by Maximilian Uriarte © 2012

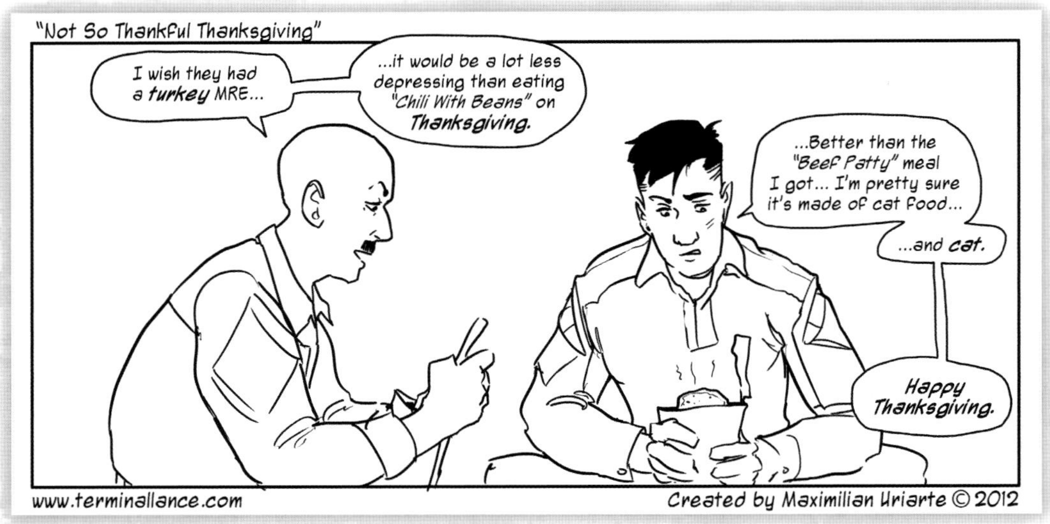
"Not So Thankful Thanksgiving"
I wish they had a ***turkey*** MRE...
...it would be a lot less depressing than eating *"Chili With Beans"* on ***Thanksgiving.***
...Better than the *"Beef Patty"* meal I got... I'm pretty sure it's made of cat food...
...and ***cat.***
Happy Thanksgiving.
www.terminallance.com
Created by Maximilian Uriarte © 2012

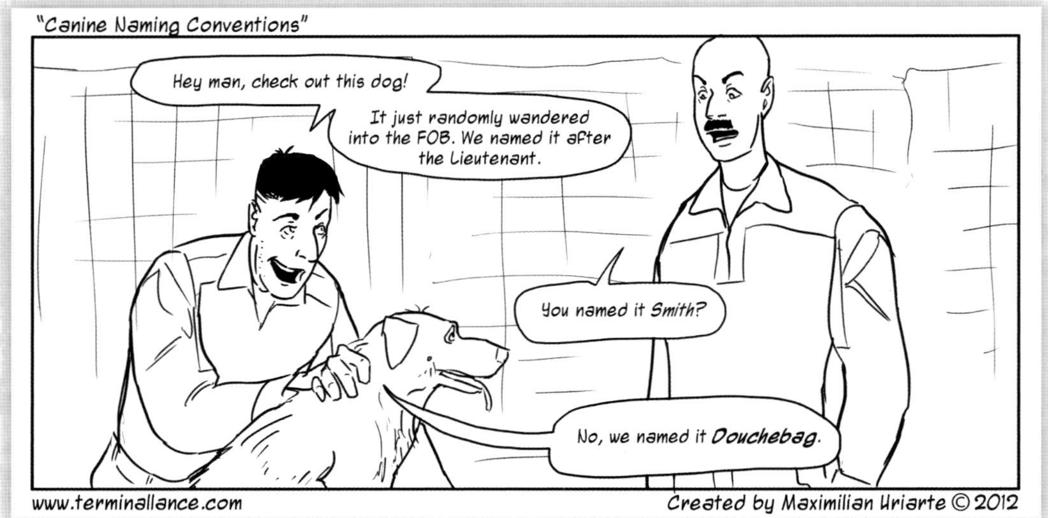
"Canine Naming Conventions"
Hey man, check out this dog!
It just randomly wandered into the FOB. We named it after the Lieutenant.
You named it *Smith?*
No, we named it ***Douchebag.***
www.terminallance.com
Created by Maximilian Uriarte © 2012

"Mail Call of Duty"

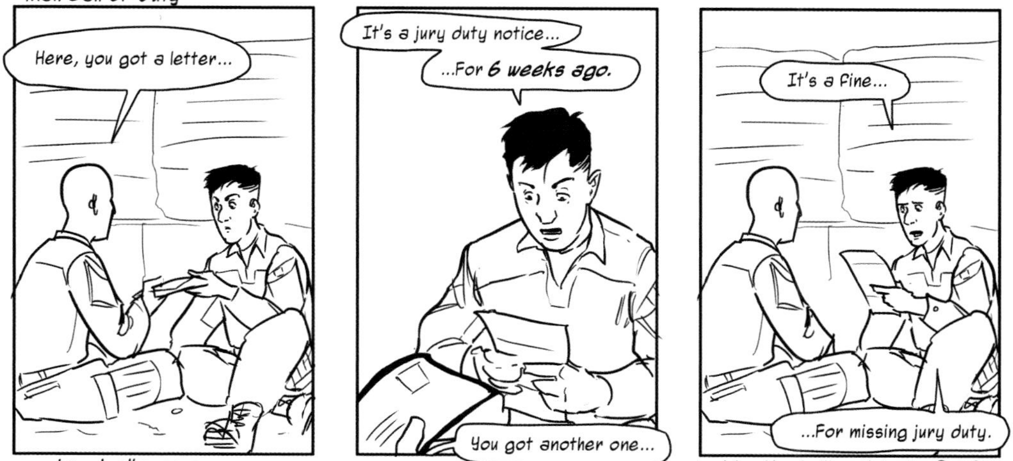
Here, you got a letter...
It's a jury duty notice...
...For 6 weeks ago.
You got another one...
It's a fine...
...For missing jury duty.

www.terminallance.com Created by Maximilian Uriarte © 2012

"Friday Night Barracks Logic"

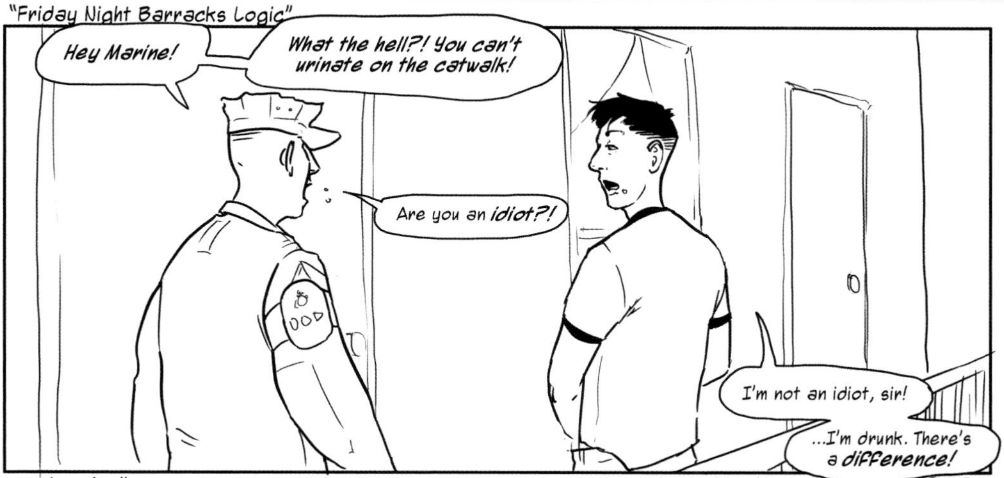
Hey Marine!
What the hell?! You can't urinate on the catwalk!
Are you an idiot?!
I'm not an idiot, sir!
...I'm drunk. There's a difference!

www.terminallance.com Created by Maximilian Uriarte © 2012

"Standing for the Cause"

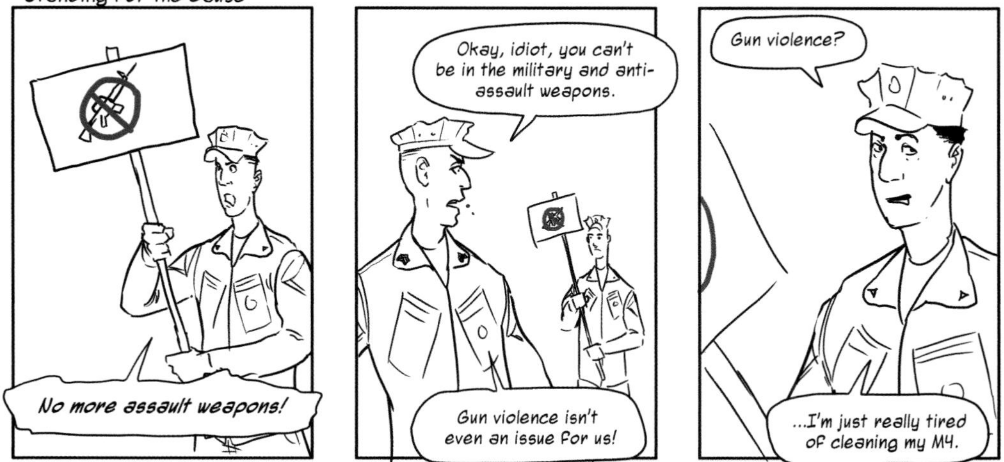
No more assault weapons!
Okay, idiot, you can't be in the military and anti-assault weapons.
Gun violence isn't even an issue for us!
Gun violence?
...I'm just really tired of cleaning my M4.

www.terminallance.com Created by Maximilian Uriarte © 2012

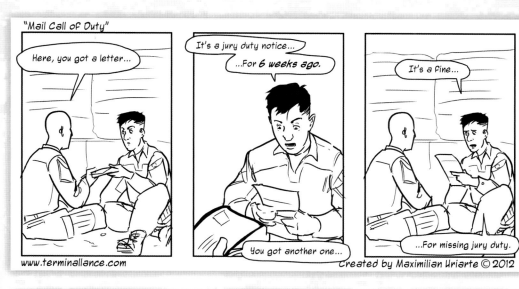

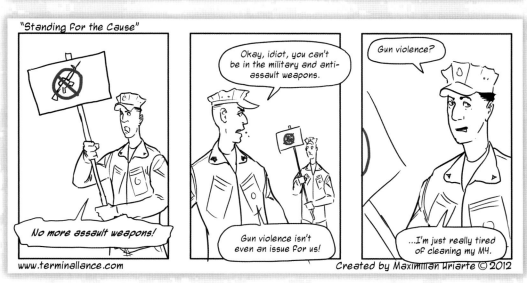

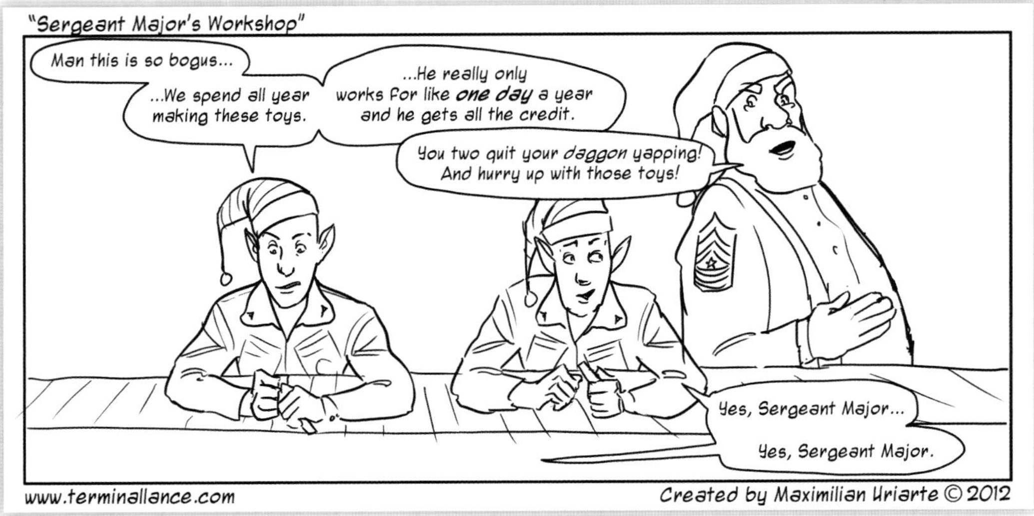
"Sergeant Major's Workshop"
Man this is so bogus...
...We spend all year making these toys.
...He really only works for like *one day* a year and he gets all the credit.
You two quit your *daggon* yapping! And hurry up with those toys!
Yes, Sergeant Major...
Yes, Sergeant Major.
www.terminallance.com
Created by Maximilian Uriarte © 2012

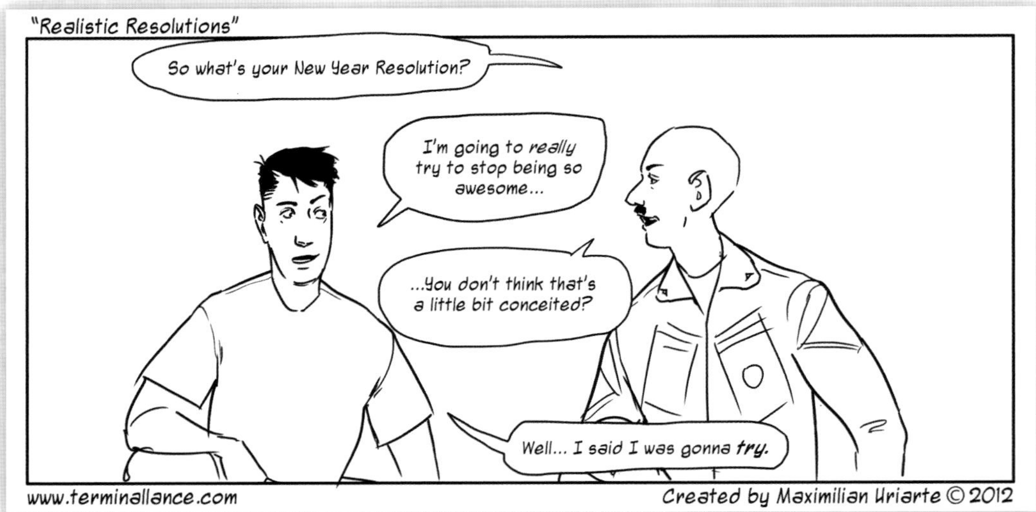
"Realistic Resolutions"
So what's your New Year Resolution?
I'm going to *really* try to stop being so awesome...
...You don't think that's a little bit conceited?
Well... I said I was gonna ***try.***
www.terminallance.com
Created by Maximilian Uriarte © 2012

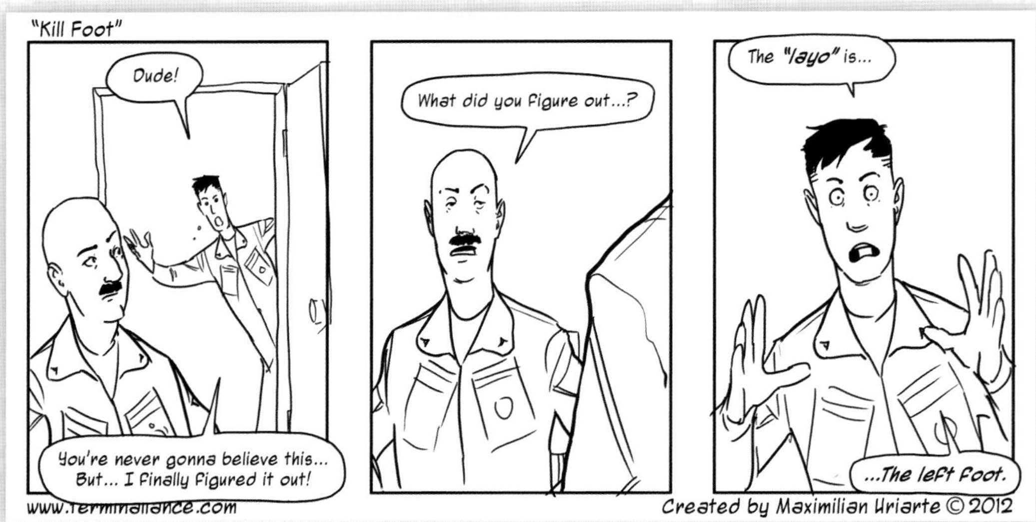
"Kill Foot"
Dude!
You're never gonna believe this... But... I finally figured it out!
What did you figure out...?
The *"layo"* is...
...The left foot.
www.terminallance.com
Created by Maximilian Uriarte © 2012

"Looking Professional II: Service Uniform Fridays"

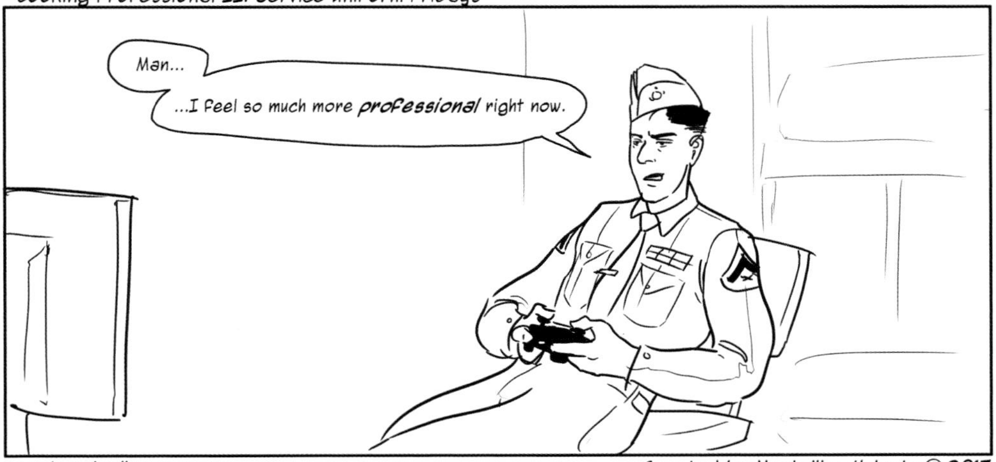
Man...
...I feel so much more ***professional*** right now.

www.terminallance.com Created by Maximilian Uriarte © 2013

"Gunny-Timed"

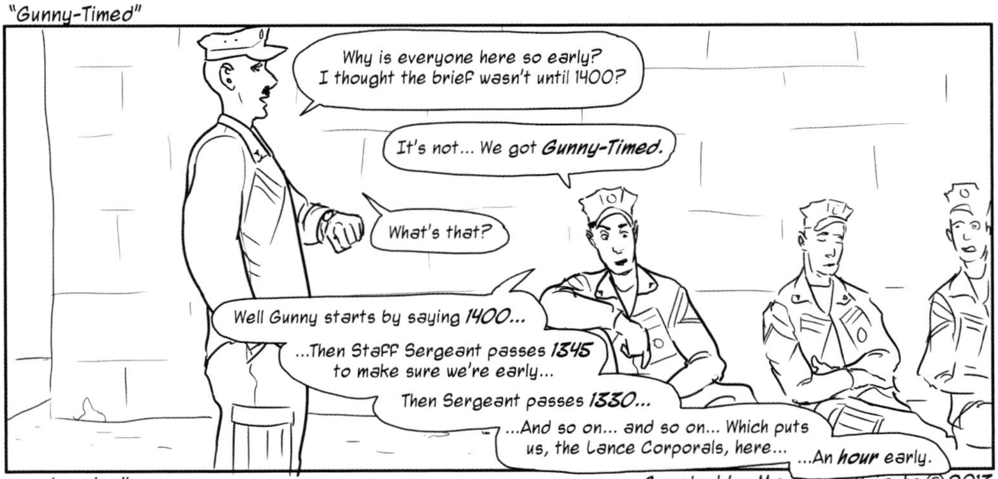
Why is everyone here so early? I thought the brief wasn't until 1400?
It's not... We got ***Gunny-Timed.***
What's that?
Well Gunny starts by saying *1400...*
...Then Staff Sergeant passes *1345* to make sure we're early...
Then Sergeant passes *1330...*
...And so on... and so on... Which puts us, the Lance Corporals, here...
...An ***hour*** early.

www.terminallance.com Created by Maximilian Uriarte © 2013

"The Day My Marine Corps Came Alive"

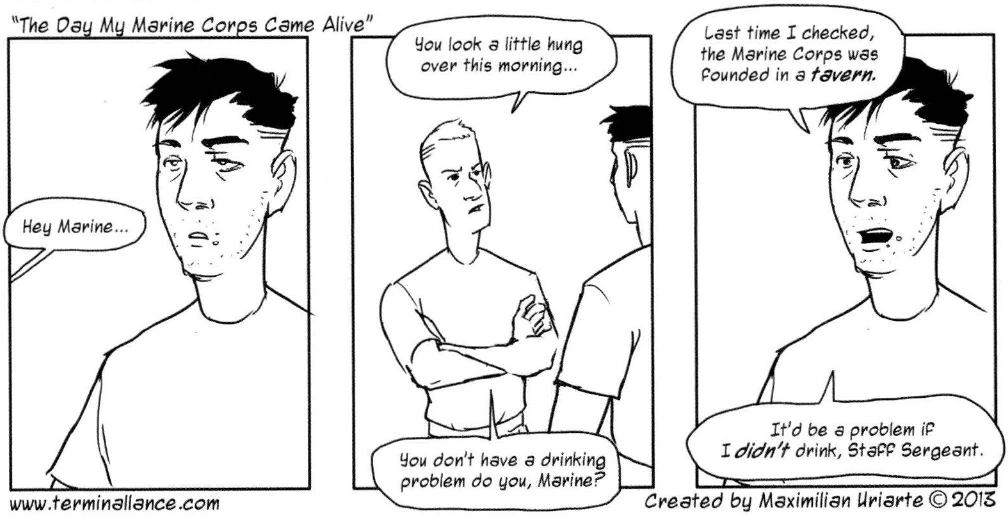
Hey Marine...
You look a little hung over this morning...
You don't have a drinking problem do you, Marine?
Last time I checked, the Marine Corps was founded in a ***tavern.***
It'd be a problem if I ***didn't*** drink, Staff Sergeant.

www.terminallance.com Created by Maximilian Uriarte © 2013

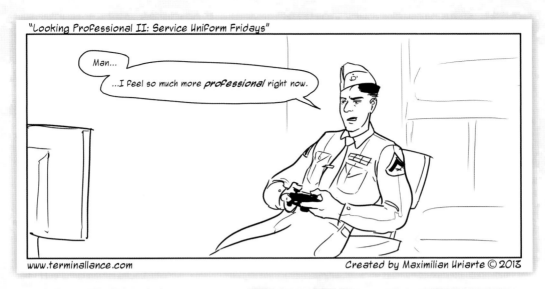

"Old Dog Learning a New Trick"

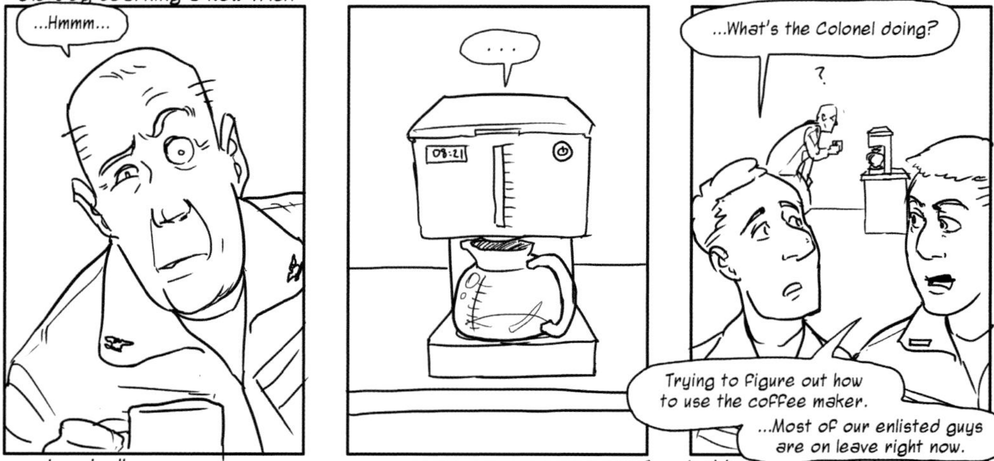

...Hmmm...
. . .
...What's the Colonel doing?
?
Trying to figure out how to use the coffee maker.
...Most of our enlisted guys are on leave right now.

www.terminallance.com Created by Maximilian Uriarte © 2013

"Too Close"

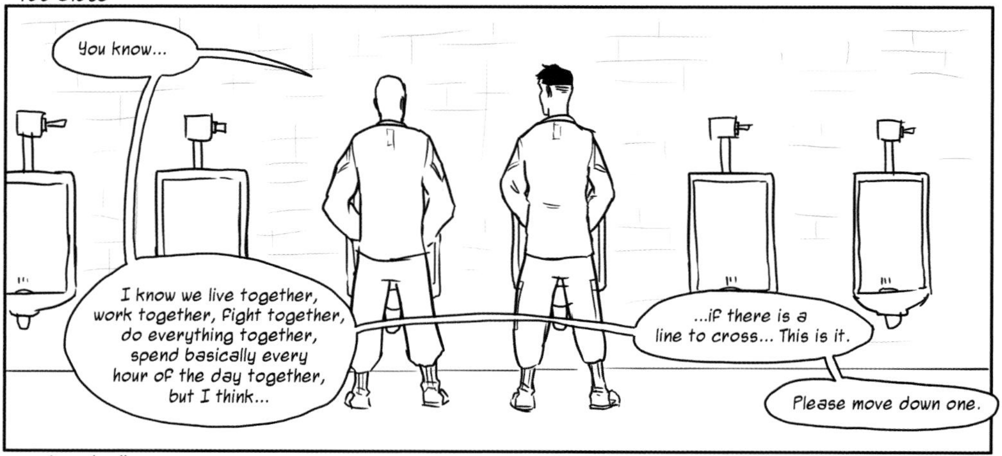

You know...
I know we live together, work together, fight together, do everything together, spend basically every hour of the day together, but I think...
...if there is a line to cross... This is it.
Please move down one.

www.terminallance.com Created by Maximilian Uriarte © 2013

"Follow My Lead"

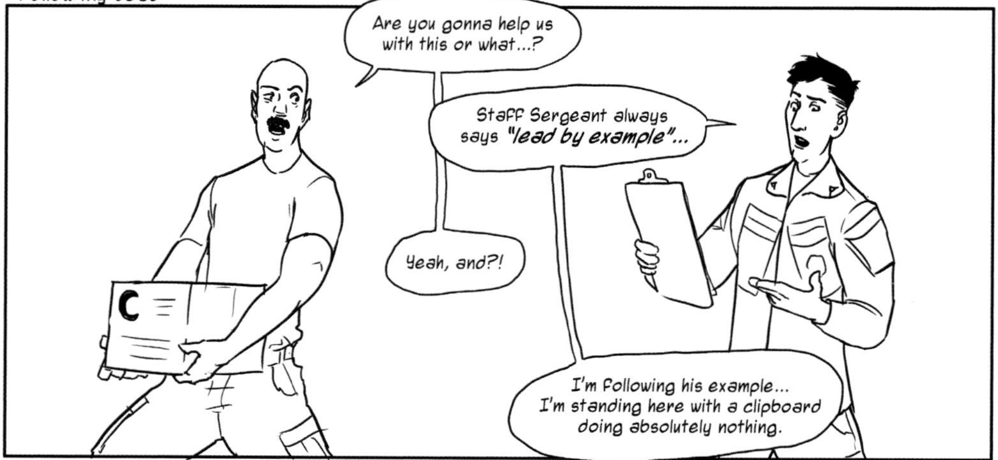

Are you gonna help us with this or what...?
Staff Sergeant always says *"lead by example"*...
Yeah, and?!
I'm following his example... I'm standing here with a clipboard doing absolutely nothing.

www.terminallance.com Created by Maximilian Uriarte © 2013

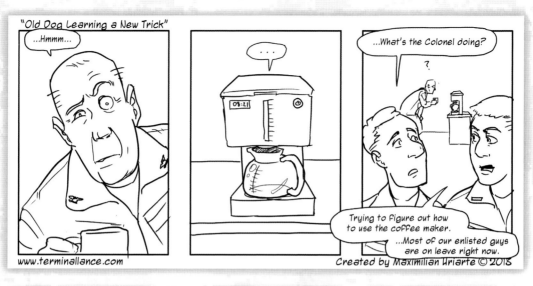

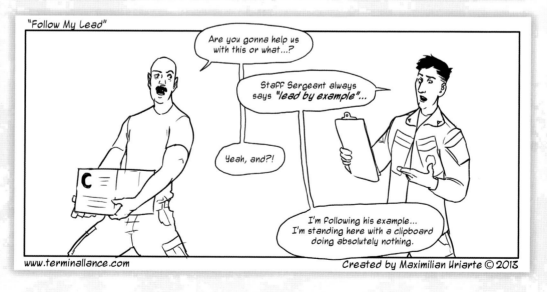

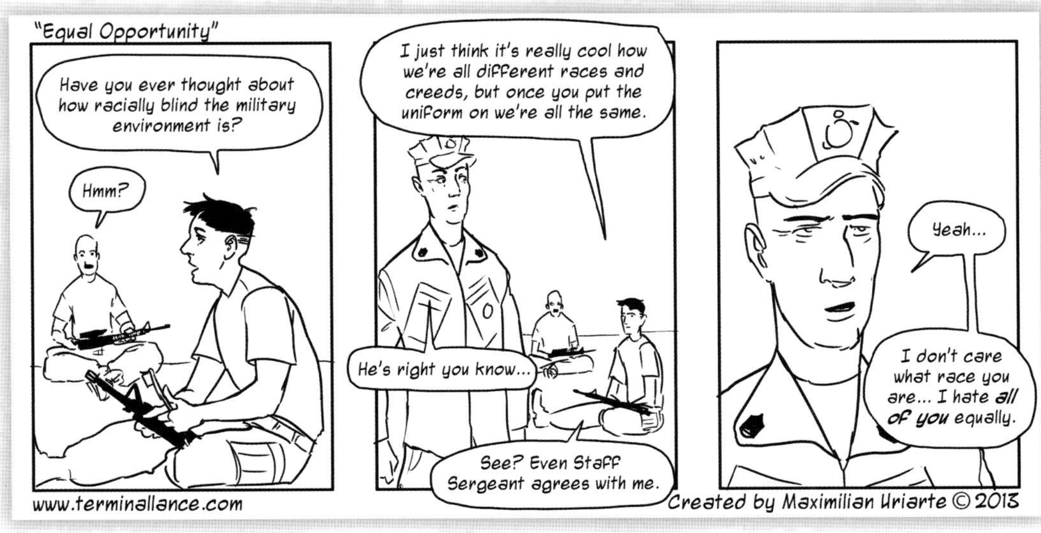
"Equal Opportunity"
Have you ever thought about how racially blind the military environment is?
Hmm?
I just think it's really cool how we're all different races and creeds, but once you put the uniform on we're all the same.
He's right you know...
See? Even Staff Sergeant agrees with me.
Yeah...
I don't care what race you are... I hate ***all of you*** equally.
www.terminallance.com
Created by Maximilian Uriarte © 2013

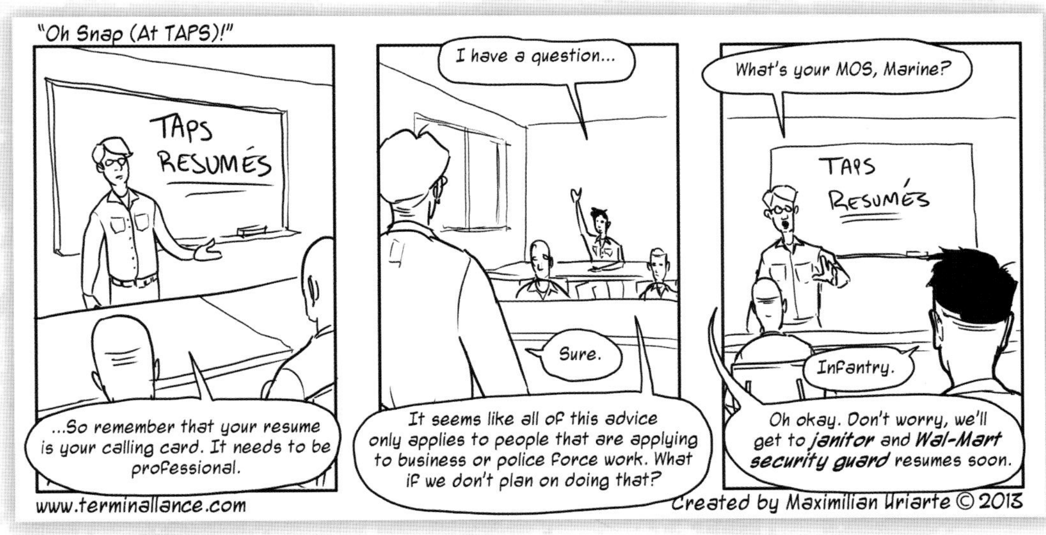
"Oh Snap (At TAPS)!"
TAPS RESUMÉS
...So remember that your resume is your calling card. It needs to be professional.
I have a question...
Sure.
It seems like all of this advice only applies to people that are applying to business or police force work. What if we don't plan on doing that?
What's your MOS, Marine?
TAPS RESUMÉS
Infantry.
Oh okay. Don't worry, we'll get to ***janitor*** and ***Wal-Mart security guard*** resumes soon.
www.terminallance.com
Created by Maximilian Uriarte © 2013

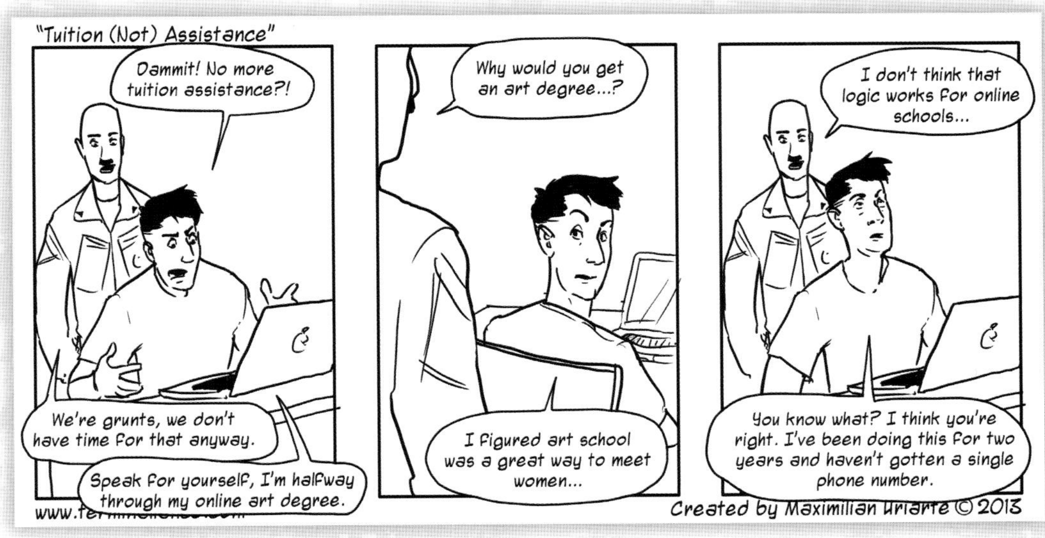
"Tuition (Not) Assistance"
Dammit! No more tuition assistance?!
We're grunts, we don't have time for that anyway.
Speak for yourself, I'm halfway through my online art degree.
Why would you get an art degree...?
I figured art school was a great way to meet women...
I don't think that logic works for online schools...
You know what? I think you're right. I've been doing this for two years and haven't gotten a single phone number.
Created by Maximilian Uriarte © 2013

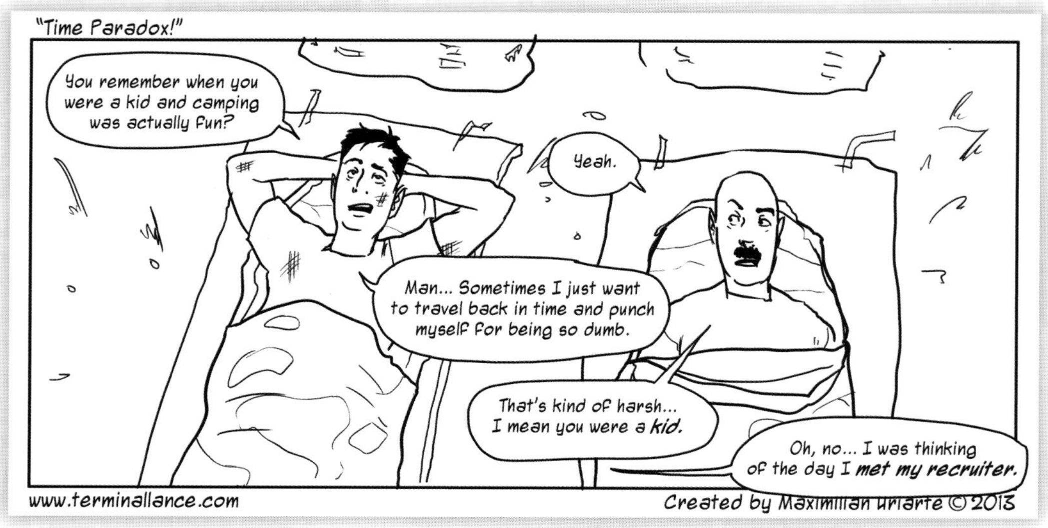
"Time Paradox!"
You remember when you were a kid and camping was actually fun?
Yeah.
Man... Sometimes I just want to travel back in time and punch myself for being so dumb.
That's kind of harsh... I mean you were a *kid.*
Oh, no... I was thinking of the day I ***met my recruiter.***
www.terminallance.com
Created by Maximilian Uriarte © 2013

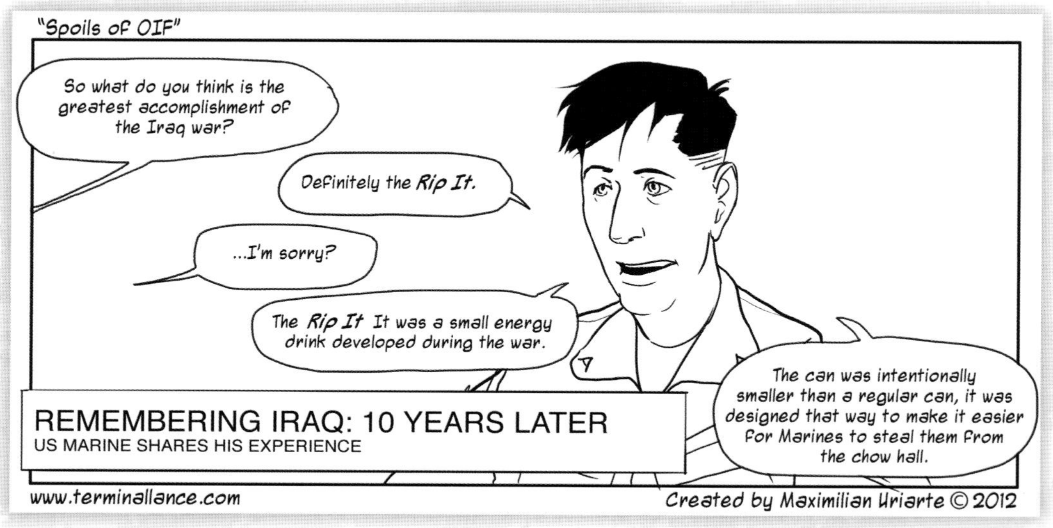
"Spoils of OIF"
So what do you think is the greatest accomplishment of the Iraq war?
Definitely the *Rip It.*
...I'm sorry?
The *Rip It* It was a small energy drink developed during the war.
REMEMBERING IRAQ: 10 YEARS LATER
US MARINE SHARES HIS EXPERIENCE
The can was intentionally smaller than a regular can, it was designed that way to make it easier for Marines to steal them from the chow hall.
www.terminallance.com
Created by Maximilian Uriarte © 2012

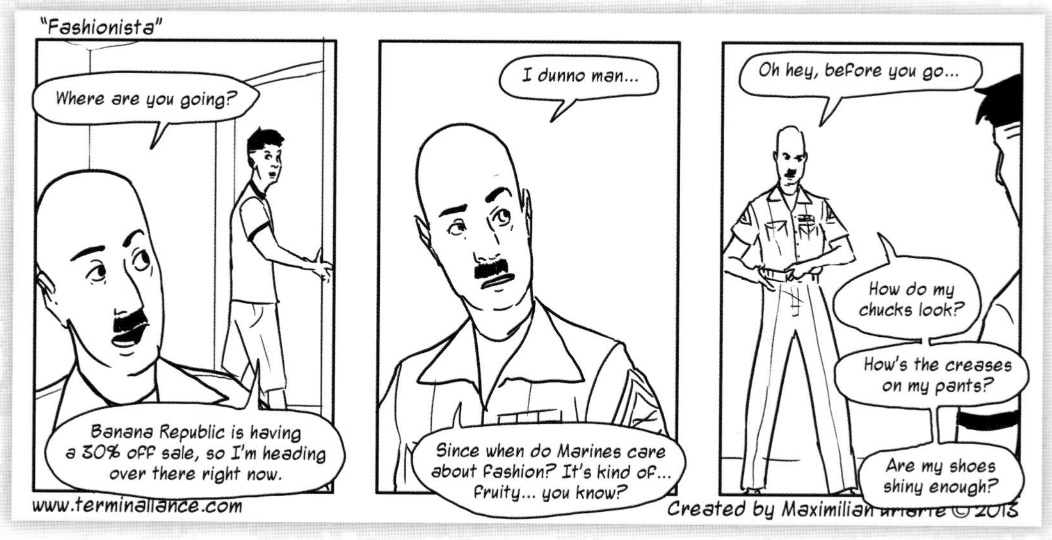
"Fashionista"
Where are you going?
Banana Republic is having a 30% off sale, so I'm heading over there right now.
I dunno man...
Since when do Marines care about fashion? It's kind of... fruity... you know?
Oh hey, before you go...
How do my chucks look?
How's the creases on my pants?
Are my shoes shiny enough?
www.terminallance.com
Created by Maximilian Uriarte © 2013

"Cleaning House"

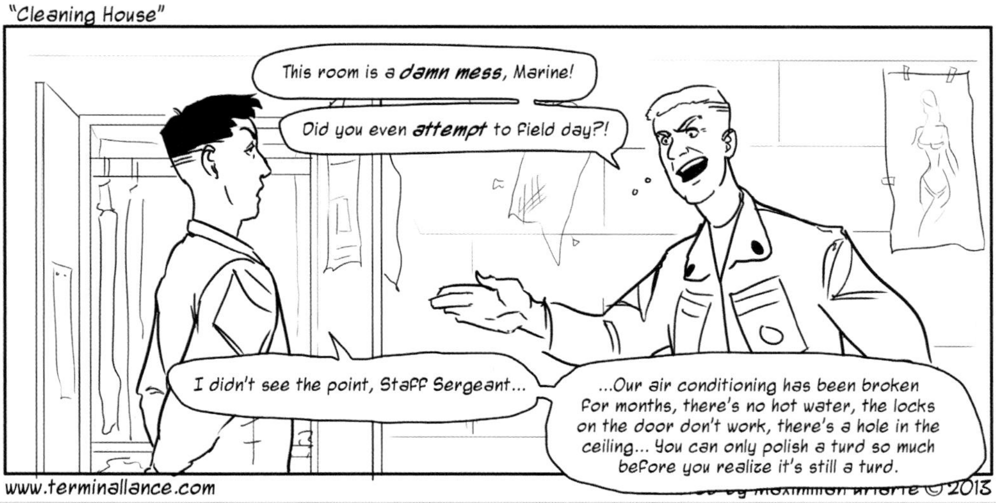

This room is a *damn mess*, Marine!
Did you even *attempt* to field day?!
I didn't see the point, Staff Sergeant...
...Our air conditioning has been broken for months, there's no hot water, the locks on the door don't work, there's a hole in the ceiling... You can only polish a turd so much before you realize it's still a turd.

www.terminallance.com

"Texting Old People"

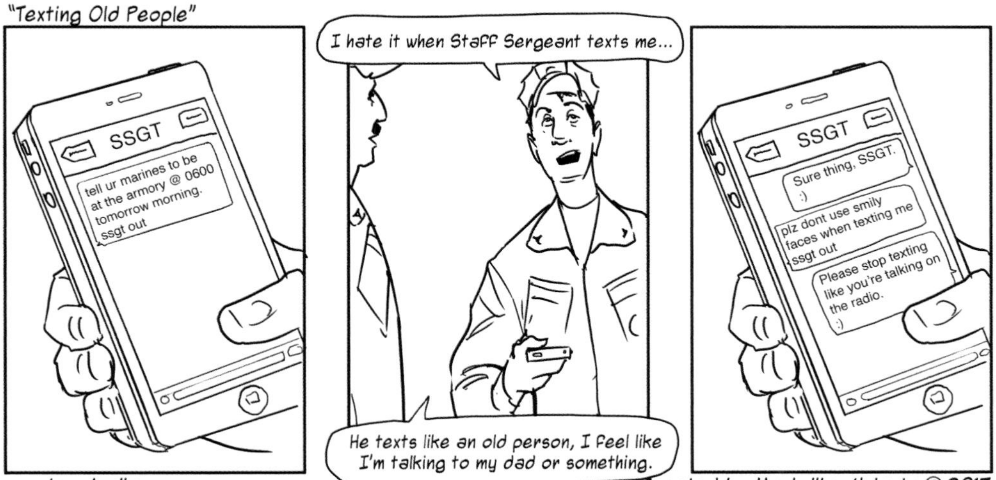

SSGT
tell ur marines to be at the armory @ 0600 tomorrow morning. ssgt out
I hate it when Staff Sergeant texts me...
He texts like an old person, I feel like I'm talking to my dad or something.
SSGT
Sure thing, SSGT. :)
plz dont use smily faces when texting me ssgt out
Please stop texting like you're talking on the radio. :)

www.terminallance.com Created by Maximilian Uriarte © 2013

"Hazardous to Your Health"

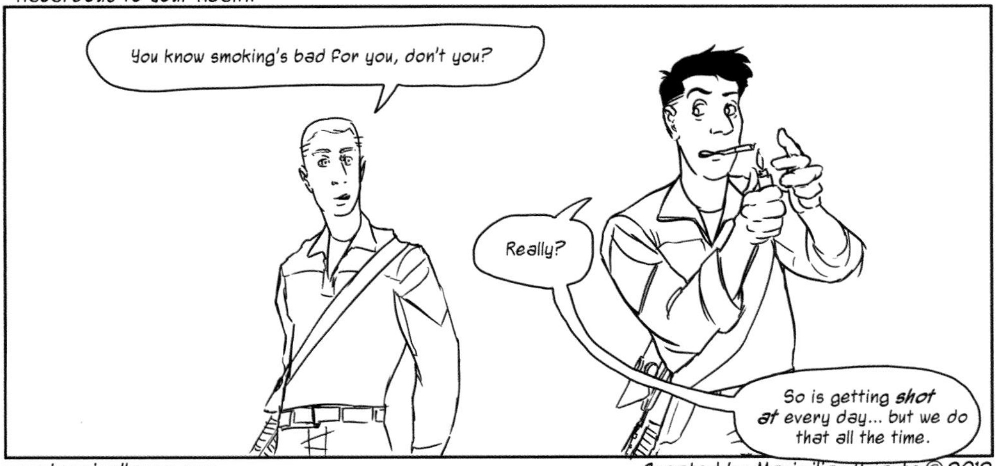

You know smoking's bad for you, don't you?
Really?
So is getting *shot at* every day... but we do that all the time.

www.terminallance.com Created by Maximilian Uriarte © 2012

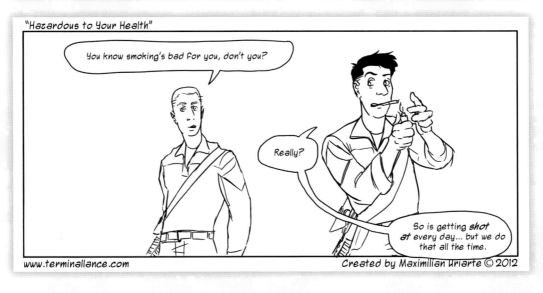

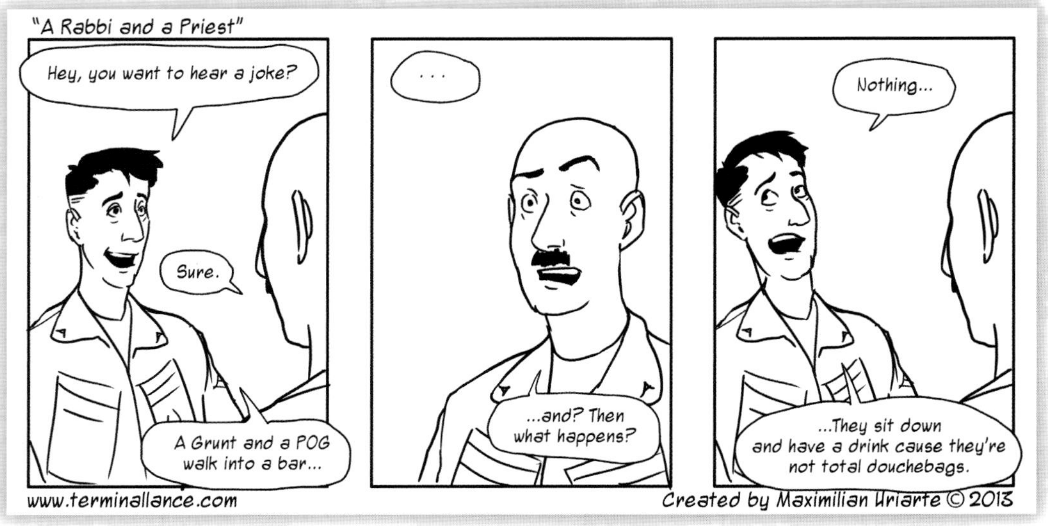
"A Rabbi and a Priest"
Hey, you want to hear a joke?
Sure.
A Grunt and a POG walk into a bar...
. . .
...and? Then what happens?
Nothing...
...They sit down and have a drink cause they're not total douchebags.
www.terminallance.com
Created by Maximilian Uriarte © 2013

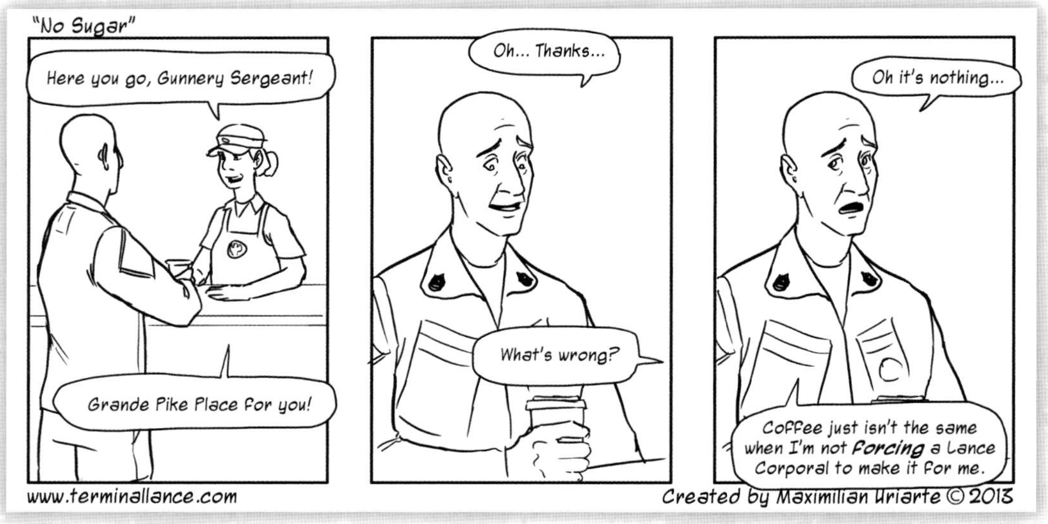
"No Sugar"
Here you go, Gunnery Sergeant!
Grande Pike Place for you!
Oh... Thanks...
What's wrong?
Oh it's nothing...
Coffee just isn't the same when I'm not *forcing* a Lance Corporal to make it for me.
www.terminallance.com
Created by Maximilian Uriarte © 2013

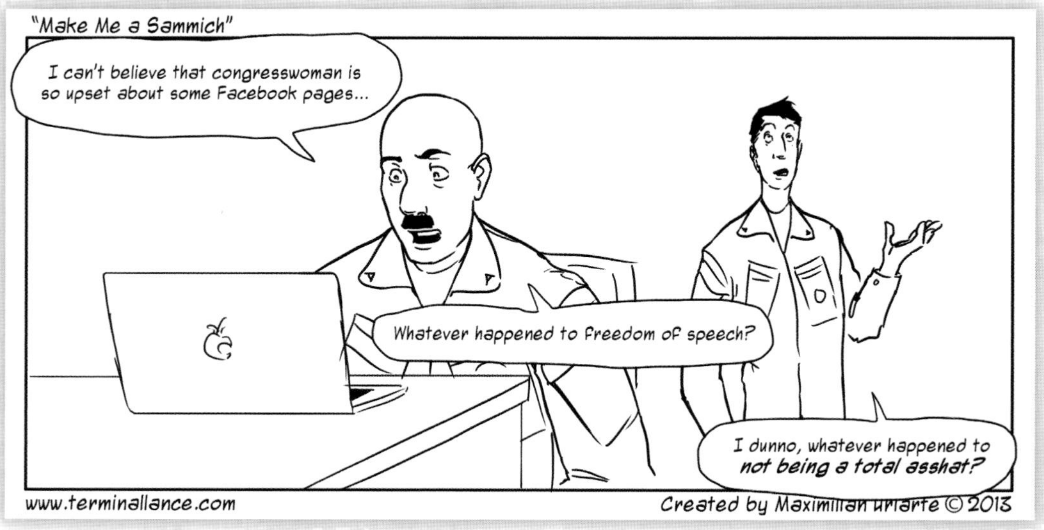
"Make Me a Sammich"
I can't believe that congresswoman is so upset about some Facebook pages...
Whatever happened to freedom of speech?
I dunno, whatever happened to ***not being a total asshat?***
www.terminallance.com
Created by Maximilian Uriarte © 2013

"Fly Home Fly"

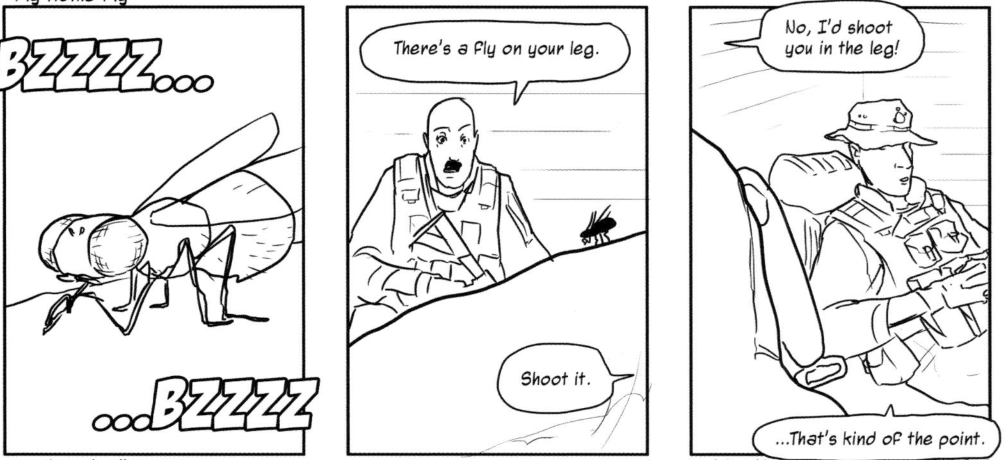
BZZZZ...
...BZZZZ
There's a fly on your leg.
Shoot it.
No, I'd shoot you in the leg!
...That's kind of the point.

www.terminallance.com Created by Maximilian Uriarte © 2013

"Perspiration Inspiration"

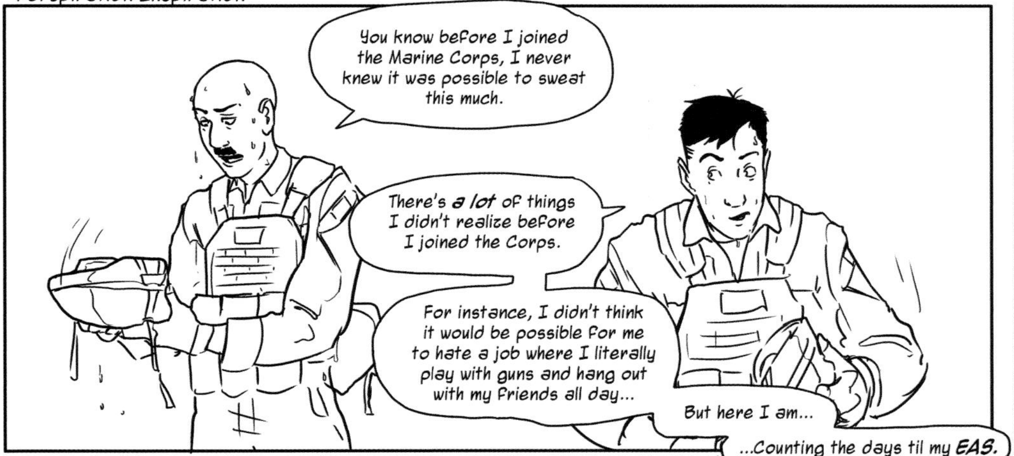
You know before I joined the Marine Corps, I never knew it was possible to sweat this much.
There's *a lot* of things I didn't realize before I joined the Corps.
For instance, I didn't think it would be possible for me to hate a job where I literally play with guns and hang out with my friends all day...
But here I am...
...Counting the days til my *EAS*.

www.terminallance.com Created by

"The Clinton Years"

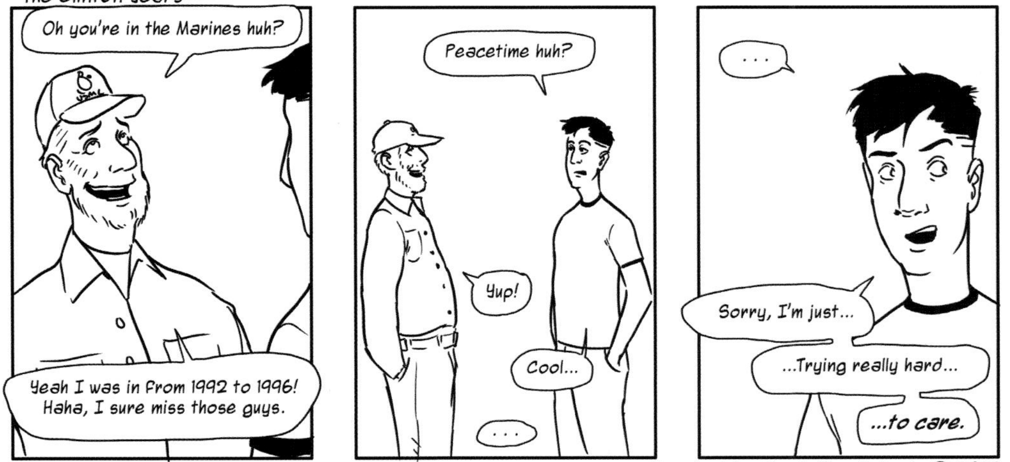
Oh you're in the Marines huh?
Yeah I was in from 1992 to 1996! Haha, I sure miss those guys.
Peacetime huh?
Yup!
Cool...
. . .
. . .
Sorry, I'm just...
...Trying really hard...
...to care.

www.terminallance.com Created by Maximilian Uriarte © 2013

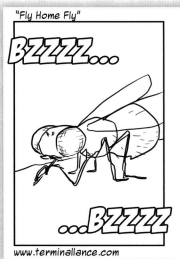

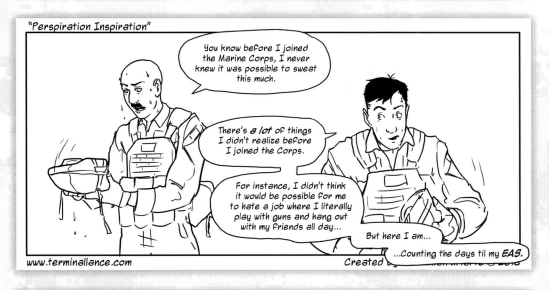

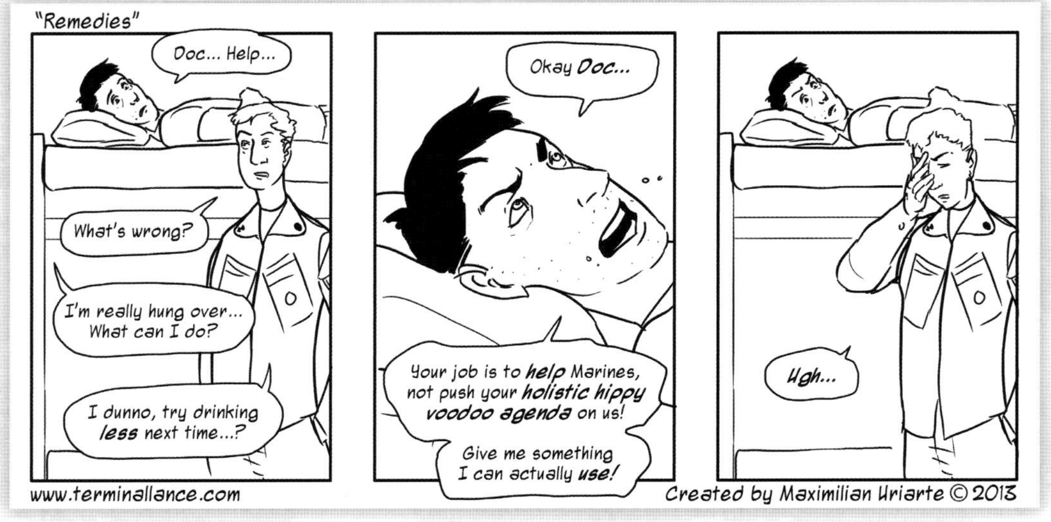
"Remedies"
Doc... Help...
What's wrong?
I'm really hung over... What can I do?
I dunno, try drinking *less* next time...?
Okay *Doc...*
Your job is to *help* Marines, not push your *holistic hippy voodoo agenda* on us!
Give me something I can actually *use!*
Ugh...
www.terminallance.com
Created by Maximilian Uriarte © 2013

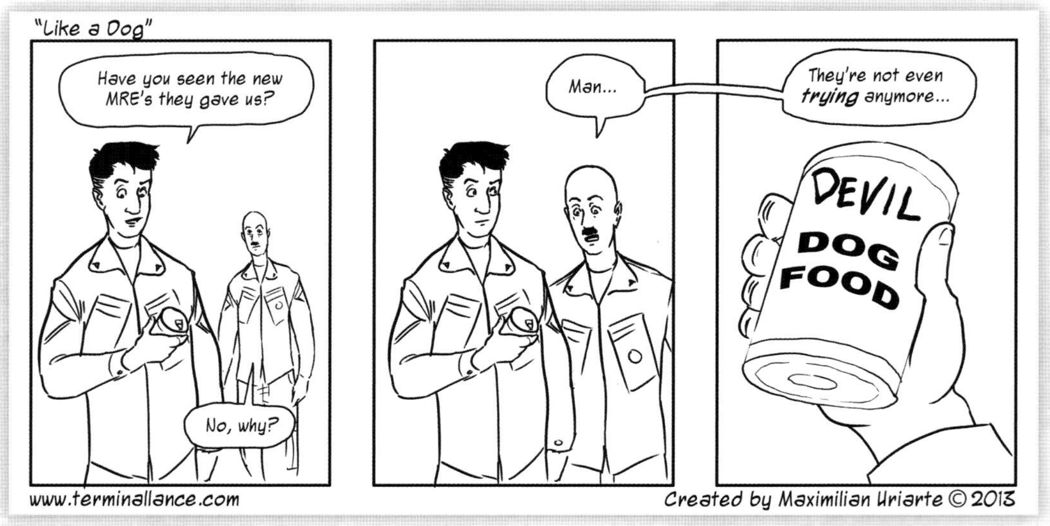
"Like a Dog"
Have you seen the new MRE's they gave us?
No, why?
Man...
They're not even *trying* anymore...
DEVIL
DOG
FOOD
www.terminallance.com
Created by Maximilian Uriarte © 2013

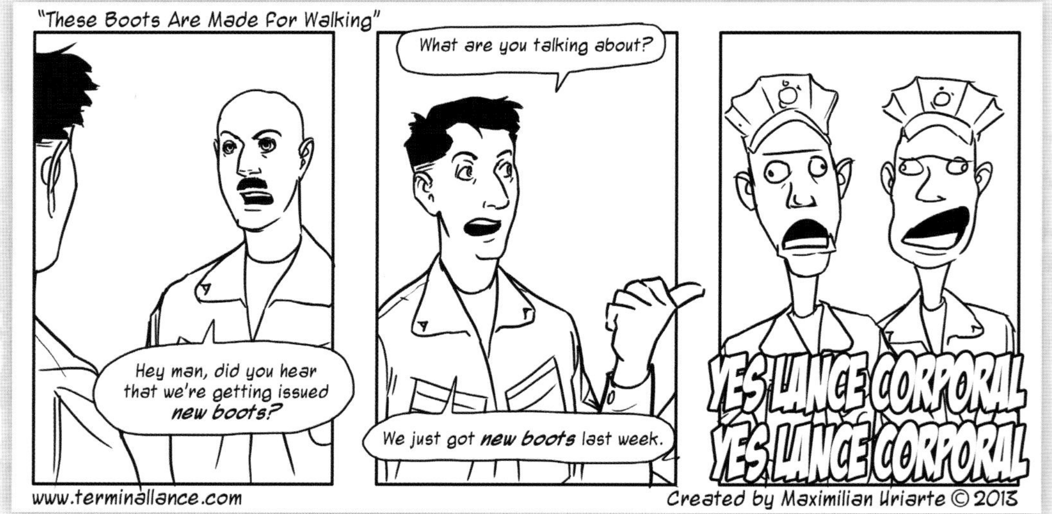
"These Boots Are Made For Walking"
Hey man, did you hear that we're getting issued *new boots?*
What are you talking about?
We just got *new boots* last week.
YES LANCE CORPORAL
YES LANCE CORPORAL
www.terminallance.com
Created by Maximilian Uriarte © 2013

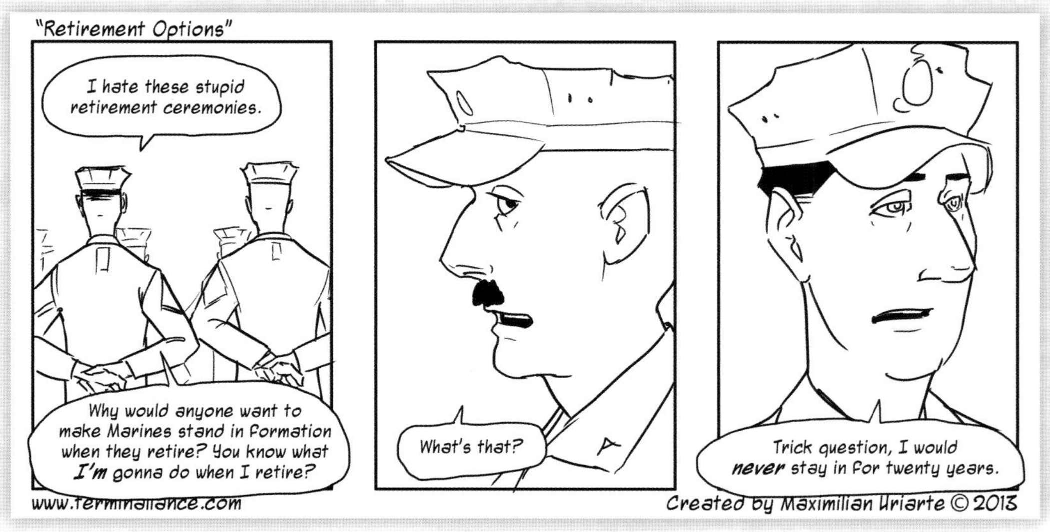
"Retirement Options"
I hate these stupid retirement ceremonies.
Why would anyone want to make Marines stand in formation when they retire? You know what I'm gonna do when I retire?
What's that?
Trick question, I would never stay in for twenty years.
www.terminallance.com
Created by Maximilian Uriarte © 2013

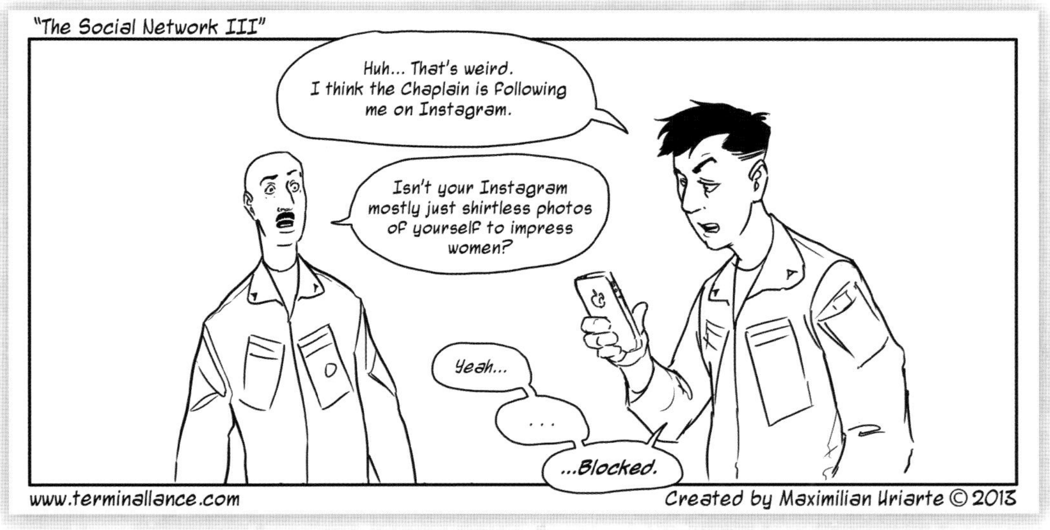
"The Social Network III"
Huh... That's weird. I think the Chaplain is following me on Instagram.
Isn't your Instagram mostly just shirtless photos of yourself to impress women?
Yeah...
. . .
...Blocked.
www.terminallance.com
Created by Maximilian Uriarte © 2013

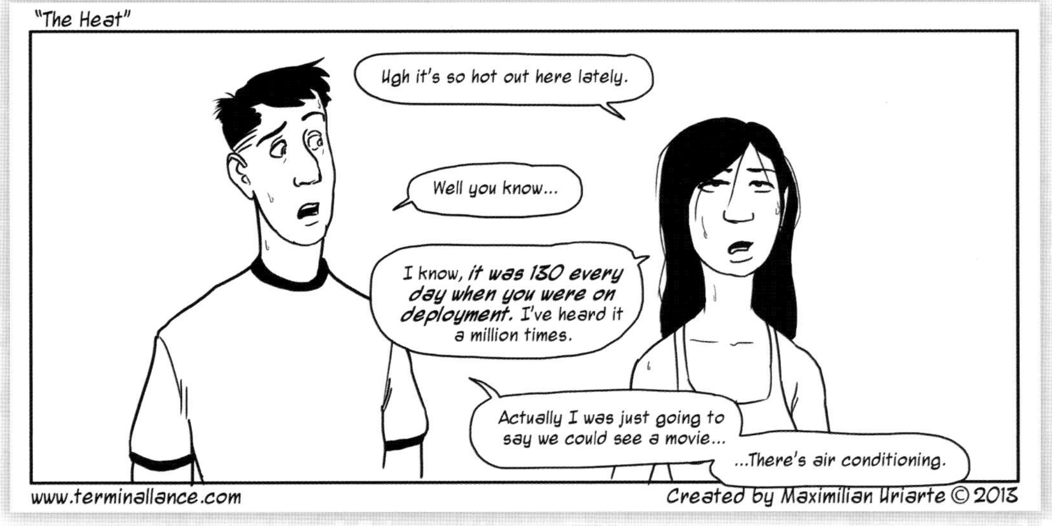
"The Heat"
Ugh it's so hot out here lately.
Well you know...
I know, it was 130 every day when you were on deployment. I've heard it a million times.
Actually I was just going to say we could see a movie...
...There's air conditioning.
www.terminallance.com
Created by Maximilian Uriarte © 2013

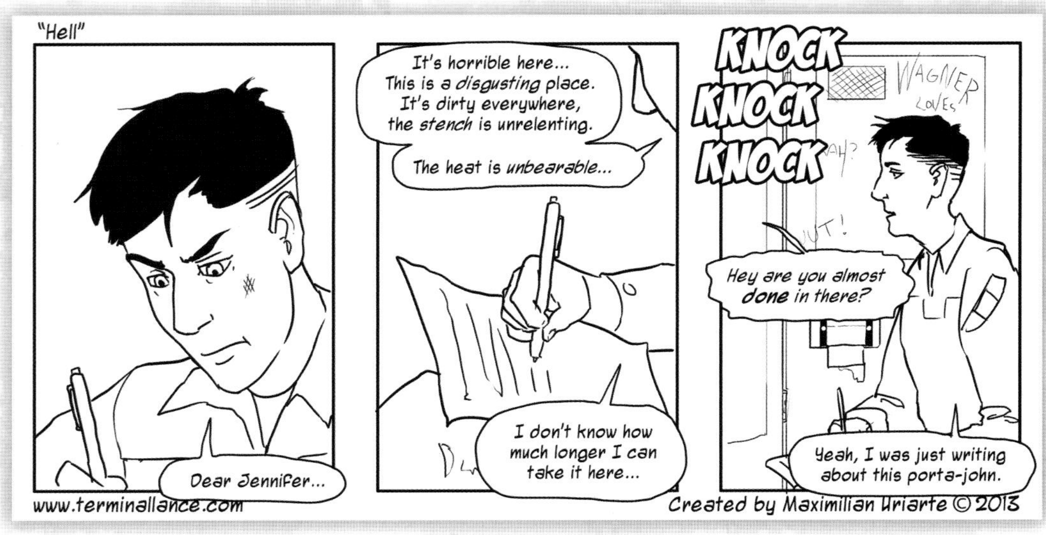
"Hell"
Dear Jennifer...
It's horrible here... This is a disgusting place. It's dirty everywhere, the stench is unrelenting.
The heat is unbearable...
I don't know how much longer I can take it here...
KNOCK KNOCK KNOCK
Hey are you almost done in there?
Yeah, I was just writing about this porta-john.
www.terminallance.com
Created by Maximilian Uriarte © 2013

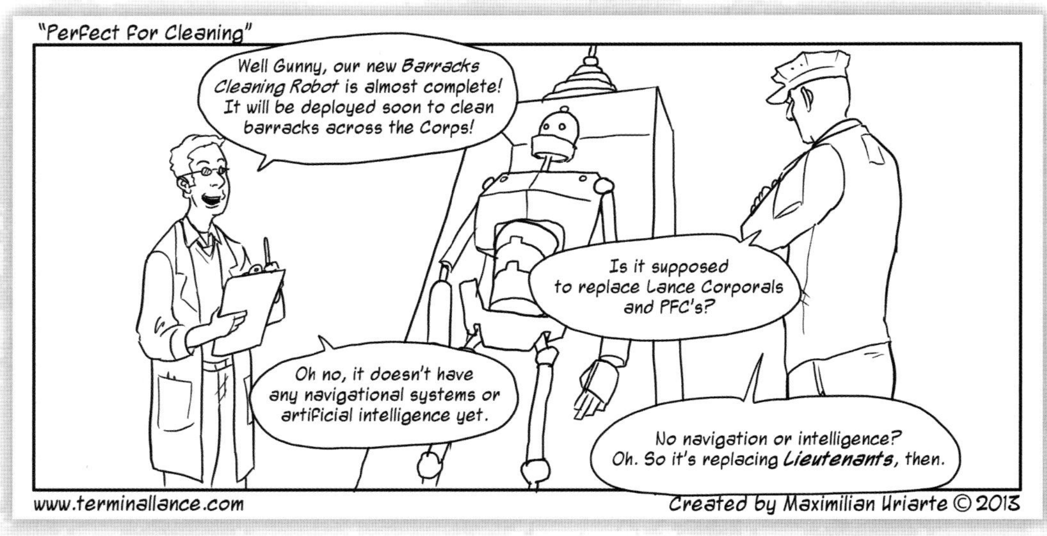
"Perfect for Cleaning"
Well Gunny, our new Barracks Cleaning Robot is almost complete! It will be deployed soon to clean barracks across the Corps!
Is it supposed to replace Lance Corporals and PFC's?
Oh no, it doesn't have any navigational systems or artificial intelligence yet.
No navigation or intelligence? Oh. So it's replacing Lieutenants, then.
www.terminallance.com
Created by Maximilian Uriarte © 2013

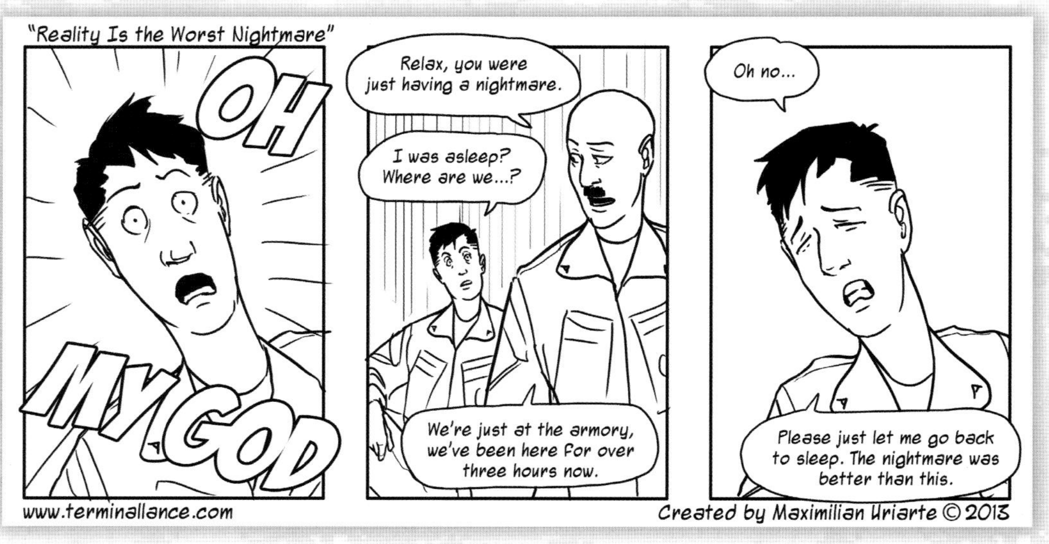
"Reality Is the Worst Nightmare"
OH
MY GOD
Relax, you were just having a nightmare.
I was asleep? Where are we...?
We're just at the armory, we've been here for over three hours now.
Oh no...
Please just let me go back to sleep. The nightmare was better than this.
www.terminallance.com
Created by Maximilian Uriarte © 2013

"Sending Out an SMS"

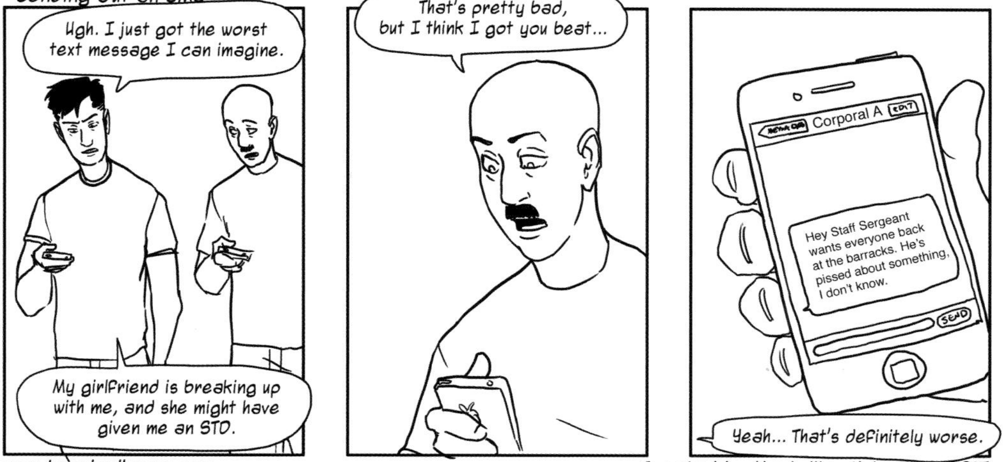
Ugh. I just got the worst text message I can imagine.
My girlfriend is breaking up with me, and she might have given me an STD.
That's pretty bad, but I think I got you beat...
Corporal A
EDIT
Hey Staff Sergeant wants everyone back at the barracks. He's pissed about something, I don't know.
SEND
Yeah... That's definitely worse.

www.terminallance.com Created by Maximilian Uriarte © 2013

"Insomniac"

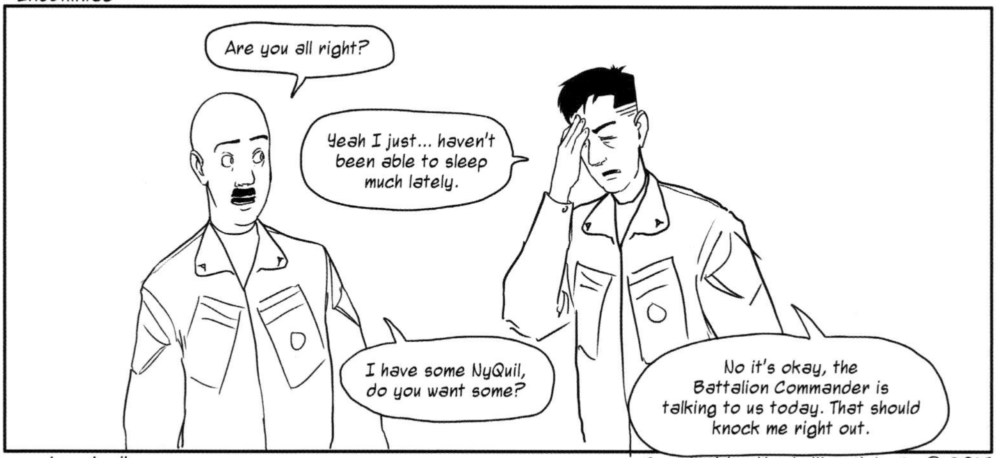
Are you all right?
Yeah I just... haven't been able to sleep much lately.
I have some NyQuil, do you want some?
No it's okay, the Battalion Commander is talking to us today. That should knock me right out.

www.terminallance.com Created by Maximilian Uriarte © 2013

"Crustaceous Confusion"

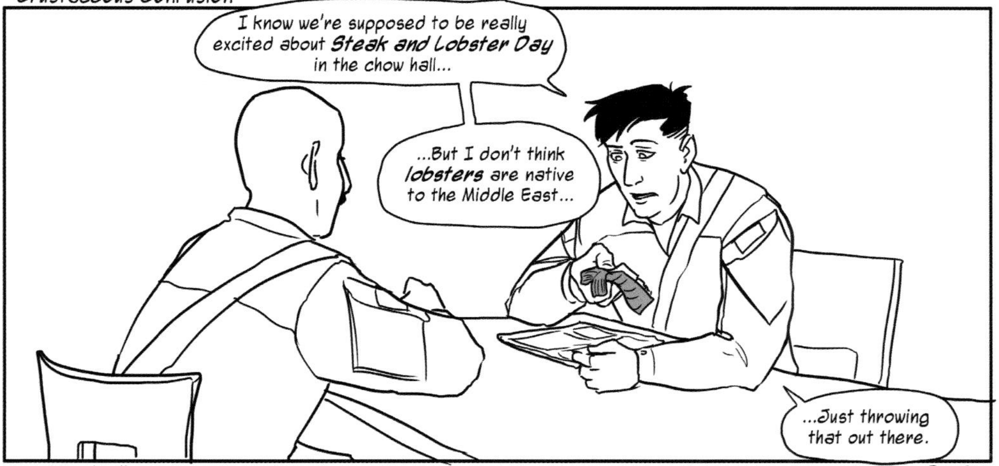
I know we're supposed to be really excited about Steak and Lobster Day in the chow hall...
...But I don't think lobsters are native to the Middle East...
...Just throwing that out there.

www.terminallance.com Created by Maximilian Uriarte © 2013

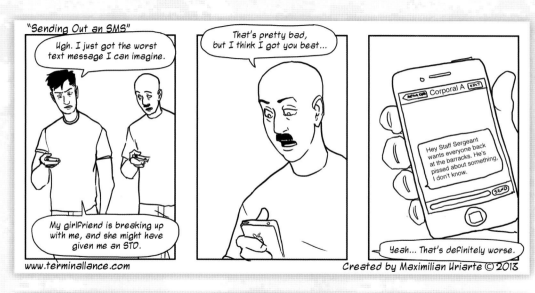

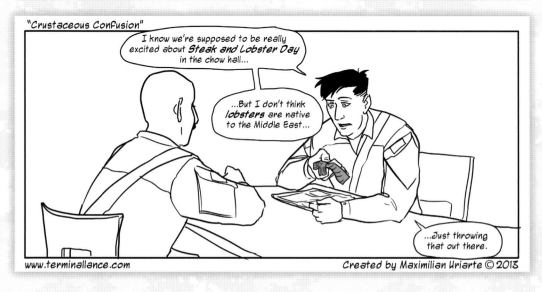

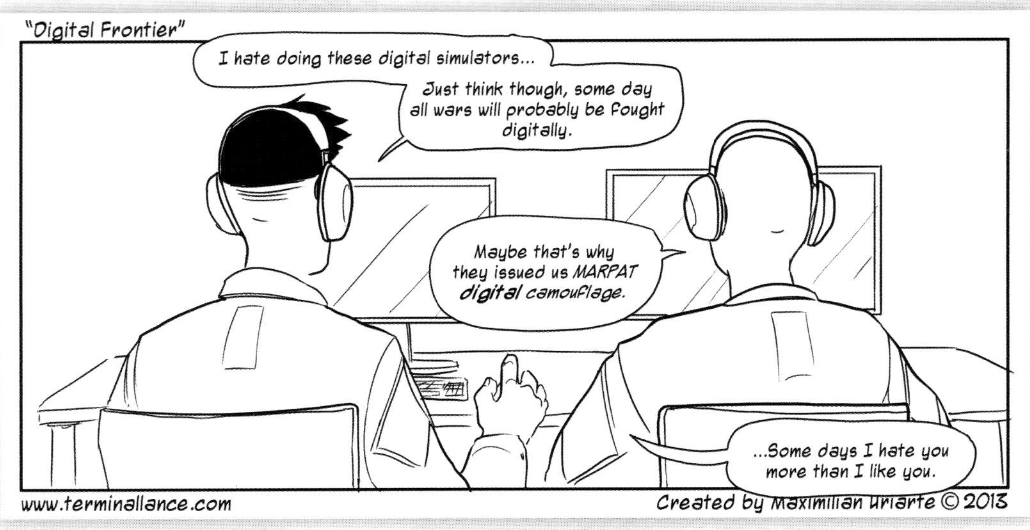
"Digital Frontier"
I hate doing these digital simulators...
Just think though, some day all wars will probably be fought digitally.
Maybe that's why they issued us MARPAT **digital** camouflage.
...Some days I hate you more than I like you.
www.terminallance.com
Created by Maximilian Uriarte © 2013

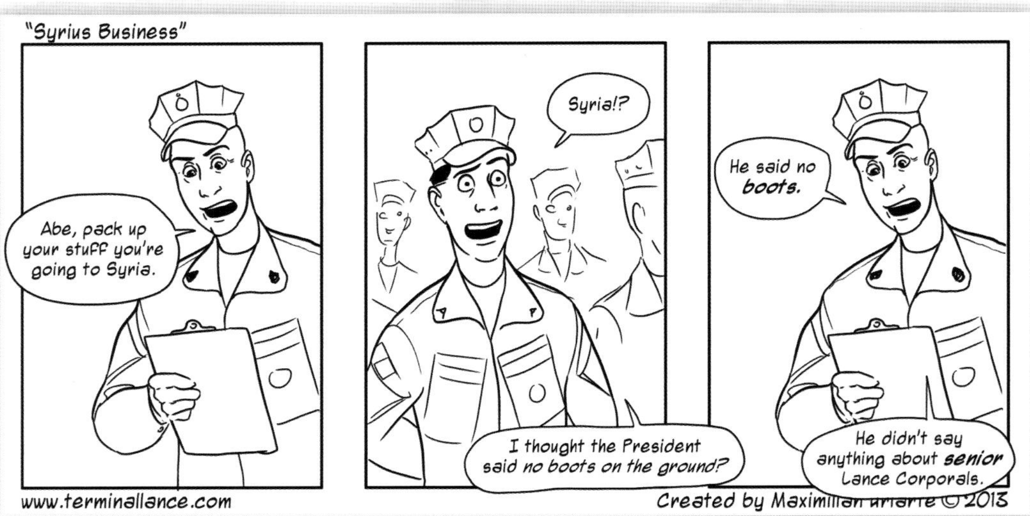
"Syrius Business"
Abe, pack up your stuff you're going to Syria.
Syria!?
I thought the President said no boots on the ground?
He said no **boots.**
He didn't say anything about ***senior*** Lance Corporals.
www.terminallance.com
Created by Maximilian Uriarte © 2013

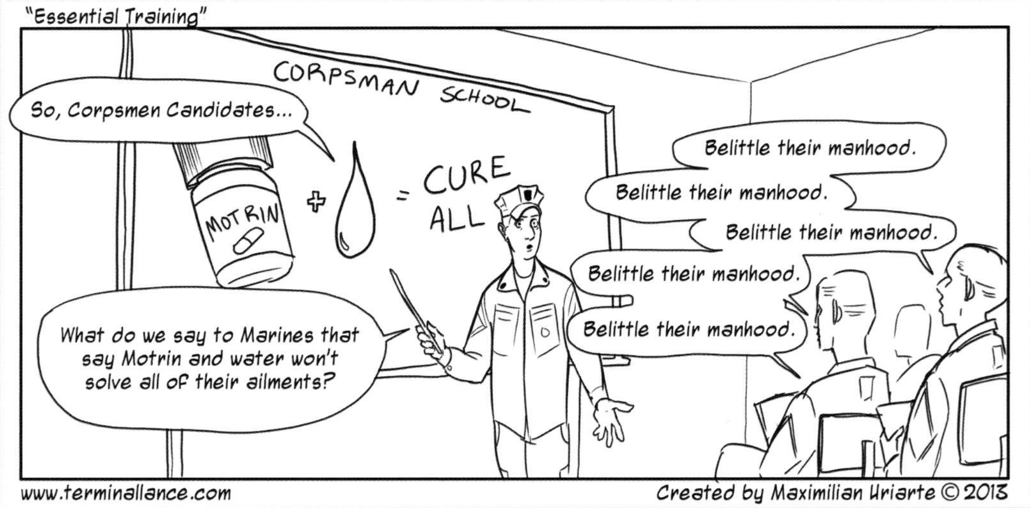
"Essential Training"
CORPSMAN SCHOOL
So, Corpsmen Candidates...
MOTRIN
+
= CURE ALL
What do we say to Marines that say Motrin and water won't solve all of their ailments?
Belittle their manhood.
Belittle their manhood.
Belittle their manhood.
Belittle their manhood.
Belittle their manhood.
www.terminallance.com
Created by Maximilian Uriarte © 2013

"Due for an Upgrade II"

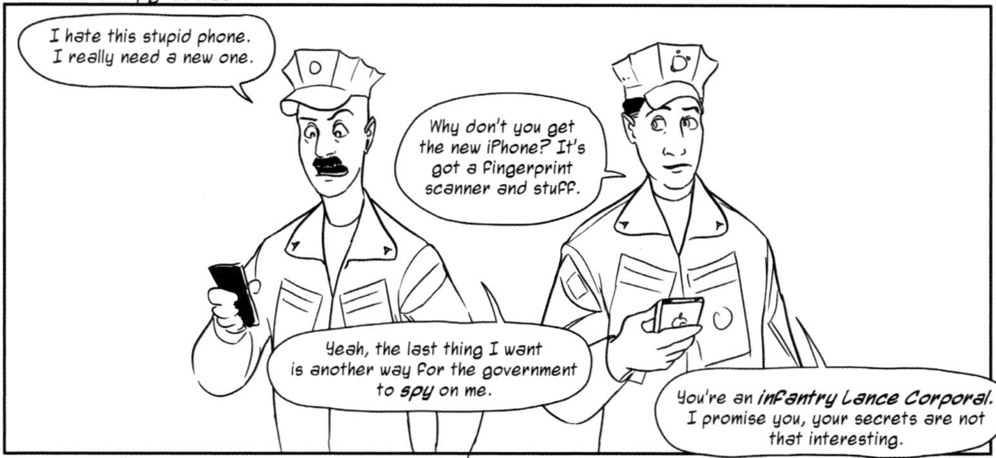
I hate this stupid phone. I really need a new one.
Why don't you get the new iPhone? It's got a fingerprint scanner and stuff.
Yeah, the last thing I want is another way for the government to **spy** on me.
You're an **infantry Lance Corporal.** I promise you, your secrets are not that interesting.

www.terminallance.com Created by Maximilian Uriarte © 2013

"Stacked"

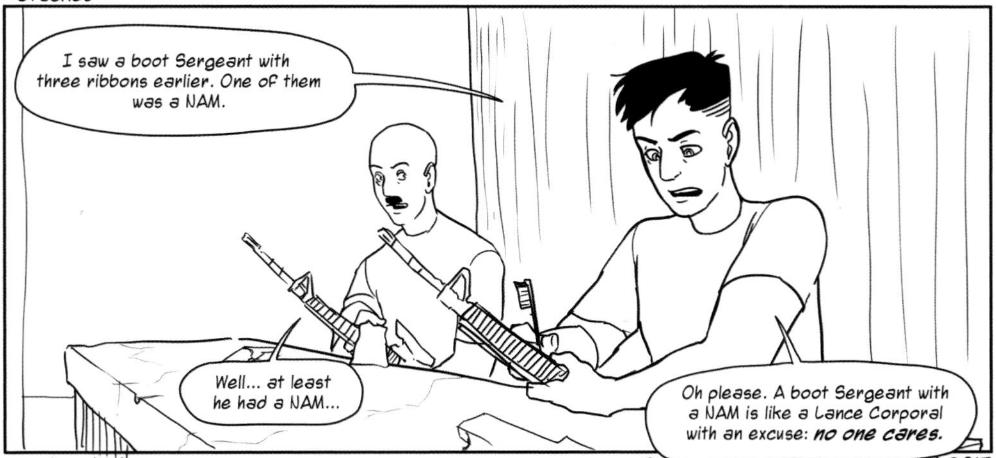
I saw a boot Sergeant with three ribbons earlier. One of them was a NAM.
Well... at least he had a NAM...
Oh please. A boot Sergeant with a NAM is like a Lance Corporal with an excuse: **no one cares.**

www.terminallance.com Created by Maximilian Uriarte © 2013

"Barracks House Rules"

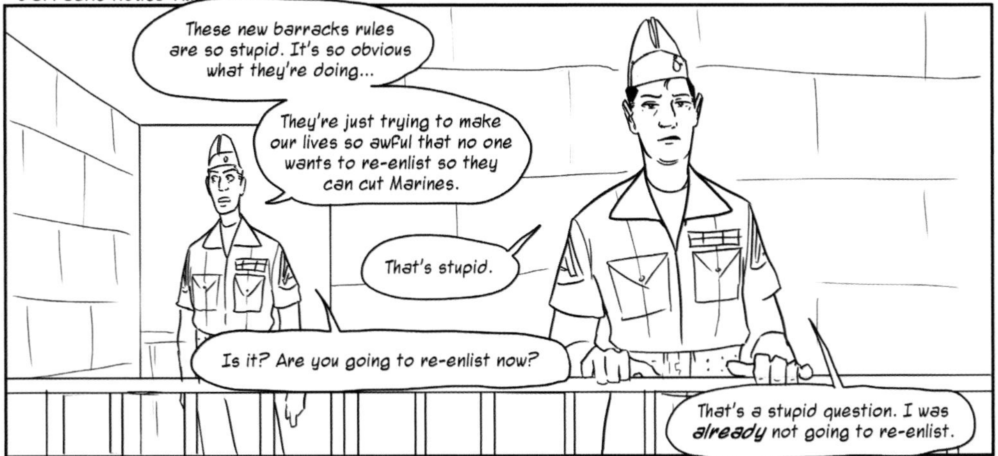
These new barracks rules are so stupid. It's so obvious what they're doing...
They're just trying to make our lives so awful that no one wants to re-enlist so they can cut Marines.
That's stupid.
Is it? Are you going to re-enlist now?
That's a stupid question. I was **already** not going to re-enlist.

www.terminallance.com Created by Maximilian Uriarte © 2013

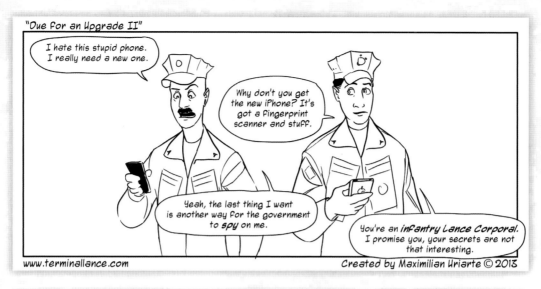

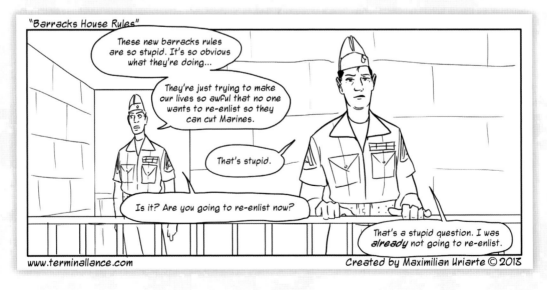

"Justified Viewpoints"

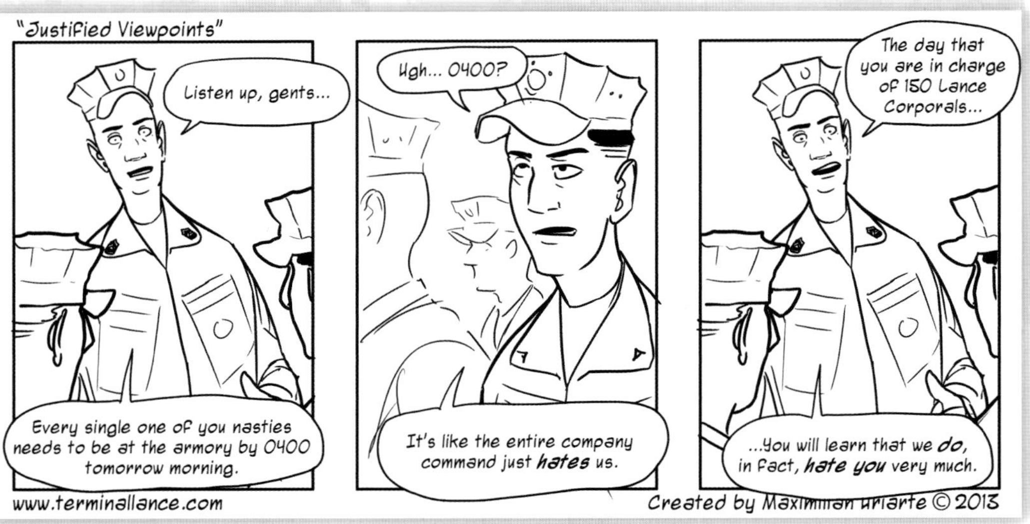
Listen up, gents...
Every single one of you nasties needs to be at the armory by 0400 tomorrow morning.
Ugh... 0400?
It's like the entire company command just *hates* us.
The day that you are in charge of 150 Lance Corporals...
...You will learn that we *do*, in fact, *hate you* very much.

www.terminallance.com Created by Maximilian Uriarte © 2013

"Shutdown Showdown"

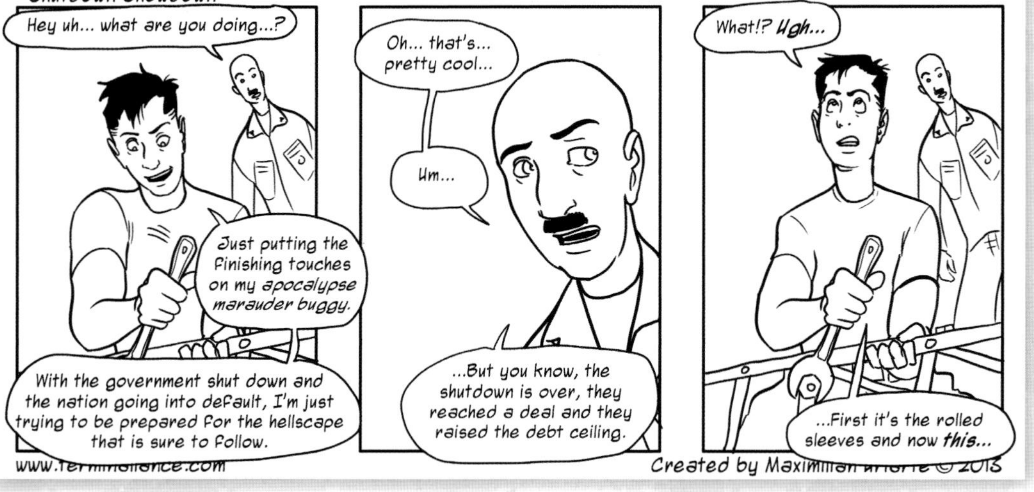
Hey uh... what are you doing...?
Just putting the finishing touches on my *apocalypse marauder buggy.*
With the government shut down and the nation going into default, I'm just trying to be prepared for the hellscape that is sure to follow.
Oh... that's... pretty cool...
Um...
...But you know, the shutdown is over, they reached a deal and they raised the debt ceiling.
What!? *Ugh...*
...First it's the rolled sleeves and now *this...*

www.terminallance.com Created by Maximilian Uriarte © 2013

"Hats Off"

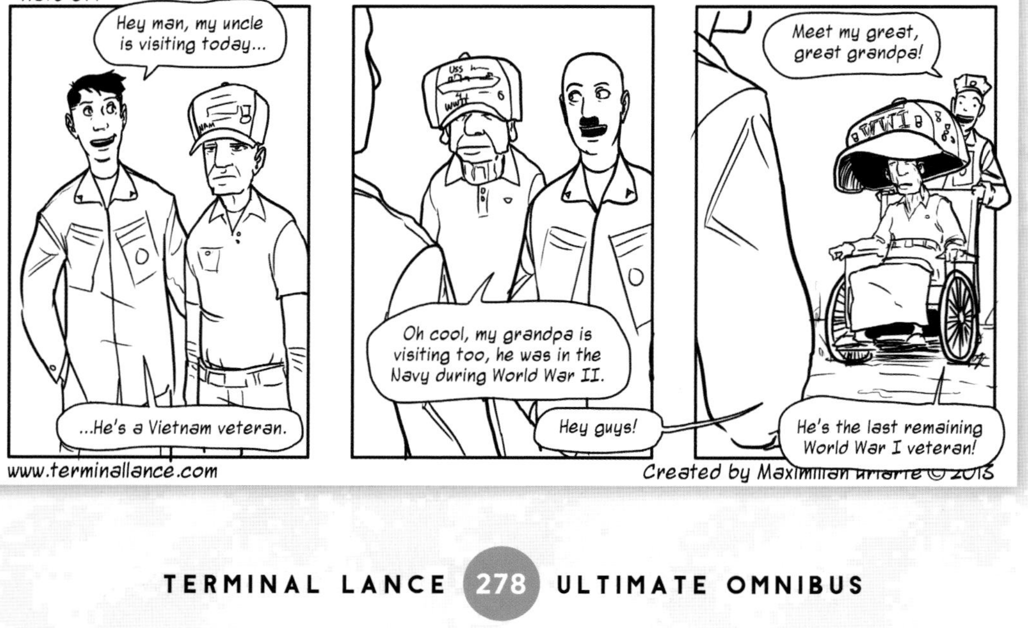
Hey man, my uncle is visiting today...
...He's a Vietnam veteran.
Oh cool, my grandpa is visiting too, he was in the Navy during World War II.
Hey guys!
Meet my great, great grandpa!
He's the last remaining World War I veteran!

www.terminallance.com Created by Maximilian Uriarte © 2013

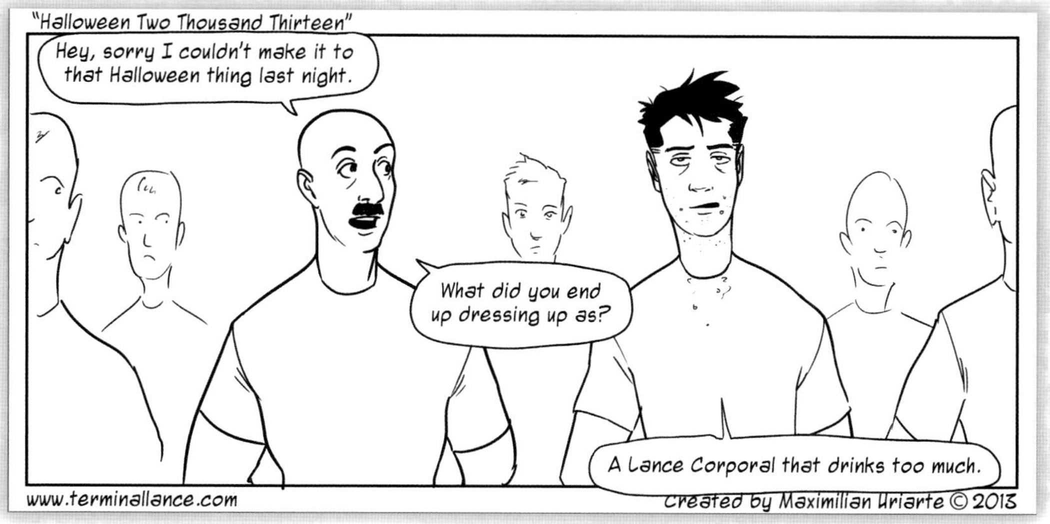
"Halloween Two Thousand Thirteen"
Hey, sorry I couldn't make it to that Halloween thing last night.
What did you end up dressing up as?
A Lance Corporal that drinks too much.
www.terminallance.com
Created by Maximilian Uriarte © 2013

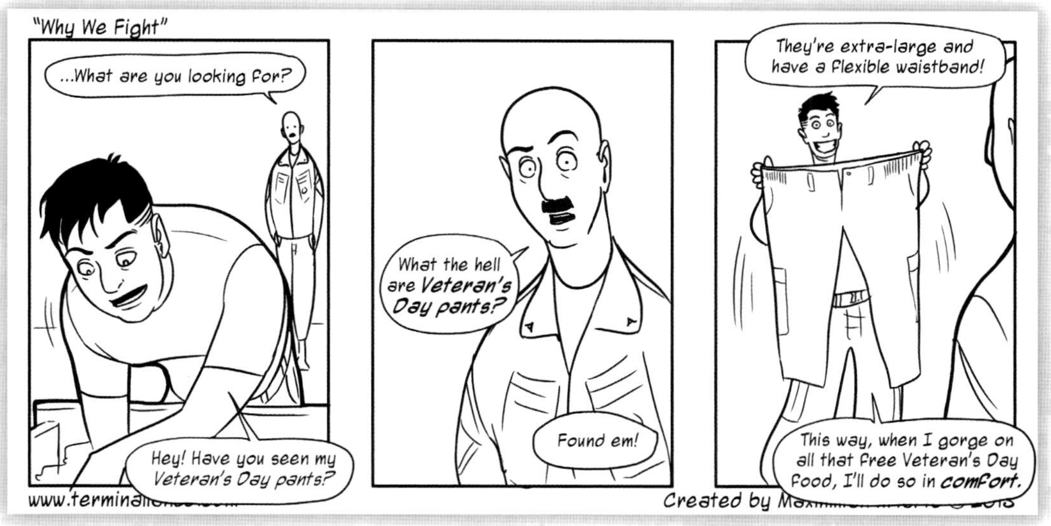
"Why We Fight"
...What are you looking for?
Hey! Have you seen my Veteran's Day pants?
What the hell are Veteran's Day pants?
Found em!
They're extra-large and have a flexible waistband!
This way, when I gorge on all that free Veteran's Day food, I'll do so in comfort.
www.termina
Created by Ma

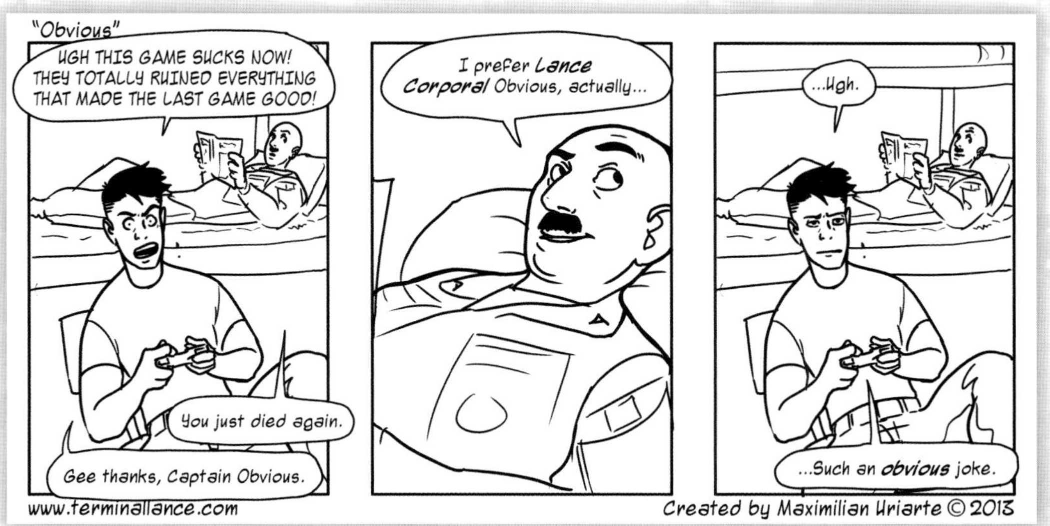
"Obvious"
UGH THIS GAME SUCKS NOW! THEY TOTALLY RUINED EVERYTHING THAT MADE THE LAST GAME GOOD!
You just died again.
Gee thanks, Captain Obvious.
I prefer Lance Corporal Obvious, actually...
...Ugh.
...Such an obvious joke.
www.terminallance.com
Created by Maximilian Uriarte © 2013

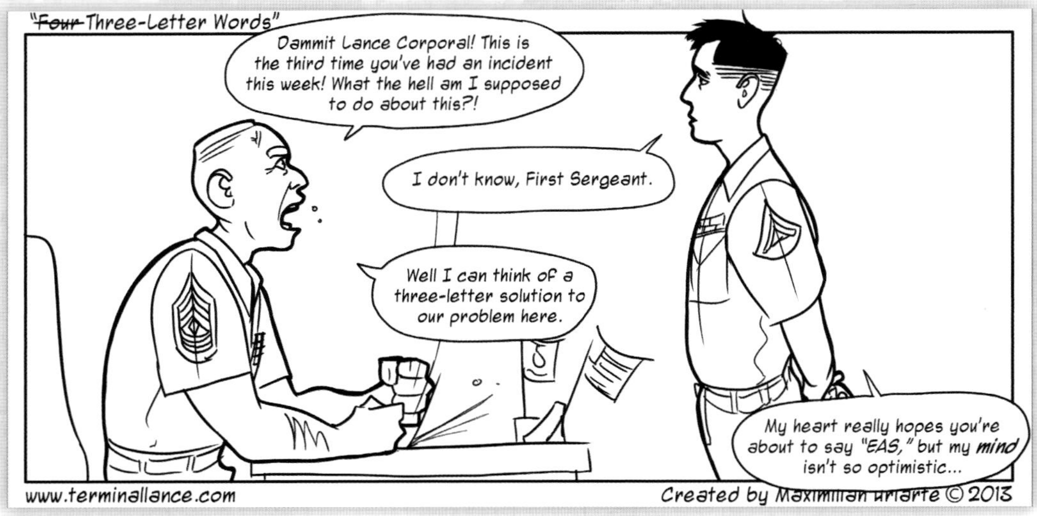
"~~Four~~ Three-Letter Words"
Dammit Lance Corporal! This is the third time you've had an incident this week! What the hell am I supposed to do about this?!
I don't know, First Sergeant.
Well I can think of a three-letter solution to our problem here.
My heart really hopes you're about to say "EAS," but my ***mind*** isn't so optimistic...
www.terminallance.com
Created by Maximilian Uriarte © 2013

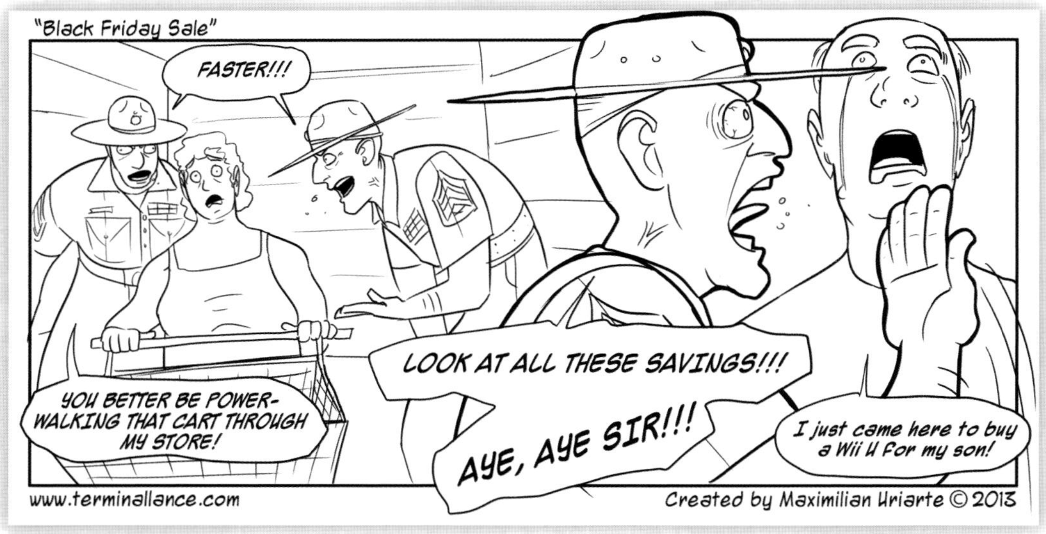
"Black Friday Sale"
FASTER!!!
YOU BETTER BE POWER-WALKING THAT CART THROUGH MY STORE!
LOOK AT ALL THESE SAVINGS!!!
AYE, AYE SIR!!!
I just came here to buy a Wii U for my son!
www.terminallance.com
Created by Maximilian Uriarte © 2013

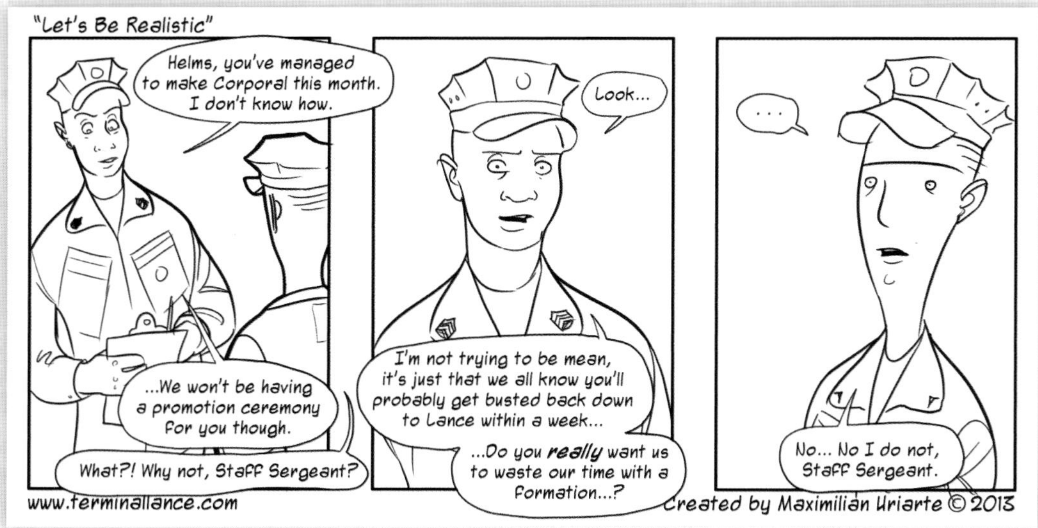
"Let's Be Realistic"
Helms, you've managed to make Corporal this month. I don't know how.
...We won't be having a promotion ceremony for you though.
What?! Why not, Staff Sergeant?
Look...
I'm not trying to be mean, it's just that we all know you'll probably get busted back down to Lance within a week...
...Do you ***really*** want us to waste our time with a formation...?
. . .
No... No I do not, Staff Sergeant.
www.terminallance.com
Created by Maximilian Uriarte © 2013

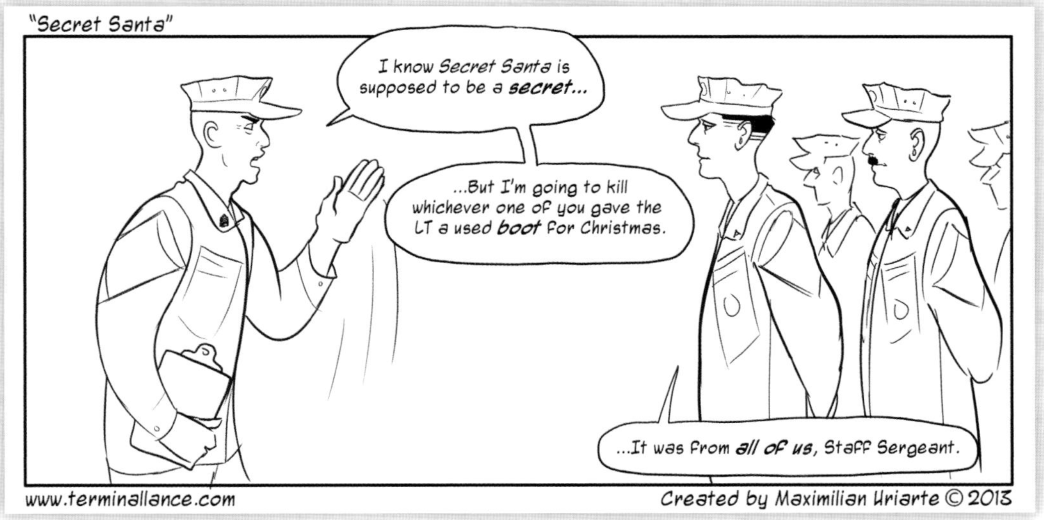
"Secret Santa"
I know Secret Santa is supposed to be a secret...
...But I'm going to kill whichever one of you gave the LT a used boot for Christmas.
...It was from all of us, Staff Sergeant.
www.terminallance.com
Created by Maximilian Uriarte © 2013

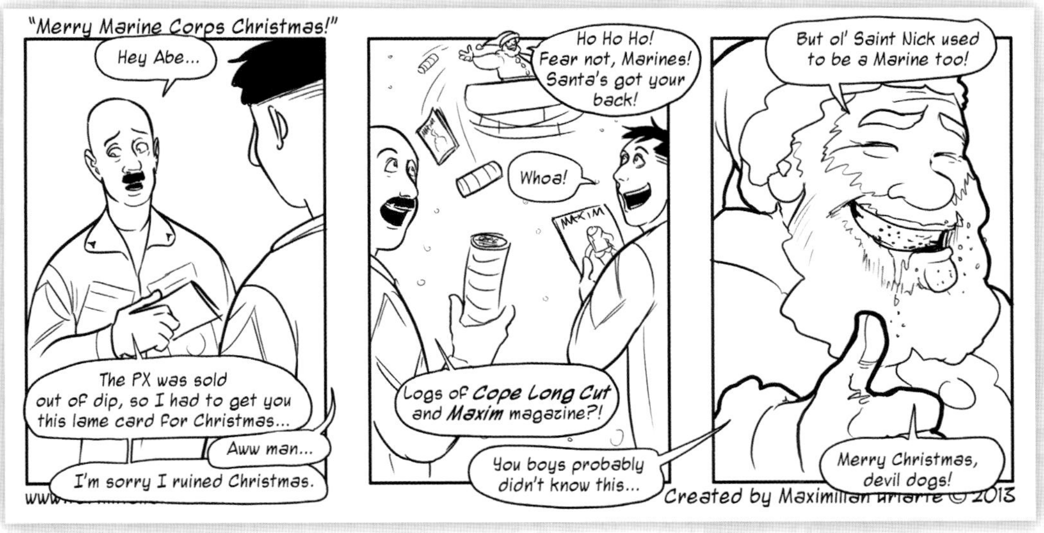
"Merry Marine Corps Christmas!"
Hey Abe...
The PX was sold out of dip, so I had to get you this lame card for Christmas...
Aww man...
I'm sorry I ruined Christmas.
Ho Ho Ho! Fear not, Marines! Santa's got your back!
Whoa!
MAXIM
Logs of Cope Long Cut and Maxim magazine?!
You boys probably didn't know this...
But ol' Saint Nick used to be a Marine too!
Merry Christmas, devil dogs!

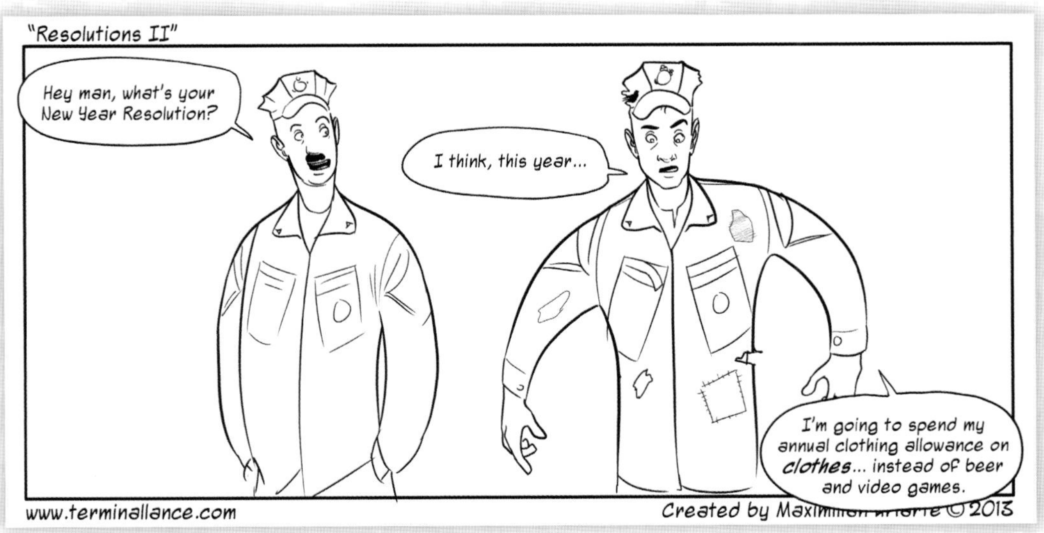
"Resolutions II"
Hey man, what's your New Year Resolution?
I think, this year...
I'm going to spend my annual clothing allowance on clothes... instead of beer and video games.
www.terminallance.com

"Tact"

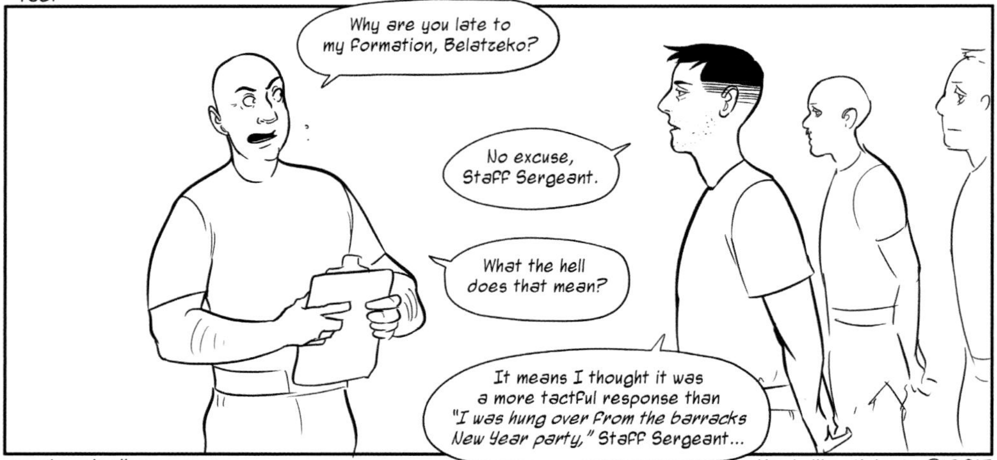
Why are you late to my formation, Belatzeko?
No excuse, Staff Sergeant.
What the hell does that mean?
It means I thought it was a more tactful response than "I was hung over from the barracks New Year party," Staff Sergeant...

www.terminallance.com Created by Maximilian Uriarte © 2013

"Mellow Yellow"

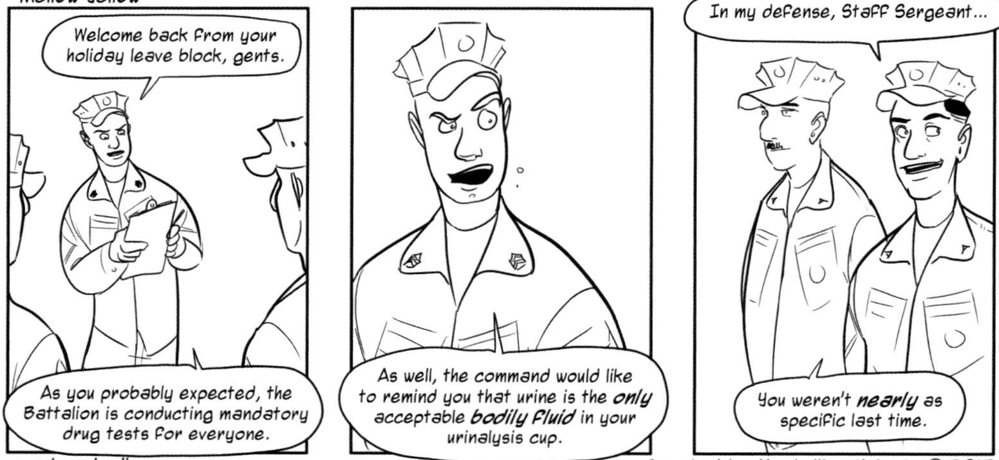
Welcome back from your holiday leave block, gents.
As you probably expected, the Battalion is conducting mandatory drug tests for everyone.
As well, the command would like to remind you that urine is the *only* acceptable *bodily fluid* in your urinalysis cup.
In my defense, Staff Sergeant...
You weren't *nearly* as specific last time.

www.terminallance.com Created by Maximilian Uriarte © 2013

"Cut From the Score"

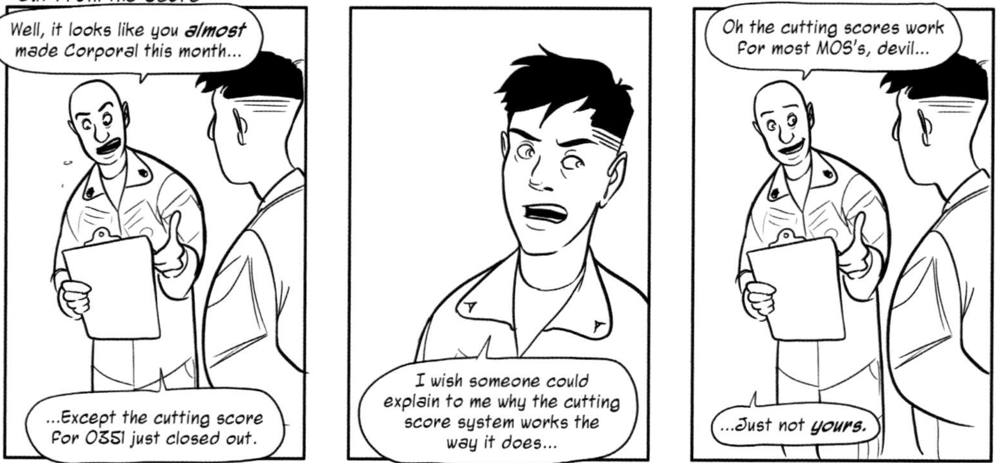
Well, it looks like you *almost* made Corporal this month...
...Except the cutting score for 0351 just closed out.
I wish someone could explain to me why the cutting score system works the way it does...
Oh the cutting scores work for most MOS's, devil...
...Just not *yours.*

www.terminallance.com Created by Maximilian Uriarte © 2013

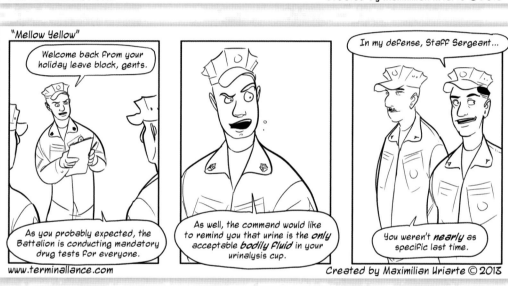

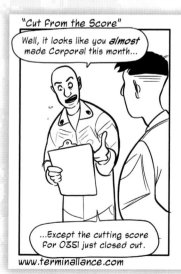

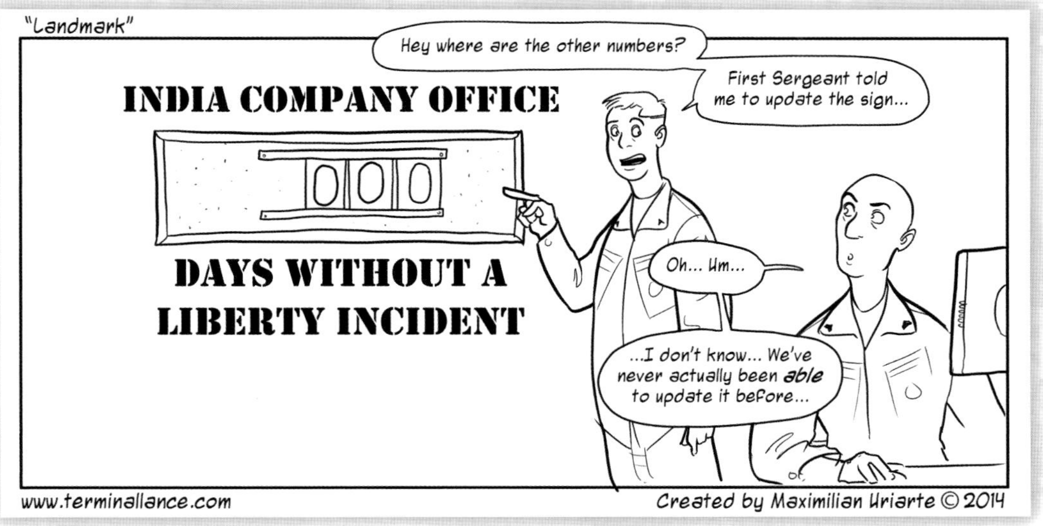
"Landmark"
Hey where are the other numbers?
First Sergeant told me to update the sign...
INDIA COMPANY OFFICE
000
DAYS WITHOUT A LIBERTY INCIDENT
Oh... Um...
...I don't know... We've never actually been *able* to update it before...
www.terminallance.com
Created by Maximilian Uriarte © 2014

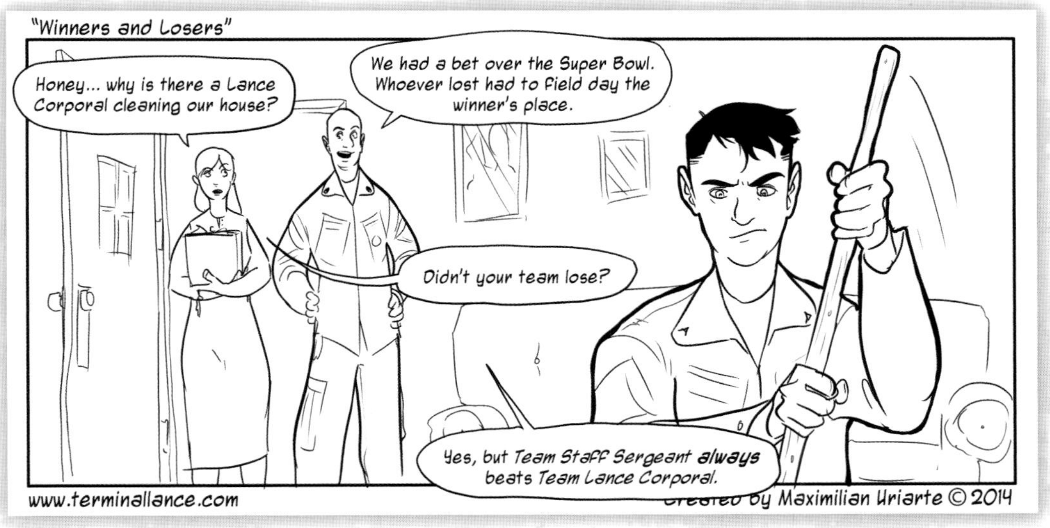
"Winners and Losers"
Honey... why is there a Lance Corporal cleaning our house?
We had a bet over the Super Bowl. Whoever lost had to field day the winner's place.
Didn't your team lose?
Yes, but *Team Staff Sergeant* ***always*** beats *Team Lance Corporal.*
www.terminallance.com
Created by Maximilian Uriarte © 2014

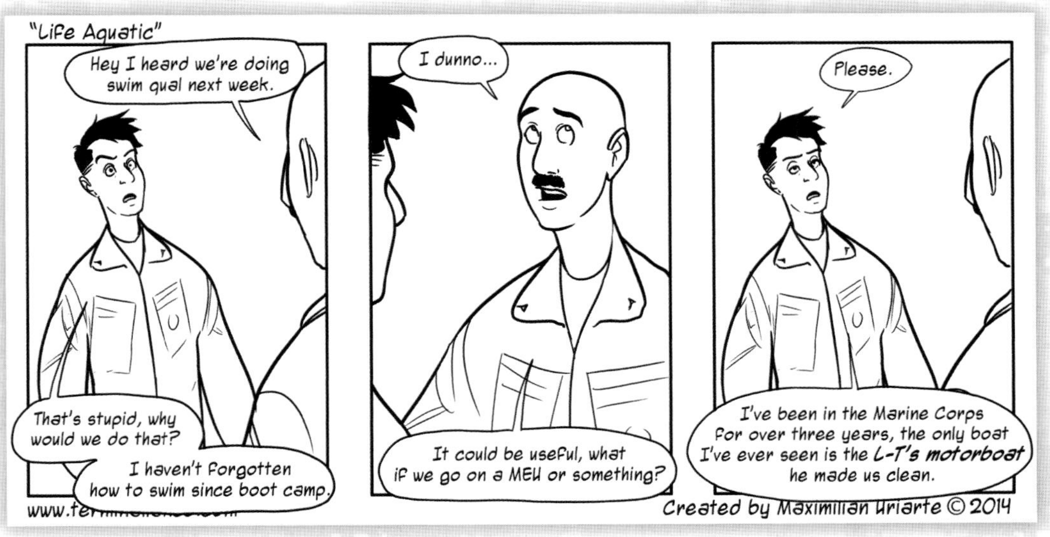
"Life Aquatic"
Hey I heard we're doing swim qual next week.
That's stupid, why would we do that?
I haven't forgotten how to swim since boot camp.
I dunno...
It could be useful, what if we go on a MEU or something?
Please.
I've been in the Marine Corps for over three years, the only boat I've ever seen is the ***L-T's motorboat*** he made us clean.
Created by Maximilian Uriarte © 2014

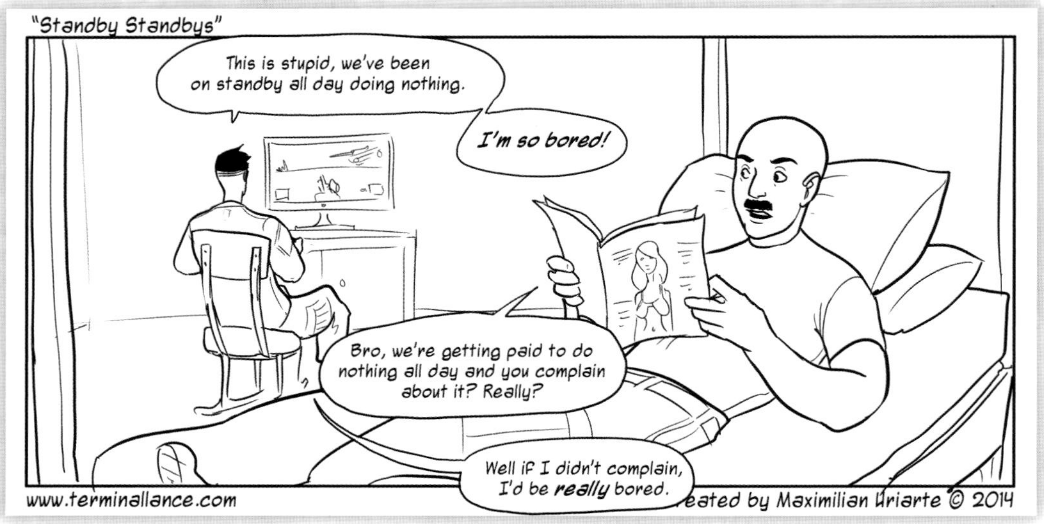
"Standby Standbys"
This is stupid, we've been on standby all day doing nothing.
I'm so bored!
Bro, we're getting paid to do nothing all day and you complain about it? Really?
Well if I didn't complain, I'd be really bored.
www.terminallance.com
Created by Maximilian Uriarte © 2014

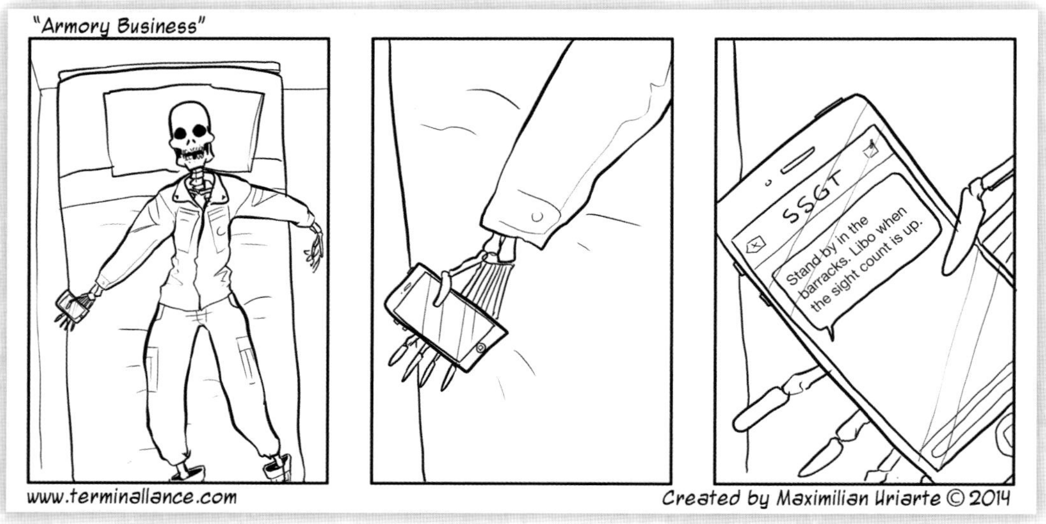
"Armory Business"
SSGT
Stand by in the barracks. Libo when the sight count is up.
www.terminallance.com
Created by Maximilian Uriarte © 2014

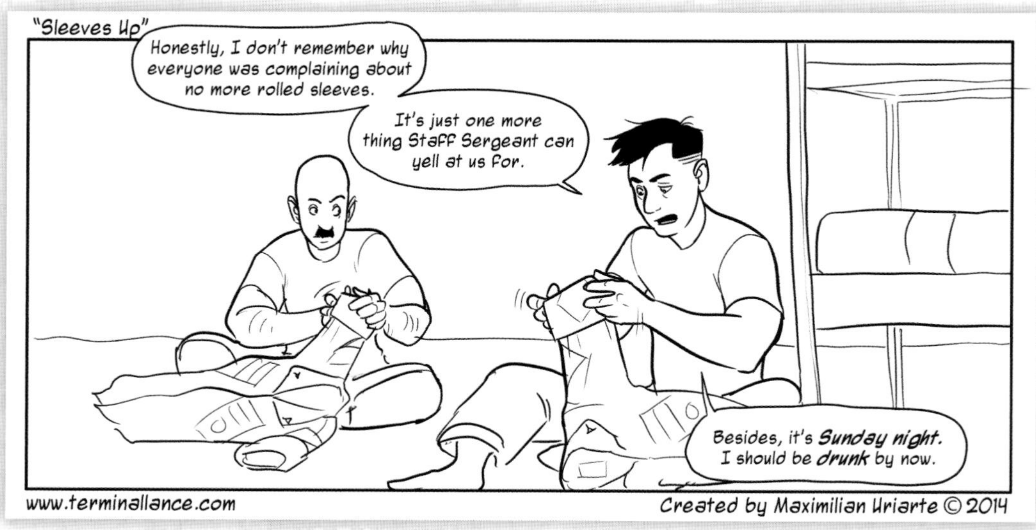
"Sleeves Up"
Honestly, I don't remember why everyone was complaining about no more rolled sleeves.
It's just one more thing Staff Sergeant can yell at us for.
Besides, it's Sunday night. I should be drunk by now.
www.terminallance.com
Created by Maximilian Uriarte © 2014

"A Joke"

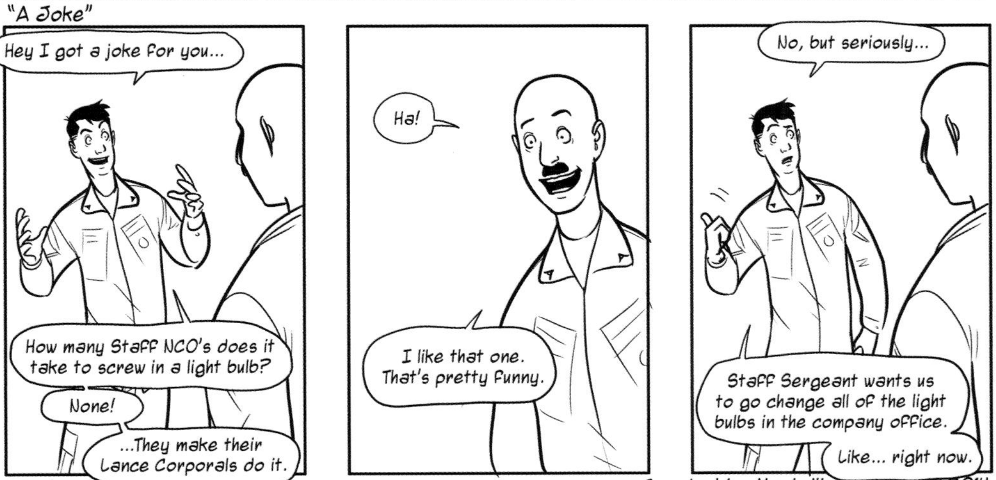

Hey I got a joke for you...
How many Staff NCO's does it take to screw in a light bulb?
None!
...They make their Lance Corporals do it.
Ha!
I like that one. That's pretty funny.
No, but seriously...
Staff Sergeant wants us to go change all of the light bulbs in the company office.
Like... right now.

www.terminallance.com Created by Maximilian Uriarte © 2014

"Don't Ask, Don't Tell Another One, Please"

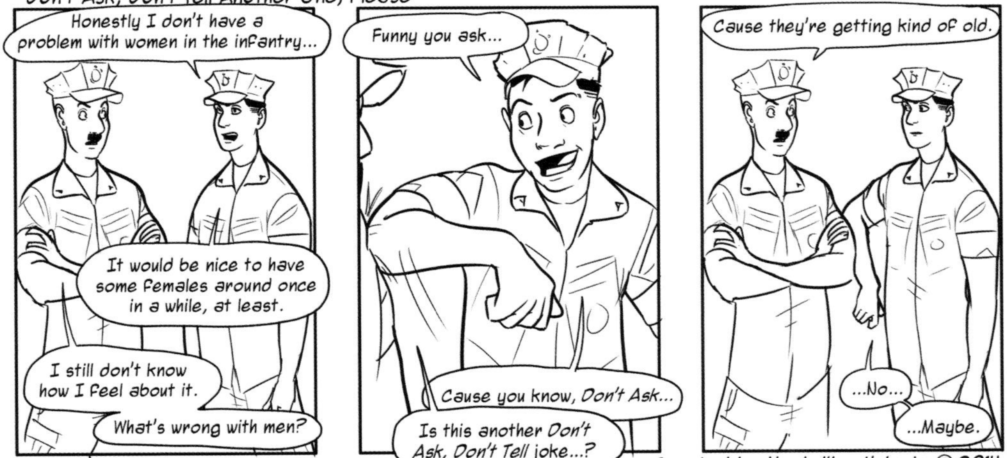

Honestly I don't have a problem with women in the infantry...
It would be nice to have some females around once in a while, at least.
I still don't know how I feel about it.
What's wrong with men?
Funny you ask...
Cause you know, Don't Ask...
Is this another Don't Ask, Don't Tell joke...?
Cause they're getting kind of old.
...No...
...Maybe.

www.terminallance.com Created by Maximilian Uriarte © 2014

"Faster Than Light"

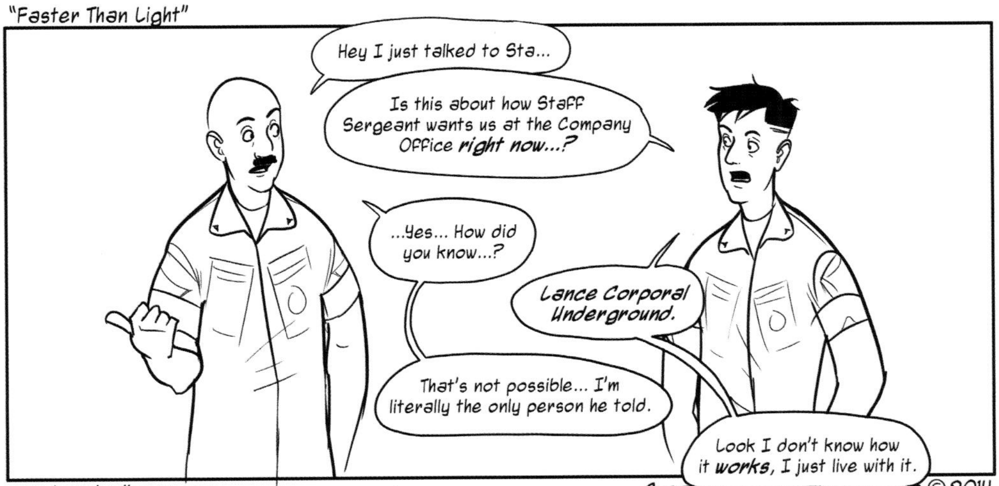

Hey I just talked to Sta...
Is this about how Staff Sergeant wants us at the Company Office ***right now...?***
...Yes... How did you know...?
Lance Corporal Underground.
That's not possible... I'm literally the only person he told.
Look I don't know how it ***works***, I just live with it.

www.terminallance.com Created by Maximilian Uriarte © 2014

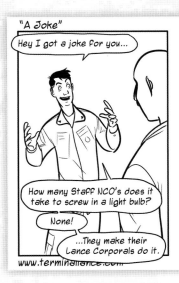

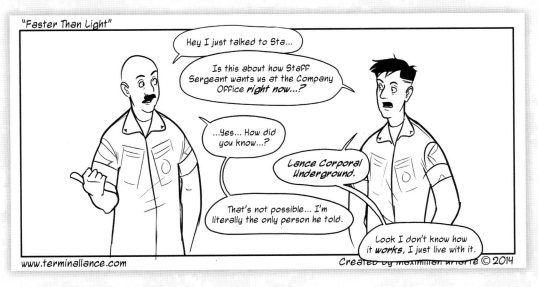

"The Drinking Problem"

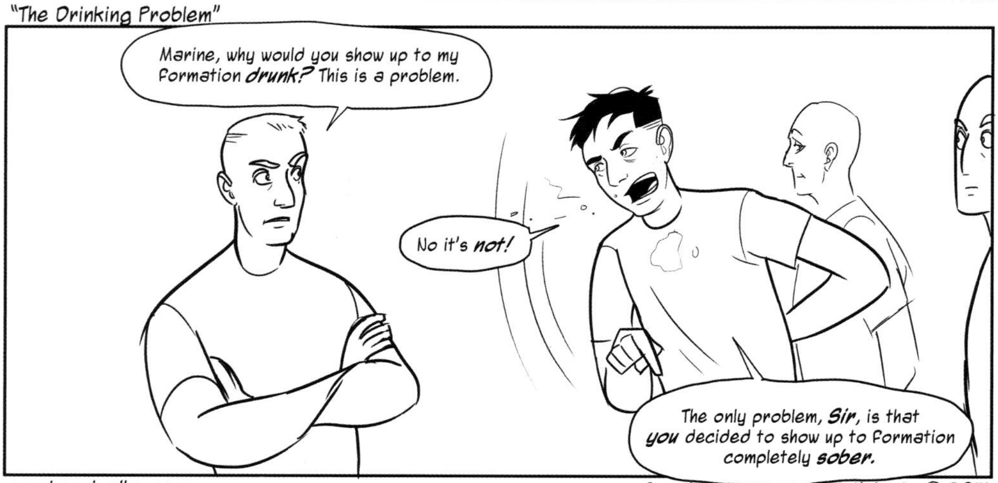
Marine, why would you show up to my formation *drunk?* This is a problem.
No it's *not!*
The only problem, *Sir*, is that *you* decided to show up to formation completely *sober.*

www.terminallance.com Created by Maximilian Uriarte © 2014

"Hair Reg Rage"

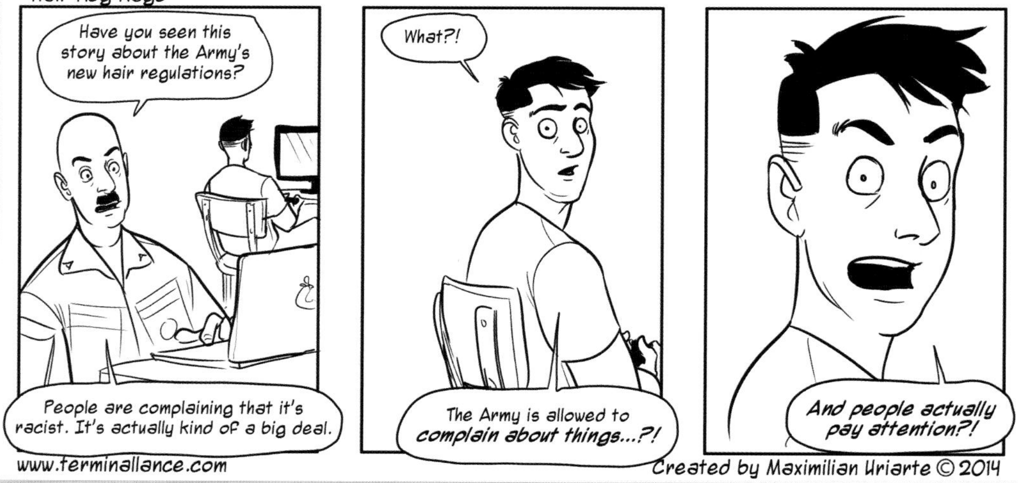
Have you seen this story about the Army's new hair regulations?
People are complaining that it's racist. It's actually kind of a big deal.
What?!
The Army is allowed to *complain about things...?!*
And people actually pay attention?!

www.terminallance.com Created by Maximilian Uriarte © 2014

"Economic Discipline"

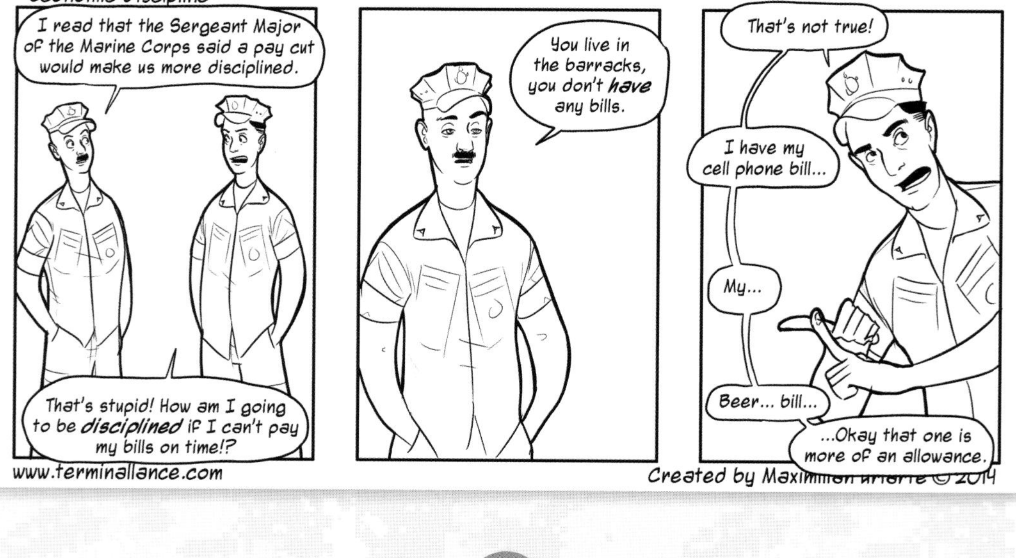
I read that the Sergeant Major of the Marine Corps said a pay cut would make us more disciplined.
That's stupid! How am I going to be *disciplined* if I can't pay my bills on time!?
You live in the barracks, you don't *have* any bills.
That's not true!
I have my cell phone bill...
My...
Beer... bill...
...Okay that one is more of an allowance.

www.terminallance.com Created by Maximilian Uriarte © 2014

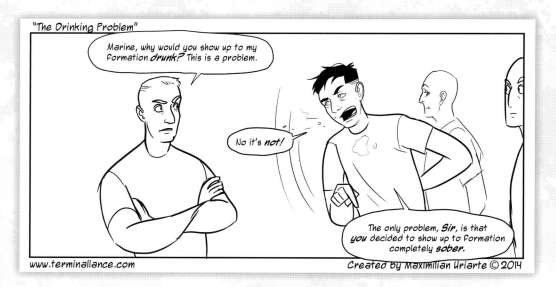

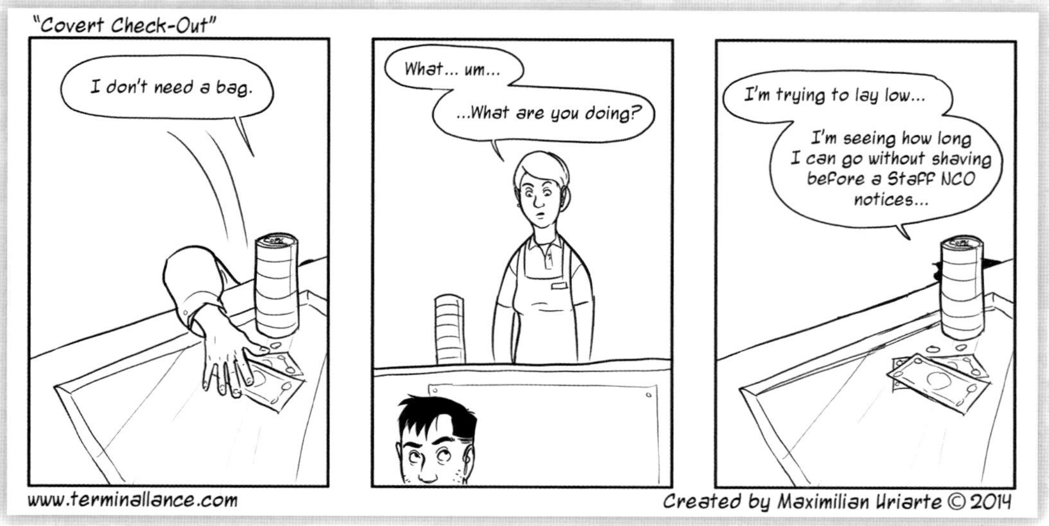
"Covert Check-Out"
I don't need a bag.
What... um...
...What are you doing?
I'm trying to lay low...
I'm seeing how long I can go without shaving before a Staff NCO notices...
www.terminallance.com
Created by Maximilian Uriarte © 2014

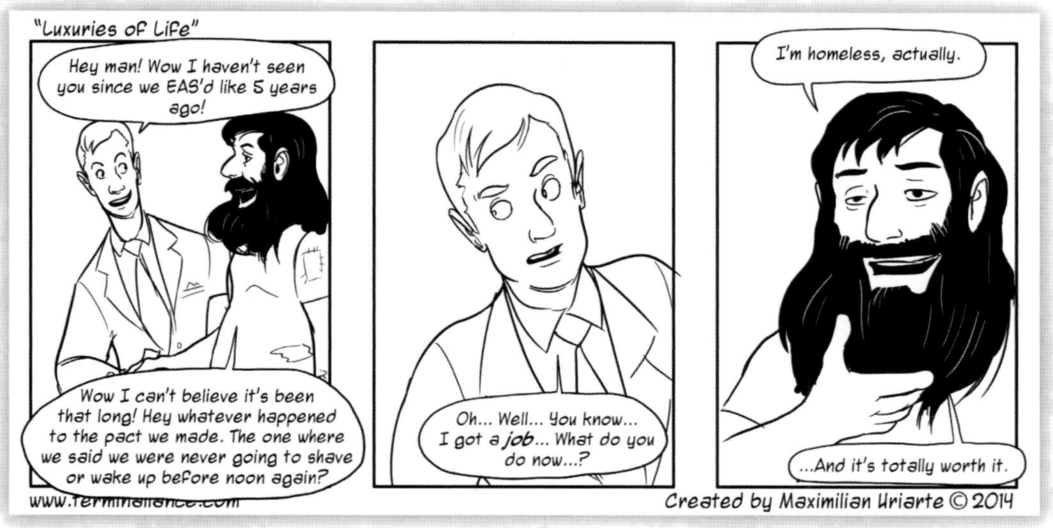
"Luxuries of Life"
Hey man! Wow I haven't seen you since we EAS'd like 5 years ago!
Wow I can't believe it's been that long! Hey whatever happened to the pact we made. The one where we said we were never going to shave or wake up before noon again?
Oh... Well... You know... I got a job... What do you do now...?
I'm homeless, actually.
...And it's totally worth it.
www.terminallance.com
Created by Maximilian Uriarte © 2014

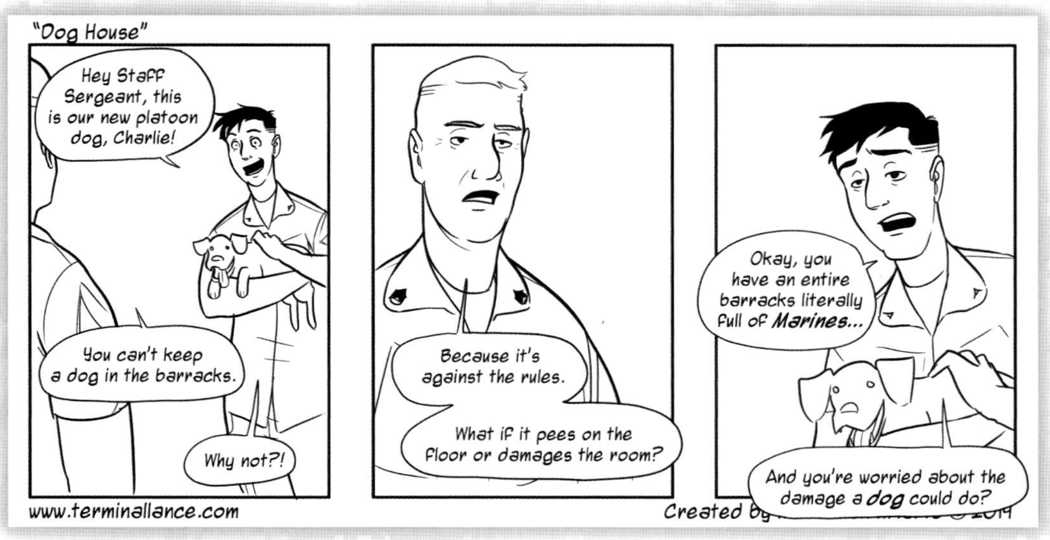
"Dog House"
Hey Staff Sergeant, this is our new platoon dog, Charlie!
You can't keep a dog in the barracks.
Why not?!
Because it's against the rules.
What if it pees on the floor or damages the room?
Okay, you have an entire barracks literally full of Marines...
And you're worried about the damage a dog could do?
www.terminallance.com
Created by

"Discounted Discount"

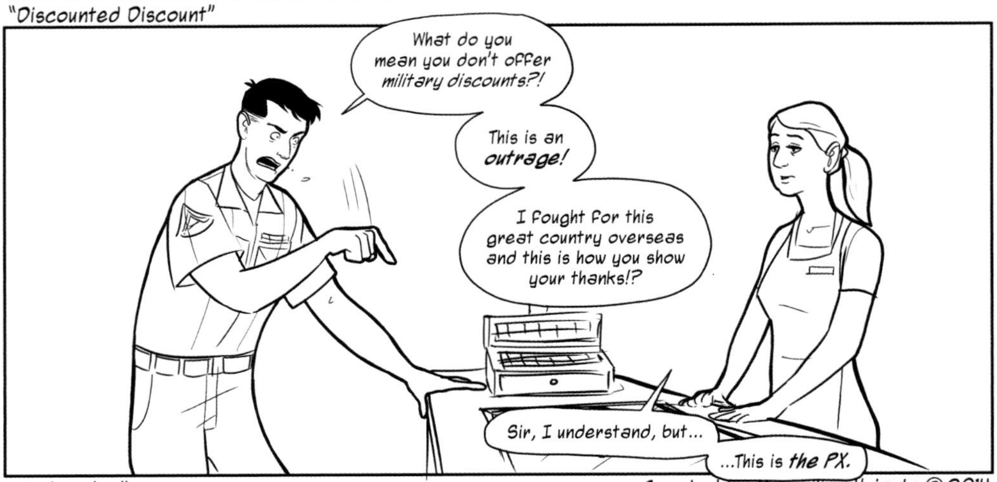
What do you mean you don't offer military discounts?!
This is an *outrage!*
I fought for this great country overseas and this is how you show your thanks!?
Sir, I understand, but...
...This is *the PX.*

www.terminallance.com

"Trailblazers"

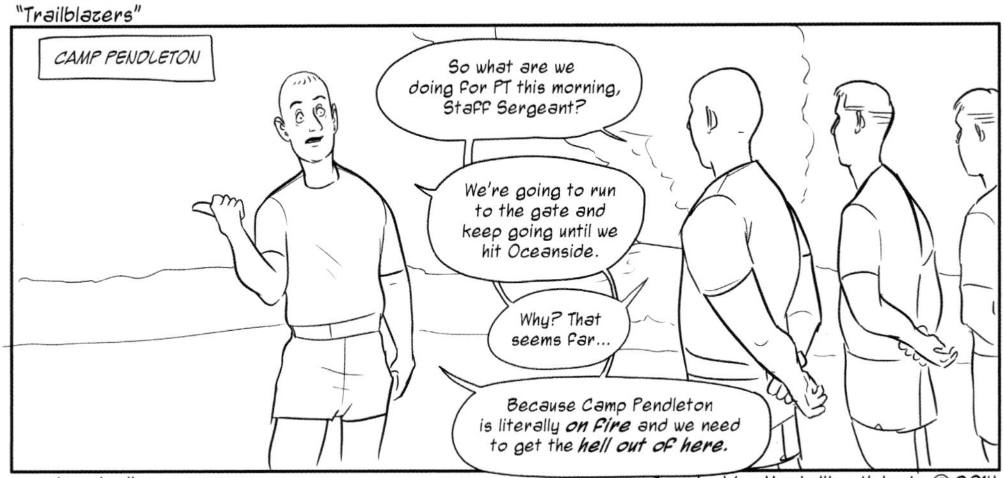
CAMP PENDLETON
So what are we doing for PT this morning, Staff Sergeant?
We're going to run to the gate and keep going until we hit Oceanside.
Why? That seems far...
Because Camp Pendleton is literally *on fire* and we need to get the *hell out of here.*

www.terminallance.com

"A Word"

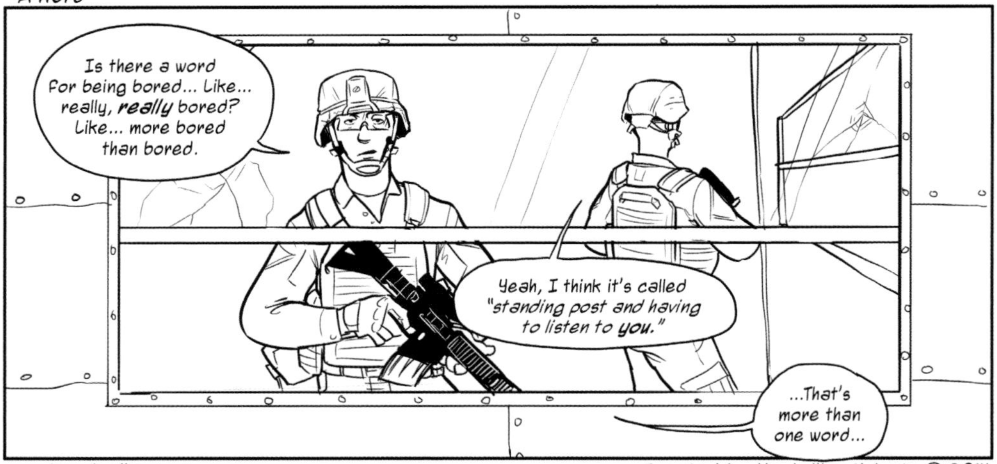
Is there a word for being bored... Like... really, *really* bored? Like... more bored than bored.
Yeah, I think it's called "standing post and having to listen to *you.*"
...That's more than one word...

www.terminallance.com

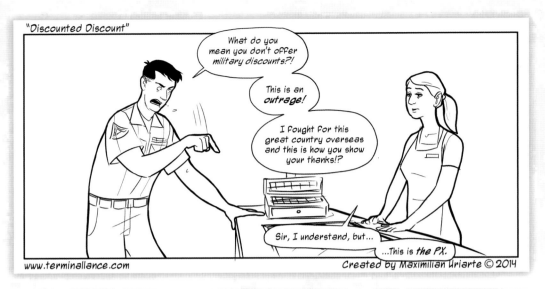

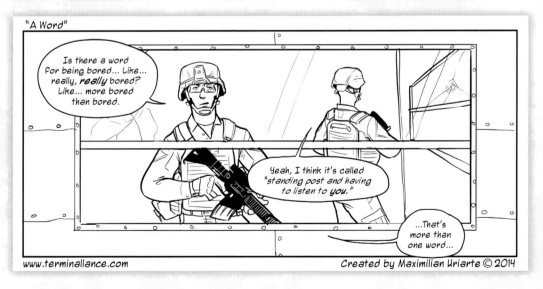

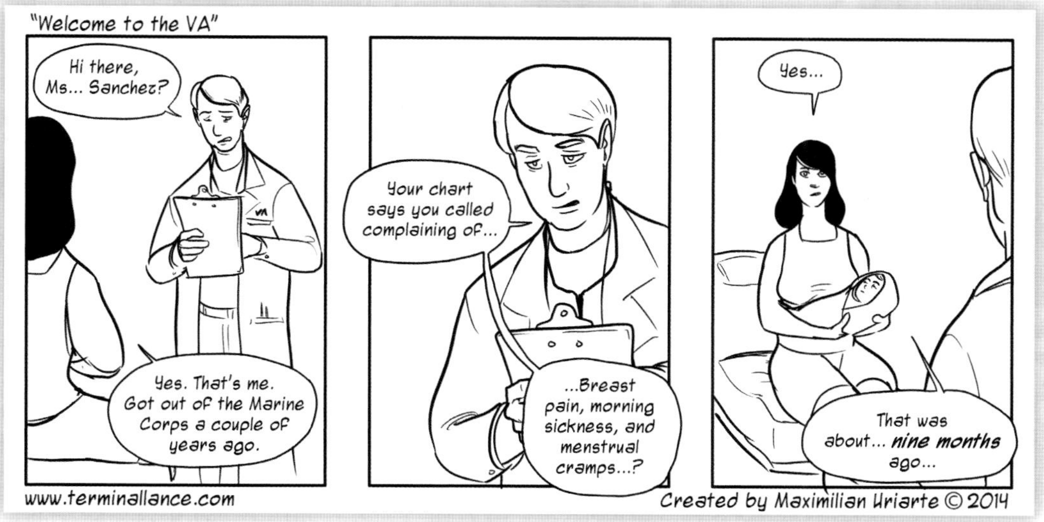
"Welcome to the VA"
Hi there, Ms... Sanchez?
Yes. That's me. Got out of the Marine Corps a couple of years ago.
Your chart says you called complaining of...
...Breast pain, morning sickness, and menstrual cramps...?
Yes...
That was about... nine months ago...
www.terminallance.com
Created by Maximilian Uriarte © 2014

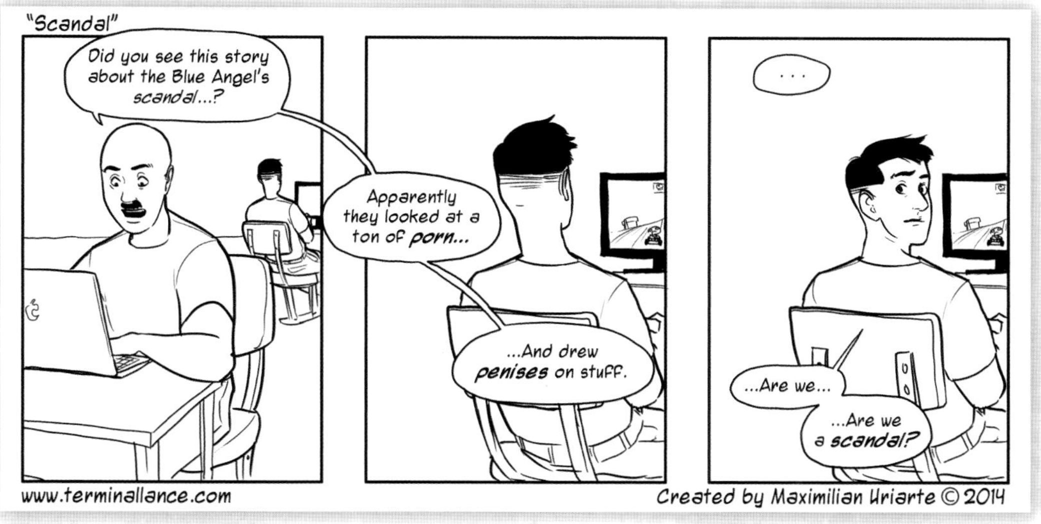
"Scandal"
Did you see this story about the Blue Angel's scandal...?
Apparently they looked at a ton of porn...
...And drew penises on stuff.
. . .
...Are we...
...Are we a scandal?
www.terminallance.com
Created by Maximilian Uriarte © 2014

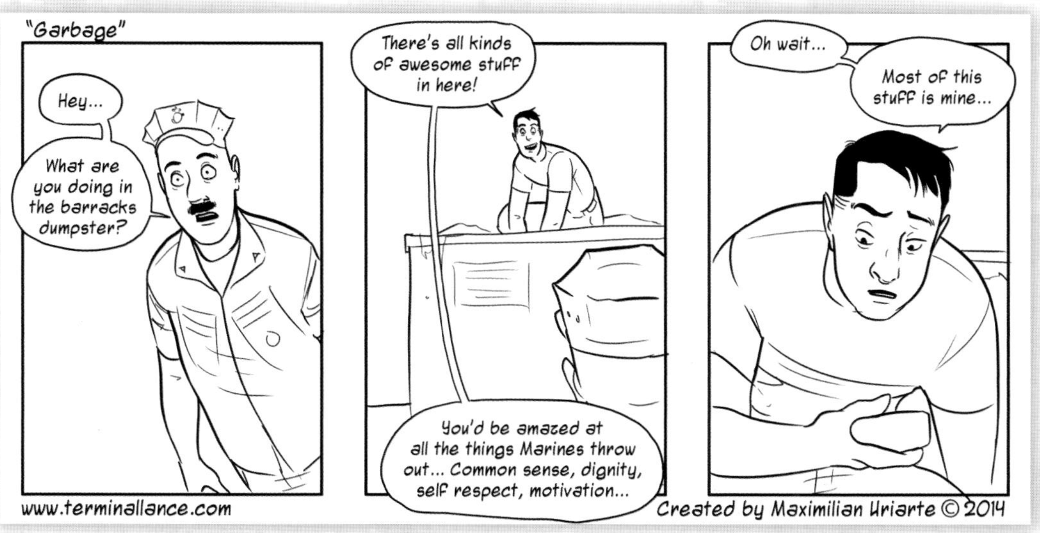
"Garbage"
Hey...
What are you doing in the barracks dumpster?
There's all kinds of awesome stuff in here!
You'd be amazed at all the things Marines throw out... Common sense, dignity, self respect, motivation...
Oh wait...
Most of this stuff is mine...
www.terminallance.com
Created by Maximilian Uriarte © 2014

"Sodium"

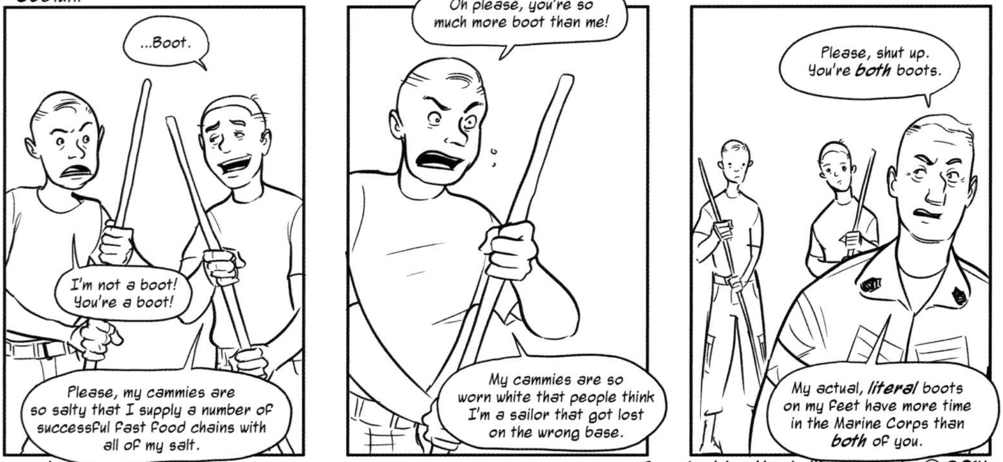

...Boot.
I'm not a boot! You're a boot!
Please, my cammies are so salty that I supply a number of successful fast food chains with all of my salt.
Oh please, you're so much more boot than me!
My cammies are so worn white that people think I'm a sailor that got lost on the wrong base.
Please, shut up. You're both boots.
My actual, literal boots on my feet have more time in the Marine Corps than both of you.

www.terminallance.com Created by Maximilian Uriarte © 2014

"Suspense"

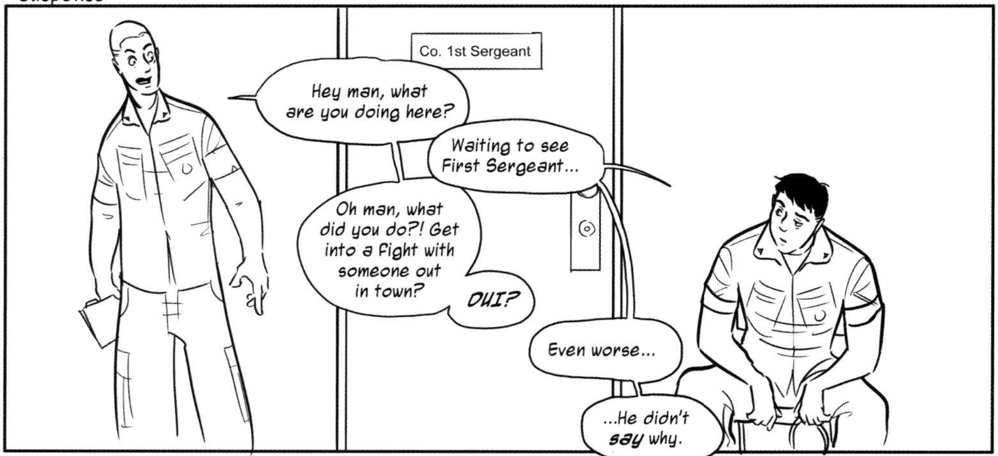

Co. 1st Sergeant
Hey man, what are you doing here?
Waiting to see First Sergeant...
Oh man, what did you do?! Get into a fight with someone out in town?
DUI?
Even worse...
...He didn't say why.

www.terminallance.com Created by Maximilian Uriarte © 2014

"Stars and Stripes"

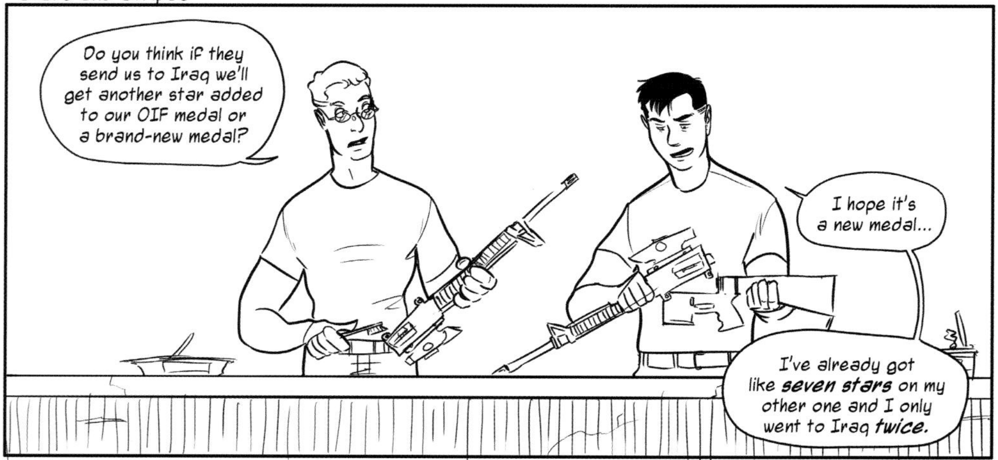

Do you think if they send us to Iraq we'll get another star added to our OIF medal or a brand-new medal?
I hope it's a new medal...
I've already got like seven stars on my other one and I only went to Iraq twice.

www.terminallance.com Created by Maximilian Uriarte © 2014

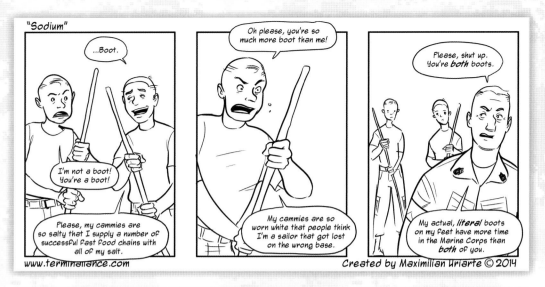

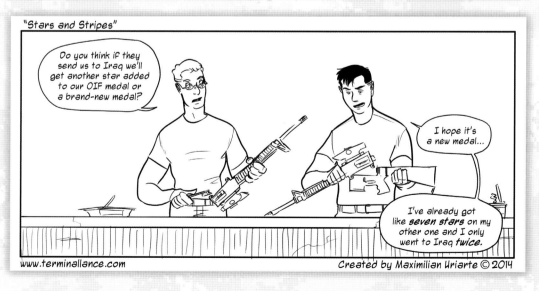

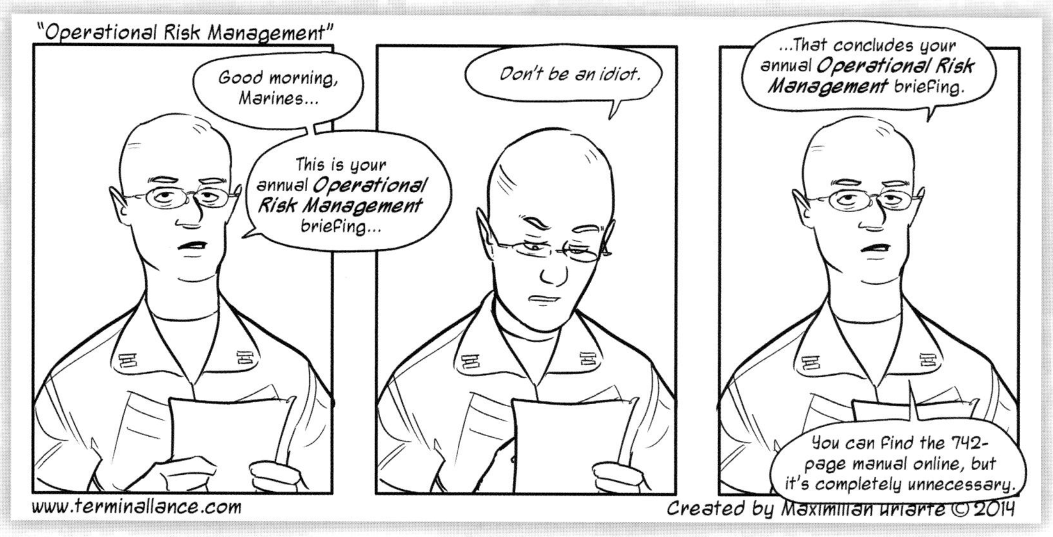
"Operational Risk Management"
Good morning, Marines...
This is your annual Operational Risk Management briefing...
Don't be an idiot.
...That concludes your annual Operational Risk Management briefing.
You can find the 742-page manual online, but it's completely unnecessary.
www.terminallance.com
Created by Maximilian Uriarte © 2014

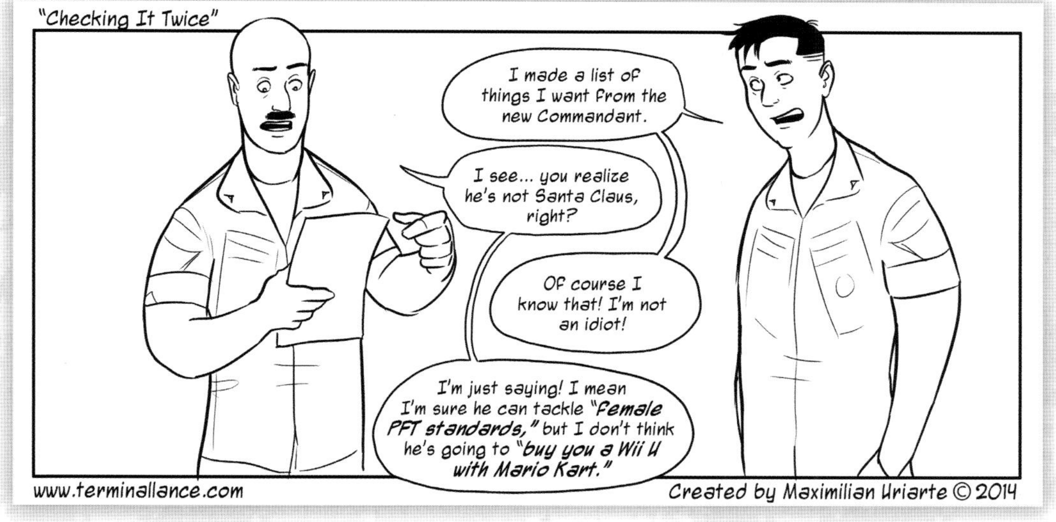
"Checking It Twice"
I made a list of things I want from the new Commandant.
I see... you realize he's not Santa Claus, right?
Of course I know that! I'm not an idiot!
I'm just saying! I mean I'm sure he can tackle "female PFT standards," but I don't think he's going to "buy you a Wii U with Mario Kart."
www.terminallance.com
Created by Maximilian Uriarte © 2014

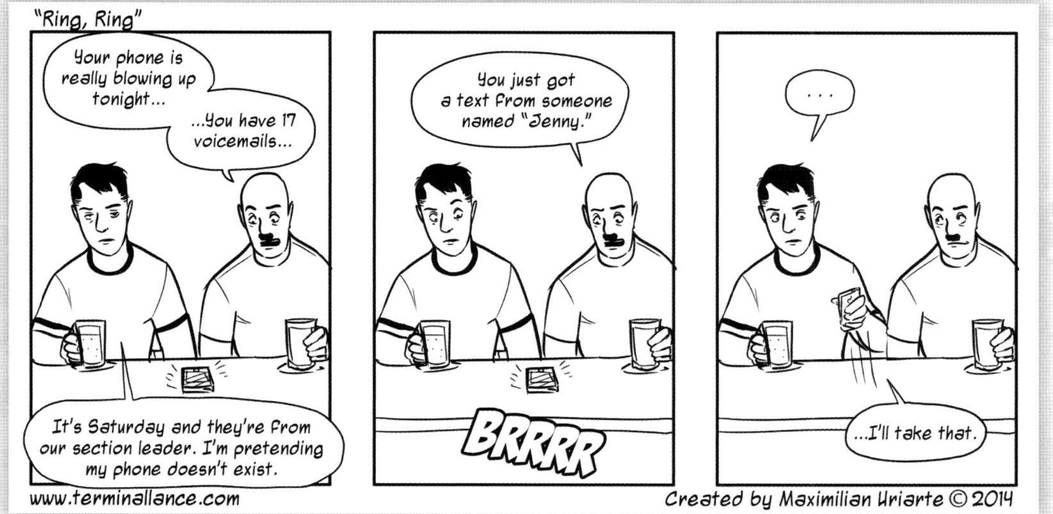
"Ring, Ring"
Your phone is really blowing up tonight...
...You have 17 voicemails...
It's Saturday and they're from our section leader. I'm pretending my phone doesn't exist.
You just got a text from someone named "Jenny."
BRRRR
. . .
...I'll take that.
www.terminallance.com
Created by Maximilian Uriarte © 2014

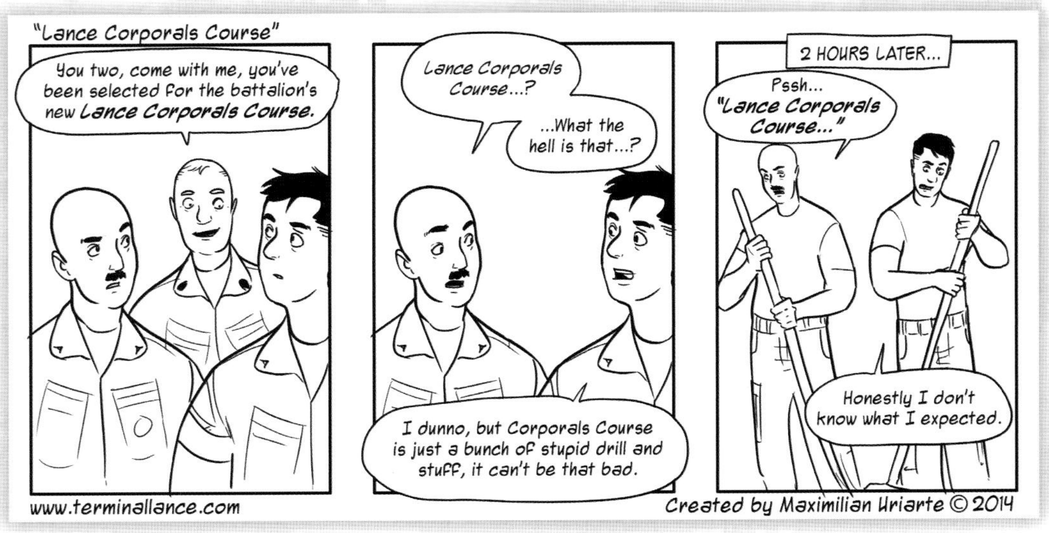
"Lance Corporals Course"
You two, come with me, you've been selected for the battalion's new *Lance Corporals Course.*
Lance Corporals Course...?
...What the hell is that...?
I dunno, but Corporals Course is just a bunch of stupid drill and stuff, it can't be that bad.
2 HOURS LATER...
Pssh... *"Lance Corporals Course..."*
Honestly I don't know what I expected.
www.terminallance.com
Created by Maximilian Uriarte © 2014

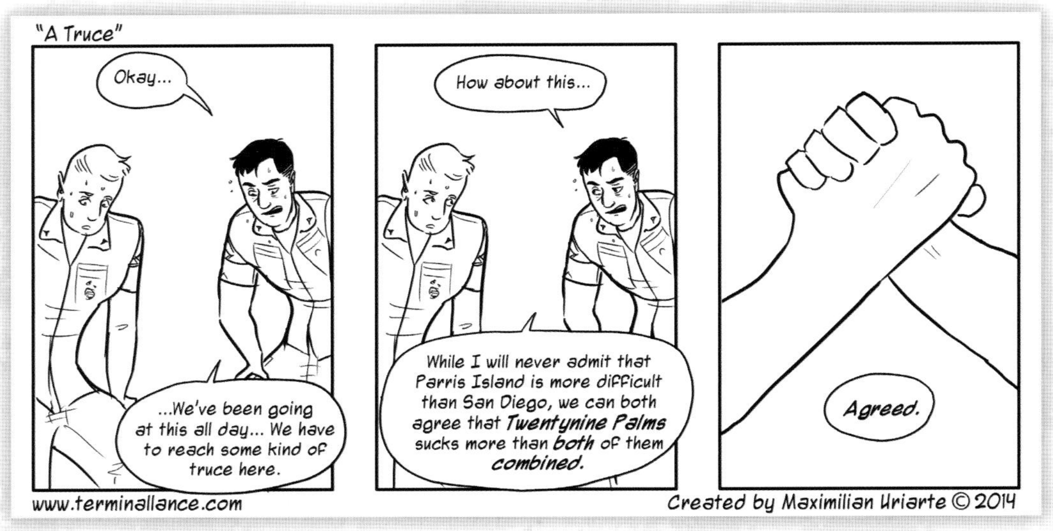
"A Truce"
Okay...
...We've been going at this all day... We have to reach some kind of truce here.
How about this...
While I will never admit that Parris Island is more difficult than San Diego, we can both agree that *Twentynine Palms* sucks more than *both* of them *combined.*
Agreed.
www.terminallance.com
Created by Maximilian Uriarte © 2014

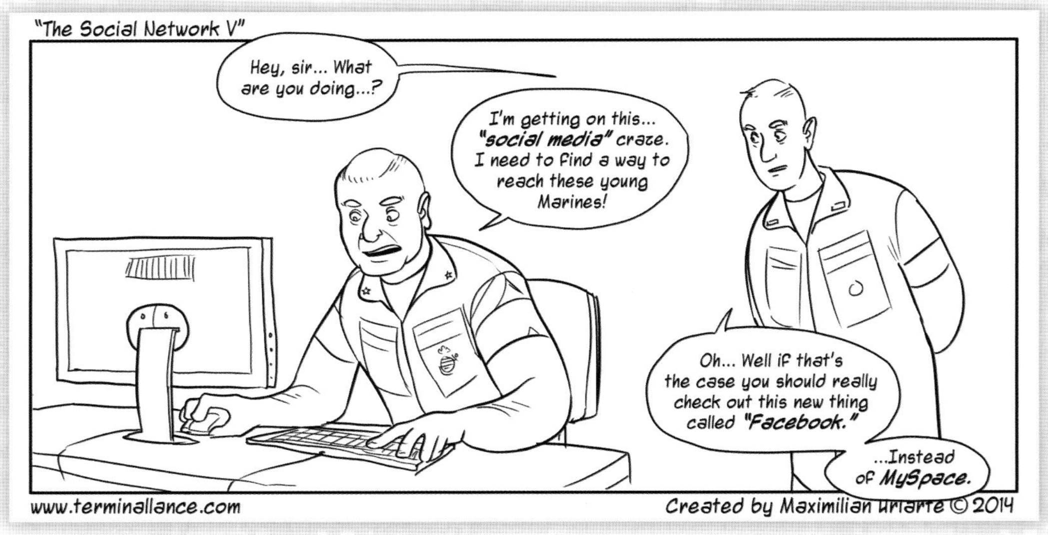
"The Social Network V"
Hey, sir... What are you doing...?
I'm getting on this... *"social media"* craze. I need to find a way to reach these young Marines!
Oh... Well if that's the case you should really check out this new thing called *"Facebook."*
...Instead of *MySpace.*
www.terminallance.com
Created by Maximilian Uriarte © 2014

"Funding the Fun"

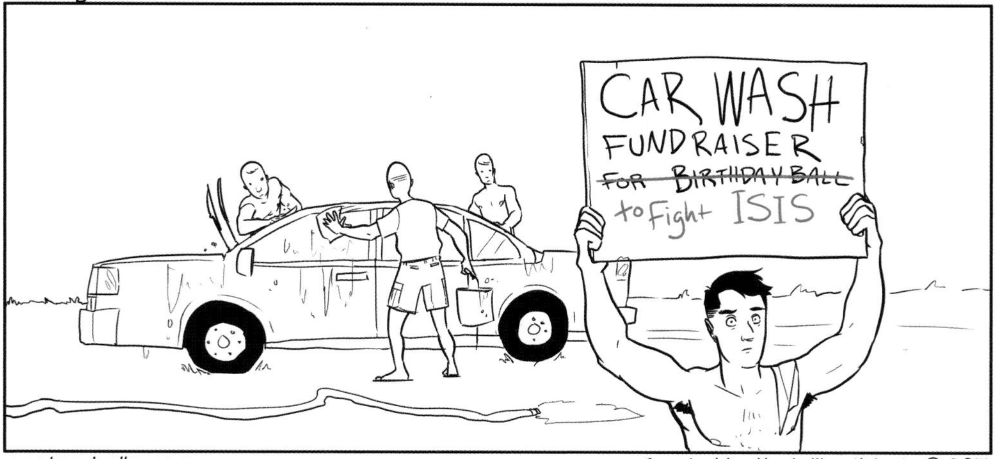
CAR WASH
FUNDRAISER
~~FOR BIRTHDAY BALL~~
to Fight ISIS

www.terminallance.com Created by Maximilian Uriarte © 2014

"Fun For Everyone"

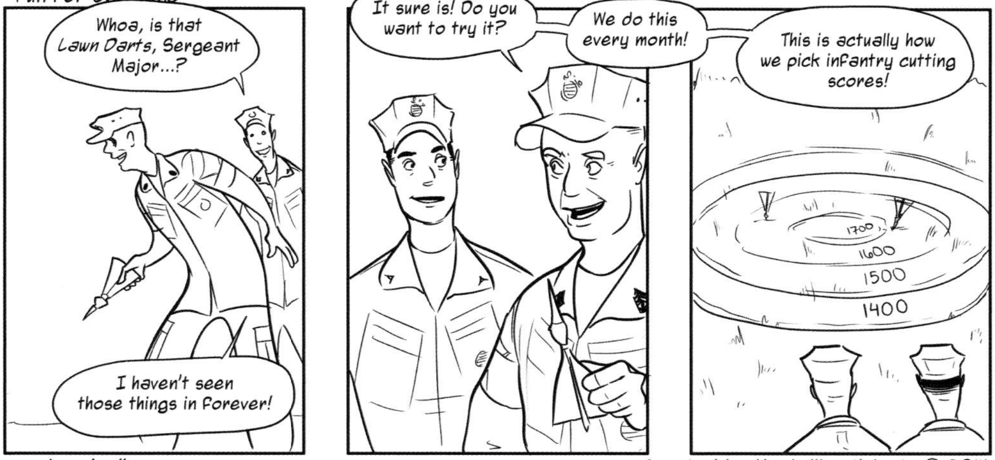
Whoa, is that Lawn Darts, Sergeant Major...?
I haven't seen those things in forever!
It sure is! Do you want to try it?
We do this every month!
This is actually how we pick infantry cutting scores!
1700
1600
1500
1400

www.terminallance.com Created by Maximilian Uriarte © 2014

"Chow Talk"

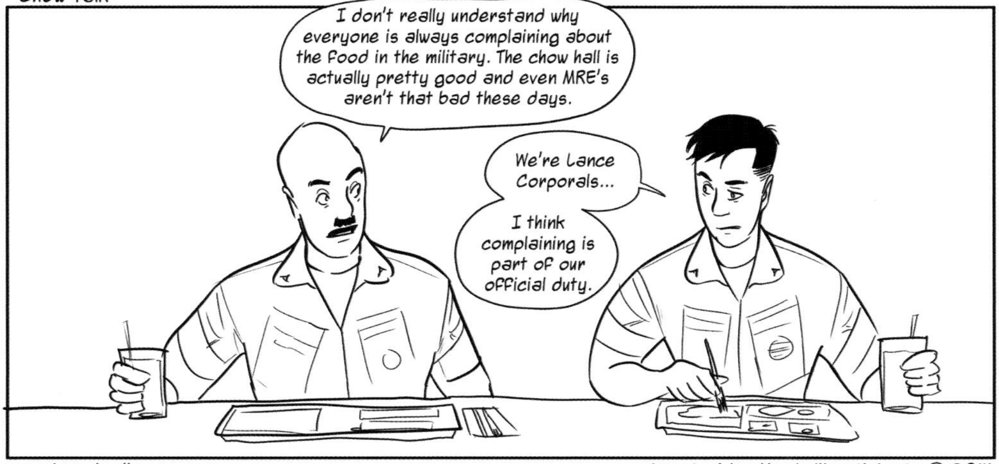
I don't really understand why everyone is always complaining about the food in the military. The chow hall is actually pretty good and even MRE's aren't that bad these days.
We're Lance Corporals...
I think complaining is part of our official duty.

www.terminallance.com Created by Maximilian Uriarte © 2014

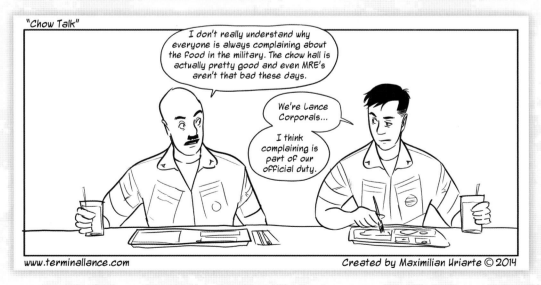

"Back to Iraq"

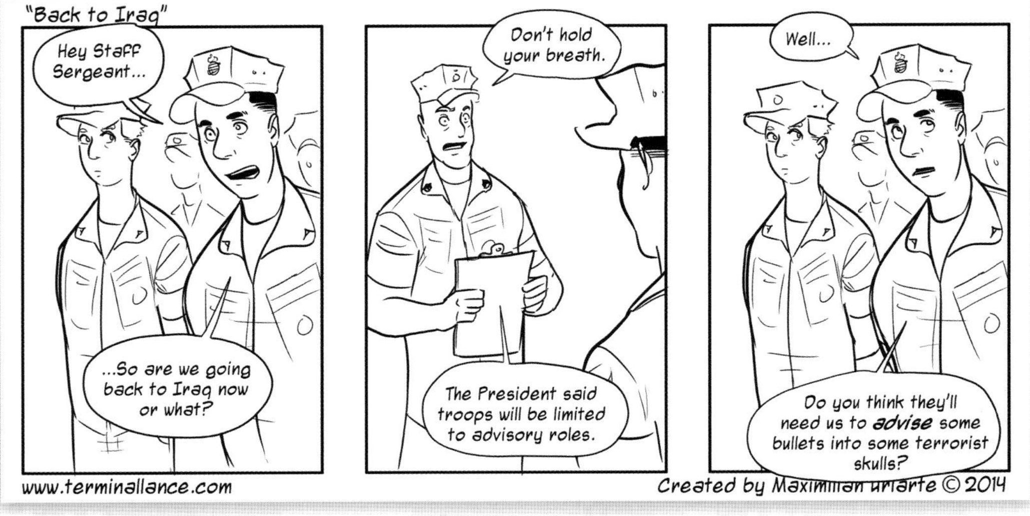
Hey Staff Sergeant...
...So are we going back to Iraq now or what?
Don't hold your breath.
The President said troops will be limited to advisory roles.
Well...
Do you think they'll need us to *advise* some bullets into some terrorist skulls?
www.terminallance.com
Created by Maximilian Uriarte © 2014

"Freedom Isn't Free"

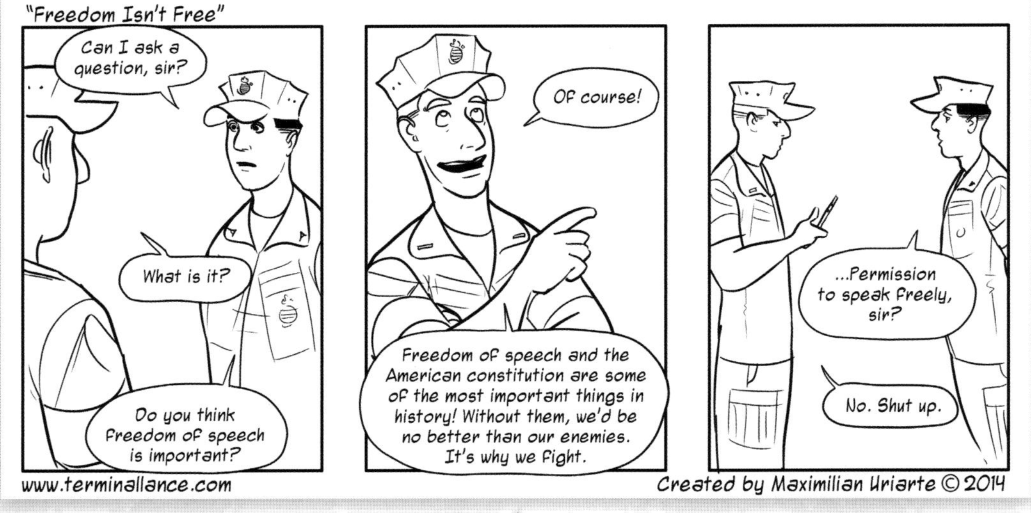
Can I ask a question, sir?
What is it?
Do you think freedom of speech is important?
Of course!
Freedom of speech and the American constitution are some of the most important things in history! Without them, we'd be no better than our enemies. It's why we fight.
...Permission to speak freely, sir?
No. Shut up.
www.terminallance.com
Created by Maximilian Uriarte © 2014

"Latte Salute"

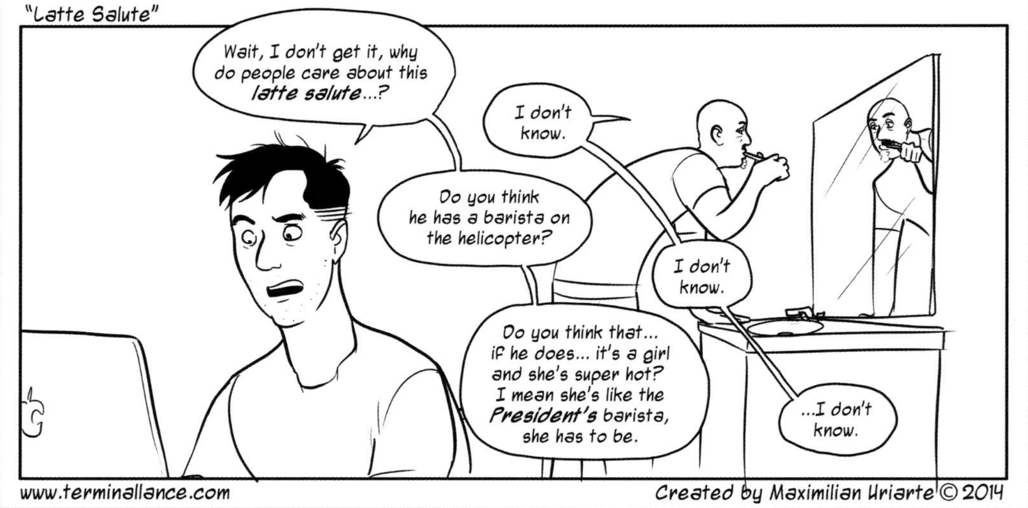
Wait, I don't get it, why do people care about this *latte salute*...?
I don't know.
Do you think he has a barista on the helicopter?
I don't know.
Do you think that... if he does... it's a girl and she's super hot? I mean she's like the *President's* barista, she has to be.
...I don't know.
www.terminallance.com
Created by Maximilian Uriarte © 2014

"Outbreak"

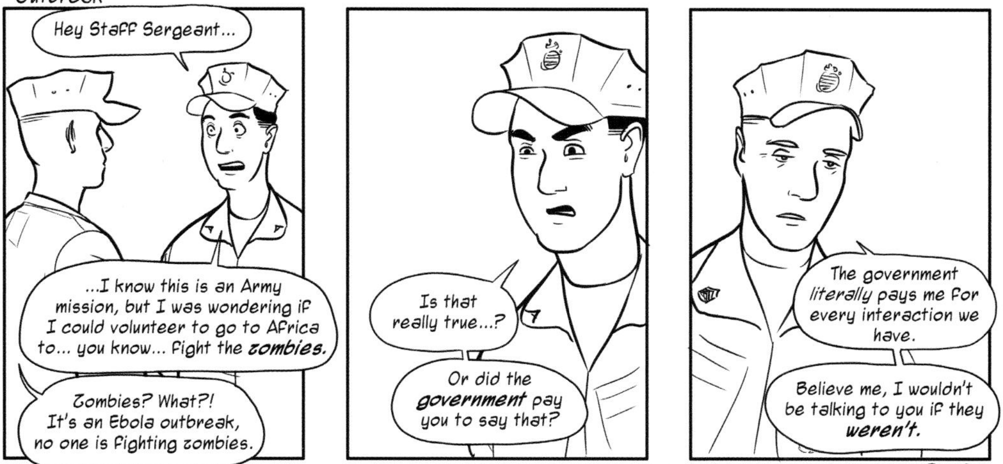
Hey Staff Sergeant...
...I know this is an Army mission, but I was wondering if I could volunteer to go to Africa to... you know... fight the ***zombies.***
Zombies? What?! It's an Ebola outbreak, no one is fighting zombies.
Is that really true...?
Or did the ***government*** pay you to say that?
The government *literally* pays me for every interaction we have.
Believe me, I wouldn't be talking to you if they ***weren't.***

www.terminallance.com

Created by Maximilian Uriarte © 2014

"Powering the Point"

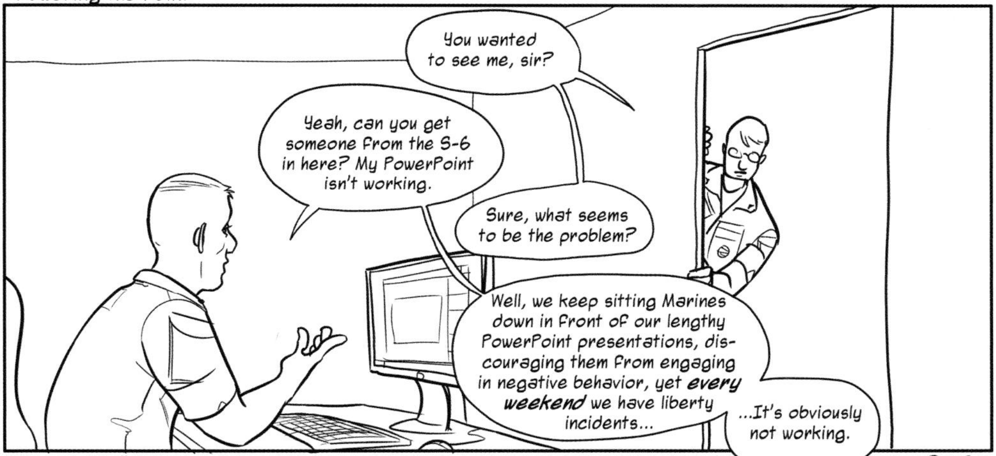
You wanted to see me, sir?
Yeah, can you get someone from the S-6 in here? My PowerPoint isn't working.
Sure, what seems to be the problem?
Well, we keep sitting Marines down in front of our lengthy PowerPoint presentations, discouraging them from engaging in negative behavior, yet ***every weekend*** we have liberty incidents...
...It's obviously not working.

www.terminallance.com

Created by Maximilian Uriarte © 2014

"Peer Promotions"

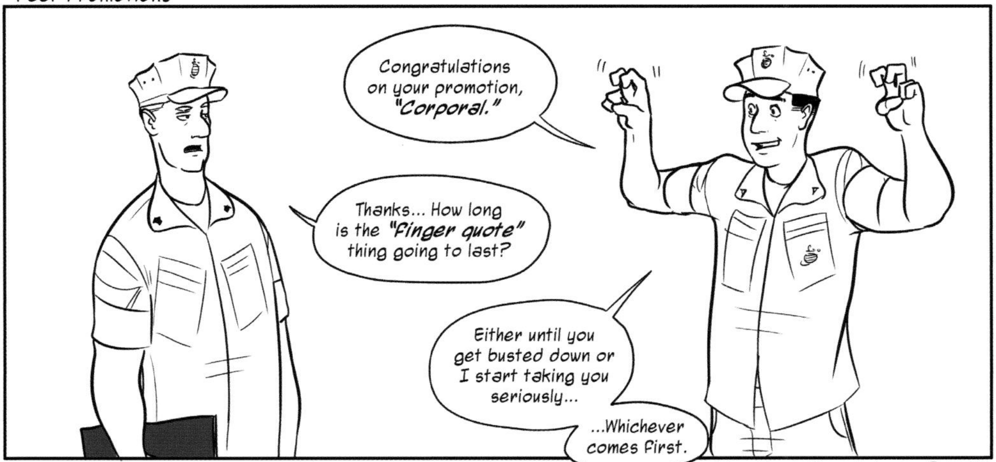
Congratulations on your promotion, ***"Corporal."***
Thanks... How long is the ***"finger quote"*** thing going to last?
Either until you get busted down or I start taking you seriously...
...Whichever comes first.

www.terminallance.com

Created by Maximilian Uriarte © 2014

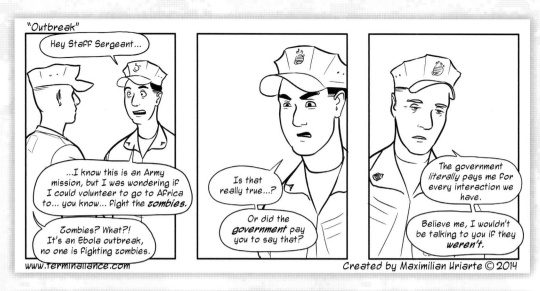

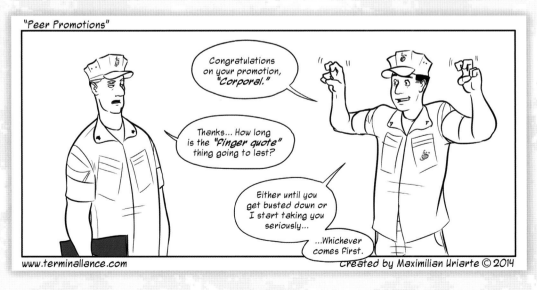

"Furious Fury"

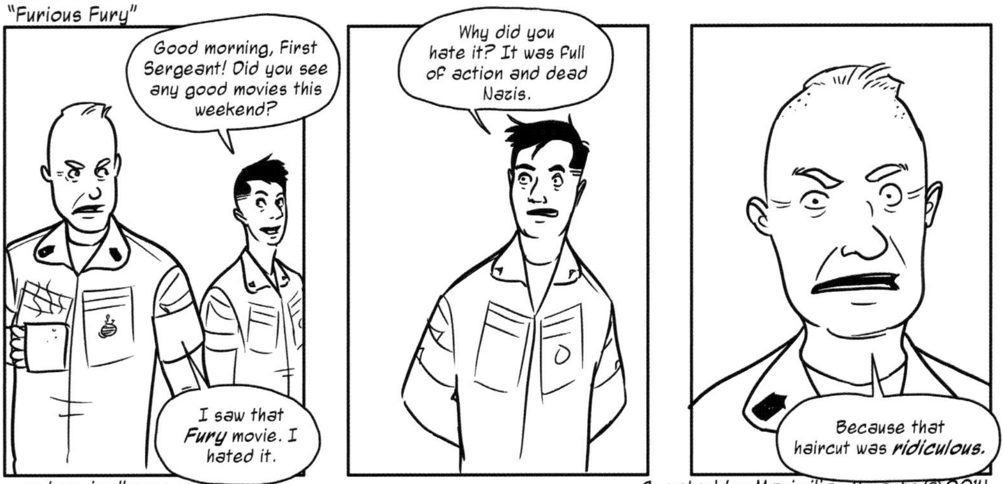
Good morning, First Sergeant! Did you see any good movies this weekend?
I saw that *Fury* movie. I hated it.
Why did you hate it? It was full of action and dead Nazis.
Because that haircut was ***ridiculous.***

www.terminallance.com Created by Maximilian Uriarte © 2014

"Afghanistan, Over"

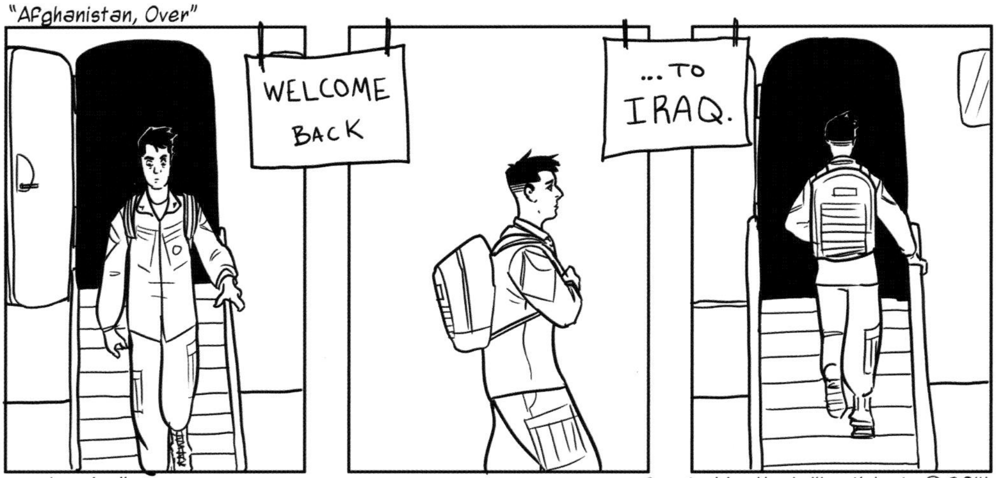
WELCOME BACK
...TO IRAQ.

www.terminallance.com Created by Maximilian Uriarte © 2014

"Birthday Bash"

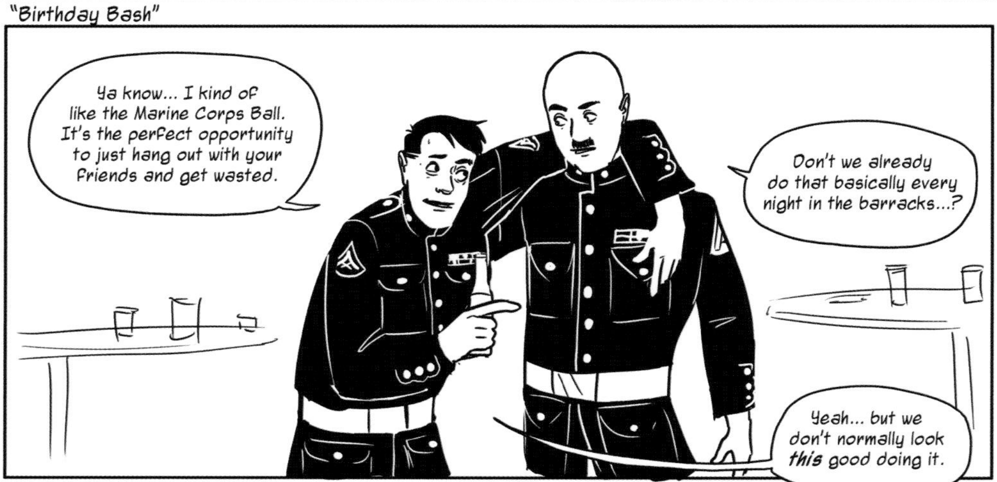
Ya know... I kind of like the Marine Corps Ball. It's the perfect opportunity to just hang out with your friends and get wasted.
Don't we already do that basically every night in the barracks...?
Yeah... but we don't normally look *this* good doing it.

www.terminallance.com Created by Maximilian Uriarte © 2014

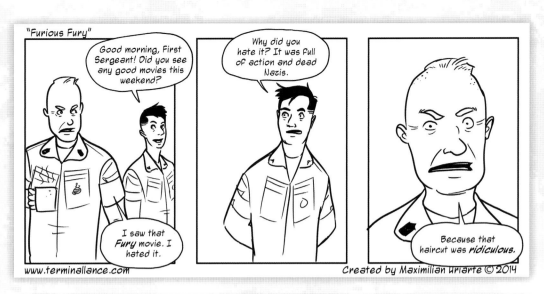

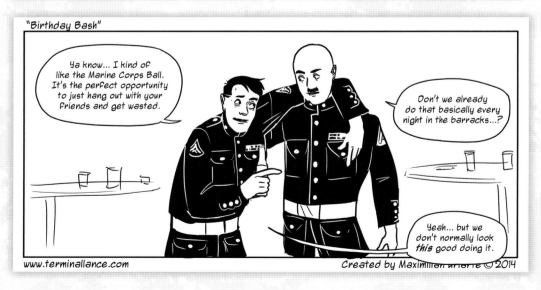

"Smooth as Silk"

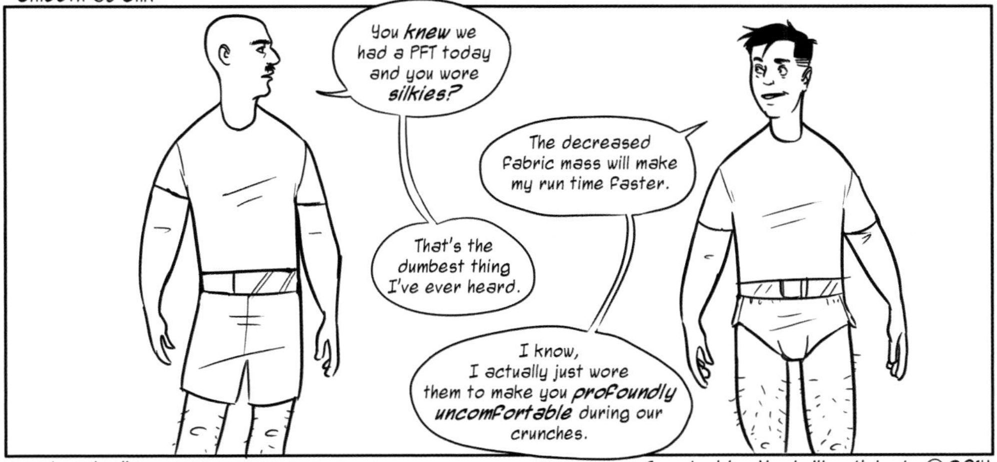
You **knew** we had a PFT today and you wore ***silkies?***
The decreased fabric mass will make my run time faster.
That's the dumbest thing I've ever heard.
I know, I actually just wore them to make you ***profoundly uncomfortable*** during our crunches.

www.terminallance.com

Created by Maximilian Uriarte © 2014

"Metaphorically"

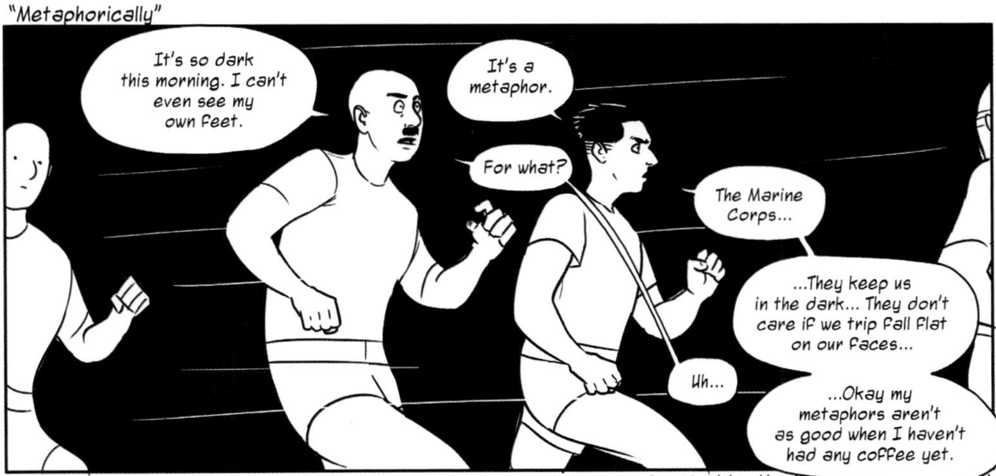
It's so dark this morning. I can't even see my own feet.
It's a metaphor.
For what?
The Marine Corps...
...They keep us in the dark... They don't care if we trip fall flat on our faces...
Uh...
...Okay my metaphors aren't as good when I haven't had any coffee yet.

www.terminallance.com

Created by Maximilian Uriarte © 2014

"Left Over"

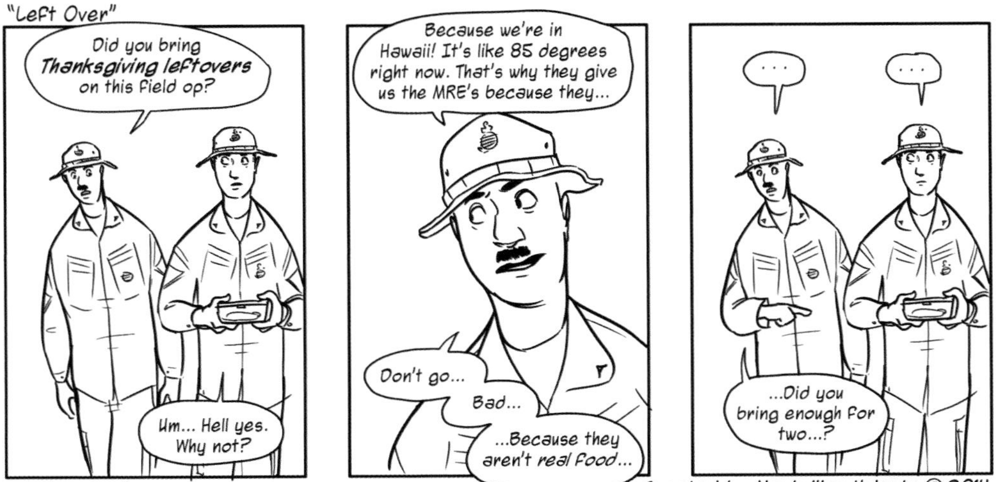
Did you bring ***Thanksgiving leftovers*** on this field op?
Um... Hell yes. Why not?
Because we're in Hawaii! It's like 85 degrees right now. That's why they give us the MRE's because they...
Don't go...
Bad...
...Because they aren't *real* food...
...
...
...Did you bring enough for two...?

www.terminallance.com

Created by Maximilian Uriarte © 2014

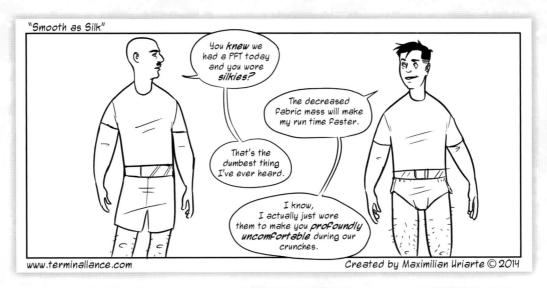

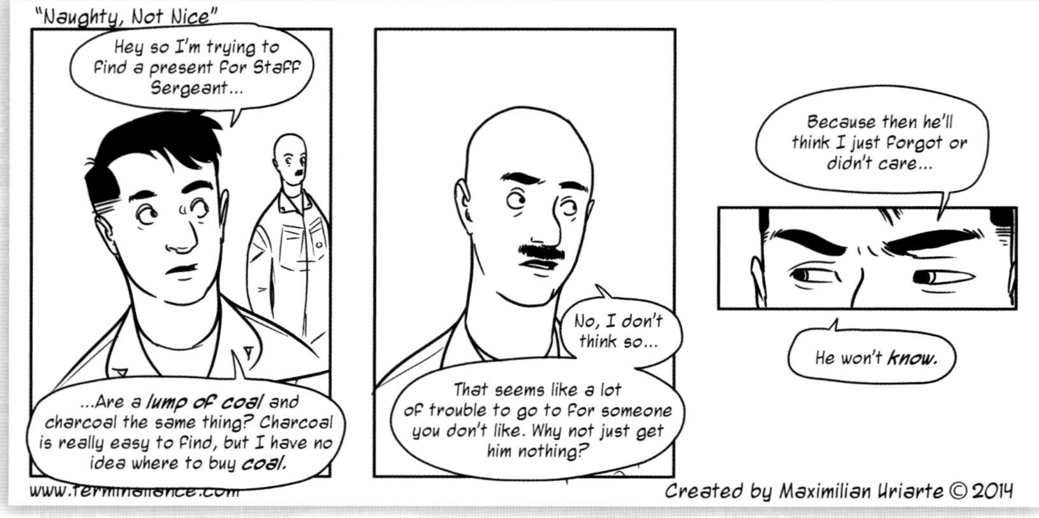
"Naughty, Not Nice"
Hey so I'm trying to find a present for Staff Sergeant...
...Are a *lump of coal* and charcoal the same thing? Charcoal is really easy to find, but I have no idea where to buy *coal.*
No, I don't think so...
That seems like a lot of trouble to go to for someone you don't like. Why not just get him nothing?
Because then he'll think I just forgot or didn't care...
He won't *know.*
www.terminallance.com
Created by Maximilian Uriarte © 2014

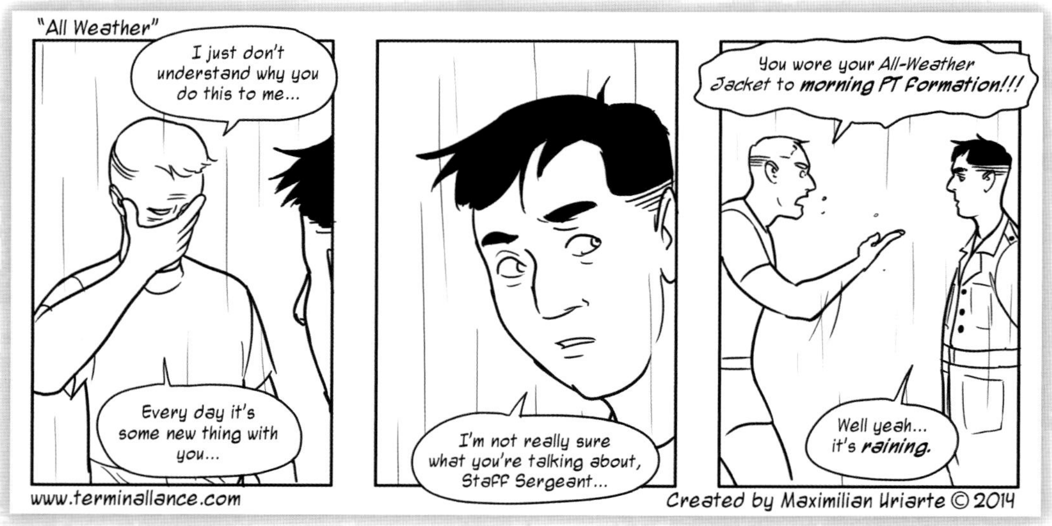
"All Weather"
I just don't understand why you do this to me...
Every day it's some new thing with you...
I'm not really sure what you're talking about, Staff Sergeant...
You wore your *All-Weather Jacket* to **morning PT formation!!!**
Well yeah... it's *raining.*
www.terminallance.com
Created by Maximilian Uriarte © 2014

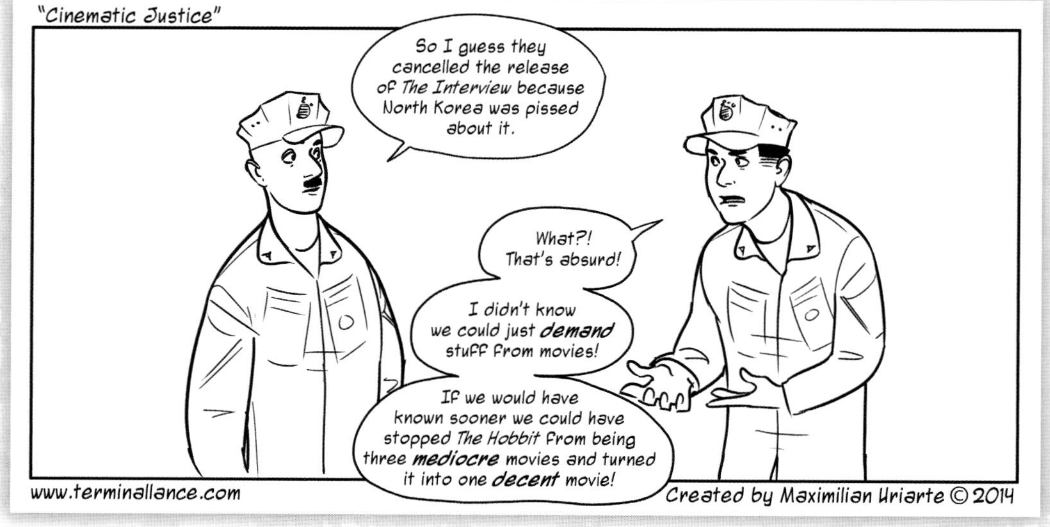
"Cinematic Justice"
So I guess they cancelled the release of *The Interview* because North Korea was pissed about it.
What?! That's absurd!
I didn't know we could just *demand* stuff from movies!
If we would have known sooner we could have stopped *The Hobbit* from being three *mediocre* movies and turned it into one *decent* movie!
www.terminallance.com
Created by Maximilian Uriarte © 2014

"The New Year"

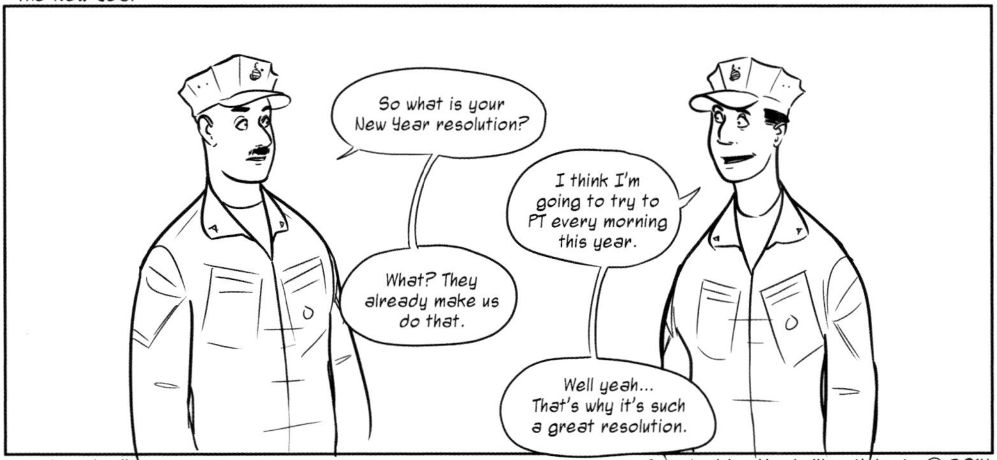
So what is your New Year resolution?
I think I'm going to try to PT every morning this year.
What? They already make us do that.
Well yeah... That's why it's such a great resolution.

www.terminallance.com Created by Maximilian Uriarte © 2014

"Je Suis Charlie"

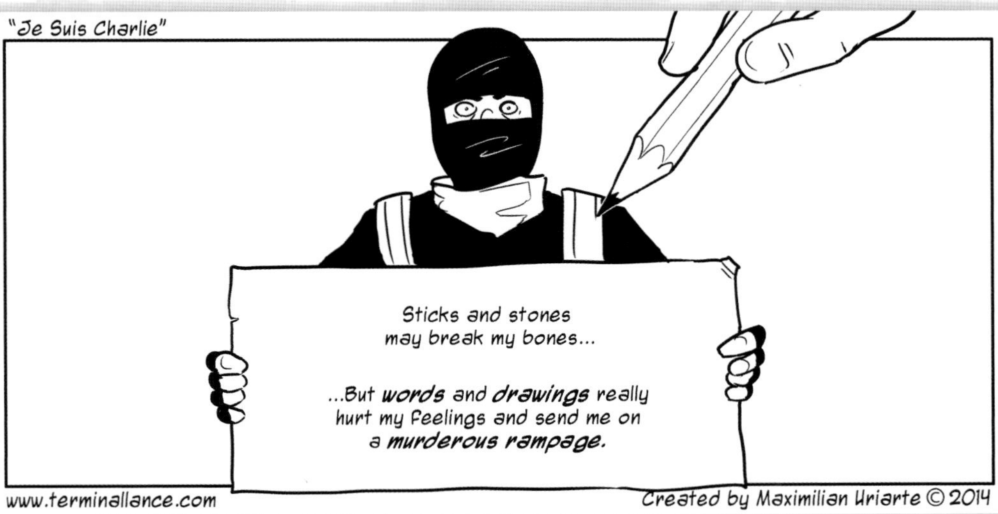
Sticks and stones may break my bones...
...But *words* and *drawings* really hurt my feelings and send me on a *murderous rampage.*

www.terminallance.com Created by Maximilian Uriarte © 2014

"Anywhere but Here"

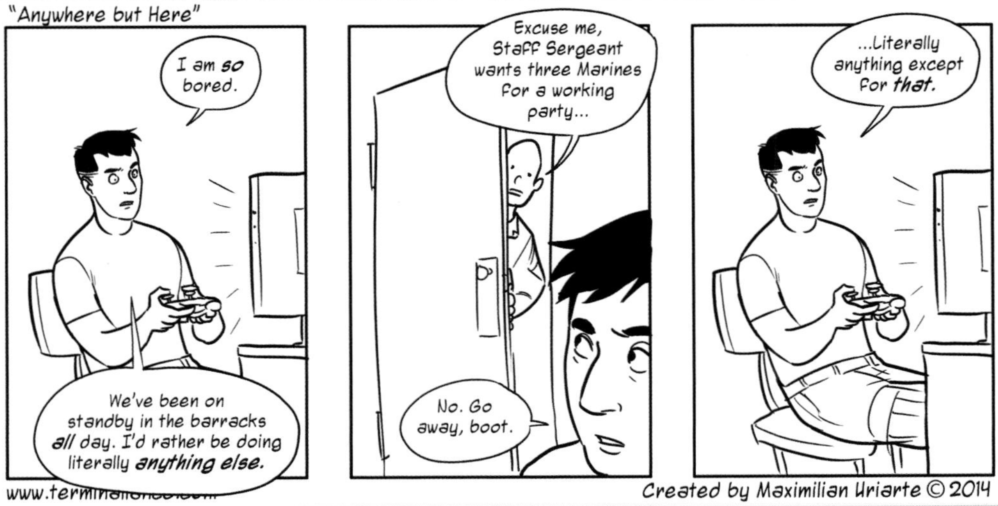
I am *so* bored.
We've been on standby in the barracks *all* day. I'd rather be doing literally *anything else.*
Excuse me, Staff Sergeant wants three Marines for a working party...
No. Go away, boot.
...Literally anything except for *that.*

www.terminallance.com Created by Maximilian Uriarte © 2014

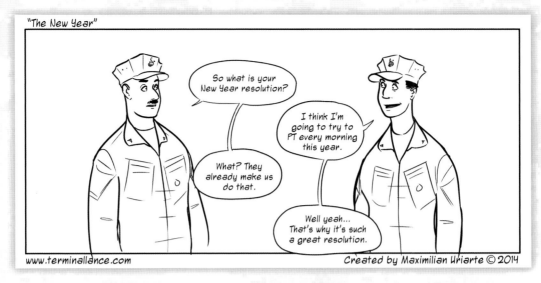

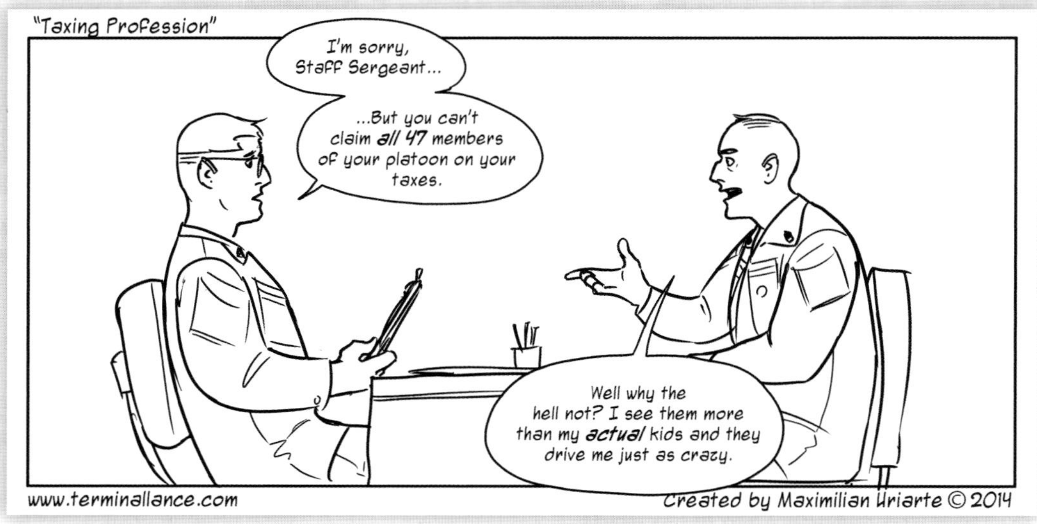
"Taxing Profession"
I'm sorry, Staff Sergeant...
...But you can't claim all 47 members of your platoon on your taxes.
Well why the hell not? I see them more than my actual kids and they drive me just as crazy.
www.terminallance.com
Created by Maximilian Uriarte © 2014

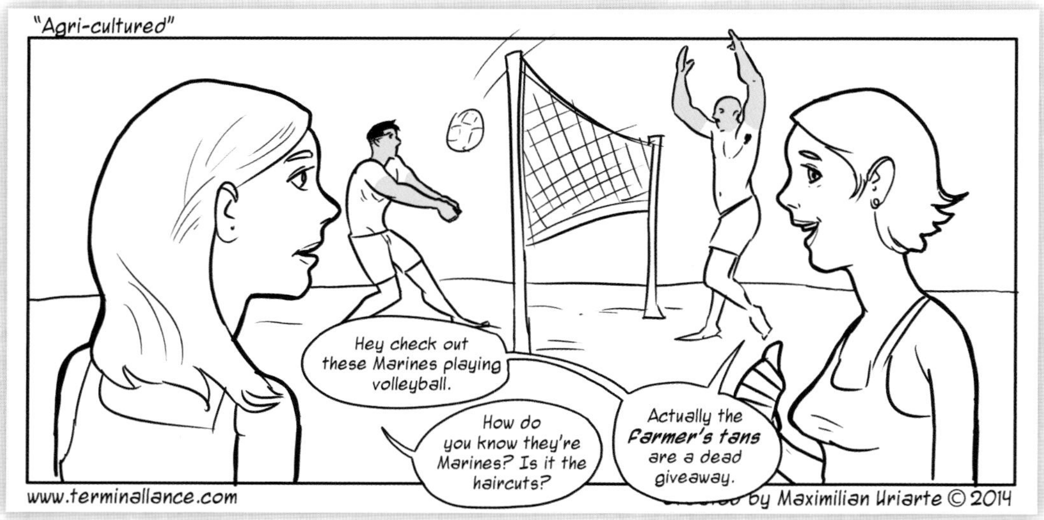
"Agri-cultured"
Hey check out these Marines playing volleyball.
How do you know they're Marines? Is it the haircuts?
Actually the Farmer's tans are a dead giveaway.
www.terminallance.com
by Maximilian Uriarte © 2014

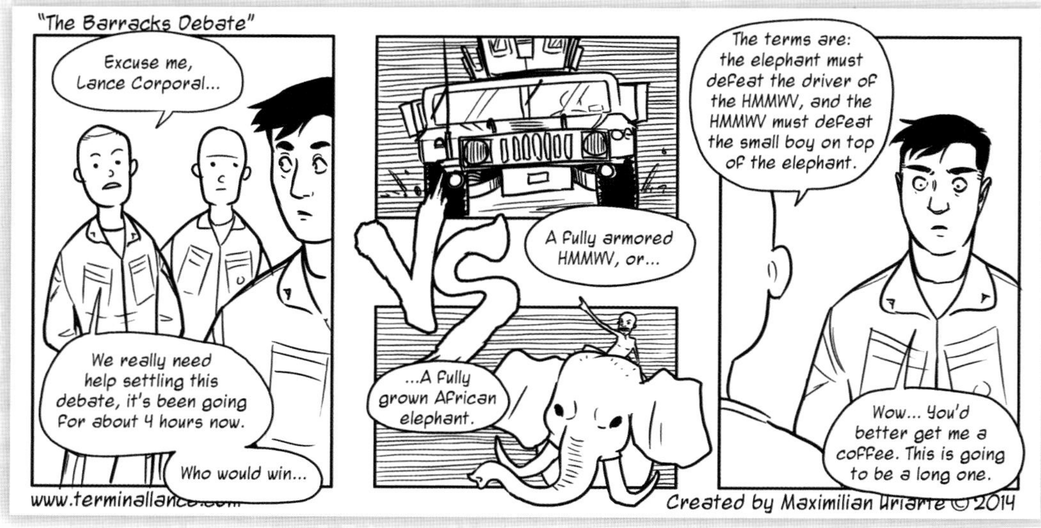
"The Barracks Debate"
Excuse me, Lance Corporal...
We really need help settling this debate, it's been going for about 4 hours now.
Who would win...
A fully armored HMMWV, or...
VS
...A fully grown African elephant.
The terms are: the elephant must defeat the driver of the HMMWV, and the HMMWV must defeat the small boy on top of the elephant.
Wow... You'd better get me a coffee. This is going to be a long one.
Created by Maximilian Uriarte © 2014

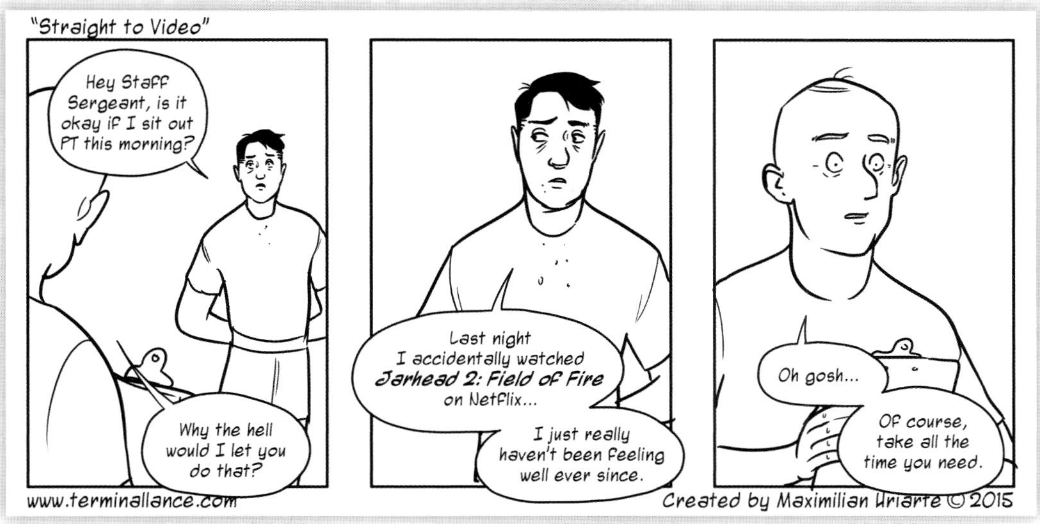
"Straight to Video"
Hey Staff Sergeant, is it okay if I sit out PT this morning?
Why the hell would I let you do that?
Last night I accidentally watched Jarhead 2: Field of Fire on Netflix...
I just really haven't been feeling well ever since.
Oh gosh...
Of course, take all the time you need.
www.terminallance.com
Created by Maximilian Uriarte © 2015

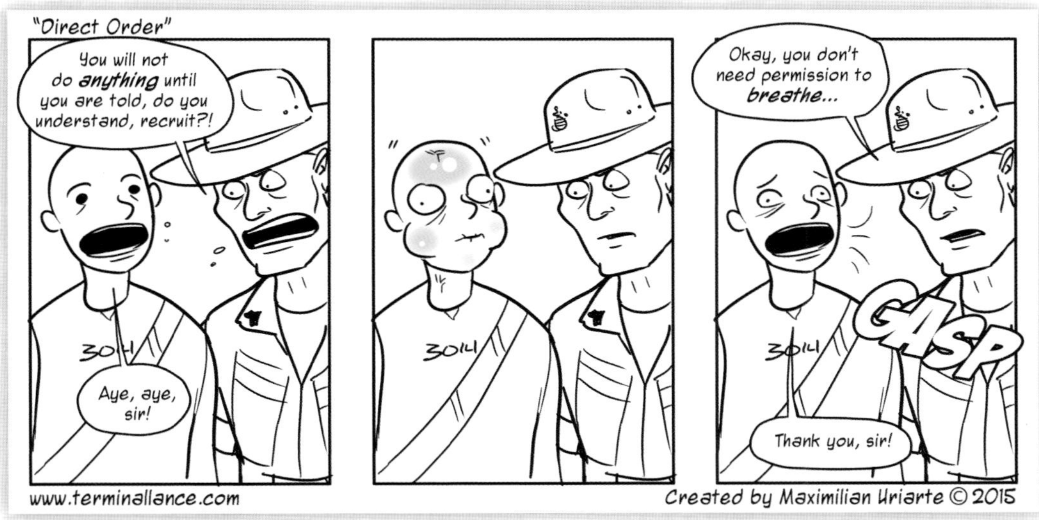
"Direct Order"
You will not do anything until you are told, do you understand, recruit?!
Aye, aye, sir!
Okay, you don't need permission to breathe...
GASP
Thank you, sir!
www.terminallance.com
Created by Maximilian Uriarte © 2015

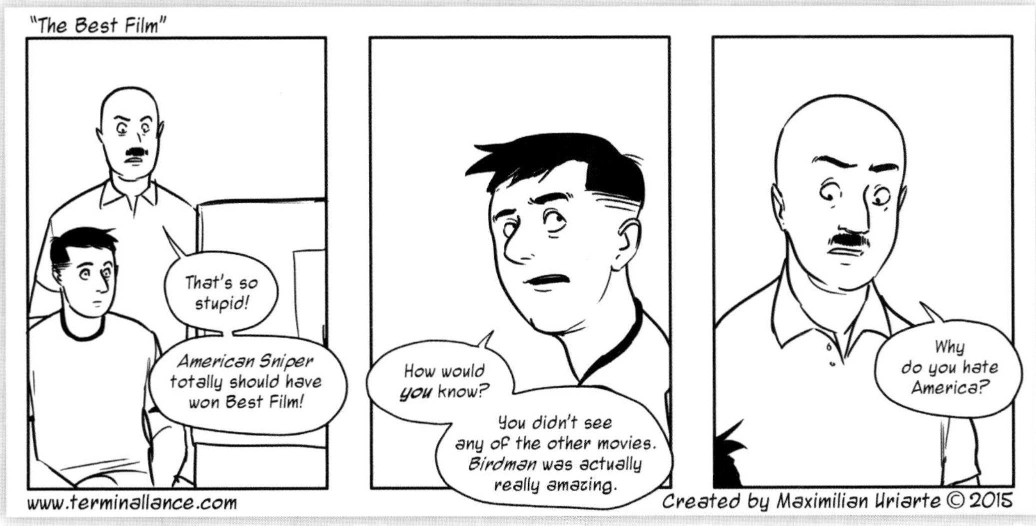
"The Best Film"
That's so stupid!
American Sniper totally should have won Best Film!
How would you know?
You didn't see any of the other movies. Birdman was actually really amazing.
Why do you hate America?
www.terminallance.com
Created by Maximilian Uriarte © 2015

"No Ragrets"

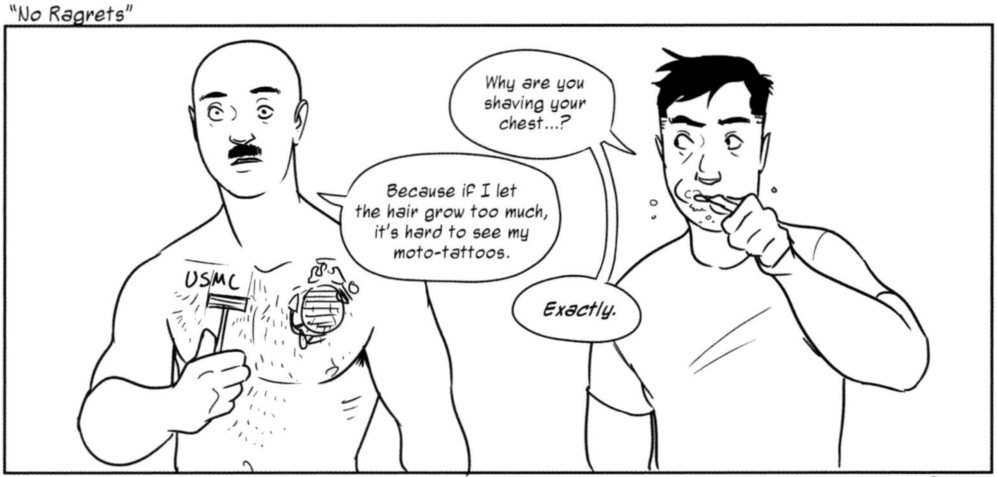
Why are you shaving your chest...?
Because if I let the hair grow too much, it's hard to see my moto-tattoos.
Exactly.
USMC

www.terminallance.com Created by Maximilian Uriarte © 2015

"Limerick"

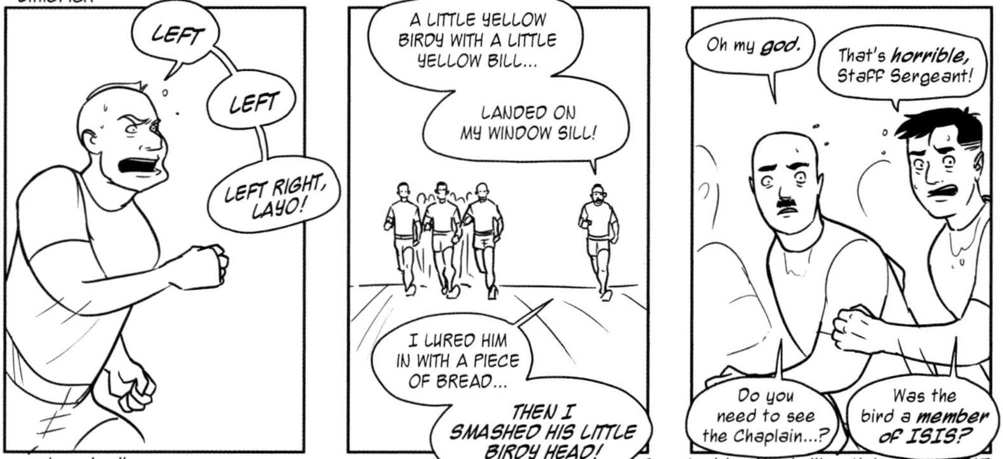
LEFT
LEFT
LEFT RIGHT, LAYO!
A LITTLE YELLOW BIRDY WITH A LITTLE YELLOW BILL...
LANDED ON MY WINDOW SILL!
I LURED HIM IN WITH A PIECE OF BREAD...
THEN I SMASHED HIS LITTLE BIRDY HEAD!
Oh my god.
That's horrible, Staff Sergeant!
Do you need to see the Chaplain...?
Was the bird a member of ISIS?

www.terminallance.com Created by Maximilian Uriarte © 2015

"War Stories II"

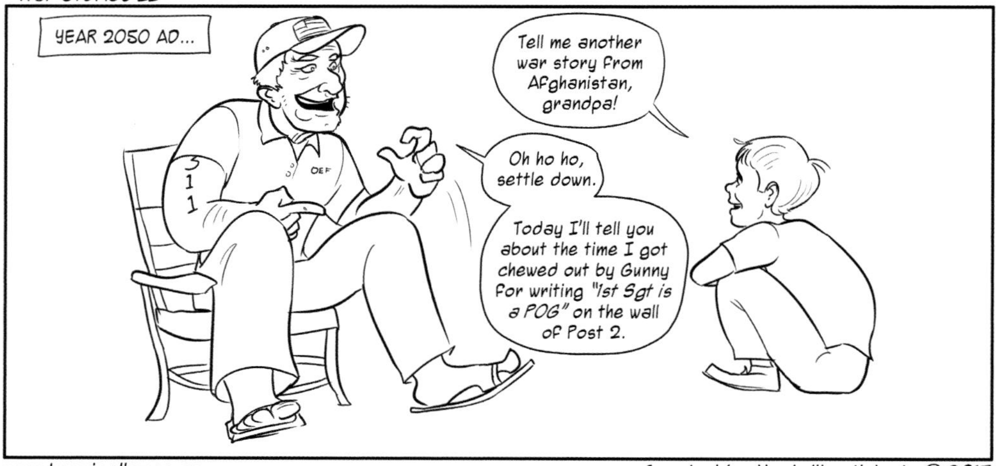
YEAR 2050 AD...
Tell me another war story from Afghanistan, grandpa!
Oh ho ho, settle down.
Today I'll tell you about the time I got chewed out by Gunny for writing "1st Sgt is a POG" on the wall of Post 2.
OEF
311

www.terminallance.com Created by Maximilian Uriarte © 2015

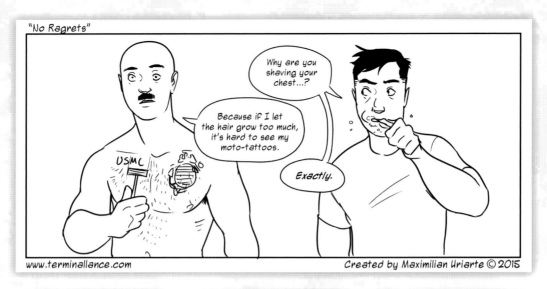

"Equidae"

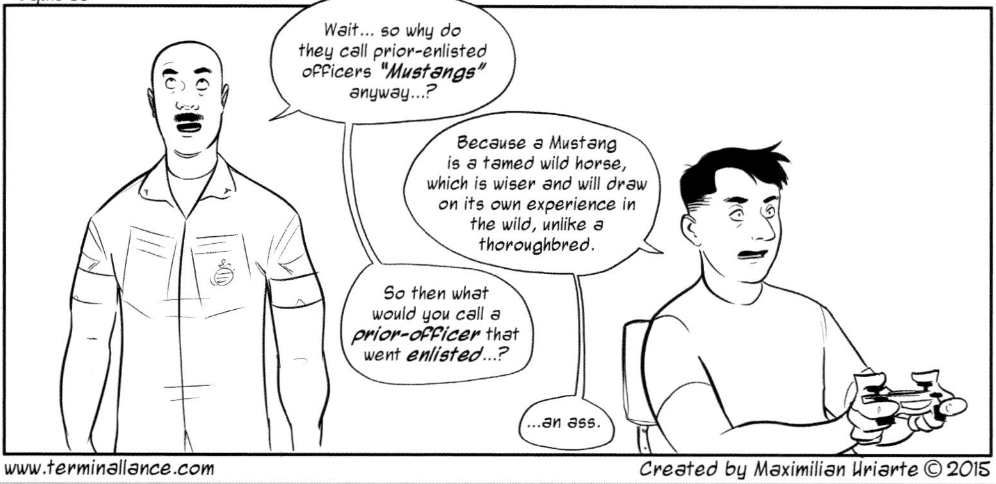
Wait... so why do they call prior-enlisted officers **"Mustangs"** anyway...?
Because a Mustang is a tamed wild horse, which is wiser and will draw on its own experience in the wild, unlike a thoroughbred.
So then what would you call a ***prior-officer*** that went ***enlisted***...?
...an ass.
www.terminallance.com
Created by Maximilian Uriarte © 2015

"Now on the App Store"

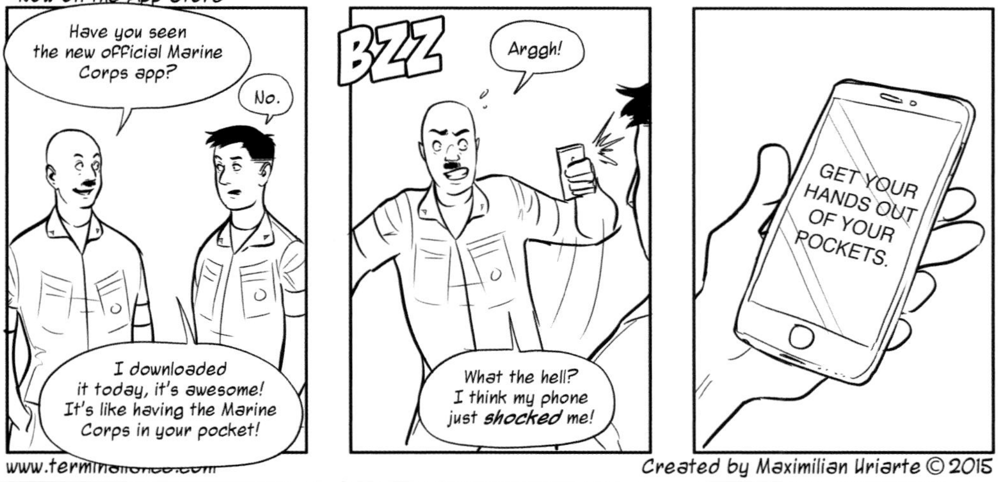
Have you seen the new official Marine Corps app?
No.
I downloaded it today, it's awesome! It's like having the Marine Corps in your pocket!
BZZ
Arggh!
What the hell? I think my phone just ***shocked*** me!
GET YOUR HANDS OUT OF YOUR POCKETS.
www.terminallance.com
Created by Maximilian Uriarte © 2015

"New Corps"

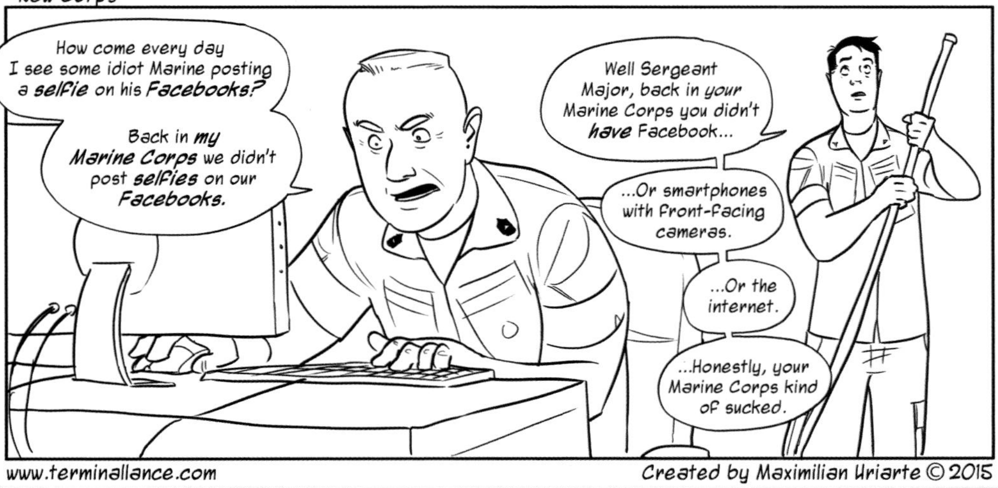
How come every day I see some idiot Marine posting a ***selfie*** on his ***Facebooks?***
Back in ***my Marine Corps*** we didn't post ***selfies*** on our ***Facebooks.***
Well Sergeant Major, back in *your* Marine Corps you didn't ***have*** Facebook...
...Or smartphones with front-facing cameras.
...Or the internet.
...Honestly, your Marine Corps kind of sucked.
www.terminallance.com
Created by Maximilian Uriarte © 2015

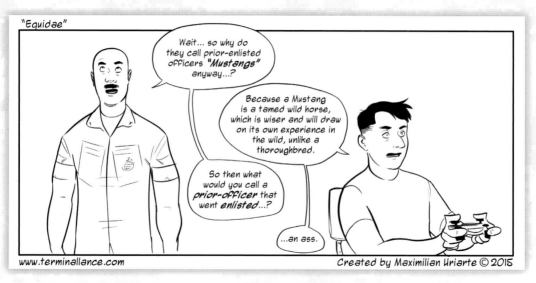

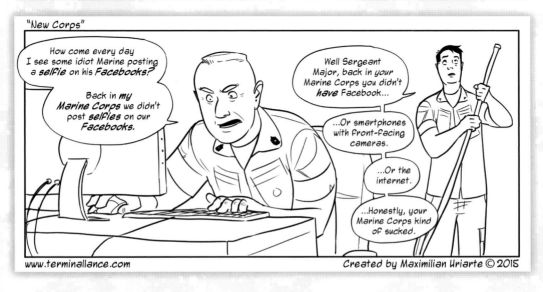

"Hump Day"

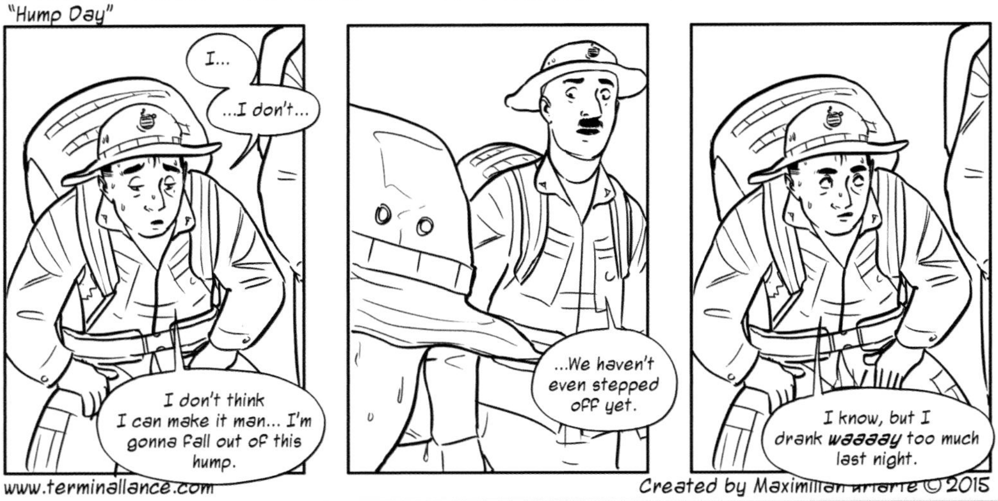
I...
...I don't...
I don't think I can make it man... I'm gonna fall out of this hump.
...We haven't even stepped off yet.
I know, but I drank *waaaay* too much last night.
www.terminallance.com
Created by Maximilian Uriarte © 2015

"B[A]S"

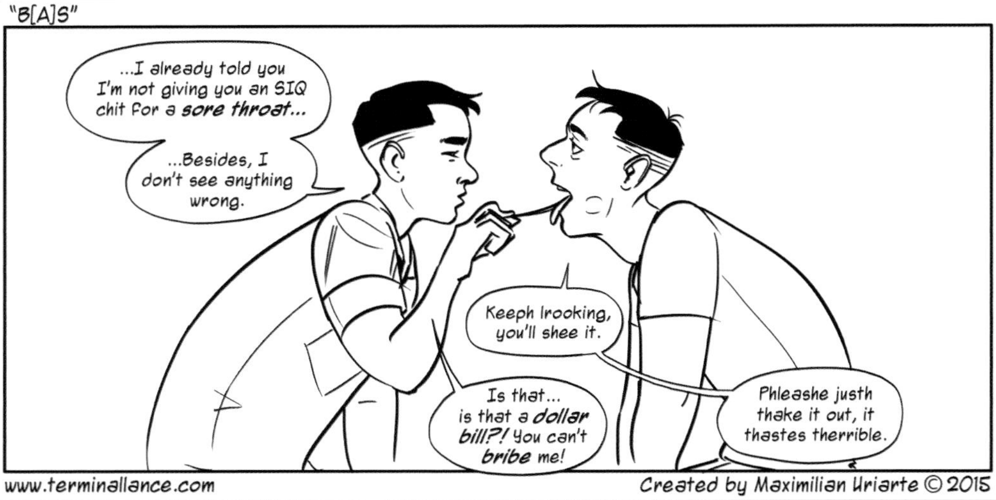
...I already told you I'm not giving you an SIQ chit for a *sore throat...*
...Besides, I don't see anything wrong.
Keeph lrooking, you'll shee it.
Is that... is that a *dollar bill?!* You can't *bribe* me!
Phleashe justh thake it out, it thastes therrible.
www.terminallance.com
Created by Maximilian Uriarte © 2015

"Parenthood"

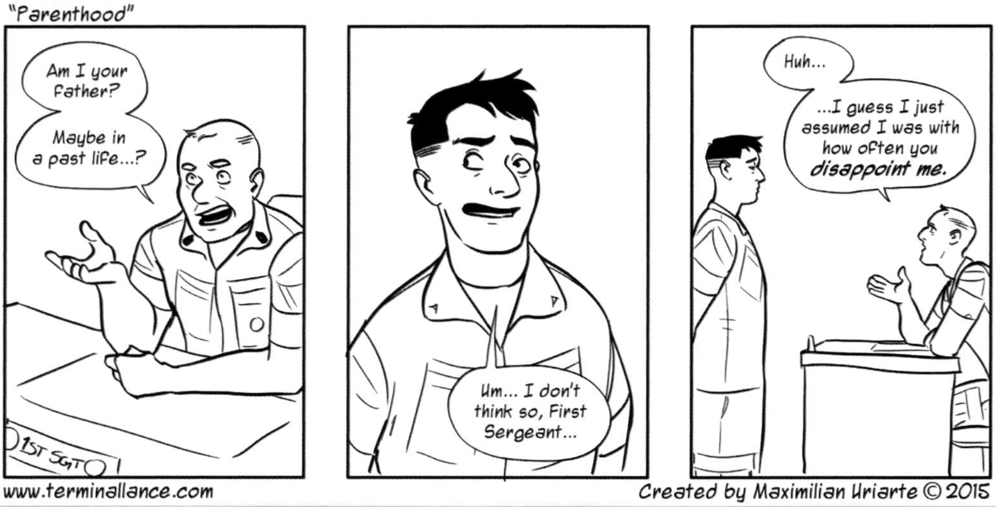
Am I your father?
Maybe in a past life...?
1ST SGT
Um... I don't think so, First Sergeant...
Huh...
...I guess I just assumed I was with how often you *disappoint me.*
www.terminallance.com
Created by Maximilian Uriarte © 2015

"Breakups"

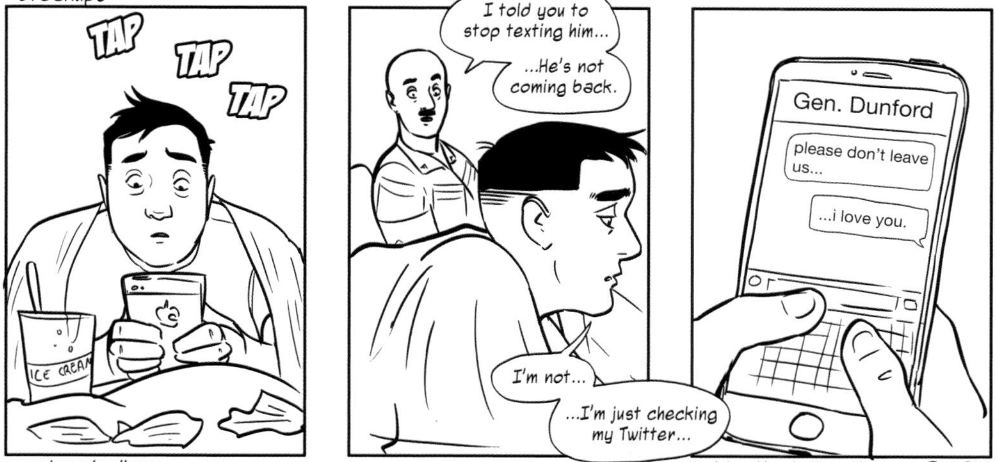
TAP
TAP
TAP
ICE CREAM
I told you to stop texting him...
...He's not coming back.
I'm not...
...I'm just checking my Twitter...
Gen. Dunford
please don't leave us...
...i love you.

www.terminallance.com

Created by Maximilian Uriarte © 2015

"Watching *Jarhead 2*"

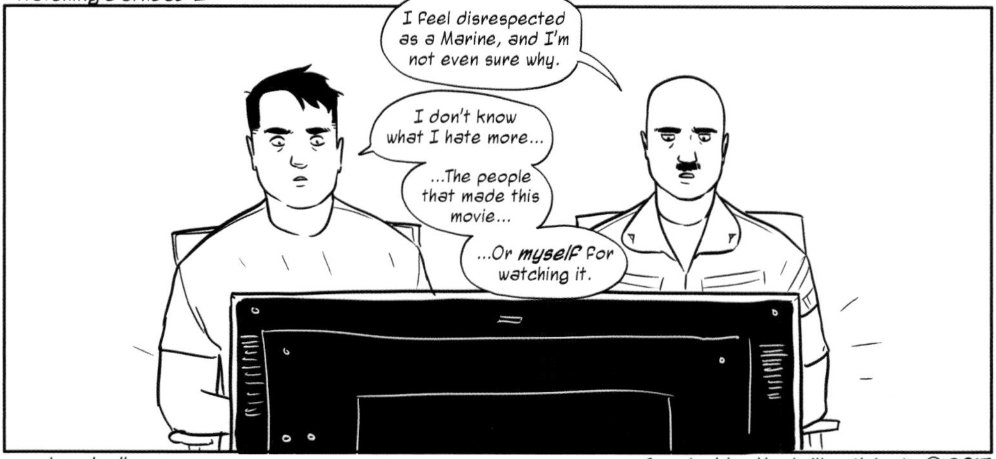
I feel disrespected as a Marine, and I'm not even sure why.
I don't know what I hate more...
...The people that made this movie...
...Or *myself* for watching it.

www.terminallance.com

Created by Maximilian Uriarte © 2015

"Long Distance"

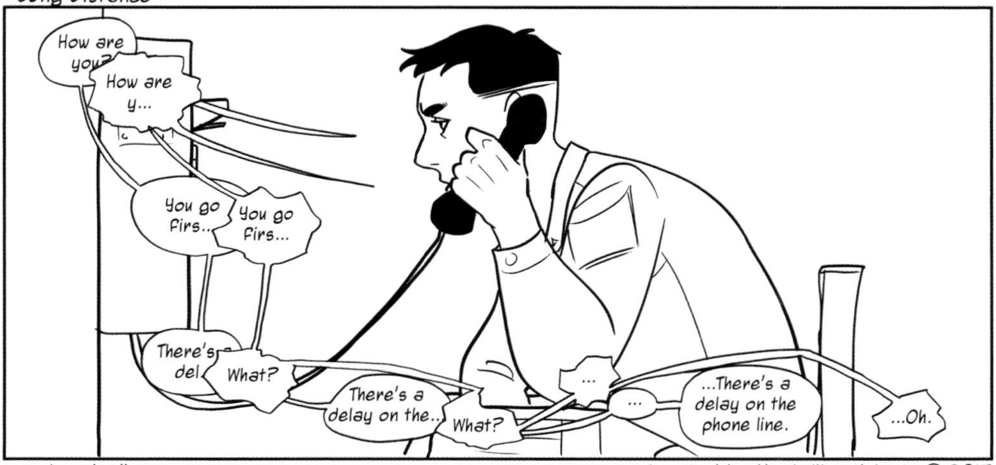
How are you?
How are y...
You go firs...
You go firs...
There's a del
What?
There's a delay on the..
What?
...
...
...There's a delay on the phone line.
...Oh.

www.terminallance.com

Created by Maximilian Uriarte © 2015

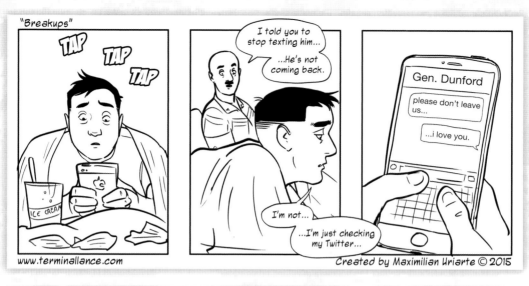

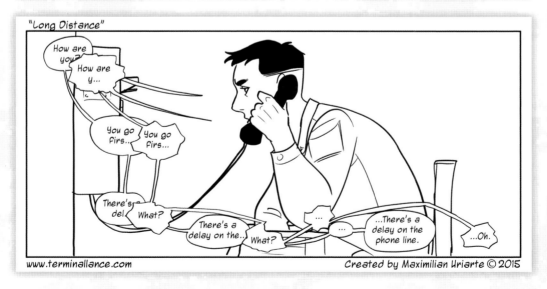

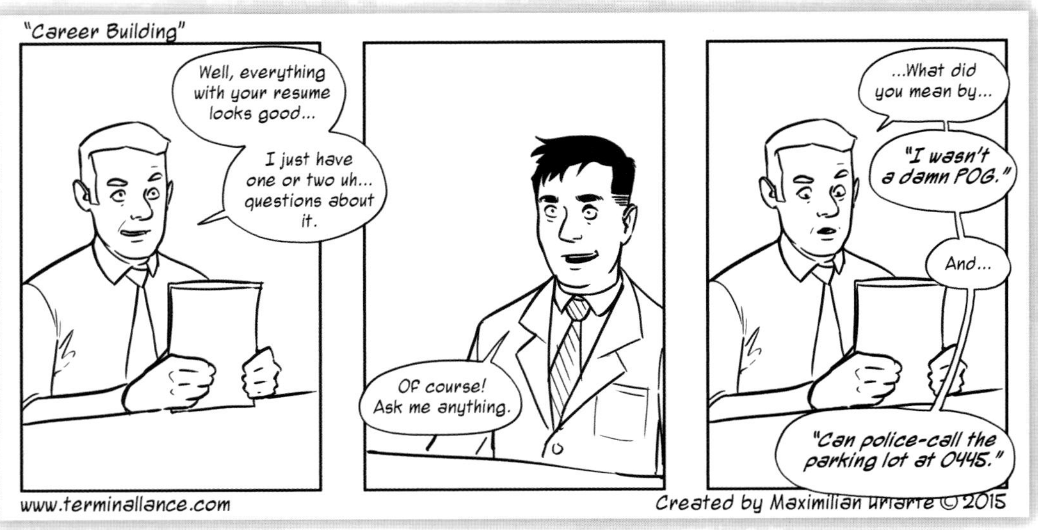
"Career Building"
Well, everything with your resume looks good...
I just have one or two uh... questions about it.
Of course! Ask me anything.
...What did you mean by...
"I wasn't a damn POG."
And...
"Can police-call the parking lot at 0445."
www.terminallance.com
Created by Maximilian Uriarte © 2015

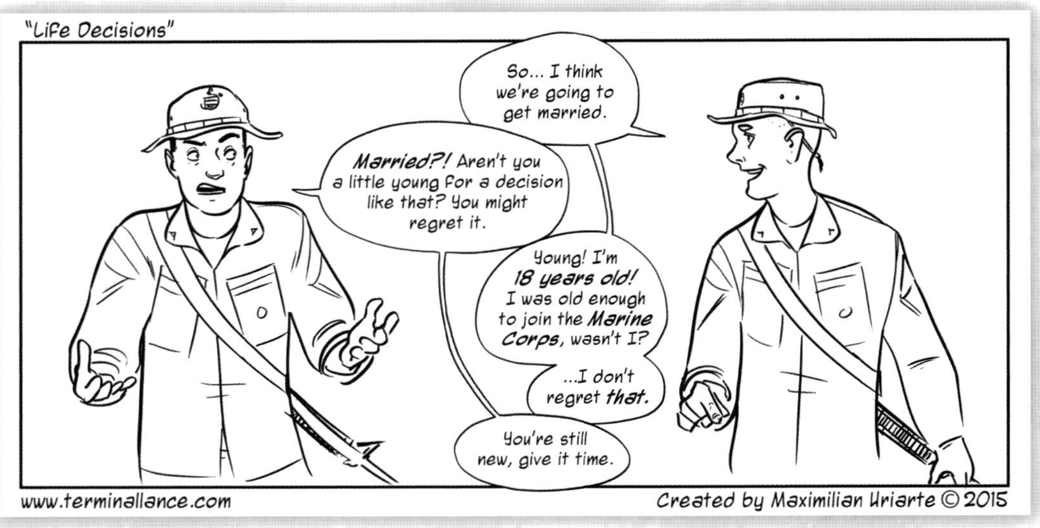
"Life Decisions"
So... I think we're going to get married.
Married?! Aren't you a little young for a decision like that? You might regret it.
Young! I'm 18 years old! I was old enough to join the Marine Corps, wasn't I?
...I don't regret that.
You're still new, give it time.
www.terminallance.com
Created by Maximilian Uriarte © 2015

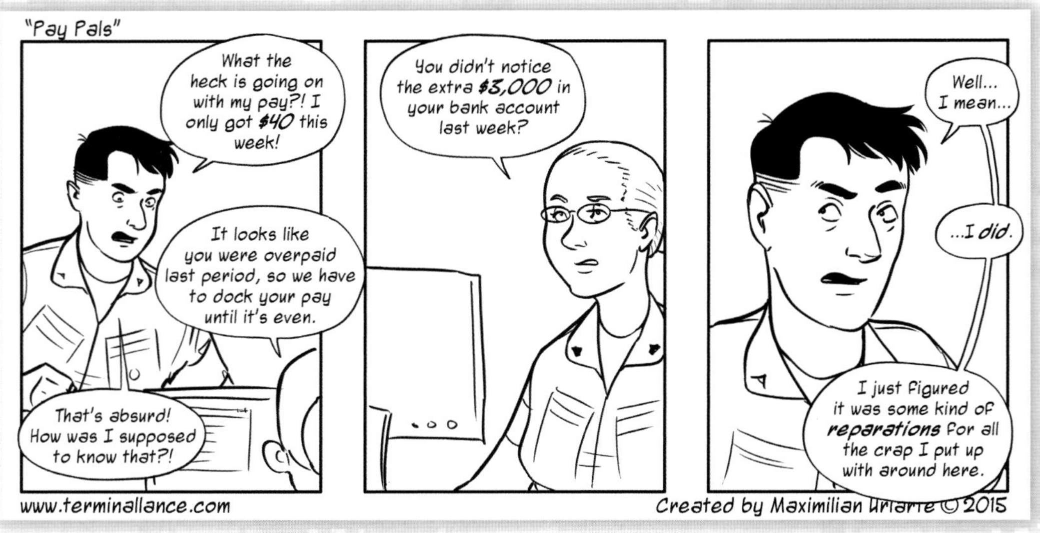
"Pay Pals"
What the heck is going on with my pay?! I only got $40 this week!
It looks like you were overpaid last period, so we have to dock your pay until it's even.
That's absurd! How was I supposed to know that?!
You didn't notice the extra $3,000 in your bank account last week?
Well... I mean...
...I did.
I just figured it was some kind of reparations for all the crap I put up with around here.
www.terminallance.com
Created by Maximilian Uriarte © 2015

"E3"

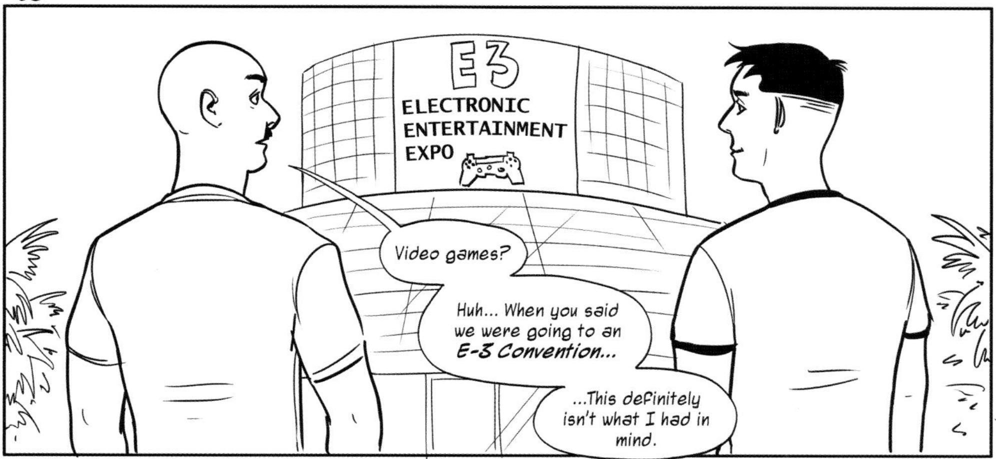
E3
ELECTRONIC
ENTERTAINMENT
EXPO
Video games?
Huh... When you said we were going to an ***E-3 Convention...***
...This definitely isn't what I had in mind.

www.terminallance.com Created by Maximilian Uriarte © 2015

"Cretaceous Corps"

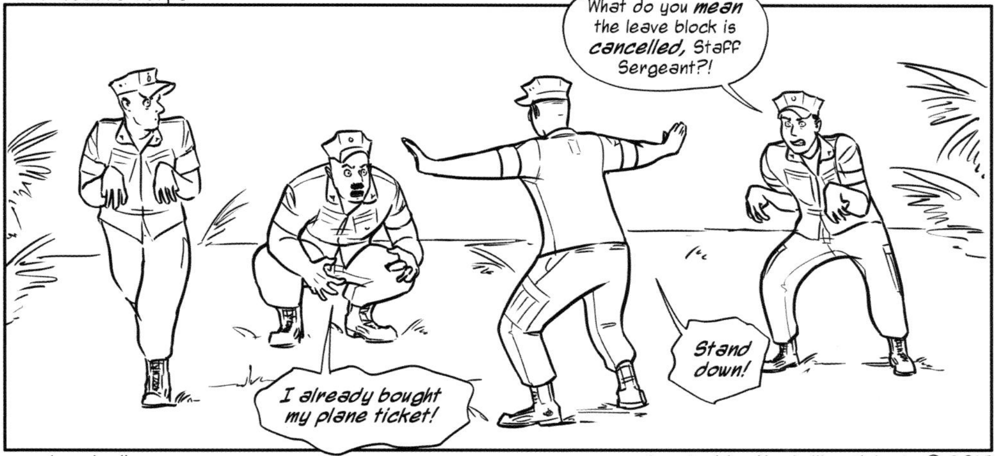
What do you ***mean*** the leave block is ***cancelled,*** Staff Sergeant?!
Stand down!
I already bought my plane ticket!

www.terminallance.com Created by Maximilian Uriarte © 2015

"Vote for Abe"

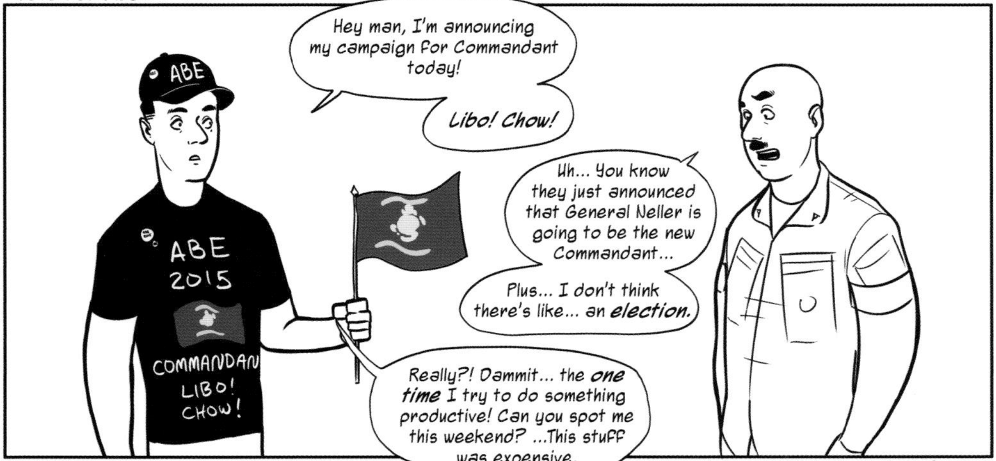
ABE
ABE 2015
COMMANDAN
LIBO! CHOW!
Hey man, I'm announcing my campaign for Commandant today!
Libo! Chow!
Uh... You know they just announced that General Neller is going to be the new Commandant...
Plus... I don't think there's like... an ***election.***
Really?! Dammit... the ***one time*** I try to do something productive! Can you spot me this weekend? ...This stuff was expensive.

www.terminallance.com Created by Maximilian Uriarte © 2015

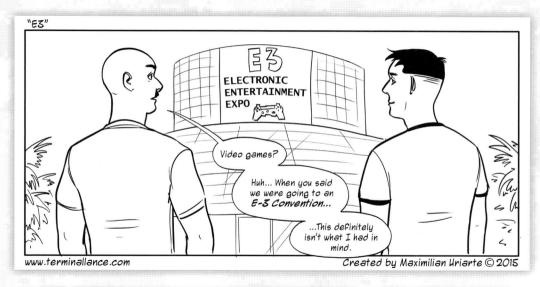

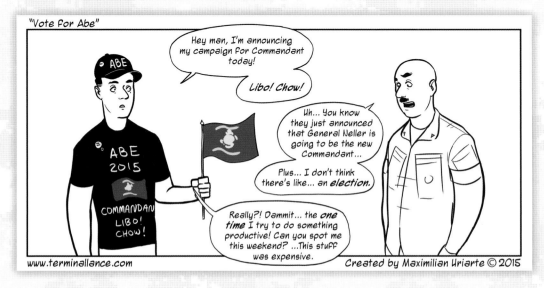

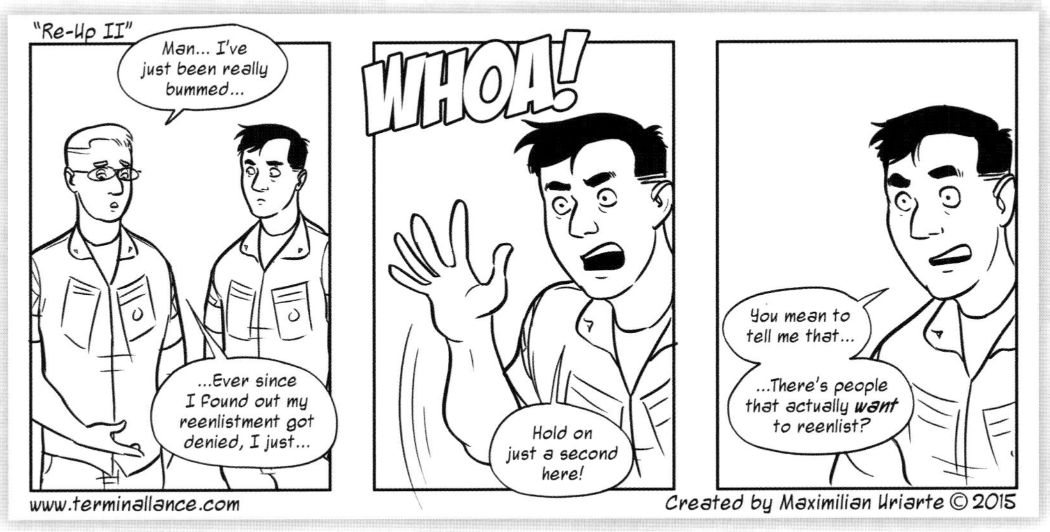
"Re-Up II"
Man... I've just been really bummed...
...Ever since I found out my reenlistment got denied, I just...
WHOA!
Hold on just a second here!
You mean to tell me that...
...There's people that actually **want** to reenlist?
www.terminallance.com
Created by Maximilian Uriarte © 2015

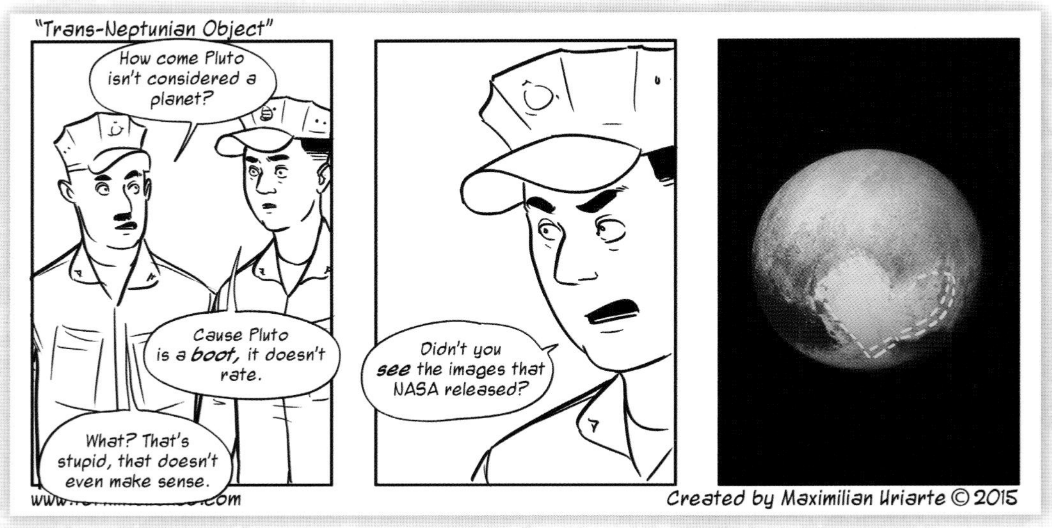
"Trans-Neptunian Object"
How come Pluto isn't considered a planet?
Cause Pluto is a **boot,** it doesn't rate.
What? That's stupid, that doesn't even make sense.
Didn't you **see** the images that NASA released?
Created by Maximilian Uriarte © 2015

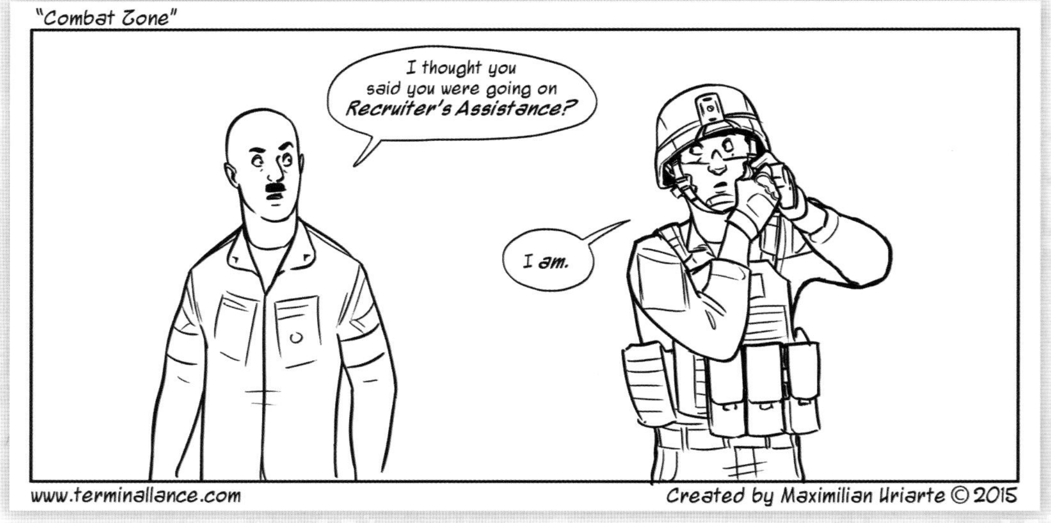
"Combat Zone"
I thought you said you were going on **Recruiter's Assistance?**
I **am.**
www.terminallance.com
Created by Maximilian Uriarte © 2015

"Samesies"

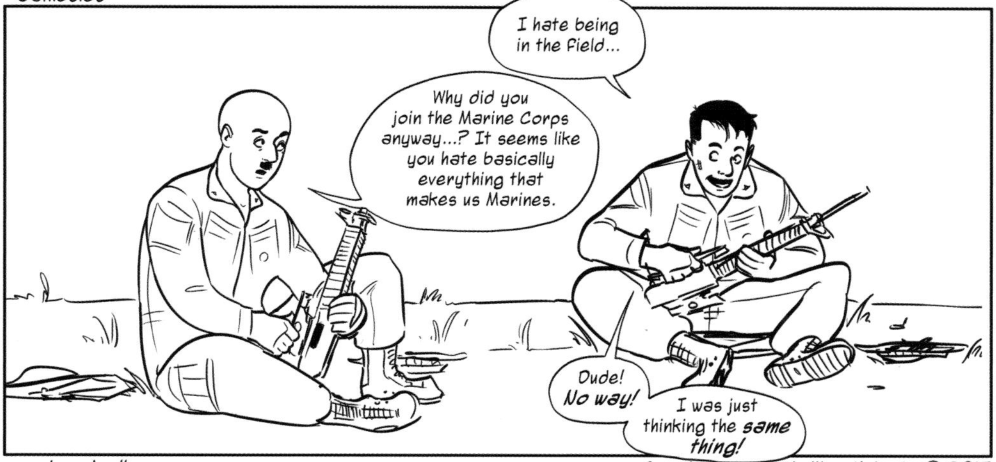
I hate being in the field...
Why did you join the Marine Corps anyway...? It seems like you hate basically everything that makes us Marines.
Dude! No way!
I was just thinking the same thing!

www.terminallance.com Created by Maximilian Uriarte © 2015

"Hydrate or Die"

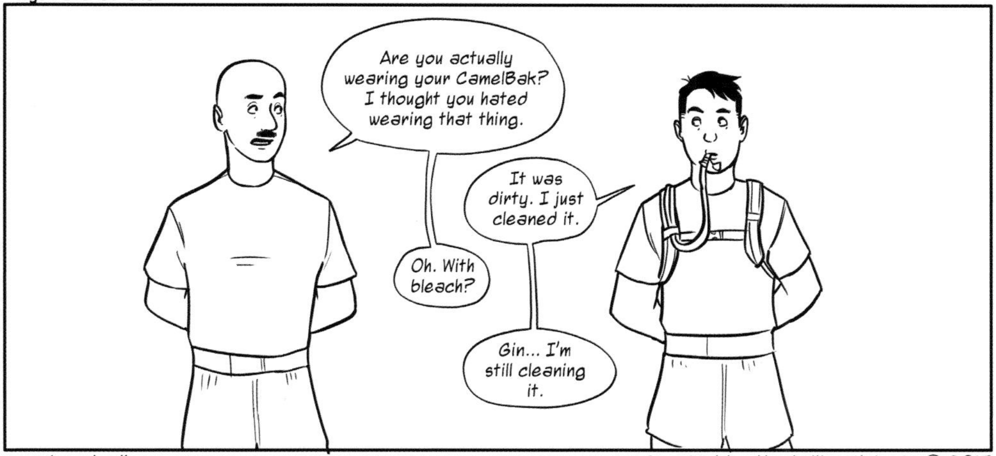
Are you actually wearing your CamelBak? I thought you hated wearing that thing.
It was dirty. I just cleaned it.
Oh. With bleach?
Gin... I'm still cleaning it.

www.terminallance.com Created by Maximilian Uriarte © 2015

"Meat Lovers"

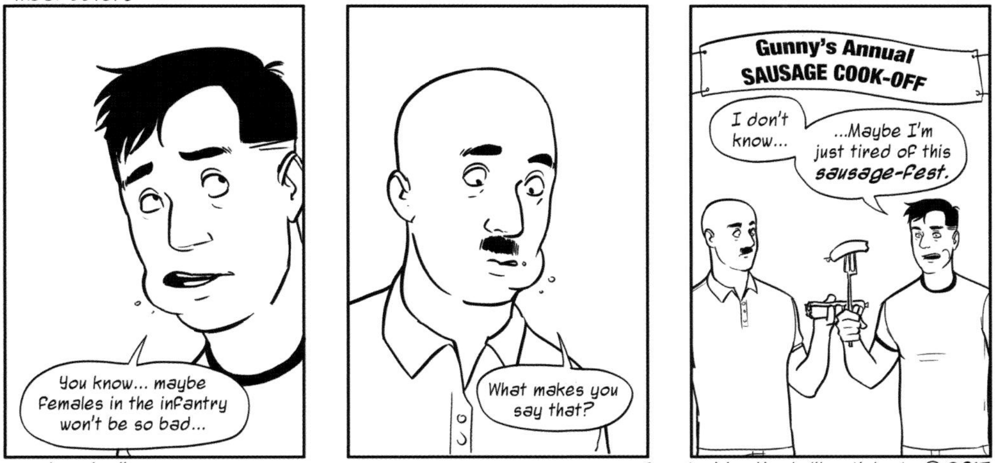
You know... maybe females in the infantry won't be so bad...
What makes you say that?
Gunny's Annual SAUSAGE COOK-OFF
I don't know...
...Maybe I'm just tired of this sausage-fest.

www.terminallance.com Created by Maximilian Uriarte © 2015

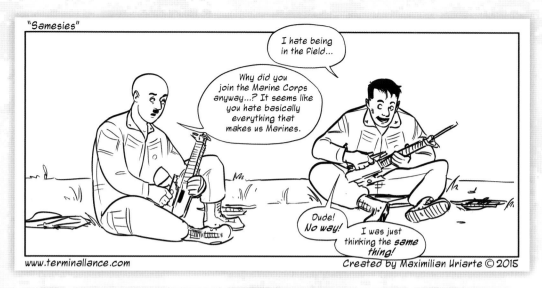

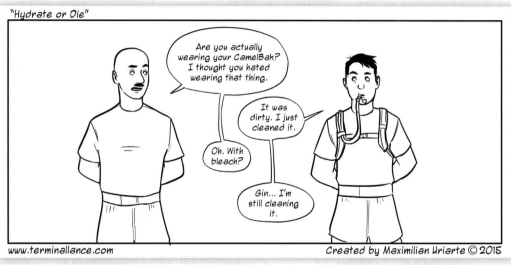

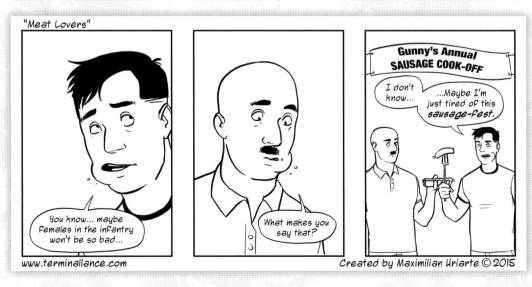

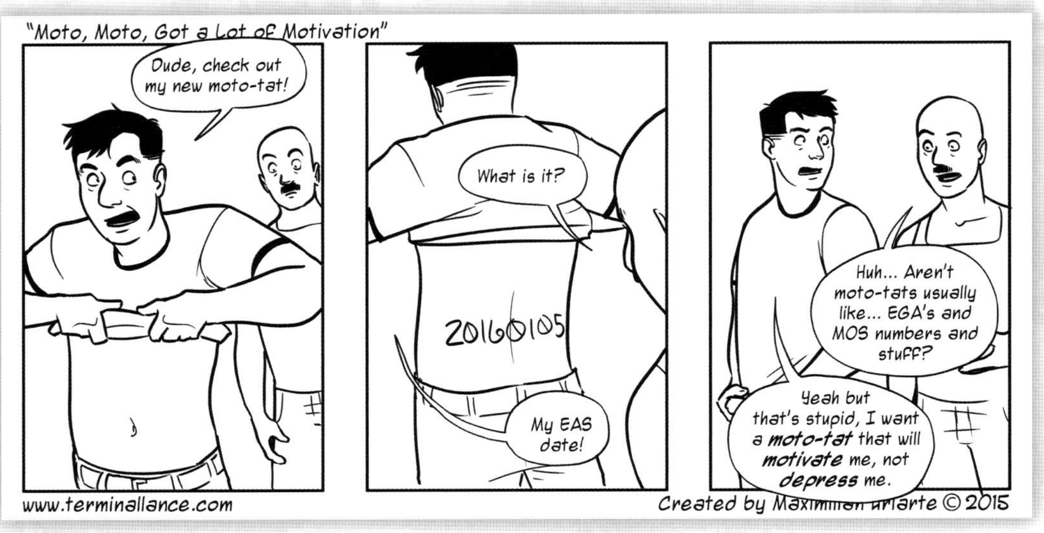
"Moto, Moto, Got a Lot of Motivation"
Dude, check out my new moto-tat!
What is it?
20160105
My EAS date!
Huh... Aren't moto-tats usually like... EGA's and MOS numbers and stuff?
Yeah but that's stupid, I want a *moto-tat* that will *motivate* me, not *depress* me.
www.terminallance.com
Created by Maximilian Uriarte © 2015

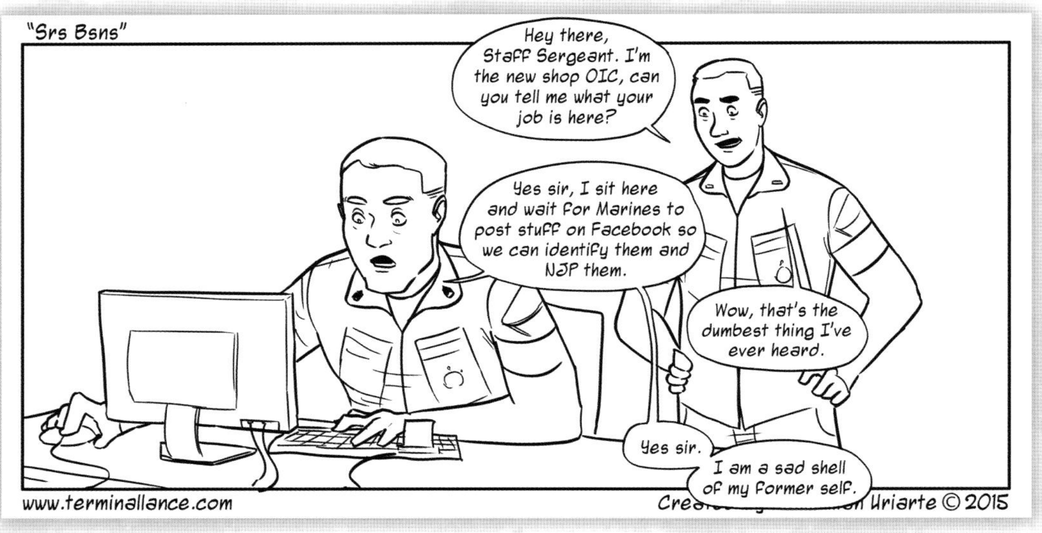
"Srs Bsns"
Hey there, Staff Sergeant. I'm the new shop OIC, can you tell me what your job is here?
Yes sir, I sit here and wait for Marines to post stuff on Facebook so we can identify them and NJP them.
Wow, that's the dumbest thing I've ever heard.
Yes sir.
I am a sad shell of my former self.
www.terminallance.com

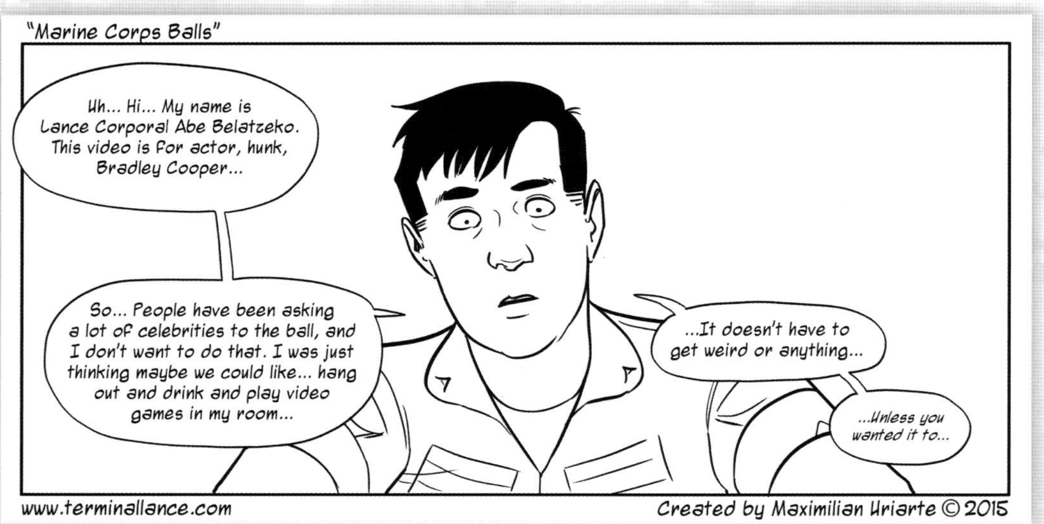
"Marine Corps Balls"
Uh... Hi... My name is Lance Corporal Abe Belatzeko. This video is for actor, hunk, Bradley Cooper...
So... People have been asking a lot of celebrities to the ball, and I don't want to do that. I was just thinking maybe we could like... hang out and drink and play video games in my room...
...It doesn't have to get weird or anything...
...Unless you wanted it to...
www.terminallance.com
Created by Maximilian Uriarte © 2015

"Seniority"

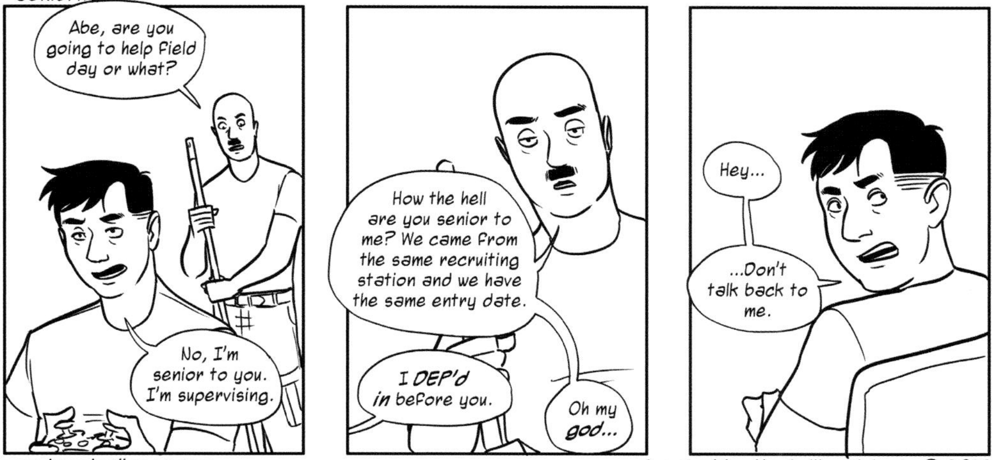

Abe, are you going to help field day or what?
No, I'm senior to you. I'm supervising.
How the hell are you senior to me? We came from the same recruiting station and we have the same entry date.
I DEP'd in before you.
Oh my god...
Hey...
...Don't talk back to me.

www.terminallance.com Created by Maximilian Uriarte © 2015

"Presidential Primary Colors"

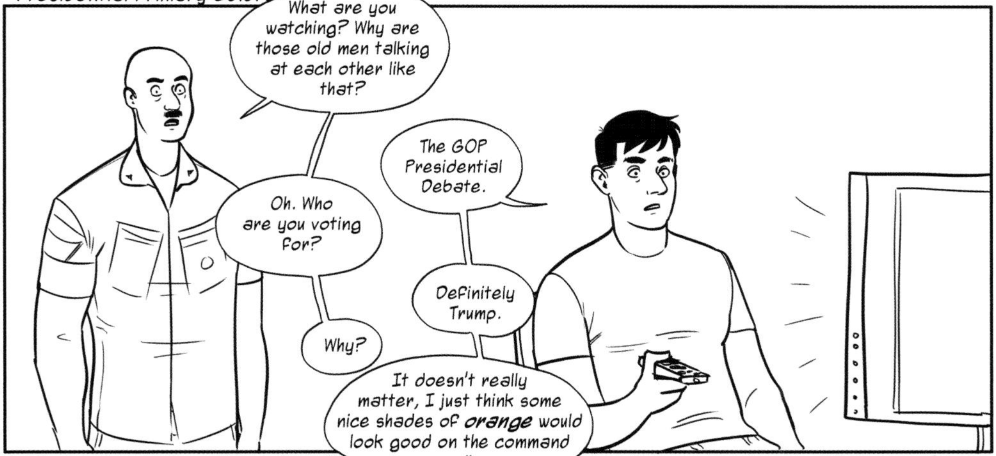

What are you watching? Why are those old men talking at each other like that?
The GOP Presidential Debate.
Oh. Who are you voting for?
Definitely Trump.
Why?
It doesn't really matter, I just think some nice shades of orange would look good on the command wall.

www.terminallance.com Created by Maximilian Uriarte © 2015

"Did Anyone Actually Read It? II"

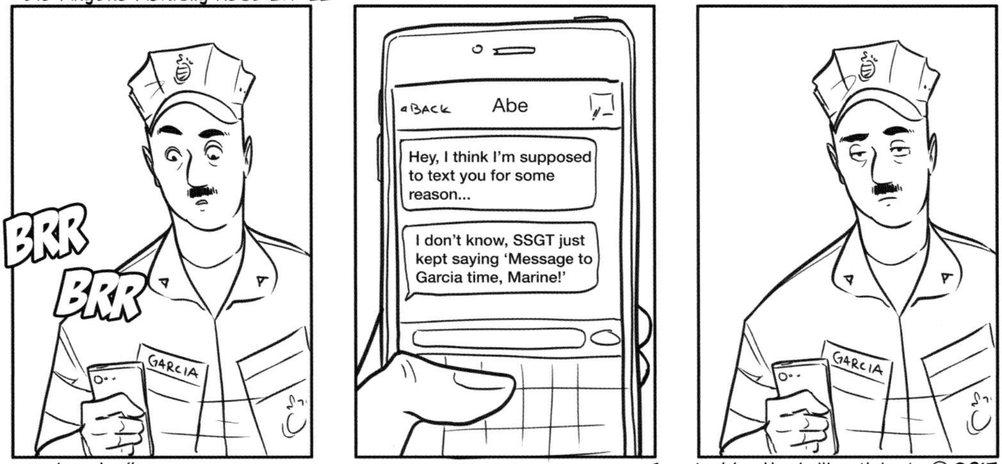

BRR
BRR
GARCIA
BACK
Abe
Hey, I think I'm supposed to text you for some reason...
I don't know, SSGT just kept saying 'Message to Garcia time, Marine!'
GARCIA

www.terminallance.com Created by Maximilian Uriarte © 2015

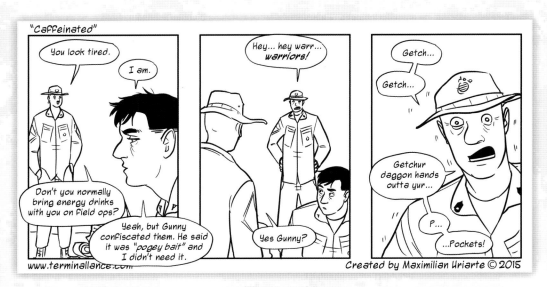

"Caffeinated"

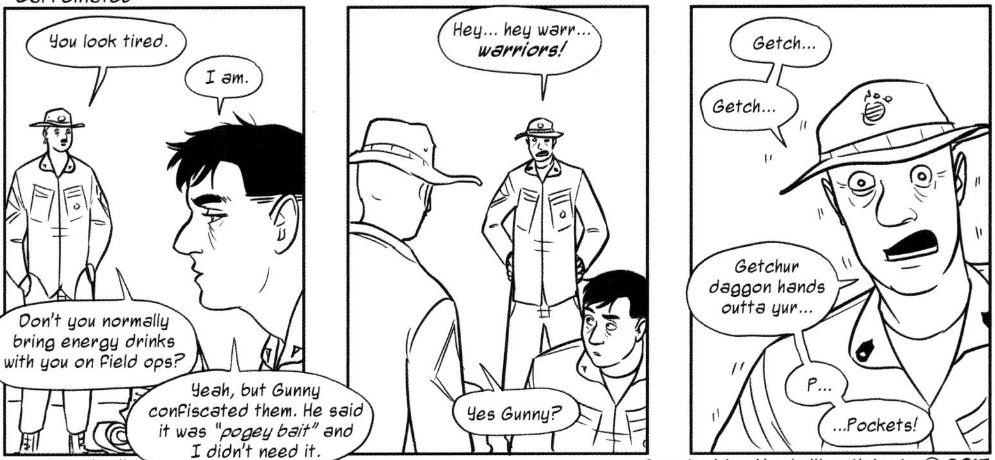
You look tired.
I am.
Don't you normally bring energy drinks with you on field ops?
Yeah, but Gunny confiscated them. He said it was "pogey bait" and I didn't need it.
Hey... hey warr... **warriors!**
Yes Gunny?
Getch...
Getch...
Getchur daggon hands outta yur...
P...
...Pockets!

www.terminallance.com

Created by Maximilian Uriarte © 2015

"McDouble Rat"

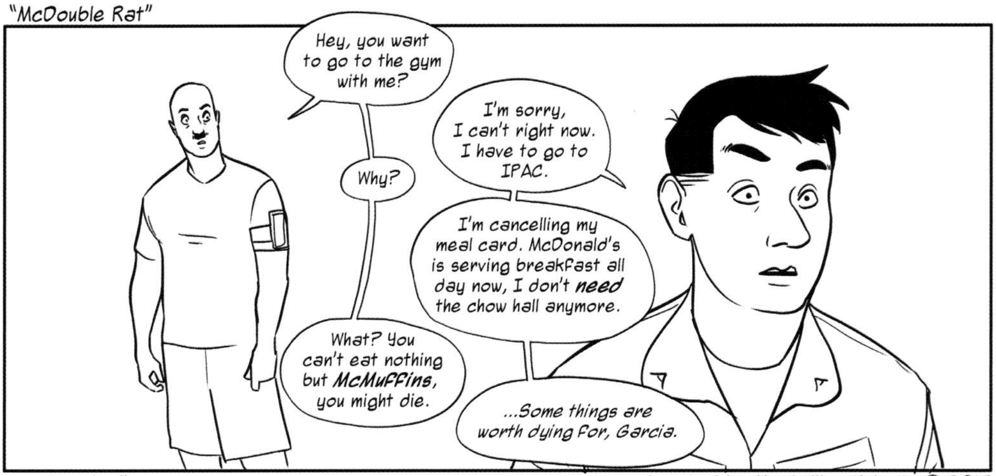
Hey, you want to go to the gym with me?
I'm sorry, I can't right now. I have to go to IPAC.
Why?
I'm cancelling my meal card. McDonald's is serving breakfast all day now, I don't *need* the chow hall anymore.
What? You can't eat nothing but *McMuffins*, you might die.
...Some things are worth dying for, Garcia.

www.terminallance.com

Created by Maximilian Uriarte © 2015

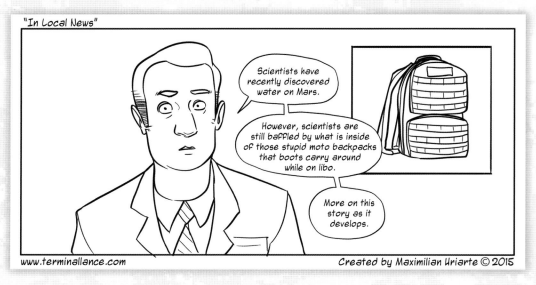

"In Local News"

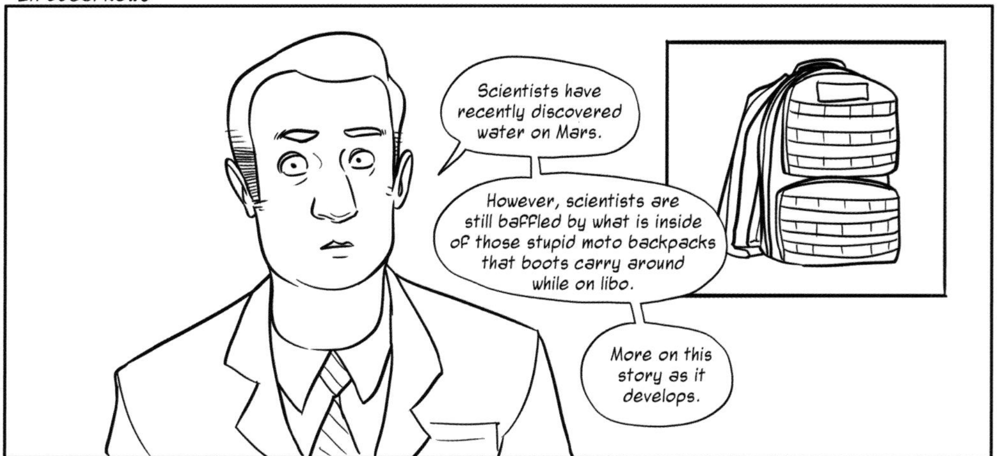
Scientists have recently discovered water on Mars.
However, scientists are still baffled by what is inside of those stupid moto backpacks that boots carry around while on libo.
More on this story as it develops.

www.terminallance.com

Created by Maximilian Uriarte © 2015

"Grunt Lyfe"

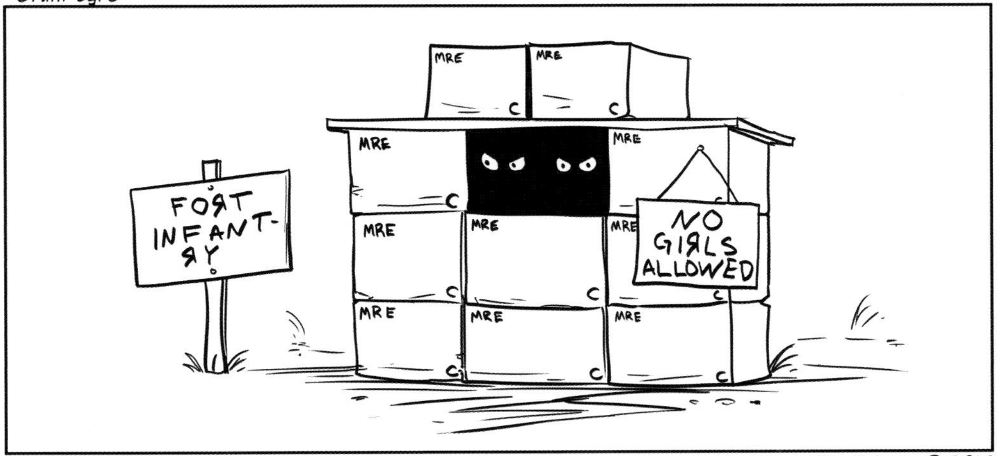
MRE
MRE
MRE
MRE
FORT INFANT-RY
MRE
MRE
MRE
NO GIRLS ALLOWED
MRE
MRE
MRE

www.terminallance.com Created by Maximilian Uriarte © 2015

"Happy 240th Birthday!"

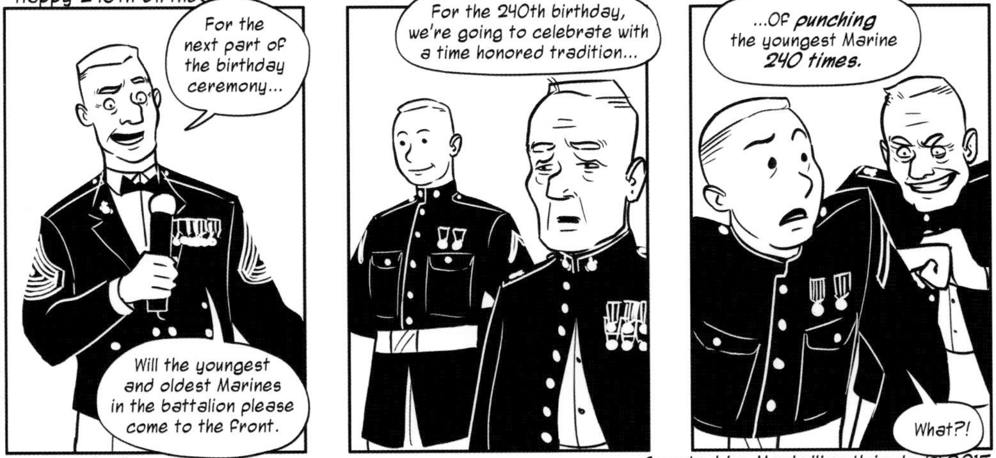
For the next part of the birthday ceremony...
Will the youngest and oldest Marines in the battalion please come to the front.
For the 240th birthday, we're going to celebrate with a time honored tradition...
...of *punching* the youngest Marine **240 times.**
What?!

www.terminallance.com Created by Maximilian Uriarte © 2015

"Very Thankful"

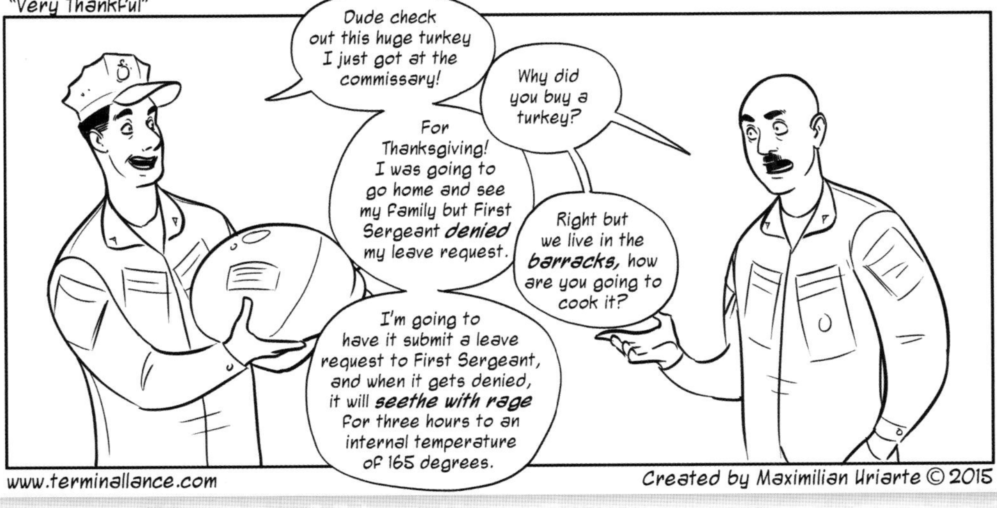
Dude check out this huge turkey I just got at the commissary!
Why did you buy a turkey?
For Thanksgiving! I was going to go home and see my family but First Sergeant *denied* my leave request.
Right but we live in the *barracks,* how are you going to cook it?
I'm going to have it submit a leave request to First Sergeant, and when it gets denied, it will *seethe with rage* for three hours to an internal temperature of 165 degrees.

www.terminallance.com Created by Maximilian Uriarte © 2015

"Small Victories"

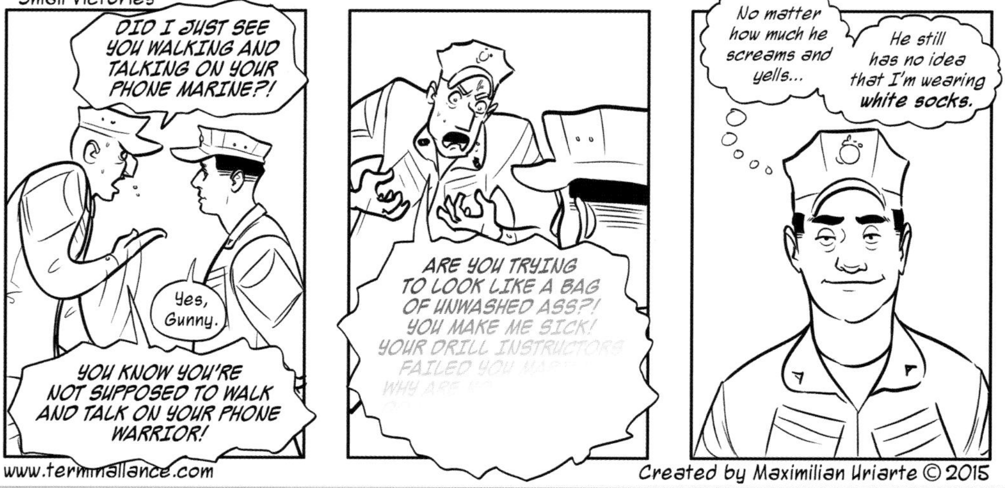
DID I JUST SEE YOU WALKING AND TALKING ON YOUR PHONE MARINE?!
Yes, Gunny.
YOU KNOW YOU'RE NOT SUPPOSED TO WALK AND TALK ON YOUR PHONE WARRIOR!
ARE YOU TRYING TO LOOK LIKE A BAG OF UNWASHED ASS?! YOU MAKE ME SICK! YOUR DRILL INSTRUCTORS
No matter how much he screams and yells...
He still has no idea that I'm wearing **white socks.**
www.terminallance.com
Created by Maximilian Uriarte © 2015

"Checking It Twice"

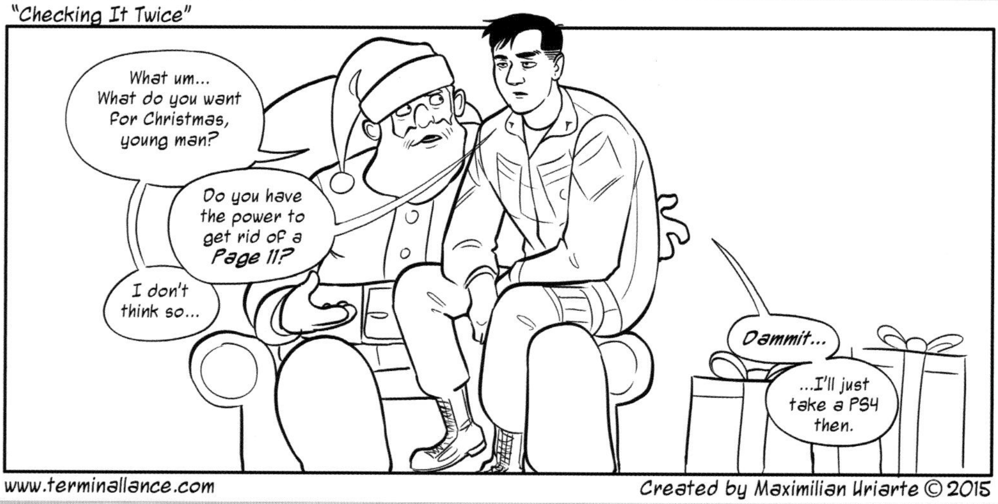
What um... What do you want for Christmas, young man?
Do you have the power to get rid of a *Page 11?*
I don't think so...
Dammit...
...I'll just take a PS4 then.
www.terminallance.com
Created by Maximilian Uriarte © 2015

"Aloha Tobacco"

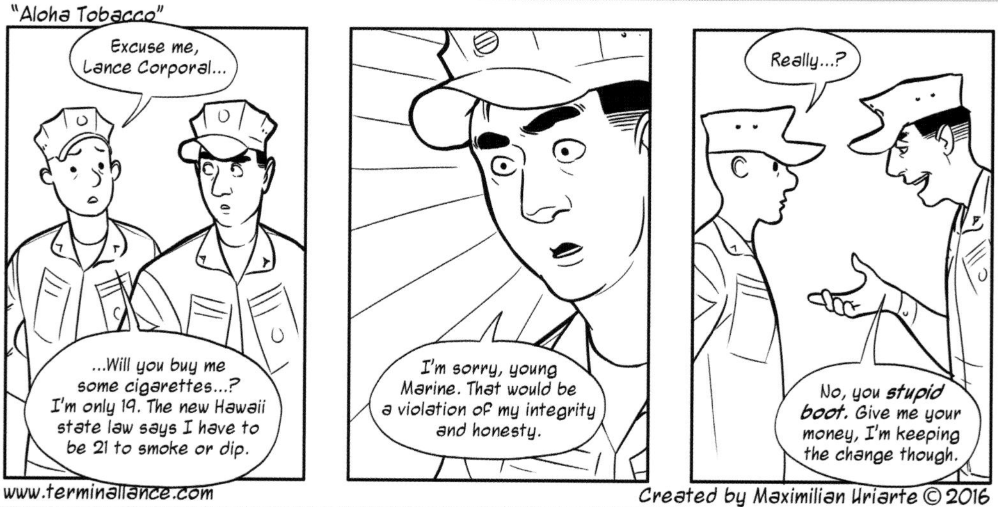
Excuse me, Lance Corporal...
...Will you buy me some cigarettes...? I'm only 19. The new Hawaii state law says I have to be 21 to smoke or dip.
I'm sorry, young Marine. That would be a violation of my integrity and honesty.
Really...?
No, you *stupid boot.* Give me your money, I'm keeping the change though.
www.terminallance.com
Created by Maximilian Uriarte © 2016

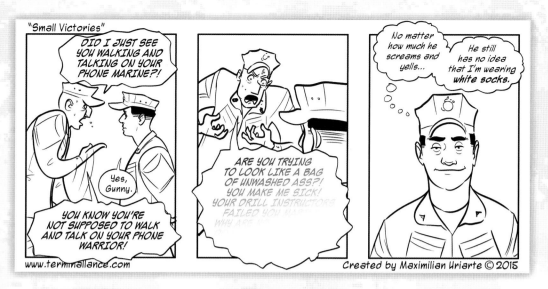

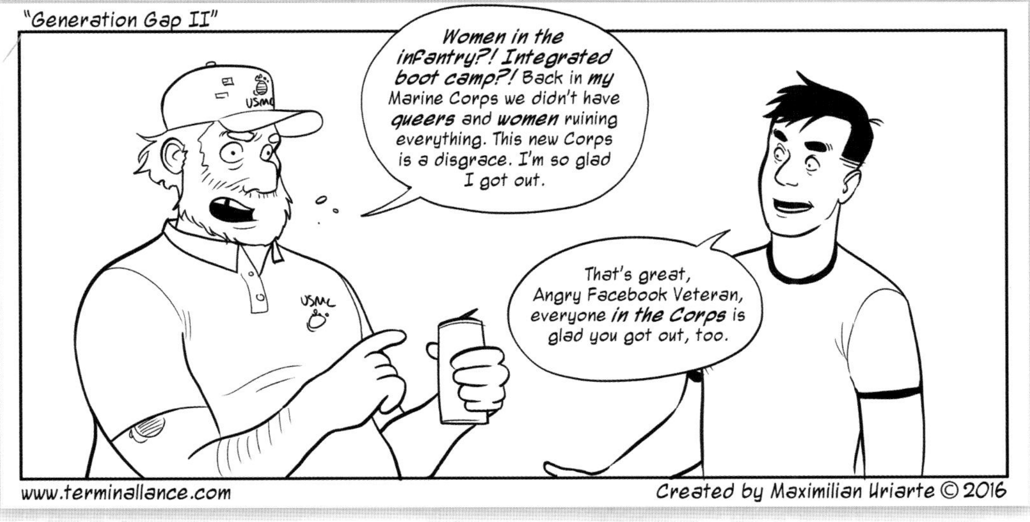
"Generation Gap II"
Women in the infantry?! Integrated boot camp?! Back in my Marine Corps we didn't have queers and women ruining everything. This new Corps is a disgrace. I'm so glad I got out.
That's great, Angry Facebook Veteran, everyone in the Corps is glad you got out, too.
www.terminallance.com
Created by Maximilian Uriarte © 2016

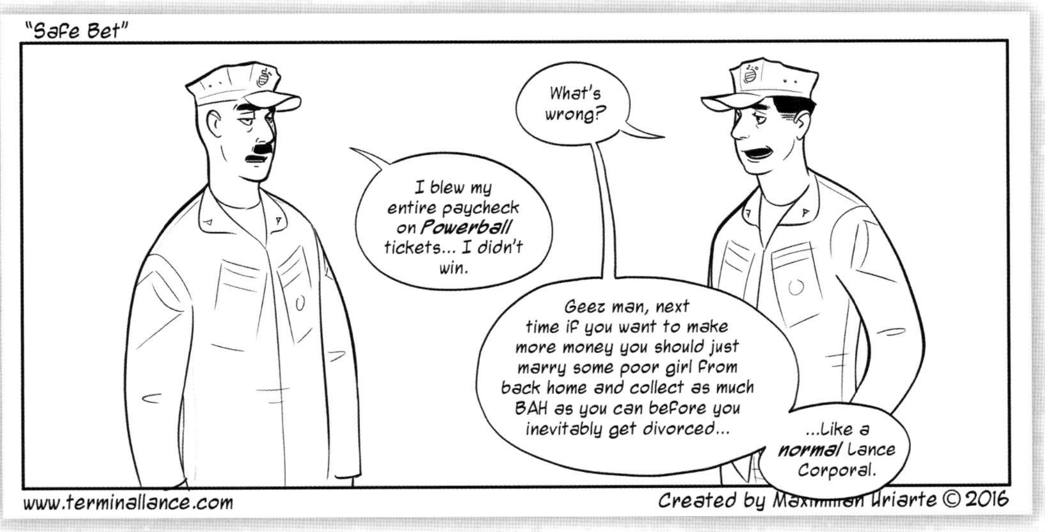
"Safe Bet"
What's wrong?
I blew my entire paycheck on Powerball tickets... I didn't win.
Geez man, next time if you want to make more money you should just marry some poor girl from back home and collect as much BAH as you can before you inevitably get divorced...
...Like a normal Lance Corporal.
www.terminallance.com
Created by Maximilian Uriarte © 2016

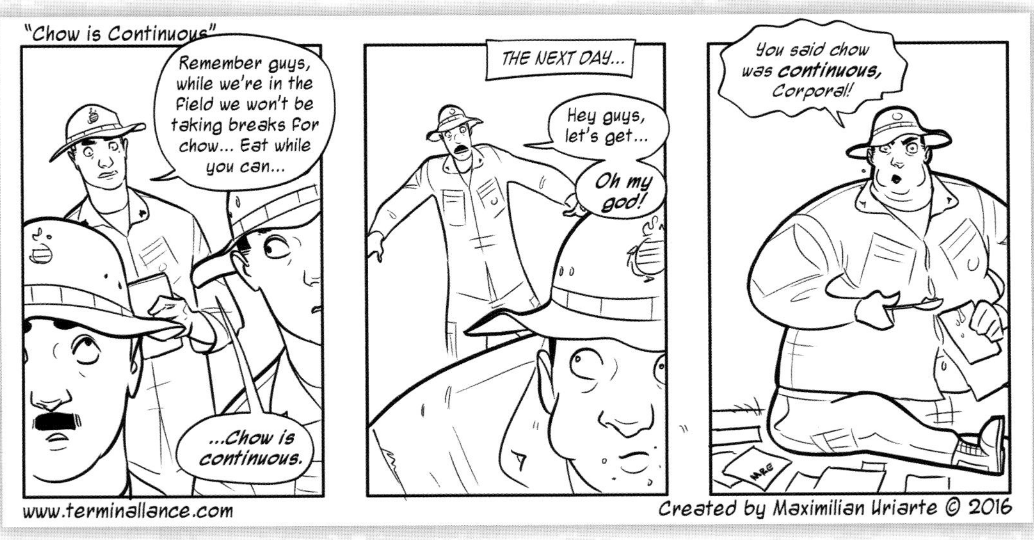
"Chow is Continuous"
Remember guys, while we're in the field we won't be taking breaks for chow... Eat while you can...
...Chow is continuous.
THE NEXT DAY...
Hey guys, let's get...
Oh my god!
You said chow was continuous, Corporal!
www.terminallance.com
Created by Maximilian Uriarte © 2016

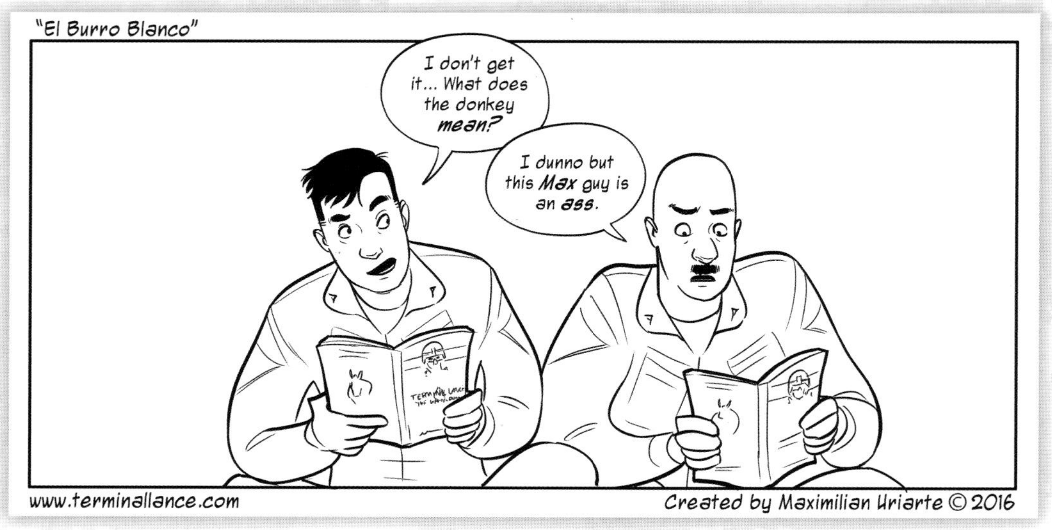
"El Burro Blanco"
I don't get it... What does the donkey *mean?*
I dunno but this *Max* guy is an *ass*.
www.terminallance.com
Created by Maximilian Uriarte © 2016

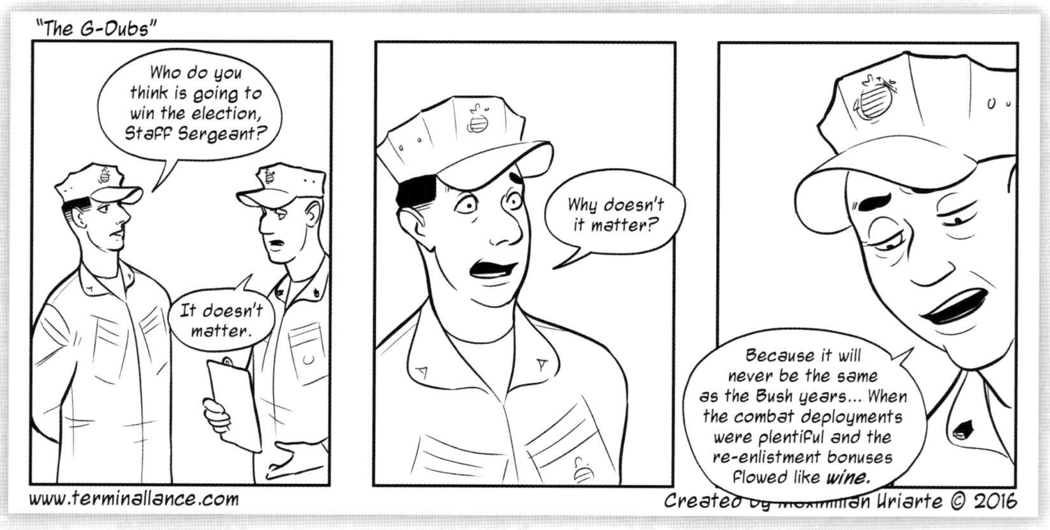
"The G-Dubs"
Who do you think is going to win the election, Staff Sergeant?
It doesn't matter.
Why doesn't it matter?
Because it will never be the same as the Bush years... When the combat deployments were plentiful and the re-enlistment bonuses flowed like *wine.*
www.terminallance.com
Created by Maximilian Uriarte © 2016

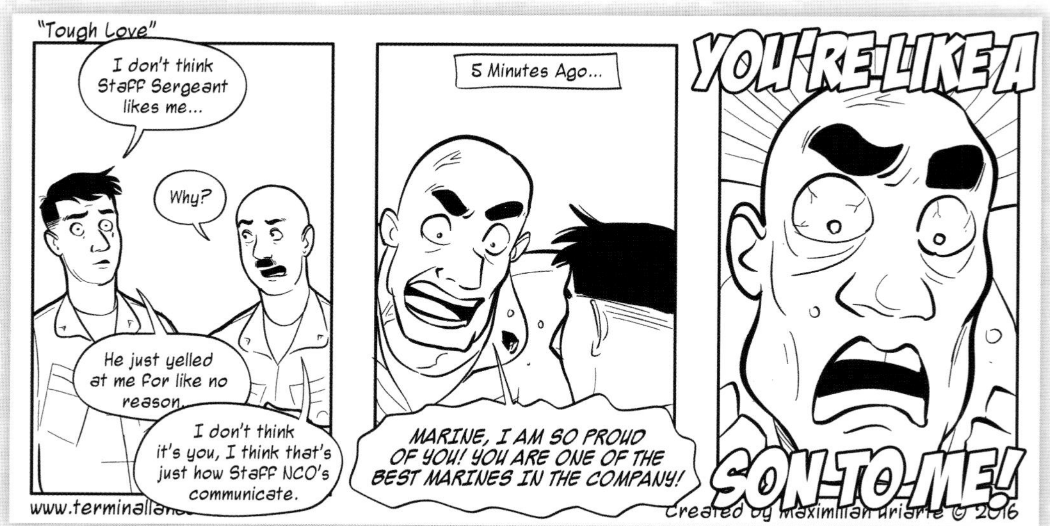
"Tough Love"
I don't think Staff Sergeant likes me...
Why?
He just yelled at me for like no reason.
I don't think it's you, I think that's just how Staff NCO's communicate.
5 Minutes Ago...
MARINE, I AM SO PROUD OF YOU! YOU ARE ONE OF THE BEST MARINES IN THE COMPANY!
YOU'RE LIKE A
SON TO ME!
Created by Maximilian Uriarte © 2016

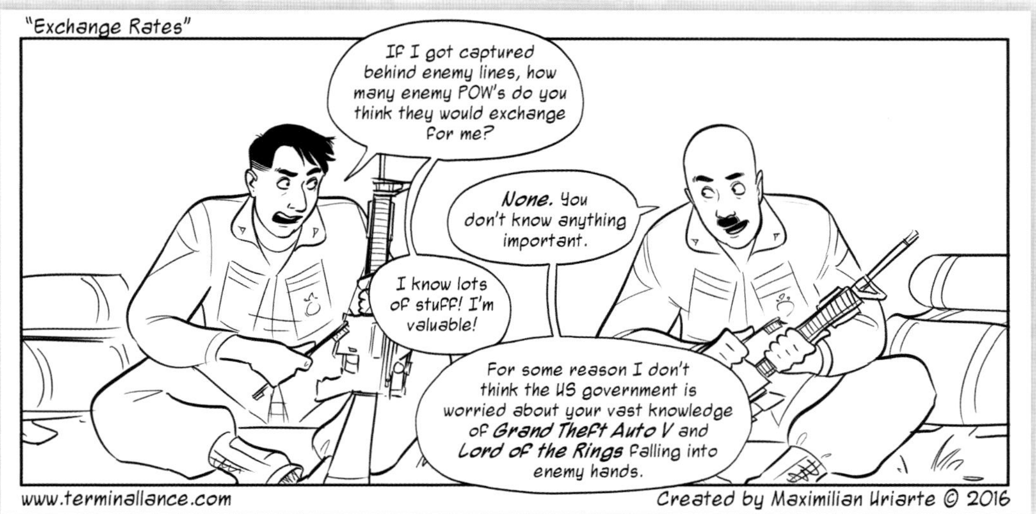
"Exchange Rates"
If I got captured behind enemy lines, how many enemy POW's do you think they would exchange for me?
None. You don't know anything important.
I know lots of stuff! I'm valuable!
For some reason I don't think the US government is worried about your vast knowledge of Grand Theft Auto V and Lord of the Rings falling into enemy hands.
www.terminallance.com
Created by Maximilian Uriarte © 2016

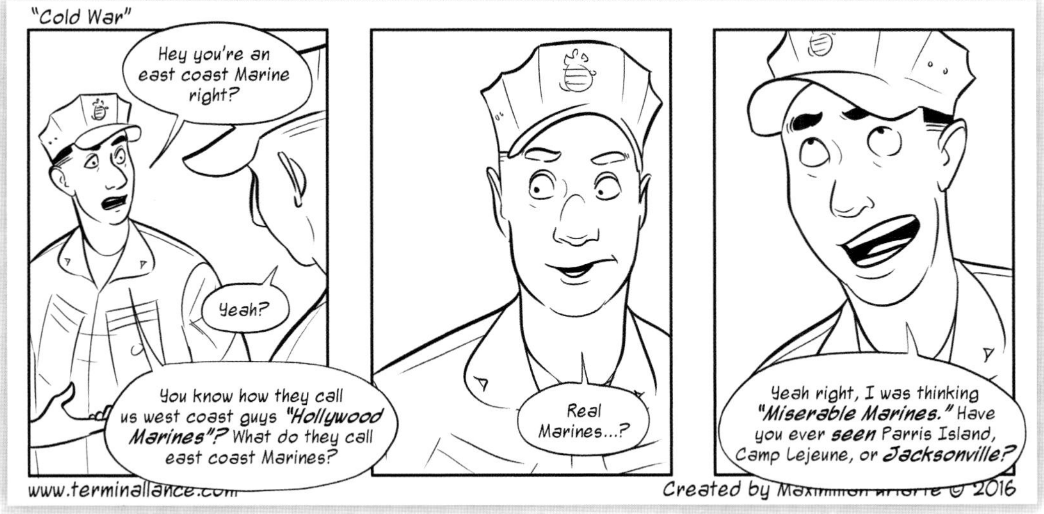
"Cold War"
Hey you're an east coast Marine right?
Yeah?
You know how they call us west coast guys "Hollywood Marines"? What do they call east coast Marines?
Real Marines...?
Yeah right, I was thinking "Miserable Marines." Have you ever seen Parris Island, Camp Lejeune, or Jacksonville?
www.terminallance.com
Created by Maximilian Uriarte © 2016

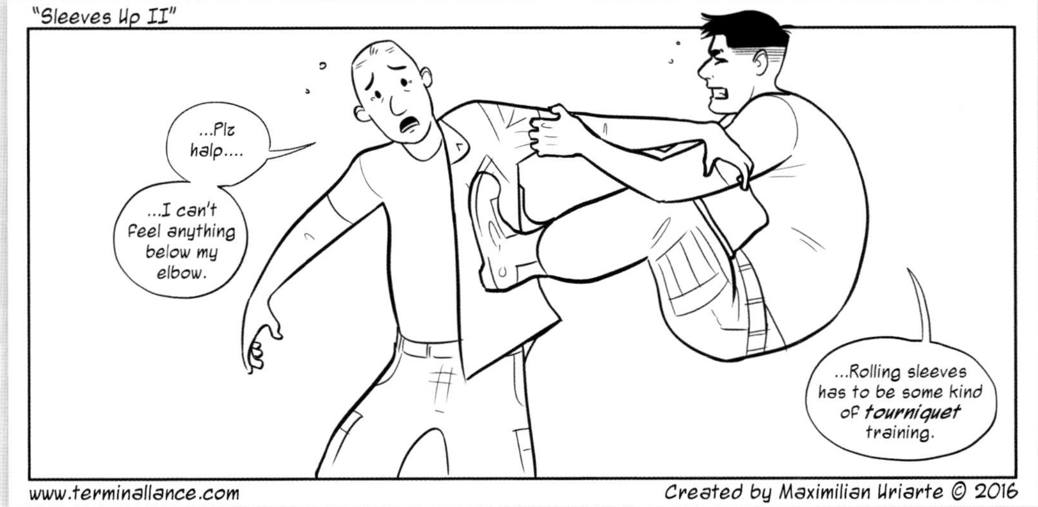
"Sleeves Up II"
...Plz halp....
...I can't feel anything below my elbow.
...Rolling sleeves has to be some kind of tourniquet training.
www.terminallance.com
Created by Maximilian Uriarte © 2016

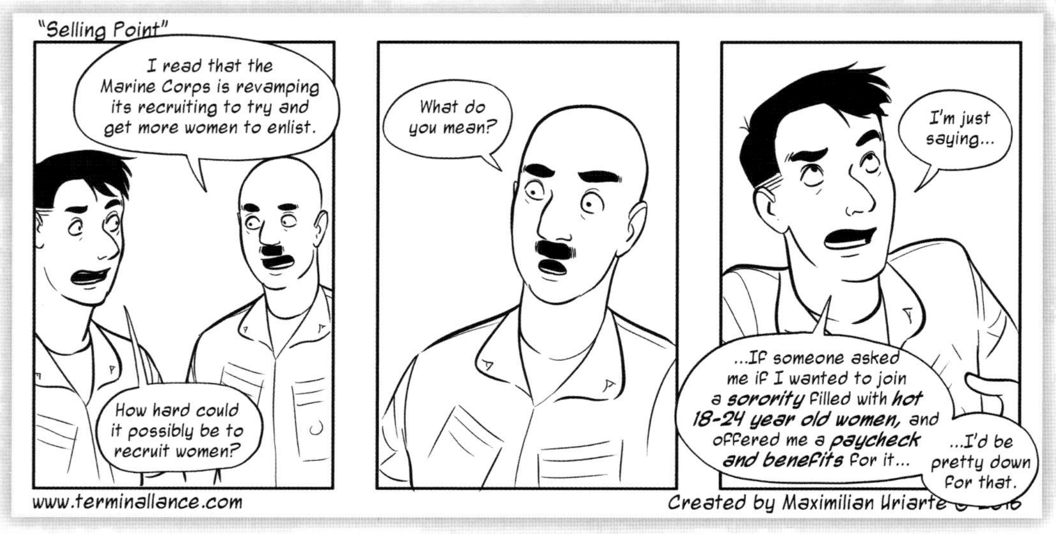
"Selling Point"
I read that the Marine Corps is revamping its recruiting to try and get more women to enlist.
How hard could it possibly be to recruit women?
What do you mean?
I'm just saying...
...If someone asked me if I wanted to join a *sorority* filled with *hot 18-24 year old women,* and offered me a *paycheck and benefits* for it...
...I'd be pretty down for that.
www.terminallance.com
Created by Maximilian Uriarte © 2016

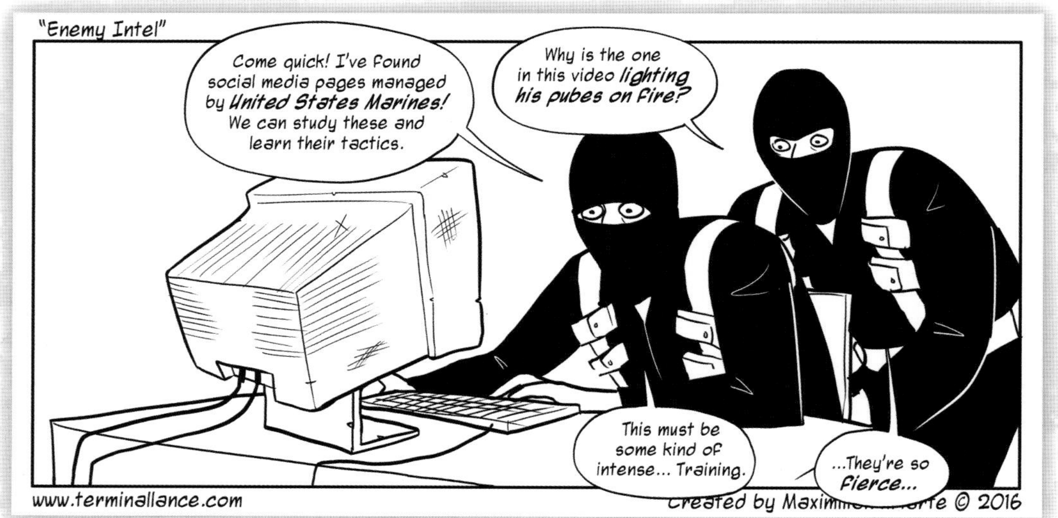
"Enemy Intel"
Come quick! I've found social media pages managed by *United States Marines!* We can study these and learn their tactics.
Why is the one in this video *lighting his pubes on fire?*
This must be some kind of intense... Training.
...They're so *fierce...*
www.terminallance.com
Created by Maxim

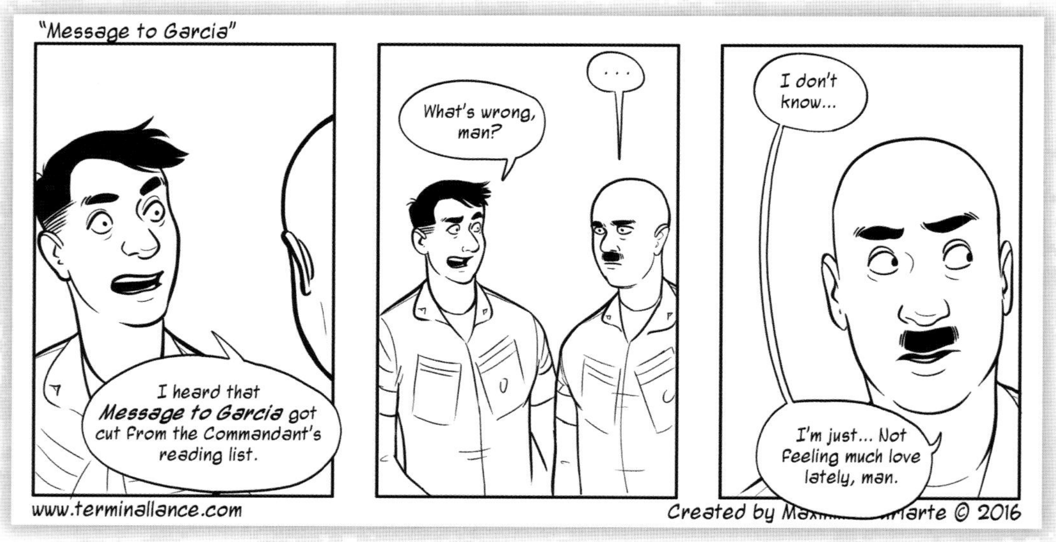
"Message to Garcia"
I heard that *Message to Garcia* got cut from the Commandant's reading list.
What's wrong, man?
. . .
I don't know...
I'm just... Not feeling much love lately, man.
www.terminallance.com
Created by Maxim

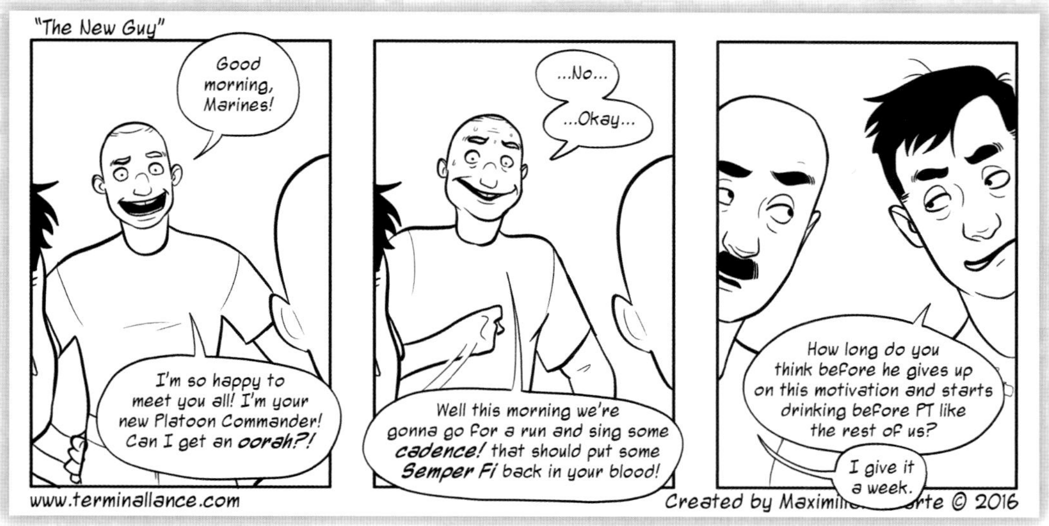
"The New Guy"
Good morning, Marines!
I'm so happy to meet you all! I'm your new Platoon Commander! Can I get an **oorah?!**
...No...
...Okay...
Well this morning we're gonna go for a run and sing some ***cadence!*** that should put some ***Semper Fi*** back in your blood!
How long do you think before he gives up on this motivation and starts drinking before PT like the rest of us?
I give it a week.
www.terminallance.com
Created by Maximilian Uriarte © 2016

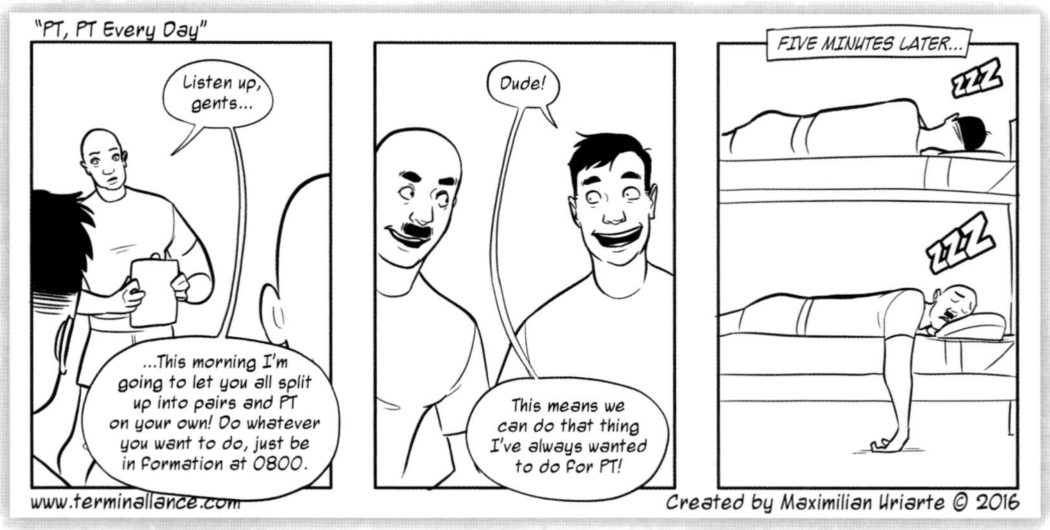
"PT, PT Every Day"
Listen up, gents...
...This morning I'm going to let you all split up into pairs and PT on your own! Do whatever you want to do, just be in formation at 0800.
Dude!
This means we can do that thing I've always wanted to do for PT!
FIVE MINUTES LATER...
ZZZ
ZZZ
www.terminallance.com
Created by Maximilian Uriarte © 2016

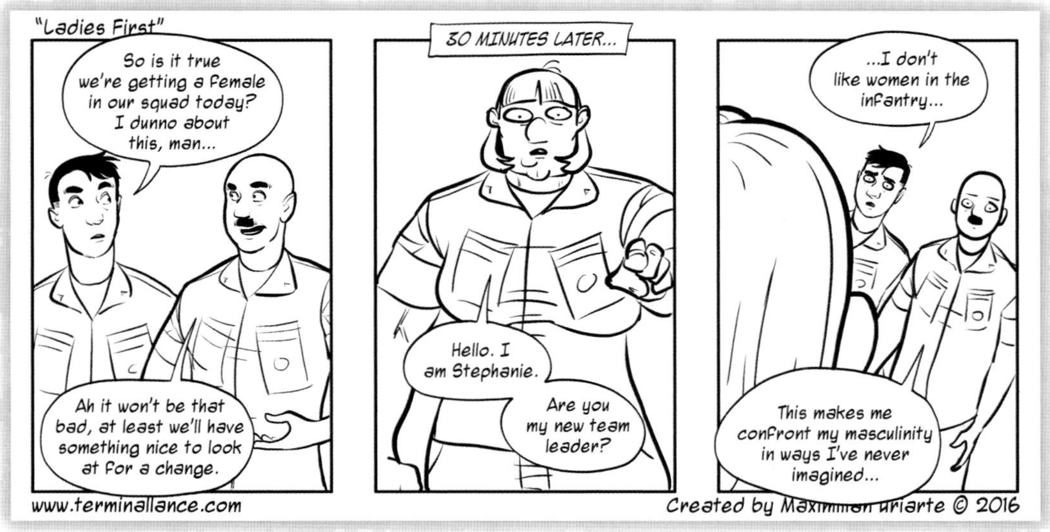
"Ladies First"
So is it true we're getting a female in our squad today? I dunno about this, man...
Ah it won't be that bad, at least we'll have something nice to look at for a change.
30 MINUTES LATER...
Hello. I am Stephanie.
Are you my new team leader?
...I don't like women in the infantry...
This makes me confront my masculinity in ways I've never imagined...
www.terminallance.com
Created by Maximilian Uriarte © 2016

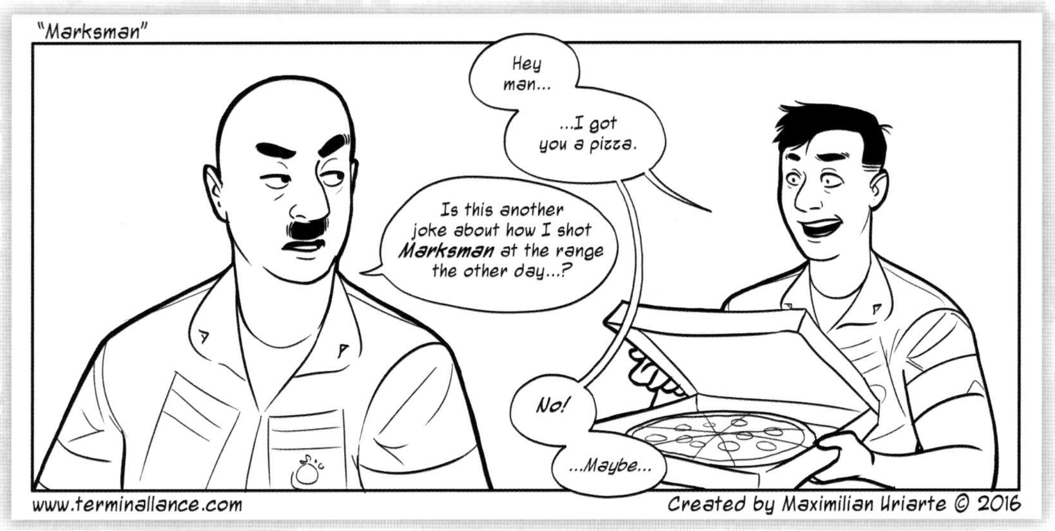
"Marksman"
Hey man...
...I got you a pizza.
Is this another joke about how I shot Marksman at the range the other day...?
No!
...Maybe...
www.terminallance.com
Created by Maximilian Uriarte © 2016

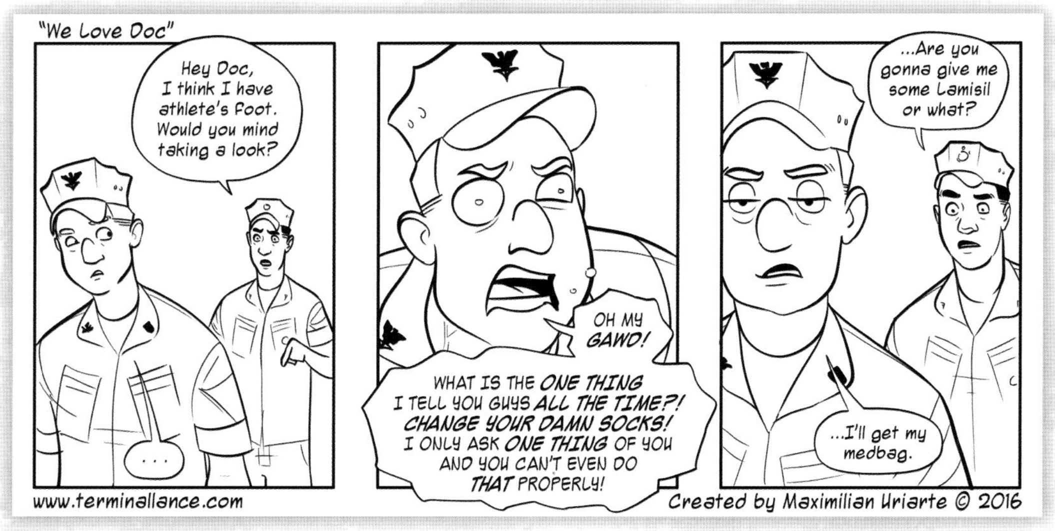
"We Love Doc"
Hey Doc, I think I have athlete's foot. Would you mind taking a look?
...
OH MY GAWD!
WHAT IS THE ONE THING I TELL YOU GUYS ALL THE TIME?! CHANGE YOUR DAMN SOCKS! I ONLY ASK ONE THING OF YOU AND YOU CAN'T EVEN DO THAT PROPERLY!
...Are you gonna give me some Lamisil or what?
...I'll get my medbag.
www.terminallance.com
Created by Maximilian Uriarte © 2016

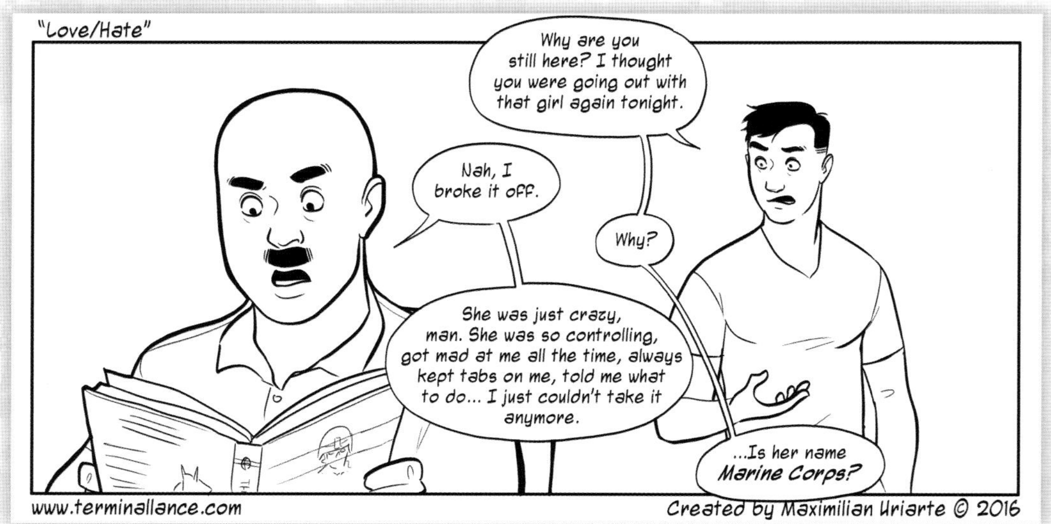
"Love/Hate"
Why are you still here? I thought you were going out with that girl again tonight.
Nah, I broke it off.
Why?
She was just crazy, man. She was so controlling, got mad at me all the time, always kept tabs on me, told me what to do... I just couldn't take it anymore.
...Is her name Marine Corps?
www.terminallance.com
Created by Maximilian Uriarte © 2016

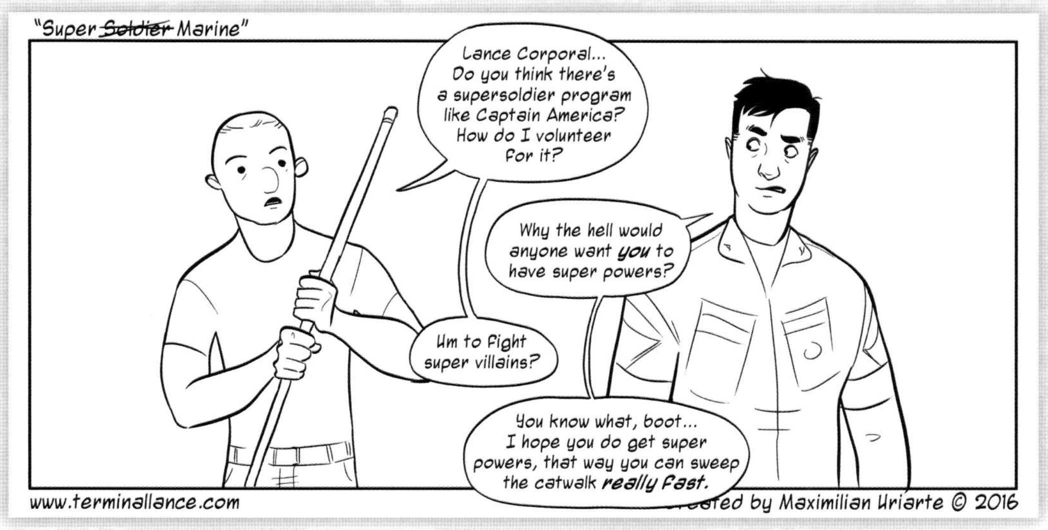
"Super ~~Soldier~~ Marine"
Lance Corporal... Do you think there's a supersoldier program like Captain America? How do I volunteer for it?
Why the hell would anyone want *you* to have super powers?
Um to fight super villains?
You know what, boot... I hope you do get super powers, that way you can sweep the catwalk *really fast.*
www.terminallance.com
Created by Maximilian Uriarte © 2016

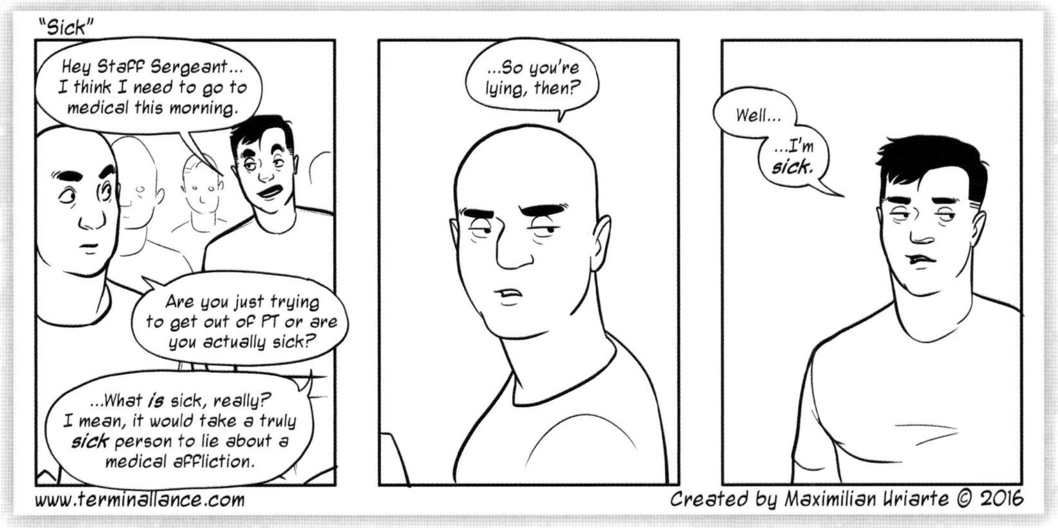
"Sick"
Hey Staff Sergeant... I think I need to go to medical this morning.
Are you just trying to get out of PT or are you actually sick?
...What *is* sick, really? I mean, it would take a truly *sick* person to lie about a medical affliction.
...So you're lying, then?
Well...
...I'm *sick.*
www.terminallance.com
Created by Maximilian Uriarte © 2016

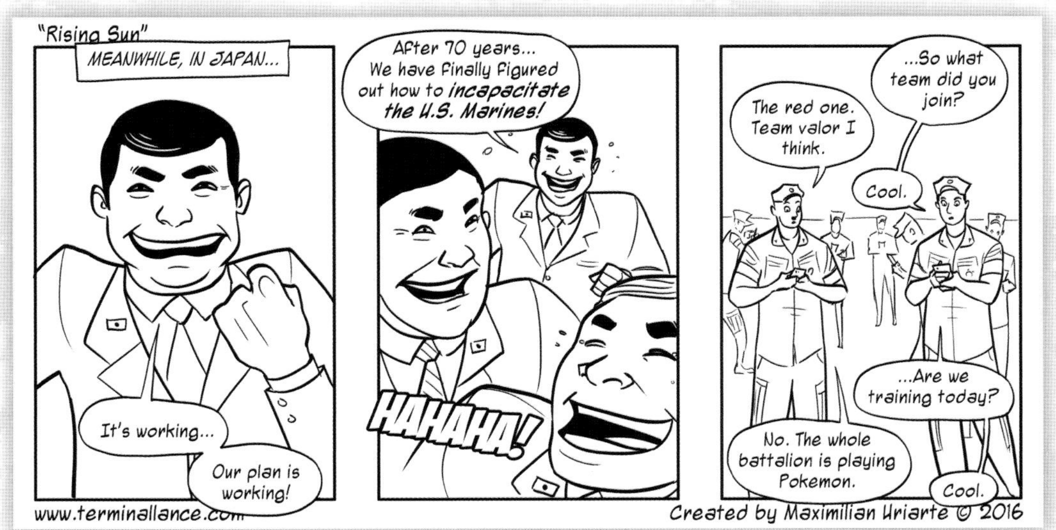
"Rising Sun"
MEANWHILE, IN JAPAN...
It's working...
Our plan is working!
After 70 years... We have finally figured out how to *incapacitate the U.S. Marines!*
HAHAHA!
...So what team did you join?
The red one. Team valor I think.
Cool.
...Are we training today?
No. The whole battalion is playing Pokemon.
Cool.
www.terminallance.com
Created by Maximilian Uriarte © 2016

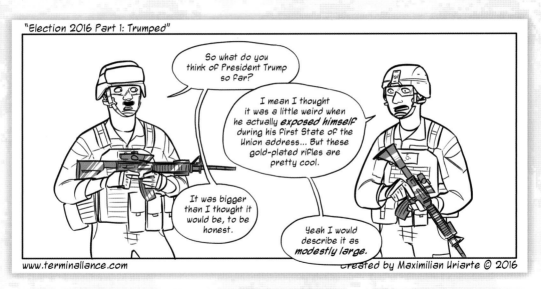

"Election 2016 Part I: Trumped"

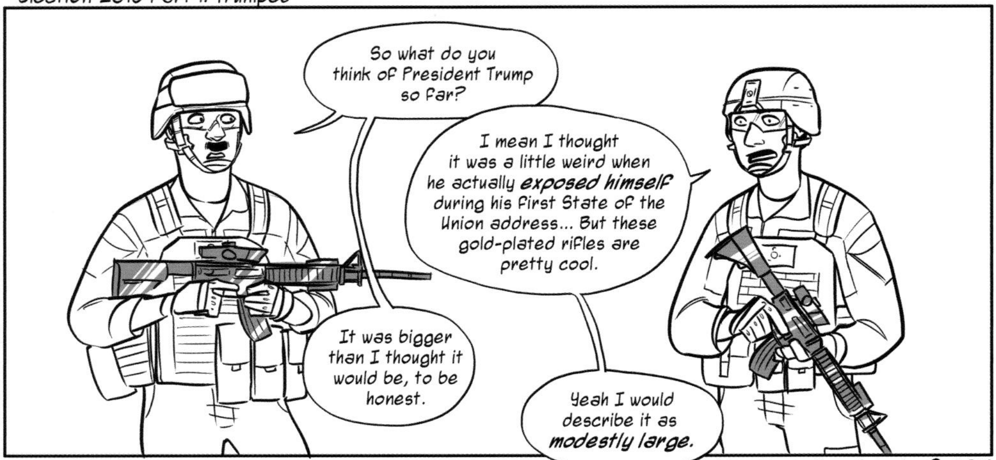

So what do you think of President Trump so far?
I mean I thought it was a little weird when he actually **exposed himself** during his first State of the Union address... But these gold-plated rifles are pretty cool.
It was bigger than I thought it would be, to be honest.
Yeah I would describe it as **modestly large.**

www.terminallance.com

Created by Maximilian Uriarte © 2016

"Election 2016 Part II: Hillary"

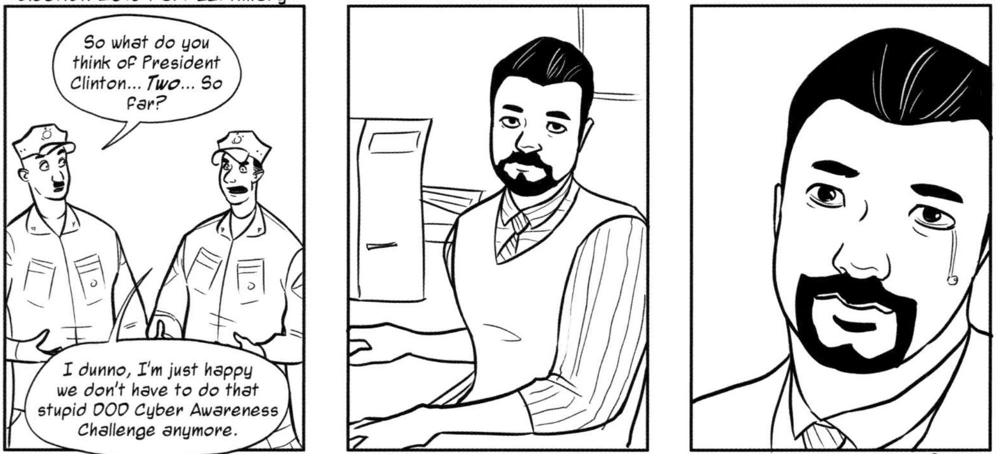

So what do you think of President Clinton... **Two**... So far?
I dunno, I'm just happy we don't have to do that stupid DOD Cyber Awareness Challenge anymore.

www.terminallance.com

Created by Maximilian Uriarte © 2016

"New Corps II"

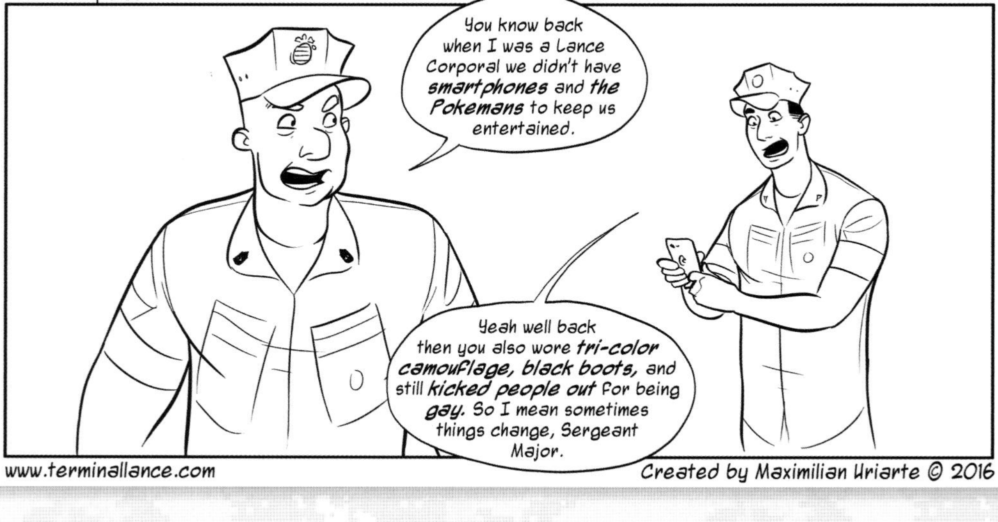

You know back when I was a Lance Corporal we didn't have **smartphones** and **the Pokemans** to keep us entertained.
Yeah well back then you also wore **tri-color camouflage, black boots,** and still **kicked people out** for being **gay.** So I mean sometimes things change, Sergeant Major.

www.terminallance.com

Created by Maximilian Uriarte © 2016

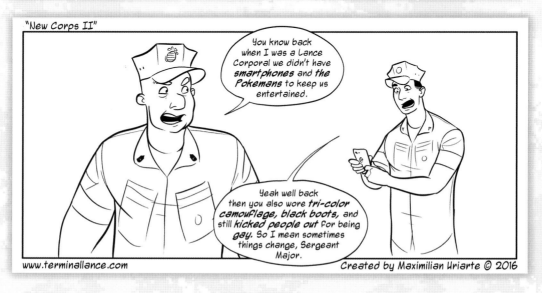

"Special Insignia"

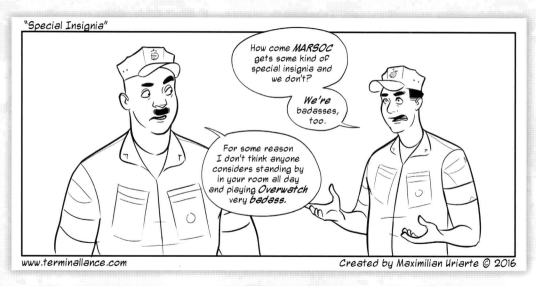

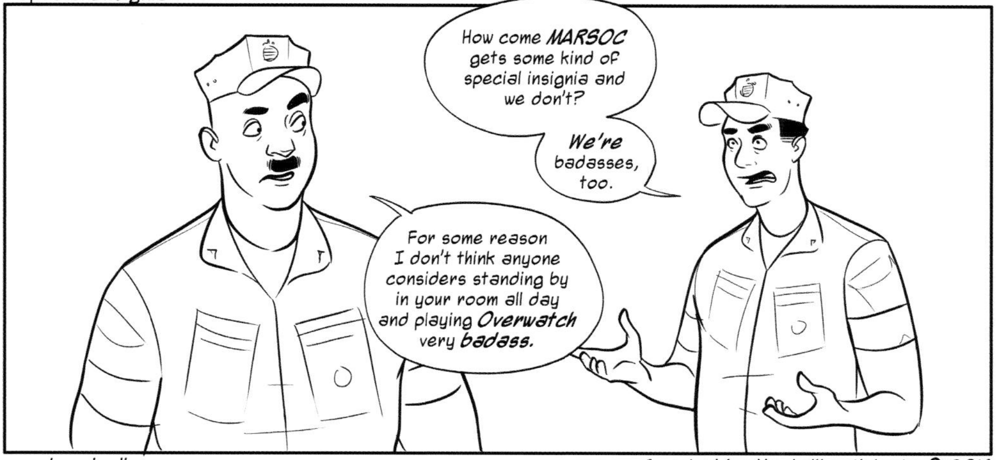
How come MARSOC gets some kind of special insignia and we don't?
We're badasses, too.
For some reason I don't think anyone considers standing by in your room all day and playing Overwatch very badass.

www.terminallance.com Created by Maximilian Uriarte © 2016

"Founded in a Tavern"

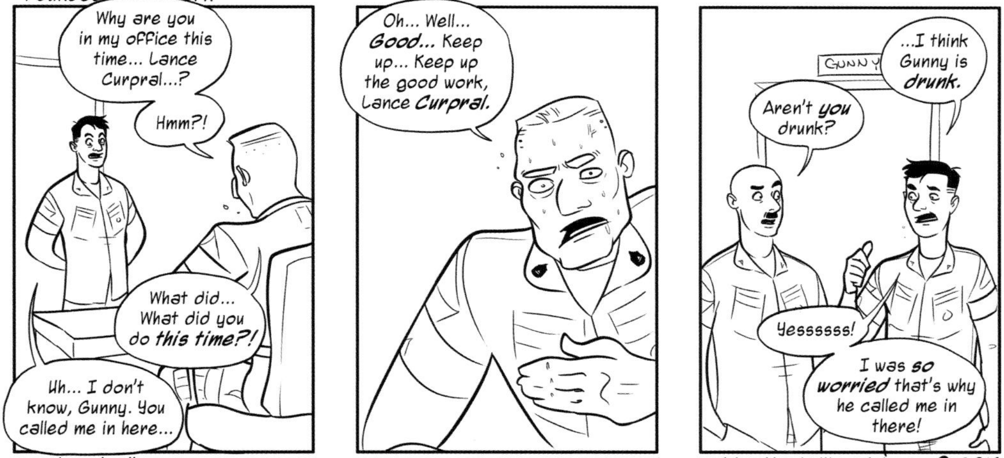
Why are you in my office this time... Lance Curpral...?
Hmm?!
What did... What did you do this time?!
Uh... I don't know, Gunny. You called me in here...
Oh... Well... Good... Keep up... Keep up the good work, Lance Curpral.
GUNNY
...I think Gunny is drunk.
Aren't you drunk?
Yesssss!
I was so worried that's why he called me in there!

www.terminallance.com Created by Maximilian Uriarte © 2016

"High-Tech"

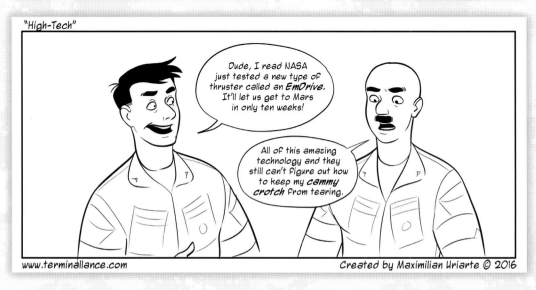

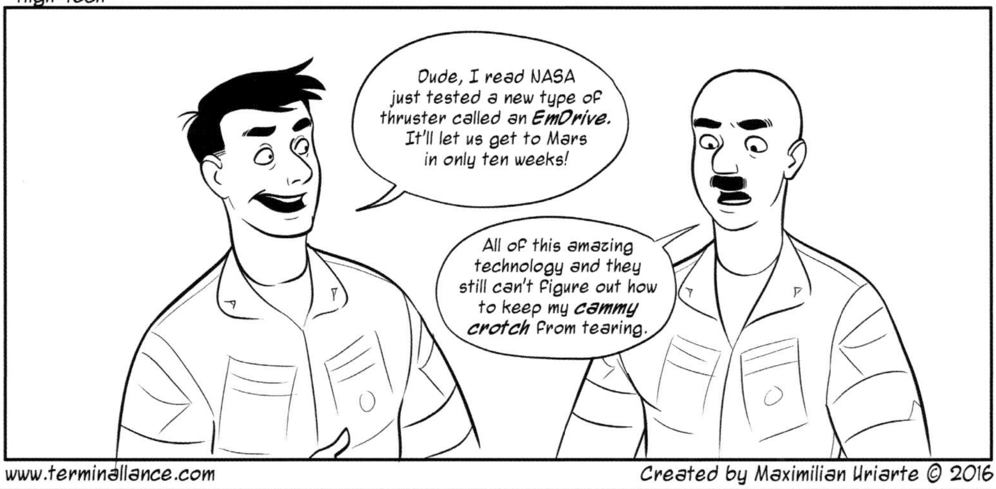
Dude, I read NASA just tested a new type of thruster called an EmDrive. It'll let us get to Mars in only ten weeks!
All of this amazing technology and they still can't figure out how to keep my cammy crotch from tearing.

www.terminallance.com Created by Maximilian Uriarte © 2016

"PT Stud"

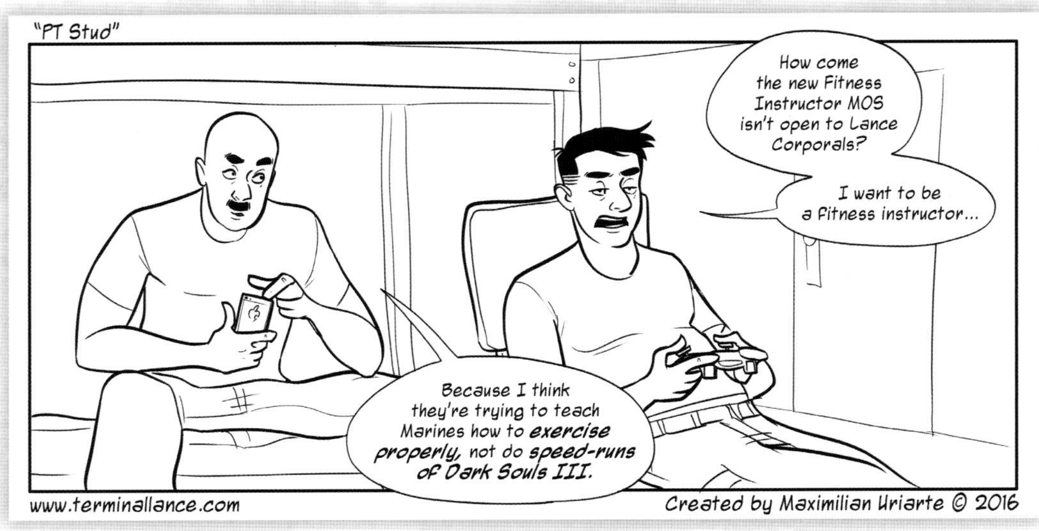
How come the new Fitness Instructor MOS isn't open to Lance Corporals?
I want to be a fitness instructor...
Because I think they're trying to teach Marines how to **exercise properly,** not do **speed-runs of Dark Souls III.**
www.terminallance.com
Created by Maximilian Uriarte © 2016

"Debatable"

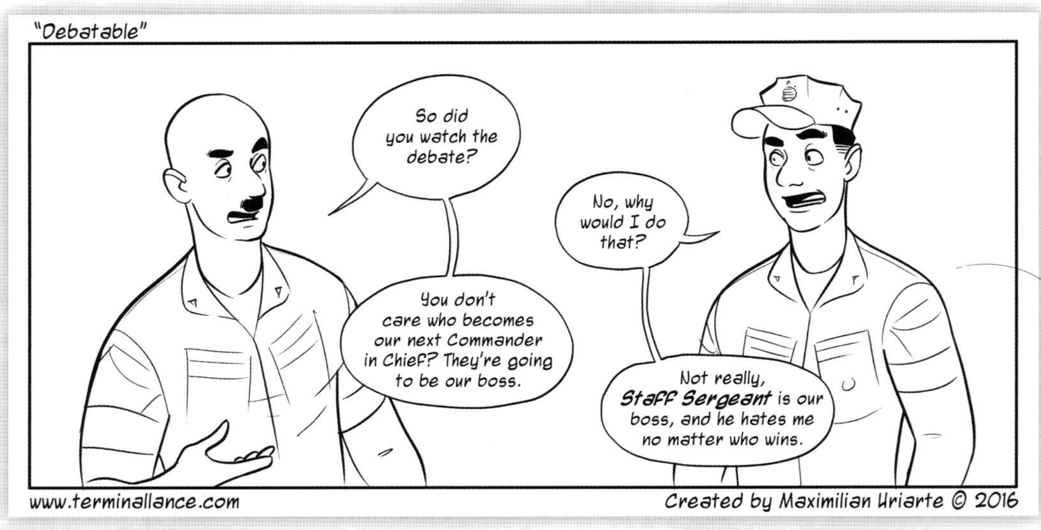
So did you watch the debate?
No, why would I do that?
You don't care who becomes our next Commander in Chief? They're going to be our boss.
Not really, **Staff Sergeant** is our boss, and he hates me no matter who wins.
www.terminallance.com
Created by Maximilian Uriarte © 2016

"Page Master"

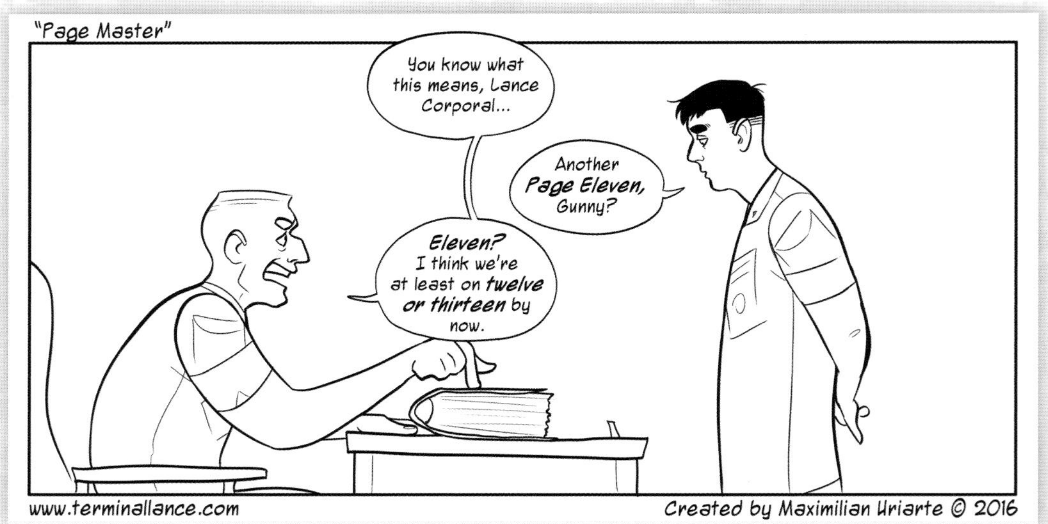
You know what this means, Lance Corporal...
Another **Page Eleven,** Gunny?
Eleven? I think we're at least on **twelve or thirteen** by now.
www.terminallance.com
Created by Maximilian Uriarte © 2016

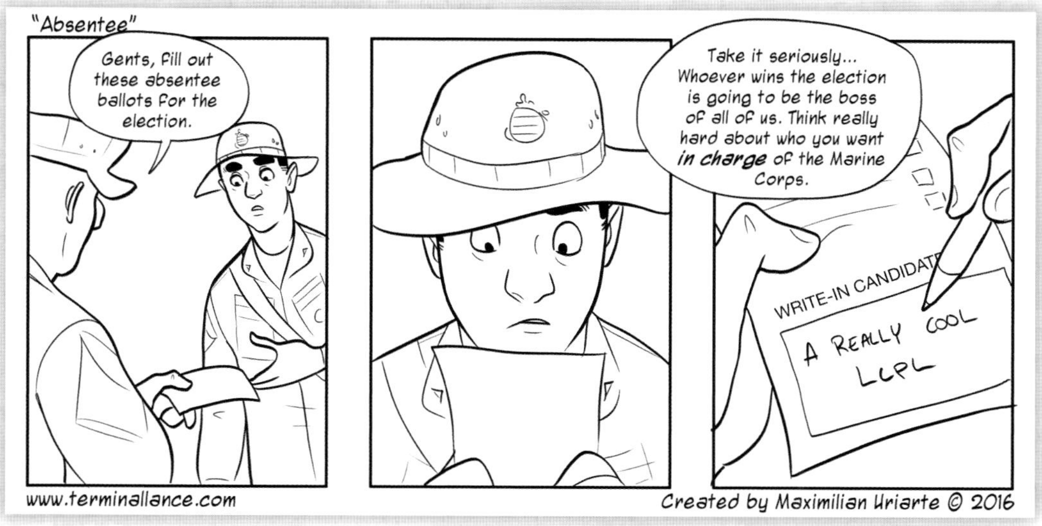
"Absentee"
Gents, fill out these absentee ballots for the election.
Take it seriously... Whoever wins the election is going to be the boss of all of us. Think really hard about who you want *in charge* of the Marine Corps.
WRITE-IN CANDIDATE
A REALLY COOL LCPL
www.terminallance.com
Created by Maximilian Uriarte © 2016

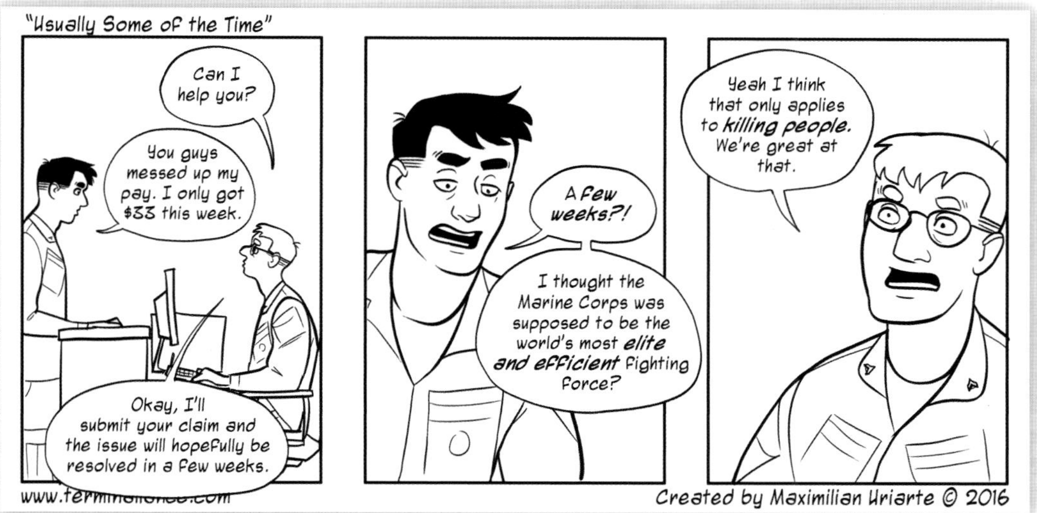
"Usually Some of the Time"
Can I help you?
You guys messed up my pay. I only got $33 this week.
Okay, I'll submit your claim and the issue will hopefully be resolved in a few weeks.
A *few weeks?!*
I thought the Marine Corps was supposed to be the world's most *elite and efficient* fighting force?
Yeah I think that only applies to *killing people.* We're great at that.
www.terminallance.com
Created by Maximilian Uriarte © 2016

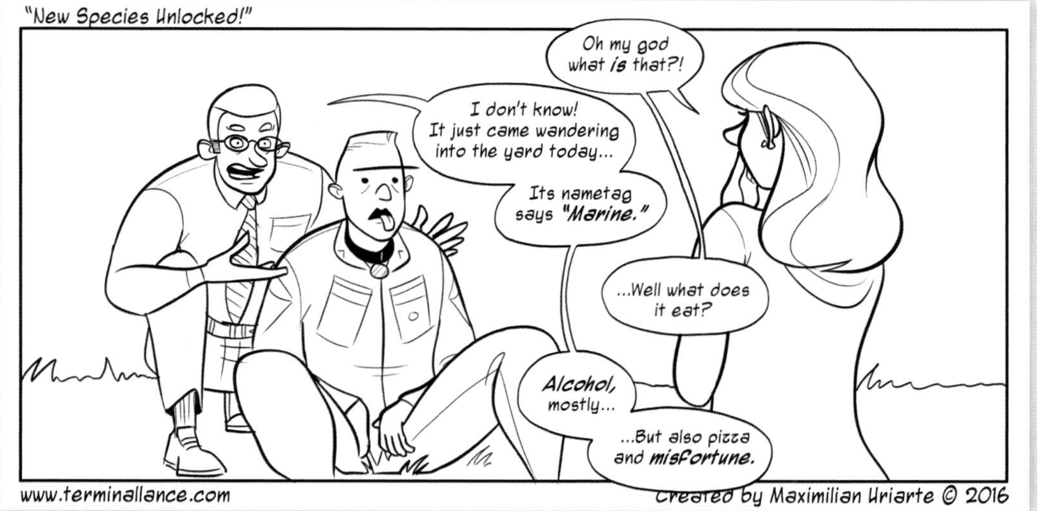
"New Species Unlocked!"
Oh my god what *is* that?!
I don't know! It just came wandering into the yard today...
Its nametag says *"Marine."*
...Well what does it eat?
Alcohol, mostly...
...But also pizza and *misfortune.*
www.terminallance.com
Created by Maximilian Uriarte © 2016

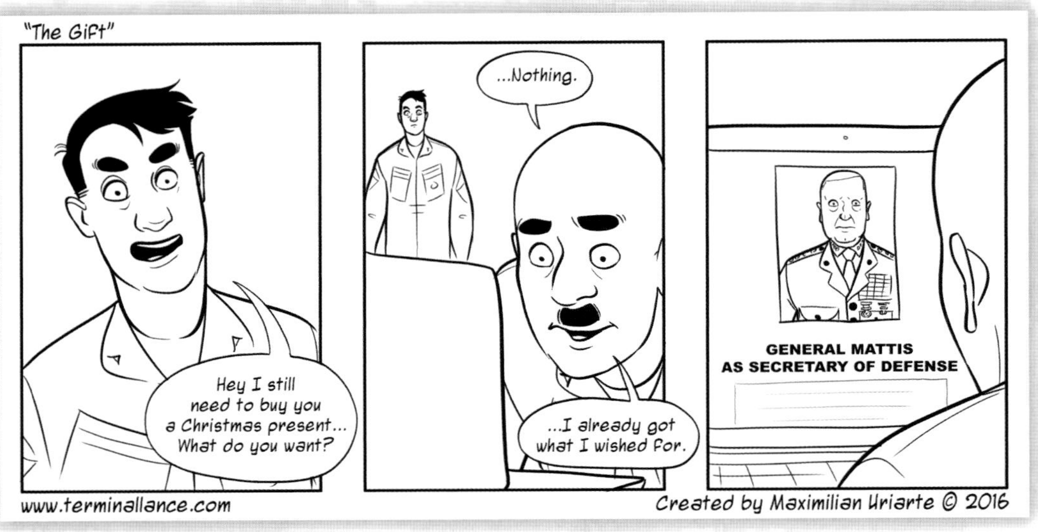
"The Gift"
Hey I still need to buy you a Christmas present... What do you want?
...Nothing.
...I already got what I wished for.
GENERAL MATTIS AS SECRETARY OF DEFENSE
www.terminallance.com
Created by Maximilian Uriarte © 2016

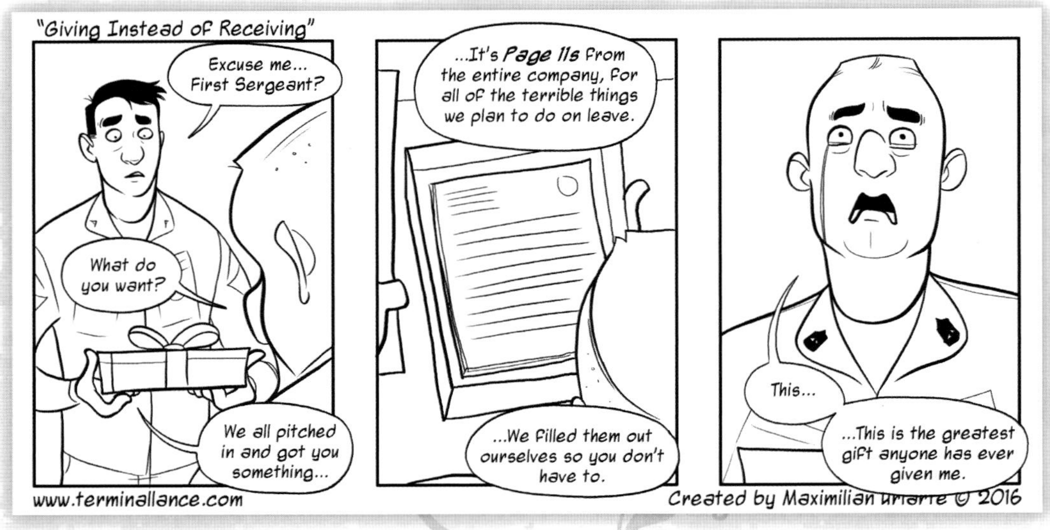
"Giving Instead of Receiving"
Excuse me... First Sergeant?
What do you want?
We all pitched in and got you something...
...It's **Page 11s** from the entire company, for all of the terrible things we plan to do on leave.
...We filled them out ourselves so you don't have to.
This...
...This is the greatest gift anyone has ever given me.
www.terminallance.com
Created by Maximilian Uriarte © 2016

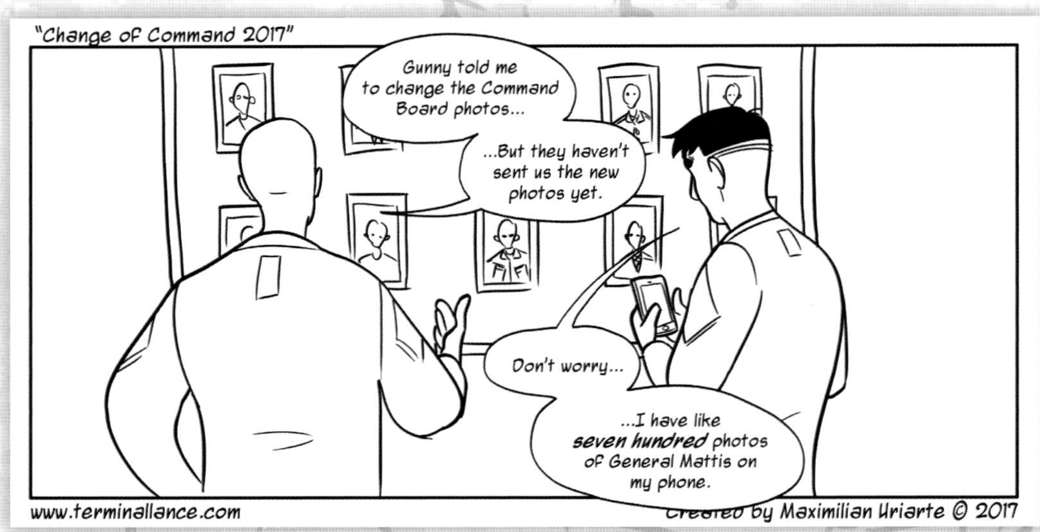
"Change of Command 2017"
Gunny told me to change the Command Board photos...
...But they haven't sent us the new photos yet.
Don't worry...
...I have like **seven hundred** photos of General Mattis on my phone.
www.terminallance.com
Created by Maximilian Uriarte © 2017

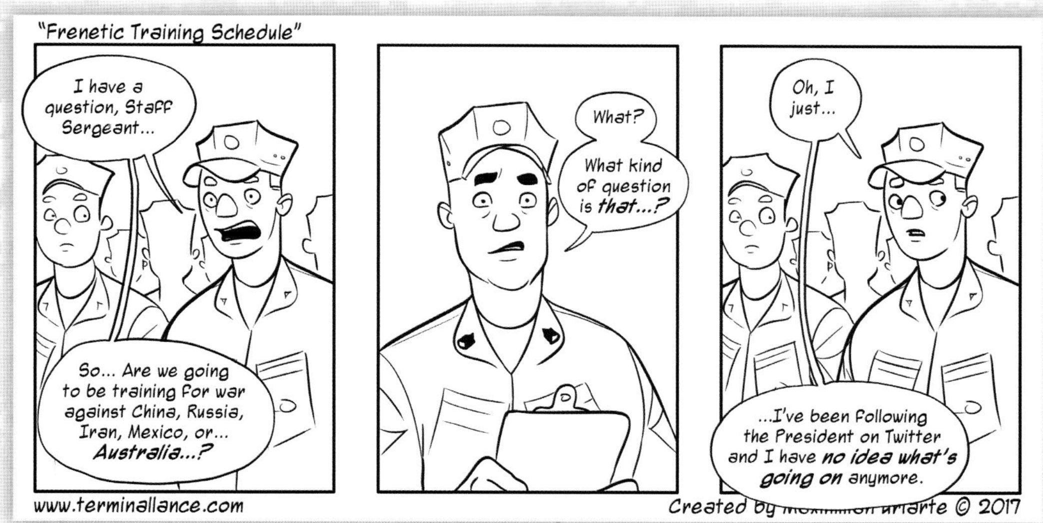
"Frenetic Training Schedule"
I have a question, Staff Sergeant...
So... Are we going to be training for war against China, Russia, Iran, Mexico, or... **Australia...?**
What?
What kind of question is **that...?**
Oh, I just...
...I've been following the President on Twitter and I have **no idea what's going on** anymore.
www.terminallance.com
Created by © 2017

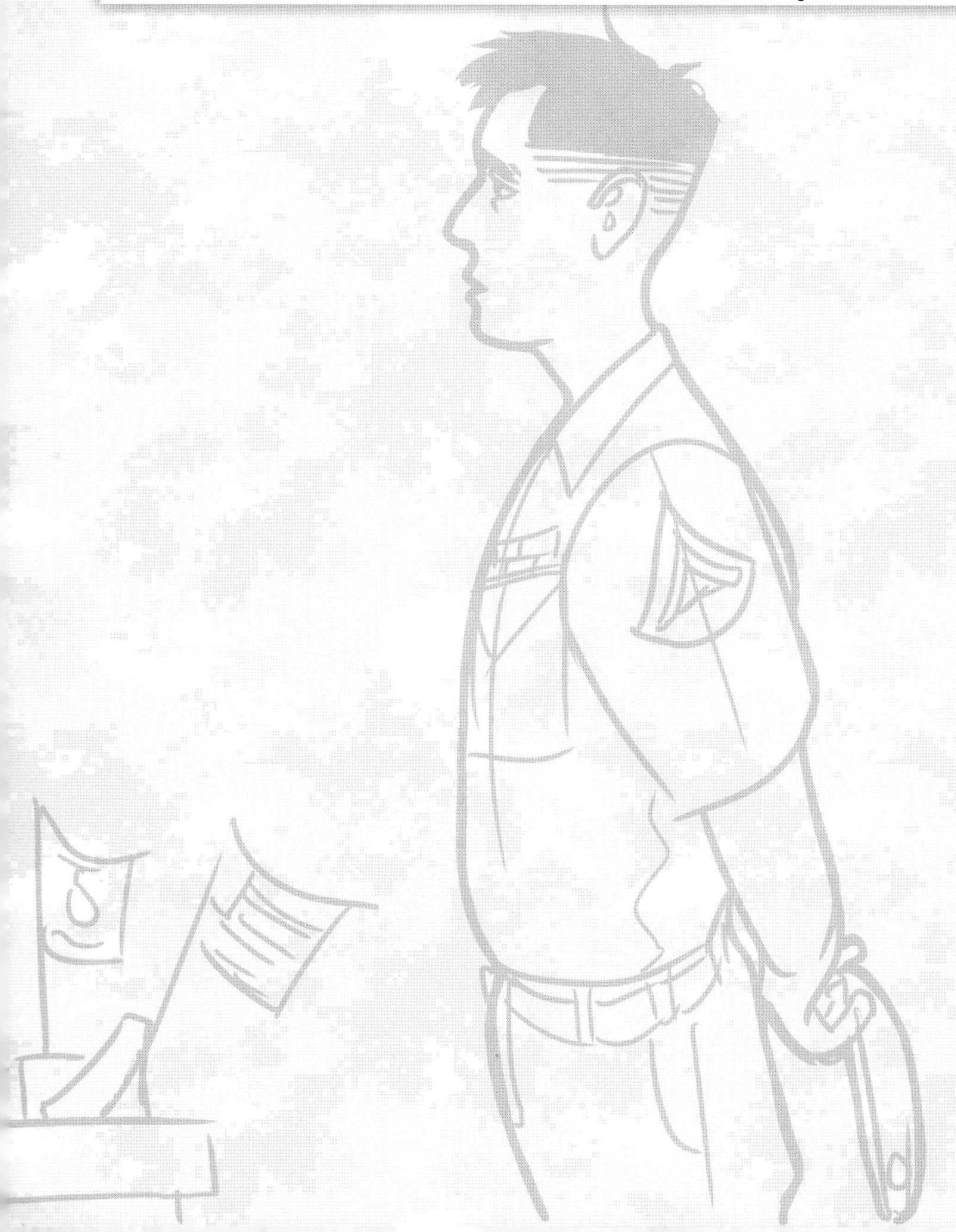

Honestly, Staff Sergeant, I figured I would have gotten busted down by now...

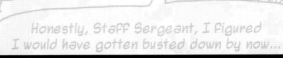

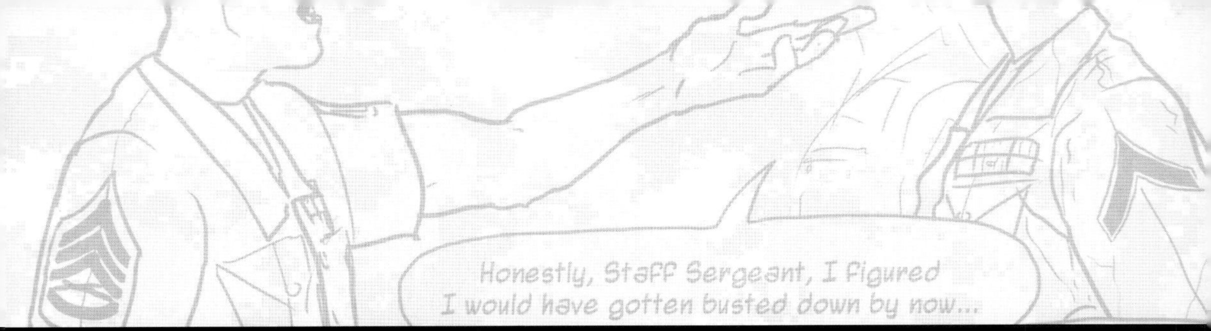

The Characters of Terminal Lance

A number of characters have graced the panels of *Terminal Lance* comics over the years. Here are some of the recurring ones you will run across throughout the *Terminal Lance* lexicon!

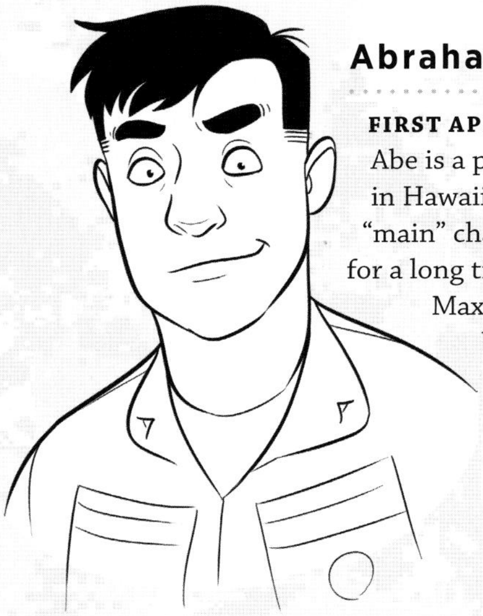

Abraham Belatzeko

FIRST APPEARANCE: #1 "How Nicknames Are Born"
Abe is a plucky, smartass 0351 Infantry Assaultman stationed in Hawaii. For all intents and purposes, Abe is considered the "main" character of *Terminal Lance*. Abe went without a name for a long time, simply acting as an avatar of sorts for creator Maximilian Uriarte. It wasn't until Max began writing *The White Donkey* that Abe was graced with a name. Abe and Max still share a lot of similarities—"Abe" is even Max's platoon nickname because his last name is too difficult for other Marines to pronounce properly.

Jesus Garcia

FIRST APPEARANCE: #93 "POG's Impressing the Grunts"
Garcia is Abe's barracks roommate as well as his best friend. As with Abe, it wasn't until *The White Donkey* that Garcia became a named, recurring character of the strip. Since then, the strip has primarily been about the Marine Corps adventures of Abe and Garcia. Garcia, with his relaxed demeanor and willingness to suck it up, often acts as a voice of reason for Abe. Garcia thrives in the Marine Corps lifestyle because, unlike Abe, he tends to roll with the punches instead of complain about them.

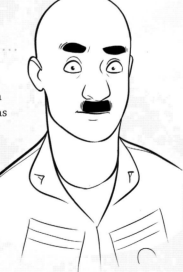

Boot

FIRST APPEARANCE: #363 "Boot (Camp) Stories"
While boots have been featured in *Terminal Lance* since the beginning, the character really didn't take shape in his current form until #363. It was at this point that boots were to be forever denoted with their characteristic beady eyes, which serve as a metaphor for their unenlightened state. Always wearing his CamelBak and high and tight haircut, Boot exists at the whim of his senior Lance Corporals and leadership. His life is terrible, but no one cares because he's a fucking boot.

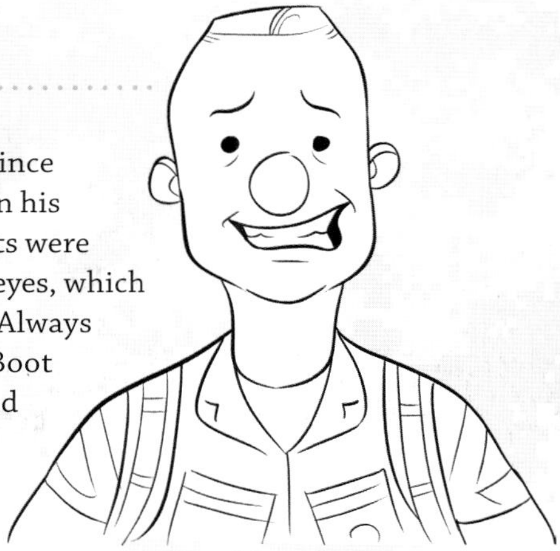

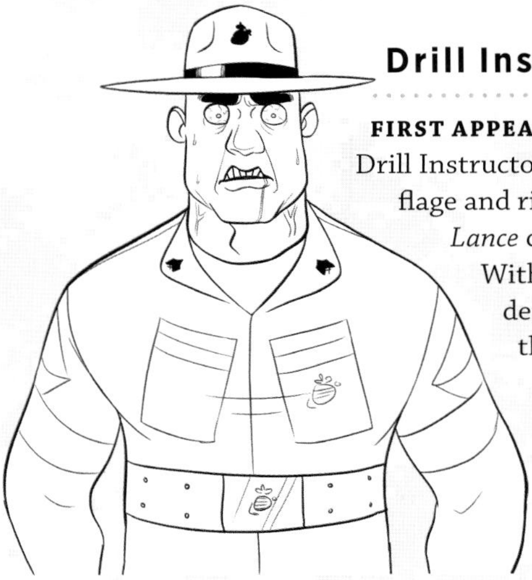

Drill Instructor

FIRST APPEARANCE: #59 "Knife-Hand Anger Gauge"
Drill Instructors are as iconic to the Marine Corps as camouflage and rifles, and make frequent appearances in *Terminal Lance* comics surrounding the subject of boot camp. With their frogged voices and overall angry, sweaty demeanor, Drill Instructors practically caricature-ize themselves. While there's no single recurring Drill Instructor character, you'll find them frequently throughout the comic.

First Sergeant

FIRST APPEARANCE: #446 "Logged"
First Sergeant has had many appearances throughout the panels of *Terminal Lance,* but it is only recently that he has been locked into a recurring character design. First Sergeant is vindictive, dark, and openly hateful of the Lance Corporals under his command. Perhaps he was once a normal Marine, but the corruption of the green weenie has seeped into the very fiber of his soul. He no longer remembers the taste of wine, or the smell of fresh flowers. He just knows the hate he has for his Marines.

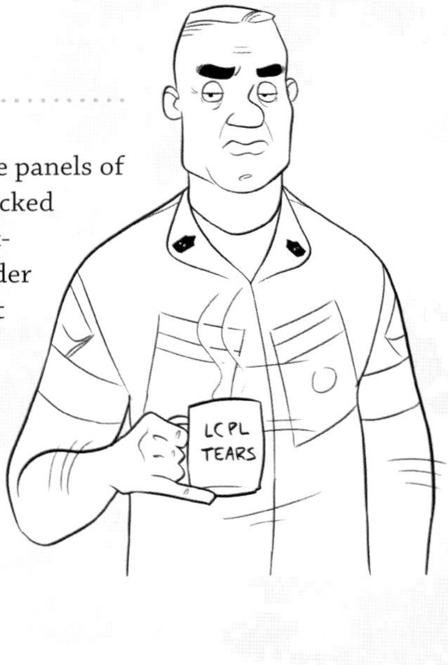
LCPL
TEARS

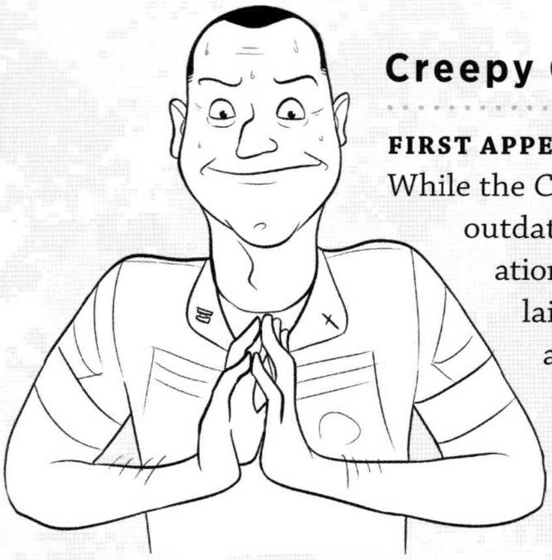

Creepy Chaplain

FIRST APPEARANCE: #160 "Working (It) at the Car Wash"
While the Creepy Chaplain character is undoubtedly somewhat outdated at this point, he remains a fan favorite. The inspiration for the Creepy Chaplain was simply the fact that Chaplains are often just a little bit creepy. Frequently loitering about the base swimming pool and ball fundraiser car washes, the Creepy Chaplain creeps everyone out on the regular, but he's all the battalion has for their religious leadership.

Chongo and Old Man

FIRST APPEARANCE: #214 "Meritorious"
Throughout the *Terminal Lance* library, Chongo serves as a representation of the military's often absurd culture in a "real world" business environment. Chongo is not smart, but he's the perfect Marine. He can run really fast, do lots of pull-ups, and shoot really good. For whatever reason, Old Man serves as his handler, often verbally making the case for him since Chongo can't speak English properly.

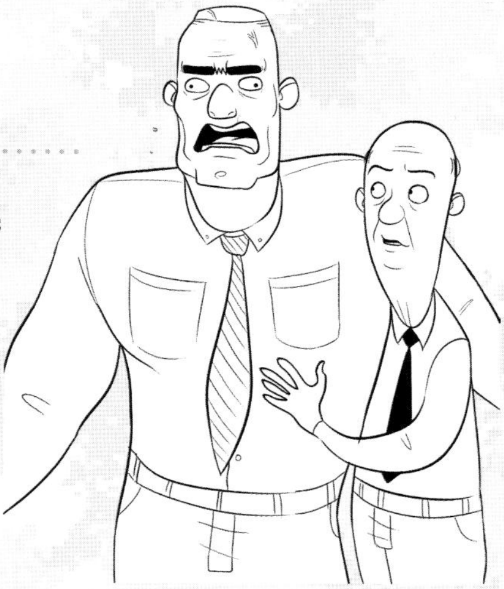

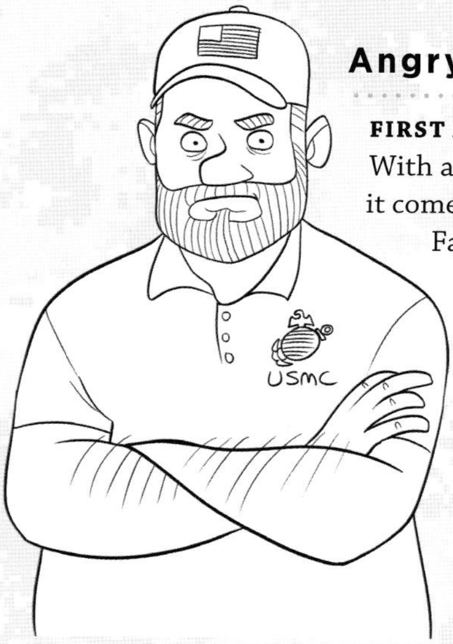
USMC

Angry Facebook Veteran

FIRST APPEARANCE: "Offended"
With a social media footprint as large as *Terminal Lance,* it comes as no surprise that we get our fair share of Angry Facebook Veterans. The Angry Facebook Veteran is that douchebag everyone knows who uses his veteran status as a qualifier for every terrible opinion he has. He has declared himself an authority on all things patriotic and believes himself to be an expert on foreign policy due to his extensive four years of being lower enlisted. He bitched about the Marine Corps every day, but now that he's out, he makes sure you know he was a Marine by wearing a moto hat and setting all his profile pictures to Eagle, Globe, and Anchors.

1171 Water Dog

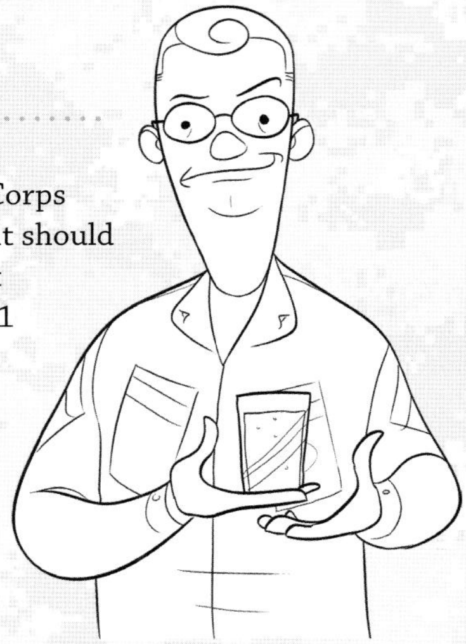

FIRST APPEARANCE: #106 "The Water Dog"
The 1171 Water Dog is colloquially known throughout the Corps as "The Most POG MOS in Existence." Okay, not really, but it should be. You'll find throughout the *Terminal Lance* collection that creator Maximilian has a personal vendetta against the 1171 Water Dog. This was due to one real-life incident where he was stuck on the rifle range next to the only one he's ever met, who was obnoxiously overconfident and hit on every woman around him despite the fact that they were painfully uninterested in him. Because of this, Max never skips an opportunity to shit on them and encourages everyone else to as well.

The Ghost of Chesty Puller

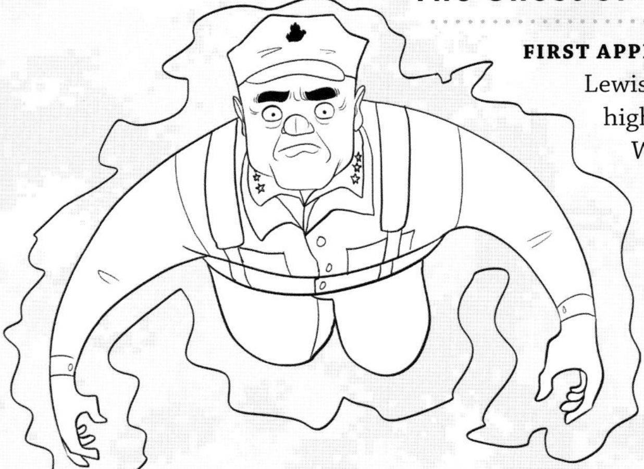

FIRST APPEARANCE: #98 "Unexpected Guest"
Lewis B. (Chesty) Puller was a revered and highly decorated Marine officer of World War II and the Korean War. He is beloved throughout the Corps culture and often referred to in times of great motivation. It is because of this that his ghost occasionally appears to impart upon Marines the wisdom of the Old Corps. The Ghost of Chesty Puller recurs in *Terminal Lance* to settle petty arguments and to bring peace to the Corps.

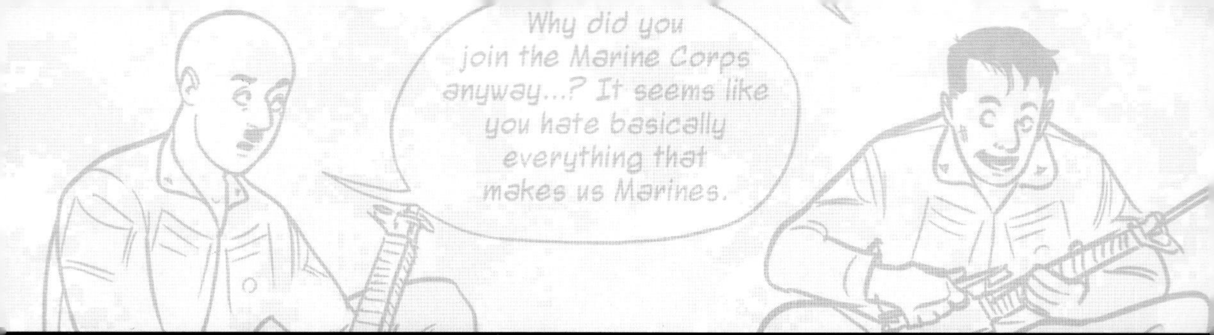
Why did you join the Marine Corps anyway...? It seems like you hate basically everything that makes us Marines.

The Evolution of Terminal Lance Artwork

As both the artist and writer behind *Terminal Lance,* I've spent a lot of time over the years crafting comic strips from start to finish. As you may have noticed from reading the comics, the artwork has changed considerably since the beginning. There's a lot of reasons for this, including the tools I use as well as my own improvement as an illustrator. Below I've broken down the artwork into the various "eras" of *Terminal Lance* art.

The First Comics

The first thirty-four comics are notable because they were all done while I was active duty aboard Marine Corps Base Hawaii, Kaneohe Bay. They are also the only comic strips in the *Terminal Lance* collection that were done with real media (ink on bristol vellum).

The linework in these first thirty-four strips tends to be a bit cleaner and more uniform because it was done with micron pens. While there is always something to be said about doing work in real media, it ultimately ended up being unnecessarily time consuming since all the text was done digitally anyway.

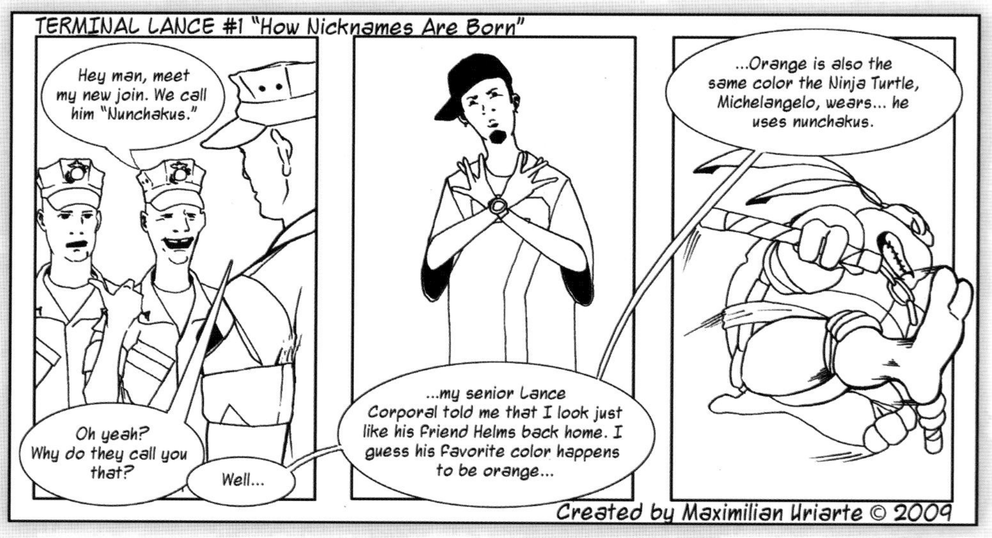
TERMINAL LANCE #1 "How Nicknames Are Born"
Hey man, meet my new join. We call him "Nunchakus."
Oh yeah? Why do they call you that?
Well...
...my senior Lance Corporal told me that I look just like his friend Helms back home. I guess his favorite color happens to be orange...
...Orange is also the same color the Ninja Turtle, Michelangelo, wears... he uses nunchakus.
Created by Maximilian Uriarte © 2009

Fresh Out

Right after leaving the Marine Corps, I spent the summer with my mom in Oregon and had to put most of my stuff in storage. This meant that I didn't really have anywhere to sit down and draw my comic, so I began drawing them 100 percent digitally with a WACOM Intuos tablet.

For whatever reason, this meant that a lot of the artwork drifted into a much looser area. The brushstrokes are scattered and more gestural, mostly because I didn't particularly like drawing tight ink work on the screenless drawing device. However, from this time forward all of the *Terminal Lance* comics became completely digital.

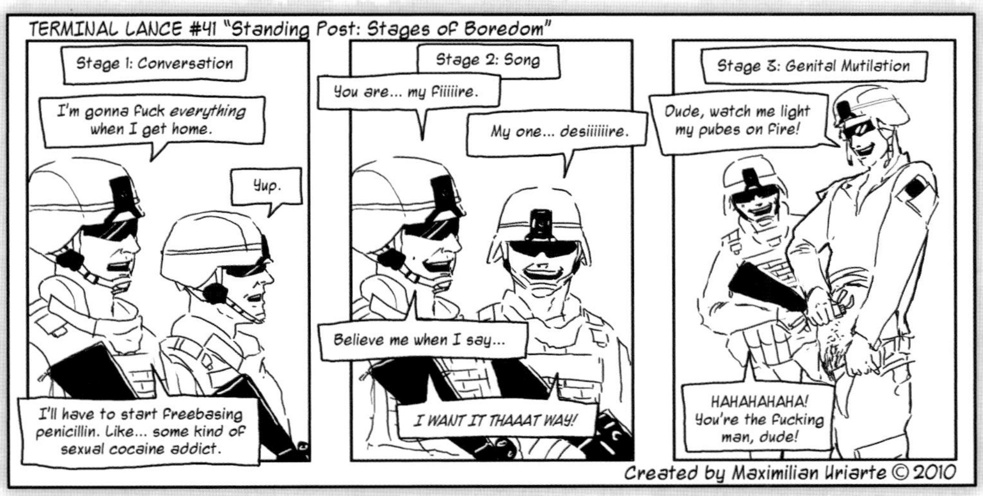
TERMINAL LANCE #41 "Standing Post: Stages of Boredom"
Stage 1: Conversation
I'm gonna fuck everything when I get home.
Yup.
I'll have to start freebasing penicillin. Like... some kind of sexual cocaine addict.
Stage 2: Song
You are... my fiiiiire.
My one... desiiiiiire.
Believe me when I say...
I WANT IT THAAAT WAY!
Stage 3: Genital Mutilation
Dude, watch me light my pubes on fire!
HAHAHAHAHA! You're the fucking man, dude!
Created by Maximilian Uriarte © 2010

The Loose Ages

Utilizing the wonderful Post-9/11 GI Bill to attend animation school at the California College of Arts in Oakland, I started making the artwork for *Terminal Lance* increasingly loose and, frankly, a little sloppy. As a fan of gestural animation art, I had a lot of trouble locking down a visual style for the comic. As a result, the comics from this period were drawn without much focus, making them visually inconsistent from strip to strip.

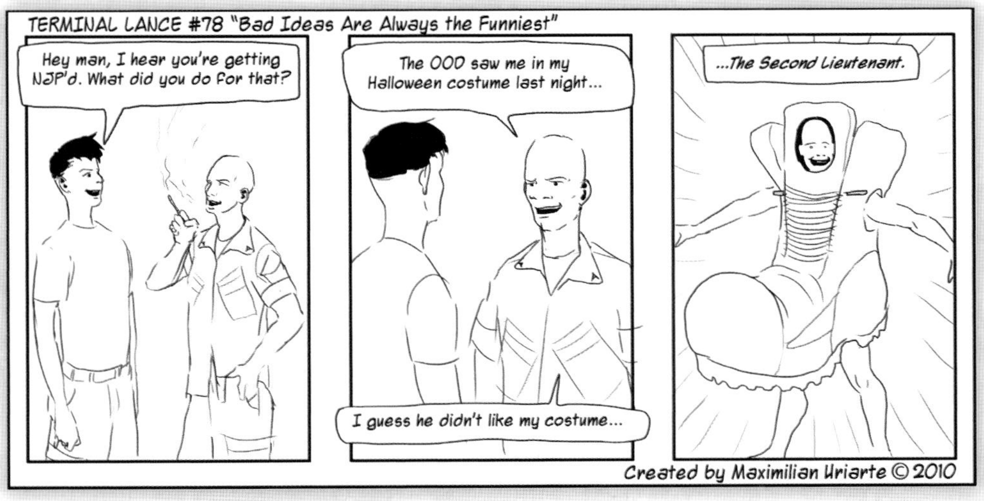
TERMINAL LANCE #78 "Bad Ideas Are Always the Funniest"
Hey man, I hear you're getting NJP'd. What did you do for that?
The OOD saw me in my Halloween costume last night...
I guess he didn't like my costume...
...The Second Lieutenant.
Created by Maximilian Uriarte © 2010

Foundations

The early half of 2013 saw me refining the *Terminal Lance* style into a vestigial version of what you see today. You'll notice the linework is a little bit less sloppy, but still looser, with a consistent line width that is visually easier on the eyes.

I always considered myself more of a naturalist artist, and at this point I was still fighting the need to get more stylized and cartoony with the comic.

TERMINAL LANCE #254 "The Clipboard"
You ever notice that Staff Sergeant always has that clipboard, at every formation?
So?
You ever wonder what's on it...?
Not really...
...It's probably just a call sheet with our names and socials and stuff.
PENIS DRAGON!

Style

In the latter part of 2013, I began working on the graphic novel *The White Donkey*. This came with the purchase of some new equipment, notably a WACOM Cintiq monitor that allowed me to draw directly on the screen. This was a game changer for *Terminal Lance,* as it allowed me to focus less on my technical limitations and more on nailing a consistent look for the comic strip.

The artwork in this period tends to be a bit cleaner, leaning closer to a more stylized cartoon look.

TERMINAL LANCE #298 "Bird of Prey"
CA-CAW!
POOP
SHOOOOOOOOM
Hey Abe, I know your girlfriend is flying out this weekend, but I volunteered you for duty so I wouldn't be bored.
SPLAT
...Don't worry, I gave her number to Sanchez and Stephens. They said they'd show her around.
Created by Maximilian Uriarte © 2013

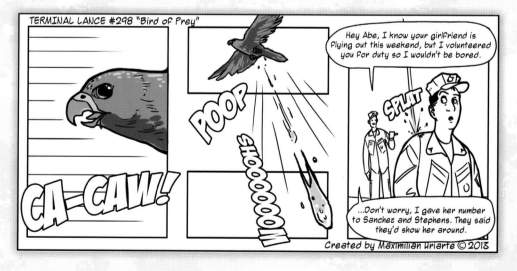

Flow

The modern look of *Terminal Lance* was developed in conjunction with my own development of some character designs meant for animation. The focus was mostly on what I like to refer to as the flow of lines, all done in singular sweeping gestures with the pen. This greatly informed the comic, giving everything a more polished and "animated" look that you could see in a TV cartoon series.

I fought doing cartoon art for a long time, but the more I worked with this style the more I enjoyed it. It also made me realize that cartoon work requires a lot of discipline and skill, which I was only able to accomplish after years and hundreds of comics.

We'll see where the comic goes from here, but this is a look that I am quite happy with. It is uniquely my own as well as uniquely *Terminal Lance*.

TERMINAL LANCE #442 "Boot Camp: The Care Package"
RECRUIT TOMS!
YES SIR!
YOU HAVE A CARE PACKAGE! GET OVER HERE AND OPEN IT!
3014
Oh no...
It's a... Dildo...
...With a note...
"Loved your last letter, give this to the Drill Instructor that you told to go fuck himself!"
ONE WEEK AGO...
Oh are you sending a care package to your poolee friend?
That's so sweet, what a good friend you are.
I hate him.
Created by Maximilian Uriarte © 2016

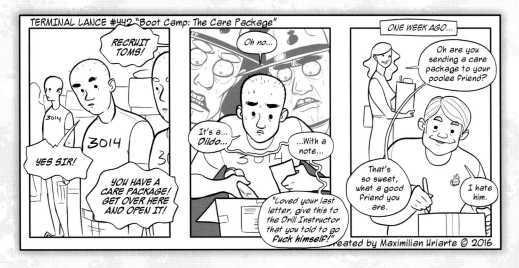

Acknowledgments

Terminal Lance has been a long journey from my active duty days in Hawaii to now, and I owe its success to many people that have helped me along the way.

First and foremost, the fans of *Terminal Lance* who have supported the comic and keep it going with enthusiasm and love. Additionally, the Marine Corps itself for embracing the comic and continuing to read my weekly rants online and otherwise.

The editorial staff over at the *Marine Corps Times,* while shifting through different members over the years, has always maintained a great relationship with me and *Terminal Lance.* Notably, Andrew DeGrandpre (who now resides at the *Washington Post*), was a vocal proponent of *Terminal Lance* in its early days and really helped me by putting the comic in front of a wider audience.

There are many more notable individuals I could name here, but I want to give special attention to my literary agent, Katie Boyle, and my lawyer, Susan Grode, for taking chances on my work and helping me take it all to the next level.

And, of course, the people of Little, Brown, for allowing me to grace their fine brand with a lot of very terrible jokes and crudely drawn phalluses.

About the Author

Photograph by Gabor Szantai

Terminal Lance Ultimate Omnibus was written and illustrated by infantry Marine and Iraq veteran Maximilian Uriarte, creator of the hit comic strip *Terminal Lance* and author of *New York Times* bestseller *The White Donkey*. Uriarte enlisted in the United States Marine Corps in 2006 at the age of nineteen and served for four years. During his first deployment to Iraq in 2007 he served as an MRAP turret gunner and dismount of India Company's "Jump" platoon in the Zaidon region southeast of Fallujah. He deployed to Iraq again in 2009 as a billeted Combat Photographer and Combat Artist, then enrolling in California College of the Arts. In 2010 Uriarte created *Terminal Lance* while still on active duty. The strip is now published in *The Marine Corps Times* and has grown immensely in popularity.